Contracts

Carolina Academic Press Context and Practice Series

Michael Hunter Schwartz
Series Editor

Administrative Law
Richard Henry Seamon

Advanced Torts
Alex B. Long and Meredith J. Duncan

Antitrust Law
Steven Semeraro

Civil Procedure
Gerald F. Hess, Theresa M. Beiner, and Scott R. Bauries

Civil Procedure for All States
Benjamin V. Madison, III

Constitutional Law
David Schwartz and Lori Ringhand

A Context and Practice Global Case File:
An Intersex Athlete's Constitutional Challenge,
Hastings v. USATF, IAAF, and IOC
Olivia M. Farrar

A Context and Practice Global Case File:
A Mother's International Hague Petition for the Return of Her Child,
Thorpe v. Lightfoot
Olivia M. Farrar

Contracts
Second Edition
Michael Hunter Schwartz and Adrian Walters

Current Issues in Constitutional Litigation
Second Edition
Sarah E. Ricks, with contributions by Evelyn M. Tenenbaum

Employment Discrimination
SECOND EDITION
Susan Grover, Sandra F. Sperino, and Jarod S. Gonzalez

Energy Law
Joshua P. Fershee

Evidence
Pavel Wonsowicz

International Business Transactions
Amy Deen Westbrook

International Women's Rights, Equality, and Justice
Christine M. Venter

The Lawyer's Practice
Kris Franklin

Professional Responsibility
Barbara Glesner Fines

Sales
Edith R. Warkentine

Secured Transactions
Edith R. Warkentine and Jerome A. Grossman

Torts
Paula J. Manning

Workers' Compensation Law
Michael C. Duff

Your Brain and Law School
Marybeth Herald

Contracts

A Context and Practice Casebook

SECOND EDITION

Michael Hunter Schwartz
William H. Bowen School of Law
University of Arkansas at Little Rock

Adrian Walters
IIT Chicago-Kent College of Law

CAROLINA ACADEMIC PRESS
Durham, North Carolina

ISBN 978-1-61163-554-6
LCCN 2015937481

Carolina Academic Press
700 Kent Street
Durham, NC 27701
Telephone (919) 489-7486
Fax (919) 493-5668
www.cap-press.com

Printed in the United States of America

Contents

PART TWO
CONTRACT FORMATION
Do the parties even have a deal?

PART THREE
CONTRACT DEFENSES
Can either party get out of the deal?

PART FOUR
CONTRACT REMEDIES
What does a party who sues for breach get if she wins?

PART FIVE
CONTRACT MEANING
What, exactly, has each of the parties agreed to do?

PART SIX
CONTRACT PERFORMANCE AND NON-PERFORMANCE
In what order were the parties to perform, and is there any justification for any non-performance?

PART SEVEN

Non-Party Contract Rights

Other than the parties, who else can enforce a deal?

PART EIGHT
Contract Law Problems
How do contract lawyers use contract law to analyze and solve client problems?

Table of Principal Cases

Series Editor's Preface

Welcome to a new type of casebook. Designed by leading experts in law school teaching and learning, Context and Practice casebooks assist law professors and their students to work together to learn, minimize stress, and prepare for the rigors and joys of practicing law. **Student learning and preparation for law practice are the guiding ethics of these books.**

Why would we depart from the tried and true? Why have we abandoned the legal education model by which we were trained? Because legal education can and must improve.

In Spring 2007, the Carnegie Foundation published *Educating Lawyers: Preparation for the Practice of Law* and the Clinical Legal Education Association published *Best Practices for Legal Education*. Both works reflect in-depth efforts to assess the effectiveness of modern legal education, and both conclude that legal education, as presently practiced, falls quite short of what it can and should be. Both works criticize law professors' rigid adherence to a single teaching technique, the inadequacies of law school assessment mechanisms, and the dearth of law school instruction aimed at teaching law practice skills and inculcating professional values. Finally, the authors of both books express concern that legal education may be harming law students. Recent studies show that law students, in comparison to all other graduate students, have the highest levels of depression, anxiety and substance abuse.

The problems with traditional law school instruction begin with the textbooks law teachers use. Law professors cannot implement *Educating Lawyers* and *Best Practices* using texts designed for the traditional model of legal education. Moreover, even though our understanding of how people learn has grown exponentially in the past 100 years, no law school text to date even purports to have been designed with educational research in mind.

The Context and Practice Series is an effort to offer a genuine alternative. Grounded in learning theory and instructional design and written with *Educating Lawyers* and *Best Practices* in mind, Context and Practice casebooks make it easy for law professors to change.

I welcome reactions, criticisms, and suggestions; my e-mail address is mhschwartz@ualr.edu. Knowing the author(s) of these books, I know they, too, would appreciate your input; we share a common commitment to student learning. In fact, students, if your professor cares enough about your learning to have adopted this book, I bet s/he would welcome your input, too!

Michael Hunter Schwartz, Series Designer and Editor
Consultant, Institute for Law Teaching and Learning
Dean and Professor of Law, William H. Bowen School of Law,
University of Arkansas at Little Rock

Preface to the Second Edition

Six years ago, when I launched the Context and Practice Casebook Series by publishing the first edition of this book (with Denise Riebe), the world of legal education was in in the middle of a boom era. Although the Carnegie Foundation's EDUCATING LAWYERS: PREPARATION FOR THE PRACTICE OF LAW[1] and Roy Stuckey's BEST PRACTICES FOR LEGAL EDUCATION[2] had made compelling arguments for legal education reform, legal education, as a field, was feeling pretty good about itself and not so eager to change. Why fix it if it ain't broke?

Legal education in 2015 looks quite a bit different. We are in the middle of a perfect storm of: greatly declined applications, increased pressure from the state bars and legal employers to produce more practice-ready lawyers, and newly-adopted ABA standards that require law schools to provide more formative and summative assessment and to adopt and measure student learning outcomes. Law schools are closing, merging, and shrinking, and law professor hiring has slowed to a trickle.

This changed landscape has made books like this contracts text and book series like the Context and Practice series a necessity. Legal educators need turnkey tools that allow them to teach more effectively, teach students more about the actual practice of law, and provide multiple formative and summative assessments. Consequently, while my new co-author, Professor Adrian Walters of Chicago Kent, and I concluded that a second edition was necessary and valuable, we were not inclined to change the essential structure and features of the original version. Accordingly, we have retained the first edition's heavy emphasis on good teaching, multiple assessments, visual learning aids, professional identity development, and practical lawyering. We also have kept most of the cases from the first edition, and, as to the cases we did eliminate or replace, we moved them to the teachers' edition so that no former user will suffer withdrawals. We even retained the preface from the first edition because we believe everything it says is still true.

So, what did we change and why did we change it? The most significant changes we made involved replacing or editing many of the chapter problems and a large number of the other problems sprinkled throughout the book. At some point, the internet had made answers to the first edition's problems so readily available to our digital generation students that the problems became less valuable as teaching tools. We also changed some of the cases. For example, Professor Walters abhors the *Lefkowitz* case, and I caved in when confronted by his marked distaste for this terrific, old case. Third, we expanded and clarified the materials on contract reading and contract terms, and we made it clear that, while the Schmo contract is a wonderful teaching tool, it is not a well-drafted contract. Finally, we cleaned up typos and other editing errors in the first edition; at least, we *believe* we caught all or nearly all of the typos this time. Experience tells me, however, that students and faculty users will still find a few and, for those errors, we apologize.

---

1. William M. Sullivan, Anne Colby, Judith Welch Wegner, Lloyd Bond, & Lee S. Shulman, EDUCATING LAWYERS: PREPARATION FOR THE PROFESSION OF LAW (2007).

2. Roy Stuckey & Others, BEST PRACTICES FOR LEGAL EDUCATION (2007).

A word or two about my new co-author. Professor Walters was an early adopter of the text, and I had found myself drawn to his blog. He is a wonderful legal thinker and a great teacher (and, in fact, this year, he won a teaching honor). He is funny, gregarious, and hard working, and, because he is British, everything he says sounds smarter than it really is. I am honored by his choice to add his name to the book.

I hope you find the book useful and wish you wonderful contracts students and professors.

~Michael Hunter Schwartz, May 2015

Second Edition Acknowledgments

Adrian Walters thanks Mike Schwartz for inviting him to co-author this edition and for trusting him not to ruin all the good work! He also thanks the following for their help and support: Rachel and Alice Walters, Shohreh Davoodi (Chicago-Kent class of 2015), Sarah Harding, Steve Harris, Hal Krent, Nicole Lechuga, Matthew Smart (Chicago-Kent class of 2016), and Scott Vanderlin.

Michael Hunter Schwartz thanks Adrian, his administrative teammate Patti Bell, his wife Stacey, his daughters Samantha and Kendra, and his colleagues at the University of Arkansas at Little Rock, William H. Bowen School of law. He thanks the folks at Carolina Academic Press, including Tim, Linda, Keith, Ryland, and Meredith, for their patience and support.

Preface to the First Edition

By our count, there are at least 20 other contracts casebooks out there. And legal publishers offer a wide variety of casebook series. Why write another casebook? Why create a new casebook series?

Because legal education can and must improve.

For years, law professors have complained that, no matter how hard they tried to be effective educators, their students' performance fell short of their goals. In 2000, the editor of this series, Professor Michael Hunter Schwartz, took a community college class in learning theory and instructional design. It changed his whole outlook on legal education. He learned there are better ways to teach what we wanted our students to learn.

In the meantime, a series of studies found that, while law students come to law school with the same levels of depression, anxiety and substance abuse as their graduate and professional school peers, by the end of their first year, law students are more depressed and more anxious and abuse substances at a greater rate.[1]

The problems with traditional law school instruction begin with the textbooks law teachers use. Law professors are like members of fraternities or sororities who, having been through an initiation process that included hazing, continue hazing all new initiates. Professors often think, "If it was good enough for me, it should be good enough for my students." In this way, legal education is disturbingly similar to the fraternity paddling rituals depicted in the movies.

In Spring 2007, the Carnegie Foundation's EDUCATING LAWYERS: PREPARATION FOR THE PRACTICE OF LAW[2] and Roy Stuckey's BEST PRACTICES FOR LEGAL EDUCATION[3] measured the effectiveness of modern legal education and concluded that legal education, as presently practiced, falls quite short of what it can and should be. Both works severely criticize the rigid adherence to a single teaching technique and the absence of law practice and professional identity development in legal education.

Inspired by the call to action reflected in these works and by the absence of teaching materials designed in light of these studies and of the hundreds of educational studies in the instructional design field, law teaching experts from around the country have gathered as a group and envisioned a casebook series responsive to the research on teaching and

---

1. G. Andrew H. Benjamin et al., *The Role of Legal Education in Producing Psychological Distress Among Law Students and Lawyers*, 1986 AM. B. FOUND. RES. J. 225; Kennon M. Sheldon & Lawrence S. Krieger, *Does Legal Education Have Undermining Effects on Law Students? Evaluating Changes in Motivation, Values, and Well-Being*, 22 BEHAV. SCI. & L. 261 (2004); Kennon M. Sheldon & Lawrence S. Krieger, *Understanding the Negative Effects of Legal Education on Law Students: A Longitudinal Test of Self-Determination Theory*, 33 J. PERSONALITY & SOC. PSYCHOL. 883 (2007).

2. William M. Sullivan, Anne Colby, Judith Welch Wegner, Lloyd Bond, & Lee S. Shulman, EDUCATING LAWYERS: PREPARATION FOR THE PROFESSION OF LAW (2007).

3. Roy Stuckey & Others, BEST PRACTICES FOR LEGAL EDUCATION (2007).

learning and to the Carnegie and Stuckey studies. The result is this series. We hope this book and the series serve as tools to allow law professors and their students to work together to improve students' learning, reduce students' stress, and better prepare students for the rigors and joys of practicing law.

Overview and Structure of This Text

You will notice from the outset that this text, like all the books in the Context and Practice Casebook series, is unlike other law school texts in significant ways. Whereas most law school texts consist mostly of cases with some textual materials and problems thrown in, this text provides a different mix of cases and contextual material, plus thousands of problems.

This text also uses cases in a very different way from traditional law school texts. Most law school texts provide little to no background knowledge and require you to derive rules of law from cases in a way that is very different from how practicing lawyers do so. When they can, practicing lawyers read secondary resources summarizing an area of law before they start reading the cases. That background provides lawyers with a context for understanding the cases. In contrast to traditional model casebooks, this text provides students with the background knowledge a practicing lawyer would develop before considering reading the cases.

Unlike other texts, this casebook has been designed to give students the tools they need to understand the law and the cases. The book guides students through activities that will make it more likely they will remember what they have learned. For example, the book focuses extensively on helping students learn to use rules, to apply rules and cases to analyze legal problems.

In addition, this text provides many exercises to help students build law learning skills as they study contract law. All contract law professors agree that they cannot possibly teach their students every rule of contract law. So, every contract law professor tries to cover the most important aspects of contract law while also hoping students somehow develop a more general skill for learning contract law. This book has been explicitly designed to train contracts students to become expert at learning in the field. In fact, we hope the text becomes a more general resource for students. Students who internalize the expert learning skills taught in this book will be able to use the skills to help them learn in their other law school courses and to become life-long, expert learners of the law.

By and large, law practice requires that lawyers be expert legal readers and writers. All existing casebooks make challenging reading demands on students. This casebook also emphasizes legal reading skills, and it probably places a greater emphasis on legal writing than most casebooks. In addition, the book provides learning experiences that allow students to make sense of what they are learning from a visual perspective, and learning experiences that are as close to authentic law practice as possible, experiences that allow students to see how practicing lawyers would use the concepts in practice.

The book is also carefully sequenced. Early in the book, the primary focus is on building basic lawyering and legal analysis skills, such as reading and understanding cases and statutes, identifying legal issues, applying rules, and applying and distinguishing cases. Consequently, the first few chapters provide substantial guidance in your development of these skills and, where appropriate, examples, hints and cues to help students succeed.

As students proceed through the book, we gradually decrease the guidance and increase the expectations. The last several chapters increasingly put students in the role of a lawyer who not only must understand and account for the application of somewhat indeterminate law to somewhat indeterminate facts but also must account for client interests and goals and the lawyers' professional responsibilities and values. In fact, the final chapter of the book, Chapter 15, focuses on helping you develop problem-solving skills, both in the context of the types of problems you are likely to encounter on your final exams and in the much more contextual, ambiguous and challenging problems contract lawyers handle. Chapter 15 reflects the research on learning that indicates that students learning in new fields learn best if they are taught both the trees (the individual concepts) in the forest (the field) and the how experts work in the forest (how experts combine and use the concepts to solve real-world problems).

Finally, you may notice that this text contemplates a higher level of class preparation and practice in solving problems than texts you have encountered in your past educational experiences. The upside for you is that if you do the work presented along the way, you will learn more effectively and will not need to study as much for your examinations.

Contracts Course Objectives

This book has been designed to help students develop skills and knowledge in four areas: (1) contract law and its application to legal problems; (2) expert learning skills applicable not only to learning contracts but also applicable to learning any body of law; (3) contract reading skills; and (4) the beginnings of contract drafting skills. The discussion below explains each of these skills and what you should be learning with respect to each.

Objectives Relating to Learning Contract Doctrine and Its Application

By the end of your study of contract law, if you are given the facts and relevant documents that form the basis of a contract dispute, you will be able to analyze such "closed universe" problems:

1. Identify the contract law litigation or drafting issues implicated by the facts;
2. Know and articulate, at a mastery level, the relevant contract rules and the rationales that support those rules;
3. Develop arguments that reasonable lawyers representing all involved parties would make with respect to the litigation issues and draft contract terms addressing the drafting issues; and
4. Predict how a court would evaluate the arguments to resolve the litigation dispute or how a court would interpret the draft language were it ever disputed.

Objectives Relating to Expert Learning Skills

In addition, by the end of your study of contract law, you should have increased your level of independent, expert learning skills. Accordingly, you should be better able to self-regulate your law school learning and know when and how to use the skills law students and lawyers need to succeed in law school, on the bar examination, and in practice.

Objectives Relating to Learning Contract Reading Skills

This text is not designed to help you become an expert in reading contracts, but it is designed to move you closer to that designation. That skill takes a few more years to develop. However, by the end of your study of contracts, if you are given a contract and asked to evaluate it, you should be able to:

1. Identify a wide variety of commonly-used clauses;
2. Evaluate the strengths and weaknesses of the particular versions of the commonly-used clauses;
3. Find ambiguities in both the language used in the commonly-used clauses and in the contract's other clauses; and
4. Evaluate the implications of the ambiguities in light of a set of client goals.

Objectives Relating to Learning Contract Drafting Skills

Finally, you will be familiar with and begin to develop contract drafting skills. This text also does not purport to make you a master draftsperson. You can expect to learn to:

1. Describe how contracts lawyers think about and approach drafting problems;
2. Be able to use others' "form contracts" thoughtfully, actively and creatively; and
3. Be able to competently draft some contract clauses.

Some of the Underlying Objectives

To achieve the above goals, you will need to develop the following base-level knowledge and skills:

1. Knowledge of the principles of contract law;
2. Knowledge of basic contract drafting principles;
3. The skill of applying principles of contract law to facts;
4. Knowledge of the context within which each of the contract principles arises;
5. The skill of identifying and distinguishing among contract law issues;
6. Knowledge of common argument patterns in contract law analyses;
7. The skill of brainstorming and articulating arguments contract lawyers make;
8. The skill of organizing your thoughts; and
9. The skill of clearly, precisely, and concisely expressing your thoughts in writing.

Of course, hundreds of sub-sub-goals underlie each objective and sub-goal listed above.

Organization of This Text and of Each Chapter

We have structured this text into eight parts: an introduction; the six broad subjects in contract law (formation, defenses, interpretation, performance, third-party rights, and remedies for breach); and, an additional part that focuses on solving the types of problems that contract lawyers need to be able to analyze and solve. Each of the broad subject areas includes several subtopics, each of which is assigned its own chapter. For example, Part II, Contract Formation, includes three chapters: Chapter 2, Mutual Assent; Chapter 3, Consideration; and Chapter 4, Promissory Estoppel.

Each chapter follows a similar format. Each chapter starts with a problem you should be able to analyze and resolve by the end of your study of that chapter. For each new body of law, we summarize or otherwise introduce the law you will be learning and, in many instances, provide a simple example. In particular, in almost every instance, you will learn a rule from the text or from a secondary source that the text instructs you to consult, *before* you read cases in which courts have applied that rule. The chapters also include an overview so that you have a sense of how you will be learning what you need to learn.

The introductions are most often followed by a series of cases, with problems and active learning exercises interspersed throughout. Many of the cases in the first half of the book include commentary alongside designed to increase your understanding of the cases or to teach you something about legal method. Many of the problems and exercises suggest you write a response, and we encourage you to do so. In class, you can expect your professor will ask you many of the questions included in this text.

The chapters also include graphics designed to give you a visual sense of the concepts and the overall body of law. Toward the end of each chapter, we include hints for analyzing and solving the problem presented at the beginning of the chapter. Many chapters also ask you to find the law of the state in which you currently are planning to practice law. Finally, each chapter concludes with reflection questions designed to further your professional development.

PART ONE

INTRODUCTION TO CONTRACT LAW

Chapter 1

Introduction to Contract Law

In our society, we devote enormous amounts of resources to contracts. For example, we use courtrooms, judges, lawyers, courtroom personnel, arbitrators, and mediators to resolve contract disputes. Why do we devote so many resources to what are primarily private dealings between private parties? (Hint: Think economics. What would happen to our free market economy if agreements were not legally enforceable?)

To make sense of society's allocation of resources, as well as your personal resources in connection with this course, this introduction explores the reasons underlying the allocation and the implications of it. This discussion lays a foundation in public policy that you need both for this course and for the practice of contract law. The study of contracts assumes you possess this knowledge base, and practicing lawyers have learned how to strategically deploy this knowledge to assist their clients.

Our legal system does not concern itself with all agreements. Consider the following two situations: (1) an exchange of a promise to provide an inexpensive watch for the act of opening an envelope, and (2) a promise to give a homeless person a free meal. Our courts label situations like the first one a "contract" and are willing to address them. In contrast, our courts do not label promises like the second one a "contract" and do not address them. Why do our courts concern themselves with situations like the first one labeled a "contract," but ignore situations like the second one?

This text focuses on the analysis of disputes regarding situations we label "contracts" as well as disputes about whether to attach the contract label at all. Two of the biggest problems contracts students have in mastering this material are: (1) not understanding the big picture of contract law so that they lose sight of the relationships among the rules they are studying, and (2) not being able to use the rules to analyze contract disputes. To address the criticism that law school teaching methods are biased towards a litigation or dispute resolution perspective, this text also aims to provide you with a foundational awareness of contracts from the perspective of a transactional attorney.

Students who lack an understanding of the big picture tend to miss issues on their law school and bar exams. They write essay answers in which each paragraph may sound good, but overall their essays fail to demonstrate an understanding of contracts. Moreover, students' lack of understanding carries over into legal practice and, as attorneys, they struggle to recognize and articulate the significance of the issues they analyze.

You will be learning contract law from two principal sources: (1) the common law, a body of law developed by judges in response to particular disputes, and (2) the Uniform Commercial Code ("U.C.C.") Article 2, a body of statutory law drafted by lawyers, law professors, and judges and adopted in almost every state.

In this chapter, you will learn to determine whether a given contract is governed by the common law of contracts or U.C.C. Article 2. This distinction is a crucial one for students and lawyers alike. Because the applicable rules of law are different depending on which body of law governs, students risk failing their law school exams and the bar exam if they do not understand the distinction. Lawyers who fail to recognize the distinction risk even greater embarrassment. One of the single most embarrassing experiences a lawyer can have is to appear in court and make a thoughtful and well-reasoned argument, and then hear the judge say, "Well, counsel, that would be a great argument if we were talking about a common law contract — but, we're not."

Overview

The overarching goal of this chapter is to lay a foundation for the remainder of this text. For this reason, unlike subsequent chapters, this chapter only really holds together as a unit of study because it has been labeled "Introduction to Contract Law." Otherwise, you should feel free to consider this chapter as four subunits, which are described below.

1. The "Why" of Contract Law

The first subunit examines why we, as a society, choose to insert ourselves in private deal-making. In other words, the first subunit explores the underlying rationales that influence contract law, what lawyers call contract policies. You will read contextual materials regarding contract policies and then answer questions (first in the text and then in class) to make sure you understand the policies. These questions will require you to identify the policy rationales underlying particular rules of contract law.

2. The "Big Picture" of Contract Law

The second subunit will provide you with a glimpse of the big picture of contract law. This subunit will also involve reading contextual materials. At this stage, our goal is to ensure that you understand how all the material we will be studying fits together. Throughout this text, we will keep returning to this big picture and flesh out the details.

3. Contract Law in Practice

The third subunit gives you the opportunity to learn about what contracts lawyers actually do in practice. The aim of this subunit is to help you begin to think about contract law not just from the perspective of a litigation attorney who only becomes involved once the parties are in dispute, but also from the perspective of a transactional attorney assisting his or her client to close a deal on favorable terms.

4. Common Law Contracts versus U.C.C. Article 2 Contracts

The fourth subunit addresses the distinction between our two bodies of contract law, the common law and U.C.C. Article 2. In this subunit, you will be presented with a series of problems that involve contracts subject to either the common law or U.C.C. Article 2. You will be told which contracts are common law contracts and which contracts are U.C.C. Article 2 contracts. Then, you will derive the principles upon which the distinction between the two is made. You also will come up with your own examples of each type of contract and explain your classifications. Finally, you will practice the process of articulating and predicting what body of law courts would apply to a given contract.

Contract Law Policy

Policy provides the "why" of law: why courts have created the particular rules they have created and decided cases the way they have decided them. For example, in most states, tort law does not let people use deadly force to protect personal property, such as cars. This rule, like any rule, is not inherently so; it is a policy choice. We might choose to allow deadly force. In your torts class, you will learn the policy that underlies the no deadly force rule: society values a life, even a wrongdoer's life, more than property.

Think of contract law policy as the foundation for many of the rules that make up the body of contract law and as a collection of arguments lawyers commonly deploy to persuade courts to resolve a contract dispute in a particular way. In other words, contract lawyers need to know both the "whys" of contract doctrine and how to deploy those "whys" to serve their clients.

Note that the policies discussed in this chapter do not comprise an exclusive list of all contract policy. Rather, this chapter presents the four policies most frequently used by lawyers and courts in contract cases. The four policies are: (1) *predictability*, (2) *freedom of contract*, (3) *fairness*, and (4) *efficiency*.

A. Predictability

In most, if not all, of your first-year courses, one underlying policy is predictability (also known as "certainty"). As a general goal, the law strives to structure human relations so that people can predict the consequences of their actions. For example, criminal law generally strives to punish only those parties who knowingly or recklessly violate the law, thereby allowing parties to anticipate the consequences of their conduct.

In the context of contract law, predictability promotes our free market economy by providing certainty for those involved in exchanging goods and services. If a merchant knows the legal consequences of her negotiating efforts or of the language she selects for her contracts, she can act accordingly. This predictability encourages people to enter into contracts, secure in the knowledge that those contracts will be enforced. Thus, if one party to a contract refuses to perform, society, through our judicial system, will step in and assure that the aggrieved party can get what she expected—or, at least, something close to what she expected.[1]

Predictability as a goal underlies much of contract doctrine. For example, courts generally dislike changing contract law at all because parties make contracts on the premise that their bargain will be governed by existing law. In other words, courts want to provide predictable consequences for parties entering contracts.

Similarly, in Chapter 2, you will learn that courts are disinclined to conclude that parties have entered into a contract unless the parties both express their desire to contract using unqualified language. This rule allows parties to predict the consequences of their negotiating behavior and, therefore, to negotiate freely and with confidence as to the

---

1. For this reason, you may perceive that this course requires you to buy into a particular political-economic perspective—notably, that of the United States. You are not required, however, to agree with this perspective. If you wish to be a lawyer in a country in which the legal system, particularly its law of contracts, reinforces a market economy, you will need to learn, understand, and be able to do legal work within that system.

range of possible outcomes. However, sometimes, for strategic business reasons, parties choose to negotiate with each other in a way that is right on the border between negotiation and contract and, as a result, obtain a result they did not intend.

As another example, later in this text, you will learn that courts typically do not let parties out of their contracts. In other words, nearly all contracts are enforced. This rule allows parties to predict the consequence of making contracts—the obligation to perform.

B. Freedom of Contract

Freedom of contract may be viewed as an outgrowth of our society's emphasis on individualism. Our culture assumes people are individual actors with free will whose freely made choices should be respected. Contract law promotes that assumption by emphasizing that we have, in general, the freedom to make whatever contracts we choose to make.

Freedom of contract serves the larger goal of encouraging contract-making in our market economy. The more likely courts are to respect the parties' autonomy and uphold what they agree to in their contracts, the more likely parties are to continue to make contracts. And, like predictability, freedom of contract can be seen as a basis for courts' reluctance to allow parties to avoid fulfilling the contracts they make.

Finally, freedom of contract is promoted when courts enforce contracts, even if those contracts seem unfair. In those situations, courts are respecting parties' freedom to voluntarily make their own contractual bargains and are refraining from imposing their own view about what the parties' contract should have been.

C. Fairness

Another policy you will learn about in this text and in your other courses is fairness. A legal system fails altogether if, as a general matter, it does not reach results that society believes are fair and legitimate. The fairness policy is often expressed by words such as "just" or "equitable." "Protection" is another term sometimes used to express this idea.

Fairness encourages contract-making. When parties believe the legal system will treat them fairly, they are more likely to enter contracts. Conversely, parties also feel more comfortable entering contracts if they know that unfair contracts will not be enforced by our legal system. For example, it would be unfair to enforce a contract signed at gunpoint or based on a lie. Accordingly, a party who signs a contract at gunpoint may use duress as a defense to a lawsuit seeking to enforce the contract, and a party who signs a contract based on a lie may use misrepresentation as a defense.

As you begin your legal studies, you will also notice that many times a situation raises conflicting policy concerns. For example, at times, fairness concerns conflict with predictability and freedom of contract. Situations raising fairness concerns often create blurry lines and require flexible, case-by-case, justice-oriented—and unpredictable—standards. In contrast, predictability dictates clear lines and unambiguous rules. Nonetheless, as you will learn in later chapters of this text, courts have developed contract defenses to allow parties an escape from unfair contracts despite the policies of predictability and freedom of contract. Contract law provides a framework for trade-offs to be made between conflicting policies.

D. Efficiency

Efficiency is a frequently cited policy, especially in the areas of tort law and civil procedure. For example, in tort cases, courts usually hold that a party who is in the best position to avoid a loss assumes the risk of that loss. In civil procedure, a motion to dismiss promotes efficiency (i.e., the best use of scarce public resources) by allowing a court to dismiss a lawsuit that fails to state a cause of action.

In contract law, efficiency also plays a significant role. As noted above, contract law promotes our market economy by encouraging contractual exchange. Contractual exchange is desirable because it facilitates each party to make an exchange that gives that party something she values more greatly than what she currently possesses. For example, when a person buys a car, she does so because she values having the car more than she values having the money. In this sense, contract law as a whole can be viewed as facilitating exchanges that economists would regard as efficient because those exchanges lead to an allocation of resources that maximizes the parties' welfare (buyer gets the car she wants for a price she is prepared to pay; seller gets the money she wants in return for the car).

Specific contract rules also promote efficiency. For example, contract rules might be said to promote "efficient breaches" of contract. These rules encourage a party to breach a contract and pay damages if that party can do so in an economically efficient manner (*i.e.*, that party would end up better off economically by paying damages rather than fulfilling his contractual obligations). Similarly, courts interpret contracts against the party who wrote them, reasoning that the drafter was best placed to make the contract unambiguous at least cost.

In sum, in any given case, lawyers may assert conflicting policies. For example, a lawyer seeking to enforce a contract on behalf of her client might assert that enforcing the contract will promote predictability and freedom of contract. Conversely, the opposing lawyer might seek to avoid contractual liability based on fairness concerns. Exercise 1-1 gives you an opportunity to practice the skill of identifying and using policy arguments.

Exercise 1-1: Identifying Policy Rationales

For each of the following contract law rules, circle the policy rationale(s) that best explain(s) the rule. More than one policy may apply to each rule. Be prepared to discuss your choice(s). Note that the name for each rule is provided in parentheses as a preview of concepts you will learn later in this text.

1. Courts refuse to enforce contracts if the parties had greatly unequal bargaining power and the bargain they made was particularly one-sided ("unconscionability").

   predictability   freedom of contract   fairness   efficiency

2. Courts generally allow a person who is not a party to a contract (a "third party") to enforce the contract if the parties to that contract intended to confer the benefits of the contract on that third party ("third-party beneficiary").

   predictability   freedom of contract   fairness   efficiency

3. Courts do not require a contracting party who has breached a contract to pay damages based on harm suffered by the other party if the breaching

party could not have anticipated such harm at the time the parties entered into their contract ("foreseeability").

predictability   freedom of contract   fairness   efficiency

4. Courts generally do not hold a party in breach of a contract where the party's performance has been made impossible by an unexpected event ("impossibility").

predictability   freedom of contract   fairness   efficiency

5. Courts generally do not allow parties to testify about contractual terms not contained in their written agreement (the "parol evidence rule").

predictability   freedom of contract   fairness   efficiency

6. Courts limit the damages non-breaching parties to a contract may recover if they have failed to make reasonable efforts to minimize the resulting harm they suffer ("avoid avoidable consequences" or "mitigate damages").

predictability   freedom of contract   fairness   efficiency

7. Courts do not require most types of contracts to be in writing or signed (these contracts are not subject to a "statute of frauds").

predictability   freedom of contract   fairness   efficiency

The "Big Picture" of Contract Law

Every course has its own internal organizational scheme. In criminal law, for example, criminal offenses are distinguished from defenses, group crimes (such as solicitation and conspiracy) are distinguished from individual crimes, and crimes against property are distinguished from crimes against people. Similarly, in tort law, causes of action may be grouped into several classifications such as intentional torts, negligence, and strict liability.

Contract law may be an even more highly structured body of law than criminal law or torts. As Diagram 1-1, the "Contracts Law Graphic Organizer," reflects, contract doctrine has a cradle-to-grave structure. Contract law not only fits together as a whole, but also reflects a logical order (left to right in Diagram 1-1). In other words, contract topics logically flow from contract formation (the requirements for making contracts) to defenses (the requirements for escaping contracts) to meaning (the process of interpreting contracts) to performance and breach (the law governing the performance and breach of contracts) to third-party issues (the circumstances where courts will afford contract rights to people who were not the original contracting parties) and, finally, to remedies (what a party gets if she wins a lawsuit for breach of contract). As Diagram 1-1 indicates, each of these topics can be framed as a question.

As you study each of these topics in depth, you will discover that each topic incorporates many subtopics. For example, contract formation includes mutual assent, consideration and promissory estoppel. Contract meaning includes the parol evidence rule, implied contract terms, and interpretation of express and implied terms. In subsequent chapters in this text, you will be provided more detailed versions of the contract law graphic organizer, which include these and other subtopics. At this point, it is only important to see and understand the big picture.

Diagram 1-1: Contract Law Graphic Organizer

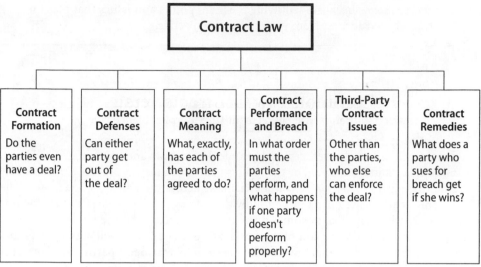

You may also have noted that the order of the topics in the graphic organizer is different from the order of the chapters in this text. Most significantly, the materials on contract remedies appear in Chapters 6 to 9. This organization of the text reflects intentional choices about the process of building your knowledge and legal skills. Understanding the stakes involved in contract disputes, i.e., the remedies, will help you better understand the other topics.

As you proceed in this course (and your other courses), you will want to organize and compile a course outline that contains all of the principles of substantive law. Note that the graphic organizer can assist you in that task. For example, the graphic organizer suggests how many roman-numeral headings your course outline should possess. You can then organize the substantive law you learn in each chapter under the appropriate heading.

Contract Law in Practice

In order to learn the law, it is inevitable that we have to read cases because case law (a.k.a. the common law) is a primary source of legal rules and authoritative interpretations of statutes. But the study of case law can create the false impression that the only thing lawyers do is argue cases at trial and on appeal.[2] As most cases settle without the need for a trial, we need a richer picture of what lawyers in general, and contracts lawyers in particular, actually do.

Exercise 1-2: What Contracts Lawyers Do

1. What tasks do you think contract lawyers perform for clients? Make a list containing at least five items.

---

2. Walters has written some more about this on his blog. *See* 'Some brief thoughts on the case method', *available at* http://bit.ly/1qQUA9C.

2. Your client is setting up a car rental business. The client asks you to draft a contract with standard terms that each customer will sign when they rent a car. Create a checklist identifying the main points and issues that the contract should address from your client's perspective.

Common Law Contracts versus U.C.C. Article 2 Contracts

As mentioned above, lawyers can find contract law in cases and in statutes. The U.C.C. is a uniform law jointly produced by the Uniform Law Commission and the American Law Institute that aims to harmonize commercial laws across the entire United States. The U.C.C. only acquires the force of law if individual states choose to enact it. Our focus is on Article 2, which applies to some, but not all, contracts. All the states apart from Louisiana have enacted a version of Article 2. The exercise below will allow you to discover for yourself the rule that governs the question of whether a particular contract is governed by the common law or by U.C.C. Article 2. While in many circumstances the legal result under the common law and Article 2 will be the same, Article 2 does sometimes dictate a different outcome. For this reason, you need to be able to figure out when a contract is governed by the U.C.C. rather than state common law.

Exercise 1-3: Distinguishing Common Law Contracts from U.C.C. Article 2 Contracts

Each of the contracts described below is either a common law contract or a U.C.C. Article 2 contract. After each description, the proper classification appears in parentheses. After reviewing all these examples, you should be able to derive the principles courts use to distinguish common law contracts and Article 2 contracts. After reading all of the descriptions, answer the three questions at the end of this list. Among other things, you will be synthesizing all the classification conclusions into a single, unifying rule.[3]

- A contract between a first-year law student and an upper-division law student for tutoring services in contract law (common law).

- A contract between two lawyers for the sale of a new Jaguar automobile (U.C.C. Article 2).

- A contract between two high school students for the sale of a new Schwinn bicycle (U.C.C. Article 2).

- A sale of an airline ticket by an airline to a passenger (common law).

- A contract to build an apartment building between a landowner and a contractor (common law).

---

3. This exercise is a discovery sequence exercise. The mental effort required to determine a rule that synthesizes all the results will help you better remember the rule. This book has a number of discovery sequence exercises.

- A contract between two wealthy landowners for the sale of Schwartzacre, a large tract of undeveloped land zoned for a factory (common law).

- A contract for the sale of two tons of apples (U.C.C. Article 2).

- A contract for the purchase and sale of an apple farm (common law).

- A contract for the purchase and sale of an ocean liner (U.C.C. Article 2).

- A contract between the owner of a soda vending machine and a person who deposits $1.00 to purchase a soda from the machine (U.C.C. Article 2).

- A contract for the sale of a factory (common law).

- A contract for the sale of $10 million of car manufacturing equipment (U.C.C. Article 2).

- A contract between McDonald's and a businessperson to grant and purchase a McDonald's franchise (common law).

- A contract between a child and a candy store for the sale of a piece of licorice (U.C.C. Article 2).

- A contract between two children to open up a lemonade stand together and to share the start-up costs and the profits (common law).

Exercise 1-4: The U.C.C.

Based on what you have learned from the descriptions of common law and U.C.C. Article 2 contracts in this exercise, answer the following questions:

1. Article 2 of the U.C.C. applies to … (*complete this sentence*).

2. Why did the lawyers, judges, and law professors who drafted the U.C.C. choose to single out certain types of contracts for distinct treatment?

3. Challenge question: Decide whether the common law or U.C.C. Article 2 applies to the following contract. DCI and Wachter entered into a contract. Wachter agreed to pay DCI $3,000,000. DCI agreed to supply Wachter with software to be used by construction companies, to customize and install that software, to provide employee training and assistance in transition between systems, to provide ongoing technical assistance, and to provide annual software maintenance. *See Wachter Mgmt. Co. v. Dexter Chaney, Inc.*, 282 Kan. 365, 366, 144 P.3d 747, 749 (2006). Be prepared to discuss your answer in class.

4. Find the version of the U.C.C. enacted by the state in which you plan to practice law. Provide a citation.

Professional Development Reflection Questions

1. Imagine that you are an attorney who has been retained to represent David, a defendant in a breach-of-contract lawsuit brought by Peter. After filing your answer, you learned that another lawyer in your law firm had previously represented Peter in a real estate closing. (This information should have already been known when your

firm conducted a conflicts check.) Can you, and should you, proceed with your representation of David?

2. Legal practice requires lawyers to continually learn and use new information. Accordingly, one characteristic of effective lawyers is that they are expert, self-regulated learners. Does this surprise you? Why or why not?

3. Educational research demonstrates that there are three key components of being an expert, self-regulated learner: (1) planning, (2) implementing your plans with self-monitoring to ensure you stay on task, and (3) reflecting on your learning process.[4] As you begin the next chapter in this text, how can you ensure that you use your study time as effectively as possible?

4. Spend a few minutes reflecting about how well you learned the material in this chapter. Did you plan your study time effectively? Did you self-monitor to ensure your studying was effective? What will you do the same or differently to master the material in Chapter 2?

---

4. *See, e.g.,* Reinhard W. Lindner & Bruce Harris, *Self-Regulated Learning: Its Assessment and Instructional Implications,* 16(2) EDUC. RES. Q. 29 (1992); Barry J. Zimmerman & Andrew Paulson, *Self-Monitoring During Collegiate Studying: An Invaluable Tool for Academic Self-Regulation, in* NEW DIRECTIONS FOR TEACHING AND LEARNING: UNDERSTANDING SELF-REGULATED LEARNING 63, at 13–14 (1995).

PART TWO

CONTRACT FORMATION
Do the parties even have a deal?

Chapter 2

Mutual Assent

Chapter Problem*

Here is a memorandum from your supervisor. Read it carefully, and then try to predict how a court would resolve the dispute and why. By the end of this chapter, you will be able to fully analyze this problem. For now, develop a hypothesis you will test as you work your way through the chapter. Thus, as you read this chapter, keep this problem in mind and look for hints about how to go about solving it.

JONES & MALLOY
Intra-Office Memorandum

Date: August 27

To: Alex Associate

From: Senior Partner Amy Jones

Subject: Pizarro Machinery Company, # 1125-1-3

This memorandum summarizes my interview with Paula Pizarro, the president of Pizarro Machinery Company ("Pizarro"). Ms. Pizarro would like our opinion as to whether Pizarro and Diamond Car Company ("Diamond") are bound by contract to Attachment A, entitled "Letter of Intent." Ms. Pizarro reports that Diamond is threatening to sue Pizarro for breach of contract.

In addition to the facts provided in the Letter of Intent, Ms. Pizarro provided me with the following information:

Ms. Pizarro is the president of Pizarro, a manufacturer of car manufacturing equipment. Pizarro's equipment allows a car manufacturer to build cars using one-tenth the personnel needed by its competitors' equipment by using robots and other computer technology. Pizarro's machinery is huge, requiring a car manufacturer to allocate a three-acre plant solely to the machinery. Debra Diamond is the president of Diamond, the fastest growing car manufacturer in the world. Ms. Pizarro hopes to convince Ms. Diamond to adopt Pizarro's equipment for all of Diamond's car manufacturing efforts.

---

* This problem is based in part on materials provided to Professor Schwartz by his former colleague, Professor Edith Warkentine of Western State University College of Law, and is used with her permission and with gratitude for her never-ending willingness to share her great teaching ideas and materials.

In February, Ms. Diamond and Ms. Pizarro entered into negotiations for the purchase and sale of three of Pizarro's machines. Both parties were very interested in the transaction. Ms. Pizarro wanted to be able to present a contract to her bank so she could get a construction loan for her planned expansion of her business next year. Ms. Diamond wanted to be able to announce a contract to the public because she was planning on incorporating her company and selling its stock to the general public in early May.

The negotiations proved slow and difficult. Both Ms. Pizarro and Ms. Diamond are known in the industry as ruthless, relentless negotiators. Although Ms. Pizarro invited Ms. Diamond to her plant to see the machines they were discussing, Ms. Diamond repeatedly refused Ms. Pizarro's invitations, saying she had "no need to see the machines at this time." After two and one-half months of negotiations, Ms. Pizarro and Ms. Diamond held a meeting at which they signed Attachment A, entitled "Letter of Intent." Each party brought her in-house counsel to the meeting. After a signing ceremony during which they sipped champagne and then simultaneously signed a giant copy of the Letter of Intent, Ms. Diamond and Ms. Pizarro shook hands and left the room. As they were leaving, Ms. Diamond and Ms. Pizarro said, "We're off to celebrate. You attorneys iron out the fine print."

Two months later, and after several hundred more hours of discussions, Ms. Pizarro called off the discussions, saying, "You people are impossible to deal with. I'm glad we never finalized our deal." Ms. Diamond replied, "What do you mean? We have a deal! We signed a contract." Ms. Pizarro then said, "That Letter of Intent? It doesn't even address how you would have financed the purchase; it doesn't define what would be a breach of contract by either of us, and it has no attorney's fees clause. It's no contract."

Ms. Pizarro reports that, if forced to perform the contract, Pizarro will lose between $500,000 and $1,000,000.

Attachment A
Letter of Intent

This document confirms our intent to purchase and sell the equipment described below on the following terms and conditions:

1. **Parties to the Transaction.** The parties to the transaction described in this Letter of Intent are Pizarro Machinery Company ("Pizarro") and Diamond Car Company ("Diamond").

2. **Description of Machinery.** Three identical versions of Pizarro's car manufacturing machine No. 875-2345.

3. **Purchase Price.** $7,000,000 per machine, $21,000,000 total.

4. **Risk of Loss.** Liability for and risk of loss or damage in transit or otherwise to the machinery described above shall remain with Pizarro until completion of the installation of the machinery.

5. **Completion of Installation.** Installation of the machinery shall be completed no later than two years from the signing of this document.

6. **Arbitration.** The parties agree to submit all ensuing disputes, whether sounding in tort, in contract, or in both, to binding arbitration in accordance with the normal procedures of the American Arbitration Association.

7. **Disclaimer.** This Letter of Intent is the only and entire agreement between us with respect to the machinery described above. The purpose of this Letter of Intent is to confirm our mutual consent with respect to the terms described in this document. Although we have set forth our agreements to date here, both parties contemplate signing a subsequent, more detailed agreement.

8. **Dated.** April 18.

9. **Signed.**

Paula Pizarro

Paula Pizarro, President

Pizarro Machinery Company

Debra Diamond

Debra Diamond, President

Diamond Car Company

Introduction

In this chapter, and also in Chapters 3 and 4, you will be learning about **contract formation**. The specific focus of this chapter is on a broad concept called "*mutual assent*." Chapter 3 will focus on **consideration** and Chapter 4 will focus on **promissory estoppel**.

Before you study the specific concepts relevant to mutual assent, it is helpful to understand where these subtopics fit within the big picture of contract law. Diagram 2-1 depicts where these subtopics fit in. As Diagram 2-1 shows, mutual assent and consideration are subtopics under the more general contract formation topic and are linked together as aspects of **traditional formation**. You should note that promissory estoppel appears to be distinct from traditional formation.

As you learned in Chapter 1, contract law encompasses many topics, and each of those topics has many subtopics. Make sure you always understand how and where each new topic and subtopic fits into contracts as a body of law.

Diagram 2-1: Contract Law Graphic Organizer

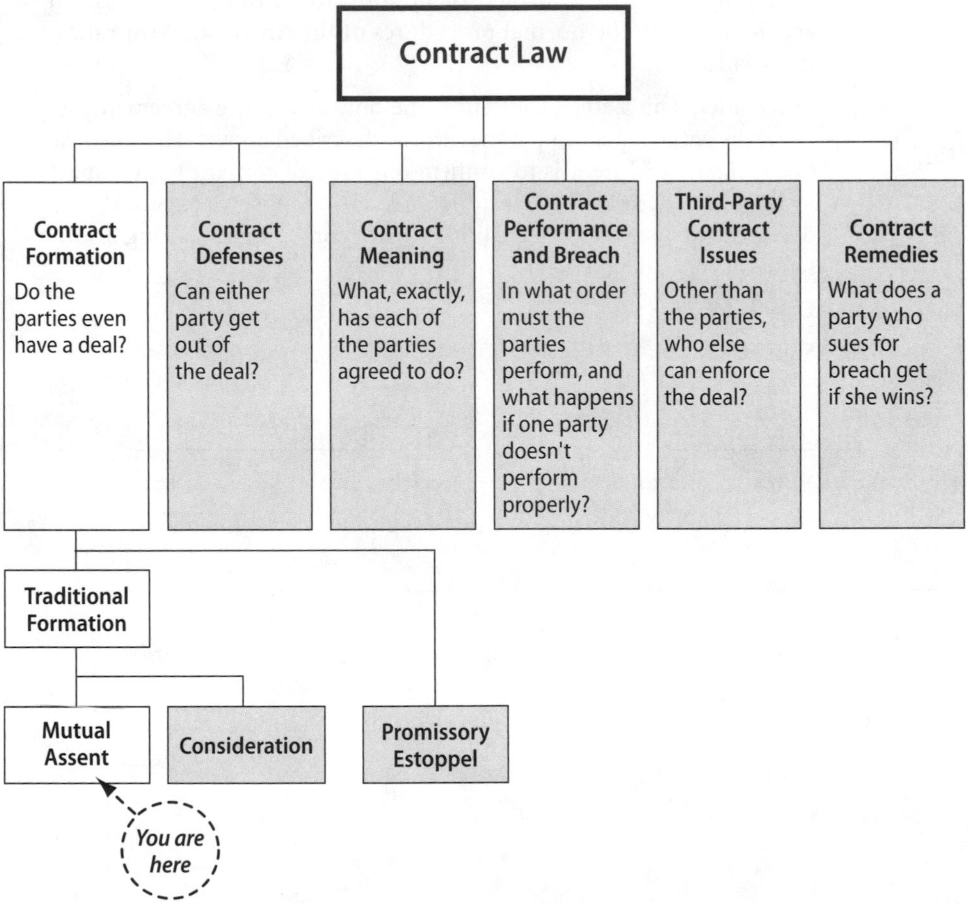

Overview of Chapter 2

This chapter focuses on the law relating to contract formation and, more specifically, the requirement that each party express mutual assent. You will learn about these concepts in seven subunits:

1. Communication of a Present Commitment
2. Certainty of Terms
3. Special Offer Rules
4. Manner of Acceptance
5. Termination of the Power to Accept
6. The Mailbox Rules
7. Mutual Assent under U.C.C. Article 2

Because this is the first area of substantive contract law you will be learning, this chapter also provides you with guidance about the process of learning the law and the process of analyzing legal problems. Remember, your professor is likely to ask you in class many of the questions in this book.

Communication of Present Commitment

Exercise 2-1: Amy-Betty Contract Formation Hypo

Amy, who desperately needed a job to pay for her next meal, noticed that the floor of Betty's store was quite dirty. She approached Betty and said, "I will sweep and mop your floor for $20." Betty responded, "The floor is a mess. I really ought to let you do it." Then Betty walked away. Do you think that Amy and Betty communicated a present commitment to form a contract? Why or why not?

If the hypo above were an exam question or a court argument, neither "yes" nor "no" would be a sufficient answer. While law students and lawyers are often asked to provide their professional judgment regarding the outcome of a case, it is rare that a simple "yes" or "no" will provide a complete response.

Both when writing law school exams and arguing cases, the most effective law students and lawyers do more than just predict outcomes—they provide logical legal analyses. Accordingly, to be an effective student (and earn high grades) or an effective lawyer (and solve problems for clients), you need to learn the process of performing legal analysis.

The information in this chapter will begin to train you to analyze legal issues the way lawyers do so. Table 2-1 provides an example of how a lawyer might answer the question posed in Exercise 2-1. The legal analysis in Table 2-1 is artificially limited to the question of whether Betty communicated the requisite present commitment to form a contract. (There may be other legal issues relevant to Exercise 2-1, but those are intentionally not addressed.)

Table 2-1: Sample Legal Analysis

The legal issue presented is whether Amy and Betty communicated a present commitment to form a contract. To form a contract, both parties must communicate a present commitment. This commitment often takes the form of an offer followed by an acceptance. An acceptance is a manifestation of assent by the offeree to the terms of an offer in a proper manner.

Here, Amy almost certainly made an offer. The word "will," as used by Amy, communicates an unequivocal plan of future action and therefore the requisite commitment. Because Amy spoke directly to Betty, Betty was the offeree. Amy's offer did not address the manner of acceptance; so, it was reasonable for Betty to use the same manner as Amy, speaking. Betty responded by saying, "I really ought to let you do it." It is possible that a reasonable person in Amy's situation might understand "ought" to mean "must." But, it is more likely that a reasonable person would interpret "ought" as expressing Betty's belief about what could be a desirable course of action without unequivocally committing to that course of action. As such, "ought" does not communicate a present commitment to go forward with a specific action.

Consequently, Betty probably did not communicate the requisite present commitment necessary to form a contract.

Note that the legal analysis focuses on one legal issue: whether the parties communicated a present commitment to form a contract. *The requirement that parties express present commitment is a rule.* Next, note that the tone of the analysis appears objective and dispassionate. At the same time, the analysis has a persuasive feel to it; the writer is trying to be convincing. In other words, the author wants the reader to agree with his conclusion. Finally, note that, although the analysis adopts a dispassionate tone, neither law students nor lawyers need to be dispassionate. It is appropriate for a lawyer to believe that Amy should win and to try to develop arguments to support that position.

Background Information

An Introduction to the Restatement (Second) of Contracts. Exercise 2-2 below requires you to read and paraphrase select sections from the Restatement (Second) of Contracts. A restatement is a collection of statements that purports to articulate the rules that constitute a particular body of law. The Restatement (Second) of Contracts is, therefore, the second such effort to describe the rules of contract law.

Restatements are written by judges, law professors, and expert lawyers. In general, restatements describe the law as it currently exists, but some restatement sections go further and describe what the authors think the law should be. Restatements are not binding law; courts may ignore them. Restatements, however, are often very influential. Courts frequently cite to restatements to support their decisions. Watch for courts using the Restatement (Second) of Contracts to support their decisions as you read cases in this text.

Exercise 2-2: Rules Addressing the Commitment Requirement in the Restatement (Second) of Contracts

Read sections 17, 22, 24, and 50 in the Restatement (Second) of Contracts and answer the following questions. (*Note: When you are done, you will have identified a set of legal rules you need to know for this class.*)

1. What is required to form a contract? Answer this question based solely on the listed Restatement sections. Cite a section of the Restatement in support of your answer.

2. What does section 22 add to your understanding of contract formation?

3. What is an offer? First, quote the Restatement definition. Then, rewrite that definition in your own words.

4. What is an acceptance? First, quote the Restatement definition. Note that the definition references more than one requirement. Rewrite the definition as a list of requirements.

5. What do the definitions of offer and acceptance have in common?

A glimpse ahead at "consideration." Chapter 3, the next chapter in this text, addresses the vast and complex body of consideration law. Consideration is one requirement for forming a valid contract. This short discussion about consideration is intended to provide you with enough information about consideration so that you will be able to understand the cases and materials in this chapter and so that you will not be troubled by the various, unexplained references to consideration.

In a nutshell, consideration law requires that each party to a contract promise to perform or actually perform "something" in exchange for "something" from the other party. This something may be very little and of slight value, or it may be quite valuable. As a general rule, courts allow parties the freedom to make their own contracts, whether they are "good" or "bad" deals, as long as each party gets something.

Thus, if we promise to give you a new laptop computer in exchange for a promise from you to give us a ten-dollar pair of sandals, a court would conclude that each of us received consideration. In contrast, if we promise to give you a gift of a new laptop computer, a court would conclude that we received no consideration for our promise and no contract has been formed.

The Present Commitment Requirement for Contract Formation

The first two cases you will read deal with one requirement for forming a contract: that each party communicate a **present commitment** to forming the contract. In most instances, one party's expression of commitment is called an *offer* and the other party's expression of commitment is called an *acceptance*. The present commitment requirement applies to both offers and acceptances. When both parties, usually through an offer and acceptance, communicate a present commitment, there is *mutual assent* to form a contract.

For each of these first two cases, this text provides you with guidance to make sure you focus on the most important aspects of the cases. The first case, *Lucy v. Zehmer*, addresses the question of what perspective courts should use to determine whether a present commitment to contract exists. There are basically two choices: (1) focusing on what lawyers refer to as a person's **subjective intention**, what the person claims she meant by the words she used, or (2) focusing on what lawyers refer to as a person's **objective intention**, how a reasonable person would understand the words the person used. These two perspectives, as *Lucy* reveals, can lead to opposite results. Exercise 2-3 provides some guidance for your efforts to identify the lessons of *Lucy*.

Exercise 2-3: *Lucy v. Zehmer* and Case Reading Skills

As you read *Lucy*, look for answers to each of the questions in this exercise. These questions are designed to help you extract the key points out of the case. The questions in the next exercise, 2-4, will ensure that you understand *Lucy* by asking you to apply the lessons of the case to additional problems. This pattern of pre-case questions to focus your case reading and post-case questions focusing on applying what you have learned is continued throughout this text.

1. The *Lucy* case introduces you to a lot of new terminology. Look up the following terms in a legal dictionary:

   a. complainants
   b. specific performance
   c. instrument
   d. answer
   e. decree
   f. assignment of error

2. What are the key facts in this case? (Hint: The key facts include every piece of evidence on which the court relied in deciding the case. When reading contract cases, the specific words used by the parties are often key facts.)

3. Look again at your definitions of offer and acceptance in Exercise 2-2. Why are the specific words the parties used important in deciding whether an offer or acceptance has been made?

4. Quote the *rule* the *Lucy* court stated about whether a subjective or objective approach should be taken to determine whether a present commitment exists. Then, write your own paraphrased version of the rule.

5. Did the *Lucy* court conclude that courts should adopt a subjective or objective approach to deciding whether a party has expressed the required present commitment to form a contract? Why do you say so?

6. What does the rule the court stated add to the definitions of offer and acceptance that you already learned?

7. The court assumes a reasonable person looking at the instrument written by Zehmer would conclude that the document expresses commitment. Why?

8. Explain why and how the circumstances surrounding Lucy's and Zehmer's interactions influenced the court's decision.

9. Identify any circumstances that support the losing party's preferred result and articulate the losing party's argument as to why those circumstances support the losing party's position.

10. What policy supports the result in this case? (Hint: Pick one of the four policies you learned in Chapter 1.)

Lucy v. Zehmer

84 S.E.2d 516 (1954)

(Ed.'s note: Please note that, because you are at least somewhat new to reading cases like a lawyer, we have provided you with guidance in margin notes to facilitate development of your case reading skills. These skills are essential to your success in law school and law practice.)

Buchanan, J. This suit was instituted by W.O. Lucy and J.C. Lucy, complainants, against A.H. Zehmer and Ida S. Zehmer, his wife, defendants, to have specific performance of a contract by which it was alleged the Zehmers had sold to W.O. Lucy a tract of land owned by A.H. Zehmer known as the Ferguson farm, for $50,000. J.C. Lucy, the other complainant, is a brother of W.O. Lucy, to whom W.O. Lucy transferred a half interest in his alleged purchase.

The instrument sought to be enforced was written by A.H. Zehmer on December 20, 1952, in these words: "We hereby agree to sell to W.O. Lucy the Ferguson Farm complete for $50,000.00, title satisfactory to buyer" and signed by the defendants, A.H. Zehmer and Ida S. Zehmer.

> To an expert case reader, this paragraph jumps out because it describes what seems to be a written, signed contract. Your initial reaction should be to ask yourself, "Given this document, why is there any dispute about the existence of a contract at all?"

The answer of A.H. Zehmer admitted that at the time mentioned W.O. Lucy offered him $50,000 cash for the farm, but that he, Zehmer, considered that the offer was made in jest; that so thinking, and both he and Lucy having had several drinks, he wrote out "the memorandum" quoted above and induced his wife to sign it; that he did not deliver the memorandum to Lucy, but that Lucy picked it up, read it, put it in his pocket, attempted to offer Zehmer $5 to bind the bargain, which Zehmer refused to accept, and realizing for the first time that Lucy was serious, Zehmer assured him that he had no intention of selling the farm and that the whole matter was a joke. Lucy left the premises insisting that he had purchased the farm.

> Now the point in dispute jumps out: Zehmer claims he wasn't serious when he signed the alleged contract.

Depositions were taken and the decree appealed from was entered holding that the complainants had failed to establish their right to specific performance, and dismissing their bill. The assignment of error is to this action of the court.

W.O. Lucy, a lumberman and farmer, thus testified in substance: He had known Zehmer for fifteen or twenty years and had been familiar with the Ferguson farm for ten years. Seven or eight years ago he had offered Zehmer $20,000 for the farm which Zehmer had accepted, but the agreement was verbal and Zehmer backed out. On the night of December 20, 1952, around eight o'clock, he took an employee to McKenney, where Zehmer lived and operated a restaurant, filling station and motor court. While there he decided to see Zehmer and again try to buy the Ferguson farm. He entered the restaurant and talked to Mrs. Zehmer until Zehmer came in. He asked Zehmer if he had sold the Ferguson farm. Zehmer replied that he had not. Lucy said, "I bet you wouldn't take $50,000.00 for that place." Zehmer replied, "Yes, I would too; you wouldn't give fifty." Lucy said he would and told Zehmer to write up an agreement to that effect. Zehmer took a restaurant check and wrote on the back of it, "I do hereby agree to sell to W.O. Lucy the Ferguson Farm for $50,000 complete." Lucy told him he had better change it to "We" because Mrs. Zehmer would have to sign it too. Zehmer then tore up what he had written, wrote the agreement quoted above and asked Mrs. Zehmer, who was at the other end of the counter ten or twelve feet away, to sign it. Mrs. Zehmer said she would for $50,000 and signed it. Zehmer brought it back and gave it to Lucy, who offered him $5 which Zehmer refused, saying, "You don't need to give me any money, you got the agreement there signed by both of us."

The discussion leading to the signing of the agreement, said Lucy, lasted thirty or forty minutes, during which Zehmer seemed to doubt that Lucy could raise $50,000. Lucy suggested the provision for having the title examined and Zehmer made the suggestion that he would sell it "complete, everything there," and stated that all he had on the farm was three heifers....

December 20 was on Saturday. The next day Lucy telephoned to J.C. Lucy and arranged with the latter to take a half interest in the purchase and pay half of the consideration. On Monday he engaged an attorney to examine the title. The attorney reported favorably on December 31 and on January 2 Lucy wrote Zehmer stating that the title was satisfactory, that he was ready to pay the purchase price in cash and asking when Zehmer would be ready to close the deal. Zehmer replied by letter, mailed on January 13, asserting that he had never agreed or intended to sell.

Mr. and Mrs. Zehmer were called by the complainants as adverse witnesses. Zehmer testified in substance as follows:

He bought this farm more than ten years ago for $11,000. He had had twenty-five offers, more or less, to buy it, including several from Lucy, who had never offered any specific sum of money. He had given them all the same answer, that he was not interested in selling it. On this Saturday night before Christmas it looked like everybody and his brother came by there to have a drink....

After they had talked a while Lucy asked whether he still had the Ferguson farm. He replied that he had not sold it and Lucy said, "I bet you wouldn't take $50,000.00 for it." Zehmer asked him if he would give $50,000 and Lucy said yes. Zehmer replied, "You haven't got $50,000 in cash." Lucy said he did and Zehmer replied that he did not believe it. They argued "pro and con for a long time," mainly about "whether he had $50,000 in cash that he could put up right then and buy that farm."

Finally, said Zehmer, Lucy told him if he didn't believe he had $50,000, "you sign that piece of paper here and say you will take $50,000.00 for the farm." He, Zehmer, "just grabbed the back off of a guest check there" and wrote on the back of it. At that point in his testimony Zehmer asked to see what he had written to "see if I recognize my own handwriting." He examined the paper and exclaimed, "Great balls of fire, I got 'Firgerson' for Ferguson. I have got satisfactory spelled wrong. I don't recognize that writing if I would see it, wouldn't know it was mine."

After Zehmer had, as he described it, "scribbled this thing off," Lucy said, "Get your wife to sign it." Zehmer walked over to where she was and she at first refused to sign but did so after he told her that he "was just needling him [Lucy], and didn't mean a thing in the world, that I was not selling the farm." Zehmer then "took it back over there ... and I was still looking at the dern thing. I had the drink right there by my hand, and I reached over to get a drink, and he said, 'Let me see it.' He reached and picked it up, and when I looked back again he had it in his pocket and he dropped a five dollar bill over there, and he said, 'Here is five dollars payment on it.'... I said, 'Hell no, that is beer and liquor talking. I am not going to sell you the farm. I have told you that too many times before.' " [Mrs. Zehmer's testimony was similar to her husband's testimony. She did add that, after Lucy said], "All right, get your wife to sign it," Zehmer came back to where she was standing and said, "You want to put your name to this?" She said "No," but he said in an undertone, "It is nothing but a joke," and she signed it....

The defendants insist that the evidence was ample to support their contention that the writing sought to be enforced was prepared as a bluff or dare to force Lucy to admit that he did not have $50,000; that the whole matter was a joke; that the writing was not delivered to Lucy and no binding contract was ever made between the parties.

It is an unusual, if not bizarre, defense. When made to the writing admittedly prepared by one of the defendants and signed by both, clear evidence is required to sustain it.

In his testimony Zehmer claimed that he "was high as a Georgia pine," and that the transaction "was just a bunch of two doggoned drunks bluffing to see who could talk the biggest and say the most." ... The record is convincing that Zehmer was not intoxicated to the extent of being unable to comprehend the nature and consequences of the instrument he executed, and hence that instrument is not to be invalidated on that ground.

The evidence is convincing also that Zehmer wrote two agreements, the first one beginning "I hereby agree to sell." Zehmer first said he could not remember about that, then that "I don't think I wrote but one out." Mrs. Zehmer said that what he wrote was "I hereby agree," but that the "I" was changed to "We" after that night. The agreement that was written and signed is in the record and indicates no such change. Neither are the mistakes in spelling that Zehmer sought to point out readily apparent.

The appearance of the contract, the fact that it was under discussion for forty minutes or more before it was signed; Lucy's objection to the first draft because it was written in the singular, and he wanted Mrs. Zehmer to sign it also; the rewriting to meet that objection and the signing by Mrs. Zehmer; the discussion of what was to be included in the sale, the provision for the examination of the title, the completeness of the instrument that was executed, the taking possession of it by Lucy with no request or suggestion by either of the defendants that he give it back, are facts which furnish persuasive evidence that the execution of the contract was a serious business transaction rather than a casual, jesting matter as defendants now contend....

If it be assumed, contrary to what we think the evidence shows, that Zehmer was jesting about selling his farm to Lucy and that the transaction was intended by him to be a joke, nevertheless the evidence shows that Lucy did not so understand it but considered it to be a serious business transaction and the contract to be binding on the Zehmers as well as on himself....

Not only did Lucy actually believe, but the evidence shows he was warranted in believing, that the contract represented a serious business transaction and a good faith sale and purchase of the farm.

In the field of contracts, as generally elsewhere, "We must look to the outward expression of a person as manifesting his intention rather than to his secret and unexpressed intention. 'The law imputes to a person an intention

Note: Court opinions usually include a summary of the relevant facts, but few opinions devote as much space as this court does to summarizing and quoting the parties' testimony. Why do you think the court does so?

Note: These paragraphs provide most of the court's argument as to why Lucy should win. Notice that the court is engaged in the act of persuasive writing. What fact or facts does the court ignore that might lead to the conclusion that Zehmer should win?

corresponding to the reasonable meaning of his words and acts.'" [Citation omitted] ...

At no time prior to the execution of the contract had Zehmer indicated to Lucy by word or act that he was not in earnest about selling the farm. They had argued about it and discussed its terms, as Zehmer admitted, for a long time. Lucy testified that if there was any jesting it was about paying $50,000 that night. The contract and the evidence show that he was not expected to pay the money that night. Zehmer said that after the writing was signed he laid it down on the counter in front of Lucy. Lucy said Zehmer handed it to him. In any event there had been what appeared to be a good faith offer and a good faith acceptance, followed by the execution and apparent delivery of a written contract. Both said that Lucy put the writing in his pocket and then offered Zehmer $5 to seal the bargain. Not until then, even under the defendants' evidence, was anything said or done to indicate that the matter was a joke. Both of the Zehmers testified that when Zehmer asked his wife to sign he whispered that it was a joke so Lucy wouldn't hear and that it was not intended that he should hear....

These paragraphs state the applicable rules of law. Highlight the rules and then try restating the rules in your own words. Why does the court conclude that these rules compel a conclusion that Lucy should prevail? (Hint: Consider what facts match up with the rules.)

If the words or other acts of one of the parties have but one reasonable meaning, his undisclosed intention is immaterial except when an unreasonable meaning which he attaches to his manifestations is known to the other party....

An agreement or mutual assent is of course essential to a valid contract but the law imputes to a person an intention corresponding to the reasonable meaning of his words and acts. If his words and acts, judged by a reasonable standard, manifest an intention to agree, it is immaterial what may be the real but unexpressed state of his mind. 17 C.J.S., Contracts, § 32, p. 361; 12 Am. Jur., Contracts, § 19, p. 515.

So a person cannot set up that he was merely jesting when his conduct and words would warrant a reasonable person in believing that he intended a real agreement. 17 C.J.S., Contracts, § 47, p. 390; Clark on Contracts, 4 ed., § 27, p. 54.

Whether the writing signed by the defendants and now sought to be enforced by the complainants was the result of a serious offer by Lucy and a serious acceptance by the defendants, or was a serious offer by Lucy and an acceptance in secret jest by the defendants, in either event it constituted a binding contract of sale between the parties....

The complainants are entitled to have specific performance of the contracts sued on. The decree appealed from is therefore reversed and the cause is remanded for the entry of a proper decree requiring the defendants to perform the contract in accordance with the prayer of the bill.

Reversed and remanded.

Exercise 2-4: *Lucy v. Zehmer* Revisited

Based on what you have learned from the *Lucy* case, respond to the following questions:

1. Change the words in the instrument signed by Lucy and Zehmer so that Zehmer would win.

2. What would the result in *Lucy* have been if Lucy had known that Zehmer was kidding? Justify your answer by quoting a specific statement from the case.

3. Analyze the following problem: Dana walks into a cafe obviously upset and angry. For the next half hour, she sips her soda and complains about her laptop to the other customers in the cafe. To each person, she says, "If you fix this thing and find my report so I can e-mail the report to my boss, I will sell you the laptop for $50." Because Dana is well known to most of the customers as a blowhard and a pathological liar, and because the laptop is an expensive laptop worth $2,000, no one, apart from Pedro takes her seriously. Pedro has never met Dana and he has no idea what the laptop is worth, but he is good at fixing computers. Pedro says to Dana, "Let me have a look at it for you." He works on it for ten minutes, retrieves the document Dana needs, and e-mails the document to Dana's boss at an e-mail address Dana provides. He then hands Dana $50 in cash, and insists that Dana give him the laptop. Do Dana and Pedro have a contract? To answer this question, consider the hints below.

   a. One form of reasoning lawyers use to reach a conclusion is called **analogical reasoning**. To use analogical reasoning here, try arguing why this problem is sufficiently similar to *Lucy* that the court should reach the same result the *Lucy* court reached.

   b. Another form of reasoning lawyers use to reach a conclusion is called **counter-analogical reasoning**. To use counter-analogical reasoning, try arguing why this problem is sufficiently different from *Lucy* that the court should reach the opposite result from the result the *Lucy* court reached.

Exercise 2-5: *Harvey v. Facey*

The next case, *Harvey v. Facey*, focuses more specifically on the particular language a party's statement must possess for a court to conclude that a reasonable person would find what the rule you have learned requires: **a present commitment.** Before reading the case, read the five questions in this exercise as cues for what is important in the case. After reading the case, work backward from the court's conclusions and respond to the questions in this exercise.

1. Look at the first telegram. According to the court, what was the legal significance of that telegram? Why? Why might you argue that the court was wrong about that point?

2. Look at the second telegram. According to the court, what was the legal significance of that telegram? Why? Why might you argue that the court was wrong as to that point?

3. Look at the third telegram. According to the court, what was the legal significance of that telegram? Why?

4. If a party intends an acceptance, can a court call it an offer? Why?

5. *Harvey v. Facey* can be cited for the proposition that courts are reluctant to conclude that a party has expressed the requisite commitment to contract

unless that party has unambiguously done so. What is the policy rationale for this reluctance?

Harvey v. Facey

[1893] A.C. 552 (United Kingdom Privy Council)

Appeal from a decree of the Supreme Court of Judicature of Jamaica ... setting aside a decree of Curran, J., ... which dismissed the suit, which was one for specific performance of an alleged contract in writing.

The facts are stated in the judgment of their Lordships.

The respondents, Facey and his wife, denied the [existence of a] contract....

The question decided in appeal was whether the three telegrams set out in the pleadings constituted a binding agreement of sale and purchase.

Lord Morris: The appellants instituted an action against the respondents to obtain specific performance of an agreement alleged to have been entered into by the respondent Larchin M. Facey for the sale of a property named Bumper Hall Pen. The respondent L. M. Facey was alleged to have had power and authority to bind his wife the respondent Adelaide Facey in selling the property.

The case came on for hearing before Mr. Justice Curran who dismissed the action with costs, on the ground that the agreement alleged by the appellants did not disclose a concluded contract for the sale and purchase of the property. The Court of Appeal reversed the judgment of Curran, J., and declared that a binding agreement for the sale and purchase of the property had been proved as between the appellants and the respondent L. M. Facey....

The appellants are solicitors carrying on business in partnership at Kingston, and it appears that in the beginning of October, 1891, negotiations took place between the respondent L. M. Facey and the Mayor and Council of Kingston for the sale of the property in question, that Facey had offered to sell it to them for the sum of £900, that the offer was discussed by the council at their meeting on the 6th of October, 1891, and the consideration of its acceptance deferred; that on the 7th of October, 1891, L. M. Facey was traveling [sic]in the train from Kingston to Porus, and that the appellants caused a telegram to be sent after him from Kingston addressed to him "on the train for Porus," in the following words: "Will you sell us Bumper Hall Pen? Telegraph lowest cash price—answer paid;" That on the same day L. M. Facey replied by telegram to the appellants in the following words: "Lowest price for Bumper Hall Pen £900;" that on the same day the appellants replied to the last-mentioned telegram by a telegram addressed to L. M. Facey "on train at Porus" in the words following: "We agree to buy Bumper Hall Pen for the sum of nine hundred pounds asked by you. Please send us your title deed in order that we may get early possession."

The above telegrams were duly received by the appellants and by L. M. Facey.... [T]heir Lordships concur in the judgment of Mr. Justice Curran that there was no concluded contract between the appellants and L. M. Facey

Do you think this court opinion provides a good example of effective legal writing? If not, why not? Note that effective legal writing — like good writing in general — should be clear, straightforward, precise, and concise.

Excellent case readers talk to the text. For example, they look for aspects of court opinions with which they disagree. Reasonable minds could disagree with the conclusion reached in this case. Do you agree or disagree with the court's conclusion? Why or why not?

"Answer paid" refers to the fact that Harvey was promising to pay for the cost of Facey's telegram response.

to be collected from the aforesaid telegrams. The first telegram asks two questions. The first question is as to the willingness of L. M. Facey to sell to the appellants; the second question asks the lowest price, and the word "Telegraph" is in its collocation addressed to that second question only. L. M. Facey replied to the second question only, and gives his lowest price. The third telegram from the appellants treats the answer of L. M. Facey stating his lowest price as an unconditional offer to sell to them at the price named....

[T]he reply telegram from the appellants cannot be treated as an acceptance of an offer to sell to them; it is an offer that required to be accepted by L. M. Facey. The contract could only be completed if L. M. Facey had accepted the appellant's last telegram. It has been contended for the appellants that L. M. Facey's telegram should be read as saying "yes" to the first question put in the appellants' telegram, but there is nothing to support that contention. L. M. Facey's telegram gives a precise answer to a precise question, viz., the price.

The contract must appear by the telegrams, whereas the appellants are obliged to contend that an acceptance of the first question is to be implied. Their Lordships are of opinion that the mere statement of the lowest price at which the vendor would sell contains no implied contract to sell at that price to the persons making the inquiry. [T]he judgment of the Supreme Court should be reversed and the judgment of Curran, J., restored. The appellants must pay to the respondents the costs of the appeal to the Supreme Court and of this appeal.

Exercise 2-6: Application of *Harvey v. Facey*

Read the problem presented in this exercise and determine whether Mr. & Mrs. Richards and Ms. Flowers formed a contract. Be prepared to apply or distinguish *Harvey*. In other words, use analogical or counter-analogical reasoning.

Mr. & Mrs. Richards wrote Ms. Flowers the following letter: "We would be interested in buying your lot on Gravatt Drive in Oakland, California, if we can deal with you directly and not through a realtor. If you are interested, please advise us by return mail the cash price you would expect to receive." Flowers replied, "Thank you for your inquiry regarding my lot on Gravatt Drive. Considering what I paid for the lot, and the taxes which I have paid, I expect to receive $4,500 for this property. Please let me know what you decide."

The Richards then wrote, "Agree to buy your lot on your terms. Will handle transaction through local title company."

Types of Legal Reasoning

As you have quickly discovered as you tried to apply and distinguish *Lucy* and *Harvey*, one of the most important skills you should develop as a law student are the legal reasoning skills necessary to perform effective legal analyses. Effective law students and effective lawyers use four primary types of legal reasoning. Watch for the use of these four types of legal reasoning as you read cases in this text and in your other courses.

1. **Rule-based reasoning** (also known as **syllogistic** or **deductive reasoning**): Rule-based reasoning involves applying rules to relevant facts to reach a conclusion. The next section of this chapter will explore rule-based reasoning in greater detail.

2. **Analogical reasoning**: You were introduced to analogical (and counter-analogical reasoning) in Exercises 2-4 and 2-6. Analogical reasoning involves arguing that a factual situation is similar to a situation in another case so that the conclusion reached should be the same as the conclusion in the other case.

3. **Counter-analogical reasoning**: Counter-analogical reasoning involves arguing that a factual situation is different from a situation in another case so that the conclusion reached should be different from the conclusion in the other case.

4. **Policy-based reasoning**: Policy-based reasoning involves arguing that a given policy should dictate a certain conclusion in a given legal problem.

Applying Rules to Facts

Learning how to apply rules to facts—in other words, to engage in **rule-based reasoning**—is essential for success on law school exams and in practice. This section of the text will provide you with information and examples about how to apply rules to facts. Then, you will be given a chance to use what you know and cement your understanding in Exercise 2-7.[1]

A **legal rule** is simply a statement of an abstract set of facts (often called requirements or elements) that a court, legislature, or administrative agency has determined must be present to produce a specified legal consequence. In other words, if a court finds that the facts of a particular situation (the facts of a dispute or alleged crime) match up sufficiently to the required abstract set of facts, the court will attach the specified legal consequence. For example, the common law rule of burglary can be broken into six elements:

1. a nighttime
2. breaking
3. and entering
4. into the dwelling house
5. of another
6. with the intent to commit a felony

As an example of a legal rule, focus specifically on the second element, "breaking." Courts define breaking as "the application of force, however slight." That rule is an abstract description of the required action (using force, even a little bit, to get into a dwelling). Courts could, therefore, apply the breaking rule to a wide range of conduct, such as: blowing up a door with a bomb, knocking down a door, pushing a door open, or even just turning a doorknob (because of the ambiguity of the word "slight").

Again, notice that the rule for breaking describes the requisite conduct abstractly ("the application of force, however slight"). To apply the rule to a set of facts, you must match the facts of a particular situation (*e.g.,* turning a doorknob) to the abstract rule.

---

1. This discussion is a modified version of the discussion about applying rules to facts in MICHAEL HUNTER SCHWARTZ, EXPERT LEARNING FOR LAW STUDENTS (2d ed. 2008).

Law students and law professors often refer to the process of applying rules to facts with the mnemonic **"IRAC"** (also called "IRACing" or "using IRAC"). IRAC is simply shorthand for applying rules to facts. Some professors and practicing lawyers use slightly different mnemonics such as "CRAC" or "CIRAC." The use of an initial C is a reminder to provide a conclusion (an explicit answer to the issue presented). Do not be troubled by these different formulations. They are all accomplishing the same purpose.

IRAC is deceptively simple. IRAC is a powerful tool to use as you organize and write answers to legal problems because it ensures that you are: (1) touching all the bases you must touch to get available points on exams or to conduct effective legal analyses in practice, and (2) engaging in logical, coherent legal analyses. Table 2-2 provides further information about the IRAC mnemonic and provides suggestions for using it effectively.

Table 2-2: IRAC

Issue Start by identifying and explicitly stating the precise legal issue you are about to discuss. In nearly all instances, the issue will not be a broad topic such as "contract" (or even "contract formation") or "crime" or "burglary." Rather, the precise legal issue should be one narrow aspect of the broader legal rule you plan to analyze, such as communicating a present commitment to contract or the "entering" element of burglary. Professors vary in the degree of specificity they want in students' issue statements. Some professors simply want you to identify the issue presented as a topical heading (*e.g.*, Present Commitment to Contract or Entering). Other professors will want a complete and precise statement of the legal issue in a sentence (*e.g.*, "The issue presented is whether Chuck Criminal's conduct satisfied the second element of burglary, entering, when he turned the doorknob and entered the house.").

Rule Next, accurately state the specific rule you plan to apply. Again, professors have a range of preferences — and it is perfectly acceptable to ask your professors about their preferences. Some professors want exact statements of rules. Most professors accept — and some prefer — accurate paraphrases of rules.

Analysis Immediately following your statement of the rule, apply the rule to the specific relevant facts presented in the legal problem you are analyzing. Because the analysis portions of your IRACs are given the most weight in grading your exams, the next section of this text details the steps involved in applying rules to facts in your legal analyses.

Conclusion After your analysis, state an explicit conclusion — your specific prediction as to how a court would decide the particular issue you discussed. Your conclusion should flow directly from your analysis. Thus, if your analysis identifies arguments for both parties, your conclusion should explain why you believe one set of arguments is more persuasive.

Although the IRAC mnemonic is commonly used and very effective when used appropriately, many law professors tell their students that they hate IRAC. Notwithstanding professorial statements of disdain for IRAC, however, exams that utilize the IRAC mnemonic almost always receive good marks.

The dislike many law professors express for IRAC does not stem from proper uses of it; rather, the dislike is based on students' misuse and overuse of IRAC. In other words, when law professors complain about IRAC, they are really saying they dislike poor, inappropriate, and thoughtless uses of IRAC. You can avoid poor use of IRAC by understanding the points in Table 2-3, a list of seven common errors in students' use of IRAC. Note that this list may be even more meaningful after you have some practice IRACing. Therefore, we encourage you to mark this list and return to review it as you practice IRACing.

Table 2-3: Seven Common Errors in Students' Use of IRAC

1. Labeling each component of your IRAC. Some students literally write the IRAC components in their answers to lawyering problems (for example, "Issue," "Rule," "Analysis," "Conclusion"). Like any mnemonic, **IRAC should generally be used as a guide inside your head, not as a set of labels written in an answer to a lawyering problem, unless your professor explicitly instructs you otherwise.**

2. Making your entire answer to a lawyering problem one gigantic IRAC (for example, stating all the issues in one paragraph, stating all applicable rules in the next paragraph, etc.). As mentioned in Table 2-2, each IRAC you write should address a precise legal issue—only one narrow aspect of the broader legal rule you are analyzing. Accordingly, you should **use a separate IRAC for every precise legal issue that you address.**

3. Making each IRAC or each component of your IRACs the same length. There is no rule about how long each IRAC should be. You will need to develop the legal judgment and discretion to determine how much to write to answer a specific lawyering problem. Some IRACs are short (one paragraph, four sentences) and some IRACs are long (two pages and seven paragraphs). Substance should trump form. In other words, **the length of your IRACs should reflect the complexity of the legal issue you're addressing in a given lawyering problem.**

4. Giving equal weight, length, and time to each component of IRAC. For example, some students assume each piece of IRAC should be one sentence long. This assumption is incorrect. You should make each component as long as needed to address a specific problem. The "I" and "C" components of your IRACs will almost always be relatively short. The real "meat" of your IRACs will be the "R" and "A" components. In fact, when answering lawyering problems on your law school exams, the "A" component will usually count for 66%–80% of your grade. Therefore, **usually your analysis should be the most extensive portion of your IRAC.**

5. Ignoring all other principles of exam taking, organizing, and writing. IRAC is not intended to replace more general principles of exam taking. For example, some law students erroneously include only IRAC paragraphs in their exam answers and never actually respond to the questions posed. As with exam taking in general, you must answer the questions posed on your law school exams (in addition to IRACing). Similarly, some students erroneously include only IRAC paragraphs in their exam answers and omit introductions and conclusions in their exam answers. **The IRAC mnemonic provides guid-**

ance about bases that are important to touch when responding to lawyering problems in addition to more general exam taking, organizing, and writing strategies.

6. Trying to use IRAC to address questions solely about rules of law. Sometimes exam questions ask students to discuss questions solely about what the applicable rules of law are or should be. **IRAC is not applicable to questions solely about rules of law;** follow your professor's instructions and **only address the merits and implications of the rules of law under scrutiny.** You should distinguish questions solely about the law from situations where a lawyering problem is presented and multiple distinct rules of law are relevant and should be applied (for example, a rule adopted by most states, a "majority rule," and a rule adopted by fewer states, a "minority rule"). When discussing application of law to facts problems, it is appropriate to use IRAC. Provide the multiple distinct rules of law in the "R" section of your IRAC (for example, the majority and minority rules). Apply the distinct rules of law in the "A" section of your IRAC (for example, the relevant facts and results under both the majority and minority rules).

7. Trying to use IRAC to address questions solely about policy. Sometimes exam questions ask students to discuss questions solely about public policy. **IRAC is not applicable to questions solely about public policy;** follow your professor's instructions and **only address the relevant policy issues.** You should distinguish questions solely about policy from situations where a lawyering problem is presented and there is a relevant policy consideration that should be discussed (for example, predictability). When discussing lawyering problems, it is appropriate to use IRAC. Provide the relevant policy consideration under the "R" section of your IRAC (for example, that an objective approach to determining whether there is a present commitment to contract furthers the policy of predictability). Apply the policy consideration to the facts in the "A" section of your IRAC. In other words, use policy-based reasoning. For example, under the facts presented in a specific lawyering problem, argue that a court should find a present commitment to contract using an objective approach in order to further the policy of predictability.

The IRAC mnemonic is somewhat flawed in the sense that it inadequately explains the most important part—the "A." In other words, knowing that you need to complete something labeled an "analysis" is not the same as understanding how to complete an analysis—how exactly to apply rules to facts. Applying rules to facts requires you to engage in a further, four-step process, which is detailed in Table 2-4 on the next page.

By following three additional pieces of advice, you can ensure that you are engaging in sound legal analyses.

First, always discuss the applicable rules before ever discussing any relevant fact. If you have not first identified an applicable rule, it is a waste of time to argue the justice or injustice, rightness or wrongness, or fairness or unfairness of the facts. Discussion of the facts without a proper framing of the applicable law is like a ship without a rudder.

Second, assume that a judge or jury will evaluate the arguments you are making. If you could not make the arguments to a judge or jury with a straight face, they should not be made in a legal analysis.

Table 2-4: Completing the "A" in IRAC

1. Identify and list all facts in a lawyering problem that tend to prove or disprove the state of facts required by the rule.

** Hints **

✓ Read the facts carefully and repeatedly.

✓ Try to avoid thinking of yourself as an advocate for any one party. Look for facts that any party could rely on or that help any party.

✓ Facts are in the fact pattern either for you to recognize as relevant and use or to recognize as irrelevant and ignore. Consciously decide to use or disregard each fact.

2. State one fact (or set of facts) that tends to prove or disprove the existence of the state of facts required by the rule.

3. Explain why the fact (or set of facts) tends to prove or disprove the existence of the abstract set of facts required by a rule. Your goal is to explain the relevance of the significant facts. This step usually requires you to draw inferences from the facts and link them to the rule's requirements with arguments as to why the facts satisfy a rule's requirements. You can remember this approach by knowing you should "FIL(L)" your exams with analysis — provide Facts, Inferences, and Links.

4. Repeat steps 1–3 for each relevant fact (or set of facts).

** Hints **

✓ Imagine your reader is someone like the stereotypical three year-old who keeps asking you "why" in response to whatever you say. This will ensure you explain every step of your reasoning.

✓ Make sure you identify arguments that could be made by any party involved (there may be more than two). Note that many facts can be used by opposing parties in different ways. Watch out for and explain how to apply facts that both parties may use but from which they would draw opposite inferences.

Third, explicitly explain your reasoning process. Do not assume your reader will know what is in your mind. Explaining why relevant facts are legally significant is key to both good grades on exams and effective legal analyses in practice. As your math teacher may have said on more than one occasion, you need to "show your work." Many law students find it helpful to use imagery (such as the image in Diagram 2-2) to make sure they include explanations every time they mention legally significant facts. Diagram 2-2 shows the explanation as the largest part of the IRAC process (because it is the most important part) and what happens if the explanation is missing from your analysis (you fall).

A sample legal analysis (IRAC) is provided in Table 2-5. That analysis responds to a lawyering problem raising one narrow issue, the "nighttime" requirement for burglary. The problem stated that police were unable to determine the time of day when the events oc-

Diagram 2-2: The Explanation Gap

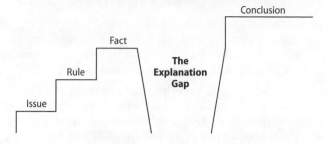

Table 2-5: Sample Legal Analysis (IRAC)

IRAC	Annotations
Nighttime element The first element of burglary requires that the alleged conduct has occurred during the "nighttime." Common law courts define "nighttime" as "the period between sunset and sunrise when there is not enough light to discern a face."	*Issue*: Note that both the heading and the first sentence of text identify the legal issue. *Rule*: The rule is stated after the issue.
Here, on the one hand, the facts do not state the time of day so it is difficult to know whether the acts occurred after sundown or when there was not enough light to see a face. On the other hand, the facts state that defendant carried a lit torch both before she entered the alleged victim's house and while she was inside the house. Lit torches only have utility if a place is dark enough such that the person carrying it feels she cannot see without it. If it was dark enough to need a torch to see, it likely was too dark to see much of anything, including a face.	*Analysis*: Note the transition ("Here, on the one hand") that is used to signal the start of the analysis and that the analysis will argue both sides. Steps 2–3 are used by identifying the absence of a key fact (time of day) and explaining its significance (unclear whether element is met). A transition is also used to signal the beginning of a counter-argument ("On the other hand"). Then, steps 2–3 are used again to identify a relevant fact (lit torch carried) and explain its significance. Step 3 is also used, in part, to draw an inference from that fact and connect it to the "too dark to discern a face" standard.
Moreover the facts state that she carried the lit torch **before** she entered the house, suggesting that, even outside, she perceived a need for light to be able to see. This suggests it was dark outside and was after sunset.	Another transition ("Moreover") is used to signal the start of an additional argument. Steps 2–3 are used again to identify another relevant fact and connect it to the abstract requirements of the rule.
Therefore, because it almost certainly was after sunset and too dark to discern a face, it seems likely a court would conclude the nighttime element was met.	*Conclusion*: Note that the writer uses the key language from the rule and predicts a result.

curred, but they found strong evidence that the alleged burglar carried a lit torch both before she entered the alleged victim's house and while she was inside the house.

For purposes of instruction, Table 2-5 includes annotations that explicitly identify each of the IRAC components and each of the four steps for legal analyses outlined in Table 2-4. Note that these annotations are provided to help you understand the legal analysis. You should not include IRAC labels or annotations in your legal writing.

Also note in the Table 2-5 example that there are conventions of legal writing that make it easier for readers to follow the writer. While each of these conventions is no doubt unoriginal, using them makes sense because they complement one of the purposes of using IRAC—making it easy for a reader to follow your analysis.

For example, you should have noticed that a heading is used ("Nighttime element"). Using headings is a recommended practice because headings serve as signposts that make it easier for a reader to know what topic you are about to address and to follow your writing.

In a similar vein, transitional phrases are used as signals to the reader. For example, "Here" is used to signal the beginning of the analysis section. Other transitions that also signal analysis are "In this case" or "Under these facts." Two sides of the analysis are signaled by using the transitional phrases "On the one hand" and "On the other hand." The writer signals that she is concluding the analysis with the transition "Therefore."

Finally, the sample IRAC in Table 2-5 can be used to understand the differences between objective and persuasive writing and how the two overlap. Table 2-6 highlights the primary differences between objective and persuasive writing. The sample IRAC is primarily objective because its purpose is to inform and predict and it presents opposing sides of an argument. Law professors often refer to IRACing and exam writing as objective. That assertion is correct in the sense that students must analyze facts somewhat unemotionally and try to accurately predict what a court would conclude. You will notice, however, that the sample IRAC is also somewhat persuasive. The author's goal is to convince the reader that the author has correctly analyzed the facts and has accurately predicted how a court would decide the issue.

Table 2-6: Objective Versus Persuasive Writing

	Objective Writing	Persuasive Writing
Purpose:	To inform, educate, predict	To persuade, advocate
Tone:	Objective	Persuasive
Analysis:	Presents both sides of an argument	Provides an argument for one party and uses counter-arguments to head off the other party's arguments

Exercise 2-7: IRAC Application

1. Define in your own words each of the four IRAC components.

2. Answer fully and in writing problems a–d below. Each problem requires you to apply the communication of present commitment requirement (for offers or acceptances) to a discrete set of facts. Below is a template you can use that might help. Note that the template reflects the discussion in the

section of this chapter entitled, "Applying Rules to Facts." Template components are in bold. Hints are in italics. If you get stuck along the way, it may help to reread the analysis of the Betty-Amy problem (Exercise 2-1 and Table 2-1).

Issue:

The issue presented is whether _____ .

Rule:

An offer (or an acceptance) requires a communication of present commitment. To determine whether a party has expressed the requisite commitment, courts interpret the language used by the parties in the context in which they used it from the perspective of a hypothetical reasonable person.

Analysis:

In this case, _____ (*speaker's name*) said, "_____." [S]he said so when _____ (*state any relevant facts about the context*). On the one hand, _____ (*state an interpretation of the words in the context (using dictionary definitions if necessary*). If the court were to interpret _____'s words in this way, the court would conclude _____(*link your language interpretation to the rule*).

On the other hand, _____ (*state an alternative interpretation of the words in the context (using dictionary definitions if necessary*). If the court were to interpret _____'s words in this way, the court would conclude _____ (*link your language interpretation to the rule*).

Conclusion:

Therefore, because _____ (*state why one party's argument is more convincing than the other party's argument*), a court probably would conclude that _____ (*speaker's name*) (*did/did not*) (*make an offer/ accept the offer*).

a. "I might sell you the car for $5,000." Assume this statement was made to a person interested in buying the speaker's car. Analyze whether it is an offer.

b. "I promise to sell you the car for $5,000." Assume this statement was made to a person interested in buying the speaker's car. Analyze whether it is an offer.

c. Jose says to Thu, "I want that one."

   i. If Jose has just come to Thu's home as a guest for dinner and is pointing at Thu's Jaguar automobile, on which there is a sign stating "For Sale— $45,000," has Jose made an offer?

   ii. If Thu owns a liquor store and is standing next to a display of cigarettes underneath a sign that says, "All cigarettes—$1.00 each," and Jose is pointing at a specific pack, has Jose made an offer?

d. Betty offered to sell Abe stale bread and a cup of water for $10. Abe responded, "Betty, you slime. You know that I do not have anywhere else I can go for food and water because of the earthquake. You are a cheat, but I have no choice. I'll pay you the $10." Did Abe accept Betty's offer?

Certainty of Terms

Introduction and Section Example

An expression of commitment may not be enough to be an offer, an acceptance, or an expression of assent. For example, imagine someone says to you, "I will sell you my computer."

1. Can you guess why every court would conclude that those words, standing alone, could not possibly be an offer?

2. Why would you assume that the person making that statement has not bound herself?

3. Read section 33 of the RESTATEMENT (SECOND) OF CONTRACTS. Restate it in your own words.

Essential Terms

No fixed list of terms required by the certainty rule will allow you to resolve every case. When you paraphrased section 33, you should have realized that the common law certainty rule is very flexible. Courts generally agree, however, that the most important terms (the essential ones that absolutely must be present) are a quantity (how many of an specific item) and the parties, price, and subject matter (*e.g.,* a specific house). Two other important (but not essential) terms are the time and place for performance. Law students frequently recall these terms with the mnemonic "**Q-TPPPS**":

> Q: Quantity
>
> T: Time for performance
>
> P: Parties to the contract
>
> P: Price
>
> P: Place for performance
>
> S: Subject matter

Even this list, however, is imperfect. For example, if parties agree a buyer will pay a "reasonable" price, courts will interpret "reasonable" to mean fair market value and will conclude that the contract is sufficiently certain. Likewise, if a contract is silent regarding the time or place of performance, a court will construe that contract to mean a reasonable time or place. Reasonable certainty of terms is therefore not a difficult standard to meet.

Exercise 2-8: Certainty of Terms

1. Create an example of a communication regarding a possible contract that includes all of the "Q-TPPPS" terms, but nevertheless is not an offer.

2. Study sections 2-204(3), 2-305, and 2-308 to 2-310 in U.C.C. Article 2. Is the certainty rule under U.C.C. Article 2 different from the common law certainty rule? If so, in what ways? If not, why not?

3. A and B mutually agree that each will render her performance due under their agreement "immediately." Is the contract sufficiently certain?

4. A and B mutually agree that each will render her performance due under their agreement "promptly." Is the contract sufficiently certain?

5. A promises to sell and B promises to buy goods at "A's cost plus ten percent profit." Is the price term sufficiently certain?

6. A promises to sell and B promises to buy goods at "A's cost plus a fair profit." Is the price term sufficiently certain?

Special Offer Rules

Introduction

In this section, you will learn about a set of special offer rules that courts have layered onto the general principles you have already learned (that an offer must communicate a present commitment to contract and must include sufficiently certain terms).

The rules detailed in this section only apply if a problem falls within one of the several categories enumerated in this section, such as advertisements, quotes, requests for bids, and letters of intent. In other words, you should only apply the rules in this section if a problem falls within one of the enumerated categories.

Practicing lawyers need to know how to apply rules as well as how to develop arguments about whether a given problem falls within a particular category at all. Accordingly, you will be presented opportunities to both apply the rules in this section of the text as well as opportunities to develop arguments about whether particular problems fall into particular categories.

As you learn the new material in this section of the text, keep in mind that these rules apply in addition to the rules you have already learned about present commitment and certainty of terms. Consequently, even if the facts of a particular problem would lead you to conclude that a particular communication is presumptively not an offer under the rules in this section, if it expresses a present commitment and includes sufficient certainty of terms it could still be construed as an offer.

Note about "General Rules"

Many of the rules you are learning in this text might be classified as "**general rules**." This phrase has a special meaning in the legal context. A "general rule" is a legal principle that governs most situations, but, under particular circumstances, is not determinative. For example, as a general rule, advertisements are not offers. Nonetheless, there may be exceptional cases where courts will conclude that the advertisement at issue was an offer.

Advertisements, Circulars, and Quotes as Possible Offers

As a general rule, newspaper advertisements, circulars, and price quotes are not offers; rather, they are invitations for offers. The rationale most commonly given by the courts in support of this rule is that there is neither a specific offeree (because an advertisement is communicated to everyone in the public who reads it) nor a specific quantity (because advertisements do not usually state specific quantities). Accordingly, advertisements lack the requisite certainty of terms.

Moreover, think about what would happen if advertisements were considered offers. An advertiser would be liable in contract to each person who comes to the business and says, "I accept," and would be liable for an unlimited quantity of the item advertised. For all of these reasons, courts would not, without more, consider the advertisement in Table 2-7 an offer.

Table 2-7: Sample Advertisement

COMPUTER UNIVERSE
Your Home Computer Store

FOR SALE
HewPack BCDE 222 Computers

120 GB hard drive	Amplified stereo speakers
4 GB ram	Pentagon 16 Quad-Core Processor
Burns CDs and DVDs	Macrohard Software Included

The next well-known case illustrates the formulation and application of the general rule.

Exercise 2-9: *Leonard v. Pepsico, Inc.*

1. Identify all the statements of the general rule about advertisements that the court makes in *Leonard* and then restate the rule in your own words.

2. The key to understanding why the *Lefkowitz* and *Carlill* courts concluded that the advertisements at issue in those cases were offers is the specific language used in the advertisements. Look closely at the words used in the advertisements. What words in those advertisements distinguish them from the *Leonard* advertisement and the computer advertisement in Table 2-7? (Hint: Consider why the words used in the *Lefkowitz* and *Carlill* advertisements are inconsistent with the rationale courts traditionally use to conclude that advertisements are not offers.)

3. Based on your answer to question 2 and your reading of *Leonard*, try to create a rule that states when an exception will be made to the general rule that advertisements are not offers. Note: Your answer to this question will give you a rule you can use in evaluating whether other advertisements are offers.

4. Explain how this case illustrates the application of the rule in *Lucy v. Zehmer*.

Leonard v. Pepsico, Inc.

88 F.Supp.2d 116, S.D.N.Y. (1999)

KIMBA M. WOOD, District Judge.

Plaintiff brought this action seeking, among other things, specific performance of an alleged offer of a Harrier Jet, featured in a television advertisement for defendant's "Pepsi Stuff" promotion. Defendant has moved for summary judgment ... For the reasons stated below, defendant's motion is granted.

...

This case arises out of a promotional campaign conducted by defendant, the producer and distributor of the soft drinks Pepsi and Diet Pepsi ... The promotion, entitled "Pepsi Stuff," encouraged consumers to collect "Pepsi Points" from specially marked packages of Pepsi or Diet Pepsi and redeem these points for merchandise featuring the Pepsi logo ... Plaintiff saw the Pepsi Stuff commercial ... that he contends constituted an offer of a Harrier Jet.

...

Because whether the television commercial constituted an offer is the central question in this case, the Court will describe the commercial in detail. The commercial opens upon an idyllic, suburban morning, where the chirping of birds in sun-dappled trees welcomes a paperboy on his morning route. As the newspaper hits the stoop of a conventional two-story house, the tattoo of a military drum introduces the subtitle, "MONDAY 7:58 AM." The stirring strains of a martial air mark the appearance of a well-coiffed teenager preparing to leave for school, dressed in a shirt emblazoned with the Pepsi logo, a red-white-and-blue ball. While the teenager confidently preens, the military drumroll again sounds as the subtitle "T–SHIRT 75 PEPSI POINTS" scrolls across the screen. Bursting from his room, the teenager strides down the hallway wearing a leather jacket. The drumroll sounds again, as the subtitle "LEATHER JACKET 1450 PEPSI POINTS" appears. The teenager opens the door of his house and, unfazed by the glare of the early morning sunshine, puts on a pair of sunglasses. The drumroll then accompanies the subtitle "SHADES 175 PEPSI POINTS." A voiceover then intones, "Introducing the new Pepsi Stuff catalog," as the camera focuses on the cover of the catalog ...

The scene then shifts to three young boys sitting in front of a high school building. The boy in the middle is intent on his Pepsi Stuff Catalog, while the boys on either side are each drinking Pepsi. The three boys gaze in awe at an object rushing overhead, as the military march builds to a crescendo. The Harrier Jet is not yet visible, but the observer senses the presence of a mighty plane as the extreme winds generated by its flight create a paper maelstrom in a classroom devoted to an otherwise dull physics lesson. Finally, the Harrier Jet swings into view and lands by the side of the school building, next to a bicycle rack. Several students run for cover, and the velocity of the wind strips one hapless faculty member down to his underwear. While the faculty member is being deprived of his dignity, the voiceover announces: "Now the more Pepsi you drink, the more great stuff you're gonna get."

The teenager opens the cockpit of the fighter and can be seen, helmetless, holding a Pepsi. "[L]ooking very pleased with himself," (Pl. Mem. at 3,) the teenager exclaims, "Sure beats the bus," and chortles. The military drumroll sounds a final time, as the following words appear: "HARRIER FIGHTER 7,000,000 PEPSI POINTS." A few seconds later, the following appears in more stylized script: "Drink Pepsi—Get Stuff." With that message, the music and the commercial end with a triumphant flourish.

Inspired by this commercial, plaintiff set out to obtain a Harrier Jet. Plaintiff explains that he is "typical of the 'Pepsi Generation'... he is young, has an adventurous spirit, and the notion of obtaining a Harrier Jet appealed to him enormously." ... Plaintiff consulted the Pepsi Stuff Catalog. The Catalog features youths dressed in Pepsi Stuff regalia or enjoying Pepsi Stuff accessories, such as "Blue Shades" ("As if you need another reason to look forward to sunny days."), "Pepsi Tees" ("Live in 'em. Laugh in 'em. Get in 'em."), "Bag of Balls" ("Three balls. One bag. No rules."), and "Pepsi Phone Card" ("Call your mom!"). The Catalog specifies the number of Pepsi Points required to obtain promotional merchandise. (*See* Catalog, at rear foldout pages.) The Catalog includes an Order Form which lists, on one side, fifty-three items of Pepsi Stuff merchandise redeemable for Pepsi Points ... Conspicuously absent from the Order Form is any entry or description of a Harrier Jet ... The amount of Pepsi Points required to obtain the listed merchandise ranges from 15 (for a "Jacket Tattoo" ("Sew 'em on your jacket, not your arm.")) to 3300 (for a "Fila Mountain Bike" ("Rugged. All-terrain. Exclusively for Pepsi.")). It should be noted that plaintiff objects to the implication that because an item was not shown in the Catalog, it was unavailable ...

The rear foldout pages of the Catalog contain directions for redeeming Pepsi Points for merchandise ... These directions note that merchandise may be ordered "only" with the original Order Form ... The Catalog notes that in the event that a consumer lacks enough Pepsi Points to obtain a desired item, additional Pepsi Points may be purchased for ten cents each; however, at least fifteen original Pepsi Points must accompany each order ...

Although plaintiff initially set out to collect 7,000,000 Pepsi Points by consuming Pepsi products, it soon became clear to him that he "would not be able to buy (let alone drink) enough Pepsi to collect the necessary Pepsi Points fast enough." ... Reevaluating his strategy, plaintiff "focused for the first time on the packaging materials in the Pepsi Stuff promotion," ... and realized that buying Pepsi Points would be a more promising option. Through acquaintances, plaintiff ultimately raised about $700,000 ...

B. *Plaintiff's Efforts to Redeem the Alleged Offer*

On or about March 27, 1996, plaintiff submitted an Order Form, fifteen original Pepsi Points, and a check for $700,008.50 ... Plaintiff appears to have been represented by counsel at the time he mailed his check; the check is drawn on an account of plaintiff's first set of attorneys ... At the bottom of the Order Form, plaintiff wrote in "1 Harrier Jet" in the "Item" column and "7,000,000" in the "Total Points" column ... In a letter accompanying his submission, plaintiff stated that the check was to purchase additional Pepsi Points "expressly for obtaining a new Harrier jet as advertised in your Pepsi Stuff commercial." ...

On or about May 7, 1996, defendant's fulfillment house rejected plaintiff's submission and returned the check ...

...

In a letter dated May 30, 1996, BBDO Vice President Raymond E. Mc-Govern, Jr., explained to plaintiff that:

> I find it hard to believe that you are of the opinion that the Pepsi Stuff commercial ("Commercial") really offers a new Harrier Jet. The use of the Jet was clearly a joke that was meant to make the Commercial more humorous and entertaining. In my opinion, no reasonable person would agree with your analysis of the Commercial.

[The judge at this point explained the procedural history and posture. There were two lawsuits. The first brought by Pepsico seeking a declaratory judgment stating that it had no obligation to furnish the plaintiff with a Harrier Jet. The second brought by Leonard seeking to enforce Pepsico's alleged contractual commitment to provide him with a Harrier Jet in return for the Pepsi Points or cash equivalent that he had tendered].

...

The general rule is that an advertisement does not constitute an offer. The *Restatement (Second) of Contracts* explains that:

> Advertisements of goods by display, sign, handbill, newspaper, radio or television are not ordinarily intended or understood as offers to sell. The same is true of catalogues, price lists and circulars, even though the terms of suggested bargains may be stated in some detail. It is of course possible to make an offer by an advertisement directed to the general public (see §29), but there must ordinarily be some language of commitment or some invitation to take action without further communication.

Restatement (Second) of Contracts §26 cmt. b (1979). Similarly, a leading treatise notes that:

> It is quite possible to make a definite and operative offer to buy or sell goods by advertisement, in a newspaper, by a handbill, a catalog or circular or on a placard in a store window. *It is not customary to do this, however; and the presumption is the other way....* Such advertisements are understood to be mere requests to consider and examine and negotiate; and no one can reasonably regard them as otherwise unless the circumstances are exceptional and the words used are very plain and clear.

1 Arthur Linton Corbin & Joseph M. Perillo, *Corbin on Contracts* §2.4, at 116–17 (rev. ed.1993) (emphasis added); *see also* 1 E. Allan Farnsworth, *Farnsworth on Contracts* §3.10, at 239 (2d ed.1998); 1 Samuel Williston & Richard A. Lord, *A Treatise on the Law of Contracts* §4:7, at 286–87 (4th ed.1990). New York courts adhere to this general principle. *See Lovett v. Frederick Loeser & Co.,* 124 Misc. 81, 207 N.Y.S. 753, 755 (N.Y.Mun.Ct.1924) (noting that an "advertisement is nothing but an invitation to enter into negotiations, and is not an offer which may be turned into a contract by a person who signifies his intention to purchase some of the articles mentioned in the advertisement"); *see also Geismar v. Abraham & Strauss,* 109 Misc.2d 495, 439 N.Y.S.2d 1005, 1006 (N.Y.Dist.Ct.1981) (reiterating *Lovett* rule); *People v. Gimbel Bros.,* 202 Misc. 229, 115 N.Y.S.2d 857, 858 (N.Y.Sp.Sess.1952) (because an "[a]dvertisement does not constitute an offer of sale but is solely an

invitation to customers to make an offer to purchase," defendant not guilty of selling property on Sunday).

An advertisement is not transformed into an enforceable offer merely by a potential offeree's expression of willingness to accept the offer through, among other means, completion of an order form. In *Mesaros v. United States,* 845 F.2d 1576 (Fed.Cir.1988), for example, the plaintiffs sued the United States Mint for failure to deliver a number of Statue of Liberty commemorative coins that they had ordered. When demand for the coins proved unexpectedly robust, a number of individuals who had sent in their orders in a timely fashion were left empty-handed. *See id.* at 1578–80. The court began by noting the "well-established" rule that advertisements and order forms are "mere notices and solicitations for offers which create no power of acceptance in the recipient." ... ; *Restatement (Second) of Contracts* § 26 ("A manifestation of willingness to enter a bargain is not an offer if the person to whom it is addressed knows or has reason to know that the person making it does not intend to conclude a bargain until he has made a further manifestation of assent."). The spurned coin collectors could not maintain a breach of contract action because no contract would be formed until the advertiser accepted the order form and processed payment. *See id.* at 1581; *see also Alligood v. Procter & Gamble,* 72 Ohio App.3d 309, 594 N.E.2d 668 (1991) (finding that no offer was made in promotional campaign for baby diapers, in which consumers were to redeem teddy bear proof-of-purchase symbols for catalog merchandise); *Chang v. First Colonial Savings Bank,* 242 Va. 388, 410 S.E.2d 928 (1991) (newspaper advertisement for bank settled the terms of the offer once bank accepted plaintiffs' deposit, notwithstanding bank's subsequent effort to amend the terms of the offer). Under these principles, plaintiff's letter of March 27, 1996, with the Order Form and the appropriate number of Pepsi Points, constituted the offer. There would be no enforceable contract until defendant accepted the Order Form and cashed the check.

The exception to the rule that advertisements do not create any power of acceptance in potential offerees is where the advertisement is "clear, definite, and explicit, and leaves nothing open for negotiation," in that circumstance, "it constitutes an offer, acceptance of which will complete the contract." *Lefkowitz v. Great Minneapolis Surplus Store,* 251 Minn. 188, 86 N.W.2d 689, 691 (1957). In *Lefkowitz,* defendant had published a newspaper announcement stating: "Saturday 9 AM Sharp, 3 Brand New Fur Coats, Worth to $100.00, First Come First Served $1 Each." *Id.* at 690. Mr. Morris Lefkowitz arrived at the store, dollar in hand, but was informed that under defendant's "house rules," the offer was open to ladies, but not gentlemen. *See id.* The court ruled that because plaintiff had fulfilled all of the terms of the advertisement and the advertisement was specific and left nothing open for negotiation, a contract had been formed ...

The present case is distinguishable from *Lefkowitz.* First, the commercial cannot be regarded in itself as sufficiently definite, because it specifically reserved the details of the offer to a separate writing, the Catalog. The commercial itself made no mention of the steps a potential offeree would be required to take to accept the alleged offer of a Harrier Jet. The advertisement in *Lefkowitz,* in contrast, "identified the person who could accept." Corbin, *supra,* § 2.4, at 119. *See generally United States v. Braunstein,* 75 F.Supp. 137, 139 (S.D.N.Y.1947) ("Greater precision of expression may be required, and less

Here the court makes reference to the problem of multiple acceptances, which is a rationale for the general rule.

Note the technique used by the court here. Having stated the general rule and the exception, the court now uses legal reasoning to explain why the case falls within the rule rather than the exception.

help from the court given, when the parties are merely at the threshold of a contract."); Farnsworth, *supra*, at 239 ("The fact that a proposal is very detailed suggests that it is an offer, while omission of many terms suggests that it is not."). Second, even if the Catalog had included a Harrier Jet among the items that could be obtained by redemption of Pepsi Points, the advertisement of a Harrier Jet by both television commercial and catalog would still not constitute an offer. As the *Mesaros* court explained, the absence of any words of limitation such as "first come, first served," renders the alleged offer sufficiently indefinite that no contract could be formed. *See Mesaros,* 845 F.2d at 1581. "A customer would not usually have reason to believe that the shopkeeper intended exposure to the risk of a multitude of acceptances resulting in a number of contracts exceeding the shopkeeper's inventory." Farnsworth, *supra*, at 242. There was no such danger in *Lefkowitz,* owing to the limitation "first come, first served."

The Court finds, in sum, that the Harrier Jet commercial was merely an advertisement. The Court now turns to the line of cases upon which plaintiff rests much of his argument.

...

In opposing the present motion, plaintiff largely relies on a different species of unilateral offer, involving public offers of a reward for performance of a specified act. Because these cases generally involve public declarations regarding the efficacy or trustworthiness of specific products, one court has aptly characterized these authorities as "prove me wrong" cases. *See Rosenthal v. Al Packer Ford,* 36 Md.App. 349, 374 A.2d 377, 380 (1977). The most venerable of these precedents is the case of *Carlill v. Carbolic Smoke Ball Co.,* 1 Q.B. 256 (Court of Appeal, 1892), a quote from which heads plaintiff's memorandum of law: "[I]f a person chooses to make extravagant promises ... he probably does so because it pays him to make them, and, if he has made them, the extravagance of the promises is no reason in law why he should not be bound by them." *Carbolic Smoke Ball,* 1 Q.B. at 268 (Bowen, L.J.).

Long a staple of law school curricula, *Carbolic Smoke Ball* owes its fame ... to its role in developing the law of unilateral offers. The case arose during the London influenza epidemic of the 1890s. Among other advertisements of the time ... appeared solicitations for the Carbolic Smoke Ball. The specific advertisement that Mrs. Carlill saw, and relied upon, read as follows:

> 100 £ reward will be paid by the Carbolic Smoke Ball Company to any person who contracts the increasing epidemic influenza, colds, or any diseases caused by taking cold, after having used the ball three times daily for two weeks according to the printed directions supplied with each ball. 1000 £ is deposited with the Alliance Bank, Regent Street, shewing our sincerity in the matter.

> During the last epidemic of influenza many thousand carbolic smoke balls were sold as preventives against this disease, and in no ascertained case was the disease contracted by those using the carbolic smoke ball.

Carbolic Smoke Ball, 1 Q.B. at 256–57. "On the faith of this advertisement," *id.* at 257, Mrs. Carlill purchased the smoke ball and used it as directed, but contracted influenza nevertheless. The lower court held that she was entitled to recover the promised reward.

Affirming the lower court's decision, Lord Justice Lindley began by noting that the advertisement was an express promise to pay £ 100 in the event that a consumer of the Carbolic Smoke Ball was stricken with influenza. *See id.* at 261. The advertisement was construed as offering a reward because it sought to induce performance, unlike an invitation to negotiate, which seeks a reciprocal promise. As Lord Justice Lindley explained, "advertisements offering rewards ... are offers to anybody who performs the conditions named in the advertisement, and anybody who does perform the condition accepts the offer." *Id.* at 262; *see also id.* at 268 (Bowen, L.J.). Because Mrs. Carlill had complied with the terms of the offer, yet contracted influenza, she was entitled to £100.

Like *Carbolic Smoke Ball,* the decisions relied upon by plaintiff involve offers of reward ... Other "reward" cases underscore the distinction between typical advertisements, in which the alleged offer is merely an invitation to negotiate for purchase of commercial goods, and promises of reward, in which the alleged offer is intended to induce a potential offeree to perform a specific action, often for noncommercial reasons. In *Newman v. Schiff,* 778 F.2d 460 (8th Cir.1985), for example, the Fifth Circuit held that a tax protestor's assertion that, "If anybody calls this show ... and cites any section of the code that says an individual is required to file a tax return, I'll pay them $100,000," would have been an enforceable offer had the plaintiff called the television show to claim the reward while the tax protestor was appearing. *See id.* at 466–67. The court noted that, like *Carbolic Smoke Ball,* the case "concerns a special type of offer: an offer for a reward." *Id.* at 465 ...

In the present case, the Harrier Jet commercial did not direct that anyone who appeared at Pepsi headquarters with 7,000,000 Pepsi Points on the Fourth of July would receive a Harrier Jet. Instead, the commercial urged consumers to accumulate Pepsi Points and to refer to the Catalog to determine how they could redeem their Pepsi Points. The commercial sought a reciprocal promise, expressed through acceptance of, and compliance with, the terms of the Order Form. As noted previously, the Catalog contains no mention of the Harrier Jet. Plaintiff states that he "noted that the Harrier Jet was not among the items described in the catalog, but this did not affect [his] understanding of the offer." ... It should have.

Carbolic Smoke Ball itself draws a distinction between the offer of reward in that case, and typical advertisements, which are merely offers to negotiate. As Lord Justice Bowen explains:

> It is an offer to become liable to any one who, before it is retracted, performs the condition.... It is not like cases in which you offer to negotiate, or you issue advertisements that you have got a stock of books to sell, or houses to let, in which case there is no offer to be bound by any contract. Such advertisements are offers to negotiate — offers to receive offers — offers to chaffer, as, I think, some learned judge in one of the cases has said.

Carbolic Smoke Ball, 1 Q.B. at 268 ...

Plaintiff's understanding of the commercial as an offer must also be rejected because the Court finds that no objective person could reasonably have concluded that the commercial actually offered consumers a Harrier Jet.

Note how in this paragraph the court characterizes the Pepsi advert to distinguish it from the adverts in the "reward" cases.

. . .

In evaluating the commercial, the Court must not consider defendant's subjective intent in making the commercial, or plaintiff's subjective view of what the commercial offered, but what an objective, reasonable person would have understood the commercial to convey. *See Kay–R Elec. Corp. v. Stone & Webster Constr. Co.,* 23 F.3d 55, 57 (2d Cir.1994) ("[W]e are not concerned with what was going through the heads of the parties at the time [of the alleged contract]. Rather, we are talking about the objective principles of contract law."); *Mesaros,* 845 F.2d at 1581 ("A basic rule of contracts holds that whether an offer has been made depends on the objective reasonableness of the alleged offeree's belief that the advertisement or solicitation was intended as an offer."); Farnsworth, *supra,* § 3.10, at 237; Williston, *supra,* § 4:7 at 296–97.

If it is clear that an offer was not serious, then no offer has been made:

> What kind of act creates a power of acceptance and is therefore an offer? It must be an expression of will or intention. It must be an act that leads the offeree reasonably to conclude that a power to create a contract is conferred. This applies to the content of the power as well as to the fact of its existence. *It is on this ground that we must exclude* invitations to deal or acts of mere preliminary negotiation, and *acts evidently done in jest* or without intent to create legal relations.

Corbin on Contracts, § 1.11 at 30 (emphasis added). An obvious joke, of course, would not give rise to a contract. *See, e.g., Graves v. Northern N.Y. Pub. Co.,* 260 A.D. 900, 22 N.Y.S.2d 537 (1940) (dismissing claim to offer of $1000, which appeared in the "joke column" of the newspaper, to any person who could provide a commonly available phone number). On the other hand, if there is no indication that the offer is "evidently in jest," and that an objective, reasonable person would find that the offer was serious, then there may be a valid offer. *See Barnes,* 549 P.2d at 1155 ("[I]f the jest is not apparent and a reasonable hearer would believe that an offer was being made, then the speaker risks the formation of a contract which was not intended."); *see also Lucy v. Zehmer,* 196 Va. 493, 84 S.E.2d 516, 518, 520 (1954) (ordering specific performance of a contract to purchase a farm despite defendant's protestation that the transaction was done in jest as " 'just a bunch of two doggoned drunks bluffing' ").

. . .

Plaintiff's insistence that the commercial appears to be a serious offer requires the Court to explain why the commercial is funny. Explaining why a joke is funny is a daunting task; as the essayist E.B. White has remarked, "Humor can be dissected, as a frog can, but the thing dies in the process. . . ." . . . The commercial is the embodiment of what defendant appropriately characterizes as "zany humor." . . .

In sum, [the] plaintiff's demand cannot prevail as a matter of law. First, the commercial was merely an advertisement, not a unilateral offer. Second, the tongue-in-cheek attitude of the commercial would not cause a reasonable person to conclude that a soft drink company would be giving away fighter planes as part of a promotion . . .

For the reasons stated above, the Court grants defendant's motion for summary judgment . . .

Exercise 2-10: *Leonard* Revisited

1. In 2014, a car dealer published an advertisement on its Web site which stated (with slight modifications):

> Year: 2014
> Make: Range Rover
> Model: 5.0L Supercharged Autobiography
> Mileage: 100
> Body Style: SUV
> Exterior Color: Santorini Black Metal
> Interior Color: Ebony
> Stock #: 253960
> Vin #: SALGV2RS1BC253960
> Price: $210,995
> Email dealer.

Use the rules and facts from *Leonard,* along with rule-based, analogical, or counter-analogical reasoning, to analyze whether the advertisement is an offer.

2. Find a newspaper advertisement that you believe is an offer. Be prepared to justify your conclusion that the advertisement is an offer.

Exercise 2-11: *Fairmount Glass Works v. Crunden-Martin Wooden Ware Co.*

The next case, *Fairmount Glass Works*, involves a price quote. As you read the case, consider the following questions:

1. What are the key facts? (Remember that, in contract cases, the specific language used by the parties is frequently key.)

2. What general rule does the court state?

3. When you read *Fairmount Glass Works,* you will see that the facts include an April 23 letter. What statement in the April 23 letter is especially important? Why did the court conclude that that statement was important?

4. What additional statement in the April 23 letter supports the court's conclusion?

Fairmount Glass Works v. Crunden-Martin Wooden Ware Co.

106 Ky. 659, 51 S.W. 196 (1899)

Hobson, J.

On April 20, 1895, appellee wrote appellant the following letter:

"St. Louis, Mo., April 20, 1895.

Gentlemen: Please advise us the lowest price you can make us on our order for ten car loads of Mason green jars, complete, with caps,

packed one dozen in a case, either delivered here, or f. o. b. cars your place, as you prefer. State terms and cash discount.
Very truly, Crunden-Martin W. W. Co."

To this letter appellant answered as follows:

"Fairmount, Ind., April 23, 1895.
Crunden-Martin Wooden Ware Co., St. Louis, Mo.
Gentlemen: Replying to your favor of April 20, we quote you Mason fruit jars, complete, in one-dozen boxes, delivered in East St. Louis, Ill.: Pints $4.50, quarts $5.00, half gallons $6.50, per gross, for immediate acceptance, and shipment not later than May 15, 1895; sixty days' acceptance, or 2 off, cash in ten days.
Yours, truly, Fairmount Glass Works.

Please note that we make all quotations and contracts subject to the contingencies of agencies or transportation, delays or accidents beyond our control."

For reply thereto, appellee sent the following telegram on April 24, 1895:

"Fairmount Glass Works, Fairmount, Ind.:
Your letter twenty-third received. Enter order ten car loads as per your quotation. Specifications mailed.
Crunden-Martin W. W. Co."

In response to this telegram, appellant sent the following:

"Fairmount, Ind., April 24, 1895.
Crunden-Martin W. W. Co., St. Louis, Mo.: Impossible to book your order. Output all sold. See letter.
Fairmount Glass Works."

Appellee insists that, by its telegram sent in answer to the letter of April 23rd, the contract was closed for the purchase of ten car loads of Mason fruit jars.

Appellant insists that the contract was not closed by this telegram, and that it had the right to decline to fill the order at the time it sent its telegram of April 24th. This is the chief question in the case. The court below gave judgment in favor of appellee, and appellant has appealed, earnestly insisting that the judgment is erroneous.

We are referred to a number of authorities holding that a quotation of prices is not an offer to sell, in the sense that a completed contract will arise out of the giving of an order for merchandise in accordance with the proposed terms. There are a number of cases holding that the transaction is not completed until the order so made is accepted. [Citations omitted.] But each case must turn largely upon the language there used.

In this case we think there was more than a quotation of prices, although appellant's letter uses the word "quote" in stating the prices given. The true meaning of the correspondence must be determined by reading it as a whole. Appellee's letter of April 20th, which began the transaction, did not ask for a quotation of prices. It reads: "Please advise us the lowest price you can make us on our order for ten car loads of Mason green jars. State terms and cash discount." From this appellant could not fail to understand that appellee wanted to know at what price it would sell it ten car loads of these jars; so

The April 23 letter contains the language the court later says is crucial to its conclusion that there was an offer. Try to predict what is the crucial language in the letter.

This paragraph also supports the court's conclusion. The court, however, does not address it. How does the paragraph support the court's conclusion?

The last sentence in this paragraph states a principle crucial to contract law. Explain what this principle means.

when, in answer, it wrote: "We quote you Mason fruit jars ... pints $4.50, quarts $5.00, half gallons $6.50, per gross, for immediate acceptance; ... 2 off, cash in ten days," — it must be deemed as intending to give appellee the information it had asked for. We can hardly understand what was meant by the words "for immediate acceptance," unless the latter was intended as a proposition to sell at these prices if accepted immediately. In construing every contract, the aim of the court is to arrive at the intention of the parties. In none of the cases to which we have been referred on behalf of appellant was there on the face of the correspondence any such expression of intention to make an offer to sell on the terms indicated. In ... [one case], the use of the expression that the buyer should reply as soon as possible, in case he was disposed to *accede* to the terms offered, was held sufficient to show that there was a definite proposition, which was closed by the buyer's acceptance. The expression in appellant's letter, "for immediate acceptance," taken in connection with appellee's letter, in effect, at what price it would sell it the goods, is, it seems to us, much stronger evidence of a present offer, which, when accepted immediately, closed the contract. Appellee's letter was plainly an inquiry for the price and terms on which appellant would sell it the goods, and appellant's answer to it was not a quotation of prices, but a definite offer to sell on the terms indicated, and could not be withdrawn after the terms had been accepted....

Judgment affirmed.

Exercise 2-12: *Fairmount Glass Works* Revisited

1. What is the basis of the *Fairmount Glass Works* decision? Did the court conclude that the April 23rd letter was not really a "quote" or that the general rule applicable to quotes should not apply?

2. In *Chicago & Alton Railroad Company v. Benjamin F. Jones*, 53 Ill.App.431 (1893) the plaintiff grain shipper wrote to the defendant railroad company as follows (with slight modifications) on January 15:

    "H.H. Cartwright, General Freight Agent, Chicago & Alton Railroad— Dear Sir: I want rates to Springfield, Ohio and Middletown, Conn. Yours respectfully, B.F. Jones."

    Cartwright replied the next day stating:

    "Dear Sir: In replying to your favor of 15th inst., I beg to name you the following rates from Pontiac, Ill. On grain and on hay: Springfield, Ohio, 13 cents per 100 lbs; Middletown, Conn., 22 1/2 cents per 100 lbs."

    On January 24, Jones sent Cartwright the following letter:

    "Dear Sir: I accept the rates you gave me on January 16."

    When the railroad refused to ship plaintiff's grain to Middletown unless plaintiff paid 32 1/2 cents per 100 lbs., plaintiff sued the railroad for breach of contract.

    The court concluded that there was no contract. Why not?

Letters of Intent

So far, the transactions in this chapter have been relatively simple exchanges. For example, *Lucy v. Zehmer* involved an exchange of money for land and *Fairmount Glass Works* involved an exchange of money for personal property. While the negotiations for such exchanges can be long and involved, they typically are not.

Some transactions, however, are considerably more complicated. For example, when one large company agrees to buy all or a part of another company, the negotiations may take months or years and the final contract between the parties may be dozens or even hundreds of pages in length.

In complex transactions involving an enormous number of issues that must be addressed in an eventual contract, parties often choose to document their progress toward a contract in something called a "letter of intent" which makes it clear that they only intend to be formally bound at a future point once a final contract has been drawn up or executed. Sometimes, though, the parties agree all of the main terms relatively informally in a letter (or email) of intent in a manner that is legally binding and later memorialize their agreement in a formal written document that they intend as a mere formality. As you can imagine, these two distinct uses of letters of intent raise legal issues because it is often difficult to determine whether the parties intended to document their progress towards a deal without yet being bound or to create binding contractual obligations with any subsequent formal document serving merely as a memorial of an agreement already reached.

Sections 26–27 of the RESTATEMENT (SECOND) OF CONTRACTS address letters of intent. The Restatement provides that letters of intent may or may not be binding depending on whether the parties intend a letter to be binding or intend that neither party will be bound until they negotiate and execute final documentation of their deal. Try to predict what facts would be relevant in ascertaining what parties intend when they execute a letter of intent.

Exercise 2-13: *Store Properties v. Neal*

Store Properties v. Neal involves a letter of intent. As you read the case, think about the following questions:

1. Why aren't sophisticated parties, like both parties in *Neal*, more careful in delineating the boundary between contract and non-contract? Consider whether there are any advantages or business reasons for leaving things unclear.

2. Identify all the language in the letter of intent in *Neal* that the court regarded as determinative of the outcome. Why did the court consider that language so crucial?

Store Properties v. Neal

72 Cal.App.2d 112, 164 P.2d 38 (1945)

MOORE, Presiding Justice.

From a judgment of dismissal entered pursuant to an order sustaining a demurrer to its second amended complaint plaintiff appeals. The action is one for the specific performance of a contract which plaintiff contends was created by its acceptance of the offer of defendants as follows:

"Coldwell, Banker & Company,
523 West Sixth Street L
Los Angeles 14, California

"Gentlemen:

"We, as lessors, propose to lease to Store Properties, Inc., as lessee, the property at the southeasterly corner of Brighton Way and Beverly Drive in Beverly Hills, California, lot size 100 by 150 , upon the following terms and conditions:

"(1) The lease shall run for a term of 99 years, commencing on the first day of November, 1944.

"(2) The rental for said term shall be at the rate of $750.00 monthly for the first 15 years of the lease; $800.00 monthly for the following 10 years; $850.00 monthly for the following 24 years; $1,000.00 monthly for the following 50 years.

"Upon execution and delivery of the lease the lessee shall pay to the lessor the sum of $18,000.00, $9,000.00 of which shall be as consideration for the execution of the lease, and the remaining $9,000.00 shall cover the first year's rental.

"(3) In addition to the above rental, Lessee will pay all taxes, assessments, insurance, and maintenance; in other words, the above rental will be net to the lessor.

"(4) Upon execution and delivery of the lease, the lessee will place in trust of escrow the sum of $30,000.00 as a guarantee that the lessee will make building improvements or alterations at a total cost of not less than $30,000.00. Said sum of $30,000.00 shall be released to the lessee when such improvements or alterations are completed.

"(5) The lessor shall furnish at the expense of the lessor at the time of execution and delivery of lease, a leasehold policy of title insurance with liability of $39,000.00 showing title to said property vested in the lessor, free and clear of any and all liens, except taxes not delinquent, and such conditions, restrictions, reservations, easements, rights and rights of way of record as the purchaser may approve, and insuring the leasehold interest of the lessee under said lease.

"(6) The property shall be delivered to the lessee subject to presently existing leases and such month-to-month tenancies as may exist at the date of commencement of lease, and all written leases shall be subject to the approval of the lessee, and the lessor's interest therein shall be assigned to the lessee.

"(7) Taxes, rents and insurance shall be prorated as of the date of execution of the lease.

"(8) Terms and conditions of the lease not covered by this proposal shall be subject to the approval of both parties.

"(9) Lessee shall deposit with Coldwell, Banker & Company the sum of $5,000.00 as evidence of good faith. If this offer is accepted by the lessee of said property and a lease is prepared and mutually agreed upon, the lessee shall, upon execution and delivery of said lease, pay to the lessor of said property this sum of $5,000.00 to apply on the first payment under said lease. If a lease upon the above terms and conditions has not been executed within thirty (30) days from date hereof, both parties reserve the right at any time thereafter, but prior to the execution of such a lease, to terminate this offer and the above sum of $5,000.00 shall thereupon be returned to the lessee upon demand.

"(10) This proposal shall become null and void unless accepted in writing by the lessee on or before 12 o'clock noon October 23d, 1944.

"John W. Neal
"Clara B. Neal"

"October 20, 1944

"We agree to enter into a lease on the above described property on the terms as set forth above.

"Store Properties, Inc.
"Samuel Genis
"President."

> The last three paragraphs of the letter of intent in this case seem to point in opposite directions in terms of the legal issue of whether the parties intended that this letter be binding. Can you see why we say so?

By appropriate allegations plaintiff declared that the offer and acceptance constitute a valid, binding contract for a 99-year lease. The complaint includes many formal allegations, alleges plaintiff's deposit of $5,000, the reasonable value of the leasehold, its agreement to deposit $30,000 as a guaranty that the improvements and alterations would be completed, its receipt from defendants of a form of formal lease, and its execution thereof at the request of defendants. The pleading includes a number of argumentative allegations, which cannot add to the value of the factual declarations relative to the alleged contract. The offer and acceptance are attached as Exhibit A and the proposed formal lease as Exhibit B.

Defendants contend that by reason of its indefiniteness and uncertainty the writing is not an enforceable contract; that it lacks mutuality; that even though Exhibit B be considered as one of a series of acts with Exhibit A still there is no contract susceptible of enforcement; that Exhibit B is ineffectual in that it contravenes the statute of frauds. On the other hand, plaintiff argues: (1) That defendants' proposal to execute a lease incorporated all the terms necessary to constitute a valid instrument; (2) that defendants' offer having been accepted in writing and the acceptance of such offer having been delivered to defendants, the result is a binding contract to lease on the terms specified in the offer; (3) that defendants cannot maintain uncertainty in the contract with reference to the improvements to be made for the reason that they left the nature of such improvements to the judgment of plaintiff, which was to enjoy their exclusive use; (4) that Exhibit A contains no clause reserving to defendants the right to refuse to sign a proper form of lease after its acceptance by plaintiff.

Inasmuch as we have concluded that the offer and acceptance do not constitute an enforcible [sic] contract, we confine our discussion to that attack upon the sufficiency of the pleading....

Where a contract appears to be a preliminary agreement 'embodying only the spirit of a contemplated supplementary contract ... and it is perfectly clear ... that the minds of the parties never met upon the details,' then it is not enforceable. [Citation omitted.] When it is the understanding that the terms of a contract are to be reduced to writing and signed by the parties, assent to its terms must be evidenced by a writing subscribed by all of them; otherwise it does not become a completed contract. [Citations omitted.] When only the principal provisions of a lease are agreed upon, leaving the details and conditions to be expressed in a writing to be executed by the parties, and such writing is never signed by those to be charged, it never becomes a binding obligation upon either. [Citation omitted.] If parties contemplate a reduction to writing of their agreement before it can be considered complete, there is no contract until the writing is signed. [Citation omitted.] If a writing is viewed as the consummation of the negotiations there is no contract until the written draft is finally signed. [Citation omitted.]

Notice how similar these rules are to the assigned rules from the restatement.

Under the principles established by the foregoing decisions it is clear that no agreement enforceable at equity was made by the parties herein. There was a promise by defendants to lease their property to plaintiff for 99 years provided that if "a lease upon the above terms and conditions has not been executed within 30 days from date hereof, both parties reserve the right at anytime thereafter, but prior to the execution of such a lease, to terminate this offer." The proposal also provides that the terms and conditions of the lease not specified therein shall be subject to the approval of both parties; that "upon execution and delivery of the lease, the lessee shall pay" etc.; that "upon execution and delivery of the lease, the lessee will place in escrow the sum of $30,000"; that "taxes, rents and insurance shall be prorated as of the date of the execution of the lease"; that "if this offer is accepted and a lease is prepared and mutually agreed upon, the lessee shall upon execution and delivery of said lease, pay ..." Such language clearly implies that the parties contemplated the execution of a formal lease as a necessary act towards the culmination of their proposed transaction. Moreover, the provision in paragraph 9 of the offer is a definite reservation of each party to be released from every obligation under the contract if the lease shall not have been executed within 30 days from the date of the offer.

It was evidently the numerous provisions contemplated as indispensable to a competent 99-year lease that caused defendants to include those provisions in paragraphs 8 and 9, providing for their own approval of the lease thereafter to be prepared and for their reservation of the right to terminate the offer if a lease should not be executed within 30 days after the offer.

Further to demonstrate the soundness of our thesis that the parties must have intended the execution of a lease as a condition precedent to the consummation of the negotiations we return to a consideration of the covenants that should be agreed upon before it can be said that the minds of the parties have met upon all of the essentials of a contract of such importance as a 99-year lease. Absent from Exhibit A are provisions for (1) the kind of a building and the nature of its construction; (2) the nature of its foundation; (3) the type of its roof, its conformance with restrictions, zoning ordinances and other legal requirements pertaining to a permanent structure; (4) methods for preventing an abandonment and of enforcing the obligations of the lease in event of lessee's insolvency and means of determining the extent or nature of repairs; and (5) the character and financial responsibility of an assignee. Covenants bearing upon these and many other subjects must be agreed upon before it can be said that a contract for a 99-year lease has been made. But in this case in order to determine that the offer is not enforceable it is unnecessary to go further than paragraphs 8 and 9 to observe that the offer merely adumbrates the instrument contemplated. It is merely one step in the negotiations for a lease. The offer, which was addressed to a broker, indicates that the parties contemplated further study and conferences with reference to the terms of the lease. It cannot be said, therefore, that the parties contracted for a 99-year lease....

The judgment is affirmed.

Exercise 2-14: *Diesel Power Equipment, Inc. v. ADDCO, Inc.*

The next case provides a further illustration of the perils and pitfalls associated with letters of intent in the context of complex commercial transactions.

1. What was the purpose of the proposed deal between Diesel Power and ADDCO?

2. What key deal terms were included in the Letter of Intent? How did the draft Asset Purchase Agreements differ from the Letter of Intent? Why did the court regard these differences as significant?

Diesel Power Equipment, Inc. v. ADDCO, Inc.

377 F.3d 853 (2004)

HANSEN, Circuit Judge.

Following a bench trial, the district court awarded $809,396 to Diesel Power Equipment, Inc. (Diesel Power) in its breach-of-contract claim against ADDCO, Inc., and ADDCO appeals. Because the parties' agreements were not sufficiently definite to form a binding contract under Nebraska law, we reverse the district court's judgment.

I.

Diesel Power is a Deutz engine distributor based in Omaha, Nebraska, whose distributorship covered Nebraska, Iowa, Missouri, Illinois, Indiana, parts of Kansas, and most of Kentucky. ADDCO is a Minnesota company that owned a division called the Nicholson Engine Group (NEG), which primarily engaged in the sale and distribution of Deutz engines and products in Minnesota, South Dakota, North Dakota, and parts of Wisconsin. This case involves Diesel Power's failed attempt to purchase NEG from ADDCO.

Diesel Power's owner, Bill Engler, began negotiating the purchase of the NEG division with Tim Nicholson, ADDCO's president, in early 2001. Engler and his business consultant, Morley Zipursky, met with Nicholson several times over the summer and Engler sent a preliminary offer letter to Nicholson on

August 24, 2001, detailing values for the inventory, fixed assets, and furniture that Diesel Power was interested in purchasing. The letter stated that it was not the entire offer and listed goodwill, consulting, and noncompete payments, as well as other elements, as items that needed to be discussed. The parties met on August 30 to finalize specific inventory and fixed-asset items to be included in the purchase. Engler offered $275,000 for goodwill, or $350,000 to be paid in installments, and Nicholson indicated he wanted more money for goodwill. Engler agreed to draft a joint letter to be sent to Deutz for its approval of the sale. The men discussed closing the sale in October or November 2001.

The next day, Nicholson called Engler and stated that he accepted the offer, and Engler agreed to draft a letter of intent. Zipursky drafted a proposed letter of intent, which specified amounts for various assets and discussed how to handle the purchase of accounts receivables. The letter of intent offered to pay for goodwill in one of two ways: either $275,000 paid at closing, or $100,000 at closing with five annual installments of $50,000 for a total of $350,000. Zipursky forwarded the letter of intent to Nicholson on September 4. Nicholson responded that one item was missing from the list of fixed assets and that one amount was not as agreed. Zipursky forwarded a revised letter of intent correcting these items on September 6. After reviewing the revised letter of intent, Nicholson called Zipursky and discussed changing the goodwill price to $350,000 due in full at closing. Engler offered to pay $300,000 at closing and $25,000 per year over the next two years. Nicholson responded "we've got a deal."

A third revised letter of intent was forwarded to Nicholson on September 11, which Nicholson signed. The total purchase price contemplated in the Letter of Intent was $1,290,400. The Letter of Intent stated that closing "will depend on when we get the agreements in place" and assured ADDCO that Diesel Power's "efforts should we be successful in purchasing the NEG company will [in] no way have a diliterious [sic] affect [sic] on your reputation." ... Nicholson also signed the joint letter to Deutz, which stated that Diesel Power had "agreed in principle" to buy NEG from ADDCO and requested Deutz's approval of the transfer of the distributorship. On September 18, Deutz sent a letter to both parties stating it approved of the sale with the conditions that Diesel Power maintain a facility in the Minneapolis area, Diesel Power comply with its distributorship contract, there be a separate contract for the NEG territory, and the accounts of both Diesel Power and NEG be brought current.

Zipursky prepared a draft Asset Purchase Agreement and forwarded it to Nicholson on September 27. The draft agreement contained terms similar to the September 11 Letter of Intent, with the addition of closing procedures and other miscellaneous provisions. Nicholson asked that various prices be shifted between the goodwill figure and the other assets. A second draft Asset Purchase Agreement was forwarded on October 24. The October 24 agreement varied from the September 27 draft in the following respects: the October 24 agreement allocated $180,000 toward the Deutz distributorship, whereas the September 27 agreement placed no value on the distributorship; the October 24 agreement provided for a noncompete agreement for the three principals of ADDCO and allocated $50,000 (payable in two installments of $25,000 over a two-year period) toward the value of the noncompete, whereas the September 27 agreement did not mention a noncompete agreement; the October 24 agreement made no mention of a goodwill payment, whereas the

September 27 agreement allocated $350,000 to goodwill, to be paid $300,000 at closing and two $25,000 annual payments; and the October 24 agreement allocated full value to the inventory, whereas the September 27 agreement discounted older inventory. Neither of the draft Asset Purchase Agreements was ever signed.

In late October 2001, Interstate Companies, Inc., which had attempted to purchase the NEG division in 1999, contacted Nicholson about buying NEG. Nicholson sought and received approval from Deutz to sell NEG to Interstate. On November 6, Nicholson informed Engler that he had another offer that was $1 million higher and asked Engler if he would increase his offer. Engler tried to enforce the Letter of Intent, but ADDCO subsequently entered an Asset Purchase Agreement with Interstate on November 20 for a total price of $2,181,896, and the sale closed on November 30.

Diesel Power sued ADDCO for breach of contract. In a trial to the bench, the district court determined that the parties entered an oral agreement on August 31, which was memorialized by the September 11 Letter of Intent. The court found that the commitments and agreements were certain and definite and that the parties' conduct evinced an objective intent to be bound by the terms of the Letter of Intent. The court found that the October 24 draft Asset Purchase Agreement did not materially alter the terms of the September 11 Letter of Intent, concluding that any terms referred to in the draft Asset Purchase Agreement but not in the Letter of Intent were either implied in the Letter of Intent, were not essential to the agreement, or were reallocated at Nicholson's request for purposes of maximizing tax benefits.

The court found that ADDCO breached the contract by selling NEG to Interstate and assessed Diesel Power's damages at the difference between the sale price to Interstate and the contract price specified in the September 11 Letter of Intent, with adjustments for a few minor differences between the property included in the Interstate sale and that contemplated by the Letter of Intent. The court also reduced the damage award by $50,000, the amount that ADDCO disputedly owed to Deutz to bring its account current, to avoid having to deal with any issues arising out of Deutz's September 18 condition that both ADDCO and Diesel Power bring their accounts current before Deutz would approve the sale to Diesel Power. The court entered judgment for Diesel Power for $809,396, and ADDCO appeals.

II.

...

We review the district court's factual findings for clear error ...

"[I]n order to establish an express contract [under Nebraska law,] there must be a definite proposal and an unconditional and absolute acceptance thereof." *Viking Broad.*, 497 N.W.2d at 386. Further, there must be a meeting of the minds "at every point; nothing can be left open for future arrangement." *Cimino v. FirsTier Bank, N.A.*, 247 Neb. 797, 530 N.W.2d 606, 614 (1995). "A contract is not formed if the parties contemplate that something remains to be done to establish contractual arrangements or if elements are left for future arrangement." *Neb. Nutrients, Inc.*, 626 N.W.2d at 499. An informal agreement may be binding, despite the parties' intentions to enter a formal agreement at a later time, only if the later, formal agreement contains no new provisions not contained in or inferred from the prior informal agreement. *Reynolds & Maginn v. Omaha Gen. Iron Works*, 105 Neb. 361, 180 N.W. 584, 586 (1920) ... The district court concluded that ADDCO and Diesel Power entered a binding verbal agreement on August 31, when Nicholson called Engler after meeting with him at the ADDCO facilities the day before. Under Nebraska law, the parties' agreement was not sufficiently definite as of August 31 to form a binding contract. Nicholson and Engler continued negotiations about the amount and timing of the goodwill payment at least up until execution of the September 11 Letter of Intent. Those negotiations did not include merely re-allocating the total price among various assets, but a real change in the timing of the goodwill payment, from an initial offer of $275,000 at closing or $100,000 at closing with $50,000 annual payments over five years, to $300,000 at closing and $25,000 annual payments over two years. Thus, the parties had not reached agreement on that vital term, as well as others, before September 11. *See Sayer v. Bowley*, 243 Neb. 801, 503 N.W.2d 166, 170 (1993) ("[T]he conduct of the parties during the drafting of these [subsequent] documents indicates that several important terms had not been discussed or agreed upon at the time of the alleged oral agreement."). The district court erred in concluding that the August 30 and 31 negotiations formed a binding agreement.

The district court also determined that the parties were bound by the September 11 Letter of Intent. The Supreme Court of Nebraska quoted the Seventh Circuit in construing a Letter of Intent in *Viking Broadcasting*.

> We have a pattern common in commercial life. Two firms reach concord on the general terms of their transaction. They sign a document, captioned "agreement in principle" or "letter of intent," memorializing these terms but anticipating future negotiations and decisions-an appraisal of the assets, the clearing of a title, the list is endless. One of these terms proves divisive, and the deal collapses. The party that perceives itself the loser then claims that the preliminary document has legal force independent of the definitive contract.

Viking Broadcasting, 497 N.W.2d at 385 ... The letter of intent in *Viking Broadcasting* stated that any information gained during the due diligence investigation must be kept confidential "in the event the merger is not consummated," and provided that neither party would disclose the fact of the merger until the deal was consummated. *Id.* at 384. The court found that the letter of intent was so cursory, indefinite, and conditional that it failed as a matter of law to establish the parties' objective intent to be bound by it. *Id.* at 386.

Given the definiteness required under Nebraska law, we conclude that the September 11 Letter of Intent did not bind the parties. The parties continued to negotiate and prepare subsequent documents, including at least two versions of a draft Asset Purchase Agreement, neither of which was ever signed. The Supreme Court of Nebraska has looked at subsequent draft documents as a sign that the parties did not intend to be bound by an earlier document. *See Hawkins Const. Co. v. Reiman Corp.*, 245 Neb. 131, 511 N.W.2d 113, 116–17 (1994) (holding that parties did not enter a binding contract when a contractor accepted a subcontractor's bid where the parties continued to exchange draft agreements containing terms not previously addressed, such as liability insurance requirements, time for submitting shop drawings, billing and pay-

Notice the weight that the court places on the draft Asset Purchase Agreement in discerning the intention of the parties.

ment terms, and who was responsible for a dewatering problem). The September 11 Letter of Intent contained language similar to that found in *Viking Broadcasting, see* 497 N.W.2d at 385, that revealed the tenuous nature of the negotiations when it stated that Diesel Power's "efforts *should we be successful in purchasing the NEG company* will [in] no way have a diliterious [sic] affect [sic] on [ADDCO's] reputation." (Appellant's App. at 92 (emphasis added).)

Despite the district court's conclusion that the September 11 Letter of Intent and the October 24 draft Purchase Agreement were identical in all material respects, our review reveals that there are material differences of substance between the documents. One material difference between the two documents is the total price. Diesel Power does not adequately address ADDCO's assertion that the October 24 draft Asset Purchase Agreement contemplated a total purchase price $57,000 less than the September 11 Letter of Intent. The reallocation of prices among the various assets cannot account for the significant difference in the total price. Additionally, the draft Asset Purchase Agreement detailed what was to be included in the purchase of the Deutz distributorship, including "job records, customer lists, vendor lists, outstanding purchase orders, project records, and supporting documents and quotation lists." … The Letter of Intent listed only Deutz inventory and engines. The detailed listing in the draft Asset Purchase Agreement reveals that the negotiations involved more than the mere transfer of physical assets. Diesel Power was attempting to purchase the whole of the NEG business, including the confidential records included in the draft Asset Purchase Agreement. These particulars are more than mere closing procedures.

A key material item included in the draft Asset Purchase Agreement not discussed in the Letter of Intent is the noncompete agreement. The parties had contemplated the existence of a noncompete provision as revealed in the August 24 letter. While the Letter of Intent made no reference to a noncompete agreement, the October 24 draft Asset Purchase Agreement valued it at $50,000, named the individuals to whom it applied, two of whom were not signatories to any of the foregoing negotiations, and provided that the terms of the noncompete would be included as an attachment. Although the value assigned to the noncompete might have been a mere reallocation of the purchase price at ADDCO's request, the existence and the terms of the noncompete go well beyond a dollar amount. A noncompete agreement is a valuable tool used by parties in the purchase of a business to prevent the seller from competing against the purchaser. The temporal and geographic limitations are critical to both sides of the agreement, as revealed by the frequency with which we see them challenged in court. Although Diesel Power was attempting to buy an exclusive distributorship for Deutz engines, which presumably would hamper any attempts by the ADDCO principals to directly compete with Diesel Power without a Deutz distributorship, NEG did more than distribute Deutz engines. Noncompetes are generally much broader than a single brand of a product. Given the discussion of a noncompete in the August 24 letter, the absence of any mention of it in the September 11 Letter of Intent, and the reintroduction and valuation of it in the October 24 draft Asset Purchase Agreement, we cannot say that a noncompete agreement was immaterial to the transaction.

Both parties agree that the purchase was conditioned on Deutz's approval and transfer of the distributorship, yet the September 11 Letter of Intent did not mention the condition. Deutz conditionally approved the transfer on September 18, after the Letter of Intent was signed, and the October 24 draft Asset Purchase Agreement specifically provided that the transaction was contingent on the assignment of the distributor contract to Diesel Power and Deutz's approval of the assignment. We fail to see how the Letter of Intent can be said to include all of the material terms of the agreement when this very material term is not mentioned. Further, as the district court recognized when it adjusted the damage calculation by the $50,000 in dispute between ADDCO and Deutz, Deutz's approval was conditional and that condition had not been satisfied when ADDCO ended negotiations in late October.

One can easily sympathize with Diesel Power's plight. It spent nearly a year negotiating the purchase of NEG only to have its efforts come to naught when ADDCO was effectively wooed by another buyer willing to pay substantially more money. The continuing negotiations did not turn sour, which is generally what happens in cases involving letters of intent; rather, ADDCO just received a better offer. Diesel Power, as the drafter of the relevant documents, could have easily protected itself by including a good-faith or similar provision in the Letter of Intent that would have precluded ADDCO from entertaining other offers until the continuing negotiations between them broke down, and one party or the other formally withdrew from the Letter of Intent. But it did not. Given the particular definiteness required by Nebraska law, as demonstrated in *Viking Broadcasting,* we must reverse the district court's judgment.

> Pay attention to how the court rationalizes its conclusion here. It focuses on what steps Diesel Power and its lawyers could have taken to protect Diesel Power's position.

Exercise 2-15: *Store Properties v. Neal* and *Diesel Power v. ADDCO* Revisited

1. What should Store Properties have done to better protect itself? Revise the letter of intent in *Neal* to make it clear that the parties did not intend to bind themselves.

2. What could Diesel Power have done to better protect itself?

3. In another letter of intent case, *Billings v. Wilby*, 175 N.C. 571, 96 S.E. 50 (1918), the court held that parties to a letter of intent had formed a contract. The key facts in that case were:

   Plaintiff received a letter from defendant building contractor inviting plaintiff to submit a proposal for work on a federal building project according to survey and specifications which had been already made by the federal government

   On January 13, plaintiff replied by telegram: "Will put in sewer line according to specifications for five hundred dollars, you furnish pipe and material ... Wire at once if you accept this. [Signed] A. U. Billings."

   On same date defendant wrote (by a particular form of telegram called a "night letter"):

   "Forty cents per running foot is best I can do, I furnish pipe and you cement, I can do it myself for less than this, but want it put in before my man comes. If I cannot get it for the above amount, will wait and put it in myself. [Signed] William Wilby."

On January 14, plaintiff replied:

"Night letter received. Will accept. Send contract signed at once."

Neither party ever signed any additional document.

The court nevertheless concluded that the parties formed a contract. Look the case up. Why did the court conclude a contract was formed? Do you agree? How would you distinguish this case from *Store Properties* and *Diesel Power*?

4. If two parties sign a letter of intent at the same time, and a court concludes the parties intend to bind themselves to a contract, which party would a court say made the offer?

Requests for Bids

Many of the cases you will be reading in this text involve contracts relating to large-scale construction projects. Because of this, and because courts have developed the law governing requests for bids in the context of large-scale construction contracts, it is helpful to understand the way such contracts commonly are made.

When an owner of land decides to do a large-scale construction project, she first hires architects and engineers to design the project. Once the plans and specifications for the project are final, the owner asks construction companies (called "general contractors") to bid on the project.[2] General contractors are directly responsible for completing the project in accord with the project plans and specifications and at the price agreed upon.

Large-scale construction projects require a wide variety of experts, including experts in pouring concrete, building walls, installing windows, plumbing, electricity, and painting. Accordingly, general contractors almost always hire subcontractors, who are experts in each of these areas, to work on their projects.

The process of selecting a general contractor often involves a competitive bidding process in which each general contractor interested in competing for a job submits a bid. Each general contractor collects bids from multiple subcontractors in an effort to make its overall bid as low as possible. General contractors add the subcontractors' bids together, the general contractors' expenses, and a profit margin. Usually the general contractor who submits the lowest bid is awarded a contract.

Courts generally hold that, when a general contractor seeks bids from subcontractors, the general contractor's request for bids is an invitation for offers. The subcontractors' bids are considered offers.

Exercise 2-16: Requests for Bids

1. What policy rationales explain the general rule that requests for bids are not considered offers?

---

2. If a general contractor is working on a government contract, that contractor is called a "prime contractor."

2. Do you think the following request for bids is an offer? Consider the request in light of the policy rationales you identified in question 1 that support the general rule that requests for bids are not considered offers. (Hint: The hypothetical is complicated, could go either way, and requires an in-depth analysis.)

    Farideh Construction, a general contractor, sent the following request for bids:

    > Request for bids: Farideh Construction has been awarded a contract to build a courthouse for the State of Olympia. To complete the contract, Farideh requires the services of a painting subcontractor and hereby solicits bids to perform the courthouse painting in accordance with the attached specifications [assume the specifications were attached]. Bids must be sealed and delivered to Farideh no later than 5:00 p.m. on August 1, 2015. Bids will be opened in a bid opening ceremony on August 3, 2015 at 9:00 a.m. When the bids are read, the lowest conforming bid, if less than $100,000, will be deemed to have been given the contract. Farideh reserves the right to approve all bidders.

3. Challenge question—Auctions. Sandra Seller decided to sell a sculpture she owned that was made by the famous sculptor, Michelle Ann Gello. According to most experts, the sculpture was worth $5,000,000. Sandra arranged for the sculpture to be auctioned off by a professional auction house "without reserve." At the auction, the highest bid was $1,000,000. Must Sandra perform by closing the sale at that price? The answer to this question is controlled by U.C.C. Article 2. Find the applicable section and subsection in U.C.C. Article 2.

Manner of Acceptance

Introduction

You have already learned earlier in this chapter that, to form a contract, both parties must manifest commitment and the terms must be sufficiently certain. You have also learned that, in particular factual contexts, courts apply special rules to determine whether particular communications are offers. In this section of the text you will learn about additional requirements that only apply to acceptances.

Exercise 2-17: Introductory Exercise

1. Review what you have already learned by listing the four requirements to accept an offer in your own words.

2. Read section 30 of the RESTATEMENT (SECOND) OF CONTRACTS. Under that section, which party has the power to control how an offer is accepted (in other words, who controls the manner of acceptance)?

3. Section 30 refers to either inviting or requiring an answer in words or through action. What is the difference between inviting or requiring something? (Hint: Think about the consequence of failing to comply with something

that is invited. Then, think about the consequence of failing to comply with something that is required.)

4.   Under section 30, what happens if the offeror's communication does not include any reference to a manner of acceptance?

Offeror's Control over the Manner of Acceptance

Courts often say that an offeror is the **master of the offer** and, therefore, has the right to insist that an acceptance be made only in one particular way. Thus, an offeror may **require** that an offeree accept by signing, by delivering the completed performance sought by the offeror, or by dancing a jig. The classic question that arises is whether the offer calls for acceptance by promise or performance. We return to this question below because it is the touchstone of the distinction between bilateral and unilateral contracts. But the offeror can also dictate other aspects of the process of acceptance. Assume that the offeror stipulates that acceptance must be by return promise. The offeror could also require that the offeree furnish the promise in writing, or by electronic means such as email, rather than orally. The key point to keep in mind is that the common law says that an acceptance must strictly comply with the terms of the offer, including any prescribed manner of acceptance.

Offerors, however, seldom insist on a particular manner of acceptance when they make an offer. But, *if the offer does insist on a particular manner of acceptance, an offeree can only accept by complying with the insisted upon manner of acceptance. In contrast, if an offeror only suggests a preferred method of acceptance, acceptance by any reasonable means will suffice. See* RESTATEMENT (SECOND) OF CONTRACTS § 60.

An offeror's right to control the manner of acceptance gives rise to three potential issues in analyzing whether a valid acceptance exists:

1.   Does the offer require, suggest, or not address a particular manner of acceptance? If the manner is not addressed at all, that fact will be obvious. To decide whether a particular reference to manner in an offer requires or merely suggests the manner necessitates a close examination and analysis of the specific language used.

2.   If an offer does require a particular manner of acceptance, has the offeree complied with the required manner? If so, and an offeree otherwise accepts an offer, the parties have satisfied the mutual assent requirement. If not, the parties did not form a contract. If the offeree indicates assent to the offer but does not do so in the manner the offeree requires, the offeree has made a counter-offer, which the offeror can decide whether or not to accept.

3.   If an offeror suggested a particular manner of acceptance, and an offeree accepts using a different manner, has the offeree accepted? If the offeree adopts a reasonable manner and otherwise accepts, the parties have satisfied the mutual assent requirement. If not, the parties did not form a contract.

Exercise 2-18: *Kuzmeskus v. Pickup Motor Co.*

The next case in this chapter, *Kuzmeskus v. Pickup Motor Co.*, is a somewhat tricky case that involves an offeror's control over the manner of acceptance. As you read *Kuzmeskus*, consider the following questions:

1. Identify the key facts in this case. Be sure to focus on the specific language used by the parties.

2. To understand the result in this case, you need to know which party was the offeror and which was the offeree. Which party is the offeror? Why do you say so? (Hint: This question is somewhat tricky. Try not to be distracted by the fact that the parties were using Pickup Motor Co.'s forms.)

3. Why was the question about the legal status of the purchase orders outcome determinative?

4. Why did Pickup Motor Co. create a set of forms that made it vulnerable to the type of problem that happened in this case? In other words, was there a business rationale for the way Pickup did business?

5. Why did the court rule in favor of the plaintiff?

Kuzmeskus v. Pickup Motor Co.

330 Mass. 490, 115 N.E.2d 461 (1953)

Williams, Justice. This is an action of contract to recover the amount of a money deposit made by the plaintiff with the defendant on orders for the purchase of four motor buses. The defendant claims in "recoupment and set-off" damages for failure by the plaintiff to complete the purchase of the buses. The facts, as reported by an auditor whose findings are final, are summarized as follows.

The plaintiff, a resident of the town of Montague, was the successful bidder for a contract with the town to furnish transportation for school children. The contract was awarded on July 28, 1949, one of its terms being that the plaintiff should provide five new school buses. The defendant was a dealer in Dodge trucks and buses in Holyoke and in pursuance of its "sales promotion" had assisted the plaintiff in obtaining information respecting school buses and in preparing his bid for the contract. Late in the evening of July 28, and within an hour after the plaintiff had been informed of the acceptance of his bid, the general manager and a salesman of the defendant called on the plaintiff and discussed with him the terms of a purchase by him from the defendant of five new Dodge school buses. Following the determination of price, model, and date of delivery of the buses the plaintiff signed five orders to the defendant on forms presented by the general manager, each of which was an order for the purchase of a Dodge school bus. After discussion one of the orders was then and there cancelled. The remaining orders were on printed forms with the words "Pickup Motor Company, Inc. Holyoke, Mass." at the top of each form. Each contained the words "Enter my order for one New Dodge School Bus" or "one New Dodge Bus" with a statement of the price and a description of the vehicle. Each concluded with the provision, "this order is not binding unless authorized by an officer of the company, and purchaser's credit has been OK'd by Finance Company." Immediately be-

Pay special attention to the language that the court quotes from the order form. Based on the quoted language, try to predict what the outcome of the case will be and why.

neath this clause was the word "Purchaser" with a place for a signature and below that the words "Authorized by" with a line for a signature.

The plaintiff gave his check drawn in the amount of $1,000 to the defendant's agents, this amount representing a deposit of $250 on each of the four buses. At about 9 o'clock on the following morning the plaintiff telephoned the defendant's general manager that he was canceling the orders of the previous evening and requested that he be refunded his $1,000. He confirmed the cancellation by telegram within an hour and attempted to stop payment on his check but found that the defendant had caused it to be certified. The plaintiff moved for judgment on the auditor's report, and a judge of the Superior Court entered a finding for the plaintiff in the sum of $1,180 and also a finding for him as defendant in set-off. An appeal by the defendant … brings the case here. The issue between the parties is whether there were binding agreements of purchase and sale. The defendant contends that the written orders were only memoranda of oral contracts which previously had been completed, but, if not, that the orders became contracts when physically received with the deposit by the general manager.…

Although it appears that before the award the defendant was interested in having the plaintiff obtain the transportation contract from the town and engaged in preliminary negotiations with him as to the purchase of school buses if he were successful in his bid, the defendant makes no contention that these negotiations constituted any agreement of purchase and sale. Immediately after the plaintiff was notified that he had been awarded the contract the parties negotiated further and determined what the terms of the proposed sales should be. Although it appears that the basis of an agreement was then arrived at, there were no completed oral contracts because the defendant required the contracts to be executed in writing. Such contracts previously drawn by the defendant in the form of orders were presented to the plaintiff for his signature. Therein it was stated that the defendant was not bound to sell in accordance with the terms of the orders until their acceptance had been authorized by an officer of the company. A place for the authorizing official's signature was provided. On these facts no contracts were completed by the delivery of the orders to the defendant. The defendant made it clear to the plaintiff that it did not intend to be presently bound, and on his part the plaintiff could not have expected to be bound until the proposed sales were subsequently authorized in accordance with the imposed conditions. A promise made with an understood intention that it is not to be legally binding, but only expressive of a present intention, is not a contract. [Citations omitted.] The presentation of the forms for the plaintiff to sign was no more than an invitation or request to give orders on the terms and conditions therein stated. [Citations omitted.] The indication by the defendant of a willingness to receive proposals did not ripen into any contract or contracts until the proposals were accepted. [Citation omitted.] Before such acceptance had been communicated to the plaintiff his orders had been withdrawn or revoked. [Citations omitted.] If the general manager was an officer of the company with power to authorize the sales, he said or did nothing to inform the plaintiff that he was taking favorable action. [Citations omitted.] The negotiations having fallen short of a binding agreement, … the plaintiff is entitled to the return of his deposit with interest. The defendant cannot recover on its declaration in recoupment and set-off even if the pleading can legally be supported, which we do not intimate.... The findings of the Superior Court are to be treated as orders for judgment. [Citation omitted.] As such they are affirmed.

So ordered.

Exercise 2-19: *Kuzmeskus* Revisited

1. If the *Kuzmeskus* court had applied section 60 of the Restatement (Second) of Contracts, would the result in this case have been any different? Why or why not?

2. Power Tool Company (PTC) was a distributor for Echo, Inc. (Echo). The distributorship agreement provided that "All orders for Products shall be subject to acceptance by Echo at Lake Zurich, Illinois" (the location of its headquarters). Echo's regional sales manager and PTC's president negotiated and signed an Order for delivery of equipment during the following Spring. Shortly after, Echo's customer services department (based at Lake Zurich) wrote a standard letter to all its distributors "recapping your Spring equipment orders" and requesting that distributors verify that the information in the letter matched their records because "mistakes and omissions can sometimes occur" when entering orders into Echo's computer. Echo refused to ship any of the equipment requested in PTC's Order because PTC's account was delinquent. Did the parties form a contract for the sale and delivery of the equipment? What language is most significant to your conclusion? Why?

3. Buyer submitted an offer to Seller for Seller to build a machine for Buyer's factory on Buyer's property. The offer concluded with the following statement: "This purchase order agreement is not binding until accepted. Acceptance should be executed on acknowledgment copy which should be returned to Buyer." Seller did not sign anything, but did begin building the machine. The court held Buyer and Seller formed a contract. Can you see why? (Hint: Focus on the language.) *See Allied Steel & Conveyers, Inc. v. Ford Motor Co.*, 277 F.2d 907 (1960).

4. Re-read section 60 of the Restatement (Second) of Contracts. What is the policy rationale for section 60?

5. Give an unambiguous example of a prescription as to the manner of acceptance and an unambiguous example of a suggestion of the manner of acceptance. *This question is the first one in which you are asked to come up with your own examples of concepts you have learned in this book. If you understand the materials well enough to generate original examples, you have mastered the subject. Hence, the extra mental effort is worth it. Moreover, contracts lawyers draft contracts; this question is your first, small step towards developing that skill.*

6. Give an example of an ambiguous reference to manner of acceptance — in other words, a situation where it is not clear whether the manner is prescribed or suggested.

7. If the purchase order in question 3 in this exercise had been silent as to the manner of acceptance, what would the result have been?

8. If the *Allied* court (referred to in question 3 of this exercise) had concluded that the manner of acceptance was prescribed, would the court still have concluded the parties formed a contract?

Unilateral and Bilateral Contracts

This section introduces you to a significant distinction: the distinction between unilateral and bilateral contracts. Many offerors do not specify whether an acceptance must be in the form of making a promise or performing an act. When an offeror does specify a manner of acceptance, however, it makes a difference whether a contract is considered unilateral or bilateral.

A **unilateral contract** is one in which the offeror unambiguously requires that acceptance in the form of performing the very act the offeror is seeking when making her offer is the only manner of acceptance. "Unilateral" refers to the fact that only one party, the offeror, is making a promise. In contrast, a **bilateral contract** is one in which the offeror requires an acceptance to be in the form of a return promise. "Bilateral" refers to the fact that both parties are making promises.

You can test whether you understand the basic difference between unilateral and bilateral contracts by trying to answer the two questions below:

- If I offer to sell you my car for $400 and say, "You can only accept my offer by promising to buy the car," have I made an offer of a unilateral or a bilateral contract?

- If I offer to sell you my car for $400 and say, "You can only accept my offer by handing me $400," have I made an offer of a unilateral or a bilateral contract?

The first question presents an example of a bilateral contract because the offeror insists on a promise. The second question presents an example of a unilateral contract because the offeror insists that the offeree accept by a performance (handing over money).

Exercise 2-20: *Davis v. Jacoby*

Parties do not always use language that is unambiguous when discussing potential contracts. Consequently, some cases present complex and interesting questions with regard to whether a contract is unilateral or bilateral. The next case in this section, *Davis v. Jacoby*, presents a challenging question of whether a contract is unilateral or bilateral in an interesting context. It also accurately reflects the modern tendency to view contracts as bilateral unless the offer unequivocally calls for the offeree to accept by performing an act rather than making a promise. As you read *Davis*, look for the answers to the following questions:

1. What are the key facts?
2. Why does the distinction between offers of unilateral and bilateral contracts matter in this case?
3. On what rule does the court rely in its analysis of the case?
4. What policy rationale does the court offer for that rule? Does that rationale make sense?
5. What arguments does the court make in support of its conclusion that Whitehead made an offer of a bilateral contract?

6. What counter-arguments could be made to support a conclusion opposite from the one that the court reached?

7. How does the fact that Whitehead committed suicide affect the unilateral-bilateral issue? (Hint: Are there any inferences we can draw from the fact and timing of Whitehead's suicide that might reinforce a "bilateral contract" or "unilateral contract" classification?)

8. What would the result be in *Davis* under section 32 of the RESTATEMENT (SECOND) OF CONTRACTS?

Davis v. Jacoby
1 Cal. 2d 370, 34 P.2d 1026 (1934)

As you read this case (and others), notice the tone used. The tone often enables you to predict the result of a case. What is your prediction about the result in this case?

Per curiam. Plaintiffs appeal from a judgment refusing to grant specific performance of an alleged contract to make a will. The facts are not in dispute and are as follows:

The plaintiff, Caro M. Davis, was the niece of Blanche Whitehead, who was married to Rupert Whitehead. Prior to her marriage in 1913 to her co-plaintiff Frank M. Davis, Caro lived for a considerable time at the home of the Whiteheads, in Piedmont, Cal. The Whiteheads were childless and extremely fond of Caro. The record is replete with uncontradicted testimony of the close and loving relationship that existed between Caro and her aunt and uncle. During the period that Caro lived with the Whiteheads, she was treated as and often referred to by the Whiteheads as their daughter. In 1913, when Caro was married to Frank Davis, the marriage was arranged at the Whitehead home and a reception held there. After the marriage, Mr. and Mrs. Davis went to Mr. Davis' home in Canada, where they have resided ever since. During the period 1913 to 1931 Caro made many visits to the Whiteheads, several of them being of long duration. The Whiteheads visited Mr. and Mrs. Davis in Canada on several occasions. After the marriage and continuing down to 1931 the closest and most friendly relationship at all times existed between these two families. They corresponded frequently, the record being replete with letters showing the loving relationship.

By the year 1930 Mrs. Whitehead had become seriously ill. She had suffered several strokes and her mind was failing. Early in 1931 Mr. Whitehead had her removed to a private hospital. The doctors in attendance had informed him that she might die at any time or she might linger for many months. Mr. Whitehead had suffered severe financial reverses. He had had several sieges of sickness and was in poor health. The record shows that during the early part of 1931 he was desperately in need of assistance with his wife, and in his business affairs, and that he did not trust his friends in Piedmont. On March 18, 1931, he wrote to Mrs. Davis telling her of Mrs. Whitehead's condition and added that Mrs. Whitehead was very wistful. "Today I endeavored to find out what she wanted. I finally asked her if she wanted to see you. She burst out crying and we had great difficulty in getting her to stop. Evidently, that is what is on her mind. It is a very difficult matter to decide. If you come it will mean that you will have to leave again, and then things may be serious. I am going to see the doctor, and get his candid opinion and will then write you again.... Since writing the above, I have seen the doctor, and he thinks it will help considerably if you come." Shortly thereafter, Mr. Whitehead wrote to Caro Davis further explaining the physical condition of Mrs. Whitehead and himself. On March 24, 1931, Mr. Davis, at the request of his wife, telegraphed to Mr. Whitehead as follows: "Your letter received. Sorry to hear Blanche not so well. Hope you are feeling better yourself. If you wish Caro to go to you can arrange for her to leave in about two weeks. Please wire me if you think it advisable for her to go." On March 30, 1931, Mr. Whitehead wrote a long letter to Mr. Davis, in which he explained in detail the condition of Mrs. Whitehead's health and also referred to his own health. He pointed out that he had lost a considerable portion of his cash assets but still owned considerable realty, that he needed some one to help him with his wife and some friend he could trust to help him with his business affairs and suggested that perhaps Mr. Davis might come to California. He then pointed out that all his property was community property; that under his will all the property was to go to Mrs. Whitehead; that he believed that under Mrs. Whitehead's will practically everything was to go to Caro. Mr. Whitehead again wrote to Mr. Davis under date of April 9, 1931, pointing out how badly he needed some one he could trust to assist him, and giving it as his belief that if properly handled he could still save about $150,000. He then stated: "Having you [Mr. Davis] here to depend on and to help me regain my mind and courage would be a big thing." Three days later, on April 12, 1931, Mr. Whitehead again wrote, addressing his letter to "Dear Frank and Caro," and in this letter made the definite offer, which offer it is claimed was accepted and is the basis of this action. In this letter he first pointed out that Blanche, his wife, was in a private hospital and that "she cannot last much longer ... my affairs are not as bad as I supposed at first. Cutting everything down I figure $150,000 can be saved from the wreck." He then enumerated the values placed upon his various properties and then continued:

> "My trouble was caused by my friends taking advantage of my illness and my position to skin me. Now if Frank could come out here and be with me, and look after my affairs, we could easily save the balance I mention, provided I don't get into another panic and do some more foolish things. The next attack will be my end, I am 65 and my health had been bad for years, so, the Drs. don't give me much longer to live. So if you can come, Caro will inherit everything and you will make our lives happier and see Blanche is provided for to the end. My eyesight had gone back on me, I can't read only for a few lines at a time. I am at the house alone with Stanley [the chauffeur] who does everything for me and is a fine fellow. Now, what I want is some one who will take charge of my affairs and see I don't lose any more. Frank can do it, if he will and cut out the booze. Will you let me hear from you as soon as possible, I know it will be a sacrifice but times are still bad and likely to be, so by settling down you can help me and Blanche and gain in the end. If I had you here my mind would get better and my courage return, and we could work things out."

The court considers the April 12 letter an offer and, later, bases its decision on the language in that letter. Try to predict the specific language in the letter that the court will rely on in reaching its decision.

This letter was received by Mr. Davis at his office in Windsor, Canada, about 9:30 a. m. April 14, 1931. After reading the letter to Mrs. Davis over the telephone, and after getting her belief that they must go to California, Mr. Davis immediately wrote Mr. Whitehead a letter, which, after reading it to his wife, he sent by air mail. This letter was lost, but there is no doubt that it was sent by Davis and received by Whitehead; in fact, the trial court expressly so found. Mr. Davis testified in substance as to the contents of this letter. After acknowledging receipt of the letter of April 12, 1931, Mr. Davis unequivocally stated that he and Mrs. Davis accepted the proposition of Mr. Whitehead and both would leave Windsor to go to him on April 25. This letter of acceptance also contained the information that the reason they could not leave prior to April 25 was that Mr. Davis had to appear in court on April 22 as one of the executors of his mother's estate. The testimony is uncontradicted and ample to support the trial court's finding that this letter was sent by Davis and received by Whitehead....

Between April 14, 1931, the date the letter of acceptance was sent by Mr. Davis, and April 22, Mr. Davis was engaged in closing out his business affairs, and Mrs. Davis in closing up their home and in making other arrangements to leave. On April 22, 1931, Mr. Whitehead committed suicide. Mr. and Mrs. Davis were immediately notified and they at once came to California. From almost the moment of her arrival Mrs. Davis devoted herself to the care and comfort of her aunt, and gave her aunt constant attention and care until Mrs. Whitehead's death on May 30, 1931. On this point the trial court found: "From the time of their arrival in Piedmont, Caro M. Davis administered in every way to the comforts of Blanche Whitehead and saw that she was cared for and provided for down to the time of the death of Blanche Whitehead on May 30, 1931; during said time Caro M. Davis nursed Blanche Whitehead, cared for her and administered to her wants as a natural daughter would have done toward and for her mother."

Again, notice the tone used by the court. The tone should allow you to predict how the court will rule in this case.

This finding is supported by uncontradicted evidence and in fact is conceded by respondents to be correct. In fact, the record shows that after their arrival in California Mr. and Mrs. Davis fully performed their side of the agreement.

After the death of Mrs. Whitehead, for the first time it was discovered that the information contained in Mr. Whitehead's letter of March 30, 1931, in reference to the contents of his and Mrs. Whitehead's wills was incorrect. By a duly witnessed will dated February 28, 1931, Mr. Whitehead, after making several specific bequests, had bequeathed all of the balance of his estate to his wife for life, and upon her death to respondents Geoff Double and Rupert Ross Whitehead, his nephews. Neither appellant was mentioned in his will. It was also discovered that Mrs. Whitehead by a will dated December 17, 1927, had devised all of her estate to her husband. The evidence is clear and uncontradicted that the relationship existing between Whitehead and his two nephews, respondents herein, was not nearly as close and confidential as that existing between Whitehead and appellants.

After the discovery of the manner in which the property had been devised was made, this action was commenced upon the theory that Rupert Whitehead had assumed a contractual obligation to make a will whereby "Caro Davis would inherit everything;" that he had failed to do so; that plaintiffs had fully performed their part of the contract; that damages being insufficient, quasi specific performance should be granted in order to remedy the alleged wrong, upon the equitable principle that equity regards that done which ought to have been done. The requested relief is that the beneficiaries under the will of Rupert Whitehead, respondents herein, be declared to be involuntary trustees for plaintiffs of Whitehead's estate.

It should also be added that the evidence shows that as a result of Frank Davis leaving his business in Canada he forfeited not only all insurance business he might have written if he had remained, but also forfeited all renewal commissions earned on past business. According to his testimony this loss was over $8,000.

The trial court found that the relationship between Mr. and Mrs. Davis and the Whiteheads was substantially as above recounted and that the other facts above stated were true....

The theory of the trial court and of respondents on this appeal is that the letter of April 12 was an offer to contract, but that such offer could only be accepted by performance and could not be accepted by a promise to perform, and that said offer was revoked by the death of Mr. Whitehead before performance. In other words, it is contended that the offer was an offer to enter into a unilateral contract, and that the purported acceptance of April 14 was of no legal effect.

The distinction between unilateral and bilateral contracts is well settled in the law...." A unilateral contract is one in which no promisor receives a promise as consideration for his promise. A bilateral contract is one in which there are mutual promises between two parties to the contract; each party being both a promisor and a promisee." [§ 12 Restatement of Contracts]....

In the case of unilateral contracts no notice of acceptance by performance is required....

Although the legal distinction between unilateral and bilateral contracts is thus well settled, the difficulty in any particular case is to determine whether the particular offer is one to enter into a bilateral or unilateral contract. Some cases are quite clear cut. Thus an offer to sell which is accepted is clearly a bilateral contract, while an offer of a reward is a clear-cut offer of a unilateral contract which cannot be accepted by a promise to perform, but only by performance. [Citation omitted.] Between these two extremes is a vague field where the particular contract may be unilateral or bilateral depending upon the intent of the offer and the facts and circumstances of each case. The offer to contract involved in this case falls within this category. By the provisions of the Restatement of the Law of Contracts it is expressly provided that there is a *presumption* that the offer is to enter into a bilateral contract. Section 31 provides: "In case of doubt it is presumed that an offer invites the formation of a bilateral contract by an acceptance amounting in effect to a promise by the offeree to perform what the offer requests, rather than the formation of one or more unilateral contracts by actual performance on the part of the offeree."

Professor Williston, in his Treatise on Contracts, volume 1, § 60, also takes the position that a presumption in favor of bilateral contracts exists.

In the comment following § 31 of the Restatement the reason for such presumption is stated as follows: "It is not always easy to determine whether an offeror requests an act or a promise to do the act. As a bilateral contract immediately and fully protects both parties, the interpretation is favored that a bilateral contract is proposed...."

Keeping these principles in mind, we are of the opinion that the offer of April 12 was an offer to enter into a bilateral as distinguished from a unilateral contract. Respondents argue that Mr. Whitehead had the right as offeror to designate his offer as either unilateral or bilateral. That is undoubtedly the law. It is then argued that from all the facts and circumstances it must be implied that what Whitehead wanted was performance and not a mere promise to perform. We think this is a non sequitur, in fact the surrounding circumstances lead to just the opposite conclusion. These parties were not dealing at arm's length. Not only were they related, but a very close and intimate friendship existed between them. The record indisputably demonstrates that Mr. Whitehead had confidence in Mr. and Mrs. Davis, in fact that he had lost all confidence in everyone else. The record amply shows that by an accumulation of occurrences Mr. Whitehead had become desperate, and that what he wanted was the promise of appellants that he could look to them for assistance. He knew from his past relationship with appellants that if they gave their promise to perform he could rely upon them. The correspondence between them indicates how desperately he desired this assurance. Under these circumstances he wrote his offer of April 12, above quoted, in which he stated, after disclosing his desperate mental and physical condition, and after setting forth the terms of his offer: "*Will you let me hear from you as soon as possible*—I know it will be a sacrifice but times are still bad and likely to be, so by settling down you can help me and Blanche and gain in the end." By thus specifically requesting an immediate reply Whitehead expressly indicated the nature of the acceptance desired by him, namely, appellants' promise that they would come to California and do the things requested by him. This promise was immediately sent by appellants upon receipt of the offer, and was received by Whitehead. It is elementary that when an offer has indicated the mode and means of acceptance, an acceptance in accordance with that mode or means is binding on the offeror.

Another factor which indicates that Whitehead must have contemplated a bilateral rather than an unilateral contract, is that the contract required Mr. and Mrs. Davis to perform services until the death of both Mr. and Mrs. Whitehead. It is obvious that if Mr. Whitehead died first some of these services were to be performed after his death, so that he would have to rely on the promise of appellants to perform these services. It is also of some evidentiary force that Whitehead received the letter of acceptance and acquiesced in that means of acceptance....

Do you think that this case is a good example of effective legal writing? Why or why not? Although imitation may be flattery, you probably do not want to imitate the writing in many older cases. Older cases often use archaic language and adopt cumbersome constructions. You should strive for clear, direct, concise, and precise writing.

For the foregoing reasons we are of the opinion that the offer of April 12, 1931, was an offer to enter into a bilateral contract which was accepted by the letter of April 14, 1931. Subsequently appellants fully performed their part of the contract. Under such circumstances it is well settled that damages are insufficient and specific performance will be granted. [Citation omitted.] Since the consideration has been fully rendered by appellants the question as to mutuality of remedy becomes of no importance. 6 Cal. Jur. § 140....

For the foregoing reasons the judgment appealed from is reversed.

Exercise 2-21: Unilateral versus Bilateral Contracts

Determine whether the following offers propose a unilateral or a bilateral contract:

1. "I will pay you $100 if you find my lost dog, Fido."

2. "I will pay you $50 to search for my lost dog, Fido."

3. "I will pay you $30 to baby-sit my two children next Friday night."

4. An uncle writes to his favorite nephew, who is sixteen years old, "If you refrain from drinking, smoking, swearing, and playing cards until age twenty-one, I will pay you $5,000."

Exercise 2-22: Knowledge of an Offer

An additional, relatively minor issue relating to the manner of acceptance is whether an offeree can accept an offer if the offeree is unaware of that offer. As a general rule, a contract can only be formed if the offeree knew of the offer at the time of the purported acceptance. This is particularly relevant in the context of reward offers. But read section 51 of the RESTATEMENT (SECOND) OF CONTRACTS. Then, analyze the following hypothetical using that rule: D offers a reward for the capture of Connie Criminal. P sees Connie robbing a bank and chases Connie into a dead-end alley. P then notices a poster at the entrance to the alley offering $50,000 for the capture of Connie. P captures Connie and turns her over to the police and sues D for the $50,000. What is the result?

Exercise 2-23: Silence as Acceptance

Another relatively minor issue relating to the manner of acceptance is whether silence may constitute an acceptance. Are there any circumstances under which an offeree should be able to accept by doing nothing? To answer this question, read section 69 of the RESTATEMENT (SECOND) OF CONTRACTS. *Section 69 states the rules you need to apply to analyze these problems.* Respond to the questions below:

1. I say, "I offer to buy your car for $500. If I haven't heard from you by this time tomorrow, I will assume that you accept." If there is no further contact between us by this time tomorrow, do we have a contract?

2. What would be the result if you intended, by your silence, to accept my offer?

3. What would be the result if you did not intend to accept by your silence, but you took my car keys, drove the car home, and parked it in your garage?

4. Inna Insurance Co. insured Peggy Policyholder's business under a one-year policy. After the policy expired, Inna sent Peggy a renewal form offering to insure Peggy. Peggy never replied. Later, when Inna billed Peggy for one year of insurance at the end of the year, Peggy paid the bill without objection. The next year, Inna again sent Peggy a renewal form and, two months later, a bill for two months of insurance. Peggy refused to pay, saying she had purchased insurance elsewhere. Must Peggy pay for the two months?

Termination of the Power to Accept

Introduction

Exercise 2-24: Termination of the Power to Accept

This exercise serves as an introduction to this topic using restatement rules to provide the necessary guidance. Read sections 36–43 and 48 of the RESTATE-MENT (SECOND) OF CONTRACTS.

1. Assume that an offer has been made. Assume that the requirements to accept have been met. Can you say conclusively that the parties have formed a contract?

2. What does the phrase "the power to accept" mean?

3. What does it mean to say that the power to accept has been terminated?

4. Can an offeror terminate the power to accept an offer after an offeree has already accepted the offer?

5. According to the assigned sections, list all the ways a party's power to accept may be terminated.

6. To prepare for your law school exams, it is helpful to have in mind a checklist of issues that might arise on your exams. To prepare for your contracts exam, we recommend that you create issue checklists. For example, one area where it is helpful to have an issues checklist is the body of rules regarding the ways a party's power to accept an offer may be terminated. To memorize your checklist, it is helpful to develop a mnemonic device that will remind you of each item on your list. Accordingly, create your own mnemonic to help you remember your issues checklist for termination of the power to accept. If you would like information about the four different types of mnemonic devices you can use in your law studies, read Michael Hunter Schwartz, EXPERT LEARNING FOR LAW STUDENTS (Carolina Academic Press 2008), pp. 178–183.

Death or Incapacity

An offeree's power to accept an offer terminates upon the death or incapacity of the offeror. This rule could have been determinative in *Davis v. Jacoby*. If the court had concluded that Mr. Whitehead's offer was an offer of a unilateral contract, his death by suicide would have terminated the Davises' power to accept. Therefore, when the Davises showed up in California and cared for Mrs. Whitehead after Mr. Whitehead's death, their acceptance would have been too late. Of course, the *Davis* court held Mr. Whitehead offered a bilateral contract that the Davises accepted by letter before Whitehead committed suicide while they still had the power to accept.

Revocation

In this section of the text you will learn about revocation of offers and the difference between a revocable offer and an irrevocable offer. First, you will learn the common law rules regarding when offers cannot be revoked. Then you will learn two ways in which offerors can revoke offers.

The relationship between these issues may already be obvious to you: an irrevocable offer cannot be revoked. Therefore, when analyzing a revocation issue, first consider whether the offer is irrevocable. Only after resolving that issue should you analyze whether an alleged revocation really is an effective revocation.

Irrevocable offers in the bilateral contract context. There are two ways an offer can be made irrevocable in the bilateral contract context. The first way, which only applies to contracts made under U.C.C. Article 2, is by making a "firm offer" that meets the requirements set out in section 2-205 of the U.C.C. Firm offers are discussed later in this chapter, in the section entitled, "Mutual Assent Under U.C.C. Article 2."

The second way to make an offer irrevocable in the bilateral contract context is with an "**option contract**." An option contract is a tool used by undecided buyers and sellers to meet their respective needs. For example, sometimes a buyer knows she is interested in buying a particular piece of land or personal property, but has not yet made up her mind about making a purchase. In such circumstances, the buyer may worry that, while she is deciding whether to make the purchase, another buyer may come along who is ready and willing to make a purchase. Buyers, therefore, desire a mechanism that will allow them to buy time to make a decision. In contrast, a seller, unless he has a contract with the buyer, is usually reluctant to take his property off the market because other potential buyers may be lost.

Option contracts allow buyers to buy time. The buyer pays the seller an agreed-upon sum to ensure that, for a specified time, the seller will not sell property to someone else. In other words, an option contract is simply a contract in which a buyer and seller exchange time for money.

To form an option contract, the same requirements that are necessary to form any contract must be met—*mutual assent and consideration.* The only difference between option contracts and other contracts is that the consideration requirement is more lenient. Specifically, *while courts will generally conclude there is no consideration (calling the consideration "nominal") if the amount stated in a contract is $1 or less, courts accept $1 as consideration for an option.* Chapter 3 of this text addresses consideration in depth. For now, you just need to understand that an option contract requires mutual assent and consideration and that the consideration requirement is less stringent than it is for other contracts.

Irrevocable Offers in the Unilateral Contract Context. The best way to understand irrevocable offers in the unilateral contract context is with a hypothetical problem, the Brooklyn Bridge hypothetical, developed by Professor Maurice Wormser in a well-known law review article, *The True Conception of Unilateral Contracts.*[3]

Exercise 2-25: "The Brooklyn Bridge Hypothetical"

Here's a slightly modified version of Professor Wormser's problem: A makes an offer of a unilateral contract to B by stating, "I will pay you $50 if you walk across the Brooklyn Bridge." When B gets halfway across the bridge, A says, "I revoke my offer." If B walks the rest of the way across the bridge, must A pay B the $50?

---

3. 26 YALE L. J 139 (1926).

1. Professor Wormser argues that, *if an offeror of a unilateral contract revokes the offer after the offeree starts performance, but before performance is complete, no contract has been formed.* Why not?

2. Section 45 of the RESTATEMENT (SECOND) OF CONTRACTS changes the rule asserted by Professor Wormser. How so? Is the change a good one?

3. Under section 45, can A successfully sue B for breach of contract in the Brooklyn Bridge hypothetical if B walks halfway across the bridge, decides he wants to go back, and never makes it across the bridge?

Two Ways an Offeror May Revoke

In this section you will learn about the two ways in which an offeror can revoke an offer. The two ways are discussed in two well-known cases, *Petterson v. Pattberg* and *Dickinson v. Dodds*.

Exercise 2-26: *Petterson v. Pattberg*

The first case, *Petterson v. Pattberg*, addresses the most common method used to revoke offers: the offeror communicates her revocation directly to the offeree. Before you read *Petterson*, re-read section 42 of the RESTATEMENT (SECOND) OF CONTRACTS. Then, as you read *Petterson*, consider the following questions. (Warning: *Petterson* is a tricky case and you may need to read it multiple times.)

1. The court assumes that Pattberg made an offer. Why?

2. What type of contract did the court conclude that Pattberg offered Petterson, a unilateral or bilateral one? Why?

3. The court also concludes, without much discussion, that what Pattberg said would revoke his offer as long as it was timely. Explain why the court felt that Pattberg's communication was a revocation under section 42. *Section 42 states the rule courts use for determining whether an offeror's communication revokes her offer.*

4. The real issue in the case is whether Pattberg revoked his offer before Petterson accepted. Why does the order of these events matter?

5. What did the majority opinion conclude on this point? Why did the majority reach that conclusion?

6. What did the dissent conclude on this issue? Why did the dissenting judge reach the conclusion he reached? (Hint: Focus on the language of the offer.)

Petterson v. Pattberg
248 N.Y. 86, 161 N.E. 428 (1928)

Kellogg, J. The evidence given upon the trial sanctions the following statement of facts: John Petterson, of whose last will and testament the plaintiff is the executrix, was the owner of a parcel of real estate in Brooklyn, known as 5301 6th Avenue. The defendant was the owner of a bond executed by Petterson, which was secured by a third mortgage upon the parcel. On April 4, 1924, there remained unpaid upon the principal the sum of $5,450. This amount was payable in installments of $250 on April 25, 1924, and upon a like monthly date every three months thereafter. Thus the bond and mortgage had more than five years to run before the entire sum became due. Under date of the 4th of April, 1924, the defendant wrote Petterson as follows:

> "I hereby agree to accept cash for the mortgage which I hold against premises 5301 6th Ave., Brooklyn, N.Y. It is understood and agreed as a consideration I will allow you $780 providing said mortgage is paid on or before May 31, 1924, and the regular quarterly payment due April 25, 1924, is paid when due."

On April 25, 1924, Petterson paid the defendant the installment of principal due on that date. Subsequently, on a day in the latter part of May, 1924, Petterson presented himself at the defendant's home, and knocked at the door. The defendant demanded the name of his caller. Petterson replied: "It is Mr. Petterson. I have come to pay off the mortgage." The defendant answered that he had sold the mortgage. Petterson stated that he would like to talk with the defendant, so the defendant partly opened the door. Thereupon Petterson exhibited the cash, and said he was ready to pay off the mortgage according to the agreement. The defendant refused to take the money. Prior to this conversation, Petterson had made a contract to sell the land to a third person free and clear of the mortgage to the defendant. Meanwhile, also, the defendant had sold the bond and mortgage to a third party. It therefore became necessary for Petterson to pay to such person the full amount of the bond and mortgage. It is claimed that he thereby sustained a loss of $780, the sum which the defendant agreed to allow upon the bond and mortgage, if payment in full of principal, less that sum, was made on or before May 31, 1924. The plaintiff has had a recovery for the sum thus claimed, with interest.

Clearly the defendant's letter proposed to Petterson the making of a unilateral contract, the gift of a promise in exchange for the performance of an act. The thing conditionally promised by the defendant was the reduction of the mortgage debt. The act requested to be done, in consideration of the offered promise, was payment in full of the reduced principal of the debt prior to the due date thereof. "If an act is requested, that very act, and no other, must be given." WILLISTON ON CONTRACTS, §73. "In case of offers for a consideration, the performance of the consideration is always deemed a condition." [Citation omitted.] It is elementary that any offer to enter into a unilateral contract may be withdrawn before the act requested to be done has been performed. [Citations omitted.]....

An interesting question arises when, as here, the offeree approaches the offeror with the intention of proffering performance and, before actual tender is made, the offer is withdrawn. Of such a case, Williston says:

> "The offeror may see the approach of the offeree and know that an acceptance is contemplated. If the offeror can say 'I revoke' before the offeree accepts, however brief the interval of time between the two

acts, there is no escape from the conclusion that the offer is terminated." WILLISTON ON CONTRACTS, § 60b.

In this instance Petterson, standing at the door of the defendant's house, stated to the defendant that he had come to pay off the mortgage. Before a tender of the necessary moneys had been made, the defendant informed Petterson that he had sold the mortgage. That was a definite notice to Petterson that the defendant could not perform his offered promise, and that a tender to the defendant, who was no longer the creditor, would be ineffective to satisfy the debt. "An offer to sell property may be withdrawn before acceptance without any formal notice to the person to whom the offer is made. It is sufficient if that person has actual knowledge that the person who made the offer has done some act inconsistent with the continuance of the offer, such as selling the property to a third person." [Citation to *Dickinson v. Dodds*, *below*, and another case omitted.] Thus it clearly appears that the defendant's offer was withdrawn before its acceptance had been tendered. It is unnecessary to determine, therefore, what the legal situation might have been had tender been made before withdrawal. It is the individual view of the writer that the same result would follow. This would be so, for the act requested to be performed was the completed act of payment, a thing incapable of performance, unless assented to by the person to be paid. WILLISTON ON CONTRACTS, § 60b. Clearly an offering party has the right to name the precise act performance of which would convert his offer into a binding promise. Whatever the act may be until it is performed, the offer must be revocable. However, the supposed case is not before us for decision. We think that in this particular instance the offer of the defendant was withdrawn before it became a binding promise, and therefore that no contract was ever made for the breach of which the plaintiff may claim damages.

The judgment of the Appellate Division and that of the Trial Term should be reversed, and the complaint dismissed, with costs in all courts.

Lehman, J. (dissenting). The defendant's letter to Petterson constituted a promise on his part to accept payment at a discount of the mortgage he held, provided the mortgage is paid on or before May 31, 1924. Doubtless, by the terms of the promise itself, the defendant made payment of the mortgage by the plaintiff, before the stipulated time, a condition precedent to performance by the defendant of his promise to accept payment at a discount. If the condition precedent has not been performed, it is because the defendant made performance impossible by refusing to accept payment, when the plaintiff came with an offer of immediate performance. "It is a principle of fundamental justice that if a promisor is himself the cause of the failure of performance either of an obligation due him or of a condition upon which his own liability depends, he cannot take advantage of the failure." WILLISTON ON CONTRACTS, § 677. The question in this case is not whether payment of the mortgage is a condition precedent to the performance of a promise made by the defendant, but, rather, whether, at the time the defendant refused the offer of payment, he had assumed any binding obligation, even though subject to condition.

The promise made by the defendant lacked consideration at the time it was made. Nevertheless, the promise was not made as a gift or mere gratuity to the plaintiff. It was made for the purpose of obtaining from the defendant something which the plaintiff desired. It constituted an offer which was to become binding whenever the plaintiff should give, in return for the defendant's promise, exactly the consideration which the defendant requested.

Here the defendant requested no counter promise from the plaintiff. The consideration requested by the defendant for his promise to accept payment was, I agree, some act to be performed by the plaintiff. Until the act requested was performed, the defendant might undoubtedly revoke his offer. Our problem is to determine from the words of the letter, read in the light of surrounding circumstances, what act the defendant requested as consideration for his promise.

The defendant undoubtedly made his offer as an inducement to the plaintiff to "pay" the mortgage before it was due. Therefore, it is said, that "the act requested to be performed was the completed act of payment, a thing incapable of performance, unless assented to by the person to be paid." In unmistakable terms the defendant agreed to accept payment, yet we are told that the defendant intended, and the plaintiff should have understood, that the act requested by the defendant, as consideration for his promise to accept payment, included performance by the defendant himself of the very promise for which the act was to be consideration. The defendant's promise was to become binding only when fully performed; and part of the consideration to be furnished by the plaintiff for the defendant's promise was to be the performance of that promise by the defendant. So construed, the defendant's promise or offer, though intended to induce action by the plaintiff, is but a snare and delusion. The plaintiff could not reasonably suppose that the defendant was asking him to procure the performance by the defendant of the very act which the defendant promised to do, yet we are told that, even after the plaintiff had done all else which the defendant requested, the defendant's promise was still not binding because the defendant chose not to perform....

I recognize that in this case only an offer of payment, and not a formal tender of payment, was made before the defendant withdrew his offer to accept payment. Even the plaintiff's part in the act of payment was then not technically complete. Even so, under a fair construction of the words of the letter, I think the plaintiff had done the act which the defendant requested as consideration for his promise. The plaintiff offered to pay, with present intention and ability to make that payment. A formal tender is seldom made in business transactions, except to lay the foundation for subsequent assertion in a court of justice of rights which spring from refusal of the tender. If the defendant acted in good faith in making his offer to accept payment, he could not well have intended to draw a distinction in the act requested of the plaintiff in return, between an offer which, unless refused, would ripen into completed payment, and a formal tender. Certainly the defendant could not have expected or intended that the plaintiff would make a formal tender of payment without first stating that he had come to make payment. We should not read into the language of the defendant's offer a meaning which would prevent enforcement of the defendant's promise after it had been accepted by the plaintiff in the very way which the defendant must have intended it should be accepted, if he acted in good faith.

The judgment should be affirmed.

To facilitate learning specific legal doctrine, casebook authors typically excise portions of opinions that are irrelevant to the point the authors wish to make and frequently leave out dissenting opinions altogether. Why do you think we have included a dissenting opinion for you to read in this case? Casebook authors choose to include dissenting opinions for a variety of reasons. Dissents: (1) may reflect outdated views of the law, (2) may foreshadow the future of the law, (3) help you build lawyering skills by showing you relevant counter-arguments, and (4) by revealing facts or arguments omitted by the majority, help you learn that court opinions reflect views of individual judges and are not statements of truth handed down from on high.

Exercise 2-27: *Petterson* Revisited

1. Why did we include the dissent for you to read in *Petterson*?

2. What would the result have been in *Petterson* if the only thing Pattberg had said before Petterson accepted was: "I might not want to go through with this deal"? (Hint: Consider this issue in light of section 42 of the Restatement (Second) of Contracts, and the policy rationales that support courts' reluctance to find commitment in alleged offers and acceptances.)

3. What would the result have been in *Petterson* if Pattberg had promised a $780 discount in return for Petterson's promise to repay the mortgage debt by the end of May and Petterson had replied "I agree to your terms and hereby promise to repay the mortgage on or before May 31."

Exercise 2-28: *Dickinson v. Dodds*

The next case in this chapter is *Dickinson v. Dodds*. As you read *Dickinson*, consider the following questions:

1. What does this case add to your understanding about how one may revoke an offer (in addition to what you learned from *Petterson*)?

2. Read section 43 of the Restatement (Second) of Contracts. What are the elements of this type of revocation?

3. In what sense was what Dickinson learned inconsistent with Dodds's intent to enter into the proposed contract?

4. *Dickinson* fails to clarify exactly what Dickinson was told about Dodds. Specifically, it is not clear whether Dickinson was told that Dodds was "offering" to sell the property to Allan or was "selling" the property to Allan. Look at section 43 again. Why might it matter what Dickinson was told?

5. If the court had considered the issue, it seems likely that the court would have concluded that the information Dickinson learned from Berry was reliable. Why? What specific facts suggest that a reasonable person in Dickinson's circumstances would have regarded the information as reliable?

6. What does the *Dickinson* case teach you about irrevocability?

Dickinson v. Dodds

L.R. 2 Ch. D 463 (1876)

On Wednesday, the 10th of June, 1874, the Defendant, John Dodds, signed and delivered to the Plaintiff, George Dickinson, a memorandum, of which the material part was as follows:

> "I hereby agree to sell to Mr. George Dickinson the whole of the dwelling—houses, garden ground, stabling, and outbuildings thereto belonging, situate at Croft, belonging to me, for the sum of £800. As witness my hand this tenth day of June, 1874.

[Signed] John Dodds

P.S. — This offer to be left over until Friday, 9 o'clock, A.M. J. D. (the twelfth), 12th June, 1874. [Signed] J. Dodds"

The bill alleged that Dodds understood and intended that the Plaintiff should have until Friday 9 A.M. within which to determine whether he would or would not purchase, and that he should absolutely have until that time the refusal of the property at the price of £800, and that the Plaintiff in fact determined to accept the offer on the morning of Thursday, the 11th of June, but did not at once signify his acceptance to Dodds, believing that he had the power to accept it until 9 A.M. on the Friday.

In the afternoon of the Thursday the Plaintiff was informed by a Mr. Berry that Dodds had been offering or agreeing to sell the property to Thomas Allan, the other Defendant. Thereupon the Plaintiff, at about half-past seven in the evening, went to the house of Mrs. Burgess, the mother-in-law of Dodds, where he was then staying, and left with her a formal acceptance in writing of the offer to sell the property. According to the evidence of Mrs. Burgess this document never in fact reached Dodds, she having forgotten to give it to him.

On the following (Friday) morning, at about seven o'clock, Berry, who was acting as agent for Dickinson, found Dodds at the Darlington railway station, and handed to him a duplicate of the acceptance by Dickinson, and explained to Dodds its purport. He replied that it was too late, as he had sold the property. A few minutes later Dickinson himself found Dodds entering a railway carriage, and handed him another duplicate of the notice of acceptance, but Dodds declined to receive it, saying, "You are too late. I have sold the property."

It appeared that on the day before, Thursday, the 11th of June, Dodds had signed a formal contract for the sale of the property to the Defendant Allan for £800, and had received from him a deposit of £40.

The bill in this suit prayed that the Defendant Dodds might be decreed specifically to perform the contract of the 10th of June, 1874; that he might be restrained from conveying the property to Allan; that Allan might be restrained from taking any such conveyance; that, if any such conveyance had been or should be made, Allan might be declared a trustee of the property for, and might be directed to convey the property to, the Plaintiff; and for damages.

The cause came on for hearing before Vice Chancellor Bacon on the 25th of January, 1876. [He opined that because Dodds could only withdraw the offer by giving notice to Dickinson (which he did not), there was a contract between Dickinson and Dodds. Specific performance was ordered and from that decision the defendants appealed.]

The document, though beginning "I hereby agree to sell," was nothing but an offer, and was only intended to be an offer, for the Plaintiff himself tells us that he required time to consider whether he would enter into an agreement or not. Unless both parties had then agreed there was no concluded agreement then made; it was in effect and substance only an offer to sell. The Plaintiff, being minded not to complete the bargain at that time, added this memorandum — "this offer to be left over until Friday, 9 o'clock A.M., 12th June, 1874." That shows it was only an offer. There was no consideration given for

Why would all courts agree that the June 10 letter quoted in this case is an offer?

the undertaking or promise, to whatever extent it may be considered binding, to keep the property unsold until 9 o'clock on Friday morning; but apparently Dickinson was of [the] opinion, and probably Dodds was of the same opinion, that he (Dodds) was bound by that promise, and could not in any way withdraw from it, or retract it, until 9 o'clock on Friday morning, and this probably explains a good deal of what afterwards took place. But it is clear settled law, on one of the clearest principles of law, that this promise, being a mere *nudum pactum*, was not binding, and that at any moment before a complete acceptance by Dickinson of the offer, Dodds was as free as Dickinson himself. Well, that being the state of things, it is said that the only mode in which Dodds could assert that freedom was by actually and distinctly saying to Dickinson, "Now I withdraw my offer." It appears to me that there is neither principle nor authority for the proposition that there must be an express and actual withdrawal of the offer, or what is called a retraction. It must, to constitute a contract, appear that the two minds were at one, at the same moment of time, that is, that there was an offer continuing up to the time of the acceptance. If there was not such a continuing offer, then the acceptance comes to nothing. Of course it may well be that the one man is bound in some way or other to let the other man know that his mind with regard to the offer has been changed; but in this case, beyond all question, the Plaintiff knew that Dodds was no longer minded to sell the property to him as plainly and clearly as if Dodds had told him in so many words, "I withdraw the offer." This is evident from the Plaintiff's own statements in the bill.

The Plaintiff says in effect that, having heard and knowing that Dodds was no longer minded to sell to him, and that he was selling or had sold to someone else, thinking that he could not in point of law withdraw his offer, meaning to fix him to it, and endeavoring to bind him, "I went to the house where he was lodging, and saw his mother-in-law, and left with her an acceptance of the offer, knowing all the while that he had entirely changed his mind. I got an agent to watch for him at 7 o'clock the next morning, and I went to the train just before 9 o'clock, in order that I might catch him and give him my notice of acceptance just before 9 o'clock, and when that occurred he told my agent, and he told me, you are too late, and he then threw back the paper." It is to my mind quite clear that before there was any attempt at acceptance by the Plaintiff, he was perfectly well aware that Dodds had changed his mind, and that he had in fact agreed to sell the property to Allan. It is impossible, therefore, to say there was ever that existence of the same mind between the two parties, which is essential in point of law to the making of an agreement. I am of [the] opinion, therefore, that the Plaintiff has failed to prove that there was any binding contract between Dodds and himself....

The bill will be dismissed with costs.

[The concurring opinions of Mellish, L.J., and Baggalay, J.A., are omitted.]

Exercise 2-29: *Dickinson* Revisited

If you were the attorney for Dodds, would you have recommended that Dodds revoke the offer in the way that Dodds revoked it? Why or why not?

Margin note: Because the court relies on the Latin phrase *"nudum pactum"* in its decision, it is worth looking that term up in a law dictionary. What does that term mean?

Lapse and Rejection

Lapse and rejection are two methods of terminating an offer that are not inherently linked in any way. In fact, the choice to combine these two topics in this section stems solely from the fact that both happen to be addressed in the next case, *Akers v. J. B. Sedberry, Inc.* Most often, each of these topics arises separately.

Exercise 2-30: *Akers v. J. B. Sedberry, Inc.*

Before you read *Akers*, re-read section 41 of the RESTATEMENT (SECOND) OF CONTRACTS. Then, as you read *Akers*, consider the following questions:

1. What does it mean to say that an offer has lapsed?

2. What is the general rule as to when offers lapse?

3. What is the general lapse rule for offers sent by mail?

4. What is the general lapse rule for offers made during face-to-face conversations?

5. How did the court apply that rule to the facts of *Akers*?

Re-read section 38 of the RESTATEMENT (SECOND) OF CONTRACTS. Then answer the following questions relating to the rejection issue in *Akers*:

1. What is a rejection? Both the RESTATEMENT and the opinion below offer definitions. Either suffices to explain the court's conclusion.

2. Why did the court conclude there was a rejection in this case?

Akers v. J. B. Sedberry, Inc.
286 S.W.2d 617 (1955)

Felts, Judge. These two consolidated causes are before us upon a writ of error sued out by J.B. Sedberry, Inc., and Mrs. M.B. Sedberry, defendants below, to review a decree of the Chancery Court, awarding a recovery against them in favor of each of the complainants, Charles William Akers and William Gambill Whitsitt, for damages for breach of a contract of employment....

J. B. Sedberry, Inc., was a Tennessee corporation with its principal place of business at Franklin, Tennessee. Mrs. M. B. Sedberry owned practically all of its stock and was its president and in active charge of its affairs. It was engaged in the business of distributing "Jay Bee" hammer mills, which were manufactured for it under contract by Jay Bee Manufacturing Company, a Texas corporation, whose plant was in Tyler, Texas, and whose capital stock was owned principally by L.M. Glasgow and B.G. Byars.

On July 1, 1947, J.B. Sedberry, Inc., by written contract, employed complainant Akers as Chief Engineer for a term of five years at a salary of $12,000 per year, payable $1,000 per month, plus 1% of its net profits for the first year, 2% the second, 3% the third, 4% the fourth, and 5% the fifth year. His duties were to carry on research for his employer, and to see that the Jay Bee Manufacturing Company, Tyler, Texas, manufactured the mills and parts according to proper specifications. Mrs. M.B. Sedberry guaranteed the employer's performance of this contract.

On August 1, 1947, J.B. Sedberry, Inc., by written contract, employed complainant Whitsitt as Assistant Chief Engineer for a term of five years at a salary of $7,200 per year, payable $600 per month, plus 1% of the corporation's net profits for the first year, 2% for the second, 3% for the third, 4% for the fourth, and 5% for the fifth year. His duties were to assist in the work done by the Chief Engineer. Mrs. M.B. Sedberry guaranteed the employer's performance of this contract.

Under Mrs. Sedberry's instructions, Akers and Whitsitt moved to Tyler, Texas, began performing their contract duties in the plant of the Jay Bee Manufacturing Company, continued working there, and were paid under the contracts until October 1, 1950, when they ceased work, under circumstances hereafter stated.

[Mrs. Sedberry acquired the stock of Jay Bee and hired A.M. Sorenson to manage the business.] There soon developed considerable friction between Sorenson and complainants Akers and Whitsitt. The Jay Bee Manufacturing Company owed large sums to the Tyler State Bank & Trust Co.; and the bank's officers, fearing the company might fail under Sorenson's management, began talking to Akers and Whitsitt about the company's financial difficulties....

While these matters were pending, Akers and Whitsitt flew to Nashville and went to Franklin to talk with Mrs. Sedberry about them. They had a conference with her at her office on Friday, September 29, 1950, lasting from 9:30 a.m. until 4:30 p.m. As they had come unannounced, and unknown to Sorenson, they felt Mrs. Sedberry might mistrust them; and at the outset, to show their good faith, they offered to resign, but she did not accept their offer. Instead, she proceeded with them in discussing the operation and refinancing of the business.

Testifying about this conference, Akers said that, at the very beginning, to show their good faith, he told Mrs. Sedberry that they would offer their resignations on a ninety-day notice, provided they were paid according to the contract for that period; that she pushed the offers aside — "would not accept them," but went into a full discussion of the business; that nothing was thereafter said about the offers to resign; and that they spent the whole day discussing the business, Akers making notes of things she instructed him to do when he got back to Texas.

[Whitsitt also testified Mrs. Sedberry would not accept their resignations but continued to discuss the business and nothing else was mentioned about resigning.]

Mrs. Sedberry testified that Akers and Whitsitt came in and "offered their resignations"; that they said they could not work with Sorenson and did not believe the bank would go along with him; and that "they said if it would be of any help to the organization they would be glad to tender their resignation and pay them what was due them." She further said that they "did not accept the resignation," that she "felt it necessary to contact Mr. Sorenson and give consideration to the resignation offer." But she said nothing to complainants about taking the offer under consideration.

On cross-examination she said that in the offer to resign "no mention was made of any ninety-day notice." Asked what response she made to the offer she said, "I treated it rather casually because I had to give it some thought and had to contact Mr. Sorenson." She further said she excused herself from the conference with complainants, went to another room, tried to telephone Sorenson in Tyler, Texas, but was unable to locate him.

She then resumed the conference, nothing further was said about the offers to resign, nothing was said by her to indicate that she thought the offers were left open or held under consideration by her. But the discussion proceeded as if the offers had not been made. She discussed with complainants future plans for refinancing and operating the business, giving them instructions, and Akers making notes of them.

Following the conference, complainants, upon Mrs. Sedberry's request, flew back to Texas to proceed to carry out her instructions....

On Monday, October 2, 1950, Mrs. Sedberry sent to complainants similar telegrams, signed by "J. B. Sedberry, Inc., by M. B. Sedberry, President," stating that their resignations were accepted, effective immediately. We quote the telegram to Akers, omitting the formal parts:

> "Account present unsettled conditions which you so fully are aware we accept your kind offer of resignation effective immediately. Please discontinue as of today with everyone employed in Sedberry, Inc., Engineering Department, discontinuing all expenses in this department writing."

While this said she was "writing," she did not write. Akers wrote her ... [and], in his letter, Akers said that he was amazed to get her telegram, and called her attention to the fact that no offer to resign by him was open or outstanding when she sent the telegram; that while he had made a conditional offer to resign at their conference on September 29, she had immediately rejected the offer, and had discussed plans for the business and had instructed him and Whitsitt as to things she wanted them to do in the business on their return to Tyler.

This letter further stated that Akers was expecting to be paid according to the terms of his contract until he could find other employment that would pay him as much income as that provided in his contract, and that if he had to accept a position with less income, he would expect to be paid the difference, or whatever losses he suffered by her breach of the contract. Whitsitt's letter contained a similar statement of his position.

On November 10, 1950, Mrs. Sedberry wrote a letter addressed to both Akers and Whitsitt in which she said that "no one deplored the action taken more than the writer," but she did not recede from her position as expressed in the telegram. She stated her contention that the offers to resign had been without condition; and though she also said she would like to make an amicable settlement, no settlement was made.

As it takes two to make a contract, it takes two to unmake it. It cannot be changed or ended by one alone, but only by mutual assent of both parties. A contract of employment for a fixed period may be terminated by the employee's offer to resign, provided such offer is duly accepted by the employer.

An employee's tender of his resignation, being a mere offer is, of course, not binding until it has been accepted by the employer. Such offer must be accepted according to its terms and within the time fixed. The matter is governed by the same rules as govern the formation of contracts.

An offer may be terminated in a number of ways, as, for example, where it is rejected by the offeree, or where it is not accepted by him within the time fixed, or, if no time is fixed, within a reasonable time. An offer terminated in either of these ways ceases to exist and cannot thereafter be accepted. 1 Williston on Contracts (1936), §§ 50A, 51, 53, 54; 1 Corbin on Contracts (1950), §§ 35, 36; 1 Rest., Contracts, §§ 35, 40.

The question what is a reasonable time, where no time is fixed, is a question of fact, depending on the nature of the contract proposed, the usages of business and other circumstances of the case. Ordinarily, an offer made by one to another in a face to face conversation is deemed to continue only to the close of their conversation, and cannot be accepted thereafter.

The rule is illustrated by Restatement of Contracts, § 40, Illustration 2, as follows:

> "2. While A and B are engaged in conversation, A makes B an offer to which B then makes no reply, but a few hours later meeting A again, B states that he accepts the offer. There is no contract unless the offer or the surrounding circumstances indicate that the offer is intended to continue beyond the immediate conversation...."

Professor Corbin says: "When two negotiating parties are in each other's presence, and one makes an offer to the other without indicating any time for acceptance, the inference that will ordinarily be drawn by the other party is that an answer is expected at once.... If, when the first reply is not an acceptance, the offeror turns away in silence, the proper inference is that the offer is no longer open to acceptance." 1 Corbin on Contracts (1950), § 36, p. 111.

The only offer by Akers and Whitsitt to resign was the offer made by them in their conversation with Mrs. Sedberry. They made that offer at the outset, and on the evidence it seems clear that they expected an answer at once. Certainly, there is nothing in the evidence to show that they intended the offer to continue beyond that conversation; and on the above authorities, we think the offer did not continue beyond that meeting.

Indeed, it did not last that long, in our opinion, but was terminated by Mrs. Sedberry's rejection of it very early in that meeting. While she did not expressly reject it, and while she may have intended, as she says, to take the offer under consideration, she did not disclose such an intent to complainants; but, by her conduct, led them to believe she rejected the offer, brushed it aside, and proceeded with the discussion as if it had not been made.

"An offer is rejected when the offeror is justified in inferring from the words or conduct of the offeree that the offeree intends not to accept the offer or to take it under further advisement (Rest. Contracts § 36). 1 Williston on Contracts, section 51.

So, we agree with the Trial Judge that when defendants sent the telegrams, undertaking to accept offers of complainants to resign, there was no such offer in existence; and that this attempt of defendants to terminate their contract was unlawful and constituted a breach for which they are liable to complainants....

All of the assignments of error are overruled and the decree of the Chancellor is affirmed.... The causes are remanded to the Chancery Court for further proceedings not inconsistent with this opinion.

Notice that, after the court concludes that the power to accept the offer had lapsed, the court nevertheless goes on to analyze whether the power to accept was terminated by rejection. Why do you think the court does so? Consider the following two points: (1) the discussion of rejection is probably *dicta* (look up that term in your law dictionary), and (2) the court's choice to give two grounds for its decision minimizes the likelihood that its decision would be reversed by an appellate court.

Exercise 2-31: More on Lapse and Rejection

1. What would the result have been in *Dickinson v. Dodds* if Dodds had not made the contract with Allan until 10:00 am on Friday, June 12, 1874, and Dickinson had communicated his acceptance of the original offer to Dodds on Saturday, June 13, 1874?

2. Analyze the following lapse questions:

   a. Why might a court conclude that an offer made during a face-to-face conversation did not lapse at the end of the conversation? In other words, under what circumstances might the general rule not apply?

   b. A makes B an offer by mail to sell her house to B. B receives the offer two days later at the close of business. B accepts the offer by mail first thing the next morning. Is B's acceptance in the proper manner and timely? What if B waited three days?

   c. A sends B a telegraphic offer two hours before the end of the business day to sell B gold at a time when gold is subject to rapid fluctuations in price. B sends an acceptance the next day, ten minutes after a sharp rise in the price of gold is announced. Is B's acceptance timely? What if the offer was for gold "at the market price at the time of acceptance"?

   d. Monte, Cindi, and April Monteleone were insured under an automobile liability policy issued by Allstate in December 1991. The policy was renewed June 21, 1992, for an additional six months. November 16, 1992, thirty-five days before the expiration of the second six-month policy term, Allstate mailed an offer to renew for a third six-month term from December 21, 1992, to June 21, 1993. The offer stated: "Important ... this is a renewal offer only. Insurance described on this document will not go into effect unless the premium is paid by the due date shown on the payment notice below...." The due date on the payment notice was December 21, 1992. The notice stated a total premium due of $912 but gave the option of installment payments. The notice also stated: "Renewal coverage will not go into effect if we do not receive payment by your due date."

      The Monteleones did not pay the premium by the due date. December 31, 1992, appellants received a notice from Allstate which stated: "Your insurance coverages have terminated. You are eligible for reinstatement of your policy, with a short lapse in coverage. Please read the enclosed letter for more information." Mrs. Monteleone stated that the letter informed them that they were able to reinstate the policy by paying the first premium installment of $230.50 by January 7, 1993. She called her Allstate agent on December 31, 1992, and left a message that she wanted April (her daughter) added to the policy. January 3, 1993, April drove the family vehicle and was involved in an accident which became the basis for a personal injury claim and lawsuit by Charles Nelson. January 4, 1993, Mrs. Monteleone mailed the installment premium payment to Allstate. Allstate received the late premium payment of $230.50 on January 6, 1993, and reinstated the policy effective January 4, 1993, the date the premium was mailed and one day after the accident. Allstate denied coverage for the accident and the court ruled that Allstate was entitled to deny coverage. How come?

3. Analyze the following rejection hypotheticals:

   a. Yvonne offers to buy Zina's home for $200,000. Zina responds, "I don't know. I may decide to keep the house and rent it out if all I can get for it is $200,000." Has Zina rejected Yvonne's offer? Why or why not?

   b. Would Zina's statements be a revocation if Zina had made the initial offer (*i.e.,* if Zina had offered to sell Zina's house to Yvonne for $200,000)? Why or why not?

Counter-Offers

In many instances, an offeree is not willing to be bound by the terms stated in an offeror's offer, but wishes to continue her discussions with the offeror. In this situation, an offeree may propose an alternative deal, a counter-offer. When an offeree chooses to make a counter-offer, that choice seems to imply a rejection of the original offer.

Exercise 2-32: *Livingstone v. Evans*

Livingstone v. Evans addresses counter-offers and adds an interesting wrinkle. As you read *Livingstone*, consider the following questions:

1. What are the key facts in *Livingstone*?

2. Read the RESTATEMENT (SECOND) OF CONTRACTS, section 39, subsection 1. What are the elements of a counter-offer according to that subsection?

   a. Apply the elements from section 39, subsection 1, to the facts of the *Livingstone* case.

   b. The *Livingstone* court says the issue is "whether plaintiff's counter-offer was in law a rejection of the defendant's offer." Re-read section 39. Are counter-offers always rejections?

3. The court also addresses the effect of Mr. Evans' response, "Cannot reduce price." What did the court say was the legal effect of that response? Why? What is the best counter-argument to the court's conclusion about the legal effect of that response?

Livingstone v. Evans

4 D.L.R. 169 (Alberta Supreme Court, 1925)

Walsh, J. The defendant, T.J. Evans, through his agent, wrote to the plaintiff offering to sell him the land in question for $1,800 on terms. On the day that he received this offer the plaintiff wired this agent as follows: "Send lowest cash price. Will give $1,600 cash. Wire." The agent replied to this by telegram as follows "Cannot reduce price." Immediately upon the receipt of this telegram the plaintiff wrote accepting the offer. It is admitted by the defendants that this offer and the plaintiff's acceptance of it constitute a contract for the sale of this land to the plaintiff by which he is bound unless the intervening telegrams above set out put an end to his offer so that the plaintiff could not thereafter bind him to it by his acceptance of it.

It is quite clear that when an offer has been rejected it is thereby ended and it cannot be afterwards accepted without the consent of him who made it. The simple question and the only one argued before me is whether the plaintiff's counter-offer was in law a rejection of the defendant's offer which freed them from it.

Hyde v. Wrench, 3 Beav. 334, 49 E.R. 132 (1840), a judgment of Lord Langdale, M.R., pronounced in 1840, is the authority for the contention that it was. The defendant offered to sell for $1,000. The plaintiff met that with an offer to pay $950 and (to quote from the judgment at p. 337) "he thereby rejected the offer previously made by the Defendant. I think that it was not competent for him to revive the proposal of the Defendant, by tendering an acceptance of it."

Stevenson v. McLean, 5 Q.B.D. 346 (1880), a later case relied upon by Mr. Grant is easily distinguishable from *Hyde v. Wrench, supra,* as it is in fact distinguished by Lush, J., who decided it. He held (p. 350) that the letter there relied upon as constituting a rejection of the offer was not a new proposal "but a mere inquiry, which should have been answered and not treated as a rejection" but the Judge said that if it had contained an offer it would have likened the case to *Hyde v. Wrench*.

Hyde v. Wrench has stood without question for 85 years. It is adopted by the text writers as a correct exposition of the law and is generally accepted and recognized as such. I think it not too much to say that it has firmly established it as a part of the law of contracts that the making of a counter-offer is a rejection of the original offer.

The plaintiff's telegram was undoubtedly a counter-offer. True, it contained an inquiry as well but that clearly was one which called for an answer only if the counter-offer was rejected. In substance it said: "I will give you $1,600 cash. If you won't take that wire your lowest cash price." In my opinion it put an end to the defendants' liability under their offer unless it was revived by the telegram in reply to it.

The real difficulty in the case, to my mind, arises out of the defendants' telegram "cannot reduce price." If this was simply a rejection of the plaintiff's counter-offer it amounts to nothing. If, however, it was a renewal of the original offer it gave the plaintiff the right to bind the defendants to it by his subsequent acceptance of it.

With some doubt I think that it was a renewal of the original offer or at any rate an intimation to the plaintiff that he was still willing to treat on the basis of it. It was, of course, a reply to the counter-offer and to the inquiry in the plaintiff's telegram. But it was more than that. The price referred to in it was unquestionably that mentioned in his letter. His statement that he could not reduce that price strikes me as having but one meaning, namely, that he was still standing by it and, therefore, still open to accept it. . . .

I am, therefore, of the opinion that there was a binding contract for the sale of this land to the plaintiff of which he is entitled to specific performance. It was admitted by his counsel that if I reached this conclusion his subsequent agreement to sell the land to the defendant Williams would be of no avail as against the plaintiff's contract.

There will, therefore, be judgment for specific performance with a declaration that the plaintiff's rights under his contract have priority over those of the defendant Williams under his ...

Exercise 2-33: *Livingstone* Revisited

1. A purported acceptance that changes any of the terms of an offer and/or adds additional terms is a counter-offer. This concept is sometimes referred to as the "mirror-image rule." Why?

2. What could Livingstone have said differently if he wanted to make a counter-offer, but also wanted to keep Evans's offer open?

3. Would Livingstone and Evans have had a contract if Evans had not replied to Livingstone's telegram at all?

4. If Evans had wanted to reply in some way, but did not want to risk liability, what should Evans have said?

5. Read section 37 of the RESTATEMENT (SECOND) OF CONTRACTS. Why are counter-offers and rejections treated differently if the offer is irrevocable by virtue of a separate option contract?

Much business today is conducted on standard forms with pre-printed terms and conditions. It is common practice—especially in goods transactions—for the buyer to submit a purchase order containing the buyer's standard terms and the seller to issue an acknowledgment containing the seller's standard terms. Consider the following hypothetical (based with slight modifications on *Diamond Fruit Growers, Inc. v. Krack Corp.*, 794 F.2d 1440 (1986)):

Krack manufactured commercial refrigeration units. Metal-Matic supplied Krack with steel tubing components for the refrigeration units. Krack placed an order for steel tubing on its standard purchase order. There was a clause in the purchase order which stated that "Seller will indemnify Krack against all loss and damage suffered by Krack attributable to defects in goods supplied by Seller." Metal-Matic responded to the purchase order by sending Krack an acknowledgment form which stated in bold-capitals: "METAL-MATIC, INC.'S ACCEPTANCE OF PURCHASER'S OFFER OR ITS OFFER TO PURCHASER IS HEREBY EXPRESSLY MADE CONDITIONAL TO PURCHASER'S ACCEPTANCE OF THE TERMS AND CONDITIONS IN THIS ACKNOWLEDGMENT FORM. METAL-MATIC DISCLAIMS ALL LIABILITY FOR CONSEQUENTIAL DAMAGES ATTRIBUTABLE TO DEFECTS IN TUBING. METAL-MATIC'S LIABILITY FOR DEFECTS IN TUBING IS LIMITED TO REFUND OF PURCHASE PRICE OR COST OF REPLACEMENT/REPAIR." Krack took delivery of the tubing and then sold a unit containing some of the tubing to Diamand Fruit Growers. The unit leaked ammonia because the tubing was defective. Diamond sued Krack to recover the loss in value of fruit that it was forced to remove from the unit because of the ammonia leak. Krack sought an indemnity from Metal-Matic for the full amount of Diamond's loss in accordance with the term in Krack's purchase order. Metal-Matic argued that its liability is limited to the purchase price in accordance with the term in its acknowledgment form.

Assume that the "mirror-image" rule applies. Who would win?

The steps in the analysis can be tabulated as follows:

Chronology	Analysis
1. Krack offers to purchase on terms that include full indemnity	Offer
2 Metal-Matic agrees to sell but on terms that limit liability for defective tubing	Not mirror image therefore counter-offer
3. Krack takes delivery of the tubing	Acceptance of counter-offer by conduct

It appears that Metal-Matic would win because Krack impliedly accepted its counter-offer by taking delivery of the tubing without objecting to the disclaimer of liability introduced in Metal-Matic's acknowledgment form. The result is dictated by what is known in this context as the "last shot" rule. Metal-Matic fired the last shot because it was the last to put a set of terms on the table before the deal went ahead.

The eagle-eyed among you will have noticed that the hypothetical involves a goods transaction and you have learned already that goods transactions are governed by U.C.C. Article 2. You will learn later in this chapter that section 2-207 of the U.C.C. substantially modifies the application of the common law "mirror-image" and "last shot" rules.

The Mailbox Rule

Exercise 2-34: The Mailbox Rule

Read sections 63, 66, 67, 40, and 42 of the RESTATEMENT (SECOND) OF CONTRACTS. Then use those sections to answer the problems in this exercise. When doing so, cite the Restatement sections that you rely on in your answers. (Hint: There is one right answer to each hypothetical; that answer can be found by applying one of the rules stated in the four referenced Restatement sections.) This exercise is the first of several that focuses on rule reading skills. Try to synthesize what you learn from this exercise into four rules. It can be done.

1. A sent B the following letter: "I will sell you five contract law books for $2 each." The letter was deposited in the mail on September 2 and received on September 4. B then sent the following letter to A: "I accept your offer." B's letter was deposited in the mail on September 5 and received on September 7. A then sent the following fax to B: "Offer is rescinded." The fax was both sent and received on September 6. What is the result of these communications?

2. Assume the same situation as in question 1, except A's revocation was sent September 4 and received September 6. What is the result?

3. Assume the same situation as in question 1, except that A never received B's acceptance. What is the result?

4. Assume the same situation as in question 1, except that A's offer was governed by an option contract. What is the result?

5. A sent B the following telegram: "I will sell you five contract law books for $2 each. Telegram your acceptance a.s.a.p." A's telegram was sent and received on September 2. B then sent A the following letter: "I accept."

The letter was deposited in the mail on September 5 and received on September 7. A then sent B the following telegram: "Offer is rescinded." A's telegram was sent and received on September 6. What is the result of these communications?

6. Assume the same situation as that presented in question 5, except A's original telegram ended with: "We would prefer that you telegram your acceptance."

7. A sent B the following letter: "I will sell you five contract law books for $2 each." That letter was deposited in the mail on September 2 and received on September 4. B sent A the following letter: "I reject your offer." B's letter was deposited in the mail on September 5 and received on September 7. B then sent the following fax to A: "On second thought, I accept your offer." The fax was sent and received on September 6. What is the result of these communications?

8. Assume the same situation as that presented in question 7 except that A received the letter before A received the fax. What would the result be?

9. A sent B the following letter: "I will sell you five contract law books for $2 each." The letter was deposited in the mail on September 2 and received on September 4. B then sent A the following letter: "I accept your offer." B's letter was deposited on September 5 and received on Sept. 7. B then sent A the following fax: "I reject your offer." The fax was sent and received on September 6. What is the result of these communications?

10. Redraft A's letter in question 1 to avoid the application of the mailbox rule and change the outcome.

Electronic Transactions

Exercise 2-35: Timing of Acceptance in Electronic Transactions

The mailbox rule was devised for a world in which communication between parties who were geographically distant from one another was not instantaneous. Now read section 64 of the RESTATEMENT (SECOND) OF CONTRACTS and compare it with section 63.

1. Where and when does an acceptance communicated via the internet become effective under the default rule in section 64?

2. How does this rule differ from the mailbox rule?

Synthesis of Common Law Mutual Assent Law

Exercise 2-36: Synthesis of Common Law Mutual Assent Law

1. Create an outline depicting what you have learned about mutual assent. Diagrams 2-3 and 2-4 on the following pages are two partially completed hierarchy charts that you may find helpful as you create your outline. Complete those charts.

Diagram 2-3: Synthesis of Mutual Assent Law

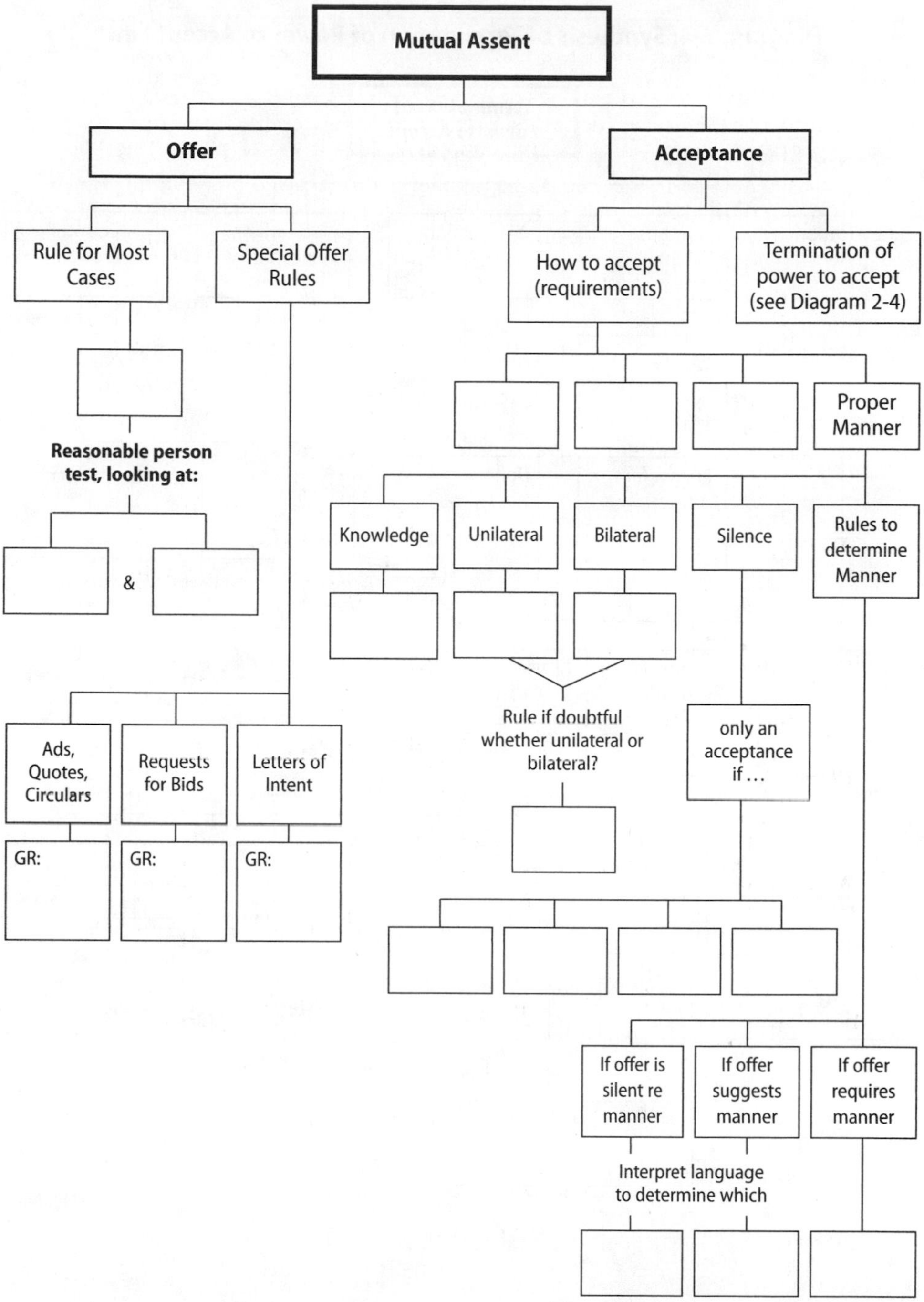

```
                        ┌─────────────────┐
                        │  Mutual Assent  │
                        └─────────────────┘
              ┌───────────────────┴───────────────────┐
        ┌───────────┐                           ┌─────────────┐
        │   Offer   │                           │  Acceptance │
        └───────────┘                           └─────────────┘
       ┌──────┴──────┐                     ┌──────────┴──────────┐
  ┌──────────┐ ┌──────────┐         ┌──────────────┐    ┌──────────────┐
  │ Rule for │ │ Special  │         │ How to accept│    │ Termination of│
  │   Most   │ │  Offer   │         │(requirements)│    │ power to accept│
  │  Cases   │ │  Rules   │         └──────────────┘    │(see Diagram 2-4)│
  └──────────┘ └──────────┘                             └──────────────┘
```

Reasonable person test, looking at:

&

Ads, Quotes, Circulars — GR:

Requests for Bids — GR:

Letters of Intent — GR:

Proper Manner

Knowledge | Unilateral | Bilateral | Silence | Rules to determine Manner

Rule if doubtful whether unilateral or bilateral?

only an acceptance if ...

If offer is silent re manner | If offer suggests manner | If offer requires manner

Interpret language to determine which

Diagram 2-4: Synthesis of Termination of Power to Accept Law

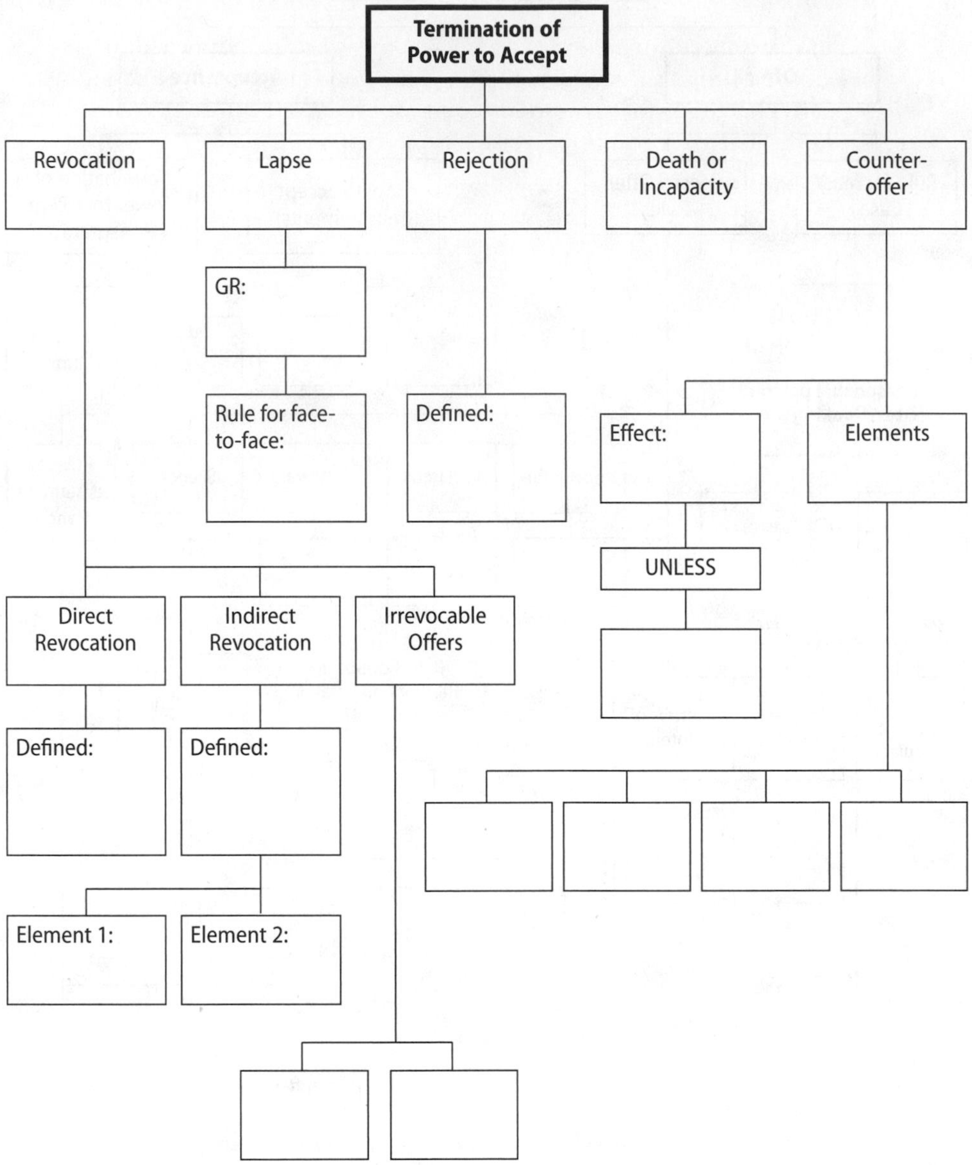

```
                              ┌─────────────────────┐
                              │    Termination of    │
                              │  Power to Accept     │
                              └─────────────────────┘
                                        │
     ┌──────────────┬─────────────┬─────────────┬──────────────┐
┌─────────┐  ┌─────────┐  ┌─────────┐  ┌─────────┐  ┌─────────┐
│Revocation│  │  Lapse  │  │Rejection│  │Death or │  │Counter- │
│         │  │         │  │         │  │Incapacity│  │ offer   │
└─────────┘  └─────────┘  └─────────┘  └─────────┘  └─────────┘
     │            │            │                         │
     │       ┌─────────┐       │                         │
     │       │  GR:    │       │                         │
     │       └─────────┘       │           ┌─────────────┴──────┐
     │            │            │       ┌─────────┐        ┌─────────┐
     │     ┌──────────┐  ┌──────────┐  │ Effect: │        │Elements │
     │     │Rule for face-│ │Defined: │  └─────────┘        └─────────┘
     │     │to-face:   │  └──────────┘       │                   │
     │     └──────────┘                 ┌─────────┐             │
     │                                  │ UNLESS  │             │
     │                                  └─────────┘             │
  ┌──┴────────┬─────────────┐              │                    │
┌─────────┐ ┌─────────┐ ┌─────────┐   ┌─────────┐              │
│ Direct  │ │Indirect │ │Irrevocable│ │         │              │
│Revocation│ │Revocation│ │ Offers  │ └─────────┘              │
└─────────┘ └─────────┘ └─────────┘                            │
     │          │           │      ┌─────────┬─────────┬───────┴──┐
┌─────────┐ ┌─────────┐     │   ┌─────┐ ┌─────┐ ┌─────┐ ┌─────┐
│Defined: │ │Defined: │     │   │     │ │     │ │     │ │     │
└─────────┘ └─────────┘     │   └─────┘ └─────┘ └─────┘ └─────┘
     │          │           │
┌─────────┐ ┌─────────┐     │
│Element 1:│ │Element 2:│    │
└─────────┘ └─────────┘     │
                      ┌──────┴──────┐
                   ┌─────┐    ┌─────┐
                   │     │    │     │
                   └─────┘    └─────┘
```

2. After you have completed your mutual assent outline, prepare a complete and thoughtful written answer to the problem below. (Hint: You must analyze the multiple legal implications of each paragraph.)

One morning, Bill, a homeowner, clad in his robe and slippers, walked out to his driveway to get his newspaper. As he reached over to pick up the newspaper, Bill said, in a very loud voice, "I need to hire a gardener who will take $65 to cut my lawn."

Bill's neighbor, Anna, who is a gardener and who also happened to be outside getting her newspaper, said, "I am good at gardening and I regularly charge $65 for my work. I accept your offer and will do the entire lawn, including clean-up, for $65."

Bill responded, "I don't know. I forgot how easy my yard is. I don't think I could let anyone do it for any more than $30."

Anna then said, "I accept."

Bill replied, "I will pay you $25 if you will cut my lawn. I would like you to accept this offer by cutting the lawn."

Anna then said, "I promise I will cut your lawn." Three days later, Anna cut Bill's lawn.

Did Bill and Anna enter into a contract? Discuss the legal issues presented.

Mutual Assent under U.C.C. Article 2

Introduction

This section presents your first extended discussion of U.C.C. Article 2. U.C.C. Article 2 is a collection of model statutes drafted by a team of lawyers, professors, and judges. The U.C.C. has been enacted in nearly every state. For this reason, the U.C.C. has become the governing law for all deals within its scope. Reading statutes, like reading cases, involves learning special skills. Accordingly, in this section you will be introduced to some basic techniques for reading statutes. At the same time, this section will also introduce you to some fundamental Article 2 rules that govern U.C.C. mutual assent issues.

Exercise 2-37: A Further Introduction to the U.C.C.

1. Has the state where you plan to practice law enacted the U.C.C.? Nearly all states have done so. Find the U.C.C. in the code books for your state.

2. Take a moment to look up and read section 1-103 of the U.C.C. Try to summarize 1-103 in your own words before you continue reading.

There are a few things in section 1-103 that should "jump out" at you:

- The word "unless" at the start of section 1-103(b): "Unless" is a cue that indicates that the section will contain a general principle limited by the category of things in the "unless" clause.

- The word "including" through the word "cause": "Including" is a cue indicating that a list is not exhaustive. Therefore, it is helpful to first read the statutory language while ignoring the words in the "including" clause.

- The phrase "Unless displaced by the particular provisions of this act, the principles of law and equity ... shall supplement its provisions": This use of "Unless displaced" means that lawyers should apply U.C.C. rules in all instances where there are applicable U.C.C. rules; conversely, lawyers should apply common law rules if the U.C.C. does not address a particular issue.[4]

The Relevant U.C.C. Rules

Exercise 2-38: U.C.C. Mutual Assent Rules

The U.C.C. rules that address mutual assent are sections 2-204, 2-205, 2-206, and 2-207. These sections are addressed below. As you read each of the U.C.C. sections, try using the following techniques to build your statute reading skills:

- Try to translate each section into your own words.

- If there are subsections, treat each subsection as a separate rule you need to understand and translate it into your own words.

- When you first start reading each section, ignore non-essential words (such as the words in an "including" clause).

- Look for the key connecting words:
  - "And" signals multiple elements of a rule
  - "Or" signals requirements that can be met in alternative ways
  - "Unless" signals an exception to a rule
  - "Including" signals a non-exclusive list of examples

- If a section provides cross-references to definitions of terms, be sure to look up and read those definitions. You can find definitions in Article 1 (sections 1-201, 1-204, and 1-205) and in Article 2 (sections 2-103, 2-104, 2-105, and 2-106).

- Try to diagram section 2-205. For example, Diagram 2-5 provides an outline for section 2-205.

- Look for common law analogies. For example, section 2-204(3) is similar to section 33 in the RESTATEMENT (SECOND) OF CONTRACTS.

2-205. The subject matter of section 2-205 is irrevocable offers. For instructional purposes, this is the first U.C.C. provision you will be introduced to in depth (even though, earlier in this chapter, the topic of irrevocable offers came after the discussion of the communication of a commitment and the certainty requirements).

---

4. For this reason, you may find it helpful to keep a list of common law rules for which there is no parallel U.C.C. rule.

You will see that section 2-205 is labeled "**Firm Offers**." It is a special U.C.C. rule for making offers irrevocable. One way to make sense of this statute, like other statutes, is to outline it. Outlining is an effective technique because it allows you to see the structure of a rule, to identify specific requirements, and to identify the effect of meeting or not meeting those requirements.

Take a moment to look at section 2-205. You should notice that section 2-205 is written as a single sentence. But, even a quick glance should tell you that the section has multiple elements.

Read the first line of section 2-205. You should see that the first five words state: "**An offer by a merchant....**" Thus, in just the first five words of 2-205 you are presented with two specific requirements: (1) there must be an offer, and (2) the offeror must be a merchant.

As you read on in section 2-205, you should note that the section describes the effect of a court concluding that something is a "firm offer": the offer is "not revocable ... during the time stated or if no time is stated for a reasonable time...." Consequently, if something is a firm offer, the offeror cannot revoke it for the time stated in the offer or for a reasonable time.

As you examine the rest of section 2-205, you will see that all the remaining parts of the section can be classified either as additional requirements or as limits on the effect of the section. These two broad categories can help you understand the section and outline it.

The outline depicted in Diagram 2-5 is one possible outline for section 2-205. As you can likely tell, you need to engage in a careful, sequential, step-by-step process to outline a rule. Once you complete your own outline of section 2-205, check to make sure it is accurate. To do so, match each part of your outline to words in the statute and highlight those words in the statute. When you are done with this task, each part of the statute should be highlighted and addressed in your outline. Finally, note that the mental effort required to outline a rule will also help you encode it in your memory and remember it.

Diagram 2-5: Outline of 2-205

Below is an outline of 2-205. Note that we have provided information in italics in the outline to give you insight into the thinking process you should be engaging in as you outline rules.

I. Requirements

    A. **An offer** (*This requirement is the first identified above. We looked for a U.C.C. definition of offer; finding none, we know from 1-103 that a court will apply the common law definition.*) **and** (*For now we have added the word "and" and made it bold to remind ourselves that this rule states a list of requirements.*)

    B. **By a merchant** (*This requirement is the second identified above. We quickly discover that the term "merchant" is defined in 2-104 so we now need to diagram 2-104. 2-104(1) defines what a merchant is, and it is a rule stated in alternatives. Thus, we will make those alternatives 2a-2c and place an "or" between the alternatives, both because the rule uses "or" and as a reminder that the items are alternatives.*) **and** (*This "and" again reminds us that we are dealing with a list of requirements.*)

       1. A person, corporation or other entity (*1-201 defines a person in this way.*)

       2. Who either

     a. Deals in such goods **or**

     b. By his occupation presents himself as having knowledge or skills particular to the field **or**

     c. By his employment of others who have knowledge or skill particular to the field

  C. **Contains assurances that it will be held open and**

  D. **Those assurances are in a signed writing and**

     1. "Signed" includes any symbol adopted by a party with present intent to authenticate (validate) a writing (*1-201 defines signed in this way.*)

     2. Writing includes printing, typewriting, or any other intentional reduction to tangible form (*1-201 defines writing in this way.*)

  E. **If the assurances are on a form supplied by the offeree, the assurances are separately signed by the offeror and**

  F. **[There's no additional requirement of consideration — <u>contrast</u> a common law option contract]**

II. **Effect of being a firm offer: offer is irrevocable**

  A. **For time stated or**

  B. **A reasonable time if no time is stated** (*1-205 says a reasonable time depends on the nature, purpose, and circumstances.*)

  C. **Up to a maximum of three months**

2-204 and 2-206. U.C.C. sections 2-204 and 2-206 are relatively simple statutory provisions. Complete Exercise 2-39 to learn about these two sections.

Exercise 2-39: U.C.C. Sections 2-204 and 2-206

    1. Section 2-204 makes minor adjustments to the common law formation rules. Paraphrase each subsection of 2-204 and try to determine how 2-204 modifies the common law.

    2. Section 2-206 contains two subsections. Outline subsection (1) (because it is slightly complex). Paraphrase subsection (2).

2-207. Section 2-207 is considerably more complicated than the previous sections you just read. The next case, *Wachter Management Co. v. Dexter & Chaney, Inc.*, addresses 2-207 in a context familiar to anyone who has ever purchased computer software or hardware. The purchaser buys the software or hardware at the store and then discovers, either in the box or when he or she loads the software or starts the computer, that the manufacturer is claiming additional rights. When these additional contract terms are in the box, they are referred to as "shrinkwrap" agreements. When the terms pop up on the computer screen and the buyer is asked to agree to the terms by clicking somewhere on the screen, the terms are called "clickwrap" agreements.

Exercise 2-40: *Wachter Management Co. v. Dexter & Chaney, Inc.*

    To understand 2-207 and the *Wachter* case, complete the task in 1., below, and answer the questions in 2. and 3.

1. Convert 2-207 into an outline or flowchart. If you need to refresh your understanding as to what is involved in converting a statute into an outline, review the discussion of 2-205 above. The section 2-207 rule is very complicated; it may take you as long as one hour to outline it. (Hint: Outline each subsection separately.)

2. What does *Wachter* teach you about the meaning of 2-207?

3. What does *Wachter* teach you about the meaning of 2-204 and 2-206?

Wachter Management Co. v. Dexter & Chaney, Inc.
282 Kan. 365, 144 P.3d 747 (2006)

[*Editor's note: All citations to sections of the U.C.C. have been altered to reflect the standardized form: 2-207 (first the article number, followed by a dash and section number).*]

Rosen, J. Wachter Management Company (Wachter) filed an action for breach of contract, [etc.] ... against Dexter & Chaney, Inc. (DCI).... [DCI moved to dismiss Wachter's lawsuit based on a choice of venue provision in a "shrinkwrap" agreement enclosed with the software DCI sold Wachter. Choice of venue refers to the court in which a party can be sued. The trial court denied DCI's motion.]

Facts

Wachter is a construction management company incorporated in Missouri with its principal place of business in Lenexa, Kansas. DCI is a software services company that develops, markets, and supports construction software, project management software, service management software, and document imaging software for construction companies like Wachter. DCI is incorporated in Washington with its principal place of business in Seattle.

Beginning in April 2002, DCI approached Wachter for the purpose of marketing its software to Wachter. Wachter expressed some interest in DCI's software but delayed negotiations to purchase the software until August 2003. After detailed negotiations, DCI issued a written proposal to Wachter on October 15, 2003, for the purchase of an accounting and project management software system. The proposal included installation of the software, a full year of maintenance, and a training and consulting package. The proposal did not contain an integration clause or any provision indicating that it was the final and complete agreement of the parties, nor did the proposal contain any provision indicating that additional terms might be required. An agent for Wachter signed DCI's proposal at Wachter's Lenexa office on October 17, 2003.

Thereafter, DCI shipped the software and assisted Wachter in installing it on Wachter's computer system. Enclosed with the software, DCI included a software licensing agreement, also known as a "shrinkwrap" agreement, which provided:

"This is a legal agreement between you (the 'CUSTOMER') and Dexter & Chaney, Inc. ('DCI'). By opening this sealed disk package, you agree to be bound by this agreement with respect to the enclosed software as well as any updates and/or applicable custom programming related thereto which you may have purchased or to which you may be entitled. If you do not accept the terms of this agreement, promptly return the unopened disk package and all accompanying documentation to DCI...."

The software license agreement also contained a choice of law/venue provision providing that the agreement would be governed by the laws of the State of Washington and that any disputes would be resolved by the state courts in King County, Washington.

In February 2005, after encountering problems with the software, Wachter sued DCI in Johnson County, Kansas ... seeking damages in excess of $350,000. DCI moved to dismiss Wachter's petition, alleging improper venue based on the provision of the software licensing agreement, which provided that King County, Washington, was the proper venue. In response, Wachter argued that the software licensing agreement was an unenforceable addition to the parties' original contract.

The district court denied DCI's motion, finding that the parties entered into a contract when Wachter signed DCI's proposal and concluding that the software license agreement contained additional terms that Wachter had not bargained for or accepted....

Analysis

DCI argues that the district court erred when it refused to recognize the applicability of "shrinkwrap" license agreements. DCI raises four arguments. First, DCI contends that Wachter accepted the terms of the license agreement by opening and using the software. Second, DCI argues that other courts have upheld the terms of shrinkwrap agreements. Third, DCI claims that the district court's refusal to apply the licensing agreement provides Wachter with an undeserved windfall because its use of the software was unfettered by any license terms. Fourth, DCI asserts that the venue clause in its license agreement is applicable to noncontract claims that are related to or limited by the contract.

Wachter counters by arguing that DCI's license agreement is a unilateral alteration of the contract created when Wachter accepted DCI's proposal. Disputing DCI's contention that it assented to the additional terms by opening, installing, and using the software, Wachter claims that it received no independent consideration for the amendments to the contract....

Pursuant to [2-204], a contract for the sale of goods is formed "in any manner sufficient to show agreement, including conduct by both parties which recognizes the existence of such a contract." Unless otherwise unambiguously indicated by the language or circumstances, an offer to make a contract shall be construed as inviting acceptance in any manner and by any medium reasonable in the circumstances. [2-206.] The Kansas Comment to [2-206] provides that the offeror is the master of the offer and may require a specific manner of acceptance if it is unambiguously conveyed in the language of the offer or other circumstances.

In this case, DCI issued a written proposal to Wachter containing an itemized list of the software to be purchased, the quantity to be purchased, the price of the software, the time period for execution, and the cost for the incidental maintenance, training, and consulting services. DCI's proposal requested Wachter to accept its offer to sell Wachter software by signing the proposal above the words "[p]lease ship the software listed above." Accordingly, Wachter accepted DCI's offer to sell the software to it by signing the proposal at Wachter's office in Lenexa. Thus, a contract was formed when Wachter accepted DCI's offer to sell it the software, indicating agreement between the parties. *See* [2-204].

The cover letter with DCI's proposal stated that it included "modules and licenses." However, DCI did not attach a copy of its Software Licensing Agreement to the proposal or incorporate it by reference in the proposal to indicate that there would be additional contract language regarding the licenses. Consequently, the parties' contract did not contain the terms of the Software Licensing Agreement. Wachter was advised of the terms of the Software Licensing Agreement after DCI shipped the software in partial performance of its duties under the contract. Because the Software Licensing Agreement was attached to the software rather than the original contract, it must be considered as an attempt to amend the contract.

The U.C.C. addresses the modification of a contract. [2-207] provides in pertinent part:

> "(1) A definite and seasonable expression of acceptance or a written confirmation which is sent within a reasonable time operates as an acceptance even though it states terms additional to or different from those offered or agreed upon, unless acceptance is expressly made conditional on assent to the additional or different terms.

> (2) The additional terms are to be construed as proposals for addition to the contract....

> (3) Conduct by both parties which recognizes the existence of a contract is sufficient to establish a contract for sale although the writings of the parties do not otherwise establish a contract. In such case the terms of the particular contract consist of those terms on which the writings of the parties agree, together with any supplementary terms incorporated under any other provisions of this act...."

DCI argues that Wachter expressly consented to the shrinkwrap agreement when it installed and used the software rather than returning it. However, continuing with the contract after receiving a writing with additional or different terms is not sufficient to establish express consent to the additional or different terms.

[Another court facing a similar issue] applied the principles of U.C.C. 2-207 to conclude that the parties must expressly intend to modify a previous agreement.... [That court] stated that U.C.C. 2-207 provides a default rule in the absence of a party's express assent to proposed changes in an agreement. According to the default rule, the terms of the agreement include the terms both parties have agreed upon and any terms implied by the provisions of the U.C.C. Treating the shrinkwrap license as a "written confirmation containing additional terms," the ... court concluded that continuing with the contract after receiving the shrinkwrap license was not sufficient to establish an express assent to the new or additional terms contained in the shrinkwrap license. Because the plaintiff never expressly agreed to the additional terms contained in the shrinkwrap license, the terms did not become part of the parties' agreement.... The court also found that the integration clause in the license agreement and the "consent by opening" language did not render the software provider's acceptance conditional because it gave no real indication that it was willing to forgo the transaction if [the other party] rejected the additional terms.

[A different case] addressed the validity of an arbitration clause contained in a shrinkwrap-type agreement. In [that case], a consumer purchased a Gateway computer. Gateway included its Standard Terms and Conditions Agreement (Agreement) inside the box with the computer. When the consumer sued for breach of contract and breach of warranty, Gateway filed a motion to dismiss, claiming that the consumer was bound by the arbitration clause in its Agreement. Assuming that the consumer offered to purchase the computer and Gateway accepted the offer by agreeing to ship or shipping the computer, the ... court treated Gateway's Agreement as an expression of acceptance or written confirmation of the consumer's offer to purchase and applied 2-207. According to Gateway's Agreement, retaining the computer for more than 5 days constituted an acceptance of its Agreement. Gateway argued that the consumer assented to the arbitration clause by retaining the computer for more than 5 days.... [T]he ... court rejected Gateway's argument, finding that the consumer was unaware that the transaction depended on his acceptance of the Agreement and concluding that the consumer had not expressly agreed to Gateway's terms....

DCI relies on *Hill v. Gateway 2000, Inc.,* 105 F.3d 1147 (7th Cir. 1997); *ProCD v. Zeidenberg,* 86 F.3d 1447 (7th Cir. 1996); and *Mortenson Co. v. Timberline Software,* 140 Wash.2d 568, 998 P.2d 305 (2000), for the proposition that shrinkwrap agreements are valid, and the terms contained within them are enforceable, because the purchaser accepts the terms when it uses the product.

In *ProCD,* a consumer purchased a software database program at a retail store. A license enclosed in the package with the software limited its use to noncommercial applications. The software also required a user to accept the license agreement by clicking an on-screen button before activating the software. Contrary to the license, the consumer made the database available on the internet at a reduced price. ProCD sued, seeking an injunction against further dissemination of its database.

The *ProCD* court determined that the *vendor* is the master of the offer under the U.C.C. and may invite acceptance by conduct or limit the kind of conduct that constitutes acceptance. The court found that ProCD proposed a contract that invited acceptance by using the software after having an opportunity to review the license. If the buyer disagreed with the terms of the contract, he or she could return the software. Holding that the consumer was bound by the terms of the license agreement, the *ProCD* court stated that "[n]otice on the outside, terms on the inside, and a right to return the software for a refund if the terms are unacceptable (a right the license expressly extends), may be a means of doing business valuable to buyers and sellers alike." [Citation omitted.]

In *Hill,* a consumer ordered a Gateway computer over the telephone. When the computer arrived, the box contained Gateway's standard terms governing the sale. According to Gateway's standard terms, the consumer accepted the terms by retaining the computer for 30 days. When the consumer was not satisfied with the operation of the computer, he sued Gateway on behalf of a class of similarly situated consumers. Relying on the *ProCD* court's analysis that the *vendor* is the master of the offer, the *Hill* court enforced the arbitration clause found in Gateway's standard terms even though the consumer was not aware of the terms until he received the computer. The *Hill* court noted that there are many commercial transactions in which money is exchanged for products with disclosure of certain terms of the sale following the execution of the sale. [Citations omitted.] The *Hill* court announced its policy that "[p]ractical considerations support allowing vendors to enclose the full legal terms with their products.... Customers as a group are better off when vendors skip costly and ineffectual steps such as telephonic recitation [of standard terms], and use a simple approve-or-return device." [Citation omitted.]

Both *ProCD* and *Hill* can be distinguished from this case. The buyers in *ProCD* and *Hill* were both consumers who did not enter into negotiations with the vendors prior to their purchases. Wachter, on the other hand, participated in detailed negotiations with DCI before accepting DCI's proposal to sell Wachter the software. The *ProCD* and *Hill* courts concluded that the offer to sell software to the consumers was not accepted until the consumers opened the packaging with the terms of the sale enclosed and retained the product after having an opportunity to read the terms of the sale. Accordingly, the contract was not formed until the last act indicating acceptance occurred. Here, however, the last act indicating acceptance of DCI's offer to sell software to Wachter occurred when Wachter signed DCI's proposal. Thus, the contract was formed before DCI shipped the software and Wachter had an opportunity to consider the licensing agreement.

Although *ProCD* and *Hill* are distinguishable, the third case cited by DCI is factually similar to this case. In *Mortenson*, a construction contractor purchased software to assist with its bid preparation. The contractor issued a purchase order and the developer shipped the software accompanied by a shrinkwrap license, which included a limitation of remedies clause. Applying U.C.C. 2-204, the *Mortenson* court held that the initial purchase order and the shrinkwrap license were part of a "layered contract" where the initial purchase order was not an integrated contract because it did not contain an integration clause and required additional terms to be determined later. The *Mortenson* court adopted the contract formation analysis from *ProCD* and *Hill* and concluded that Mortenson's use of the software constituted its assent to the terms of the shrinkwrap license. [Citation omitted.]

Although the facts in *Mortenson* are similar to the facts in this case, we disagree with the *Mortenson* court's analysis of when the contract was formed. We adhere to the traditional contract principles outlined by the dissenting justices in *Mortenson* and the decisions in [other cases cited by the court]. The offeror, whether the seller or the buyer, is the master of the offer.

In this case, DCI and Wachter negotiated prior to entering into a contract for the sale of software. DCI's written proposal following the parties' negotiations constituted an offer to sell. Wachter accepted that offer when it signed the proposal, requesting shipment of the software. The contract was formed when Wachter accepted DCI's proposal. *See* [2-204]. Because the contract was

What is the difference between the *Wachter* court's view as to how to apply 2-204 and 2-207 and the *Mortenson* court's view?

formed before DCI shipped the software with the enclosed license agreement, the Software Licensing Agreement must be treated as a proposal to modify the terms of the contract. There is no evidence that Wachter expressly agreed to the modified terms, and Wachter's actions in continuing the preexisting contract do not constitute express assent to the terms in the Software Licensing Agreement. Thus, the forum selection clause in the Software Licensing Agreement is not enforceable against Wachter. We affirm the district court's denial of DCI's motion to dismiss and remand the matter for further proceedings.

Luckert, J., dissenting. I would reverse the district court's conclusion that the choice of venue provision in the software licensing agreement was not enforceable. I disagree with the majority's analysis that the license agreement was a modification of the contract. Rather, the original offer included the license or, at least, expressed the intent of the parties that a license was a part of the offer. Wachter assented to and accepted these terms by its conduct.

DCI's letter transmitting the proposal notified Wachter that "[t]he proposal includes modules and licenses." Wachter did not question, object to, or offer an alternative to the proposal. Instead Wachter signed the proposal, thus accepting the offer which included licenses. See [2-204] ("A contract for sale of goods may be made in any manner sufficient to show agreement, including conduct by both parties which recognizes the existence of such a contract."). In turn, DCI sent the software. Wachter opened the software and installed it. In doing so, it accepted the goods. If Wachter felt that the goods were nonconforming because of the license agreement, Wachter was required by [2-204] to reject the goods. Wachter's failure to object after a reasonable time for inspection constituted an acceptance of the goods. See ProCD, Inc. v. Zeidenberg, 86 F.3d 1447, 1452–53 (7th Cir. 1996); [citation omitted].

Alternatively, by DCI's referring to "licenses" in the proposal, there was an expression of intent either that there was to be a layered contract or that a contract was not formed until Wachter accepted the license agreement. When sending the software, DCI gave Wachter the option of accepting the terms of the license or "promptly return[ing] the unopened disk package." DCI, as the offeror, could invite acceptance by conduct and could propose limitations on the kind of conduct that constitutes acceptance. [2-204.] The notice on the shrinkwrap advised Wachter of the specifics of the license agreement and notified Wachter that by opening the software it was accepting the terms. Again, Wachter did not question or object to the terms and did not offer alternative terms. Rather, it accepted the terms of the license with notice through DCI's communication that the proposal included licenses that were a part of the contract. Wachter could have prevented formation of the contract by returning the software. Instead, Wachter opened the software. Wachter's conduct was sufficient to evidence its agreement with the terms of the contract. See [2-204].

Under the facts of this case, where the negotiations included a clear communication that the proposal included licenses and the parties' contract did not include an integration provision, the rationale of these cases does not apply. This case does not involve contract modification but contract formation. Furthermore, even if the issue were one of modification, Wachter's acceptance, made with notice that the license was a part of the proposal, was an assent to the modification. The communication made Wachter aware that the continuation of the contract depended upon its acceptance of the terms of the license....

Under the facts of this case on this issue of contract formation rather than contract modification, I find persuasive the analysis of *Hill v. Gateway 2000, Inc.,* 105 F.3d 1147, 1149–50 (7th Cir.), *cert. denied* 522 U.S. 808, 118 S.Ct. 47, 139 L.Ed.2d 13 (1997); *ProCD, Inc. v. Zeidenberg,* 86 F.3d at 1452–53; *Brower v. Gateway 2000,* 246 A.D.2d 246, 250–51, 676 N.Y.S.2d 569 (1998); and *Mortenson Co. v. Timberline Software,* 140 Wash.2d 568, 583–84, 998 P.2d 305 (2000).

Nuss and Beier, JJ., join in the foregoing dissent.

Exercise 2-41: *Wachter* Revisited and Chapter Wrap-Up

1. Assume the *Wachter* court held that the dispute was governed by 2-207 and a contract was formed under 2-207(1). What are the terms of the parties' contract under 2-207(2)?

2. Assume the *Wachter* court held that the dispute was goverened by 2-207 and no contract was formed under 2-207(1). What are the terms of the parties' contract under 2-207(3)?

3. If the initial contract in *Wachter* had clearly communicated that the software would include additional terms to which Wachter had to agree if Wachter wished to buy the software, would that disclosure have changed the result?

4. Revisit the Krack / Metal-Matic hypothetical (immediately after Exercise 2-33). Analyze how 2-207 would apply to that hypothetical and try to predict the result.

5. Create a comparison chart in which you identify all the similarities and differences between common law formation and U.C.C. Article 2 formation.

Chapter Problem Revisited

You now know enough to fully analyze the chapter problem introduced at the beginning of this chapter. The problem is similar to one you might be asked to analyze on a law school exam or in law practice. Here are a few hints to help you complete the problem:

- Make sure you start by determining what law governs the problem.

- There is no obviously correct conclusion as to whether the letter of intent in the problem is binding. Thus, your task is to identify the precise issues presented, state the applicable rules you have learned, and analyze the problem, including the arguments reasonable lawyers representing each of the parties might make. To assist you in this task, it may help to refer back to Table 2-2 (IRAC), Table 2-4 (Completing the "A" in IRAC), and the IRAC template above.

- At this point, you may be surprised to hear that you should also consider non-legal matters implicated in the chapter problem. While clients come to lawyers for our insight regarding legal issues, clients want legal advice that is practical and attuned to their business needs. Be creative!

Professional Development Reflection Questions

1. Picture yourself when you were taking the LSAT, completing law school applications, and deciding which law school to attend. Why did you want to attend law school? What did you visualize yourself doing after law school? What were your ultimate goals and dreams? Use those dreams as a touchstone when you are struggling to stay motivated in law school.

2. Have your goals and dreams changed since you started law school?

3. Do you feel law school is changing you? Some students worry that law school changes them in negative ways. Be aware of how you are changing and stay grounded by focusing on your goals and dreams.

4. Letters of intent are often drafted in a way that may make it seem as if they bind both parties when, in fact, they do not contractually bind the parties. Imagine that a client asks you, as her lawyer, to draft a letter of intent that *appears* to bind both parties, but doesn't actually bind either party. Doing so is lawful, but should you engage in such a practice? Is it "good lawyering"?

Chapter 3

The Consideration Requirement for Contract Formation

Exercise 3-1: Chapter Problem

Your client, Daniela, Inc., has come to you for help and has handed you the complaint provided in Table 3-1. As you have learned by now, in civil cases, complaints are documents filed by plaintiffs to initiate lawsuits. Complaints state the facts and bases for legal relief which justify the courts' intervention and the enforcement of legal rights. In the contract law context, the contract at issue in a dispute is almost always attached to the complaint (as it is in Table 3-1).

After a quick review of Daniela's complaint, you determine that you have one month in which to file an answer. Your answer should allege that your client is not liable because he did not receive "*consideration*" and, therefore, did not enter into a contract. Accordingly, you need to learn the factual basis for asserting lack of consideration as a defense.

Your specific tasks in this exercise are to identify the consideration issue implicated by the contract attached to Daniela's complaint, accurately predict whether a court will conclude the contract lacks consideration, plan a strategy for handling the dispute, and draft an answer to the complaint. By the end of this chapter, you will be able to do so.

As you read this chapter, keep your client's case in mind. The materials at the end of this chapter will provide guidance for drafting an answer to the complaint. So, until the end of this chapter, you just need to focus on identifying and analyzing the consideration issue.

Finally, please note that in all jurisdictions, your signature on legal papers represents that you have engaged in a reasonable inquiry and are certifying that your allegations: (1) are not being presented for any improper purpose; (2) are warranted by either existing law or a non-frivolous argument for modification of existing law; and (3) have evidentiary support or are likely to have evidentiary support after a reasonable opportunity for further investigation.[1]

Consequently, we urge you to consider the signing of any document a serious matter that represents your level of credibility and reputation as an attorney. Now is the time to set a high professional standard for how you will conduct yourself and what type of attorney you will be. Thus, think about the importance of the standard you set for yourself as a legal professional as you draft the answer for your client at the end of this chapter.

---

1. For example, for cases filed in federal court, the applicable procedural rule provides that all papers filed by an attorney shall be signed and that unsigned papers will be stricken. The rule states that an attorney's signature provides a certification that the allegations being made are based on a reasonable inquiry and are appropriate. Finally, the rules provide for sanctions, such as fines, payment of attorneys' fees, the striking of pleadings, and other nonmonetary consequences, for papers filed in violation of the rule's requirement. FED. R. CIV. P. R. 11.

Table 3-1: Breach of Contract Complaint

As you read this complaint, note that, for instructional purposes, we have added notes in the margins with explanations about the complaint. Obviously, a real complaint would not include such notes. Also, note that this complaint has been filed in a fictional state, Jefferson. Treat the complaint as if it were filed in the state in which you are in law school.

The heading of a legal document, which contains the names of the parties, the court, and the case number, is called a "caption."

A court must have "jurisdiction," the power to hear and determine a case, before adjudicating a case.

A "cause of action" states the facts that give rise to a particular legal claim, such as a claim for breach of contract. If a complaint fails to state a cause of action, it will be dismissed. Most complaints allege multiple causes of action.

In most states, a cause of action for a breach of contract must allege: (1) the parties had a contract; (2) the plaintiff performed all of his obligations; (3) the defendant breached the contract; and (4) the plaintiff suffered damages as a result.

You have probably already noticed that the language of legal pleadings, as you see in this complaint, is frequently stilted and overly formal. Don't be intimidated.

State of Jefferson, County of Lincoln

Pietro Corp., Inc.,	)	
Plaintiff	)	
	)	
v.	)	**Complaint for Breach of Contract**
	)	
	)	**Case No.: BC29783543**
Daniela, Inc.,	)	
Defendant.	)	
_____	)	

Plaintiff, by and through its attorney, Lindsey Lawyer, hereby alleges as follows:

Parties and Jurisdiction

1. This action is filed pursuant to Chapter 22 of the Jefferson Code Annotated.

2. Plaintiff Pietro Corp., Inc., is a resident of Madison City, Lincoln County, in Jefferson State.

3. Defendant Daniela, Inc., is also a resident of Madison City, Lincoln County, in Jefferson State.

4. All of the events described in this complaint occurred in Madison City, Lincoln County, in Jefferson State.

5. Accordingly, this court has jurisdiction of the above-captioned matter.

Cause of Action: Breach of Contract

6. On or about June 1, Plaintiff and Defendant entered into a contract whereby Defendant agreed to serve as a marketing consultant to Plaintiff, and Plaintiff agreed to pay $175 per hour. A copy of the contract is attached hereto as Attachment A and incorporated by reference herein.

7. At all relevant times, Plaintiff has been ready, willing, and able to pay Defendant for Defendant's services.

8. On June 20 and continuously thereafter, Defendant breached the contract described in paragraph six by expressly and unequivocally denying that Plaintiff and Defendant entered into a valid and enforceable contract and by refusing to perform the contract or provide any marketing consulting services.

9. As a result, Plaintiff has suffered damages in the amount of $250,000 for loss of the benefit of its bargain, for lost profits, and for other incidental expenses.

Wherefore, Plaintiff prays for judgment against Defendant as follows:

1. Damages in the amount of $250,000.

2. Costs and such other relief as the court may deem proper.

This, the 1st day of August, 20___.

Lindsey Lawyer

Law Offices of Lindsey Lawyer, LLC
Attorneys for Plaintiff
1111 State Street
Madison, Jefferson 99999-0001
(519) 677-8999
State Bar No. 10985

A party's request for what he wants a court to do is called a "prayer for relief."

Procedural rules require attorneys to sign all papers filed with a court, and unsigned papers will be stricken. The rules also state that an attorney's signature provides a certification the allegations are based on a reasonable inquiry and are appropriate.

Attachment A
Consulting Agreement

This agreement made the first day of June by and between Pietro Corp, Inc., a corporation organized and existing under the laws of Jefferson State, with its principal place of business located at 2222 City Street, Madison City, Jefferson 99999 ("Company"), and Daniela, Inc., with its principal place of business located at 1112 State Street, Madison City, Jefferson 99999 ("Consultant").

Recitals

Company wishes to contract with Consultant for Consultant's marketing services. Consultant is willing and qualified to perform such services. In consideration of the matters described above, and of the mutual benefits and obligations set forth in this agreement, the parties agree as follows:

Services

Consultant agrees to perform such services as may be requested in writing by Company including, but not limited to, developing and implementing a marketing plan satisfactory to Company. It is understood that Company shall have the unrestricted, instantaneous right to cancel this agreement.

Compensation

Company shall compensate Consultant as follows: (1) $175 per hour and (2) all actual expenses incurred by Consultant directly related to Consultant's performance of this agreement. Consultant shall provide Company with monthly invoices reflecting services rendered to Company. These invoices shall be due and payable within ten days of their making.

Confidentiality

Consultant agrees that: (1) all knowledge and information that Consultant may receive from Company or from its employees or by virtue of the performance of services under and pursuant to this agreement belongs to Company; and (2) all information provided by Consultant to Company shall be regarded by Consultant as strictly confidential and shall be solely for Company's benefit and use. Consultant shall not use or disclose any such knowledge or information directly or indirectly to any person.

Consultant Representations

Consultant represents and warrants that Consultant has the right to perform the services required under this agreement.

Effective Date

This agreement shall become effective on the date stated above.

Entire Agreement

This agreement shall constitute the entire agreement between the parties and any prior understanding or representation of any kind preceding the date of this agreement shall not be binding upon either party.

Modification of Agreement

Any modification of this agreement or additional obligation assumed by either party in connection with this agreement shall be binding only if evidenced in writing signed by each party.

Notices

Any notice provided for or concerning this agreement shall be in writing and be deemed sufficiently given when sent by certified or registered mail if sent to the respective address of each party as set forth at the beginning of this agreement.

Governing Law

This agreement shall be governed by, construed, and enforced in accordance with the laws of the State of Jefferson.

Signatures

Each party to this agreement has caused it to be executed at Madison, Jefferson.

This, the first day of June, 20___,

Pietro Peterberg
_____
Pietro Peterberg, President
Pietro Corp, Inc.

Daniela Dubois
_____
Daniela Dubois, President
Daniela, Inc.

Introduction

Preliminary Questions

Answer the following two questions by re-reading RESTATEMENT (SECOND) OF CONTRACTS, Section 17.

1. How do you form a contract?

2. What is the effect of a finding that an agreement lacks consideration?

Diagram 3-1 depicts where consideration fits within the big picture of contract law. As Diagram 3-1 shows, both mutual assent and consideration are linked together as aspects of "Traditional Formation" under the more general "Contract Formation" topic.

Diagram 3-1: Contract Law Graphic Organizer

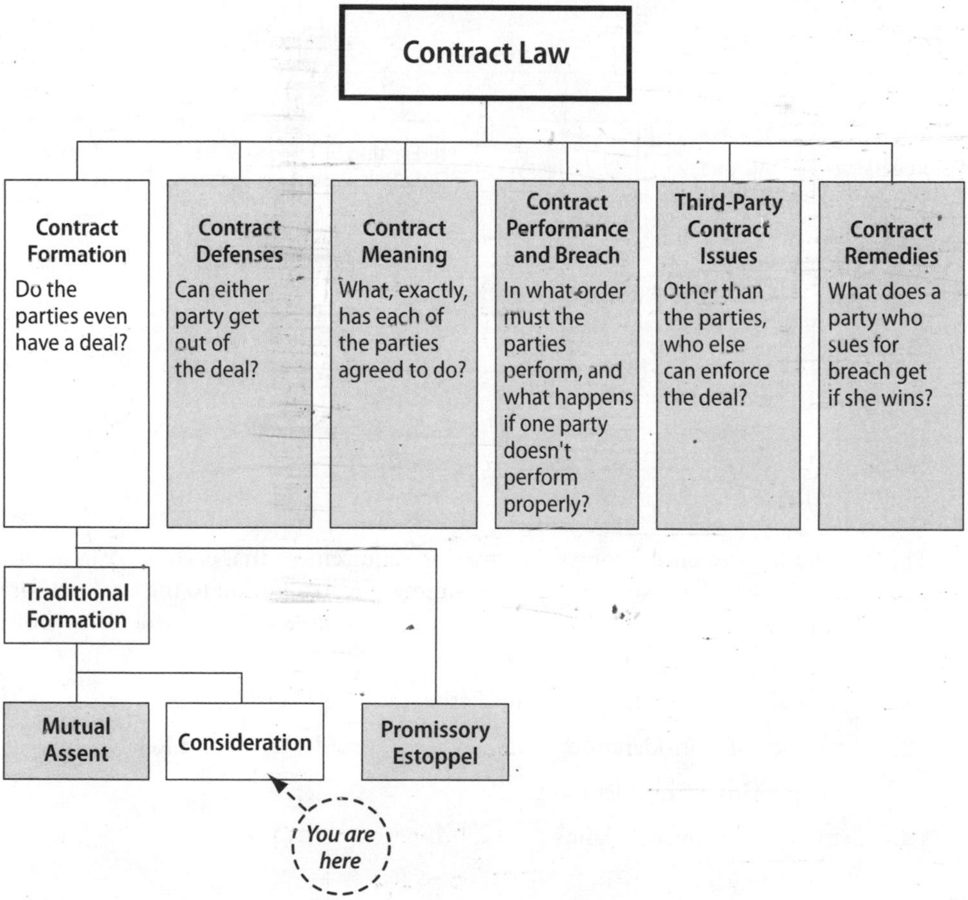

Contract Law

Contract Formation	Contract Defenses	Contract Meaning	Contract Performance and Breach	Third-Party Contract Issues	Contract Remedies
Do the parties even have a deal?	Can either party get out of the deal?	What, exactly, has each of the parties agreed to do?	In what order must the parties perform, and what happens if one party doesn't perform properly?	Other than the parties, who else can enforce the deal?	What does a party who sues for breach get if she wins?

Traditional Formation

Mutual Assent · Consideration · Promissory Estoppel

You are here

Consideration, like mutual assent, has many subtopics. Diagram 3-2 depicts how all of consideration's subtopics fit together. At the outset of your study of consideration, it is worth noting that, as reflected in Diagram 3-2, all contracts must meet the general rule requiring a **"bargained-for exchange."** Additionally, there are a series of consideration problems that may arise in contract cases.

Diagram 3-2: Consideration Law Graphic Organizer

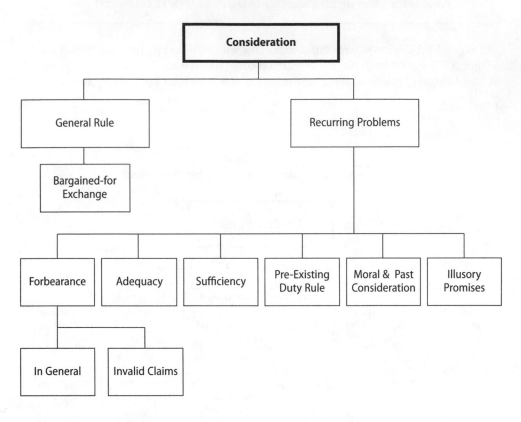

Overview of Chapter 3

This chapter focuses on the contract formation requirement that each party to a contract receive consideration. Note that this requirement is in addition to the contract formation requirement that you studied in Chapter 2, mutual assent. You will learn about consideration in six subsections:

1. The Basic Consideration Rule and Forbearance as Consideration
2. Adequacy of Consideration, Sufficiency of Consideration, and Related Topics
3. Past and Moral Consideration
4. Settlement of Invalid Claims
5. The Pre-Existing Duty Rule
6. Illusory Promises

The Basic Consideration Rule and Forbearance as Consideration

Exercise 3-2: The Basic Consideration Rule and Forbearance as Consideration

In the RESTATEMENT (SECOND) OF CONTRACTS, read section 71, subsections 1 and 2. Then answer the following questions:

1. What is the general rule regarding consideration? State the rule in your own words.

2. Why do courts require anything beyond mutual assent and certainty to form a contract? In other words, what is the policy rationale for requiring consideration?

3. Educational research demonstrates that students who are the most effective at learning during class are students who prepare before class by engaging in activities like completing their assignments and preparing to take notes during class. This exercise is designed to help you prepare to take notes in class by creating a structure for organizing your notes. Create a skeletal outline of consideration law based on your course syllabus, Diagram 3-2, the information in this set of questions, and section 71. Your skeletal outline should identify the major consideration topics and leave plenty of space under each topic for filling in notes during class.

4. Compare problems 4a and 4b. Problem 4a is an agreement that has consideration. Problem 4b is an agreement that lacks consideration. Based on section 71, explain why the former agreement has consideration and the latter agreement does not. When you finish, compare your analysis with the analysis in Table 3-2.

   a. Anna agrees to pay Bill $500, and Bill agrees to tutor Anna in contract law for five hours.
   b. Out of sympathy for Anna, Bill agrees to tutor Anna in contract law for five hours.

Table 3-2: Sample Consideration Analysis for Exercise 3-2, Problem 4

Each party to a contract must receive consideration. A return promise or performance is consideration if it is "bargained for"—for example, sought by the promisor and given by the promisee in exchange for the promisor's promise.

In problem 4a, Anna linked her promise to pay to Bill's promise to tutor her in contracts. Therefore, she bargained for the exchange. Similarly, Bill linked his promise to tutor to Anna's promise to pay. Therefore, Bill also bargained for the exchange. Anna's and Bill's promises are reciprocal inducements and thus constitute consideration.

In contrast, in problem 4b, while Anna received Bill's promise to be tutored, Bill does not appear to have sought anything and Anna does not appear to have given anything in exchange for Bill's promise. Therefore, Bill has not received any consideration.

Exercise 3-3: *Hamer v. Sidway*

The first consideration case you will read in this chapter, *Hamer v. Sidway*, addresses whether a court will find consideration where one party agrees to pay money and the other agrees to not do certain things. As you read *Hamer*, consider the following questions:

1. What are the relevant facts?

2. Who are Hamer and Sidway?

3. What was the offer in this case? (Hint: Exercise 2-21, Question 4 in Chapter 2 recited many of the facts of *Hamer* and asked you to analyze whether the offer was an offer of a unilateral or bilateral contract. Review your analysis of that question.)

4. Was the offer accepted? How?

5. The court seems to assume, without discussion, that there is no question that there was consideration passing from the uncle to the nephew. What was that consideration?

6. Why did the court conclude that there was consideration passing from the nephew to the uncle? How does the court deal with the fact that the nephew presumably benefited from giving up the specified activities and the uncle does not appear to have gained anything?

Hamer v. Sidway

124 N.Y. 538, 27 N.E. 256 (1898)

As you read this case, make sure you figure out who Hamer and Sidway are.

This action was brought upon an alleged contract.

The plaintiff presented a claim to the executor of William E. Story, Sr., for $5,000 and interest from the 6th day of February, 1875. She acquired it through several mesne assignments from William E. Story, 2d. The claim being rejected by the executor, this action was brought. It appears that William E. Story, Sr., was the uncle of William E. Story, 2d; that at the celebration of the golden wedding of Samuel Story and wife, father and mother of William E. Story, Sr., on the 20th day of March, 1869, in the presence of the family and invited guests he promised his nephew that if he would refrain from drinking, using tobacco, swearing and playing cards or billiards for money until he became twenty-one years of age he would pay him a sum of $5,000. The nephew assented thereto and fully performed the conditions inducing the promise. When the nephew arrived at the age of twenty-one years and on the 31st day of January, 1875, he wrote to his uncle informing him that he had performed his part of the agreement and had thereby become entitled to the sum of $5,000. The uncle received the letter and a few days later and on the sixth of February, he wrote and mailed to his nephew the following letter:

"Buffalo, Feb. 6, 1875.
W. E. Story, Jr.:

Dear Nephew—Your letter of the 31st ult. came to hand all right, saying that you had lived up to the promise made to me several years ago. I have no doubt but you have, for which you shall have five thousand dollars as I promised you. I had the money in the bank the day you was 21 years old that I intend for you, and you shall have the money certain. Now, Willie I do not intend to interfere with this money in any way till I think you are capable of taking care of it and the sooner that time comes the better it will please me. I would hate very much to have you start out in some adventure that you thought all right and lose this money in one year.... Willie, you are 21 and you have many a thing to learn yet. This money you have earned much easier than I did besides acquiring good habits at the same time and you are quite welcome to the money; hope you will make good use of it....
Truly Yours,
W.E. Story
P. S.—You can consider this money on interest."

The nephew received the letter and thereafter consented that the money should remain with his uncle in accordance with the terms and conditions of the letters. The uncle died on the 29th day of January, 1887, without having paid over to his nephew any portion of the said $5,000 and interest....

The question which provoked the most discussion by counsel on this appeal, and which lies at the foundation of plaintiff's asserted right of recovery, is whether by virtue of a contract defendant's testator William E. Story became indebted to his nephew William E. Story, 2d, on his twenty-first birthday in the sum of five thousand dollars. The trial court found as a fact that "on the 20th day of March, 1869, ... William E. Story agreed to and with William E. Story, 2d, that if he would refrain from drinking liquor, using tobacco, swearing, and playing cards or billiards for money until he should become 21 years of age then he, the said William E. Story, would at that time pay him, the said William E. Story, 2d, the sum of $5,000 for such refraining, to which the said William E. Story, 2d, agreed," and that he "in all things fully performed his part of said agreement."

The defendant contends that the contract was without consideration to support it, and, therefore, invalid. He asserts that the promisor, by refraining from the use of liquor and tobacco, was not harmed but benefited; that that which he did was best for him to do independently of his uncle's promise, and insists that it follows that unless the promisor was benefited, the contract was without consideration. A contention, which if well founded, would seem to leave open for controversy in many cases whether that which the promisee did or omitted to do was, in fact, of such benefit to him as to leave no consideration to support the enforcement of the promisor's agreement. Such a rule could not be tolerated, and is without foundation in the law. The Exchequer Chamber, in 1875, defined consideration as follows: "A valuable consideration in the sense of the law may consist either in some right, interest, profit or benefit accruing to the one party, or some forbearance, detriment, loss or responsibility given, suffered or undertaken by the other." Courts "will not ask whether the thing which forms the consideration does in fact benefit the promisee or a third party, or is of any substantial value to anyone. It is enough that something is promised, done, forborne or suffered by the party to whom the promise is made as consideration for the promise made to him."

"In general a waiver of any legal right at the request of another party is a sufficient consideration for a promise." PARSONS ON CONTRACTS, 444.

Why do you think that the court states the applicable rule several times and in several different ways?

"Any damage, or suspension, or forbearance of a right will be sufficient to sustain a promise." KENT, vol. 2, 465, 12th ed.

Pollock, in his work on contracts, page 166, after citing the definition given by the Exchequer Chamber already quoted, says: "The second branch of this judicial description is really the most important one. Consideration means not so much that one party is profiting as that the other abandons some legal right in the present or limits his legal freedom of action in the future as an inducement for the promise of the first."

Now, applying this rule to the facts before us, the promisee used tobacco, occasionally drank liquor, and he had a legal right to do so. That right he abandoned for a period of years upon the strength of the promise of the testator that for such forbearance he would give him $5,000. We need not speculate on the effort which may have been required to give up the use of those stimulants. It is sufficient that he restricted his lawful freedom of action within certain prescribed limits upon the faith of his uncle's agreement, and now having fully performed the conditions imposed, it is of no moment whether such performance actually proved a benefit to the promisor, and the court will not inquire into it, but were it a proper subject of inquiry, we see nothing in this record that would permit a determination that the uncle was not benefited in a legal sense. Few cases have been found which may be said to be precisely in point, but such as have been support the position we have taken....

The order appealed from should be reversed and the judgment of the Special Term affirmed, with costs payable out of the estate.

Exercise 3-4: *Hamer* Revisited

1. If the court had applied the rule stated in section 71 of the RESTATEMENT (SECOND) OF CONTRACTS, would the result in *Hamer* have changed?

2. Are there any facts in *Hamer* that indicate that the only thing the uncle really intended was a gift?

3. Stacey, who was about to perform in a play, approached her favorite adult niece, Kendra, and said, "If you come to the play, I will pay you $4,000. I will even leave you free tickets at the door." Kendra, who already was planning to attend the play, said, "Sure. I'll come, Auntie." Is Kendra's statement consideration for Stacey's promise? Why or why not? Be sure your analysis addresses the *Hamer* court's reference to relinquishing a right.

4. Would the result in *Hamer* have changed if all the activities from which the uncle asked the nephew to refrain were illegal for someone, like the nephew, who was under age twenty-one?

5. Dalton, Inc. decided to downsize its workforce by initiating a voluntary layoff program through which permanent employees were offered six months'

salary in return for severance. All participating employees were required to sign an agreement which contained the following clause:

> "In exchange for the consideration described above [six months' net salary], which the Employee acknowledges to be good and valuable consideration for [his/her] obligations hereunder, the Employee hereby fully and forever releases and discharges any and all claims [he/she] may have, have ever had, or may in the future have against Dalton, Inc. that may lawfully be waived and released arising out of or in any way related to [his/her] hire, benefits, employment or separation from employment with the Employer."

A Dalton employee who is considering whether or not to take the layoff deal asks for your advice. Advise her on her options having regard to *Hamer*.

Adequacy of Consideration, Sufficiency of Consideration, and Related Topics

The next two cases, *Lucht's Concrete Pumping, Inc. v. Horner* and *Schnell v. Nell*, address the issue of adequacy of consideration. The general rule, providing the backdrop against which both cases are decided, is that courts will not inquire into the adequacy of consideration. Consider both cases in this light.

Exercise 3-5: *Lucht's Concrete Pumping, Inc. v. Horner*

1. What are the key facts of *Lucht's*?
2. What was Horner's argument?
3. What was the court's ruling?
4. Paraphrase in your own words the rule the court formulated and applied with regard to adequacy of consideration.
5. What exception to its "adequacy" rule did the court identify?
6. Explain why the court's determination of the consideration issue did not fully dispose of the litigation between Lucht's and Horner.

Lucht's Concrete Pumping, Inc. v. Horner
255 P.3d 1058 (2011)

Justice Eid delivered the Opinion of the Court.

We granted certiorari to determine whether continuing the employment of an existing at-will employee is adequate consideration to support a noncompetition agreement. Petitioner Lucht's Concrete Pumping seeks to enforce a noncompetition agreement signed by respondent Tracy Horner, a former at-will employee. Because Horner was an existing at-will employee when he signed the agreement, Lucht's argues that its forbearance from terminating Horner constitutes adequate consideration for the noncompetition agreement.

The court of appeals held that continued employment does not constitute adequate consideration for a noncompetition agreement once an employee has begun working for an employer because the employee is in the same position as he was before he signed the noncompetition agreement. *Lucht's Concrete Pumping, Inc. v. Horner,* 224 P.3d 355 (Colo.App.2009).

We granted certiorari [footnote omitted] and now reverse the court of appeals. We hold that an employer that forbears from terminating an existing at-will employee forbears from exercising a legal right, and that therefore such forbearance constitutes adequate consideration for a noncompetition agreement. We have recognized that continuation of at-will employment is adequate consideration in the context of an employee's receipt of a benefit, *Continental Air Lines, Inc. v. Keenan,* 731 P.2d 708, 711 (Colo.1987), and now apply that reasoning to the context of consideration for a noncompetition agreement.

I.

The case before us arises from an employment dispute between respondent Tracy Horner ("Horner"), an individual, and his former employer, petitioner Lucht's Concrete Pumping, Inc. ("Lucht's"). Respondent Everist Materials, LLC ("Everist"), a competitor of Lucht's and subsequent employer of Horner, is also a party to the case.

Lucht's is a Colorado corporation in the concrete pumping business with approximately seventy employees. While it is based out of Denver where it does much of its business, Lucht's began expansion into the Summit County area in 2001.

To implement its expansion, Lucht's hired Horner as mountain division manager on an at-will basis beginning in 2001. Lucht's primarily hired Horner as its "key person" with connections to the industry. As such, Horner was solely responsible for establishing and maintaining the relationships in the mountain region upon which Lucht's relied for business.

On April 15, 2003, Horner was asked to sign, and did sign, a noncompetition agreement. Among other things, the agreement stated that in the event that Horner left his position, he would not "directly or indirectly solicit, induce, recruit or encourage any of [Lucht's] employees or customers to leave [Lucht's]" for twelve months following his termination, and he would not divulge any trade secrets or other confidential information to any future employer. Horner was not offered any pay increase, promotion, or additional benefits at the time he signed the agreement.

Horner resigned from Lucht's on March 12, 2004, and began working for Everist three days later on March 15, 2004. Everist is a supplier of ready-mix concrete and had many of the same customers in the mountain region as Lucht's. Shortly after Horner started, Everist entered the concrete pumping business in the mountain region, directly competing with Lucht's, with Horner as its pumping manager.

Lucht's sued Horner for breach of contract, breach of duty of loyalty, breach of fiduciary duty, and misappropriation of trade value. It also sued Everist for intentional interference with contract, aiding and abetting a breach of duty of loyalty, aiding and abetting a breach of fiduciary duty, and misappropriation of trade value.

The trial court granted summary judgment against Lucht's on its claims for breach of contract and intentional interference with contract, concluding that the noncompetition agreement was unenforceable due to lack of consideration ...

Lucht's appealed ... [I]t argued that summary judgment was improperly entered on its breach of contract and interference with contract claims because Horner's continued employment constituted adequate consideration to support the noncompetition agreement.

The court of appeals concluded that continued employment of an at-will employee cannot, by itself, constitute consideration for a noncompetition agreement if the employee had already begun working for an employer. *Lucht's,* 224 P.3d at 358. The court of appeals reasoned that, even though an employer may agree to continue an at-will employee's employment if the employee agrees to sign the covenant, nothing prevents the employer from discharging the employee at a future date and therefore the employee receives nothing more than what was already promised in the original at-will agreement.

We granted certiorari and now reverse the court of appeals. We hold that an employer that forbears from terminating an existing at-will employee forbears from exercising a legal right, and that therefore such forbearance constitutes adequate consideration for a noncompetition agreement. We have recognized that continuation of at-will employment is adequate consideration in the context of an employee's receipt of a benefit, *Continental Air Lines,* 731 P.2d at 711, and now apply that reasoning to the context of consideration for a noncompetition agreement.

II.

Today we address the validity of a covenant not to compete when an at-will employee signs the agreement after his initial hiring. A covenant not to compete, like any other contract, must be supported by consideration. *Freudenthal v. Espey,* 45 Colo. 488, 497–500, 102 P. 280, 283–84 (1909). This court has long held that any benefit to a promisor or any detriment to a promisee at the time of the contract—no matter how slight—constitutes adequate consideration. *W. Fed. Sav. & Loan Ass'n of Denver v. Nat'l Homes Corp.,* 167 Colo. 93, 103, 445 P.2d 892, 897–98 (1968); *see also* 2 Joseph M. Perillo & Helen H. Bender, *Corbin on Contracts* § 5.14 at 70 (1995) (concluding that a "peppercorn" is sufficient). Except in extreme circumstances, such as those involving allegations of unconscionability, a court should not judge or attempt to assess the adequacy of the consideration. *Freudenthal,* 45 Colo. at 499–500, 102 P. at 284 (holding that "the court will not inquire into [the adequacy of the consideration].... the exact value of the consideration the court ought not, and in the nature of things cannot, undertake to measure"). Therefore, we need only find some consideration, regardless of its relative value, to support a covenant not to compete.

The court formulates and discusses the general rule in this paragraph.

Consideration may take the form of forbearance by one party to refrain from doing something that it is legally entitled to do. *Troutman v. Webster,* 82 Colo. 93, 97, 257 P. 262, 264 (1927); *Int'l Paper Co. v. Cohen,* 126 P.3d 222,

225 (Colo.App.2005) (quoting *Black's Law Dictionary* 324 (8th ed. 2004)); *see also Jones v. Jones,* 1 Colo.App. 28, 32, 27 P. 85, 86 (1891) ("[V]aluable consideration … may consist either in some right, interest, profit, or benefit accruing to one party, or some forbearance, detriment, loss, or responsibility given, suffered, or undertaken by the other."). In the context of employment, an employer has a legal right to terminate an at-will employee at any time because employment at-will is a continuing contract between an employer and an employee that is terminable at the will of either the employer or the employee. *Continental Air Lines,* 731 P.2d at 711. Thus, an employer may terminate an at-will employee at any time without incurring any legal liability. *See Garcia v. Aetna Fin. Co.,* 752 F.2d 488, 491 (10th Cir.1984) (applying Colorado law); *Coors Brewing Co. v. Floyd,* 978 P.2d 663, 666 (Colo.1999) ("Under common law, either an employer or an employee can terminate an at-will employment relationship without incurring legal liability for this termination.").

What, if anything, do you think this case adds to what you learned from *Hamer*?

Because an employer may terminate an at-will employee at any time during the employment relationship as a matter of right, its forbearance from terminating that employee is the forbearance of a legal right. As such, we find that such forbearance constitutes adequate consideration to support a noncompetition agreement with an existing at-will employee. In so holding, we join several other jurisdictions that conclude that an employer's forbearance of the right to terminate an existing at-will employee constitutes adequate consideration to support a noncompetition agreement. *See, e.g., Ackerman v. Kimball Int'l, Inc.,* 652 N.E.2d 507, 509 (Ind.1995); *Sherman v. Pfefferkorn,* 241 Mass. 468, 135 N.E. 568, 569 (1922); *Brignull v. Albert,* 666 A.2d 82, 84 (Me.1995); *Camco, Inc. v. Baker,* 113 Nev. 512, 936 P.2d 829, 831–32 (1997); *Lake Land Emp't Grp. of Akron, LLC v. Columber,* 101 Ohio St.3d 242, 804 N.E.2d 27, 31–32 (2004); *Summits 7, Inc. v. Kelly,* 178 Vt. 396, 886 A.2d 365, 373 (2005); *Research & Trading Corp. v. Powell,* 468 A.2d 1301, 1305 (Del.Ch.1983).

We have utilized this same reasoning in the context of an at-will employee's acceptance of a benefit offered by the employer. In *Continental Air Lines,* we held that an at-will employee could enforce the termination procedures specified in an employee manual on the theory that the employee's decision to continue to work constituted "acceptance" of the offer as well as "consideration for those procedures." 731 P.2d at 711, 712; *see also id.* at 713 (holding that an at-will employee would have to demonstrate that his willingness to work "provided the requisite consideration"). Accordingly, when the at-will employee continued to work, he not only accepted the employer's offer of termination procedures, he provided consideration for the exchange to the employer. *Id.* at 711. Stated differently, by continuing to work, the at-will employee decided to forbear from his right to discontinue working … If an at-will employee's continuation of work constitutes adequate consideration for the acceptance of an employer's benefit, by the same reasoning, an employer's forbearance from terminating the at-will employee constitutes adequate consideration for an employee's acceptance of an employer's noncompetition agreement. In both cases, consideration is found in the continuation of the at-will relationship.

The court of appeals came to a different conclusion based on the rationale that an employee's continuation of work is "nothing more than [what] was already promised in the original at-will agreement." *Lucht's,* 224 P.3d at

358. The court of appeals reasoned that, even though an employer may agree to continue an at-will employee's employment if the employee agrees to sign the noncompetition agreement, nothing prevents the employer from discharging the employee at a future date. Therefore, the court of appeals reasoned, the employee receives nothing more than what was already promised at the beginning of the employment relationship ...

There appears to be no question that an employee's acceptance of an at-will employment arrangement at the time of initial employment is sufficient consideration for a noncompetition agreement. *See, e.g., Precision Walls, Inc. v. Servie,* 152 N.C.App. 630, 568 S.E.2d 267, 272 (2002). The question becomes whether the result is changed by the fact that the noncompetition agreement is presented to the employee after that initial employment period has ended. We do not believe it is.

At initial employment and during existing employment, both the employer and the employee must decide whether an employment relationship will exist. *See Copeco, Inc. v. Caley,* 91 Ohio App.3d 474, 632 N.E.2d 1299, 1301 (1992) ("As a practical matter every day is a new day for both employer and employee in an at-will relationship."). For both an initial and an existing at-will employee, the employee and employer have the ability to negotiate. Just as an at-will employee may refuse to accept initial employment if the employer's conditions are unacceptable, so too may an existing employee leave employment if she does not assent to the terms of a noncompetition agreement. In fact, our case law has made no distinction between the adequacy of consideration made at the initial hiring and consideration made during the relationship. *See Continental Air Lines,* 731 P.2d at 711 (noting that an employee's *"initial or continued employment* [may] constitute[ ] acceptance of and consideration for" the termination procedures) (emphasis added). Accordingly, we find no distinction between a decision to agree to a noncompetition agreement offered at the initial hiring period and a decision to agree to such an agreement subsequent to that period ...

Horner had the option of either accepting the agreement and continuing his employment, or rejecting the agreement and leaving Lucht's. By virtue of the nature of at-will employment itself, the presentation of the agreement was an offer to renegotiate the terms of Horner's at-will employment, which Horner accepted by continuing to work [footnote omitted].

Drawing a distinction between covenants not to compete signed on the first day of hire and covenants signed during employment would only induce employers to terminate employees and then rehire them the next day with a covenant not to compete ... Therefore, to distinguish between noncompetition agreements signed as a condition of employment and noncompetition agreements signed after employment would create a perverse incentive for employers.

Importantly, we note that all noncompetition agreements must be assessed for reasonableness. *Zeff, Farrington & Assocs., Inc. v. Farrington,* 168 Colo. 48, 49, 449 P.2d 813, 814 (1969) (holding that all covenants not to compete must be assessed for reasonableness). And, as with all restrictive covenants, "[w]hat is reasonable depends upon the facts of each case." *Id.* For instance, "legitimate consideration for the covenant exists as long as the employer does not act in bad faith by terminating the employee shortly after the employee signs the covenant." *Summits 7,* 886 A.2d at 373. To the extent that an employer enters into a noncompetition agreement with an employee with the intention of terminating the employee immediately afterwards, the agreement may fail for lack of consideration. *See, e.g., Simko, Inc. v. Graymar Co.,* 55 Md.App. 561, 464 A.2d 1104, 1107 (1983) ("Were an employer to discharge an employee without cause in an unconscionably short length of time after extracting the employee's signature to a restrictive covenant through a threat of discharge, there would be a failure of the consideration."). In this case, because the district court declared the noncompetition agreement invalid due to lack of consideration, no reasonableness assessment has been performed. We therefore remand the case for consideration of whether the noncompetition agreement was reasonable and for further proceedings consistent with this opinion.

Exercise 3-6: *Lucht's Concrete Pumping* Revisited

1. Revisit the Dana & Pedro problem (Exercise 2-4, Q3). Even if we assume that there was mutual assent, would Dana & Pedro's agreement be unenforceable for lack of consideration?

2. Peter agreed with Delilah that he would pay $20,000 in return for her transferring 50% of her stock in her start up company to him. At the time, the company had no significant assets but was actively negotiating a number of potentially lucrative contracts with customers. The company quickly burned through its cash and was unable to win any of the contracts it was negotiating. It ended up filing for bankruptcy. Peter sues Delilah to recover his $20,000 claiming that he received no consideration from Delilah under the stock transfer agreement. Will his claim succeed?

Exercise 3-7: *Schnell v. Nell*

Schnell is a useful case because, in addition to adequacy, it also addresses related consideration issues and foreshadows later cases that deal with moral consideration. As you read *Schnell*, consider the following questions:

1. What were the three possible items of consideration at issue in *Schnell*?

2. Why did each possible item of consideration fail? Explain your answer for each item both in terms of the consideration rules referenced in the case and in terms of the basic consideration rule stated in section 71 of the RESTATEMENT (SECOND) OF CONTRACTS.

Schnell v. Nell

17 Ind. 29 (1861)

Perkins, J. Action by J. B. Nell against Zacharias Schnell, upon the following instrument:

Read this contract carefully. Note all the ways the parties attempted to supply consideration for Schnell's promise.

This agreement, entered into this 13th day of February, 1856, between Zach. Schnell, of Indianapolis, Marion county, State of Indiana, as party of the first part, and J. B. Nell, of the same place, Wendelin Lorenz, of Stilesville,

Hendricks county, State of Indiana, and Donata Lorenz, of Frickinger, Grand Duchy of Baden, Germany, as parties of the second part, witnesseth: The said Zacharias Schnell agrees as follows: whereas his wife, Theresa Schnell, now deceased, has made a last will and testament, in which, among other provisions, it was ordained that every one of the above named second parties, should receive the sum of $200; and whereas the said provisions of the will must remain a nullity, for the reason that no property, real or personal, was in the possession of the said Theresa Schnell, deceased, in her own name, at the time of her death, and all property held by Zacharias and Theresa Schnell jointly, therefore reverts to her husband; and whereas the said Theresa Schnell has also been a dutiful and loving wife to the said Zach. Schnell, and has materially aided him in the acquisition of all property, real and personal, now possessed by him; for, and in consideration of all this, and the love and respect he bears to his wife; and, furthermore, in consideration of one cent, received by him of the second parties, he, the said Zach. Schnell, agrees to pay the above named sums of money to the parties of the second part, to wit: $200 to the said J. B. Nell; $200 to the said Wendelin Lorenz; and $200 to the said Donata Lorenz, in the following installments, viz., $200 in one year from the date of these presents; $200 in two years, and $200 in three years; to be divided between the parties in equal portions of $66 2/3 each year, or as they may agree, till each one has received his full sum of $200.

And the said parties of the second part, for, and in consideration of this, agree to pay the above named sum of money [one cent], and to deliver up to said Schnell, and abstain from collecting any real or supposed claims upon him or his estate, arising from the said last will and testament of the said Theresa Schnell, deceased.

In witness whereof, the said parties have, on this 13th day of February, 1856, set hereunto their hands and seals.

Zacharias Schnell, [seal]

J. B. Nell, [seal]

Wen. Lorenz, [seal]

The complaint contained no averment of a consideration for the instrument, outside of those expressed in it; and did not aver that the one cent agreed to be paid, had been paid or tendered.

A demurrer to the complaint was overruled.

The defendant answered that the instrument sued on was given for no consideration whatever.

He further answered, that it was given for no consideration, because his said wife, Theresa, at the time she made the will mentioned, and at the time of her death, owned, neither separately, nor jointly with her husband, or anyone else (except so far as the law gave her an interest in her husband's property), any property, real or personal, etc.

The will is copied into the record, but need not be into this opinion.

The Court sustained a demurrer to these answers, evidently on the ground that they were regarded as contradicting the instrument sued on, which particularly set out the considerations upon which it was executed. But the instrument is latently ambiguous on this point. *See* Ind. Dig., p. 110.

The case turned below, and must turn here, upon the question whether the instrument sued on does express a consideration sufficient to give it legal obligation, as against Zacharias Schnell. It specifies three distinct considerations for his promise to pay $600:

1. A promise, on the part of the plaintiffs, to pay him one cent.

2. The love and affection he bore his deceased wife, and the fact that she had done her part, as his wife, in the acquisition of property.

3. The fact that she had expressed her desire, in the form of an inoperative will, that the persons named therein should have the sums of money specified.

> The court rejects each possible argument that consideration supported Schnell's promise. Should courts find an absence of consideration in cases where the parties seem to try to create consideration?

The consideration of one cent will not support the promise of Schnell. It is true, that as a general proposition, inadequacy of consideration will not vitiate an agreement. *Baker v. Roberts*, 14 Ind. 552. But this doctrine does not apply to a mere exchange of sums of money, of coin, whose value is exactly fixed, but to the exchange of something of, in itself, indeterminate value, for money, or, perhaps, for some other thing of indeterminate value. In this case, had the one cent mentioned, been some particular one cent, a family piece, or ancient, remarkable coin, possessing an indeterminate value, extrinsic from its simple money value, a different view might be taken. As it is, the mere promise to pay six hundred dollars for one cent, even had the portion of that cent due from the plaintiff been tendered, is an unconscionable contract, void, at first blush, upon its face, if it be regarded as an earnest one. *Hardesty v. Smith*, 3 Ind. 39. The consideration of one cent is, plainly, in this case, merely nominal, and intended to be so. As the will and testament of Schnell's wife imposed no legal obligation upon him to discharge her bequests out of his property, and as she had none of her own, his promise to discharge them was not legally binding upon him, on that ground. A moral consideration, only, will not support a promise. Ind. Dig., p. 13. And for the same reason, a valid consideration for his promise can not be found in the fact of a compromise of a disputed claim; for where such claim is legally groundless, a promise upon a compromise of it, or of a suit upon it, is not legally binding. [Citation omitted.] There was no mistake of law or fact in this case, as the agreement admits the will inoperative and void. The promise was simply one to make a gift. The past services of his wife, and the love and affection he had borne her, are objectionable as legal considerations for Schnell's promise, on two grounds:

1. They are past considerations. Ind. Dig., p. 13.

2. The fact that Schnell loved his wife, and that she had been industrious, constituted no consideration for his promise to pay J. B. Nell, and the Lorenzes, a sum of money. Whether, if his wife, in her lifetime, had made a bargain with Schnell, that, in consideration of his promising to pay, after her death, to the persons named, a sum of money, she would be industrious, and worthy of his affection, such a promise would have been valid and consistent with public policy, we need not decide. Nor is the fact that Schnell now venerates the memory of his deceased wife, a legal consideration for a promise to pay any third person money.

The instrument sued on, interpreted in the light of the facts alleged in the second paragraph of the answer, will not support an action. The demurrer to the answer should have been overruled. *See Stevenson* v. *Druley,* 4 Ind. 519.

Per Curiam. The judgment is reversed.

Exercise 3-8: *Schnell* Revisited

1. What does the term "nominal consideration" mean? Does the idea of "nominal consideration" conflict with the general rule that courts will not inquire into the adequacy of consideration?

2. What if, instead of one cent, the amount recited was ten cents? One dollar?

3. What if the contract falsely recited that the plaintiffs had jointly given Schnell a horse worth $600?

4. A young boy received an envelope in the mail from a magazine publisher. The front of the envelope contained a window through which the boy read, "We'll give you this versatile new calculator watch free just for opening this envelope before Feb. 15, 2012." Beneath the offer was a picture of the calculator watch itself. The boy tore open the envelope only to discover that, according to the publisher, the boy also had to subscribe to a magazine. Instead of subscribing, the boy sued. In *Harris v. Time, Inc.,* 191 Cal. App. 3d 449 (1987), the court concluded that the act of opening the envelope was adequate consideration for the promise of the watch. Why did the court reach that conclusion?

5. Given the result in *Harris* (Q4 above), what is the point of even having a consideration requirement? What role does consideration play in a market economy?

6. Read section 87(1) of the RESTATEMENT (SECOND) OF CONTRACTS. How does this affect the *Schnell* exception to the general rule?

7. Paula agrees to give Dana three new, standard baseballs in exchange for Dana giving Paula seven new, standard baseballs. Under these facts, has each party received consideration? Apply and distinguish *Lucht's* and *Schnell.*

8. The following two problems raise an issue that might be labeled "sufficiency of consideration." Analyze both problems.

    a. David signs a written document by which he agrees to pay Peter, who holds himself out as a psychic, $5,000 for revealing the name of the woman who will be David's wife. Is there consideration for David's promise? Apply and distinguish *Lucht's* and *Schnell.*

    b. Timorei contracts to pay Madeline $25 to buy ownership of the "multiplication facts" (*e.g.,* ownership of the fact that $6 \times 7 = 42$ and $9 \times 8 = 72$, etc.). Note that Timorei is not purchasing a particular depiction of those facts; but, rather, the facts themselves. Is there consideration for Timorei's promise? Apply and distinguish *Lucht's* and *Schnell.*

9. Try to generalize a principle of law from your conclusions about problems 8a and b above.

Past and Moral Consideration

Exercise 3-9: *Mills v. Wyman*

The next case, *Mills v. Wyman*, further develops one of the issues discussed in *Schnell v. Nell*—that of past and moral consideration. As you read *Mills v. Wyman*, consider the following questions:

1. Why did the *Mills* court conclude there was no consideration?

2. Explain the result in *Mills* based on the general definition of consideration stated in section 71 of the RESTATEMENT (SECOND) OF CONTRACTS.

3. What if the father had requested the Plaintiff's services before the services were rendered to Levi (the sick son)?

4. In what sense does this case stand for the proposition that past consideration is not good consideration?

Mills v. Wyman

20 Mass. 207 (1825)

This is the headnote.

This was an action of *assumpsit* brought to recover a compensation for the board, nursing, &c., of Levi Wyman, son of the defendant, from the 5th to the 20th of February, 1821. The plaintiff then lived at Hartford, in Connecticut; the defendant, at Shrewsbury, in this county. Levi Wyman, at the time when the services were rendered, was about 25 years of age, and had long ceased to be a member of his father's family. He was on his return from a voyage at sea, and being suddenly taken sick at Hartford, and being poor and in distress, was relieved by the plaintiff in the manner and to the extent above stated. On the 24th of February, after all the expenses had been incurred, the defendant wrote a letter to the plaintiff, promising to pay him such expenses.

The opinion starts here.

Parker C. J. General rules of law established for the protection and security of honest and fair-minded men, who may inconsiderately make promises without any equivalent, will sometimes screen men of a different character from engagements which they are bound in *foro conscientiae* to perform. This is a defect inherent in all human systems of legislation. The rule that a mere verbal promise, without any consideration, cannot be enforced by action, is universal in its application, and cannot be departed from to suit particular cases in which a refusal to perform such a promise may be disgraceful.

The promise declared on in this case appears to have been made without any legal consideration. The kindness and services towards the sick son of the defendant were not bestowed at his request. The son was in no respect under the care of the defendant. He was twenty-five years old, and had long left his father's family. On his return from a foreign country, he fell sick among strangers, and the plaintiff acted the part of the good Samaritan, giving him shelter and comfort until he died. The defendant, his father, on being informed of this event, influenced by a transient feeling of gratitude, promises in writing to pay the plaintiff for the expenses he had incurred. But he has determined to break this promise, and is willing to have his case appear on record as a strong example of particular injustice sometimes necessarily resulting from the operation of general rules.

It is said a moral obligation is a sufficient consideration to support an express promise; and some authorities lay down the rule thus broadly; but upon examination of the cases we are satisfied that the universality of the rule cannot be supported, and that there must have been some preexisting obligation, which has become inoperative by positive law, to form a basis for an effective promise. The cases of debts barred by the statute of limitations, of debts incurred by infants, of debts of bankrupts, are generally put for illustration of the rule. Express promises founded on such preexisting equitable obligations may be enforced; there is a good consideration for them; they merely remove an impediment created by law to the recovery of debts honestly due, but which public policy protects the debtors from being compelled to pay. In all these cases there was originally a *quid pro quo;* and according to the principles of natural justice the party receiving ought to pay; but the legislature has said he shall not be coerced; then comes the promise to pay the debt that is barred, the promise of the man to pay the debt of the infant, of the discharged bankrupt to restore to his creditor what by the law he had lost. In all these cases there is a moral obligation founded upon an antecedent valuable consideration. These promises therefore have a sound legal basis. They are not promises to pay something for nothing; not naked pacts; but the voluntary revival or creation of obligation which before existed in natural law, but which had been dispensed with, not for the benefit of the party obliged solely, but principally for the public convenience.

If moral obligation, in its fullest sense, is a good substratum for an express promise, it is not easy to perceive why it is not equally good to support an implied promise. What a man ought to do, generally he ought to be made to do, whether he promise or refuse. But the law of society has left most of such obligations to the *interior* forum, as the tribunal of conscience has been aptly called. Is there not a moral obligation upon every son who has become affluent by means of the education and advantages bestowed upon him by his father, to relieve that father from pecuniary embarrassment, to promote his comfort and happiness, and even to share with him his riches, if thereby he will be made happy? And yet such a son may, with impunity, leave such a father in any degree of penury above that which will expose the community in which he dwells, to the danger of being obliged to preserve him from absolute want. Is not a wealthy father under strong moral obligation to advance the interest of an obedient, well disposed son, to furnish him with the means of acquiring and maintaining a becoming rank in life, to rescue him from the horrors of debt incurred by misfortune? Yet the law will uphold him in any degree of parsimony, short of that which would reduce his son to the necessity of seeking public charity.

Without doubt there are great interests of society which justify withholding the coercive arm of the law from these duties of imperfect obligation, as they are called; imperfect, not because they are less binding upon the con-

The first two paragraphs of *Mills* seem to include an effort by the court to send a particular message to the defendant. What is that message? What language supports your answer?

science than those which are called perfect, but because the wisdom of the social law does not impose sanctions upon them.

A deliberate promise, in writing, made freely and without any mistake, one which may lead the party to whom it is made into contracts and expenses cannot be broken without a violation of moral duty. But if there was nothing paid or promised for it, the law, perhaps wisely, leaves the execution of it to the conscience of him who makes it. It is only when the party making the promise gains something, or he to whom it is made loses something, that the law gives the promise validity. And in the case of the promise of the adult to pay the debt of the infant, of the debtor discharged by the statute of limitations or bankruptcy, the principle is preserved by looking back to the origin of the transaction, where an equivalent is to be found. An exact equivalent is not required by the law; for there being a consideration, the parties are left to estimate its value: though here the courts of equity will step in to relieve from gross inadequacy between the consideration and the promise.

These principles are deduced from the general current of decided cases upon the subject, as well as from the known maxims of the common law. The general position, that moral obligation is a sufficient consideration for an express promise, is to be limited in its application, to cases where at some time or other a good or valuable consideration has existed.

A legal obligation is always a sufficient consideration to support either an express or an implied promise; such as an infant's debt for necessaries, or a father's promise to pay for the support and education of his minor children. But when the child shall have attained to manhood, and shall have become his own agent in the world's business, the debts he incurs, whatever may be their nature, create no obligation upon the father; and it seems to follow, that his promise founded upon such a debt has no legally binding force.

The cases of instruments under seal and certain mercantile contracts, in which considerations need not be proved, do not contradict the principles above suggested. The first import a consideration in themselves, and the second belong to a branch of the mercantile law, which has found it necessary to disregard the point of consideration in respect to instruments negotiable in their nature and essential to the interests of commerce....

It has been attempted to show a legal obligation on the part of the defendant by virtue of our statute, which compels lineal kindred in the ascending or descending line to support such of their poor relations as are likely to become chargeable to the town where they have their settlement. But it is a sufficient answer to this position, that such legal obligation does not exist except in the very cases provided for in the statute, and never until the party charged has been adjudged to be of sufficient ability thereto. We do not know from the report any of the facts which are necessary to create such an obligation. Whether the deceased had a legal settlement in this commonwealth at the time of his death, whether he was likely to become chargeable had he lived, whether the defendant was of sufficient ability, are essential facts to be adjudicated by the court to which is given jurisdiction on this subject. The legal liability does not arise until these facts have all been ascertained by judgment, after hearing the party intended to be charged.

For the foregoing reasons we are all of opinion that the nonsuit directed by the Court of Common Pleas was right, and that judgment be entered thereon for costs for the defendant.

Exercise 3-10: *Mills* Revisited

1. How do you reconcile the three exceptions that the *Mills* court identifies with the denial of relief in the *Mills* case? (Hint: Consider both logic and public policy.)

2. Read section 82 of the RESTATEMENT (SECOND) OF CONTRACTS and analyze the following problems:

   a. Debtor owed a debt that is unenforceable because the applicable statute of limitations has run. Debtor sent a check that reflected some of the interest that would be due on the debt if it were enforceable. Can the creditor enforce the debt?

   b. Debtor owed a debt that is unenforceable because the applicable statute of limitations has run. Debtor said to the creditor, "Don't worry—I will not assert the statute of limitations as a defense if you sue me." Can the creditor enforce the debt?

3. Would the result in *Mills* be the same if the son had lived and made the promise?

4. In *Webb v. McGowin*, 27 Ala. App. 82, 168 So. 196 (1935), plaintiff worked at a lumber mill. To clean the upper floor of the mill, in order to prevent a logjam, plaintiff prepared to drop a seventy-five pound pine block from the upper floor to the ground below (according to the court, this method was the typical method used to clean a mill floor and prevent logjams). As plaintiff was about to drop the block, he realized that, if he dropped it, it would fall on and seriously injure (or even kill) McGowin. To save McGowin, plaintiff diverted the fall of the pine block away from McGowin by falling with the block. While McGowin was saved, plaintiff was seriously injured and became permanently disabled.

   McGowin then agreed to pay plaintiff $15 every two weeks for the rest of plaintiff's life. McGowin indeed paid plaintiff until McGowin died approximately nine years later. McGowin's heirs stopped paying plaintiff within a month of McGowin's death and a lawsuit ensued. The court held that plaintiff saving McGowin's life was good consideration for McGowin's promise to pay plaintiff. Can you reconcile *Mills* and *Webb*?

5. What is the position of the RESTATEMENT (SECOND) OF CONTRACTS on the issue raised in *Mills* and *Webb*?

6. According to the commentary in the RESTATEMENT if A finds B's escaped bull and feeds and cares for it, B's subsequent promise to pay reasonable compensation to A is binding. How so when Wyman's promise to reimburse Mills was not binding?

Settlement of Invalid Claims

This section of Chapter 3 addresses the settlement of invalid claims. In a settlement contract, a party against whom a claim is asserted agrees to resolve that claim by paying the other party money. Settlement contracts are commonly made and enforced.

For example, assume that A files a claim to recover from B who ran a red light and crashed into A's car. B and A then agree that B will pay A $10,000 to settle the claim. Note that both A and B made promises: A promised not to sue B, and B promised to pay A $10,000. Accordingly, there is no issue of mutual assent. The exchange also, on its face, has consideration on both sides: A exchanged a promise to relinquish her right to seek legal redress against B for B's promise to pay A $10,000 and vice versa.[2]

In this situation, sometimes a problem arises if B later comes to believe that, if he had not settled, he would have prevailed in the lawsuit. For example, B may later learn that an eyewitness took a picture of B's car at the moment the car entered the intersection and the picture shows that B had a green light. In other words, B may later come to believe that, if he had not settled, he would not have had to pay A anything. As you may imagine, B would not be happy that he had agreed to pay money and, in his view, received nothing in return because it later turns out that there may have been no case to answer.

B might then sue to rescind the settlement contract, or B might refuse to perform the settlement contract causing A to sue B to enforce the contract. Courts face conflicting rationales in trying to decide whether to hold parties like B to their settlement contracts. On the one hand, courts do not want to encourage people to assert frivolous claims to extort money from each other. On the other hand, courts want to encourage settlements. Even though approximately ninety-five percent of all lawsuits settle, the courts are overcrowded. If it were easy to undo settlements, parties would be less likely to settle and the courts would be hopelessly overcrowded.

Because of these conflicting policy rationales, many courts adopt a compromise position. Under that position, a settlement of a claim which later turns out to be invalid is enforced if: (1) the settling plaintiff had a genuine belief that the claim was valid at the time of the settlement, and (2) the claim was, at worst, doubtful (as opposed to obviously invalid) from the perspective of a reasonable person. Thus, in the above example, B could get out of his settlement contract with A if either A did not genuinely believe B caused the accident or if A's claim is doubtful from the perspective of a reasonable person.

Other courts take the position that a genuine belief in the validity of the claim alone suffices as consideration and enforce settlements based on that genuine belief. The RE-STATEMENT (SECOND) OF CONTRACTS takes yet another position and states that courts should enforce a settlement of an invalid claim if either the plaintiff had a genuine belief or if the claim was doubtful. *See* RESTATEMENT (SECOND) OF CONTRACTS § 74.

Exercise 3-11: *Fiege v. Boehm*

The *Fiege v. Boehm* case addresses the settlement of an invalid claim in a colorful context. As you read the *Fiege* case, consider the following questions:

---

2. For a slightly more complex example, see *Swimelar v. Baker*, 604 F.3d 727 (release of wrongful death claim by Mr. Baker was good consideration for an annuity purchased by an insurance company to settle a lawsuit based on the claim). The scenario in question 5 of Exercise 3-4 is also analogous.

1.   What rule does the court adopt?

2.   What evidence suggests that the plaintiff had a genuine belief in her claim?

3.   What evidence suggests that the plaintiff had a reasonable belief in the possible validity of her claim? What facts made her claim no worse than doubtful?

4.   Could you make a policy argument for enforcing settlements of invalid claims based on the four contract law policies you learned in Chapter 1?

Fiege v. Boehm
210 Md. 352, 123 A.2d 316 (1956)

This suit was brought in the Superior Court of Baltimore City by Hilda Louise Boehm against Louis Gail Fiege to recover for breach of a contract to pay the expenses incident to the birth of his bastard child and to provide for its support upon condition that she would refrain from prosecuting him for bastardy.

Plaintiff alleged in her declaration substantially as follows: (1) that early in 1951 defendant had sexual intercourse with her although she was unmarried, and as a result thereof she became pregnant, and defendant acknowledged that he was responsible for her pregnancy; (2) that on September 29, 1951, she gave birth to a female child; that defendant is the father of the child; and that he acknowledged on many occasions that he is its father; (3) that before the child was born, defendant agreed to pay all her medical and miscellaneous expenses and to compensate her for the loss of her salary caused by the child's birth, and also to pay her ten dollars per week for its support until it reached the age of 21, upon condition that she would not institute bastardy proceedings against him as long as he made the payments in accordance with the agreement; (4) that she placed the child for adoption on July 13, 1954, and she claimed the following sums: Union Memorial Hospital, $110; Florence Crittenton Home, $100; Dr. George Merrill, her physician, $50; medicines, $70.35; miscellaneous expenses, $20.45; loss of earnings for 26 weeks, $1,105; support of the child, $1,440; total, $2,895.80; and (5) that defendant paid her only $480, and she demanded that he pay her the further sum of $2,415.80, the balance due under the agreement, but he failed and refused to pay the same.

Defendant demurred to the declaration on the ground that it failed to allege that in September, 1953, plaintiff instituted bastardy proceedings against him in the Criminal Court of Baltimore, but since it had been found from blood tests that he could not have been the father of the child, he was acquitted of bastardy. The Court sustained the demurrer with leave to amend.

Plaintiff then filed an amended declaration, which contained the additional allegation that, after the breach of the agreement by defendant, she filed a charge with the State's Attorney that defendant was the father of her bastard child; and that on October 8, 1953, the Criminal Court found defendant not guilty solely on a physician's testimony that "on the basis of certain blood tests made, the defendant can be excluded as the father of the said child, which testimony is not conclusive upon a jury in a trial court."

Defendant also demurred to the amended declaration, but the Court overruled that demurrer.

Plaintiff, a typist, now over 35 years old, who has been employed by the Government in Washington and Baltimore for over thirteen years, testified in the Court below that she had never been married, but that at about midnight on January 21, 1951, defendant, after taking her to a moving picture theater on York Road and then to a restaurant, had sexual intercourse with her in his automobile. She further testified that he agreed to pay all her medical and hospital expenses, to compensate her for loss of salary caused by the pregnancy and birth, and to pay her ten dollars per week for the support of the child upon condition that she would refrain from instituting bastardy proceedings against him. She further testified that between September 17, 1951, and May, 1953, defendant paid her a total of $480.

Defendant admitted that he had taken plaintiff to restaurants, had danced with her several times, had taken her to Washington, and had brought her home in the country; but he asserted that he had never had sexual intercourse with her. He also claimed that he did not enter into any agreement with her. He admitted, however, that he had paid her a total of $480. His father also testified that he stated "that he did not want his mother to know, and if it were just kept quiet, kept principally away from his mother and the public and the courts, that he would take care of it."

Defendant further testified that in May, 1953, he went to see plaintiff's physician to make inquiry about blood tests to show the paternity of the child; and that those tests were made and they indicated that it was not possible that he could have been the child's father. He then stopped making payments. Plaintiff thereupon filed a charge of bastardy with the State's Attorney....

Although defendant was acquitted by the Criminal Court, the Superior Court overruled his motion for a directed verdict. In the charge to the jury the Court instructed them that defendant's acquittal in the Criminal Court was not binding upon them. The jury found a verdict in favor of plaintiff for $2,415.80, the full amount of her claim.

Defendant filed a motion for judgment n. o. v. or a new trial. The Court overruled that motion also, and entered judgment on the verdict of the jury. Defendant appealed from that judgment.

Defendant contends that, even if he did enter into the contract as alleged, it was not enforceable, because plaintiff's forbearance to prosecute was not based on a valid claim, and hence the contract was without consideration....

[W]here statutes are in force to compel the father of a bastard to contribute to its support, the courts have invariably held that a contract by the putative father with the mother of his bastard child to provide for the support of the child upon the agreement of the mother to refrain from invoking the bastardy statute against the father, or to abandon proceedings already commenced, is supported by sufficient consideration....

We have thus adopted the rule that the surrender of, or forbearance to assert, an invalid claim by one who has not an honest and reasonable belief in its possible validity is not sufficient consideration for a contract. 1 RESTATEMENT, CONTRACTS, sec. 76(b). We combine the subjective requisite that the claim be *bona fide* with the objective requisite that it must have a reasonable basis of support. Accordingly a promise not to prosecute a claim which is not

This case is somewhat disturbing given the fact that the plaintiff is seeking money from the defendant for a child who isn't the defendant's child. Don't let that fact distract you from learning what this case has to teach you.

founded in good faith does not of itself give a right of action on an agreement to pay for refraining from so acting, because a release from mere annoyance and unfounded litigation does not furnish valuable consideration.

Professor Williston was not entirely certain whether the test of reasonableness is based upon the intelligence of the claimant himself, who may be an ignorant person with no knowledge of law and little sense as to facts; but he seemed inclined to favor the view that "the claim forborne must be neither absurd in fact from the standpoint of a reasonable man in the position of the claimant, nor, obviously unfounded in law to one who has an elementary knowledge of legal principles." 1 WILLISTON ON CONTRACTS, Rev. Ed., sec. 135. We agree that while stress is placed upon the honesty and good faith of the claimant, forbearance to prosecute a claim is insufficient consideration if the claim forborne is so lacking in foundation as to make its assertion incompatible with honesty and a reasonable degree of intelligence. Thus, if the mother of a bastard knows that there is no foundation, either in law or fact, for a charge against a certain man that he is the father of the child, but that man promises to pay her in order to prevent bastardy proceedings against him, the forbearance to institute proceedings is not sufficient consideration.

On the other hand, forbearance to sue for a lawful claim or demand is sufficient consideration for a promise to pay for the forbearance if the party forbearing had an honest intention to prosecute litigation which is not frivolous, vexatious, or unlawful, and which he believed to be well founded. *Snyder v. Cearfoss*, 187 Md. 635, 643, 51 A.2d 264; *Pullman Co. v. Ray*, 201 Md. 268, 94 A.2d 266. Thus the promise of a woman who is expecting an illegitimate child that she will not institute bastardy proceedings against a certain man is sufficient consideration for his promise to pay for the child's support, even though it may not be certain whether the man is the father or whether the prosecution would be successful, if she makes the charge in good faith. The fact that a man accused of bastardy is forced to enter into a contract to pay for the support of his bastard child from fear of exposure and the shame that might be cast upon him as a result, as well as a sense of justice to render some compensation for the injury he inflicted upon the mother, does not lessen the merit of the contract, but greatly increases it....

In the case at bar there was no proof of fraud or unfairness. Assuming that the hematologists were accurate in their laboratory tests and findings, nevertheless plaintiff gave testimony which indicated that she made the charge of bastardy against defendant in good faith. For these reasons the Court acted properly in overruling the demurrer to the amended declaration and the motion for a directed verdict....

It is immaterial whether defendant was the father of the child or not.... The court is rather vague in its analysis. Make sure to figure out why plaintiff won this appeal.

As we have found no reversible error in the rulings and instructions of the trial Court, we will affirm the judgment entered on the verdict of the jury....

Exercise 3-12: *Fiege* Revisited

1. Would the result in *Fiege* be the same if the plaintiff believed the defendant was the father—even though she had sex with the defendant and another

man an equal number of times in the relevant time frame? What if the plaintiff had sex with the defendant once and with the other man nine times in the relevant time frame?

2. The following problem includes both a settlement of claims issue and an issue based on materials covered in Chapter 2. Elizabeth and Hannah both applied to be on a game show. As they were waiting in line to audition, they discussed what would happen if one of them made it and the other did not. Elizabeth said, "I know. We ought to share the winnings." Without thinking much about it (because she didn't think either she (Hannah) or Elizabeth would get on the show or would win), Hannah said, "Great idea." Elizabeth did not get on the show. Hannah did and won $100,000. Elizabeth demanded half of the money, asserting she and Hannah had a contract. Assume that Elizabeth genuinely believed this assertion. Hannah eventually agreed to pay Elizabeth $25,000 as a settlement.

    a. If Hannah later claimed that Elizabeth's claim was invalid and sued to rescind the contract, what should Hannah argue to justify her position?

    b. Do you think Hannah's argument would be successful?

    c. Assume that, if Hannah litigated the issue, Elizabeth's claim would be held invalid. Could Hannah get out of the settlement agreement under *Fiege*?

The Pre-Existing Duty Rule

This section addresses the ***"pre-existing duty rule."*** Courts phrase the pre-existing duty rule in a relatively straightforward way: a promise to do what one already is legally obligated to do is not good consideration. At this point in your legal education, you won't likely be surprised to learn that the application of this rule is not always so straightforward.

For an example of a problem raising a pre-existing duty issue, consider the following: Two friends (Albert and Betty) are trading baseball cards. They agree to trade the card of one famous player for the card of another famous player. After Albert has handed over his card, Betty says, "I'll give you the card I promised to give you **only if** you agree to give me a second card." Betty then asks for a specific card. Albert, although upset, agrees to hand over the second card because of his passionate desire for the card for which he originally had bargained. While Albert might agree to the second deal and even perform, he almost certainly will feel cheated.

The pre-existing duty rule, applied to the baseball card exchange, nicely justifies Albert getting his second card back. The rule also works well to solve a similar problem in the case following Exercise 3-13: *Alaska Packers' Association v. Domenico*.

Exercise 3-13: The Pre-Existing Duty Rule

The application of the pre-existing duty rule becomes more complicated, however, in more complex contexts. Consider how courts should apply the rule to these alternate versions of the Albert-Betty problem. At this point, you should make sure you hypothesize why Betty's chances of prevailing in these problems are much better than in the original problem at the beginning of this section. It is useful when attempting these problems to distinguish carefully between the concepts of *obligation* (what a party promised or agreed to do) and *performance* (what a party actually did to meet his or her obligation).

1. What if Betty's reason for demanding a second card was that, after she looked at the first card from Albert, she discovered the card was in much worse condition than she had been led to believe?

2. What if Betty agreed to throw in a second card to get Albert's second card?

3. Would it matter in problem 2 if Albert's second card were considerably more valuable than Betty's second card?

4. What if Betty agreed to pay $1 to get Albert's second card? (So imagine now that Betty had said, "I'll give you the card I promised to give you **only if** you agree to sell me a second card of my choice for $1.")

5. Imagine that Betty, instead of agreeing to the trade, had agreed to buy Albert's first card for $10 and, after getting the card, handed Albert a check for $8 with the notation "paid in full" on it. If Albert cashed the check, could he then assert the pre-existing duty rule and successfully sue for the remaining $2?

6. Imagine that Betty agreed to wash Albert's convertible car in exchange for Albert's first baseball card. After getting the card, a truckload of manure is dumped onto and into Albert's car. If Betty then demands, and Albert agrees to give her, a second baseball card, will the pre-existing duty rule prevent Betty from collecting the second card?

One hint will help you understand the pre-existing duty issue (and, thus, the cases and materials in this section). This issue frequently arises when two parties have made one contract, and then make a second contract. The question then becomes whether there is consideration for the second contract so that the second contract is enforceable.

You should also be aware that many courts now address many pre-existing duty rule issues under a contract defense called "economic duress." Economic duress is discussed in Chapter 5. When you get to that chapter, consider which approach to the problem is superior.

As you consider which avenue is most appropriate for resolving pre-existing duty issues, also look at section 2-209(1) of the U.C.C. Do you think that 2-209(1) means the U.C.C. drafters were unconcerned with the problem addressed by the pre-existing duty rule? Why do you say so? Find another U.C.C. section to cite to support your conclusion.

Exercise 3-14: *Alaska Packers' Assn. v. Domenico*

The first case you will read in this section is *Alaska Packers' Association v. Domenico*. As you read that case, consider the following questions:

1. What are the key facts of the *Alaska Packers* case? Make sure you note how many alleged contracts were formed.

2. What is the rule the court applies? (Hint: The court states the rule most clearly in its quotation from the *Lingenfelder* case.)

3. How did the court apply the rule to the facts in *Alaska Packers*?

4. What is the policy rationale for the pre-existing duty rule? In other words, why do courts choose to interfere with parties' private dealings in these cases?

Alaska Packers' Association v. Domenico
117 F. 99 (1902)

The court uses the admiralty law term "libel" to refer to what non-admiralty courts call a "complaint" and the admiralty law term "libelants" to refer to what non-admiralty courts call "plaintiffs."

Ross, Circuit Judge. The libel in this case was based upon a contract alleged to have been entered into between the libelants and the appellant corporation on the 22d day of May, 1900, at Pyramid Harbor, Alaska, by which it is claimed the appellant promised to pay each of the libelants, among other things, the sum of $100 for services rendered and to be rendered. In its answer the respondent denied the execution, on its part, of the contract sued upon, averred that it was without consideration, and for a third defense alleged that the work performed by the libelants for it was performed under other and different contracts than that sued on, and that, prior to the filing of the libel, each of the libelants was paid by the respondent the full amount due him thereunder, in consideration of which each of them executed a full release of all his claims and demands against the respondent.

The evidence shows without conflict that on March 26, 1900, at the city and county of San Francisco, the libelants entered into a written contract with the appellants, whereby they agreed to go from San Francisco to Pyramid Harbor, Alaska, and return, on board such vessel as might be designated by the appellant, and to work for the appellant during the fishing season of 1900, at Pyramid Harbor, as sailors and fishermen, agreeing to do 'regular ship's duty, both up and down, discharging and loading; and to do any other work whatsoever when requested to do so by the captain or agent of the Alaska Packers' Association. By the terms of this agreement, the appellant was to pay each of the libelants $50 for the season, and two cents for each red salmon in the catching of which he took part.

On the 15th day of April, 1900, 21 of the libelants of the libelants signed shipping articles by which they shipped as seamen on the Two Brothers, a vessel chartered by the appellant for the voyage between San Francisco and Pyramid Harbor, and also bound themselves to perform the same work for the appellant provided for by the previous contract of March 26th; the appellant agreeing to pay them therefor the sum of $60 for the season, and two cents each for each red salmon in the catching of which they should respectively take part. Under these contracts, the libelants sailed on board the Two Brothers for Pyramid Harbor, where the appellants had about $150,000 invested in a salmon cannery. The libelants arrived there early in April of the year mentioned, and began to unload the vessel and fit up the cannery. A few days thereafter, to wit, May 19th, they stopped work in a body, and demanded of the company's superintendent there in charge $100 for services in operating the vessel to and from Pyramid Harbor, instead of the sums stipulated for in and by the contracts; stating that unless they were paid this additional wage they would stop work entirely, and return to San Francisco. The evidence showed, and the court below found, that it was impossible for the appellant to get other men to take the places of the libelants, the place being remote, the season short and just opening; so that, after endeavoring for several days without success to induce the libelants to proceed with their work in accordance with their contracts, the company's superintendent, on the 22d day of May, so far yielded to their demands as to instruct his clerk to copy the contracts executed in San Francisco, including the words 'Alaska Packers' Association' at the end, substituting, for the $50 and $60 payments, respectively, of those contracts, the sum of $100, which document, so prepared, was signed by the libelants before a shipping commissioner whom they had requested to be brought from Northeast Point; the superintendent, however, testifying that he at the time told the libelants that he was without authority to enter into any such contract, or to in any way alter the contracts made between them and the company in San Francisco. Upon the return of the libelants to San Francisco at the close of the fishing season, they demanded pay in accordance with the terms of the alleged contract of May 22d, when the company denied its validity, and refused to pay other than as provided for by the contracts of March 26th and April 5th, respectively. Some of the libelants, at least, consulted counsel, and, after receiving his advice, those of them who had signed the shipping articles before the shipping commissioner at San Francisco went before that officer, and received the amount due them thereunder, executing in consideration thereof a release in full, and the others paid at the office of the company, also receipting in full for their demands.

On the trial in the court below, the libelants undertook to show that the fishing nets provided by the respondent were defective, and that it was on that account that they demanded increased wages. On that point, the evidence was substantially conflicting, and the finding of the court was against the libelants the court saying:

"The contention of libelants that the nets provided them were rotten and unserviceable is not sustained by the evidence. The defendants' interest required that libelants should be provided with every facility necessary to their success as fishermen, for on such success depended the profits defendant would be able to realize that season from its packing plant, and the large capital invested therein. In view of this self-evident fact, it is highly improbable that the defendant gave libelants rotten and unserviceable nets with which to fish. It follows from this finding that libelants were not justified in refusing performance of their original contract." 112 Fed. 554.

The evidence being sharply conflicting in respect to these facts, the conclusions of the court, who heard and saw the witnesses, will not be disturbed. [Citations omitted.]

The court says that it will not disturb the trial court's conclusion that the nets were not, as claimed by the plaintiffs, rotten and unserviceable. Why do you think the court made this choice?

The real questions in the case as brought here are questions of law, and, in the view that we take of the case, it will be necessary to consider but one of those. Assuming that the appellant's superintendent at Pyramid Harbor was authorized to make the alleged contract of May 22d, and that he executed it on behalf of the appellant, was it supported by a sufficient consideration? From the foregoing statement of the case, it will have been seen that the libelants agreed in writing, for certain stated compensation, to render their services to the appellant in remote waters where the season for conducting fishing operations is extremely short, and in which enterprise the appellant had a large amount of money invested; and, after having entered upon the discharge of their contract, and at a time when it was impossible for the appellant to secure other men in their places, the libelants, without any valid cause, absolutely refused to continue the services they were under contract to perform unless the appellant would consent to pay them more money. Consent to such a demand, under such circumstances, if given, was, in our opinion, without consideration, for the reason that it was based solely upon the libelants' agreement to render the exact services, and none other, that they were already under contract to render. The case shows that they willfully and arbitrarily broke that obligation. As a matter of course, they were liable to the appellant in damages, and it is quite probable, as suggested by the court below in its opinion, that they may have been unable to respond in damages....

In *Lingenfelder v. Brewing Co.*, 103 Mo. 578, 15 S.W. 844, the court, in holding void a contract by which the owner of a building agreed to pay its architect an additional sum because of his refusal to otherwise proceed with the contract, said:

> It is urged upon us by respondents that this was a new contract. New in what? Jungenfeld was bound by his contract to design and supervise this building. Under the new promise, he was not to do anything more or anything different. What benefit was to accrue to Wainwright? He was to receive the same service from Jungenfeld under the new, that Jungenfeld was bound to tender under the original, contract. What loss, trouble, or inconvenience could result to Jungenfeld that he had not already assumed? No amount of metaphysical reasoning can change the plain fact that Jungenfeld took advantage of Wainwright's necessities, and extorted the promise of five percent on the refrigerator plant as the condition of his complying with his contract already entered into....

That a promise to pay a man for doing that which he is already under contract to do is without consideration is conceded by respondents. The rule has been so long imbedded in the common law and decisions of the highest courts of the various states that nothing but the most cogent reasons ought to shake it. [Citations omitted.] But it is "carrying coals to Newcastle" to add authorities on a proposition so universally accepted, and so inherently just and right in itself. The learned counsel for respondents do not controvert the general proposition. They contention is, and the circuit court agreed with them, that, when Jungenfeld declined to go further on his contract, the defendant then had the right to sue for damages, and not having elected to sue Jungenfeld, but having acceded to his demand for the additional compensation defendant cannot now be heard to say his promise is without consideration. While it is true Jungenfeld became liable in damages for the obvious breach of his contract, we do not think it follows that defendant is estopped from showing its promise was made without consideration ...

> What we hold is that, when a party merely does what he has already obligated himself to do, he cannot demand an additional compensation therefore; and although, by taking advantage of the necessities of his adversary, he obtains a promise for more, the law will

Note the court's phrase "carrying coals to Newcastle." What must that phrase mean given how the court uses it?

regard it as *nudum pactum*, and will not lend its process to aid in the wrong....

It results from the views above expressed that the judgment must be reversed, and the cause remanded, with directions to the court below to enter judgment for the respondent, with costs. It is so ordered.

Exercise 3-15: *Alaska Packers* Revisited

1. If, in *Alaska Packers*, both parties had agreed to rip up their agreement and then signed the new agreement for the extra compensation, would the result have been different?

2. For two years, Kendra was in default on a $100 debt she owed her sister, Samantha. One day, Samantha said to Kendra, "That $100 you owe me is way overdue, but I don't want to sue you. You don't use your old DVR very much. I can use it to make sure I never miss any of my favorite television shows. If you give me the DVR, I will agree you have paid me in full." Kendra agreed to the proposal. Assume the DVR is worth $50. Did the parties form a contract? Why or why not?

3. Mike is a police officer. Elizabeth is a business owner whose business is robbed at gunpoint by Robert. Elizabeth offers Mike $10,000 to capture Robert. If Mike captures Robert while on duty, Elizabeth will not have to pay Mike the $10,000. Why not? If Mike captures Robert while on vacation in another state, Elizabeth will have to pay. Why?

4. Read sections 73 and 89 of the RESTATEMENT (SECOND) OF CONTRACTS and then complete a through e below:

   a. Create a graphic organizer depicting the order in which you would analyze the requirements and exceptions stated in section 73 on an exam.

   b. Take a look again at the hypothetical problems in Exercise 3-13. Can you see how those problems relate to the legal principles you depicted in your graphic organizer?

   c. Assume that, in *Alaska Packers*, the packers and the packing company had a dispute as to whether the packers had the right to sleep on board while the boat was in the harbor or had to pay to stay at a hotel. What would the result be under section 73? What would the packers argue to try to fit within the exception to the general rule? Why would the appellate court reject that argument?

   d. Assume that, in *Alaska Packers*, the packers agreed, in the contract on which they sued, to help deliver the canned fish to the various supermarkets that purchased it. What would the result be under section 73?

   e. Assume that, in *Alaska Packers*, the weather in the harbor, for the first time in history, was unseasonably rough so that the packers had to work sixteen-hour days both fishing and keeping the ship afloat (whereas under normal conditions they only had to work eight hours a day). What would the result be under section 89?

Exercise 3-16: *AFC Interiors v. DiCello*

The next case, *AFC Interiors v. DiCello*, addresses a recurring problem: what happens if a party who owes money under a contract sends the other party a check labeled "payment in full" and the other party, while disputing the fact that the check reflects full payment, nevertheless cashes it? As you read *AFC Interiors*, answer the following questions:

1. What do the following terms mean? (Look them up in a legal dictionary.)

    a. satisfaction

    b. accord and satisfaction

    c. liquidated claim

2. For what principle does *AFC Interiors* stand?

3. Why have most courts agreed with the dissent in *AFC Interiors* rather than with the majority opinion?

AFC Interiors v. DiCello

46 Ohio St. 3d 1, 544 N.E.2d 869 (1989)

Syllabus by the Court

1. R.C. 1301.13, which embodies section 1-207 of the Uniform Commercial Code, supersedes the common-law doctrine of accord and satisfaction in the "full payment" or "conditional check" situation.

2. Pursuant to R.C. 1301.13, where a debtor tenders a check to a creditor as payment in full for less than the amount alleged to be owed on the debt, the creditor may accept the check as partial payment on the debt so long as the creditor explicitly reserves all rights by endorsing the check "under protest" or any legend sufficient to apprise the debtor that the check is not accepted as full payment on the debt. In so doing, the creditor does not thereby prejudice any rights reserved on the balance alleged to be due.

In June 1984, plaintiff-appellant, AFC Interiors ("AFC"), and defendant-appellee, Nicholas DiCello, d.b.a. Ohio State Home Services ("DiCello"), entered into an oral contract whereby AFC would perform certain interior decorating services for DiCello. These services were performed by AFC, and furnishings were thereafter purchased by AFC and delivered to DiCello. Invoices reflecting the amount due on the furnishings were sent to DiCello. However, payment from DiCello was not forthcoming. Subsequently, on or about November 7, 1984, AFC filed this action against DiCello in the court of common pleas alleging breach of contract on the amount due for the furnishings. AFC thereafter filed a motion for summary judgment to which defendant responded that it should be denied. Thereafter, the matter was referred to arbitration, and on October 28, 1986, the arbitrators found in favor of AFC in the amount of $15,421, and further found that defendant was entitled to the return of the goods, except for a desk.

Meanwhile, on or about July 3, 1985, DiCello sent a letter to AFC stating that he was returning the specific items that he no longer wanted pursuant to their oral contract, and enclosed a check containing a notation on the back, "[p]ayment in full for any and all claims against Nick DiCello." Kenneth Henderson, Vice-President of AFC, testified that he received the merchandise and the check, but that he crossed out the notation on the back of the check and inserted the words "Payment on Account." Henderson thereafter negotiated the check.

On October 22, 1987, DiCello filed a motion for summary judgment with the trial court on the ground that AFC's negotiation of the check amounted to an accord and satisfaction of the underlying debt. After due consideration, the trial court agreed, and granted DiCello's motion for summary judgment.

Upon appeal, the court of appeals affirmed, finding that the trial court was correct in finding that an accord and satisfaction had taken place under Ohio law....

Sweeney, Justice.

The dispositive question presented in this cause is whether an accord and satisfaction has taken place with regard to the debt owed by DiCello to AFC. The appellee, DiCello, contends that an accord and satisfaction has taken place under the instant facts. The appellant, AFC, argues however that R.C. 1301.13, which embodies section 1-207 of the Uniform Commercial Code ("U.C.C."), should supersede the doctrine of accord and satisfaction in the "full payment" or "conditional check" situation where the payee reserves his or her rights to pursue the balance of the debt alleged to be owed.

Accord and satisfaction is a common-law doctrine where there is a contract between a creditor and debtor for settlement of a claim by some performance other than that which is due. [Citations omitted.]

In the cause *sub judice*, DiCello tendered a check for an amount apparently less than what AFC expected. The check carried the notation that it constituted payment in full for any and all claims that AFC may have against DiCello. AFC crossed out the notation and inserted the words "Payment on Account" and further negotiated the check. Under Ohio law, it has been held that in such a situation the creditor had " ... but one alternative; he must accept the amount tendered upon the terms of the condition, unless the condition be waived, or he must reject it entirely, or if he has received the amount by check in a letter, he must return it." [Citations omitted.] Thus, the precise question before this court is whether the special endorsement of the check by AFC with knowledge of a dispute as to the amount due, and with knowledge of the conditional statement on the check, constituted an acceptance of the conditional check, *i.e.*, an accord and satisfaction. In light of the language of R.C. 1301.13, we do not believe that the special endorsement by AFC reserving its rights and subsequent negotiation of the check should continue to be recognized as an accord and satisfaction. Therefore, we reverse the decision of the court of appeals below and remand the cause for further proceedings.

R.C. 1301.13 (U.C.C. 1-207) provides:

> A party who with explicit reservation of rights performs or promises performance or assents to performance in a manner demanded or offered by the other party does not thereby prejudice the rights reserved. Such words as "without prejudice," "under protest," or the like are sufficient.

The Official Comment to this section provides in part:

> This section provides machinery for the continuation of performance along the lines contemplated by the contract despite a pending dispute, by adopting the mercantile device of going ahead with delivery, acceptance, or payment "without prejudice," "under protest," "under reserve," "with reservation of all our rights," and the like. All of these phrases completely reserve all rights within the meaning of this section. The section therefore contemplates that limited as well as general reservations and acceptance by a party may be made "subject to satisfaction of our purchaser," "subject to acceptance by our customers," or the like.

The issue of whether U.C.C. 1-207 should apply to supersede the doctrine of accord and satisfaction has been the subject of much scholarly debate. Courts in different jurisdictions are split with regard to the effect of U.C.C. 1-207 in this context. [Citations omitted.]

We are of the opinion, however, that the drafters of the U.C.C., and Ohio's General Assembly, promulgated U.C.C. 1-207 in response to a perceived injustice to creditors that occurs where a creditor, under protest, deposits a check marked "paid in full" or the like, and later discovers that an accord and satisfaction has taken place which extinguished the right to demand further payment on the debt.

While this court has not applied R.C. 1301.13 (U.C.C. 1-207) in factual situations similar to the case at bar, it appears that a discernible trend has developed whereby U.C.C. 1-207 is used to supersede the common-law doctrine of accord and satisfaction in "full payment" or "conditional check" situations. Subsequent to the adoption of the U.C.C., at least two other jurisdictions dealt with the subject, albeit in dicta. *See Hanna v. Perkins* 2 UCC Rep. Serv. 1044 (1965); *Baillie Lumber Co. v. Kincaid Carolina Corp.*, 4 N.C. App. 342, 167 S.E.2d 85 (1969).

In *Baillie, supra,* the court stated that its version of U.C.C. 1-207 would prevent an accord and satisfaction where a conditional check was endorsed "With reservation of all our rights." *Id.* at 353, 167 S.E.2d at 93. In *Hanna, supra,* the court did not rely on U.C.C. 1-207 because it found no accord and satisfaction based on the fact that there was a triable issue therein. However, the court cited U.C.C. 1-207 and opined that "[i]f it were not that this court finds that triable issues of fact are present, this court would deny the motion by holding this particular section of the code would seem to favor plaintiff's overriding endorsement of 'Deposited under protest' as a reservation of his right to collect payment of [the] balance." *Id.* at 1046....

In addition to the above-cited precedents, it appears that four other jurisdictions (Delaware, Florida, Massachusetts and New Hampshire) have embraced the view that the U.C.C. 1-207 supersedes the common-law doctrine of accord and satisfaction in the local comments to their respective versions of U.C.C. 1-207....

[W]e believe that the framers of the U.C.C. drafted Section 1-207 in order to balance the interests of debtors and creditors in a more equitable manner. In any event, we are persuaded that U.C.C. 1-207 was intended to apply in the situation confronting us in the cause *sub judice*.

At least one Ohio appellate judge has recognized the perspicaciousness of the [old] interpretation of U.C.C. 1-207 by noting that if such a rationale were adopted in Ohio, " '... a creditor would no longer be at the mercy of the debtor facing the dilemma of either accepting the lesser amount as full settlement or returning the check and gambling his chances of collecting anything. Instead, the risk of loss would be upon the debtor who, after having received protest from the creditor, could stop payment on the check. Even if it were too late for the debtor to stop payment, he would still have the opportunity to protest the remainder the creditor claimed to be due on the debt....' " *Inger Interiors, supra*, 30 Ohio App.3d at 98, 30 OBR at 196, 506 N.E.2d at 1202–1203 (Patton, J., dissenting). [Citations omitted.]

In applying the provisions of R.C. 1301.13 to the facts of the cause sub judice, we find that appellant explicitly reserved its rights by crossing out DiCello's notation on the back of the check and substituting its own notation, "Payment on Account." By putting DiCello on notice in such a manner, AFC reserved its rights to collect the balance alleged to be due.

Therefore, based on the foregoing, we hold that R.C. 1301.13, which embodies U.C.C. 1-207, supersedes the common-law doctrine of accord and satisfaction in the "full payment" or "conditional check" situation.

Moreover, we ... hold that pursuant to R.C. 1301.13, where a debtor tenders a check to a creditor as payment in full for less than the amount alleged to be owed on the debt, the creditor may accept the check as partial payment on the debt so long as the creditor explicitly reserves all rights by endorsing the check "under protest" or any legend sufficient to apprise the debtor that the check is not accepted as full payment on the debt. In so doing, the creditor does not thereby prejudice any rights reserved on the balance alleged to be due.

Accordingly, the judgment of the court of appeals is reversed, and the cause is remanded to the trial court for further proceedings not inconsistent with this opinion.

Judgment reversed and cause remanded....

Herbert R. Brown, Justice, dissenting.

To reach its decision, the majority has misread and misapplied the Uniform Commercial Code, ignored the overwhelming weight of authority in other jurisdictions, and overruled the long-standing decisional law of this state.... Further, the majority reverses the unanimous decision of the court of appeals and the judgment granted in the trial court. I respectfully, but vigorously, dissent.

At common law, an accord and satisfaction is accomplished when a creditor accepts and deposits a check which the debtor offers as full payment for an unliquidated or disputed debt. By cashing the check, the creditor manifests assent to the terms of a new contract which extinguishes the debtor's prior contractual obligation. This holds true even if the creditor erases the full-payment language on the check, endorses the check with partial-payment language (or some other language indicating a reservation of rights), or later informs the debtor he intends to collect the full amount....

The case before us satisfies the elements of accord and satisfaction. A bona-fide dispute existed as to whether DiCello has the option to return the furniture he did not want for full credit. Moreover, DiCello claimed he was being charged for furniture he did not receive. Along with the returned items and a letter explaining his actions, DiCello delivered a check to AFC marked **"Payment in Full for Any and All Claims against Nick DiCello."** The deposition of Kenneth Henderson, AFC's vice-president, demonstrates he understood DiCello's intention was to fully settle the account. Henderson took the check, crossed out the words "Payment in full for any and all claims against Nick DiCello," inserted "Payment on Account," and deposited the check before giving notice to DiCello that AFC intended to collect the full amount.

AFC contends (and the majority finds) that R.C. 1301.13 (U.C.C. 1-207) supersedes the common-law doctrine of accord and satisfaction in the "full payment" or "conditional check" situation. For the following reasons, I disagree.

R.C. 1301.13 (U.C.C. 1-207) provides: "A party who with explicit reservation of rights performs or promises performance or assents to performance in a manner demanded or offered by the other party does not thereby prejudice the rights reserved. Such words as 'without prejudice,' 'under protest,' or the like are sufficient."

First, full-payment checks are a widely recognized means of implementing settlements. An interpretation of R.C. 1301.13 (U.C.C. 1-207) altering common-law accord and satisfaction on full-payment checks "would make informal settlements of disputes more difficult and would effect a substantial shift in the balance of power between disputatious creditors and debtors." [Citations omitted.]

Second, the language of R.C. 1301.13 (U.C.C. 1-207) and its Official Comment indicate the statute is intended to provide a means by which a party to an executory contract can accept defective performance under the contract without prejudicing his right to adequate performance. The Official Comment to R.C. 1301.13 states in part:

> 1. This section provides machinery for the continuation of performance along the lines contemplated by the contract despite a pending dispute, by adopting the mercantile device of going ahead with delivery, acceptance, or payment "without prejudice," "under protest," "under reserve," "with reservation of all our rights," and the like....
>
> 2. This section does not add any new requirement of language of reservation where not already required by law, but merely provides a specific measure on which a party can rely as he makes or concurs in any interim adjustment in the course of performance....

Accord and satisfaction, on the other hand, involves the creation and execution of a new contract, not performance (or even payment) pursuant to an executory contract. The creditor cannot accept the new contract, a material term of which is the extinguishment of the debtor's obligation, and simultaneously reserve rights to collect the full amount under the original contract. *See Flambeau Prod. Corp. v. Honeywell Information Sys., Inc.*, 116 Wis. 2d 95, 111, 341 N.W.2d 655, 663 (1984) ("The interests of fairness dictate that a creditor who cashes a check offered in full payment should be bound by the terms of the offer. The debtor's intent is known, and allowing the creditor to keep the money disregarding the debtor's conditions seems unfair and violative of the obligation of good faith which the U.C.C. makes applicable to every contractor duty.").

This reading of R.C. 1301.13 (U.C.C. 1-207) and its Official Comment is supported by numerous courts and commentators. [Citations omitted.]

Third, common-law rules governing commercial transactions remain in effect unless displaced by the provisions of the Ohio Uniform Commercial Code. R.C. 1301.03. Neither R.C. 1301.13 nor its Official Comment indicates that the statute was intended to displace common-law accord and satisfaction. Rather, the absence of any mention of such a widely used and long-standing commercial device as accord and satisfaction is a strong indication the statute was not intended to negate its use. This inference is strengthened by the co-existence without cross-reference of both Section 1-207 and a section explicitly recognizing full-payment checks in early drafts of the U.C.C....

Finally, the great majority of courts and legal scholars which have addressed the relationship between full-payment checks and Section 1-207 have held that Section 1-207 does not affect common-law accord and satisfaction.... [3]

Although problems will arise because of overreaching debtors, the doctrine of accord and satisfaction provides sufficient safeguards: there must be a good-faith dispute about the debt and the creditor must have reasonable notice that the check is intended to be in full satisfaction of the debt. *Flambeau Products Corp., supra*, 116 Wis. 2d at 111, 341 N.W.2d at 663. In addition, the Ohio Uniform Commercial Code allows a court to refuse to enforce an unconscionable contract. R.C. 1302.15 (U.C.C. 2-302).

I would affirm the decision of the court of appeals which affirmed the judgment of the trial court.

Moyer, C.J., and Wright, J., concur in the foregoing dissenting opinion.

---

3. The majority cites three other cases which have "dealt with the subject, albeit in dicta." In each of these cases, the facts indicate that no common-law accord and satisfaction existed because the claims were not disputed. *See Majestic Bldg. Material Corp. v. Gateway Plumbing, Inc.*, 694 S.W.2d 762, 764 (1985) ("... Gateway's check was partial payment of an undisputed and liquidated claim."); *Hanna v. Perkins*, 2 UCC Rep. Serv. 1044, 1045 (1985) ("In the instant case, defendant does not dispute plaintiff's claim...."); *Baillie Lumber Co. v. Kincaid Carolina Corp.*, 4 N.C. App. 342, 351, 167 S.E.2d 85, 91 (1969) ("In the present case the account of Baillie for the lumber sold and delivered by Kincaid was both liquidated and undisputed.")....

Exercise 3-17: *AFC Interiors* Revisited

1. Explain the result in *AFC Interiors* in terms of section 73 of the Restatement (Second) of Contracts.

2. Would the majority and dissent have disagreed about the result if there was no dispute as to whether DiCello still could return some of the furnishings and only pay for the furnishings he kept? Why or why not?

3. Read section 1-308 of the U.C.C. If section 1-308 (rather than section 1-207) had been in force when *AFC Interiors* was decided, would the result have been different. If so, why? If not, why not?

Illusory Promises

A. Introduction

The last topic in this chapter is "**illusory promises**." To paraphrase Arthur Corbin, a well-known contract law expert, an illusory promise really is not a promise at all. In other words, the speaker has not bound herself to any obligation.

To put this topic in context, recall a few basic ideas about breach of contract. Any party to a contract can choose to breach the contract and suffer the consequences of doing so. A breach of contract occurs when a party refuses to perform the contract or a party's promised performance is defective in some way. The consequences that a breaching party faces usually involve paying a sum of money as damages to the non-breaching party.

Often in breach of contract actions, a party will try to avoid liability by arguing that, for some specific reason, there was no performance due. For example, a party could defend herself in a breach of contract action by arguing that the alleged promise made was illusory. Illusory promises are one basis on which courts may choose not to enforce alleged contracts. Why do you think that courts are concerned about illusory promises?

Before you read more about illusory promises, it may be helpful to recall your prior study of consideration. Both courts and the Restatement (Second) of Contracts define consideration as a bargained-for promise, act, or forbearance.

In this section about illusory promises, your focus will be on bargained-for promises (contracts that involve exchanges of promises). Parties bargain for a promise when one party seeks a promise in exchange for her promise and the other party gives a promise in exchange for the first promisor's promise.

To see if you still understand consideration, write an answer to the following problem:

After several hours of negotiating, Peggy Sue says to Demetrius: "I will pay you $50 per week if you clean my house once per week for the next year." Demetrius replies: "I accept your offer." Why would a court likely hold that there is consideration to both parties to this transaction?

After you are done analyzing this problem, continue reading for an explanation of the answer to the problem.

In this problem, Peggy Sue asked for cleaning services from Demetrius and promised $50 per week as an inducement, thereby proposing an exchange of a promise of services for a promise of money. Demetrius promised his services to induce Peggy Sue's promise of money. Peggy Sue promised her money to obtain Demetrius' promise of services. In other words, both parties bargained for each other's promises. Therefore, a court would conclude that both parties received consideration.

Recall that, even if a particular promise has been bargained for, a court may nevertheless conclude that the promise does not suffice as consideration. For example, if Peggy Sue had offered to pay Demetrius only one cent per week, and Demetrius had accepted, a court would deem the consideration inadequate because it was nominal (even though courts do not generally inquire into the inadequacy of consideration).

Similarly, a court would conclude that there is no consideration if Peggy Sue offers and Demetrius accepts an offer to exchange Peggy Sue's $50 per week for Demetrius' $100 per week. That exchange would involve a like-kind exchange of items known to be of different value and, therefore, really a gift.

There are a few other instances when, despite the fact that parties have bargained for an exchange, courts will not find consideration and will not enforce a promise, including: (1) a promise for actions or forbearances rendered in the past (past consideration), (2) a promise based solely on moral grounds (moral consideration); and (3) a promise for a settlement or release (forbearance) of an invalid claim without an honest or reasonable belief that the claim has a colorable basis.

B. Illusory Promises

Imagine you are a parent. Your seventeen-year-old daughter comes to you on Thursday and asks to use your car on Saturday night. You know the car needs washing, so you say, "If you wash the car today, I will let you use it on Saturday if I determine not to use it." Your seventeen-year-old does not say a word and leaves the room in a huff. After a moment or two, you hear the door to her room slam, making a sound somewhat similar to the sound made by a firing gun.

Why is your daughter so angry? She feels you have set her up. She has to agree to wash the car in exchange for the mere possibility of being allowed to drive the car. You have reserved, for later decision, the right to either allow her to use the car—or not. In other words, while she must wash the car, you have not committed yourself at all, and you have done so while making it sound like you are promising something ("I will let you use it"). In this section, you will study illusory promises and what happens when problems of apparent, but not real, promises move from parent-child conflicts to real-world contract disputes.

Now imagine another interaction. Thu owed Juanita $500 and lacked sufficient funds to repay Juanita on the due date. Thu begged Juanita for extra time to pay. Juanita said, "If you agree to pay me an extra $50, I will not demand that you pay me all the money you owe me until I, using my sole discretion, decide to demand it." What is your reaction to this promise? Do you think Juanita is really giving anything at all (in other words, is there consideration), or has she made an illusory promise?

Continuing the same problem, imagine that Thu replied, "Thanks, I promise to pay you an extra $50." Juanita waited one month, and then demanded payment. Thu paid Juanita $500, but refused to pay the extra $50. In a suit brought by Juanita against Thu for breach of contract to recover the extra $50, Thu raises the defense that Juanita's promise was illusory so there was no consideration. What do you think a court would decide?

All courts would agree that Juanita's promise is illusory and, therefore, there is no consideration for Thu's promise to pay the extra $50. Because there is no consideration, there is no enforceable contract for the extra $50. With no enforceable contract, Juanita would lose her lawsuit.

Now imagine a similar, but slightly different, interaction. Once again, Thu owed Juanita $500 and could not repay it on the due date. Thu begged for extra time to pay. But, this time, Juanita said, "If you agree to pay me an extra $50, I will not demand that you pay me all the money you owe me until one month from today." Do you think Juanita has given anything this time? In other words, is there consideration or has Juanita made an illusory promise?

Continuing the same problem, imagine that Thu replied, "Thanks, I promise to pay you an extra $50." In one month, Juanita demands payment. Thu pays $500, but refuses to pay the extra $50. Juanita then sues Thu for breach of contract to recover the extra $50. Do you think there is an enforceable contract for the extra $50?

All courts would agree that Juanita's promise is not illusory, that there is consideration, and, therefore, there is an enforceable contract obligation for the extra $50. Consequently, assuming Juanita's lawsuit did not raise any other contract issues, Juanita would win her lawsuit.

At this point, you should understand that when a court refuses to enforce a promise deemed illusory, that conclusion is the result reached after analyzing a given problem. In law school and in practice, you will need to know how to analyze whether a promise is illusory. To do so, make sure that you understand why Juanita's promise in the first example is illusory and why Juanita's promise in the second example is not illusory.

C. What Makes Promises Illusory

Because illusory promise is an abstract and difficult concept, legal commentators have exerted considerable effort trying to develop the definitive definition. No definitive definition yet exists but three useful alternatives are:

1. **a promise is illusory if it does not restrict the promisor's future right of action;**
2. **a promise is illusory if it gives the promisor unfettered discretion to perform or not perform the promise; or**
3. **a promise is illusory if it does not restrict the promisor's autonomy.**

Each of these alternatives is equally serviceable, yet none captures the full complexity required for an illusory promise analysis.

Two other concepts that influence courts' determinations of whether particular promises are illusory are: (1) good faith, and (2) reasonableness or reasonable efforts. Courts uniformly agree that every contract includes an implied duty of good faith, often defined as "honesty in fact," and courts have used this implied duty as a mechanism to enforce what otherwise appear to be illusory promises. Similarly, courts have held that contracting parties have a duty of reasonableness or reasonable efforts and have used these implied obligations to enforce promises that otherwise appear to be illusory. However, some promises, those that justify the conclusion that they are illusory, cannot be saved by either of these techniques. To understand the above definitions and how they work with the implied duties, it is helpful to revisit the Juanita-Thu problem.

In the Juanita-Thu problem, Juanita made an illusory promise when she stated, "If you agree to pay me an extra $50, **I will** not demand that you pay me all the money you owe me

until I, using my sole discretion, decide to demand it." As you previously learned, "I will," if linked to an action or forbearance (here a forbearance from demanding), expresses the requisite commitment to be a promise. The word "until" suggests that what is to follow is a time restriction on the speaker — that is, the period of time before the speaker can demand repayment.

What follows, however, is "I, using my sole discretion, decide." This is the phrase that makes Juanita's promise illusory. Because Juanita can demand payment at any time, according to her "sole discretion," she may demand payment immediately or at a later date. She has not necessarily agreed to delay the payment. She has the right to decide when to demand payment.

A court could not make Juanita's promise non-illusory by implying either good faith or reasonable efforts. A good faith requirement would not save the promise from being illusory because Juanita could act honestly in deciding to demand the money right away (because she's greedy or wants to buy a new dress). In other words, a good faith requirement would not eliminate Juanita's absolute discretion.

Similarly, a reasonable efforts requirement would not save the promise from being illusory because using one's discretion does not involve taking any kind of action. It is an internal, mental, decisional process. Thus, although Juanita's promise included the language of a promise, it was illusory because: (1) it did not restrict Juanita's discretion to choose, and (2) it could not be restricted by implying good faith or a requirement of reasonable effort.

In contrast, Thu's promise to pay money (the extra $50) is not illusory. Thu has no discretion whether to pay the extra $50 or not. So, Juanita received consideration from Thu, but Thu did not receive consideration from Juanita. As a result, a court would not enforce the contract.

In the other Juanita-Thu problem, Juanita said: "If you agree to pay me an extra $50, **I will** not demand that you pay me all the money you owe me **until one month from today**." Note that "I will" are words of promise. The word "until" suggests Juanita is agreeing to postpone collection. The stated time for postponement, "one month from today," is critical. Juanita has no discretion to demand payment before one month. Indeed, if Juanita demands payment sooner than one month, she will have breached her promise. The promise, therefore, is non-illusory and did make an enforceable contract: Thu gets an additional month to repay his loan in return for his promise to pay the extra $50.

Exercise 3-18: Illusory–Non-Illusory Promises

One trait of successful law students is that they read actively. One way they do so is by engaging in a dialogue with the material they are reading. Intentionally practice this technique as you read and think through the problems in this exercise.

The problems in this exercise present examples of illusory or non-illusory promises. Your goal is to correctly classify them. Please do so before reading on because the answers are discussed immediately following the problems. This exercise is an opportunity for you to assess your own understanding of the illusory promise concept. If you are able to correctly categorize six out of the eight problems, then you should feel confident that you understand the concept.

1. "I will buy your car for $5,000 cash if I feel like it."

2. "I will buy your car for $5,000 cash."

3. "If I wake up in a good mood tomorrow, I will clean your house in exchange for $100."

4. "Unless I win the lottery tonight, I will clean your house in exchange for $100."

5. From a baseball league to a baseball manufacturer: "We will buy, at $1 per ball, all of the baseballs we require."

6. From a baseball league to a baseball manufacturer: "We will buy, at $1 per ball, as many baseballs as we choose to buy."

7. "I covenant to pay you $4,000 for this washing machine if I am satisfied with it."

8. "I covenant to pay you $4,000 for this washing machine if I desire to do so."

Table 3-3: Answers to Exercise 3-18

Answers to and explanations for these problems are provided below:

1. "I will buy your car for $5,000 cash if I feel like it."

This promise is illusory. Although "I will" is the language of a promise, "feel like it" does not restrict the speaker's discretion in any way. The speaker could either feel like or not feel like buying the car without breaching the promise. Moreover, implying a good faith duty to feel like buying the car would not save the promise from being illusory because a person can either honestly feel like doing something or honestly not feel like doing something. Likewise, implying a duty to make a reasonable effort to feel like it would not save the promise from being illusory because the only relevant efforts would occur in the speaker's head.

2. "I will buy your car for $5,000 cash."

This promise is not illusory. Again, "I will" is the language of a promise. There is no discretion reserved or contingency expressed. If the speaker failed to pay $5,000, he would breach the contract.

3. "If I wake up in a good mood tomorrow, I will clean your house in exchange for $100."

This promise is illusory. Again, "I will" is language of a promise. "If I wake up in a good mood tomorrow," however, does not restrict the speaker's discretion. The speaker could either be in a good mood or not be in a good mood and not breach the promise. Further, implying a good faith duty to be in a good mood would not make this promise non-illusory because a person can honestly be or not be in a good mood. Similarly, implying a duty to make a reasonable effort to be in a good mood would not make the promise non-illusory because the only relevant efforts would occur in the speaker's head.

4. "Unless I win the lottery tonight, I will clean your house in exchange for $100."

This promise is not illusory. Again, "I will" is the language of a promise. The fact that the promise is contingent on the speaker not winning the lottery raises a question as to whether the speaker's discretion has been restricted. On the one hand, the speaker seems to be able to avoid liability simply by not buying a lottery ticket, and because he has full control over whether that purchase occurs, he can avoid liability altogether if he wins the lottery. Courts, however, would imply a duty to make a reasonable effort to buy the ticket. Therefore, the speaker has no discretion because he has to try to buy the ticket and he has no control over whether he wins the lottery. Consequently, the promise is not illusory. It follows that a promise that is made conditional on the happening of some defined event is not illusory just because the defined event never happens.

5. From a baseball league to a baseball manufacturer: "**We will buy** at $1 per ball all of the baseballs we **require**."

This promise is not illusory. "We will buy" is language of a promise. "Require" suggests the speaker has complete control over whether the league orders the baseballs or not. However, section 2-306 of the U.C.C. implies a duty of good faith in such contracts, known as "requirement contracts." Accordingly, the baseball league must require or not require baseballs in good faith. If the league's orders were much lower or much higher than in previous years, a court would analyze closely whether the league breached its duty to require baseballs in good faith. A court could assess objectively whether any such deviation from the league's normal requirements was honest.

6. From a baseball league to a baseball manufacturer: "**We will buy**, at $1 per ball, as many baseballs as **we choose to buy**."

This promise is illusory. "We will buy" is language of a promise. However, "we choose to buy" has the same connotation as the phrase "feel like it" in problem 1. There is no restriction on the league's discretion. Moreover, implying a good faith or a reasonable efforts requirement would not save the promise from being illusory.

7. "**I covenant** to pay you $4,000 for this washing machine **if I am satisfied** with it."

This promise is not illusory. Although "I covenant" is the language of a promise, "if I am satisfied," suggests the promisor may choose to perform or withdraw based simply on whether she feels satisfied with the washer. Courts, however, imply a duty of good faith satisfaction in matters of taste or judgment and a reasonable satisfaction requirement in matters of utility. Here, the effectiveness of the washing machine is a matter of utility (whether the machine works properly). Therefore, a court would imply a duty of reasonable satisfaction. The speaker could only avoid liability if she has a reasonable basis for claiming dissatisfaction.

8. "**I covenant** to pay you $4,000 for this washing machine **if I desire to do so**."

This promise is illusory. "I covenant" is the language of a promise. However, "if I desire to do so" is like the phrase "feel like it" in problem 1. There is no restriction on the speaker's discretion. Additionally, implying a good faith or reasonable efforts requirement would not save the promise from being illusory.

The next three cases in this chapter, *Harris v. Blockbuster Inc.*, *Omni Group, Inc. v. Seattle-First National Bank*, and *Wood v. Lucy, Lady Duff-Gordon*, address illusory promise issues. The material you have already learned in this chapter should allow you to predict the outcomes in the cases before you read the courts' analyses. Try to do so.

Exercise 3-19: *Harris v. Blockbuster Inc.*

As you read *Harris*, also consider the following questions:

1. What did the parties agree?

2.   Why did the court conclude that the agreement was or was not illusory? Identify each step of the court's reasoning.

3.   Would the result in *Harris* be different if the court implied a duty to act in good faith or to use reasonable efforts? Why or why not?

Harris v. Blockbuster Inc.

622 F. Supp. 2d 396 (2009)

BARBARA M.G. LYNN, District Judge.

This Opinion sets forth the grounds for the Court's denial of Defendant's Motion to Compel Individual Arbitration.

Background

This case arises out of alleged violations of the Video Privacy Protection Act by Defendant Blockbuster Inc. ("Blockbuster"). Blockbuster operates a service called Blockbuster Online, which allows customers to rent movies through the internet. Blockbuster entered into an agreement with Facebook ("the Blockbuster contract") which caused Blockbuster's customers' movie rental choices to be disseminated on the customers' Facebook accounts through Facebook's "Beacon" program. In short, when a customer rented a video from Blockbuster Online, the Beacon program would transmit the customer's choice to Facebook, which would then broadcast the choice to the customer's Facebook friends.

Plaintiff claims that this arrangement violated the Video Privacy Protection Act, 18 U.S.C. § 2710, which prohibits a videotape service provider from disclosing personally identifiable information about a customer unless given informed, written consent at the time the disclosure is sought. The Act provides for liquidated damages of $2,500 for each violation.

Blockbuster attempted to invoke an arbitration provision in its "Terms and Conditions," which includes a paragraph governing "Dispute Resolution" that states, in pertinent part: "[a]ll claims, disputes or controversies ... will be referred to and determined by binding arbitration." It further purportedly waives the right of its users to commence any class action. As a precondition to joining Blockbuster Online, customers were required to click on a box certifying that they had read and agreed to the Terms and Conditions.

On August 30, 2008, before the case was transferred to this Court, the Defendant moved to enforce the arbitration provision. The Plaintiffs argued that the arbitration provision is unenforceable, principally for two reasons: (1) it is illusory; and (2) it is unconscionable. Because the Court concludes that the arbitration provision is illusory, the Court does not reach the unconscionability issue.

Legal Standard

In Texas, a contract must be supported by consideration, and if it is not, it is illusory and cannot be enforced. In *Morrison v. Amway Corp.*, the Fifth Circuit analyzed a very similar arbitration provision to that in the subject

Terms and Conditions and held it to be illusory [footnote citation omitted]. In *Morrison*, defendant, a seller of household products marketed through a chain of distributors, was sued by its distributors for a variety of torts, including racketeering and defamation. The defendant sought to enforce an arbitration provision in which each distributor agreed:

> "[T]o conduct [his or her] business according to the Amway Code of Ethics and Rules of Conduct, as they are amended and published from time to time in official Amway literature.... I agree I will give notice in writing of any claim or dispute arising out of or relating to my Amway distributorship, or the Amway Sales and Marketing Plan or Rules of Conduct to the other party or parties.... I agree to submit any remaining claim or dispute arising out of or relating to any Amway distributorship, the Amway Sales and Marketing Plan, or the Amway Rules of Conduct ... to binding arbitration in accordance with the Amway Arbitration rules, which are set forth in the Amway Business Compendium." [footnote citation omitted]

The *Morrison* court held that the provision was illusory because "[t]here is no express exemption of the arbitration provisions from Amway's ability to unilaterally modify all rules, and the only express limitation on that unilateral right is published notice. While it is inferable that an amendment thus unilaterally made by Amway to the arbitration provision would not become effective until published, there is nothing to suggest that once published the amendment would be inapplicable to disputes arising, or arising out of events occurring, *before* such publication." [footnote citation omitted].

Why might a unilateral contractual right to modify all the terms of a contract be illusory?

The *Morrison* court distinguished *In re Halliburton Co.*, in which the Texas Supreme Court rejected an argument that an arbitration clause was illusory [footnote citation omitted]. The provision in *Halliburton* specifically limited the defendant's ability to apply changes to the agreement as follows:

> [N]o amendment shall apply to a Dispute of which the Sponsor [Halliburton] had actual notice on the date of amendment.... termination [of the arbitration agreement] shall not be effective until 10 days after reasonable notice of termination is given to Employees or as to Disputes which arose prior to the date of termination [footnote citation omitted].

In *Morrison,* the Fifth Circuit held that the limitation on the ability to unilaterally modify or terminate the agreement in *Halliburton* is what caused the Texas Supreme Court to rule that it was enforceable [footnote citation omitted]. Because the *Morrison* agreement contained no "*Halliburton* type savings clauses," which would "preclude application of such amendments to disputes which arose (or of which Amway had notice) before the amendment," the agreement in *Morrison* was illusory.

Analysis

The basis for the Plaintiffs' claim that the arbitration provision is illusory is that Blockbuster reserves the right to modify the Terms and Conditions, including the section that contains the arbitration provision, "at its sole discretion" and "at any time," and such modifications will be effective immediately upon being posted on the site. Under the heading "Changes to Terms and Conditions," the contract states:

Blockbuster may at any time, and at its sole discretion, modify these Terms and Conditions of Use, including without limitation the Privacy Policy, with or without notice. Such modifications will be effective immediately upon posting. You agree to review these Terms and Conditions of Use periodically and your continued use of this Site following such modifications will indicate your acceptance of these modified Terms and Conditions of Use. If you do not agree to any modification of these Terms and Conditions of Use, you must immediately stop using this Site.

The Court concludes that the Blockbuster arbitration provision is illusory for the same reasons as that in *Morrison*. Here, as in *Morrison*, there is nothing in the Terms and Conditions that prevents Blockbuster from unilaterally changing any part of the contract other than providing that such changes will not take effect until posted on the website. There are likewise no "*Halliburton* type savings clauses," as there is "nothing to suggest that once published the amendment would be inapplicable to disputes arising, or arising out of events occurring, before such publication." [footnote citation omitted]. The Fifth Circuit in *Morrison* noted the lack of an "express exemption" of the ability to unilaterally modify all rules, which the Blockbuster agreement also does not contain [footnote citation omitted]. The Blockbuster contract only states that modifications "will be effective immediately upon posting," and the natural reading of that clause does not limit application of the modifications to earlier disputes.

The Court addresses two differences between the Blockbuster contract and that in *Morrison*. Under Texas law, where, as here, an arbitration provision is incorporated within a larger contract, the benefits of the underlying contract can serve as consideration [footnote citation omitted]. The *Morrison* contract was a stand-alone agreement, and as such required independent consideration. Second, in *Morrison*, the defendant was actually attempting to retroactively apply the arbitration agreement to events that had happened before it was in effect, and there is no such suggestion here.

Neither distinction affects this Court's determination that the Blockbuster contract is illusory ... [T]he rule in *Morrison* applies to cases where there was no attempt to apply a contract modification to prior events. In *Simmons v. Quixtar, Inc.*, the court stated that "a close reading of the Fifth Circuit's opinion [in *Morrison*] is not predicated on that sole ground [of applying modification to earlier actions]. The Court's reasoning applies to the Rules of Conduct and Amway's (Quixtar's) ability to unilaterally change the rules of the game." [footnote citation omitted].

The court continued: "[t]he language of the Circuit's [*Morrison*] opinion ... decided the issue on the basis that the ability to change the rules at any time made the contract merely illusory." The Court agrees with that analysis and finds that the *Morrison* rule applies even when no retroactive modification has been attempted.

Conclusion

For these reasons, the Court concludes that the arbitration provision of the Blockbuster contract is illusory and unenforceable, and accordingly, Defendant's Motion to compel individual arbitration is denied.

What difference would it have made if the contract had said that modifications to the terms and conditions would not apply retroactively?

Exercise 3-20: *Omni Group, Inc. v. Seattle-First National Bank*

The next case, *Omni Group, Inc. v. Seattle-First National Bank*, involves a contract that raises illusory promise issues in two different ways. The court concludes that the promise was non-illusory and there is an enforceable contract. As you read *Omni Group*, consider the following questions:

1. What did the buyer promise?

2. What did the seller promise?

3. Whose promise was allegedly illusory?

4. What two aspects of that promise made it appear illusory? Why?

5. Why did the court conclude that the promise was not illusory? Identify each step of the court's reasoning. If you believe the court did not explicitly state any part of its reasoning, determine what the court must have reasoned.

Omni Group, Inc. v. Seattle-First National Bank

32 Wash. App. 22, 645 P.2d 727 (1982)

James, Judge. Plaintiff Omni Group, Inc. (Omni), a real estate development corporation, appeals entry of a judgment in favor of John B. Clark, individually, and as executor of the estate of his late wife, in Omni's action to enforce an earnest money agreement for the purchase of realty owned by the Clarks. We reverse.

In December 1977, Mr. and Mrs. Clark executed an exclusive agency listing agreement with the Royal Realty Company of Bellevue (Royal) for the sale of approximately 59 acres of property. The list price was $3,000 per acre. In early May, Royal offered the Clark property to Omni. On May 17, following conversations with a Royal broker, Omni signed an earnest money agreement offering $2,000 per acre. Two Royal brokers delivered the earnest money agreement to the Clarks. The Clarks signed the agreement, but directed the brokers to obtain further consideration in the nature of Omni's agreement to make certain improvements on adjacent land not being offered for sale. Neither broker communicated these additional terms to Omni.

In pertinent part, the earnest money agreement provides:

> This transaction is subject to purchaser receiving an engineer's and architect's feasibility report prepared by an engineer and architect of the purchaser's choice. Purchaser agrees to pay all costs of said report. If said report is satisfactory to purchaser, purchaser shall so notify seller in writing within fifteen (15) days of seller's acceptance of this offer. If no such notice is sent to seller, this transaction shall be considered null and void.

Omni's purpose was to determine, prior to actual purchase, if the property was suitable for development.

On June 2, an Omni employee personally delivered to the Clarks a letter advising that Omni had decided to forgo a feasibility study. They were further advised that a survey had revealed that the property consisted of only 50.3 acres. The Clarks agreed that if such were the case, they would accept Omni's offer of $2,000 per acre but with a minimum of 52 acres ($104,000). At this meeting, the Clarks' other terms (which had not been disclosed by Royal nor included in the earnest money agreement signed by the Clarks) were discussed. By a letter of June 8, Omni agreed to accept each of the Clarks' additional terms. The Clarks, however, refused to proceed with the sale after consulting an attorney.

The Clarks argued and the trial judge agreed, that, by making its obligations subject to a satisfactory "engineer's and architect's feasibility report" in paragraph 6, Omni rendered its promise to buy the property illusory. Omni responds that paragraph 6 created only a condition precedent to Omni's duty to buy, and because the condition was for its benefit, Omni could waive the condition and enforce the agreement as written. We conclude Omni's promise was not illusory.

A promise for a promise is sufficient consideration to support a contract. [Citations omitted.] If, however, a promise is illusory, there is no consideration and therefore no enforceable contract between the parties. [Citation omitted.] Consequently, a party cannot create an enforceable contract by waiving the condition which renders his promise illusory. But that a promise given for a promise is dependent upon a condition does not necessarily render it illusory or affect its validity as consideration. [Citations omitted.]

Furthermore, "a contractor can, by the use of clear and appropriate words, make his own duty expressly conditional upon his own personal satisfaction with the quality of the performance for which he has bargained and in return for which his promise is given. Such a limitation on his own duty does not invalidate the contract as long as the limitation is not so great as to make his own promise illusory." [Citation omitted.]

Paragraph 6 may be analyzed as creating two conditions precedent to Omni's duty to buy the Clarks' property. First, Omni must receive an "engineer's and architect's feasibility report." Undisputed evidence was presented to show that such "feasibility reports" are common in the real estate development field and pertain to the physical suitability of the property for development purposes. Such a condition is analogous to a requirement that a purchaser of real property obtain financing, which imposes upon the purchaser a duty to make a good faith effort to secure financing. [Citation omitted.] In essence, this initial language requires Omni to attempt, in good faith, to obtain an "engineer's and architect's feasibility report" of a type recognized in the real estate trade.

The second condition precedent to Omni's duty to buy the Clarks' property is that the feasibility report must be "satisfactory" to Omni. A condition precedent to the promisor's duty that the promisor be "satisfied" may require performance personally satisfactory to the promisor or it may require performance acceptable to a reasonable person. Whether the promisor was actually satisfied or should reasonably have been satisfied is a question of fact. In neither case is the promisor's promise rendered illusory. [Citation omitted.]

In *Mattei v. Hopper*, 51 Cal.2d 119, 121, 330 P.2d 625 (1958), plaintiff real estate developer contracted to buy property for a shopping center "'(s)ubject

Why does the court conclude that the earnest money agreement creates two illusory promise issues? What are those two issues?

to Coldwell Banker & Company obtaining leases satisfactory to the purchaser.'" Plaintiff had 120 days to consummate the purchase, including arrangement of satisfactory leases for shopping center buildings, before he was committed to purchase the property. The trial judge found the agreement "illusory." The California Supreme Court reversed. The court's language is apposite:

> [I]t would seem that the factors involved in determining whether a lease is satisfactory to the lessor are too numerous and varied to permit the application of a reasonable man standard as envisioned by this line of cases. Illustrative of some of the factors which would have to be considered in this case are the duration of the leases, their provisions for renewal options, if any, their covenants and restrictions, the amounts of the rentals, the financial responsibility of the lessees, and the character of the lessees' businesses.
>
> Comparable factors doubtless determine whether an "engineer's and architect's feasibility report" is satisfactory. But (t)his multiplicity of factors which must be considered in evaluating a lease shows that this case more appropriately falls within the second line of authorities dealing with "satisfaction" clauses, being those involving fancy, taste, or judgment. Where the question is one of judgment, the promisor's determination that he is not satisfied, when made in good faith, has been held to be a defense to an action on the contract.... Although these decisions do not expressly discuss the issues of mutuality of obligation or illusory promises, they necessarily imply that the promisor's duty to exercise his judgment in good faith is an adequate consideration to support the contract. None of these cases voided the contracts on the ground that they were illusory or lacking in mutuality of obligation. Defendant's attempts to distinguish these cases are unavailing, since they are predicated upon the assumption that the deposit receipt was not a contract making plaintiff's performance conditional on his satisfaction. As seen above, this was the precise nature of the agreement.
>
> Further, even though the "satisfaction" clauses discussed in the above-cited case dealt with performances to be received as parts of the agreed exchanges, the fact that the leases here which determined plaintiff's satisfaction were not part of the performance to be rendered is not material. The standard of evaluating plaintiff's satisfaction-good faith-applies with equal vigor to this type of condition and prevents it from nullifying the consideration otherwise present in the promises exchanged.

Mattei v. Hopper, supra at 123–24, 330 P.2d 625. Thus, even the fact that "[i]t was satisfaction with the leases that (the purchaser) was himself to obtain" was immaterial. 3A A. CORBIN, CONTRACTS section 644 at 84. [Citations omitted.] We conclude that the condition precedent to Omni's duty to buy requiring receipt of a "satisfactory" feasibility report does not render Omni's promise to buy the property illusory.

Paragraph 6 further provides, "If said report is satisfactory to purchaser, purchaser shall so notify seller in writing within fifteen (15) days of seller's acceptance of this offer;" otherwise, the transaction "shall be considered null and void." We read this language to mean that Omni is required ("shall") to notify the Clarks of its acceptance if the feasibility report was "satisfactory." As we have stated, this determination is not a matter within Omni's unfettered discretion.

Omni has, by the quoted language, reserved to itself a power to cancel or terminate the contract. [Citation omitted.] Such provisions are valid and do not render the promisor's promise illusory, where the option can be exercised upon the occurrence of specified conditions. [Citations omitted.] Here, Omni can cancel by failing to give notice only if the feasibility report is not "satisfactory." Otherwise, Omni is bound to give notice and purchase the property. Accordingly, we conclude paragraph 6 does not render Omni's promise illusory. The May 18 earnest money agreement was supported by consideration. . . .

The judgment is reversed and remanded with instructions to enter a decree ordering specific performance of the earnest money agreement.

Exercise 3-21: *Omni* Revisited

In *Omni*, the court states: "Omni has, by the quoted language, reserved to itself a power to cancel or terminate the contract. Such provisions are valid and do not render the promisor's promise illusory, where the option can be exercised upon the occurrence of specified conditions."

All courts agree that, if a party promises to perform but reserves a right to terminate the contract without notice, the promise is illusory. Reconcile the quoted statement from *Omni* and the result in *Omni* with the rule that a promise which includes a reservation of the right to terminate without notice is illusory. (Hint: How did the promisor in *Omni* restrict his discretion to choose whether to perform?)

The next illusory promise case is *Wood v. Lucy, Lady Duff-Gordon*. Many students have a hard time understanding *Lucy*. The case is easier to understand once you understand what its author was trying to accomplish. The author of the opinion, Benjamin Cardozo, is regarded as one of the greatest jurists of all time and had an enormous influence on the development of American law. One of Cardozo's great skills was to present new law as inevitable and thus not really new at all. Pay particular attention to Cardozo's writing choices. From the beginning of the opinion, you will see that Cardozo sets the stage so that you will believe that the only possible conclusion is that the plaintiff should win.

Exercise 3-22: *Wood v. Lucy, Lady Duff-Gordon*

As you read *Lucy*, consider the following questions:

1. What did the employer promise?
2. What did the employee promise?
3. Whose promise was allegedly illusory?
4. What created the illusory promise issue?

5. What did the court conclude as to whether the promise was illusory or not?

6. Why did the court conclude that the promise was or was not illusory? Identify each step of the court's reasoning. If you believe the court did not explicitly state any part of its reasoning, determine what the court must have reasoned.

7. In both *Lucy* and *Omni Group*, the courts seem to invest great effort to find ways to enforce the parties' alleged contracts. Why?

Wood v. Lucy, Lady Duff-Gordon
222 N.Y. 88, 118 N.E. 214 (1917)

Cardozo, J. The defendant styles herself 'a creator of fashions.' Her favor helps a sale. Manufacturers of dresses, millinery, and like articles are glad to pay for a certificate of her approval. The things which she designs, fabrics, parasols, and what not, have a new value in the public mind when issued in her name. She employed the plaintiff to help her to turn this vogue into money. He was to have the exclusive right, subject always to her approval, to place her endorsements on the designs of others. He was also to have the exclusive right to place her own designs on sale, or to license others to market them. In return she was to have one-half of "all profits and revenues" derived from any contracts he might make. The exclusive right was to last at least one year from April 1, 1915, and thereafter from year to year unless terminated by notice of 90 days. The plaintiff says that he kept the contract on his part, and that the defendant broke it. She placed her endorsement on fabrics, dresses, and millinery without his knowledge, and withheld the profits. He sues her for the damages, and the case comes here on demurrer.

The agreement of employment is signed by both parties. It has a wealth of recitals. The defendant insists, however, that it lacks the elements of a contract. She says that the plaintiff does not bind himself to anything. It is true that he does not promise in so many words that he will use reasonable efforts to place the defendant's endorsements and market her designs. We think, however, that such a promise is fairly to be implied. The law has outgrown its primitive stage of formalism when the precise word was the sovereign talisman, and every slip was fatal. It takes a broader view today. A promise may be lacking, and yet the whole writing may be "instinct with an obligation," imperfectly expressed.... If that is so, there is a contract.

The implication of a promise here finds support in many circumstances. The defendant gave an exclusive privilege. She was to have no right for at least a year to place her own endorsements or market her own designs except through the agency of the plaintiff. The acceptance of the exclusive agency was an assumption of its duties. [Citations omitted.] We are not to suppose that one party was to be placed at the mercy of the other. [Citations omitted.] Many other terms of the agreement point the same way. We are told at the outset by way of recital that, "The said Otis F. Wood possesses a business organization adapted to the placing of such endorsements as the said Lucy, Lady Duff-Gordon, has approved."

The implication is that the plaintiff's business organization will be used for the purpose for which it is adapted. But the terms of the defendant's compensation are even more significant. Her sole compensation for the grant of an exclusive agency is to be one-half of all the profits resulting from the plaintiff's efforts. Unless he gave his efforts, she could never get anything. Without an implied promise, the transaction cannot have such business "efficacy, as both parties must have intended that at all events it should have…." But the contract does not stop there. The plaintiff goes on to promise that he will account monthly for all moneys received by him, and that he will take out all such patents and copyrights and trade-marks as may in his judgment be necessary to protect the rights and articles affected by the agreement. It is true, of course, as the Appellate Division has said, that if he was under no duty to try to market designs or to place certificates of endorsement, his promise to account for profits or take out copyrights would be valueless. But in determining the intention of the parties the promise has a value. It helps to enforce the conclusion that the plaintiff had some duties. His promise to pay the defendant one-half of the profits and revenues resulting from the exclusive agency and to render accounts monthly was a promise to use reasonable efforts to bring profits and revenues into existence. For this conclusion the authorities are ample. [Citations omitted.]

The judgment of the Appellate Division should be reversed, and the order of the Special Term affirmed, with costs in the Appellate Division and in this court.

Exercise 3-23: Illusory Promise Problems

Analyze the following problems using what you have learned about illusory promises. Determine whether each statement is an illusory or non-illusory promise. Be prepared to explain your analyses.

1. "Pay me $25 per month as premiums. If you keep current with your premium payments and become physically or mentally unable to work at your current employment, I will pay you half of your monthly salary each month."

2. "We will pay you $5 per brick for all of the bricks our architect determines that we need for this construction project."

3. From a widget manufacturer to a widget retailer: "We will sell you at $.50 per widget all the widgets we produce."

4. "If you give me one dollar, and if I draw your name from this fishbowl from among all of the names of others from whom I have collected a dollar, I will give you all of the money I have collected."

5. "Unless I accept the job offer I received to be a law clerk with the Law Offices of Darrow & Smith, I promise to tutor you in contracts."

6. "I covenant to pay you $25 per hour to tutor me in contracts, but I may terminate this contract at any time."

7. "I will buy your home if I get a thirty-year, $200,000 loan from the Bank of Trust at an 8% interest rate."

8. "We will pay you $5 per brick for 50,000 used bricks. We may cancel this contract at any time without notice."

9. "We will pay you $5 per brick for 50,000 used bricks. We may cancel this contract at any time."

Exercise 3-24: Recurring Illusory Promise Issues

One effective technique for preparing for your law school exams is to create issue checklists that match the information you have covered during your courses. Issue checklists make it easier for you to identify legal issues presented in problems on your exams.

This exercise is intended to help you create an issue checklist for illusory promises. You have now learned about eight recurring illusory promise issues. These eight issues arise in the context of eight specific fact patterns. Re-read all of the illusory promise problems in this chapter and make a list of those eight specific fact patterns.

Chapter Problem Revisited

You now know enough to fully analyze Exercise 3-1 which was introduced at the beginning of this chapter. The problem presented in Exercise 3-1 is similar to one you might be asked to analyze on a law school exam or in law practice. Here are a few hints for analyzing and completing the problem:

1. Re-read Exercise 3-1 and make sure you understand the exact tasks you were asked to accomplish.

2. Start by identifying the consideration law issue implicated by the contract attached to the complaint.

3. Because you are a novice in drafting pleadings, it is most important to make thoughtful decisions about what you write (and less important that you create a perfect answer to the complaint). Accordingly, as you draft your answer, also write comments which explain your thinking process (either within your answer or on a separate sheet of paper).

4. Before you try writing your answer, you may find it helpful to look at sample answers in a form book for the state in which your law school is located or for federal practice.

5. Table 3-4 is a sample answer to a complaint. Assume that the complaint asserted that the defendant committed the tort of battery. It is reproduced here to give you an idea as to how to draft an answer. There are text boxes added to provide explanations for different aspects of the sample answer. Note that the text boxes are only provided to assist your understanding and should not actually appear in any legal pleadings.

Table 3-4: Sample Answer to Battery Complaint

State of Jefferson, County of Lincoln

Jane Smith,	)	
Plaintiff	)	
	)	
v.	)	Answer to Complaint
	)	
	)	Case No.: TB43434343
Tom Jones,	)	
Defendant.	)	
_____	)	

Defendant Tom Jones, by and through his attorney, Alice Attorney, hereby responds to the complaint filed by Jane Smith in the above-captioned matter as follows:

Responses to Allegations of the Complaint

An answer admits allegations known to be true, denies allegations known to be false, denies allegations believed to be false based "on information and belief," and denies allegations for which a party has a complete lack of relevant information.

1. Defendant lacks sufficient information or belief to admit or deny the allegations contained in paragraphs 1-2 of the complaint and denies those allegations on that ground.

2. In answer to paragraph 3 of the complaint, defendant admits that defendant is a resident of the city of Madison, the County of Lincoln, state of Jefferson.

3. Defendant denies on information and belief the allegations contained in paragraph 4 of the complaint.

4. Defendant denies the allegations contained in paragraphs 5-10 of the complaint.

5. On information and belief, Defendant denies the allegations contained in paragraph 11 of the complaint.

Affirmative Defenses

An affirmative defense is a defense which serves as a basis for providing new facts which would allow a defendant to avoid a judgment against him, even assuming all the allegations of a complaint are true.

As affirmative defenses, defendant alleges:

1. Affirmative Defense 1: Statute of Limitations. Even assuming, for argument's sake, all of the allegations of the complaint are true, all of the events described in the complaint occurred more than two years before the filing of the complaint and therefore the statute of limitations for this cause of action has run.

2. Affirmative Defense 2: Self-Defense. Even assuming, for argument's sake, all of the allegations of the complaint are true, defendant's actions were taken as a response to the plaintiff approaching the defendant with a loaded gun and pointing the gun at defendant and therefore the defendant reasonably believed in the need to act in self-defense and the defendant's actions were proportionate to the threat posed by the plaintiff.

Just as plaintiffs include prayers for relief in their complaints, defendants include prayers for relief in their answers.

Wherefore, defendant requests a judgment by the court:

1. Ordering that plaintiff take nothing by the complaint filed in the above-entitled matter, and that the same be dismissed with prejudice;

2.   Awarding defendant costs; and

3.   Granting defendant such other and further relief as the court deems just and proper.

September 28, 20___   *Betty Barrister, Esq.*

Betty Barrister, Esq.
Law Offices of Betty Barrister & Associates
1212 State Street
Madison, Jefferson 99999-0001
984-689-7979
State Bar No. 398760

Professional Development Reflection Questions

1.   Imagine that Carl Client asks you to draft a contract for him and include an illusory promise, which appears to bind both parties. Doing so is lawful, but should you engage in such a practice? Is it "good lawyering"? Would you want to represent Carl?

2.   In Chapter 1, you were introduced to the three key components of being an expert learner (planning, implementing your plans with self-monitoring, and reflecting on your learning process). As you revisit this learning model with the questions that follow, focus on strengthening your expert learning skills.

3.   In the planning phase, you should set mastery learning goals (for example, "By the end of the day, I'll be able to recite and explain the elements of promissory estoppel") and not task-completion goals (for example, "I will read pages 80–100 of my text").[4] Take a few minutes to set mastery learning goals for Chapter 4 before you begin your study of that chapter.

4.   In the planning phase, it is also important to make careful decisions about when, how long, where, and how you'll study. It's best to study at set, regular times (one to two hours each) with regular, short breaks (ten minutes each) and to give yourself occasional rewards if you stick to your plans. Most students study best in locations that are quiet, clean, and free from distractions, and where they have easy access to help if they're struggling with material (for example, from a library, peer, former professor, or friend). As you plan to learn the materials in Chapter 4, plan carefully how you'll study.

5.   As you study Chapter 4, also try to bring a heightened level of awareness to the implementation phase by maintaining focused attention and monitoring your comprehension and learning pace. For example, regularly ask yourself whether you understand what you're learning and whether your learning strategies are work-

---

4. Educational studies have found that students who set mastery learning goals get higher grades than those who set results-oriented goals. *See* Michael Hunter Schwartz, *Teaching Law Students to Be Self-Regulated Learners*, 2003 MICH. ST. D.C.L. L. REV. 447, 479.

ing. You may benefit by taking a learning self-assessment to ensure you are using learning strategies that are a good fit for you. We recommend taking the short, five-minute assessment at Vark-learn.com to ensure you are using strategies that will be effective for you.

6. For the third phase, reflection, evaluate how well you've learned the consideration rules in this chapter, identify any deficiencies in your studying of consideration, and plan how you'll study more effectively when you begin Chapter 4. It's tempting to skip this step; however, if you don't engage in reflection, you won't know when and how you've gone astray or be able to make a plan to improve your studying. In contrast, by reflecting and adapting your study approaches as you work, you can discard strategies that aren't working and retain the ones that are—resulting in better overall learning.

Chapter 4

Promissory Estoppel

Exercise 4-1: Chapter Problem

You now know enough contract law to begin writing practice answers in preparation for your law school exams. Accordingly, instead of providing you a legal task to complete (similar to the introductory problems in the previous chapters), we are giving you an opportunity to write exam answers to begin preparing yourself for your first set of law school exams.

Tables 4-1 through 4-3 present three sample contract law exam questions we will ask you to complete at the end of this chapter. The materials at the end of the chapter will provide you more guidance for answering these questions. For now, read the questions and keep them in mind as you read this chapter. Because this problem is one of your first experiences with law school exam questions, we added text boxes to the first two problems to give you a few hints to think about.

Table 4-1: Practice Exam Question 1

On June 21, Pierre hand-delivered a signed letter to Debra that said, "I will buy your screenplay, *Wedgwood Blues*, from you for $200,000 on July 30, but only if I can persuade myself that a musical about a law school study group can succeed. Remember: I give preferential treatment to written answers because I like to keep my business matters private."

> Focus on the meaning of the language used and what reasonable lawyers representing each party would argue it means.

On June 22, while driving to a business meeting, Debra saw Pierre eating lunch at an outdoor café. She quickly pulled out a bullhorn and said, "Pierre, this is Debra. I am thrilled to get *Wedgwood Blues* off my hands for $200,000. I originally bought it for $150,000 so you just guaranteed me a $50,000 profit." Assume Pierre heard every word.

On June 29, Debra and Pierre got into an argument as to whether they had formed a binding contract. After hours of yelling and threats, they signed a document in which Pierre expressed his promise to buy *Wedgwood Blues* from Debra for $210,000 and Debra expressed her promise to sell *Wedgwood Blues* to Pierre at that price.

> This paragraph raises a new set of issues.

On July 29, Debra informed Pierre that she decided not to sell *Wedgwood Blues* to Pierre. Pierre sued Debra for breach of contract. Discuss the legal issues presented.

Table 4-2: Practice Exam Question 2

You are a legislative analyst for Columbia State Senator Hannah Leigh. Below is a proposed statute and the legislative commentary to the proposed statute pre-

This question would be classified as one that only presents a policy question.

pared by the sponsors of the bill. Senator Leigh has not decided whether to support or oppose the bill. She therefore has asked you to write her a memorandum in which you critically evaluate both the statute and the assertions in the legislative commentary.

Proposed Statute

Columbia Civil Code Section 100: The formation of a contract requires only mutual manifestations of assent. Consideration no longer shall be a prerequisite to the formation of a contract.

Legislative Commentary

Don't assume that this commentary is accurate or convincing. Be critical.

1. Few, if any, courts decide cases today based on an absence of consideration. Rather, consideration is a meaningless requirement, and courts regularly engage in legal and rhetorical gymnastics to avoid concluding that a contract is unenforceable because it lacks consideration. *See, e.g., Omni Group, Inc. v. Seattle-First National Bank; Ricketts v. Scothorn.*

2. Most of the public policy concerns supporting a consideration requirement are adequately addressed by the mutual assent requirement.

3. The public policies supporting a consideration requirement which are not addressed by the mutual assent requirement are paternalistic and conflict with this state's public policy of encouraging contract-making.

Discuss the strengths and weaknesses of the proposed statute, the accuracy and persuasiveness of the assertions in the commentary, and the appropriateness and persuasiveness of the citations of authority in the commentary. Cite and discuss relevant cases, statutes, and other authority not cited in the commentary. You also are encouraged to make policy arguments not addressed in the commentary.

Table 4-3: Practice Exam Question 3

Artie, a collector of classic cars, is the owner and curator of Artie's Auto Museum. Last month, he saw an ad on ClassicCars.net, placed by Barry, a car dealer, listing a 1967 Cadillac Eldorado Convertible for sale at an asking price of $30,000. The listing described the car as follows:

"A 'must see' American classic. Odometer reading: 95,000 miles. Mechanically sound both within and out. Red metallic exterior. Automatic transmission, power steering, and air conditioning all in perfect working order. Serious inquiries only. Call or email Barry."

Artie thought the asking price was way too high but was determined to add the '67 Eldorado to his collection. He emailed Barry as follows:

"I hereby agree to buy the 1967 Cadillac Eldorado you have for sale on ClassicCars.net. I will pay you no more than $25,000. Let me know when you can deliver and I'll organize the cash."

Artie's email contained a hypertext link to Barry's ad so there could be no doubt about which car he was referring to. Barry replied immediately:

"Great. Thanks. I'll call by your place tomorrow with the car and we can figure the rest out."

The next day, Barry set off to deliver the car to Artie. Just as he was pulling up in front of the Auto Museum, Artie called Barry on Barry's cell phone to say that he'd reconsidered and was no longer interested in buying the car at $25,000. Barry said: "But I've just arrived with the car. I thought we had a deal."

Artie replied: "I don't think we have a deal yet but, as you're here, I'll tell you what I'll do. I'll still take the car, but I'm afraid you'll have to be content with $20,000. That's my final offer." Because he is in financial trouble, Barry reluctantly agreed to drop the price, even though $20,000 was well below market value. Barry now regrets selling the car for such a low price and claims that Artie owes him an additional $5,000. Discuss the legal issues presented.

Introduction to Promissory Estoppel

The fundamental goal of promissory estoppel is to protect a party if that party legitimately relies on another party's promise, even though the technical requisites for contract formation have not been met. In this sense, promissory estoppel may be thought of as a doctrine based on a completely separate theory of contract formation (the "reliance theory") that contrasts with the formation theory you learned about in previous chapters (the "bargain theory").

Accordingly, the doctrine of promissory estoppel reflects two departures: (1) a departure by you as a contract student from your study of traditional contract formation to an alternative doctrine by which courts may enforce promises, and (2) a departure within contract law from the relatively formal approach of early contract law to more modern approaches advocated for by lawyers, law professors, and judges based on different policy rationales.

Diagram 4-1, the Contract Law Graphic Organizer on the next page, depicts where promissory estoppel fits within the big picture of contract law. As the graphic organizer shows, promissory estoppel is an alternative to "Traditional Formation" under the more general topic of "Contract Formation."

Overview of Chapter 4

This chapter focuses on promissory estoppel. First, you will learn the elements of promissory estoppel. Then, you will learn how courts use promissory estoppel to enforce otherwise unenforceable promises in a variety of contexts, including the use of promissory estoppel as:

1. A substitute for consideration;
2. A substitute for a required writing;
3. A mechanism for making certain offers irrevocable; and
4. A mechanism for policing unfair bargaining behavior.

The Elements of Promissory Estoppel

Exercise 4-2: Promissory Estoppel

Read section 90(1) of the RESTATEMENT (SECOND) OF CONTRACTS. Then, answer the following questions:

1. What are the elements of promissory estoppel? (Hint: There are four.)

Diagram 4-1: Contract Law Graphic Organizer

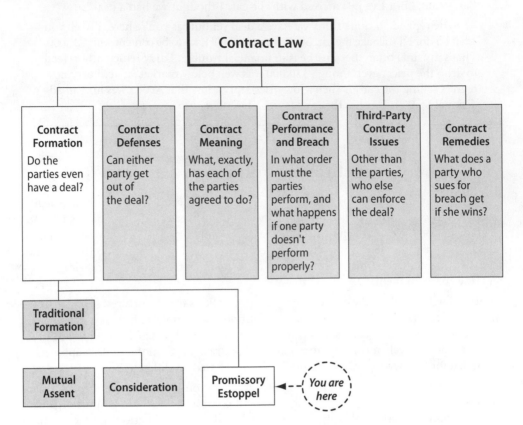

2. What does the last sentence in 90(1) tell you? What do you think the drafters intended by this sentence? Read comment d., which clarifies the drafters' intentions, to revise or confirm your understanding of section 90(1).

3. Re-read the extract from *Hamer v. Sidway* in Chapter 3. Analyze the facts of the case using section 90(1). Which do you think is the better theory of the uncle's liability in the case: bargain theory or reliance theory?

Promissory Estoppel as a Substitute for Consideration

Exercise 4-3: *Ricketts v. Scothorn*

The next case, *Ricketts v. Scothorn*, is an early milestone on the way to courts' current, wholesale adoption of promissory estoppel. As you read *Ricketts*, consider the following questions:

1. Why did the *Ricketts* court conclude there was no consideration for the promissory note?

2. How can you reconcile *Hamer v. Sidway* with the conclusion regarding consideration in *Ricketts*?

3. Assume the *Ricketts* courts had adopted what is now section 90 of the Restatement (Second) of Contracts. How would the courts have applied section 90 to the facts of the case?

4. What is the policy rationale for enforcing otherwise unenforceable promises based on reliance?

5. Does promissory estoppel conflict with another policy rationale?

6. In *Ricketts*, why didn't it matter to the court that Scothorn went back to work?

7. Why didn't the *Ricketts* court use promissory estoppel?

8. In what sense is *Ricketts* more like a contract law case than a tort law case? [Hint: we can assume that Katie Scothorn obtained judgment for the full amount of the note plus interest]

Ricketts v. Scothorn

57 Neb. 51, 77 N.W. 365 (1898)

Sullivan, J. In the district court of Lancaster County the plaintiff, Katie Scothorn, recovered judgment against the defendant, Andrew D. Ricketts, as executor of the last will and testament of John C. Ricketts, deceased. The action was based upon a promissory note, of which the following is a copy: "May the first, 1891. I promise to pay to Katie Scothorn on demand, $2,000, to be at 6 per cent. per annum. J. C. Ricketts." In the petition the plaintiff alleges that the consideration for the execution of the note was that she should surrender her employment as bookkeeper for Mayer Bros., and cease to work for a living. She also alleges that the note was given to induce her to abandon her occupation, and that, relying on it, and on the annual interest, as a means of support, she gave up the employment in which she was then engaged. These allegations of the petition are denied by the administrator.

The material facts are undisputed. They are as follows: John C. Ricketts, the maker of the note, was the grandfather of the plaintiff. Early in May—presumably on the day the note bears date—he called on her at the store where she was working. What transpired between them is thus described by Mr. Flodene, one of the plaintiff's witnesses:

> "A. Well, the old gentleman came in there one morning about nine o'clock, probably a little before or a little after, but early in the morning, and he unbuttoned his vest, and took out a piece of paper in the shape of a note; that is the way it looked to me; and he says to Miss Scothorn, 'I have fixed out something that you have not got to work any more.' He says, none of my grandchildren work, and you don't have to. Q. Where was she? A. She took the piece of paper and kissed him, and kissed the old gentleman, and commenced to cry."

Pay attention to the specific words used by the grandfather, the promisor.

It seems Miss Scothorn immediately notified her employer of her intention to quit work, and that she did soon after abandon her occupation. The mother of the plaintiff was a witness, and testified that she had a conversation with her father, Mr. Ricketts, shortly after the note was executed, in which he informed her that he had given the note to the plaintiff to enable her to quit work; that none of his grandchildren worked, and he did not think she ought to. For something more than a year the plaintiff was without an occupation, but in September, 1892, with the consent of her grandfather, and by his assistance, she secured a position as bookkeeper with Messrs. Funke & Ogden. On June 8, 1894, Mr. Ricketts died.... We quite agree with counsel for the defendant that upon this evidence there was nothing to submit to the jury, and that a verdict should have been directed peremptorily for one of the parties. The testimony of Flodene and Mrs. Scothorn, taken together, conclusively establishes the fact that the note was not given in consideration of the plaintiff pursuing, or agreeing to pursue, any particular line of conduct. There was no promise on the part of the plaintiff to do, or refrain from doing, anything. Her right to the money promised in the note was not made to depend upon an abandonment of her employment with Mayer Bros., and future abstention from like service. Mr. Ricketts made no condition, requirement, or request. He exacted no quid pro quo. He gave the note as a gratuity, and looked for nothing in return. So far as the evidence discloses, it was his purpose to place the plaintiff in a position of independence, where she could work or remain idle, as she might choose. The abandonment of Miss Scothorn of her position as bookkeeper was altogether voluntary. It was not an act done in fulfillment of any contract obligation assumed when she accepted the note. The instrument in suit, being given without any valuable consideration, was nothing more than a promise to make a gift in the future of the sum of money therein named.

Ordinarily, such promises are not enforceable, even when put in the form of a promissory note. [Citations omitted.] But it has often been held that an action on a note given to a church, college, or other like institution, upon the faith of which money has been expended or obligations incurred, could not be successfully defended on the ground of a want of consideration. [Citations omitted.] In this class of cases the note in suit is nearly always spoken of as a gift or donation, but the decision is generally put on the ground that the expenditure of money or assumption of liability by the donee on the faith of the promise constitutes a valuable and sufficient consideration. It seems to us that the true reason is the preclusion of the defendant, under the doctrine of estoppel, to deny the consideration. Such seems to be the view of the matter taken by the supreme court of Iowa in the case of *Simpson Centenary College v. Tuttle*, 71 Iowa, 596, 33 N.W. 74, where Rothrock, J., speaking for the court, said: "Where a note, however, is based on a promise to give for the support of the objects referred to, it may still be open to this defense [want of consideration], unless it shall appear that the donee has, prior to any revocation, entered into engagements, or made expenditures based on such promise, so that he must suffer loss or injury if the note is not paid. This is based on the equitable principle that, after allowing the donee to incur obligations on the faith that the note would be paid, the donor would be estopped from pleading want of consideration...."

Under the circumstances of this case, is there an equitable estoppel which ought to preclude the defendant from alleging that the note in controversy is lacking in one of the essential elements of a valid contract? We think there is. An *estoppel in pais* is defined to be "a right arising from acts, admissions, or conduct which have induced a change of position in accordance with the real or apparent intention of the party against whom they are alleged." Mr. Pomeroy has formulated the following definition: "Equitable estoppel is the effect of the voluntary conduct of a party whereby he is absolutely precluded, both at law and in equity, from asserting rights which might, perhaps, have otherwise existed, either of property, of contract, or of remedy, as against another person who in good faith relied upon such conduct, and has been led thereby to change his position for the worse, and who on his part acquires some corresponding right, either of property, of contract, or of remedy." 2 POM. EQ. JUR. 804. According to the undisputed proof, as shown by the record before us, the plaintiff was working, holding a position in which she earned a salary of $10 per week. Her grandfather, desiring to put her in a position of independence, gave her the note, accompanying it with the remark that his other grandchildren did not work, and that she would not be obliged to work any longer. In effect, he suggested that she might abandon her employment, and rely in the future upon the bounty which he promised. He doubtless desired that she should give up her occupation, but, whether he did or not, it is entirely certain that he contemplated such action on her part as a reasonable and probable consequence of his gift. Having intentionally influenced the plaintiff to alter her position for the worse on the faith of the note being paid when due, it would be grossly inequitable to permit the maker, or his executor, to resist payment on the ground that the promise was given without consideration. The petition charges the elements of an equitable estoppel, and the evidence conclusively establishes them. If errors intervened at the trial, they could not have been prejudicial. A verdict for the defendant would be unwarranted. The judgment is right, and is affirmed.

> The court does a good job making its decision seem inevitable. However, the result was not at all inevitable at the time the court decided this case.

Exercise 4-4: *Ricketts v. Scothorn* Revisited

1. Under section 90(1) of the RESTATEMENT (SECOND) OF CONTRACTS, what if Scothorn had used the promise of the money to convince a gambling establishment to extend her credit and then lost $5,000 gambling at the establishment?

2. Under section 90(1) of the RESTATEMENT (SECOND) OF CONTRACTS, what if Scothorn, in anticipation of getting the money, had purchased an inexpensive piece of art for $25 that she says she would not otherwise have purchased?

3. If Scothorn's grandfather had said, "You are working so hard I want to give you a little something extra," could Scothorn claim promissory estoppel if she quit her job?

4. Dan lived with his granddaughter, Petra, in her apartment for 15 years rent-free. She helped to take care of him. Dan decided to buy Greenacre for Petra, a property consisting of a house and an apartment to give them more space. On July 2, Dan executed an instrument which stated: "For good and valuable consideration, I do hereby convey and assign to Petra the sum of $17,000 to be payable when purchase of Greenacre closes." On July 3, Petra entered into a contract to purchase Greenacre with Greenacre's owner for a price of $17,000. The contract provided that closing would take place on July 30. Petra paid a deposit of $1,700 out of her personal savings. Dan died on July 15. His estate refuses to pay out the $17,000 to Petra? Is Dan's promise enforceable?

5. Why do you think section 90(2) states a special rule for charitable sub-
    scriptions? Why don't courts require reliance by a charity before the char-
    ity can enforce a promise to make a donation?

Exercise 4-5: *East Providence Credit Union v. Geremia*

The next case, *East Providence Credit Union v. Geremia*, gives you an additional opportunity to see how courts apply promissory estoppel to solve potential consideration problems. As you read *East Providence Credit Union*, consider
the following questions:

1. What are the key facts?

2. The court concludes there was consideration for the bank's promise to pay
    the insurance premium for the Geremias. Why?

3. The court also concludes that the promise was enforceable on the basis of
    promissory estoppel.

    a. Having decided that the promise was enforceable on the basis of consid-
        eration, why did the court go on to analyze promissory estoppel?

    b. Assign a letter grade to the court's analysis of the promissory estoppel issue.
        What's wrong with the court's analysis of the promissory estoppel issue?

    c. Complete a more effective analysis of the promissory estoppel issue.

East Providence Credit Union v. Geremia
103 R.I. 597, 239 A.2d 725 (1968)

Kelleher, Justice. This is a civil action to collect from the defendants the balance due on a promissory note. The defendants filed a counterclaim. The case
was heard by a justice of the superior court. He dismissed the plaintiff's complaint and found for the defendants on their counterclaim. The case is before
us on the plaintiff's appeal.

On December 5, 1963, defendants, who are husband and wife, borrowed
$2,350.28 from plaintiff for which they gave their promissory note. The pay-
ment of the note was secured by a chattel mortgage on defendants' 1962 ranch
wagon. The mortgage contained a clause which obligated defendants to maintain insurance on the motor vehicle in such amounts as plaintiff required
against loss by fire, collision, upset or overturn of the automobile and similar
hazards. This provision also stipulated that if defendants failed to maintain
such insurance, plaintiff could pay the premium and " … any sum so paid
shall be secured hereby and shall be immediately payable." The defendants had
procured the required insurance and had designated plaintiff as a loss payee on
its policy. The premium therefore was payable in periodic installments.

On October 11, 1965, defendants received a notice from the insurance carrier informing them that the premium then payable was overdue and that,
unless it was paid within the ensuing twelve days, the policy would be cancelled. A copy of this notice was also sent by the insurer to plaintiff who there-

upon sent a letter to defendants. The pertinent portion thereof reads as follows: "We are in receipt of a cancellation notice on your Policy. If we are not notified of a renewal Policy within 10 days, we shall be forced to renew the policy for you and apply this amount to your loan."

Upon receiving this communication, defendant wife testified that she telephoned plaintiff's office and talked to the treasurer's assistant; that she told this employee to go ahead and pay the premium; that she explained to the employee that her husband was sick and they could not pay the insurance premium and the payment due on the loan; and that the employee told her that the call would be referred to plaintiff's treasurer. The employee testified that she told defendant to contact this officer. We deem this difference in testimony insignificant. It is clear from the record that defendants communicated their approval of and acquiescence in plaintiff's promise to pay the insurance due on the car and that this employee notified the treasurer of such fact.

On December 17, 1965, defendants' motor vehicle was demolished in a mishap the nature of which cannot be learned from the record. It is obvious, however, that the loss was within the coverage of the policy. The automobile was a total loss. The evidence shows that at the time of the loss, the outstanding balance of the loan was $987.89 and the value of the ranch wagon prior to the loss exceeded the balance due on the loan.

Sometime after this unfortunate incident, all the parties became aware that the insurer would not indemnify them for the loss because the overdue premium had not been paid and defendants' policy had been canceled prior to the accident.

The defendants had on deposit with plaintiff over $200 in savings shares. The plaintiff, in accordance with the terms of the note, had deducted therefrom certain amounts and applied them to defendants' indebtedness so that at the time this litigation was instituted defendants allegedly owed plaintiff $779.53.

In finding for defendants on their counterclaim, the trial justice awarded them all the moneys which plaintiff had applied after the date of defendants' accident to the then outstanding balance of the loan. The justice, at the conclusion of the evidence, made certain findings which were in accordance with the testimony as set forth above. He found from the evidence that plaintiff, in pursuance of its right under the mortgage contract and its letter to defendants, had agreed to renew the policy and charge and premiums paid by it on behalf of defendants to the outstanding balance on their loan....

The sole issue raised by this appeal is whether or not plaintiff is precluded from recovering on its loan contract by reason of its failure to fulfill a promise to defendants to pay the overdue insurance premium. In urging that the trial justice erred in finding for defendants, plaintiff directs our attention to *Hazlett v. First Fed. Sav. & Loan Assn.*, 14 Wash. 2d 124, 127 P.2d 273, in which the court refused to apply the doctrine of promissory estoppel to enforce a gratuitous promise made by a mortgagee to procure fire insurance for mortgaged property even though the mortgagor suffered serious detriment in reliance on the mortgagee's promise....

In the instant case, however, after a careful review of the facts, we are of the opinion that plaintiff made more than a mere gratuitous or unrecompensed promise. Instead, we believe that the promise by plaintiff to pay the insurance premium on defendants' car was one made in exchange for valid consideration. The mortgage contract provided that in the event plaintiff paid a premium for defendants, it would add such expended sums to the outstanding balance of defendants' loan. We are satisfied from a close examination of plaintiff's reply to defendants' interrogatories and of the chattel mortgage agreement that plaintiff intended to compute interest on any money it expended in keeping the insurance on defendants' car active. Hence, in our opinion, the interest due on any sums paid out by plaintiff on behalf of defendants for insurance represents valid consideration and converts their promise into a binding contract. The plaintiff's failure to successfully carry out its promise must be deemed a breach of that contract....

We would point out that, even if it could be shown by plaintiff that it never intended to compute any interest on amounts paid by it for insurance premiums on defendants' car and that its promise was truly a pure gratuitous undertaking, we believe such a showing would be of no avail to it since we would not hesitate in finding from this record evidence sufficient to establish a case for the application of promissory estoppel. The conditions precedent for the invocation of this doctrine are well set forth by Dean Boyer in his oft-cited article, *Promissory Estoppel: Requirements and Limitations of the Doctrine*, 98 U. Pa. L. Rev. 459. He enumerates the conditions as follows:

(1) Was there a promise which the promisor should reasonably expect to induce action or forbearance of a definite and substantial character on the part of the promisee?

(2) Did the promise induce such action or forbearance?

(3) Can injustice be avoided only by enforcement of the promise?

After a study of the facts in this case, our reply to each of the above inquiries is a definite 'yes.' Promissory estoppel as a legal theory is gaining in prominence as a device used by an increasing number of courts to provide a much needed remedy to alleviate the plight of those who suffer a serious injustice as a result of their good-faith reliance on the unfulfilled promises of others. As the Arkansas supreme court has so appropriately commented in *Peoples Nat'l Bank of Little Rock v. Linebarger Constr. Co.*, 219 Ark. 11, at 17, 240 S.W.2d 12, at 16, the law of promissory estoppel exhibits " ... an attempt by the courts to keep remedies abreast of increased moral consciousness of honesty and fair representations in all business dealings...." We subscribe to those sentiments.

The plaintiff's appeal is denied and dismissed and the judgment appealed from is affirmed.

Exercise 4-6: *Valley Bank v. Dowdy*

The final case in this section provides you with another example of a simple secured transaction involving a motor vehicle and further illustrates the workings of the promissory estoppel doctrine. As you read *Dowdy*, consider the following questions:

1. What are the key facts?

2. The court concludes that Dowdy was not entitled to recover the costs incurred repairing the truck. Why?

3. How does the theory of detrimental reliance described by the court relate to section 90(1) of the RESTATEMENT (SECOND) OF CONTRACTS? (Hint: It is in substance a different way of expressing some of the elements of section 90(1).)

Valley Bank v. Dowdy

337 N.W.2d 164 (1983)

MORGAN, Justice.

This appeal arises from an action commenced by Valley Bank, appellant (Bank), for repossession of a tractor/trailer, pursuant to Larry Dowdy's, appellee (Dowdy), default on a promissory note. Trial court awarded Bank possession of the tractor/trailer but ordered Bank to pay Dowdy for repair costs to the tractor/trailer. Bank appeals from that portion of the judgment awarding repair costs to Dowdy ...

Bank is a commercial bank organized and operated under the laws of the state of Idaho. In June, 1981, Dowdy was employed by Weeks Brothers, Inc., an Idaho ranching corporation, which was a customer of Bank. Dowdy and Weeks Brothers agreed that Dowdy would purchase, for $16,000.00, the tractor/trailer then owned by Weeks Brothers. Bank agreed to finance the purchase, provided that Weeks Brothers would co-sign the note. On June 17, 1981, Dowdy and Weeks Brothers executed a promissory note and security agreement for $16,000.00. The note was to be paid by Dowdy in six months. Bank paid the $16,000.00 proceeds to Weeks Brothers but did not transfer the title to Dowdy. Title to the tractor/trailer was held at the bank in the name of Weeks Brothers, subject to all security interests of Bank. Dowdy had possession of the tractor/trailer from June 17, 1981, until trial. During this time, Dowdy maintained and repaired the truck, spending $4,658.98 for parts and claiming $2,000.00 for his labor. After approximately three months, Dowdy moved from Idaho to South Dakota bringing the truck with him. Dowdy did not make any payment on principal or interest and Bank brought suit for repossession of the tractor/trailer. Dowdy counterclaimed for the repairs on the [theory of] detrimental reliance and promissory estoppel ... seeking recovery of the $6,658.98 spent on maintenance and repairs. Trial was held on July 23, 1982, with the trial court ruling that Bank was entitled to possession but Dowdy was entitled to his repair costs based upon detrimental reliance and promissory estoppel.

Both parties appeal. Bank contends Dowdy was not entitled to repair costs under the equitable theories of detrimental reliance and promissory estoppel. Dowdy contends that if he was not entitled to equitable relief he was entitled to repair costs under a possessory mechanic's lien ...

We first examine the propriety of the trial court's judgment in favor of Dowdy for repairs to the truck on the theory of detrimental reliance and promissory estoppel. Detrimental reliance is an equitable relief emanating from equitable estoppel. J. Murray, *Law of Contracts,* §91 at 195–97 (2d ed. 1974). When cases first appeared involving agreements lacking the element of consideration and the promisee reasonably relied upon a promise to his detriment, courts held the detrimental reliance substituted for the consideration and enforced the contract under equitable estoppel.[1] Equitable estoppel, however, was not quite the appropriate theory since it refers to a situation "in which a party made a false representation to, or knowingly concealed material facts from, another party with the intention that the innocent party should act upon the false representation or concealment." *Id.,* §91 at 196–97. Courts then subsequently developed the broader theory of detrimental reliance, which is usually referred to as the doctrine of promissory estoppel. *Id.;* Simpson, *Contracts,* §61 at 112-19 (2d ed. 1965). *See also* Henderson, *Promissory Estoppel and Traditional Contract Doctrine,* 78 Yale L.J. 343, 376 (1969).

> *Here the court provides a concise and useful account of the promissory estoppel doctrine.*

This court in *Northwest Engineering Co. v. Ellerman,* 69 S.D. 397, 10 N.W.2d 879 (1943), adopted the doctrine of promissory estoppel as stated in Restatement of the Law of Contracts §90. As revised by the Restatement (Second) of Contracts §90, the doctrine of promissory estoppel provides:

> A promise which the promisor should reasonably expect to induce action or forbearance on the part of the promisee or a third person and which does induce such action or forbearance is binding if injustice can be avoided only by enforcement of the promise. The remedy granted for breach may be limited as justice requires.

[Citations omitted].

We now examine whether Dowdy established the elements of the theory of detrimental reliance by clear and convincing evidence. *Cromwell v. Hosbrook,* 81 S.D. 324, 134 N.W.2d 777 (1965). Our standard of review is whether the evidence is sufficient to support the trial court's conclusions that based upon these theories Dowdy was entitled to repair costs. In our opinion the trial court erred.

The crux of the trial court's decision rests on certain findings of fact which can be summarized as follows:

> Bank promised that it would transfer title to Dowdy.

> Bank did not arrange for transfer of title from Weeks Brothers Inc. to Dowdy.

> Bank never transferred title to Dowdy.

> When Dowdy concluded Bank had not and was not going to transfer title he thereafter refused to make additional repairs or improvements to the truck; refused to return the truck to the Bank, or to pay the note.

> Dowdy reasonably believed title to the motor vehicle would be transferred by Bank.

---

1. One of the best known cases regarding the development of this doctrine is *Ricketts v. Scothorn,* 57 Neb. 51, 77 N.W. 365 (1898), in which a court enforced a grandfather's promise of $2,000.00 to his granddaughter in return for her leaving her employment.

Dowdy reasonably relied on Bank's promise, making improvements and expenditures in the amount of $6,658.98.

The improvements were to the detriment of Dowdy and would not have been made if he had known the Bank would not perform.

From these findings of fact the trial court concluded, as a matter of law:

The Bank voluntarily assumed the duty of properly transferring title to Dowdy, subject only to Bank's security interest.

The detrimental reliance of Dowdy upon the Bank's promise serves as consideration for promise of the Bank to transfer title.

To refuse enforcement of obligation created by Bank's promise would cause injustice because Dowdy would not receive the benefit of his bargain with Bank.

Our disagreement with the trial court comes from the fact that on the entire record we can find no detriment to Dowdy arising from the failure of Bank to require Weeks Brothers to assign the title to Dowdy. Under Idaho law, where this transaction took place, as under South Dakota law [citation omitted] the first lienholder is entitled to retain the title in its possession. Dowdy was not entitled to receive that motor vehicle title until he had paid the amount due on the loan to Bank, which he never did or attempted to do. Dowdy had the beneficial use of the vehicle during the period of the time of the loan regardless of the names on the title. What possible detriment did he suffer? Of course, Dowdy has lost the $6,658.98 that he says went into repairs; however, he is out that amount because he did not pay the amount due on the note. Had Dowdy tendered payment of the promissory note and had Bank then been unable to deliver to him a properly assigned title he would have had a valid claim for detrimental reliance. Under the present circumstances, Dowdy simply does not. In the ancient maxim of equity jurisprudence, Dowdy does not come into court with clean hands.

...

All the Justices concur.

Promissory Estoppel as a Substitute for a Required Writing

As you will learn in Chapter 5, courts will not enforce certain types of contracts unless they are in writing and signed. Statutes which require signed writings are called "statutes of fraud." Promissory estoppel has made inroads into this body of law by providing a mechanism to enforce promises that do not comply with signed writing requirements.

Exercise 4-7: Promissory Estoppel and Statutes of Fraud

Read section 139 of the RESTATEMENT (SECOND) OF CONTRACTS and then analyze the following problem: Mike orally agreed with Elizabeth to buy HannahAcre, a vacant tract of land, for $500,000 due six months after he takes possession.

To be enforceable, a statute of frauds requires this type of agreement to be in a signed writing. Mike takes possession, builds a house on HannahAcre, and signs a $500,000 promissory note. If Elizabeth refuses to perform, asserting the statute of frauds, will Mike succeed with a promissory estoppel argument?

Promissory Estoppel as a Mechanism for Making Certain Offers Irrevocable

Exercise 4-8: *Drennan v. Star Paving Co.*

Before you read the next case, *Drennan v. Star Paving Co.*, it may be helpful to re-read the discussion of large-scale construction contracts in Chapter 2 (under the section entitled "Requests for Bids"). *Drennan* is authored by Roger Traynor, one of the most respected jurists of his generation. *Drennan* takes the promissory estoppel doctrine one step further than you have already seen: it uses promissory estoppel as an alternative way to make an offer irrevocable. As you read *Drennan*, consider the following:

1. The *Drennan* court notes that the trial court concluded that Star Paving made an offer. Why do you think the trial court reached this conclusion?

2. What is the normal rule as to when offers can be revoked? If the court had applied the normal rule to the facts of this case, what would have been the result?

3. Was there any basis for the court to conclude that the parties created an option contract?

4. Why, then, did the court conclude that the offer was irrevocable? Identify the rule the court relied on and how the court applied that rule to the facts.

5. Why did the court focus on whether Star Paving's offer was irrevocable as opposed to whether the offer was accepted by Drennan's use of the offer in calculating its bid?

Drennan v. Star Paving Co.

51 Cal. 2d 409, 333 P.2d 757 (1958)

Traynor, J. Defendant appeals from a judgment for plaintiff in an action to recover damages caused by defendant's refusal to perform certain paving work according to a bid it submitted to plaintiff.

On July 28, 1955, plaintiff, a licensed general contractor, was preparing a bid on the "Monte Vista School Job" in the Lancaster school district. Bids had to be submitted before 8 p.m. Plaintiff testified that it was customary in that area for general contractors to receive the bids of subcontractors by telephone on the day set for bidding and to rely on them in computing their own bids. Thus on that day plaintiff's secretary, Mrs. Johnson, received by telephone between 50 and 75 subcontractors' bids for various parts of the school job. As each bid came in, she wrote it on a special form, which she brought into plaintiff's office. He then posted it on a master cost sheet setting forth the names and bids of all subcontractors. His own bid had to include the names of subcontractors who were to perform one-half of one per cent or more of the construction work, and he had also to provide a bidder's bond of 10 per cent of his total bid of $317,385 as a guarantee that he would enter the contract if awarded the work.

Late in the afternoon, Mrs. Johnson had a telephone conversation with Kenneth R. Hoon, an estimator for defendant. He gave his name and telephone number and stated that he was bidding for defendant for the paving work at the Monte Vista School according to plans and specifications and that his bid was $7,131.60. At Mrs. Johnson's request he repeated his bid. Plaintiff listened to the bid over an extension telephone in his office and posted it on the master sheet after receiving the bid form from Mrs. Johnson. Defendant's was the lowest bid for the paving. Plaintiff computed his own bid accordingly and submitted it with the name of defendant as the subcontractor for the paving. When the bids were opened on July 28th, plaintiff's proved to be the lowest, and he was awarded the contract.

On his way to Los Angeles the next morning plaintiff stopped at defendant's office. The first person he met was defendant's construction engineer, Mr. Oppenheimer. Plaintiff testified: "I introduced myself and he immediately told me that they had made a mistake in their bid to me the night before, they couldn't do it for the price they had bid, and I told him I would expect him to carry through with their original bid because I had used it in compiling my bid and the job was being awarded them. And I would have to go and do the job according to my bid and I would expect them to do the same."

In an omitted portion of the court's opinion, the court rejected the defendant's argument based on unilateral mistake. We will revisit this case in Chapter 5 to consider the unilateral mistake issue.

Defendant refused to do the paving work for less than $15,000. Plaintiff testified that he "got figures from other people" and after trying for several months to get as low a bid as possible engaged L & H Paving Company, a firm in Lancaster, to do the work for $10,948.60.

The trial court found on substantial evidence that defendant made a definite offer to do the paving on the Monte Vista job according to the plans and specifications for $7,131.60, and that plaintiff relied on defendant's bid in computing his own bid for the school job and naming defendant therein as the subcontractor for the paving work. Accordingly, it entered judgment for plaintiff in the amount of $3,817 (the difference between defendant's bid and the cost of the paving to plaintiff) plus costs.

Defendant contends that there was no enforceable contract between the parties on the ground that it made a revocable offer and revoked it before plaintiff communicated his acceptance to defendant.

There is no evidence that defendant offered to make its bid irrevocable in exchange for plaintiff's use of its figures in computing his bid. Nor is there evidence that would warrant interpreting plaintiff's use of defendant's bid as the acceptance thereof, binding plaintiff, on condition he received the main contract, to award the subcontract to defendant. In sum, there was neither an option supported by consideration nor a bilateral contract binding on both parties.

Justice Traynor starts by rejecting alternative theories for making the defendant's promise binding.

Plaintiff contends, however, that he relied to his detriment on defendant's offer and that defendant must therefore answer in damages for its refusal to perform. Thus the question is squarely presented: Did plaintiff's reliance make defendant's offer irrevocable?

Section 90 of the RESTATEMENT OF CONTRACTS states: "A promise which the promisor should reasonably expect to induce action or forbearance of a definite and substantial character on the part of the promisee and which does induce such action or forbearance is binding if injustice can be avoided only by enforcement of the promise." This rule applies in this state. [Citations omitted.]

Defendant's offer constituted a promise to perform on such conditions as were stated expressly or by implication therein or annexed thereto by operation of law. *See* 1 WILLISTON, CONTRACTS [3d ed.], § 24A, p. 56, § 61, p. 196. Defendant had reason to expect that if its bid proved the lowest, it would be used by plaintiff. It induced "action ... of a definite and substantial character on the part of the promisee."

Had defendant's bid expressly stated or clearly implied that it was revocable at any time before acceptance, we would treat it accordingly. It was silent on revocation, however, and we must therefore determine whether there are conditions to the right of revocation imposed by law or reasonably inferable in fact. In the analogous problem of an offer for a unilateral contract, the theory is now obsolete that the offer is revocable at any time before complete performance. Thus section 45 of the RESTATEMENT OF CONTRACTS provides: "If an offer for a unilateral contract is made, and part of the consideration requested in the offer is given or tendered by the offeree in response thereto, the offeror is bound by a contract, the duty of immediate performance of which is conditional on the full consideration being given or tendered within the time stated in the offer, or, if no time is stated therein, within a reasonable time." In explanation, comment b states that the "main offer includes as a subsidiary promise, necessarily implied, that if part of the requested performance is given, the offeror will not revoke his offer, and that if tender is made it will be accepted. Part performance or tender may thus furnish consideration for the subsidiary promise. Moreover, merely acting in justifiable reliance on an offer may in some cases serve as sufficient reason for making a promise binding (*see* § 90)."

Whether implied in fact or law, the subsidiary promise serves to preclude the injustice that would result if the offer could be revoked after the offeree had acted in detrimental reliance thereon. Reasonable reliance resulting in a foreseeable prejudicial change in position affords a compelling basis also for implying a subsidiary promise not to revoke an offer for a bilateral contract.

The absence of consideration is not fatal to the enforcement of such a promise. It is true that in the case of unilateral contracts the Restatement finds consideration for the implied subsidiary promise in the part performance of the bargained-for exchange, but its reference to section 90 makes clear that consideration for such a promise is not always necessary. The very purpose of section 90 is to make a promise binding even though there was no consideration "in the sense of something that is bargained for and given in exchange." *See* 1 CORBIN, CONTRACTS 634 et seq. Reasonable reliance serves to hold the offeror in lieu of the consideration ordinarily required to make the offer binding. . . .

When plaintiff used defendant's offer in computing his own bid, he bound himself to perform in reliance on defendant's terms. Though defendant did not bargain for this use of its bid neither did defendant make it idly, indifferent to whether it would be used or not. On the contrary, it is reasonable to suppose that defendant submitted its bid to obtain the subcontract. It was bound to realize the substantial possibility that its bid would be the lowest, and that it would be included by plaintiff in his bid. It was to its own interest that the contractor be awarded the general contract; the lower the subcontract bid, the lower the general contractor's bid was likely to be and the greater its chance of acceptance and hence the greater defendant's chance of getting the paving subcontract. Defendant had reason not only to expect plaintiff to rely on its bid but to want him to. Clearly defendant had a stake in plaintiff's reliance on its bid. Given this interest and the fact that plaintiff is bound by his own bid, it is only fair that plaintiff should have at least an opportunity to accept defendant's bid after the general contract has been awarded to him. . . .

The judgment is affirmed.

Exercise 4-9: *Drennan* Revisited

1. Assume the same facts as in *Drennan*, except that the general contractor hired a different subcontractor after using the first subcontractor's bid in calculating the bid to the owner. Could the first subcontractor sue the general contractor for breach?

2. You are sent by your firm to take part in a "beauty parade" at a large electrical subcontracting company that is looking to hire new outside counsel to help manage its bid processes. The company has asked that all participating firms make a presentation outlining what they can do to help it to manage risks arising from the submission of bids to general contractors. What would be the key points in your presentation?

Promissory Estoppel as a Mechanism for Policing Unfair Bargaining Behavior

Exercise 4-10: *Hoffman v. Red Owl Stores, Inc.*

The next case, *Hoffman v. Red Owl Stores, Inc.*, represents a further extension of promissory estoppel. In *Hoffman*, promissory estoppel is applied to enforce a statement that is not even an offer. As you read the case, answer the following questions:

1. What promise formed the basis for the court applying promissory estoppel?

2. How did the court apply the elements of promissory estoppel to the facts?

Hoffman v. Red Owl Stores, Inc.

26 Wis.2d 683, 133 N.W.2d 267 (1965)

Action by Joseph Hoffman (hereinafter 'Hoffman') and wife, plaintiffs, against defendants Red Owl Stores, Inc. (hereinafter 'Red Owl') and Edward Lukowitz.

The complaint alleged that Lukowitz, as agent for Red Owl, represented to and agreed with plaintiffs that Red Owl would build a store building in Chilton and stock it with merchandise for Hoffman to operate in return for which plaintiffs were to put up and invest a total sum of $18,000; that in reliance upon the above mentioned agreement and representations plaintiffs sold their bakery building and business and their grocery store and business; also in reliance on the agreement and representations Hoffman purchased the building site in Chilton and rented a residence for himself and his family in Chilton; plaintiffs' actions in reliance on the representations and agreement disrupted their personal and business life; plaintiffs lost substantial amounts of income and expended large sums of money as expenses. Plaintiffs demanded recovery of damages for the breach of defendants' representations and agreements.

The action was tried to a court and jury. The facts hereafter stated are taken from the evidence adduced at the trial. Where there was a conflict in the evidence the version favorable to plaintiffs has been accepted since the verdict rendered was in favor of plaintiffs.

Hoffman assisted by his wife operated a bakery at Wautoma from 1956 until sale of the building late in 1961. The building was owned in joint tenancy by him and his wife. Red Owl is a Minnesota corporation having its home office at Hopkins, Minnesota. It owns and operates a number of grocery supermarket stores and also extends franchises to agency stores which are owned by individuals, partnerships and corporations. Lukowitz resides at Green Bay and since September, 1960, has been divisional manager for Red Owl in a territory comprising Upper Michigan and most of Wisconsin in charge of 84 stores. Prior to September, 1960, he was district manager having charge of approximately 20 stores.

In November, 1959, Hoffman was desirous of expanding his operations by establishing a grocery store and contacted a Red Owl representative by the name of Jansen, now deceased. Numerous conversations were had in 1960 with the idea of establishing a Red Owl franchise store in Wautoma. In September, 1960, Lukowitz succeeded Jansen as Red Owl's representative in the negotiations. Hoffman mentioned that $18,000 was all the capital he had available to invest and he was repeatedly assured that this would be sufficient to set him up in business as a Red Owl store. About Christmastime, 1960, Hoffman thought it would be a good idea if he bought a small grocery store in Wautoma and operated it in order that he gain experience in the grocery business prior to operating a Red Owl store in some larger community. On February 6, 1961, on the advice of Lukowitz and Sykes, who had succeeded Lukowitz as Red Owl's district manager, Hoffman bought the inventory and fixtures of a small grocery store in Wautoma and leased the building in which it was operated.

After three months of operating this Wautoma store, the Red Owl representatives came in and took inventory and checked the operations and found the store was operating at a profit. Lukowitz advised Hoffman to sell the store to his manager, and assured him that Red Owl would find a larger store from him elsewhere. Acting on this advice and assurance, Hoffman sold the fixtures and inventory to his manager on June 6, 1961. Hoffman was reluctant to sell at that time because it meant losing the summer tourist business, but he sold on the assurance that he would be operating in a new location by fall and that he must sell this store if he wanted a bigger one. Before selling, Hoffman told the Red Owl representatives that he had $18,000 for "getting set up in business" and they assured him that there would be no problems in establishing him in a bigger operation. The makeup of the $18,000 was not discussed; it was understood plaintiff's father-in-law would furnish part of it. By June, 1961, the towns for the new grocery store had been narrowed down to two, Kewaunee and Chilton. In Kewaunee, Red Owl had an option on a building site. In Chilton, Red Owl had nothing under option, but it did select a site to which plaintiff obtained an option at Red Owl's suggestion. The option stipulated a purchase price of $6,000 with $1,000 to be paid on election to purchase and the balance to be paid within 30 days. On Lukowitz's assurance that everything was all set plaintiff paid $1,000 down on the lot on September 15th.

On September 27, 1961, plaintiff met at Chilton with Lukowitz and Mr. Reymund and Mr. Carlson from the home office who prepared a projected financial statement. Part of the funds plaintiffs were to supply as their investment in the venture were to be obtained by sale of their Wautoma bakery building.

On the basis of this meeting, Lukowitz assured Hoffman: "… [E]verything is ready to go. Get your money together and we are set." Shortly after this meeting Lukowitz told plaintiffs that they would have to sell their bakery business and bakery building, and that their retaining this property was the only 'hitch' in the entire plan. On November 6, 1961, plaintiffs sold their bakery building for $10,000. Hoffman was to retain the bakery equipment as he contemplated using it to operate a bakery in connection with his Red Owl store. After sale of the bakery Hoffman obtained employment on the night shift at an Appleton bakery.

The record contains different exhibits which were prepared in September and October, some of which were projections of the fiscal operation of the business and others were proposed building and floor plans. Red Owl was to procure some third party to buy the Chilton lot from Hoffman, construct the building, and then lease it to Hoffman. No final plans were ever made, nor were bids let or a construction contract entered. Some time prior to November 20, 1961, certain of the terms of the lease under which the building was to be rented by Hoffman were understood between him and Lukowitz. The lease was to be for 10 years with a rental approximating $550 a month calculated on the basis of 1 percent per month on the building cost, plus 6 percent of the land cost divided on a monthly basis. At the end of the 10-year term he was to have an option to renew the lease for an additional 10-year period or to buy the property at cost on an installment basis. There was no discussion as to what the installments would be or with respect to repairs and maintenance.

On November 22nd or 23rd, Lukowitz and plaintiffs met in Minneapolis with Red Owl's credit manager to confer on Hoffman's financial standing and on financing the agency. Another projected financial statement was there drawn up entitled, "Proposed Financing For An Agency Store." This showed Hoffman contributing $24,100 of cash capital of which only $4,600 was to be cash possessed by plaintiffs. Eight thousand was to be procured as a loan from a Chilton bank secured by a mortgage on the bakery fixtures, $7,500 was to be obtained on a 5 percent loan from the father-in-law, and $4,000 was to be obtained by sale of the lot to the lessor at a profit.

A week or two after the Minneapolis meeting Lukowitz showed Hoffman a telegram from the home office to the effect that if plaintiff could get another $2,000 for promotional purposes the deal could go through for $26,000. Hoffman stated he would have to find out if he could get another $2,000. He met with his father-in-law, who agreed to put $13,000 into the business provided he could come into the business as a partner. Lukowitz told Hoffman the partnership arrangement "sounds fine" and that Hoffman should not go into the partnership arrangement with the "front office." On January 16, 1962, the Red Owl credit manager teletyped Lukowitz that the father-in-law would have to sign an agreement that the $13,000 was either a gift or a loan subordinate to all general creditors and that he would prepare the agreement. On January 31, 1962, Lukowitz teletyped the home office that the father-in-law would sign one or other of the agreements. However, Hoffman testified that it was not until the final meeting some time between January 26th and February 2nd, 1962, that he was told that his father-in-law was expected to sign an agreement that the $13,000 he was advancing was to be an outright gift. No mention was then made by the Red Owl representatives of the alternative of the father-in-law signing a subordination agreement. At this meeting the Red Owl agents presented Hoffman with [a] projected financial statement [that indicated that Hoffman would require $62,000 for the "operation"].

Hoffman interpreted the ... statement to require of plaintiffs a total of $34,000 cash made up of $13,000 gift from his father-in-law, $2,000 on mortgage, $8,000 on Chilton bank loan, $5,000 in cash from plaintiff, and $6,000 on the resale of the Chilton lot. Red Owl claims $18,000 is the total of the unborrowed or unencumbered cash, that is, $13,000 from the father-in-law and $5,000 cash from Hoffman himself. Hoffman informed Red Owl he could not go along with this proposal, and particularly objected to the requirement that his father-in-law sign an agreement that his $13,000 advancement was an absolute gift. This terminated the negotiations between the parties.

The case was submitted to the jury on a special verdict with the first two questions answered by the court. This verdict, as returned by the jury, was as follows:

> Question No. 1: Did the Red Owl Stores, Inc. and Joseph Hoffman on or about mid-May of 1961 initiate negotiations looking to the establishment of Joseph Hoffman as a franchise operator of a Red Owl Store in Chilton? Answer: Yes. (Answered by the Court.)

> Question No. 2: Did the parties mutually agree on all of the details of the proposal so as to reach a final agreement thereon? Answer: No. (Answered by the Court.)

It is common for jury verdicts to take the form of a series of questions and answers. Other times, though, jury verdicts just state which party wins and, if applicable, the amount of damages.

Question No. 3: Did the Red Owl Stores, Inc., in the course of said negotiations, make representations to Joseph Hoffman that if he fulfilled certain conditions that they would establish him as franchise operator of a Red Owl Store in Chilton? Answer: Yes.

Question No. 4: If you have answered Question No. 3 'Yes,' then answer this question: Did Joseph Hoffman rely on said representations and was he induced to act thereon? Answer: Yes.

Question No. 5: If you have answered Question No. 4 'Yes,' then answer this question: Ought Joseph Hoffman, in the exercise of ordinary care, to have relied on said representations? Answer: Yes.

Question No. 6: If you have answered Question No. 3 'Yes' then answer this question: Did Joseph Hoffman fulfill all the conditions he was required to fulfill by the terms of the negotiations between the parties up to January 26, 1962? Answer: Yes....

The instant appeal and cross-appeal present these questions: (1) Whether this court should recognize causes of action grounded on promissory estoppel as exemplified by sec. 90 of the RESTATEMENT OF CONTRACTS? and (2) Do the facts in this case make out a cause of action for promissory estoppel? ...

Recognition of a Cause of Action Grounded on Promissory Estoppel

Sec. 90 of the RESTATEMENT OF CONTRACTS, provides (at p. 110):

A promise which the promisor should reasonably expect to induce action or forbearance of a definite and substantial character on the part of the promisee and which does induce such action of forbearance is binding if injustice can be avoided only by enforcement of the promise....

Many courts of other jurisdictions have seen fit over the years to adopt the principle of promissory estoppel, and the tendency in that direction continues.... [T]he development of the law of promissory estoppel "is an attempt by the courts to keep remedies abreast of increased moral consciousness of honesty and fair representations in all business dealings." [Citation omitted.] ...

Because we deem the doctrine of promissory estoppel, as stated in sec. 90 of the RESTATEMENT OF CONTRACTS, is one which supplies a needed tool which courts may employ in a proper case to prevent injustice, we endorse and adopt it.

Applicability of Doctrine to Facts of this Case

The record here discloses a number of promises and assurances given to Hoffman by Lukowitz in behalf of Red Owl upon which plaintiffs relied and acted upon to their detriment.

Foremost were the promises that for the sum of $18,000 Red Owl would establish Hoffman in a store. After Hoffman had sold his grocery store and paid the $1,000 on the Chilton lot, the $18,000 figure was changed to $24,100. Then in November, 1961, Hoffman was assured that if the $24,100 figure were increased by $2,000 the deal would go through. Hoffman was induced to sell his grocery store fixtures and inventory in June, 1961, on the promise that he would be in his new store by fall. In November, plaintiffs sold their bakery building on the urging of defendants and on the assurance that this was the last step necessary to have the deal with Red Owl go through.

We determine that there was ample evidence to sustain the answers of the jury to the questions of the verdict with respect to the promissory representations made by Red Owl, Hoffman's reliance thereon in the exercise of ordinary care, and his fulfillment of the conditions required of him by the terms of the negotiations had with Red Owl.

There remains for consideration the question of law raised by defendants that agreement was never reached on essential factors necessary to establish a contract between Hoffman and Red Owl. Among these were the size, cost, design, and layout of the store building; and the terms of the lease with respect to rent, maintenance, renewal, and purchase options. This poses the question of whether the promise necessary to sustain a cause of action for promissory estoppel must embrace all essential details of a proposed transaction between promisor and promisee so as to be the equivalent of an offer that would result in a binding contract between the parties if the promisee were to accept the same.

Originally the doctrine of promissory estoppel was invoked as a substitute for consideration rendering a gratuitous promise enforceable as a contract. *See* WILLISTON, CONTRACTS (1st ed.), p. 307, sec. 139. In other words, the acts of reliance by the promisee to his detriment provided a substitute for consideration. If promissory estoppel were to be limited to only those situations where the promise giving rise to the cause of action must be so definite with respect to all details that a contract would result were the promise supported by consideration, then the defendants' instant promises to Hoffman would not meet this test. However, see section 90 of the RESTATEMENT OF CONTRACTS, does not impose the requirement that the promise giving rise to the cause of action must be so comprehensive in scope as to meet the requirements of an offer that would ripen into a contract if accepted by the promisee. Rather the conditions imposed are:

(1) Was the promise one which the promisor should reasonably expect to induce action or forbearance of a definite and substantial character on the part of the promisee?

(2) Did the promise induce such action or forbearance?

(3) Can injustice be avoided only by enforcement of the promise?

We deem it would be a mistake to regard an action grounded on promissory estoppel as the equivalent of a breach of contract action.... While the first two of the above listed three requirements of promissory estoppel present issues of fact which ordinarily will be resolved by a jury, the third requirement, that the remedy can only be invoked where necessary to avoid injustice, is one that involves a policy decision by the court. Such a policy decision necessarily embraces an element of discretion.

In an omitted portion of this opinion, the court addresses the measure of plaintiff's damages. In Chapter 6, you will learn about damages and revisit this case.

We conclude that injustice would result here if plaintiffs were not granted some relief because of the failure of defendants to keep their promises which induced plaintiffs to act to their detriment....

Order affirmed. Because of the cross-appeal, plaintiffs shall be limited to taxing but two-thirds of their costs.

Chapter Problem Revisited

Exercise 4-1 presented three exam-like problems for you to consider while you learned the material in this chapter. You now know enough to fully analyze those problems. Below are some recommendations to help you analyze the Exercise 4-1 problems.[2]

1. We encourage you to work with peers as you complete the exam questions. First, try to answer the questions on your own. Then, compare your answers with your peers' answers.

2. Begin each question by reading the call of the question so that you will focus on the task or question presented.

3. You should notice that the second question is dramatically different from the first and third questions because it asks you to only analyze the law from a policy standpoint. You are not asked to apply the law to a factual situation.

4. Just as we have encouraged you to actively read this text, try to actively read the problems.

5. In exam questions, it is common for all or almost all of the stated facts to be important. Therefore, don't simply highlight facts you think are important because you are likely to highlight most of the facts (and thus be no further along than when you started reading the question). To a large extent, law school exams test how well you *use* the facts presented. Accordingly, next to each fact try to write comments about why the fact is legally significant. For example, Table 4-4 lists facts from the first paragraph in Table 4-1 and indicates why those facts are legally significant.

Table 4-4: Facts and Their Legal Significance

Facts	Legal Significance (Matching Rules)
"Will buy" "Give preferential treatment to written answers" Signed writing Hand-delivered	Mutual assent: Offers
Quantity (single item, *Wedgewood Blues*) Time for performance (July 30) Parties (P and D) Price ($200,000) Subject (screenplay)	Certainty

6. It is crucial that you organize your essay. There are many effective ways to organize your essays, although some ways are simply wrong. As a general rule, it works well to organize by keeping the parties, claims, and legal issues separate.

7. Use non-legal writing conventions that make writing reader-friendly. For example, use introductory paragraphs, headings, and transitions to help your reader follow your substance. It is helpful to start your essays with an introduc-

---

2. For a more thorough discussion of exam writing, see Michael Hunter Schwartz, Expert Learning for Law Students, Chapters 15 and 16 (Carolina Academic Press 2008).

tory paragraph that connects to the call of the question (*e.g., "The question presented is whether the Plaintiff and Defendant formed a contract."*).

8. Populate your answers with IRAC paragraphs for each narrow legal issue. For each narrow legal issue, explicitly state the issue and the applicable rule. Then, apply the rules to the facts presented. Specifically, your task is to explain the significance of each fact by drawing inferences from the fact and linking those inferences to the requirements of the applicable rule.

9. For the first and second essays, give yourself unlimited time and focus on creating excellent essays. For the third essay, limit your time to one and one-half hours.

Professional Development Reflection Questions

1. Take a moment to step back and consider what the "law" is and why law matters to our society. For example, what is the purpose of contract law? What would be the impact on society if we didn't have contract law?

2. We—the authors of this text as well as legal educators and legal professionals—have a special responsibility to prepare you as future professionals "with enough understanding, skill and judgment to support the vast and complicated system of the law needed to sustain the United States as a free society."[3] A recent text written by a group of respected legal educators and published by the Carnegie Foundation, Educating Lawyers: Preparation for the Profession of Law (2007), asserts that "There is a compelling need to change legal education in the United States in significant ways. Law schools are doing some things well, but they do some things poorly or not at all."[4] Take a few minutes to think about what the strengths of your legal education have been thus far. What have been the weaknesses? How well do you think legal education is working?

3. Educating Lawyers proposes a three-part model of effective professional development, including learning to (1) think like a lawyer (knowledge); (2) perform like a lawyer (skills); and (3) behave like a lawyer (professional identity and professionalism). Identify at least two ways you can focus on each of the three components during the next month to enhance your development as a legal professional.

4. Paula has consulted you about representing her in a contract lawsuit against Devin. Paula alleges that David breached their contract. You have conducted a preliminary review of the case and believe that Paula has a strong case and will likely prevail with a promissory estoppel argument. Paula would like to retain you and would like to know how you will bill her for your services. What type of fee agreement will you offer for your services?

---

3. Sullivan et al., Educating Lawyers: Preparation for the Profession of Law (2007)
4. *Id.*

PART THREE

CONTRACT DEFENSES
Can either party get out of the deal?

Chapter 5

Contract Defenses

Chapter Problems

For this chapter, you are provided with two introductory problems. Both problems present contract defense issues similar to ones you may be asked to analyze on law school exams or in legal practice. In the first problem, you are asked to conduct a case evaluation. The second problem asks you to prepare to interview a client and provide legal advice. You should be able to analyze both problems by the time you complete this chapter.

Exercise 5-1: Case Evaluation

Two months ago, Elizabeth test-drove a car. While examining the car, she noticed a piece of paper in the glove compartment dated six months earlier. The paper reflected minor repairs done on the car and listed the name of the owner of the car as "Stacy Landon." Elizabeth exclaimed, "I cannot believe this car was owned by Stacy Landon!" Assume that Stacey (with an "e") Landon is a famous actress whereas Stacy (without an "e") Landon is an unknown tax accountant. Responding to Elizabeth, the car salesman nodded his head and enthusiastically said, "Yes!"

Elizabeth and the salesman then quickly entered into a contract to buy and sell the car for $10,000. Elizabeth thought the car would only be worth $8,000 if it had not been owned by a famous person. Elizabeth paid the $10,000 and drove the car home.

Two months after Elizabeth's purchase, she discovered the truth about the identity of the previous owner. Elizabeth has hired you to analyze her case. Consider what legal issues the case presents and the applicable rules. Then, analyze whether a lawsuit would succeed and whether it would make sense to pursue this claim. When doing so, also consider whether you need any additional information to accurately analyze the case.

Exercise 5-2: Client Interview and Advice

Table 5-1 presents an inter-office memorandum that you, a law firm associate, received from your supervising partner about a new client. Read the memorandum and prepare to conduct a client interview and to give your client legal advice. The information presented in this chapter will help you do so.

Table 5-1: Inter-Office Memorandum

SERVUM & WELL

Memorandum

Date: November 13
To: Associate
From: Senior Partner Amy Servum
Subject: Plymouth Shipping Supply Co., # 1125-1-3

I spoke on the phone today with a new client, Stacey Plymouth, the owner of Plymouth Supply Company. She contacted me about the possibility of Servum & Well representing her in a lawsuit against the state. She entered into a contract with the state a few months ago and now wants to get out of the contract. She asserts she and the state entered into the contract based on an error as to the nature of what the state was selling and she was buying.

During our conversation, Ms. Plymouth told me the following information. Plymouth buys and sells used government property, primarily property used by shipping companies. Plymouth makes hundreds of contracts every year with the government to buy such property, and makes hundreds of contracts every year to re-sell that property to other businesses.

Ms. Plymouth says this dispute is her first with the government. She said she mistakenly understood she was getting one type of net used in shipping and actually received a different type of net that was worth much less.

Be prepared to interview Ms. Plymouth at her appointment at the end of this week. To prepare for your interview, consider the legal issues raised and applicable rules as well as what additional information you need to evaluate the case. Also be prepared to objectively analyze the case and provide Ms. Plymouth with your advice. She faxed me the two documents attached to this memorandum; make sure you review them before you meet with her.

The following document is an excerpt from the October issue of *Shipping International*, a trade magazine for the international shipping industry catering to shipowners, builders, and operators.

> **For Sale by the State Government of California**
> Items 65 through 83:
>
> 180 Nets, Cargo, 20' × 40', Manila rope, Used.
>
> **WARNING: Read the "General Sale Terms and Conditions"**
> **document available where the property is stored at the**
> **California State Warehouse located at 2520 State Street,**
> **Sacramento, CA 94205.**

The following is an excerpt (paragraph 6) from the "General Sales Terms and Conditions" document available at the California State Warehouse located at 2520 State Street, Sacramento, CA 94205.

General Sales Terms and Conditions

6.   Bidders should inspect the property carefully before buying it. The California State Government based the descriptions in the advertisement on the best available information, but much of the property has been in storage for years so that not all of the information in the advertisement is certain.

Introduction to Contract Defenses

This chapter is your first major change of topics in your study of contracts. In the previous chapters, you learned about contract formation—that is, how parties get into contracts. In this chapter, you will learn about a range of **contract defenses** that, if established, enable parties to get out of contracts. Some of the defenses discussed in this chapter allow parties to get out of contracts on the theory that the parties did not truly assent, for example, because one party was induced to make the contract by deception or duress, or because both parties were laboring under a fundamentally mistaken apprehension about the subject matter of the deal. Other defenses discussed in this chapter allow parties to get out of contracts on the rationale that the terms are fundamentally unfair or undesirable from a public policy perspective. The common thread is that there is some legally cognizable ground to doubt that the parties gave their voluntary and fully informed consent to the deal in question.

As you already recognize, contracts facilitate the movement of goods, money, services, and other forms of wealth among members of our society. They also, however, limit contracting parties' freedom of action. In most cases, the choice to bind oneself by contract is voluntarily and knowingly made. Therefore, we as a society (and courts) do not object to this restriction of freedom.

In some cases, though, it doesn't seem fair to restrict parties' freedom by contract. For example, what if someone uses a loaded gun to force another person to sign a contract or if someone lies to another person to induce the other to sign a contract? In the first situation, it does not appear that the victim made the contract voluntarily. In the latter situation, it does not appear that the victim made the contract knowingly. If either of the victims were sued for breach of contract, it would seem fair to allow them to assert contract defenses and avoid enforcement of the contracts. Alternatively, it would seem fair to allow the victims to rescind (undo) their contracts.

In many other cases, parties want out of their contracts. This desire to get out of contracts happens frequently enough that our culture has developed the phrases "buyers' remorse" and "sellers' remorse" to capture the sentiment. When parties enter into bargains that, with hindsight, don't turn out to be good deals, they feel remorse. If I agree to buy a car for $20,000 and a few days later I discover I could have bought the exact same make and model in the exact same condition for $15,000 from another seller, I may well feel remorse about the contract I made. In such a state of remorse, parties are tempted to say anything to try to get out of their contracts. Courts therefore have to tread carefully and, as a rule of thumb, they are not very receptive to parties' attempts to assert defenses as a way to avoid contractual obligations. As you learned in Chapter 1, enforcing contracts promotes some important public policy rationales such as predictability and freedom of contract. Indeed, long ago courts adopted a Latin phrase, *pacta sunt servanda*, which means "agreements are to be observed" to express the position that contracts should generally be enforced.

As you read this chapter, you will see tension between these public policy rationales — predictability and freedom of contract on the one hand, and the fairness concerns underlying contract defenses on the other. As you read the cases and materials in this chapter, watch how these rationales come into play.

Diagram 5-1, the Contract Law Graphic Organizer, depicts where contract defenses fit within the big picture of contract law. Take a moment to look where "Contract Defenses" are listed on the diagram. Also look at the defenses listed in the boxes under "Contract Defenses." You will see that there are many defenses. You should also notice that two categories, "Deception" and "Mistake," contain multiple defenses. It would be atypical for any law school exam question or client situation to raise all of the contract defenses. Accordingly, as you read this chapter it is important to learn the facts which give rise to each of the defenses. You will also need to be able to readily recall the defenses. The problems in this chapter will help you accomplish both tasks.

Overview of Chapter 5

In this chapter, you will learn about each contract defense depicted in Diagram 5-1. You will first learn about the multiple defenses categorized as deception. You will then proceed to learn about mistake and the other contract defenses. You will learn about each defense separately, but you should note the similarities and differences among the defenses as you learn about each one.

Deception

This section discusses the first contract defense listed in Diagram 5-1: **deception**.

Exercise 5-3: Deception Example

Imagine a client, Bob Buyer, comes to you with the following problem: Two weeks ago, Bob purchased a used car from Sally Seller. Bob liked the car because

Diagram 5-1: Contract Law Graphic Organizer

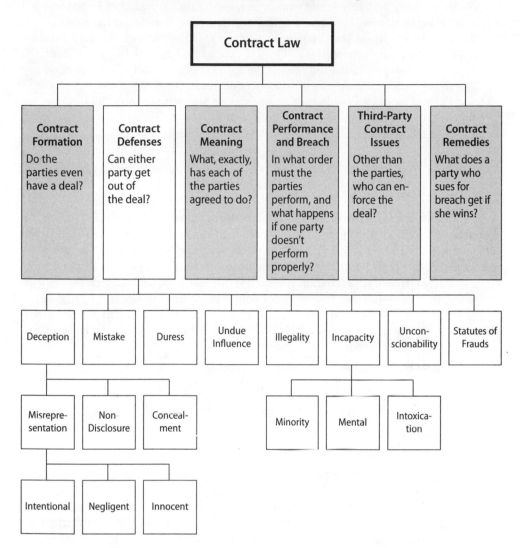

it had low mileage and appeared to be in good condition. Sally was asking what Bob determined to be a fair price, $6,000. Bob and Sally agreed that Bob would pay Sally three weeks after delivery of the car. During negotiations, Sally showed Bob documents indicating she was the original owner of the car and truthfully told Bob that she was the only person who ever drove the car. Sally also told Bob that the car had never been in a car accident. The car had actually been in two major car accidents, a fact that Bob discovered two days ago when he took the car to his mechanic. Because of the accidents, Bob's mechanic said the car is only worth $4,000. Bob returned the car to Sally and told her he is unwilling to buy it. Sally threatened to sue Bob for breach of contract. Bob has asked you whether Sally is likely to win her lawsuit.

In Exercise 5-3, it is likely that Sally would lose her lawsuit. Bob will likely be able to successfully assert misrepresentation as a defense. If, however, the facts were different, Bob might not be able to successfully assert misrepresentation as a defense. For example, if the car had only grazed a bicycle on each of the two occasions, Sally probably would win. In fact, even if the car had been in two significant accidents but the accidents had not significantly reduced the value of the car, and if Sally had not lied but had simply failed to mention the accidents to Bob, Sally probably would win. Or, if the car had a large, highly visible dent at the time Bob purchased the car so that it was obvious that the car had been in a major accident, Sally might win. Why do you think Bob's misrepresentation defense would probably succeed in Exercise 5-3, but probably fail in these alternative scenarios?

Misrepresentation

This section discusses the first deception defense depicted in Diagram 5-1, **misrepresentation.** Misrepresentation law can be a little difficult to pin down because courts in different states use a bewildering array of terminology to capture the same concepts. You will learn that a misrepresentation can be intentional (fraudulent) or unintentional (negligent or innocent). But courts nationwide do not necessarily express the elements of misrepresentation in consistent and uniform language. What follows is our attempt to synthesize the law of misrepresentation at a high level of generality and to provide a simplified yet representative framework that is designed to help you grasp the basics. Generally speaking, misrepresentation has **five elements:**

1.   **A false statement of fact, intention, or opinion;**
2.   **Addressing a fact, intention or opinion material to the contract;**
3.   **Made with the requisite state of mind (intentional, negligent or innocent);**
4.   **Actually and justifiably relied on by the other party; and**
5.   **Caused damage to the other party.**

There are cases in which the party trying to get out of the contract will not need to establish all of these elements. If the misrepresentation is intentional (element 3), it is not usually necessary to establish that the misrepresentation was material (element 2). However, where the misrepresentation is unintentional (negligent or innocent) then all the elements, including the requirement of materiality, will need to be made out. Thus, for example, section 162 of the Restatement (Second) of Contracts distinguishes between "fraudulent" and "material" misrepresentation and Comment a. to that section asserts that a fraudulent (mis)representation is actionable even if it is not material.

Before you even started law school, you already knew a considerable amount of information about these elements. Below, you will learn what each element means in the legal context. Each element is explained in detail and many examples are provided. Then, you will read a case, *Cousineau v. Walker,* in which several of the elements are at issue so that you can get a feel for how courts apply the elements.

1. False Statements of Fact, Intentions, and Opinions

Categorizing a statement as false and as either a fact, an intention, or an opinion makes a difference to your legal analysis. "**False**" means untrue, inaccurate, or erroneous. A "**fact**" is something that exists or occurs. An "**intention**" is a determination to act in a certain way in the future. An "**opinion**" is an expression of a person's belief or viewpoint, but not a matter of positive knowledge.

All misrepresentations of fact and intention are actionable. Only certain types of opinions, however, are actionable. Specifically, only opinions that imply specific underlying facts are actionable.

For example, if Hannah lies and says she thinks a particular painting is beautiful when she thinks it is ugly, she has not made an actionable misrepresentation because the representation does not suggest any underlying facts. In contrast, if Elizabeth, a known car expert, lies and says a car is fast when she knows it is not, she has made an actionable misrepresentation. Elizabeth's characterization of the car as fast falsely implies that the car can obtain higher maximum speeds than most cars or that the car can accelerate faster than most cars. The following exercise will help you develop your ability to identify and distinguish actionable false statements of fact, intention, and opinion.

Exercise 5-4: False Statements of Fact, Intentions, and Opinions

Determine whether each of the misrepresentations below is a false statement of fact, intention, or opinion and develop an argument about whether each would be actionable under the standards you just learned.

1. The seller of a used car lies about the car's maintenance record.

2. The seller of a used car lies about the age of the car's tires.

3. The seller of a used car lies and says, in her opinion, the car is a "good buy."

4. The seller of a used car lies and says she thinks the car is "gorgeous."

5. The seller of a used car lies and says she intends to buy a new version of the same make/model car. She actually intends to buy an entirely different kind of car.

6. The seller of an office building lies and says that a major manufacturer is planning to move its business nearby.

7. An art expert who is selling a painting lies and says, in her opinion, the painting is a "masterpiece."

---

2. Materiality

A fact is "**material**" if a reasonable person in the same circumstances would regard the fact as important in deciding whether or not to make a contract. Section 162 of the RESTATEMENT (SECOND) OF CONTRACTS, captures the concept in similar terms, stating that a misrepresentation is material "if it would be likely to induce a reasonable person to manifest his assent". Whenever you see the word "reasonable" in your law school texts, it should jump out at you. "Reasonable" usually indicates that you are dealing with an objective standard. The majority of courts apply an objective, reasonable person test to determine if a fact is material. In other words, these courts would not ask what you or a particular person would think; rather, the vantage point is that of a hypothetical person with the ordinary level of knowledge and prudence that our society imputes to its citizens. A minority of courts applies a subjective test: a fact is material if a particular party relied on the fact in making her decision to enter into a contract.

The first case you will read later in this section, *Cousineau*, involves a materiality issue. In exercises after that case, you will have an opportunity to assess your understanding of this concept.

3. The Requisite State of Mind

"**Requisite state of mind**" refers to the knowledge of a party making a misrepresentation at the time the party makes the misrepresentation. There is no single state of knowledge required to assert the defense of misrepresentation. Rather, a contracting party can avoid liability under a contract by showing one of the three states of mind listed under misrepresentation in Diagram 5-1 at the beginning of this chapter. Specifically, a party claiming misrepresentation can show that the speaker either:

1. **knew or believed the representation was not true (an "intentional misrepresentation" or "fraud");**

2. **unreasonably believed the representation to be true (a "negligent misrepresentation"); or**

3. **reasonably believed the representation to be true (an "innocent misrepresentation").**

Some commentators have observed that allowing the defense of misrepresentation for innocent misrepresentations is a form of strict liability. In other words, a speaker cannot enforce a contract if the speaker made a false statement believing it to be true even if, under the circumstances, a reasonable person would believe the statement to be true.

In addition, allowing parties to use the defense of misrepresentation even for innocent misrepresentations may appear to make differentiating among the three states of mind a distinction without a difference. The distinction is important, however, for several reasons. First, as we already mentioned, for intentional misrepresentations, courts do not require any showing of materiality. Second, only victims of intentional misrepresentation are entitled to punitive damages. Third, only victims of intentional or negligent misrepresentation are entitled to damages as an additional or alternative remedy to getting out of (rescinding) the contract. In the case of an innocent misrepresentation, a victim is not entitled to any money damages at all; he can only use the defense of misrepresentation as a way to avoid his contractual obligations by rescinding the contract made.

Before reading further, stop and consider why courts allow parties to avoid contract liability in the case of innocent misrepresentations, but do not usually award damages for innocent misrepresentations. What public policy rationale does this approach promote?

As you learned in Chapter 1, one important policy rationale in contract law is efficiency. It is considered efficient to place losses on the parties who are in the best position to avoid the problems causing losses—in other words, on the "**better loss avoider.**" In the case of an innocent misrepresentation, the party who made the innocent misrepresentation is the better loss avoider. The false speaker is in the better position to avoid a problem because he can choose whether to make the representation. Because speakers who make innocent representations act honestly and reasonably, however, courts limit the speakers' liability by not awarding damages for innocent misrepresentations.

To understand the distinctions among the three misrepresentation states of mind, consider the Sally-Bob problem you already read in Exercise 5-3. In that problem, Bob could successfully assert misrepresentation as a defense. The key aspect to understand at this point is how the facts satisfy the state-of-mind requirement. Take a moment to re-read Exercise 5-3 and try to figure out which state of mind applies. After you do so, read the state-of-mind analysis in Table 5-2 to see whether you correctly understood the concept.

Table 5-2: Sample Analysis

The issue presented is whether Sally made an intentional misrepresentation. An intentional misrepresentation is a representation made by a party who knows the representation is false.

Here, Sally was the original owner of the car and truthfully told Bob she was the only person who ever drove the car. Sally falsely told Bob, however, that the car never had been in an accident. In fact, the car had been in two major accidents. A person who was the only owner and driver of a car would be aware whether the car had been in two major accidents. Indeed, as the owner of the car, Sally would have had to arrange for the repair of damages caused by the accidents and would, therefore, be aware of them. These facts provide an inference that Sally's misrepresentation was intentional, an inference that seems especially strong because Bob did not see any visible indications that the car had been in the accidents.

Therefore, Bob will be able to show that Sally made an intentional misrepresentation and successfully defend against Sally's lawsuit. Bob will also have a counterclaim for damages if he incurred any additional costs in entering into the contract.

In Table 5-2, note that the sample analysis uses the IRAC approach recommended in Chapter 2. You should have also noticed that the analysis only addresses intentional misrepresentation; it does not address negligent or innocent misrepresentation. In most cases, careful lawyers consider all three types of misrepresentation. That approach was not needed here, though, because there is no colorable argument that the misrepresentation was merely negligent or innocent. You will have an opportunity to analyze all three types of misrepresentation in Exercise 5-5, a modification of the Sally-Bob problem.

Exercise 5-5: State-of-Mind Problem

Two weeks ago, Bob purchased a used car from Sally Seller. Bob determined that Sally's asking price, $6,000, was fair. Bob and Sally agreed that Bob would pay Sally three weeks after delivery of the car. During negotiations, Bob explained that he was unable to use his legs in driving and, consequently, needed to install a device on the car that would allow him to accelerate and brake using hand controls. Sally then told Bob that there would be no problem installing the device on the car. Sally and Bob made a contract. Then, Bob took the car to his installer and was informed that the car was the only model of car into which hand controls could not be installed. Bob returned the car to Sally and told her he is unwilling to buy it. Sally sued Bob for breach of contract. Will Sally prevail?

The fact pattern in Exercise 5-5 is more typical than that in Exercise 5-3 because it is unclear what state of mind Sally had when she made the representation. As you already learned, Bob can successfully assert misrepresentation as a defense even if Sally did not know her representation was false and even if she reasonably believed her representation to be true. The critical issue is: What was Sally's state of mind? Analyze that issue before reading the sample analysis in Table 5-3.

Table 5-3: Sample State-of-Mind Analysis

The issue presented is what type of misrepresentation Sally made. A misrepresentation can either be intentional, negligent, or innocent. First, intentional misrepresentation involves a situation where a party knows a representation to be false. Here, there are no facts suggesting Sally required hand controls when she drove the car or knows anyone who requires such a device. There are also no facts suggesting Sally possesses any expertise regarding such devices or cars in general. Finally, there are no facts suggesting Sally was particularly desperate to sell to Bob such that she would want to lie to Bob. Sally's lack of relevant knowledge suggests she could not tell, one way or the other, whether the device could be installed. Her lack of desperation suggests she was not motivated to lie. For these reasons, it seems unlikely Bob will be able to show Sally knew the device could not be installed. Therefore, Bob will not be able to prove intentional misrepresentation.

Second, negligent misrepresentation involves a situation where a party makes a false statement of fact unreasonably believing the statement to be true. On the one hand, the car was the only model of car into which the device could not be installed and there are no facts suggesting there was anything unique about the car that would suggest such a device could not be installed into it. These facts suggest that even a careful seller might not know that this car was the only model of car into which the device could not be installed.

There are no facts, however, suggesting Sally was aware the device could be installed in most car models, in no car models, or in some car models. Moreover, there are no facts suggesting Sally required such a device when she drove the car or knows anyone who requires such a device. There are also no facts suggesting Sally possesses any expertise regarding such devices or cars in general or ever conducted any inquiry about the possibility of installing the device. For these reasons, Sally does not appear to have had any basis for believing the device could or could not be installed. Even a careful person in Sally's position would not believe she possessed sufficient expertise to know, one way or the other, whether the device could be installed into the car. Therefore, because Sally probably could not have reasonably believed the device could be installed, her misrepresentation was negligent.

Third, even if Sally's misrepresentation is not deemed negligent, it would at least be deemed innocent because Sally nevertheless made a false representation.

Therefore, Sally likely made a negligent misrepresentation. In any event, it was at least an innocent misrepresentation. Bob will thus succeed in using misrepresentation as a defense to Sally's breach of contract action.

Note that the sample analysis in Table 5-3 again uses the IRAC approach recommended in Chapter 2. Also note that the length of any given part of an IRAC will vary with the circumstances. For example, the negligent misrepresentation discussion was relatively long, and the innocent misrepresentation discussion was only a single, simple sentence. The negligent misrepresentation discussion was balanced and addressed all reasonable arguments regarding innocent misrepresentation, too. Therefore, the writer appropriately decided not to provide a lengthy, duplicative analysis under innocent misrepresentation.

Exercise 5-6: State-of-Mind Problems

Analyze the state-of-mind issues in the following two hypotheticals.

1. Bonnie Buyer, who is in the business of developing undeveloped land and building single-family homes, entered into negotiations to buy from Soledad Seller a large tract of undeveloped land called DevelopAcre in New City, Olympia (a new state). Soledad was also a developer and had developed nine nearby tracts into single-family homes. DevelopAcre was the last tract of land owned by Soledad in New City. During negotiations, Bonnie told Soledad that, if she purchased DevelopAcre, she would subdivide the land into 100 lots and build 100 single-family homes on the land for sale to the general public. Soledad assured Bonnie there was more than enough water underneath the land to supply the water needed for Bonnie's planned development. During escrow, Bonnie discovered the representation was false. In fact, there was only enough water to supply 75 single-family homes. Bonnie therefore refused to close the deal. Soledad sued Bonnie for breach of contract.

2. Sandra Seller entered into negotiations with Baldo Buyer for the sale of Sandra's vacant lot. Sandra had owned the lot for the past 30 years. During negotiations, Sandra told Baldo, "This land has been entirely unused since the day I bought it." Baldo then entered into a contract to buy the land. After Baldo took possession of the land, he discovered 25 large metal canisters containing oil and gas buried ten feet below the surface of the ground. The canisters had labels on them indicating they were less than ten years old. The labels also indicated the canisters belonged to a gas station located one mile away. Bob immediately returned the deed to the land to Sandra and demanded she return his money.

---

4. Actual and Justifiable Reliance

A party's reliance is "**actual**" if the party acted because of a representation. In other words, a person actually relies on a representation if the representation caused her to make a contract. This element is reflected in Section 167 of the RESTATEMENT (SECOND) OF CONTRACTS.

A party's reliance is "**justifiable**" if it is not completely irrational, preposterous, or absurd. In other words, if a party has any basis for believing another party's representation, even if a reasonable person would not have done so, courts deem reliance justifiable. When you read this definition, you should be asking yourself, "When would a court ever find reliance not justifiable?" Indeed, the standard for finding justifiable reliance is very low. Public policy, and sympathy for victims, supports the low standard. The rationale, as expressed by one court, is that "no rogue should enjoy his ill-gotten plunder for the simple reason that his victim by chance is a fool." [1] You will learn more about the actual and justifiable reliance elements when you read the *Cousineau* case below

---

1. *Chamberlin v. Fuller*, 9 A. 832, 836 (Vt. 1887).

5. Damage

"**Damage**" means some type of loss, harm, or injury. In general, courts require some type of harm to be shown before a party is entitled to a remedy in a legal action. Exercise 5-7 provides you an opportunity to understand how the damage element, as well as the falsity and reliance elements, may arise and be analyzed in a legal problem.

Exercise 5-7: Falsity, Reliance, and Damages

Re-read the problem presented in Exercise 5-3. As you do so, think about the elements of falsity, reliance, and damages. Consider how you would analyze these three issues in that problem. Specifically, think about the applicable rules and how they would apply to the facts presented. Then, try to write your analysis of those three issues using the IRACing suggestions you learned in Chapter 2. After you are done, read the sample analysis in Table 5-4. Note the ways in which your analysis is similar to or different from the sample analysis. Then, reflect on what you should do the next time you conduct a similar analysis to ensure that your analysis is as effective as possible.

Table 5-4: Sample Analysis of the Falsity, Reliance, and Damage Elements of Bob's Misrepresentation Claim Against Sally

False Statement of Fact

The first issue presented is whether there is a false statement of fact. One element of misrepresentation is a false statement of fact. Here, Sally asserted the car had never been in an accident. The car actually had been in two accidents. Sally's assertion that the car never had been in an accident is both a fact and false because it was an inaccurate characterization of the situation. Therefore, the false statement of fact element of misrepresentation is met.

Actual Reliance

The second issue presented is whether there was actual reliance. A party claiming misrepresentation must have actually relied on the misrepresentation. Here, the facts do not state the basis on which Bob made his purchase. However, the facts state that Sally made the misrepresentation during negotiations and that Bob later entered into the contract with Sally. Further, there is a significant difference in value and attractiveness between a car that has never been in an accident and one that has been in an accident. Bob made his decision to buy after he heard that the car never had been in an accident. Accordingly, it appears that one causal factor in Bob's decision to buy the car was the assurance that it had never been in an accident. Therefore, it is likely a court will conclude that the actual reliance element of misrepresentation is met.

Damages

The third issue presented is whether Bob suffered damage. Damage is another element that must be proven to establish a misrepresentation claim. Here, the facts state the car would have been worth at least $6,000, the contract price, if the car had not been in any accident. However, the car was only worth $4,000 in its actual condition. Accordingly, Bob paid $2,000 more for the car because of Sally's misrepresentation than he would have if he had known the true facts. Moreover, Bob was also harmed by being deprived of the car he thought he was purchasing. Thus, the damage element of misrepresentation is met.

There are several things that you should notice about the sample analysis in Table 5-4. First, note that the analysis is limited to only three elements of misrepresentation (there is no discussion of materiality, state of mind, or justifiable reliance). Second, for each element discussed, the analysis follows the IRAC format recommended in Chapter 2. Third, the discussion about actual reliance identifies a lack of information (that the facts did not state the basis on which Bob made his purchase). Students are often hesitant to identify such factual gaps when answering exam questions because they are afraid that they missed something. If you believe crucial information is missing, however, you will write more effective exam answers by saying so. Noting the absence of relevant facts is an important part of a complete legal analysis and will impress your professor. At worst, even if the information really was there and you missed it, at least the professor will know you were looking for it.

Exercise 5-8: *Cousineau v. Walker*

In the next case, *Cousineau*, several misrepresentation elements are at issue. As you read the case, consider how the court applies the elements. Also, consider the following questions:

1. What are the key facts?

2. Which elements of misrepresentation does the court address? How does the court analyze each of those elements?

3. Why doesn't the court decide whether the misrepresentation was intentional, negligent, or innocent? How would you decide that issue? Why?

Cousineau v. Walker

613 P.2d 608 (1980)

Boochever, Justice. The question in this case is whether the appellants are entitled to rescission of a land sale contract because of false statements made by the sellers. The superior court concluded that the buyers did not rely on any misrepresentations made by the sellers, that the misrepresentations were not material to the transaction, and that reliance by the buyers was not justified. Restitution of money paid under the contract was denied. We reverse and remand the case to the superior court to determine the amount of damages owed the appellants.

In 1975, Devon Walker and his wife purchased 9.1 acres of land in Eagle River, Alaska, known as Lot 1, Cross Estates. They paid $140,000.00 for it. A little over a year later, in October, 1976, they signed a multiple listing agreement with Pat Davis, an Anchorage realtor. The listing stated that the property had 580 feet of highway frontage on the Old Glenn Highway and that "Engineer Report Says Over 1 Million in Gravel on Prop." The asking price was $245,000.00.

When the multiple listing expired, Walker signed a new agreement to retain Davis as an exclusive agent. In the broker's contract, the property was again described as having 580 feet of highway frontage, but the gravel content was listed as "minimum 80,000 cubic yds of gravel." The agreement also stated that 2.6 acres on the front of the parcel had been proposed for B-3 zoning (a commercial use), and the asking price was raised to $470,000.00.

An appraisal was prepared to determine the property's value as of December 31, 1976. Walker specifically instructed the appraiser not to include the value of gravel in the appraisal. A rough draft of the appraisal and the appraiser's notes were introduced at trial. Under the heading, "Assumptions and Limiting Conditions," the report stated the appraisal "does not take into account any gravel...." But later in the report the ground was described as "all good gravel base ... covered with birch and spruce trees." The report did not mention the highway footage of the lot.

Wayne Cousineau, a contractor who was also in the gravel extraction business, became aware of the property when he saw the multiple listing. He consulted Camille Davis, another Anchorage realtor, to see if the property was available. In January, Cousineau and Camille Davis visited the property and discussed gravel extraction with Walker, although according to Walker's testimony commercial extraction was not considered. About this time Cousineau offered Walker $360,000.00 for the property. Cousineau tendered a proposed sales agreement which stated that all gravel rights would be granted to the purchaser at closing.

Sometime after his first offer, Cousineau attempted to determine the lot's road frontage. The property was covered with snow, and he found only one boundary marker. At trial the appraiser testified he could not find any markers. Cousineau testified that he went to the borough office to determine if any regulations prevented gravel extraction.

Despite Walker's reference to an "Engineer Report" allegedly showing "over 1 million in gravel," Walker admitted at trial that he had never seen a copy of the report. According to Walker's agent, Pat Davis, Camille Davis was told that if either she or Cousineau wanted the report they would have to pay for it themselves. It was undisputed that Cousineau never obtained the report.

In February, 1977, the parties agreed on a purchase price of $385,000.00 and signed an earnest money agreement. The sale was contingent upon approval of the zoning change of the front portion of the lot to commercial use. The amount of highway frontage was not included in the agreement. Paragraph 4(e) of the agreement conditionally granted gravel rights to Cousineau.[2] According to the agreement, Cousineau would be entitled to remove only so much gravel as was necessary to establish a construction grade on the commercial portion of the property. To remove additional gravel, Cousineau would be required to pay releases on those portions of ground where gravel was removed. This language was used to prevent Walker's security interest in the property from being impaired before he was fully paid.

---

2. Paragraph IX of the judge's factual findings states that there was no mention of the amount of gravel or road frontage in the purchase agreement. This statement is correct insofar as the agreement did not mention specific amounts of gravel or frontage, but the agreement plainly does provide for the transfer of gravel rights.

Soon after the earnest money agreement was signed, the front portion of the property was rezoned and a month later the parties closed the sale.

There is no reference to the amount of highway frontage in the final purchase agreement. An addendum to a third deed of trust incorporates essentially the same language as the earnest money agreement with regard to the release of gravel rights.

After closing, Cousineau and his partners began developing the commercial portion of the property. They bought a gravel scale for $12,000.00 and used two of Cousineau's trucks and a loader. The partners contracted with South Construction to remove the gravel. According to Cousineau's testimony, he first learned of discrepancies in the real estate listing which described the lot when a neighbor threatened to sue Cousineau because he was removing gravel from the neighbor's adjacent lot. A recent survey shows that there is 415 feet of highway frontage on the property not 580 feet, as advertised.

At the same time Cousineau discovered the shortage in highway frontage, South Construction ran out of gravel. They had removed 6,000 cubic yards. To determine if there was any more gravel on the property, a South Construction employee bulldozed a trench about fifty feet long and twenty feet deep. There was no gravel. A soils report prepared in 1978 confirmed that there were no gravel deposits on the property.

After December, 1977, Cousineau and his partners stopped making monthly payments. At that time they had paid a total of $99,000.00 for the property, including a down payment and monthly installments. In March, 1978, they informed Walker of their intention to rescind the contract. A deed of trust foreclosure sale was held in the fall of 1978, and Walker reacquired the property. At a bench trial in December, Cousineau and his partners were denied rescission and restitution....

Rescission of the Contract

Numerous cases hold and the Restatement provides that an innocent misrepresentation may be the basis for rescinding a contract. There is no question, as the trial judge's findings of fact state, that the statements made by Walker and his real estate agent in the multiple listing were false.[3] Three questions must be resolved, however, to determine whether Cousineau is entitled to rescission and restitution of the amount paid for the property on the basis of the misrepresentations. First, it must be determined whether Cousineau in fact relied on the statements. Second, it must be determined whether the statements were material to the transaction that is, objectively, whether a reasonable person would have considered the statements important in deciding whether to purchase the property. Finally, assuming that Cousineau relied

---

3. The statements made regarding highway frontage and gravel content in the two listing agreements cannot be characterized as "puffing." They were positive statements "susceptible of exact knowledge" at the time they were made. *Young & Cooper, Inc. v. Vestring*, 214 Kan. 311, 521 P.2d 281, 290 (1974). Although not applicable to real property sales, it is revealing that under the Uniform Commercial Code, where it is frequently necessary to distinguish "sales talk" from those statements which create express warranties, such definite statements as those made in the listing agreements would most probably be construed as creating an express warranty. *See* Annot., 94 A.L.R.3d 729 (1979).

on the statements and that they were material, it must be determined whether his reliance was justified.[4]

A. Reliance on the False Statements

… [I]n his findings of fact, the trial judge stated, "The plaintiffs did not rely on any misinformation or misrepresentations of defendants." Because this case was decided by a judge without a jury, our standard of review of factual findings is the "clearly erroneous" standard. Alaska R. Civ. P. 52(a). When a finding leaves the court with the definite and firm conviction on the entire record that a mistake has been made, it is clearly erroneous. [Citation Omitted.] In our opinion, the trial judge's finding that Cousineau and his partners did not rely on the statements made by Walker is clearly erroneous.…

In the remaining sections of this opinion, this appellate court concludes that the trial judge's conclusions as to the elements are wrong. Because those trial court conclusions were based on factual determinations, the court's decision is unusual. Why is it unusual?

[T]he uncontroverted facts are that Wayne Cousineau was in the gravel extraction business. He first became aware of the property through a multiple listing that said "1 Million in Gravel." The subsequent listing stated that there were 80,000 cubic yards of gravel. Even if Walker might have taken the position that the sale was based on the appraisal, rather than the listings, the appraisal does not disclaim the earlier statements regarding the amount of highway frontage and the existence of gravel. In fact, the appraisal might well reaffirm a buyer's belief that gravel existed, since it stated there was a good gravel base. All the documents prepared regarding the sale from the first offer through the final deed of trust make provisions for the transfer of gravel rights. Cousineau's first act upon acquiring the property was to contract with South Construction for gravel removal, and to purchase gravel scales for $12,000.00. We conclude that the court erred in finding that Cousineau did not rely on Walker's statement that there was gravel on the property.

We are also convinced that the trial court's finding that Cousineau did not rely on Walker's statement regarding the amount of highway frontage was clearly erroneous. The Cousineaus were experienced and knowledgeable in real estate matters. In determining whether to purchase the property, they would certainly have considered the amount of highway frontage to be of importance. Despite Walker's insistence that Cousineau knew the location of the boundary markers, neither Cousineau nor the appraiser ever found them. It is improbable that Cousineau would have started removing gravel from a neighbor's property had he known the correct location of his boundary line.

B. Materiality of the Statements

Materiality is a mixed question of law and fact. A material fact is one "to which a reasonable man might be expected to attach importance in making his choice of action." W. Prosser, LAW OF TORTS section 108, at 719 (4th ed. 1971). It is a fact which could reasonably be expected to influence someone's judgment or conduct concerning a transaction. [Citations omitted.] Under §306

---

4. RESTATEMENT (SECOND) OF CONTRACTS section 306, comment (a), (Tent. Draft no. 11, 1976) states: "A misrepresentation may make a contract voidable under the rule stated in this Section, even though it does not prevent the formation of a contract under the rule stated in the previous section. Three requirements must be met in addition to the requirement that there must have been a misrepresentation. First, the misrepresentation must have been either fraudulent or material.… Second, the misrepresentation must have induced the recipient to make the contract.… Third, the recipient must have been justified in relying on the misrepresentation."

of the tentative draft of the RESTATEMENT (SECOND) OF CONTRACTS, a misrepresentation may be grounds for voiding a contract if it is either fraudulent or material. RESTATEMENT (SECOND) OF CONTRACTS § 306 (Tent. Draft No. 11, 1976). The reason behind the rule requiring proof of materiality is to encourage stability in contractual relations. The rule prevents parties who later become disappointed at the outcome of their bargain from capitalizing on any insignificant discrepancy to void the contract.

We conclude as a matter of law that the statements regarding highway frontage and gravel content were material. A reasonable person would be likely to consider the existence of gravel deposits an important consideration in developing a piece of property. Even if not valuable for commercial extraction, a gravel base would save the cost of obtaining suitable fill from other sources. Walker's real estate agent testified that the statements regarding gravel were placed in the listings because gravel would be among the property's "best points" and a "selling point."[5] It seems obvious that the sellers themselves thought a buyer would consider gravel content important.

The buyers received less than three-fourths of the highway frontage described in the listings. Certainly the amount of highway frontage on a commercial tract would be considered important. Numerous cases from other jurisdictions have held discrepancies to be material which were similar in magnitude to those here. [Footnoted citations omitted].

C. Justifiable Reliance

The trial judge concluded as a matter of law that the plaintiffs "were not entitled to rely on the alleged misrepresentation."

The bulk of the appellee's brief is devoted to the argument that Cousineau's unquestioning reliance on Walker and his real estate agent was imprudent and unreasonable. Cousineau failed to obtain and review the engineer's report. He failed to obtain a survey or examine the plat available at the recorder's office. He failed to make calculations that would have revealed the true frontage of the lot. Although the property was covered with snow, the plaintiffs, according to Walker, had ample time to inspect it. The plaintiffs were experienced businessmen who frequently bought and sold real estate. Discrepancies existed in the various property descriptions which should have alerted Cousineau and his partners to potential problems. In short, the appellees urge that the doctrine of caveat emptor precludes recovery.

In fashioning an appropriate rule for land sale contracts, we note initially that, in the area of commercial and consumer goods, the doctrine of caveat emptor has been nearly abolished by the Uniform Commercial Code and imposition of strict products liability. In real property transactions, the doctrine is also rapidly receding. Alaska has passed the Uniform Land Sales Practices Act, AS 34.55.004-.046, which imposes numerous restrictions on vendors of subdivided property. Criminal penalties may be imposed for violations. The Uniform Residential Landlord and Tenant Act, AS 34.03.010-

---

5. Walker testified that gravel was not a "selling point." This testimony obviously conflicts with the testimony of his real estate agent, who thought the information was of some importance. A person experienced in real estate sales would seem to be in a better position to evaluate what a buyer would be likely to consider important.

.380, has greatly altered the common law of landlord and tenant in favor of tenants. Many states now imply warranties of merchantability in new home sales. Wyoming has recently extended this warranty beyond the initial purchaser to subsequent buyers. [Citation Omitted.]

There is a split of authority regarding a buyer's duty to investigate a vendor's fraudulent statements, but the prevailing trend is toward placing a minimal duty on a buyer. Recently, a Florida appellate court reversed long-standing precedent which held that a buyer must use due diligence to protect his interest, regardless of fraud, if the means for acquiring knowledge concerning the transaction were open and available. In the context of a building sale the court concluded: "A person guilty of fraudulent misrepresentation should not be permitted to hide behind the doctrine of caveat emptor." [Citation omitted.]

The Supreme Court of Maine has also recently reversed a line of its prior cases, concluding that a defense based upon lack of due care should not be allowed in land sales contracts where a reckless or knowing misrepresentation has been made. [Citation omitted.] This is also the prevailing view in California, Idaho, Kansas, Massachusetts, and Oregon. [Footnoted citations omitted]. On the other hand, some jurisdictions have reaffirmed the doctrine of caveat emptor, but as noted in WILLISTON ON CONTRACTS,

> The growing trend and tendency of the courts will continue to move toward the doctrine that negligence in trusting in a misrepresentation will not excuse positive willful fraud or deprive the defrauded person of his remedy.

W. Jaeger, WILLISTON ON CONTRACTS § 1515B at 487 (3d ed. 1970).

There is also authority for not applying the doctrine of caveat emptor even though the misrepresentation is innocent. The Restatements, case law, and a ready analogy to express warranties in the sale of goods support this view.

The recent draft of the RESTATEMENT OF CONTRACTS allows rescission for an innocent material misrepresentation unless a buyer's fault was so negligent as to amount to "a failure to act in good faith and in accordance with reasonable standards of fair dealing."[6] RESTATEMENT (SECOND) OF CONTRACTS section 314, Comment b (Tent. Draft. no. 11, 1976)....

A buyer of land, relying on an innocent misrepresentation, is barred from recovery only if the buyer's acts in failing to discover defects were wholly irrational, preposterous, or in bad faith.

Although Cousineau's actions may well have exhibited poor judgment for an experienced businessman, they were not so unreasonable or preposterous in view of Walker's description of the property that recovery should be denied. Consequently, we reverse the judgment of the superior court....

---

6. As an illustration of "fair dealing," the proposed Restatement suggests the following example: "A, seeking to induce B to make a contract to buy land, tells B that the land is free from encumbrances. Unknown to either A or B, C holds a recorded and unsatisfied mortgage on the land. B could easily learn this by walking across the street to the register of deeds in the courthouse but does not do so. B is induced by A's statement to make the contract. B's reliance is justified since his fault does not amount to a failure to act in good faith and in accordance with reasonable standards of fair dealing, and the contract is voidable by B." RESTATEMENT (SECOND) OF CONTRACTS section 314, Comment b, Illustration 2 (Tent. Draft no. 11, 1976).

Walker received a total of $99,000.00 from Cousineau and his partners, but the appellants are not entitled to restitution of this amount. Cousineau apparently caused extensive damage to one building on the property, and he removed 6,000 cubic yards of gravel. Walker should be allowed some recoupment for these items ...

It is necessary to remand this case to the trial court to determine the correct amount of damages. Reversed and remanded.

Exercise 5-9: *Cousineau* Revisited

1. Change the facts in *Cousineau* in a way that would change the result on the justifiable reliance element.

2. Assume that a jurisdiction has a statute that excludes liability for representations made in good faith by sellers in real estate transactions. How might that affect the outcome of cases like *Cousineau* in that jurisdiction?

3. Analyze the material fact element in the following problems:[7]

    a. Larry Landowner was negotiating with Betty Buyer for Betty to buy, for $50,000, PurpleAcre, a tract of farmland on which a corn crop is growing. Betty, who owns a chain of ice skating rinks, was planning to use the land to open an ice skating rink. During negotiations, Larry told Betty that, within the next two years, his brother, Ken was planning to build a shopping mall on a nearby tract of land that Ken owned. Betty thereafter agreed to buy the land from Larry. At the time he made this statement, Larry was unaware that Ken had been forced to abandon his plan to build the shopping mall because he (Ken) had been unable to raise the necessary finance. He was also unaware that Ken had promised the city council (in return for a substantial payment) that he would not develop his land for at least the next fifteen years. Three weeks before the sale was due to close, Betty discovered the truth. She refused to close. Larry sued Betty for breach of contract. Is the fact that Larry misrepresented material so that Betty would not be liable for breaching the contract?

    b. Larry Landowner was negotiating with Betty Buyer for Betty to buy, for $50,000, PurpleAcre, a tract of farmland on which a corn crop is growing. Betty, who owns a chain of ice skating rinks, was planning to use the land to open an ice skating rink. During negotiations, Larry told Betty that the land had only ever been used for farming. Betty thereafter agreed to buy the land from Larry. Three weeks before the sale was due to close, Betty discovered that, without Larry knowing, his brother Ken had buried several hundred large metal containers twenty feet underground on a portion of the property Betty did not intend to use. The containers were not harming the property and an expert with whom Betty consulted told Betty that he did not expect the containers to cause any harm to the property. However, the expert also noted that no one could say with certainty the

---

7. These problems are reprinted with permission from MICHAEL HUNTER SCHWARTZ, EXPERT LEARNING FOR LAW STUDENTS WORKBOOK(Carolina Academic Press 2008).

containers would not deteriorate and then begin to harm the land because the particular metal used for the containers had only been in existence for a few years. Betty refused to close the deal. Larry sued Betty for breach of contract. Is the fact that Larry misrepresented material so that Betty would not be liable for breaching the contract?

4. Analyze the justifiable reliance element in the following problem: Two weeks ago, Bob purchased a used car from Sally Seller. Sally was asking what Bob determined to be a fair price for the car, $6,000. The car was very popular and, as Bob knew, there were tens of thousands of identical versions of the car in existence. During negotiations, Sally told Bob the deal was a great one because Fred Filmmaker was planning to use this particular car in one of Filmmaker's next films. After Bob took delivery of the car, Bob asked Filmmaker when he wanted to borrow the car. Filmmaker told Bob he never intended to use the car in a film and had never even met Sally. Bob returned the car to Sally and told her he is unwilling to buy it. Sally sued Bob for breach of contract. Was Bob's reliance on Sally's misrepresentation justifiable?

Now that you have learned about the misrepresentation elements and practiced applying them, you need to be aware of a common student error. Students often confuse the material fact, actual reliance, and justifiable reliance elements. These three elements impose distinct requirements which are graphically depicted in Table 5-5 and explained below:

Table 5-5: Material Fact versus Justifiable Reliance versus Actual Reliance

Element	Focus of Analysis	Test	Type of Test	Assumptions for Analysis
Material Fact	The factors that would lead a hypothetical reasonable person to decide the transaction would be worth making	Would a reasonable person consider the fact important in deciding whether to enter a contract?	Objective	Assume the facts are true
Justifiable Reliance	The types of assertions and sources of information that a hypothetical reasonable person would consider sufficiently reliable to count on	Was the victim's reliance wholly irrational, preposterous, or absurd?	Mostly objective	Assume the facts are false and that those who deceive gullible people should be held liable
Actual Reliance	What actually happened	Did the representation cause the victim to make the contract?	Subjective	Assume misrepresented facts are false

1. The material fact requirement focuses on the importance of a fact to a party's decision to enter into a contract. To analyze this element, assume that the misrepresented fact is true and take an objective perspective.

2. The actual reliance element focuses on the causal basis for a party's decision to enter into a contract. To analyze this element, assume the misrepresented fact is false and use a subjective perspective.

3. The justifiable reliance requirement focuses on the reasonableness of a party's decision to believe a representation. To analyze this element, assume the mis-

represented fact is false and determine whether the decision to believe the misrepresented fact was wholly irrational from a mostly objective perspective.

Exercise 5-10: Material Fact versus Justifiable Reliance versus Actual Reliance

In each of the problems in this exercise, Dan makes a misrepresentation before entering a contract of sale with Patty. Determine whether each problem presents an issue regarding the material fact element, the justifiable reliance element, or the actual reliance element. Circle your answers. A few questions have more than one possible answer.

1. Dan argues that a reasonable person would never have believed him because he is a known liar.

    material fact   justifiable reliance   actual reliance

2. Dan argues that Patty did not believe him.

    material fact   justifiable reliance   actual reliance

3. Dan argues that Patty bought property from him for reasons other than the misrepresentation.

    material fact   justifiable reliance   actual reliance

4. Dan argues that no one possibly could have believed such a ridiculous misrepresentation.

    material fact   justifiable reliance   actual reliance

5. Dan argues that buyers would not care whether what he said was true or not.

    material fact   justifiable reliance   actual reliance

6. Dan argues that the subject of his statement would have no effect on the fair market value of the property.

    material fact   justifiable reliance   actual reliance

7. Dan argues that a buyer who was buying the property for the use planned by the buyer would find the misrepresented fact irrelevant.

    material fact   justifiable reliance   actual reliance

8. Dan argues that the buyer knew, from an outside source, information that squarely contradicted what he said.

    material fact   justifiable reliance   actual reliance

Exercise 5-11: Distinguishing Between Representations and Warranties

It is common in standard form contracts for sellers to "represent and warrant" the truth of statements about the subject matter of the contract. The following case, *CBS Inc. v. Ziff-Davis Publishing Co.*, illustrates the importance of the distinction. Consider the following questions as you read the extract:

1. What are the key facts?

2. What do you think was the commercial purpose of CBS's letter of February 4, 1985?

3. Why couldn't CBS rescind the contract on the basis that Ziff-Davis had misrepresented the financial condition of the consumer magazines business?

4. What is the difference between a representation and a warranty?

5. Why did it matter that Ziff-Davis had warranted as well as represented that the audited accounts had been prepared in accordance with generally accepted accounting principles and presented a fair view of the financial condition of the consumer magazines business?

CBS Inc. v. Ziff-Davis Publishing Co.

75 N.Y.2d 496 (1990)

HANCOCK, Judge.

A corporate buyer made a bid to purchase certain businesses based on financial information as to their profitability supplied by the seller. The bid was accepted and the parties entered into a binding bilateral contract for the sale which included, specifically, the seller's express warranties as to the truthfulness of the previously supplied financial information. Thereafter, pursuant to the purchase agreement, the buyer conducted its own investigation which led it to believe that the warranted information was untrue. The seller dismissed as meritless the buyer's expressions of disbelief in the validity of the financial information and insisted that the sale go through as agreed. The closing took place with the mutual understanding that it would not in any way affect the previously asserted position of either party. Did the buyer's manifested lack of belief in and reliance on the truth of the warranted information prior to the closing relieve the seller of its obligations under the warranties? This is the central question presented in the breach of express warranty claim brought by CBS Inc. (CBS) against Ziff–Davis Publishing Co. (Ziff–Davis). The courts below concluded that CBS's lack of reliance on the warranted information was fatal to its breach of warranty claim and, accordingly, dismissed that cause of action on motion ... We granted leave to appeal and, for reasons stated hereinafter, disagree with this conclusion and hold that the warranty claim should be reinstated.

I

The essential facts pleaded—assumed to be true for the purpose of the dismissal motion—are these. In September 1984, Goldman Sachs & Co., acting as Ziff–Davis's investment banker and agent, solicited bids for the sale of the assets and businesses of 12 consumer magazines and 12 business publications. The offering circular, prepared by Goldman Sachs and Ziff–Davis, described Ziff–Davis's financial condition and included operating income statements for the fiscal year ending July 31, 1984 prepared by Ziff–Davis's accountant, Touche Ross & Co. Based on Ziff–Davis's representations in the offering circular, CBS, on November 9, 1984 submitted a bid limited to the purchase of the 12 consumer magazines in the amount of $362,500,000. This was the highest bid.

On November 19, 1984 CBS and Ziff–Davis entered into a binding bilateral purchase agreement for the sale of the consumer magazine businesses for the price of $362,500,000. Under section 3.5 of the purchase agreement, Ziff–Davis warranted that the audited income and expense report of the businesses for the 1984 fiscal year, which had been previously provided to CBS in the offering circular, had "been prepared in accordance with generally accepted accounting principles" (GAAP) and that the report "present[ed] fairly the items set forth". Ziff–Davis agreed to furnish an interim income and expense report (Stub Report) of the businesses covering the period after the end of the 1984 fiscal year, and it warranted under section 3.6 that from July 31, 1984 until the closing, there had "not been any material adverse change in Seller's business of publishing and distributing the Publications, taken as a whole". Section 6.1(a) provided that "all representations and warranties of Seller to Buyer shall be true and correct as of the time of the closing", and in section 8.1, the parties agreed that all "representations and warranties shall survive the closing, notwithstanding any investigation made by or on behalf of the other party." In section 5.1 Ziff–Davis gave CBS permission to "make such investigation" of the magazine businesses being sold "as [it might] desire" and agreed to give CBS and its accountants reasonable access to the books and records pertaining thereto and to furnish such documents and information as might reasonably be requested.

Thereafter, on January 30, 1985 Ziff–Davis delivered the required Stub Report. In the interim, CBS, acting under section 5.1 of the purchase agreement, had performed its own "due diligence" examination of Ziff–Davis's financial condition. Based on this examination and on reports by its accountant, Coopers & Lybrand, CBS discovered information causing it to believe that Ziff–Davis's certified financial statements and other financial reports were not prepared according to GAAP and did not fairly depict Ziff–Davis's financial condition.

In a January 31, 1985 letter, CBS wrote Ziff–Davis that, "[b]ased on the information and analysis provided [to it, CBS was] of the view that there [were] material misrepresentations in the financial statements provided [to CBS] by Touche Ross & Co., Goldman, Sachs & Co. and Ziff–Davis". In response to this letter, Ziff–Davis advised CBS by letter dated February 4, 1985 that it "believe[d] that all conditions to the closing were fulfilled", that "there [was] no merit to the position taken by CBS in its [Jan. 31, 1985] letter" and that the financial statements were properly prepared and fairly presented Ziff–Davis's financial condition. It also warned CBS that, since all conditions to closing were satisfied, closing was required to be held that day, February 4, 1985, and that, if it "should fail to consummate the transactions as provided Ziff–Davis intend[ed] *to pursue all of its rights and remedies as provided by law.*" (Emphasis added.)

CBS responded to Ziff–Davis's February 4, 1985 letter with its own February 4 letter, which Ziff–Davis accepted and agreed to. In its February 4 letter, CBS acknowledged that "a clear dispute" existed between the parties. It stated that it had decided to proceed with the deal because it had "spent considerable time, effort and money in complying with [its] obligations and recogniz[ed] that [Ziff–Davis had] considerably more information available". Accordingly, the parties agreed "to close [that day] on a mutual understanding that the decision to close, and the closing, [would] not *constitute a waiver of any rights or defenses either of us may have*" (emphasis added) under the purchase agreement. The deal was consummated on February 4.

Make sure you understand the basic deal here. Lawyers call this kind of deal a "mergers and acquisitions" or "M & A" transaction.

CBS then brought this action claiming … that Ziff–Davis had breached the warranties made as to the magazines' profitability. Based on that breach, CBS alleged that "the price bid and the price paid by CBS were in excess of that which would have been bid and paid by CBS had Ziff–Davis not breached its representation and warranties." …

II

In addressing the central question whether the failure to plead reliance is fatal to CBS's claim for breach of express warranties, it is necessary to examine the exact nature of the missing element of reliance which Ziff–Davis contends is essential. This critical lack of reliance, according to Ziff–Davis, relates to CBS's disbelief in the truth of the warranted financial information which resulted from its investigation *after* the signing of the agreement and *prior to* the date of closing. The reliance in question, it must be emphasized, does not relate to whether CBS relied on the submitted financial information in making its bid or relied on Ziff–Davis's express warranties as to the validity of this information when CBS committed itself to buy the businesses by signing the purchase agreement containing the warranties.

Under Ziff–Davis's theory, the reliance which is a necessary element for a claim of breach of express warranty is essentially that required for a tort action based on fraud or misrepresentation — i.e., a belief in the truth of the representations made in the express warranty and a change of position in reliance on that belief. Thus, because, prior to the closing of the contract on February 4, 1985, CBS demonstrated its lack of belief in the truth of the warranted financial information, it cannot have closed in reliance on it and its breach of warranty claim must fail. This is so, Ziff–Davis maintains, despite its unequivocal rejection of CBS's expressions of its concern that the submitted financial reports contained errors, despite its insistence that the information it had submitted complied with the warranties and that there was "no merit" to CBS's position, and despite its warnings of legal action if CBS did not go ahead with the closing …

CBS, on the other hand, maintains that the decisive question is whether it purchased the express warranties as bargained-for contractual terms that were part of the purchase agreement (*see, e.g., Ainger v. Michigan Gen. Corp.*, 476 F.Supp. 1209, 1225 [S.D.N.Y.1979], *affd.* 632 F.2d 1025 [2d Cir.1980]). It alleges that it did so and that, under these circumstances, the warranty provisions amounted to assurances of the existence of facts upon which CBS relied in committing itself to buy the consumer magazines. Ziff–Davis's assurances of these facts, CBS contends, were the equivalent of promises by Ziff–Davis to indemnify CBS if the assurances proved unfounded. Thus, as continuing promises to indemnify, the express contractual warranties did not lose their operative force when, prior to the closing, CBS formed a belief that the warranted financial information was in error. Indeed, CBS claims that it is precisely because of these warranties that it proceeded with the closing, despite its misgivings.

As authority for its position, CBS cites, *inter alia, Ainger v. Michigan Gen. Corp. (supra)* and Judge Learned Hand's definition of warranty as "an assurance by one party to a contract of the existence of a fact upon which the other party may rely. It is intended precisely to relieve the promisee of any duty to

Pay close attention to this segment of the opinion. It explains the difference between a claim for misrepresentation and a claim for breach of a contractual promise.

ascertain the fact for himself; *it amounts to a promise to indemnify the promisee for any loss if the fact warranted proves untrue, for obviously the promisor cannot control what is already in the past."* [citations omitted].

We believe that the analysis of the reliance requirement in actions for breach of express warranties adopted in *Ainger v. Michigan Gen. Corp. (supra)* and urged by CBS here is correct. The critical question is not whether the buyer believed in the truth of the warranted information, as Ziff–Davis would have it, but "whether [it] believed [it] was purchasing the [seller's] promise [as to its truth]." (*Ainger v. Michigan Gen. Corp., supra,* at 1225) [other citations omitted]. This view of "reliance" — i.e., as requiring no more than reliance on the express warranty as being a part of the bargain between the parties — reflects the prevailing perception of an action for breach of express warranty as one that is no longer grounded in tort, but essentially in contract. (*See, Ainger v. Michigan Gen. Corp., supra,* at 1225) [other citations omitted]. The express warranty is as much a part of the contract as any other term. Once the express warranty is shown to have been relied on as part of the contract, the right to be indemnified in damages for its breach does not depend on proof that the buyer thereafter believed that the assurances of fact made in the warranty would be fulfilled. The right to indemnification depends only on establishing that the warranty was breached [citations omitted].

If, as is allegedly the case here, the buyer has purchased the seller's promise as to the existence of the warranted facts, the seller should not be relieved of responsibility because the buyer, after agreeing to make the purchase, forms doubts as to the existence of those facts (*see, Ainger v. Michigan Gen. Corp., supra,* at 1234) [other citations omitted]. Stated otherwise, the fact that the buyer has questioned the seller's ability to perform as promised should not relieve the seller of his obligations under the express warranties when he thereafter undertakes to render the promised performance.

The cases which Ziff–Davis cites as authority for the application of its tort-action type of reliance requirement do not support the proposition it urges. None are similar to the case at bar where the warranties sued on are bargained-for terms in a binding bilateral purchase contract. In most, the basis for the decision was a factor other than the buyer's lack of reliance such as, for example, insufficient proof of the existence of the alleged express warranty [citations omitted] or that the warranty sued upon was expressly excluded by terms of the contract [citations omitted] or that there was insufficient proof that the express warranty had been breached [citations omitted] and some involve implied rather than express warranties [citations omitted] ...

Viewed as a contract action involving the claimed breach of certain bargained-for express warranties contained in the purchase agreement, the case may be summarized this way. CBS contracted to buy the consumer magazine businesses in consideration, among other things, of the reciprocal promises made by Ziff–Davis concerning the magazines' profitability. These reciprocal promises included the express warranties that the audited reports for the year ending July 31, 1984 made by Touche Ross had been prepared according to GAAP and that the items contained therein were fairly presented, that there had been no adverse material change in the business after July 31, 1984, and that all representations and warranties would "be true and correct as of the time of the closing" and would "survive the closing, notwithstanding any investigation" by CBS.

Unquestionably, the financial information pertaining to the income and expenses of the consumer magazines was relied on by CBS in forming its opinion as to the value of the businesses and in arriving at the amount of its bid; the warranties pertaining to the validity of this financial information were express terms of the bargain and part of what CBS contracted to purchase. CBS was not merely buying identified consumer magazine businesses. It was buying businesses which it believed to be of a certain value based on information furnished by the seller which the seller warranted to be true. The determinative question is this: should Ziff–Davis be relieved from any contractual obligation under these warranties, as it contends that it should, because, prior to the closing, CBS and its accountants questioned the accuracy of the financial information and because CBS, when it closed, did so without *believing in* or *relying on* the truth of the information?

We see no reason why Ziff–Davis should be absolved from its warranty obligations under these circumstances. A holding that it should because CBS questioned the truth of the facts warranted would have the effect of depriving the express warranties of their only value to CBS—i.e., as continuing promises by Ziff–Davis to indemnify CBS if the facts warranted proved to be untrue [citation omitted]. Ironically, if Ziff–Davis's position were adopted, it would have succeeded in pressing CBS to close despite CBS's misgivings and, at the same time, would have succeeded in *defeating* CBS's breach of warranties action because CBS harbored these *identical misgivings....*

Non-Disclosure

This section discusses another type of deception listed in Diagram 5-1 at the beginning of this chapter: **non-disclosure**. You just learned that the focus of misrepresentation is misstating important facts. In contrast, the focus of non-disclosure is failing to speak about important facts.

Non-disclosure has five elements:

1. **Failure to disclose a fact;**

2. **A duty to disclose that fact;**

3. **The non-disclosed fact was material;**

4. **The other party actually and justifiably relied on the state of things in the absence of disclosure of the fact; and**

5. **Damage.**

The last three elements should be familiar to you because they are also elements of misrepresentation. Because you have already studied those elements, they will not be discussed again in this section.

The first two elements are unique to non-disclosure. The first element, a failure to disclose, is self-evident. A party accused of non-disclosure must have failed to tell the other party something.

The second element, a duty to disclose, is the focus in this section. The general rule is that there is no duty to disclose material facts to another party. However, there are four situations that give rise to a duty to disclose. Your objective in this section is to learn the four ways of showing that a duty to disclose exists.

Exercise 5-12: Duty to Disclose

The objective of this exercise is to help you learn the four ways of showing that a duty to disclose exists. Read the problems and answers below and then derive the four ways of showing that a duty to disclose exists. This exercise is another discovery sequence exercise. The mental effort required to identify the patterns will help you remember the concepts.

1. Sophie Seller entered into negotiations with Betty Buyer to sell Seller's house to Buyer. If Seller knows a murder was committed in the house five years ago, must Seller disclose that fact to Buyer? No, Seller would not have a duty to disclose.

2. Assume the same facts as in problem 1, except Seller is also Buyer's regular lawyer. Must Seller disclose the fact to Buyer? Yes, Seller would have a duty to disclose.

3. Assume the same facts as in problem 1, except Seller is Buyer's mother. Must Seller disclose the fact to Buyer? Yes, Seller would have a duty to disclose.

4. Assume the same facts as in problem 1, except Seller raised Buyer since she was a child and was Buyer's chief advisor with respect to all matters since Buyer was fifteen years old. Must Seller disclose the fact to Buyer? Yes, Seller would have a duty to disclose.

5. Assume the same facts as in problem 1, except Seller is Buyer's friend and has never rendered any advice or help to Buyer. Must Seller disclose the fact to Buyer? No, Seller would not have a duty to disclose.

6. Assume the same facts as in problem 1, except Seller is an employee of Buyer. Seller has never rendered any advice or help to Buyer. Must Seller disclose the fact to Buyer? No, Seller would not have a duty to disclose.

7. Sophie Seller entered into negotiations with Betty Buyer to sell Seller's house to Buyer. If Seller knows that Buyer is unaware that the house is riddled with termites such that it cannot be fixed except at a cost that represents two-thirds the value of the house, must Seller disclose that fact to Buyer? Yes, Seller would have a duty to disclose.

8. Sophie Seller entered into negotiations with Betty Buyer to sell Seller's house to Buyer. If Seller knows the neighbors are noisy on Saturday nights, must Seller disclose this fact to buyer? No, Seller would not have a duty to disclose.

9. Sophie Seller entered into negotiations with Betty Buyer to sell Seller's house to Buyer for $350,000. If Seller knows that the building and safety department has issued a warning to Seller that Seller must enclose Seller's septic tank (at a cost of $2,000) or face substantial fines (as much as $500 per day), must Seller disclose that fact to Buyer? No, Seller would not have a duty to disclose.

10. Sophie Seller entered into negotiations with Betty Buyer to sell Seller's restaurant to Buyer for $75,000. If Seller knows that the health department has issued repeated warnings that Seller must make expensive improvements to the restaurant (at a cost of as much as $50,000) or the health department will close the restaurant, must Seller disclose that fact to Buyer? Yes, Seller would have a duty to disclose.

11. Sophie Seller entered into negotiations with Betty Buyer to sell Seller's house to Buyer for $350,000. If Seller knows that the house has a well-established reputation for being inhabited by ghosts, must Seller disclose that fact to Buyer? No, Seller would not have a duty to disclose.

12. Sophie Seller, seeking to induce Betty Buyer to purchase Seller's house and land, tells Buyer that the house "has no problems." Unknown to Seller, all of the electrical wiring in the house is a fire hazard and needs to be replaced. If Seller later learns of the electrical wiring problem before the parties sign their contract, must Seller disclose that fact to Buyer? Yes, Seller would have a duty to disclose.

13. Sophie Seller, seeking to induce Betty Buyer to purchase Seller's house and land, tells Buyer that Gary Frank, a world-renowned architect, designed Seller's house. After escrow closes and Buyer takes possession, Seller learns that Frank's daughter actually designed the house after Frank died. Must Seller disclose that fact to Buyer? No, Seller would not have a duty to disclose.

14. Sophie Seller, seeking to induce Betty Buyer to purchase Seller's house and land, tells Buyer that the house "has only a few problems" and gives Buyer a list labeled "Problems With Betty's House." If Seller knows that, in addition to the problems she listed, the house needs a new roof, must Seller disclose that fact to Buyer? Yes, Seller would have a duty to disclose.

15. Assume the same facts as in problem 14, except Seller did not tell Buyer that the house had any problems at all. If Seller knows that the roof needs some repairs, must Seller disclose that fact to Buyer? No, Seller would not have a duty to disclose.

16. Sadie Spouse entered into negotiations with Crafty Creditor to pay off her husband's debts. If Creditor knows that, without expressly saying so, he has given Spouse the incorrect impression that Spouse's husband will be imminently arrested if Spouse does not agree to Creditor's demands, must Creditor disclose the true facts to Spouse? Yes, Seller would have a duty to disclose.

17. Assume the same facts as in problem 16, except Creditor did nothing to give Spouse the impression that Spouse's husband would be imminently arrested. Nevertheless, Spouse believed her husband would be arrested and Creditor knew of Spouse's belief. Must Creditor disclose the true facts to Spouse? No, Seller would not have a duty to disclose.

Exercise 5-13: Duty to Disclose

Andy Applicant applied for a position as a bank teller with Careful Bank. In his application, Andy did not disclose his criminal record. Twenty years ago, Andy was convicted and jailed for burglarizing his stepfather's house. Did Andy have a duty to disclose his criminal record? Analyze this problem and be prepared to explain your answer.

Concealment

This section discusses the third type of deception listed in Diagram 5-1 at the beginning of this chapter: **concealment**. Concealment involves one party engaging in active efforts to prevent another party from learning a fact (rather than lying about a fact).

The elements of concealment are:

1. **Active efforts to prevent another party from learning a fact;**

2. **The concealed fact was material;**

3. **The other party actually and justifiably relied on the misrepresentation; and**

4. **Damage.**

You have already learned about all these elements except the first one: engaging in active efforts to prevent another party from learning a fact. That element is relatively easy to understand. For example, that element is met if a homebuilder installs tiles on a floor to cover up a defect in the floor or if a car salesman turns a car's odometer back several thousand miles.

It is important that you understand the distinction among the three types of deception that you have just learned about: misrepresentation, non-disclosure, and concealment. While the focus of misrepresentation is misstating a fact and the focus of non-disclosure is not stating a fact, the focus of concealment is hiding a fact. On an exam, you will need to identify which type of deception a given question raises and analyze it (you will not likely have enough time to analyze all three types of deception). To know which type of deception to discuss, you need to know the distinguishing features of each type. Exercise 5-14 is designed to ensure that you understand the differences among the three types of deception.

Exercise 5-14: Misrepresentation, Non-Disclosure, or Concealment?

Read the following problems. Determine whether each presents a misrepresentation, non-disclosure, or concealment claim. Circle your answers. Some questions have more than one possible answer.

1. D unknowingly but falsely stated that his house is in excellent condition when it actually has a termite problem.

   misrepresentation   non-disclosure   concealment

2. D truthfully stated that his house is in excellent condition; but, after D said so, termites invaded his house. D learned of the termites but never informed the other party about this change.

   misrepresentation   non-disclosure   concealment

3. D painted the ceiling of his house white because it had become gray in color from a roof leak, but did not repair the roof leak or mention it to the other party.

misrepresentation   non-disclosure   concealment

4. D, a borrower, never mentioned to the other party, a lender, that D had declared bankruptcy on two prior occasions.

misrepresentation   non-disclosure   concealment

5. D told the other party that his house has a roof leak, needs paint, needs new carpeting, and has one window that needs replacing. D failed to mention that the foundation of the house is cracked.

misrepresentation   non-disclosure   concealment

6. D stood in front of a hole in the wall of his living room when another party toured D's house.

misrepresentation   non-disclosure   concealment

7. D, who truly believed a false rumor, incorrectly told the other party that gold has been found on the tract next to the tract D is selling.

misrepresentation   non-disclosure   concealment

8. D lied about his last name in a credit application so that when the other party, the prospective creditor, ran a credit check, it did not discover D's terrible credit.

misrepresentation   non-disclosure   concealment

Exercise 5-15: Creating Hypotheticals

One trait of expert learners is that they accurately assess whether they have learned what they have attempted to learn. There are two main reasons to confirm your understanding of the material you are learning in law school. First, it is not sufficient to just memorize rules of law. Indeed, you are wasting your time if you are memorizing rules but don't understand them. You must also know how to apply rules to facts and engage in effective legal analysis. The second reason to confirm your understanding of the material is that doing so will facilitate later recall of that material.

There are several techniques you can use to ensure you understand what you have learned. One way is by creating and answering your own hypothetical problems. If you understand a legal topic well enough to create a hypothetical about which reasonable lawyers would disagree, you have mastered that topic.

Assess your understanding of deception by creating and answering a hypothetical deception problem. Your problem should contain sufficient information to analyze each element of the particular deception claim raised. Try to make the analysis of at least two of the elements debatable. Write an answer to your problem.[8]

---

8. If you struggle with this assignment, read Chapter 16 in MICHAEL HUNTER SCHWARTZ, EXPERT LEARNING FOR LAW STUDENTS (Carolina Academic Press 2008).

Mistake

This section discusses the second contract defense listed in Diagram 5-1 at the beginning of this chapter: **mistake**. There are two types of mistake defenses: "**mutual mistake**" and "**unilateral mistake**." The first type of mistake defense you will learn is mutual mistake.

A. Mutual Mistake

Mutual mistake applies to situations where parties make contracts in light of certain, crucial assumptions about particular qualities of what they are buying and selling and those assumptions prove untrue.

Exercise 5-16: Section Example

Bob and Sally were contemplating entering into a contract under which Bob would buy the right to mine Sally's property for schwartzium, a mineral known to be in plentiful supply on Sally's land. Bob and Sally are both experienced schwartzium miners and assumed Bob would have no trouble mining the schwartzium on Sally's land. The parties then signed a contract. When Bob started his mining operations, he discovered that, unknown to either Bob or Sally, the schwartzium on Sally's land was embedded in the rock in such a way that Bob could not mine it at all.

If Bob refused to pay and offered to return the mineral rights to Sally and Sally refused, Bob might be able to successfully assert mistake as a defense to a breach of contract action. If the facts were slightly different, however, Bob's mistake defense almost certainly would fail. For example, if mining the schwartzium were simply more expensive than Bob had anticipated, such that Bob would make little or no profit on selling the schwartzium, Bob's mistake defense most likely would fail. Likewise, if Bob expressly agreed he would take the mining rights regardless of whether he could mine the schwartzium, Bob's defense would fail. Why might Bob's mistake defense succeed in the first problem and probably fail in the alternative problems?

Mutual mistake has three elements:

1. A mistake by both parties about the facts surrounding a transaction at the time a contract is made;

2. concerning a basic assumption on which the contract was made; and

3. which has a material effect on the parties' contractual exchange.

Exercise 5-17: *Sherwood v. Walker*

The next case, *Sherwood v. Walker*, is a classic case that addresses one of the three elements of mutual mistake without specifically naming it. As you read *Sherwood*, consider the following questions:

1. What are the key facts? (Hint: Pay particular attention to the details in the record that relate to the parties' beliefs about "Rose 2d of Aberlone".)

2. Which element of mistake does *Sherwood* address?

3. How does the court apply the element to the facts?

4. Do the majority judges and dissenters disagree about what the applicable law is or how it applies? Which opinion is more convincing to you? Why?

Sherwood v. Walker

66 Mich. 568, 33 N.W. 919 (1887)

Morse, J. Replevin for a cow. Suit commenced in justice's court; judgment for plaintiff; appealed to circuit court of Wayne county, and verdict and judgment for plaintiff in that court. The defendants bring error, and set out 25 assignments of the same.

The main controversy depends upon the construction of a contract for the sale of the cow.... The defendants reside at Detroit, but are in business at Walkerville, Ontario, and have a farm at Greenfield, in Wayne county, upon which were some blooded cattle supposed to be barren as breeders. The Walkers are importers and breeders of polled Angus cattle. The plaintiff is a banker living at Plymouth, in Wayne county. He called upon the defendants at Walkerville for the purchase of some of their stock, but found none there that suited him. Meeting one of the defendants afterwards, he was informed that they had a few head upon their Greenfield farm. He was asked to go out and look at them, with the statement at the time that they were probably barren, and would not breed. May 5, 1886, plaintiff went out to Greenfield, and saw the cattle. A few days thereafter, he called upon one of the defendants with the view of purchasing a cow, known as "Rose 2d of Aberlone." After considerable talk, it was agreed that defendants would telephone Sherwood at his home in Plymouth in reference to the price. The second morning after this talk he was called up by telephone, and the terms of the sale were finally agreed upon. He was to pay five and one-half cents per pound, live weight, fifty pounds shrinkage....

On the twenty-first of the same month the plaintiff went to defendants' farm at Greenfield, and presented the order and letter to Graham, who informed him that the defendants had instructed him not to deliver the cow. Soon after, the plaintiff tendered to Hiram Walker, one of the defendants, $80, and demanded the cow. Walker refused to take the money or deliver the cow. The plaintiff then instituted this suit. After he had secured possession of the cow under the writ of replevin, the plaintiff caused her to be weighed by the constable who served the writ, at a place other than King's cattle-yard. She weighed 1,420 pounds.

Note that the parties' view as to what they were buying and selling is revealed in how they calculated their price.

[At trial, t]he defendants ... introduced evidence tending to show that at the time of the alleged sale it was believed by both the plaintiff and themselves that the cow was barren and would not breed; that she cost $850, and if not barren would be worth from $750 to $1,000 ... that the defendants were informed by said Graham that in his judgment the cow was with calf, and therefore they instructed him not to deliver her to plaintiff, and on the twentieth of May, 1886, telegraphed plaintiff what Graham thought about the cow being with calf, and that consequently they could not sell her. The cow had a calf in the month of October following....

It appears from the record that both parties supposed this cow was barren and would not breed, and she was sold by the pound for an insignificant sum as compared with her real value if a breeder. She was evidently sold and purchased on the relation of her value for beef, unless the plaintiff had learned of her true condition, and concealed such knowledge from the defendants. Before the plaintiff secured possession of the animal, the defendants learned that she was with calf, and therefore of great value, and undertook to rescind the sale by refusing to deliver her. The circuit judge ruled that this fact did not avoid the sale and it made no difference whether she was barren or not. I am of the opinion that the court erred in this holding. I know that this is a close question, and the dividing line between the adjudicated cases is not easily discerned. But it must be considered as well settled that a party who has given an apparent consent to a contract of sale may refuse to execute it, or he may avoid it after it has been completed, if the assent was founded, or the contract made, upon the mistake of a material fact,—such as the subject-matter of the sale, the price, or some collateral fact materially inducing the agreement; and this can be done when the mistake is mutual. [Citations omitted.]

If there is a difference or misapprehension as to the substance of the thing bargained for; if the thing actually delivered or received is different in substance from the thing bargained for, and intended to be sold,—then there is no contract; but if it be only a difference in some quality or accident, even though the mistake may have been the actuating motive to the purchaser or seller, or both of them, yet the contract remains binding. "The difficulty in every case is to determine whether the mistake or misapprehension is as to the substance of the whole contract, going, as it were, to the root of the matter, or only to some point, even though a material point, an error as to which does not affect the substance of the whole consideration." *Kennedy v. Panama, etc., Mail Co.*, L.R. 2 Q.B. 580, 587. It has been held, in accordance with the principles above stated, that where a horse is bought under the belief that he is sound, and both vendor and vendee honestly believe him to be sound, the purchaser must stand by his bargain, and pay the full price, unless there was a warranty.

It seems to me, however, in the case made by this record, that the mistake or misapprehension of the parties went to the whole substance of the agreement. If the cow was a breeder, she was worth at least $750; if barren, she was worth not over $80. The parties would not have made the contract of sale except upon the understanding and belief that she was incapable of breeding, and of no use as a cow. It is true she is now the identical animal that they thought her to be when the contract was made; there is no mistake as to the identity of the creature. Yet the mistake was not the mere quality of the animal, but went to the very nature of the thing. A barren cow is substantially a different creature than a breeding one. There is as much difference between them for all purposes of use as there is between an ox and a cow that is capable of breeding and giving milk. If the mutual mistake had simply related to the fact whether she was with calf or not for one season, then it might have been a good sale, but the mistake affected the character of the animal for all time, and for its present and ultimate use. She was not in fact the animal, or the kind of animal, the defendants intended to sell or the plaintiff to buy. She

Be sure you understand why the hypothetical horse contract discussed by the court is distinguishable from the actual case.

was not a barren cow, and, if this fact had been known, there would have been no contract. The mistake affected the substance of the whole consideration, and it must be considered that there was no contract to sell or sale of the cow as she actually was. The thing sold and bought had in fact no existence. She was sold as a beef creature would be sold; she is in fact a breeding cow, and a valuable one. The court should have instructed the jury that if they found that the cow was sold, or contracted to be sold, upon the understanding of both parties that she was barren, and useless for the purpose of breeding, and that in fact she was not barren, but capable of breeding, then the defendants had a right to rescind, and to refuse to deliver, and the verdict should be in their favor.

The judgment of the court below must be reversed, and a new trial granted, with costs of this court to defendants....

Sherwood, J. (*dissenting.*) I do not concur in the opinion given by my brethren in this case. I think the judgments before the justice and at the circuit were right.... There is no pretense there was any fraud or concealment in the case, and an intimation or insinuation that such a thing might have existed on the part of either of the parties would undoubtedly be a greater surprise to them than anything else that has occurred in their dealings or in the case.

Notice the similarities and differences between the majority and dissenting opinions' renditions of the facts. Do you think the majority would have let the seller out of the contract if it had agreed with the dissent's version of the facts?

As has already been stated by my brethren, the record shows that the plaintiff is a banker and farmer as well, carrying on a farm, and raising the best breeds of stock, and lived in Plymouth, in the county of Wayne, 23 miles from Detroit; that the defendants lived in Detroit, and were also dealers in stock of the higher grades; that they had a farm at Walkerville, in Canada, and also one in Greenfield in said county of Wayne, and upon these farms the defendants kept their stock. The Greenfield farm was about 15 miles from the plaintiff's. In the spring of 1886 the plaintiff, learning that the defendants had some "polled Angus cattle" for sale, was desirous of purchasing some of that breed, and meeting the defendants, or some of them, at Walkerville, inquired about them, and was informed that they had none at Walkerville, "but had a few head left on their farm in Greenfield, and asked the plaintiff to go and see them, stating that in all probability they were sterile and would not breed." In accordance with said request, the plaintiff, on the fifth day of May, went out and looked at the defendants' cattle at Greenfield, and found one called "Rose, Second," which he wished to purchase, and the terms were finally agreed upon at five and a half cents per pound, live weight, 50 pounds to be deducted for shrinkage. The sale was in writing, and the defendants gave an order to the plaintiff directing the man in charge of the Greenfield farm to deliver the cow to plaintiff. This was done on the fifteenth of May. On the twenty-first of May plaintiff went to get his cow, and the defendants refused to let him have her; claiming at the time that the man in charge at the farm thought the cow was with calf, and, if such was the case, they would not sell her for the price agreed upon. The record further shows that the defendants, when they sold the cow, believed the cow was not with calf, and barren; that from what the plaintiff had been told by defendants (for it does not appear he had any other knowledge or facts from which he could form an opinion) he believed the cow was farrow, but still thought she could be made to breed. The foregoing shows the entire interview and treaty between the parties as to the sterility and qualities of the cow sold to the plaintiff. The cow had a calf in the month of October.

There is no question but that the defendants sold the cow representing her of the breed and quality they believed the cow to be, and that the purchaser so understood it. And the buyer purchased her believing her to be of the breed represented by the sellers, and possessing all the qualities stated, and even more. He believed she would breed. There is no pretense that the plaintiff bought the cow for beef, and there is nothing in the record indicating that he would have bought her at all only that he thought she might be made to breed. Under the foregoing facts, and these are all that are contained in the record material to the contract, it is held that because it turned out that the plaintiff was more correct in his judgment as to one quality of the cow than the defendants, and a quality, too, which could not by any possibility be positively known at the time by either party to exist, the contract may be annulled by the defendants at their pleasure. I know of no law, and have not been referred to any, which will justify any such holding, and I think the circuit judge was right in his construction of the contract between the parties.

It is claimed that a mutual mistake of a material fact was made by the parties when the contract of sale was made. There was no warranty in the case of the quality of the animal. When a mistaken fact is relied upon as ground for rescinding, such fact must not only exist at the time the contract is made, but must have been known to one or both of the parties. Where there is no warranty, there can be no mistake of fact when no such fact exists, or, if in existence, neither party knew of it, or could know of it; and that is precisely this case. If the owner of a Hambletonian horse had speeded him, and was only able to make him go a mile in three minutes, and should sell him to another, believing that was his greatest speed, for $300, when the purchases believed he could go much faster, and made the purchase for that sum, and a few days thereafter, under more favorable circumstances, the horse was driven a mile in 2 min. 16 sec., and was found to be worth $20,000, I hardly think it would be held, either at law or in equity, by any one, that the seller in such case could rescind the contract. The same legal principles apply in each case.

In this case neither party knew the actual quality and condition of this cow at the time of the sale. The defendants say, or rather said, to the plaintiff, "they had a few head left on their farm in Greenfield, and asked plaintiff to go and see them, stating to plaintiff that in all probability they were sterile and would not breed." Plaintiff did go as requested, and found there these cows, including the one purchased, with a bull. The cow had been exposed, but neither knew she was with calf or whether she would breed. The defendants thought she would not, but the plaintiff says that he thought she could be made to breed, but believed she was not with calf. The defendants sold the cow for what they believed her to be, and the plaintiff bought her as he believed she was, after the statements made by the defendants. No conditions whatever were attached to the terms of sale by either party. It was in fact as absolute as it could well be made, and I know of no precedent as authority by which this court can alter the contract thus made by these parties in writing, interpolate in it a condition by which, if the defendants should be mistaken in their belief that the cow was barren, she could be returned to them and their contract should be annulled. It is not the duty of the courts to destroy contracts when called upon to enforce them, after they have been legally made. There was no mistake of any material fact by either of the parties in the case as would license the vendors to rescind. There was no difference between the parties, nor mis-apprehension, as to the substance of the thing bargained for, which was a cow supposed to be barren by one party, and believed not to be by the other. As to the quality of the animal, subsequently developed, both parties were equally ignorant, and as to this each party took his chances. If this were not the law, there would be no safety in purchasing this kind of stock.

I entirely agree with the brethren that the right to rescind occurs when-ever "the thing actually delivered or received is different in substance from the thing bargained for, and intended to be sold; but if it be only a difference in some quality or accident, even though the misapprehension may have been the actuating motive" of the parties in making the contract, yet it will remain binding. In this case the cow sold was the one delivered. What might or might not happen to her after the sale formed no element in the contract. [Judge Sher-wood then discussed the cases relied upon by the majority.]

The foregoing are all the authorities relied on as supporting the positions taken by my brethren in this case. I fail to discover any similarity between them and the present case; and I must say, further, in such examination as I have been able to make, I have found no adjudicated case going to the extent, either in law or equity, that has been held in this case going to the extent, ei-ther in law or equity, that has been held in this case. In this case, if either party had superior knowledge as to the qualities of this animal to the other, certainly the defendants had such advantage. I understand the law to be well settled that "there is no breach of any implied confidence that one party will not profit by his superior knowledge as to facts and circumstances" actually within the knowledge of both, because neither party reposes in any such con-fidence unless it be specially tendered or required, and that a general sale does not imply warranty of any quality, or the absence of any; and if the seller rep-resents to the purchaser what he himself believes as to the qualities of an an-imal, and the purchaser buys relying upon his own judgment as to such qualities, there is no warranty in the case, and neither has a cause of action against the other if he finds himself to have been mistaken in judgment.

The only pretense for avoiding this contract by the defendants is that they erred in judgment as to the qualities and value of the animal. I think the prin-ciples adopted by Chief Justice Campbell in *Williams v. Spurr* completely cover this case, and should have been allowed to control in its decision. [Citations omitted.] The judgment should be affirmed.

Exercise 5-18: *Sherwood* Revisited

1. Would the result in this case have been different if Rose were a horse? A pig? A mutt dog?

2. What would the result have been if Walker had agreed to sell Rose 2nd of Aber-lone to Sherwood and delivered instead a different brood cow, Daisy 2nd, that both parties mistakenly believed was Rose 2nd? For a case in point, see *Lane-Lott v. White*, 126 So.3d 1016 (Miss.App. 2013).

3. Given the ability of modern technology to ascertain whether an animal has been impregnated, would this case be decided the same way today?

4. Did the mistake in this case have a material effect on the exchange? How so?

5. Courts often consider whether a party claiming a mistake assumed the risk of that mistake in addition to applying the three elements of mutual mistake listed before the *Sherwood* case. Accordingly, assumption of risk could be viewed as an additional element of mutual mistake. It is better understood, however, as a ground on which a court can refuse in its discretion to order rescission even though the elements of mutual mistake are made out. In any event, assumption of risk is frequently an issue in mutual mistake cases. Consequently, you should consider assumption of risk in every mistake problem you analyze.

There are three situations in which a party may be found to have assumed a risk:

1. A contract allocates a risk to one party;

2. One party knows she has limited knowledge, but nonetheless treats that limited knowledge as sufficient (conscious ignorance); or

3. A court considers it is just to allocate a risk to one party.

If the *Sherwood* majority had analyzed the assumption of risk issue, would the court have reached the same result? Why or why not? (Hint: Focus on the second and third situations in which a party may be found to have assumed a risk.)

Exercise 5-19: *Lenawee County Board of Health v. Messerly*

The next case, *Lenawee County Board of Health v. Messerly*, continues to examine what constitutes a "basic assumption" and also examines the assumption of risk issue. As you read *Messerly*, consider the following questions:

1. What are the key facts of this case? Pay particular attention to the details of the alleged mistake and the terms of the land contract.

2. Why does the court conclude that the fact at issue related to a basic assumption on which the parties had made the contract?

3. The court states that the mistake had a material effect on the exchange without really explaining its reasoning. Why did the mistake have a material effect on the exchange?

4. Why does the court conclude the Pickleses assumed the risk?

5. Your textbook authors disagree with the court's assumption of risk conclusion. Develop an argument that the Pickleses did not assume the risk.

Lenawee County Board of Health v. Messerly
417 Mich. 17, 331 N.W.2d 203 (1982)

Ryan, Justice. In March of 1977, Carl and Nancy Pickles purchased from William and Martha Messerly a 600-square-foot tract of land upon which is located a three-unit apartment building. Shortly after the transaction was closed, the Lenawee County Board of Health condemned the property and obtained a permanent injunction which prohibits human habitation on the premises until the defective sewage system is brought into conformance with the Lenawee County sanitation code.

We are required to determine whether the Pickleses should prevail in their attempt to avoid this land contract on the basis of mutual mistake and failure of consideration. We conclude that the parties did entertain a mutual misapprehension of fact, but that the circumstances of this case do not warrant rescission.

The facts of the case are not seriously in dispute. In 1971, the Messerlys acquired approximately one acre plus 600 square feet of land. A three-unit apartment building was situated upon the 600-square-foot portion. The trial court found that, prior to this transfer, the Messerlys' predecessor in title, Mr. Bloom, had installed a septic tank on the property without a permit and in violation of the applicable health code. The Messerlys used the building as an income investment property ...

After inspecting the property, Mr. and Mrs. Pickles executed a new land contract with the Messerlys on March 21, 1977. It provided for a purchase price of $25,500. A clause was added to the end of the land contract form which provides:

> "17. Purchaser has examined this property and agrees to accept same
> in its present condition. There are no other or additional written or
> oral understandings."

Five or six days later, when the Pickleses went to introduce themselves to the tenants, they discovered raw sewage seeping out of the ground. Tests conducted by a sanitation expert indicated the inadequacy of the sewage system. The Lenawee County Board of Health subsequently condemned the property and initiated this lawsuit in the Lenawee Circuit Court against the Messerlys as land contract vendors, and the Pickleses, as vendees, to obtain a permanent injunction proscribing human habitation of the premises until the property was brought into conformance with the Lenawee County sanitation code. The injunction was granted.

 . . . .

The additional information provided is crucial to the court's basic assumption analysis. Why?

[Authors' note: The following additional factual information appears in a later, deleted portion of the court's opinion. 2,500 square feet of property is necessary to support a sewage system adequate to serve a three-family dwelling and it was impossible to remedy the already illegal septic system within the confines of the 600-square-foot parcel].

When no payments were made on the land contract, the Messerlys [sued] the Pickleses seeking foreclosure, sale of the property, and a deficiency judgment. Mr. and Mrs. Pickles then counterclaimed for rescission against the Messerlys....

[T]he [trial] court concluded that the Pickleses had no cause of action against ... the Messerlys ... as there was no fraud or misrepresentation. This ruling was predicated on the trial judge's conclusion that none of the parties knew of ... the resultant problem with the septic system until it was discovered by the Pickleses, and that the sanitation problem was not caused by any of the parties. The trial court held that the property was purchased "as is"....

Mr. and Mrs. Pickles appealed.... The Court of Appeals ... reversed the finding of no cause of action on the Pickleses' claims against the Messerlys. [Citations omitted.] It concluded that the mutual mistake between the Messerlys and the Pickleses went to a basic, as opposed to a collateral, element of the contract,[9] and that the parties intended to transfer income—producing rental property but, in actuality, the vendees paid $25,500 for an asset without value.

We granted the Messerlys' application for leave to appeal....

A contract may be rescinded because of a mutual misapprehension of the parties, but this remedy is granted only in the sound discretion of the court. [Citations omitted.] [The Messerlys] argue that the parties' mistake relates only to the quality or value of the real estate transferred, and that such mistakes are collateral to the agreement and do not justify rescission....

[The Pickleses] contend ... that in this case the parties were mistaken as to the very nature of the character of the consideration and claim that the pervasive and essential quality of this mistake renders rescission appropriate. They cite in support of that view *Sherwood v. Walker,* 66 Mich. 568, 33 N.W. 919 (1887), the famous "barren cow" case. In that case, the parties agreed to the sale and purchase of a cow which was thought to be barren, but which was, in reality, with calf. When the seller discovered the fertile condition of his cow, he refused to deliver her. In permitting rescission, the Court stated:

> It seems to me, however, in the case made by this record, that the mistake ... went to the whole substance of the agreement. If the cow was a breeder, she was worth at least $750; if barren, she was worth not over $80. The parties would not have made the contract of sale except upon the understanding and belief that she was incapable of breeding, and of no use as a cow. It is true she is now the identical animal that they thought her to be when the contract was made; there is no mistake as to the identity of the creature. Yet the mistake was not of the mere quality of the animal, but went to the very nature of the thing. A barren cow is substantially a different creature than a breeding one.... If the mutual mistake had simply related to the fact whether she was with calf or not for one season, then it might have been a good sale; but the mistake affected the character of the animal for all time, and for her present and ultimate use.... The thing sold and bought had in fact no existence. She was sold as a beef creature would be sold; she is in fact a breeding cow, and a valuable one....

[R]escission is indicated when the mistaken belief relates to a basic assumption of the parties upon which the contract is made, and which materially affects the agreed performances of the parties. [Citations omitted.] Rescission is not available, however, to relieve a party who has assumed the risk of loss in connection with the mistake. [Citations omitted.][10]

---

9. Mr. and Mrs. Pickles did not appeal the trial court's finding that there was no fraud or misrepresentation by the Messerlys or Mr. and Mrs. Barnes. Likewise, the propriety of that ruling is not before this Court today.

10. § 154. When a Party Bears the Risk of a Mistake. A party bears the risk of a mistake when: (a) the risk is allocated to him by agreement of the parties; or (b) he is aware, at the time the contract is

All of the parties to this contract erroneously assumed that the property transferred by the vendors to the vendees was suitable for human habitation and could be utilized to generate rental income. The fundamental nature of these assumptions is indicated by the fact that their invalidity changed the character of the property transferred, thereby frustrating, indeed precluding, Mr. and Mrs. Pickles' intended use of the real estate. Although the Pickleses are disadvantaged by enforcement of the contract, performance is advantageous to the Messerlys, as the property at issue is less valuable absent its income-earning potential. Nothing short of rescission can remedy the mistake. Thus, the parties' mistake as to a basic assumption materially affects the agreed performances of the parties.

Despite the significance of the mistake made by the parties, we reverse the Court of Appeals because we conclude that equity does not justify the remedy sought by Mr. and Mrs. Pickles ...

A court need not grant rescission in every case in which the mutual mistake relates to a basic assumption and materially affects the agreed performance of the parties.

In cases of mistake by two equally innocent parties, we are required, in the exercise of our equitable powers, to determine which blameless party should assume the loss resulting from the misapprehension they shared ...

Equity suggests that, in this case, the risk should be allocated to the purchasers. We are guided to that conclusion, in part, by the standards announced in § 154 of the RESTATEMENT (SECOND) OF CONTRACTS, for determining when a party bears the risk of mistake. Section 154(a) suggests that the court should look first to whether the parties have agreed to the allocation of the risk between themselves. While there is no express assumption in the contract by either party of the risk of the property becoming uninhabitable, there was indeed some agreed allocation of the risk to the vendees by the incorporation of an "as is" clause into the contract....

That is a persuasive indication that the parties considered that, as between them, such risk as related to the "present condition" of the property should lie with the purchaser. If the "as is" clause is to have any meaning at all, it must be interpreted to refer to those defects which were unknown at the time that the contract was executed. Thus, the parties assigned the risk of loss to Mr. and Mrs. Pickles.

We conclude that Mr. and Mrs. Pickles are not entitled to the equitable remedy of rescission and, accordingly, reverse the decision the Court of Appeals.

The "basic assumption" element discussed in *Messerly* should sound familiar to you because it is similar to the material fact element of misrepresentation. Students often struggle to understand what the basic assumption element means. Two factors make this element difficult to understand. First, courts struggle with what "basic" means. Common definitions include "core of the deal," "essence of the contract," "goes to the very nature of the property being sold," and "root of the matter." Second, courts are frequently

---

made, that he has only limited knowledge with respect to the facts to which the mistake relates but treats his limited knowledge as sufficient; or (c) the risk is allocated to him by the court on the ground that it is reasonable in the circumstances to do so.

unclear about the difference between a fact that is material and a fact that is basic. Table 5-6 clarifies the distinction between material and basic.

Table 5-6: Distinction between "Material" and "Basic" Facts

	Element of What Claim	How Defined by Courts	Focus of Analysis
Material Fact	Misrepresentation	A fact that a reasonable person would consider important in evaluating the transaction	Is this a fact a prudent person would want to know?
Basic Fact	Mistake	A fact that goes to the essence of the contract	Is this a fact that is central to the whole deal?

When a problem presents a mutual mistake issue, the parties make predictable arguments as to whether the fact was basic. The party claiming mistake will emphasize the specific details of what she was expecting. She will then argue that, because of the mistake, she is getting something entirely and radically different than what she thought she was getting. The party challenging a mistake defense will emphasize the general aspects of the deal made. Then, he will argue that the other party received that for which she bargained. Table 5-7 provides an example of these typical arguments in the context of the *Sherwood* case.

Table 5-7: Analysis of *Sherwood* Basic Assumption Issue

The issue presented is whether Rose's inability to bear calves was a basic assumption on which the contract was made. Courts define the term basic assumption in a variety of ways, including "essence of the contract" or "core of the deal." The key distinction is whether a fact is merely important or critical.

Here, the parties discussed Rose's inability to conceive and created a price based on what her weight would be after she had been slaughtered. On the one hand, the parties bargained for the purchase and sale of a particular cow, Rose. They, in fact, sold and purchased that particular cow. There was, therefore, no significant change from what they thought they were exchanging and what they exchanged.

On the other hand, the parties' choice to calculate the price based on Rose's weight suggests they regarded her as meat for sale to a butcher, not as a source of long-term future income (as she would be if she produced calves who could produce income either as meat or as calf-bearers). A cow purchased solely for slaughter is not the same thing as one that has long-term financial potential. Moreover, the parties discussed the issue of Rose's inability to conceive, which suggests that this ability was important to the transaction.

Accordingly, the core of the deal was Rose's inability to bear calves and therefore the mistake about that fact was a basic assumption on which the contract was made.

Exercise 5-20: *Messerly* Revisited

1. Would the *Messerly* court's conclusion on the basic assumption issue have been the same if the septic tank could have functioned on the lot with the

consequence that the County Board of Health had no grounds for condemning the property, but had a leak that needed repair?

2. Pierre offered to sell Dominic an old violin for $500,000. The parties agreed Dominic would pay this amount because they both believed the violin might be a Stradivarius (a very old brand of violin typically worth a few million dollars). The violin turned out not to be a Stradivarius and therefore was only worth $5,000. Does the parties' mistake about the brand of violin affect a basic assumption on which the contract was made?

3. In *Messerly*, the Pickleses were arguably aware, at the time the contract was made, that they had only limited knowledge with respect to the facts to which the mistake related. Could the court have concluded that the Pickleses assumed the risk by conscious ignorance? Why or why not?

Exercise 5-21: *Wood v. Boynton*

Your last mutual mistake case, *Wood v. Boynton*, is a bit tricky. The court does not clearly explain the reasons for its decision, but you should be able to reconcile the court's conclusion with the prior mistake cases you have read and the mistake law you have learned. As you read *Wood*, consider the following questions:

1. What are the key facts in this case? (Hint: Make sure you avoid assuming any facts not stated in the opinion. Many students think the case is wrongly decided based on a faulty assumption about the facts in this case.)

2. Synthesize this case with the prior mistake cases you have read and what you have learned about mistake law. (Hint: There are two alternative ways to understand this case, both of which are equally correct. Try to identify both.)

Wood v. Boynton

64 Wis. 265, 25 N.W. 42 (1885)

Taylor, J. This action was brought in the circuit court for Milwaukee county to recover the possession of an uncut diamond of the alleged value of $1,000. The case was tried in the circuit court, and after hearing all the evidence in the case, the learned circuit judge directed the jury to find a verdict for the defendants. The plaintiff excepted to such instruction, and, after a verdict was rendered for the defendants, moved for a new trial upon the minutes of the judge. The motion was denied, and the plaintiff duly excepted, and after judgment was entered in favor of the defendants, appealed to this court. The defendants are partners in the jewelry business. On the trial it appeared that on and before the twenty-eighth of December, 1883, the plaintiff was the owner of and in the possession of a small stone of the nature and value of which she was ignorant; that on that day she sold it to one of the defendants for the sum of one dollar. Afterwards it was ascertained that the stone was a rough diamond, and of the value of about $700. After hearing this fact the plaintiff tendered the defendants the one dollar, and ten cents as interest, and demanded a return of the stone to her. The defendants refused to deliver it, and therefore she commenced this action.

The plaintiff testified to the circumstances attending the sale of the stone to Mr. Samuel B. Boynton, as follows:

"... I thought I would ask him what the stone was, and I took it out of the box and asked him to please tell me what that was. He took it in his hand and seemed some time looking at it. I told him I had been told it was a topaz, and he said it might be. He says, 'I would buy this; would you sell it?' I told him I did not know but what I would. What would it be worth? And he said he did not know; he would give me a dollar and keep it as a specimen, and I told him I would not sell it; and it was certainly pretty to look at. He asked me where I found it, and I told him in Eagle. He asked about how far out, and I said right in the village, and I went out. Afterwards, and about the twenty-eighth of December, I needed money pretty badly, and thought every dollar would help, and I took it back to Mr. Boynton and told him I had brought back the topaz, and he says, 'Well, yes; what did I offer you for it?' and I says, 'One dollar,' and he stepped to the change drawer and gave me the dollar, and I went out."

In another part of her testimony she [said]:

"Before I sold the stone I had no knowledge whatever that it was a diamond. I told him that I had been advised that it was probably a topaz, and he said probably it was. The stone was about the size of a canary bird's egg, nearly the shape of an egg, worn pointed at one end; it was nearly straw color, a little darker."

She also testified that before this action was commenced she tendered the defendants $1.10, and demanded the return of the stone, which they refused. This is substantially all the evidence of what took place at and before the sale to the defendants, as testified to by the plaintiff herself. She produced no other witness on that point.

The evidence on the part of the defendant is not very different from the version given by the plaintiff, and certainly is not more favorable to the plaintiff. Mr. Samuel B. Boynton, the defendant to whom the stone was sold, testified that at the time he bought this stone, he had never seen an uncut diamond; had seen cut diamonds, but they are quite different from the uncut ones; "he had no idea this was a diamond, and it never entered his brain at that time." Considerable evidence was given as to what took place after the sale and purchase, but that evidence has very little if any bearing, upon the main point in the case.

This evidence clearly shows that the plaintiff sold the stone in question to the defendants, and delivered it to them in December, 1883, for a consideration of one dollar. By such sale the title to the stone passed by the sale and delivery to the defendants. How has that title been divested and again vested in the plaintiff? The contention of the learned counsel for the appellant is that the title became vested in the plaintiff by the tender to the Boyntons of the purchase money with interest, and a demand of a return of the stone to her. Unless such tender and demand revested the title in the appellant, she cannot maintain her action. The only question in the case is whether there was anything in the sale which entitled the vendor (the appellant) to rescind the sale and so revest the title in her. The only reasons we know of for rescinding a sale and revesting the title in the vendor so that he may maintain an action at law for the recovery of the possession against his vendee are (1) that the vendee was guilty of some fraud in procuring a sale to be made to him; (2) that there was a mistake made by the vendor in delivering an article which was not the article sold,—a mistake in fact as to the identity of the thing sold with the thing delivered upon the sale. This last is not in reality a rescission of the sale made, as the thing delivered was not the thing sold, and no title ever passed to the vendee by such delivery.

In this case, upon the plaintiff's own evidence, there can be no just ground for alleging that she was induced to make the sale she did by any fraud or unfair dealings on the part of Mr. Boynton. Both were entirely ignorant at the time of the character of the stone and of its intrinsic value. Mr. Boynton was not an expert in uncut diamonds, and had made no examination of the stone, except to take it in his hand and look at it before he made the offer of one dollar, which was refused at the time, and afterwards accepted without any comment or further examination made by Mr. Boynton. The appellant had the stone in her possession for a long time, and it appears from her own statement that she had made some inquiry as to its nature and qualities. If she chose to sell it without further investigation as to its intrinsic value to a person who was guilty of no fraud or unfairness which induced her to sell it for a small sum, she cannot repudiate the sale because it is afterwards ascertained that she made a bad bargain. [Citation omitted.] There is no pretense of any mistake as to the identity of the thing sold. It was produced by the plaintiff and exhibited to the vendee before the sale was made, and the thing sold was delivered to the vendee when the purchase price was paid. [Citations omitted.] Suppose the appellant had produced the stone, and said she had been told it was a diamond, and she believed it was, but had no knowledge herself as to its character or value, and Mr. Boynton had given her $500 for it, could he have rescinded the sale if it had turned out to be a topaz or any other stone of very small value? Could Mr. Boynton have rescinded the sale on the ground of mistake? Clearly not, nor could he rescind it on the ground that there had been a breach of warranty, because there was no warranty, nor could he rescind it on the ground of fraud, unless he could show that she falsely declared that she had been told it was a diamond, or, if she had been so told, still she knew it was not a diamond. [Citation omitted.]

We can find nothing in the evidence from which it could be justly inferred that Mr. Boynton, at the time he offered the plaintiff one dollar for the stone, had any knowledge of the real value of the stone, or that he entertained even a belief that the stone was a diamond. It cannot, therefore, be said that there was a suppression of knowledge on the part of the defendant as to the value of the stone which a court of equity might seize upon to avoid the sale. The following cases show that, in the absence of fraud or warranty, the value of the property sold, as compared with the price paid, is no ground for rescission of a sale. [Citations omitted.] However unfortunate the plaintiff may have been in selling this valuable stone for a mere nominal sum, she had failed entirely to make out a case either of fraud or mistake in the sale such as will entitle her to a rescission of such sale so as to recover the property sold in an action at law.

The judgment of the circuit court is affirmed.

This discussion is the court's rejection of plaintiff's mistake claim.

Exercise 5-22: *Wood* Revisited

1. Isn't a topaz more different from a diamond than a barren cow is from a fertile cow?

2. Change one fact in *Sherwood* so that the result in that case would be the same as in *Wood*.

3. Change one fact in *Wood* so that the result is the same as the result in *Sherwood*.

4. Consider again the Pierre-Dominic violin transaction in Exercise 5-20. Could that problem, which you previously analyzed as a basic assumption issue, be decided on the same basis as *Wood*? Why or why not?

5. Becky Buyer entered into negotiations with Sally Seller to buy Selleracre, a huge undeveloped tract of land. During negotiations, the parties agreed that they did not know how many acres were in Selleracre and therefore retained a surveyor to determine the acreage. The surveyor reported an acreage amount to the parties, and the parties agreed to a purchase price. During the parties' negotiations, Buyer requested that the parties insert a clause that would allow either party to withdraw from the deal without consequence if the surveyor's acreage determination proved to be erroneous. Seller refused to agree to that term. The parties then signed the contract without including the term Buyer had requested. During escrow, Buyer discovered the surveyor had overstated the acreage by fifty percent and refused to perform the contract. Could this problem be decided on the same basis as *Wood*? Why or why not?

6. On December 1, Devin crashed into Paula's car, severely damaging the car. Paula had a mild headache after the crash. Later that day, Devin and Paula agreed that Devin would pay all the repair costs for Paula's car and Paula signed a promise not to sue Devin for "all injuries, known and unknown, relating to the December 1 crash." One month later, Paula's headache was diagnosed as a brain injury. As a result, Paula incurred over $200,000 in medical treatment costs. Can Paula rescind her promise not to sue on the basis of mistake?

B. Unilateral Mistake

This section continues the discussion of the second contract defense listed in Diagram 5-1 at the beginning of this chapter: **mistake**. As you now know, there are two types of mistake defenses: mutual mistake and unilateral mistake. You have already learned about mutual mistake. You should recall that the three elements of mutual mistake are:

1. **A mistake by both parties about the facts surrounding a transaction at the time a contract is made;**

2. **Concerning a basic assumption on which the contract was made; and**

3. **Which has a material effect on the parties' contractual exchange.**

Unilateral mistake has four elements. The first three elements are the same as for mutual mistake, except, in the first element, the mistake only needs to be made by one party. The additional element for unilateral mistake is:

4.   Either: (a) the non-mistaken party knew of, should have known of, or caused the mistake, or (b) the mistake makes the contract a grossly unfair (unconscionable) bargain.

Alternative 4(a) makes mistake law consistent with non-disclosure law. As you already learned, there is a duty to disclose "basic" facts. Consequently, if a party can show a unilateral mistake as to a basic fact and the other party knows the truth or should know the truth, the other party has a duty to disclose the truth. Otherwise, the mistaken party can have the contract rescinded based on non-disclosure or mistake. Likewise, there is a duty to disclose if a representation has misled a party. Otherwise, a party whose mistake was caused by the other party may assert mistake as a defense.

Alternative 4(b) allows rescission for unilateral mistake if the mistake makes the deal grossly unfair or unconscionable. For example, consider a hypothetical case of buyers of a lake house who purchased the house for a year-round home and could not afford a second home. Unknown to them, and despite reasonable efforts to collect relevant information, the house was unsuitable for living in during the winter. A court would probably hold that the buyers' mistake made the contract unconscionable and therefore would rescind the contract. You will learn more about unconscionability in the section devoted to unconscionability later in this chapter.

As you learned in the section on mutual mistake, courts usually consider whether a party claiming mistake assumed the risk of that mistake. You will recall that there are three situations in which a party may be found to have assumed a risk:

1.   A contract allocates a risk to one party;

2.   One party knows she has limited knowledge, but nonetheless treats that limited knowledge as sufficient (conscious ignorance); or

3.   A court believes it is just to allocate a risk to one party.

Below is an excerpt from *Drennan v. Star Paving Co.* regarding unilateral mistake. You previously read *Drennan* in Chapter 4 when you learned about promissory estoppel. As you may recall, *Drennan* involved a subcontractor who inadvertently miscalculated its bid on a construction project. Before the subcontractor withdrew its bid, the general contractor used the bid in calculating its bid to the owner. After the general contractor was awarded the contract, the subcontractor purported to withdraw the bid. In the section of the court's opinion you read in Chapter 4, the court held that the doctrine of promissory estoppel prevented the subcontractor from revoking its offer because the general contractor had, in the meantime, relied on the bid in calculating its bid to the owner.

Exercise 5-23: *Drennan v. Star Paving Co.*

In the excerpt from *Drennan* below, the court addresses another one of the subcontractor's arguments: that it should be allowed out of the contract on the basis of unilateral mistake. In addition, *Drennan* raises a new ground for denying relief based on unilateral mistake: prejudice to the other party if the contract were rescinded. As you read the except from *Drennan,* consider the following questions:

1.   Which of the two alternative ways of proving the fourth unilateral mistake element was at issue?

2.   How did the court resolve that issue? Why?

3. Did the subcontractor present convincing evidence with respect to the other elements of mistake?

4. Why did the court conclude that the subcontractor could not restore the status quo?

Drennan v. Star Paving Co.
51 Cal. 2d 409, 333 P.2d 757 (1958)

... Defendant contends, however, that its bid was the result of mistake and that it was therefore entitled to revoke it. It relies on the rescission cases of *M. F. Kemper Const. Co. v. City of Los Angeles*, 37 Cal. 2d 696, and *Brunzell Const. Co. v. G. J. Weisbrod, Inc.*, 134 Cal. App. 2d 278. [Additional citations omitted.] In those cases, however, the bidder's mistake was known or should have been to the offeree, and the offeree could be placed in status quo. Of course, if plaintiff had reason to believe that defendant's bid was in error, he could not justifiably rely on it, and section 90 would afford no basis for enforcing it. [Citations omitted.] Plaintiff, however, had no reason to know that defendant had made a mistake in submitting its bid, since there was usually a variance of 160 per cent between the highest and lowest bids for paving in the desert around Lancaster. He committed himself to performing the main contract in reliance on defendant's figures. Under these circumstances defendant's mistake, far from relieving it of its obligation, constitutes an additional reason for enforcing it, for it misled plaintiff as to the cost of doing the paving....

Exercise 5-24: *Drennan* Revisited

1. Change the facts of *Drennan* in a way that will change the result on the mistake issue.

2. On the morning of February 22, 1968, Reed's employee began filling out a purchase order form for five different kinds of labels that Reed desired to buy from Monarch. In handwriting he filled in the blank spaces for four different types of labels. In the quantity column for each he noted "2M." (In the industry, "M" refers to thousands.) At that point, he was interrupted by a customer. It was not until later in the afternoon that he finished filling in the order form. He described the fifth label as "Label as Attached," attached a copy of the desired label, and in the quantity column wrote "4MM." (In the industry, "MM" refers to millions.) The fifth label became the basis of a lawsuit. The purchase order required delivery "at once." On April 10, 1968, four million labels were delivered to Reed via motor freight. Reed immediately contacted Monarch, stating that a terrible mistake had been made and that Reed only needed 4,000 copies of the fifth label. May Reed rescind the contract on the basis of unilateral mistake? Analyze the legal issue presented and be prepared to explain your answer.

Diagram 5-2: Duress

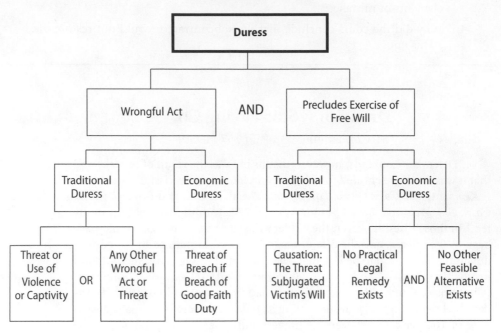

Duress

This section discusses the third contract defense listed in Diagram 5-1 at the beginning of this chapter: **duress.**

Duress has two elements:

1.   **One party must commit a wrongful act; and**

2.   **The wrongful act must preclude the other party from exercising his free will.**

There are two forms of duress claims: **traditional duress** and **economic duress.** Both are graphically depicted in Diagram 5-2. In traditional duress situations, one party uses violence or a threat of violence to preclude the other party from exercising her free will. A good example is a famous scene from the movie *The Godfather*.[11] The protagonist, Vito Corleone, holds a gun to a man's head and tells him that either his brains or his signature will appear on the contract in the next two minutes. The threat to shoot the man is a wrongful act and the fact that the man thinks he will be killed if he does not sign the contract precludes him from exercising his free will.

Traditional duress may also take the form of false imprisonment or a threat thereof to force someone to enter into a contract. For example, duress exists when one person locks another person in a room until he agrees to enter into a contract. False imprisonment, a tort, is a wrongful act and the fact that the other person can escape only by agreeing to a contract precludes him from exercising his free will. Traditional duress may also take any other form that includes a wrongful act, if that act precludes the exercise of free will. These days, traditional duress can encompass improper threats to make public embarrassing information about a person unless that person enters a contract on disadvantageous terms.

---

11. Paramount Pictures, 1972.

The second type of duress is economic duress. Economic duress includes situations where one party uses economic threats to overcome another party's will. The defense of economic duress frequently arises as an alternative to an argument that a contract has violated the pre-existing duty rule that you learned about in Chapter 3. Indeed, on your contracts exam, if you encounter facts that suggest a possible breach of the pre-existing duty rule, it is likely your professor will want you to address economic duress as well as the pre-existing duty rule.

Economic duress claims raise tricky issues such as whether a particular threat to breach a contract is in bad faith or is an appropriate demand for extra compensation for extra work. Therefore, economic duress cases require a careful analysis of whether a party's free will has been precluded. In most instances, a party can refuse to give in to a threat to breach a contract, hire someone else to fulfill the performance called for by the contract, and sue for breach.

Accordingly, to determine whether a situation raises an economic duress issue, look for a completely unjustified threat and a party who cannot afford to wait to let the legal system address the harm caused by the threatened breach.

Exercise 5-25: Duress

1. Create and write three hypotheticals in which a party uses a threat of violence or actual violence to subjugate the will of the other party to a contract.

2. Create and write three hypotheticals in which a party uses a threat of imprisonment or actual imprisonment to subjugate the will of the other party to a contract.

Exercise 5-26: *Austin Instrument, Inc. v. Loral Corp.*

The next case, *Austin Instrument, Inc. v. Loral Corporation*, provides a classic example of economic duress. Economic duress issues often arise in situations where parties make two contracts regarding the same subject matter (similar to situations in which pre-existing duty issues arise). As you read *Austin Instrument*, consider the following questions:

1. Look at Diagram 5-2, the graphic depiction of duress. Try to annotate the chart with the matching facts and holdings from *Austin Instrument*.

2. Why does the court apply a common law rule to a U.C.C. case? Why doesn't U.C.C. 2-209(1) require the court to rule in favor of Austin?

3. What is the policy for recognizing economic duress as a viable defense?

4. Is economic duress or the pre-existing duty rule a superior mechanism for analyzing these types of problems?

Austin Instrument, Inc. v. Loral Corporation
29 N.Y.2d 124, 272 N.E.2d 533 (1971)

Fuld, Chief Judge. The defendant, Loral Corporation, seeks to recover payment for goods delivered under a contract which it had with plaintiff

Austin Instrument, Inc., on the ground that the evidence establishes, as a matter of law, that it was forced to agree to an increase in price on the items in question under circumstances amounting to economic duress.

In July of 1965, Loral was awarded a $6,000,000 contract by the Navy for the production of radar sets. The contract contained a schedule of deliveries, a liquidated damages clause applying to late deliveries and a cancellation clause in case of default by Loral. The latter thereupon solicited bids for some 40 precision gear components needed to produce the radar sets, and awarded Austin a subcontract to supply 23 such parts. That party commenced delivery in early 1966.

In May, 1966, Loral was awarded a second Navy contract for the production of more radar sets and again went about soliciting bids. Austin bid on all 40 gear components but, on July 15, a representative from Loral informed Austin's president, Mr. Krauss, that his company would be awarded the subcontract only for those items on which it was low bidder. The Austin officer refused to accept an order for less than all 40 of the gear parts and on the next day he told Loral that Austin would cease deliveries of the parts due under the existing subcontract unless Loral consented to substantial increases in the prices provided for by that agreement—both retroactively for parts already delivered and prospectively on those not yet shipped—and placed with Austin the order for all 40 parts needed under Loral's second Navy contract. Shortly thereafter, Austin did, indeed, stop delivery. After contacting 10 manufacturers of precision gears and finding none who could produce the parts in time to meet its commitments to the Navy,[12] Loral acceded to Austin's demands; in a letter dated July 22, Loral wrote to Austin that "We have feverishly surveyed other sources of supply and find that because of the prevailing military exigencies, were they to start from scratch as would have to be the case, they could not even remotely begin to deliver on time to meet the delivery requirements established by the Government.... Accordingly, we are left with no choice or alternative but to meet your conditions."

Loral thereupon consented to the price increases insisted upon by Austin under the first subcontract and the latter was awarded a second subcontract making it the supplier of all 40 gear parts for Loral's second contract with the Navy. Although Austin was granted until September to resume deliveries, Loral did, in fact, receive parts in August and was able to produce the radar sets in time to meet its commitments to the Navy on both contracts. After Austin's last delivery under the second subcontract in July, 1967, Loral notified it of its intention to seek recovery of the price increases.

On September 15, 1967, Austin instituted this action against Loral to recover an amount in excess of $17,750 which was still due on the second subcontract. On the same day, Loral commenced an action against Austin claiming damages of some $22,250—the aggregate of the price increases under the first subcontract—on the ground of economic duress. The two actions were consolidated and, following a trial, Austin was awarded the sum it requested and Loral's complaint against Austin was dismissed on the ground that it was not shown that "it could not have obtained the items in question from other

---

12. The best reply Loral received was from a vendor who stated he could commence deliveries sometime in October.

sources in time to meet its commitment to the Navy under the first contract." A closely divided Appellate Division affirmed. [Citation omitted.] There was no material disagreement concerning the facts; as Justice Steuer stated in the course of his dissent below, "[the] facts are virtually undisputed, nor is there any serious question of law. The difficulty lies in the application of the law to these facts." [Citation omitted.]

The applicable law is clear and, indeed, is not disputed by the parties. A contract is voidable on the ground of duress when it is established that the party making the claim was forced to agree to it by means of a wrongful threat precluding the exercise of his free will. [Citations omitted.] The existence of economic duress or business compulsion is demonstrated by proof that "immediate possession of needful goods is threatened," [citation omitted], or, more particularly, in cases such as the one before us, by proof that one party to a contract has threatened to breach the agreement by withholding goods unless the other party agrees to some further demand. [Citations omitted.] However, a mere threat by one party to breach the contract by not delivering the required items, though wrongful, does not in itself constitute economic duress. It must also appear that the threatened party could not obtain the goods from another source of supply and that the ordinary remedy of an action for breach of contract would not be adequate.

We find without any support in the record the conclusion reached by the courts below that Loral failed to establish that it was the victim of economic duress. On the contrary, the evidence makes out a classic case, as a matter of law, of such duress.

It is manifest that Austin's threat to stop deliveries unless the prices were increased deprived Loral of its free will. As bearing on this, Loral's relationship with the Government is most significant. As mentioned above, its contract called for staggered monthly deliveries of the radar sets, with clauses calling for liquidated damages and possible cancellation on default. Because of its production schedule, Loral was, in July, 1966, concerned with meeting its delivery requirements in September, October and November, and it was for the sets to be delivered in those months that the withheld gears were needed. Loral had to plan ahead, and the substantial liquidated damages for which it would be liable, plus the threat of default, were genuine possibilities. Moreover, Loral did a substantial portion of its business with the Government, and it feared that a failure to deliver as agreed upon would jeopardize its chances for future contracts. These genuine concerns do not merit the label "'self-imposed, undisclosed and subjective'" which the Appellate Division majority placed upon them. It was perfectly reasonable for Loral, or any other party similarly placed, to consider itself in an emergency, duress situation.

Austin, however, claims that the fact that Loral extended its time to resume deliveries until September negates its alleged dire need for the parts. A Loral official testified on this point that Austin's president told him he could deliver some parts in August and that the extension of deliveries was a formality. In any event, the parts necessary for production of the radar sets to be delivered in September were delivered to Loral on September 1, and the parts needed for the October schedule were delivered in late August and early September. Even so, Loral had to "work ... around the clock" to meet its commitments. Considering that the best offer Loral received from the other vendors it contacted was commencement of delivery sometime in October, which, as the record shows, would have made it late in its deliveries to the Navy in both September and October, Loral's claim that it had no choice but to accede to Austin's demands is conclusively demonstrated.

We find unconvincing Austin's contention that Loral, in order to meet its burden, should have contacted the Government and asked for an extension of its delivery dates so as to enable it to purchase the parts from another vendor. Aside from the consideration that Loral was anxious to perform well in the Government's eyes, it could not be sure when it would obtain enough parts from a substitute vendor to meet its commitments. The only promise which it received from the companies it contacted was for *commencement* of deliveries, not full supply, and, with vendor delay common in this field, it would have been nearly impossible to know the length of the extension it should request. It must be remembered that Loral was producing a needed item of military hardware. Moreover, there is authority for Loral's position that nonperformance by a subcontractor is not an excuse for default in the main contract. [Citations omitted.] In light of all this, Loral's claim should not be held insufficiently supported because it did not request an extension from the Government.

Loral, as indicated above, also had the burden of demonstrating that it could not obtain the parts elsewhere within a reasonable time, and there can be no doubt that it met this burden. The 10 manufacturers whom Loral contacted comprised its entire list of "approved vendors" for precision gears, and none was able to commence delivery soon enough.[13] As Loral was producing a highly sophisticated item of military machinery requiring parts made to the strictest engineering standards, it would be unreasonable to hold that Loral should have gone to other vendors, with whom it was either unfamiliar or dissatisfied, to procure the needed parts. As Justice Steuer noted in his dissent, Loral "contacted all the manufacturers whom it believed capable of making these parts," 35 A.D.2d at 393, and this was all the law requires.

It is hardly necessary to add that Loral's normal legal remedy of accepting Austin's breach of the contract and then suing for damages would have been inadequate under the circumstances, as Loral would still have had to obtain the gears elsewhere with all the concomitant consequences mentioned above. In other words, Loral actually had no choice, when the prices were raised by Austin, except to take the gears at the "coerced" prices and then sue to get the excess back.…

In sum, the record before us demonstrates that Loral agreed to the price increases in consequence of the economic duress employed by Austin. Accordingly, the matter should be remanded to the trial court for a computation of its damages.

The order appealed from should be modified, with costs, by reversing so much thereof as affirms the dismissal of defendant Loral Corporation's claim and, except as so modified, affirmed.

---

13. Loral, as do many manufacturers, maintains a list of "approved vendors"; that is, vendors whose products, facilities, techniques and performance have been inspected and found satisfactory.

Exercise 5-27: *Austin Instrument* Revisited

1. Change the facts of *Austin Instrument* so that Loral Corporation would lose.

2. In cases where both the pre-existing duty rule and economic duress are implicated, either theory should lead you to the same conclusion. Skim the *Alaska Packers' Association v. Domenico* case that you previously read in Chapter 3, in the section entitled "The Pre-Existing Duty Rule." Then analyze the following problems after *Alaska Packers* as economic duress issues:

   a. Exercise 3-15, Q2.

   b. Exercise 3-15, Q4, parts b–d.

3. Tara Tenant's lease in Laura Landlord's building is set to expire on November 1. Landlord already has told Tenant that, because Landlord is planning to demolish the building on December 15 and build a shopping center on the site, Tenant will not be allowed to renew the lease and must, instead, vacate the premises. Assume Landlord's conduct is proper. Also assume, as is true in every state, a tenant who improperly refuses to vacate premises after the expiration of her lease may be removed by the landlord in a summary lawsuit called "unlawful detainer." Unlawful detainer actions typically take four weeks from start to finish. Tenant tells Landlord that she will not vacate unless Landlord agrees to pay Tenant $500. Landlord agrees and pays. After Tenant moves out, however, Landlord sues for restitution based on duress. Analyze the legal issue presented and be prepared to explain you answer.

4. Anna's brother, Chet, was a check-kiter, a fact that Anna knew. Check-kiting is a form of bank fraud that involves opening a series of checking accounts and then writing a series of checks for which you have insufficient funds and covering those checks with insufficiently funded checks from checking accounts at other banks. One day, Anna was contacted by Bob Banker who told Anna he had discovered Chet's check-kiting. Bob demanded that Anna cover Chet's checks, telling Anna that Chet would be prosecuted for check-kiting unless she agreed to pay. Unknown to Anna, who was not a legal expert, while there was a high risk that Chet would be prosecuted, Bob, who did not work for the prosecutor's office, had no control over whether Chet was prosecuted or not. Anna agreed to pay. May Anna rescind her agreement to pay?

5. A, who contracted to sell 1,000,000 widgets to B for $1.00 per widget, informs B that A will not deliver the widgets unless B agrees to pay an extra $.25 per widget. A informs B that a shortage in the world market of the metal out of which widgets are made has made the manufacture of widgets more expensive. To maintain A's planned profits, A needs the extra money. B desperately needs the widgets to build Whatchamacallits, which B has promised to deliver to C, a Whatchamacallit retailer. Another widget manufacturer, D, has enough widgets to meet B's needs but will charge B $1.10 per widget. B knows about D's supply but has had business conflicts with D in the past. B agrees to pay A the extra $.25 per widget. Must B pay A the extra $250,000?

Undue Influence

This section addresses the fourth contract defense listed in Diagram 5-1 at the beginning of this chapter: **undue influence**.

Exercise 5-28: Undue Influence

1. Read section 177 of the RESTATEMENT (SECOND) OF CONTRACTS. Try to paraphrase the requirements of section 177. Then, create a graphic organizer for the elements of undue influence.

2. Apply the undue influence rule you learned from section 177 to the following problems:

   a. Nelson, who is naïve and inexperienced in business matters, has long relied on Terry for business advice. Terry convinces Nelson to sell Nelson's car for $50,000, even though the fair market value of the car is $95,000. May Nelson get out of this contract on the basis of undue influence?

   b. Robert pesters his sickly, 88-year-old, wealthy Uncle Rich to exchange Rich's house and land for Robert's house and land. After five straight days of Robert's pestering, Rich gives in. Rich's house and land is worth much more than Robert's house and land. May Rich get out of this contract on the basis of undue influence?

   c. Assume the same problem presented in b, except Rich's house and land is worth less than Robert's house and land. May Rich get out of this contract on the basis of undue influence?

   d. What should an attorney or a relative do in circumstances such as those described in problems a through c to avoid raising an undue influence issue? In other words, what would you advise that an attorney or a relative do to ensure that no one contests a contract on the basis of undue influence?

Exercise 5-29: *Odorizzi v. Bloomfield School District*

The next case, *Odorizzi v. Bloomfield School District*, involves a complicated extension of a long line of cases holding that the exploitation by one party of another party's vulnerability is a ground for rescinding a contract. As you read *Odorizzi*, consider the following questions:

1. The case considers several theories as alternatives to undue influence. Why did the court reject duress, fraud, and mistake?

2. In several places in the *Odorizzi* opinion, the court makes comments and draws analogies that you will likely find offensive. The case also may offend you because it involves a man being arrested and being pressured to quit his job solely because he is alleged to be gay. Please don't let the prejudices in the court's opinion distract you from learning the lessons the case has to offer.

3. *Odorizzi* should refine your understanding of undue influence. Accordingly, use the case to refine and finalize your undue influence graphic organizer.

Odorizzi v. Bloomfield School District

246 Cal. App. 2d 123, 54 Cal. Rptr. 533 (1966)

Fleming, Justice. Appeal from a judgment dismissing plaintiff's amended complaint on demurrer.

Be sure you know what a "demurrer" is.

Plaintiff Donald Odorizzi was employed during 1964 as an elementary school teacher by defendant Bloomfield School District and was under contract with the District to continue to teach school the following year as a permanent employee. On June 10 he was arrested on criminal charges of homosexual activity, and on June 11 he signed and delivered to his superiors his written resignation as a teacher, a resignation which the District accepted on June 13. In July the criminal charges against Odorizzi were dismissed under Penal Code, section 995, and in September he sought to resume his employment with the District. On the District's refusal to reinstate him he filed suit for declaratory and other relief.

Odorizzi's amended complaint asserts his resignation was invalid because obtained through duress, fraud, mistake, and undue influence and given at a time when he lacked capacity to make a valid contract. Specifically, Odorizzi declares he was under such severe mental and emotional strain at the time he signed his resignation, having just completed the process of arrest, questioning by the police, booking, and release on bail, and having gone for forty hours without sleep, that he was incapable of rational thought or action. While he was in this condition and unable to think clearly, the superintendent of the District and the principal of his school came to his apartment. They said they were trying to help him and had his best interests at heart, that he should take their advice and immediately resign his position with the District, that there was no time to consult an attorney, that if he did not resign immediately the District would suspend and dismiss him from his position and publicize the proceedings, his "aforedescribed arrest" and cause him "to suffer extreme embarrassment and humiliation"; but that if he resigned at once the incident would not be publicized and would not jeopardize his chances of securing employment as a teacher elsewhere. Odorizzi pleads that because of his faith and confidence in their representations they were able to substitute their will and judgment in place of his own and thus obtain his signature to his purported resignation. A demurrer to his amended complaint was sustained without leave to amend.

By his complaint plaintiff in effect seeks to rescind his resignation pursuant to Civil Code, section 1689, on the ground that his consent had not been real or free within the meaning of Civil Code, section 1567, but had been obtained through duress, menace, fraud, undue influence, or mistake. A pleading under these sections is sufficient if, stripped of its conclusions, it sets forth sufficient facts to justify legal relief. [Citations omitted.] In our view the facts in the amended complaint are insufficient to state a cause of action for duress, menace, fraud, or mistake, but they do set out sufficient elements to justify rescission of a consent because of undue influence. We summarize our conclusions on each of these points.

No duress or menace has been pleaded. Duress consists in unlawful confinement of another's person, or relatives, or property, which causes him to consent to a transaction through fear. [Citations omitted.] Duress is often used interchangeably with menace [citation omitted] but in California menace is technically a threat of duress or a threat of injury to the person, property, or character of another. [Citations omitted.] We agree with respondent's contention that neither duress nor menace was involved in this case, because the action or threat in duress or menace must be unlawful, and a threat to take legal action is not unlawful unless the party making the threat knows the falsity of his claim. [Citation omitted.] The amended complaint shows in substance that the school representatives announced their intention to initiate suspension and dismissal proceedings under Education Code, section 13403, 13408 *et seq.*, at a time when the filing of such proceedings was not only their legal right but their positive duty as school officials. [Citations omitted.] Although the filing of such proceedings might be extremely damaging to plaintiff's reputation, the injury would remain incidental so long as the school officials acted in good faith in the performance of their duties. [Citations omitted.] Neither duress nor menace was present as a ground for rescission.

Nor do we find a cause of action for fraud.... Actual fraud involves conscious misrepresentation, or concealment, or non-disclosure of a material fact which induces the innocent party to enter the contract. [Citations omitted.] A complaint for fraud must plead misrepresentation, knowledge of falsity, intent to induce reliance, justifiable reliance, and resulting damage. [Citations omitted.] While the amended complaint charged misrepresentation, it failed to assert the elements of knowledge of falsity, intent to induce reliance, and justifiable reliance. A cause of action for actual fraud was therefore not stated....

As to mistake, the amended complaint fails to disclose any facts which would suggest that consent had been obtained through a mistake of fact or of law. The material facts of the transaction were known to both parties. Neither party was laboring under any misapprehension of law of which the other took advantage. The discussion between plaintiff and the school district representatives principally attempted to evaluate the probable consequences of plaintiff's predicament and to predict the future course of events. The fact that their speculations did not forecast the exact pattern which events subsequently took does not provide the basis for a claim that they were acting under some sort of mistake. The doctrine of mistake customarily involves such errors as the nature of the transaction, the identity of the parties, the identity of the things to which the contract relates, or the occurrence of collateral happenings. RESTATEMENT OF CONTRACTS § 502, cmt. e. Errors of this nature were not present in the case at bench.

However, the pleading does set out a claim that plaintiff's consent to the transaction had been obtained through the use of undue influence. Undue influence, in the sense we are concerned with here, is a shorthand legal phrase used to describe persuasion which tends to be coercive in nature, persuasion which overcomes the will without convincing the judgment. [Citation omitted.] The hallmark of such persuasion is high pressure, a pressure which works on mental, moral, or emotional weakness to such an extent that it approaches the boundaries of coercion. In this sense, undue influence has been called overpersuasion. [Citation omitted.] Misrepresentations of law or fact are not essential to the charge, for a person's will may be overborne without misrepresentation. By statutory definition undue influence includes "taking an unfair advantage of another's weakness of mind; or ... taking a grossly oppressive and unfair advantage of another's necessities or distress." [Citation omitted.] While most reported cases of undue influence involve persons who bear a confidential relationship to one another, a confidential or authoritative relationship between the parties need not be present when the undue influence involves unfair advantage taken of another's weakness or distress....

In essence undue influence involves the use of excessive pressure to persuade one vulnerable to such pressure, pressure applied by a dominant subject to a servient object. In combination, the elements of undue susceptibility in the servient person and excessive pressure by the dominating person make the latter's influence undue, for it results in the apparent will of the servient person being in fact the will of the dominant person.

Undue susceptibility may consist of total weakness of mind which leaves a person entirely without understanding [citation omitted]; or, a lesser weakness which destroys the capacity of a person to make a contract even though he is not totally incapacitated [citation omitted]; or, the first element in our equation, a still lesser weakness which provides sufficient grounds to rescind a contract for undue influence. [Citation omitted.] Such lesser weakness need not be longlasting nor wholly incapacitating, but may be merely a lack of full vigor due to age..., physical condition..., emotional anguish..., or a combination of such factors. [Citations omitted.] The reported cases have usually involved elderly, sick, senile persons alleged to have executed wills or deeds under pressure. [Citations omitted.] In some of its aspects this lesser weakness could perhaps be called weakness of spirit. But whatever name we give it, this first element of undue influence resolves itself into a lessened capacity of the object to make a free contract.

In the present case plaintiff has pleaded that such weakness at the time he signed his resignation prevented him from freely and competently applying his judgment to the problem before him. Plaintiff declares he was under severe mental and emotional strain at the time because he had just completed the process of arrest, questioning, booking, and release on bail and had been without sleep for forty hours. It is possible that exhaustion and emotional turmoil may wholly incapacitate a person from exercising his judgment. As an abstract question of pleading, plaintiff has pleaded that possibility and sufficient allegations to state a case for rescission.

Undue influence in its second aspect involves an application of excessive strength by a dominant subject against a servient object. Judicial consideration of this second element in undue influence has been relatively rare, for there are few cases denying persons who persuade but do not misrepresent the benefit of their bargain. Yet logically, the same legal consequences should apply to the results of excessive strength as to the results of undue weakness. Whether from weakness on one side, or strength on the other, or a combination of the two, undue influence occurs whenever there results "that kind of influence or supremacy of one mind over another by which that other is prevented from acting according to his own wish or judgment, and whereby the will of the person is over-borne and he is induced to do or forbear to do an act which he would not do, or would do, if left to act freely." *Webb v. Saunders*, 79 Cal. App. 2d 863, 871, 181 P.2d 43, 47. Undue influence involves a type of mismatch which our statute calls unfair advantage. [Citations omitted.] Whether a person of subnormal capacities has been subjected to ordinary force or a person of normal capacities subjected to extraordinary force, the match is equally out of balance. If will has been overcome against judgment, consent may be rescinded.

The difficulty, of course, lies in determining when the forces of persuasion have overflowed their normal banks and become oppressive flood waters. There are second thoughts to every bargain, and hindsight is still better than foresight. Undue influence cannot be used as a pretext to avoid bad bargains or escape from bargains which refuse to come up to expectations. A woman who buys a dress on impulse, which on critical inspection by her best friend turns out to be less fashionable than she had thought, is not legally entitled to set aside the sale on the ground that the saleswoman used all her wiles to close the sale. A man who buys a tract of desert land in the expectation that it is in the immediate path of the city's growth and will become another Palm Springs, an expectation cultivated in glowing terms by the seller, cannot rescind his bargain when things turn out differently. If we are temporarily persuaded against our better judgment to do something about which we later have second thoughts, we must abide the consequences of the risks inherent in managing our own affairs. [Citation omitted.]

However, overpersuasion is generally accompanied by certain characteristics which tend to create a pattern. The pattern usually involves several of the following elements: (1) discussion of the transaction at an unusual or inappropriate time, (2) consummation of the transaction in an unusual place, (3) insistent demand that the business be finished at once, (4) extreme emphasis on untoward consequences of delay, (5) the use of multiple persuaders by the dominant side against a single servient party, (6) absence of third-party advisers to the servient party, (7) statements that there is no time to consult financial advisers or attorneys. If a number of these elements are simultaneously present, the persuasion may be characterized as excessive. The cases are illustrative:

Moore v. Moore, 56 Cal. 89, 93, and 81 Cal. 195, 22 P. 589, 874. The pregnant wife of a man who had been shot to death on October 30 and buried on November 1 was approached by four members of her husband's family on November 2 or 3 and persuaded to deed her entire interest in her husband's estate to his children by a prior marriage. In finding the use of undue influence on Mrs. Moore, the court commented: "It was the second day after her late husband's funeral. It was at a time when she would naturally feel averse to transacting any business, and she might reasonably presume that her late husband's brothers would not apply to her at such a time to transact any important business, unless it was of a nature that would admit of no delay. And as it would admit of delay, the only reason which we can discover for their unseemly haste is, that they thought that she would be more likely to comply with their wishes then than at some future time, after she had recovered from the shock which she had then so recently experienced. If for that reason they selected that time for the accomplishment of their purpose, it seems to us that they not only took, but that they designed to take, an unfair advantage of her weakness of mind. If they did not, they probably can explain why they selected that inappropriate time for the transaction of business which might have been delayed for weeks without injury to any one. In the absence of any explanation, it appears to us that the time was selected with reference to just that condition of mind which she alleges that she was then in. "Taking an unfair advantage of another's weakness of mind is undue influence, and the law will not permit the retention of an advantage thus obtained." Civ. Code section 1575.

Weger v. Rocha, 138 Cal. App. 109, 32 P.2d 417. Plaintiff, while confined in a cast in a hospital, gave a release of claims for personal injuries for a relatively small sum to an agent who spent two hours persuading her to sign. At the time of signing plaintiff was in a highly nervous and hysterical condition and suffering much pain, and she signed the release in order to terminate the interview. The court held that the release had been secured by the use of undue influence....

The difference between legitimate persuasion and excessive pressure, like the difference between seduction and rape, rests to a considerable extent in the manner in which the parties go about their business. For example, if a day or two after Odorizzi's release on bail the superintendent of the school district had called him into his office during business hours and directed his attention to those provisions of the Education Code compelling his leave of absence and authorizing his suspension on the filing of written charges, had told him that the District contemplated filing written charges against him, had pointed out the alternative of resignation available to him, had informed him he was free to consult counsel or any adviser he wished and to consider the matter overnight and return with his decision the next day, it is extremely unlikely that any complaint about the use of excessive pressure could ever have been made against the school district.

But, according to the allegations of the complaint, this is not the way it happened, and if it had happened that way, plaintiff would never have resigned. Rather, the representatives of the school board undertook to achieve their objective by overpersuasion and imposition to secure plaintiff's signature but not his consent to his resignation through a high-pressure carrot-and-stick technique-under which they assured plaintiff they were trying to assist him, he should rely on their advice, there wasn't time to consult an attorney, if he didn't resign at once the school district would suspend and dismiss him from his position and publicize the proceedings, but if he did resign the incident wouldn't jeopardize his chances of securing a teaching post elsewhere.

Plaintiff has thus pleaded both subjective and objective elements entering the undue influence equation and stated sufficient facts to put in issue the question whether his free will had been overborne by defendant's agents at a time when he was unable to function in a normal manner. It was sufficient to pose " ... the ultimate question ... whether a free and competent judgment was merely influenced, or whether a mind was so dominated as to prevent the exercise of an independent judgment." [Citations omitted.] The question cannot be resolved by an analysis of pleading but requires a finding of fact....

The judgment is reversed.

Exercise 5-30: *Odorizzi* Revisited

1. Try eliminating each of the key facts in *Odorizzi* one by one and predicting the point at which the school district's conduct would no longer constitute

undue influence. For example, if the school district only had sent one employee instead of two, would the court have held that there was no undue influence?

2. Re-read Q2a in Exercise 5-28 (Nelson-Terry). Analyze the problem using your refined version of your undue influence rule from *Odorizzi*.

3. Many students confuse undue influence and duress cases. While some cases raise both claims, most cases raise one or the other. How will you distinguish between the two? (Hint: Focus on the core wrong of each claim.)

4. Determine whether problems a through e below raise undue influence or duress issues, or both. Be prepared to explain and support your answers. You do not need to analyze who would prevail in each of the problems.

   a. B, whom A has hired to repair A's television set, refuses to return the television set unless A agrees also to pay B to repair A's sewing machine. A agrees.

   b. A, who has no legitimate claim whatsoever to Schwartzacre, informs B that, unless B agrees to pay A $50,000, A will record and file a *lis pendens* against Schwartzacre asserting that A is entitled to an ownership interest in the property. B, who is about to sell the property to C and knows that a *lis pendens* will cause C to withdraw from the sale, agrees to pay A the money.

   c. A, who is not experienced in business matters, has always relied on B, his lawyer, for advice. One day, B urges A to sell Aacre for $500,000 to C, B's accomplice. Aacre is actually worth $750,000. A agrees to the proposed sale.

   d. Alice, a lawyer, seeks to induce her husband Bert, who has no legal expertise and who has had a history of severe emotional problems, to sign a divorce agreement. Alice tells Bert that, unless he signs, Bert will never see his children again, will not get back any of the property he owned before he married Alice, and will get no spousal support. Believing Alice, Bert signs the agreement.

   e. For two years B has visited, prepared meals for, and has generally befriended A, B's lonely, very wealthy, elderly uncle. One day B tells A that, unless A agrees to name B as the sole beneficiary of A's will, B will stop "supporting" A. A agrees to name B as his sole beneficiary.

5. Draft an undue influence problem.

6. Fully analyze problem 4d above (the Alice-Bert problem).

Illegality

This section addresses the fifth contract defense listed in Diagram 5-1 at the beginning of this chapter: **illegality**. Courts, legal commentators, and the drafters of the RESTATEMENT (SECOND) OF CONTRACTS have generally chosen to re-label this defense "**contracts against public policy.**" For example, section 178 of the RESTATEMENT (SECOND) OF CONTRACTS provides that a contract is unenforceable on the grounds of public policy if a statute says so or if a court's general interest in enforcing the contract is outweighed by public policy. As you read the materials and cases below, try to determine the rationale for using the phrase "against public policy" rather than "illegality."

There are several sources courts look to for statements of public policy when they recognize this defense. For example, courts find expressions of public policy in statutes, constitutional provisions, regulations, local ordinances, and court decisions.

The result of finding a contract illegal or against public policy is that the contract is void. In contrast, where the defenses of deception, mistake, duress, or undue influence are established, a contract is voidable by the party successfully asserting the defense. What is the difference between a contract that is "void" and a contract that is "voidable"?

Complete coverage of all of the situations where illegality might be invoked as a defense is beyond the scope of this section. Instead, we will highlight four recurring illegality problems.

1. Contracts prohibited by statute;

2. Contracts in violation of licensing statutes;

3. Covenants not to compete; and

4. Tangential illegality.

A. Contracts Prohibited by Statute

A contract is against public policy if either the contract is expressly prohibited by statute or if a party's performance would violate a statute. Examples of contracts prohibited by statute include contracts to buy and sell drugs, contracts to pay others to commit crimes (such as murder or arson), and, in most states, gambling contracts.

B. Contracts in Violation of Licensing Statutes

A license is a right granted to do something which cannot legally be done without such permission. Governmental authorities grant licenses to, among other things, carry on certain businesses or to practice certain occupations. Sometimes, parties contract to undertake work without obtaining required licenses. Such contracts may be deemed against public policy. If the sole purpose of a licensing statute is to generate income, a contract made without obtaining the required license is not considered against public policy. However, if a licensing requirement is created for the purpose of protecting the public, a contract made without obtaining the required license is against public policy: see section 181 of the RESTATEMENT (SECOND) OF CONTRACTS.

Exercise 5-31: Contracts in Violation of Licensing Statutes

Determine whether a contract made in violation of each of the following licensing requirements would be against public policy. Explain your reasoning.

1. A license to sell fruit in a street fair.

2. A license to practice law.

3. A building contractor's license.

4. A license to sell real estate.

5. A general business license.

C. Covenants Not to Compete

A covenant not to compete is a promise by one party not to work for a competing business or not to open up a competing business. Courts consider such promises troubling. Why are courts troubled by covenants not to compete? How do such covenants harm society?

There are two contexts in which non-compete covenants arise. First, in connection with the sale of a business, it is common for a buyer to require the seller to promise not to open a competing business. The buyer believes that a non-compete covenant is necessary to protect the goodwill of the business he is purchasing and for which he is paying. Courts are sympathetic to buyers in this situation because, if a seller were to open a competing business, there is a great risk that the seller's former customers would follow her to the new business and dilute the value of the business purchased.

Second, it is common for employers to require employees not to compete with the employers after the employment relationship has ended. Such promises are called post-employment covenants not to compete. On the one hand, employers have legitimate interests in protecting the investment they make in training their employees, in protecting the confidentiality of customer lists, and in protecting trade secrets. On the other hand, sometimes employers simply do not want to have to deal with competition from their former employees. Courts are less likely to enforce post-employment covenants than they are to enforce covenants made in connection with the sale of a business. Why do you think this is so? In other words, what are the public policy rationales in each context?

Exercise 5-32: *Wood v. May*

The materials below focus on post-employment covenants not to compete. In particular, *Wood v. May* details the convoluted approach adopted by courts in deciding whether and to what degree to enforce such covenants. As you read *Wood*, consider the following questions:

1. As you know, the concept of freedom of contract discourages courts from interfering with contracts freely made by both parties. How does that rationale square with courts' reluctance to enforce post-employment covenants not to compete?

2. Both the majority and dissenting opinions agree that the covenant at issue is overbroad. About what do they disagree?

3. Why is the majority so eager to salvage the former employee's promise?

4. What policy objection can you make to the majority's willingness to rewrite the contract term?

5. The court references three judicial alternatives for dealing with an overbroad covenant not to compete. What are those alternatives? What rationales support each of those alternatives?

Wood v. May

73 Wash.2d 307, 438 P.2d 587 (1968)

Finley, Chief Justice. In November 1961 appellant, Gordon S. Wood, a master horseshoer with some 15-years experience, employed respondent, William R. May, as an apprentice horseshoer. On January 3, 1962 the parties signed a written contract wherein appellant agreed to teach respondent the art of horseshoeing. Respondent agreed that:

> "[F]or a period of five years from and after the time he shall leave the first party employer, either if by resignation or by discharge, that he shall not engage directly or indirectly in any business or enterprise the nature of which is competitive to the employers business, that is to say he shall not engage in the practice of Horseshoeing or Blacksmithing, within a radius of one hundred (100) miles from the Oakwood Horseshoeing presently situated at Route 1, Box 1491, or any branch of the Oakwood Horseshoeing during the tenure of this time."

The contract further provided that in the event of breach of the agreement not to compete, respondent could be enjoined by a court of equity from engaging in the trade of horseshoeing in the territory and during the time covered by the agreement.

Respondent displayed marked aptitude for horseshoeing, and during the two years he worked for appellant he progressed rapidly from the apprenticeship stage. He was soon on his own, so to speak, in shoeing the horses of a substantial number of appellant's customers. Actually, respondent became the only contact appellant had with many of his customers, and these customers gained confidence in respondent's ability as a horseshoer. Consequently, when respondent terminated his employment in March 1964 and immediately set up his own horseshoeing business in Tacoma, five miles distance from Spanaway, he secured a substantial number of appellant's customers in Pierce County and on Vashon Island. Appellant began this action to enjoin respondent from engaging in horseshoeing in violation of the agreement.

The bulk of appellant's horseshoeing business was located in Pierce County and on Vashon Island, although he regularly shod a few horses as far north as Lynden, nearly 100 miles from Spanaway.

The trial court dismissed the case at the close of appellant's evidence, finding that although the rest of the contract was reasonable, it was unreasonable to restrict respondent from engaging in horseshoeing within a radius of 100 miles from Spanaway, an area which includes all or part of 22 counties in Washington, and parts of Oregon and Canada. The trial court determined the contract to be indivisible and for that reason refused to modify the restrictive covenants as to time and area.

There are four issues on appeal: (1) are restrictive covenants not to compete after termination of employment void for reasons of public policy? (2) if such covenants are not void, were the covenants in this contract supported by adequate consideration? (3) if supported by adequate consideration, were the restrictions reasonable as to time and areas as to both the parties and the public? (4) if the restrictions were unreasonable, can a court exercising its equity jurisdiction modify such restrictive covenants and enforce them against respondent in a more reasonable manner?

I.

In *Racine v. Bender*, 141 Wash. 606, 611, 252 P. 115 (1927), we recognized the following principles in relation to restrictive covenants in employment contracts:

In some instances, a covenant not to compete of any duration or geographic scope would be deemed invalid. In other instances, a covenant may be valid. These paragraphs lay out the test for deciding this question.

> The general rule applied in construing such contracts is that restrictions therein are upheld if they meet the test of showing that they are not greater than are reasonably necessary to protect the business or good will of the employer, even though they restrain the employee of his liberty to engage in a certain occupation or business, and deprive the public of the services, or restrain trade.

[Citation omitted.] 9 A.L.R. 1467, 1468, states the rule as follows:

> The validity of covenants by employees not to engage in a similar or competing business for a definite period of time, following the termination of the contract of employment in which the covenant is incorporated, may be sustained, although the contract is recognized to be in restraint of trade. The test generally applied in determining the validity of such a covenant is whether or not the restraint is necessary for the protection of the business or good will of the employer, and, if so, whether it imposes on the employee any greater restraint than is reasonably necessary to secure to the business of the employer, or the good will thereof, such protection, regard being had to the injury which may result to the public, by restraining the breach of the covenant, in the loss of the service and skill of the employee, and the danger of his becoming a charge upon the public. It is clear that if the nature of the employment is such as will bring the employee in personal contact with the patrons or customers of the employer, or enable him to acquire valuable information as to the nature and character of the business and the names and requirements of the patrons or customers, enabling him, by engaging in a competing business in his own behalf, or for another, to take advantage of such knowledge of or acquaintance with the patrons or customers of his former employer, and thereby gain an unfair advantage, equity will interfere in behalf of the employer and restrain the breach of a negative covenant not to engage in such competing business....

The restrictive covenants in the instant matter are not void for reasons of public policy. The evidence indicated that there are some 3000 horses in the Pierce County area, and some 8 competent horseshoers residing in the immediate area. Although customers may prefer respondent to other horseshoers in the area, his services are not indispensible. The law presumes that the services can be performed by someone else. *Racine v. Bender, supra,* at 613, 252 P. at 115. And, it was not shown that respondent will not be able to find work as a horseshoer without competing with appellant.

II.

The contract, although somewhat vague and poorly drawn, was supported by adequate consideration. Respondent promised not to compete with ap-

pellant upon termination of his employment in return for appellant's promise to teach respondent the skill of horseshoeing. Over the period of two years
during which the parties operated under the contract, appellant did indeed
teach respondent the trade or art of horseshoeing. The evidence showed that
there are two methods of becoming a skilled horseshoer. One may either attend a college course in horseshoeing, followed by experience under a master horseshoer, or he may learn by the apprenticeship method as respondent
did in this case. During the two years respondent worked for appellant he
earned approximately $3800 the first year and approximately $6500 the second year. After he left appellant's service respondent grossed from $500 to
$1800 per month, horseshoeing being somewhat seasonal in nature. Appel-
lant obviously fulfilled his part of the bargain. He taught respondent to be a
proficient horseshoer, a trade at which he has been able to earn a good living.
This is adequate consideration for a promise not to compete in a trade which
involves a unique personal relationship between tradesman and customer.

III.

The trial court correctly found the area restriction in the contract to be
unreasonable. It was correct to refuse to enforce this restriction as written,
since it is both unduly harsh to respondent in curtailing his legitimate efforts
to earn a livelihood and unnecessary for the protection of the legitimate interests of appellant. *See* 41 A.L.R.2d 314, 43 A.L.R.2d 141. The trial judge
found the time restriction to be more acceptable, stating that he felt the time
involved was "particularly lengthy," but that "[t]he Court could accept the restriction in terms of five-years."

However, on the basis of the evidence presented, we are constrained to believe that the restrictions were probably unreasonable *both* as to area and time.
The trial judge felt he was obligated to either accept or reject the restrictions *in
toto* rather than to modify them on the basis of his factual findings. We do not
believe he could properly decide the issues before him while operating under
this assumption. We are granting a new trial in this matter so that reasonable
restrictions upon respondent's competitive activities, both as to time and area,
can be determined and imposed. We note in passing that counsel for appellant admitted in oral argument that an area of 25-mile radius from Spanaway
would be reasonable. This court approved a restrictive period of three years in
the *Racine* case, *supra*. But we offer no suggestion without more evidence than
the record reveals whether a period of one year, three years or some other period of time is reasonable under the facts in this case. Neither do we suggest that
it would be improper to restrict respondent only as to those customers with
whom he came in contact while in the service of appellant. *See Columbia College of Music v. Tunberg*, 64 Wash. 19, 116 P. 280 (1911), in which such a restriction was found adequate to protect the employer. We do not limit the court
upon new trial to any given formula for determining reasonable restrictions, nor
do we read any of the cases cited in this opinion as so limiting a trial court.
While guidelines set down in similar cases are helpful, the facts of a given case
must determine the reasonableness of the restrictions imposed.

IV.

It is well settled that a court of equity will use its power to enforce a restriction
against a former employee's competition only to the extent that such restric-

tion is reasonable and necessary to protect a legitimate business interest of the employer. [Citations omitted.] But it does not follow that an entire contract must fail because of an unreasonable restriction as to time and area. One line of authority holds that unless the contract is divisible the court will not write a new contract and will refuse to grant any equitable relief against competition. [Citations omitted.] However, a substantial number of American courts in later cases have adopted a new and different rule that a contract in restraint of trade will be enforced to the extent it is reasonable and lawful. [Citations omitted.]

We adopt the reasoning in the second line of cases. The enforcement of such a contract does not depend upon mechanical divisibility, meaning that offending portions of the covenant can be lined out and still leave the remainder grammatically meaningful and thus enforceable. This is the so-called "blue pencil test." The better test is whether partial enforcement is possible without injury to the public and without injustice to the parties. [Citations omitted.]

Professor Corbin, in approving the latter test, says:

> An agreement restricting competition may be perfectly reasonable as to a part of the territory included within the restriction but unreasonable as to the rest. Will the courts enforce such an agreement in part while holding the remainder invalid? It renders no service to say that the answer depends upon whether or not the contract is "divisible." "Divisibility" is a term that has no general and invariable definition; instead the term varies so much with the subject-matter involved and the purposes in view that its use either as an aid to decision or in the statement of results tends to befog the real issue.
>
> With respect to partial illegality, the real issue is whether partial enforcement is possible without injury to the public and without injustice to the parties themselves. It is believed that such enforcement is quite possible in the great majority of cases. If a seller whose business and good will do not extend beyond the city limits of Trenton promises not to open a competing business anywhere within the state of New Jersey, the restriction is much greater than is reasonable. This is a good reason for refusing to enjoin the seller from doing business in Newark; but it is not a good reason for permitting him to open up a competing store within the same block in Trenton.

6A CORBIN, CONTRACTS § 1390 at 66 (1962).... Professor Williston's comments on the subject are as follows:

> If a sharply defined line separated a restraint which is excessive territorially from such restraint as is permissible, there seems no reason why effect should not be given to a restrictive promise indivisible in terms, to the extent that it is lawful. If it be said that the attempt to impose an excessive restraint invalidates the whole promise, a similar attempt should invalidate a whole contract, though the promises are in terms divisible. Questions involving legality of contracts should not depend on form. Public policy surely is not concerned to distinguish differences of wording in agreements of identical meaning.

5 WILLISTON, CONTRACTS § 1660 (rev. ed. 1937). We are in accord with the views expressed by Corbin and Williston. Under the circumstances of this case we find it just and equitable to protect appellant by injunction to the extent necessary to accomplish the basic purpose of the contract insofar as such contract is reasonable. The trial court erred in granting dismissal at the close of appellant's case. A new trial must be afforded to determine what is reasonable regarding time and space in limiting respondent's competitive horseshoeing activities, wherein both parties may offer evidence bearing thereon. Since we do not have the benefit of respondent's evidence, we cannot decide whether the restriction should be as to area, i.e., a certain number of miles from appellant's business, or as to those customers which respondent came to know during his employment with appellant. Neither can we decide a precise limitation as to time.

The judgment should be reversed and remanded for new trial consistent with the views expressed herein. It is so ordered....

Rosellini, Judge (dissenting). The respondent was born and raised in the small community of Cleveland, Tennessee. When he was 17 years old, he entered the United States Army and had not completed his high school studies. While in the army, he was awarded an army high school diploma.

The respondent, prior to army service, had no special training for employment and had not held any compensable employment. After his discharge from the army, the respondent married and lived with his wife at Eatonville, Pierce County, Washington. He was 25 years old at the time of trial.

Prior to beginning his apprenticeship as a horseshoer, he served four months as a deputy sheriff for Pierce County. In November 1961, the respondent began apprenticeship with the appellant and was paid $1 for each horse shod. Nothing was said in regard to an agreement not to compete. In the latter part of 1961, the appellant asked the respondent to go to his accountant's office, stating that he had a contract which he desired the respondent to sign. The respondent signed the contract described by the majority.

Evidence discloses that horseshoeing can be taught in college in a five-weeks' course. The apprenticeship under the appellant lasted from November 1961 to the middle of July 1962, approximately an eight-months' period. From July 1962, the respondent was considered a journeyman horseshoer. He was permitted to and did shoe horses without direction or advice from appellant.

The record shows that there are approximately 3,000 horses in Pierce County. The appellant had approximately 130 customers. There is no contention that these customers owned all or even a substantial percentage of these horses.

When the respondent terminated his employment with the appellant, he began shoeing horses. Eleven months after his departure, he had only 13 rotating customers who had been customers of the appellant. A rotating customer is defined as one who, by agreement, has his horse shod for a period of a year; during that period his horse will be shod every six to eight weeks without the necessity of the owner asking for the service.

The majority, in reversing the trial court, fails to note that courts are reluctant to enforce contracts which prohibit individuals from continuing to

Why does the dissent seem to believe that it's significant that one can learn horseshoeing in a five-week college course?

work. It holds that the contract is enforceable even though the restriction of engaging in the business of horseshoeing for a period of five years and within 100 miles' vicinity of Pierce County is unreasonable. The majority has failed to observe that there is a different test applied where restrictions are contained in bargains for transfer of land or business and to where they are contained in bargains for employment. A restriction which may be upheld as reasonable in the sale of land or a business, may be found unduly harsh where the relationship between the parties has been that of employer and employee. This is rightly so because by an improvident contract entered into by an employee may deny him the opportunity to earn a livelihood which is every man's right....

Lord Parker pointed out [in the English case of *Herbert Morris, Ltd.* v. *Saxelby*, [1916] A.C. 688] that there is a distinction between restrictions placed upon a vendor and equal restrictions placed upon an employee. He said, at 709:

> It is quite different in the case of an employer taking such a covenant from his employee or apprentice. The good will of his business is, under the conditions in which we live, necessarily subject to the competition of all persons (including the servant or apprentice) who choose to engage in a similar trade. The employer in such a case is not endeavoring to protect what he has, but to gain a special advantage which he could not otherwise secure. I cannot find any case in which a covenant against competition by a servant or apprentice has, as such, ever been upheld by the Court. Wherever such covenants have been upheld it has been on the ground, not that the servant or apprentice would, by reason of his employment or training, obtain the skill and knowledge necessary to equip him as a possible competitor in the trade, but that he might obtain such personal knowledge of an influence over the customers of his employer, or such an acquaintance with his employer's trade secrets as would enable him, if competition were allowed, to take advantage of his employer's trade connection or utilize information confidentially obtained....

The restriction of five years and 100 miles' vicinity are unreasonable as to time and area. The court should be slow to enforce an agreement restraining an employee from engaging in his occupation. In the instant case the respondent does not know and has never worked at any other occupation than horseshoeing. If an injunction is granted it will be necessary for respondent to sell his home and move elsewhere. The great hardship to the respondent seems oppressive and harsh when it is compared to benefits the contract bestows upon the appellant. There is no showing of irreparable harm to the appellant if the contract is not enforced. The damage he may sustain is minute in comparison to the respondent's damage. From the record it appears that the restraint is not reasonable and necessary for the protection of the appellant. This is so because there are 3,000 horses in the vicinity and the appellant has only 130 customers. Thus he has ample opportunity and potential to increase his business, which the respondent is prevented from earning his livelihood in the only manner for which he is trained.

The cross-examination of the appellant suggests that the reason some of his customers left him was because he was inattentive to his business and some of his work was not satisfactory to them. The public interest is a factor to be considered. The public has a right to obtain the best services possible and should not be forced by the court to accept services which may be inferior.

When the equity power of the court is invoked, it is the duty of the court to weigh the consideration of the contract. It must find that the bargain is fair and equitable between the parties. If it is unfair or the consideration of the party seeking injunctive relief is small in comparison to the penalty he seeks to impose on the other party, the court should refrain from using its injunctive powers.

Since horseshoeing can be taught in five weeks in college, and an apprentice can become a journeyman horseshoer in eight months, it is not an occupation that is special, unique, or extraordinary. Thus a restriction such as that imposed on the respondent is not a reasonable quid pro quo for being taught the occupation of horseshoeing.

I believe this contract should not be enforced. I would affirm the trial court. In any event if it is enforced, it should be governed by the rule in *Columbia College of Music v. Tunberg*, 64 Wash. 19, 116 P. 280 (1911), where the court refused to enforce a contract by a music teacher not to teach elsewhere except to restrain him from soliciting clients of his employer. Any other result would be unjust and would prevent the respondent from earning a livelihood by the only occupation for which he is trained.

Hale, J., concurs in the dissent.

Exercise 5-33: *Wood* Revisited

1. Would the result in *Wood* have been the same if the defendant had been an employee rather than an apprentice and his job had involved unskilled labor (such as cleaning up after horses)?

2. Would the result in *Wood* have been the same if the defendant had been an employee rather than an apprentice and was already an expert at shoeing horses?

3. If the duration and geographic scope of the covenant in *Wood* had not been overbroad, but the covenant had restricted the defendant from "working with horses," would the court have found it overbroad? If so, how could the court have altered the covenant to make it reasonable?

D. Tangential Illegality

A contract may or may not be against public policy if the illegality is only tangential to the contract. Exercise 5-34 will introduce you to this concept.

Exercise 5-34: Tangential Illegality

Debra Departmentstore employed Billy Buyer to be her buyer of sunglasses for her chain of department stores. They executed a one-year contract. One day,

Billy accepted a bribe of $10,000 from a particular manufacturer of sunglasses, Coolshades™. Billy then signed a contract on behalf of Debra's stores, which committed its entire sunglasses budget to purchasing only Coolshades sunglasses. When Debra discovered what Billy had done, she sued to rescind the contract between her company and Coolshades based on illegality. Analyze the legal issue presented.

Incapacity

This section discusses the sixth contract defense listed in Diagram 5-1 at the beginning of this chapter: **incapacity**.

Exercise 5-35: Incapacity

1. There are three types of incapacity. Read sections 12–16 of the RESTATEMENT (SECOND) OF CONTRACTS. What are the three types?

2. Outline the incapacity rules in your own words. Your roman numeral I should be "Incapacity." A, B, and C should be the three types of incapacity. Then, under each letter, provide a numbered list of the requirements of each type of incapacity.

3. For all three types of incapacity, contracts for "necessaries" are excluded from the defense. What are necessaries? Create two examples. Then create two examples of things that are not necessaries. Try to make one of your examples something about which reasonable lawyers might disagree.

4. Why do courts allow people to escape contracts based on incapacity? In other words, what social good is served by allowing people to escape contracts based on incapacity?

5. Donnie Drinker, who did not own a car, went into Bob's Bar for drinks. Donnie entered the bar complaining about having to take the bus to work every day because the bus was unreliable. After seven stiff drinks and some dickering about price, Donnie entered into a contract with Bob, the bar's owner and bartender, to buy Bob's car for $5,000 (the car's fair market value). The next morning, Donnie awakened inside the car with the car's title tucked into his pocket. Donnie sued to rescind the contract. At trial, Donnie truthfully testified that, when he awakened, he had no recollection of having discussed a contract, much less any memory of having signed the contract. All he remembered the next morning was that he had gone into the bar and complained about the bus system. Will Donnie prevail at trial? Analyze the legal issue presented.

Unconscionability

This section discusses the seventh contract defense listed in Diagram 5-1 at the beginning of this chapter: **unconscionability**. Unconscionability is a mechanism that allows courts to police extraordinarily one-sided contracts. If a court determines that a contractual term is so unfair under the circumstances as to be outrageous, the court may refuse to enforce the entire contract, enforce the contract without the unconscionable clause, or limit the application of the unconscionable clause in a way that avoids an unconscionable result. U.C.C. § 1-302; RESTATEMENT (SECOND) OF CONTRACTS § 208.

For example, in a famous case, a welfare recipient purchased a $300 freezer for $900.[14] With additional time credit charges and tax, the total price was $1439.69. A New York court concluded the contract was unconscionable. Consequently, the buyer, who had already made payments of over $600, was able to keep the refrigerator with no further payments due.

Unconscionability is a controversial contract defense. For hundreds of years, courts of equity have refused to enforce contracts that are extraordinarily one-sided and should not therefore be regarded "in conscience" as binding. The modern law of unconscionability reflects similar fairness-based concerns. As you read the materials below, see if you can discern why courts, commentators, and lawyers are so ambivalent about this defense.

Exercise 5-36: *Williams v. Walker-Thomas Furniture Co.* and *Lhotka v. Geographic Expeditions, Inc.*

Consider the next two cases together. The first, *Williams v. Walker-Thomas Furniture Co.*, is probably the most well-known modern unconscionability case. As you read the cases, consider the following points:

1. There are two elements of unconscionability: procedural and substantive unconscionability. Define each element. Note that there are two alternative ways to satisfy the procedural unconscionability element.

2. Although the *Williams* court created the two-part unconscionability test, it did not use the "procedural" and "substantive" labels applied by later courts, including the *Lhotka* court. Which aspects of the *Williams* holding would now be classified as procedural unconscionability and which aspects of the *Williams* holding would now be classified as substantive unconscionability.

3. The *Williams* court did not apply the unconscionability test in the *Williams* case. Why not? Analyze the *Williams* case applying the court's two-part test.

4. How did the *Lhotka* court apply the two-part test?

5. What are the conflicting policy rationales implicated by unconscionability law?

Williams v. Walker-Thomas Furniture Co.
350 F.2d 445 (D.C. Cir. 1965)

J. Skelly Wright, Circuit Judge. Appellee, Walker-Thomas Furniture Company, operates a retail furniture store in the District of Columbia. During the period from 1957 to 1962 each appellant in these cases purchased a number

---

14. *Jones v. Star Credit Corp.*, 298 N.Y.S.2d 264 (1969).

of household items from Walker-Thomas, for which payment was to be made in installments. The terms of each purchase were contained in a printed form contract which set forth the value of the purchased item and purported to lease the item to appellant for a stipulated monthly rent payment. The contract then provided, in substance, that title would remain in Walker-Thomas until the total of all the monthly payments made equaled the stated value of the item, at which time appellants could take title. In the event of a default in the payment of any monthly installment, Walker-Thomas could repossess the item.

The contract further provided that "the amount of each periodical installment payment to be made by [purchaser] to the Company under this present lease shall be inclusive of and not in addition to the amount of each installment payment to be made by [purchaser] under such prior leases, bills or accounts; *and all payments now and hereafter made by (purchaser) shall be credited pro rata on all outstanding leases, bills and accounts* due the Company by [purchaser] at the time each such payment is made." [Emphasis added.] The effect of this rather obscure provision was to keep a balance due on every item purchased until the balance due on all items, whenever purchased, was liquidated. As a result, the debt incurred at the time of purchase of each item was secured by the right to repossess all the items previously purchased by the same purchaser, and each new item purchased automatically became subject to a security interest arising out of the previous dealings.

The italicized contract clause is called a "dragnet" clause. What does that mean? Translate the clause into your own words.

On May 12, 1962, appellant Thorne purchased an item described as a Daveno, three tables, and two lamps, having total stated value of $391.10. Shortly thereafter, he defaulted on his monthly payments and appellee sought to replevy all the items purchased since the first transaction in 1958. Similarly, on April 17, 1962, appellant Williams bought a stereo set of stated value of $514.95.[15] She too defaulted shortly thereafter, and appellee sought to replevy all the items purchased since December, 1957. The Court of General Sessions granted judgment for appellee. The District of Columbia Court of Appeals affirmed, and we granted appellants' motion for leave to appeal to this court.

Appellants' principal contention, rejected by both the trial and the appellate courts below, is that these contracts, or at least some of them, are unconscionable and, hence, not enforceable. In its opinion in *Williams v. Walker-Thomas Furniture Company*, 198 A.2d 914, 916 (1964), the District of Columbia Court of Appeals explained its rejection of this contention as follows:

> Appellant's second argument presents a more serious question. The record reveals that prior to the last purchase appellant had reduced the balance in her account to $164. The last purchase, a stereo set, raised the balance due to $678. Significantly, at the time of this and the preceding purchases, appellee was aware of appellant's financial position. The reverse side of the stereo contract listed the name of appellant's social worker and her $218 monthly stipend from

---

15. At the time of this purchase her account showed a balance of $164 still owing from her prior purchases. The total of all the purchases made over the years in question came to $1,800. The total payments amounted to $1,400.

the government. Nevertheless, with full knowledge that appellant had to feed, clothe and support both herself and seven children on this amount, appellee sold her a $514 stereo set.

We cannot condemn too strongly appellee's conduct. It raises serious questions of sharp practice and irresponsible business dealings. A review of the legislation in the District of Columbia affecting retail sales and the pertinent decisions of the highest court in this jurisdiction disclose, however, no ground upon which this court can declare the contracts in question contrary to public policy. We note that were the Maryland Retail Installment Sales Act, Art. 83 §§ 128–153, or its equivalent, in force in the District of Columbia, we could grant appellant appropriate relief. We think Congress should consider corrective legislation to protect the public from such exploitive contracts as were utilized in the case at bar.

We do not agree that the court lacked the power to refuse enforcement to contracts found to be unconscionable. In other jurisdictions, it has been held as a matter of common law that unconscionable contracts are not enforceable. While no decision of this court so holding has been found, the notion that an unconscionable bargain should not be given full enforcement is by no means novel. In *Scott v. United States*, 79 U.S. (12 Wall.) 443, 445, 20 L. Ed. 438 (1870), the Supreme Court stated: "If a contract be unreasonable and unconscionable, but not void for fraud, a court of law will give to the party who sues for its breach damages, not according to its letter, but only such as he is equitably entitled to...."

Since we have never adopted or rejected such a rule, the question here presented is actually one of first impression. Congress has recently enacted the Uniform Commercial Code, which specifically provides that the court may refuse to enforce a contract which it finds to be unconscionable at the time it was made. 28 D.C.Code § 2-302 (Supp. IV 1965). The enactment of this section, which occurred subsequent to the contracts here in suit, does not mean that the common law of the District of Columbia was otherwise at the time of enactment, nor does it preclude the court from adopting a similar rule in the exercise of its powers to develop the common law for the District of Columbia. In fact, in view of the absence of prior authority on the point, we consider the congressional adoption of § 2-302 persuasive authority for following the rationale of the cases from which the section is explicitly derived. Accordingly, we hold that where the element of unconscionability is present at the time a contract is made, the contract should not be enforced.

Unconscionability has generally been recognized to include an absence of meaningful choice on the part of one of the parties together with contract terms which are unreasonably favorable to the other party. Whether a meaningful choice is present in a particular case can only be determined by consideration of all the circumstances surrounding the transaction. In many cases the meaningfulness of the choice is negated by a gross inequality of bargaining power. The manner in which the contract was entered is also relevant to this consideration. Did each party to the contract, considering his obvious education or lack of it, have a reasonable opportunity to understand the terms of the contract, or were the important terms hidden in a maze of fine print and minimized by deceptive sales practices? Ordinarily, one who signs an agree-

Why does the court say that a party's meaningfulness of choice can be negated by a gross inequality of bargaining power?

ment without full knowledge of its terms might be held to assume the risk that he has entered a one-sided bargain. But when a party of little bargaining power, and hence little real choice, signs a commercially unreasonable contract with little or no knowledge of its terms, it is hardly likely that his consent, or even an objective manifestation of his consent, was ever given to all the terms. In such a case the usual rule that the terms of the agreement are not to be questioned should be abandoned and the court should consider whether the terms of the contract are so unfair that enforcement should be withheld.

In determining reasonableness or fairness, the primary concern must be with the terms of the contract considered in light of the circumstances existing when the contract was made. The test is not simple, nor can it be mechanically applied. The terms are to be considered "in the light of the general commercial background and the commercial needs of the particular trade or case." Corbin suggests the test as being whether the terms are "so extreme as to appear unconscionable according to the mores and business practices of the time and place." 1 Corbin, *op. cit. supra*. We think this formulation correctly states the test to be applied in those cases where no meaningful choice was exercised upon entering the contract.

Because the trial court and the appellate court did not feel that enforcement could be refused, no findings were made on the possible unconscionability of the contracts in these cases. Since the record is not sufficient for our deciding the issue as a matter of law, the cases must be remanded to the trial court for further proceedings. So ordered.

Lhotka v. Geographic Expeditions, Inc.

181 Cal.App.4th 816 (2010)

SIGGINS, J.

Geographic Expeditions, Inc. (GeoEx) appeals from an order denying its motion to compel arbitration of a wrongful death action brought by the survivors of one of its clients who died on a Mount Kilimanjaro hiking expedition. GeoEx contends the trial court erred when it ruled that the agreement to arbitrate contained in GeoEx's release form was unconscionable....

BACKGROUND

Jason Lhotka was 37 years old when he died of an altitude-related illness while on a GeoEx expedition up Mount Kilimanjaro with his mother, plaintiff Sandra Menefee. GeoEx's limitation of liability and release form, which both Lhotka and Menefee signed as a requirement of participating in the expedition, provided that each of them released GeoEx from all liability in connection with the trek and waived any claims for liability "to the maximum extent permitted by law." The release also required that the parties would submit any disputes between themselves first to mediation and then to binding arbitration. It reads: "I understand that all Trip Applications are subject to acceptance by GeoEx in San Francisco, California, USA. I agree that in the unlikely event a dispute of any kind arises between me and GeoEx, the following conditions will apply: (a) the dispute will be submitted to a neutral third-party mediator in San Francisco, California, with both parties splitting equally the cost of such mediator. If the dispute cannot be resolved through mediation, then (b) the dispute will be submitted for binding arbitration to the American Arbitration Association in San Francisco, California; (c) the dispute will be governed by California law; and (d) the maximum amount of recovery to which I will be entitled under any and all circumstances will be the sum of the land and air cost of my trip with GeoEx. I agree that this is a fair and reasonable limitation on the damages, of any sort whatsoever, that I may suffer. I agree to fully indemnify GeoEx for all of its costs (including attorneys' fees) if I commence an action or claim against GeoEx based upon claims I have previously released or waived by signing this release." Menefee paid $16,831 for herself and Lhotka to go on the trip.

A letter from GeoEx president James Sano that accompanied the limitation of liability and release explained that the form was mandatory and that, on this point, "our lawyers, insurance carriers and medical consultants give us no discretion. A signed, unmodified release form is required before any traveler may join one of our trips. Ultimately, we believe that you should choose your travel company based on its track record, not what you are asked to sign.... My review of other travel companies' release forms suggests that our forms are not a whole lot different from theirs."

After her son's death, Menefee sued GeoEx for wrongful death and alleged various theories of liability including fraud, gross negligence and recklessness, and intentional infliction of emotional distress. GeoEx moved to compel arbitration.

The trial court found the arbitration provision was unconscionable under *Armendariz v. Foundation Health Psychcare Services, Inc.* (2000) 24 Cal.4th 83, 99 Cal.Rptr.2d 745, 6 P.3d 669 (*Armendariz*) and on that basis denied the motion. It ruled: "The agreement at issue is both procedurally and substantively unconscionable.... The Sano letter establishes that the agreement was presented as a Take It Or Leave It proposition and was also represented to be consistent with industry practice. As a consequence[,] if the plaintiff and decedent wished to go on this trip, they could do so only on these terms. Unconscionability also permeates the substantive terms of the agreement to arbitrate. The problematic terms are the limitation on damages, the indemnity of GeoEx, the requirement that GeoEx costs and attorneys' fees be paid if suit is filed related to certain claims, splitting the costs of mediation, the absence of an agreement on the cost of arbitration and the lack of mutuality as to each of these terms. As a consequence, this is not a case where the court may strike a single clause and compel arbitration."

This appeal timely followed.

DISCUSSION

The question ... posed here [is] whether the agreement to arbitrate is unconscionable and, therefore, unenforceable ... We answer [that] question ... in the affirmative.

I. *Standard of Review*

On appeal from the denial of a motion to compel arbitration, "[u]nconscionability findings are reviewed de novo if they are based on declarations that

raise 'no meaningful factual disputes.' [Citation.] However, where an unconscionability determination 'is based upon the trial court's resolution of conflicts in the evidence, or on the factual inferences which may be drawn
therefrom, we consider the evidence in the light most favorable to the court's
determination and review those aspects of the determination for substantial
evidence.' [Citation.] …"

II. *Unconscionability*

The *Lhotka* court's ex-
tended discussion of pro-
cedural and substantive
unconscionability starts
here.

We turn first to GeoEx's contention that the court erred when it found the
arbitration agreement unconscionable. Although the issue arises here in a relatively novel setting, the basic legal framework is well established. "'[U]ncon-
scionability has generally been recognized to include an absence of meaningful
choice on the part of one of the parties together with contract terms which
are unreasonably favorable to the other party.' [Citation.] Phrased another
way, unconscionability has both a 'procedural' and a 'substantive' element." (*A
& M Produce Co. v. FMC Corp.* (1982) 135 Cal.App.3d 473, 486, 186 Cal.Rptr.
114.) "'The procedural element requires oppression or surprise. [Citation.]
Oppression occurs where a contract involves lack of negotiation and meaningful choice, surprise where the allegedly unconscionable provision is hidden within a prolix printed form. [Citation.] The substantive element concerns
whether a contractual provision reallocates risks in an objectively unreasonable or unexpected manner.' [Citation.] Under this approach, both the procedural and substantive elements must be met before a contract or term will
be deemed unconscionable. Both, however, need not be present to the same
degree. A sliding scale is applied so that 'the more substantively oppressive
the contract term, the less evidence of procedural unconscionability is required to come to the conclusion that the term is unenforceable, and vice
versa.'" [Citations omitted.] This notion of a "sliding scale," as will be seen,
figures centrally in the analysis of the agreement at issue here.

A. *Procedural Unconscionability*

GeoEx argues the arbitration agreement involved neither the oppression
nor surprise aspects of procedural unconscionability. GeoEx argues the agreement was not oppressive because plaintiffs made no showing of an "industry-
wide requirement that travel clients must accept an agreement's terms without
modification" and "they fail[ed] even to attempt to negotiate" with GeoEx. We
disagree. GeoEx's argument cannot reasonably be squared with its own statements advising participants that they must sign an *unmodified* release form to
participate in the expedition; that GeoEx's "lawyers, insurance carriers and
medical consultants give [it] no discretion" on that point; and *that other travel
companies were no different.* In other words, GeoEx led the plaintiffs to understand not only that its terms and conditions were non-negotiable, but that
plaintiffs would encounter the same requirements with any other travel company. This is a sufficient basis for us to conclude the plaintiffs lacked bargaining power.

GeoEx also contends its terms were not oppressive, apparently as a matter of law, because Menefee and Lhotka could have simply decided not to trek
up Mount Kilimanjaro. It argues that contracts for recreational activities can
never be unconscionably oppressive because, unlike agreements for necessities such as medical care or employment, a consumer of recreational activi-

ties *always* has the option of foregoing the activity. The argument has some initial resonance, but on closer inspection we reject it as unsound.

While the nonessential nature of recreational activities is a factor to be taken into account in assessing whether a contract is oppressive, it is not necessarily the dispositive factor. *Szetela v. Discover Bank* (2002) 97 Cal.App.4th 1094, 118 Cal.Rptr.2d 862 is informative. The defendant, a credit card company, argued the plaintiff could not establish procedural unconscionability because there were "market alternatives" to its product—i.e., the plaintiff had the option of taking his business to a different bank. The court disagreed, and held the customer's ability to walk away rather than sign the offending contract was not dispositive. "The availability of similar goods or services elsewhere may be relevant to whether the contract is one of adhesion, but even if the clause at issue here is not an adhesion contract, it can still be found unconscionable. Moreover, 'in a given case, a contract might be adhesive even if the weaker party could reject the terms and go elsewhere. [Citation.]' [Citation.] Therefore, whether Szetela could have found another credit card issuer who would not have required his acceptance of a similar clause *is not the deciding factor.*" (*Id.* at p. 1100, 118 Cal.Rptr.2d 862, italics added....) The focus of procedural unconscionability in *Szetela,* rather, was on the manner in which the disputed clause was presented. Faced with the options of either closing his account or accepting the credit card company's "take it or leave it" terms, Szetela established the necessary element of procedural unconscionability despite the fact that he could have simply taken his business elsewhere. (*Szetela, supra,* at p. 1100, 118 Cal.Rptr.2d 862.)

The cases on which GeoEx relies do not hold otherwise. GeoEx relies on *Morris v. Redwood Empire Bancorp, supra,* 128 Cal.App.4th at page 1320, 27 Cal.Rptr.3d 797, for its statement that the "'procedural element of unconscionability may be defeated ... if the complaining party has a meaningful choice of reasonably available alternative sources of supply from which to obtain the desired goods and services free of the terms claimed to be unconscionable.'" "[M]ay be defeated," true—but not "must," in all cases and as a matter of law. *Morris* takes its premise from *Dean Witter Reynolds, Inc. v. Superior Court* (1989) 211 Cal.App.3d 758, 772, 259 Cal.Rptr. 789, in which Division Two of this court expressly declined to hold or suggest "that *any* showing of competition in the marketplace as to the desired goods and services defeats, as a matter of law, *any* claim of unconscionability." Indeed, *Morris* itself recognizes that some contracts may be oppressive despite the availability of market alternatives, albeit in the context of employment or medical care— i.e., contracts for "'life's necessities.'" (*Morris, supra,* at p. 1320, 27 Cal.Rptr.3d 797, quoting *West v. Henderson* (1991) 227 Cal.App.3d 1578, 1587, 278 Cal.Rptr. 570; see *Armendariz, supra,* 24 Cal.4th at p. 115, 99 Cal.Rptr.2d 745, 6 P.3d 669 [employment].)

Many of the other authorities cited by GeoEx are inapposite because they concern challenges to release of liability clauses under the rule that invalidates exculpatory provisions that affect the public interest. (See *Tunkl v. Regents of University of California* (1963) 60 Cal.2d 92, 96–97 & fn. 6, 32 Cal.Rptr. 33, 383 P.2d 441; Civ.Code, § 1668.) In this specific context, our courts consistently hold that recreation does not implicate the public interest, and therefore approve exculpatory provisions required for participation in recreational activities. (See, e.g., *Randas v. YMCA of Metropolitan Los Angeles* (1993) 17 Cal.App.4th 158, 161–162, 21 Cal.Rptr.2d 245 [swim class]; *Saenz v. Whitewater Voyages, Inc.* (1990) 226 Cal.App.3d 758, 764, 276 Cal.Rptr. 672 [river rafting]; *Madison v. Superior Court* (1988) 203 Cal.App.3d 589, 597–599, 250 Cal.Rptr. 299 [scuba diving]; *Paralift, Inc. v. Superior Court* (1993) 23 Cal.App.4th 748, 756, 29 Cal.Rptr.2d 177 [skydiving]; *Buchan v. United States Cycling Federation, Inc.* (1991) 227 Cal.App.3d 134, 277 Cal.Rptr. 887 [cycle racing]; *Coates v. Newhall Land & Farming, Inc.* (1987) 191 Cal.App.3d 1, 8, 236 Cal.Rptr. 181 [riding dirtbike]; *Kurashige v. Indian Dunes, Inc.* (1988) 200 Cal.App.3d 606, 611–612, 246 Cal.Rptr. 310 [motorcycle dirtbike].) But these cases do not focus on unconscionability, and they do not hold that contracts for recreational activities are immune from analysis for procedural unconscionability.

Here, certainly, plaintiffs could have chosen not to sign on with the expedition. That option, like any availability of market alternatives, is relevant to the existence, and degree, of oppression. (See *Szetela v. Discover Bank, supra,* 97 Cal.App.4th at p. 1100, 118 Cal.Rptr.2d 862; *Laster v. T–Mobile USA, Inc.* (S.D.Cal.2005) 407 F.Supp.2d 1181, 1188 & fn. 1; see also *Allan v. Snow Summit, Inc.* (1996) 51 Cal.App.4th 1358, 1376, 59 Cal.Rptr.2d 813 [nonessential, recreational nature of skiing was one of several factors that indicated a release clause was not substantively unconscionable]; but see *Belton v. Comcast Cable Holdings, LLC* (2007) 151 Cal.App.4th 1224, 1246, 60 Cal.Rptr.3d 631 [dictum that availability of other cable providers defeated claim of unconscionability].) But we must also consider the other circumstances surrounding the execution of the agreement. GeoEx presented its limitation of liability and release form as mandatory and unmodifiable, and essentially told plaintiffs that any other travel provider would impose the same terms. "Oppression arises from an inequality of bargaining power which results in no real negotiation and an absence of meaningful choice...." (*Crippen v. Central Valley RV Outlet* (2004) 124 Cal.App.4th 1159, 1165, 22 Cal.Rptr.3d 189 [finding no oppression where evidence showed no circumstances surrounding the execution of the agreement, so no showing of unequal bargaining power, lack of negotiation, or lack of meaningful choice].) Here, in contrast to *Crippen,* GeoEx presented its terms as both nonnegotiable and *no different than what plaintiffs would find with any other provider.* Under these circumstances, plaintiffs made a sufficient showing to establish at least a minimal level of oppression to justify a finding of procedural unconscionability. (See *Morris v. Redwood Empire Bancorp, supra,* 128 Cal.App.4th at p. 1319, 27 Cal.Rptr.3d 797 ["our task is not only to determine *whether* procedural unconscionability exists, but more importantly, *to what degree* it may exist"].)

B. *Substantive Unconscionability*

With the "sliding scale" rule firmly in mind (*Armendariz, supra,* 24 Cal.4th at p. 114, 99 Cal.Rptr.2d 745, 6 P.3d 669), we address whether the substantive unconscionability of the GeoEx contract warrants the trial court's ruling. *Harper v. Ultimo, supra,* 113 Cal.App.4th 1402, 7 Cal.Rptr.3d 418, is analogous. The Harpers hired a contractor to perform work on their property. The contractor allegedly broke a sewer pipe, causing concrete to infiltrate the plaintiffs' soil, plumbing and sewer and wreak havoc on their backyard drainage system. Unfortunately for the Harpers, the arbitration provision in the construction contract limited the remedies against their contractor to a refund, completion of work, costs of repair or any out-of-pocket loss or property damage—and then capped any compensation at $2,500 unless the parties agreed otherwise in writing.

In the words of Justice Sills, substantive unconscionability was "so present that it is almost impossible to keep from tripping" over it. (*Harper v. Ultimo, supra,* 113 Cal.App.4th at p. 1407, 7 Cal.Rptr.3d 418.) "Substantive unconscionability focuses on the one-sidedness or overly harsh effect of the contract term or clause. [Citations.] In the present case, the operative effect of the arbitration is even more one-sided against the customer than the clauses in any number of cases where the courts have found substantive unconscionability. (E.g., *Little v. Auto Stiegler, Inc.* (2003) 29 Cal.4th 1064 [130 Cal.Rptr.2d 892, 63 P.3d 979] [either party could appeal any award of more than $50,000 to second arbitrator]; *Szetela v. Discover Bank* [, *supra*] 97 Cal.App.4th 1094 [118 Cal.Rptr.2d 862] [arbitration clause absolutely barred class actions]; *Saika v. Gold* (1996) 49 Cal.App.4th 1074 [56 Cal.Rptr.2d 922] [arbitration award could be rejected if it exceeded $25,000].) As in *Little, Szetela* and *Saika,* the limitation of damages provision here is yet another version of a 'heads I win, tails you lose' arbitration clause that has met with uniform judicial opprobrium." The arbitration provision in the Harpers' contract did not allow even a theoretical possibility that they could be made whole, because there was no possibility of obtaining meaningful compensation unless the contractor agreed—which, not surprisingly, it did not. (*Harper v. Ultimo, supra,* at p. 1407, [7 Cal.Rptr.3d 418].)

The arbitration provision in GeoEx's release is similarly one-sided as that considered in *Harper.* It guaranteed that plaintiffs could not possibly obtain anything approaching full recompense for their harm by limiting any recovery they could obtain to the amount they paid GeoEx for their trip. In addition to a limit on their recovery, plaintiffs, residents of Colorado, were required to mediate and arbitrate in San Francisco—all but guaranteeing both that GeoEx would never be out more than the amount plaintiffs had paid for their trip, and that any recovery plaintiffs might obtain would be devoured by the expense they incur in pursing their remedy. The release also required plaintiffs to indemnify GeoEx for its costs and attorney fees for defending any claims covered by the release of liability form. Notably, there is no reciprocal limitation on damages or indemnification obligations imposed on GeoEx. Rather than providing a neutral forum for dispute resolution, GeoEx's arbitration scheme provides a potent disincentive for an aggrieved client to pursue any claim, in any forum—and may well guarantee that GeoEx wins even if it loses. Absent reasonable justification for this arrangement—and none is apparent—we agree with the trial court that the arbitration clause is so one-sided as to be substantively unconscionable. (See *Armendariz, supra,* 24 Cal.4th at p. 121, 99 Cal.Rptr.2d 745, 6 P.3d 669 [damages remedy unilaterally limited]; *Pinedo v. Premium Tobacco Stores, Inc.* (2000) 85 Cal.App.4th 774, 781, 102 Cal.Rptr.2d 435 [damages remedy limited, plaintiff required to pay all costs, and required hearing location was in Oakland].)

DISPOSITION

The order denying GeoEx's motion to compel arbitration is affirmed.

We concur: McGUINESS, P.J., and POLLAK, J.

Exercise 5-37: *Williams* and *Lhotka* Revisited

1. Bill and Fred were the sole shareholders of a corporation that owned an amusement park. Immediately after the park suffered damage from a fire, a fire prevention services company approached the amusement park and the park entered into a contract for the installation of a fire prevention system. The fire prevention company was a large, national corporation. There were fourteen competing fire prevention companies listed in the phone book. Although the fire prevention company did not prevent bargaining, the parties did not discuss terms. The amusement park owners neither fully read the contract nor "shopped around" for alternative fire prevention systems. The contract included a clause that limited the fire prevention company's liability for breach to ten percent of the annual charge for the system (the annual charge was $2,500) or $250, whichever was greater. The value of the fixtures in the park (such as the rides and the concession stands) was in excess of $1,500,000. After another fire destroyed the amusement park, the owners of the park sued the fire prevention company for breach and asked the court to strike the clause limiting damages as unconscionable. Analyze the legal issue presented.

2. Plaintiff's decedent entered into a contract with a ski resort to participate in a ski race. The contract contained a clause entitled "Release of Claim" in hard-to-follow legalese that purported to absolve the defendant of all potential liability for any injury to the decedent. The contract also released the defendant from liability for personal injury or property damage claims unrelated to the race. The contract, which was drafted by the ski resort's attorney, was presented to the decedent on a "take-it-or-leave-it" basis. After the decedent died in the race, the plaintiff sued the ski resort for negligence. Analyze whether the release clause is unconscionable.

3. Chemical Co. purchased resin oil from Oil Co. to use in its business which involves the production of resins for use by manufacturers in consumer products such as paint, adhesive, floor tiles, and matting. Oil was supplied on Oil Co.'s standard terms which state that the buyer unqualifiedly accepts all shipments and waives all claims in respect thereto unless he gives notice of a claim within fifteen days of delivery and further limit any claim timely notified to the contract price. The resin oil in one particular shipment had become exposed during Oil Co.'s production process to a highly reactive contaminant. The contract price for this shipment was $50,000. Chemical Co. used the contaminated oil to manufacture resins, which its customers, in turn, used to manufacture consumer products. It was only after the end products had been manufactured and passed into the hands of the consumers that the chemical compound formed by the introduction of the contaminant began to break down into its components. One of the components was an acid which emitted a persistent foul odour. All the end products containing the affected resin had to be destroyed and Chemical Co. faces multimillion dollar liabilities to its customers and end consumers as a result. Chemical Co. seeks a full indemnity from Oil Co. Oil Co. argues that, under its standard terms, it has either no liability because the claim was not timely

notified or, in the alternative, its liability is limited to $50,000. Can Chemical Co. successfully plead unconscionability?

Statute of Frauds

A. Introduction

This section addresses the eighth and final contract defense listed in Diagram 5-1 at the beginning of this chapter: the **statute of frauds**. This section is structured consistently with how this topic should be analyzed on an exam and to provide you with the most efficient and effective means to learn this material.

Statute of frauds problems raise three potential issues:

1. Is the contract subject to a statute of frauds?

2. Does the contract comply with the writing requirement of the applicable statute of frauds?

3. Is the contract enforceable notwithstanding its failure to comply with the writing requirement of an applicable statute of frauds?

If your answer to the first question is no, you are done with the analysis. Many contracts do not need to be in writing. For these contracts, there is no need to analyze the statute of frauds any further. If, however, your answer is yes, you need to analyze the second question.

If your answer to the second question is yes, you are done with the analysis. The contract complies with the applicable statute and is enforceable. If, however, your answer is no, you need to analyze the third question.

In connection with the third question, be aware that courts and the drafters of the U.C.C. have developed a number of mechanisms for preventing unfair outcomes even if a contract fails to comply with an applicable statute of frauds. For example, as you learned in Chapter 4, the promissory estoppel doctrine allows a party who has relied on the existence of an assumed contract to recover notwithstanding a failure to comply with an applicable statute of frauds.

B. Statute of Frauds Example

Imagine the following problem. On October 5, 2013, Jan and Ranae entered into an oral contract for the purchase and sale of a vacant tract of land for $200,000. They agreed that Jan was free to start building her planned home on the land, but Ranae would provide the title to the land and Jan would pay Ranae the money on October 10, 2014. Between October 5, 2013, and October 10, 2014, Jan spent over $100,000 and hundreds of hours building a house on the land. Ranae, however, refused to perform the contract and now asserts that the contract is not enforceable. If Jan were to sue Ranae for breach, would a court enforce the contract?

Your starting points in analyzing the Jan-Ranae contract are the applicable statutes of frauds. Contracts for the sale of land and contracts that, by their terms, cannot be performed within a year of their making must be in writing. Here, the contract was for the sale of land (the vacant tract) and was not scheduled to be performed for over a year (the contract was made October 5, 2013, yet was not scheduled to be performed until October 10, 2014). Because the contract involved a sale of land and because neither party could fully perform the contract within one year, the contract was subject to two statutes of frauds.

To be enforceable, a contract subject to a common law statute of frauds must be in writing (at least as its essential terms) and must be signed by the party against whom enforcement is sought. Here, the contract was not in writing and Jan, the party against whom Ranae is seeking enforcement, did not sign a writing. Accordingly, this contract does not comply with the common law writing requirement and is not enforceable unless another theory applies.

If a contract is not enforceable because it fails to comply with an applicable statute of fraud, it may be enforceable if a party seeking to enforce the contract can satisfy the elements of promissory estoppel. Promissory estoppel requires a promise inducing reliance, reliance on that promise, and a showing that injustice can only be avoided by enforcing the promise. In addition, older cases enforce unwritten land sale contracts if a party has significantly improved the property.

Here, Ranae made a promise that induced reliance. Ranae could foresee that she would induce Jan's reliance on that promise. Ranae could foresee Jan's reliance because the parties' contract specifically permitted Jan to rely by building on the land. Jan in fact relied on Ranae's promise by building on the land. Injustice can only be prevented by enforcing the contract. Otherwise, Ranae would get the benefit of Jan's expenditures of time and money in the form of the increased value of the land. Jan's efforts would be wasted as far as Jan would be concerned. Accordingly, a court would apply promissory estoppel and enforce Jan and Ranae's deal.

C. Is a contract subject to a statute of frauds?

Statutes of frauds apply to the following types of contracts:

1. Land sale contracts;

2. Suretyship contracts;

3. Contracts that cannot be performed within one year;

4. Contracts for the sale of goods for $500 or more;

5. Contracts made in consideration of marriage; and

6. Contracts by executors to answer for a duty owed by their decedents.

In this section, you will learn about the first three types of contracts subject to statutes of fraud because they are the types you will most frequently encounter in practice. The fourth type of contract, involving a sale of goods, is governed by the U.C.C. and will be dealt with separately in part F below. The fifth type of contract, one made in consideration of marriage, is rare. The sixth type of contract, involving executors, is governed by rules similar to those applicable to suretyship contracts.

Land sale contracts. A contract to buy, transfer, or pay for any interest in land is subject to a statute of frauds. "Interest" includes any right, power, privilege, or immunity with respect to land. Land sale contracts are usually in writing, so this issue is seldom litigated. What is the rationale for requiring land sale contracts to be in signed writings?

Suretyship contracts. A "surety" is a person who promises to pay or perform on behalf of another party to a contract. For example, assume that Elizabeth and Hannah enter into a loan contract. Hannah agrees to loan Elizabeth money and Elizabeth promises to pay Hannah back at a certain time. Sam Surety promises to pay Hannah in the event that Elizabeth does not. The parties have made a suretyship contract which must satisfy the statute of frauds or it cannot be enforced.

The statute of frauds applies if the person who is owed money or some performance (Hannah in the above example) knows or has reason to know of the suretyship relation or if the surety's promise is conditioned on a default by the other party to the contract (Elizabeth).

The statute of frauds does not apply if the promisor (Sam) owed a duty to perform to either of the other parties to the contract: see, e.g., RESTATEMENT (SECOND) OF CONTRACTS § 114. It also does not apply if the promisor's (Sam's) reason for making the promise is mainly to serve his own economic advantage rather than to benefit the party to the contract (Elizabeth): see, e.g., RESTATEMENT (SECOND) OF CONTRACTS § 116.

Exercise 5-38: Suretyship Contracts

1. When dealing with suretyship contracts or other three-party situations, it is helpful to diagram the relationships between the parties. Draw a diagram that shows the relationships among Sam, Hannah, and Elizabeth. Use arrows to designate who must perform what obligations to whom.

2. What is the rationale for requiring suretyship contracts to be in signed writings?

3. Mike agrees to guarantee a loan to convince Bank to loan Hannah money so that Hannah can purchase a house. Is this contract within the suretyship provision?

4. Arthur agrees to personally guarantee a loan by Bank to Captive Corp., Arthur's closely held business. Arthur owns 75% of the stock. Is this contract within the suretyship provision?

5. Assume the same facts as in problem 4, except that the corporation's stock is publically traded and Arthur owns only 15% of the stock. Is this contract within the suretyship provision?

Contracts not to be performed within one year. If a promise in a contract cannot possibly be performed within one year from the day on which the contract was made, the contract must comply with the statute of frauds. This provision is liberally applied so that, if it is in any way possible that performance could be completed within one year, the contract does not need to comply with the statute of frauds.

Exercise 5-39: One-Year Provision

1. What is the rationale for requiring contracts that cannot be performed within one year to be in signed writings?

2. A contract for services for life is not subject to a statute of frauds. Why not?

3. A contract for services for thirteen months must comply with the statute of frauds. Why?

4. A contract to build a skyscraper that the parties believe should take fifteen months to complete does not fall within the statute of frauds. Why not?

D. Does a contract comply with the writing requirement of the applicable statute of frauds?

A contract complies with the common law statute of frauds[16] if:

1. The contract is evidenced by any writing that:

    a. Identifies the subject of the contract, and

    b. Is sufficient to indicate a contract has been made, and

    c. Includes the essential terms, and

2. Is signed by the party against whom enforcement is sought.

As you can see, these requirements do not require a formal, executed contract. There are several ways to satisfy the signed writing requirement. For example, the requirements can be satisfied with several writings if they clearly indicate that they relate to the same transaction. The writings can be made and signed at any time, even after the asserted contract was made. Further, if a writing once existed but has been lost or destroyed, courts will accept as sufficient testimony about the writing. On the writing requirement see, e.g., RESTATEMENT (SECOND) OF CONTRACTS §§ 131–137. Consider also the effect of the UNIFORM ELECTRONIC TRANSACTIONS ACT § 7.

Exercise 5-40: The Signed Writing Requirement

1. The definition of "signed" in the U.C.C. is the same as the definition that applies to common law contracts. Find the U.C.C. definition.

2. Paula and Donna enter into an oral contract for the purchase and sale of Donna-land for $200,000. Two weeks after entering the contract, Donna sends Paula an e-mail in which she thanks Paula for agreeing to buy Donnaland for $200,000. Paula replies by e-mail, "You're welcome."

    a. Is there a sufficient signed writing that Paula can use to enforce the contract against Donna? Why or why not?

    b. Is there a sufficient signed writing that Donna can use to enforce the contract against Paula? Why or why not?

E. Is a contract enforceable notwithstanding its failure to comply with the writing requirement of an applicable statute of frauds?

Some contracts that are subject to statutes of frauds are enforceable even if they do not satisfy the signed writing requirement. For example, as noted in the section exam-

---

16. The U.C.C. Article 2 statute of frauds is different and is addressed in section F.

ple (part B above, "Statute of Fraud Example"), courts enforce contracts if the party seeking enforcement can make out the elements of promissory estoppel. Similarly, even before adoption of the promissory estoppel doctrine, full performance by both parties allowed either to enforce the contract without meeting a signed writing requirement. Assuming the rationales for statutes of frauds are good ones, why have courts developed rules that allow parties to enforce unwritten contracts that are supposed to be in writing?

F. U.C.C. Statute of Frauds

Exercise 5-41: U.C.C. Statute of Frauds

Read section 2-201 of the U.C.C. and then outline the rule using the three statute of frauds issues listed at the beginning of this section:

1. Is a contract subject to a statute of frauds?

2. Does a contract comply with the writing requirement of the applicable statute of frauds?

3. Is a contract enforceable notwithstanding its failure to comply with the writing requirement of an applicable statute of frauds? (Make sure to determine whether promissory estoppel applies to U.C.C. contracts.)

Chapter Recap

You have now finished your study of contract defenses. Complete Exercise 5-42 and the problems presented at the beginning of this chapter to solidify your understanding of contract defenses.

Exercise 5-42: Contract Defenses

1. To be able to identify contract defense issues in lawyering problems, and to avoid confusing the defenses, you need to understand the essence of each defense. Create a list of all the contract defenses. Then, for each, write, in five words or less, the essence of the defense.

2. To be able to identify contract defense issues on your law school exams or in legal practice, it is helpful to create a defense checklist. Create something to help you remember your checklist. For example, you could create a mnemonic, flashcards, or draw a picture. If you are a visual learner, creating a picture that is personally meaningful to you is a particularly effective tool. For example, you could draw a fortress, and depict each contract defense as a way by which an army might attack the fortress (*e.g.*, misrepresentation as a Trojan Horse, non-disclosure as a spy in a trench coat, duress as a person making a telephone call threatening to blow up the fortress).

3. Blake was poor for the first thirty years of his life. He only had one year of high school education and had only worked as a laborer. His average yearly income was $19,000. Then, on his thirtieth birthday, Blake won $5,000,000

in the state lottery. Blake then decided to become a land developer. He loved Palm Springs and decided to purchase desert land in his home state of Columbia. He wanted to build a golf course and condominium community and to be the "father of Columbia's Palm Springs." Blake contacted Big Developer Co., the largest developer in the state of Columbia, and asked about purchasing DesertAcre. DesertAcre was owned by Big Developer and located in the westernmost part of the Great Columbia Desert.

The parties entered into negotiations. They discussed their belief that the area would be developed into a Palm Springs-like community within ten years. The area was beautiful, and there were no similar resorts anywhere in the State of Columbia. They also discussed the risks involved in purchasing undeveloped property. Blake, who did not retain an attorney, asked Big Developer's attorneys to include a clause that allowed Blake to rescind the contract if, within one year of the contract date, the project was not "economically feasible." Big Developer's attorneys refused, truthfully stating that they had represented Big Developer for thirty years and never had included such a clause in a land sale contract. They also truthfully stated that Big Developer always sold its land using its form agreement and that Big Developer did not negotiate terms with new developers. Finally, one of the attorneys said, "Look, Blake, if you want to play with the big boys and get rich, you have to take some risks."

The parties then signed a contract. Blake agreed to pay Big Developer $3,000,000, and Big Developer agreed to transfer DesertAcre to Blake. Unknown to Blake, the contract included, in tiny print, a clause requiring the property to be appraised within one year of the contract date and providing that Blake would pay Big Developer seventy-five percent of Blake's profits if the new appraised value exceeded $4,000,000. The contract contained no other relevant clauses. Both parties performed their contractual obligations.

Unknown to either party, six months before Blake and Big Developer signed their contract, Nancy Able had begun construction of her own Palm Springs-like resort on a tract located 200 miles away from DesertAcre in the easternmost part of the Great Columbia Desert. When the information about Nancy's development became public knowledge, Blake was unable to obtain construction financing or to convince other developers to build near DesertAcre. By any definition, Blake's project became unfeasible and the value of his land plummeted to less than $1,000,000. When Blake discovered this information, he sued to rescind the contract. Analyze the legal issues presented.

Chapter Problems Revisited

You now know enough to fully analyze the two problems introduced at the beginning of this chapter (Exercises 5-1 and 5-2). The problems are similar to problems you might be asked to analyze on a law school exam or in law practice. In sections A and B below, you are provided with some hints for completing these exercises.

The exercises are somewhat different from the chapter problems in previous chapters because they ask you to perform new tasks. Exercise 5-1 asks you to act as an attorney conducting a case evaluation. Exercise 5-2 asks you to perform a client interview and provide legal advice. Both of these tasks are common in legal practice. Clients' cases do not come pre-packaged with labels that identify the legal issues presented, the applicable law, or the relevant and irrelevant facts. Rather, cases come to lawyers as peoples' stories.

A. Exercise 5-1: Stacy Landon Car Problem

For this exercise, your task is to provide a case evaluation. To do so, identify the legal issues presented and the applicable law. Then, analyze the application of the law to your client's case and consider whether there is any additional information you need to evaluate the case. Also determine where you can get the additional information you need to evaluate the case.

B. Exercise 5-2: Plymouth Shipping Supply Problem

For this problem, your task is to conduct a client interview, gather factual information, and provide legal advice. We have given you this problem for two reasons: First, interviewing clients and gathering factual information are essential, everyday skills that all competent attorneys must possess. Second, it is important that, at this early stage of your legal training, you understand the key role that gathering facts plays in lawyering.[17]

As you have likely already experienced, most doctrinal law school courses present you with specific sets of facts in appellate opinions. This approach does not expose you to the ambiguities present in most cases or to your role in gathering facts. It's also unlikely that you can fully understand appellate cases if you do not have insight into how lawyers interview clients and gather facts. Moreover, the specific facts presented in appellate opinions may leave you with the impression that lawyers deal with a tidy set of objective facts that all parties agree on. However, that is seldom the case.[18]

Start your preparation for the interview by identifying the legal issues presented and the applicable law. Also preliminarily consider the application of the law to the facts you have already been provided. You should never assume that the facts you are provided are accurate and complete. You should also never assume that a client's framing of an issue (here, whether Plymouth can get out of the contract based on an error) is the precise legal issue presented. It's your job as a lawyer to develop legal theories for your cases. Accordingly, when you conduct your client interview, you will want to flesh out the information you have been provided and revise your understanding of the facts and issues.

Before you conduct your client interview, you should prepare by making a checklist for your interview. If you have never conducted a client interview, it is helpful to read a good article about client interviews.[19] Be aware that the mod-

---

17. Alan M. Lerner, *Law and Lawyering in the Work Place: Building Better Lawyers by Teaching Students to Exercise Critical Judgment as Creative Problem Solvers*, 32 Akron L. Rev. 107, 127–28 (1999).

18. Id.

19. For a quick and straightforward approach to interviewing clients, see Marlene Pontrelli Maerowitz, *A Three-Step Approach to Effective Client/Witness Interviews*, 33 Ariz. Attorney 17 (1997). For more detailed insight into interviewing clients, see Linda F. Smith, *Interviewing Clients: A Linguistic Comparison of the "Traditional" Interview and the "Client-Centered" Interview*, 1 Clinical L.

ern approach to interacting with clients is a collaborative one with active listening and encouragement of client participation. Be prepared to begin your interview by explaining what will happen during the interview. Your primary goals should be fact-gathering and issue identification, but it is equally important to understand the difficulties your client is experiencing and the result your client desires in addition to inviting your client to discuss how you can best serve her.[20]

You have been told that your client desires an objective evaluation of her case and that she is likely to ask for it during your interview. Be prepared to respond to your client, but balance your need to conduct research and reflect on the case.

Also, make sure to consider the non-legal implications of pursuing the case and be prepared to discuss those implications with your client. Most problems have both legal and non-legal dimensions. Accordingly, any solution involves balancing both dimensions as well as understanding what is important to your client.[21]

Finally, when you meet with your client, you are engaging in a professional encounter. Make sure to act accordingly.

Professional Development Reflection Questions

1. Once students get in the "fishbowl" of law school, they quickly forget how talented and amazing they are. What percent of the population do you think even gets a college degree? What percent of the population do you think gets admitted to law school?

2. As a legal professional, you will enjoy the status of "professional privilege." In what sense is it a privilege to be a member of our profession?

3. Why does society give legal professionals a privileged status? In other words, what is the benefit to society?

4. As a member of this privileged profession, what are your individual responsibilities to society?

5. Imagine that you have been retained by Pam to represent her in a lawsuit against Debbie for breach of contract. As far as Pam or you know, Debbie has not consulted and has not retained an attorney. Is it appropriate for you, as Pam's lawyer, to communicate directly with Debbie?

Rev. 541 (Spring 1995) (examining client-centered model for interviewing and counseling clients as opposed to more traditional, attorney-dominated and attorney-controlled approach).

20. Smith, 1 CLINICAL L. REV. at 542–553.

21. Smith, 1 CLINICAL L. REV. at 542, 552.

PART FOUR

Contract Remedies
*What does a party who sues for breach
get if she wins?*

Chapter 6

Contract Damages

Chapter Problems

In this chapter, there are two introductory problems. The first problem is similar to Exercise 5-2 in that it asks you to prepare for a meeting with a client in a way that ensures that you will have all the information you need to advise her on the quantum of damages. The second problem requires you to evaluate specific contract language and advise on its effectiveness (or otherwise).

Exercise 6-1: Information Gathering

Elizabeth, a new client, contacted you with a breach of contract claim. At your intake interview, Elizabeth said that she entered into a contract with Jerk to purchase Jerkacre. Elizabeth and Jerk signed a contract that is proper in all respects, but Jerk refused to perform. You conclude that Jerk breached the contract and the only issue between Elizabeth and Jerk are Elizabeth's damages.

Elizabeth retained you as her attorney to recover her damages. You scheduled a follow-up meeting with Elizabeth to gather specific information about her damages. Elizabeth has asked you to send her a list of questions she should be prepared to answer at the meeting and a list of documents she should bring. Prepare for your client meeting with Elizabeth, including making a list of documents she should bring to your meeting and a list of questions you plan to ask Elizabeth to determine damages.

Exercise 6-2: Contract Evaluation

Your firm's client, Biotechnic, Inc. is a manufacturer of medical devices. Three years ago, before your firm was retained, it entered into a five-year exclusive distribution agreement with Wholeheart, Inc. in relation to a coronary stent called the CS25. Under the terms of the agreement, Wholeheart has exclusive rights to sell the CS25 in the U.S. and Canada. The agreement required Wholeheart to pay Biotechnic a price each quarter calculated as 50% of Wholeheart's net sales in the previous quarter. Biotechnic, Inc. has now developed and obtained FDA approval for a new stent. Recent medical trials suggest that the new stent works much better in emergency coronary care situations than does the CS25. Biotechnic therefore wishes to withdraw the CS25 from the market immediately and sell the new stent through a different distributor. Biotechnic's CEO wants to know how much it would cost Biotechnic to get out of the agreement with Wholeheart. She is hopeful that it would cost them nothing because of the following damage waiver clause in the agreement:

"Neither party shall be liable to the other for any indirect, special, or consequential damage with respect to any claim arising out of this agreement (including without limitation its performance or breach of this agreement) for any reason."

At this stage, the CEO asks you to make a preliminary evaluation of Biotechnic's potential exposure (if any) and, in particular, the impact of the damage waiver clause. Having made this evaluation, please then consider what (if any) improvements you would recommend to the damage waiver clause were you to be asked to draft distribution agreements for Biotechnic in the future.

Introduction to Contract Remedies

A. Chapter Introduction

In the last chapter, you learned about contract defenses. In other words, you learned the circumstances under which a party who has made a contract can avoid performing the contract without incurring any liability. In this chapter, you will learn about one type of contract remedy: **damages**. In other words, you will learn about how damages are calculated if a party breaches a contract and does not have any defenses that would allow her to avoid liability.

Diagram 6-1, the Contract Law Graphic Organizer on the next page, depicts where you are in your study of contracts. You just finished the second major contract law topic, "Contract Defenses." This chapter begins your study of "Contract Remedies." In this chapter you will learn about the first category of contract remedies, "Contract Damages." In subsequent chapters you will learn about the other three categories of remedies: restitution, agreed damages, and coercive equitable remedies.

So far, you have likely spent most of your law school career studying liability—what a party must show to win a lawsuit. The topic of remedies is a major shift in focus. The subject of remedies focuses on the consequences of liability. Specifically, when studying contract remedies, you should assume that a defendant breached a contract and a plaintiff has proven it. The only question you now care about is: what does the plaintiff get?

Many students also find it confusing that remedies, the "end of the story" (what a party gets if she sues for breach and wins), is taught before addressing all other contract law topics. The rationale for this approach is that the subject of remedies is foundational for all of contracts law. For example, when parties try to prove they formed a contract, they are doing so because they want to recover remedies for breach. When parties try to convince a court to interpret a contract in a particular way, they are doing so in the hope of having a court conclude that the other party breached and should be required to provide a remedy. When parties argue about the adequacy of each other's performance, they do so hoping they will recover damages for any deficiency. Remedies are thus the goal in contract law. For this reason, you will likely understand and learn contract law better as a whole if you understand remedies early on.

B. Types of Contract Breaches

Before studying contract remedies, it is helpful to understand that a contract breach may take one of two forms. First, a party may breach by not performing her obligations

Diagram 6-1: Contract Law Graphic Organizer

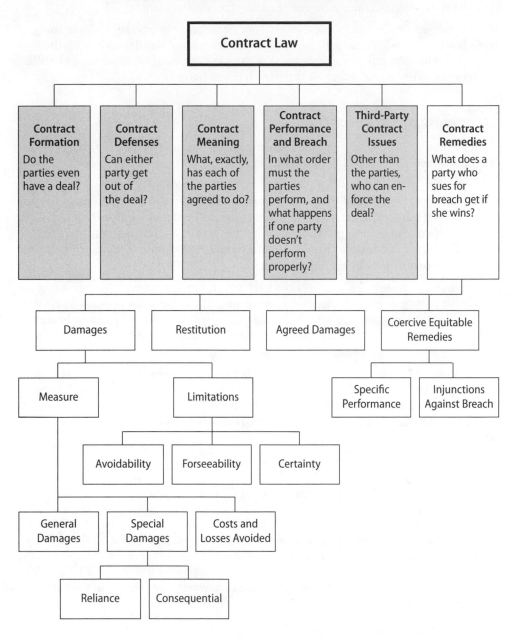

at all, which is called "**breach by non-performance.**" For example, imagine Chrissie Contractor promises to build Lynette Landowner a house for $100,000, and Lynette promises to pay Chrissie $100,000. If Chrissie never shows up at all, Chrissie has committed a breach by non-performance.

Second, a party may breach by rendering a "**defective performance.**" For example, assume the same situation as in the Chrissie-Lynette problem, except Chrissie built the house without a fireplace although she had promised one and installed the plumbing in a sloppy way that resulted in a leak. Or, perhaps Chrissie finished the house two months later than promised. Again, Chrissie breached the contract, but the breach is a different type. Chrissie's performance is defective rather than non-existent.

The distinction between these two types of breaches is important to your study of remedies. As you might guess, the applicable remedies can differ depending on the type of breach. Different remedies apply because these two types of breaches are two different types of wrongdoing and cause different types of harm.

Overview of Chapter 6

In this chapter, you will learn about one category of contract remedies: damages. There is an introductory note in the RESTATEMENT (SECOND) OF CONTRACTS which contains the following useful statement:

> "The traditional goal of contract remedies has not been compulsion of the promisor but compensation of the promise for the loss resulting from breach ... punitive damages have not been awarded for breach of contract, and specific performance has also not been granted where compensation in damages is an adequate substitute for the injured party."

The ordinary remedy for breach of contract is therefore an award of damages designed to give the party a monetary substitute equivalent to the value of the promised performance. Although, in some circumstances, the courts will compel the party in breach to perform — through the remedy of specific performance which you will encounter in Chapter 9 — this is not the norm. Hence, we start with damages.

The topic of damages involves two main sub-topics: the measure of damages and limitations on damages. Your study of the measure of damages will focus on identifying each potential item of recovery available to a party that sues for breach of contract. Your study of the topic of limitations on damages will focus on what a defendant must prove to justify reducing a plaintiff's recovery.

Introduction to Damages

Damages are depicted in Diagram 6-1 as the first type of contract remedy. The core goal in awarding damages for a breach of contract is to award a plaintiff a sum of money sufficient to place him in the exact same economic situation he would be in if the breaching party had fully and perfectly performed. This goal reflects our society's policy decision that it is "good" to ensure that parties to contracts receive the "**benefit of the bargains**" they make. You can remember this core goal with the "Four Ps":

1. Put the
2. Plaintiff in the
3. Performance
4. Position.

Damages are a sum of money given as compensation and as a substitute for harm suffered. Note that, although damages are awarded with a sum of money, not all awards of money are damages. For example, a different remedy, restitution, frequently involves awarding money, too. Next, note that damages are only awarded for harms suffered. So, a party who sues for breach of contract cannot recover any damages if he did not suffer any harm. For example, if a party were to agree to pay $10,000 for an automobile worth $8,000, and the seller were to perform, in economic terms the buyer would lose approximately $2,000.[1] If the seller did not perform, but, instead, breached the contract, the buyer would actually be better off. Accordingly, no damages would be awarded.

Finally, damages are a substitute for a suffered loss. In other words, damages do not restore what the plaintiff lost and what the other party promised to deliver—for example, a specific cow, horse, or contract price. Rather, damages are the economic equivalent of the harm the plaintiff suffered. By awarding an economic equivalent, a plaintiff's position should be economically identical to what it would have been if the other party properly performed the contract.

You may have noticed that contract damages are similar to tort damages. As you are learning in your torts course, tort damages do not restore a plaintiff to the same physical situation the plaintiff was in before being damaged by a tort. It is not possible to travel backwards in time and undo the tort. Instead, the goal with both tort and contract damages is to provide a plaintiff with an economic substitute.

There is a critical difference, however, between the goal in awarding breach of contract damages and the goal in awarding tort damages: the point in time used as the measuring stick. As you have already learned, in contract law, the relevant point in time when awarding damages is the party's "**post-performance position.**" In awarding damages for breach of contract, courts seek to give the party what he bargained for. In torts, the relevant point in time when awarding damages is the party's "**pre-tort position.**" In awarding damages for torts, courts strive to make the party whole. This difference stems from society's belief that the harm from a tort is the tort itself. In contrast, the harm from a breach of contract is not the contract itself (which society considers a "good" thing); rather, the harm is the failure to perform the contract properly—the breach.

The Measure of Damages

As depicted in Diagram 6-1 at the beginning of this chapter, the subject of damages involves analyzing both the measure of damages and limitations on damages. This section will address the **measure of damages**. Diagram 6-1 further shows that the measure of damages itself involves three subtopics: "General Damages," "Special Damages," and "Costs and Losses Avoided." To give a plaintiff the benefit of the bargain, a court awards him general damages—the damages that any party who suffered a similar wrong would incur. Courts also award special damages—damages necessary under the particular circumstances to ensure the plaintiff ends up in the same economic position that he or she would have reached had the breaching party fully and properly performed the contract. Finally, courts deduct any costs or losses a plaintiff is able to avoid because of the breach so that the plaintiff does not end up in a better economic position than he would have been in if the contract had been fully and properly performed. The aim is to give the plaintiff the economic equivalent of performance—no more, no less—not to give the plaintiff a windfall. These three subtopics are discussed in separate sections below.

---

1. The term "approximately" is used because, under specific circumstances, a buyer may suffer harm greater than $2,000. More than $2,000 would need to be awarded to give a buyer the economic equivalent of performance if, for example, he already paid a down payment or the full contract price or if he already purchased a custom car seat or car cover for the car.

A. General Damages[2]

"**General damages**" is the first subtopic depicted under "Measure" in Diagram 6-1 at the beginning of this chapter. This section explains the rules for measuring general damages for the most common contracts. These rules are also graphically depicted in Table 6-1, at the end of this section.

The measure of general damages almost always takes the form of an award of the plaintiff's loss of value because of the breach, the cost of giving the plaintiff what he was promised, or the profit the plaintiff expected from full performance of the contract. General damages are sometimes referred to as "direct" damages. The measure of general damages works slightly differently, depending on whether a breach is by non-performance or defective performance. Accordingly, the measure of general damages is discussed separately for these two types of breaches.

General damages for breach by non-performance. In many cases, plaintiffs recover general damages measured by their loss of value. For example, in the Chrissie-Lynette problem, the contractor, Chrissie, promised to build the landowner, Lynette, a house for $100,000, and Lynette promised to pay Chrissie $100,000. Chrissie never showed up at all and breached the contract by non-performance. The measure of general damages for Chrissie's non-performance would be the fair market value ("FMV") of Chrissie's services less the price Lynette agreed to pay. This rule can be expressed with the following formula:

Damages = FMV of Defendant's Performance – Contract Price

In this formula, the damages relate to a specific type of breach: non-performance. "FMV of the defendant's performance" refers to what a hypothetical willing buyer would pay a hypothetical willing seller for the defendant's performance. Contract price refers to the dollar amount the landowner agreed to pay the contractor.

For example, imagine that the FMV of Chrissie's services was $125,000. You would arrive at that figure by obtaining evidence about the prevailing price for a similar project among contractors in the local area. Now imagine that the contract price was $100,000, perhaps because Lynette is a good negotiator or perhaps because Chrissie believed she could perform more efficiently than her competitors and earn a profit even at a below-market price. Applying the formula, Lynette's damages for Chrissie's non-performance would be $25,000 ($125,000 – $100,000).

The same formula (FMV minus contract price) would apply if Lynette were buying land from Sarah Seller and Sarah breached by refusing to deliver the land. Assume the FMV of the land was $250,000 and the contract price was $235,000. The general damages would be $15,000 ($250,000 – $235,000). Note that the measure of damages redresses Lynette's economic loss caused by Sarah's non-performance. When Lynette executed the contract to buy the land, she knew that, after both parties performed, she would have gained an asset (the land) and relinquished an asset (the money she paid). When Sarah breached, Lynette's loss was the difference between the value of what she expected to get (the value

---

2. Note that this is an area of contract law that lacks an agreed, uniform taxonomy. Some courts and commentators refer to general damages using the term "expectation damages" thus equating the two concepts. However, other courts and commentators use the term "expectation damages" to refer to all of a plaintiff's items of damage, or at least those items that might loosely be called the plaintiff's "expected profit" on the contract. Because of these different uses of the term "expectation damages," we believe it is less confusing to call this category of damages "general damages."

of the land, $250,000) and what she expected to give up (the amount of money she had agreed to pay, $235,000). The difference between what she expected to get and what she expected to give up, the net gain or "profit" she expected had the contract been performed, comprises Lynette's general damages ($15,000).

Returning to the Chrissie-Lynette problem, the general damages amount, $25,000, reflects the difference between what Lynette would have to pay to replace Chrissie's services ($125,000) and what Lynette agreed to pay Chrissie ($100,000). Accordingly, the formula for general damages for non-performance could be simplified as follows:

Damages = Value Plaintiff Expected to Get – Value Plaintiff Expected to Give

or, even more simply, the formula could be expressed as:

Damages = Get – Give

Sometimes, of course, it is the buyer (*e.g.*, Lynette) who breaches a contract to buy land. Using the get minus give formula, the seller (Sarah) would recover the difference between what she expected to get and what she expected to give. Sarah expected to get money (the contract price) and expected to give up her land. Sarah's general damages could be calculated with the following formula:

Damages = Contract Price – FMV of Plaintiff's Performance

If the contract price was $250,000 and the FMV was $235,000, the general damages would be $15,000. You may have begun to wonder why contract prices and fair market values ever differ. Don't parties agree to fair prices? In fact, there are often disparities between contract prices and FMVs. These disparities can result from an inequality of bargaining skills or bargaining power, from discrepancies in parties' information about the market or about the property being purchased, or from just plain luck.

If, however, Lynette and Sarah had agreed on a contract price of $235,000 and the FMV was $250,000, and if Lynette breached by non-performance, Sarah would have no general damages. Sarah expected to get $235,000 but expected to give up an asset worth $250,000. Lynette behaved foolishly by breaching an advantageous contract.

Returning to the Chrissie-Lynette problem, if Lynette were the party who breached the contract, the measure of damages would get a bit trickier. Using the get-give concept, Chrissie expected to be paid a sum of money and expected to give up the total cost of performing her obligation. Chrissie's measure of general damages for non-performance would be:

Damages = Contract Price – Contractor's Cost to Perform

In other words, the general damages are Chrissie's anticipated profit (what she was going to be paid less what she was going to spend performing). A contractor is unlikely to make a contract unless she believes she can make a profit on the deal. Thus, assume that Chrissie would only accept a contract price of $50,000 if she would have to spend less than $50,000 to perform. For example, if we assume that Chrissie's cost of performance is $45,000, Chrissie's general damages would be $5,000 ($50,000 – $45,000).

It is important to note that while we have introduced a variety of different formulas, they are all just different ways of expressing the same basic concept, i.e. that plaintiffs are entitled to receive general damages that reflects their loss in value and gives them the net gain or profit they would have earned had the breaching party fully performed.

General damages for breach by defective performance. If a breach takes the form of a defective performance rather than non-performance, loss in value caused by the breach and the cost of repair ("COR") provide alternative measures of general damages. As you will learn later, sometimes the COR may be grossly disproportionate to the diminution in value ("DIV") (the value as promised less the value as received) caused by a breach. In such cases, courts may use the DIV as the measure of damages.

For example, consider the Chrissie-Lynette problem where Chrissie performed, but her performance was defective because she did not perform as promised. Chrissie would be required to pay the cost of correcting the work or the difference between the market value of the house if it had been built exactly to the contract specifications and the value of the house as it was actually built.

Note that it is possible that the COR and DIV would be the same because market values often reflect the cost of fixing defects in property. Or, those numbers may be different. For example, consider the omitted fireplace in the Chrissie-Lynette problem. A house that lacks a fireplace is worth less than one that has a fireplace. That difference, however, would be less than the cost of demolishing a part of the newly constructed house to make space for a fireplace, building the fireplace, and fixing anything that was demolished in order to build the fireplace.

One way to measure damages for the failure to include the fireplace is the difference between the market value of the house with the fireplace and the value of the house without it. The following formula expresses this measure:

$$\text{Damages} = \text{FMV as Promised} - \text{FMV as Received}$$

Damages refers to the damages for the particular type of breach: breach by defective performance. FMV as promised means the FMV of the defendant's promised performance. FMV as received refers to the fair market value of the house in the actual condition in which it was received.

Table 6-1: General Damages for Commonly Made Contracts

Nature of Contract	Breaching Party and Nature of Breach	Non-Breaching Party	Measure of General Damages
Purchase and sale of land	Buyer: breach by non-performance	Seller	K price – FMV of land
Purchase and sale of land	Seller: breach by non-performance	Buyer	FMV of land – K price
Construction contract	Contractor: breach by non-performance	Owner	FMV of contractor's services – K price
Construction contract	Owner: breach by non-performance	Contractor	K price – contractor's cost of performing
Employment contract for specific term	Employer: breach by non-performance	Employee	K price
Employment contract for specific term	Employee: breach by non-performance	Employer	FMV of employee's services – K price
Construction contract	Contractor: breach by defective performance	Owner	COR. If COR is grossly disproportionate to DIV, some states use DIV.

B. Special Damages

"**Special damages**" is the second subtopic depicted under "Measure" in Diagram 6-1 at the beginning of this chapter. Special damages refer to all losses, other than general damages, caused by a breach. Special damages are sometimes called "indirect" damages. This category is broader than general damages because it incorporates a wide spectrum of possible harms. There are two main categories of special damages: (1) **reliance damages**, and (2) **consequential damages**.

Reliance damages include expenditures made while preparing to perform or performing a contract. For example, for a contract to install a swimming pool, reliance damages could potentially include the expense of renting an excavator to dig into the ground and the expense of paying an employee to dig the pool. Reliance damages include wasted expenditures such as a seller's purchase of a special car cover to cover a car that the seller, in breach of contract, failed to deliver to the buyer. Reliance damages also include additional expenditures caused by a breach such as advertising costs incurred to try to find a replacement buyer. Extra costs incurred in response to a breach are also referred to as "incidental" damages or "incidental reliance".

In some cases, reliance damages will not be recoverable because the plaintiff will be fully compensated by an award of general damages. Let's say I'm a painting contractor and I have a contract to paint a large building for a contract price of $50,000. Assume that my anticipated costs of performing will be $35,000 and that includes $25,000 for pots of paint. If I buy the pots of paint from my supplier and the other party then cancels the contract before I start painting, I stand to recover the $15,000 profit I would have made on the contract as per the **Contract Price** ($50,000) – **Contractor's Cost to Perform** ($35,000) formula (see above). But I won't necessarily recover the $25,000 I spent on paint, although it is an expenditure I made "while preparing to perform or performing a contract". Why not? Well, it's because the $25,000 I spent on paint is part of my costs of performing. In other words, it's money I had to spend anyway in order to earn my profit on the contract. To award me my profit *and* my expenditure in this type of situation (a total of $45,000 — virtually the full contract price) would overcompensate me because it reimburses the $25,000 and leaves me with lots of valuable paint (with an apparent wholesale value of $25,000) that I could presumably reuse or resell. The law doesn't allow you to recover twice for the same loss.[3] In other cases, a non-breaching party is limited to recovering only reliance damages. That situation is addressed in a separate section at the end of this chapter.

Consequential damages are indirect losses resulting from a breach of contract. Consequential damages include items such as loss of profits because the buyer is deprived of the use of the item contracted, loss of profits on resale transactions with third parties, or personal injuries or property damage caused by some defect in the defendant's performance.

C. Costs and Losses Avoided

"**Costs and Losses Avoided**" is the third subtopic depicted under "Measure" in Diagram 6-1 at the beginning of this chapter. In many instances, a breach of contract saves a non-breaching party money. For example, if a seller repudiates a contract before a buyer has paid any money, the buyer saves the money she would have paid the seller. Sometimes a breach may even save a party from the consequences of his poor bargaining. Consider a situation where a buyer contracts to purchase a house worth $180,000 for $200,000.

---

3. This is not to say that I could *never* recover reliance damages in this situation. For example, if I could prove that I could not use the paint on any of my other contracts or I could only sell it back to my supplier for less than what I paid for it or if I have to pay extra to store the paint, I will have suffered a loss over and above the loss of the anticipated profit on the contract.

If the contract were performed, the buyer would lose $20,000 (the difference between the contract price and the value he was getting). This loss avoided would be deducted from the buyer's overall damage award.

Exercise 6-3: Measure of Damages

1. In this chapter, you have learned that the goal of contract damages is to award a non-breaching party the economic equivalent of the benefit of her bargain. Explain what this means in your own words.

2. What's the difference between putting non-breaching parties in the pre-contract position and putting non-breaching parties in the post-performance position? Why have courts chosen the performance position as the goal for contract damages?

3. In this chapter you have also learned that courts often measure damages in terms of fair market values. What policy does this choice promote?

4. To analyze measure of damages questions, consider damages from as broad a perspective as possible. Step back and identify all of the harm suffered by the non-breaching party and the dollar value of that harm. Practice this approach with the cases below. After you read the cases, identify and make a list of each item of damages.

5. Paula entered into a contract to purchase land from David for $250,000, which is the appraised market value of the land. Paula made a $25,000 down payment, and further of payments of $750 for a survey and $500 on title investigations. David breached. At the time of David's breach, Paula was under contract to resell the land to Eric for $275,000. Identify and classify each item of damage Paula might recover. Based on what you have learned so far, what do you think her total dollar recovery would be?

The first three damage cases you will read deal with breaches by non-performance (*Donovan v. Bachstadt*, *Neri v. Retail Marine Corp.*, and *Wilson Salvage Co. v. Hays*). Then, the next two damage cases you will read deal with breaches by defective performance (*S.J. Groves & Sons v. John Wunder Company* and *Peevyhouse v. Garland Coal & Mining Company*).

Exercise 6-4: *Donovan v. Bachstadt*

The first case, *Donovan*, includes statements somewhat inconsistent with the damage rules you have already learned in this chapter. *Donovan* responds to a body of law in England and some states that did not require a seller of land to pay benefit-of-the-bargain damages if the court concludes that the breach was in good faith. Commentators suggest this rule stemmed from a view that sellers should not be punished for failing to deliver good title to property because title was so difficult to ascertain. The rule is not followed in many states and seems likely to die out altogether because technology has made it easier to ascertain titleholders. As you read *Donovan*, consider the following questions:

1. For what losses did the plaintiffs seek recovery?

2. For what losses did the court say the plaintiffs could recover?

3. Which items of damage approved by the court are general damages?

4. Which items of damage approved by the court are special damages?

5. Which items of damage approved by the court are reliance damages?

6. Which items of damage approved by the court are consequential damages?

Donovan v. Bachstadt
91 N.J. 434, 453 A.2d 160 (1982)

Schreiber, J. The central legal issue in this case concerns the damages to which a buyer of realty is entitled upon the breach of the executory agreement by the seller. The procedural circumstances under which the question arose are unique. The buyers, Edward Donovan and Donna Donovan, husband and wife, prevailed in a suit for specific performance in which the venue was laid in the Superior Court, Middlesex County. When the seller, Carl Bachstadt, could not perform because of a defect in title, the Donovans instituted this action for damages in the Superior Court, Monmouth County. The Donovans partially succeeded in their action for damages. On their motion for summary judgment they were awarded reimbursement of their expenditures of $145.00 for a survey and $142.85 for title searches. Having been denied compensatory damages, they appealed to the Appellate Division, which reversed and remanded for a trial on that issue. We granted the seller's petition for certification. 89 N.J. 403 (1982).

The plaintiffs' motion for summary judgment recited that reliance for the motion was predicated only on a memorandum submitted by counsel. However, both parties during the oral argument before the trial court relied on the pleadings, depositions of the seller and exhibits marked on the depositions. Though the record is sparse, the following uncontroverted facts appear.

On December 1, 1977, Joan Lowden acquired a deed from Middletown Township to Lots 25 and 26 in Block F as shown on a certain map duly filed in the Monmouth Clerk's Office. The defendant, Bachstadt, advanced the funds for the purchase of land. Ms. Lowden gave Bachstadt a deed to the property that he never recorded. Bachstadt constructed a house on the property and on January 19, 1980 entered into a contract to sell the premises to the Donovans.

The contract was on a standard form prepared by an association of realtors. Bachstadt had no attorney. The record does not disclose if the Donovans were represented at the time the contract was executed. Indeed, Bachstadt never met the Donovans until after the contract had been signed, the realtor having been the only link between the parties.

The contract recited that the purchase price was $58,900. A deposit of $5,890 was paid to and held by the broker. At the closing scheduled for May 1, 1980, the Donovans were to pay an additional $9,010 in cash and the balance was to consist of a purchase money bond or note and mortgage in the principal amount of $44,000, for 30 years, at an interest rate of [10.5%].[4] The conveyance was to be made subject to easements and restrictions of record and facts disclosed in an accurate survey, provided that these would not render the title unmarketable. The contract also stated that title "shall be marketable and insurable ... by any reputable title insurance company...." There was no liquidated damage provision.

A title search obtained by the Donovans from Lawyers Title Insurance Corporation disclosed that title was presently in Anthony and Jane Mettrich, and not in Middletown Township or Joan Lowden. This was brought to Bachstadt's attention. Middletown had foreclosed its tax lien on other property owned by the Mettrichs, but it had inadvertently failed to foreclose on Lots 25 and 26 in Block F, the land sold to Joan Lowden....

When defendant could not obtain marketable title, the Donovans commenced this suit for compensatory and punitive damages. As previously observed the trial court granted plaintiffs' motion for summary judgment. It was indisputable that the defendant had breached the agreement. The only issue was damages. The trial court held that plaintiffs were entitled under N.J.S.A. 2A:29-1 to recovery of their costs for the title search and survey.[5] Plaintiffs had apparently in the interim purchased a home in Middlesex County and obtained a mortgage loan bearing interest at the rate of [13.25%] per annum. Plaintiffs sought the difference between [10.5%] and [13.25%] as compensatory damages, representing their loss of the benefit of the bargain. The trial court denied recovery because the contract was for the sale of the property and the financing "was only incidental to the basic concept."...

There is no sound basis why benefit-of-the-bargain damages should not be awarded whether the subject matter of the contract is realty or personalty. Serious losses should not be borne by the vendee of real estate to the benefit of the defaulting vendor. This is particularly so when an installment purchase contract is involved that extends over a period of years during which the vendee makes substantial payments upon the principal, as well as extensive improvements to the property.

The innocent purchaser should be permitted to recover benefit-of-the-bargain damages irrespective of the good or bad faith of the seller. Contract culpability depends on the breach of the contractual promise. 4 CORBIN, CONTRACTS §§ 943–44, at 806–08 (1951). Where, as here, the seller agreed that title would be marketable, the seller's liability should depend upon his breach of that promise....

We are satisfied that a buyer should be permitted to recover benefit-of-the-bargain damages when the seller breaches an executory contract to convey real property. Here the defendant agreed to convey marketable title. He made that bargained-for promise and breached it and is responsible to the

---

4. The interest rate stipulated in the loan contract was actually 13%. However, New Jersey has laws that cap the interest that lenders can charge. The true rate of interest by virtue of the cap then applicable was 10.5%.

5. Notice that the legal basis for the recovery of these expenses was a New Jersey statute. That statute currently provides that where a seller who contracts to sell real estate subsequently fails to perform because of a title defect, the buyer may recover the reasonable expenses of examining the title and making a survey of the property, unless the contract provides otherwise.

plaintiff for the damages occasioned thereby. The next question is how to compute those compensatory damages.

Judicial remedies upon breach of contract fall into three general categories: restitution, compensatory damages and performance. Separate concepts undergird each of these remedial provisions. The rationale for restitution is to return the innocent party to his status before the contract was executed. Compensatory damages are intended to recompense the injured claimant for losses due to the breach, that is, to give the innocent party the benefit of the bargain. Performance is to effect a result, essentially other than in terms of monetary reparation, so that the innocent party is placed in the position of having had the contract performed. We have now adopted the American rule providing for compensatory damages upon the seller's breach of an executory contract to sell realty and we must examine the appropriate elements that should properly be included in an award.

"Compensatory damages are designed 'to put the injured party in as good a position as he would have had if performance had been rendered as promised.' 5 *Corbin, Contracts* § 992, p. 5 (1951)." [Citations omitted.] What that position is depends upon what the parties reasonably expected. It follows that the defendant is not chargeable for loss that he did not have reason to foresee as a probable result of the breach when the contract was made. *Hadley v. Baxendale*, 9 Ex. 341, 156 Eng. Rep. 145 (1854); *accord Crater v. Binninger*, 33 N.J.L. 513 (E. & A. 1869). The oft-quoted language in *Hadley* for this proposition is:

> Where two parties have made a contract, which one of them has broken, the damages which the other party ought to receive, in respect of such breach, should be such as may fairly be considered either arising naturally, *i.e.*, according to the usual course of things, from such breach of contract itself, or such as may reasonably be supposed to have been in the contemplation of both parties at the time they made the contract, as the probable result of the breach of it. [Citation omitted.]

See RESTATEMENT (SECOND) OF CONTRACTS § 351 (1981); [Secondary citation omitted.]. Further the loss must be a reasonably certain consequence of the breach although the exact amount of the loss need not be certain. [Citations omitted.]

The specific elements to be applied in any given case of a seller's breach of an executory agreement to sell realty may vary in order to achieve the broad purposes of reparations; some items, however, will almost invariably exist. Thus the purchaser will usually be entitled to the return of the amount paid on the purchase price with interest thereon. Costs and expenses incurred in connection with the proposed acquisition, such as for the title search and survey, would fall in the same category. The traditional test is the difference between the market price of the property at the time of the breach and the contract price. [Citations omitted.] ...

The difference between market and contract price may not be suitable in all situations. Thus where a buyer had in turn contracted to sell the realty, it is reasonable to measure his damages in terms of the actual lost profit. [Citations omitted.] What the proper elements of damage are depend upon the particular circumstances surrounding the transaction, especially the terms, conditions and nature of the agreement.

The plaintiffs here assert that their damages are equivalent to the difference in interest costs incurred by them in purchasing a different home at another location. This claim assumes that the financial provision of the contract concerning the purchase money mortgage that the defendant agreed to accept was independent and divisible from the purchase of the land and house. The defendant contends that he did not agree to loan these funds in connection with the purchase of some other property, but that this provision was incidental to the sale of the house. Neither position is entirely sound. This financing was an integral part of the transaction. It can be neither ignored nor viewed as an isolated element.

The relationship of the financing to the purchase of a home has changed in recent years. As interest rates rose and the availability of first mortgage funds was sharply reduced, potential homeowners ... found financing difficult to obtain ... The rise in interest rates, the expense of mortgage credit and the availability of funds has rendered traditional methods of financing acquisition of homes impractical ... Favorable vendor financing could lead to increased market value ...

In some circumstances interest rate differentials are an appropriate measure of damages. Where the buyer has obtained specific performance, but because of the delay has incurred higher mortgage rates, then his loss clearly should include the higher financing cost. *Godwin v. Lindbert*, 101 Mich. App. 754, 300 N.W.2d 514 (1981), is illustrative. The buyers lost their commitment for a mortgage with an interest rate of [8.75%] when the seller refused to convey. The buyers succeeded in obtaining specific performance but were compelled to borrow funds at [11.5%]. They were awarded the difference reduced to present value. [Citation omitted.] Moreover, we are not unmindful of the possibility that a buyer might demonstrate that a lending institution's commitment to advance the funds initially at a certain interest rate was due to the buyer's financial condition. The particular realty might well be a secondary and incidental consideration for the loan. Therefore an interest differential occasioned by the seller's default might be a proper factor in fixing damages where the buyer shortly thereafter purchased another property financed at a higher interest rate.

This is not such a situation. The defendant's motive was to sell a house and not to lend money. In measuring the plaintiffs' loss there should be a determination of the fair market value of the property and house that could be acquired with a purchase money mortgage in the principal amount of $44,000 at an interest rate of [10.5%] ... for a 30-year term. The valuation should be at the time the defendant failed to comply with the judgment of specific performance. The plaintiffs would be entitled to the difference between $58,900 and that fair market value. If the fair market value was not more than the contract price, the plaintiffs would not have established any damage ascribable to the loss of the bargain. They are also entitled to their expenditures for the survey, search, and counsel fees for services rendered in preparation of the aborted closing. The plaintiffs have hitherto received the return of the deposit.

The judgment of the Appellate Division is modified and, as so modified, remanded to the trial court for further proceedings consistent with this opinion.

The second damages case you will read, *Neri v. Retail Marine Corp.*, addresses a complicated point of U.C.C. Article 2 damages law. It is included here for several reasons: to help you understand the benefit-of-the-bargain measure and how the U.C.C. alters common law damages rules, and to give you examples of special damages.

Neri involves a contract for a boat. The buyers are consumers who encountered personal difficulties and repudiated the contract. Although the buyers are sympathetic parties, that fact is essentially irrelevant. Liability for breach of contract attaches regardless of whether a breach is intentional or negligent—or even for a good, honest reason.

Exercise 6-5: *Neri v. Retail Marine Corp.*

The Neris filed suit even though they were the ones who breached the contract. They paid a significant down payment and sued to get it back. As the court explains, a breaching party can get restitution of any performance bestowed on the non-breaching party, but only to the extent the bestowed performance exceeds the amount of damages caused by the breach. Accordingly, the court analyzed Retail Marine's damages to determine if the Neris can recover any of their down payment. As you read *Neri*, consider the following questions:

1. What injuries did the non-breaching party claim it suffered?

2. What damages did the court conclude the non-breaching party was entitled to? Why?

3. The non-breaching party was awarded "incidental damages" under section 2-710 of the U.C.C., but no consequential damages. Why not? Why do you think that sellers of goods, land, or services almost never recover consequential damages?

Neri v. Retail Marine Corp.
30 N.Y.2d 393, 285 N.E.2d 311 (1972)

Gibson, J. The appeal concerns the right of a retail dealer to recover loss of profits and incidental damages upon the buyer's repudiation of a contract governed by the Uniform Commercial Code. This is, indeed, the correct measure of damage in an appropriate case and to this extent the code (§ 2-708, subsection 2) effected a substantial change from prior law, whereby damages were ordinarily limited to "the difference between the contract price and the market or current price." Upon the record before us, the courts below erred in declining to give effect to the new statute and so the order appealed from must be reversed.

The plaintiffs contracted to purchase from defendant a new boat of a specified model for the price of $12,587.40, against which they made a deposit of $40. They shortly increased the deposit to $4,250 in consideration of the de-

The court references the common law damages rule you have already learned: the contract price minus the FMV.

fendant dealer's agreement to arrange with the manufacturer for immediate delivery on the basis of "a firm sale," instead of the delivery within approximately four to six weeks originally specified. Some six days after the date of the contract plaintiffs' lawyer sent to defendant a letter rescinding the sales contract for the reason that plaintiff Neri was about to undergo hospitalization and surgery, in consequence of which, according to the letter, it would be "impossible for Mr. Neri to make any payments." The boat had already been ordered from the manufacturer and was delivered to defendant at or before the time the attorney's letter was received. Defendant declined to refund plaintiffs' deposit and this action to recover it was commenced. Defendant counterclaimed, alleging plaintiffs' breach of the contract and defendant's resultant damage in the amount of $4,250, for which sum defendant demanded judgment. Upon motion, defendant had summary judgment on the issue of liability tendered by its counterclaim; and Special Term directed an assessment of damages, upon which it would be determined whether plaintiffs were entitled to the return of any portion of their down payment.

Upon the trial so directed, it was shown that the boat ordered and received by defendant in accordance with plaintiffs' contract of purchase was sold some four months later to another buyer for the same price as that negotiated with plaintiffs. From this proof the plaintiffs argue that defendant's loss on its contract was recouped, while defendant argues that but for plaintiffs' default, it would have sold two boats and have earned two profits instead of one. Defendant proved, without contradiction, that its profit on the sale under the contract in suit would have been $2,579 and that during the period the boat remained unsold incidental expenses aggregating $674 for storage, upkeep, finance charges and insurance were incurred. Additionally, defendant proved and sought to recover attorneys' fees of $1,250.

The trial court found "untenable" defendant's claim for loss of profit, inasmuch as the boat was later sold for the same price that plaintiffs had contracted to pay; found, too, that defendant had failed to prove any incidental damages; further found "that the terms of section 2-718, subsection 2(b), of the Uniform Commercial Code are applicable and same make adequate and fair provision to place the sellers in as good a position as performance would have done" and, in accordance with paragraph (b) of subsection (2) thus relied upon, awarded defendant $500 upon its counterclaim and directed that plaintiffs recover the balance .of their deposit, amounting to $3,750. The ensuing judgment was affirmed, without opinion, at the Appellate Division and defendant's appeal to this court was taken by our leave.

The court explains the rule you learned in the introduction to this case: the breaching buyers can recover their deposit as restitution less damages caused to the seller by the breach.

The issue is governed in the first instance by section 2-718 of the Uniform Commercial Code which provides, among other things, that the buyer, despite his breach, may have restitution of the amount by which his payment exceeds: (a) reasonable liquidated damages stipulated by the contract, or (b) absent such stipulation, 20% of the value of the buyer's total performance or $500, whichever is smaller (§ 2-718, subsection 2, para. a, b). As above noted, the trial court awarded defendant an offset in the amount of $ 500 under paragraph (b) and directed restitution to plaintiffs of the balance. Section 2-718, however, establishes, in paragraph (a) of subsection (3), an alternative right of offset in favor of the seller, as follows: "The buyer's right to restitution under subsection (2) is subject to offset to the extent that the seller establishes (a) a right to recover damages under the provisions of this Article other than subsection (1)."

Among "the provisions of this Article other than subsection (1)" are those to be found in section 2-708, which the courts below did not apply. Subsection (1) of that section provides that "the measure of damages for non-acceptance or repudiation by the buyer is the difference between the market price at the time and place for tender and the unpaid contract price together with any incidental damages provided in this Article (section 2-710), but less expenses saved in consequence of the buyer's breach." However, this provision is made expressly subject to subsection (2), providing: "If the measure of damages provided in subsection (1) is inadequate to put the seller in as good a position as performance would have done then the measure of damages is the profit (including reasonable overhead) which the seller would have made from full performance by the buyer, together with any incidental damages provided in this Article (section 2-710), due allowance for costs reasonably incurred and due credit for payments or proceeds of resale."

The provision of the code upon which the decision at Trial Term rested (§ 2-718, subsection 2, para. b) does not differ greatly from the corresponding provisions of the prior statute (Personal Property Law, § 145-a, subsection 1, para. b) except as the new act includes the alternative remedy of a lump sum award of $500. Neither does the present reference (in § 2-718, subsection 3, para. a) to the recovery of damages pursuant to other provisions of the article differ from a like reference in the prior statute (Personal Property Law, § 145, subsection 2, para. a) to an alternative measure of damages under section 145 of that act; but section 145 made no provision for recovery of lost profits as does section 2-708 (subsection 2) of the code. The new statute is thus innovative and significant and its analysis is necessary to the determination of the issues here presented.

Prior to the code, the New York cases "applied the 'profit' test, contract price less cost of manufacture, only in cases where the seller [was] a manufacturer or an agent for a manufacturer" (1955 Report of N.Y. Law Rev. Comm., vol. 1, p. 693). Its extension to retail sales was "designed to eliminate the unfair and economically wasteful results arising under the older law when fixed price articles were involved. This section permits the recovery of lost profits in all appropriate cases, which would include all standard priced goods." Official Comment 2, McKinney's Con. Laws of N.Y., Book 62½, Part 1, p. 605, under Uniform Commercial Code, § 2-708. Additionally, and "[in] all cases the seller may recover incidental damages." *Id.*, comment 3. The buyer's right to restitution was established at Special Term upon the motion for summary judgment, as was the seller's right to proper offsets, in each case pursuant to section 2-718; and, as the parties concede, the only question before us, following the assessment of damages at Special Term, is that as to the proper measure of damage to be applied. The conclusion is clear from the record — indeed with mathematical certainty — that "the measure of damages provided in subsection (1) is inadequate to put the seller in as good a position as performance would have done" (Uniform Commercial Code, § 2-708, subsection 2) and hence — again under subsection (2) — that the seller is entitled to its "profit (including reasonable overhead) ... together with any incidental damages..., due allowance for costs reasonably incurred and due credit for payments or proceeds of resale."

It is evident, first, that this retail seller is entitled to its profit and, second, that the last sentence of subsection (2), as hereinbefore quoted, referring to "due credit for payments or proceeds of resale" is inapplicable to this retail sales contract. Closely parallel to the factual situation now before us is that hypothesized by Dean Hawkland as illustrative of the operation of the rules:

> Thus, if a private party agrees to sell his automobile to a buyer for $2,000, a breach by the buyer would cause the seller no loss (except incidental damages, *i.e.,* expense of a new sale) if the seller was able to sell the automobile to another buyer for $2000. But the situation is different with dealers having an unlimited supply of standard-priced goods. Thus, if an automobile dealer agrees to sell a car to a buyer at the standard price of $2000, a breach by the buyer injures the dealer, even though he is able to sell the automobile to another for $2000. If the dealer has an inexhaustible supply of cars, the resale to replace the breaching buyer costs the dealer a sale, because, had the breaching buyer performed, the dealer would have made two sales instead of one. The buyer's breach, in such a case, depletes the dealer's sales to the extent of one, and the measure of damages should be the dealer's profit on one sale. Section 2-708 recognizes this, and it rejects the rule developed under the Uniform Sales Act by many courts that the profit cannot be recovered in this case.

Hawkland, Sales and Bulk Sales (1958 ed.), pp. 153–54; *see Comment*, 31 Fordham L. Rev. 749, 755–56.

The record which in this case establishes defendant's entitlement to damages in the amount of its prospective profit, at the same time confirms defendant's cognate right to "any incidental damages provided in this Article (Section 2-710)," Uniform Commercial Code, § 2-708, subsection 2. From the language employed it is too clear to require discussion that the seller's right to recover loss of profits is not exclusive and that he may recoup his "incidental" expenses as well. [Citation omitted.] Although the trial court's denial of incidental damages in the uncontroverted amount of $674 was made in the context of its erroneous conclusion that paragraph (b) of subsection (2) of section 2-718 was applicable and was "adequate ... to place the sellers in as good a position as performance would have done," the denial seems not to have rested entirely on the court's mistaken application of the law, as there was an explicit finding "that defendant completely failed to show that it suffered any incidental damages." We find no basis for the court's conclusion with respect to a deficiency of proof inasmuch as the proper items of the $674 expenses (being for storage, upkeep, finance charges and insurance for the period between the date performance was due and the time of the resale) were proven without objection and were in no way controverted, impeached or otherwise challenged, at the trial or on appeal. Thus the court's finding of a failure of proof cannot be supported upon the record and, therefore, and contrary to plaintiffs' contention, the affirmance at the Appellate Division was ineffective to save it ...

It follows that plaintiffs are entitled to restitution of the sum of $4,250 paid by them on account of the contract price less an offset to defendant in the amount of $3,253 on account of its lost profit of $2,579 and its incidental damages of $674. The order of the Appellate Division should be modified, with costs in all courts, in accordance with this opinion, and, as so modified, affirmed. Ordered accordingly.

Exercise 6-6: *Wilson Salvage Co. v. Hays*

The next case, *Wilson Salvage Co. v. Hays*, involves a straightforward application of basic damage principles. As you read the case, consider the following:

1. Read sections 2-711, 2-712, 2-713, and 2-715 of the U.C.C. carefully. What options does a buyer in the position of Hays have under these provisions?

2. How did the trial court calculate the plaintiff's damages?

3. Identify and classify each item of damage awarded by the trial court.

4. Why did the court conclude that the plaintiff could not recover all the damages claimed?

Wilson Salvage Co. v. Hays
544 S.W.2d 833 (1976)

James, J. This is a suit by the buyer against the seller for breach of an oral contract to sell and deliver used bricks. Trial was had to a jury, which rendered a verdict favorable to the Plaintiff buyer, pursuant to which verdict the trial court entered judgment. We affirm in part and reverse and render in part.

Plaintiff-Appellee W. D. Hays was in the business of buying and selling used building materials. Defendant-Appellant Bobby Wilson doing business as Wilson Salvage Co. was in the business of wrecking or demolishing buildings. In March 1972, Defendant Wilson was in the process of wrecking some buildings in Midland, Texas. Plaintiff Hays became interested in buying the used, uncleaned brick from Defendant Wilson's demolition work. Whereupon, Hays and Wilson entered into an oral agreement whereby Wilson agreed to sell and deliver 600,000 used uncleaned bricks to Hays at a price of one cent per brick, and Hays agreed to buy said bricks at said price. Hays paid Wilson $6,000.00 in advance. Wilson delivered the uncleaned brick to a designated area where Hays had people hired to clean and stack the brick. Wilson delivered a lesser number of brick than 600,000, thereby precipitating this suit.

Plaintiff-Appellee Hays brought this suit for the return of the proportionate part of the purchase price paid for the bricks he did not get, plus damages. In answer to special issues the jury found:

(1) That Bobby Wilson orally agreed with Hays that he, Bobby Wilson, would sell and deliver to Hays at least 600,000 bricks at a price of one cent per brick; ...

(6) That Bobby Wilson did not deliver 600,000 uncleaned bricks to Hays (but);

(6A) Bobby Wilson delivered only 400,000 bricks to Hays;

(7) The market value of used bricks in Midland, Texas, in April 1972 was five cents per brick;

(8) Hays suffered lost profits in the amount of $6250.00 by virtue of the failure of Bobby Wilson to deliver to Hays at least 600,000 bricks; and

(9) That Hays saved $2605.00 in expenses in consequence of the failure of Bobby Wilson to deliver to him (Hays) at least 600,000 bricks.

Pursuant to the jury verdict, the trial court entered judgment in favor of Plaintiff Hays against Defendant Bobby Wilson in the amount of $13,645.00, plus accrued interest at 6% per annum from and after May 15, 1972, up to Jan. 27, 1976, same being the date of the trial court's judgment, plus interest at 9% per annum from and after the date of said judgment. From this judgment, Defendant Wilson appeals....

Plaintiff-Appellee Hays's remedies and measures of damages as a buyer of goods in the case at bar are governed by sections 2.711, 2.712, 2.713, and 2.715 of the Texas Business and Commerce Code. We herewith quote the portions of said sections that bear upon the case at bar:

Sec. 2.711. Buyer's Remedies in General

(a) Where the seller fails to make delivery or repudiates ... the buyer may cancel and whether or not he has done so may in addition to recovering so much of the price as has been paid.

(1) "Cover" and have damages under the next section as to all the goods affected whether or not they have been identified to the contract; or

(2) Recover damages for non-delivery as provided in this chapter (section 2.713).

Section 2.712. "Cover"; Buyer's Procurement of Substitute Goods

(a) After a breach within the preceding section the buyer may cover by making in good faith and without unreasonable delay any reasonable purchase of or contract to purchase goods in substitution for those due from the seller.

(b) The buyer may recover from the seller as damages the difference between the cost of cover and the contract price together with any incidental or consequential damages as hereinafter defined (section 2.715), but less expenses saved in consequence of the seller's breach.

(c) Failure of the buyer to effect cover within this section does not bar him from any other remedy.

Section 2.713. Buyer's Damages for Non-Delivery or Repudiation

(a) The measure of damages for non-delivery or repudiation by the seller is the difference between the market price at the time when the buyer learned of the breach and the contract price together with any incidental and consequential damages provided in this chapter (section 2.715), but less expenses saved in consequence of the seller's breach.

Section 2.715. Buyer's Incidental and Consequential Damages

(a) Incidental damages....

(b) Consequential damages resulting from the seller's breach include:

(1) Any loss resulting from general or particular requirements and needs of which the seller at the time of contracting had reason to know and which could not reasonably be prevented by cover or otherwise....

Let us analyze the verdict and judgment in the light of the foregoing statutory provisions. In the first place, it is established that Plaintiff Hays paid $6000.00 for 600,000 used brick at the rate of one cent per brick, whereas he received only 400,000 brick. Therefore he paid $2000 for 200,000 brick that he never got, and he is thereby entitled to recover $2000.00 under Section 2.711 for "recovering so much of the price as has been paid."

Next, under Section 2.713, he is entitled to damages for "non-delivery or repudiation," and here his measure of damages is the difference between the market price and the contract price. The contract price of the 200,000 brick not delivered is established at $2000.00. The market price at the appropriate time and place of the undelivered brick was five cents per brick or $10,000.00. This jury finding of market value (five cents per brick) although challenged by Appellant for legal and factual insufficiency, is amply supported by the evidence and is well within the range of probative testimony. Therefore under Section 2.713 and appropriate jury findings, Plaintiff is entitled to $8000.00 damages (or $10,000.00 market price less $2000.00 contract price) for non-delivery.

Now we come to the problem of "consequential damages ... less expenses saved in consequence of the seller's breach" as mentioned in section 2.713 and which damages are provided for in section 2.715. As stated, the jury found Hays sustained lost profits of $6250.00 (Special Issue No. 8) and saved $2605.00 expenses (No. 9), thereby suffering a lost-profit net of $3645.00, which last-named amount was included in the $13,645.00 judgment total. This $3645.00 lost-profits amount has no support in the evidence. Under section 2.715, "consequential damages" includes "any loss ... which could not reasonably be prevented by cover or otherwise."

There is no evidence in the record whatever that Plaintiff Hays at any time made any effort to cover or in any other manner attempt to prevent or mitigate a loss resulting from the Defendant Wilson's non-delivery of the 200,000 brick in question. In the absence of such a showing these consequential damages are unauthorized under section 2.715. The burden of proving the extent of loss incurred by way of consequential damage is on the buyer. See committee comment to Section 2.715; *General Supply and Equipment Co. v. Phillips*, 490 S.W.2d 913, 920 (1972). This being so, we are of the opinion that there is no evidence to support these jury findings concerning consequential damages, and that the trial court's judgment insofar as it awarded Plaintiff Hays $3645.00 lost profits is improper and this amount should be deleted from said judgment.

As stated before, the judgment is proper and should be affirmed for the amount of $10,000.00, same being composed of $2000.00 paid by Plaintiff for which he received no bricks plus $8000.00 damages for non-delivery.

We therefore affirm in part and reverse and render in part the trial court's judgment as follows: Plaintiff-Appellee Hays is hereby awarded judgment against Defendant-Appellant Wilson in the amount of $10,000.00, plus interest at six percent per annum from and after May 15, 1972 up until January 27, 1976, the date of entry of the trial court's judgment, together with interest from the date of the trial court's judgment upon the amount then due at the rate of nine percent per annum until paid. Costs of the trial court and of this appeal are taxed one-half each to Appellant and Appellee. Affirmed in part and reversed and rendered in part.

Exercise 6-7: *Groves* and *Peevyhouse*

Consider the next two cases, *Groves* and *Peevyhouse*, together. Both deal with measuring general damages for defective performance breaches. As you read the cases, consider the following questions:

1. What is the relationship between the two cases?

2. What rule does the *Groves* court apply? What rule does the *Peevyhouse* court apply? Find and paraphrase the RESTATEMENT (SECOND) OF CONTRACTS approach to such problems.

3. How did the *Groves* and *Peevyhouse* courts apply the rules they adopted?

4. Why do you think that courts prefer to award the cost of repairing breaches rather than the loss in value caused by breaches?

5. Are there any facts in *Peevyhouse* that suggest that *Peevyhouse* presented a stronger case for awarding the cost of repair than *Groves*?

Groves & Sons v. John Wunder Co.

205 Minn. 163, 286 N.W. 235 (1939)

Stone, Justice. Action for breach of contract. Plaintiff got judgment for a little over $15,000. Sorely disappointed by that sum, he appeals.

In August, 1927, S. J. Groves & Sons Company, a corporation (hereinafter mentioned simply as Groves), owned a tract of 24 acres of Minneapolis suburban real estate. It was served or easily could be reached by railroad trackage. It is zoned as heavy industrial property. But for lack of development of the neighborhood its principal value thus far may have been in the deposit of sand and gravel which it carried. The Groves company had a plant on the premises for excavating and screening the gravel. Nearby defendant owned and was operating a similar plant.

In August, 1927, Groves and defendant made the involved contract. For the most part it was a lease from Groves, as lessor, to defendant, as lessee; its term seven years. Defendant agreed to remove the sand and gravel and to leave the property "at a uniform grade, substantially the same as the grade now existing at the roadway ... on said premises, and that in stripping the overburden ... it will use said overburden for the purpose of maintaining and establishing said grade."

Under the contract defendant got the Groves screening plant. The transfer thereof and the right to remove the sand and gravel made the consideration moving from Groves to defendant, except that defendant incidentally got rid of Groves as a competitor. On defendant's part it paid Groves $105,000. So that from the outset, on Groves' part the contract was executed except for defendant's right to continue using the property for the stated term. (Defendant had a right to renewal which it did not exercise.)

Defendant breached the contract deliberately. It removed from the premises only "the richest and best of the gravel" and wholly failed, according to the findings, "to perform and comply with the terms, conditions, and provisions of said lease ... with respect to the condition in which the surface of the demised premises was required to be left." Defendant surrendered the premises, not substantially at the grade required by the contract "nor at any uniform grade." Instead, the ground was "broken, rugged, and uneven." Plaintiff sues as assignee and successor in right of Groves.

As the contract was construed below, the finding is that to complete its performance 288,495 cubic yards of overburden would need to be excavated, taken from the premises, and deposited elsewhere. The reasonable cost of doing that was found to be upwards of $60,000. But, if defendant had left the premises at the uniform grade required by the lease, the reasonable value of the property on the determinative date would have been only $12,160. The judgment was for that sum, including interest, thereby nullifying plaintiff's claim that cost of completing the contract rather than difference in value of the land was the measure of damages. The gauge of damage adopted by the decision was the difference between the market value of plaintiff's land in the condition it was when the contract was made and what it would have been if defendant had performed. The one question for us arises upon plaintiff's assertion that he was entitled, not to that difference in value, but to the reasonable cost to him of doing the work called for by the contract which defendant left undone....

In reckoning damages for breach of a building or construction contract, the law aims to give the disappointed promisee, so far as money will do it, what he was promised. 9 Am. Jur., Building and Construction Contracts § 152. It is so ruled by a long line of decisions in this state, beginning with *Carli v. Seymour, Sabin & Co.* 26 Minn. 276, 3 N.W. 348, where the contract was for building a road. There was a breach. Plaintiff was held entitled to recover what it would cost to complete the grading as contemplated by the contract. For our other similar cases, see 2 Dunnell, Minn. Dig. (2 ed. & Supps.) §§ 2561, 2565.

Never before, so far as our decisions show, has it even been suggested that lack of value in the land furnished to the contractor who had bound himself to improve it any escape from the ordinary consequences of a breach of the contract....

[I]t is error to instruct that the measure of damage is "the difference in value between the house as it was and as it would have been if constructed according to contract." The "correct doctrine" is that the cost of remedying the defect is the "proper" measure of damages. [Citation omitted.] ...

To diminish damages recoverable against him in proportion as there is presently small value in the land would favor the faithless contractor. It would also ignore and so defeat plaintiff's right to contract and build for the future. To justify such a course would require more of the prophetic vision than judges possess. This factor is important when the subject matter is trackage property in the margin of such an area of population and industry as that of the Twin Cities....

It is suggested that because of little or no value in his land the owner may be unconscionably enriched by such a reckoning. The answer is that there can be no unconscionable enrichment, no advantage upon which the law will frown, when the result is but to give one party to a contract only what the other has promised; particularly where, as here, the delinquent has had full payment for the promised performance.

It is said by the RESTATEMENT OF CONTRACTS, § 346, Comment b: "Sometimes defects in a completed structure cannot be physically remedied without tearing down and rebuilding, at a cost that would be imprudent and unreasonable. The law does not require damages to be measured by a method requiring such economic waste. If no such waste is involved, the cost of remedying the defect is the amount awarded as compensation for failure to render the promised performance."

The "economic waste" declaimed against by the decisions applying that rule has nothing to do with the value in money of the real estate, or even with the product of the contract. The waste avoided is only that which would come from wrecking a physical structure completed, or nearly so, under the contract. The cases applying that rule go no further ... Absent such waste, as it is in this case, the rule of the RESTATEMENT OF CONTRACTS § 346, is that "the cost of remedying the defect is the amount awarded as compensation for failure to render the promised performance." That means that defendants here are liable to plaintiff for the reasonable cost of doing what defendants promised to do and have willfully declined to do....

The judgment must be reversed with a new trial to follow. So ordered.

> The court states an exception to the principles it has been explaining: the "economic waste" exception. Why doesn't that exception justify reducing plaintiff's damages in this case?

Peevyhouse v. Garland Coal & Mining Co.
382 P.2d 109 (1962)

Jackson, Justice. In the trial court, plaintiffs Willie and Lucille Peevyhouse sued the defendant, Garland Coal and Mining Company, for damages for breach of contract. Judgment was for plaintiffs in an amount considerably less than was sued for. Plaintiffs appeal and defendant cross-appeals.

In the briefs on appeal, the parties present their argument and contentions under several propositions; however, they all stem from the basic question of whether the trial court properly instructed the jury on the measure of damages.

Briefly stated, the facts are as follows: plaintiffs owned a farm containing coal deposits, and in November, 1954, leased the premises to defendant for a period of five years for coal mining purposes. A "strip-mining" operation was contemplated in which the coal would be taken from pits on the surface of the ground, instead of from underground mine shafts. In addition to the usual covenants found in a coal mining lease, defendant specifically agreed to perform certain restorative and remedial work at the end of the lease period. It is unnecessary to set out the details of the work to be done, other than to say that it would involve the moving of many thousands of cubic yards of dirt, at a cost estimated by expert witnesses at about $29,000.00. However, plaintiffs sued for only $25,000.00.

During the trial, it was stipulated that all covenants and agreements in the lease contract had been fully carried out by both parties, except the remedial work mentioned above; defendant conceded that this work had not been done.

Plaintiffs introduced expert testimony as to the amount and nature of the work to be done, and its estimated cost. Over plaintiffs' objections, defendant thereafter introduced expert testimony as to the "diminution in value" of plaintiffs' farm resulting from the failure of defendant to render performance as agreed in the contract—that is, the difference between the present value of the farm, and what its value would have been if defendant had done what it agreed to do.

At the conclusion of the trial, the court instructed the jury that it must return a verdict for plaintiffs, and left the amount of damages for jury determination. On the measure of damages, the court instructed the jury that it might consider the cost of performance of the work defendant agreed to do, "together with all of the evidence offered on behalf of either party."

It thus appears that the jury was at liberty to consider the "diminution in value" of plaintiffs' farm as well as the cost of "repair work" in determining the amount of damages. It returned a verdict for plaintiffs for $ 5000.00—only a fraction of the "cost of performance," *but more than the total value of the farm even after the remedial work is done.*

On appeal, the issue is sharply drawn. Plaintiffs contend that the true measure of damages in this case is what it will cost plaintiffs to obtain performance of the work that was not done because of defendant's default. Defendant argues that the measure of damages is the cost of performance "limited, however, to the total difference in the market value before and after the work was performed."

It appears that this precise question has not heretofore been presented to this court. In *Ardizonne v. Archer*, 72 Okl. 70, 178 P. 263, this court held that the measure of damages for breach of a contract to drill an oil well was the reasonable cost of drilling the well, but here a slightly different factual situation exists. The drilling of an oil well will yield valuable geological information, even if no oil or gas is found, and of course if the well is a producer, the value of the premises increases. In the case before us, it is argued by defendant with some force that the performance of the remedial work defendant agreed to do will add at the most only a few hundred dollars to the value of plaintiffs' farm, and that the damages should be limited to that amount because that is all plaintiffs have lost.

Plaintiffs rely on *Groves v. John Wunder Co.*, 205 Minn. 163, 286 N.W. 235. In that case, the Minnesota court, in a substantially similar situation, adopted the "cost of performance" rule as opposed to the "value" rule. The result was to authorize a jury to give plaintiff damages in the amount of $60,000, where the real estate concerned would have been worth only $12,160, even if the work contracted for had been done.

It may be observed that *Groves v. John Wunder Co., supra*, is the only case which has come to our attention in which the cost of performance rule has been followed under circumstances where the cost of performance greatly exceeded the diminution in value resulting from the breach of contract. Incidentally, it appears that this case was decided by a plurality rather than a majority of the members of the court.

Defendant relies principally upon *Sandy Valley & E. R. Co., v. Hughes*, 175 Ky. 320, 194 S.W. 344; *Bigham v. Wabash-Pittsburg Terminal Ry. Co.*, 223 Pa. 106, 72 A. 318; and *Sweeney v. Lewis Const. Co.*, 66 Wash. 490, 119 P. 1108. These were all cases in which, under similar circumstances, the appellate courts followed the "value" rule instead of the "cost of performance" rule. Plaintiff points out that in the earliest of these cases (*Bigham*) the court cites as authority on the measure of damages an earlier Pennsylvania tort case, and that the other two cases follow the first, with no explanation as to why a measure of damages ordinarily followed in cases sounding in tort should be used in contract cases. Nevertheless, it is of some significance that three out of four appellate courts have followed the diminution in value rule under circumstances where, as here, the cost of performance greatly exceeds the diminution in value.

The explanation may be found in the fact that the situations presented are artificial ones. It is highly unlikely that the ordinary property owner would agree to pay $29,000 (or its equivalent) for the construction of "improvements" upon his property that would increase its value only about ($300) three hundred dollars. The result is that we are called upon to apply principles of law theoretically based upon reason and reality to a situation which is basically unreasonable and unrealistic....

Even in the case of contracts that are unquestionably building and construction contracts, the authorities are not in agreement as to the factors to be considered in determining whether the cost of performance rule or the value rule should be applied. The American Law Institute's RESTATEMENT OF CONTRACTS, volume 1, sections 346(1)(a)(i) and (ii) submits the proposition that the cost of performance is the proper measure of damages "if this is possible and does not involve *unreasonable economic waste;*" and that the diminution in value caused by the breach is the proper measure "if construction and completion in accordance with the contract would involve *unreasonable economic waste.*" (Emphasis supplied.) In an explanatory comment immediately following the text, the Restatement makes it clear that the "economic waste" referred to consists of the destruction of a substantially completed building or other structure. Of course no such destruction is involved in the case now before us.

On the other hand, in McCORMICK, DAMAGES, section 168, it is said with regard to building and construction contracts that " ... in cases where the defect is one that can be repaired or cured without *undue expense*" the cost of performance is the proper measure of damages, but where ..."the defect in material or construction is one that cannot be remedied without *an expenditure for reconstruction disproportionate to the end to be attained"* (emphasis supplied) the value rule should be followed. The same idea was expressed in *Jacob & Youngs, Inc. v. Kent,* 230 N.Y. 239, 129 N.E. 889, as follows:

> The owner is entitled to the money which will permit him to complete, unless the cost of completion is grossly and unfairly out of proportion to the good to be attained. When that is true, the measure is the difference in value.

It thus appears that the prime consideration in the Restatement was "economic waste"; and that the prime consideration in MCCORMICK, DAMAGES and in *Jacob & Youngs, Inc. v. Kent, supra,* was the relationship between the expense involved and the "end to be attained"—in other words, the "relative economic benefit."

In view of the unrealistic fact situation in the instant case, and certain Oklahoma statutes to be hereinafter noted, we are of the opinion that the "relative economic benefit" is a proper consideration here. This is in accord with the recent case of *Mann v. Clowser,* 190 Va. 887, 59 S.E.2d 78, where, in applying the cost rule, the Virginia court specifically noted that "the defects are remediable from a practical standpoint and the costs *are not grossly disproportionate to the results to be obtained*" (emphasis supplied). 23 O.S.1961 §§ 96 and 97 provide as follows:

> § 96.... Notwithstanding the provisions of this chapter, no person can recover a greater amount in damages for the breach of an obligation, than he would have gained by the full performance thereof on both sides....

> § 97.... Damages must, in all cases, be reasonable, and where an obligation of any kind appears to create a right to unconscionable and grossly oppressive damages, contrary to substantial justice no more than reasonable damages can be recovered.

Although it is true that the above sections of the statute are applied most often in tort cases, they are by their own terms, and the decisions of this court, also applicable in actions for damages for breach of contract. It would seem that they are peculiarly applicable here where, under the "cost of performance" rule, plaintiffs might recover an amount about nine times the total value of their farm. Such would seem to be "unconscionable and grossly oppressive damages, contrary to substantial justice" within the meaning of the statute. Also, it can hardly be denied that if plaintiffs here are permitted to recover under the "cost of performance" rule, they will receive a greater benefit from the breach than could be gained from full performance, contrary to the provisions of section 96....

We therefore hold that where, in a coal mining lease, lessee agrees to perform certain remedial work on the premises concerned at the end of the lease period, and thereafter the contract is fully performed by both parties except that the remedial work is not done, the measure of damages in an action by lessor against lessee for damages for breach of contract is ordinarily the reasonable cost of performance of the work; however, where the contract provision breached was merely incidental to the main purpose in view, and where the economic benefit which would result to lessor by full performance of the work is grossly disproportionate to the cost of performance, the damages

Note that McCormick's view has carried the day in the Second Restatement. As you read on, see if you can figure out why.

which lessor may recover are limited to the diminution in value resulting to the premises because of the non-performance.

We believe the above holding is in conformity with the intention of the Legislature as expressed in the statutes mentioned, and in harmony with the better-reasoned cases from the other jurisdictions where analogous fact situations have been considered. It should be noted that the rule as stated does not interfere with the property owner's right to "do what he will with his own," [citation omitted], or his right, if he chooses, to contract for "improvements" which will actually have the effect of reducing his property's value. Where such result is in fact contemplated by the parties, and is a main or principal purpose of those contracting, it would seem that the measure of damages for breach would ordinarily be the cost of performance.

The above holding disposes of all of the arguments raised by the parties on appeal.

Under the most liberal view of the evidence herein, the diminution in value resulting to the premises because of non-performance of the remedial work was $300.00. After a careful search of the record, we have found no evidence of a higher figure, and plaintiffs do not argue in their briefs that a greater diminution in value was sustained. It thus appears that the judgment was clearly excessive, and that the amount for which judgment should have been rendered is definitely and satisfactorily shown by the record. . . .

We are of the opinion that the judgment of the trial court for plaintiffs should be, and it is hereby, modified and reduced to the sum of $300.00, and as so modified it is affirmed.

Exercise 6-8: *Groves* and *Peevyhouse* Revisited

1. Under the Restatement (Second) of Contracts rules, what would the result have been if the cost of repair in *Peevyhouse* had been only $10,000? $5,000? $1,000? $500? $300?

2. What constitutes "economic waste"?

3. What policy rationale explains the *Groves* court's willingness to allow the plaintiff to recover COR damages so greatly in excess of the DIV caused by the breach?

4. What policy rationale explains the *Peevyhouse* court's opposite result?

5. How far does this principle go? Consider *Chatlos v. NCR*, 670 F.2d 1304 (3d Cir. 1982), in which the defendant sold plaintiff a computer system for $46,000, and warranted what functions it would perform. To obtain a machine elsewhere that would perform the warranted functions would have cost approximately $207,000. The machine only performed functions that a $30,000 machine would perform. What are the benefit-of-the-bargain damages?

6. Baila decided to add an office building to a parcel of undeveloped land she owned. After receiving five bids, Baila selected Sally because her bid was the lowest by $50,000. Sally and Baila thereafter entered into a contract whereby Sally agreed to build an office building for Baila for a total of $500,000. Sally and Baila agreed that payments would be in five installments:

- $100,000 before construction begins;
- $100,000 when the building is 25% complete;
- $100,000 when the building is 50% complete;
- $100,000 when the building is 75% complete; and
- $100,000 after the building has obtained final approval from the local construction inspection authority.

Sally calculated her bid by adding $100,000 to her estimated construction costs, which included what Sally estimated she would have to pay others for materials and labor on the job and the value she allocated to her own expected time in supervising the project.

Analyze each of the problems below based on these facts and the benefit-of-the-bargain principle you have learned.

a. Baila refuses to perform before Sally began any work and before Baila paid Sally anything. What amount, if any, may Sally recover as damages?

b. Baila makes the first payment, but then refuses to pay Sally any more even though Sally completed 25% of the project. What amount, if any, may Sally recover as damages?

c. Sally completes the project, but Baila refuses to make the last payment. What amount, if any, may Sally recover as damages?

d. Sally refuses to perform before either party begins performance. What amount, if any, may Baila recover as damages?

e. After receiving Baila's first payment, but before Sally begins any construction, Sally refuses to perform. What amount, if any, may Baila recover as damages?

f. Sally fully performs, but uses a cheap grade of paint (instead of the promised grade) which makes the building worth $50,000 less than it would have been worth as promised. Baila makes all but the final payment because of the paint grade used. What would the result be in a lawsuit between Baila and Sally?

g. Sally refuses to perform before either party begins performance. Baila loses $150,000 worth of monthly rental income she would otherwise have obtained because it took Baila one month to replace Sally (a reasonable amount of time to find a replacement). What amount, if any, may Baila recover as damages?

h. Baila makes the first payment, but Sally refuses to complete the job after completing 25% of the project. What amount, if any, may Baila recover as damages? Hint: This problem involves an advanced application of the concepts you have been studying. Focus on making sure that the amount of damages you award achieves the overall goal of awarding benefit-of-the-bargain damages (damages which will put Baila in the position she would be in had Sally fully performed).

7. You have now finished studying "Measure" under "Damages" as depicted in Diagram 6-1 at the beginning of this chapter. Accordingly, you should now complete the portion of your course outline dealing with the measure of damages for breaches of contract. Your outline should include the rules of

law you have learned, the applicable policy rationales, and examples from the cases you have read. Follow proper outlining procedure. (For example, you should use roman numerals for major concepts, you should never have an A without at least a B, and you should never have a 1 without at least a 2.) Your outline should look similar to the sample provided in Table 6-2, a partial outline for contract defenses. Please note that the Table 6-2 outline is an excerpt intended to show you how to set up your outline. The excerpt is incomplete; it does not include case examples and only covers one contract defense (misrepresentation, one type of deception).

Table 6-2: Contract Course Outline

I. Formation
II. K Defenses
   A. Mistake
   B. Deception
      1. Misrepresentation
         a. Elements
            (1) Misstatement of:
                (a) a fact,
                (b) an opinion if it implies underlying facts, or
                (c) an intention
            (2) Fact is material, one that a reasonable person would consider important (objective standard)
            (3) State of mind
                (a) Intentional
                    i.   Knowledge of falsity
                    ii. a/k/a Fraud
                    iii. Punitive damages possible
                    iv. No materiality required in many states
                (b) Negligent
                    i.   Lack of due care re: truth (may be honest but unreasonable)
                    ii. Basis for damages
                      iii. No punitives allowed
                (c) Innocent
                    i.   Honest, reasonable, and incorrect belief in truth
                    ii. Only remedy rescission
             (4) Actual reliance: D's conduct causes P to make K
            (5) Justifiable reliance: not wholly irrational or absurd
            (6) Injury: harm to P
         b. Policy
            (1) Fairness b/c allows deceived parties to escape Ks
            (2) Ks less predictable b/c may be an escape
      2. Non-disclosure

Limitations on Damages

"**Limitations**" is the second topic depicted under "Damages" in Diagram 6-1 at the beginning of this chapter. As Diagram 6-1 indicates, there are three types of limitations on damages: (1) avoidability (or avoidable consequences), often also referred to as "mitigation of damage," (2) foreseeability (or reasonable contemplation), and (3) certainty.

As you already learned earlier in this chapter, when analyzing contract damage problems your first step should be to consider the measure of all possible items of damage. Your second step should be to consider whether any of the limitations on damages justify reducing a plaintiff's damage recovery. Given the fact that our legal system awards damages to non-breaching parties to encourage promise keeping and contract making, why do you think there are any limitations on the recovery of damages? As you learn about the three types of limitations below, consider what policy rationales are served by limiting damages.

A. Avoidability

This section addresses the first limitation on damages depicted in Diagram 6-1 at the beginning of this chapter: **avoidability**.

Exercise 6-9: Avoidability

Read section 350 of the RESTATEMENT (SECOND) OF CONTRACTS. Then, state the rule for avoidability in your own words.

Exercise 6-10: *Rockingham County v. Luten Bridge Co.*

The first avoidability case you will read is *Rockingham County v. Luten Bridge Co.* This case provides an example of an application of the avoidability rule as well as another example of a measure analysis (a benefit-of-the-bargain award). When you read the case, make sure you understand both the avoidability and measure analyses. Further, specifically consider the following questions:

1. In what sense is this case an application of the avoidability rule from section 350 that you stated in Exercise 6-9?

2. What more specific rule relating to avoidability does the court state?

3. What policy rationale supports the result in this case?

4. How do the avoidability doctrine and the result in this case relate to the idea of causation?

Exercise 6-10: *Rockingham County v. Luten Bridge Co.*

The first avoidability case you will read is *Rockingham County v. Luten Bridge Co.* This case provides an example of an application of the avoidability rule as well as another example of a measure analysis (a benefit-of-the-bargain award). When you read the case, make sure you understand both the avoidability and measure analyses. Further, specifically consider the following questions:

1. In what sense is this case an application of the avoidability rule from section 350 that you stated in Exercise 6-9?

2. What more specific rule relating to avoidability does the court state?

3. What policy rationale supports the result in this case?

4. How do the avoidability doctrine and the result in this case relate to the idea of causation?

Rockingham County v. Luten Bridge Co.

35 F.2d 301 (4th Cir. 1929)

Parker, Circuit Judge. This was an action at law instituted in the court below by the Luten Bridge Company, as plaintiff, to recover of Rockingham County, North Carolina, an amount alleged to be due under a contract. [Rockingham County] contends that notice of cancellation was given the bridge company before the erection of the bridge was commenced, and that it is liable only for the damages which the company would have sustained, if it had abandoned construction at that time. The judge below refused to strike out an answer filed by certain members of the board of commissioners of the county, admitting liability in accordance with the prayer of the complaint, allowed this pleading to be introduced in evidence as the answer of the county, excluded evidence offered by the county in support of its contentions as to notice of cancellation and damages, and instructed a verdict for plaintiff for the full amount of its claim. From judgment on this verdict the county has appealed.

The facts out of which the case arises, as shown by the affidavits and offers of proof appearing in the record, are as follows: On January 7, 1924, the board of commissioners of Rockingham county voted to award to plaintiff a contract for the construction of the bridge in controversy. Three of the five commissioners favored the awarding of the contract and two opposed it. Much feeling was engendered over the matter, with the result that on February 11, 1924, W. K. Pruitt, one of the commissioners who had voted in the affirmative, sent his resignation to the clerk of the superior court of the county. The clerk received this resignation on the same day, and immediately accepted same and noted his acceptance thereon. Later in the day, Pruitt called him over the telephone and stated that he wished to withdraw the resignation, and later sent him written notice to the same effect. The clerk, however, paid no attention to the attempted withdrawal, and proceeded on the next day to appoint one W. W. Hampton as a member of the board to succeed him.

After his resignation, Pruitt attended no further meetings of the board, and did nothing further as a commissioner of the county. Likewise Pratt and McCollum, the other two members of the board who had voted with him in favor of the contract, attended no further meetings. Hampton, on the other hand, took the oath of office immediately upon his appointment and entered upon the discharge of the duties of a commissioner. He met regularly with the two remaining members of the board, Martin and Barber, in the courthouse at the county seat, and with them attended to all of the business of the county. Between the 12th of February and the first Monday in December following, these three attended, in all, 25 meetings of the board.

At one of these meetings, a regularly advertised called meeting held on February 21st, a resolution was unanimously adopted declaring that the contract for the building of the bridge was not legal and valid, and directing the clerk of the board to notify plaintiff that it refused to recognize same as a valid contract, and that plaintiff should proceed no further thereunder. This resolution also rescinded action of the board theretofore taken looking to the construction of a hard-surfaced road, in which the bridge was to be a mere connecting link. The clerk duly sent a certified copy of this resolution to plaintiff.

At the regular monthly meeting of the board on March 3d, a resolution was passed directing that plaintiff be notified that any work done on the bridge would be done by it at its own risk and hazard, that the board was of the opinion that the contract for the construction of the bridge was not valid and legal, and that, even if the board were mistaken as to this, it did not desire to construct the bridge, and would contest payment for same if constructed. A copy of this resolution was also sent to plaintiff. At the regular monthly meeting on April 7th, a resolution was passed, reciting that the board had been informed that one of its members was privately insisting that the bridge be constructed. It repudiated this action on the part of the member and gave notice that it would not be recognized. At the September meeting, a resolution was passed to the effect that the board would pay no bills presented by plaintiff or anyone connected with the bridge. At the time of the passage of the first resolution, very little work toward the construction of the bridge had been done, it being estimated that the total cost of labor done and material on the ground was around $1,900; but, notwithstanding the repudiation of the contract by the county, the bridge company continued with the work of construction.

On November 24, 1924, plaintiff instituted this action against Rockingham County, and against Pruitt, Pratt, McCollum, Martin, and Barber, as constituting its board of commissioners. Complaint was filed, setting forth the execution of the contract and the doing of work by plaintiff thereunder, and alleging that for work done up until November 3, 1924, the county was indebted in the sum of $18,301.07. On November 27th, three days after the filing of the complaint, and only three days before the expiration of the term of office of the members of the old board of commissioners, Pruitt, Pratt, and McCollum met with an attorney at the county seat, and, without notice to or consultation with the other members of the board, so far as appears, had the attorney prepare for them an answer admitting the allegations of the complaint. This answer, which was filed in the cause on the following day, did not purport to be an answer of the county, or of its board of commissioners, but of the three commissioners named.

On December 1, 1924, the newly elected board of commissioners held its first meeting and employed attorneys to defend the action which had been instituted by plaintiff against the county. These attorneys immediately moved to strike out the answer which had been filed by Pruitt, Pratt, and McCollum, and entered into an agreement with opposing counsel that the county should have 30 days from the action of the court on the motion within which to file answer. The court denied the motion on June 2, 1927, and held the answer filed by Pruitt, Pratt, and McCollum to be the answer of the county. An order was then entered allowing the county until August 1st to file answer, pursuant to stipulation, within which time the answer of the county was filed. This answer denied that the contract sued on was legal or binding, and for a further defense set forth the resolutions of the commissioners with regard to the building of the bridge, to which we have referred, and their communication to plaintiff. A reply was filed to this, and the case finally came to trial.

At the trial, plaintiff, over the objection of the county, was allowed to introduce in evidence, the answer filed by Pruitt, Pratt, and McCollum, the contract was introduced, and proof was made of the value under the terms of the contract of the work done up to November 3, 1924. The county elicited on cross-examination proof as to the state of the work at the time of the passage of the resolutions to which we have referred. It then offered these resolutions in evidence, together with evidence as to the resignation of Pruitt, the acceptance of his resignation, and the appointment of Hampton; but all of this evidence was excluded, and the jury was instructed to return a verdict for plaintiff for the full amount of its claim. The county preserved exceptions to the rulings which were adverse to it, and contends that there was error on the part of the judge below in denying the motion to strike out the answer filed by Pruitt, Pratt, and McCollum; in allowing same to be introduced in evidence; in excluding the evidence offered of the resignation of Pruitt, the acceptance of his resignation, and the appointment of Hampton, and of the resolutions attempting to cancel the contract and the notices sent plaintiff pursuant thereto; and in directing a verdict for plaintiff in accordance with its claim.

As the county now admits the execution and validity of the contract, and the breach on its part, the ultimate question in the case is one as to the measure of plaintiff's recovery, and the exceptions must be considered with this in mind.... [The court then discussed issues relating to the membership and authority of the board of commissioners.]

Coming, then, to the third question — *i.e.,* as to the measure of plaintiff's recovery — we do not think that, after the county had given notice, while the contract was still executory, that it did not desire the bridge built and would not pay for it, plaintiff could proceed to build it and recover the contract price. It is true that the county had no right to rescind the contract, and the notice given plaintiff amounted to a breach on its part; but, after plaintiff had received notice of the breach, it was its duty to do nothing to increase the damages flowing therefrom. If A enters into a binding contract to build a house for B, B, of course, has no right to rescind the contract without A's consent. But if, before the house is built, he decides that he does not want it, and notifies A to that effect, A has no right to proceed with the building and thus pile up damages. His remedy is to treat the contract as broken when he receives the notice, and sue for the recovery of such damages, as he may have sustained from the breach, including any profit which he would have realized upon performance, as well as any other losses which may have resulted to him. In the case at bar, the county decided not to build the road of which the bridge was to be a part, and did not build it. The bridge, built in the midst of the forest, is of no value to the county because of this change of circumstances. When, therefore, the county gave notice to the plaintiff that it would not proceed with the project, plaintiff should have desisted from further work. It had no right thus to pile up damages by proceeding with the erection of a useless bridge....

The American rule and the reasons supporting it are well stated by Prof. Williston as follows:

> There is a line of cases running back to 1845 which holds that, after
> an absolute repudiation or refusal to perform by one party to a con-

tract, the other party cannot continue to perform and recover damages based on full performance. This rule is only a particular application of the general rule of damages that a plaintiff cannot hold a defendant liable for damages which need not have been incurred; or, as it is often stated, the plaintiff must, so far as he can without loss to himself, mitigate the damages caused by the defendant's wrongful act. The application of this rule to the matter in question is obvious. If a man engages to have work done, and afterwards repudiates his contract before the work has been begun or when it has been only partially done, it is inflicting damage on the defendant without benefit to the plaintiff to allow the latter to insist on proceeding with the contract. The work may be useless to the defendant, and yet he would be forced to pay the full contract price. On the other hand, the plaintiff is interested only in the profit he will make out of the contract. If he receives this it is equally advantageous for him to use his time otherwise.

The leading case on the subject in this country is the New York case of *Clark v. Marsiglia*, 1 Denio (N.Y.) 317, 43 Am. Dec. 670. In that case defendant had employed plaintiff to paint certain pictures for him, but countermanded the order before the work was finished. Plaintiff, however, went on and completed the work and sued for the contract price. In reversing a judgment for plaintiff, the court said:

> The plaintiff was allowed to recover as though there had been no countermand of the order; and in this the court erred. The defendant, by requiring the plaintiff to stop work upon the paintings, violated his contract, and thereby incurred a liability to pay such damages as the plaintiff should sustain. Such damages would include a recompense for the labor done and materials used, and such further sum in damages as might, upon legal principles, be assessed for the breach of the contract; but the plaintiff had no right, by obstinately persisting in the work, to make the penalty upon the defendant greater than it would otherwise have been....

It follows that there was error in directing a verdict for plaintiff for the full amount of its claim. The measure of plaintiff's damage, upon its appearing that notice was duly given not to build the bridge, is an amount sufficient to compensate plaintiff for labor and materials expended and expense incurred in the part performance of the contract, prior to its repudiation, plus the profit which would have been realized if it had been carried out in accordance with its terms....

The judgment below will accordingly be reversed, and the case remanded for a new trial. Reversed.

Exercise 6-11: *Luten Bridge* Revisited

1. Why might the Luten Bridge Company have had a desire to continue building the project even after it knew the county did not want the bridge? Why aren't such desires given consideration?

2. Assume that, at the time the county first repudiated the contract, Luten Bridge had already entered into subcontracts under which it would be liable for breach of contract if it refused to go forward. Assume also that Luten Bridge could not fully predict how much it would have to pay in damages to those subcontractors if it were to repudiate those contracts. If Luten Bridge determined that the cost of finishing the bridge would only be a thousand dollars more than it would have to pay in damages to the subcontractors, could Luten Bridge recover the full contract price if it finished the bridge?

Exercise 6-12: *Parker*

The next case, *Parker v. Twentieth Century-Fox Film Corp.*, also address the avoidability rule. *Parker* involves an employment contract in a specialized field, movie making, and involves a famous actress (although you will not see her screen name in the opinion). As you read the case, consider the following:

1. The starting point for an award of benefit-of-the-bargain damages in the employment context is the full contract price, not a FMV-contract price differential. Why?

2. Explain the sense in which the case involves an application of the avoidability rule.

3. The *Parker* court states and relies on a specific avoidability rule. What is that rule?

4. The dissenting opinion in *Parker* seems to criticize at least part of the majority's analysis as too superficial.

a. Which aspect of the majority's analysis is superficial? In other words, what step of applying rules did the majority omit?

b. Develop a proper analysis of your own. Your analysis should include identifying each difference between the two offers of employment and arguing why each difference is legally significant.

Parker v. Twentieth Century-Fox Film Corp.

3 Cal. 3d 176, 474 P.2d 689 (1970)

Burke, Justice. Defendant Twentieth Century-Fox Film Corporation appeals from a summary judgment granting to plaintiff the recovery of agreed compensation under a written contract for her services as an actress in a motion picture. As will appear, we have concluded that the trial court correctly ruled in plaintiff's favor and that the judgment should be affirmed.

Plaintiff is well known as an actress, and in the contract between plaintiff and defendant is sometimes referred to as the "Artist." Under the contract, dated August 6, 1965, plaintiff was to play the female lead in defendant's contemplated production of a motion picture entitled "Bloomer Girl." The contract provided that defendant would pay plaintiff a minimum "guaranteed compensation" of $53,571.42 per week for 14 weeks commencing May 23, 1966, for a total of $750,000. Prior to May 1966 defendant decided not to produce the picture and by a letter dated April 4, 1966, it notified plaintiff of that decision and that it would not "comply with our obligations to you under" the written contract.

By the same letter and with the professed purpose "to avoid any damage to you," defendant instead offered to employ plaintiff as the leading actress in another film tentatively entitled "Big Country, Big Man" (hereinafter, "Big Country"). The compensation offered was identical, as were 31 of the 34 numbered provisions or articles of the original contract.[1] Unlike "Bloomer Girl," however, which was to have been a musical production, "Big Country" was a dramatic "western type" movie. "Bloomer Girl" was to have been filmed in California; "Big Country" was to be produced in Australia. Also, certain terms in the proffered contract varied from those of the original.[2] Plaintiff was given one week within which to accept; she did not and the offer lapsed. Plaintiff then commenced this action seeking recovery of the agreed guaranteed compensation.

The complaint sets forth two causes of action. The first is for money due under the contract; the second, based upon the same allegations as the first, is for damages resulting from defendant's breach of contract. Defendant in its answer admits the existence and validity of the contract, that plaintiff complied with all the conditions, covenants and promises and stood ready to complete the performance, and that defendant breached and "anticipatorily repudiated" the contract. It denies, however, that any money is due to plaintiff either under the contract or as a result of its breach, and pleads as an af-

---

1. Among the identical provisions was the following found in the last paragraph of Article 2 of the original contract: "We (defendant) shall not be obligated to utilize your (plaintiff's) services in or in connection with the Photoplay hereunder, our sole obligation, subject to the terms and conditions of this Agreement, being to pay you the guaranteed compensation herein provided for."

2. Article 29 of the original contract specified that plaintiff approved the director already chosen for "Bloomer Girl" and that in case he failed to act as director plaintiff was to have approval rights of any substitute director. Article 31 provided that plaintiff was to have the right of approval of the "Bloomer Girl" dance director, and Article 32 gave her the right of approval of the screenplay. Defendant's letter of April 4 to plaintiff, which contained both defendant's notice of breach of the "Bloomer Girl" contract and offer of the lead in "Big Country," eliminated or impaired each of those rights. It read in part as follows:

The terms and conditions of our offer of employment are identical to those set forth in the "Bloomer Girl" Agreement, Articles 1 through 34 and Exhibit A to the Agreement, except as follows:

1. Article 31 of said Agreement will not be included in any contract of employment regarding "Big Country, Big Man" as it is not a musical and it thus will not need a dance director.

2. In the "Bloomer Girl" agreement, in Articles 29 and 32, you were given certain director and screenplay approvals and you had preapproved certain matters. Since there simply is insufficient time to negotiate with you regarding your choice of director and regarding the screenplay and since you already expressed an interest in performing the role in "Big Country, Big Man," we must exclude from our offer of employment in "Big Country, Big Man" any approval rights as are contained in said Articles 29 and 32; however, we shall consult with you respecting the director to be selected to direct the photoplay and will further consult with you with respect to the screenplay and any revisions or changes therein, provided, however, that if we fail to agree ... the decision of ... (defendant) with respect to the selection of a director and to revisions and changes in the said screenplay shall be binding upon the parties to said agreement.

firmative defense to both causes of action plaintiff's allegedly deliberate failure to mitigate damages, asserting that she unreasonably refused to accept its offer of the leading role in "Big Country."

Plaintiff moved for summary judgment under Code of Civil Procedure section 437c, the motion was granted, and summary judgment for $750,000 plus interest was entered in plaintiff's favor. This appeal by defendant followed.

The familiar rules are that the matter to be determined by the trial court on a motion for summary judgment is whether facts have been presented which give rise to a triable factual issue. The court may not pass upon the issue itself. Summary judgment is proper only if the affidavits or declarations in support of the moving party would be sufficient to sustain a judgment in his favor and his opponent does not by affidavit show facts sufficient to present a triable issue of fact. The affidavits of the moving party are strictly construed, and doubts as to the propriety of summary judgment should be resolved against granting the motion. Such summary procedure is drastic and should be used with caution so that it does not become a substitute for the open trial method of determining facts. The moving party cannot depend upon allegations in his own pleadings to cure deficient affidavits, nor can his adversary rely upon his own pleadings in lieu or in support of affidavits in opposition to a motion; however, a party can rely on his adversary's pleadings to establish facts not contained in his own affidavits. [Citation omitted.] Also, the court may consider facts stipulated to by the parties and facts which are properly the subject of judicial notice. [Citations omitted.]

As stated, defendant's sole defense to this action which resulted from its deliberate breach of contract is that in rejecting defendant's substitute offer of employment plaintiff unreasonably refused to mitigate damages.

The general rule is that the measure of recovery by a wrongfully discharged employee is the amount of salary agreed upon for the period of service, less the amount which the employer affirmatively proves the employee has earned or with reasonable effort might have earned from other employment.[4] [Citations omitted.] However, before projected earnings from other employment opportunities not sought or accepted by the discharged employee can be applied in mitigation, the employer must show that the other employment was comparable, or substantially similar, to that of which the employee has been deprived; the employee's rejection of or failure to seek other available employment of a different or inferior kind may not be resorted to in order to mitigate damages. [Citations omitted.]

In the present case defendant has raised no issue of reasonableness of efforts by plaintiff to obtain other employment; the sole issue is whether plaintiff's refusal of defendant's substitute offer of "Big Country" may be used in mitigation. Nor, if the "Big Country" offer was of employment different or inferior when compared with the original "Bloomer Girl" employment, is there an issue as to whether or not plaintiff acted reasonably in refusing the substitute offer. Despite defendant's arguments to the contrary, no case cited or

---

4. Although it would appear that plaintiff was not discharged by defendant in the customary sense of the term, as she was not permitted by defendant to enter upon performance of the "Bloomer Girl" contract, nevertheless the motion for summary judgment was submitted for decision upon a stipulation by the parties that "plaintiff Parker was discharged."

which our research has discovered holds or suggests that reasonableness is an element of a wrongfully discharged employee's option to reject, or fail to seek, different or inferior employment lest the possible earnings therefrom be charged against him in mitigation of damages.[5]

Applying the foregoing rules to the record in the present case, with all intendments in favor of the party opposing the summary judgment motion—here, defendant—it is clear that the trial court correctly ruled that plaintiff's failure to accept defendant's tendered substitute employment could not be applied in mitigation of damages because the offer of the "Big Country" lead was of employment both different and inferior, and that no factual dispute was presented on that issue. The mere circumstance that "Bloomer Girl" was to be a musical review calling upon plaintiff's talents as a dancer as well as an actress, and was to be produced in the City of Los Angeles, whereas "Big Country" was a straight dramatic role in a "Western Type" story taking place in an opal mine in Australia, demonstrates the difference in kind between the two employments; the female lead as a dramatic actress in a western style motion picture can by no stretch of imagination be considered the equivalent of or substantially similar to the lead in a song-and-dance production.

Additionally, the substitute "Big Country" offer proposed to eliminate or impair the director and screenplay approvals accorded to plaintiff under the original "Bloomer Girl" contract, and thus constituted an offer of inferior employment. No expertise or judicial notice is required in order to hold that the deprivation or infringement of an employee's rights held under an original employment contract converts the available "other employment" relied upon by the employer to mitigate damages, into inferior employment which the employee need not seek or accept. [Citation omitted.]

Statements found in affidavits submitted by defendant in opposition to plaintiff's summary judgment motion, to the effect that the "Big Country" offer was not of employment different from or inferior to that under the "Bloomer Girl" contract, merely repeat the allegations of defendant's answer to the complaint in this action, constitute only conclusionary assertions with respect to undisputed facts, and do not give rise to a triable factual issue so as to defeat the motion for summary judgment. [Citations omitted.]

In view of the determination that defendant failed to present any facts showing the existence of a factual issue with respect to its sole defense—plaintiff's rejection of its substitute employment offer in mitigation of damages— we need not consider plaintiff's further contention that for various reasons, including the provisions of the original contract set forth in footnote 1, ante, plaintiff was excused from attempting to mitigate damages.

---

5. Instead, in each case the reasonableness referred to was that of the efforts of the employee to obtain other employment that was not different or inferior; his right to reject the latter was declared as an unqualified rule of law. Thus, *Gonzales v. Internat. Assn. of Machinists, supra*, 213 Cal. App. 2d 817, 823–24, 29 Cal. Rptr. 190, 194, holds that the trial court correctly instructed the jury that plaintiff union member, a machinist, was required to make "such *efforts* as the average (member of his union) desiring employment would make at that particular time and place" (italics added); but, further, that the court *properly rejected* defendant's *offer of proof of the availability of other kinds of employment* at the same or higher pay than plaintiff usually received and all outside the jurisdiction of his union, as plaintiff could not be required to accept different employment or a nonunion job....

The judgment is affirmed.

Sullivan, Acting Chief Justice (dissenting). The basic question in this case is whether or not plaintiff acted reasonably in rejecting defendant's offer of alternate employment. The answer depends upon whether that offer (starring in "Big Country, Big Man") was an offer of work that was substantially similar to her former employment (starring in "Bloomer Girl") or of work that was of a different or inferior kind. To my mind this is a factual issue which the trial court should not have determined on a motion for summary judgment. The majority have not only repeated this error but have compounded it by applying the rules governing mitigation of damages in the employer-employee context in a misleading fashion. Accordingly, I respectfully dissent.

The familiar rule requiring a plaintiff in a tort or contract action to mitigate damages embodies notions of fairness and socially responsible behavior which are fundamental to our jurisprudence. Most broadly stated, it precludes the recovery of damages which, through the exercise of due diligence, could have been avoided. Thus, in essence, it is a rule requiring reasonable conduct in commercial affairs. This general principle governs the obligations of an employee after his employer has wrongfully repudiated or terminated the employment contract. Rather than permitting the employee simply to remain idle during the balance of the contract period, the law requires him to make a reasonable effort to secure other employment.[1] He is not obliged, however, to seek or accept any and all types of work which may be available. Only work which is in the same field and which is of the same quality need be accepted.[2]

Over the years the courts have employed various phrases to define the type of employment which the employee, upon his wrongful discharge, is under an obligation to accept. Thus in California alone it has been held that he must accept employment which is "substantially similar" (citations omitted); employment "in the same general line of the first employment," [citation omitted]; "equivalent to his prior position" [citation omitted]; "employment in a similar capacity," [citations omitted]; employment which is "not ... of a different or inferior kind." [Citation omitted.]

For reasons which are unexplained, the majority cite several of these cases yet select from among the various judicial formulations which contain one particular phrase, "Not of a different or inferior kind," with which to analyze this case. I have discovered no historical or theoretical reason to adopt this phrase, which is simply a negative restatement of the affirmative standards set out in the above cases, as the exclusive standard. Indeed, its emergence is an exam-

---

1. The issue is generally discussed in terms of a duty on the part of the employee to minimize loss. The practice is long-established and there is little reason to change despite Judge Cardozo's observation of its subtle inaccuracy. "The servant is free to accept employment or reject it according to his uncensored pleasure. What is meant by the supposed duty is merely this: That if he unreasonably reject, he will not be heard to say that the loss of wages from then on shall be deemed the jural consequence of the earlier discharge. He has broken the chain of causation, and loss resulting to him thereafter is suffered through his own act." *McClelland v. Climax Hosiery Mills* (1930) 252 N.Y. 347, 359, 169 N.E. 605, 609 (concurring).

2. This qualification of the rule seems to reflect the simple and humane attitude that it is too severe to demand of a person that he attempt to find and perform work for which he has no training or experience. Many of the older cases hold that one need not accept work in an inferior rank or position nor work which is more menial or arduous. This suggests that the rule may have had its origin in the bourgeois fear of resubmergence in lower economic classes.

ple of the dubious phenomenon of the law responding not to rational judicial choice or changing social conditions, but to unrecognized changes in the language of opinions or legal treatises. However, the phrase is a serviceable one and my concern is not with its use as the standard but rather with what I consider its distortion.

The relevant language excuses acceptance only of employment which is of a different kind. [Citations omitted.] It has never been the law that the mere existence of differences between two jobs in the same field is sufficient, as a matter of law, to excuse an employee wrongfully discharged from one from accepting the other in order to mitigate damages. Such an approach would effectively eliminate any obligation of an employee to attempt to minimize damage arising from a wrongful discharge. The only alternative job offer an employee would be required to accept would be an offer of his former job by his former employer.

Although the majority appear to hold that there was a difference "in kind" between the employment offered plaintiff in "Bloomer Girl" and that offered in "Big Country" (opn. at p. 10), an examination of the opinion makes crystal clear that the majority merely point out differences between the two films (an obvious circumstance) and then apodictically assert that these constitute a difference in the kind of employment. The entire rationale of the majority boils down to this: that the "mere circumstances" that "Bloomer Girl" was to be a musical revue while "Big Country" was a straight drama "demonstrates the difference in kind" since a female lead in a western is not "the equivalent of or substantially similar to" a lead in a musical. This is merely attempting to prove the proposition by repeating it. It shows that the vehicles for the display of the star's talents are different but it does not prove that her employment as a star in such vehicles is of necessity different in kind and either inferior or superior.

I believe that the approach taken by the majority (a superficial listing of differences with no attempt to assess their significance) may subvert a valuable legal doctrine.[5] The inquiry in cases such as this should not be whether differences between the two jobs exist (there will always be differences) but whether the differences which are present are substantial enough to constitute differences in the kind of employment or, alternatively, whether they render the substitute work employment of an inferior kind.

It seems to me that this inquiry involves, in the instant case at least, factual determinations which are improper on a motion for summary judgment. Resolving whether or not one job is substantially similar to another or whether, on the other hand, it is of a different or inferior kind, will often (as here) require a critical appraisal of the similarities and differences between them in light of the importance of these differences to the employee. This necessitates a weighing of the evidence, and it is precisely this undertaking which is forbidden on summary judgment. [Citation omitted.]

---

5. The values of the doctrine of mitigation of damages in this context are that it minimizes the unnecessary personal and social (*e.g.*, nonproductive use of labor, litigation) costs of contractual failure. If a wrongfully discharged employee can, through his own action and without suffering financial or psychological loss in the process, reduce the damages accruing from the breach of contract, the most sensible policy is to require him to do so. I fear the majority opinion will encourage precisely opposite conduct.

This is not to say that summary judgment would never be available in an action by an employee in which the employer raises the defense of failure to mitigate damages. No case has come to my attention, however, in which summary judgment has been granted on the issue of whether an employee was obliged to accept available alternate employment. Nevertheless, there may well be cases in which the substitute employment is so manifestly of a dissimilar or inferior sort, the declarations of the plaintiff so complete and those of the defendant so conclusionary and inadequate that no factual issues exist for which a trial is required. This, however, is not such a case.

It is not intuitively obvious, to me at least, that the leading female role in a dramatic motion picture is a radically different endeavor from the leading female role in a musical comedy film. Nor is it plain to me that the rather qualified rights of director and screenplay approval contained in the first contract are highly significant matters either in the entertainment industry in general or to this plaintiff in particular....

I cannot accept the proposition that an offer which eliminates any contract right, regardless of its significance, is, as a matter of law, an offer of employment of an inferior kind. Such an absolute rule seems no more sensible than the majority's earlier suggestion that the mere existence of differences between two jobs is sufficient to render them employment of different kinds. Application of such per se rules will severely undermine the principle of mitigation of damages in the employer-employee context.

I remain convinced that the relevant question in such cases is whether or not a particular contract provision is so significant that its omission create employment of an inferior kind. This question is, of course, intimately bound up in what I consider the ultimate issue: whether or not the employee acted reasonably. This will generally involve a factual inquiry to ascertain the importance of the particular contract term and a process of weighing the absence of that term against the countervailing advantages of the alternate employment. In the typical case, this will mean that summary judgment must be withheld.

In the instant case, there was nothing properly before the trial court by which the importance of the approval rights could be ascertained, much less evaluated. Thus, in order to grant the motion for summary judgment, the trial court misused judicial notice. In upholding the summary judgment, the majority here rely upon per se rules which distort the process of determining whether or not an employee is obliged to accept particular employment in mitigation of damages.

I believe that the judgment should be reversed so that the issue of whether or not the offer of the lead role in "Big Country, Big Man" was of employment comparable to that of the lead role in "Bloomer Girl" may be determined at trial....

Exercise 6-13: *Parker* Revisited

1. Imagine you are a lawyer for Twentieth Century-Fox. The president of the company informs you that the company has decided not to produce "Bloomer Girl" notwithstanding its contract with MacLaine. The company has not yet

informed MacLaine about its decision. Advise the president about how to handle the contract with MacLaine. Consider both the avoidability issue you have learned about and non-legal issues. As a practicing lawyer, your clients will expect you to offer more than just technical legal advice. Clients want their attorneys to help them solve problems and litigation is seldom an economically efficient solution.

2. BPS Guard Services ("BPS") provided security for a nuclear generating station. BPS employed Sullivan as a senior nuclear security officer. BPS terminated Sullivan's employment in breach of contract and, after court proceedings, it was determined that she had been wrongfully discharged. During the course of the proceedings, BPS made two offers to re-employ Sullivan. The first offer was for a guard position at a manufacturing plant. This position had a lower rate of pay than Sullivan's previous job, and no benefits. The second offer was for watch person position at BPS's headquarters, which was located approximately 80 miles from Sullivan's home. That position included the same rate of pay and benefits as Sullivan's original job. Sullivan declined both offers. BPS argues that her rejection of the offers constitutes an unreasonable failure to mitigate her damages.

   a. Analyze whether BPS has a case in the light of section 350 of the RE-STATEMENT (SECOND) OF CONTRACTS and *Parker.*

   b. Would it make any difference to the outcome if BPS had offered Sullivan a position as a security officer at the nuclear generating officer on the same pay and benefits, but reporting to the senior nuclear security officer that had been appointed to replace her after she was fired?

   c. Had BPS offered Sullivan her old job back on the exact same terms, could she still turn them down and successfully argue that she is entitled to full damages?

B. Foreseeability

This section addresses the second limitation on damages depicted in Diagram 6-1 at the beginning of this chapter: **foreseeability**.

Exercise 6-14: Foreseeability

Read section 351 of the RESTATEMENT (SECOND) OF CONTRACTS. Then, state the rule for foreseeability in your own words.

The next three cases, *Hadley v. Baxendale, Victoria Laundry Ltd. v. Newman Industries Ltd.*, and *Prutch v. Ford Motor Co.* all address the foreseeability rule. As you will see, this rule does not really tell you how any particular case will come out. Many lawyers and law professors believe that rules often fail as tools for predicting outcomes because many cases are policy-driven. In any event, we expect you will find the indeterminacy of the applicable standards in foreseeability law particularly vexing. The factual contexts of cases raising foreseeability issues are key. Accordingly, as you read the cases below, pay careful attention to how the foreseeability rule is applied and develop fact-specific holdings for each case. If your contracts exam includes a foreseeability issue, you will need to analogize to or distinguish these cases.

Exercise 6-15: *Hadley v. Baxendale*

The first case, *Hadley*, is a famous English case that most lawyers and law students know by name. As you read *Hadley*, consider the following:

1. What is a "rule nisi"?

2. What is a "rule absolute"?

3. Explain how the case involves an application of the rule you stated in response to Exercise 6-14.

4. How does the foreseeability rule promote the predictability and efficiency policies you have already learned?

Hadley v. Baxendale
9 Ex. Ch. 341; 156 Eng. Rep. 145 (Court of Exchequer, 1854)

At the trial before Crompton, J., at the last Gloucester Assizes, it appeared that the plaintiffs carried on an extensive business as millers at Gloucester; and that, on the 11th of May, their mill was stopped by a breakage of the crank shaft by which the mill was worked. The steam-engine was manufactured by Messrs. Joyce & Co., the engineers, at Greenwich, and it became necessary to send the shaft as a pattern for a new one to Greenwich. The fracture was discovered on the 12th, and on the 13th the plaintiffs sent one of their servants to the office of the defendants, who are the well-known carriers trading under the name of Pickford & Co., for the purpose of having the shaft carried to Greenwich. The plaintiffs' servant told the clerk that the mill was stopped, and that the shaft must be sent immediately; and in answer to the inquiry when the shaft would be taken, the answer was, that if it was sent up by twelve o'clock an day, it would be delivered at Greenwich on the following day. On the following day the shaft was taken by the defendants, before noon, for the purpose of being conveyed to Greenwich, and the sum of [two pounds and four shillings] was paid for its carriage for the whole distance; at the same time the defendants' clerk was told that a special entry, if required, should be made to hasten its delivery. The delivery of the shaft at Greenwich was delayed by some neglect; and the consequence was, that the plaintiffs did not receive the new shaft for several days after they would otherwise have done, and the working of their mill was thereby delayed, and they thereby lost the profits they would otherwise have received.

On the part of the defendants, it was objected that these damages were too remote, and that the defendants were not liable with respect to them. The learned Judge left the case generally to the jury, who found a verdict with [twenty five pounds] damages beyond the amount paid into Court.

Whateley, in last Michaelmas Term, obtained a rule nisi for a new trial, on the ground of misdirection.

The judgment of the Court was now delivered by Alderson, B. We think that there ought to be a new trial in this case; but, in so doing, we deem it to be expedient and necessary to state explicitly the rule which the Judge, at the next trial, ought, in our opinion, to direct the jury to be governed by when they estimate the damages. It is, indeed, of the last importance that we should do this; for, if the jury are left without any definite rule to guide them, it will, in such cases as these, manifestly lead to the greatest injustice....

Now we think the proper rule is such as the present is this: Where two parties have made a contract which one of them has broken, the damages which the other party ought to receive in respect of such breach of contract should be such as may fairly and reasonably be considered either arising naturally, *i.e.*, according to the usual course of things, from such breach of contract itself, or such as may reasonably be supposed to have been in the contemplation of both parties, at the time they made the contract, as the probable result of the breach of it.

Now, if the special circumstances under which the contract was actually made where communicated by the plaintiffs to the defendants, and thus known to both parties, the damages resulting from the breach of such a contract, which they would reasonably contemplate, would be the amount of injury which would ordinarily follow from a breach of contract under these special circumstances so known and communicated. But, on the other hand, if these special circumstances were wholly unknown to the party breaking the contract, he, at the most, could only be supposed to have had in his contemplation the amount of injury which would arise generally, and in the great multitude of cases not affected by any special circumstances, from such a breach of contract. For, had the special circumstances bee known, the parties might have specially provided for the breach of contract by special terms as to the damages in that case; and of this advantage it would be very unjust to deprive them....

Now, in the present case, if we are to apply the principles laid down, we find the only circumstances here communicated by the plaintiffs to the defendants at the time the contract was made, were, that the article to be carried was the broken shaft of a mill, and that the plaintiffs were the millers of that mill. But how do these circumstances show reasonably that the profits of the mill must be stopped by an unreasonable delay in the delivery of the broken shaft by the carrier to the third person? Suppose the plaintiffs had another shaft in their possession put up or putting up at the time, and that they only wished to send back the broken shaft to the engineer who made it; it is clear that this would be quite consistent with the above circumstances, and yet the unreasonable delay in the delivery would have no effect on the intermediate profits of the mill. Or, again, suppose, that, at the time of the delivery to the carrier, the machinery in the mill had been in other respects defective, then, also, the same results would follow.

Here it is true that the shaft was sent back to serve as a model for a new one, and that the want of a new one was the only cause of the stoppage of the mill, and that the loss of profits really arose from not sending down the new shaft in proper time, and that this arose from the delay in delivering the broken one to serve as a model. But it is obvious that, in the great multitude of cases of millers sending off broken shafts to third persons by a carrier under ordinary circumstances, such consequence would not, in all probability, have occurred; and these special circumstances were never communicated by the plaintiffs to the defendants. It follows, therefore, that the loss of profits here cannot be considered such a consequence of the breach of contract as could have been fairly and reasonably contemplated by the parties when they made this contract. For such loss would neither have flowed naturally from the breach of this contract in the great multitude of such cases occurring under ordinary circumstances, nor were the special circumstances, which, perhaps, would have made it a reasonable and natural consequence of such breach of contract, communicated to or known by the defendants.

The Judge ought, therefore, to have told the jury, that, upon the facts then before them, they ought not to take the loss of profits into consideration at all in estimating the damages. There must therefore be a new trial in this case. Rule absolute.

Exercise 6-16: *Hadley* Revisited

1. Imagine that, in *Hadley*, the defendants were told not only that the plaintiffs' mill was stopped, but also that the mill was stopped because of the damage to the shaft the defendants would be carrying. Would the result in the case be any different?

2. To prevail on the foreseeability issue, what should the plaintiffs have said to the defendants?

Exercise 6-17: *Victoria Laundry v. Newman*

The second foreseeability case, *Victoria Laundry*, makes an effort to summarize and expand upon *Hadley*. As you read the case, consider the following questions:

1. What new standards does the court introduce to help explain the idea of foreseeability?

2. The court distinguishes the plaintiff's normal laundering and dyeing contracts from the especially lucrative dyeing contracts with the Ministry of Supply, holding that loss of profits on the former are recoverable but loss of profits on the latter are not. Explain the court's distinction.

Victoria Laundry (Windsor) Ltd. v. Newman Industries Ltd.

Coulson & Co. Ltd. (Third Parties)
[1949] 2 KB 528

Asquith, L.J. delivered the judgment of the court. This is an appeal by the plaintiffs against a judgment of Streatfeild J. in so far as that judgment limited the damages to £110 in respect of an alleged breach of contract by the defendants, which is now uncontested. The breach of contract consisted in the delivery of a boiler sold by the defendants to the plaintiffs some twenty odd weeks after the time fixed by the contract for delivery. The short point is whether, in addition to the £110 awarded, the plaintiffs were entitled to claim in respect of loss of profits which they say they would have made if the boiler had been delivered punctually.

Seeing that the issue is as to the measure of recoverable damage and the application of the rules in *Hadley v. Baxendale*, it is important to inquire what information the defendants possessed at the time when the contract was made, as to such matters as the time at which, and the purpose for which, the plaintiffs required the boiler. The defendants knew before, and at the time of the contract, that the plaintiffs were laundrymen and dyers, and required the boiler for purposes of their business as such. They also knew that the plaintiffs wanted the boiler for immediate use.

On the latter point the correspondence is important. The contract was concluded by, and is contained in, a series of letters. In the earliest phases of the correspondence—that is, in letters of January 31 and February 1, 1946 (which letters, as appears from their terms, followed a telephone call on the earlier date)—the defendants undertook to make the earliest possible arrangements for the dismantling and removal of the boiler. The natural inference from this is that in the telephone conversation referred to the plaintiffs had conveyed to the defendants that they required the boiler urgently. Again, on February 7 the plaintiffs write to the defendants: "We should appreciate your letting us know how quickly your people can dismantle it"; and finally, on April 26, in the concluding letter of the series by which the contract was made: "We are most anxious that this" (that is, the boiler) "should be put into use in the shortest possible space of time." Hence, up to and at the very moment when a concluded contract emerged, the plaintiffs were pressing upon the defendants the need for expedition; and the last letter was a plain intimation that the boiler was wanted for immediate use.

This is none the less so because when, later, the plaintiffs encountered delays in getting the necessary permits and licences [sic], the exhortations to speed come from the other side, who wanted their money, which in fact they were paid in advance of delivery. The defendants knew the plaintiffs needed the boiler as soon as the delays should be overcome, and they knew by the beginning of June that such delays had by then in fact been overcome. The defendants did not know at the material time the precise role for which the boiler was cast in the plaintiffs' economy, *e.g.* whether (as the fact was) it was to function in substitution for an existing boiler of inferior capacity, or in replacement of an existing boiler of equal capacity, or as an extra unit to be operated side by side with and in addition to any existing boiler.

It has indeed been argued strenuously that, for all they knew, it might have been wanted as a "spare" or "standby," provided in advance to replace an existing boiler when, perhaps some time hence, the latter should wear out; but such an intention to reserve it for future use seems quite inconsistent with the intention expressed in the letter of April 26, to "put it into use in the shortest possible space of time."

In this connection, certain admissions made in the course of the hearing are of vital importance. The defendants formally admitted what in their defense they had originally traversed, namely, the facts alleged in para. 2 of the statement of claim. That paragraph reads as follows: "At the date of the contract hereinafter mentioned the defendants well knew as the fact was that the plaintiffs were launderers and dyers carrying on business at Windsor and required the said boiler for use in their said business and the said contract was made upon the basis that the said boiler was required for the said purpose." ...

Delivery was taken by the plaintiffs on November 8 and the boiler was erected and working by early December. The plaintiffs claim, as part — the disputed part — of the damages, loss of the profits they would have earned if the machine had been delivered in early June instead of November. Evidence was led for the plaintiffs with the object of establishing that if the boiler had been punctually delivered, then, during the twenty odd weeks between then and the time of actual delivery: (1) they could have taken on a very large number of new customers in the course of their laundry business, the demand for laundry services at that time being insatiable, they did in fact take on extra staff in the expectation of its delivery, and (2) that they could and would have accepted a number of highly lucrative dyeing contracts for the Ministry of Supply. In the statement of claim, para. 10, the loss of profits under the first of these heads was quantified at £16. a week and under the second at £262 a week.

The evidence, however, which promised to be voluminous, had not gone very far when Mr. Paull, for the defendants, submitted that in law no loss of profits was recoverable at all, and that to continue to hear evidence as to its quantum was merely waste of time. He suggested that the question of remoteness of damage under this head should be decided on the existing materials, including the admissions to which we have referred. The learned judge accepted Mr. Paull's submission, and on that basis awarded £110 damages under certain minor heads, but nothing in respect of loss of profits, which he held to be too remote. It is from that decision that the plaintiffs now appeal.

The ground of the learned judge's decision, which we consider more fully later, may be summarized as follows: He took the view that the loss of profit claimed was due to special circumstances and therefore recoverable, if at all, only under the second rule in *Hadley v. Baxendale* and not recoverable in this case because such special circumstances were not at the time of the contract communicated to the defendants. He also attached much significance to the fact that the object supplied was not a self-sufficient profit-making article, but part of a larger profit-making whole, and cited in this connection the cases of *Portman v. Middleton* and *British Columbia Sawmills v. Nettleship*. Before commenting on the learned judge's reasoning, we must refer to some of the authorities.

Three of the authorities call for more detailed examination. First comes *Hadley v. Baxendale* itself. Familiar though it is, we should first recall the memorable sentence in which the main principles laid down in this case are enshrined: "Where two parties have made a contract which one of them has broken, the damages which the other party ought to receive in respect of such breach of contract should be such as may fairly and reasonably be considered as either arising naturally, *i.e.*, according to the usual course of things, from such breach of contract itself, or such as may reasonably be supposed to have been in the contemplation of both parties, at the time they made the contract, as the probable result of the breach of it." The limb of this sentence prefaced by "either" embodies the so-called "first" rule; that prefaced by "or" the "second."

In considering the meaning and application of these rules, it is essential to bear clearly in mind the facts on which *Hadley v. Baxendale* proceeded. The headnote is definitely misleading in so far as it says that the defendant's clerk, who attended at the office, was told that the mill was stopped and that the shaft must be delivered immediately. The same allegation figures in the statement of facts which are said on page 344 to have "appeared" at the trial before Crompton J. If the Court of Exchequer had accepted these facts as established, the court must, one would suppose, have decided the case the other way round; must, that is, have held the damage claimed was recoverable under the second rule. But it is reasonably plain from Alderson B's judgment that the court rejected this evidence, for on page 355 he says: "We find that the only circumstances here communicated by the plaintiffs to the defendants at the time when the contract was made were that the article to be carried was the broken shaft of a mill and that the plaintiffs were the millers of that mill," and it is on this basis of fact that he proceeds to ask, "How do these circumstances show reasonably that the profits of the mill must be stopped by an unreasonable delay in the delivery of the broken shaft by the carrier to the third person?"

British Columbia Sawmills v. Nettleship [citation omitted] annexes to the principle laid down in *Hadley v. Baxendale* ... a rider to the effect that where knowledge of special circumstances is relied on as enhancing the damage recoverable that knowledge must have been brought home to the defendant at the time of the contract and in such circumstances that the defendant impliedly undertook to bear any special loss referable to a breach in those special circumstances. The knowledge which was lacking in that case on the part of the defendant was knowledge that the particular box of machinery negligently lost by the defendants was one without which the rest of the machinery could not be put together and would therefore be useless.

Cory v. Thames Ironworks Company, a case strongly relied on by the plaintiffs, presented the peculiarity that the parties contemplated respectively different profit-making uses of the chattel sold by the defendant to the plaintiff. It was the hull of a boom derrick, and was delivered late. The plaintiffs were coal merchants, and the obvious use, and that to which the defendants believed it was to be put, was that of a coal store. The plaintiffs, on the other hand, the buyers, in fact intended to use it for transhipping coals from colliers to barges, a quite unprecedented use for a chattel of this kind, one quite unsuspected by the sellers and one calculated to yield much higher profits. The case accordingly decides, inter alia, what is the measure of damage recoverable when the parties are not ad idem in their contemplation of the use for which the article is needed. It was decided that in such a case no loss was recoverable beyond what would have resulted if the intended use had been that reasonably within the contemplation of the defendants, which in that case was the "obvious" use. This special complicating factor, the divergence between the knowledge and contemplation of the parties respectively, has somewhat obscured the general importance of the decision, which is in effect that the facts of the case brought it within the first rule of *Hadley v. Baxendale* ... and enabled the plaintiff to recover loss of such profits as would have arisen from the normal and obvious use of the article. The "natural consequence," said Blackburn J., of not delivering the derrick was that £420 representing those normal profits was lost. Cockburn C.J., interposing during the argument, made the significant observation: "No doubt in order to recover damage arising from a special purpose the buyer must have communicated the special purpose to the seller; but there is one thing which must always be in the knowledge of both parties, which is that the thing is bought for the purpose of being in some way or other profitably applied." This observation is apposite to the present case ...

What propositions applicable to the present case emerge from the authorities as a whole, including those analyzed above? We think they include the following:

1. It is well settled that the governing purpose of damages is to put the party whose rights have been violated in the same position, so far as money can do so, as if his rights had been observed. [Citation omitted.] This purpose, if relentlessly pursued, would provide him with a complete indemnity for all loss de facto resulting from a particular breach, however improbable, however unpredictable. This, in contract at least, is recognized as too harsh a rule.

2. Hence, in cases of breach of contract the aggrieved party is only entitled to recover such part of the loss actually resulting as was at the time of the contract reasonably foreseeable as liable to result from the breach.

3. What was at that time reasonably so foreseeable depends on the knowledge then possessed by the parties or, at all events, by the party who later commits the breach.

4. For this purpose, knowledge "possessed" is of two kinds; one imputed, the other actual. Everyone, as a reasonable person, is taken to know the "ordinary course of things" and consequently what loss is liable to result from a breach of contract in that ordinary course. This is the subject matter of the "first rule" in *Hadley v. Baxendale*. But to this knowledge, which a contract-breaker is assumed to possess whether he actually possesses it or not, there may have to be added in a particular case knowledge which he actually possesses, of special circumstances outside the "ordinary course of things," of such a kind that a breach in those special circumstances would be liable to cause more loss. Such a case attracts the operation of the "second rule" so as to make additional loss also recoverable.

5. In order to make the contract-breaker liable under either rule it is not necessary that he should actually have asked himself what loss is liable to result from a breach. As has often been pointed out, parties at the time of contracting contemplate not the breach of the contract, but its performance. It suffices that, if he had considered the question, he would as a reasonable man have concluded that the loss in question was liable to result.

6. Nor, finally, to make a particular loss recoverable, need it be proved that upon a given state of knowledge the defendant could, as a reasonable man, foresee that a breach must necessarily result in that loss. It is enough if he could foresee it was likely so to result. It is indeed enough, to borrow from the language of Lord du Parcq in the same case, at page 158, if the loss (or some factor without which it would not have occurred) is a "serious possibility "or a "real danger." For short, we have used the word "liable" to result. Possibly the colloquialism "on the cards" indicates the shade of meaning with some approach to accuracy.

If these, indeed, are the principles applicable, what is the effect of their application to the facts of this case? We have, at the beginning of this judgment, summarized the main relevant facts. The defendants were an engineering company supplying a boiler to a laundry. We reject the submission for the defendants that an engineering company knows no more than the plain man about boilers or the purposes to which they are commonly put by different classes of purchasers, including laundries. The defendant company were not, it is true, manufacturers of this boiler or dealers in boilers, but they gave a highly technical and comprehensive description of this boiler to the plaintiffs by letter of January 19, 1946, and offered both to dismantle the boiler at Harpenden and to re-erect it on the plaintiffs' premises. Of the uses or purposes to which boilers are put, they would clearly know more than the uninstructed layman. Again, they knew they were supplying the boiler to a company carrying on the business of laundrymen and dyers, for use in that business. The obvious use of a boiler, in such a business, is surely to boil water for the purpose of washing or dyeing. A laundry might conceivably buy a boiler for some other purpose; for instance, to work radiators or warm bath water for the comfort of its employees or directors, or to use for research, or to exhibit in a museum.

All these purposes are possible, but the first is the obvious purpose which, in the case of a laundry, leaps to the average eye. If the purpose then be to wash or dye, why does the company want to wash or dye, unless for purposes of business advantage, in which term we, for the purposes of the rest of this judgment, include maintenance or increase of profit, or reduction of loss? (We shall speak henceforward not of loss of profit, but of "loss of business.") No commercial concern commonly purchases for the purposes of its business a very large and expensive structure like this—a boiler 19 feet high and costing over £2,000—with any other motive, and no supplier, let alone an engineering company, which has promised delivery of such an article by a particular date, with knowledge that it was to be put into use immediately on delivery, can reasonably contend that it could not foresee that loss of business (in the sense indicated above) would be liable to result to the purchaser from a long delay in the delivery thereof.

Since we are differing from a carefully reasoned judgment, we think it due to the learned judge to indicate the grounds of our dissent. In that judgment, after stressing the fact that the defendants were not manufacturers of this boiler or of any boilers (a fact which is indisputable), nor (what is disputable) people possessing any special knowledge not common to the general public of boilers or laundries as possible users thereof, he goes on to say: "That is the general principle and I think that the principle running through the cases is this—and to this extent I agree with Mr. Beney—that if there is nothing unusual, if it is a normal user of the plant, then it may well be that the parties must be taken to contemplate that the loss of profits may result from non-delivery, or the delay in delivery, of the particular article.

On the other hand, if there are, as I think there are here, special circumstances, I do not think that the defendants are liable for loss of profits unless these special circumstances were drawn to their notice. In looking at the cases, I think there is a distinction as Mr. Paull has pointed out and insists upon, between the supply of the part of the profit-making machine, as against the profit-making machine itself." Then, after referring to *Portman v. Middleton*, he continues: "It is to be observed that not only must the circumstances be known to the supplier, but they must be such that the object must be taken to have been within the contemplation of both parties. I do not think that on the facts of the case as I have heard them, and upon the admissions, it can be said that it was within the contemplation of the supplier, namely, the defendants, that any delay in the delivery of this boiler was going to lead necessarily to loss of profits. There was nothing that I know of in the evidence to indicate how it was to be used or whether delivery of it by a particular day would necessarily be vital to the earning of these profits.

I agree with the propositions of Mr. Paull that it was no part of the contract, and it cannot be taken to have been the basis of the contract, that the laundry would be unable to work if there was a delay in the delivery of the boiler, or that the laundry was extending its business, or that it had any special contracts which they could fulfill only by getting delivery of this boiler. In my view, therefore, this case falls within the second rule of *Hadley v. Baxendale* under which they are not liable for the payment of damages for loss of profits unless there is evidence before the court—which there is not—that the special object of this boiler was drawn to their attention and that they contracted upon the basis that delay in the delivery of the boiler would make them liable to payment of loss of profits."

The answer to this reasoning has largely been anticipated in what has been said above, but we would wish to add: First, that the learned judge appears to infer that because certain "special circumstances" were, in his view, not "drawn to the notice of" the defendants and therefore, in his view, the operation of the "second rule" was excluded, ergo nothing in respect of loss of business can be recovered under the "first rule." This inference is, in our view, no more justified in the present case than it was in the case of *Cory v. Thames Ironworks Company*.

Secondly, that while it is not wholly clear what were the "special circumstances" on the non-communication of which the learned judge relied, it would seem that they were, or included, the following: (a) the "circumstance" that delay in delivering the boiler was going to lead "necessarily" to loss of profits. But the true criterion is surely not what was bound "necessarily" to result, but what was likely or liable to do so, and we think that it was amply conveyed to the defendants by what was communicated to them (plus what was patent without express communication) that delay in delivery was likely to lead to "loss of business"; (b) the "circumstance" that the plaintiffs needed the boiler "to extend their business." It was surely not necessary for the defendants to be specifically informed of this, as a precondition of being liable for loss of business. Reasonable, persons in the shoes of the defendants must be taken to foresee without any express intimation, that a laundry which, at a time when there was a famine of laundry facilities, was paying £2,000 odd for plant and intended at such a time to put such plant "into use" immediately, would be likely to suffer in pocket from five months' delay in delivery of the plant in question, whether they intended by means of it to extend their business, or merely to maintain it, or to reduce a loss; (c) the "circumstance" that the plaintiffs had the assured expectation of special contracts, which they could only fulfill by securing punctual delivery of the boiler. Here, no doubt, the learned judge had in mind the particularly lucrative dyeing contracts to which the plaintiffs looked forward and which they mention in para. 10 of the statement of claim.

We agree that in order that the plaintiffs should recover specifically and as such the profits expected on these contracts, the defendants would have had to know, at the time of their agreement with the plaintiffs, of the prospect and terms of such contracts. We also agree that they did not in fact know these things. It does not, however, follow that the plaintiffs are precluded from recovering some general (and perhaps conjectural) sum for loss of business in respect of dyeing contracts to be reasonably expected, any more than in respect of laundering contracts to be reasonably expected.

Thirdly, the other point on which Streatfeild J. largely based his judgment was that there is a critical difference between the measure of damages applicable when the defendant defaults in supplying a self-contained profit-earning whole and when he defaults in supplying a part of that whole. In our view, there is no intrinsic magic, in this connection, in the whole as against a part. The fact that a part only is involved is only significant in so far as it bears on the capacity of the supplier to foresee the consequences of non-delivery. If it is clear from the nature of the part (or the supplier of it is informed) that its non-delivery will have the same effect as non-delivery of the whole, his liability will be the same as if he had defaulted in delivering the whole....

We are therefore of opinion that the appeal should be allowed and the issue referred to an official referee as to what damage, if any, is recoverable in addition to the £110 awarded by the learned trial judge. The official referee would assess those damages in consonance with the findings in this judgment as to what the defendants knew or must be taken to have known at the material time, either party to be at liberty to call evidence as to the quantum of the damage in dispute.

Exercise 6-18: *Prutch v. Ford Motor Co.*

The third foreseeability case, *Prutch*, also makes an effort to summarize and expand upon *Hadley*. As you read the case, consider the following questions:

1. What two limitations on damages did Ford assert in this case? Why did each fail?

2. How can you reconcile *Hadley, Victoria Laundry*, and *Prutch*?

Prutch v. Ford Motor Co.
618 P.2d 657 (1980)

Per Curiam. Petitioners Carl and Sam Prutch (the "Prutches") were plaintiffs below. They sued for alleged breaches of express and implied warranties arising out of their purchases of a tractor, plow, disc harrow, and hay baler. The defendants in the lawsuit were the Ford Motor Company ("Ford"), manufacturer of all four farm implements, and its dealer, Baldridge Implement Company ("Baldridge"), which had sold the equipment to Prutches.

The first trial ended in a mistrial. At the conclusion of the second trial, the jury rendered a verdict for $60,200 in favor of the plaintiffs against Ford. The jury, however, held Baldridge not liable.

Ford appealed. The court of appeals overturned the jury verdict and remanded the case for a third trial. *Prutch v. Ford Motor Co.*, 40 Colo. App. 129, 574 P.2d 102 (1977). The court of appeals ruled that the plaintiffs had the burden of proving: (1) the particular items of equipment which caused the specific damages, (2) that each item found defective was defective when it left the manufacturer's control, and (3) that the plaintiffs gave the manufacturer timely, direct notice of the claimed breach of warranty. We granted certiorari and now reverse the court of appeals' decision and reinstate the jury verdict.

The facts are summarized in the opinion of the court of appeals....

The plaintiffs' claim for damages was based upon the contention that the failure of the Ford implements to comply with warranties adversely affected the crops which were produced or harvested by use of those implements in the year of sale ...

Ford contends that it cannot be charged with the crop damages incurred by the Prutches. Colorado law authorizes consequential damages for "any loss resulting from general or particular requirements and needs of which the seller at the time of contracting had reason to know and which could not reasonably be prevented by cover or otherwise." Section 4-2-715(2)(a), C.R.S. 1973. The court of appeals noted that the Colorado statutory scheme rejects the "tacit agreement" test that would permit consequential damages only if the seller specifically contemplated or actually assumed the risk of such damages. *Id.*, official comment 2. Rather, as the court of appeals observed, recovery of consequential damages is determined by the test of "foreseeability" of consequences.

Ford would have us construe "foreseeability" to generate liability only if a manufacturer had some prior actual knowledge as a basis for anticipating damage. But the defendant, in trying to add the ingredient of prior knowledge to the foreseeability concept, confuses foreseeable with actually foreseen. A standard that would require actual prior knowledge by the defendant would impose liability only upon proof that the defendant actually foresaw consequential damages. Such a test would be excessively restrictive. The statutory "reason to know" standard, in our view, triggers liability for consequences that may not have been actually foreseen but which were foreseeable.

A manufacturer knowing that its products will be used for crop production reasonably can be expected to foresee that defects in those products may cause crop losses. [Citation omitted.] In such circumstances, therefore, the manufacturer should not escape liability by arguing that it did not actually foresee probable consequences which it should have foreseen.

Ford also seeks to avoid liability for consequential damages by claiming that the plaintiffs' own actions increased their losses and thus became an intervening cause of damages. The defendant correctly states the rule that consequential damages created by a buyer's use of the product after discovery of the defect may not be recovered in a breach of warranty action. [Citations omitted.] But unlike the facts in the cases the defendant has cited, Ford's failure to provide the Prutches properly functioning equipment left them a narrow range of alternatives. The plaintiffs' only choice was between reduced crops and no crops at all. Contrary to Ford's contention, the record does not support a conclusion that the plaintiffs could have mitigated their damages further by shifting the onion crop to lands prepared for planting by use of the Prutches' old John Deere equipment, and planting vegetables for which proper seedbed preparation is less critical on the lands prepared by use of the Ford implements.

The plaintiffs, in deciding to continue farming with the knowledge that their Ford equipment might continue to malfunction, actually mitigated their losses. This they were required by statute to do. Section 4-2-715(2)(a), C.R.S. 1973. Their decision to try to produce at least part of a normal crop, rather than no crop at all, was required by their "duty to lessen, rather than increase," their damages. [Citation omitted.]

The judgment of the court of appeals is reversed and the cause is remanded with directions that it be returned to the district court for reinstatement of the jury verdict.

Exercise 6-19: Foreseeability

1. P chartered a ship from a ship owner for one year with an option to renew for a further year at a time when market charter rates were very low. P later sub-chartered the ship to a third party at market rates, which were double the rates fixed in the charter. The contract between ship owner and P provided that P should make payments monthly in advance and entitled ship owner to terminate the contract if any payment was not made on time. P made payments by wire transfer from its account with the Continental Illinois National Bank in Chicago ("Continental"). On P's instructions, Continental would debit P's account, and, in turn, instruct its correspondent bank, Swiss Bank, to transfer funds to ship owner's account with the Banque de Paris in Geneva, Switzerland. After successfully making a number of payments using this method, P failed to make a monthly payment ($27,000) on time because Swiss Bank failed to comply with Continental's instructions due to a mix up. Ship owner terminated the charter. In a lawsuit brought by P against

Swiss Bank, the court held that P's lost profits based on the difference between the charter and subcharter rates ($2 million) were insufficiently foreseeable. Why?

2. P, a mining company, paid D, a railroad, thousands of dollars to transport an enormous piece of mining equipment to P's work site. The piece of equipment was so large that it had to be loaded on to five separate railroad cars. The bill of lading described the machinery as "used mining equipment." D breached the contract by delivering the equipment late. P sued, seeking as damages what it had paid to rent a piece of machinery between the date when D should have delivered P's machine and the date when D actually delivered P's machine. The court held this loss was foreseeable. Why?

3. P purchased a tractor-trailer and insured it against theft and other risks with D insurer. The policy noted on its front page that the vehicle would be used for commercial purposes and that P's occupation was a hauler of dry freight. P used the tractor in his business for 14 months until it was stolen. P reported the theft to the police and to D. D delayed in settling the policy and as a result P suffered lost profits. The court held that the lost profits were foreseeable. Why?

4. P contracted to sell his house to D in Maine in January, the sale to close in May. D failed to raise the purchase money and breached the contract. P was unable to sell the house for another year and had to incur extra costs repurchasing winter equipment and for snow removal. The court held that the extra costs were not foreseeable. Why not?

5. P contracted to work for D. When P was hired, D told him he had "job security," a term D never defined and P never asked D to define. Shortly after P starting working, D terminated P's employ. P sued D for breach, seeking, among other things, damages for emotional distress. D asserted foreseeability as a limitation on P's recovery of damages for emotional distress. Discuss D's foreseeability defense. Be sure to consider section 353 of the RESTATEMENT (SECOND) OF CONTRACTS.

C. Certainty

This section addresses the third limitation on damages depicted in Diagram 6-1 at the beginning of this chapter: **certainty**.

Exercise 6-20: Certainty

Section 352 of the RESTATEMENT (SECOND) OF CONTRACTS states that damages must be established with "reasonable certainty." Many courts view certainty as referring to two rules; a plaintiff must prove: (1) the fact of damage (that she suffered a loss) by a preponderance of the evidence, and (2) the amount of damages by submitting enough data to allow a reasonable estimate of damages. Paraphrase both rules in your own words.

To illustrate the different functions that the foreseeability and certainty limitations serve, recall Question 6g. in Exercise 6-8. If a contractor is going to build an office complex for an owner, it will not be difficult to establish that, at the time the contractor and the owner made the contractor, it is foreseeable that the owner will lose rental income if contractor fails to perform or does not perform on time. But what if, at the relevant time, the market is saturated with office space in a down economy? What if there's lots of empty office space in the area? In this scenario, the loss is foreseeable but the owner will have to prove that she could have rented out at least some of the office space with reasonable certainty.

Exercise 6-21: *Freund* and *Mindgames, Inc.*

The next two cases, *Freund v. Washington Square Press* and *Mindgames, Inc. v. Western Publishing Co.,* deal with certainty. As you read them, consider the following questions:

1. In *Freund*, the court states that the plaintiff was not entitled to the royalties he would have earned had the defendant not breached. Why not? Was the problem a failure to prove the fact of damage or the amount of damages or both?

2. *Mindgames* refers to what courts and commentators call the "new business rule." What is that rule?

3. What rule did the *Mindgames* court apply?

4. Why did the plaintiffs in both cases lose on the certainty issue?

5. Do you agree with the majority or the dissent in *Mindgames*?

Freund v. Washington Square Press, Inc.
34 N.Y.2d 379, 314 N.E.2d 419 (1974)

In this action for breach of a publishing contract, we must decide what damages are recoverable for defendant's failure to publish plaintiff's manuscript. In 1965, plaintiff, an author and a college teacher, and defendant, Washington Square Press, Inc., entered into a written agreement which, in relevant part, provided as follows. Plaintiff ("author") granted defendant ("publisher") exclusive rights to publish and sell in book form plaintiff's work on modern drama. Upon plaintiff's delivery of the manuscript, defendant agreed to complete payment of a nonreturnable $2,000 "advance." Thereafter, if defendant deemed the manuscript not "suitable for publication," it had the right to terminate the agreement by written notice within 60 days of delivery. Unless so terminated, defendant agreed to publish the work in hardbound edition within 18 months and afterwards in paperbound edition.

The contract further provided that defendant would pay royalties to plaintiff, based upon specified percentages of sales. (For example, plaintiff was to receive 10% of the retail price of the first 10,000 copies sold in the continental United States.) If defendant failed to publish within 18 months, the contract provided that "this agreement shall terminate and the rights herein granted to the Publisher shall revert to the Author. In such event all payments theretofore made to the Author shall belong to the Author without prejudice to any other remedies which the Author may have." The contract also provided that controversies were to be determined pursuant to the New York simplified procedure for court determination of disputes. [Citation omitted.]

Plaintiff performed by delivering his manuscript to defendant and was paid his $2,000 advance. Defendant thereafter merged with another publisher and ceased publishing in hardbound. Although defendant did not exercise its 60-day right to terminate, it has refused to publish the manuscript in any form.

Plaintiff commenced the instant action pursuant to the simplified procedure practice and initially sought specific performance of the contract. The Trial Term Justice denied specific performance but, finding a valid contract and a breach by defendant, set the matter down for trial on the issue of monetary damages, if any, sustained by the plaintiff. At trial, plaintiff sought to prove: (1) delay of his academic promotion; (2) loss of royalties which would have been earned; and (3) the cost of publication if plaintiff had made his own arrangements to publish. The trial court found that plaintiff had been promoted despite defendant's failure to publish, and that there was no evidence that the breach had caused any delay. Recovery of lost royalties was denied without discussion. The court found, however, that the cost of hardcover publication to plaintiff was the natural and probable consequence of the breach and, based upon expert testimony, awarded $10,000 to cover this cost. It denied recovery of the expenses of paperbound publication on the ground that plaintiff's proof was conjectural.

The Appellate Division affirmed (three to two) finding that the cost of publication was the proper measure of damages. In support of its conclusion, the majority analogized to the construction contract situation where the cost of completion may be the proper measure of damages for a builder's failure to complete a house or for use of wrong materials. The dissent concluded that the cost of publication is not an appropriate measure of damages and consequently, that plaintiff may recover nominal damages only. We agree with the dissent. In so concluding, we look to the basic purpose of damage recovery and the nature and effect of the parties' contract.

It is axiomatic that, except where punitive damages are allowable, the law awards damages for breach of contract to compensate for injury caused by the breach—injury which was foreseeable, *i.e.,* reasonably within the contemplation of the parties at the time the contract was entered into. *Swain* v. *Schieffelin*, 134 N.Y. 471, 473. Money damages are substitutional relief designed in theory "to put the injured party in as good a position as he would have been put by full performance of the contract, at the least cost to the defendant and without charging him with harms that he had no sufficient reason to foresee when he made the contract." 5 CORBIN, CONTRACTS § 1002, pp. 31–32; 11 WILLISTON, CONTRACTS (3d ed.) § 1338, p. 198. In other words, so far as possible, the law attempts to secure to the injured party the benefit of his bargain, subject to the limitations that the injury—whether it be losses suffered or gains prevented—was foreseeable, and that the amount of damages claimed be measurable with a reasonable degree of certainty and, of course, adequately proven. *See generally* DOBBS, LAW OF REMEDIES, p. 148; *see also* FARNSWORTH, LEGAL REMEDIES FOR BREACH OF CONTRACT, 70 COL. L. REV. 1145, 1159. But it is equally fundamental that the injured party should not recover more from the breach than he would have gained had the contract been fully performed. [Citations omitted.]

Measurement of damages in this case according to the cost of publication to the plaintiff would confer greater advantage than performance of the contract would have entailed to plaintiff and would place him in a far better position than he would have occupied had the defendant fully performed. Such measurement bears no relation to compensation for plaintiff's actual loss or anticipated profit. Far beyond compensating plaintiff for the interests he had in the defendant's performance of the contract—whether restitution, reliance or expectation, *see* Fuller & Perdue, *Reliance Interest in Contract Damages*, 46 YALE L.J. 52, 53–56—an award of the cost of publication would enrich plaintiff at defendant's expense.

Pursuant to the contract, plaintiff delivered his manuscript to the defendant. In doing so, he conferred a value on the defendant which, upon defendant's breach, was required to be restored to him. Special Term, in addition to ordering a trial on the issue of damages, ordered defendant to return the manuscript to plaintiff and plaintiff's restitution interest in the contract was thereby protected. *Cf.* 5 CORBIN, CONTRACTS § 996, p. 15.

At the trial on the issue of damages, plaintiff alleged no reliance losses suffered in performing the contract or in making necessary preparations to perform. Had such losses, if foreseeable and ascertainable, been incurred, plaintiff would have been entitled to compensation for them. [Citation omitted.]

As for plaintiff's expectation interest in the contract, it was basically twofold—the "advance" and the royalties. (To be sure, plaintiff may have expected to enjoy whatever notoriety, prestige or other benefits that might have attended publication, but even if these expectations were compensable, plaintiff did not attempt at trial to place a monetary value on them.) There is no dispute that plaintiff's expectancy in the "advance" was fulfilled— he has received his $2,000. His expectancy interest in the royalties—the profit he stood to gain from sale of the published book—while theoretically compensable, was speculative. Although this work is not plaintiff's first, at trial he provided no stable foundation for a reasonable estimate of royalties he would have earned had defendant not breached its promise to publish. In these circumstances, his claim for royalties falls for uncertainty. [Citation omitted.]

Since the damages which would have compensated plaintiff for anticipated royalties were not proved with the required certainty, we agree with the dissent in the Appellate Division that nominal damages alone are recoverable. [Citation omitted.] Though these are damages in name only and not at all compensatory, they are nevertheless awarded as a formal vindication of plaintiff's legal right to compensation which has not been given a sufficiently certain monetary valuation. [Citations omitted.]

In our view, the analogy by the majority in the Appellate Division to the construction contract situation was inapposite. In the typical construction contract, the owner agrees to pay money or other consideration to a builder and expects, under the contract, to receive a completed building in return. The value of the promised performance to the owner is the properly constructed building. In this case, unlike the typical construction contract, the value to plaintiff of the promised performance—publication—was a percentage of sales of the books published and not the books themselves. Had the plaintiff contracted for the printing, binding and delivery of a number of hardbound copies of his manuscript, to be sold or disposed of as he wished, then perhaps the construction analogy, and measurement of damages by the cost of replacement or completion, would have some application.

Here, however, the specific value to plaintiff of the promised publication was the royalties he stood to receive from defendant's sales of the published book. Essentially, publication represented what it would have cost the defendant to confer that value upon the plaintiff, and, by its breach, defendant saved that cost. The error by the courts below was in measuring damages not by the value to plaintiff of the promised performance but by the cost of that performance to defendant. Damages are not measured, however, by what the defaulting party saved by the breach, but by the natural and probable consequences of the breach *to the plaintiff*. In this case, the consequence to plaintiff of defendant's failure to publish is that he is prevented from realizing the gains promised by the contract—the royalties. But, as we have stated, the amount of royalties plaintiff would have realized was not ascertained with adequate certainty and, as a consequence, plaintiff may recover nominal damages only.

Accordingly, the order of the Appellate Division should be modified to the extent of reducing the damage award of $10,000 for the cost of publication to six cents, but with costs and disbursements to the plaintiff. Order modified, with costs and disbursements to plaintiff-respondent, in accordance with opinion herein and, as so modified, affirmed.

MindGames, Inc. v. Western Publishing Co., Inc.
218 F.3d 652 (7th Cir. 2000)

Posner, Chief Judge. This is a diversity suit for breach of contract, governed by Arkansas law because of a choice of law provision in the contract. The plaintiff, MindGames, was formed in March of 1988 by Larry Blackwell to manufacture and sell an adult board game, "Clever Endeavor," that he had invented. The first games were shipped in the fall of 1989 and by the end of the year, 75 days later, 30,000 had been sold. In March of 1990, MindGames licensed the game to the defendant, Western, a major marketer of games. Western had marketed the very successful adult board games "Trivial Pursuit" and "Pictionary" and thought "Clever Endeavor" might be as successful. The license contract, on which this suit is premised, required Western to pay MindGames a 15 percent royalty on all games sold. The contract was by its terms to remain in effect until the end of January of 1993, or for another year if before then Western paid MindGames at least $1.5 million in the form of royalties due under the contract or otherwise, and for subsequent years as well if Western paid an annual renewal fee of $300,000.

During the first year of the contract, Western sold 165,000 copies of "Clever Endeavor" and paid MindGames $600,000 in royalties. After that, sales fell precipitously (though we're not told by how much) but the parties continued under the contract through January 31, 1994, though Western did not pay the $900,000 ($1.5 million minus $600,000) that the contract would have required it to pay in order to be entitled to extend the contract for a year after its expiration. In February of 1994 the parties finally parted. Later that year MindGames brought this suit, which seeks $900,000, plus lost royalties of some $40 million that MindGames claims it would have earned had not Western failed to carry out the promotional obligations that the contract imposed on it, plus $300,000 on the theory that Western renewed the contract for a third year, beginning in February of 1994; Western sold off its remaining inventory of "Clever Endeavor" in that year.

The more difficult issue is MindGames' right to recover lost profits for Western's alleged breach of its duty to promote "Clever Endeavor." A minority of states have or purport to have a rule barring a new business, as distinct from an established one, from obtaining damages for lost profits as a result of a tort or a breach of contract.... The rule of *Hadley v. Baxendale* often prevents the victim of a breach of contract from obtaining lost profits, but that rule is not invoked here. [Citation omitted.] Neither the "new business" rule nor the rule of *Hadley v. Baxendale* stands for the general proposition that lost profits are never a recoverable item of damages in a tort or breach of contract case.

Arkansas is said to be one of the "new business" rule states on the strength of a case decided by the state's supreme court many years ago. The appellants in *Marvell Light & Ice Co. v. General Electric Co.,* 162 Ark. 467, 259 S.W. 741 (1924), sought to recover the profits that they claimed to have lost as a result of a five and a half month delay in the delivery of icemaking machinery; the delay, the appellants claimed, had forced them to delay putting their ice factory into operation. The court concluded, however, that because there was no indication "that the manufacture and sale of ice by appellants was an established business so that proof of the amount lost on account of the delay ... might be made with reasonable certainty," "the anticipated profits of the new business are too remote, speculative, and uncertain to support a judgment for their loss." It quoted an earlier decision in which another court had said that "he who is prevented from embarking in a new business can recover no profits, because there are no provable data of past business from which the fact that anticipated profits would have been realized can be legally deduced." *Central Coal & Coke Co. v. Hartman,* 111 F. 96, 99 (8th Cir. 1901). That quotation is taken to have made Arkansas a "new business" state, although the rest of the *Marvell* opinion indicates that the court was concerned that the anticipated profits of the *particular* new business at issue, rather than of every new business, were too speculative to support an award of damages.

On its facts, moreover, *Marvell* was a classic *Hadley v. Baxendale* type of case—in fact virtually a rerun of *Hadley,* except that the appellants alleged that they had notified the seller of the icemaking machinery of the damages that they would suffer if delivery was delayed, and the seller had agreed to be liable for those damages. The decision is puzzling in light of that allegation; it is doubly puzzling because, assuming that by the time of the trial the ice factory was up and running, it should not have been difficult to compute the damages that the appellants had lost by virtue of the five and a half month delay in placing the factory in operation. Presumably it would have had five-and-a-half months of additional profits.

Marvell has never been overruled; and federal courts ordinarily take a nonoverruled decision of the highest court of the state whose law governs a controversy by virtue of the applicable choice of law rule to be conclusive on the law of the state. [Citations omitted.] But this is a matter of practice or presumption, not of rule. The rule is that in a case in federal court in which state law provides the rule of decision, the federal court must predict how the state's highest court would decide the case, and decide it the same way. [Citations omitted.] Law, Holmes said, in a controversial definition that is, however, a pretty good summary of how courts apply the law of other jurisdictions, is just a prediction of what the courts of that jurisdiction would do with the case if they got their hands on it. Oliver Wendell Holmes, *The Path of the Law*, 10 Harv. L. Rev. 457, 461 (1897). Since state courts like federal courts do occasionally overrule their decisions, there will be occasional, though rare, instances in which the best prediction of what the state's highest court will do is that it will not follow its previous decision. [Citations omitted.]

That is the best prediction in this case. *Marvell* was decided more than three quarters of a century ago, and the "new business" rule which it has been thought to have announced has not been mentioned in a published Arkansas case since. The opinion doesn't make a lot of sense on its facts, as we have seen, and the Eighth Circuit case on which it relied has long been superseded in that circuit. *See, e.g., Central Telecommunications, Inc. v. TCI Cablevision, Inc.*, 800 F.2d 711, 727–28 (8th Cir. 1986).

The Arkansas cases decided since *Marvell* that deal with damages issues exhibit a liberal approach to the estimation of damages that is inconsistent with a flat rule denying damages for lost profits to all businesses that are not well established. [Citations omitted.] The *Ozark* decision, for example, allowed an orchard farmer to recover for the damages to a new orchard. The "new business" rule has, moreover, been abandoned in most states that once followed it. [Citations omitted.]

Western tries to distinguish *Ozark* by pointing to the fact that the plaintiff there was an established orchard farmer, albeit the particular orchard represented a new venture for him. This effort to distinguish that case brings into view the primary objection to the "new business" rule, an objection of such force as to explain its decline and make it unlikely that Arkansas would follow it if the occasion for its supreme court to choose arose. The objection has to do with the difference between *rule* and *standard* as methods of legal governance. A rule singles out one or a few facts and makes it or them conclusive of legal liability; a standard permits consideration of all or at least most facts that are relevant to the standard's rationale. A speed limit is a rule; negligence is a standard. Rules have the advantage of being definite and of limiting factual inquiry but the disadvantage of being inflexible, even arbitrary, and thus overinclusive, or of being underinclusive and thus opening up loopholes (or of being *both* over- and underinclusive!). Standards are flexible, but vague and open-ended; they make business planning difficult, invite the sometimes unpredictable exercise of judicial discretion, and are more costly to adjudicate —and yet when based on lay intuition they may actually be more intelligible, and thus in a sense clearer and more precise, to the persons whose behavior they seek to guide than rules would be.

No sensible person supposes that rules are always superior to standards, or vice versa, though some judges are drawn to the definiteness of rules and others to the flexibility of standards. But that is psychology; the important point is that some activities are better governed by rules, others by standards. States that have rejected the "new business" rule are content to control the award of damages for lost profits by means of a standard — damages may not be awarded on the basis of wild conjecture, they must be proved to a reasonable certainty, [Citations omitted.] — that is applicable to proof of damages generally. [Citations omitted.] The "new business" rule is an attempt now widely regarded as failed to control the award of such damages by means of a rule.

The rule doesn't work because it manages to be at once vague and arbitrary. One reason is that the facts that it makes determinative. "New," "business," and "profits," are not facts, but rather are the conclusions of a reasoning process that is based on the rationale for the rule and that as a result turns the rule into an implicit standard. What, for example, is a "new" business? What, for that matter, is a "business"? And are royalties what the rule means by "profits"?

MindGames was formed more than a year before it signed the license agreement with Western, and it sold 30,000 games in the six months between the first sales and the signing of the contract. MindGames' only "business," moreover, was the licensing of intellectual property. An author who signs a contract with a publisher for the publication of his book would not ordinarily be regarded as being engaged in a "business," or his royalties or advance described as "profits." He would be surprised to learn that if he sued for unpaid royalties he could not get them because his was a "new business." Suppose a first-time author sued a publisher for an accounting, and the only issue was how many copies the publisher had sold. Under the "new business" rule as construed by Western, the author could not recover his lost royalties even though there was no uncertainty about what he had lost. So construed and applied, the rule would have no relation to its rationale, which is to prevent the award of speculative damages.

Western goes even further, arguing that even if it, Western, a well-established firm, were the plaintiff, it could not recover its lost profits because the sale of "Clever Endeavor" was a new business. On this construal of the rule, "business" does not mean the enterprise; it means any business activity. So Western's sale of a new game is a new business, yet we know from the Ozark decision that an orchard farmer's operation of a new orchard is an old business.

The rule could be made sensible by appropriate definition of its terms, but we find it hard to see what would be gained, given the existence of the serviceable and familiar standard of excessive speculativeness. The rule may have made sense at one time; the reduction in decision costs and uncertainty brought about by avoiding a speculative mire may have swamped the increased social costs resulting from the systematically inadequate damages that a "new business" rule decrees. But today the courts have become sufficiently sophisticated in analyzing lost-earnings claims, and have accumulated sufficient precedent on the standard of undue speculativeness in damages awards, to make the balance of costs and benefits tip against the rule. In any event we are far in this case, in logic as well as time, from the ice factory whose opening was delayed by the General Electric Company. We greatly doubt that there is a "new business" rule in the common law of Arkansas today, but if there is it surely does not extend so far beyond the facts of the only case in which the rule was ever invoked to justify its invocation here. There is no authority for, and no common sense appeal to, such an extension.

But that leaves us with the question of undue speculation in estimating damages. Abrogation of the "new business" rule does not produce a free-for-all. What makes MindGames' claim of lost royalties indeed dubious is not any "new business" rule but the fact that the success of a board game, like that of a book or movie, is so uncertain. Here newness enters into judicial consideration of the damages claim not as a rule but as a factor in applying the standard. Just as a start-up company should not be permitted to obtain pie-in-the-sky damages upon allegations that it was snuffed out before it could begin to operate (unlike the ice factory in *Marvell*, which did begin production, albeit a little later than planned), capitalizing fantasized earnings into a huge present value sought as damages, so a novice writer should not be permitted to obtain damages from his publisher on the premise that but for the latter's laxity he would have had a bestseller, when only a tiny fraction of new books achieve that success. Damages must be proved, and not just dreamed, though "some degree of speculation is permissible in computing damages, because reasonable doubts as to remedy ought to be resolved against the wrongdoer." [Citations omitted.]

This is not to suggest that damages for lost earnings on intellectual property can never be recovered; that "entertainment damages" are not recoverable in breach of contract cases. That would just be a variant of the discredited "new business" rule. What is important is that Blackwell had no track record when he created "Clever Endeavor." He could not point to other games that he had invented and that had sold well. He was not in the position of the bestselling author who can prove from his past success that his new book, which the defendant failed to promote, would have been likely—not certain, of course—to have enjoyed a success comparable to that of the average of his previous books if only it had been promoted as promised. That would be like a case of a new business launched by an entrepreneur with a proven track record.

In the precontract sales period and the first year of the contract a total of 195,000 copies of "Clever Endeavor" were sold; then sales fizzled. The public is fickle. It is possible that if Western had marketed the game more vigorously, more would have been sold, but an equally if not more plausible possibility is that the reason that Western didn't market the game more vigorously was that it correctly sensed that demand had dried up.

Even if that alternative is rejected, we do not see how the number of copies that would have been sold but for the alleged breach could be determined given the evidence presented in the summary judgment proceedings (a potentially important qualification, of course); and so MindGames' proof of damages is indeed excessively speculative.... Those proceedings were completed with no evidence having been presented from which a rational trier of fact could conclude on this record that some specific quantity, or for that matter some broad but bounded range of alternative estimates, of copies of "Clever Endeavor" would have been sold had Western honored the contract. MindGames obtained $600,000 in royalties on sales of 165,000 copies of the game, implying that Western would have had to sell more than 10 million copies to generate the $40 million in lost royalties that MindGames seeks to recover. [Citation omitted.]

When the breach occurred, MindGames should have terminated the contract and sought distribution by other means. *See* FARNSWORTH, *supra*, § 12.12, pp. 806–08. The fact that it did not do so—that so far as appears it has made no effort to market "Clever Endeavor" since the market for the game collapsed in 1991—is telling evidence of a lack of commercial promise unrelated to Western's conduct.

Although Western in its brief in this court spent most of its time misguidedly defending the "new business" rule, clinging to *Marvell* for dear life (a case seemingly on point, however vulnerable, is a security blanket that no lawyer feels comfortable without), it did argue that in any event MindGames' claim for lost royalties was too speculative to ground an award of damages for that loss. The argument was brief but not so brief as to fail to put MindGames on notice of a possible alternative ground for upholding the district court's judgment; we may of course affirm an award of summary judgment on any ground that has not been forfeited or waived in the district court. [Citation omitted.] MindGames did not respond to the argument in its reply brief. It pointed to no evidence from which lost royalties could be calculated to even a rough approximation. We find its silence eloquent and Western's argument compelling, and so the judgment in favor of Western is affirmed.

Fairchild, Circuit Judge, dissenting in part. I agree that: (1) MindGames' claim for a renewal fee for the year following the initial term of the Licensing Agreement was properly dismissed, and (2) we are not bound by *Marvell*... to affirm the dismissal of MindGames' claim for loss of royalties caused by breach of contract. I do, however, respectfully disagree with the conclusion that, as a matter of law, that claim is too speculative to support an award of damages.

This was never a claim in which MindGames sought to recover lost profits from the operation of a business. The damages sought would be measured by the royalties which Western would have been obliged to pay on sales which did not occur because of Western's alleged failure to perform its contract. Western's obligation to pay royalties arose from the sales of games manufactured, promoted and sold by it, and whether MindGames showed a profit, as well as MindGames' lack of history, was wholly irrelevant. The ultimate questions would be whether there was a breach by Western and whether the breach caused a loss of sales.

Sales did not meet expectations. In the period from March 30, 1990 to January 31, 1991, 165,000 games were sold; in the year ending January 31, 1992, 58,113; in the year ending January 31, 1993, 26,394; and in the year after the initial term, 7,438. The sales in the initial term totaled approximately $4,000,000 and royalties $600,000. Soon after January 31, 1993, Western was sufficiently interested in continuing as licensee to agree to pay a minimum royalty of $27,500 for the coming year. MindGames' complaint alleged that a substantial number of games produced by Western failed to meet quality standards; Western failed to promote and make reasonable efforts to sell; and its efforts did not meet standards under the agreement or those recognized in the industry. It is MindGames' position that these failures caused loss of sales.

Western's motion for partial summary judgment was premised on the new business rule which Western perceived as announced in *Marvell*, and the district court granted the motion on that basis. If, as we all agree, *Marvell* does not control this case, then the applicable Arkansas doctrine is that MindGames is entitled to recover any royalties on sales which MindGames can prove to a reasonable certainty would have been made had Western carried out the contract. The rule that damages which are uncertain cannot be recovered does not apply to uncertainty as to the value of the benefits to be derived, but to uncertainty as to whether any benefit would be derived at all. [Citations omitted.]

In my opinion we cannot say on this record, as a matter of law, that MindGames cannot prove to a reasonable certainty that Western's failures to perform, if proved, caused a loss of sales.

I would not hold that MindGames has waived or forfeited its opportunity to produce evidence of damages. It is true that in responding to Western's motion for partial summary judgment MindGames did not provide evidentiary material tending to show the breaches by Western nor that such breaches caused a loss of sales. This should not be deemed a waiver or forfeiture of an opportunity to do so because of Western's complete reliance in its motion on the new business rule and *Marvell,* which, if applied, would prevent proof of breach and causation of loss. Western's motion did not reach the issue of breach, and establishing damages would require MindGames to prove that the breach occurred and caused loss of sales. Although Western, in its memorandum in support of its motion did include a section making the point that the success of a new product in the entertainment industry is especially difficult to predict, it used that point to support an argument that the new business rule was particularly appropriate in this case, and that the Arkansas Supreme Court would be unlikely to retreat from the new business rule under circumstances like these. Western did not squarely assert, as an alternative ground, that MindGames could not prove to a reasonable certainty that any breach by Western caused loss of sales. Rather, Western urged that the district court should strictly apply the new business rule.

In this court, Western again relied on *Marvell* and the new business rule, also arguing, as it had in the district court, that this type of case, involving a new product in the entertainment industry, is not one where the Arkansas Supreme Court would retreat from its application of the new business rule. Although at pages 30–32 of its brief it asserted the inherently speculative nature of a claim for lost profits in the entertainment industry, and cited cases, it failed squarely to assert, as an alternative ground, that its alleged failures to perform, if proved, could not have been proved to a reasonable certainty to have caused lost sales. On page 5 of its reply brief, MindGames referred to pages 29–32 of Western's brief, and challenged as contrary to Arkansas law "non-Arkansas cases [cited by Western] in arguing that businesses in the entertainment industry are barred *per se* from claiming lost profits." Again I do not think it is appropriate to rely on waiver or forfeiture.

I would remand for further proceedings on this part of MindGames' complaint.

Exercise 6-22: Limitations on Damages

1. You have now finished the section of this chapter regarding limitations, the second topic under "Damages" in Diagram 6-1 at the beginning of this chap-

ter. Accordingly, you should review the limitation materials and create an outline, graphic organizer, or other learning aid to summarize what you have learned. Create a learning aid of your choice to summarize what you have learned about damage limitations.

2. In December, Paulo, a car manufacturer whose principal place of business was located in downtown Centerville, and Demitrius, a landowner, entered into negotiations for the purchase, by Paulo, of Businessacre, a parcel of land owned by Demitrius. Businessacre was the last unused parcel in downtown Centerville zoned for manufacturing. There are a few appropriately zoned and much less expensive parcels of land located in rural areas within a hundred miles of Centerville. Paulo and Demitrius were introduced by a mutual friend, who told Demitrius that Paulo thought that Businessacre was an ideal location for a manufacturing plant given its location in downtown Centerville.

On January 1, Paulo and Demitrius entered into a valid and enforceable written contract whereby Demitrius agreed to sell Paulo Businessacre, and Paulo agreed to pay Demitrius $100,000. After the contract was signed, Paulo spent $50,000 obtaining an architectural design for a minivan manufacturing plant.

On January 30, the scheduled day for closing the sale, Demitrius refused to perform because he felt he had made a bad bargain. The market value of Businessacre had risen to $150,000. Paulo filed suit and sought $1,100,000 in damages as his remedy.

At trial, Paulo introduced the foregoing facts and introduced the following additional evidence:

(1) Paulo has been in the car manufacturing business for thirty years. He makes 100,000 cars per year and he makes $100 in profit on each car ($10,000,000 total); and

(2) Paulo had planned to use Businessacre to expand into minivan manufacturing. He planned to make 10,000 minivans using Businessacre, and he anticipated making $100 in profit on each minivan ($1,000,000 total).

Demitrius contends that Paulo is entitled to $50,000 or, at most, $100,000. Analyze the measure of damages and limitation issues raised in this problem. (Hint: All three limitations on damages are implicated by this problem.)

Reliance Damages

A. Introduction

You were introduced to "**reliance damages**" at the beginning of this chapter in the section entitled "Special Damages." As depicted in Diagram 6-1 at the beginning of this chapter, reliance damages are one category of special damages. "Special Damages" are one category under "Measure."

So far, you have learned to analyze the measure of damages by considering: (1) general damages (usually loss of value or cost), (2) special damages (including both reliance and consequential damages), and (3) costs and losses avoided. In most cases, plaintiffs can recover both general damages and reliance damages. In some cases, however, a non-breaching party is limited to recovering only reliance damages — and that topic is the focus of this section.

Reliance damages may take one of two forms: (1) "**essential reliance damages**," and (2) "**incidental reliance damages**." Essential reliance damages include the cost of preparing to perform or performing a contract. Imagine a buyer who contracts to buy an apple for $1. She pays the $1 when due, but the seller never delivers the apple. Assume that the FMV of the apple was $2. The buyer could recover not only her $1 anticipated profit (the FMV of $2 less the contract price of $1), but also her $1 payment. The loss of the $1 payment constitutes reliance damages.[7] More specifically, the payment constitutes essential reliance damages because it involved an expenditure of money made in performing the contract. If the buyer also paid her bank $.10 in interest to borrow the $1, that payment would also constitute essential reliance damages because it reflects an expenditure made while preparing to perform.

Second, incidental reliance damages include all other expenditures made in reliance on a contract or in reliance on a breach. For example, if the apple buyer breached the contract and the apple seller had spent money storing, insuring, or reselling the apple, those expenditures made in reliance on the breach are incidental reliance damages. Likewise, if the seller had spent money transporting the apple from the seller's place of business to the buyer's place of business, that expenditure in reliance on the contract would be recoverable as incidental reliance damages. The main point of distinction between essential and incidental reliance damages is that essential reliance damages reflect costs incurred by the non-breaching party in and toward performance of contractual obligations whereas incidental reliance damages reflect costs that the non-breaching party is not required to incur by the contract but are reasonable expenditures that are indirectly related to it. To take another example, a buyer of real estate is not usually *obliged* by the contract of sale to incur costs investigating the seller's title. But there is no doubt that it is prudent as a matter of normal practice for the buyer to incur these costs. Damages awarded to reimburse the buyer's loss in incurring the costs of investigating the seller's title would therefore be incidental reliance damages.

Both of these labels — essential and incidental reliance damages — are worth learning. Understanding these labels as separate recoverable damages will help ensure that you consider all possible items of damages in evaluating an exam question or a client's case in practice. In other words, these labels will help ensure that you spot all possible items of recovery in a given problem.

Note that reliance damages do not put a plaintiff in a post-performance position (as she would be under the general benefit-of-the-bargain approach). Reliance damages put a plaintiff in a pre-contract position, restoring any losses or expenditures made because of a contract or its breach. Earlier in this text, we recommended that you remember benefit-of-the-bargain damages with the "4 Ps" ("Put the Plaintiff in the Performance Position"). In a similar way, you can remember reliance damages with the "3 Bs": "Bring her Back to the Beginning."

The materials that follow will help you understand the circumstances in which a plaintiff's recovery may be restricted to only reliance damages and further develop your ability to identify items as reliance damages.

---

7. We can further subdivide essential reliance damages into damages that have either a restitutionary or a compensatory function. In this example, the damages serve both functions by reimbursing the $1 the buyer spent in performing the contract while, at the same time, preventing the breaching seller from making an unjust gain.

Exercise 6-23: Reliance Damages

1. Earlier in this chapter, you read several cases in which the plaintiffs recovered both benefit-of-the-bargain damages and reliance damages: *Donovan, Neri,* and *Luten Bridge Co.* For each of those cases, identify each item of reliance damages and classify each item as essential or incidental.

2. For the Paulo-Demitrius problem in Exercise 6-22 identify each item of reliance damages and classify each item as essential or incidental.

3. The comment to section 349 of the RESTATEMENT (SECOND) OF CONTRACTS indicates that uncertainty as to the measure of a plaintiff's expectancy damages may justify a court in limiting the plaintiff to reliance damages. Read that section of the comment and then paraphrase it.

4. Assume you are the lawyer for Mr. Freund in the *Freund* case and you know that Mr. Freund will be denied his lost royalties. What might you argue Mr. Freund should recover instead? (Hint: The correct answer is not an item of damages mentioned at all in the *Freund* court's opinion.)

Exercise 6-24: *Reimer v. Badger*

The next case, *Reimer v. Badger Wholesale Co.*, provides additional guidance about limiting a plaintiff to reliance damages based on uncertainty. As you read the case, consider the following questions:

1. Why didn't the plaintiff seek or recover benefit-of-the-bargain damages?

2. What was wrong with the plaintiff's proof for incidental and consequential damages?

Reimer v. Badger Wholesale Co., Inc.
147 Wis. 2d 389 · 433 N.W.2d 592 (1988)

Scott, Chief Judge. Badger Wholesale Company, Inc. ("Badger"), appeals from a judgment awarding its former employee, Dennis Reimer, $16,500 on a breach of contract claim. Badger argues that Reimer was an employee-at-will and therefore could not bring a breach of contract claim after his termination. In the alternative, Badger argues that the measure of damages was incorrect. We conclude that the contractual breach was unrelated to the term or duration of employment; therefore, a breach of contract claim will lie. Further, we conclude that the measure of damages was correct; however, credible evidence, in the light most favorable to Reimer, only supports a judgment of $16,245.81. We therefore modify the judgment to reflect this amount. The order denying the motion for a new trial is affirmed.

Facts

We state the facts in the light most favorable to the jury verdict. Reimer worked in Missouri as a wholesale foods salesperson. Following a death in the family in Wisconsin, Reimer considered moving back to the area if he received an offer of suitable employment.

Over the course of several meetings between Badger representatives and Reimer, an agreement evolved whereby Reimer would receive a minimum wage base salary plus commission. He also was offered an exclusive territory in the Neenah-Menasha area and an opportunity to expand Badger's business into the Oshkosh area. Badger representatives further told Reimer that he would have a ninety-day trial period to make $10,000 in sales. Based on Reimer's experience, he was told that he could expect to earn between $20,000 and $25,000 a year.

After accepting Badger's offer, Reimer quit his previous employment where he earned $350 per week without commission. He and his family incurred moving expenses of slightly over $2000. After beginning work for Badger, Reimer discovered that other sales representatives already handled twenty-six accounts in the Neenah-Menasha area. When he pressed Badger about opening up territory near Oshkosh, it established a minimum number of sales, under which it would not make deliveries, forcing Reimer to deliver goods himself.

Badger terminated Reimer after seventeen and a half working days for lack of sales. Reimer had made thirteen sales in his brief employ, considered by an expert witness to be very good for a salesperson in new territory.

Reimer brought suit against Badger, alleging breach of contract, misrepresentation, promissory estoppel and wrongful dismissal. The last two causes of action were dismissed on Badger's motion for summary judgment. Prior to submission of the case to the jury, Reimer elected to proceed on the contract theory.... The jury found a breach and awarded $16,500 in damages. Badger appealed....

[W]e note that in dismissing Reimer's wrongful discharge claim the trial court made a finding that this was an employment-at-will situation. This fact does not, however, relieve Badger of its responsibility for any and all promises made to Reimer as a prospective employee [citation omitted] ... Reimer alleged and proved that Badger's failure to provide him with the promised exclusive territory and opportunity for expansion prevented him from doing his job to the expectations of himself and others. As a result, he was terminated for these "poor sales". Because Reimer's claim was not dependent on his status as an at-will employee or otherwise, this was a legitimate breach of contract case.

Damages

The jury awarded $16,500 to Reimer as damages on the breach of contract claim. A summary of damages prepared by Reimer as an exhibit broke down damages as follows:

Loss of income while employed at Badger (Difference between salary at Badger and previous salary in Missouri)	$1,188.00
Loss of income following termination until time of trial (Based on salary in Missouri)	$12,950.00
Moving expenses	$2,107.81
Incidental and consequential damages	$5,000.00
Total	$21,245.81

We take note that the damages award approximated Reimer's summary with the exception of the incidental and consequential damages.

Badger argues that the damages should be limited to what Reimer would have earned at Badger had he stayed there for the term of his employment—ninety days. It relies on *Wassenaar v. Panos*, 111 Wis. 2d 518, 331 N.W.2d 357 (1983), which states:

> According to black-letter law, when an employee is wrongfully discharged, damages are the salary the employee would have received during the unexpired term of the contract plus the expenses of securing other employment reduced by the income which he or she has earned, will earn, or could with reasonable diligence earn, during the unexpired term.

Id. at 534, 331 N.W.2d at 365 (footnote omitted).

The fallacy in Badger's argument is that, as previously noted, this is not a wrongful discharge case but a breach of contract action. Remedies for breach of contract protect three interests: the expectation interest, the reliance interest, and the restitution interest. [Citations omitted.] We consider the damages proven by Reimer to be based upon his reliance interest.

Remedies for injury to a reliance interest are defined as "being reimbursed for loss caused by reliance on the contract by being put in as good a position as he would have been in had the contract not been made." Restatement (Second) of Contracts sec. 344 (1981). Had the contract between Reimer and Badger not been made, he would not have had moving expenses and would still be employed in Missouri. These reliance damages are particularly appropriate where proof of the expectation interest, *i.e.*, profit, is uncertain. *Id.* at sec. 349 comment a. Reimer's profit would have been difficult to determine because of his short sales history with Badger.

Badger also disputes the calculation of damages in that it is based on the time period between Reimer's termination and the date of trial. Our review of the record reveals no attempt by Badger to prove that Reimer failed to mitigate his damages with respect to seeking or obtaining employment prior to trial. If the damages here reflected Reimer's expectation interest, there would be a concern about the length of time for which damages would be awarded, particularly since this was an at-will employment situation. However, Reimer chose to present his reliance interest as the measure of damages. As a result, the relevant inquiry, as contained in the Restatement cited earlier, is what sum of money would put Reimer in the position he would have been had the contract not been made....

Badger moved for a new trial on the bases that the verdict was contrary to the law of damages in Wisconsin and that the damages were excessive. We have already dealt with the first ground alleged and concluded that the measure of damages was appropriate.

If there is any credible evidence which, under any reasonable view, supports the jury's damage figure, we will not disturb the finding unless the award shocks judicial conscience, especially where the verdict has the trial court's approval. [Citation omitted.] We initially express our opinion that the amount of the jury verdict, $16,500, does not shock judicial conscience. Therefore, we turn to the question of whether credible evidence supports this amount.

After examining the record, we cannot find support for an award which exceeds $16,245.81. The only evidence on damages was presented by Reimer. In addition to lost wages of $14,138 and moving expenses of $2107.81, Reimer made a claim of $5,000 for incidental and consequential damages. No proof of this figure was received other than Reimer's statement when referring to his "summary of damages" exhibit that he was claiming this amount. Mere conclusions of a witness that he has been damaged to a certain extent without stating the facts on which the estimate is made is too uncertain. [Citation omitted.] We therefore reduce the award from $16,500 to $16,245.81 and affirm the judgment as modified.

Exercise 6-25: *Reimer* Revisited

Paula entered into a contract with David to buy a tract of land. The contract price was $250,000 and the FMV of the land was $240,000. Paula paid David a down payment of $25,000 and paid inspectors $5,000 to inspect the land. Before escrow closed on the deal, David breached by refusing to perform the contract. Re-read section 349 of the RESTATEMENT (SECOND) OF CONTRACTS (especially the last clause). Then, analyze Paula's damages.

Exercise 6-26: *Designer Direct, Inc. v. DeForest Redevelopment Authority*

The next case, *Designer Direct, Inc. v. DeForest Redevelopment Authority*, raises a reliance damage issue in a complex transactional setting. As you read the case, consider the following:

1. What breaches of contract did the court identify? (Be sure to consider the relevant terms of the contract and the factual basis of the DRA's various breaches of these terms).

2. Why do you think that the court did not characterize the awards of the $50,000 (earnest money) and $35,270.02 (unpaid fees) as reliance damages?

3. Why did the court conclude that Levin was entitled to reliance damages? Were they essential reliance damages or incidental reliance damages?

Designer Direct, Inc. v.
DeForest Redevelopment Authority
313 F.3d 1036 (2002)

BAUER, Circuit Judge.

This case arises out of a contractual relationship between Designer Direct, Inc. d/b/a/ Levin Associates Architects ("Levin") and the DeForest Redevelopment Authority ("DRA"). The contract between the parties involved the redevelopment of the downtown area of DeForest, Wisconsin. Levin brought a breach of contract claim against the DRA after the DRA failed to provide certain services required by the contract. The DRA filed a counter-claim alleging that Levin's actions constituted a breach of contract. After a bench trial, the district court found the DRA breached the contract but limited damages to only certain aspects of the breach. The district court entered a judgement in favor of Levin for $85,270.02 and dismissed the DRA's counterclaim. Both parties filed notices of appeal. Levin bases its appeal on the district court's denial of reliance damages. The DRA contends that the district court erred when it granted judgement in favor of Levin and denied its counterclaim. For the reasons set forth below, we reverse and remand in part, and affirm in part.

BACKGROUND

In 1995, the Village of DeForest ("Village") devised a plan to revitalize its downtown area. The Village sought to create a downtown district that, as the center of community life, would generate increased property, sales, and income taxes for the town. To accomplish this, the Village created a separate entity, the DRA, which was responsible for the redevelopment. The Village also established a Tax Incremental Financing District, which would encourage investment in the downtown. The DRA chose Levin to create a redevelopment plan to achieve the goals of the DRA. The parties entered into a redevelopment plan agreement and a Phase I sub-agreement in October 1996.

Phase I consisted primarily of the creation of a redevelopment plan. Phase I established Levin as the developer. As developer, Levin was responsible for finishing the remainder of the redevelopment plan. The parties entered into a second agreement in August 1998 reflecting the new arrangement. This contract consisted of two more phases. Phase II concerned the construction of the infrastructure which would support Levin's plan and Phase III dealt with the sale of the land and the subsequent construction.

A synopsis of the agreement is as follows: Levin was required to purchase land obtained by the DRA and construct buildings on it. These buildings would increase the value of the property to at least $12,000,000.00. Assuming everything went according to plan, this increase in property value would result in increased tax revenues for the Village.

The plan ran into snags. To begin with, the DRA had a contractual obligation to provide a full-time liaison to work with Levin but failed to do so. The DRA assigned one Joan Laine to be the designated liaison, but she worked only two days a week. To meet the problem, Levin hired outside sources to provide liaison services at a cost of $20,000.00. The DRA reimbursed Levin but Levin objected to the DRA's failure to appoint a full-time liaison. Levin presented amendments to the contract in an attempt to negotiate a resolution of the liaison problem but without success.

Another area of dispute between the parties involved an area of land known as Carriage Way. The contract required the DRA to acquire parcels of land identified in the redevelopment plan. The agreement also required the DRA to prepare the parcels for development and convey them to Levin at the appropriate time. The redevelopment area known as Carriage Way, experienced problems from the start. Plans were behind schedule and the parcel sizes were constantly being changed by the DRA. This confusion hampered Levin's ability to perform infrastructure work on Carriage Way and resulted in costs to

Levin of approximately $490,000.00 in architectural design, drawings, and engineering changes in the Phase III property development. In addition, the modifications frustrated Levin's ability to purchase the land when the DRA demanded payment on the original closing date. Levin objected to the closing date because there was, among other things, a lack of infrastructure, a lack of zoning, and a lack of building permits. The DRA refused to extend the closing date and notified Levin that it was in breach but took no other action.

The parties' relationship finally broke under the strain of a disagreement over plans to build a public library. A major goal of the redevelopment project was to find an entity to serve as an anchor tenant. It became apparent that a public library in the downtown area would be a plausible anchor tenant. The DRA authorized Levin to contact the DeForest Library Board about the construction of a new library in the downtown area of the city. Under the agreement, Levin had the right to purchase and develop the land where the DRA wanted to put the library. The DRA wanted Levin to give up its right to purchase the land so that the library could be developed on that site. Levin agreed to this on the condition that it would be given the job of overseeing the design and construction of the library. Levin prepared a four-party agreement concerning the proposed library site. The DeForest Library Board was willing to sign the agreement; the DRA refused. Levin contends, and the district court found, that there was a secret meeting between the DeForest Library Board and the DRA in which the DRA suggested that the Board delay the library development plan. The DRA contends that Levin's construction manager was present and thus the meeting was not secret. The secrecy of the meeting notwithstanding, Levin became aware that the Library Board would likely delay a month before signing any agreement. At this point Levin elected to terminate all contacts with the DRA.

Levin filed a complaint against the DRA for failure to pay fees and expenses, failure to return earnest money, and contractual breaches of the Phase II and III agreement. The DRA filed a counterclaim against Levin for failure to develop a new tax base, failure to purchase land, and failure to construct infrastructure improvements as provided for in the contract.

After a bench trial, the district court entered judgment in favor of Levin in the amount of $85,270.02 and dismissed the DRA's counterclaim. The damages awarded to Levin consisted of the return of $50,000 of earnest money and approximately $35,000 in billed fees. While the district court found the DRA breached the Phase II and III agreements, the court did not award Levin damages for the breach of contract claims.

ANALYSIS

I. *The Liaison Requirement*

One of the main disputes in this case is the liaison requirement under Section 2.5 of the contract. This provision states in part:

> In the event the DRA shall default on its obligation to provide a designated representative to perform the required tasks, and failure to cure the default upon reasonable written notice from the Developer, Developer shall be entitled to a change order authorizing the necessary work by Developer and making appropriate adjustments to

the deadlines and compensation as provided in secs. 4.1, 4.2, 4.3, and/or 5.9.

...

The district court determined the DRA breached the contract when it failed to provide a designated liaison. The DRA does not dispute its failure to provide a liaison. The DRA does argue that its failure to appoint a liaison was remedied by its willingness to refund Levin for any costs it incurred for liaison services ...

While it is true that the DRA faithfully repaid Levin for any costs incurred as a result of paying for liaison services, the DRA fails to recognize that there was more than just failing to comply with the liaison provision. Levin was forced to work in a climate rife with disorganization and inefficiency. Levin had to deal with the additional headaches of finding outside resources, negotiating costs, and evaluating the efficiency and ability of these outside sources. These problems created additional costs which deprived Levin of what it expected from the contractual relationship. For these reasons, we find the district court's determination that the DRA breached the agreement by failing to provide liaison services was correct ...

Levin expected and continuously requested the DRA to appoint a full-time liaison. The absence of such a person had a particularly significant effect on Levin's ability to perform. The DRA's failure to provide a full-time liaison deprived Levin of the right to purchase and develop land because it substantially delayed and interfered with the redevelopment. An effective liaison was necessary for Levin to fulfill its duties under the contract. The district court specifically found a lack of good faith on the part of the DRA, and we cannot find fault with this decision.

II. *Carriage Way Property*

The second point of contention between the parties involved a parcel of land known as Carriage Way. Section 5.1 of the Phase II and III agreement required the DRA to acquire parcels of land identified in the redevelopment plan. The contract also provided that the DRA prepare the land for development and convey the land to Levin. Both parties agreed that Carriage Way would be developed first. However, with the problems above recited, the project stalled, and the land was never redeveloped. The district court determined that the DRA further materially breached the contract when it insisted on the closing of the Carriage Way property before Levin was ready and when it failed to negotiate in good faith with Levin over the purchase price or the closing time ...

In its finding that the DRA breached the contract with regard to the Carriage Way property, the district court found that the DRA breached the expressed good-faith requirements of the contract. The testimony of Kerry Levin, the owner of Levin, reveals the difficulties Levin had with Carriage Way. A project as complex as this one must be planned well in advance. Yet the size of the final parcel for Carriage Way had been in question up until the closing date, forcing Levin to modify its designs. The modifications included eliminating garages and changing master bedroom units. In addition, Levin had to change engineering drawings for the infrastructure work and the architectural drawings. Despite this major overhaul the DRA caused by its actions, the DRA still expected Levin to close in November though Levin had not finished its architectural drawings and other designs. Kerry Levin also testified that building permits had not yet been obtained, the land was not rezoned, and the infrastructure was not yet built because Levin was still modifying the engineering.

The district court also found the price charged by the DRA was in excess of the amount required by the contract. The DRA defends its actions regarding the purchase price of Carriage Way as stemming from the change of the status of a road from public to private. Thus, it claims to be merely demanding adherence to specific contract requirements. A closer inspection reveals that there was more to this situation than the DRA suggests....

For these reasons, we find the DRA violated the express provisions in the contract requiring good faith. The DRA's demand for a November closing when its own actions placed Levin in the position of being unable to meet this date exemplifies the DRA's failure to fulfill the good-faith requirements of the contract. The DRA's delays and failure to cooperate with Levin on the Carriage Way closing date and price confirm the DRA's lack of good faith. For these reasons, we agree with the district court's finding that the DRA breached the express provisions requiring good faith.

III. *The Public Library*

The third point of contention between the parties concerns the plans to construct a public library in downtown DeForest. Levin attempted to secure a right to design and build a library on land promised to it for redevelopment. The DRA wanted Levin to give up its right to buy the land so that a library could be developed on the site. Under this proposal, Levin agreed to give up its right to purchase the land if it could design and build the library. As this proposal was about to be formally agreed to, Levin became aware that the Library Board planned to hold out on signing the agreement for another month after a secret meeting it had with the DRA.

The district court found that the DRA failed to act in good faith with respect to the library negotiations. The court based its decision on the fact that a secret meeting occurred involving all the interested parties except Levin. The district court noted that if good-faith negotiations are to exist, all parties should be present. The DRA claims that the district court erred and that the contract did not require it to negotiate in good faith with regard to the library negotiations.

Whether the DRA had a contractual duty to negotiate in good faith is a matter of contract interpretation and a question of law. *Harris v. Metro. Mall,* 112 Wis.2d 487, 503, 334 N.W.2d 519 (1983). We review questions of law de novo.

The provisions of the Phase II & III Sub–Agreement relevant to the library negotiations include the following:

> Section 5.1. Notwithstanding the foregoing, if due to environmental contamination or other conditions or circumstances DRA cannot obtain any parcel at what it deems a reasonable cost, Developer agrees to meet with DRA or its representative and negotiate in good faith for adjustment of the Redevelopment Plan and the terms of this Agreement to avoid, if possible, the need to acquire such parcel(s).

Section 5.10. In the event the Redevelopment Plan is modified resulting in a positive economic benefit to the project (including, but not limited to, inclusion of a new public library or a new restaurant), ... the parties shall meet and negotiate in good faith for appropriate adjustments to the amount of guaranteed development value as provided in sec. 5.8, the development phasing as provided in sec. 5.9 and/or the promotional efforts and expenditures as provided by secs. 3.2 and 4.1, considering such factors as the ... reasonable expectation of the parties at the time of execution of this Agreement and any other factors which have, or are expected to, increase or decrease the overall expense or benefits from the project to the Developer or DRA from any other previously unanticipated changes in circumstances.

The DRA misreads the plain language of Section 5.10 and attempts to devise an interpretation of it that simply ignores the unambiguous nature of Section 5.10. We agree with the DRA that Levin had no contractual right to build a library. But this does not preclude the DRA from acting in good faith when it negotiated with Levin about the library. Contractual language is ambiguous only when it is "reasonably or fairly susceptible of more than one construction." [citation omitted]. Unambiguous contractual language must be enforced as written. [citation omitted]. We cannot agree that the contractual language at issue is ambiguous. Section 5.10 specifically asserts that the parties are to "negotiate in good faith" if a new public library is included in the plan.

After finding these good-faith provisions of the agreement apply, we must consider whether the DRA breached them in its negotiations concerning the library. The district court found that there was a secret meeting between the DRA, the DeForest Village Board, and the Library Board and that this meeting constituted bad faith negotiations. The determination that a secret meeting occurred is a question of fact ...

We agree with the district court that backroom deals between parties conspiring to outmaneuver the other party to the contract do not epitomize good-faith negotiations. The district court found that no representative of Levin was present at the meeting, and given the factual surroundings, we find no error in its assessment.

IV. *Implied Covenant of Good Faith*

... [In this section of the opinion the court affirms the district court's ruling that the DRA had also breached an implied covenant of good faith and fair dealing.] ...

V. *Damages*

Not surprisingly, the parties also disagree over the district court's decisions regarding damages. The district court found that Levin was entitled to receive damages and awarded Levin damages consisting of unpaid invoices of $35,270.02 and the return of earnest money totaling $50,000.00. In this appeal, Levin argues that the district court erred when it refused to grant it reliance damages. The DRA, on the other hand, claims that the district court erred when it awarded Levin the $50,000.00 in earnest money and the

$35,270.02 in unpaid fees. We review the determination of damages for clear error. [citation omitted].

We will first consider the DRA's argument that Levin is not entitled to the damages awarded by the district court. The district court awarded Levin $50,000.00 of earnest money because the failure to close on the purchase of Carriage Way was not Levin's fault. The DRA argues that Levin is not entitled to the earnest money because it never purchased any parcels of land.

The DRA attempts to deflect attention away from its conduct during Phase I and II by arguing that Levin's inaction in Phase III supports the finding that it is not entitled to the $50,000.00. According to the DRA, Levin is not entitled to recover the $50,000.00 because it never purchased any parcels during Phase III. This argument fails to consider the real reason for this outcome. The very reason the parties never reached Phase III, the actual development, was due to the evasive conduct of the DRA. To place blame on Levin for something that it not only had no control over, but was also in actuality the fault of the DRA, is an argument that we reject.

The DRA next claims that, in addition to the factual basis noted above, there is a legal basis for its argument that Levin is not entitled to the earnest money. It cites, as support for its position, *Schwartz v. Syver*, 264 Wis. 526, 529, 59 N.W.2d 489 (1953) (*quoting* 55 Am.Jur., Vendor and Purchaser, §535, p. 927), which notes: "So long as the vendor is not in default and is willing and able to perform, the purchaser cannot wrongfully refuse to complete the transaction and recover what he has paid toward the purchase money." The DRA fails to consider that the relationship in this case was not the typical buyer-seller relationship that this statement envisions. The DRA and Levin were more akin to partners in a business venture. Thus, the traditional vendor type analysis which the DRA refers to is legally inapposite to the underlying situation and we, therefore, find it unpersuasive. Levin's failure to close on the purchase price of Carriage Way was not its fault because the property was not available for conveyance before the termination of the contract and the trial court so found.

The DRA also contests the district court's ruling that Levin was entitled to recover $35,270.02 in billing fees. The DRA argues that the unpaid invoices were miscalculated. It claims Levin is not entitled to $35,270.02 because Levin did not consider contractor inefficiency in its calculation of the invoices. Thus, it merely disputes the accuracy of the numbers, not the validity of awarding the damages itself ...

... [W]e find the district court did not err in its determination of damages for the unpaid invoices.

The last issue relating to damages concerns the district court's denial of reliance damages to Levin. The district court denied Levin its reliance damages because its expenses were not incurred in reliance on any contractual obligation. The reliance damages requested by Levin would reimburse it for those expenses made in anticipation of Phase III property development. The district court's underlying reasoning for its decision centered around its finding that Levin subjectively believed it could terminate the contract without cause at anytime. On appeal, Levin argues the court erred and that it is entitled to its reliance damages.

Wisconsin law recognizes the propriety of reliance damages when proof of an expectation interest (profit) is uncertain. *Reimer v. Badger Wholesale Co.*, 147 Wis.2d 389, 433 N.W.2d 592, 594 (1988). The case at bar fits that description.

The purpose behind reliance damages is to reimburse the injured party so that he is put in "as good a position as he would have been in had the contract not been made." Restatement (Second) of Contracts § 344 (1981). The district court and the DRA give the definition of reliance damages a narrow reading. The district court noted, "Certainly the plaintiff incurred expenses in anticipation of development. But he did not do so in reliance on any contractual obligation of the defendant to proceed under the contract because he did not believe the DRA was obligated to proceed." The district court puts heavy emphasis on the phrase "contractual obligation," as if there must be some specific provision spelled out in the contract that must be relied upon for a party to recover expenses. The Restatement and case law are clear that an injured party has a right to damages based on expenditures "made in preparation for performance." Restatement (Second) of Contracts § 349(b) (1981); *Glendale Fed. Bank, FSB v. United States*, 239 F.3d 1374, 1383 (Fed.Cir.2001). Thus, reliance damages are not limited to those expenses made in relation to duties spelled out in the contractual agreement. The second vulnerable point in the district court's reasoning is that Levin is not entitled to reliance damages because it did not believe the DRA was obligated to proceed. The expenses at issue were not incurred before it made the contract. *See* Farnsworth, Contracts § 12.16, at 928 n. 2 (2d ed. 1990) ("Reliance damages are limited to those expenses incurred after an agreement has been reached"). We also believe that Levin would not perform the services and work it did (over $490,000 worth) without thinking the DRA would proceed with its end of the deal. The services Levin performed were the type that would have no value to them in another project or with a future client.

The district court analyzed the issue in a divisible time frame context. However, this project, like most complex ventures, cannot be viewed in such a fashion. Tasks such as infrastructure preparation, architectural design, and final construction plans must be developed far in advance of when they are actually to be worked on. Levin should not be punished simply for preparing for Phase III of the contract. The district court's position of viewing the contractual relationship in neat time frames led it to reject Levin's claim for reliance damages. Design, engineering, construction, and promotion costs were all incurred by Levin for its Phase III work. The precise reason the parties never reached Phase III was due to the various contract breaches of the DRA. These costs are a classic example of why reliance damages exist: to put the party in as good a position as he would have been in had the contract not been made. *See* Restatement (Second) of Contracts § 349(b) (1981).

We are not holding that any costs incurred before the contractual relationship was terminated comes under the guise of reliance damages. However, the expenses Levin incurred were made in reliance to its duties under Phase III of the redevelopment plan. If Levin had not undertaken these expenses when it did, the project would have been severely delayed. This redevelopment project was a complex, expensive, long-term undertaking. The parties interacted frequently and relied upon each other to achieve the goals of the redevelopment plan. Levin's duties included architectural work, infrastructure work, and design work which is highly technical and arduous. The expenses it incurred are a reflection of this process and the nature of the work. Without reliance damages, Levin would suffer a loss of expenses made in preparation for the Phase III redevelopment. Thus, we find the district court erred in denying reliance damages to Levin. We reverse and remand for a determination of an award of reliance damages consistent with the facts of the record.

CONCLUSION

For the foregoing reasons, we AFFIRM the district court's decision as it relates to the judgment in favor of Levin, and REVERSE and REMAND the matter concerning the denial of reliance damages to Levin.

Costs to be assessed against defendant-appellant.

Exercise 6-27: *Designer Direct* Revisited

1. D agreed to buy P's only boat (P was not a boat manufacturer or retailer). The boat had a FMV of $12,000; D agreed to pay $12,500. D breached. P reasonably resold the boat for $12,000 and, during the time P was looking for a new buyer, P spent $50 for upkeep on the boat, $200 for storage, and $75 for insurance. What damages can P recover?

2. In problem 1, what damages could P recover if P was able to reasonably resell the boat for $12,500? (Hint: This problem should suggest to you an additional situation where courts limit plaintiffs to reliance damages. What is that situation?)

3. D, a famous actor, entered into a contract with P film company to star in a film. At the time the parties made their contract, P already had hired a director ($2,000,000) and cinematographer ($500,000) and had rented some equipment needed for the film ($100,000). D was aware of these expenditures at the time the parties signed their contract. After the contract was signed, P hired a costume director ($50,000). D repudiated the contract. After six months of approaching every other possible famous actor and being rejected, P decided not to go forward with the project. Assume P made a reasonable effort to minimize damages.

   a. Why would P be unlikely to seek or recover benefit-of-the-bargain damages?

   b. Should P be allowed to recover damages based on expenditures made before the contract was signed?

   c. To what damages would P be entitled?

You have now learned about several situations in which a party may be limited to reliance damages. A party may also be limited to reliance damages in promissory estoppel cases. Before reading the relevant excerpt from the *Hoffman* case below, re-read the portion of the *Hoffman* opinion in Chapter 4. Also re-read section 90 of the RESTATEMENT (SECOND) OF CONTRACTS.

Hoffman v. Red Owl Stores, Inc.
26 Wis. 683, 133 N.W.2d 267 (1965)

Parnell, J. The complaint alleged that Lukowitz, as agent for Red Owl, represented to and agreed with plaintiffs that Red Owl would build a store building in Chilton and stock it with merchandise for Hoffman to operate in return for which plaintiffs were to put up and invest a total sum of $18,000; that in reliance upon the above mentioned agreement and representations plaintiffs sold their bakery building and business and their grocery store and business; also in reliance on the agreement and representations Hoffman purchased the building site in Chilton and rented a residence for himself and his family in Chilton; plaintiffs' actions in reliance on the representations and agreement disrupted their personal and business life; plaintiffs lost substantial amounts of income and expended large sums of money as expenses. Plaintiffs demanded recovery of damages for the breach of defendants' representations and agreements....

Damages

Defendants attack all the items of damages awarded by the jury.

The bakery building at Wautoma was sold at defendants' instigation in order that Hoffman might have the net proceeds available as part of the cash capital he was to invest in the Chilton store venture. The evidence clearly establishes that it was sold at a loss of $2,000. Defendants contend that half of this loss was sustained by Mrs. Hoffman because title stood in joint tenancy. They point out that no dealings took place between her and defendants as all negotiations were had with her husband. Ordinarily only the promisee and not third persons are entitled to enforce the remedy of promissory estoppel against the promisor. However, if the promisor actually foresees, or has reason to foresee, action by a third person in reliance on the promise, it may be quite unjust to refuse to perform the promise. 1A CORBIN, CONTRACTS, p. 220, sec. 200. Here not only did defendants foresee that it would be necessary for Mrs. Hoffman to sell her joint interest in the bakery building, but defendants actually requested that this be done. We approve the jury's award of $2,000 damages for the loss incurred by both plaintiffs in this sale.

Defendants attack on two grounds the $1,000 awarded because of Hoffman's payment of that amount on the purchase price of the Chilton lot. The first is that this $1,000 had already been lost at the time the final negotiations with Red Owl fell through in January, 1962, because the remaining $5,000 of purchase price had been due on October 15, 1961. The record does not disclose that the lot owner had foreclosed Hoffman's interest in the lot for failure to pay this $5,000. The $1,000 was not paid for the option, but had been paid as part of the purchase price at the time Hoffman elected to exercise the option. This gave him an equity in the lot which could not be legally foreclosed without affording Hoffman an opportunity to pay the balance. The second ground of attack is that the lot may have had a fair market value of $6,000, and Hoffman should have paid the remaining $5,000 of purchase price. We determine that it would be unreasonable to require Hoffman to have invested an additional $5,000 in order to protect the $1,000 he had paid. Therefore, we find no merit to defendants' attack upon this item of damages.

We also determine it was reasonable for Hoffman to have paid $125 for one month's rent of a home in Chilton after defendants assured him everything would be set when plaintiff sold the bakery building. This was a proper item of damage.

Plaintiffs never moved to Chilton because defendants suggested that Hoffman get some experience by working in a Red Owl store in the Fox River Valley. Plaintiffs, therefore, moved to Neenah instead of Chilton. After moving, Hoffman worked at night in an Appleton bakery but held himself available for work in a Red Owl store. The $140 moving expense would not have been incurred if plaintiffs had not sold their bakery building in Wautoma in reliance upon defendants' promises. We consider the $140 moving expense to be a proper item of damage.

We turn now to the damage item with respect to which the trial court granted a new trial, (*i. e.,* that arising from the sale of the Wautoma grocery store fixtures and inventory for which the jury awarded $16,735). The trial court ruled that Hoffman could not recover for any loss of future profits for the summer months following the sale on June 6, 1961, but that damages would be limited to the difference between the sales price received and fair market value of the assets sold, giving consideration to any goodwill attaching thereto by reason of the transfer of a going business. There was no direct evidence presented as to what this fair market value was on June 6, 1961. The evidence did disclose that Hoffman paid $9,000 for the inventory, added $1,500 to it and sold it for $10,000 or a loss of $500. His 1961 federal income tax return showed that the grocery equipment had been purchased for $7,000 and sold for $7,955.96. Plaintiffs introduced evidence of the buyer that during the first eleven weeks of operation of the grocery store his gross sales were $44,000 and his profit was $6,000 or roughly 15 percent. On cross-examination he admitted that this was gross and not net profit. Plaintiffs contend that in a breach of contract action damages may include loss of profits. However, this is not a breach of contract action.

The only relevancy of evidence relating to profits would be with respect to proving the element of goodwill in establishing the fair market value of the grocery inventory and fixtures sold. Therefore, evidence of profits would be admissible to afford a foundation for expert opinion as to fair market value.

Where damages are awarded in promissory estoppel instead of specifically enforcing the promisor's promise, they should be only such as in the opinion of the court are necessary to prevent injustice. Mechanical or rule of thumb approaches to the damage problem should be avoided. In discussing remedies to be applied by courts in promissory estoppel we quote the following views of writers on the subject:

> Enforcement of a promise does not necessarily mean specific performance. It does not necessarily mean damages for breach. Moreover the amount allowed as damages may be determined by the plaintiff's expenditures or change of position in reliance as well as by the value to him of the promised performance. Restitution is also an "enforcing" remedy, although it is often said to be based upon some kind of a rescission. In [determining] what justice requires, the court must remember all of its powers, derived from equity, law

merchant, and other sources, as well as the common law. Its decree should be molded accordingly.

1A CORBIN, CONTRACTS, p. 221, sec. 200.

> The wrong is not primarily in depriving the plaintiff of the promised reward but in causing the plaintiff to change position to his detriment. It would follow that the damages should not exceed the loss caused by the change of position, which would never be more in amount, but might be less, than the promised reward.

Seavey, *Reliance on Gratuitous Promises or Other Conduct*, 64 HARV. L. REV. 913, 926 (1951).

> There likewise seems to be no positive legal requirement, and certainly no legal policy, which dictates the allowance of contract damages in every case where the defendant's duty is consensual.

Shattuck, *Gratuitous Promises-A New Writ?*, 35 MICH. L. REV. 908, 912 (1936).

At the time Hoffman bought the equipment and inventory of the small grocery store at Wautoma he did so in order to gain experience in the grocery store business. At that time discussion had already been had with Red Owl representatives that Wautoma might be too small for a Red Owl operation and that a larger city might be more desirable. Thus Hoffman made this purchase more or less as a temporary experiment. Justice does not require that the damages awarded him, because of selling these assets at the behest of defendants, should exceed any actual loss sustained measured by the difference between the sales price and the fair market value.

Since the evidence does not sustain the large award of damages arising from the sale of the Wautoma grocery business, the trial court properly ordered a new trial on this issue. Order affirmed.

Exercise 6-28: *Hoffman* Revisited

Look at the other promissory estoppel cases you read in Chapter 4. In which of those cases would an award of only reliance damages have been an appropriate remedy? In which of those cases would benefit-of-the-bargain damages plus reliance damages seem most appropriate? Explain your answers.

Chapter Problem Revisited

You now know enough to fully analyze Exercises 6-1 and 6-2, which were introduced to you at the beginning of this chapter. The problems presented in Exercise 6-1 and 6-2 are similar to one you might be asked to analyze on a law school exam or in law practice. The first problem is a contract damage problem that asks you to prepare for a meeting with your client, Elizabeth. Your preparation should include making a list of documents to ask Elizabeth to bring to your meeting and a list of questions you plan to ask Elizabeth to determine damages. Although your client meeting is not an initial intake meeting like the meeting in Exercise 5-2 in Chapter 5, many of the skills discussed in connection with that exercise are equally applicable here. Accordingly, you may find it helpful to re-read the information provided for client interviews at the end of Chapter 5 (under "Chapter Problem Revisited," section B, "Exercise 5-2: Plymouth Shipping Supply Problem").

The second problem requires you to consider contract damages from the perspective of a client who wants to get out of (and so breach) an existing contract. You need to think about all the categories of damages you have encountered in this chapter in order to make a preliminary evaluation of the client's exposure and then analyze the legal effect of a damage waiver clause.

Professional Development Reflection Questions

1. Reflect on a positive experience that you've had so far in law school. What made the experience positive? What did you do that made the experience positive?

2. Reflect on a negative experience that you've had so far in law school. What made the experience negative? What did you do that made the experience negative? What would you do differently?

3. Imagine that you have been retained by Paula to represent her in a lawsuit against Dana for breach of contract. You successfully identify all of the facts, review the contract, and conclude that Pam has no case whatsoever on the merits. You advise her accordingly. Pam yells at you: "I'm the client here. I don't care if I have a case or not. I just know she'd rather settle with me than get involved in defending a lawsuit. So get busy preparing the papers. That's what I pay you for." What would you do?

Chapter 7

Restitution

Exercise 7-1: Chapter Problem

You are a lawyer who works for a law firm representing Priscilla Perkins in a lawsuit. The parties to the lawsuit, Danielle Dunworth and Perkins, have entered into the "Stipulation of Undisputed Facts" provided in Table 7-1 on the next page. Dunworth has moved for summary judgment regarding the following three issues:

1. As a matter of law, Perkins cannot recover any damages.

2. As a matter of law, Perkins cannot recover restitution.

3. As a matter of law, if Perkins were to recover restitution, Perkins's restitutionary recovery should be limited to $35,000.

You may assume that the State of Columbia recently unequivocally reaffirmed the New Business Rule and will not abandon that rule.

Your supervising partner has asked you to write the argument section of a "Memorandum in Opposition to Defendant's Motion for Summary Judgment," arguing that Perkins may recover damages, that she may recover restitution, and, if she does recover restitution, that the measure of her restitutionary recovery should be $45,000.

Remember that, as a practicing attorney, you should exercise your independent professional judgment and ensure that any work product you produce is either warranted by existing law or by a modification of existing law. If you believe that any or all of your supervising partner's positions are unwarranted and should not be argued to the court, write a separate inter-office memorandum to your supervising partner explaining why Perkins should concede each such issue.

Table 7-1: Stipulation of Undisputed Facts

United States District Court
Northern District of Columbia

Priscilla Perkins,
    Plaintiff
      v.   Case no: 2015-12345
Danielle Dunworth,
    Defendant

Stipulation of Undisputed Facts

Pursuant to the direction of the Court, the parties hereby submit the following stipulation of undisputed facts in connection with Danielle Dunworth's motion for summary judgment. This stipulation exclusively contains facts that are undisputed for purposes of the pending motion only. The parties reserve the right to argue whether certain facts are material to the legal issues before the Court. The parties also refer the Court to their respective pleadings, memoranda, declarations or affidavits, citations to authority, and other evidence that the parties have submitted for the record in connection with the pending motions.

The parties hereby stipulate and agree that the following facts are undisputed:

1.   After weeks of negotiations, Danielle Dunworth ("Dunworth") and Priscilla Perkins ("Perkins") were close to finalizing a deal by which Dunworth would sell Dunworth's land and home (known as "Orangeacre") to Perkins. On March 1, 20__, Perkins went to view the house one last time before making her final decision. During Perkins's final visit, Dunworth, hoping to convince Perkins to buy, said, "This house is so beautiful and is in such a restful spot that I feel like I am living in a bed & breakfast inn. Over the years, I have had four or five people express an interest in buying the place so they could convert it into a B & B." Perkins, who had already decided to convert Orangeacre into a Bed & Breakfast-style hotel, responded by saying, "That's a great idea! Given how much you are charging me for this place, I probably will have no choice but to do that."

2.   Later that day, Perkins and Dunworth signed a written, valid, and enforceable agreement whereby Danielle agreed to sell Orangeacre to Priscilla for $350,000. As part of the deal, Perkins agreed to pay and did pay Dunworth $35,000 as a down payment. Both parties' performances were due on May 1, 20__. The contract also provided that Perkins would hire a professional to conduct an inspection of the premises and that Dunworth would

cooperate with Perkins's architect, who was drawing up plans to remodel Orangeacre.

3.   On March 15, Perkins paid $2,000 for an inspection of Orangeacre, paid $5,000 to repave the driveway of Orangeacre, and paid $3,000 for an architect to draw up plans for converting Orangeacre into a Bed & Breakfast-style hotel.

4.   Dunworth, who was unaware that Perkins planned to repave the driveway, personally watched while the repaving company repaved the driveway (which greatly needed it), but she never said anything to the company or to Perkins about it.

5.   On April 1, 20__, Dunworth unequivocally and wrongfully repudiated the contract.

6.   After six months of trying, Perkins determined there were no other local properties appropriate for developing a Bed & Breakfast-style hotel.

7.   Perkins has sued Dunworth for breach of contract, seeking damages and restitution as alternative remedies.

8.   At all relevant times, the fair market value of Orangeacre was $300,000.

For Defendant Danielle Dunworth	**For Plaintiff Priscilla Perkins**
October 15, 20__	October 15, 20__
Law Offices of Lawyer & Solicitor	Law Offices of Barrister & Attorney
By: _Experienced Lawyer_	By: _Gifted Barrister_
Experienced Lawyer	Gifted Barrister
State Bar No. MHS-1289	State Bar No. DR-0932
1111 Columbia Street, Suite 1	1111 Columbia Street, Suite 10
Columbia City, Columbia 12345	Columbia City, Columbia 12345
Tel. (Voice): (007) 007-2222	Tel. (Voice): (007) 007-1111
(FAX): (007) 007-2221	(FAX): (007) 007-1112

Introduction to Restitution

Restitution is a unique topic in your study of contracts. Restitution is both a remedy for a breach of contract (and therefore part of the body of contract law) and its own, separate body of law. In fact, many law schools offer entire courses focused on restitution, or at least devote a substantial part of their remedies courses to a study of restitution. Given this fact, an in-depth study of restitution is impossible here. Rather, in this chapter you will learn mostly about the intersections between restitution and contract law.

At the outset, it will help you understand this area of law if you understand restitution-related terminology. Restitution is commonly referred to as "quasi-contract," "contract implied in law," "assumpsit," and "unjust enrichment." The first three terms exist largely as a by-product of the historical development of restitution. The early cases that recognized restitution as a separate theory of relief (in addition to contract and tort theories), disguised the innovation by describing restitution as a type of contract claim. The contract terminology is confusing, however, because restitution is not a type of contract claim. Restitution is the remedy for unjust enrichment, similar to how damages and specific performance are remedies for breaches of contracts. To avoid further confusion, we will only use the term "restitution" in this chapter.

We also will use the term "unjust enrichment" because unjust enrichment is the substantive claim on which a request for restitution must be based. In other words, unjust enrichment is a theory of recovery similar to tort or breach of contract. Although lawyers often label unjust enrichment claims as "common counts," claims "for money had and received," or "*quantum meruit*," we will use the term unjust enrichment in this chapter.

A claim for unjust enrichment has two elements: (1) a defendant obtained a benefit at a plaintiff's expense (an "enrichment"); and (2) defendant's retention of that benefit without compensating the plaintiff would be unfair ("unjust"). Look for both elements in each of the cases you read in this chapter.

You need to learn two skills with respect to restitution (similar to what you learned in the context of reliance damages). First, you need to learn to identify items as restitutionary recoveries. Second, you need to learn to analyze specific fact patterns to determine whether a plaintiff's recovery should be limited to restitution as the plaintiff's sole remedy. In addition, you will learn that the measure of restitution depends on the basis for awarding a plaintiff restitution. Accordingly, you will need to learn to state and apply differing measures of restitution.

Diagram 7-1 depicts where restitution fits in within the big picture of contract law. As you will see in Diagram 7-1, restitution is the second topic under "Contract Remedies." Below "Restitution" in Diagram 7-1, you will also see the major conceptual issues you will learn in this chapter.

As Diagram 7-1 reflects, restitution is available only if a defendant has been unjustly enriched. In this chapter, you will learn that courts distinguish parties who confer benefits under circumstances warranting restitution from parties referred to as "officious intermeddlers"—those who gratuitously confer benefits on others and who are not entitled to restitution. As Diagram 7-1 further reflects, there are four main circumstances under which a party is entitled to restitution:

1. A party has performed a contractual obligation, but normal damages for breach of contract would not be an efficacious remedy;

Diagram 7-1: Contract Law Graphic Organizer

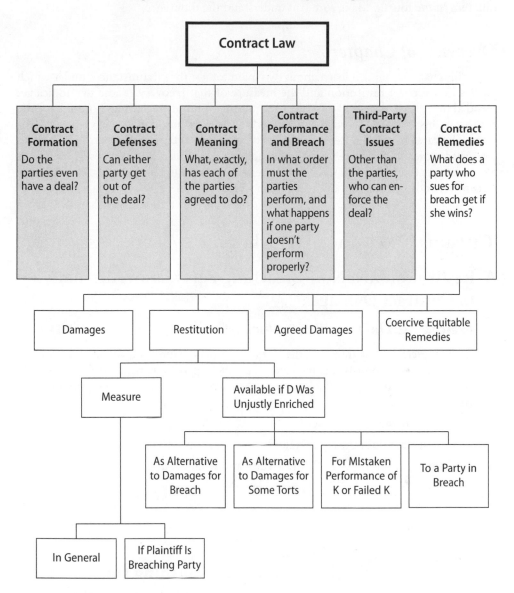

2. A party is a victim of a tort that not only harmed the victim but also benefitted the tortfeasor;

3. A party mistakenly over-performed a contract or mistakenly performed under an alleged contract a court has deemed unforeseeable or nonexistent; or

4. A party has partially performed a contract and then breached it, but the benefit to the non-breaching party of the party's partial performance exceeds the harm the breaching party caused.

The cases and materials in this chapter examine these four categories. The cases also explain the measure of restitution in each of these contexts. You will learn that the measure—the value of the wrongdoer's gain—is the same in the first three categories, but is different in the fourth. Make sure you understand the difference.

Overview of Chapter 7

In this chapter, you will learn about two main topics: the circumstances under which parties may recover restitution and the measure of that recovery. These two topics get blended together in nearly all published restitution opinions, including those you will be reading in this chapter. You will see that courts award restitution in a wide variety of contexts. The cases in this chapter are organized according to the four most common bases for awarding restitution as depicted in Diagram 7-1. As you read the cases in this chapter, make sure to identify and understand the circumstance under which the courts award restitution and the measures of restitutionary recovery.

Circumstances under Which Courts Award Restitution

A. Restitution to a Non-Breaching Party as an Alternative to Contract Damages

Exercise 7-2: *Chodos v. West Publishing Co.*

As depicted in Diagram 7-1, the first restitution situation you will learn about is restitution to a non-breaching party as an alternative to damages for breach of contract. *Chodos v. West Publishing Co.* provides an example of this situation. As you read *Chodos*, consider the following questions:

1. What are the relevant facts?

2. What rules does the court state?

3. How does the court apply those rules and what result does it reach?

Chodos v. West Publishing Co.

92 Fed. App. 471 (9th Cir. 2004)

Browning, J., Reinhardt, J. and Wardlaw, J. In an earlier case, *Chodos v. West Publishing Co.*, 292 F.3d 992 (9th Cir. 2002), this Court held that West Publishing Co. ("West") breached its contract with Rafael Chodos when it refused to publish his manuscript on the law of fiduciary duties and that Chodos was entitled to restitution. Chodos now appeals a jury verdict awarding him $300,000....

Chodos's main claim in this appeal is that the district court's jury instruction on the proper method for measuring recovery in *quantum meruit* was erroneous under California law....

In California, "[t]he measure of recovery in *quantum meruit* is the reasonable value of the services rendered, provided they were of direct benefit to the defendant." [Citations omitted.] California courts have adopted a subsidiary definition of the reasonable value of a plaintiff's services: the amount that it would have cost the defendant to obtain the services from another person. [Citation omitted.] Alternatively, California courts have formulated this measure as the amount the defendant would have had to pay on the "open market" to obtain the same services, or the "comparable charge" for such services. [Citations omitted]; *See* Restatement (Second) of Contracts § 371, cmt. a....

Chodos further argues that his recovery in *quantum meruit* must be measured by the value to him of the time and effort he reasonably invested in preparing the manuscript, which he contends is the amount he could have earned in legal fees as a practitioner over the two years he devoted to writing his manuscript. However, the case upon which Chodos relies, *Earhart v. William Low Co.* [Full case cites omitted], "merely held ... that where the defendant urged the plaintiff to render services to a third party the plaintiff could still be compensated in *quantum meruit* for those services." [Citation omitted.] *Earhart* did not address the proper measure of compensation for those who have made out a valid claim for recovery in *quantum meruit*. Chodos has pointed to no California precedent measuring recovery in *quantum meruit* by the plaintiff's lost business opportunities. The district court properly allowed Chodos to present evidence of his lost business opportunities to the jury, since such evidence was relevant to a determination of what Chodos would have received if the parties had negotiated a lump sum payment for the services rendered. However, the trial judge was also correct in rejecting Chodos's proposed jury instruction, which would have required the jury to equate restitution with Chodos's lost business opportunities....

Finally, Chodos claims that the jury verdict of $300,000 was not supported by substantial evidence. The jury considered evidence on the expected value of the contract at its inception, supplemented by Chodos's and West's conflicting testimony as to the compensation that West would have offered to pay and a practicing attorney like Chodos would have accepted to produce the treatise. The jury's estimation of the reasonable value of Chodos's services based on the extensive testimony presented was within its discretion.

Because West's claims on cross-appeal are conditioned on a reversal of the jury verdict, we do not address them.

Affirmed.

Exercise 7-3: *United States v. Algernon Blair, Inc.*

The next case you will read, *United States v. Algernon Blair, Inc.*, is tricky and, at least arguably, incorrectly decided. As you read this case, consider the following questions:

1. Who was claiming restitution?

2. What are the key facts?

3. What rules does the court state?

4.   How does the court apply those rules and what result does it reach?

United States v. Algernon Blair, Inc.
479 F.2d 638 (4th Cir. 1973)

Craven, J. May a subcontractor, who justifiably ceases work under a contract because of the prime contractor's breach, recover in *quantum meruit* the value of labor and equipment already furnished pursuant to the contract irrespective of whether he would have been entitled to recover in a suit on the contract? ...

The subcontractor, Coastal Steel Erectors, Inc., brought this action ... in the name of the United States against Algernon Blair, Inc., and its surety, United States Fidelity and Guaranty Company. Blair had entered a contract with the United States for the construction of a naval hospital in Charleston County, South Carolina. Blair had then contracted with Coastal to perform certain steel erection and supply certain equipment in conjunction with Blair's contract with the United States. Coastal commenced performance of its obligations, supplying its own cranes for handling and placing steel. Blair refused to pay for crane rental, maintaining that it was not obligated to do so under the subcontract. Because of Blair's failure to make payments for crane rental, and after completion of approximately 28 percent of the subcontract, Coastal terminated its performance. Blair then proceeded to complete the job with a new subcontractor. Coastal brought this action to recover for labor and equipment furnished.

The district court ... found that under the contract the amount due Coastal, less what had already been paid, totaled approximately $37,000. Additionally, the court found Coastal would have lost more than $37,000 if it had completed performance. Holding that any amount due Coastal must be reduced by any loss it would have incurred by complete performance of the contract, the court denied recovery to Coastal. While the district court correctly stated the "'normal' rule of contract damages," we think Coastal is entitled to recover in *quantum meruit*.

In *United States for Use of Susi Contracting Co. v. Zara Contracting Co* ... the court was faced with a situation similar to that involved here—the prime contractor had unjustifiably breached a subcontract after partial performance by the subcontractor. [Citation omitted.] The court stated:

> For it is an accepted principle of contract law, often applied in the case of construction contracts, that the promisee upon breach has the option to forego any suit on the contract and claim only the reasonable value of his performance.

...

Quantum meruit recovery is not limited to an action against the prime contractor but may also be brought against the Miller Act surety, as in this case. [Citation omitted.] Further, that the complaint is not clear in regard to the theory of a plaintiff's recovery does not preclude recovery under *quantum meruit*....

In the present case, Coastal has, at its own expense, provided Blair with labor and the use of equipment. Blair, who breached the subcontract, has retained these benefits without having fully paid for them. On these facts, Coastal is entitled to restitution in *quantum meruit*.

The "restitution interest," involving a combination of unjust impoverishment with unjust gain, presents the strongest case for relief. If ... we regard the purpose of justice as the maintenance of an equilibrium of goods among members of society, the restitution interest presents twice as strong a claim to judicial intervention as the reliance interest....

The impact of *quantum meruit* is to allow a promisee to recover the value of services he gave to the defendant irrespective of whether he would have lost money on the contract and been unable to recover in a suit on the contract. [Citation omitted.] The measure of recovery for *quantum meruit* is the reasonable value of the performance, Restatement of Contracts § 347 (1932); and recovery is undiminished by any loss which would have been incurred by complete performance. 12 Williston on Contracts § 1485, at 312 (3d ed. 1970). While the contract price may be evidence of reasonable value of the services, it does not measure the value of the performance or limit recovery.[7] Rather, the standard for measuring the reasonable value of the services rendered is the amount for which such services could have been purchased from one in the plaintiff's position at the time and place the services were rendered.

Since the district court has not yet accurately determined the reasonable value of the labor and equipment use furnished by Coastal to Blair, the case must be remanded for those findings. When the amount has been determined, judgment will be entered in favor of Coastal, less payments already made under the contract. Accordingly, for the reasons stated above, the decision of the district court is reversed and remanded with instructions.

Exercise 7-4: *Algernon Blair* Revisited

1. Why was the United States the named plaintiff?

2. What is the relationship between restitution and what the court calls *quantum meruit*?

3. Why couldn't the claimant in this case recover benefit-of-the-bargain damages?

4. Why didn't the claimant in this case want reliance damages?

5. In what sense was Algernon Blair unjustly enriched? (Apply the two elements of unjust enrichment.)

6. How did the court measure the claimant's restitutionary recovery?

---

7. [Citations omitted.] It should be noted, however, that in suits for restitution there are many cases permitting the plaintiff to recover the value of benefits conferred on the defendant, even though this value exceeds that of the return performance promised by the defendant. In these cases it is no doubt felt that the defendant's breach should work a forfeiture of his right to retain the benefits of an advantageous bargain. [Citation omitted.]

7. Why do you think many commentators and courts have asserted that the recovery by the claimant in this case was a bad decision? Do you agree with the decision or with its critics? Why?

8. What is the policy basis for the court's decision? What policy does the court's decision undermine?

9. The claimant in this case would have recovered nothing by way of restitution if, at the time of breach, all the claimant had done was gather the materials and rent the machinery it was planning to use in performing the contract. *See* section 370, illustration 2, in the RESTATEMENT (SECOND) OF CONTRACTS. Reconcile the result in illustration 2 with the result in *Algernon Blair*.

10. Paula and David entered into a contract to buy and sell for $100,000 an abstract painting painted by David. Paula paid David $10,000 as a down payment. David breached the contract. If the fair market value of the painting is $100,000, what would Paula recover as damages? What would she recover as restitution? Which remedy should she choose?

B. Restitution as an Alternative to Suing for a Tort

As depicted in Diagram 7-1, the second restitution situation is restitution as an alternative to suing for a tort. It is well settled that, if a defendant obtains a benefit by committing a tort, such as conversion or trespass to land, the defendant may be required to pay restitution based on the value obtained. *See, e.g., Olwell v. Nye & Nissen Co.*, 26 Wash.2d 282 (1946) (benefit obtained by defendant's conversion of plaintiff's egg-washing machine); *Edwards v. Lee's Administrator*, 265 Ky. 418 (1936) (benefit obtained by defendant's unauthorized use, *i.e.*, trespass, of a portion of a cave under plaintiff's land as a for-profit tourist attraction).

Exercise 7-5: Restitution as an Alternative to Suing for a Tort

1. Dave converts Riley's car, worth $10,000, and sells it to Cindy for $12,000. What may Riley recover as damages? May Riley recover restitution? If so, what may Riley recover as restitution?

2. Danielle accidentally crashes her car into Ben's car, causing Ben's car to need $5,000 in repairs. What may Ben recover as damages? May Ben recover restitution? If so, what may Ben recover as restitution?

3. Darci operates Darci's cement factory in a way that causes cement dust to rain on Jeff's property. Jeff sues for restitution, seeking Darci's profits from operating the factory in this way. Most courts would deny Jeff's request. Why?

C. Restitution for Mistaken Performance of an Alleged Contract

As depicted in Diagram 7-1, the third restitution situation is for the mistaken performance of an alleged contract. A party can obtain restitution if she mistakenly over performs an existing contract or if she performs pursuant to a contract which turns out to be unenforceable. For instance, if a tenant inadvertently pays her rent twice, most courts would allow the tenant to recover the overpayment. Or, if a contract is unenforceable due to a failure to comply with an applicable statute of frauds, most courts would allow a party to recover money paid. So, if a land buyer enters into an oral contract to buy land for $200,000 and pays a $20,000 down payment, most courts would allow the buyer to recover the down payment as restitution. In a similar vein, if the buyer had already taken possession of the land and improved the land by adding a building, the buyer could recover the increase in value caused by the improvement.

Exercise 7-6: *Earhart v. William Low Co.*

While it is relatively easy to understand the concept of restitution for the mistaken performance of a contract in the abstract, the principle can be tricky to apply to actual factual situations — especially where it is hard to discern any benefit to the party from whom restitution is sought. The next case, *Earhart v. William Low Co.*, provides you an example of this situation. As you read *Earhart*, consider the following questions:

1. What are the relevant facts?

2. What distinction does the court make between the work the plaintiff did on the Pillow property and the work the plaintiff did on the Low property?

3. What was the significance of that distinction as far as the trial court was concerned?

4. What does the *Earhart* court conclude about the significance of that distinction? Why?

5. Most experts agree that the court's conclusions with respect to the work the plaintiff did on the Pillow property reflect an expansive approach to restitutionary liability. Explain why.

Earhart v. William Low Co.

25 Cal.3d 503, 600 P.2d 1344 (1979)

Tobriner, Justice. In this case we must determine whether a party who expends funds and performs services at the request of another, under the reasonable belief that the requesting party will compensate him for such services, may recover in *quantum meruit* although the expenditures and services do not directly benefit property owned by the requesting party.

In the instant case, plaintiff asserts that, at defendant's request, he expended sums in commencing the construction of a mobile home park on land owned by defendant and on an adjacent parcel owned by a third party. When defendant refused to compensate plaintiff for any of the services so rendered, plaintiff sued in *quantum meruit*.

While permitting plaintiff to recover the sums which he expended on the parcel actually owned by defendant, the trial court denied plaintiff recovery for the expenses incurred in construction on the adjoining parcel, reasoning that under past California cases defendant received no direct "benefit" from construction on the property that he did not own. Plaintiff now appeals from the trial court's adverse judgment limiting his recovery, contending that he should be permitted to recover in *quantum meruit* despite the absence of defendant's ownership of the adjoining parcel.

As we shall explain, plaintiff is entitled to prove defendant's liability for the reasonable value of plaintiff's services rendered on both parcels of land. The trial court in the instant case apparently felt constrained to limit plaintiff's recovery because of this court's decision in *Rotea v. Izuel,* 14 Cal. 2d 605, 95 P.2d 927 (1939). In that case the court denied quasi-contractual recovery on the ground that the only "benefit" received by the defendant was the "incidental benefit" which he may have found in the satisfaction of obtaining compliance with his request.

In view of the facts of the present case, we reject such a broad limitation of the remedy of *quantum meruit*. Here, plaintiff claims that defendant urged him to begin work on the mobile home park for which he and defendant had long been negotiating. Plaintiff further asserts that, under defendant's supervision, he immediately commenced construction, justifiably relying on his belief that defendant would pay for the requested performance. If the trial court finds these facts to be true and, thus, that plaintiff rendered the very performance that defendant requested, we believe that principles of fairness support plaintiff's recovery for the reasonable value of his labor....

Plaintiff Fayette L. Earhart is the president and owner of Earhart Construction Company. For approximately two months in early 1971, plaintiff and defendant William Low, on behalf of defendant William Low Company, engaged in negotiations for the construction of the Pana Rama Mobile Home Park. These negotiations culminated in a construction contract which was to become binding when defendant obtained the requisite financing to build the park and when plaintiff secured a labor and material or performance bond for the work. Neither condition was ever fulfilled.

The proposed park was to cover a number of acres, some of which defendant owned, and the balance of which were owned by Ervie Pillow. In May 1971 defendant and Pillow entered into an escrow agreement in which Pillow agreed to sell her tract to defendant on the condition that defendant obtain financing for the mobile home park. According to plaintiff, a "special use permit" allowing the construction of a mobile home park on Pillow's land was of particular interest to defendant. Plaintiff claimed that the permit would expire on May 27, 1971, without possibility of renewal, unless work on the property were "diligently under way" by that date.

Plaintiff maintained that on May 25, 1971, defendant telephoned him to inform him that he had secured the necessary financing for the park, and, waiving all conditions to the contract, urged plaintiff to move equipment onto the property and commence work immediately in order to "save" the special use permit. Plaintiff's crew began work at once and continued to work for one week, often in the presence of defendant. On June 1, 1971, plaintiff submitted a progress bill to defendant and at that time learned that defendant had not secured the requisite financing. Defendant refused to pay plaintiff's bill, revealing that in the interim he had signed a construction contract for the park with another firm.

At trial, defendant took issue with a number of plaintiff's assertions. According to defendant, the validity of the Pillow permit was irrelevant to his plan to construct a mobile home park since he had obtained a permit himself, and, as he testified, "As long as I had my permit, [Pillow's auto] court could be developed." Furthermore, defendant denied telephoning plaintiff and asserted that he had never asked plaintiff to work "specifically" on the Pillow property. Rather, defendant claimed that plaintiff began construction before either of the conditions to the written agreement had been met, in order to get "kind of a leg up there in [defendant's] eyes towards getting the contract eventually.... [Plaintiff] was going to take a gamble in there subject to requisite financing" and without charge to defendant.

At the conclusion of the trial, the court determined that plaintiff was entitled to recover from defendant on a theory of *quantum meruit*. Stating that "[g]enerally speaking, the court has a tendency to believe the testimony of Mr. Earhart and to disbelieve the testimony of Mr. Low," the trial court specifically found that plaintiff had furnished machinery, labor, and materials to defendant's property "at the special instance and request of defendant."

In assessing the amount of the ... [restitution] to which plaintiff was entitled under *quantum meruit*, however, the court limited plaintiff's recovery to the reasonable value of the work done on defendant's tract, declining to award damages for the reasonable value of services rendered in construction on the Pillow property. Acknowledging that plaintiff's services "were furnished both to the Pillow property and to the Low property," the trial court interpreted this court's decision in *Rotea v. Izuel, supra*, 14 Cal. 2d 605, 95 P.2d 927, as precluding plaintiff's recovery with respect to the work on the Pillow property. The court stated in this regard:

> [I]t is an established proposition of law in California ... that you can't get recovery for services furnished to a third person, even though the services were furnished at the request of the defendant....
> So the plaintiff can't recover for services furnished Mrs. Pillow....
> [E]ven though the plaintiff renders services or delivers a product, if it is of no value to the defendant, then the defendant doesn't pay for it. All he pays for is the value of what he got, notwithstanding how much it cost the plaintiff to produce it. That's the proper measure in this case.

Because the court construed the governing cases as barring recovery for work on the Pillow property as a matter of law, the court made no factual findings as to whether plaintiff had actually furnished labor and materials to the Pillow property at defendant's request nor as to the value of any work that may have been done. Plaintiff now appeals from the trial court judgment insofar as it denied him recovery for services allegedly rendered with regard to the adjoining Pillow parcel....

While the result which the court reached in *Rotea* is understandable in light of the mutual exchange of familial support which the record indicates, the court's statement that the satisfaction of obtaining compliance with one's request will not support *quantum meruit* recovery has ever since its rendition been criticized for its harshness. Commentators have attacked the requirement of a "direct benefit" to the defendant as "purely an historical one...."

While the unfair receipt of a tangible benefit to the defendant may have inspired the common law courts to order restitution, the court in *Rotea* need not have interpreted the ancient principle of unjust enrichment so literally. Even under contemporary authorities, the court could have recognized, consistent with the orthodox principle of unjust enrichment, that a defendant who receives the satisfaction of obtaining another person's compliance with the defendant's request to perform services incurs an obligation to pay for labor and materials expended in reliance on that request.

Section 1 of the Restatement of Restitution, which predates the decision in *Rotea*, provides that "[a] person who has been unjustly enriched at the expense of another is required to make restitution to the other." Rest., Restitution (1937) section 1. A person is enriched if he has "received a benefit." *Id.*, com. a., p. 12. Furthermore, "[a] person confers a benefit upon another if he ... performs services Beneficial to or at the request of the other...." *Id.*, com. b., p. 12 (emphasis added). While the Restatement does not establish that performance of services at the request of another uniformly results in the unjust retention of "benefit," the Restatement recognizes, unlike the decision in *Rotea*, that performance of services at another's behest may itself constitute "benefit" such that an obligation to make restitution may arise....[5]

Finally, section 90 of the Restatement of Contracts the so-called "promissory estoppel" section provides that reasonably expected reliance may under some circumstances make binding a promise for which nothing has been given or promised in exchange....

In view of the equitable considerations lying at the foundation of these several doctrines ... we conclude that compensation for a party's performance should be paid by the person whose request induced the performance. In light of this conclusion, the portion of the judgment denying plaintiff recovery with respect to the Pillow property must be reversed. As we have explained, plaintiff's evidence indicated that he had performed services and furnished materials in work on the Pillow property at the urgent request of defendant. Moreover, according to plaintiff, the work was performed under circumstances in which plaintiff reasonably relied upon the belief that defendant would pay for it....

The judgment is reversed and the case is remanded to the trial court for further proceedings consistent with this opinion.

---

5. We note that while restitution ordinarily connotes the return of something which one party has "received" from another, the term may also refer to a broader obligation to pay. Thus, "(i)t is enough that the plaintiff has rendered the very performance for which the defendant bargained.... Service or forbearance rendered at the defendant's request is regarded as having been received by him; and the fair price that it would have cost to obtain this service or forbearance from a person in the plaintiff's position can be recovered. Judgment will be given for the value of services so rendered, ... even though there never was any product created by the service that added to the wealth of the defendant." [Citations omitted.]

D. Restitution to a Party Who Has Breached a Contract

Exercise 7-7: *Kutzin v. Pirnie*

As depicted in Diagram 7-1, the fourth situation when restitution is granted is when a party has breached a contract and that breaching party sues for restitution. The next case, *Kutzin v. Pirnie,* provides an example of this situation. As you read *Kutzin,* answer the following questions:

1. What are the relevant facts?

2. The court notes the traditional common law rule that a party who breaches a contract cannot recover restitution. The court then abandons that rule. Why?

3. Is the court's decision to abandon the traditional rule useful from a policy perspective? Why or why not?

4. What is the measure of restitutionary relief for a party in breach of contract according to the *Kutzin* court?

5. Why is that measure different from the measure in other restitution cases?

Kutzin v. Pirnie

124 N.J. 500, 591 A.2d 932 (1991)

Clifford, J. This is an action on a contract for the sale of residential property. The sellers' real-estate agent prepared the contract, after which defendants, the prospective buyers, signed it, paid a deposit of nearly ten percent of the purchase price, and then decided not to go through with the purchase. In the trial court the buyers argued that the contract had been rescinded because attorneys for both parties had sought to amend it during the three-day period provided by the contract's attorney-review clause. The court found the contract to be valid and awarded the sellers compensatory damages, albeit in an amount less than the deposit. The Appellate Division agreed that the contract is binding but held that the sellers are entitled to keep the entire deposit as damages. We granted certification ... to determine whether the contract is enforceable and, if so, whether the sellers should be allowed to keep the deposit. We affirm the Appellate Division holding that the contract is valid but modify that court's judgment on the issue of damages and reinstate the damage award of the trial court.

[I.] On September 1, 1987, defendants, Duncan and Gertrude Pirnie, and plaintiffs, Milton and Ruth Kutzin, signed a contract for the sale of the Kutzins' house in Haworth for $365,000. The contract, which is the standard-form real-estate sales contract adopted by the New Jersey Association of Realtors, had been prepared by Weichert Realtors (Weichert), the sellers' real-estate agent. Under its terms, the Pirnies agreed to pay a partial deposit of $1,000 on signing the contract and the remainder of the deposit, $35,000, within seven days. In compliance therewith, the Pirnies made out a check for $1,000 to the trust account of Russo Real Estate (Russo), their real-estate agent. The contract does not contain a "forfeiture" or "liquidated damages" clause; with reference to the disposition of the deposit should the sale not take place, the contract merely states, "If this contract is voided by either party, the escrow monies shall be disbursed pursuant to the written direction of both parties."

[The Pirnies decided not to make the purchase and communicated that decision to the Kutzins.]

The Kutzins refused to return the deposit and promptly sued for specific performance of the contract. The Pirnies counterclaimed for return of their $36,000 deposit, contending that the contract had been validly rescinded either pursuant to the attorney-review provision or by agreement of the parties. Because the Kutzins sold the house to another buyer for $352,500 while the case was pending, they amended their complaint to seek only damages.

The trial court ruled that the parties had entered into a binding contract that had not been rescinded either by agreement or pursuant to the attorney-review clause. Consequently, the court held that the sellers were entitled to $17,325 in damages. That amount consisted of the $12,500 difference between the $365,000 the Pirnies had contracted to pay and the $352,500 for which the house eventually sold; $3,825 in utilities, real-estate taxes, and insurance expenses the Kutzins had incurred during the six-month period between the originally-anticipated closing date and the date of actual sale; and $1,000 the Kutzins had paid for a new basement carpet, which their realtor had recommended they buy to enhance the attractiveness of their house to prospective buyers. The court ordered the Kutzins to return the $18,675 balance of the deposit to the Pirnies.

On appeal, the Kutzins argued that ... they should be allowed to retain the deposit. On cross-appeal the Pirnies claimed entitlement to the entire deposit, again asserting that the contract had been validly rescinded. In an unreported opinion, the Appellate Division found that the contract between the parties "was enforceable according to its terms...." The court then noted that "the Kutzins' loss as determined by the trial court was less than the Pirnies' $36,000 deposit," and concluded that "the Kutzins are entitled to retain the [entire] deposit, but they may not recover any additional amount as damages...."

[III.] We next determine whether the Kutzins are entitled to retain the entire $36,000 deposit as damages. The issue of whether a seller should be entitled to retain a deposit when a buyer breaches a contract that does not contain a liquidated-damages or forfeiture clause has long troubled courts. As Professor Williston has observed, "Few questions in the law have given rise to more discussion and difference of opinion than that concerning the right of one who has materially broken his contract without legal excuse to recover for such benefit [here, the deposit] as he may have conferred on the other party...." 12 S. Williston, A Treatise on the Law of Contracts § 1473 at 220 (3d ed. 1961).

A. "[T]he common-law rule, which has been very generally followed..., [was] that where the vendee of real property makes a part payment on the purchase price, but fails to fulfill the contract without lawful excuse, he cannot recover the payment ... even though the vendor may have made a profit by reason of the default." [Citations omitted.] The thought behind that rule is that "restitution should always be refused, for the good and sufficient reason that the [buyer] is guilty of a breach of contract and should never be allowed to have advantage from his own wrong." [Citations omitted.]

New Jersey traditionally has adhered to the common-law rule....

Following that long line of cases, the Appellate Division held that the Kutzins are entitled to retain the deposit even though the court was "sympathetic to the trial judge's ruling that the Pirnies were entitled to the return of the balance of their $36,000 contract deposit in excess of the Kutzins' actual damages."

B. Despite the ample authority supporting the Appellate Division's disposition of the damages question, "there has been a growing recognition of the injustice that often results from the application of the rule permitting total forfeiture of part payments under a contract of sale." *Great United Realty Co. v. Lewis*, 203 Md. 442, 448, 101 A.2d 881, 883 (1954). *See also Quillen v. Kelley, supra*, 216 Md. at 402, 140 A.2d at 520 ("In applying [the common-law] rule, there have been instances of harshness and injustice, which have caused a reconsideration of the same, in recent years, by the courts and by learned and renowned scholars and text-writers on the subject of contracts.").

Professor Corbin led the movement favoring departure from the strict common-law rule. In *The Right of a Defaulting Vendee to the Restitution of Installments Paid*, 40 Yale L.J. 1013, 1013 (1931), he stated:

> If a contractor has committed a total breach of his contract, having rendered no performance whatever thereunder, no penalty or forfeiture will be enforced against him; he will be required to do no more than to make the injured party whole by paying full compensatory damages. In like manner, a contractor who commits a breach after he has rendered part performance must also make the injured party whole by payment of full compensatory damages. The part performance rendered, however, may be much more valuable to the defendant than the amount of the injury caused by the breach; and in such case, to allow the injured party to retain the benefit of the part performance so rendered, without making restitution of any part of such value, is the enforcement of a penalty or forfeiture against the contract-breaker.

Corbin went on to declare that if a plaintiff "can and does show by proper evidence that the defendant is holding an amount of money as a penalty rather than as compensation for injury, he should be given judgment for restitution of that amount." *Id.* at 1025–26 (footnote omitted). He then concluded that

> [t]he cases denying restitution can ... be justified on one or more of the following grounds: (1) The defendant has not rescinded and remains ready and willing to perform, and still has a right to specific performance by the vendee; (2) the plaintiff has not shown that the injury caused by his breach is less than the installments received by the defendant; (3) there is an express provision that the money may be retained by the vendor and the facts are such as to make this a genuine provision for liquidated damages, and not one for a penalty or forfeiture. If the facts are such that none of these justifications exists, restitution should be allowed. Id. at 1032–33 (footnote omitted)....

Section 374(1) of the Restatement (Second) of Contracts is based on section 357 but "is more liberal in allowing recovery in accord with the policy behind Uniform Commercial Code §2-718(2)." Restatement (Second) of Contracts §374 reporter's note (1981). That section sets forth the rule as follows:

> [I]f a party justifiably refuses to perform on the ground that his remaining duties of performance have been discharged by the other party's breach, the party in breach is entitled to restitution for any benefit that he has conferred by way of part performance or reliance in excess of the loss that he has caused by his own breach. *Id.* §374(1).

Particularly relevant to this case is the following illustration:

> A contracts to sell land to B for $100,000, which B promises to pay in $10,000 installments before transfer of title. After B has paid $30,000 he fails to pay the remaining installments and A sells the land to another buyer for $95,000. B can recover $30,000 from A in restitution less $5,000 damages for B's breach of contract, or $25,000. If A does not sell the land to another buyer and obtains a decree of specific performance against B, B has no right to restitution. *Id.* §374 illustration 1....

With the issue squarely presented in this case, we overrule those New Jersey cases adhering to the common-law rule and adopt the modern approach set forth in section 374(1) of the Restatement (Second) of Contracts. In Professor Williston's words, "to deny recovery [in this situation] often gives the [seller] more than fair compensation for the injury he has sustained and imposes a forfeiture (which the law abhors) on the [breaching buyer]." 12 Williston, *supra*, §1473 at 222. The approach that we adopt is suggested to have the added benefit of promoting economic efficiency: penalties deter "efficient" breaches of contract "by making the cost of the breach to the contract breaker greater than the cost of the breach to the victim." R. Posner, Economic Analysis of Law §4.10 at 116 (3d ed. 1986).

C. We conclude that the Pirnies are entitled, under the Restatement formulation of damages, to restitution for any benefit that they conferred by way of part performance or reliance in excess of the loss that they caused by their own breach. *See* Restatement (Second) of Contracts, *supra*, §374(1). We stress, however, that "[o]ne who charges an unjust enrichment has the burden of proving it...."

The trial court found that the Kutzins had suffered $17,325 in damages, a figure that we accept because it is not challenged in this Court. The Pirnies' deposit of $36,000 exceeded the injury caused by their breach by $18,675, and they are thus entitled to recovery of that amount.

Our holding is not affected by the fact that the $36,000 deposit was less than ten percent of the $365,000 purchase price. [Citation omitted.] Whenever the breaching buyer proves that the deposit exceeds the seller's actual damages suffered as a result of the breach, the buyer may recover the difference.

[IV.] To ensure that our opinion not be misread, we emphasize that the contract at issue does not contain a forfeiture or liquidated-damages clause; it merely states, "If this contract is voided by either party, the escrow monies shall be disbursed pursuant to the written direction of both parties." The contract is otherwise silent on the subject of what would happen to the deposit were the sale not to occur. Had the contract contained a liquidated-damages clause, this case would have been governed by section 374(2) of the Restatement (Second) of Contracts, which states:

> To the extent that, under the manifested assent of the parties, a party's performance is to be retained in the case of breach, that party is not entitled to restitution if the value of the performance as liquidated damages is reasonable in the light of the anticipated loss caused by the breach and the difficulties of proof of loss....

[V.] The Pirnies are entitled to restitution of their deposit less the amount of the injury to the Kutzins caused by the Pirnies' breach. To allow retention of the entire deposit would unjustly enrich the Kutzins and would penalize the Pirnies contrary to the policy behind our law of contracts.

The judgment of the Appellate Division is modified to reinstate the trial court's damage award. As modified the judgment is affirmed.

Exercise 7-8: Restitution Wrap-Up

1.   Jacob contracted with Dawn to build Dawn a church edifice. Jacob finished the building and Dawn took possession. The building's ceiling was two feet lower than promised, the windows were shorter and narrower than promised, and the seats were narrower than promised. Jacob's breach was in good faith. Dawn objected to the errors, although Dawn was able to make full use of the building. The building could not be fixed without taking partially demolishing and rebuilding it. Because the building was designed to be a church and was fully functional as a church, the defects had no effect on the value of the building. Jacob sued for restitution based on the reasonable value of his services. Analyze whether Jacob's restitution claim will succeed.

2.   Create a chart depicting the various circumstances under which a party can get restitution and the measure of recovery under each of those circumstances.

Chapter Problem Revisited

In Exercise 7-1 at the beginning of the chapter, your supervising partner asked you to draft the argument section for a brief in opposition to Danielle's motion for summary judgment. Review the problem presented in Exercise 7-1. You should now understand restitution well enough complete your assigned task.

The following tips will help you draft your argument:

1.   You may recall from your civil procedure course that granting a motion for summary judgment requires meeting a two-pronged test: (1) demonstrating that there are no material facts in dispute, and (2) demonstrating that a party is entitled to judgment as a matter of law. In this case, the parties have stipulated that there are no disputed facts. Therefore, your argument should only address

the second summary judgment prong: that a party is entitled to judgment as a matter of law.

2. Organize your argument using the three points your supervising partner has asked you to address. Use each of the three points as headings and develop an argument for each point, or, if you conclude there isn't a good faith basis for making a particular argument, omit that point from your argument and explain your position in an inter-office memorandum to your supervising partner.

3. In each section of your argument, make sure that you touch all the following bases:

    a. Begin each section by asserting your conclusion for that section.

    b. After your conclusion, state the applicable legal rules that you have learned in your contracts course.

    c. Next, apply the rules to the factual situation presented.

    d. Provide an explicit conclusion for each section of your argument.

4. Carefully edit your argument to ensure that your writing is clear, concise, and precise.

Professional Development Reflection Questions

1. Earlier in this text, you learned the importance of becoming an expert learner and about the self-regulated model of learning. You may recall that the third step in the self-regulated learning model is reflecting on your learning. To what extent do you already engage in regular self-reflection about your learning?

2. Educational research demonstrates that there are several benefits to taking the time to self-assess your own learning: students who do so learn more effectively, better recall what they have learned, and also develop higher-level analytical skills. Take the time to reflect on your learning while you were studying this chapter. Identify three take-home points you can use to ensure that your learning is more effective as you start the next chapter.

3. Self-assessment is also critical as a practicing attorney: "Throughout an attorney's professional life, success in practice will depend on the ability to self-assess professional performance, behavior, and attitudes. An indispensable trait of the truly competent lawyer, at whatever stage of career development, is that of knowing the extent and limits of one's competence: what one can do and what requires the assistance of others."[1] To develop the habit of this type of self-assessment, regularly ask yourself: (1) what am I doing well? (2) what can I do differently next time to improve my performance? and (3) what did I learn?

4. Imagine that you have been retained by Peyton to represent him in a breach-of-contract lawsuit against Daniel. Daniel has offered to settle the lawsuit by making restitution. As Peyton's attorney, is it appropriate for you to immediately accept the settlement? If Peyton does not want to settle the case, and you believe he should, is it appropriate for you to have the final say and accept the settlement anyway?

---

1. Roy Stuckey et al., Best Practices for Legal Education: A Vision and a Road Map (2007).

Chapter 8

Agreed Damages

Exercise 8-1: Chapter Problem

You are a new associate in a law firm. The senior partner in your law firm has just dropped a project in your lap. She told you that the firm represents a small motorcycle manufacturing company and she asked you to draft what she calls a "bullet-proof liquidated damages clause."

By using the term "bullet-proof liquidated damages clause," the partner means that she wants you to draft a clause that is so unquestionably enforceable that no rational lawyer would challenge the clause. The partner told you that the assignment of drafting the entire contract has been divided up among several associates. Your only task is to draft the liquidated damages clause.

The clause will be used as part of a contract between your client and a construction company that is building the client a new manufacturing factory. The partner provided you with the following additional information about the deal:

- The contract will have a construction completion date of July 1, 2015.

- The client wants the project finished on time and, therefore, wants the clause to address what will happen if the construction company does not complete construction on time.

- The client estimates that the new plant will save the client $4,000,000 per year over the fifteen-year useful life of the plant. These savings stem from a number of factors; specifically, the new factory will allow the client to reduce its number of employees because it will automate more of the client's manufacturing processes, and the new machinery will require less power to operate than the machinery in the existing factory.

- The client also believes that the new factory will allow the client to produce better, more reliable motorcycles—thereby increasing the client's profits, although the client has stated that it cannot determine how much its profits will increase.

Introduction to Agreed Damages

You are about to learn about a particular type of contract clause frequently included in contracts: "**agreed**" or "**liquidated**" damages clauses. Lawyers use these two terms interchangeably and so will we in this chapter.

Diagram 8-1 depicts where this topic fits within the bigger picture of contract law. As you will see, "Agreed Damages" is the third box under the sixth major contract subject, "Contract Remedies."

Diagram 8-1: Contract Law Graphic Organizer

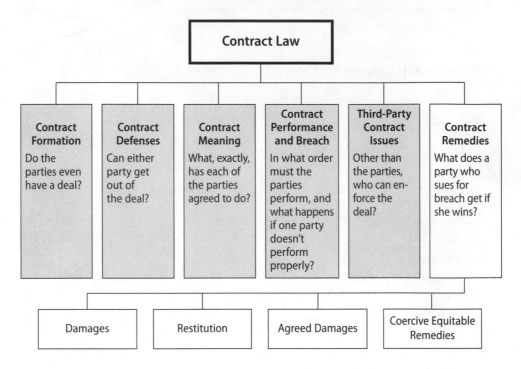

You need to learn about liquidated damage clauses because they are a common type of clause that lawyers draft and use. There are also many other types of commonly used contract clauses. For example, earlier in this text you were introduced to covenants not to compete and damages waiver clauses. To give you more insight into commonly used clauses, Table 8-1 on the next page provides a non-exhaustive list of common contract terms and a summary explanation of each type of clause. As you work your way through your study of contract law, look for all of these clauses and make sure you understand the effect of each.

Introduction to the Validity of Liquidated Damages Clauses

Courts use a set of specialized rules to determine the validity of liquidated damages clauses, although courts vary greatly in how they frame their tests. Liquidated damages clauses are generally enforceable, but courts strike down such clauses if they are found to be a "penalty." "Penalty" is just a label attached by a court when it concludes that a clause is unenforceable. The "penalty" label does not provide a rule.

Courts generally use a two-part test to determine if a liquidated damages clause is valid (not a "penalty"):

Table 8-1: Common Contract Clauses

Name of Clause	Goal of Clause
Covenant not to compete	Communicates that an employee or a seller of a business cannot compete (for a specified period of time and within a specified locale) with the employer or buyer.
Liquidated damages	States an amount a party should be awarded by a court if the other party breaches the contract.
Merger	Communicates that the written document contains all of the terms to which the parties have agreed and that prior agreements that are not reflected in the written document are not part of the parties' contract.
No oral modification	Indicates the parties only can modify the contract in writing.
Force majeure	Lists circumstances, usually natural disasters and wars, under which a party can avoid having to perform the contract without penalty.
Time is of the essence	Uses the words "time is of the essence" to communicate an expectation about timely performance of the parties' contract promises.
Choice of law	States the body of law that will govern any dispute between the parties. May also limit the state or city in which either party may file suit. (Lawyers may refer to this latter provision as a "jurisdiction clause.")
Arbitration	States that disputes under the contract will not be decided by a court but, rather, by an arbitrator. Usually includes a specified process for the arbitration (*i.e.*, what rules will be followed and how the arbitrator will be selected).
Indemnification	Communicates that, if one party is sued for a matter relating to the contract, the other party will pay for the costs of defending the suit and will pay any award of damages ordered by the court.
No assignments	States that the rights conferred under the contract (and, in some instances, the duties imposed under the contract) cannot be transferred to someone else.
Savings	Indicates the parties have agreed that, if a court invalidates a particular term of the parties' contract, the rest of the contract will remain enforceable.

1.   Were the damages difficult to ascertain when the contract was made; and

2.   Is the amount stated as liquidated damages reasonable in light of the actual and/or anticipated damages?

In the second prong of the test, the terms "and/or" reflect the fact that courts are split in their articulations of the rule. Also note that the two prongs tend to have an inverse relationship; the more difficult damages are to ascertain, the more leeway courts give parties' efforts to estimate damages (and, conversely, the easier damages are to ascertain, the less leeway courts give parties' efforts to estimate damages). The cases and materials below illustrate the application of these principles.

Overview of Chapter 8

In this chapter, you will learn the tests used to evaluate liquidated damages clauses and how courts apply those tests. You will also learn how to draft a valid and enforceable liquidated damages clause.

Evaluating the Enforceability of an Agreed Damages Clause

Exercise 8-2: *Leeber v. Deltona Corp.*

The first case you will read in this chapter, *Leeber v. Deltona Corp.*, examines the enforceability of an agreed damages clause. As you read *Leeber*, consider the following questions:

1. What are the key facts?

2. Why did the real estate developer in this case (like parties to many other contracts) include a liquidated damage clause in its contract?

3. The *Leeber* court says that liquidated damages clauses are favored under Florida law. Why?

4. Why are some courts hostile to liquidated damages clauses?

5. What was the *Leeber* court's holding and reasoning? Is it right that Deltona gets to keep the Leebers' deposit after successfully reselling the condo for $17,300 more than what the Leebers had agreed to pay for it?

6. How come the Supreme Judicial Court of Maine ends up deciding a question of Florida contract law?

Leeber v. Deltona Corp.

546 A.2d 452 (1988)

Clifford, Justice. Defendants, The Deltona Corporation and Marco Surfside, Inc., appeal from a judgment for the plaintiffs, Donald A. Leeber, Jeremy Morton and Jan Drewry, on Count I of their complaint entered in the Superior Court, Cumberland County, following a jury-waived trial....

This case arises out of a dispute involving a Florida real estate transaction. Defendant Marco Surfside, Inc., a wholly owned subsidiary of defendant The Deltona Corporation, was the developer of a condominium real estate development on Marco Island in Florida. The plaintiffs, Portland area residents, decided to invest as a group in one of the condominium units being constructed by Deltona. On May 14, 1980, the plaintiffs, dealing with defendant Maine-Florida Properties, the exclusive sales agent in Maine for Deltona, signed a Subscription and Purchase Agreement ("the Agreement") to buy a condominium unit in the Marco Island project, designated as unit

711. The price for the unit was $150,200, with 15% of this amount, $22,530, paid at the time the Agreement was signed and the balance due at the closing date, to be specified by Deltona within four years from the time of the Agreement. Under the express terms of the Agreement, the $22,530 was to be retained by Deltona as liquidated damages in the event of a breach by the plaintiffs.

Beginning in May 1982, Deltona notified the plaintiffs several times that they would be required to close on the condominium on certain dates or the liquidated damages deposit would be retained by Deltona. After each notice, the plaintiffs were able to obtain an extension from Deltona. Deltona sent the plaintiffs a final closing notice on July 8, 1982, which set a closing date of July 20, 1982. The July 8 letter advised the plaintiffs that the Agreement would be cancelled if they did not close on unit 711. The plaintiffs did not close on the July 20 date. On July 27, 1982, Deltona informed the plaintiffs in writing that the Agreement had been cancelled and the liquidated damages deposit would be retained by Deltona. Deltona then sold unit 711 to another party on July 31, 1982, for what the trial court found to be $167,500. That party paid a 15% deposit of $25,125.

Deltona refused to return the plaintiffs' deposit, and this suit was initiated in the Superior Court. Plaintiffs' complaint contained three counts: Count I, directed against Deltona and Marco Surfside, alleged that the liquidated damages provision was unenforceable. Plaintiffs further alleged that David Cloutier, president of Maine-Florida, had promised plaintiffs that he would find a buyer for their condominium allowing them to resell the unit prior to the closing, and that a buyer was found but no notice of that given to plaintiffs. Count II, treated by the court as being directed against Maine-Florida, alleged a breach of contract because of the failure to find a buyer for unit 711 before the closing date. Count III, also treated by the court as being directed against Maine-Florida, alleged a breach of fiduciary duty by Maine-Florida, based on its alleged status as real estate agent for the plaintiffs and its failure to notify the plaintiffs of the buyer who had been found for the condominium.

At the close of the plaintiffs' evidence in the nonjury trial in this case, the trial justice granted the defendants' motion for dismissal with respect to Counts II and III, and in his subsequent written decision, concluded that the plaintiffs "failed to meet the burden of proof" on those counts and entered judgment for defendant Maine-Florida Properties. As to Count I, the trial justice determined that the enforcement of the liquidated damages provision was unconscionable. The trial justice found that Deltona had proved it incurred actual damages consisting of some administrative costs and a $5,704 commission paid to Maine-Florida from the deposit and awarded plaintiffs $15,020—the balance of the deposit. A subsequent motion by the defendants to amend the trial justice's written findings of fact and conclusions of law under M.R. Civ. P. 52(b) was denied. Defendants Deltona and Marco Surfside then appealed on Count I to this court in timely fashion....

The defendants contend that the liquidated damages provision in the Agreement was valid and enforceable under Florida law. The Agreement provided for the retention by Deltona of the 15% deposit in the event of a breach of the Agreement on the part of the plaintiffs. The validity of a liquidated damages clause is assessed in the following way under Florida law:

> If the damages are ascertainable on the date of the contract, the clause is a penalty and unenforceable; if they are not so ascertainable, the clause is truly one for liquidated damages and enforceable; however, if subsequent circumstances demonstrate it would be unconscionable to allow the seller to retain the sum in question as liquidated damages, equity may relieve against the forfeiture. [Citations omitted.]

The plaintiffs do not dispute that damages were not ascertainable at the time the Agreement was entered into. Thus, the issue placed before us in this case is whether the Superior Court erred in its determination that retention of money by the sellers under an otherwise valid liquidated damage provision was unconscionable under the standard set out in [the authorities] ...

Under Florida law, if the liquidated damages provision is not a penalty, it is enforceable unless the plaintiff proves the existence of one or more of the following factors:

(1) an intimation of fraud on the seller's part;

(2) misfortune beyond his control accounting for the buyer's failure to fulfill the contract;

(3) a mutual rescission of the contract; or

(4) a benefit to the seller "the retention of which [when compared to the total contract price would be] shocking to the conscience of the court."

[Citations omitted.][4] Here, there was no showing of fraud on Deltona's part, nor evidence that plaintiffs' failure to buy was caused by misfortune beyond their control, nor evidence of mutual rescission. Only Deltona's retention of $22,530, 15% of the purchase price, examined under a "shocking to the conscience" standard, is properly considered by the court. *Id.*

Liquidated damages are favored under Florida law ... and Florida courts have uniformly viewed liquidated damage sums in the range of 15% as reasonable. [Citations omitted.]

The Superior Court, despite its recitation that it found defendants' retention of the liquidated damages to be unconscionable, did not apply a true "shock the conscience" standard in overriding the liquidated damage provision in this case. The court considered the fact of the resale of the condominium unit by Deltona several days after the default but several months after the originally designated closing date, and allowed the plaintiff buyers to recover from Deltona all of the previously paid deposit except what Deltona

---

4. Plaintiffs cite *Multitech Corp. v. St. Johns Bluff Inv. Corp.*, 518 So.2d 427, 433 (Fla. App. 1988), for the proposition that another factor to be considered in an unconscionability analysis under Florida law is "whether or not the sellers actually suffered any damage as a result of the breach." We are reluctant to accept this as a valid factor for assessing unconscionability under Florida law. The *Multitech* court, only one of several District Courts of Appeal in Florida, failed to cite any precedent for that holding and we can find no case decided by Florida's highest court, the Florida Supreme Court, that incorporates this factor. Moreover, to routinely allow such a consideration ... would unduly undermine one of the purposes of liquidated damages, namely to avoid the difficulties and uncertainties of proof of actual damages. [Citations omitted.] In any event, *Multitech* is distinguishable from the instant case because the court found unconscionability in a case where the liquidated damage amount was $120,000 and the seller suffered no damage.

convinced the court were its actual out of pocket losses resulting from plaintiffs' breach. Such an approach nullified the effect of the liquidated damages provision and made this case indistinguishable from one of ordinary breach of contract. This result undercut the traditional role of liquidated damages provisions, which have always served as an economical alternative to the costly and lengthy litigation involved in a conventional breach of contract action. [Citations omitted.]

Efforts by contracting parties to avoid litigation and to equitably resolve potential conflicts through the mechanism of liquidated damages should be encouraged. [Citations omitted] Prompt resale of real estate units by sellers upon breach of contract by buyers likewise should be encouraged. However, the Superior Court ruling in this case, if allowed to stand, would have the opposite effect.

Florida law provides that, under a real estate contract containing a liquidated damages clause similar in language to the instant contract, sellers are denied the remedy of specific performance. [Citation omitted.]. Moreover, their damage recovery is limited to the liquidated damage amount. [Citations omitted.] Buyers breaching such contracts, not being subject to specific performance nor to liability for excess damages should the sellers' losses exceed the amount of liquidated damages, would have nothing to lose in challenging the amount of liquidated damages retained or sought to be recovered by the sellers in every case where the buyers suspected the actual losses of the sellers to be less than the liquidated damage amount.

Under Florida law, the determination of the unconscionability of allowing a seller to retain liquidated damages under an otherwise valid liquidated damage provision should be based on the circumstances existent "at the time of breach"....[5] A case of liquidated damages, when the liquidated damage amount is not unreasonable on its face, is not converted as a matter of course to one of ordinary breach of contract by the seller's fortuitous resale of the contract real estate subsequent to the buyer's breach. Sellers are inescapably bound by the liquidated damage provisions in such contracts. Buyers should be bound as well unless the plaintiff proves that the circumstances are so extraordinary that the sellers' retention of the liquidated damage amount would truly shock the conscience of the court. [Citation omitted.]

It is undisputed that this liquidated damage amount of $22,530, 15% of the total contract price of the Florida real estate, was reasonable on its face and not a penalty. The retention of that sum by the sellers in this case, when plaintiff buyers delayed closing on the project for several months before breaching the contract, and sellers subsequently were able to resell the real estate through their own efforts and in doing so reduced their actual losses flowing from plaintiffs' breach, is not so extraordinary or unfair as to shock the conscience of the court. [Citation omitted.] The plaintiffs having failed to demonstrate circumstances sufficiently extraordinary to meet the shock the conscience test..., defendants must be allowed to retain the liquidated damage amount....

---

5. Some states, including Maine, measure the soundness of a liquidated damage provision as of the time the contract is made and not at the time of the breach. [Citations omitted.]

Judgment vacated as to Count I. Remanded to the Superior Court for entry of judgment in favor of defendants The Deltona Corporation, Inc., and Marco Surfside, Inc. Judgment affirmed as to Counts II and III.

Exercise 8-3: *Leeber* Revisited

1. Under the two-part test outlined at the start of this chapter, would the clause in *Leeber* have been deemed invalid?

2. Drummer agrees to play the drums with Rock Band for three weeks' worth of concerts for $10,000. The contract includes the following term, "If either party breaches this contract, the other will pay $15,000 as liquidated damages and not as a penalty." After two weeks, Drummer takes a job with another band. The concerts for the third week were sold out before the parties ever signed their contract. Rock Band hires a suitable replacement for Drummer for $10,000. Is the clause a valid liquidated damages clause or a penalty clause? As you evaluate this clause, please consider the following statement from a recent Missouri case, "While the label the parties attach to a [liquidated damages] provision is not conclusive, it is a circumstance to be considered when deciding whether the provision is to be considered liquidated damages or a penalty." *See Diffley v. Royal Papers, Inc.*, 948 S.W.2d 244, 47 (Mo. Ct. App. 1997).

3. Physician agreed to provide health care services to patients who are members of Wellbeing HMO. Under the terms of the agreement between Physician and the HMO, Physician received compensation from Wellbeing in return. The agreement contained the following term:

    > In the event that any Member disenrolls from Wellbeing's health plan to be treated by you [Physician] under some other financial arrangement other than Wellbeing's health plan, then you shall pay to HMO the amount of $700 for each such Member who is treated by you. You hereby agree to waive any claim that this amount is a penalty.

    Physician became affiliated with Feelgood, a competing HMO, and 100 of his patients left Wellbeing and enrolled with Feelgood. Wellbeing seeks $70,000 from Physician under the term in the agreement. Is the clause a valid liquidated damages clause or a penalty clause?

Exercise 8-4: *United States v. Hayes*

The next case, *United States v. Hayes,* also addresses the enforceability of an agreed damages clause. As you read *Hayes*, consider the following questions:

1. What are the key facts?

2. What is the plaintiff's best argument that the liquidated damages amount is not a reasonable attempt to estimate the plaintiff's damages? (Hint: Consider the fact that the amount applies to all contracts regardless of a doctor's area of specialty, cost of education, or amount borrowed.)

3. Why did the doctor lose in this case (as did the doctors in the other five cases that have raised the same issue)? Do you think the court reached the right outcome?

United States v. Hayes

633 F. Supp. 1183 (1986)

Erwin, District Judge. This matter is before the court on motion by the United States for summary judgment pursuant to Rule 56 of the Federal Rules of Civil Procedure. The United States seeks to recover treble damages plus accrued interest for an alleged breach of contract by the defendant pursuant to 42 U.S.C. § 254o.

The basic facts of the case are uncontroverted. The defendant is a medical doctor residing in Chapel Hill, North Carolina. In June 1978, the defendant applied pursuant to 42 U.S.C. § 254l for an award under the National Health Service Corps ("NHSC") Scholarship Program to fund her study of medicine at Tufts University School of Medicine. Defendant stated in her application that she intended to specialize in family medicine and work in a rural area. Upon acceptance of her application, defendant became obligated under the terms of the scholarship contract to perform one year of service in the NHSC for each year of scholarship awarded or two years, whichever was greater. 42 U.S.C. § 254l (f)(1)(B)(iv). Defendant was awarded a scholarship in the amount of $13,115 for the 1978–1979 school year. In June 1979, defendant received an extension of her scholarship award to include the 1979–1980 school year in the amount of $16,430. Subsequently, the defendant was granted a deferment by the Secretary of Health and Human Services to complete a three-year residency in internal medicine at North Carolina Memorial Hospital in Chapel Hill, North Carolina.

During the second year of the defendant's residency, she notified the NHSC Scholarship Program that she had abandoned her internal medicine residency and had initiated a three-year residency in dermatology. The defendant requested permission to serve in the NHSC as a dermatologist. This request was denied, and defendant was requested to prepare for placement. Defendant failed to participate in placement procedures and failed to perform her service under the scholarship contract. On March 25, 1985, the Government instituted this action.

The defendant admits that she is in breach of her scholarship contract and that she is indebted to the Government. However, the defendant disputes the amount of the debt and argues that 42 U.S.C. § 254o, the treble damages provision of the NHSC Scholarship Program, is penal in nature and thus is unenforceable, as it is an invalid liquidated damages provision. The defendant argues that this provision creates a genuine issue of material fact and asserts, therefore, that the case should survive the Government's motion for summary judgment. The motion has been briefed by both parties and is ready for a ruling.

Discussion

To sustain a motion pursuant to Rule 56 of the Federal Rules of Civil Procedure, the movant must demonstrate that there is no genuine issue as to any material fact. [Citation omitted.] This is a strict standard, and any doubts as to the existence of a genuine issue of material fact are to be resolved against the movant. [Citation omitted.]

In the instant case, the defendant does not dispute the contractual validity of the scholarship agreement. Defendant contends that a genuine issue of material fact exists as to the validity of the treble damages provision of the statute and scholarship contract. Unfortunately, the court cannot agree. Under the NHSC Scholarship Program, if an individual, for any reason, breaches her written contract by failing to either begin or complete her scholarship service obligation,

> [T]he United States shall be entitled to recover from the individual [three times the amount given by the United States to the scholarship recipient as a scholarship]. Any amount of such damages which the United States is entitled to recover under this subsection shall, within the one year period beginning on the date of the breach of the written contract, be paid to the United States. 42 USC § 254*o*(b)(1).

This provision appears in the NHSC scholarship contract and is referenced in the NHSC Scholarship Program regulations, 42 C.F.R. § 62.10(c).

Ordinarily, when construing liquidated damages provisions in government contracts, the courts turn to general principles of contract law. [Citation omitted.] Generally, it has been the modern trend to allow liquidated damages clauses in contracts. [Citation omitted.]

Today the law does not look with disfavor upon "liquidated damages" provisions in contracts. When they are fair and reasonable attempts to fix just compensation for anticipated loss caused by breach of contract, they are enforced.... They serve a particularly useful function when damages are uncertain in nature or amount or are unmeasurable, as is the case in many government contracts.... And the fact that the damages suffered are shown to be less than the damages contracted for is not fatal. These provisions are to be judged as of the time of making the contract. [Citations omitted.]

The setting of civil damages as multiples of actual damages is not uncommon and has long been upheld by the courts. [Citations omitted.]

In applying the above criterion to the case *sub judice*, this court can only conclude that the liquidated damages provision contained in the scholarship application is valid and enforceable and does not constitute a penalty. There is no dispute that the parties bargained at arm's length. The defendant certainly had notice of the potential for damages upon breach at the time she signed the application. It is clear to the court that a binding contract was formed at the time of acceptance and approval of the defendant's application by the Secretary on September 1, 1978.

There is no question that Congress has the authority to promulgate statutes and regulations to accomplish and further the purposes of statutes and other congressional acts. *See generally McCulloch v. Maryland*, 17 U.S. (4 Wheat.) 316, 4 L. Ed. 579 (1819). Further, it is uncontradicted that the statutes in question were created for the purpose of serving a proper governmental function. Clearly the scholarship program exists to help students with financial aid, who, in turn, help the government by performing their part of the bargain—rendering medical assistance in areas where health services and personnel are inadequate or in need. The district courts have been quick to enforce similar service provisions under the Armed Forces Professions Scholarship Program, 10 U.S.C. §2120 *et seq.* [Citations omitted.] The congressional history of the statute in question is replete with references to the national maldistribution of health services. *See* H.R. Rep. No. 266, 94th Cong., 2d Sess. 22–31 (1976), *reprinted in* 1976 U.S. Code Cong. & Ad. News 4947, 4964–73. Legislative history makes it clear that the NHSC Scholarship Program was not created solely to subsidize the medical education of future health care practitioners:

> The Committee wishes to emphasize in the strongest possible terms that it does not view the National Health Service Corps scholarship program as a mechanism solely intended to subsidize health professional education. Rather, in return for substantial subsidization of the costs of education, the committee views the National Health Service Corps Scholarship program as a means to overcome a geographic maldistribution of health professionals.

United States v. Swanson, 618 F. Supp. 1231, 1235–36 (E.D. Mich. 1985).... Thus, the scholarship contract is a two-way street. In exchange for the funds to further their medical education, students are expected to serve their fellow citizens through the NHSC upon completion of their studies.

The court finds that it is virtually impossible to determine the amount of damages to the government by the defendant's breach. "A physician or health care professional is not a 'fungible handyman.'" *Swanson*, 618 F. Supp. at 1243. That is, one cannot speculate in the abstract as to the value of a particular physician's services. A variety of factors, which could not be known at the time of contract formation, including ability, skills, specialties, levels of training and education, placement, etc., are all inherent in determining the value of a physician's practice; nor can it be known with what dedication a health care provider will apply herself.

Therefore, it is clear that the liquidated damages provision of the scholarship contract has a direct relation to actual damages, as it is an attempt to fairly and reasonably set just compensation in the event of a breach by the scholarship recipient. In *Swanson*, facing the same issue, the district court, per Freeman, Senior District Judge, held:

> For the above reasons, this Court holds that the liquidated damage provision does not operate as a penalty and is valid and enforceable in a court of law. In addition, to the extent that the Defendant raises the argument that the damage provision and the contract in question are unconscionable, this Court rejects this assertion in light of the previous conclusion.

Swanson, 618 F. Supp. at 1244. To this court, the holding in *Swanson* was clearly appropriate.

While the court is not without sympathy for the defendant, it is bound to follow the laws of the Congress. Therefore, this court holds that the liquidated damages provision contained in the scholarship application does not operate as a penalty and is completely valid and enforceable. Defendant is bound by the terms of the scholarship contract and must abide by them. Defendant admits that she is in breach of her scholarship contract, and this court so holds. There being no genuine issue of material fact as to the validity of the liquidated damages provision of the agreement, the Government is entitled to judgment as a matter of law. Therefore, the Government's motion for summary judgment is granted. The Government is directed to submit a judgment reflecting the opinion of the court and calculating damages as of the date of this opinion. It is so ordered.

Chapter Problem Revisited

Exercise 8-1 at the beginning of this chapter asked you to draft a liquidated damages clause. To do so, use what you have learned about liquidated damages clauses in this chapter and the drafting guidance below:

1. Implement your client's goals: Your client wants to encourage the contractor to complete the job on time; to maximize its recovery if the contractor delays completion; to have a court, if necessary, affirm the enforceability of the clause; and to have a clause that is so clearly enforceable that the contractor would not even litigate the issue.

2. Be explicit about the effect you want the contract term to have.

3. Use clear and simple language. Ineffective lawyers draft obscure contract terms, which often become the subjects of litigation.

4. Carefully edit your work product. Your work product will reflect on your level of professionalism and effectiveness as a lawyer. Ensure that any work product you produce is polished.

In addition, it may be helpful to review some sample liquidated damages clauses in formbooks and to read some articles about liquidated damages. Both are available in your law school library. For example, one article that is useful for understanding drafting principles is *How to Draft and Enforce a Liquidated Damages Clause* by Henry Luepke.[6] While we encourage you to read the entire article, below we are providing some key points and excerpts from the article:[7]

1. Express your client's intent. As Luepke states, "If the parties intended the clause to serve as compensation for the damages likely to result from a breach, the court will uphold the clause and enforce it as written. If, on the other hand, the clause was intended to serve as punishment for a breach, the court will refuse to enforce it." Thus, "when drafting a liquidated damages clause, counsel should use language demonstrating that, at the time of contracting, the parties intended the liquidated amount to fully compensate, but not punish, for a breach of the contract." Luepke specifically advises:

---

6. Henry F. Luepke III, *How to Draft and Enforce a Liquidated Damages Clause*, 61(6) J. OF THE MO. BAR (Nov.–Dec. 2005). Note that the full version of the original article, which can be accessed on Westlaw, includes endnotes with supporting citations.

7. All quotes in the list of points are from Luepke's article; citations are omitted.

The simplest way to demonstrate that the intent of a provision for liquidated damages is compensatory rather than punitive is to explicitly state this intent in the clause itself. Specifically, the clause should provide that the liquidated amount to which the parties have agreed is intended as compensation and is not intended as punishment.

2. Label the clause as a "liquidated" or "agreed" damages clause. As Luepke notes,

> It is true that labeling a liquidated damages provision as either one for compensation or as one for a penalty is not conclusive on the issue of whether it will or will not be enforced. Nevertheless, courts are generally constrained to give effect to the parties' intention as expressed by the plain terms of the contract.

3. Be cognizant of the enforceability test your clause will have to pass. As Luepke states:

> [A] court will have to answer two threshold questions, *i.e.*, 1) is the liquidated amount a reasonable forecast of just compensation in the event of a breach?; and 2) is the liquidated amount for a harm that was incapable or very difficult of accurate estimation at the time the contract was made?

Because the intent of the parties is to be ascertained from the plain language of the contract, the answers to these questions should be made explicit in the terms of the liquidated damages clause. For example, the liquidated damages clause might state explicitly and explain why the damages to be suffered in the event of breach are very difficult of accurate estimation and, for this reason, the parties have agreed that the amount fixed by the clause is a reasonable forecast of just compensation in the event of breach.

4. Specify the type of breach for which the liquidated amount is intended as compensation. Luepke explains:

> All breaches are not alike, and a liquidated damages clause should not treat them as if they were.... Where a liquidated damages clause applies equally to multiple types of breaches, regardless of the significance or magnitude of the breach, the scope of the clause is overly broad, and a court will likely find that the intent of the provision is punitive, regardless of statements indicating a contrary intent.

> The terms of the clause, therefore, should specify the types of breaches to which it applies and should clearly show that it is intended to provide compensation only for the type of breach that would result in the damages that are difficult or impossible to calculate.

5. Specify the type of harm for which the liquidated amount is intended as compensation. As Luepke notes, "the anticipated harm for which a liquidated damages clause is intended to compensate may not always be obvious to a court." Accordingly, parties to a "liquidated damages clause ... would do well to specify the types of difficult-to-quantify harm for which the clause is intended to provide compensation." For example, "where breach of a contract may result in a loss of profits ... the clause should state that the liquidated amount is intended to compensate for the difficult-to-calculate loss of anticipated profits that the parties agree would result from the type of breach in question."

6. Provide a formula for calculating the liquidated amount. A formula is preferable to a lump sum because the amount of damages will vary with the type and

duration of breach. For example, a clause could state that a certain amount is to be added to a base liquidated amount for each day contract performance is delayed. Or, where the anticipated harm is lost profits, the liquidated sum could be set as a percentage of the gross amount yet to be paid under the contract. The advantage in using a formula is that it ensures "that the liquidated amount will be adjusted according to the relative degree or magnitude of the breach." Accordingly, a court is more likely to find that "the amount to be recovered as liquidated damages is intended to bear some relationship to a reasonable forecast of the probable damages and, therefore, is intended to compensate, not punish, for a breach. On this basis, a liquidated damages clause will likely be enforced."

Professional Development Reflection Questions

1. In drafting the liquidated damages clause assigned as the Chapter Problem, you may believe that there are conflicts between two of the client's goals. Under such circumstances, what should you do?

2. Most law students find law school at least somewhat stressful. On a scale of one to ten, how stressful have you found law school so far?

3. *Educating Lawyers*[8] asserts: "Law school is the very place in which practitioners should learn to cope effectively with the demands of the profession as well as with the demands of everyday life. The development and maintenance of the psychological well-being of law students, however, may be stunted by the process of legal education; at best, it is ignored." To what extent has your psychological well-being been supported or stunted during your experience in law school?

4. Empirical research supports the assertion in *Educating Lawyers*. It shows that students begin law school with normal levels of well-being, but there is a significant decline after beginning law school which continues throughout law school and into practice (for example, with higher levels of psychopathology, alcohol and drug abuse, and suicide). Consider what you can do to protect your own well-being. What strategies are you using or could you use to protect and promote your well-being? (We will present many strategies in the reflection questions in chapters 9–15; feel free to look ahead if you want more information now about strategies to protect your well-being.)

5. Imagine that you are representing a client in a breach-of-contract lawsuit where liability is clear-cut and the key issue is damages. The contract has a liquidated-damages clause which you believe is valid and enforceable. Your client, however, wants you to argue that the clause is invalid. Will you, and should you, do so?

---

8. WILLIAM SULLIVAN ET AL., EDUCATING LAWYERS: PREPARATION FOR THE PROFESSION OF LAW (2007).

Chapter 9

Coercive Equitable Relief

Exercise 9-1: Chapter Problem

For this exercise, draft a law school final exam answer to the question that follows. After you complete your study of specific performance, you should be able to do so. Complete your answer in one-and-a-half hours.

Linda Landowner Corporation ("Linda") is one of the largest owners of commercial, high-rise office buildings in the State of Columbia. Linda owns twenty such buildings and has acquired at least one new building every year for the past ten years. From time to time, Linda sells the buildings. Claude Cleaning Co. ("CCC") is a new, start-up company engaged exclusively in the business of providing nighttime cleaning services to high-rise office buildings. CCC opened for business in December 2013, based in part on a fifteen-year loan CCC received from the New Jobs, New Businesses Fund ("The Fund"). The State of Columbia established The Fund to provide start-up loans to Columbia-based businesses founded by unemployed state residents.

On January 1, 2014, Linda and CCC entered into a valid written contract for nighttime cleaning services. The contract required and entitled CCC to clean all of Linda's buildings for the next fifteen years. In exchange, Linda agreed to pay all of CCC's home office expenses, including (but not limited to) rent, utilities, office supplies, home office employee salaries, and principal and interest on The Fund loan. The contract detailed the particular types of expenses involved, described how CCC would select its vendors, and set the salary figures for the home office employees. In addition, Linda agreed to add new buildings only at the beginning of each year of the contract and to pay CCC $10,000 per year for each additional building CCC would be required to clean. $10,000 reflects CCC's estimated average direct costs in cleaning one building for one year. The contract also included the following clause labeled "Agreed Damages":

> If Linda repudiates this contract and refuses to perform, and CCC sues Linda for damages based on the breach, Linda shall pay CCC $150,000 multiplied by the number of years remaining on the contract. If the breach occurs in the middle of any relevant year, such year will be counted proportionately to the extent of the time remaining in that year. The parties intend this clause to be a valid liquidation of damages.

Although the contract did not include any profit to CCC, it did cover all of CCC's costs of operation. Both parties knew that Linda was CCC's first client and that CCC anticipated making its profits from contracts with other clients. In fact, because the contract covered all of CCC's home office expenses, the contract would make it easier for CCC to bid low on other jobs and still make a profit on those jobs. They also knew that the contract created the stable, long-term relationship Linda had sought for years and that Linda would be paying a fair price. On January 1, 2016, Linda repudiated the contract.

1. For this question only, assume that CCC sued Linda for breach of contract, seeking to enforce the "Agreed Damages" clause as its only remedy. Discuss the enforceability of the clause.

2. For this question only, assume that CCC sued Linda for breach of contract, seeking specific performance as its only remedy. Discuss the issues relating to CCC's request for specific performance.

Coercive Equitable Relief: Introduction to Specific Performance and Injunctions against Breach

"**Coercive equitable relief**" is a broad term that refers to any order by a court requiring a party to act or to refrain from acting. When the remedy for breach of contract switches from an award of money to a court order that a party must perform a contract, the focus of analysis changes. In connection with damages, you learned to ascertain and then limit the amount of damages. In connection with equitable relief, the question is not what measure a party recovers; rather, it is whether a party can obtain a remedy at all. Thus, your task is to figure out what a plaintiff must show to obtain an equitable remedy.

The most common form of coercive equitable relief awarded in breach of contract cases is "**specific performance**." In situations involving enforcement of express or implied promises not to compete, courts label their orders "**injunctions against breach**" rather than orders for specific performance. Specific performance is a court order requiring a party to a contract to perform the contract. An injunction is a court order prohibiting a party from doing a particular act or activity.

Historically, both in England and in the United States, parties sued in courts of law if they were seeking legal remedies (such as damages) and in courts of equity if they were seeking equitable remedies (such as specific performance). Historically, in England, the "judges" in the courts of equity were ecclesiastics (not lawyers). Also, the courts of equity served as a secondary court system.

Today, in nearly all states in the United States, the two historical court systems are merged so that one judge can provide either legal or equitable relief. However, the old divide between equity and law continues to influence modern decisions. Judges only award equitable relief in cases where damages would be inadequate to fully address the nonbreaching parties' injuries. Additionally, in damages cases, a judge has no discretion to deny relief if the plaintiff proves a breach and damages. In equity cases, judges retain discretion to deny relief in a wide variety of circumstances. For example, a judge may deny relief if she deems the contract to be substantively unfair or if granting relief would require excessive court supervision.

Diagram 9-1 depicts where coercive equitable relief fits within the big picture of contract law. "Coercive Equitable Remedies" is shown as one topic under sixth major contract law topic, "Contract Remedies." Diagram 9-1 also shows three main subtopics under "Coercive Equitable Remedies": (1) "Inadequacy Requirement," (2) "13th Amendment

Diagram 9-1: Contract Law Graphic Organizer

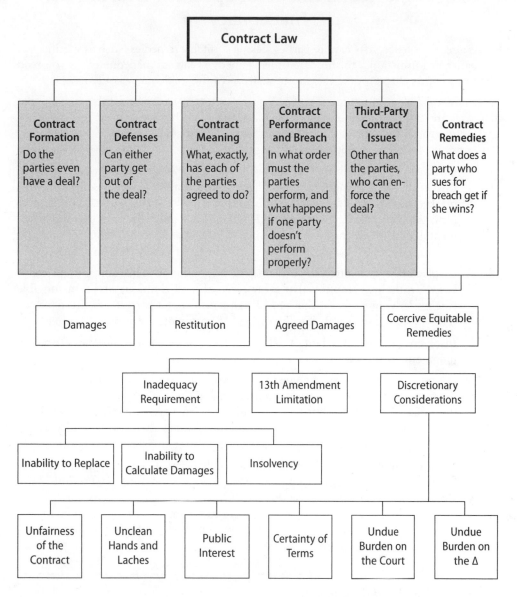

Limitation," and (3) "Discretionary Considerations." A fourth subtopic, injunctions against breaches of covenants not to compete, is not depicted but will be addressed toward the end of this chapter.

Overview of Chapter 9

In this chapter, you will learn about three main topics: (1) the fundamental requirement for obtaining specific performance of a contract; (2) the discretionary considerations courts weigh in deciding whether to grant specific performance; and (3) the requirements for obtaining an injunction to enforce a covenant not to compete.

The Basic Requirement for Specific Performance: Inadequacy

As already noted, courts require parties seeking equitable remedies (such as specific performance or injunctions) to show that their remedy at law is "inadequate." As you read the cases in this chapter, note the courts' analyses of the inadequacy issue.

In common law contract cases, the inadequacy requirement can be met by showing that damages are difficult or impossible to calculate, the subject of the contract cannot readily be replaced, or the defendant is insolvent. *See* Restatement (Second) of Contracts § 360. An example of each type of inadequacy is listed below:

- **Difficulty or impossibility of calculating damages:** A contract between two family members regarding a family heirloom. Awarding damages based on the fair market value of the item will not fully measure the loss caused by a failure to perform the contract because the market will not recognize the personal and sentimental value of the heirloom. In other words, the expected "value" of contract performance to the plaintiff cannot be measured in purely economic terms.

- **Irreplaceability:** A contract to purchase land. Courts conclude that land is irreplaceable based on the presumption that every piece of land is unique and non-fungible (the underlying notion is that one plot of land is not a perfect substitute for another plot of land even if the dimensions of both plots are exactly the same).

- **Insolvency of the defendant:** A defendant lacks sufficient assets to pay a damages judgment.

With respect to contracts for the sale of goods, the remedy at law is inadequate if the "goods are unique or in other proper circumstances." U.C.C. § 2-716. Comments to section 2-716 explain that an "inability to cover" (similar to irreplaceability) is strong evidence of "other proper circumstances." The other two common law theories, difficulty in calculating damages and insolvency, also meet the "other proper circumstances" standard.

Finally, although courts continue to state and use the inadequacy requirement, one equity expert asserts that courts no longer take the inadequacy requirement seriously and accept almost any argument that the remedy at law is inadequate.[1] Thus, an effective lawyer might argue that a court should not adhere to the inadequacy requirement at all. Nevertheless, an effective lawyer certainly also would argue why the facts of her particular case meet the inadequacy requirement.

Exercise 9-2: Inadequacy

1. Why does irreplaceability demonstrate that damages would be an inadequate remedy?

2. Why does difficulty or impossibility of calculating damages demonstrate that damages would be an inadequate remedy?

3. Why does a defendant's insolvency demonstrate that damages would be an inadequate remedy?

---

1. Douglas Laycock, *The Death of the Irreparable Injury Requirement*, 103 Harv. L. Rev. 687 (1990). For a well balanced critique of Laycock's position, see Gene R. Shreve, *The Premature Burial of the Irreparable Injury Rule*, 70 Texas L. Rev. 1063 (1992).

4. Why does inability to cover demonstrate that damages would be an inadequate remedy?

The first case you will read, *Campbell Soup Co. v. Wentz*, discusses the inadequacy requirement. As you read the case, see if you can understand what is particularly unique about carrots that will be mixed in soup and sold in cans.

Campbell Soup Co. v. Wentz
172 F.2d 80 (3rd Cir. 1948)

Goodrich, Circuit Judge. These are appeals from judgments of the District Court denying equitable relief to the buyer under a contract for the sale of carrots. The defendants in No. 9648 are the contract sellers. The defendant in No. 9649 is the second purchaser of part of the carrots which are the subject matter of the contract.

The transactions which raise the issues may be briefly summarized. On June 21, 1947, Campbell Soup Company (Campbell), a New Jersey corporation, entered into a written contract with George B. Wentz and Harry T. Wentz, who are Pennsylvania farmers, for delivery by the Wentzes to Campbell of all the Chantenay red cored carrots to be grown on fifteen acres of the Wentz farm during the 1947 season. Where the contract was entered into does not appear. The contract provides, however, for delivery of the carrots at the Campbell plant in Camden, New Jersey. The prices specified in the contract ranged from $23 to $30 per ton according to the time of delivery. The contract price for January, 1948 was $30 a ton.

The Wentzes harvested approximately 100 tons of carrots from the fifteen acres covered by the contract. Early in January, 1948, they told a Campbell representative that they would not deliver their carrots at the contract price. The market price at that time was at least $90 per ton, and Chantenay red cored carrots were virtually unobtainable. The Wentzes then sold approximately 62 tons of their carrots to the defendant Lojeski, a neighboring farmer. Lojeski resold about 58 tons on the open market, approximately half to Campbell and the balance to other purchasers.

On January 9, 1948, Campbell, suspecting that Lojeski was selling it "contract carrots," refused to purchase any more, and instituted these suits against the Wentz brothers and Lojeski to enjoin further sale of the contract carrots to others, and to compel specific performance of the contract. The trial court denied equitable relief. We agree with the result reached, but on a different ground from that relied upon by the District Court....

A party may have specific performance of a contract for the sale of chattels if the legal remedy is inadequate. Inadequacy of the legal remedy is necessarily a matter to be determined by an examination of the facts in each particular instance.

We think that on the question of adequacy of the legal remedy the case is one appropriate for specific performance. It was expressly found that at the time of the trial it was "virtually impossible to obtain Chantenay carrots in the open market." This Chantenay carrot is one which the plaintiff uses in large quantities, furnishing the seed to the growers with whom it makes contracts. It was not claimed that in nutritive value it is any better than other types of carrots. Its blunt shape makes it easier to handle in processing. And its color and texture differ from other varieties. The color is brighter than other carrots. The trial court found that the plaintiff failed to establish what proportion of its carrots is used for the production of soup stock and what proportion is used as identifiable physical ingredients in its soups. We do not think lack of proof on that point is material. It did appear that the plaintiff uses carrots in fifteen of its twenty-one soups. It also appeared that it uses these Chantenay carrots diced in some of them and that the appearance is uniform. The preservation of uniformity in appearance in a food article marketed throughout the country and sold under the manufacturer's name is a matter of considerable commercial significance and one which is properly considered in determining whether a substitute ingredient is just as good as the original.

The trial court concluded that the plaintiff had failed to establish that the carrots, "judged by objective standards," are unique goods. This we think is not a pure fact conclusion like a finding that Chantenay carrots are of uniform color. It is either a conclusion of law or of mixed fact and law and we are bound to exercise our independent judgment upon it. That the test for specific performance is not necessarily "objective" is shown by the many cases in which equity has given it to enforce contracts for articles—family heirlooms and the like—the value of which was personal to the plaintiff.

Judged by the general standards applicable to determining the adequacy of the legal remedy, we think that on this point the case is a proper one for equitable relief. There is considerable authority, old and new, showing liberality in the granting of an equitable remedy. We see no reason why a court should be reluctant to grant specific relief when it can be given without supervision of the court or other time-consuming processes against one who has deliberately broken his agreement. Here the goods of the special type contracted for were unavailable on the open market, the plaintiff had contracted for them long ahead in anticipation of its needs, and had built up a general reputation for its products as part of which reputation uniform appearance was important. We think if this were all that was involved in the case specific performance should have been granted.

The reason that we shall affirm instead of reversing with an order for specific performance is found in the contract itself. We think it is too hard a bargain and too one-sided an agreement to entitle the plaintiff to relief in a court of conscience. For each individual grower the agreement is made by filling in names and quantity and price on a printed form furnished by the buyer. This form has quite obviously been drawn by skilful draftsmen with the buyer's interests in mind.

Paragraph 2 provides for the manner of delivery. Carrots are to have their stalks cut off and be in clean sanitary bags or other containers approved by Campbell. This paragraph concludes with a statement that Campbell's determination of conformance with specifications shall be conclusive.

The defendants attack this provision as unconscionable. We do not think that it is, standing by itself. We think that the provision is comparable to the promise to perform to the satisfaction of another and that Campbell would be held liable if it refused carrots which did in fact conform to the specifications.

The next paragraph allows Campbell to refuse carrots in excess of twelve tons to the acre. The next contains a covenant by the grower that he will not sell carrots to anyone else except the carrots rejected by Campbell nor will he permit anyone else to grow carrots on his land. Paragraph 10 provides liquidated damages to the extent of $50 per acre for any breach by the grower. There is no provision for liquidated or any other damages for breach of contract by Campbell.

The provision of the contract which we think is the hardest is paragraph 9.... It will be noted that Campbell is excused from accepting carrots under certain circumstances. But even under such circumstances the grower, while he cannot say Campbell is liable for failure to take the carrots, is not permitted to sell them elsewhere unless Campbell agrees. This is the kind of provision which the late Francis H. Bohlen would call "carrying a good joke too far." What the grower may do with his product under the circumstances set out is not clear. He has covenanted not to store it anywhere except on his own farm and also not to sell to anybody else.

We are not suggesting that the contract is illegal. Nor are we suggesting any excuse for the grower in this case who has deliberately broken an agreement entered into with Campbell. We do think, however, that a party who has offered and succeeded in getting an agreement as tough as this one is, should not come to a chancellor and ask court help in the enforcement of its terms. That equity does not enforce unconscionable bargains is too well established to require elaborate citation.

The plaintiff argues that the provisions of the contract are separable. We agree that they are, but do not think that decisions separating out certain provisions from illegal contracts are in point here. As already said, we do not suggest that this contract is illegal. All we say is that the sum total of its provisions drives too hard a bargain for a court of conscience to assist.

This disposition of the problem makes unnecessary further discussion of the separate liability of Lojeski, who was not a party to the contract, but who purchased some of the carrots from the Wentzes.

The judgments will be affirmed.

Exercise 9-3: *Campbell Soup Co. v. Wentz* Revisited

1. Analyze whether the remedy at law is inadequate in each of the following hypothetical situations:

   a. Cindy Canning Company sues a farmer to enforce a contract to sell Cindy all of his tomatoes where the season for packing tomatoes is only six weeks long and Cindy hires a large, short-term work force solely to help with the packing during those six weeks.

   b. Buyer Blake sues for specific performance of a contract for a second-hand airplane where there are three other similar, but not identical, airplanes available for sale in the world.

c. Buyer Blake sues to enforce a Seller's promise to sell Buyer (a shampoo manufacturer) all of its output of lemongrass (a crop used in the manufacture of, among other things, shampoo).

d. Buyer Blake buys a new car and sues to enforce Car Dealer's promise to sell.

e. Buyer Blake buys a laptop computer rated by all the magazines as the best where the Seller/Manufacturer only sells its computers directly to consumers (like some computer manufacturers used to do).

f. Buyer Blake sues to require Seller to perform its promise to continually adjust a piece of manufacturing equipment that Seller sold to Buyer and then installed in Buyer's plant. The equipment only can be adjusted on site.

2. Why not make specific performance available on demand? Isn't the request for specific performance alone an indication that a plaintiff believes she cannot be made whole by damages?

3. The next section addresses the discretionary bases on which courts deny specific performance. While the *Campbell Soup* court concludes that the remedy at law is inadequate, it nevertheless denies relief based on one of those discretionary considerations. What is that consideration?

Discretionary Considerations in Granting Specific Performance

Exercise 9-4: Fairness

Plaintiff Pete agrees to pay Defendant Dave $200,000 for land that he later learns is worth $400,000. Can a court refuse to grant specific performance because the price is unfair? What if the land were later determined to be worth $300,000? $250,000?

Exercise 9-5: *Laclede Gas Co.* and *Van Wagner*

The next two cases, *Laclede Gas Co. v. Amoco Oil Co.* and *Van Wagner Advertising Corp. v. S & M Enterprises*, provide additional insight into the inadequacy requirement. As you read those cases, consider the follow points:

1. What is the defendant's best argument in *Laclede Gas* that the remedy at law is adequate?

2. Why did the *Laclede Gas* court conclude that the remedy at law was inadequate?

3. Why does the *Van Wagner* court conclude that the remedy at law is adequate? (Why isn't the principle that real property is presumed unique controlling?)

In addition to providing further insights regarding the inadequacy requirement, the cases also address four bases on which courts exercise their discretion to deny relief.

4. Identify each basis for denying relief addressed in *Laclede Gas*, state the rule that applies, identify the policy underpinning that rule, and explain why the *Laclede Gas* court chose not to exercise its discretion to deny relief on that basis.

5. Identify the basis on which the *Van Wagner* court denied relief, state the rule, identify the policy underpinning that rule, and explain why the *Van Wagner* court based its decision on that ground.

Laclede Gas Co. v. Amoco Oil Co.
522 F.2d 33 (8th Cir. 1975)

Ross, Circuit Judge. The Laclede Gas Company (Laclede), a Missouri corporation, brought this diversity action alleging breach of contract against the Amoco Oil Company (Amoco), a Delaware corporation. It sought relief in the form of a mandatory injunction prohibiting the continuing breach or, in the alternative, damages. The district court held a bench trial on the issues of whether there was a valid, binding contract between the parties and whether, if there was such a contract, Amoco should be enjoined from breaching it. It then ruled that the "contract is invalid due to lack of mutuality" and denied the prayer for injunctive relief. The court made no decision regarding the requested damages. *Laclede Gas Co. v. Amoco Oil Co.*, 385 F. Supp. 1332, 1336 (E.D. Mo. 1974). This appeal followed, and we reverse the district court's judgment.

On September 21, 1970, Midwest Missouri Gas Company (now Laclede), and American Oil Company (now Amoco), the predecessors of the parties to this litigation, entered into a written agreement which was designed to provide central propane gas distribution systems to various residential developments in Jefferson County, Missouri, until such time as natural gas mains were extended into these areas. The agreement contemplated that as individual developments were planned the owners or developers would apply to Laclede for central propane gas systems. If Laclede determined that such a system was appropriate in any given development, it could request Amoco to supply the propane to that specific development. This request was made in the form of a supplemental form letter, as provided in the September 21 agreement; and if Amoco decided to supply the propane, it bound itself to do so by signing this supplemental form.

Once this supplemental form was signed the agreement placed certain duties on both Laclede and Amoco. Basically, Amoco was to "install, own, maintain and operate ... storage and vaporization facilities and any other facilities necessary to provide [it] with the capability of delivering to [Laclede] commercial propane gas suitable ... for delivery by [Laclede] to its customers' facilities." Amoco's facilities were to be "adequate to provide a continuous supply of commercial propane gas at such times and in such volumes commensurate with [Laclede's] requirements for meeting the demands reasonably to be anticipated in each Development while this Agreement is in force." Amoco was deemed to be "the supplier," while Laclede was "the distributing utility."

For its part Laclede agreed to "install, own, maintain and operate all distribution facilities" from a "point of delivery" which was defined to be "the outlet of [Amoco] header piping." Laclede also promised to pay Amoco "the Wood River Area Posted Price for propane plus four cents per gallon for all amounts of commercial propane gas delivered" to it under the agreement.

Since it was contemplated that the individual propane systems would eventually be converted to natural gas, one paragraph of the agreement provided that Laclede should give Amoco 30 days written notice of this event, after which the agreement would no longer be binding for the converted development.

Another paragraph gave Laclede the right to cancel the agreement. However, this right was expressed in the following language:

> This Agreement shall remain in effect for one (1) year following the first delivery of gas by [Amoco] to [Laclede] hereunder. Subject to termination as provided in Paragraph 11 hereof [dealing with conversions to natural gas], this Agreement shall automatically continue in effect for additional periods of one (1) year each unless [Laclede] shall, not less than 30 days prior to the expiration of the initial one (1) year period or any subsequent one (1) year period, give [Amoco] written notice of termination.

There was no provision under which Amoco could cancel the agreement.

For a time the parties operated satisfactorily under this agreement, and some 17 residential subdivisions were brought within it by supplemental letters. However, for various reasons, including conversion to natural gas, the number of developments under the agreement had shrunk to eight by the time of trial. These were all mobile home parks.

During the winter of 1972–73 Amoco experienced a shortage of propane and voluntarily placed all of its customers, including Laclede, on an 80% allocation basis, meaning that Laclede would receive only up to 80% of its previous requirements. Laclede objected to this and pushed Amoco to give it 100% of what the developments needed. Some conflict arose over this before the temporary shortage was alleviated.

Then, on April 3, 1973, Amoco notified Laclede that its Wood River Area Posted Price of propane had been increased by three cents per gallon. Laclede objected to this increase also and demanded a full explanation. None was forthcoming. Instead Amoco merely sent a letter dated May 14, 1973, informing Laclede that it was "terminating" the September 21, 1970, agreement effective May 31, 1973. It claimed it had the right to do this because "the Agreement lacks 'mutuality.'"

The district court felt that the entire controversy turned on whether or not Laclede's right to "arbitrarily cancel the Agreement" without Amoco having a similar right rendered the contract void "for lack of mutuality" and it resolved this question in the affirmative. We disagree with this conclusion and hold that settled principles of contract law require a reversal....

Since he found that there was no binding contract, the district judge did not have to deal with the question of whether or not to grant the injunction prayed for by Laclede. He simply denied this relief because there was no contract....

[W]e have carefully reviewed the very complete record on appeal and conclude that the trial court should grant the injunctive relief prayed. We are satisfied that this case falls within that category in which specific performance should be ordered as a matter of right. [Citation omitted.]

Amoco contends that four of the requirements for specific performance have not been met. Its claims are: (1) there is no mutuality of remedy in the contract; (2) the remedy of specific performance would be difficult for the court to administer without constant and long-continued supervision; (3) the contract is indefinite and uncertain; and (4) the remedy at law available to Laclede is adequate. The first three contentions have little or no merit and do not detain us for long.

There is simply no requirement in the law that both parties be mutually entitled to the remedy of specific performance in order that one of them be given that remedy by the court. [Citations omitted.]

While a court may refuse to grant specific performance where such a decree would require constant and long-continued court supervision, this is merely a discretionary rule of decision, which is frequently ignored when the public interest is involved. [Citations omitted.]

Here the public interest in providing propane to the retail customers is manifest, while any supervision required will be far from onerous.

Section 370 of the Restatement of Contracts (1932) provides:

> Specific enforcement will not be decreed unless the terms of the contract are so expressed that the court can determine with reasonable certainty what is the duty of each party and the conditions under which performance is due.

We believe these criteria have been satisfied here. As discussed in part I of this opinion [not included here], as to all developments for which a supplemental agreement has been signed, Amoco is to supply all the propane which is reasonably foreseeably required, while Laclede is to purchase the required propane from Amoco and pay the contract price therefor. The parties have disagreed over what is meant by "Wood River Area Posted Price" in the agreement, but the district court can and should determine with reasonable certainty what the parties intended by this term and should mold its decree, if necessary accordingly. Likewise, the fact that the agreement does not have a definite time of duration is not fatal since the evidence established that the last subdivision should be converted to natural gas in 10 to 15 years. This sets a reasonable time limit on performance and the district court can and should mold the final decree to reflect this testimony.

It is axiomatic that specific performance will not be ordered when the party claiming breach of contract has an adequate remedy at law. [Citation omitted.] This is especially true when the contract involves personal property as distinguished from real estate.

However, in Missouri, as elsewhere, specific performance may be ordered even though personalty is involved in the "proper circumstances." Mo. Rev. Stat. § 400.2-716(1); Restatement of Contracts, *supra*, § 361. And a remedy at law adequate to defeat the grant of specific performance "must be as certain, prompt, complete, and efficient to attain the ends of justice as a decree of specific performance." [Citations omitted.]

One of the leading Missouri cases allowing specific performance of a contract relating to personalty because the remedy at law was inadequate is *Boeving v. Vandover*, 218 S.W.2d 175, 178 (1949). In that case the plaintiff sought specific performance of a contract in which the defendant had promised to sell him an automobile. At that time (near the end of and shortly after World War II) new cars were hard to come by, and the court held that specific performance was a proper remedy since a new car "could not be obtained elsewhere except at considerable expense, trouble or loss, which cannot be estimated in advance."

We are satisfied that Laclede has brought itself within this practical approach taken by the Missouri courts. As Amoco points out, Laclede has propane immediately available to it under other contracts with other suppliers. And the evidence indicates that at the present time propane is readily available on the open market. However, this analysis ignores the fact that the contract involved in this lawsuit is for a long-term supply of propane to these subdivisions. The other two contracts under which Laclede obtains the gas will remain in force only until March 31, 1977, and April 1, 1981, respectively; and there is no assurance that Laclede will be able to receive any propane under them after that time. Also it is unclear as to whether or not Laclede can use the propane obtained under these contracts to supply the Jefferson County subdivisions, since they were originally entered into to provide Laclede with propane with which to "shave" its natural gas supply during peak demand periods. Additionally, there was uncontradicted expert testimony that Laclede probably could not find another supplier of propane willing to enter into a long-term contract such as the Amoco agreement, given the uncertain future of worldwide energy supplies. And, even if Laclede could obtain supplies of propane for the affected developments through its present contracts or newly negotiated ones, it would still face considerable expense and trouble which cannot be estimated in advance in making arrangements for its distribution to the subdivisions....

For the foregoing reasons the judgment of the district court is reversed and the cause is remanded for the fashioning of appropriate injunctive relief in the form of a decree of specific performance as to those developments for which a supplemental agreement form has been signed by the parties.

Van Wagner Advertising Corp. v. S & M Enterprises et al.

492 N.E.2d 756, 67 N.Y.2d 186 (1986)

Kaye, Judge. Specific performance of a contract to lease "unique" billboard space is properly denied when damages are an adequate remedy to compensate the tenant and equitable relief would impose a disproportionate burden on the defaulting landlord ...

By agreement dated December 16, 1981, Barbara Michaels leased to plaintiff, Van Wagner Advertising, for an initial period of three years plus option periods totaling seven additional years, space on the eastern exterior wall of a building on East 36th Street in Manhattan. Van Wagner was in the business of erecting and leasing billboards, and the parties anticipated that Van Wagner would erect a sign on the leased space, which faced an exit ramp of the Midtown Tunnel and was therefore visible to vehicles entering Manhattan from that tunnel.

In early 1982 Van Wagner erected an illuminated sign and leased it to Asch Advertising, Inc. for a three-year period commencing March 1, 1982. However, by agreement dated January 22, 1982, Michaels sold the building to defendant S & M Enterprises. Michaels informed Van Wagner of the sale in early August 1982, and on August 19, 1982, S & M sent Van Wagner a letter purporting to cancel the lease as of October 18....

[The trial court] declared the lease "valid and subsisting" and found that the "demised space is unique as to location for the particular advertising purpose intended by Van Wagner and Michaels, the original parties to the Lease." However, the court declined to order specific performance in light of its finding that Van Wagner "has an adequate remedy at law for damages." Moreover, the court noted that specific performance "would be inequitable in that its effect would be disproportionate in its harm to the defendant and its assistance to plaintiff." Concluding that "[the] value of the unique qualities of the demised space has been fixed by the contract Van Wagner has with its advertising client, Asch for the period of the contract," the court awarded Van Wagner the lost revenues on the Asch sublease for the period through trial, without prejudice to a new action by Van Wagner for subsequent damages if S & M did not permit Van Wagner to reoccupy the space. On Van Wagner's motion to resettle the judgment to provide for specific performance, the court adhered to its judgment.

On cross appeals the Appellate Division affirmed, without opinion. We granted both parties leave to appeal....

S & M's cancellation of Van Wagner's lease constituted a breach of contract.

Given defendant's unexcused failure to perform its contract, we next turn to a consideration of remedy for the breach: Van Wagner seeks specific performance of the contract, S & M urges that money damages are adequate but that the amount of the award was improper.

Whether or not to award specific performance is a decision that rests in the sound discretion of the trial court, and here that discretion was not abused. Considering first the nature of the transaction, specific performance has been imposed as the remedy for breach of contracts for the sale of real property but the contract here is to lease rather than sell an interest in real property. [Citations omitted.] While specific performance is available, in appropriate circumstances, for breach of a commercial or residential lease, specific performance of real property leases is not in this State awarded as a matter of course. [Citation omitted.]

Van Wagner argues that specific performance must be granted in light of the trial court's finding that the "demised space is unique as to location for the particular advertising purpose intended." The word "uniqueness" is not, however, a magic door to specific performance. A distinction must be drawn between physical difference and economic interchangeability. The trial court found that the leased property is physically unique, but so is every parcel of real property and so are many consumer goods. Putting aside contracts for the sale of real property, where specific performance has traditionally been the remedy for breach, uniqueness in the sense of physical difference does not it-self dictate the propriety of equitable relief.

By the same token, at some level all property may be interchangeable with money. Economic theory is concerned with the degree to which consumers are willing to substitute the use of one good for another, the underlying being that "every good has substitutes, even if only very poor ones," and that "all goods are ultimately commensurable." [Citation omitted.] Such a view, how-ever, could strip all meaning from uniqueness, for if all goods are ultimately exchangeable for a price, then all goods may be valued. Even a rare manu-script has an economic substitute in that there is a price for which any pur-chaser would likely agree to give up a right to buy it, but a court would in all probability order specific performance of such a contract on the ground that the subject matter of the contract is unique.

The point at which breach of a contract will be redressable by specific per-formance thus must lie not in any inherent physical uniqueness of the prop-erty but instead in the uncertainty of valuing it:

> What matters, in measuring money damages, is the volume, refine-ment, and reliability of the available information about substitutes for the subject matter of the breached contract. When the relevant information is thin and unreliable, there is a substantial risk that an award of money damages will either exceed or fall short of the promisee's actual loss. Of course this risk can always be reduced— but only at great cost when reliable information is difficult to ob-tain. Conversely, when there is a great deal of consumer behavior generating abundant and highly dependable information about sub-stitutes, the risk of error in measuring the promisee's loss may be re-duced at much smaller cost. In asserting that the subject matter of a particular contract is unique and has no established market value, a court is really saying that it cannot obtain, at reasonable cost, enough information about substitutes to permit it to calculate an award of money damages without imposing an unacceptably high risk of un-dercompensation on the injured promisee. Conceived in this way, the uniqueness test seems economically sound: [Kronman, *Specific Performance*, 45 U Chi L Rev 351 at 362]

This principle is reflected in the case law and is essentially the position of the Restatement (Second) of Contracts, which lists "the difficulty of proving dam-ages with reasonable certainty" as the first factor affecting adequacy of dam-ages. [Citation omitted.]

Thus, the fact that the subject of the contract may be "unique as to loca-tion for the particular advertising purpose intended" by the parties does not entitle a plaintiff to the remedy of specific performance.

Here, the trial court correctly concluded that the value of the "unique qual-ities" of the demised space could be fixed with reasonable certainty and with-out imposing an unacceptably high risk of undercompensating the injured tenant. Both parties complain: Van Wagner asserts that while lost revenues on the Asch contract may be adequate compensation, that contract expired

February 28, 1985, its lease with S & M continues until 1992, and the value of the demised space cannot reasonably be fixed for the balance of the term. S & M urges that future rents and continuing damages are necessarily conjectural, both during and after the Asch contract, and that Van Wagner's damages must be limited to 60 days—the period during which Van Wagner could cancel Asch's contract without consequence in the event Van Wagner lost the demised space. S & M points out that Van Wagner's lease could remain in effect for the full 10-year term, or it could legitimately be extinguished immediately, either in conjunction with a bona fide sale of the property by S & M, or by a reletting of the building if the new tenant required use of the billboard space for its own purposes. Both parties' contentions were properly rejected.

First, it is hardly novel in the law for damages to be projected into the future. Particularly where the value of commercial billboard space can be readily determined by comparisons with similar uses—Van Wagner itself has more than 400 leases—the value of this property between 1985 and 1992 cannot be regarded as speculative. Second, S & M having successfully resisted specific performance on the ground that there is an adequate remedy at law, cannot at the same time be heard to contend that damages beyond 60 days must be denied because they are conjectural. If damages for breach of this lease are indeed conjectural, and cannot be calculated with reasonable certainty, then S & M should be compelled to perform its contractual obligation by restoring Van Wagner to the premises. Moreover, the contingencies to which S & M points do not, as a practical matter, render the calculation of damages speculative. While S & M could terminate the Van Wagner lease in the event of a sale of the building, this building has been sold only once in 40 years; S & M paid several million dollars, and purchased the building in connection with its plan for major development of the block. The theoretical termination right of a future tenant of the existing building also must be viewed in light of these circumstances. If any uncertainty is generated by the two contingencies, then the benefit of that doubt must go to Van Wagner and not the contract violator. Neither contingency allegedly affecting Van Wagner's continued contractual right to the space for the balance of the lease term is within its own control; on the contrary, both are in the interest of S & M. [Citation omitted.] Thus, neither the need to project into the future nor the contingencies allegedly affecting the length of Van Wagner's term render inadequate the remedy of damages for S & M's breach of its lease with Van Wagner.

The trial court, additionally, correctly concluded that specific performance should be denied on the ground that such relief "would be inequitable in that its effect would be disproportionate in its harm to defendant and its assistance to plaintiff." [Citations omitted.] It is well settled that the imposition of an equitable remedy must not itself work an inequity, and that specific performance should not be an undue hardship. This conclusion is "not within the absolute discretion of the Supreme Court." [Citations omitted.] Here, however, there was no abuse of discretion; the finding that specific performance would disproportionately harm S & M and benefit Van Wagner has been affirmed by the Appellate Division and has support in the proof regarding S & M's projected development of the property....

Accordingly, the order of the Appellate Division should be modified, with costs to plaintiff, and the case remitted to Supreme Court, New York County, for further proceedings in accordance with this opinion and, as so modified, affirmed.

Exercise 9-6: *Laclede Gas Co.* and *Van Wagner Advertising Corp.* Revisited

1. Can the result in *Van Wagner* be explained also on a public policy basis? In other words, what public good might explain the court's inclination to deny relief?

2. How is it possible that a court can deny a party its chosen remedy for breach merely because granting the remedy will hurt the wrongdoer too much or be against the public interest?

3. The *Laclede Gas* court granted relief even though it acknowledged that enforcing the contract would require considerable court time and effort. Courts have discretion to deny relief if relief would require excessive court supervision. This idea is sometimes referred to as "undue burden on the court." (In certain types of contracts, those involving personal relationships where the court is concerned the parties will not be able to work together cooperatively, courts may instead use the phrase "inherently unstable personal relations" to describe the problem and decide not to grant relief.) Analyze whether each of the problems below would involve excessive court supervision.

   a. Plaintiff contracted with Defendant for Defendant to build Plaintiff a widget manufacturing factory for $27.5 billion. The plans required Defendant to build a factory specifically tailored to Plaintiff's widget manufacturing process and the parties anticipated the project would take three years.

   b. Contract for Defendant to build Plaintiff a space in a shopping center for a department store where Defendant was already building two other such spaces in the same mall using the same plans.

   c. Contract for Defendant to build Plaintiff a two-story, 4,000 square foot home according to standardized plans developed by Defendant's architect.

   d. Specific performance of a McDonald's franchise contract between McDonalds, Inc., and a franchisee.

Exercise 9-7: *Travellers International*

As you read the following case, *Travellers International, AG v. Trans World Airlines, Inc.,* ask yourself:

1. Why does the court conclude the remedy at law is inadequate?

2. Given the highly interactive nature of this contract, why does the court conclude enforcing the contract would not require excessive court supervision?

Travellers Int'l, AG v.
Trans World Airlines, Inc.

722 F. Supp. 1087 (S.D.N.Y. 1989)

Ward, District Judge. Plaintiffs, Travellers International A.G. ("Travellers" or "TI") and Windsor, Inc. ("Windsor"), seek permanently to enjoin defendant, Trans World Airlines, Inc. ("TWA"), from terminating the contract of November 26, 1984 between Travellers and TWA (the "Contract"). For the reasons that follow, the request for a permanent injunction is granted....

[T]his Court conducted a bench trial on February 27–28, March 1–4 and 14–17, 1989 to determine plaintiffs' entitlement to a permanent injunction.... Based upon the evidence presented during the six days of testimony at the preliminary injunction hearing and the evidence adduced during the ten days of testimony at the bench trial, the Court makes the following findings of facts and conclusions of law pursuant to Rule 52, Fed. R. Civ. P.

Travellers, a Swiss corporation with its principal place of business in London, England, is wholly owned by Windsor, a Missouri corporation with its principal place of business in St. Louis County, Missouri. Barney Ebsworth ("Ebsworth") is the sole shareholder of Windsor. TWA is a Delaware corporation with its principal place of business in New York. Carl Icahn ("Icahn"), who acquired control of TWA in the fall of 1985, is Chairman of its Board of Directors and its Chief Executive Officer....

The relationship between Travellers and TWA began more than twenty (20) years ago, when both corporations were controlled by different owners. Travellers is in the vacation tour business. It contracts with hotels and other service providers in order to develop and operate tours in various countries. TWA is an international airline. In the early 1970's, TWA commenced its "Getaway Tours" to Europe. TWA, through the Getaway Tours, offered air transportation to passengers purchasing land tour packages. TWA owns the Getaway mark and the Getaway Tours are proprietary to it.

Beginning in 1972, Travellers sold tours to TWA, which TWA marketed as Getaway Tours. Pursuant to a written agreement between the two companies, Travellers was responsible for developing and operating the land tour packages of the Getaway Tours (the "Tours"). In 1974, Travellers and TWA entered into a Land Agreement and a Brochure Agreement, each dated April 25, 1974 (the "1974 Agreements"). The 1974 Agreements were the first in a series of successive long term contracts under which TWA was to provide air transportation for the Tours, market the Tours, wholesale the Tours to independent travel agents, and accept reservations directly for the Tours, while Travellers was to continue to develop and operate the land arrangements and to produce promotional brochures for the Tours. The brochures were to be used as selling tools by travel agents and TWA.

On or about June 6, 1979, Travellers and TWA entered into two additional agreements (the "1979 Agreements"), continuing their basic relationship. The most recent written agreement between the parties, entered into on or about November 26, 1984, relates to both Tours and brochures and is the Contract at the center of this litigation. The Contract covers the five year period from

1986 to 1991. Obligations under the Contract concerning the brochures commenced on January 1, 1986 with respect to brochures that were to be produced by Travellers and delivered to TWA for the 1987 tour season, and continued through 1990 with respect to brochures for the 1991 tour season. Obligations under the Contract concerning the Tours commenced on November 1, 1986 and continued until December 31, 1991. The parties operated pursuant to the 1979 Agreements until the effective dates specified in the Contract.

The Contract provided that Travellers was to advise TWA on marketing, advertising, development of new Tour products, preparation of promotional budgets, projection of expenses and revenues and production and distribution of brochures. The Contract also required the parties annually to reach agreement on the Tour itineraries and the prices and quality of the Tour packages.

Paragraph 5 of the Contract specified that TWA would:

> [P]roduce and distribute brochures for the Tours in such numbers as are deemed appropriate to produce the number of Tour passengers desired by TWA and TI, such desired number of Tour passengers to be mutually agreed upon for each year by TWA and TI, but in no event to be less than 100,000 per year.

Furthermore, TWA was obligated to advertise the Tours, wholesale the Tours to travel agents and make retail sales of the Tours at TWA's own sales office or through other distribution channels. The parties agreed that the Contract would be governed and construed according to New York law.

Providing the tours and the brochures as required under the Contract demanded substantial advance preparation by both parties. It had been the practice of Travellers and TWA to hold an annual planning meeting early each year to discuss the number and content of the Tours to be offered during the next calendar year, as well as the format, content, design, and number of brochures to be produced. Paragraph A.3 of the Contract provides that the final retail price for the land component of the Tours was to be agreed upon by Travellers and TWA by September 1 of the year prior to when the Tours would be offered to the public.

The prices paid by a Getaway Tour vacationer included both the cost of the Tour and the airfare to the tour destination. Travellers and TWA shared in the revenue generated by the Tours, but not the airfare, which TWA collected alone. In the past, the retail price for the land based component of a Getaway Tour was disbursed by TWA as follows: approximately fourteen percent (14%) was paid to the travel agent responsible for booking the Tour, six percent (6%) was retained by TWA as its own margin, and the balance of eighty percent (80%) was remitted to Travellers. From the percentage of the retail land tour price Travellers received, it paid the costs of operating the Tours. In addition to the 6% margin on the land-based tour aspect of the Getaway Program, TWA earned substantial revenue from the airfares it collected from Tour passengers. An internal TWA memorandum indicated that, in 1985, the Getaway Program provided incremental revenue which TWA would not have received absent its participation in the Program of over forty-nine million dollars ($49,000,000.00)....

World events in 1985 and 1986, including the hijacking of a TWA jet, highly publicized acts of terrorism, the 1986 raid on Libya by the United States and the Chernobyl nuclear disaster, as well as the TWA flight attendants' strike, combined to reduce significantly the demand for the Getaway Tours covered by the Contract.

In late 1985, Icahn acquired control of TWA. He became Chairman of the Board of TWA in January 1986. In late 1986 or early 1987, TWA began to re-examine the economics of the Getaway Tours and the Contract. In late March or early April 1987, Craig Pavlus ("Pavlus"), a vice president of TWA, was put in charge of the Getaway Program.

In early 1986, Gerald Herrod ("Herrod"), the founder, chairman and sole owner of Travellers at the time of the Contract, sought to sell Travellers. He had been the moving force behind Travellers from its inception, although since 1980 he had begun to devote more and more time to his new venture, Ocean Cruise Lines....

Subsequently, Herrod reached an understanding with Ebsworth to purchase Travellers. Prior to consummating the purchase, Ebsworth sought and obtained TWA's written consent to the acquisition. In a letter dated August 6, 1986, McHugh, on behalf of TWA, advised Ebsworth that:

> TWA acknowledges that you are negotiating for the purchase of the business of Travellers International A.G. As long as you intend to perform according to the terms and conditions of our existing contracts with Travellers International, TWA agrees to your purchase of the business.
>
> We are looking forward to working with you in the future.

Windsor and Ebsworth purchased the assets of Travellers from Herrod, including the Contract, on August 15, 1986 and the purchase of Travellers closed on August 31, 1986....

Unfortunately, the change in control of the two companies foreshadowed a change in the harmonious relationship the two companies had enjoyed for over a decade. The spring and summer of 1987 saw a series of confrontational meetings between representatives of Travellers and TWA escalate into a battle between Ebsworth and Icahn, culminating in a heated exchange between the two men at a dinner meeting on August 5, 1987.... Suffice it to say that TWA, believing the Contract unduly benefitted Travellers at its expense, sought to alter certain of the past practices between the parties.

Accordingly, in May 1987, TWA successfully renegotiated a reduction in the price paid to Travellers under the Contract for preparing the 1988 brochures, and reduced the number of brochures to be produced by Travellers. In June 1987, TWA proposed to increase its margin for the land-based tour. After stormy negotiations throughout the summer, TWA's margin was increased from six percent (6%) to ten percent (10%) of the retail land tour price ...

On September 16, 1987, Pavlus sent Travellers a letter purporting to terminate the Contract. The letter, which was also copied to both Ehrlich and Icahn, stated that the termination would be "effective December 31, 1988 with respect to Tours and as of December 31, 1987, with respect to Tour Brochures" and set forth six grounds justifying the termination.

[The court articulated and rejected each of TWA's alleged grounds for termination....]

Travellers seeks a permanent injunction requiring TWA to specifically perform the Contract. Specific performance of a contract is appropriate when (1) the contract is valid, (2) plaintiff has substantially performed under the contract and is willing and able to perform its remaining obligations, (3) defendant is able to perform its obligations, and (4) plaintiff has no adequate remedy at law. [Citations omitted.]

The evidence established that the Contract was valid and that Travellers had substantially performed its obligations. Travellers demonstrated that it will not be able to continue as a going concern at this time if the Contract, representing 90–95% of its business, is terminated. The destruction of a business has long been held to constitute the type of irreparable injury for which there is no adequate monetary remedy. [Citations omitted.]

In addition, the balance of equities tips markedly in favor of Travellers. Termination of the Contract will put Travellers out of business, while continued performance under the Contract is likely to also continue to be profitable for TWA. Regardless of the profitability of the Tours to TWA, its dealings with Travellers represent only a small fraction of its overall business, and the continuation of the Contract in no way threatens TWA's ability to remain in business.

TWA's final argument against the imposition of a permanent injunction is that compliance with the injunction would require constant judicial intervention in the business activities of the parties. [Citation omitted.] This argument, like the many that came before it, is inapposite. While Travellers and TWA are required to work together in order to agree on pricing and the substantive content of the Tours and brochures, the long history of their relationship indicates they can do just that without constant judicial intervention. In fact, the evidence indicated that the representatives of TWA involved in actually planning the Getaway Tours have had much less trouble dealing with their counterparts at Travellers than do the leaders of the respective organizations.

While there have been certain disputes regarding continued performance under the preliminary injunction and an inordinate amount of petty complaints by both sides, the parties have been able to offer Getaway Tours to the public during 1989. A continuation of the requirement that disputes under the Contract be resolved with reference to the past practices of the parties provides more than adequate direction to enable them to operate the Getaway Tours in the future without continual judicial involvement. In addition, the planning meeting for the 1990 Tours, held during the recess in the trial, was reported to have been successful, and the Court is unaware of any recent conflicts that would make continued performance under the Contract an especially onerous burden on TWA.

Plaintiffs have demonstrated that they adequately performed their obligations under the Contract and therefore that TWA's termination was unjustified. They have also proven that they will be irreparably harmed absent TWA's continued performance under the Contract. Accordingly, plaintiffs' request for a permanent injunction preventing TWA from terminating the Contract is granted....

Exercise 9-8: *Travellers International* Revisited

1. In a well-known case, *Fitzpatrick v. Michael*, 9 A.2d 639, 177 Md. 248 (1939), plaintiff agreed to work for defendant as his chauffeur, house manager, companion and nurse, and, in exchange, defendant agreed to revise his will to grant her ownership of his cars and the right to live in his house and use his furnishings for the rest of her life. Plaintiff performed her promised duties for a few years, at which time defendant more or less forced her out of the house. Plaintiff sued for specific performance. The court denied her request for specific performance. Can you see why?

2. If the plaintiff in *Fitzpatrick* was the party who breached the contract and the defendant was suing, the court would have an additional ground for denying relief. Based on the Thirteenth Amendment to the Constitution, courts generally deny specific performance of personal services contracts on the grounds that enforcement would create involuntary servitude.

The final grounds on which courts deny equitable relief are referred to as the "equitable defenses." The first equitable defense, "**laches**," is the equitable equivalent of a statute of limitations. States vary greatly as to the length of their statutes of limitations for contract claims, and, even within a state, the length of time often depends on whether the contract is written or oral. All states agree that once the time limit in a statute of limitations has expired, the plaintiff no longer can maintain her lawsuit for damages. Laches is a more flexible concept; it bars a claim if the plaintiff has delayed pursuing her claim for an unreasonable amount of time and the delay has prejudiced the defendant—for example, because of a loss of evidence or memories or because of reliance on the plaintiff's inaction.

The second equitable defense is "**unclean hands**." Unclean hands is the equitable equivalent of illegality, but it applies to a much broader range of conduct. Unclean hands is addressed in the next case.

Exercise 9-9: *Green*

As you read the next case, *Green v. Higgins*, consider the following questions:

1. Make sure you understand the rather complicated machinations created by plaintiff and defendants to deprive others of their contractual rights.

2. Why do we assert that unclean hands applies to a broader range of conduct than illegality?

Green v. Higgins

535 P.2d 446, 217 Kan. 217 (1975)

Prager, Justice. This is an action for specific performance of a contract for the sale of real estate. The facts are not in dispute and are essentially as follows: On May 7, 1969, the defendants-appellees, Damon W. Higgins and Cleo D. Higgins, sold a tract of land to Robert E. Brown and Mark S. Gilman.

At the time of this transaction and as a part of the consideration therefor, the Higgins agreed that Brown and Gilman should have a right of first refusal to purchase adjoining land from the Higgins should they desire to sell it. In addition, as a result of this same sale, a real estate agent, Lienna McCulley, obtained an agreement with the Higgins which gave Miss McCulley the right to handle any subsequent sale of the adjoining tract if the contracting or sale occurred prior to June 1, 1971. In April of 1971 the Higgins desired to sell the adjoining tract of land which was subject to the contractual rights just mentioned. The plaintiffs-appellants, Philip A. Green and Barbara A. Green, desired to purchase the adjoining tract of land from the Higgins at a proposed purchase price of $30,000. A contract for the purchase of the property for the proposed price was executed by the Greens and the Higgins on April 21, 1971. Prior to the time the contract was prepared and executed the Higgins advised the Greens that Lienna McCulley would be entitled to a commission on the sale if the contracting or sale occurred prior to June 1, 1971. The contract was dated June 2, 1971, in order to defeat Lienna McCulley's right to handle the sale of the property and to cheat her out of her real estate commission.

Plaintiff, Philip A. Green, testified in his deposition that after this contract was signed Higgins advised him that the property was subject to the right of first refusal held by Brown and Gilman pursuant to the contract of May 7, 1969. Green and Higgins apparently decided that something had to be done to avoid Higgins's obligation to give the first right of refusal to Brown and Gilman. Green testified in substance that he suggested to Higgins that a fictitious contract be prepared and delivered to Brown and Gilman with a letter giving them the opportunity to enter into a contract for the same price or otherwise the right of first refusal would be waived. The fictitious contract was dictated by Mr. Green and typed by Mrs. Green. In this fictitious contract the purchase price was stated to be $40,000 and the designated purchaser of the property was Medallion Investment Properties, Inc., a corporation of which Mr. Green was the president. It is undisputed that this fictitious contract with an inflated purchase price in the amount of $40,000 was prepared and delivered to Brown and Gilman to discourage them from exercising their right of first refusal, since the indicated purchase price of $40,000 was an excessive price for the property. This gambit was apparently successful since Brown and Gilman did not exercise their right of first refusal to purchase the property under the terms stated in the fictitious contract.

Thereafter the Higgins decided that they did not want to carry out their contract with the Greens and so advised the Greens. At that point the only money which had changed hands was the $100 given to Higgins by Green at the time the contract was executed. The Higgins offered to return this in August or September of 1971. In January of 1972 Green tendered the balance of the purchase price, $29,900 and requested a warranty deed from Higgins which Higgins refused to provide. On March 28, 1972, the Greens filed this action for specific performance of the contract. The Higgins counterclaimed for damages based upon an alleged clouding of their title and further prayed that their title to the land be quieted against the Greens. Thereafter depositions were taken of Philip A. Green and Damon W. Higgins which brought forth the facts which have been recited above. On the basis of the pleadings and depositions the plaintiffs Green filed a motion for summary judgment. The defendants Higgins then filed a motion to dismiss pursuant to K.S.A.1973

Supp. 60-212(b)(6). The Higgins motion to dismiss was based upon a number of grounds including a defense that since the plaintiffs Green had attempted to perpetrate a fraud upon a third party, the plaintiffs had not come into court with clean hands and therefore should be denied equitable relief by way of specific performance. A hearing was held on the motions filed by the parties. At the conclusion thereof the district court dismissed the petition of the Greens for specific performance and also dismissed the counterclaim of the Higgins seeking damages and a decree quieting title to their land.

In denying relief to both parties the district court found on the undisputed facts as alleged in the pleadings and as established by the depositions, that the conduct of both the plaintiffs Green and the defendants Higgins had been willful, fraudulent, illegal, and unconscionable, that neither party had come into court with clean hands, and thus neither should be granted any relief by the court. The plaintiffs Green have appealed to this court from the judgment of the district court dismissing their petition and denying them specific performance.

On this appeal the Greens contend that the motion to dismiss filed by the defendants was prematurely sustained because there were genuine issues of fact remaining in the case. We do not agree. K.S.A.1973 Supp. 60-212(b) provides that if on a motion asserting a defense of failure of the pleading to state a claim upon which relief can be granted, matters outside the pleading are presented to the court, the motion shall be treated as one for summary judgment and shall be disposed of as provided in section 60-256, provided all parties are given a reasonable opportunity to present evidentiary material pertaining thereto. In this case the plaintiffs had previously filed a motion for summary judgment based upon the undisputed facts contained in the pleadings and depositions of the parties. Here there is no complaint that the trial court did not afford to the parties every reasonable opportunity to make discovery and to obtain evidence in support of and in opposition to their respective motions. Under the provisions of K.S.A. 60-256 the trial court is authorized to render summary judgment when there is no material issue of fact. Such judgment may in fact be entered on the court's own motion. [Citation omitted.]

In this case the clean hands doctrine had been specifically raised as an affirmative defense in the defendants' answer. That defense was the basis of the defendants' motion to dismiss. The clean hands doctrine is based upon the maxim of equity that he who comes into equity must come with clean hands. The clean hands doctrine in substance provides that no person can obtain affirmative relief in equity with respect to a transaction in which he has, himself, been guilty of inequitable conduct. It is difficult to formulate a general statement as to what will amount to unclean hands other than to state it is conduct which the court regards as inequitable. Like other doctrines of equity, the clean hands maxim is not a binding rule, but is to be applied in the sound discretion of the court. The clean hands doctrine has been recognized in many Kansas cases. [Citations omitted.] The application of the clean hands doctrine is subject to certain limitations. Conduct which will render a party's hands unclean so as to deny him access to a court of equity must be willful conduct which is fraudulent, illegal or unconscionable. Furthermore the objectionable misconduct must bear an immediate relation to the subject-matter of the suit and in some measure affect the equitable relations subsisting between the parties to the litigation and arising out of the transaction. [Citations omitted.] Stated in another way the misconduct which may justify a denial of equitable relief must be related misconduct rather than collateral misconduct arising outside the specific transaction which is the subject-matter of the litigation before the court.

It should also be emphasized that in applying the clean hands maxim, courts are concerned primarily with their own integrity. The doctrine of unclean hands is derived from the unwillingness of a court to give its peculiar relief to a suitor who in the very controversy has so conducted himself as to shock the moral sensibilities of the judge. It has nothing to do with the rights or liabilities of the parties. In applying the unclean hands doctrine, courts act for their own protection, and not as a matter of 'defense' to the defendant....

The plaintiffs Green on this appeal argue that a defendant cannot invoke the protection of the clean hands maxim unless he has suffered from the misconduct of the plaintiff. They argue that here the defendants Higgins participated in the claimed misconduct and that any injury suffered would be to third parties and not to the defendants themselves. There is authority to support the plaintiffs' position. [Citations omitted.] In our judgment such an interpretation of the clean hands doctrine does not accord with its principal purpose. A court may refuse its relief to the plaintiff though the defendant himself participated in the misconduct, not because it is a privilege of such a defendant, but because the court refuses to lend its aid to either party to such a transaction. The best-reasoned cases hold that the maxim applies, even though the misconduct of the plaintiff has not injured anyone and even though the defendant himself was a participant in the misconduct. [Citations omitted.]

With these basic principles in mind we turn now to the undisputed facts in this case to determine whether or not the district court abused its discretion in denying relief to both the plaintiffs and the defendants. Here all parties have conceded that the following facts are true: That the contract entered into between the parties on April 21, 1971 was dated June 2, 1971, in order to deprive Lienna McCulley of her right to a sales commission which she had previously obtained through contract; that a fictitious contract was prepared by which it appeared the Higgins agreed to sell the real estate to Medallion Investment Properties, Inc. for $40,000; that the fraudulent contract was prepared at the suggestion of the plaintiff, Philip A. Green, and was submitted by Higgins to Brown and Gilman in order to deprive them of their right of first refusal to purchase the property at a proposed price. It simply cannot be denied that the plaintiffs Green actively and willfully participated in fraudulent and unconscionable activities to obtain title to the land and to defeat various legal rights held by third parties. The misconduct involved here was directly related to the subject-matter of the litigation and must be classified as related misconduct, not collateral misconduct. Under all the facts and circumstances we cannot say that the trial court abused its discretion in denying relief to both the plaintiffs and defendants by reason of the clean hands doctrine.

The judgment of the trial court is affirmed.

Injunctions to Enforce Covenants Not to Compete

As you learned in Chapter 5, contracting parties use covenants not to compete in three situations:

1. In connection with the sale of a business, sellers almost always promise not to compete with the business being sold.

2. In most instances, while an employee is under contract with her employer, she impliedly promises not to take the same position with a competing employer.

3. Many employment contracts restrict an employee's right to work for another employer for some period of time *after* the employment relationship has ended. Such contractual clauses are called "**post-employment covenants not to compete.**"

Exercise 9-10: Covenants Not to Compete Made *During* Employment

1. Courts distinguish and treat differently covenant-not-to-compete disputes involving employees who work for someone else *while* they are still under contract with the original employer from covenant-not-to-compete disputes involving employees who work for someone else *after* their employment contracts have ended. Why?

2. Regarding cases involving current employees, courts have held that employers cannot get specific performance based on the Thirteenth Amendment issue discussed above. However, if an employer can meet the inadequacy test and the court chooses not to exercise its discretion to deny relief, the employer can obtain an injunction prohibiting the employee from working for any other employer. Thus, in cases involving contracts with professional singers, athletes, and coaches, employers have succeeded in obtaining injunctions. In each of the following cases, assume the employee breached the contract during the term of the contract by abandoning the job and taking a job with a competing employer. In which of the following cases could an employer successfully obtain an injunction (absent a basis for the court denying relief based on any of the equitable considerations)?

    a. A contract between a music hall and an "exceptionally talented" organist where the there were "five other organists of comparable ability for hire in the ... area." *See Pingley v. Brunson*, 252 S.E.2d 560, 272 S.C. 421 (1979).

    b. A contract between a law school and a new, untenured contracts professor. What if the professor is tenured? What if she is known nationally in her field?

    c. A contract between a law firm and an associate? A contract between a law firm and a partner? What additional facts would you need to know about the partner to evaluate this problem?

Exercise 9-11: *DeSantis* and *A.N. Deringer*

The next two cases, *DeSantis v. Wackenhut Corp.* and *A.N. Deringer, Inc. v. Strough*, focus on disputes involving post-employment covenants not to compete. The *DeSantis* court describes the commonly used test to evaluate the enforceability of a post-employment covenant not to compete. Make sure to identify all the considerations courts weigh in evaluating such covenants and how courts apply those considerations.

The *A.N. Deringer* case articulates and applies the rules courts use when a covenant not to compete excessively restricts a former employee's right to work. Identify those rules and make sure you understand how the court applies them.

DeSantis v. Wackenhut Corp.

793 S.W.2d 670, 33 Tex. Sup. J. 517 (1990)

Hecht, Justice. This case involving a noncompetition agreement between an employer and employee presents [among other things, a question of] whether the noncompetition agreement is enforceable....

The trial court [held] the agreement valid but overly broad as to the geographical territory in which competition was restricted.... We hold that ... under Texas law, the noncompetition agreement is unenforceable....

Edward DeSantis has been providing international and corporate security services, both in the CIA and the private sector for his entire career. In June 1981, while employed by R.J. Reynolds Industries in North Carolina, DeSantis interviewed for a position with Wackenhut Corporation. At that time, Wackenhut, which was chartered and headquartered in Florida, was the third largest company in the nation specializing in furnishing security guards for businesses throughout the country. DeSantis met with Wackenhut's president, founder, and majority stockholder, George Wackenhut, at the company's offices in Florida, and the two agreed that DeSantis would immediately assume the position of Wackenhut's Houston area manager. According to DeSantis, George Wackenhut promised him that the area manager's position was only temporary, and that he would soon be moved into a top executive position. George Wackenhut denies that he made any such promises to DeSantis, admitting only that he mentioned advancement to an executive position as a possible opportunity.

At Wackenhut's request, DeSantis signed a noncompetition agreement at the inception of his employment. The agreement recites that it was "made and entered into" on August 13, 1981, in Florida, although DeSantis signed it in Texas. It also recites consideration "including but not limited to the Employee's employment by the Employer." In the agreement DeSantis covenanted that as long as he was employed by Wackenhut and for two years thereafter, he would not compete in any way with Wackenhut in a forty-county area in south Texas. DeSantis expressly acknowledged that Wackenhut's client list "is a valuable, special and unique asset of [Wackenhut's] business" and agreed never to disclose it to anyone. DeSantis also agreed never to divulge any confidential or proprietary information acquired through his employment with Wackenhut....

DeSantis remained manager of Wackenhut's Houston office for nearly three years, until March 1984, when he resigned under threat of termination. DeSantis contends that he was forced to quit because of disagreements with

Wackehut's senior management over the profitability of the Houston office. Wackenhut contends that DeSantis was asked to resign because of his unethical solicitation of business.

Following his resignation, DeSantis invested in a company which marketed security electronics. He also formed a new company, Risk Deterrence, Inc. ("RDI"), to provide security consulting services and security guards to a limited clientele. The month following termination of his employment with Wackenhut, DeSantis sent out letters announcing his new ventures to twenty or thirty businesses, about half of which were Wackenhut clients. He added a postscript to letters to Wackenhut clients in which he disclaimed any intent to interfere with their existing contracts with Wackenhut. Within six months, however, one of Wackenhut's clients, Marathon Oil Company, had terminated its contract with Wackenhut and signed a five-year contract with RDI, and a second Wackenhut client, TRW-Mission Drilling Products, was considering doing the same. Wackenhut claims that DeSantis was acquiring its clients in violation of the noncompetition agreement. DeSantis claims that these clients began considering other security service providers only after the quality of Wackenhut's services declined, following DeSantis' departure.

Wackenhut sued DeSantis and RDI in October 1984 to enjoin them from violating the noncompetition agreement, and to recover damages for breach of the agreement and for tortious interference with business relations. Wackenhut alleged that DeSantis and RDI were soliciting its clients' business using confidential client and pricing information which DeSantis obtained through his employment with Wackenhut. The trial court issued an ex parte temporary restraining order against DeSantis and RDI, and fixed the amount of the requisite bond which Wackenhut filed at $5,000. Following a hearing, the trial court issued a temporary injunction upon a $75,000 bond, which Wackenhut also filed. DeSantis and RDI counterclaimed against Wackenhut, alleging that Wackenhut had fraudulently induced DeSantis to sign the noncompetition agreement, that the agreement violated state antitrust laws, and that enforcement of the agreement by temporary injunction was wrongful and tortiously interfered with DeSantis and RDI's contract and business relationships. RDI claimed damages for loss of the Marathon contract, which Marathon terminated after the injunction issued, for loss of the TRW business, and for injury to its reputation. DeSantis claimed damages for lost salary, impaired reputation, and mental anguish. DeSantis and RDI both sought statutory damages under the Texas Free Enterprise and Antitrust Act, Texas Business and Commerce Code Annotated sections 15.01–15.51 (Vernon 1987 and Supp. 1990), and exemplary damages....

[T]he trial court permanently enjoined DeSantis from competing with Wackenhut, and RDI from employing DeSantis to compete with Wackenhut, for two years from the date DeSantis left Wackenhut in an area reduced by the trial court from the forty counties stated in the agreement to the thirteen counties found by the trial court to be reasonably necessary to protect Wackenhut's interest. The trial court also permanently enjoined DeSantis from divulging Wackenhut's client list or proprietary information, and RDI from using any proprietary information of Wackenhut's acquired through DeSantis. The trial court denied all relief requested by DeSantis and RDI, based upon the jury's finding that DeSantis had breached his agreement with Wackenhut. The trial court awarded Wackenhut attorney's fees and costs.

The court of appeals affirmed the judgment of the trial court in all respects....

We now consider whether the noncompetition agreement between De-Santis and Wackenhut is enforceable under Texas law. We must also consider the effect upon this case of certain legislation passed while this case has been pending before this Court.

The fundamental common law principles which govern the enforceability of covenants not to compete in Texas are relatively well established. An agreement not to compete is in restraint of trade and therefore unenforceable on grounds of public policy unless it is reasonable. [Citations omitted.] An agreement not to compete is not a reasonable restraint of trade unless it meets each of three criteria. First, the agreement not to compete must be ancillary to an otherwise valid transaction or relationship. [Citations omitted.] Such a restraint on competition is unreasonable unless it is part of and subsidiary to an otherwise valid transaction or relationship which gives rise to an interest worthy of protection. [Citations omitted.] Such transactions or relationships include the purchase and sale of a business, and employment relationships. [Citations omitted.] Second, the restraint created by the agreement not to compete must not be greater than necessary to protect the promisee's legitimate interest. [Citations omitted. Examples of legitimate, protectable interests include business goodwill, trade secrets, and other confidential or proprietary information. [Citations omitted.] The extent of the agreement not to compete must accordingly be limited appropriately as to time, territory, and type of activity. [Citations omitted.] An agreement not to compete which is not appropriately limited may be modified and enforced by a court of equity to the extent necessary to protect the promisee's legitimate interest, but may not be enforced by a court of law. [Citations omitted.] Third, the promisee's need for the protection afforded by the agreement not to compete must not be outweighed by either the hardship to the promisor or any injury likely to the public. [Citations omitted.] Before an agreement not to compete will be enforced, its benefits must be balanced against its burdens, both to the promisor and the public. Thus, such an agreement may, in a particular case, accomplish the salutary purpose of encouraging an employer to share confidential, proprietary information with an employee in furtherance of their common purpose, but must not also take unfair advantage of the disparity of bargaining power between them or too severely impair the employee's personal freedom and economic mobility. [Citations omitted.] Whether an agreement not to compete is a reasonable restraint of trade is a question of law for the court..... .

In deciding whether an ancillary agreement not to compete is reasonable, the court should focus on the need to protect a legitimate interest of the promisee and the hardship of such protection on the promisor and the public. The nature of the promisor's job—whether it is a common calling—may sometimes factor into the determination of reasonableness, but it is not the primary focus of inquiry....

There is no dispute in this case that the agreement not to compete was ancillary to an otherwise valid relationship, viz., Wackenhut's employment of De-Santis. The dispute is whether the agreement was necessary to protect some legitimate interest of Wackenhut, and whether that necessity was outweighed by the hardship of enforcement. As we have noted above, these are all questions for the court.

Wackenhut claims that the business goodwill developed for it by DeSantis was an interest protectable by an agreement not to compete. The evidence that DeSantis ever developed business goodwill for Wackenhut, however, is exceedingly slight on this record, little more than testimony that DeSantis occasionally entertained representatives of Wackenhut's clients. Indeed, Wackenhut's contention that DeSantis' unethical business solicitation led it to request his resignation tends, at least, to contradict its contention that DeSantis developed goodwill among its customers. Assuming, however, that DeSantis did develop business goodwill for Wackenhut, there is no showing that he did or even could divert that goodwill to himself for his own benefit after leaving Wackenhut. The jury found that DeSantis competed with Wackenhut after leaving its employ, and the evidence leaves little doubt that he did; but there is no finding and almost no evidence that DeSantis was able to appropriate for his own use any business goodwill that he developed for Wackenhut. Rather, the evidence is that after announcing his departure to some ten or fifteen of Wackenhut's customers, in the following six months DeSantis received business from only one of those customers and might have received business from another. There is evidence that both were considering moving their business to DeSantis' new company, RDI, because they were dissatisfied with Wackenhut's services. There is no evidence that either customer considered replacing Wackenhut with DeSantis because of the goodwill DeSantis had developed with those customers while at Wackenhut. There is simply no showing on this record that prohibiting DeSantis from competing with Wackenhut after he left its employ was necessary to keep DeSantis from trading on Wackenhut's business goodwill, much less any showing that the hardship of the agreement on DeSantis was outweighed by the need to protect any such interest.

Wackenhut also claims that it possessed confidential information protectable by an agreement not to compete. Specifically, Wackenhut contends that during his employ, DeSantis learned the identity of Wackenhut's customers, their special needs and requirements, and Wackenhut's pricing policies, cost factors and bidding strategies. Again, while confidential information may be protected by an agreement not to compete, Wackenhut has failed to show that it needed such protection in this case. Wackenhut failed to show that its customers could not readily be identified by someone outside its employ, that such knowledge carried some competitive advantage, or that its customers' needs could not be ascertained simply by inquiry addressed to those customers themselves. Also, Wackenhut failed to show that its pricing policies and bidding strategies were uniquely developed, or that information about its prices and bids could not, again, be obtained from the customers themselves. There is no evidence that DeSantis ever took advantage of any knowledge he had of Wackenhut's cost factors in trying to outbid Wackenhut or woo away its customers. Wackenhut simply has not demonstrated a need to protect any confidential information by limiting DeSantis' right to compete.

Having determined that Wackenhut has not shown that DeSantis' agreement not to compete is necessary to protect any legitimate business interest, or that the necessity of such protection outweighs the hardship of that agreement on DeSantis, we conclude that the agreement is unreasonable and therefore unenforceable.

————————

A.N. Deringer, Inc. v. Strough
103 F.3d 243 (2d Cir. 1996)

Restani, Circuit Judge. Petitioner-appellant A.N. Deringer, Inc. ("Deringer") appeals from a decision of the United States District Court (Murtha, J.) for the District of Vermont, granting summary judgment for defendants and denying enforcement of a non-competition provision in an employment agreement. For the reasons set forth below, we reverse and remand for determination of damages and attorney's fees.

Procedural and Factual Background

Deringer is a customs broker and former employer of appellee John M. Strough ("Strough"). Strough is currently employed by co-appellee Fritz Companies, Inc. ("Fritz"), a customs broker and competitor of Deringer. Strough worked for Deringer from 1984 through February 1995. In 1994 he applied for a sales position at Deringer, which he obtained in October 1994. In November 1994, Strough executed a Confidentiality and Trade Secret Agreement (hereinafter "the Agreement") in exchange for $1,000. The Agreement provided that for ninety days after the termination of his employment, Strough would not compete with Deringer, directly or indirectly, within a prohibited geographic area consisting of a 100-mile radius around any Deringer office. Deringer has at least 30 offices, many along the United States' border with Canada. Further, Deringer and Strough agreed:

> Although both of us consider the foregoing restriction to be reasonable for the protection of Deringer, if it is found by a court to be unreasonable because it is overly broad as to time period, geographic area or otherwise, then and in that case, the restriction shall nevertheless remain effective, but shall be considered amended in such manner so as to make the restriction reasonable as determined by such court and as so amended shall be enforced.

(Confidentiality and Trade Secret Agreement; App. at 11). The Agreement also provided that Deringer would be entitled to enjoin Strough from breaching the Agreement and that Strough would "pay the costs of any such proceeding, including Deringer's reasonable attorney's fees." (Confidentiality and Trade Secret Agreement; App. at 12).

In the summer of 1994, Strough applied for employment with Fritz. Fritz contacted Strough on February 15, 1995, offering him a branch manager position. Strough indicated to a Fritz official that he had signed the Agreement with Deringer, but was told that he should not worry because the Agreement was unenforceable. On February 22, 1995, Strough resigned from Deringer and the following day began working for Fritz in the immediate vicinity of his previous employment with Deringer, although not as a salesman.

On March 3, 1995, Deringer brought the present action against defendants Strough and Fritz in Vermont Superior Court, seeking enforcement of the

Agreement, damages arising out of the breach of the Agreement, and an award of attorney's fees and costs. On March 15, 1995, defendants removed the case to federal court on diversity grounds. On March 16, 1995, Deringer moved for preliminary injunction. Noting Deringer's likelihood of success on the merits based on Strough's current employment by Fritz, on March 21 the district court granted Deringer's motion for preliminary injunction and directed Strough to comply with the non-competition provision of the Agreement until the ninety day non-competition period expired on May 24, 1995. The court declined to consider hypothetical employment possibilities, but indicated that the parties might agree on an appropriate location in which Strough could work and if an agreement could not be reached, the court would hear further argument on the geographic scope of the Agreement. Fritz placed Strough outside the original geographic area of the Agreement and the parties did not return to court during the ninety day period.

On January 15, 1996, Fritz and Strough moved for summary judgment arguing that the Agreement was not enforceable. The following day, Deringer cross-moved for summary judgment and assessment of damages and attorney's fees. On February 28, 1996, the district court granted defendants' motion for summary judgment. *A.N. Deringer, Inc. v. Strough*, 918 F. Supp. 129, 133 (D. Vt. 1996). The court found that although permitted by the contract, it was not empowered to declare the contract amended to the extent of a reasonable employment restriction because the ninety-day period had expired. *Id.* The court opined that although the ninety-day period of the non-competition provision was reasonable, the provision was not enforceable because its originally unamended geographic restriction was "unreasonably broad and without adequate justification." *Id.* at 132–33.

Discussion

The threshold question in this case is whether for the purpose of awarding damages, the district court erred in declining to finally resolve whether Strough's conduct was in breach of a reasonably restrictive non-competition provision. As a preliminary matter, the district court acting through another judge (Parker, J.), concluded that Strough likely had breached the contract's non-competition provision by reason of his employment in the same industry and in the immediate vicinity of his former place of employment. Thus, the district court granted injunctive relief. *Id.* The court determined that it was premature to consider the full breadth of the non-competition provision because conduct beyond that which would be prohibited by a reasonable restriction was not at issue.

Appellee argues that the court was correct in not resolving finally the issue of whether the conduct complained of was within a reasonable restriction for damages purposes. The only case cited in support of appellee's position on this issue is *Weatherford Oil Tool Co., Inc. v. Campbell*, 161 Tex. 310, 340 S.W.2d 950, 952–53 (1960), in which the court declined to reform a non-competition agreement to permit an award of damages, although injunctive relief was permitted on such a basis. We reject the rule of *Weatherford Oil Tool* and we note this statement of the *Weatherford Oil Tool* partial dissent:

> In the case at bar plaintiff brought a suit for injunction and for damages. This invoked the jurisdiction of the court. On the injunction feature of the case, we have held the trial court should apply the test

of reasonableness to the contract, and should reduce the area set out to such area as was reasonable under all the circumstances.... It would be an anomaly to hold that in considering the question of damages to be recovered the contract could not likewise be reduced to cover a reasonable area, and, therefore, hold the contract to be valid as to such reasonable area. In this reasonable area such damages as plaintiff could show it suffered during the one year period could be recovered. To apply two entirely different rules to the construction of the same contract between the same parties in the same lawsuit would lead to a multiplicity of suits, hopeless confusion and inconsistency.

340 S.W.2d at 955 (Griffin, J., dissenting in part).

In this case the court imposed a preliminary injunction based on its view that Strough's conduct was within the range of conduct forbidden by a reasonable restriction. Damages should be awarded on the same basis, if it is finally determined that under Vermont law the contract may be so reformed and the conduct engaged in was violative of the reformed contract. The question cannot be avoided on the basis that it is too late for the court to declare finally what in essence has been declared preliminarily. Otherwise, every action for damages based on such a provision would require resolution before the expiration of the time period of the restriction. This is impractical, unnecessary, and would encourage longer temporal restrictions; whereas public policy encourages as limited a restriction as is necessary to accomplish a valid purpose. [Citation omitted.]

The issue which need not be resolved in this case is the very issue that the district court resolved against appellants. As will be discussed, the contract may be reformed and the conduct complained of breached a properly reformed contract. Thus, there is no need to determine whether the full breadth of the originally drafted non-competition clause may be enforced. The only conduct complained of is that which occurred within the first thirty days of the provision's enforcement. We need only examine the contract in relation to this conduct, not in relation to hypothetical conduct.

This brings us to the issue of whether Vermont would enforce a non-competition provision which calls for the application of the provision to the extent allowable if it is defective in any way.... [E]nforcement of non-competition clauses to the extent found reasonable is permitted in numerous other jurisdictions. [Citations omitted.]

For example, in *Central Adjustment Bureau, Inc. v. Ingram*, 678 S.W.2d 28, 36 (Tenn. 1984), the Tennessee Supreme Court examined in an analogous case the modern trend "away from the all or nothing at all rule in favor of some form of judicial modification." *Id.* In discussing the modification of an overly broad non-competition clause, the Central Adjustment Bureau court noted that there are essentially two approaches to modifying restrictive covenants. *Id.* Some courts apply the "blue pencil" rule to strike an unreasonable restriction "to the extent that a grammatically meaningful reasonable restriction remains after the words making the restriction unreasonable are stricken." *Id.*

The court also noted that the more recent trend, which it adopted, was the rule of reasonableness. *Id.* at 37. It provides that unless the circumstances indicate bad faith on the part of the employer, a court will enforce covenants not to compete to the extent that they are reasonably necessary to protect the employer's interest "without imposing undue hardship on the employee when the public interest is not adversely affected." *Id.* at 37 (quoting *Ehlers v. Iowa Warehouse Co.*, 188 N.W.2d 368, 370 (Iowa 1971)). Thus, we conclude that Vermont would permit enforcement of a defective restrictive covenant to the limit of its validity.

The last issue to be addressed is whether the conduct complained of here was within the scope of an enforceable restriction on competition. This issue was never addressed finally by the district court. As there are no factual issues to resolve and for reasons of judicial efficiency, we will apply the law to the undisputed facts, rather than remanding this issue for further consideration of the trial court.

First, there is no real dispute as to a reasonable time restriction. The ninety-day period was quite short. *See Vermont Elec. Supply Co. v. Andrus,* 132 Vt. 195, 315 A.2d 456, 458 (1974) (approving five-year restriction in non-competition agreement). It provided a reasonable time for notifying customers, to guard against involuntary disclosure of confidential information and for other organizational considerations. The district court found no defect in this aspect of the employment restriction and appellee's brief does not challenge this finding. [Citation omitted.]

The heart of appellee's position is that the geographic proscription was too broad because it prohibited employment within 100 miles of the listed Deringer offices along a broad stretch of the United States-Canada border. This provision, however, is modified easily by deleting from the list of Deringer offices all those other than the two or three offices in which Mr. Strough worked, or by merely applying a general rule of reason. The district court in finding the proscribed area unreasonable alluded to a similar result based on geographic proximity.[2] *A.N. Deringer*, 918 F. Supp. at 133. It noted that Deringer's interests would be protected by prohibiting Strough's employment near his former sales territory, but that no additional protection would be gained by expanding the area to include a 100-mile radius from all Deringer offices. *Id.*

While it is true that non-competition agreements are narrowly construed by the courts and must contain time, geographic and/or industry limitations, the Vermont Supreme Court has upheld numerous restrictive covenants in employment and related business contracts. [Citations omitted.] The Vermont rule is that "enforcement will be ordered unless the agreement is found to be contrary to public policy, unnecessary for protection of the employer, or unnecessarily restrictive of the rights of the employee, with due regard being given to the subject matter of the contract and the circumstances and conditions under which it is to be performed. The burden of establishing such facts is on the employee." [Citations omitted.] The restriction as reformed seems not to run afoul of such concerns. Factors such as Strough's voluntary departure, his training at Deringer and his knowledge of confidential material would

---

2. One of Strough's new offices was merely across the parking lot from his prior office.

weigh in favor of enforcement of the reformed provision. [Citations omitted.] The Vermont court in examining the totality of the employment relationship also likely would consider in Deringer's favor the following: that the restriction was for a short time period, that Strough was able to be placed in other Fritz offices, that he remained employed and that the disruption, if any, for ninety days was at such a low level that Strough and Fritz did not accept the court's invitation to attempt to reform the contract in a manner more to their liking. Finally, the court likely would look to evidence of bad faith, which might prevent reformation under the standards set forth in the Restatement (Second) of Contracts. *See* Restatement (Second) of Contracts § 184 (1979). No serious evidence of bad faith on Deringer's part was alleged, and in their brief appellees do not rely on "bad faith" as a reason not to reform the contract.

Accordingly, we find Strough's conduct violated a reasonable and enforceable employment restriction. The judgment of the district court is reversed and this matter remanded for calculation of damages, including attorney's fees as provided in the contract.

Exercise 9-12: *DeSantis* and *A.N. Deringer, Inc.* Revisited

1. The "all-or-nothing rule" to which the court refers holds that a covenant not to compete only can be enforced if all of its provisions are not overbroad. Some courts still adhere to this rule. Can you see why?

2. Why have other courts moved away from the "all-or-nothing rule"?

3. Do you prefer the rule adopted by the *A.N. Deringer* court or the "blue pencil" rule? Why?

4. It is now time to consolidate your knowledge of contract remedies law. Diagram 9-2 on the facing page is an incomplete graphic organizer for contract remedies. Complete it. Afterward, convert it to an outline and annotate the outline with case holdings and Restatement and U.C.C. section numbers.

Professional Development Reflection Questions

1. Some legal educators believe that the three keys to being a happy, successful practitioner are respect, responsibility, and reputation. Do you agree or disagree?

2. In what ways do you show respect for your professors? For your peers in law school? For the non-faculty people who work at your law school?

3. Why is responsibility a key to a happy, successful law practice?

4. Are you satisfied with how responsible you have been with the work assigned to you in this class?

5. Are you satisfied with your reputation at your law school? Does your reputation suggest you will be an excellent lawyer? Why or why not?

Diagram 9-2: Contract Remedies Graphic Organizer

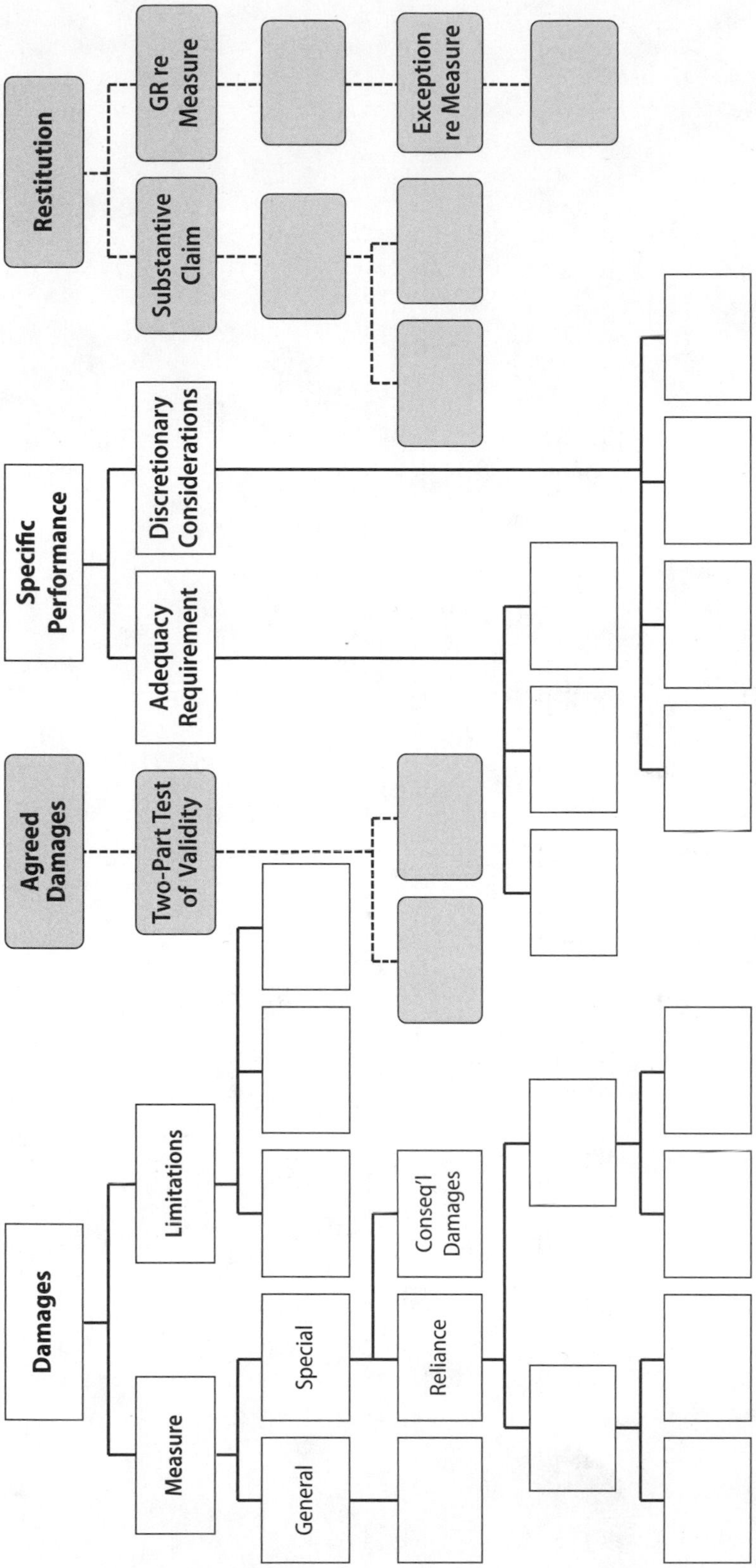

PART FIVE

CONTRACT MEANING

What, exactly, has each of the parties agreed to do?

Introduction to Part Five

Part Five of this text marks a very important transition in your study of contract law. You are moving from the study of contracts as a student to the study of contracts as a practitioner. In the previous chapters of this text, you learned how parties form contracts, how they get out of contracts, and what a contracting party may recover if the other party to the contract breaches the contract. In Parts Five and Six, you will focus on: (1) identifying the express (stated) and the implied terms of the parties' contract, (2) how courts interpret such terms, and (3) understanding a specialized set of important terms collectively referred to as "conditions." You will learn about a wide variety of terms commonly included in contracts[1] and the implications for contract performance of all contract terms. In other words, over the next several weeks, you will be asked to start thinking like a contracts lawyer. You also will start working with and studying actual contracts. When you finish your study of Parts Five and Six, your professor is likely to ask you to read a contract and explain its terms to a layperson.

Exercise: Contract Meaning

Read the Widgets, Inc.-Schmo contract in Table V-2. In class and in this text, you will be asked to re-read this contract many times. For now, imagine that you have been asked to explain the contract to a client, Josephina Schmo, Inc., that is considering entering into this contract. As you read the contract, focus on the following questions a lawyer might ask himself were he retained to evaluate this contract (although some of the questions are designed with law students in mind):

1. What is each of the parties to this contract trying to achieve with this contract? What does this contract require each party to do?

2. Are my client's interests protected against events or problems that may arise?

3. Can either party cancel this contract with or without warning?

4. Is anything you already know about contract law relevant to this contract? For example, are all the terms enforceable?

5. In Chapter 8, we provided you with a table (reproduced below and further expanded in Table V-1) of common contract clauses. The contract in Table V-2 includes many of those common clauses. As you read the contract, see how many of the clauses you can identify.

6. The Widgets, Inc.-Schmo contract is a particularly flawed contract. That choice by your authors is a deliberate one. Most often, contracts end up

---

1. Actually, your first introduction into contract terms was Chapter 8, when you learned about "liquidated damages" clauses.

being litigated because they have one or more drafting errors; the drafter failed to recognize an ambiguity in the language s/he wrote or failed to anticipate a circumstance s/he should have anticipated and draft something to address that circumstance. You need to become expert at identifying such issues, regardless of whether you end up being a contract drafter, a contract litigator, or any other type of lawyer.

While this text embeds more contract drafting experiences than others, a complete training in contract drafting requires an entire course.[2] Thus, this text does not purport to be a drafting text.

Having a poorly drafted contract, however, is an opportunity to learn a few basic principles while also learning to *read* a contract like a lawyer. **Task:** As you read the contract, see if you can identify violations of the principles listed below. The list is not an exhaustive list of the flaws in the contract, but it does capture most of the drafting-level errors. There are other mistakes you will learn about as you study the contract in connection with exercises in the chapters that follow; if you were to look at the contract again after taking a Contract Drafting course, you would discover additional errors.

    a.   A contract promise should use the word "shall."

    b.   Legalese (*e.g.*, "witnesseth," "thereof") is almost always a bad choice.

    c.   Using two words when one suffices (*e.g.*, "understands and agrees") adds little or nothing and creates a risk of conflict.

    d.   Using different words to communicate the same type of contract clause creates a significant risk; courts are likely to assume that the change in word choice was meant to convey something of significance to the parties.

    e.   Using the same word to mean two different things, *e.g.*, "Agreement" in clause 13.

---

2. We suggest you take a course in contract drafting (nearly all law schools offer one), even if you plan to be a litigator. Nearly all lawyers draft contracts; litigators draft settlement agreements. If you cannot take a course, consider purchasing, for your use as a practitioner, Tina Stark's *Drafting Contracts: How and Why Lawyers Do What They Do* (2nd ed. 2013).

Table V-1: Common Contract Clauses

Name of Clause	Goal of Clause
Covenant	A promise to perform an obligation.
Discretionary Authority	A provision that allows one party to make a choice, such as a choice about color or size.
Condition	A prerequisite created in the contract or by law to a party's duty to perform a covenant.
Representations and Warranties	A contract term that reflects a promise made to induce the other party to enter into the contract or a promise that the subject of the contract has a particular quality or set of qualities.
Covenant not to compete	Communicates that an employee or a seller of a business cannot compete (for a specified period of time and within a specified locale) with the employer or buyer.
Liquidated damages clause	States an amount a party should recover if the other party breaches the contract.
Merger clause	Communicates that the written document contains all of the terms to which the parties have agreed and that, therefore, prior agreements that are not reflected in the written document are not part of the parties' contract.
No-oral-modification clause	Indicates that the parties only can modify the contract in writing and not orally.
Force majeure clause	Lists circumstances, usually natural disasters and wars, under which a party can avoid having to perform the contract without penalty.
Time-is-of-the-essence clause	Uses the words "time is of the essence" to communicate an expectation about timely performance of the parties' contract promises.
Choice-of-law clause	States the body of law that will govern any dispute between the parties. May also limit the state or city in which either party may file suit. (Lawyers may refer to this latter provision as a jurisdiction clause.)
Arbitration clause	States an agreement that disputes under the contract will not be decided by a court but, rather, by an arbitrator. Usually includes details about the selection process for arbitrators.
Indemnification clause	Communicates that, if one party is sued for a matter relating to the contract, the other party will pay for the costs of defending the suit and will pay any award of damages ordered by the court.
No assignments clause	States that the rights conferred under the contract (and, in some instances, the duties imposed under the contract) cannot be transferred to someone else.
Savings clause	Indicates the parties have agreed that, if a court invalidates a particular term of the parties' contract, the rest of the contract will remain enforceable.

Table V-2: Independent Contractor Agreement

INDEPENDENT CONTRACTOR AGREEMENT

Dated this ___ day of February, 20__

By and between:

WIDGETS, INC., a company incorporated under the laws of the State of Delaware,

and:

JOSEPHINA SCHMO (hereinafter referred to as the "Contractor").

RECITALS

WHEREAS, Widgets, Inc. is in the business of providing temporary and permanent placement services, management consulting, marketing business methodologies, software and computer training;

AND WHEREAS, Contractor carries on business as a *corporation* under the name *Josephina Schmo, Inc.* and is experienced in public relations, which expertise is desired by Widgets, Inc.;

AND WHEREAS, Widgets, Inc. and Contractor are desirous of entering into a contractual relationship for the provision of services described below, all on the terms and conditions set forth below.

NOW, THEREFORE, this Agreement witnesseth that, in consideration of the mutual covenants and agreements hereafter contained, the parties hereby covenant and agree as follows:

1. SERVICES TO BE PERFORMED:

    1.1 Contractor shall provide her services to Widgets, Inc., and its affiliates, subsidiaries or clients in matters relating to public relations for Widgets, Inc. (hereinafter called the "Services").

    1.2 Subject to such reasonable rules and regulations which may be promulgated by Widgets, Inc. from time to time and by which the Contractor agrees to abide, Widgets, Inc. has no right to control the manner or details of how Contractor performs the Services required hereunder. Contractor is not required to work on Widgets, Inc.'s premises except to the extent necessary to provide the Services. Contractor will provide her own working materials, and Contractor is responsible for hiring, supervising, and paying her own employees.

2. TERM OF AGREEMENT:

    2.1 This Agreement shall be in effect from February ___, 20__ to February ___, 20__ (three years) within the provisions as hereinafter stated.

Page 1 of 6

2.2 Either party may terminate this Agreement at any time by giving fifteen (15) days' written notice to the other party, provided that Widgets, Inc. may terminate this Agreement without notice if the Contractor breaches any of the terms herein.

3. PAYMENT FOR SERVICES:

3.1 Contractor shall be compensated by Widgets, Inc. at the rate of $500 per hour for Services rendered. Contractor shall submit an invoice covering Services rendered during each weekly period, together with other supporting documents, which may be required from time to time by Widgets, Inc. Upon verification of Contractor's invoice, Widgets, Inc. shall make payment in full on a bi-weekly basis, it being understood and agreed that Widgets, Inc. shall at all times be in arrears of payment for Services rendered an equivalent to fourteen (14) calendar days subsequent to receipt of Contractor's invoice.

3.2 Widgets, Inc. shall reimburse Contractor for all reasonable documented travel and other out-of-pocket expenses incurred at the request of Widgets, Inc. in connection with Services rendered under this Agreement, provided that Widgets, Inc.'s approval of such expenses must be obtained prior to the expenses being incurred. Payment for travel expenses will be made upon receipt and approval of a Statement of Charges. Contractor shall produce such other supporting documents for out-of-pocket expenses as may be requested (from time to time) by Widgets, Inc.

4. INSURANCE:

4.1 Contractor recognizes that Widgets, Inc. shall not be obligated to carry insurance of any type whatsoever under this Agreement.

4.2 Widgets, Inc. shall have a duty to perform if and only if Contractor obtains liability insurance with respect to Contractor's services under this Agreement in an amount no less than $1,000,000.

5. RESPONSIBILITIES AND INDEMNIFICATION:

5.1 Contractor shall comply with all applicable municipal, state and federal laws and regulations and shall be responsible for the timely reporting and payment to the proper taxing authorities of all state, federal, and local taxes in relation to this Agreement and the Services to be provided hereunder.

5.2 Contractor agrees to indemnify and save Widgets, Inc. harmless against all claims and taxes (including interest, penalties, and any other costs) which are claimed or assessed and are attributable to the Agreement or the payments made hereunder. Contractor expressly agrees that the sole compensation under this Agreement will be the sum paid for the specific Services rendered, that neither Contractor nor any of Contractor's employees will be entitled, by virtue of this

Agreement, to participate in any of the benefit plans available to Widgets, Inc.'s employees.

5.3 It is understood that Widgets, Inc. does not bind itself to exclusively use Contractor for work required by Widgets, Inc. of the nature listed herein, nor is Contractor bound exclusively to perform work for Widgets, Inc. during the term of this Agreement, provided that Contractor shall keep all aspects of Widgets, Inc.'s products and the services being performed by Contractor for Widgets, Inc. strictly confidential.

5.4 Contractor agrees, at its own cost and expense and with counsel of its own choice, to fully defend, protect, indemnify, and hold harmless Widgets, Inc. against any liability, loss, cost, expense, damage, suit, action, claims or demands on account of Services performed by Contractor hereunder, provided such liability, loss, cost, expense, damage, suit, action, claim or demand does not arise as a result of Widgets, Inc.' negligence, fraud, dishonesty, or willful failure in the provision of the Services hereunder.

5.5 Contractor understands and agrees that all of the data and information submitted to her by Widgets, Inc., its affiliates, subsidiaries or clients, whether oral or written, is confidential and, further, that the data and information and any reports prepared by Contractor and given to Widgets, Inc., are the sole property of Widgets, Inc. and are confidential and proprietary. Contractor agrees that it will not release, disclose, or make available any of the data and information submitted to it by Widgets, Inc., its affiliates, subsidiaries or clients to any party other than Widgets, Inc. without the express prior written consent of Widgets, Inc. Upon delivery of any final work product, Contractor shall return to Widgets, Inc. all data and information delivered to it by Widgets, Inc. without retaining any copies thereof. Contractor agrees that any information received by Contractor during any furtherance of Contractor's obligations or performance under this Agreement, which concerns the affairs of Widgets, Inc. and which is not public information or generally available to the public, will be held in confidence by Contractor.

5.6 Contractor further understands and agrees all written materials and all intellectual property (including, but not limited to ideas, know-how, techniques or programs) developed by Contractor for Widgets, Inc. shall belong solely to Widgets, Inc. and is considered confidential information.

6. ACKNOWLEDGMENT OF CONTRACTOR:

6.1 During the term of this Agreement and for a period of six (6) months (or if such period is held to be excessive by a court of competent jurisdiction, then for a period of three (3) months from the termination of this Agreement), the Contractor agrees that it shall not, within the City of Columbia and the surrounding area, whether as principal, agent, employee, contractor, or in partnership or association with, any person, firm or corporation in any manner whatsoever, directly or indirectly:

(a) seek to employ or otherwise engage the staff (including temporary staff) of Widgets, Inc.

(b) seek to obtain by any means whatsoever the business of any person, firm or corporation who, at the time of the termination of this Agreement, was a customer of Widgets, Inc. with whom the Contractor had dealt with during the term of this Agreement.

(c) allow its business name to be used by any person, firm or corporation whatsoever, the business of any person, firm or corporation who, at the time of the termination of this Agreement, was a customer of Widgets, Inc. with whom the Contractor had dealt with during the term of this Agreement.

7. DISPUTE RESOLUTION:

7.1 The Parties agree that any claim or dispute between them, whether related to this agreement or otherwise, and any claim or dispute related to this agreement or to the relationship or duties contemplated under this agreement, including the validity of this arbitration clause, shall be resolved by binding arbitration by the American Arbitration Association under the Arbitration Rules then in effect. Any award of the arbitrator(s) may be entered as a judgment in any court of competent jurisdiction.

8. GENERAL:

8.1 Contractor hereby acknowledges that any actual or threatened disclosure and violation of the provisions of paragraphs 5.5, 5.6 and 6.1 could result in irreparable harm to Widgets, Inc. and that in addition to any other rights Widgets, Inc. may have, Widgets, Inc. shall be entitled to injunctive and other equitable relief to enforce the provisions of paragraphs 5.5, 5.6 and 6.1. It is further understood that the provisions contained in paragraphs 5.5, 5.6, 6.1 and 7.1 shall survive the termination or expiration of this Agreement.

8.2 It is hereby understood and agreed that the relationship created by this Agreement is not one of principal and agent, or master and servant, or employer and employee, or franchisor and franchisee, or joint venture, and that in all matters the nature of the relationship is independent contractor and contractee. Contractor covenants and agrees that it is an independent contractor to Widgets, Inc. and will not, at any time, enter into any contract, agreement or engagement whatsoever for or on behalf of Widgets, Inc. or do any other act or thing which would result in any liability or responsibility of Widgets, Inc.

8.3 This Agreement is not assignable by Contractor and shall be binding on its administrators, successors and assigns and shall inure to the benefit of and be enforceable by Widgets, Inc., its successors and assigns.

9. NOTICE:

9.1 Any notice required to be given hereunder may be given by either party to the other by delivering or mailing same by prepaid registered post at or addressed as follows:

In the case of Widgets, Inc.:

To: Corporate Secretary Department
Widgets, Inc.
9999 Center Street
Columbia City, Columbia 00001

In the case of Contractor:

To: Josephina Schmo, Inc.,
1111 Main Street
Columbia City, Columbia 00001

10. AMENDMENT OF AGREEMENT:

10.1 No amendments to this Agreement shall be valid or binding unless set forth in writing and duly executed by both parties hereto. No waiver of any breach or of any provision of this Agreement shall be effective or binding unless made in writing and signed by the party purporting to give the same and, unless otherwise provided in the written waiver, shall be limited to the specific breach waived.

11. SAVINGS CLAUSE:

11.1 If any provisions of this Agreement is determined to be invalid or unenforceable in whole or in part, such invalidity or unenforceability shall attach only to such provisions or part thereof and the remaining part of such provision and all other provisions hereof shall continue in full force and effect.

12. GOVERNING LAW:

12.1 The Agreement shall be subject to and construed in accordance with the laws of the State of Columbia.

13. PREVIOUS AGREEMENTS:

    13.1 This Agreement sets forth the entire Agreement between the parties hereto. It supersedes and cancels all previous understandings, negotiations, commitments and representation with respect hereto, whether written or oral, and constitutes the entire Agreement between the parties with respect to matters addressed herein.

IN WITNESS WHEREOF, this Agreement has been executed by the parties hereto.

SIGNED, SEALED AND DELIVERED in the presence of:

CONTRACTOR: **WIDGETS, INC.**

_____   _____

Per: Per:
Title: Title:

Chapter 10

The Parol Evidence Rule

Exercise 10-1: Chapter Problem

You are a trial lawyer in connection with a dispute regarding the performance of the contract between Widgets, Inc. and Josephina Schmo, Inc. in Table V-2. During trial, a witness for Schmo started to testify that, in addition to agreeing to all the terms listed in the Widgets-Schmo contract, the parties also agreed that, if Schmo succeeded in getting Widgets' name in an average of two newspaper or magazine articles per month during the term of the contract (and so long as the articles referred to Widgets in a positive way), Widgets' president would appear in two print and two radio advertisements for Schmo. Widgets' lawyer objected to this testimony on a timely basis. The judge has asked the lawyers to approach the bench and orally argue the admissibility of this evidence.

After you complete this chapter, you will be asked to prepare an oral argument on behalf of Widgets or Schmo. In your preparation and argument, consider the following facts:

1. Widgets, Inc. is a large, multinational corporation that has been in business for more than twenty years.

2. Josephina Schmo, the owner and sole shareholder of Josephina Schmo, Inc. is a former employee of Widgets who left the company three and a half years ago (on great terms) to start up her own consulting business. Widgets was her first customer. Schmo is a college graduate whose college major was business administration.

3. The parties had a successful and productive business relationship over the course of the Widgets-Schmo contract. Schmo succeeded in getting Widgets, Inc.'s name in an average of two newspaper or magazine articles per month during the term of the contract (and all the articles referred to Widgets in a positive way).

4. Two months ago, Widgets' president refused to appear in print and radio advertisements for Schmo. Schmo immediately sued for breach.

5. Columbia has adopted the Corbin view of the parol evidence rule.

Introduction to Contract Meaning and Contract Performance

Imagine a client has come to you. She shows you a written, signed contract whereby she agreed to buy a piece of land. She tells you the other party to the contract breached the contract because the other party refused to demolish and remove an unsightly old storage shed on the land. The promise to remove the shed is not in the written document because it was an oral promise made right before the parties signed the contract. From what you have learned so far, you should be able to predict that she would succeed in convincing a court that she really did enter into a contract. If the other party asserted a contract defense, you also should be able to assess whether the other party could successfully assert that defense. Finally, assuming the court determined that the other party breached the contract, you should be able to identify, explain and make predictions about the remedies available to your client.

You do not yet know enough, however, to predict whether a court would conclude that the oral promise to demolish and remove the storage shed was part of the parties' contract. You also do not know whether the failure to demolish and remove the storage shed was a breach of contract and, if it is a breach, whether the breach was material or minor and the legal consequences of determining that a breach is material or minor. Lawyers and law professors would say that you need to learn contract interpretation law and contract performance law. They use the term "contract interpretation" to refer to the process of identifying and understanding all of the express and implied terms of parties' contract and "contract performance law" to refer to the process of determining the proper order of performance of multiple contract obligations, of comparing the parties' performances to what they promised to do, and of evaluating those performances as well as any excuse either party may have for not performing as promised.

For the next several weeks, we will focus on these broad issues. We will look at four broad questions:

1. What terms do courts treat as part of the contract for the purposes of determining what each party has promised? (In other words, what are the contract terms?)

2. How do courts determine what the words of a contract oblige the parties to do? (In other words, what does the contract mean?)

3. Did the parties properly and fully perform? (In other words, did either party breach?)

4. Assuming either party did not properly do everything she promised to do, what is the consequence of the breach?

The first question above focuses on determining which terms are a part of the parties' contract and which terms are not. Are there other terms not contained in the written contract? If one party (such as our client referred to above) alleges that there are other terms, is evidence that those terms form part of the contract admissible? Lawyers use the parol evidence rule to address these questions.

In the context of a written contract, parol evidence rule issues may seem to have a simple answer — the contract should consist of the terms to which the parties agreed in writing and should not include terms to which the parties did not agree in writing. In many cases, this initial answer is the only and correct one: courts *do* often conclude that contracts include only the terms upon which the parties have agreed in writing. In many cases, however, the answer is more complicated. First, as we learned in connection with illusory promise law, courts imply duties of "good faith" and "reasonable efforts" into contracts even if those duties are not stated as terms in the parties' contract. Under the U.C.C., as we learned, courts will imply many more such terms. Later in Part Five, we will study other instances in which courts will imply terms not stated in contracts. Second, sometimes, it is not accurate to say that a contract includes only the terms upon which the parties have agreed in writing. As we will learn in connection with our study of the parol evidence rule, in some instances, courts will allow parties to testify about oral terms not reflected in their signed writing.

Introduction to the Parol Evidence Rule

The Basic Idea

The parol evidence rule helps determine which agreed-upon terms make up the parties' contract. The first case you will be reading, *Mitchell v. Lath*, explains that the parol evidence rule "defines the limits of the contract to be construed."

Keep in mind that the parol evidence rule is a rule governing what types of evidence a jury may hear. In other words, if the parol evidence rule applies and bars evidence of a particular term not contained in the parties' writing, the rule operates to prevent a jury from hearing about a term one party contends was part of the parties' overall arrangement. It is equally important to understand that, even if after applying the parol evidence rule, a court allows a party to testify about an unwritten contract term, all we have decided is that the jury may *hear* the evidence. Having evaluated the weight and credibility of the evidence, the jury still may conclude that the parties really did not agree to that term.

To see this point graphically, look at Diagram 10-1. It includes a label "Extrinsic Evidence." Extrinsic evidence is a term courts use to describe an alleged contract term not reflected in the parties' writing. In most instances, the extrinsic evidence that implicates a parol evidence rule issue is oral testimony about an unwritten term claimed to be a part of the parties' contract. Such evidence, however, also can be written. Diagram 10-1 also includes a shape labeled "The Parol Evidence Rule Wall." Finally, the diagram shows "The Jury" (the trier of fact) and "Extrinsic Evidence" on opposite sides of "The Parol Evidence Rule Wall." In other words, the parol evidence rule acts as a barrier that prevents the jury from seeing or hearing "Extrinsic Evidence." Thus, the diagram shows the basic operation of the parol evidence rule as a rule barring the admission of evidence.

Diagram 10-1: The Parol Evidence Rule

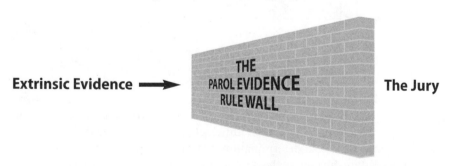

Students generally find the parol evidence rule difficult, in part because they fail to understand that the rule is a rule barring the admission of evidence and, in part, because the actual operation of the rule by courts is much more complicated than Diagram 10-1 suggests.

The parol evidence rule is premised on the belief that, when parties adopt a written document as the embodiment of their contract, it is reasonable to assume they have incorporated all of the terms of their agreement in the writing. Why bother to write the contract if you don't intend to include all the terms? And to return to our opening example, if you care that much about the demolition and removal of the shed, why not ensure that the seller's promise is included in the writing? Accordingly, the parol evidence rule initially developed to exclude evidence of agreements extrinsic to (outside of) the writing. Because contract law seeks to enforce **voluntary agreements of parties**, an important element of any parol evidence analysis is determining whether the parties intended the written document to be the final and complete expression of their agreement.

Diagram 10-2, the Contract Law Graphic Organizer, depicts where the parol evidence rule fits within the larger scheme of contract law.

Diagram 10-2: Contract Law Graphic Organizer

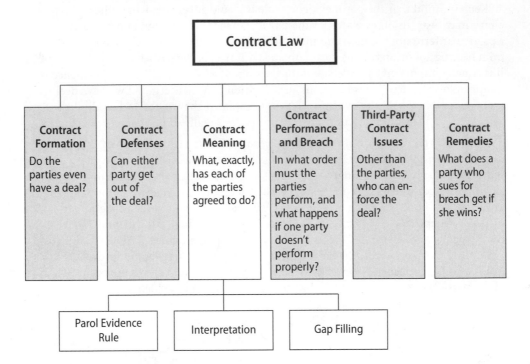

The Parol Evidence Rules

The parol evidence "rule" is actually a set of rules. In some instances, your analysis of a parol evidence problem starts and ends with the conclusion that the extrinsic evidence is of a type that does not raise a parol evidence issue: in other words, the evidence is admissible without further inquiry. There is an initial set of default rules that allows lawyers and judges to make the threshold determination that the evidence at issue is admissible *per se* without the need for further analysis under the main parol evidence rules.

Once you have determined that the evidence must be screened for admissibility under the main parol evidence rules, you will also learn how to analyze whether a written document is the final and complete expression of an agreement. Courts state this issue as a question of whether the writing is "completely integrated," "partially integrated," or "not integrated at all." For now, understand that the goal of an analysis of the "degree of integration" is to distinguish between a writing that says everything to which the parties have agreed (a completely integrated contract), a writing that completely addresses those topics it does address but does not include everything to which the parties agreed (a partially integrated contract), and a writing that really does not express a final and complete agreement as to any of the terms it states (a contract that is not integrated at all).

This distinction is a crucial one in parol evidence jurisprudence. If a court concludes that a writing is completely integrated, the court will bar extrinsic evidence. If a court concludes that a writing is only partially integrated, the court will *only* admit extrinsic evidence if the evidence is consistent with the terms in the writing. If a court concludes that a writing is not integrated at all, extrinsic evidence comes in automatically. Thus, once the judge has assessed the degree of integration, the parol evidence rule operates to: (1) exclude all extrinsic evidence if the writing is completely integrated, and (2) exclude inconsistent evidence if the writing is partially integrated. Of course, the term "inconsistent" is not self-defining or self-evident. You will, therefore, need to learn what courts mean by "inconsistent."

Even if a court is inclined to exclude evidence because a writing is completely integrated or because the evidence is inconsistent, the court still may admit evidence which falls within one of several categories, such as evidence of fraud, mistake, undue influence, or duress, and evidence to facilitate the court's interpretation of the contract. This last category, evidence to facilitate the interpretation of a contract, has generated a considerable body of law all of its own and is of great practical significance.

Like any simplistic explanation of a complex set of legal rules, this discussion of the parol evidence rule is only the tip of an iceberg. At this stage, make sure you understand the basics as reflected in Diagram 10-3, which depicts the practical application of the parol evidence rule. The rule bar some evidence (depicted by the black arrow that stops at the wall). However, some evidence — evidence which is admissible under the threshold rules — manages to sneak around the rule altogether (depicted by the gray arrow shown going around and never touching the wall). Some evidence — evidence of terms consistent with a partially integrated agreement — is subject to the main parol evidence rules but is admissible (depicted as the white arrow outlined in gray that seems to pass through the wall). Finally, some evidence is blocked by the parol evidence rule but is ultimately admissible because it falls within one of the exceptions such as evidence of fraud or mistake (illustrated by curved black arrow that depicts the evidence bouncing off the parol evidence rule and eventually making its way to the trier of fact).

Diagram 10-3: Practical Application of the Parol Evidence Rule

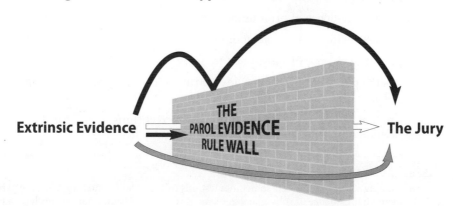

Overview of Chapter 10

Chapter 10 focuses exclusively on the parol evidence rule. The chapter is organized so that you study the materials in an order you might follow in analyzing a parol evidence rule problem. The chapter begins with foundational materials on parol evidence rule terminology. The chapter then moves to a few short exercises that will train you to identify whether the extrinsic evidence you are considering is admissible under the threshold rules so that you do not need to conduct a full analysis under the main parol evidence rules. For example, extrinsic evidence of a promise made after the parties signed their written agreement is admissible by default under the threshold rules without the need for further analysis.[1] The third part of the chapter focuses on developing and learning to apply the tests courts use to determine whether a contract is partially integrated, completely integrated, or not integrated at all. This third part will also examine what makes extrinsic evidence inconsistent with the parties' writing. The fourth part of this chapter will focus on the bases for admitting parol evidence that otherwise would be barred under the parol evidence rule. In the last part of this chapter, you will work on putting the four parts together to analyze evidentiary problems.

Basic Terminology

A significant challenge in connection with the parol evidence rule is learning the terminology and understanding the purpose of the parol evidence rule. Accordingly, this section focuses on terminology and policy.

Exercise 10-2: Basic Terminology and Policy for the Parol Evidence Rule

1. Write out definitions of the following terms based on the chapter introduction, sections 209(1), 210 (1)–(2) of the RESTATEMENT (SECOND) OF CONTRACTS, and your law dictionary:

   a. "integrated"

   b. "completely integrated"

   c. "partially integrated"

   d. "parol evidence" and "extrinsic evidence"

   e. "extrinsic evidence of prior terms"

   f. "extrinsic evidence of contemporaneous terms"

   g. "extrinsic evidence of subsequent terms"

2. What is the policy for the parol evidence rule? (*Hint: Why are courts suspicious of promises not contained in writing?*)

3. Why have courts created a large number of exceptions to the parol evidence rule?

---

1. It's worth noting that bar examiners sometimes test this rule. Students who forget that the parol evidence rule doesn't bar evidence of subsequent agreements end up missing what was really an easy question.

Determining Whether Parol Evidence of Contract Terms Not Contained in the Parties' Writing Is Admissible: The Four Steps

Diagram 10-4 at the end of this chapter maps out the steps that you should follow when analyzing whether parol evidence of a contract term that has not been included in the parties' written contract is admissible or not. The main steps are as follows:

STEP 1: Apply the threshold rules to determine whether the parol evidence rule applies to the evidence at all. If it does not apply, the evidence is **admissible** and you do not have to conduct a full-scale parol evidence rule analysis. In other words, you do not need to proceed with Steps 2-4.

STEP 2: Determine whether the parties' agreement is **integrated** at all. If it is **non-integrated**, extrinsic evidence that seeks to establish the terms of the parties' agreement is **admissible** and you do not need to proceed with Steps 3-4.

STEP 3: Having established that the parties' agreement is integrated, in Step 3, you need to determine the **degree of integration**. Is the parties' writing a **complete integration** of **all** of the terms of their agreement ("completely integrated") or is it only a **partial integration** ("partially integrated"). If it's a complete integration, the writing is treated as a comprehensive statement of all of the terms of the contract, and extrinsic evidence of other terms is **barred** without the need to proceed to Step 4.

STEP 4: Where the parties' writing is a **partial integration**, determine whether the parol term is **consistent with or contradicts** the writing. Parol evidence of terms that are consistent or non-contradictory is **admissible**. Parol evidence of terms that are inconsistent or contradictory is **inadmissible**.

Keep these steps in mind as you work through the materials that follow.

Step 1: Types of Evidence to Which the Parol Evidence Rule Applies

The first set of parol evidence rules you will study are the threshold or gate-keeping rules which determine whether the parol evidence rule applies to the evidence at all. The parol evidence rule only applies to certain types of extrinsic evidence. It is important to be clear what we mean by "applies" here. Where the parol evidence rule "applies," we need to do a full-scale parol evidence rule analysis to determine whether or not the extrinsic evidence is admissible. Where the parol evidence does not "apply" to the extrinsic evidence, then that evidence is admissible and there is no need to do a full-scale parole evidence rule analysis in Steps 2–4. These threshold or gate-keeping rules are as follows:

- The parol evidence rule applies to extrinsic evidence of a prior oral or prior written contract term, for which there is no extra consideration.

- The parol evidence rule also applies to extrinsic evidence of a contemporaneous oral term, for which there is no extra consideration.

The same rules are often stated as three rules couched in the negative:

- **The parol evidence rule does *not* apply to extrinsic evidence of a subsequent oral or subsequent written contract term.** (Evidence of subsequent oral or subsequent written contract terms is therefore admissible without further analysis).

- **The parol evidence rule does *not* apply to extrinsic evidence of an oral or written contract term if the parties agreed to separate consideration (in addition to the consideration exchanged under the writing) for that promise.** (Evidence of oral or written terms in respect of which the parties agreed to separate consideration is therefore admissible without further analysis).

- **The parol evidence rule does *not* apply to extrinsic evidence of a contemporaneous written term.** (Evidence of a contemporaneous written term is therefore admissible without further analysis).

Finally, these rules, taken together, should cause you to ask three questions every time you encounter a situation where a party is seeking to admit extrinsic evidence to vary or supplement a written contract:

1. **Is the extrinsic evidence oral or written?**

2. **Does the extrinsic evidence address an agreement made prior to, contemporaneous with, or subsequent to the making of the writing?**

3. **Is there separate consideration for the promise reflected in the extrinsic evidence?**

Exercise 10-3: Spotting Parol Evidence Issues

1. What is the policy underlying courts' refusal to apply the parol evidence rule if there is separate consideration for the parol promise?

2. What is the policy underlying courts' refusal to apply the parol evidence rule to agreements made **after** the parties signed the writing they adopted as the final version of their agreement?

3. What is the policy behind courts' refusal to apply the parol evidence rule to written parol terms made at the same time the parties signed the writing they adopted as the final version of their agreement?

4. Determine whether the parol evidence rule applies to the evidence referenced in the following hypotheticals:

   a. Abel and Betty negotiate for the purchase and sale of Abel's car. During negotiations, the parties agree that Abel will repair all the dents in the car before delivering it to Betty. The parties later sign a written document that states a price, the subject of the contract (the car), and the time and place of performance, but makes no mention of the promise to repair. Betty sues Abel for breach and seeks to testify about the promise to repair the dents. Do these facts raise a parol evidence rule issue? Why or why not?

   b. If, in the above Abel-Betty hypo, the parties had agreed that, in exchange for Abel repairing the dents, Betty would paint Abel's home, would these facts raise a parol evidence rule issue? Why or why not?

   c. If, in the above Abel-Betty hypo, the parties had agreed to increase the total price Betty was paying to an amount that reflected the cost to Abel of repairing the dents, would these facts raise a parol evidence rule issue? Why or why not?

d. If, in the above Abel-Betty hypo, Abel's promise to make the repairs was in *a* writing but not in *the* writing the parties later signed, would these facts raise a parol evidence rule issue? Why or why not?

e. If, in question d. above, the parties signed the written promise to make the repairs at the same time they signed *the* writing, would these facts raise a parol evidence rule issue? Why or why not?

f. If, in the above Abel-Betty hypo, the parties had made the repair agreement ten minutes after signing *the* writing, would these facts raise a parol evidence rule issue? Why or why not?

g. What would be the outcome in question f. above, if the subsequent repair promise was made orally and the writing contained a clause like clause 10.1 in the Widgets, Inc.-Schmo contract?

Steps 2–4: Integration, Degree of Integration and the Question of Consistency

Introduction

You are about to read a series of four cases (*Mitchill v. Lath, Lee v. Seagram & Sons, Masterson v. Sine,* and *Luria Bros. v. Pielet Bros.*). Afterward, you will have a chance to consider the version of the parol evidence rule adopted in Article 2 of the U.C.C. in Section 2-202. Together, these cases and Section 2-202 offer considerable insight into two very challenging issues:

1. Under what circumstances will courts conclude that a written document is a complete and final statement of the parties' agreement (a **complete integration**)?

2. Under what circumstances will courts conclude that extrinsic evidence is inconsistent with a partially integrated written agreement?

In particular, *Mitchill, Lee,* and *Masterson* (as well as Section 2-202) focus on the first question, whether the contract at issue is completely integrated or partially integrated. *Mitchill, Lee,* and *Luria Bros.* focus on the second question, whether evidence is consistent with the contract.

Before you get to these cases and the relatively challenging issues they analyze, it is worth pausing to address a seldom-litigated question: is it possible for a contract not to be integrated at all? This corresponds to Step 2 in the series of four steps that we outlined above. While the question seldom arises, it is worth asking because the answer is that it is possible for a contract not to be integrated at all. **A contract is not integrated at all if either it is not in writing or if it is in writing but none of its terms are final.** Some contracts are purely oral and therefore are not integrated at all. A written document that contains no final terms, however, is more rare. It only arises in two circumstances: (1) if the parties developed a document both understood to be a draft and ended up entering into an entirely oral agreement; or (2) a party is claiming that a letter or document confirming the parties' agreement (but which the other party never saw, agreed to, or signed) is a binding writing.

Summary of Doctrine in Steps 3–4

Standards courts use to determine if a contract is partially or completely integrated. Regrettably for us, there is no uniform nationwide approach to the question of whether a contract is completely or partially integrated,[2] and Article 2 of the U.C.C. includes its own parol evidence rule. For common law contracts, some courts have adopted what is known as the Williston "Four Corners" approach. Others have adopted what is known as the Corbin "All Evidence" approach.

Courts following the Williston approach first ask whether a contract contains what is known as a "merger" or as an "integration" clause. A merger clause states that the writing containing it is a final, complete, and exclusive statement of the parties' agreement. Merger clauses often also stipulate that terms not stated in the writing should not be treated as part of the parties' agreement. **If a contract contains a merger clause, Williston courts (and even many Corbin courts) conclude that the contract is completely integrated.** These courts consider that the inclusion of a merger clause demonstrates that the parties intended the writing to be a comprehensive statement of their agreement.

If a contract does not contain a merger clause, **Williston courts then ask whether a contract appears complete on its face**, *i.e.*, whether it seems to express the parties' complete respective obligations within the four corners of the document. If the agreement appears complete on its face, courts treat it as a completely integrated agreement, **unless the parties "naturally would have omitted" the extrinsic term from the writing**. The idea of the "naturally would have omitted" test is that, if the term is one the parties naturally would have omitted from their written agreement, the agreement is not completely integrated (at least as to that term).

Courts applying Corbin's "All Evidence" approach reject the "Four Corners" idea and the "naturally would have omitted" test. Instead, courts applying this approach search for the parties' actual intention with respect to integration. **Only if the parties intended the contract to be completely integrated will it be treated as such.** The rule is called the "All Evidence" rule because courts applying this rule admit all evidence, including the term at issue, in deciding whether the parties intended a complete integration.

Thus, a crucial, preliminary question you need to consider is one of approach: Does the court that is hearing a dispute tend to follow the Williston or Corbin approach?

Standards courts use to determine whether extrinsic evidence is consistent with a writing. The standards in this area are no less confusing. Some courts simply state that consistent evidence is admissible and contradictory evidence is not. These courts seem to focus on whether the extrinsic evidence and the parties' writing are "in harmony." Other courts have adopted a much narrower definition of contradiction. Such courts hold that extrinsic evidence is consistent and not contradictory so long as the evidence does not "completely negate" any term in the writing.

Exercise 10-4: U.C.C. and *Mitchill*

Read the four cases below and U.C.C. Section 2-202 as a group. As you do so, consider the following questions:

---

2. For a more extended discussion, see John D. Calamari & Joseph M. Perillo, *A Plea for a Uniform Parol Evidence Rule and Principles of Contract Interpretation*, 42 INDIANA L. REV. 333 (1967).

1. Questions that apply to all four cases and to U.C.C. Section 2-202:

   a. What rule does each case (and U.C.C. 2-202) adopt with respect to the question of complete or partial integration? Does each formulation (or the U.C.C. drafters' formulation) seem more like a Williston or a Corbin approach or is it something entirely different?

   b. What rule does each case (and U.C.C. 2-202) adopt with respect to the question of consistency? Can the various approaches be reconciled?

2. Questions focusing on the *Mitchill* case:

   a. Identify all of the key facts.

   b. The court provides an example of a situation in which an oral agreement is enforceable notwithstanding the existence of a subsequent written agreement between the parties (because the parol evidence rule does not apply to such an arrangement). What is that example?

   c. The court identifies three requirements to avoid the bar of the parol evidence rule. The first, which refers to a requirement that the agreement be, in form, collateral, is no longer good law. The second requirement is that "it must not contradict ... provisions of the written contract." The third is that "it must be one that parties would not ordinarily be expected to embody in the writing ..." To which of Steps 1–4 do the court's second and third requirements correspond?

   d. The court's third requirement is stated in three ways, each slightly different. What are the three ways the court states this requirement? In what sense are the three ways different?

   e. How does the majority of the court apply the third requirement to the facts of the *Mitchill* case? How does the dissent apply the third requirement?

   f. In dicta, the majority of the court applies its second requirement to the facts of the *Mitchill* case. Why is the court's application of the second requirement dicta? How did the majority apply the second requirement? How did the dissent apply the second requirement?

   g. Imagine you represent the plaintiff in *Mitchill* and you are trying to convince the state Supreme Court that the evidence should have been admitted. How might you use the policy for the parol evidence rule to argue that the evidence in this case should be admitted?

Mitchill v. Lath

160 N.E. 646, 247 N.Y. 377 (1928)

Andrews, Judge. In the fall of 1923 the Laths owned a farm. This they wished to sell. Across the road, on land belonging to Lieutenant Governor Lunn, they had an icehouse which they might remove. Mrs. Mitchill looked over the land with a view to its purchase. She found the icehouse objectionable. Thereupon "the defendants orally promised and agreed, for and in consideration of the purchase of their farm by the plaintiff, to remove the said icehouse in the spring of 1924." Relying upon this promise, she made a written contract to buy the property for $8,400, for cash and mortgage and containing various provisions usual in such papers. Later receiving a deed, she entered into possession, and has spent considerable sums in improving the property for use as a summer residence. The defendants have not fulfilled their promise as to the icehouse, and do not intend to do so. We are not dealing, however, with their moral delinquencies. The question before us is whether their oral agreement may be enforced in a court of equity.

This requires a discussion of the parol evidence rule—a rule of law which defines the limits of the contract to be construed. *Glackin v. Bennett*, 226 Mass. 316, 115 N.E. 490. It is more than a rule of evidence, and oral testimony, even if admitted, will not control the written contract, *O'Malley v. Grady*, 222 Mass. 202, 109 N.E. 829, unless admitted without objection, *Brady v. Nally*, 151 N.Y. 258, 45 N.E. 547. It applies, however, to attempts to modify such a contract by parol. It does not affect a parol collateral contract distinct from and independent of the written agreement. It is, at times, troublesome to draw the line. Williston, in his work on Contracts (section 637) points out the difficulty. "Two entirely distinct contracts," he says, "each for a separate consideration, may be made at the same time, and will be distinct legally. Where, however, one agreement is entered into wholly or partly in consideration of the simultaneous agreement to enter into another, the transactions are necessarily bound together.... Then if one of the agreements is oral and the other in writing, the problem arises whether the bond is sufficiently close to prevent proof of the oral agreement." That is the situation here. It is claimed that the defendants are called upon to do more than is required by their written contract in connection with the sale as to which it deals.

The principle may be clear, but it can be given effect by no mechanical rule. As so often happens it is a matter of degree, for, as Prof. Williston also says, where a contract contains several promises on each side it is not difficult to put any one of them in the form of a collateral agreement. If this were enough, written contracts might always be modified by parol. Not form, but substance, is the test.

In applying this test, the policy of our courts is to be considered. We have believed that the purpose behind the rule was a wise one, not easily to be abandoned. Notwithstanding injustice here and there, on the whole it works for good. Old precedents and principles are not to be lightly cast aside, unless it is certain that they are an obstruction under present conditions. New York has been less open to arguments that would modify this particular rule, than some jurisdictions elsewhere. Thus in *Eighmie v. Taylor*, 98 N.Y. 288, it was held that a parol warranty might not be shown, although no warranties were contained in the writing.

Under our decisions before such an oral agreement as the present is received to vary the written contract, at least three conditions must exist: (1) The agreement must in form be a collateral one; (2) it must not contradict express or implied provisions of the written contract; (3) it must be one that parties would not ordinarily be expected to embody in the writing, or, put in another way, an inspection of the written contract, read in the light of surrounding circumstances, must not indicate that the writing appears "to contain the engagements of the parties, and to define the object and measure the extent of such engagement." Or, again, it must not be so clearly connected with the principal transaction as to be part and parcel of it.

The respondent does not satisfy the third of these requirements. It may be, not the second. We have a written contract for the purchase and sale of land. The buyer is to pay $8,400 in the way described. She is also to pay her portion of any rents, interest on mortgages, insurance premiums, and water meter charges. She may have a survey made of the premises. On their part, the sellers are to give a full covenant deed of the premises as described, or as they may be described by the surveyor, if the survey is had, executed, and acknowledged at their own expense; they sell the personal property on the farm and represent they own it; they agree that all amounts paid them on the contract and the expense of examining the title shall be a lien on the property; they assume the risk of loss or damage by fire until the deed is delivered; and they agree to pay the broker his commissions. Are they to do more? Or is such a claim inconsistent with these precise provisions? It could not be shown that the plaintiff was to pay $500 additional. Is it also implied that the defendants are not to do anything unexpressed in the writing?

That we need not decide. At least, however, an inspection of this contract shows a full and complete agreement, setting forth in detail the obligations of each party. On reading it, one would conclude that the reciprocal obligations of the parties were fully detailed. Nor would his opinion alter if he knew the surrounding circumstances. The presence of the icehouse, even the knowledge that Mrs. Mitchill thought it objectionable, would not lead to the belief that a separate agreement existed with regard to it. Were such an agreement made it would seem most natural that the inquirer should find it in the contract. Collateral in form it is found to be, but it is closely related to the subject dealt with in the written agreement—so closely that we hold it may not be proved.

Where the line between the competent and the incompetent is narrow the citation of authorities is of slight use. Each represents the judgment of the court on the precise facts before it. How closely bound to the contract is the supposed collateral agreement is the decisive factor in each case. But reference may be made to *Johnson v. Oppenheim*, 55 N.Y. 280, 292.... [A]n oral stipulation, said to have been the inducing cause for the subsequent execution of the lease itself, concerning some act to be done by the landlord, or some condition as to the leased premises, might not be shown. In principle they are not unlike the case before us....

Our conclusion is that the judgment of the Appellate Division and that of the Special Term should be reversed and the complaint dismissed, with costs in all courts.

Lehman, Judge (dissenting).

I accept the general rule as formulated by Judge Andrews. I differ with him only as to its application to the facts shown in the record. The plaintiff contracted to purchase land from the defendants for an agreed price. A formal written agreement was made between the sellers and the plaintiff's husband. It is on its face a complete contract for the conveyance of the land. It describes the property to be conveyed. It sets forth the purchase price to be paid. All the conditions and terms of the conveyance to be made are clearly stated. I concede at the outset that parol evidence to show additional conditions and terms of the conveyance would be inadmissible. There is a conclusive presumption that the parties intended to integrate in that written contract every agreement relating to the nature or extent of the property to be conveyed, the contents of the deed to be delivered, the consideration to be paid as a condition precedent to the delivery of the deeds, and indeed all the rights of the parties in connection with the land. The conveyance of that land was the subject-matter of the written contract, and the contract completely covers that subject.

The parol agreement which the court below found the parties had made was collateral to, yet connected with, the agreement of purchase and sale. It has been found that the defendants induced the plaintiff to agree to purchase the land by a promise to remove an icehouse from land not covered by the agreement of purchase and sale. No independent consideration passed to the defendants for the parol promise. To that extent the written contract and the alleged oral contract are bound together. The same bond usually exists wherever attempt is made to prove a parol agreement which is collateral to a written agreement. Hence "the problem arises whether the bond is sufficiently close to prevent proof of the oral agreement." [Citation omitted.]

Judge Andrews formulated a standard to measure the closeness of the bond. Three conditions, at least, must exist before an oral agreement may be proven to increase the obligation imposed by the written agreement. I think we agree that the first condition that the agreement "must in form be a collateral one" is met by the evidence. I concede that this condition is met in most cases where the courts have nevertheless excluded evidence of the collateral oral agreement. The difficulty here, as in most cases, arises in connection with the two other conditions.

The second condition is that the "parol agreement must not contradict express or implied provisions of the written contract." Judge Andrews voices doubt whether this condition is satisfied. The written contract has been carried out. The purchase price has been paid; conveyance has been made; title has passed in accordance with the terms of the written contract. The mutual obligations expressed in the written contract are left unchanged by the alleged oral contract. When performance was required of the written contract, the obligations of the parties were measured solely by its terms. By the oral agreement the plaintiff seeks to hold the defendants to other obligations to be performed by them thereafter upon land which was not conveyed to the plaintiff. The assertion of such further obligation is not inconsistent with the written contract, unless the written contract contains a provision, express or implied, that the defendants are not to do anything not expressed in the writing. Concededly there is no such express provision in the contract, and such a provision may be implied, if at all, only if the asserted additional obligation is "so clearly connected with the principal transaction as to be part and parcel of it," and is not "one that the parties would not ordinarily be expected to embody in the writing." The hypothesis so formulated for a conclusion that the asserted additional obligation is inconsistent with an implied term of the contract is that the alleged oral agreement does not comply with the third condition as formulated by Judge Andrews. In this case, therefore, the problem reduces itself to the one question whether or not the oral agreement meets the third condition.

I have conceded that upon inspection the contract is complete. "It appears to contain the engagements of the parties, and to define the object and measure the extent of such engagement;" it constitutes the contract between them, and is presumed to contain the whole of that contract. *Eighmie v. Taylor*, 98 N.Y. 288. That engagement was on the one side to convey land; on the other to pay the price. The plaintiff asserts further agreement based on the same consideration to be performed by the defendants after the conveyance was complete, and directly affecting only other land. It is true, as Judge Andrews points out, that 'the presence of the icehouse, even the knowledge that Mrs. Mitchill though it objectionable, would not lead to the belief that a separate agreement existed with regard to it'; but the question we must decide is whether or not, assuming an agreement was made for the removal of an unsightly ice-house from one parcel of land as an inducement for the purchase of another parcel, the parties would ordinarily or naturally be expected to embody the agreement for the removal of the icehouse from one parcel in the written agreement to convey the other parcel. Exclusion of proof of the oral agreement on the ground that it varies the contract embodied in the writing may be based only upon a finding or presumption that the written contract was intended to cover the oral negotiations for the removal of the icehouse which lead up to the contract of purchase and sale. To determine what the writing was intended to cover, "the document alone will not suffice. It was intended to cover cannot be known till we know what there was to cover. The question being whether certain subjects of negotiation were intended to be covered, we must compare the writing and the negotiations before we can determine whether they were in fact covered." [Citation omitted.]

The subject-matter of the written contract was the conveyance of land. The contract was so complete on its face that the conclusion is inevitable that the parties intended to embody in the writing all the negotiations covering at least the conveyance. The promise by the defendants to remove the ice-house from other land was not connected with their obligation to convey except that one agreement would not have been made unless the other was also made. The plaintiff's assertion of a parol agreement by the defendants to remove the icehouse was completely established by the great weight of evidence. It must prevail unless that agreement was part of the agreement to convey and the entire agreement was embodied in the writing.

The fact that in this case the parol agreement is established by the overwhelming weight of evidence is, of course, not a factor which may be considered in determining the competency or legal effect of the evidence. Hardship in the particular case would not justify the court in disregarding or emasculating the general rule. It merely accentuates the outlines of our problem. The assumption that the parol agreement was made is no longer obscured by any doubts. The problem, then, is clearly whether the parties are presumed to have intended to render that parol agreement legally ineffective and nonexistent by failure to embody it in the writing. Though we are driven to say that nothing in the written contract which fixed the terms and conditions of the stipulated conveyance suggests the existence of any further parol agreement, an inspection of the contract, though it is complete on its face in regard to the subject of the conveyance, does not, I think, show that it was intended to embody negotiations or agreements, if any, in regard to a matter so loosely bound to the conveyance as the removal of an icehouse from land not conveyed.

The rule of integration undoubtedly frequently prevents the assertion of fraudulent claims. Parties who take the precaution of embodying their oral agreements in a writing should be protected against the assertion that other terms of the same agreement were not integrated in the writing. The limits of the integration are determined by the writing, read in the light of the surrounding circumstances. A written contract, however complete, yet covers only a limited field. I do not think that in the written contract for the conveyance of land here under consideration we can find an intention to cover a field so broad as to include prior agreements, if any such were made, to do other acts on other property after the stipulated conveyance was made....

Exercise 10-5: *Masterson v. Sine*

The next case you will read is *Masterson v. Sine*. As you read Masterson, revisit question 1 in Exercise 10-4 and consider also the following questions:

1. Why does the court conclude that the agreement is not completely integrated? Why else might you argue that it would have been natural for these parties to have omitted the term? Why does the dissent disagree with the majority's conclusion on the complete integration issue?

2. The consistency question in this case is somewhat different than in the previous case. How so? (Hint: Focus on the allegedly contradictory term in the writing.)

3. Why does the court conclude that the parol evidence of the "no assignment" agreement does not contradict the parties' written contract?

Masterson v. Sine

436 P.2d 561, 68 Cal. 2d 222 (1968)

Traynor, Chief Justice. Dallas Masterson and his wife Rebecca owned a ranch as tenants in common. On February 25, 1958, they conveyed it to Medora and Lu Sine by a grant deed "Reserving unto the Grantors herein an option to purchase the above described property on or before February 25, 1968" for the "same consideration as being paid heretofore plus their depreciation value of any improvements Grantees may add to the property from and after two and a half years from this date." Medora is Dallas' sister and Lu's wife. Since the conveyance Dallas has been adjudged bankrupt. His trustee in bankruptcy and Rebecca brought this declaratory relief action to establish their right to enforce the option.

The case was tried without a jury. Over defendants' objection the trial court admitted extrinsic evidence that by "the same consideration as being paid heretofore" both the grantors and the grantees meant the sum of $50,000 and by "depreciation value of any improvements" they meant the depreciation value of improvements to be computed by deducting from the total amount of any capital expenditures made by defendants grantees the amount of depreciation allowable to them under United States income tax regulations as of the time of the exercise of the option.

The court also determined that the parol evidence rule precluded admission of extrinsic evidence offered by defendants to show that the parties wanted the property kept in the Masterson family and that the option was therefore personal to the grantors and could not be exercised by the trustee in bankruptcy.

The court entered judgment for plaintiffs, declaring their right to exercise the option, specifying in some detail how it could be exercised, and reserving jurisdiction to supervise the manner of its exercise and to determine the amount that plaintiffs will be required to pay defendants for their capital expenditures if plaintiffs decide to exercise the option.

Defendants appeal. They contend that the option provision is too uncertain to be enforced and that extrinsic evidence as to its meaning should not have been admitted. The trial court properly refused to frustrate the obviously declared intention of the grantors to reserve an option to repurchase by an overly meticulous insistence on completeness and clarity of written expression. [Citations omitted.] It properly admitted extrinsic evidence to explain the language of the deed] to the end that the consideration for the option would appear with sufficient certainty to permit specific enforcement. [Citations omitted.] The trial court erred, however, in excluding the extrinsic evidence that the option was personal to the grantors and therefore non-assignable.

When the parties to a written contract have agreed to it as an "integration"—a complete and final embodiment of the terms of an agreement—parol evidence cannot be used to add to or vary its terms. [Citations omitted.] When only part of the agreement is integrated, the same rule applies to that part, but parol evidence may be used to prove elements of the agreement not reduced to writing. [Citations omitted.]

The crucial issue in determining whether there has been an integration is whether the parties intended their writing to serve as the exclusive embodiment of their agreement. The instrument itself may help to resolve that issue. It may state, for example, that "there are no previous understandings or agreements not contained in the writing," and thus express the parties' "intention to nullify antecedent understandings or agreements." [Citation omitted.] Any such collateral agreement itself must be examined, however, to determine whether the parties intended the subjects of negotiation it deals with to be included in, excluded from, or otherwise affected by the writing. Circumstances at the time of the writing may also aid in the determination of such integration. [Citations omitted.]

California cases have stated that whether there was an integration is to be determined solely from the face of the instrument, and that the question for the court is whether it "appears to be a complete ... agreement...." [Citations omitted.] Neither of these strict formulations of the rule, however, has been consistently applied. The requirement that the writing must appear incomplete on its face has been repudiated in many cases where parol evidence was admitted "to prove the existence of a separate oral agreement as to any matter on which the document is silent and which is not inconsistent with its terms"—even though the instrument appeared to state a complete agreement. [Citations omitted.] Even under the rule that the writing alone is to be consulted, it was found necessary to examine the alleged collateral agreement before concluding that proof of it was precluded by the writing alone. [Citation omitted.] It is therefore evident that "The conception of a writing as wholly and intrinsically self-determinative of the parties' intent to make it a sole memorial of one or seven or twenty-seven subjects of negotiation is an impossible one." [Citation omitted.] For example, a promissory note given by a debtor to his creditor may integrate all their present contractual rights and obligations, or it may be only a minor part of an underlying executory contract that would never be discovered by examining the face of the note.

In formulating the rule governing parol evidence, several policies must be accommodated. One policy is based on the assumption that written evidence is more accurate than human memory. [Citation omitted.] This policy, however, can be adequately served by excluding parol evidence of agreements that directly contradict the writing. Another policy is based on the fear that fraud or unintentional invention by witnesses interested in the outcome of the litigation will mislead the finder of facts. [Citations omitted.] McCormick has suggested that the party urging the spoken as against the written word is most often the economic underdog, threatened by severe hardship if the writing is enforced. In his view the parol evidence rule arose to allow the court to control the tendency of the jury to find through sympathy and without a dispassionate assessment of the probability of fraud or faulty memory that the parties made an oral agreement collateral to the written contract, or that preliminary tentative agreements were not abandoned when omitted from the writing. [Citation omitted.] He recognizes, however, that if this theory were adopted in disregard of all other considerations, it would lead to the exclusion of testimony concerning oral agreements whenever there is a writing and thereby often defeat the true intent of the parties. [Citation omitted.]

Evidence of oral collateral agreements should be excluded only when the fact finder is likely to be misled. The rule must therefore be based on the credibility of the evidence. One such standard, adopted by section 240(1)(b) of the RESTATEMENT OF CONTRACTS, permits proof of a collateral agreement if it "is such an agreement as might naturally be made as a separate agreement by parties situated as were the parties to the written contract." [Citations omitted.] The draftsmen of the Uniform Commercial Code would exclude the evidence in still fewer instances: "If the additional terms are such that, if agreed upon, they would certainly have been included in the document in the view of the court, then evidence of their alleged making must be kept from the trier of fact." [Citations omitted.]

The option clause in the deed in the present case does not explicitly provide that it contains the complete agreement, and the deed is silent on the question of assignability. Moreover, the difficulty of accommodating the formalized structure of a deed to the insertion of collateral agreements makes it less likely that all the terms of such an agreement were included. [Citations omitted.] The statement of the reservation of the option might well have been placed in the recorded deed solely to preserve the grantors' rights against any possible future purchasers, and this function could well be served without any mention of the parties' agreement that the option was personal. There is nothing in the record to indicate that the parties to this family transaction, through experience in land transactions or otherwise, had any warning of the disadvantages of failing to put the whole agreement in the deed. This case is one, therefore, in which it can be said that a collateral agreement such as that alleged "might naturally be made as a separate agreement." A fortiori, the case is not one in which the parties "would certainly" have included the collateral agreement in the deed....

In the present case defendants offered evidence that the parties agreed that the option was not assignable in order to keep the property in the Masterson family. The trial court erred in excluding that evidence.

The judgment is reversed.

Burke, Justice. I dissent. The majority opinion:

(1) Undermines the parol evidence rule as we have known it in this state since at least 1872 by declaring that parol evidence should have been admitted by the trial court to show that a written option, absolute and unrestricted in form, was intended to be limited and nonassignable;

(2) Renders suspect instruments of conveyance absolute on their face;

(3) Materially lessens the reliance which may be placed upon written instruments affecting the title to real estate; and

(4) Opens the door, albeit unintentionally, to a new technique for the defrauding of creditors.

The opinion permits defendants to establish by parol testimony that their grant to their brother (and brother-in-law) of a written option, absolute in terms, was nevertheless agreed to be nonassignable by the grantee (now a bankrupt), and that therefore the right to exercise it did not pass, by operation of the bankruptcy laws, to the trustee for the benefit of the grantee's creditors.

And how was this to be shown? By the proffered testimony of the bankrupt optionee himself! Thereby one of his assets (the option to purchase defendants' California ranch) would be withheld from the trustee in bankruptcy and from the bankrupt's creditors. Understandably the trial court, as required by the parol evidence rule, did not allow the bankrupt by parol to so contradict the unqualified language of the written option.

The court properly admitted parol evidence to explain the intended meaning of the "same consideration" and "depreciation value" phases of the written option to purchase defendants' land, as the intended meaning of those phrases was not clear. However, there was nothing ambiguous about the granting language of the option and not the slightest suggestion in the document that the option was to be nonassignable. Thus, to permit such words of limitation to be added by parol is to contradict the absolute nature of the grant, and to directly violate the parol evidence rule.

Just as it is unnecessary to state in a deed to "lot X" that the house located thereon goes with the land, it is likewise unnecessary to add to "I grant an option to Jones" the words "*and his assigns*" for the option to be assignable. As hereinafter emphasized in more detail, California statutes expressly declare that it is assignable, and only if I add language in writing showing my intent to withhold or restrict the right of assignment may the grant be so limited. Thus, to seek to restrict the grant by parol is to contradict the written document in violation of the parol evidence rule.

The majority opinion arrives at its holding via a series of false premises which are not supported either in the record of this case or in such California authorities as are offered.

The parol evidence rule is set forth in clear and definite language in the statutes of this state. [Citations omitted.] It "is not a rule of evidence but is one of substantive law.... The rule as applied to contracts is simply that as a matter of substantive law, a certain act, the act of embodying the complete terms of an agreement in a writing (the 'integration'), becomes the contract of the parties." [Citations omitted.] The rule is based upon the sound principle that the parties to a written instrument, after committing their agreement to or evidencing it by the writing, are not permitted to add to, vary or *contradict* the terms of the writing by parol evidence....

At the outset the majority in the present case reiterate that the rule against contradicting or varying the terms of a writing remains applicable when only part of the agreement is contained in the writing, and parol evidence is used to prove elements of the agreement not reduced to writing. But having restated this established rule, the majority opinion inexplicably proceeds to subvert it....

The contract of sale and purchase of the ranch property here involved was carried out through a title company upon written escrow instructions executed by the respective parties after various preliminary negotiations. The deed to defendant grantees, in which the grantors expressly reserved an option to repurchase the property within a ten-year period and upon a specified consideration, was issued and delivered in consummation of the contract. In neither the written escrow instructions nor the deed containing the option is there any language even suggesting that the option was agreed or intended by the parties to be personal to the grantors, and so nonassignable. The trial judge, on at least three separate occasions, correctly sustained objections to efforts of defendant optionors to get into evidence the testimony of Dallas Masterson (the bankrupt holder of the option) that a part of the agreement of sale of the parties was that the option to repurchase the property was personal to him, and therefore unassignable for benefit of creditors. But the majority hold that that testimony should have been admitted, thereby permitting defendant optionors to limit, detract from and contradict the plain and unrestricted terms of the written option in clear violation of the parol evidence rule and to open the door to the perpetration of fraud....

The majority opinion attempts to buttress its approach by asserting ... that "California cases have stated that whether there was an integration is to be determined solely from the face of the instrument, and that the question for the court is whether it 'appears to be a complete ... agreement ...'" but that "Neither of these strict formulations of the rule ... has been consistently applied." [Citations omitted.]

The majority's claim of inconsistent application of the parol evidence rule by the California courts fails to find support in the examples offered....

Upon [a] structure of incorrect premises and unfounded assertions the majority opinion arrives at its climax: The pronouncement of "several policies [to] be accommodated ... [*i*]*n formulating the rule governing parol evidence.*" (Italics added.) Two of the "policies" as declared by the majority are: Written evidence is more accurate than human memory; fraud or unintentional invention by interested witnesses may well occur.

I submit that these purported "policies" are in reality two of the basic and obvious reasons for adoption by the Legislature of the parol evidence rule as the policy in this state. Thus the speculation of the majority (ante, pp. 227–228) concerning the views of various writers on the subject and the advisability of following them in this state is not only superfluous but flies flatly in the face of established California law and policy. It serves only to introduce uncertainty and confusion in a field of substantive law which was codified and made certain in this state a century ago. . . .

Comment hardly seems necessary on the convenience to a bankrupt of such a device to defeat his creditors. He need only produce parol testimony that any options (or other property, for that matter) which he holds are subject to an oral "collateral agreement" with family members (or with friends) that the property is nontransferable "in order to keep the property in the family" or in the friendly group. In the present case the value of the ranch which the bankrupt and his wife held an option to purchase has doubtless increased substantially during the years since they acquired the option. The initiation of this litigation by the trustee in bankruptcy to establish his right to enforce the option indicates his belief that there is substantial value to be gained for creditors from this asset of the bankrupt . . .

I would hold that the trial court ruled correctly on the proffered parol evidence, and would affirm the judgment.

Exercise 10-6: *Lee v. Joseph E. Seagram & Sons*

The next case you will read is *Lee v. Joseph E. Seagram & Sons, Inc.* As you read *Lee*, revisit question 1 in Exercise 10-4 and consider also the following questions:

1. Why does the court conclude that the agreement is not completely integrated?

2. Why does the court conclude that the evidence is not contradictory?

Lee v. Joseph E. Seagram & Sons, Inc.
552 F.2d 447 (2d Cir. 1977)

Gurfein, Circuit Judge. This is an appeal by defendant Seagram & Sons, Inc. from a judgment in favor of the plaintiffs on a claim asserting common law breach of an oral contract. The plaintiffs are Harold S. Lee (now deceased) and his two sons, Lester and Eric ("the Lees"). Jurisdiction is based on diversity of citizenship . . .

The Lees owned a 50% interest in Capitol City Liquor Company, Inc., a wholesale liquor distributorship located in Washington, D.C. The other 50% was owned by Harold's brother, Henry D. Lee, and his nephew, Arthur Lee. Seagram is a distiller of alcoholic beverages. Capitol City carried numerous Seagram brands and a large portion of its sales were generated by Seagram lines.

The Lees and the other owners of Capitol City wanted to sell their respective interests in the business and, in May 1970, Harold Lee, discussed the possible sale of Capitol City with Jack Yogman, then Executive Vice President of Seagram, whom he had known for many years. Lee offered to sell Capitol City to Seagram but conditioned the offer on Seagram's agreement to relocate Harold and his sons, the 50% owners of Capitol City, in a new distributorship of their own in a different city.

About a month later, another officer of Seagram, John Barth, an assistant to Yogman, visited the Lees and their co-owners in Washington and began negotiations for the purchase of the assets of Capitol City by Seagram on behalf of a new distributor, one Carter, who would take it over after the purchase. The purchase of the assets of Capitol City was consummated on September 30, 1970 pursuant to a written agreement. The promise to relocate the father and sons thereafter was not reduced to writing.

Harold Lee had served the Seagram organization for thirty-six years in positions of responsibility before he acquired the half interest in the Capitol City distributorship. From 1958 to 1962, he was chief executive officer of Calvert Distillers Company, a wholly-owned subsidiary. During this long period he enjoyed the friendship and confidence of the principals of Seagram.

In 1958, Harold Lee had purchased from Seagram its holdings of Capitol City stock in order to introduce his sons into the liquor distribution business, and also to satisfy Seagram's desire to have a strong and friendly distributor for Seagram products in Washington, D.C. Harold Lee and Yogman had known each other for 13 years.

The plaintiffs claimed a breach of the oral agreement to relocate Harold Lee's sons, alleging that Seagram had had opportunities to procure another distributorship for the Lees but had refused to do so. The Lees brought this action fifteen months after the sale of the Capitol City distributorship to Seagram. They contended that they had performed their obligation by agreeing to the sale by Capitol City of its assets to Seagram, but that Seagram had failed to perform its obligation under the separate oral contract between the Lees and Seagram. The agreement was "an oral agreement with defendant which provided that if they agreed to sell their interest in Capitol City, defendant in return, within a reasonable time, would provide the plaintiffs a Seagram distributorship whose price would require roughly an amount equal to the capital obtained by the plaintiffs for the sale of their interest in Capitol City, and which distributorship would be in a location acceptable to plaintiffs." No specific exception was taken to this portion of the charge. By its verdict for the plaintiffs, we must assume as Seagram notes in its brief that this is the agreement which the jury found was made before the sale of Capitol City was agreed upon.[3]

---

3. The complaint alleged that Seagram agreed to "obtain" or "secure" or "provide" a "similar" distributorship within a reasonable time, and plaintiffs introduced some testimony to that effect. Although other testimony suggested that Seagram agreed merely to provide an opportunity for the Lees to negotiate with third parties, and the judge indicated that Seagram merely agreed "to notify plaintiffs as they learned of distributors who were considering the sale of their businesses," 413 F. Supp. at

Appellant urges several grounds for reversal. It contends that, as a matter of law, (1) plaintiffs' proof of the alleged oral agreement is barred by the parol evidence rule; and (2) the oral agreement is too vague and indefinite to be enforceable....

The District Court, in its denial of the defendant's motion for summary judgment, treated the issue as whether the written agreement for the sale of assets was an "integrated" agreement not only of all the mutual agreements concerning the sale of Capitol City assets, but also of all the mutual agreements of the parties. Finding the language of the sales agreement "somewhat ambiguous," the court decided that the determination of whether the parol evidence rule applies must await the taking of evidence on the issue of whether the sales agreement was intended to be a complete and accurate integration....

Appellant contends that, as a matter of law, the oral agreement was "part and parcel" of the subject-matter of the sales contract and that failure to include it in the written contract barred proof of its existence. *Mitchill v. Lath*, 247 N.Y. 377, 380, 160 N.E. 646 (1928). The position of appellant, is that the oral agreement was either an inducing cause for the sale or was a part of the consideration for the sale, and in either case, should have been contained in the written contract. In either case, it argues that the parol evidence rule bars its admission. Appellees maintain, on the other hand, that the oral agreement was a collateral agreement and that, since it is not contradictory of any of the terms of the sales agreement, proof of it is not barred by the parol evidence rule. The question is whether the strong policy for avoiding fraudulent claims through application of the parol evidence rule nevertheless mandates reversal on the ground that the jury should not have been permitted to hear the evidence. [Citation omitted.] ...

The District Court stated the cardinal issue to be whether the parties "intended" the written agreement for the sale of the assets to be the complete and accurate integration of all the mutual promises of the parties ...

[C]ertain oral collateral agreements, even though made contemporaneously, are not within the prohibition of the parol evidence rule "because (if) they are separate, independent, and complete contracts, although relating to the same subject.... (t)hey are allowed to be proved by parol, because they were made by parol, and no part thereof committed to writing." [Citation omitted.] ...

[T]he overarching question is whether, in the context of the particular setting, the oral agreement was one which the parties would ordinarily be expected to embody in the writing. [Citations omitted.] For example, integration is most easily inferred in the case of real estate contracts for the sale of land [citations omitted.] In more complex situations, in which customary business practice may be more varied, an oral agreement can be treated as separate and independent of the written agreement even though the written contract contains a strong integration clause. *See Gem Corrugated Box Corp. v. National Kraft Container Corp.*, 427 F.2d 499, 503 (2d Cir. 1970).

Thus, as we see it, the issue is whether the oral promise to the plaintiffs, as individuals, would be an expectable term of the contract for the sale of as-

---

698–99, the jury was permitted to find that the agreement was in the nature of a commitment to provide a distributorship.

sets by a corporation in which plaintiffs have only a 50% interest, considering as well the history of their relationship to Seagram. Here, there are several reasons why it would *not* be expected that the oral agreement to give Harold Lee's sons another distributorship would be integrated into the sales contract. In the usual case, there is an identity of parties in both the claimed integrated instrument and in the oral agreement asserted. Here, although it would have been physically possible to insert a provision dealing with only the shareholders of a 50% interest, the transaction itself was a corporate sale of assets. Collateral agreements which survive the closing of a corporate deal, such as employment agreements for particular shareholders of the seller or consulting agreements, are often set forth in separate agreements. *See Gem Corrugated Box Corp. v. National Kraft Container Corp., supra,* 427 F.2d at 503 ("it is … plain that the parties ordinarily would not embody the stock purchase agreement in a writing concerned only with box materials purchase terms"). It was expectable that such an agreement as one to obtain a new distributorship for certain persons, some of whom were not even parties to the contract, would not necessarily be integrated into an instrument for the sale of *corporate* assets....

Similarly, it is significant that there was a close relationship of confidence and friendship over many years between two old men, Harold Lee and Yogman, whose authority to bind Seagram has not been questioned. It would not be surprising that a handshake for the benefit of Harold's sons would have been thought sufficient. In point, as well, is the circumstance that the negotiations concerning the provisions of the sales agreement were not conducted by Yogman but by three other Seagram representatives, headed by John Barth. The two transactions may not have been integrated in their minds when the contract was drafted.[4]

Finally, the written agreement does not contain the customary integration clause, even though a good part of it (relating to warranties and negative covenants) is boilerplate. The omission may, of course, have been caused by mutual trust and confidence, but in any event, there is no such strong presumption of exclusion because of the existence of a detailed integration clause....

Nor do we see any contradiction of the terms of the sales agreement. [Citations omitted.] The written agreement dealt with the sale of corporate assets, the oral agreement with the relocation of the Lees. Thus, the oral agreement does not vary or contradict the money consideration recited in the contract as flowing to the selling corporation. That is the only consideration recited, and it is still the only consideration to the corporation.

We affirm [the District Court's] reception in evidence of the oral agreement …

Exercise 10-7: U.C.C. Section 2-202

Read (and either diagram or outline) section 2-202 of the U.C.C. and then answer the following questions:

---

4. Barth in a confidential memorandum to Yogman stated that "he (Harold Lee) would very much like to have another distributorship in another area for his two sons." Apparently Barth, who was not present at Harold Lee's meeting with Yogman, assumed that this was a desire on the part of Lee rather than a promise made by Yogman for Seagram.

1. Does 2-202 create a presumption that all agreements are only partially integrated? Why or why not?

2. What does 2-202 have to say about the question of consistency?

3. Section 2-202 adopts a very different approach to evidence of course of dealing, course of performance and trade usages. Define each of these terms. What makes this approach different?

Exercise 10-8: *Luria Bros v. Pielet Bros.*

Luria Bros. v. Pielet Bros. is the next case for your consideration. As you read *Luria Bros.,* revisit question 1 in Exercise 10-4 and your answers to Exercise 10-7 and also answer the following questions:

1. Why does the court conclude that the evidence is not consistent?

2. Would the result in this case have been the same had the court adopted the rule that evidence is consistent unless it "completely negates" a term of the writing?

Luria Bros. & Co., Inc. v.
Pielet Bros. Scrap Iron & Metal, Inc.
600 F.2d 103 (7th Cir. 1979)

Fairchild, Chief Judge. This is a diversity action for breach of contract. Most of the events giving rise to this litigation occurred in Illinois and we accept the parties' assumption that Illinois law is applicable. The action below was tried before a jury which returned a verdict in the amount of $600,000, having found that a contract for the purchase of barge scrap steel existed between plaintiff, Luria Brothers & Co., Inc., and defendant, Pielet Brothers Scrap Iron & Metal, Inc. (hereinafter referred to as "Pielet"), and that Luria was damaged as a consequence of Pielet's failure to deliver. Defendant appeals, arguing among other things that no enforceable agreement was ever made, and therefore, plaintiff was not entitled to damages. We affirm.

A consideration of the issues requires a statement of the facts in some detail. Luria, in its capacity as both a broker and a dealer is in the business of buying, selling, and processing scrap metal. Pielet is in the same business. The parties had done business with each other on a number of occasions prior to the transaction giving rise to this litigation. In fact, Lawrence Bloom, who represented Pielet in this matter had formerly been employed by Luria as a scrap trader....

In mid-September, 1973, Bloom, a vice-president of Pielet, telephoned Richard Fechheimer, a vice-president of Luria. Bloom informed Fechheimer that Pielet might offer a substantial quantity of scrap metal for sale. Bloom inquired as to whether Luria would be interested in purchasing the metal and Fechheimer said that it would be. Subsequent telephone conversations took place between Bloom and Fechheimer in which price quotations and other matters were discussed. The quantity was to be 35,000 net tons of scrap steel from old barges cut into sections measuring five feet by five feet by twenty feet. The shipment date was to be on or before December 31, 1973. The price was set at $42 per net ton if Luria took delivery in Houston or $49 if Luria took delivery in Brownsville (Texas). This transaction was unusual in two respects. First, the amount of scrap involved was much larger than that in a typical scrap transaction. Secondly, while the type or grade of scrap was not unusual, the dimensions were. Luria intended to process the scrap for resale as "No. 1 heavy melting" scrap by reducing it to a size that would fit into a steel furnace, generally in pieces at least 1/4 inch thick and not more than 5 feet long by 18 inches wide.

Shortly after the foregoing conversations between Bloom and Fechheimer, Fechheimer telephoned Mr. Forlani, an account executive at Luria's Chicago office, to discuss the purchase of scrap from Pielet. Forlani made some handwritten notes on a worksheet which Luria uses in connection with buying and selling scrap. These notes related to the terms of the barge scrap transaction between Pielet and Luria. Subsequently, and sometime before September 24, Forlani made a telephone call to Bloom to discuss this scrap transaction. At some point, but before September 24, Bloom made some handwritten notes on a worksheet Pielet employed in connection with buying and selling scrap.

On September 24, 1973, Bloom caused to be prepared a sales confirmation relating to the scrap transaction between Pielet and Luria. The following information was typed on the confirmation form:

Quantity:	Thirty-five thousand (35,000) net tons
Material:	Steel barges cut 5' x 5' x 20' free of non metallics
Price:	$42.00 per net ton F.O.B. Shipping point barge Houston, Texas or $49.00 per net ton delivered Brownsville, Texas
Shipment:	On or before December 31, 1973
Terms:	90% Advance on receipt of surveyor's weights and bill of lading

Bloom signed the sales confirmation and mailed the original and one copy to Forlani. The copy bore the printed words "confirmation copy." The following words are printed at the bottom of both the original and the confirmation copy of Pielet's confirmation form: "PLEASE SIGN AND RETURN THE COPY OF THIS CONFIRMATION FOR OUR FILES. FAILURE TO RETURN COPY DOES NOT VOID CONTRACT." Neither Forlani nor any officer or other employee of Luria ever signed or returned the confirmation copy to Bloom or anyone else at Pielet.

In the ordinary course of business when Luria makes a purchase of scrap, information regarding the purchase is typed or written on its own purchase confirmation form. On or about October 4, 1973, Forlani caused to be prepared a purchase confirmation containing the same terms as in Pielet's form, except with respect to the delivery date and mode of shipment. The delivery date typed on the form was by October 31, 1973 and the mode of shipment appeared to be left to the discretion of Luria. On the reverse side of this form are printed standard terms including ones referring to warranties, insurance, and taxes, as well as one stating "This order constitutes the entire contract between the parties." The original and one copy of this form are sent to the seller. These bear in red letters the words "RETURN ACCEPTANCE COPY IMMEDIATELY" in the lower right hand corner. There were no other words on this document to indicate any condition as to the existence of a contract.

Forlani sent the original and a copy of the October 4th purchase confirmation to Bloom. Bloom testified that upon receipt of this document, he immediately or shortly thereafter called Forlani to inform him that the Luria confirmation was erroneous with respect to delivery date and mode of shipment. Forlani agreed that the confirmation was erroneous in these two particulars. Bloom asked Forlani to send him an amendment correcting these errors, but Forlani never did. Neither Bloom nor any other officer or employee of Pielet ever signed or returned the acceptance copy to Luria.

During late October and November, Forlani called Bloom several times to ask why Pielet had not begun to deliver the steel. Although the delivery date stated in Pielet's confirmation form and orally agreed upon was on or before December 31, 1973, it is "common trade practice" to space deliveries out during the contract period, especially where the quantity involved is very large. On December 3, 1973, Forlani wrote a letter to Pielet saying Luria had not receiving notification of shipment and requesting that prompt attention be given. On February 6, 1974 representatives of Luria met with Bloom. Bloom stated he was having trouble with his supplier, and further mentioned that his supplier could not obtain the propane necessary for the torches used to cut the barges. On February 13, a week after the meeting, Luria wrote a letter to Bloom to make it clear that the matter had to be resolved. Luria never received a reply and Pielet never delivered the scrap. Luria filed its complaint in the district court on April 25, 1974....

Pielet contends that even if the evidence is sufficient to establish the existence of a binding contract between the parties, it was error for the district court to exclude evidence that the sales contract was expressly conditional upon Pielet obtaining the scrap metal from a particular supplier. In an offer of proof, Bloom testified that in their first conversation in September, he told Fechheimer, "I was doing business with people that I had never heard of, that they were fly-by-night people, that I was worried about shipment and if I didn't get shipment, I didn't want any big hassle, but if I got the scrap, he would get it...."[5]

The determination that the writings of the parties were intended to be a final expression of their agreement is to be made by the trial court. In light of Luria's acceptance of the terms stated in the Pielet writing, we agree with the district court's conclusion that the Pielet sales confirmation brought § 2-202 into play to bar Bloom's testimony.

Nevertheless, Pielet contends that § 2-202 is not applicable to this case. According to Pielet, Luria sued on an oral contract and therefore the parol evidence rule is not applicable because the writings of the parties were not the basis of the action but only collateral to it.

---

5. During the presentation of Luria's case, Bloom did testify on cross-examination that in conversations subsequent to the writings he told Forlani "if I get it (the scrap), you will get it." We agree with Pielet that in that context, the jury would take this statement as an excuse for not delivering rather than as a condition of the contract. Therefore, if Bloom's testimony relating to his first conversation with Fechheimer was wrongfully excluded the harm would be prejudicial.

It is true that although these writings were relied on to satisfy the Code's Statute of Frauds, §2-201, and to exclude parol evidence, Luria had to go outside these writings to prove to the jury the existence of an enforceable sales contract. But the writings are insufficient in themselves only because of two differing terms and are directly related to the contract sought to be proved.

As noted in 1 Anderson, Uniform Commercial Code §2-202:3 (2d 1970), §2-202 of the Code "extends (the operation of the parol evidence rule) to some degree to writings which are not the complete contract of the parties." The code itself refers to this fact in §2-207(3) which provides that where a contract is established by the conduct of the parties, the terms of the contract consist, at least, of those terms on which the writings agree even though "the writings of the parties do not otherwise establish a contract." Evidence of an alleged prior oral agreement cannot be used to contradict the terms on which the writings of the parties agree ...

In this case, of course, the existence of a sales contract was in issue. At first glance, it is troublesome that Luria was allowed to introduce testimony of the September conversations between the parties to help establish its case while Pielet was denied the opportunity to introduce statements made in the course of those same conversations. However, the fairness of this result becomes clear upon examination of why it was necessary for Luria to use parol evidence to prove the existence of the sales contract. Pielet's sales confirmation and Luria's purchase confirmation differed on two important terms, delivery date and mode of shipment. Luria used undisputed parol evidence that there had been a "meeting of the minds" as to these terms prior to the confirmatory memoranda to support its position that these two discrepancies were due to inadvertence and clerical error on Luria's part rather than disagreement between the parties. If the writings had agreed on these two important terms, Pielet would be hard pressed to argue that no contract for sale existed ... Allowing one party to use parol evidence to clarify a mistake in a writing, does not open the flood gates to any and all parol evidence bearing on the agreement.

Having found §2-202 applicable, the next question is whether the excluded evidence contradicts or is inconsistent with the terms of the writings. Pielet argues that the offered testimony did not "contradict" but instead "explained or supplemented" the writings with "consistent additional terms." For this contention, Pielet relies upon *Hunt Foods & Industries, Inc. v. Doliner*, 26 A.D.2d 41, 270 N.Y.S.2d 937 (1966). In reversing the trial court's summary judgment for plaintiff, the court in Hunt held that evidence of an oral condition precedent did not contradict the terms of a written stock option which was unconditional on its face. Therefore evidence of the condition precedent should not have been barred by U.C.C. §2-202. "In a sense any oral provision which would prevent the ripening of the obligations of a writing is inconsistent with the writing. But that obviously is not the sense in which the word is used. [Citation omitted.] To be inconsistent the term must contradict or negate a term of the writing." *Id.* at 43, 270 N.Y.S.2d at 940. This reasoning in *Hunt* was followed in *Michael Schiavone & Sons, Inc. v. Securalloy Co.*, 312 F. Supp. 801 (D. Conn.1970). In that case, the court found that parol evidence that the quantity in a sales contract was "understood to be up to 500 tons cannot be said to be inconsistent with the terms of the written contract which specified the quantity as '500 Gross Ton.'" *Id.* at 804.

The narrow view of inconsistency espoused in these two cases has been criticized. In *Snyder v. Herbert Greenbaum & Assoc., Inc.,* 38 Md. App. 144, 380 A.2d 618 (1977), the court held that parol evidence of a contractual right to unilateral rescission was inconsistent with a written agreement for the sale and installation of carpeting. The court defined "inconsistency" as used in § 2-202(b) as "the absence of reasonable harmony in terms of the language and respective obligations of the parties." *Id.* at 623 (emphasis in original) (citing U.C.C. § 1-205(4)). [Additional citation omitted.]

We adopt this latter view of inconsistency and reject the view expressed in *Hunt.* Where writings intended by the parties to be a final expression of their agreement call for an unconditional sale of goods, parol evidence that the seller's obligations are conditioned upon receiving the goods from a particular supplier is inconsistent and must be excluded. Had there been some additional reference such as "per our conversation" on the written confirmation indicating that oral agreements were meant to be incorporated into the writing, the result might have been different. [Citation omitted.] …

The judgment appealed from is affirmed.

Exercise 10-9: *Mitchill, Masterson, Lee,* U.C.C. § 2-202, and *Luria Bros.* Revisited

Analyze the following hypotheticals under each of the degree of integration (Step 3) and consistency tests (Step 4) outlined above:

1. Plaintiff farmer agreed to lease land according to the terms stated in a signed, written agreement dated October 16, 1974. The agreement contained only the following two terms:

   (1) "Stafford Farm [Defendant] agrees to rent to Mike Hatley [Plaintiff], Rt.1 Box 83, Halsey, Ore. Approximately 52 acres till Sept. 1st 1975 for the purpose of growing wheat with the follow[ing] condition: Stafford Farm shall have the right to buy out Mr. Mike Hatley at a figure of his cost per acre but not to exceed $70 per acre. The buyout is for the express purpose of developing a Mobile Home Park."

   (2) "Terms shall be $1800 paid on or before Jan. 20th 1975 balance due Sept. 20. 1975. The rent figure shall be $50 per acre."

   Between June 8 and 11, Defendant took possession of the land, cut the immature wheat crop, and offered to pay Plaintiff the $70 per acre under the buyout provision. Plaintiff demanded $400 per acre, which was the fair market value of the crop at that time. Plaintiff also argued (and sought to testify) that the written agreement did not include a term to which the parties had agreed. According to Plaintiff, because both parties knew that Plaintiff's farming efforts would produce wheat of considerable value, the parties had orally agreed that the buyout provision would expire 60 days after execution of the lease. Defendant objected. Should the evidence be admitted? *Cf. Hatley v. Stafford,* 588 P.2d 603, 284 Ore. 523 (1978).

2. Dawn owned two adjoining plots, each of which had a house on it. Dawn wished to retain the east plot and sell the west plot. The house on the east

plot had an unrestricted sea view from the rear of the premises. The boundary between the two plots was marked by ten very tall trees. The trees completely blocked out the sea view from the rear of the house on the west plot. After inspecting the house and land on the west plot, Pandora offered to buy the plot for a $1,000 above the asking price as long as Dawn chopped down the trees and replaced them with a low fence that would not restrict the sea view from the west plot. Dawn orally agreed.

The parties then signed a pre-printed, standard form real estate agreement that Dawn's realtor had given her. The agreement contained two pages of standard terms and left spaces for the parties to fill in their personal details, a description of the property, and the agreed price. The agreement also had a blank third page that was headed: "Additional terms and conditions." Dawn and Pandora signed the agreement but did not include any reference to Dawn's oral promise to remove the trees and replace them with a fence. Dawn is now refusing to chop down the trees. Will Pandora be able to enforce the oral term?

Exceptions to the Parol Evidence Rule

This section deals with the exceptions to the parol evidence rule. For this discussion, assume a piece of extrinsic evidence is barred either because the court deemed the contract completely integrated or because the court deemed the contract partially integrated and concluded that the extrinsic evidence was inconsistent with the written terms. In the instances explored below, while the extrinsic evidence cannot be admitted to prove the alleged contract term, courts will admit the evidence for some other purpose. For example, extrinsic evidence (be it evidence that the parties had agreed to other terms or evidence that otherwise sheds light on the parties' intentions) is always admissible if it will help a court interpret an ambiguous contract term in the parties' writing. Similarly, extrinsic evidence adduced to show that the parties entered into a contract based on a mutual mistake as to a basic assumption is always admissible. If one of the exceptions applies, two points are key: (1) **the extrinsic evidence will be admitted, and (2) the evidence will be admitted for the limited purpose reflected in the exception, not for the purpose of adding a new term to the contract.**

This section addresses the three most significant exceptions: evidence of an oral condition precedent to formation; evidence of fraud, mistake, duress, and the like; and evidence bearing on interpretation of the agreement.

An Oral Condition Precedent to Formation

Because this exception is a simple one and doesn't arise very often, we have chosen to present it by just having you read a Restatement section and analyze a problem in Exercise 10-10 below.

Exercise 10-10: Oral Condition Precedent to Formation

Please read section 217 of the RESTATEMENT (SECOND) OF CONTRACTS and answer the following hypothetical:

P and D are negotiating a contract for D to buy P's patent rights in one of P's inventions. D insists that D will not make the agreement until its two experts exam P's product, so P and D schedule a meeting with the experts. One expert shows up on time and approves the invention, but the other is delayed in traffic. After waiting one hour, the parties agree to sign the completely integrated contract and orally agree that D will not be bound if D's second expert does not approve the project. When the second expert shows up, the expert convinces D that P's product will not work and therefore D informs P it will not perform the contract.

P sues D for breach. D seeks to admit evidence of the parties' agreement, and P asserts the parol evidence rule to exclude D's testimony. Assume the evidence is admissible and explain why.

Evidence of Fraud, Mistake, and the Like

Sections 214(d) and (e) of the RESTATEMENT (SECOND) OF CONTRACTS provides that evidence to show any of the contract defenses is admissible even if the evidence otherwise would not be admissible based on the parol evidence rule.

Exercise 10-11: Introductory Questions Regarding Evidence of Invalidating Causes

1. Which of the parol evidence rule cases we have read might have come out differently had the lawyer for the party seeking to admit the evidence argued the evidence should be admitted pursuant to the rule stated in section 214(d)?

2. What would the argument in that case (those cases) have looked like? Why might the plaintiff have lost even if the evidence had been admitted for this purpose?

Exercise 10-12: *Morris v. Morris*

The following case, *Morris v. Morris,* provides an explanation of a specialized type of mistake and its implications for avoiding the bar of the parol evidence rule. As you read the case, consider the following questions:

1. How is the mistake issue in Morris different from the mistake issue in the mistake cases you read in Chapter 5?

2. Can this type of mistake be unilateral?

Morris v. Morris

637 S.E.2d 838, 282 Ga. App. 127 (2006)

Johnson, Presiding Judge. In 1966, E.E. Morris purchased approximately 548 acres of land in Randolph County. On December 30, 1993, he entered into an agreement to lease all of his farm land to his son Harold Wayne Morris for five years in exchange for annual rental payments of $22,000. Eight months later, on August 19, 1994, the father and son entered into another contract giving Harold Wayne Morris a ten-year option to buy his father's land for $260,000.

Although the option contract refers to the warranty deeds which describe all 548 acres of land bought by E.E. Morris in 1966, the option contract itself does not expressly describe all 548 acres. Rather, it describes only about 312 of those acres. The other 236 acres, identified in two paragraphs of one of the 1966 warranty deeds, are not specifically described in the option contract.

In December 1995, E.E. Morris made his last will and testament, naming as beneficiaries his children Linda Morris Peck, Marion Morris and Derrell Dean Morris. He expressly excluded Harold Wayne Morris from any inheritance under the will, providing that he was doing so because both the contract to rent the farm and the option contract to buy the farm were substantially below fair market value, and Harold Wayne Morris would thereby receive his proportionate share of the estate.

E.E. Morris passed away in 1997. On January 8, 2003, in compliance with the terms of the option contract, Harold Wayne Morris notified his brother Marion Morris, who was the executor of their father's estate, that he wanted to exercise his option to buy the land and that he had the money to do so. On March 20, 2003, Marion Morris filed a declaratory judgment action, asserting that Harold Wayne Morris had notified him that he is entitled to purchase all of their father's land, including the 236 acres that are not expressly identified in the option contract. The action sought a determination by the court as to which property the estate must convey to Harold Wayne Morris under the option contract. On April 15, 2003, Harold Wayne Morris filed an answer, counterclaim and cross-claim, asserting, among other things, that he is indeed entitled to purchase all of the land under the option contract.

A bench trial was held in Randolph County Superior Court on November 8, 2004. Harold Wayne Morris testified that he and his father had discussed the option contract and their agreement was for it to cover all of the land, just as he was working all of the land under the lease agreement. Marion Morris testified that in August 1994, his father had discussed the lease and option contracts with him, and he had no question at that time that his father had given his brother the option to buy all of the land. He testified that during the discussion his father made no distinction between all of the land that Harold Wayne Morris was working under the lease and the land that was in the option contract, and that his father never mentioned giving an option on only part of the land. He further testified that during his lifetime, his father never gave any indication that his brother did not have the option to buy all of the land.

The trial court also heard testimony from Elizabeth McDonald, who for 30 years had been the secretary to the lawyer who prepared the option contract. She testified that, per the usual office routine, she had typed the contract from notes made by the lawyer during his consultation with the client and from the lawyer's dictation of the contract terms, and that she had used the applicable warranty deeds to insert legal descriptions of the property into the contract. Based on her review of the office records, she further testified that she had no doubt that, while typing the contract, she had inadvertently left the property in question—the 236 acres described in two paragraphs of one of E.E. Morris' 1966 warranty deeds—out of the option contract.

Immediately after trial, Harold Wayne Morris filed an amendment to his pleadings to request that the option contract be reformed to include the missing land. Executor Marion Morris moved to strike that amended pleading. But in its final order, the trial court denied the motion to strike, finding that the issue of reformation of the option contract had been tried by the parties and that it was proper to amend the pleadings to conform to the evidence.

The court went on to find that this is a case of mutual mistake in that the option contract was intended to cover all of E.E. Morris' land, but that it did not due to the secretary's inadvertent omission of some of the land from the contract. . . .

[W]e find no reversible error. . . .

The estate contends that the trial court erred in finding that there was a mutual mistake in the preparation of the option contract. We disagree.

"A mutual mistake in an action for reformation means one in which both parties agree to the terms of the contract, but by mistake of the scrivener the true terms of the agreement are not set forth." [Citation omitted.] In the current case, there is clear evidence that E.E. Morris intended to give Harold Wayne Morris the option to buy all of his land, including not only Harold Wayne Morris' testimony to that effect, but also Marion Morris' own testimony that after discussing the contract with his father, he had no question that his brother had the option to purchase all of the land. Moreover, the legal secretary who typed the option contract testified without equivocation that she had inadvertently left the land in question out of the contract.

Because the evidence shows that the true terms of the agreement were not set forth in the option contract due to an inadvertent omission by the secretary, the trial court did not err in finding that there was a mutual mistake in the preparation of the contract. [Citation omitted.]

The estate contends that the trial court erred in allowing Harold Wayne Morris and Elizabeth McDonald to testify that the option contract was meant to include all of E.E. Morris' property. The contention is without merit.

"Parol evidence is admissible to prove a mistake in a deed or any other contract required by law to be in writing." [Citation omitted.] If the mistake alleged is in the contract's description and the description is unambiguous, extrinsic evidence may be resorted to for the purpose of reforming the contract so as to make it express the real intention of the parties and correct a mutual mistake of fact. [Citation omitted.] In the case at bar, since Harold Wayne Morris sought reformation of the option contract on the basis of mutual mistake of fact due to a scrivener's error mistakenly describing the property to be sold, parol evidence of the real terms of the agreement was admissible. . . .

Judgment affirmed. . . .

Evidence to Help Interpret an Ambiguous Contract

Exercise 10-13: Restatement (Second) Section 214(c) and *Bethlehem Steel*

Read section 214(c) of the RESTATEMENT (SECOND) OF CONTRACTS and translate the rule into your own words.

A crucial question in the application of section 214 is whether there is any need for evidence relating to the meaning of the writing. If a writing is unambiguous, there is no need for evidence as to the meaning of the writing because the question is one of law. The real, crucial, and difficult question is whether the agreement is ambiguous. As we will see, like many areas of the parol evidence rule, the question of how to determine whether the writing is ambiguous is the subject of an important split of authority. As you read the next case, *Bethlehem Steel Co. v. Turner Construction Co.*, consider the following questions:

1. What is the *Bethlehem Steel* court's view as to how courts should go about determining whether a writing is ambiguous?

2. What is the policy benefit of the approach adopted by the *Bethlehem Steel* court?

Bethlehem Steel Co. v. Turner Constr. Co.

141 N.E.2d 590, 2 N.Y.2d 456 (1957)

Dye, Judge. On or about July 30, 1948 the plaintiff, Bethlehem, entered into a subcontract with the defendant Turner Construction Company, to furnish, deliver and erect the structural steel for a 20-story office building on Broadway, which Turner—as general contractor—was to build for the defendant Mutual Life Insurance Company, for a fixed fee, Mutual to pay for all other costs. The contract contained a clause providing that in the event the 'prices for component materials' increased or decreased, there was to be a corresponding adjustment of the contract prices. Adjustment for increases in the price of steel in any event was limited to $15 per ton.

Pursuant to such provision, Bethlehem rendered periodic bills for materials furnished, which Mutual paid without complaint in respect to items other than the escalation portion of the price, asserting that the term 'prices for component materials' as used in the contract had reference to changes in price to Bethlehem for materials it used in progressing the work, that is, if there were increases in the prices paid by Bethlehem in order to obtain the materials necessary to produce steel which is to say the cost to Bethlehem in the manufacture of raw steel at the mill, based on the basic elements employed such as iron ore, steel scrap, limestone, etc. Bethlehem refused to accept such an interpretation and insisted that the words 'prices for component materials' included the price of steel being regularly charged to the trade which, in this instance, had been increased by $10 per ton for the aggregate of steel items known as steel shapes, plates, bars, sheets, rivets and bolts. Based on this contention, Bethlehem rendered bills aggregating $94,861.15. When Turner and Mutual persisted in their refusal to pay, Bethlehem filed a mechanic's lien against Mutual's building and brought this action for its foreclosure. The basic issue, then, is the meaning of the term "prices for component materials," as used in the price adjustment clause of the contract.

A trial is warranted only in the event that we deem the words ambiguous. No such problem faces us here. Bethlehem agreed to furnish, deliver, erect and paint all structural steel work in accordance with Class A material, A.I.S.C. Code of Standard Practice. Turner was to pay $182 per net ton for the steel, subject to the price adjustment clause in the event of increase or decrease in price. That clause made specific mention of the basis for computing the changes in steel price, viz., designing, fabrication and erection which, by the description, quite obviously has reference to the steel delivered and used on the job. The maximum increase was not to exceed $15 a ton. The increase billed was calculated on the basis of the increase of $10 per ton, which was a publicly quoted uniform price increase charged by Bethlehem to all other purchasers of steel from the mill. It appears without denial that Bethlehem increased the price of steel after the contract although the price increase was in effect before the contract was executed. As matter of undisputed fact, the parties had expressly agreed that the escalation clause was to be effective as of June 28, 1948. In support of their contention, appellants point to the testimony of Mr. Hughes, the controller of Mutual, that he understood the escalation clause to have that meaning. Such a view impresses us as straining the contract language beyond its reasonable and ordinary meaning. If "component materials" means raw materials used in the production of steel, escalation on account of labor rates would not be limited to those specifically mentioned in connection with design, fabrication and erection, but would have included labor costs at the mill as well. However, it does not. The formula employed referred to the computation of "prices for component materials, labor rates applicable to the fabrication and erection thereof and freight rates." A normal and reasonable meaning of that clause has the word "thereof" referring to the term "component materials" so that component materials signify the materials that Bethlehem contracted to provide in performing the work "furnishing, delivering, erecting and painting all structural steel work in accordance with Class 'A' material." Mere assertion by one that contract language means something to him, where it is otherwise clear, unequivocal and understandable when read in connection with the whole contract, is not in and of itself enough to raise a triable issue of fact. It has long been the rule that when a contract is clear in and of itself, circumstances, extrinsic to the document may not be considered, [citation omitted] and that where the intention of the parties may be gathered from the four corners of the instrument, interpretation of the contract is a question of law and no trial is necessary....

The judgment appealed from should be affirmed, with costs.

Conway, Chief Judge (dissenting). Plaintiff agreed to furnish, erect and paint all structural steel work in a building for defendant Mutual Life Insurance Company. The escalator or price adjustment clause in the contract provided: "The price or prices herein stated are based on prices for component materials, labor rates applicable to the fabrication and erection thereof and freight rates, in effect as of the date of this proposal. If, at any time prior to completion of performance of the work to be performed hereunder, any of said material prices, labor rates and/or freight rates shall be increased or decreased, then in respect of any of said work performed thereafter there shall be a corresponding increase or decrease in the prices herein stated."

The case turns upon the construction to be placed upon the words "component materials." It is the position of the plaintiff that by those words it meant the plain steel products such as shapes, bars, sheets and plates which were shipped from its mills to its fabricating works and that the term "prices" meant the price at which it regularly sold such products to others, so that if it increased its prices to others it could increase its price to Mutual. The defendant Mutual claims that under the disputed clause plaintiff was entitled only to increases in the cost of "component materials" which enter into the production of the structural steel to be furnished by it under the contract....

"[A]s a general rule, the construction of a written instrument is a question of law for the court to determine; but when the language employed is not free from ambiguity, or when it is equivocal and its interpretation depends upon the sense in which the words were used, in view of the subject to which they relate, the relation of the parties and the surrounding circumstances properly applicable to it, the intent of the parties becomes a matter of inquiry, and the interpretation of the language used by them is a mixed question of law and fact." [Citation omitted.]

It is suggested that the escalation clause here involved is free from ambiguity and is so clear that it is capable of but one reasonable meaning and that the one urged by Bethlehem. I cannot agree. In my opinion, the language of the contract is susceptible of more than one reasonable interpretation and so a trial must be had.

As the appellants point out, the usual purpose of an escalation clause is to *preserve*, substantially, the benefit of a bargain. Such a clause is intended to protect against unanticipated or unpredictable changes which might render the bargain unduly harsh. An escalation clause is not ordinarily intended to enable one party to render the bargain more profitable to himself. It seems to me that the words 'prices for component materials' taken in their ordinary meaning can reasonably be understood to refer to the additional prices which Bethlehem would be required to pay in order to obtain and furnish the materials necessary for the performance of the contract work. In other words, those words could reasonably mean that the contract price was to be increased pursuant to the escalation clause, if Bethlehem's costs and expenses increased. Even under *Bethlehem's interpretation* of the clause, the contract price per net ton of erected steel was to be adjusted if there was an increase or decrease in the *prices paid* by Bethlehem for labor, freight and such materials as welding rods and paint. From this, one could reasonably conclude that the clause would operate similarly insofar as other materials are concerned and that an increase could be demanded on account of steel produced by Bethlehem only if its costs with respect thereto increased, *i.e.*, if there were increases in the prices paid by Bethlehem in order to obtain the materials necessary to produce steel. In the absence of a special understanding or definition, such view is in accord with reason. It is perfectly consistent with the wording of the contract and is in keeping with the usual purpose of an escalation clause, *i.e.*, to preserve, not better, the bargain already struck.

An additional reason for adopting this interpretation, rather than Bethlehem's, is the rule that the language of a contract is to be construed strictly against the party who drafted it. The clause in question here was prepared by Bethlehem, having been taken verbatim from Bethlehem's original proposal to Mutual.

The fact that the interpretation urged by Bethlehem is other than that ordinarily given an escalation clause, and the fact that Bethlehem seeks to impress technical and uncommon meanings upon general, everyday words demonstrate, to my mind, that the clause in question is at least ambiguous and that its proper meaning cannot be summarily determined without full opportunity for inquiry into the context in which the words in dispute were used, the surrounding circumstances, the negotiations and the understanding of the individual negotiators.

In my judgment, therefore, this is not a case for the granting of summary judgment and I vote to reverse the judgment of the Appellate Division and to deny the motion for summary judgment.

Exercise 10-14: *Pacific Gas & Electric Co.*

The next case you will read is *Pacific Gas & Electric Co. v. G. W. Thomas Drayage & Rigging Co.* As you read the case, answer the following questions:

1. What are the key facts?

2. Why did the *Pacific Gas & Electric Co.* trial court conclude that the parol evidence rule bars the admission of the defendant's evidence bearing on the meaning of the clause at issue?

3. Under what circumstances would the *Pacific Gas & Electric Co.* court admit parol evidence?

4. How did the *Pacific Gas & Electric Co.* court apply the rule you stated in response to the previous question?

5. Why did the *Pacific Gas & Electric Co.* court reject the "plain meaning" rule?

6. The *Pacific Gas & Electric Co.* court suggests that the trial court should have admitted the evidence even under the "plain meaning" rule. Where? Why?

7. Assume you are a lawyer appearing the Supreme Court of a state that has not decided whether to adopt the "four corners" rule or the "all evidence" rule from the *Pacific Gas & Electric Co.* case. How might you argue the court should adopt the "Four Corners" rule? How might you argue the court should adopt the "*Pacific Gas & Electric Co.*" rule?

Pacific Gas & Elec. Co. v.
G. W. Thomas Drayage & Rigging Co.
442 P.2d 641, 69 Cal. 2d 33 (1968)

Traynor, Chief Justice. Defendant appeals from a judgment for plaintiff in an action for damages for injury to property under an indemnity clause of a contract. In 1960 defendant entered into a contract with plaintiff to furnish the labor and equipment necessary to remove and replace the upper metal cover of plaintiff's steam turbine. Defendant agreed to perform the work "at [its] own risk and expense" and to "indemnify" plaintiff "against all loss, damage, expense and liability resulting from injury to property, arising out of or in any way connected with the performance of this contract." Defendant also agreed to procure not less than $50,000 insurance to cover liability for injury to property. Plaintiff was to be an additional named insured, but the policy was to contain a cross-liability clause extending the coverage to plaintiff's property.

During the work the cover fell and injured the exposed rotor of the turbine. Plaintiff brought this action to recover $25,144.51, the amount it subsequently spent on repairs. Defendant offered to prove by admissions of plaintiff's agents, by defendant's conduct under similar contracts entered into with plaintiff, and by other proof that in the indemnity clause the parties meant to cover injury to property of third parties only and not to plaintiff's property. Although the trial court observed that the language used was "the classic language for a third party indemnity provision" and that "one could very easily conclude that ... its whole intendment is to indemnify third parties," it nevertheless held that the "plain language" of the agreement also required defendant to indemnify plaintiff for injuries to plaintiff's property. Having determined that the contract had a plain meaning, the court refused to admit any extrinsic evidence that would contradict its interpretation.

When a court interprets a contract on this basis, it determines the meaning of the instrument in accordance with the " ... extrinsic evidence of the judge's own linguistic education and experience." [Citation omitted.] The exclusion of testimony that might contradict the linguistic background of the judge reflects a judicial belief in the possibility of perfect verbal expression. [Citation omitted.] This belief is a remnant of a primitive faith in the inherent potency and inherent meaning of words.

The test of admissibility of extrinsic evidence to explain the meaning of a written instrument is not whether it appears to the court to be plain and unambiguous on its face, but whether the offered evidence is relevant to prove a meaning to which the language of the instrument is reasonably susceptible. [Citations omitted.]

A rule that would limit the determination of the meaning of a written instrument to its four-corners merely because it seems to the court to be clear and unambiguous, would either deny the relevance of the intention of the parties or presuppose a degree of verbal precision and stability our language has not attained.

Some courts have expressed the opinion that contractual obligations are created by the mere use of certain words, whether or not there was any intention to incur such obligations. Under this view, contractual obligations flow, not from the intention of the parties but from the fact that they used certain magic words. Evidence of the parties' intention therefore becomes irrelevant. In this state, however, the intention of the parties as expressed in the contract is the source of contractual rights and duties. A court must ascertain and give effect to this intention by determining what the parties meant by the words they used. Accordingly, the exclusion of relevant, extrinsic evidence to explain the meaning of a written instrument could be justified only if it were feasible to determine the meaning the parties gave to the words from the instrument alone.

If words had absolute and constant referents, it might be possible to discover contractual intention in the words themselves and in the manner in which they were arranged. Words, however, do not have absolute and constant referents. "A word is a symbol of thought but has no arbitrary and fixed meaning like a symbol of algebra or chemistry...." [Citation omitted.] The meaning of particular words or groups of words varies with the "verbal context and surrounding circumstances and purposes in view of the linguistic education and experience of their users and their hearers or readers (not excluding judges).... A word has no meaning apart from these factors; much less does it have an objective meaning, one true meaning." (Corbin, The Interpretation of Words and the Parol Evidence Rule (1965) 50 Cornell L.Q. 161, 187.)....

Although extrinsic evidence is not admissible to add to, detract from, or vary the terms of a written contract, these terms must first be determined before it can be decided whether or not extrinsic evidence is being offered for a prohibited purpose. The fact that the terms of an instrument appear clear to a judge does not preclude the possibility that the parties chose the language of the instrument to express different terms. That possibility is not limited to contracts whose terms have acquired a particular meaning by trade usage, but exists whenever the parties' understanding of the words used may have differed from the judge's understanding.

Accordingly, rational interpretation requires at least a preliminary consideration of all credible evidence offered to prove the intention of the parties. [Citations omitted.] Such evidence includes testimony as to the "circumstances surrounding the making of the agreement ... including the object, nature and subject matter of the writing ..." so that the court can "place itself in the same situation in which the parties found themselves at the time of contracting...."[6]

In the present case the court erroneously refused to consider extrinsic evidence offered to show that the indemnity clause in the contract was not intended to cover injuries to plaintiff's property. Although that evidence was not necessary to show that the indemnity clause was reasonably susceptible of the meaning contended for by defendant, it was nevertheless relevant and admissible on that issue. Moreover, since that clause was reasonably susceptible of that meaning, the offered evidence was also admissible to prove that the clause had that meaning and did not cover injuries to plaintiff's property.

Accordingly, the judgment must be reversed ...

Exercise 10-15: Restatement (Second) Section 214(c), *Bethlehem Steel* and *Pacific Gas & Elec. Co.* Revisited

1. Plaintiff and Defendant enter into a contract for the sale and purchase of horsemeat for use in dog food. The contract states that the meat "shall be

---

6. When objection is made to any particular item of evidence offered to prove the intention of the parties, the trial court may not yet be in a position to determine whether in the light of all of the offered evidence, the item objected to will turn out to be admissible as tending to prove a meaning of which the language of the instrument is reasonably susceptible or inadmissible as tending to prove a meaning of which the language is not reasonably susceptible.

50% protein." Plaintiff, the seller, delivers meat that is 49.7% protein and defendant refuses delivery. Plaintiff then sues defendant for breach and seeks to admit evidence of trade usage (a term of art in the horsemeat trade) under which the term "50% protein" is understood to mean between 49.5% and 50% protein. Analyze whether the contract is ambiguous by applying both of the above tests for determining whether a contract is ambiguous. Assume Article 2 of the U.C.C. does **not** apply.

2.   How would your approach to this problem change if Article 2 of the U.C.C. applied to the contract in the previous hypothetical?

Exercise 10-16: *Trident Center v. Connecticut General Life Insurance Co.*

In *Trident Center* case, the Ninth Circuit was sharply critical of the approach taken by the California Supreme Court in *Pacific Gas*. Read the extract and then consider the following questions:

1.   In what respects does the *Trident Center* court's approach differ from the *Pacific Gas* court's approach?

2.   Why did the *Trident Center* court nevertheless rule that the plaintiff should have the opportunity to introduce extrinsic evidence?

Trident Center v. Connecticut General Life Insurance Co.

847 F.2d 564 (1988)

KOZINSKI, Circuit Judge:

The parties to this transaction are, by any standard, highly sophisticated business people: Plaintiff is a partnership consisting of an insurance company and two of Los Angeles' largest and most prestigious law firms; defendant is another insurance company. Dealing at arm's length and from positions of roughly equal bargaining strength, they negotiated a commercial loan amounting to more than $56 million. The contract documents are lengthy and detailed; they squarely address the precise issue that is the subject of this dispute; to all who read English, they appear to resolve the issue fully and conclusively.

Plaintiff nevertheless argues here, as it did below, that it is entitled to introduce extrinsic evidence that the contract means something other than what it says. This case therefore presents the question whether parties in California can ever draft a contract that is proof to parol evidence. Somewhat surprisingly, the answer is no.

Facts

The facts are rather simple. Sometime in 1983 Security First Life Insurance Company and the law firms of Mitchell, Silberberg & Knupp and Manatt, Phelps, Rothenberg & Tunney formed a limited partnership for the purpose of constructing an office building complex on Olympic Boulevard in West

Los Angeles. The partnership, Trident Center, the plaintiff herein, sought and obtained financing for the project from defendant, Connecticut General Life Insurance Company. The loan documents provide for a loan of $56,500,000 at 12 1/4 percent interest for a term of 15 years, secured by a deed of trust on the project. The promissory note provides that "[m]aker shall not have the right to prepay the principal amount hereof in whole or in part" for the first 12 years. Note at 6. In years 13–15, the loan may be prepaid, subject to a sliding prepayment fee. The note also provides that in case of a default during years 1–12, Connecticut General has the option of accelerating the note and adding a 10 percent prepayment fee.

Everything was copacetic for a few years until interest rates began to drop. The 12 1/4 percent rate that had seemed reasonable in 1983 compared unfavorably with 1987 market rates and Trident started looking for ways of refinancing the loan to take advantage of the lower rates. Connecticut General was unwilling to oblige, insisting that the loan could not be prepaid for the first 12 years of its life, that is, until January 1996.

Trident then brought suit in state court seeking a declaration that it was entitled to prepay the loan now, subject only to a 10 percent prepayment fee. Connecticut General promptly removed to federal court and brought a motion to dismiss, claiming that the loan documents clearly and unambiguously precluded prepayment during the first 12 years. The district court agreed and dismissed Trident's complaint. The court also "*sua sponte,* sanction[ed] the plaintiff for the filing of a frivolous lawsuit." Order of Dismissal, No. CV 87–2712 JMI (Kx), at 3 (C.D. Cal. June 8, 1987). Trident appeals both aspects of the district court's ruling.

Discussion

I

Trident makes two arguments as to why the district court's ruling is wrong. First, it contends that the language of the contract is ambiguous and proffers a construction that it believes supports its position. Second, Trident argues that, under California law, even seemingly unambiguous contracts are subject to modification by parol or extrinsic evidence. Trident faults the district court for denying it the opportunity to present evidence that the contract language did not accurately reflect the parties' intentions.

A. The Contract

As noted earlier, the promissory note provides that Trident "shall not have the right to prepay the principal amount hereof in whole or in part before January 1996." Note at 6. It is difficult to imagine language that more clearly or unambiguously expresses the idea that Trident may not unilaterally prepay the loan during its first 12 years. Trident, however, argues that there is an ambiguity because another clause of the note provides that "[i]n the event of a prepayment resulting from a default hereunder or the Deed of Trust prior to January 10, 1996 the prepayment fee will be ten percent (10%)." Note at 6–7. Trident interprets this clause as giving it the option of prepaying the loan if only it is willing to incur the prepayment fee.

We reject Trident's argument out of hand. In the first place, its proffered interpretation would result in a contradiction between two clauses of the contract; the default clause would swallow up the clause prohibiting Trident from prepaying during the first 12 years of the contract. The normal rule of construction, of course, is that courts must interpret contracts, if possible, so as to avoid internal conflict. [Citation omitted.]

In any event, the clause on which Trident relies is not on its face reasonably susceptible to Trident's proffered interpretation. Whether to accelerate repayment of the loan in the event of default is entirely Connecticut General's decision. The contract makes this clear at several points. *See* Note at 4 ("in each such event [of default], the entire principal indebtedness, or so much thereof as may remain unpaid at the time, shall, *at the option of Holder,* become due and payable immediately" (emphasis added)); *id.* at 7 ("[i]n the event Holder exercises its *option to accelerate* the maturity hereof ..." (emphasis added)); Deed of Trust ¶ 2.01, at 25 ("in each such event [of default], Beneficiary *may* declare all sums secured hereby immediately due and payable ..." (emphasis added)). Even if Connecticut General decides to declare a default and accelerate, it "may rescind any notice of breach or default." *Id.* ¶ 2.02, at 26. Finally, Connecticut General has the option of doing nothing at all: "Beneficiary reserves the right at its sole option to waive noncompliance by Trustor with any of the conditions or covenants to be performed by Trustor hereunder." *Id.* ¶ 3.02, at 29.

Once again, it is difficult to imagine language that could more clearly assign to Connecticut General the exclusive right to decide whether to declare a default, whether and when to accelerate, and whether, having chosen to take advantage of any of its remedies, to rescind the process before its completion.

Trident nevertheless argues that it is entitled to precipitate a default and insist on acceleration by tendering the balance due on the note plus the 10 percent prepayment fee. The contract language, cited above, leaves no room for this construction. It is true, of course, that Trident is free to stop making payments, which may then cause Connecticut General to declare a default and accelerate. But that is not to say that Connecticut General would be required to so respond. The contract quite clearly gives Connecticut General other options: It may choose to waive the default, or to take advantage of some other remedy such as the right to collect "all the income, rents, royalties, revenue, issues, profits, and proceeds of the Property." Deed of Trust ¶ 1.18, at 22. By interpreting the contract as Trident suggests, we would ignore those provisions giving Connecticut General, not Trident, the exclusive right to decide how, when and whether the contract will be terminated upon default during the first 12 years.

In effect, Trident is attempting to obtain judicial sterilization of its intended default. But defaults are messy things; they are supposed to be. Once the maker of a note secured by a deed of trust defaults, its credit rating may deteriorate; attempts at favorable refinancing may be thwarted by the need to meet the trustee's sale schedule; its cash flow may be impaired if the beneficiary takes advantage of the assignment of rents remedy; default provisions in its loan agreements with other lenders may be triggered. Fear of these repercussions is strong medicine that keeps debtors from shirking their obligations when interest rates go down and they become disenchanted with their loans. That Trident is willing to suffer the cost and delay of a lawsuit, rather than simply defaulting, shows far better than anything we might say that these provisions are having their intended effect. We decline Trident's invitation to truncate the lender's remedies and deprive Connecticut General of its bargained-for protection.

B. Extrinsic Evidence

Trident argues in the alternative that, even if the language of the contract appears to be unambiguous, the deal the parties actually struck is in fact quite different. It wishes to offer extrinsic evidence that the parties had agreed Trident could prepay at any time within the first 12 years by tendering the full amount plus a 10 percent prepayment fee. As discussed above, this is an interpretation to which the contract, as written, is not reasonably susceptible. Under traditional contract principles, extrinsic evidence is inadmissible to interpret, vary or add to the terms of an unambiguous integrated written instrument. *See* 4 S. Williston, *supra* p. 5, §631, at 948–49; 2 B. Witkin, *California Evidence* §981, at 926 (3d ed. 1986).

Trident points out, however, that California does not follow the traditional rule. Two decades ago the California Supreme Court in *Pacific Gas & Electric Co. v. G.W. Thomas Drayage & Rigging Co.,* 69 Cal.2d 33, 442 P.2d 641, 69 Cal.Rptr. 561 (1968), turned its back on the notion that a contract can ever have a plain meaning discernible by a court without resort to extrinsic evidence. The court reasoned that contractual obligations flow not from the words of the contract, but from the intention of the parties. "Accordingly," the court stated, "the exclusion of relevant, extrinsic, evidence to explain the meaning of a written instrument could be justified only if it were feasible to determine the meaning the parties gave to the words from the instrument alone." 69 Cal.2d at 38, 442 P.2d 641, 69 Cal.Rptr. 561. This, the California Supreme Court concluded, is impossible: "If words had absolute and constant referents, it might be possible to discover contractual intention in the words themselves and in the manner in which they were arranged. Words, however, do not have absolute and constant referents." *Id.* In the same vein, the court noted that "[t]he exclusion of testimony that might contradict the linguistic background of the judge reflects a judicial belief in the possibility of perfect verbal expression. This belief is a remnant of a primitive faith in the inherent potency and inherent meaning of words." *Id.* at 37, 442 P.2d 641, 69 Cal.Rptr. 561 (citation and footnotes omitted).

Under *Pacific Gas,* it matters not how clearly a contract is written, nor how completely it is integrated, nor how carefully it is negotiated, nor how squarely it addresses the issue before the court: the contract cannot be rendered impervious to attack by parol evidence. If one side is willing to claim that the parties intended one thing but the agreement provides for another, the court must consider extrinsic evidence of possible ambiguity. If that evidence raises the specter of ambiguity where there was none before, the contract language is displaced and the intention of the parties must be divined from self-serving testimony offered by partisan witnesses whose recollection is hazy from passage of time and colored by their conflicting interests. [Citation omitted.] We question whether this approach is more likely to divulge the original intention of the parties than reliance on the seemingly clear words they agreed upon at the time. [Citation omitted.]

Pacific Gas casts a long shadow of uncertainty over all transactions negotiated and executed under the law of California. As this case illustrates, even when the transaction is very sizeable, even if it involves only sophisticated parties, even if it was negotiated with the aid of counsel, even if it results in contract language that is devoid of ambiguity, costly and protracted litigation cannot be avoided if one party has a strong enough motive for challenging the contract. While this rule creates much business for lawyers and an occasional windfall to some clients, it leads only to frustration and delay for most litigants and clogs already overburdened courts.

It also chips away at the foundation of our legal system. By giving credence to the idea that words are inadequate to express concepts, *Pacific Gas* undermines the basic principle that language provides a meaningful constraint on public and private conduct. If we are unwilling to say that parties, dealing face to face, can come up with language that binds them, how can we send anyone to jail for violating statutes consisting of mere words lacking "absolute and constant referents"? How can courts ever enforce decrees, not written in language understandable to all, but encoded in a dialect reflecting only the "linguistic background of the judge"? Can lower courts ever be faulted for failing to carry out the mandate of higher courts when "perfect verbal expression" is impossible? Are all attempts to develop the law in a reasoned and principled fashion doomed to failure as "remnant[s] of a primitive faith in the inherent potency and inherent meaning of words"?

Be that as it may. While we have our doubts about the wisdom of *Pacific Gas,* we have no difficulty understanding its meaning, even without extrinsic evidence to guide us. As we read the rule in California, we must reverse and remand to the district court in order to give plaintiff an opportunity to present extrinsic evidence as to the intention of the parties in drafting the contract. It may not be a wise rule we are applying, but it is a rule that binds us. *Erie R.R. Co. v. Tompkins,* 304 U.S. 64, 78, 58 S. Ct. 817, 822, 82 L. Ed. 1188 (1938).

II

In imposing sanctions on plaintiff, the district court stated:

> Pursuant to Fed.R.Civ.P. 11, the Court, *sua sponte,* sanctions the plaintiff for the filing of a frivolous lawsuit. The Court concludes that the language in the note and deed of trust is plain and clear. No reasonable person, much less firms of able attorneys, could possibly misunderstand this crystal-clear language. Therefore, this action was brought in bad faith.

Order of Dismissal at 3. Having reversed the district court on its substantive ruling, we must, of course, also reverse it as to the award of sanctions. While we share the district judge's impatience with this litigation, we would suggest that his irritation may have been misdirected. It is difficult to blame plaintiff and its lawyers for bringing this lawsuit. With this much money at stake, they would have been foolish not to pursue all remedies available to them under the applicable law. At fault, it seems to us, are not the parties and their lawyers but the legal system that encourages this kind of lawsuit. By holding that language has no objective meaning, and that contracts mean only what courts ultimately say they do, *Pacific Gas* invites precisely this type of lawsuit. With the benefit of 20 years of hindsight, the California Supreme Court may wish to revisit the issue. If it does so, we commend to it the facts of this case as a paradigmatic example of why the traditional rule, based on centuries of experience, reflects the far wiser approach.

Conclusion

The judgment of the district court is REVERSED. The case is REMANDED for reinstatement of the complaint and further proceedings in accordance with this opinion. The parties shall bear their own costs on appeal.

Exercise 10-17: Synthesis of Parol Evidence Rules

Look at Diagram 10-4 on the following page. Annotate the diagram with citations to the Restatement sections and cases we have read. For example, the materials regarding ambiguity, particularly the conflicting rules, should be used to annotate the reference to "evidence to help resolve an ambiguity" in Step 5.

Exercise 10-18: Parol Evidence Rule in Your State

Determine which approach your state follows for questions of complete integration, for questions of consistency, and for questions of whether a contract is ambiguous.

Exercise 10-19: Contract Editing Task

Take another look at the contract between Widgets. Inc. and Josephina Schmo. In particular focus on the merger clause. The clause has a significant flaw. Rewrite the clause to correct the error.

Chapter Problem Revisited

Prepare your oral argument on behalf of Widgets or Schmo. If your last name starts with the letters A–M, prepare an oral argument on behalf of Widgets. If your last name starts with the letters N–Z, prepare an oral argument on behalf of Schmo. Your judge will announce her or his tentative ruling before your argument begins. You will have only five minutes to make your argument.

Professional Development Reflection Questions

1. You are preparing to litigate a contract lawsuit. Your client tells you that an oral statement was made during negotiations that supports his case, but you are 99% sure the statement will be excluded from evidence under the parol evidence rule. Your client nonetheless wants you to mention the oral statement in your opening argument. Should you do so?

Diagram 10-4: "AICCA" Approach to Parol Evidence Rules

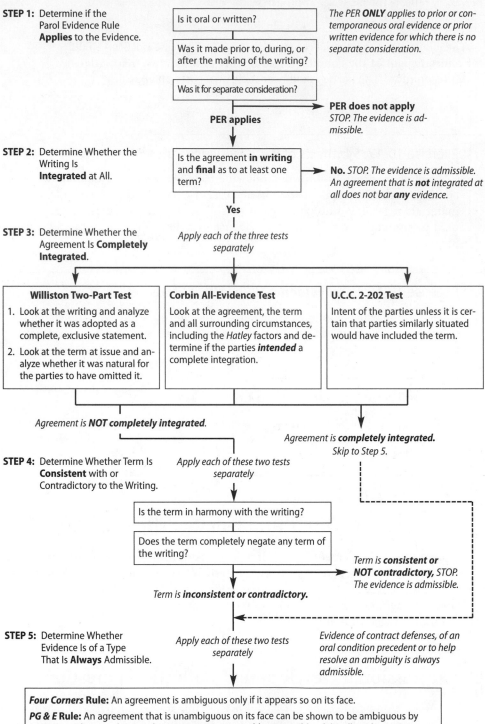

STEP 1: Determine if the Parol Evidence Rule **Applies** to the Evidence.

Is it oral or written?

Was it made prior to, during, or after the making of the writing?

Was it for separate consideration?

*The PER **ONLY** applies to prior or contemporaneous oral evidence or prior written evidence for which there is no separate consideration.*

PER does not apply
STOP. The evidence is admissible.

PER applies

STEP 2: Determine Whether the Writing Is **Integrated** at All.

Is the agreement **in writing** and **final** as to at least one term?

No. *STOP. The evidence is admissible. An agreement that is **not** integrated at all does not bar **any** evidence.*

Yes

STEP 3: Determine Whether the Agreement Is **Completely Integrated**.

Apply each of the three tests separately

Williston Two-Part Test

1. Look at the writing and analyze whether it was adopted as a complete, exclusive statement.
2. Look at the term at issue and analyze whether it was natural for the parties to have omitted it.

Corbin All-Evidence Test

Look at the agreement, the term and all surrounding circumstances, including the *Hatley* factors and determine if the parties **intended** a complete integration.

U.C.C. 2-202 Test

Intent of the parties unless it is certain that parties similarly situated would have included the term.

*Agreement is **NOT completely integrated**.*

*Agreement is **completely integrated**.*
Skip to Step 5.

STEP 4: Determine Whether Term Is **Consistent** with or Contradictory to the Writing.

Apply each of these two tests separately

Is the term in harmony with the writing?

Does the term completely negate any term of the writing?

*Term is **consistent or NOT contradictory,** STOP. The evidence is admissible.*

*Term is **inconsistent or contradictory**.*

STEP 5: Determine Whether Evidence Is of a Type That Is **Always** Admissible.

Apply each of these two tests separately

Evidence of contract defenses, of an oral condition precedent or to help resolve an ambiguity is always admissible.

***Four Corners* Rule:** An agreement is ambiguous only if it appears so on its face.

***PG & E* Rule:** An agreement that is unambiguous on its face can be shown to be ambiguous by extrinsic evidence so long as the agreement is reasonably susceptible of the alleged meaning.

If the evidence falls into any of the above categories, the evidence is admissible.

2. In the last two decades, there has been an increasing level of empirical research in the area of well-being and "happiness" and the development of a new psychological movement called "positive psychology." Note that "positive psychology" does not mean the same things as thinking positively. It is the label used to describe empirical science that focuses on positive emotions, experiences, strengths, and virtues that enable individuals, institutions, and communities to thrive. How is happiness relevant to you as a law student (and, eventually, a practicing lawyer)? Do you think happy or unhappy lawyers generate the largest proportion of disciplinary complaints? Do you think happy or unhappy lawyers function and represent clients most effectively?

3. Although rational and cerebrally oriented law students and lawyers sometimes consider topics like "happiness" light and fluffy, happiness has a relatively distinguished pedigree. For example, Aristotle stated: "Human happiness is so important, it transcends all other worldly considerations." Since the birth of our nation, the "pursuit of happiness" has been considered a primary goal and paramount right of all citizens. What does "happiness" in this sense mean? Whose responsibility is it to protect our citizens' right to pursue happiness?

4. Empirical research demonstrates that happiness is important for many reasons. As you know, happiness feels good. But, happiness is not just an epiphenomenon; it has many more benefits. What do you think the empirical research shows are the benefits of happiness?

Chapter 11

Contract Interpretation

Exercise 11-1: Chapter Problem

You are in-house counsel to Omhaha Life Insurance Company. The president of Omhaha has placed a file on your desk that includes the documents presented in Tables 11-1 through 11-4 on the following pages (the Omhaha life insurance policy purchased by Georgia Decedent; the police report from the Grand Canyon Police Department describing Ms. Decedent's death while visiting the Grand Canyon National Park; an autopsy report; and a demand letter from the attorney for Ms. Decedent's named insurance beneficiary, her daughter Alice Decedent). The president of Omhaha has asked you to evaluate the case and make and justify a recommendation. Your recommendation should state whether Omhaha should pay the amount demanded by Alice Decedent, refuse to pay the demanded amount, or try to settle the case.

As you conduct your evaluation, in addition to the purely legal questions raised, consider the following facts, which you know through your role in the company:

1. Omhaha has had some financial setbacks as of late. Over the last three months, just because of bad luck, Omhaha has had to pay out on dozens of high face-value policies.

2. The company also has been hard hit with negative publicity and lawsuits arising out of its failure to pay claims. The president, who instigated the policies that led to the lawsuits, is under fire from Omhaha's Board of Directors.

3. As a result, the company's stock price has declined.

Table 11-1: Omhaha Life Insurance Policy

Omhaha Life

Policy Number:	OL121212
Policy Date:	April 18, 2005
Insurer:	Omhaha Life Insurance Company (hereinafter "Omhaha")
Insured:	Georgia Decedent (hereinafter "Insured")
Face Amount:	$100,000.
Insuring Agreement:	Omhaha hereby agrees to pay Insured's beneficiary(ies) all amounts due under this policy within 30 days of the issuance of a death certificate confirming the death of Insured.
Exclusions:	This policy excludes coverage for a death resulting from: • Insured taking his or her own life OR • Insured dying as a result of a condition not disclosed by Insured at the time Insured entered into this contract, but this exclusion shall only apply if Insured dies within two years of the Policy Date set forth above.
Triple Indemnity:	Omhaha agrees to pay Insured's named beneficiary(ies) triple the face amount of this policy if Insured's death results from an accident, as opposed to some health reason. A death resulting from the emotional or mental reaction to an accident (such as a heart attack resulting from the Insured being frightened because an airplane in which she was flying had to crash land) shall not be an "accident" as that term is used in this policy.
Premiums:	$200 per month.
Beneficiary(ies):	Alice Decedent (daughter of Insured)
Merger Clause:	This writing embodies the entire agreement between the parties, and no terms not stated herein shall be deemed a part of this agreement.

Table 11-2: Police Report

Grand Canyon, Arizona
Police Department

Case Number:	*GCAZ 18/04/08/3462*
Incident:	*Death at Canyon East Rim*
Victim:	*Georgia Decedent*
Witnesses:	*Natasha Boris, Donatella Spirit*
Reporting Officer:	*Officer Pierre Ampere*
Date of Report:	*18 April 2015*

At about 1040 hours on 18th April 2015, I was called to the scene to investigate the death of one Georgia Decedent, a 60-year-old woman, approximately 5'8" in height with grey hair and green eyes. When I arrived at the scene, I discovered the body of Ms. Decedent on the floor of the canyon. Her body appeared to have been severely and mordantly injured when it crashed to the canyon floor.

Two women, Natasha Boris and Donatella Spirit, approached me and explained that they had witnessed the entire incident. I interviewed Ms. Boris first. Boris, Spirit and Decedent were all at the railing taking in the splendid view of the canyon from the east rim. Ms. Boris explained that she and Ms. Spirit were each standing about 10 feet on either side of Ms. Decedent. Ms. Boris reported that the three of them were calmly looking at "the wonderful view" when, suddenly, she saw Ms. Decedent grab her chest and exclaim, "I am having a heart attack!" According to Ms. Boris, Ms. Decedent's face appeared to be contorted by pain. Ms. Boris reported that Ms. Decedent toppled over the railing and fell to the canyon floor. She reported hearing Ms. Decedent's terrified screams as she fell towards the canyon floor. The screaming, according to Ms. Boris, stopped when Decedent hit the canyon floor. I then interviewed Ms. Spirit, whose report was identical.

I have no reason to doubt the accuracy of these reports.

Table 11-3: Autopsy Report

Office of the Coroner
Grand Canyon, AZ

Autopsy Report

Dated: 20 April 2015

I performed a full autopsy on Georgia Decedent, whose body was brought to the Grand Canyon, Arizona Coroner's Office on 18 April. I have determined that, shortly before death, Decedent suffered a massive heart attack. I also have determined that, while the heart attack almost certainly would have killed decedent, the actual cause of her death was a fall from a significant height, which, based on extrapolations from Decedent's massive injuries, I estimate to be two miles (the height above the canyon floor of the east rim of the canyon).

Table 11-4: Letter from Alice Decedent's Attorney

Law Offices of Honest & Trustworthy, Ltd.
1111 STATE STREET, COLUMBIA CITY, COLUMBIA 11111
(111) 111-1111

July 30, 2015

Claims Department
Omhaha Life Insurance Company
2222 1st Avenue
Columbia City, Columbia 11111

Re: Decedent v. Omhaha

To whom it may concern:

I have been retained by Alice Decedent to represent her interests in the above-referenced matter. Please direct all future correspondence regarding this matter to my attention.

As you know, Georgia Decedent and Omhaha entered into a life insurance contract on April 18, 2005. As you also know, Ms. Decedent paid all premiums due under the agreement between April 18, 2005 and her unfortunate death on April 18, 2015.

I have in my hand a letter dated July 1, 2015, in which you purport to transmit "full payment" under the policy in the amount of $100,000. Notwithstanding the fact that Ms. Decedent died of an accident when she fell to her death from the east rim to the floor of the Grand Canyon, your July 1 letter asserts that Omhaha need only pay $100,000, even though the policy unmistakably requires Omhaha to pay triple that face amount for a death that "results from an accident." As the Police Report issued by the Grand Canyon Police Department states, Georgia Decedent died when she fell to the canyon floor. There is no evidence that her fall was anything other than a tragic accident.

As a long-term practitioner in this state, I am well aware of Omhaha's recent history of denying such claims. However, you should know that I have in my possession notes made by my client's mother when she was buying the policy from Omhaha; she quotes one of your in-house agents as saying, "Omhaha does not nit-pick in its interpretation of events; we pay off our policies if the question is even close." In my opinion, the question in this case is not even close; Ms. Decedent's death was unquestionably an accident.

I expect to hear from you within 30 days. If I do not, I will have to file suit on my client's behalf. I cannot imagine Omhaha wants the kind of publicity such a suit would undoubtedly produce.

Sincerely,

I.B. Honest
I.B. Honest, Esq.

Introduction to Contract Interpretation

As explained in Chapter 10, you are now studying a crucial question in the life of a contract: what obligations each of the parties has undertaken. Your study of this question encompasses four broad questions:

1. What terms do courts treat as part of a contract for the purpose of determining what each party has promised? (In other words, what is the contract?)

2. How do courts determine what the words of a contract obligate the parties to do? (In other words, what does the contract mean?)

3. Did the parties properly and fully perform? (In other words, did either party breach?)

4. Assuming either party did not properly do everything she promised to do, what is the consequence of a breach?

The first question, which you learned about in connection with the parol evidence rule, focuses on determining which terms are parts of the parties' contract and which terms are not.

The second question, which you began to consider towards the end of Chapter 10, and return to now, involves determining what the words of the contract mean. Without question, this issue, which courts and lawyers sometimes refer to as "finding the law of the contract," is the most important part of your study of contract law. Why do you think lawyers and judges refer to this topic as "finding the law of the contract"? This point is somewhat subtle, but is worth understanding. As you probably already understand, when two parties enter into a contract, they create a set of rules that will govern their relationship. The contract tells each party what the party must do and refrain from doing. Between the parties, therefore, the contract is law. The process of interpreting those obligations involves interpreting that law (much like the process of interpreting a statute or constitution involves creating law for all those subject to that statute or constitution).

This area of law is crucial for a number of reasons. First, almost all of the rest of the subjects we will be studying, including express and constructive conditions, excuse of conditions, third-party beneficiary contracts, and assignment and delegation, are really just sub-topics within the larger topic of contract meaning. Second, contract interpretation issues are the most common problems handled by contract lawyers, regardless of whether they are litigators or transactional lawyers. In either role, lawyers must be experts at identifying and resolving problems involving contract meaning. Litigators dispute contract meaning questions. Transactional lawyers seek to identify and avoid contract meaning problems in the drafting stage so their clients can avoid litigation or at least make conscious choices to enter into contracts that have unresolved contract meaning issues. Finally, even if you never litigate, draft, or enter into a contract (which, of course, is extremely unlikely), the principles and skills you will learn in this chapter will be crucial to your success as a lawyer. The skills you will learn to use when interpreting contracts are similar, in most significant respects, to the skills used by lawyers to interpret statutes, constitutions, and regulations.

You already understand something crucial about this topic based on your study of contract formation law. There are important similarities between interpretation of language in the formation context and contract interpretation. The two processes are similar in the sense that both test your ability to identify ambiguities and to develop arguments about the interpretation of those ambiguities. Both require consideration of the specific words used by the parties. In other words, in the context of assessing whether a party has made an "offer," you would interpret that party's manifestations. For example, when you studied mutual assent, you considered the interpretation of the word "want" as in, "I want to buy...." We talked about how you would identify the word "want" as ambiguous and argue that the word could express desire (as in "I want [I desire] a Jaguar car") or selection (as in "I want [I'll take] that pack of gum"). As you will learn in this chapter, you will do the same thing with an ambiguous contractual phrase.

Note, however, that the process of resolving contractual (as opposed to formation) ambiguity is much more complicated. In the formation context, you simply examine the language used in the context in which it was expressed against a standard, *e.g.*, unequivocal present commitment. As you will see, however, resolving ambiguities of contract language requires application, where appropriate, of one (and often more than one) of the rules you are about to learn.

Your study of the parol evidence rule gave you some introduction into contract interpretation issues and law. As you learned in Chapter 10, one way to persuade a court to admit extrinsic evidence is to convince the court that the evidence is necessary to help resolve an ambiguity in the contract. You also learned, however, that the question of how courts should determine whether a contract is ambiguous is the subject of an important split of authority. Some courts follow the "plain meaning" rule in which a contract is ambiguous only if a judge determines it is ambiguous based on his or her reading of the contract. Other courts follow the "all evidence" rule in which evidence is admissible to show that a writing is ambiguous. As you will learn in this chapter, you are not done with the interpretation process just because you have concluded a court will admit evidence to help interpret the writing. Rather, you must also consider that evidence, along with all the rules of contract interpretation described in this chapter, and decide what the contract means. This chapter will walk you through this process.

Diagram 11-1, the Contract Law Graphic Organizer on the following page, shows how these principles and skills fit within the larger body of contract law. As the graphic organizer depicts, these concepts are a part of the question of contract meaning.

Overview of Chapter 11

In this chapter, you will work on developing skills and knowledge in three phases. In the first phase, you will focus on developing the skill of identifying ambiguity. To that end, you will start by learning the three ways in which a contract can be ambiguous and the intellectual processes involved in identifying ambiguities. You will then practice applying these processes in identifying ambiguities in a series of problems. In the second phase, you will be provided a list of and explanations of the rules courts use to resolve ambiguities. Then, you will be provided some examples of cases that have applied those rules to resolve particular disputes. In the third phase you will be introduced to the idea of contract gaps and will read cases in which courts have identified and resolved contract gaps.

Identification of Ambiguities

There really is only one type of ambiguity: a contract does not clearly address an issue that has arisen in its performance. To develop the skill of issue spotting, it is helpful to think of ambiguity in three categories. While these categories are, in a lot of ways, arti-

Diagram 11-1: Contract Law Graphic Organizer

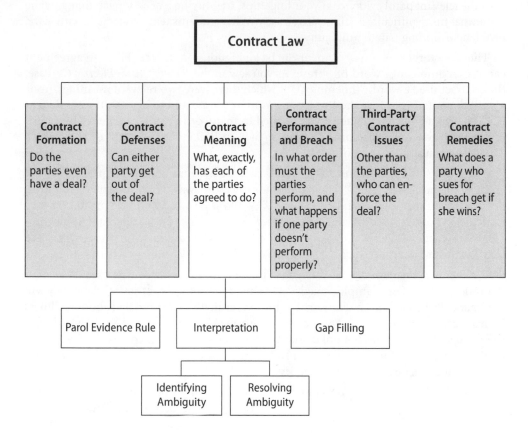

ficial, indeterminate (at least at the margins), and, to a degree, forced, they are helpful as a tool for spotting ambiguities. The three categories are:

1. patent ambiguity: an ambiguity that appears on the face of a document;

2. latent ambiguity: an ambiguity that is only revealed after learning additional information; and

3. an ambiguous "gap" in a contract: the parties' contract is silent or incomplete regarding an issue that has arisen (courts' efforts at addressing such gaps are referred to as "gap filling").

For an example of patent ambiguity, recall the *Pacific Gas & Electric Co.* court's argument that the word "indemnify" was ambiguous even without hearing the parol evidence at issue. Because the word could refer simply to paying any claim or could refer only to paying third party claims, it was, arguably, ambiguous. For an example of latent ambiguity, recall the 50% protein horsemeat hypothetical in Chapter 10. In the case on which that problem was based, the court admitted parol evidence to show a trade usage that, when parties in the industry used the term "50% protein," they really meant between 49.5% and 50% protein.

For gap-filling examples, recall *Wood v. Lucy* (in which the contract did not state what Mr. Wood would do at all and the court implied a duty of reasonable efforts to obtain endorsements on Lucy's behalf) and *Omni Group* (in which the court implied a duty of reasonable efforts in obtaining an engineer's and architect's report where the contract was silent about the buyer's duties, if any, with respect to obtaining the report).

As you might guess, identifying latent ambiguity is relatively easy because you will have the relevant parol evidence at your fingertips. Identifying a need for gap filling, while somewhat more difficult, is still relatively easy. What students tend to struggle with is the problem of finding patent ambiguity.

There are three ways an agreement can be ambiguous on its face. First, an agreement can use an ambiguous word or phrase. As you saw in the *Pacific Gas & Electric Co.* case, the contract used a word, "indemnify," for which there were two relevant meanings. Your task at the outset is to find the ambiguous word or phrase and to identify the conflicting meanings that could reasonably be attributed to that word or phrase. Standard English dictionaries are great tools for this effort. In fact, in *Pacific Gas* the court quoted definitions from statutes and dictionaries.

Second, an agreement can be ambiguous because of grammatical sloppiness. For example, imagine a promise to "wash your wife's car right away, next, your new car and all other cars you own by the end of the week." Would it be a breach if the promisor waits until the end of the week to wash the promisee's new car? The answer to that question depends on whether "by the end of the week" refers only to "all other cars you own," or to both "your new car" and "all other cars you own."

Finally, an agreement can be ambiguous because terms in the contract seem to or actually do conflict. For example, imagine a life insurance policy that states "the policy will automatically be void upon discovery by the insurer that the insured lied about an illness he had or medical treatment he received within the six months prior to the making of the policy." Also imagine the policy states "this policy shall be incontestable two years after its making." Which provision controls if the insurer discovers a lie two years and one month after the making of the policy?

To facilitate your efforts to develop the skill of identifying ambiguities, Table 11-5 provides a series of questions you can ask yourself to help you identify ambiguities.

Table 11-5: Checklist for Identifying Patent Ambiguity

Checklist for Identifying Patent Ambiguity

1. Try the easy way first. Look at the parties' contract and their dispute and try to figure out what each party would say the contract means.
2. Focus on what you know about the dispute between the parties. Look for a basis in the contract itself for either party claiming the other party breached the contract.
3. Look for ambiguous words or phrases. Use your dictionary to help you develop alternative and competing meanings for what you believe to be the key words in the contract provision at issue.
4. Look for grammatical ambiguity. Make sure you understand what word in the contract each modifying phrase is modifying. If you discover that a phrase may modify more than one word, you may have found the ambiguity.
5. Look for conflicts between terms.
6. Try to translate the contract term(s) into your own words. If you cannot find the ambiguity, the act of translating may reveal it. At least, translating the contract into your own words will ensure you can articulate one party's understanding of the contract.

Exercise 11-2: Patent Ambiguity

The best way to develop the skill of identifying ambiguity is to practice it. Read the following hypotheticals and use the checklist in Table 11-5 to identify the ambiguity. Identify the type of ambiguity as being language-based, as stemming from conflicting terms, or as being a product of an ambiguously placed modifier. If you cannot identify the ambiguity, you must at least write out responses to each of the queries reflected in the Table 11-5 checklist. To help you better understand how to perform this skill, we have provided a model answer to the first hypo. Before you read the model answer, however, see if you can analyze the problem yourself.

1. An insurance company and an insulation manufacturer entered into an insurance contract by which the insurer insured the manufacturer against legal defense costs and damage judgments in connection with any lawsuit "alleging property damage caused by the manufacturer's insulation products." During the policy period, a homeowner installed insulation in his home that was made by the manufacturer. The insulation contained asbestos (which we have since learned is a very dangerous substance). The insulation, because it is undamaged and fully functional, has not caused any health injuries, but the presence of the insulation has reduced the property value of the home. The homeowner sued the manufacturer to recover for his lost property value. The insurance company refused the manufacturer's request that the insurer defend the lawsuit and pay any judgment. The manufacturer sued the insurer for breach. What part of the contract is ambiguous and why is it ambiguous?

    Model Answer: *The word that jumps out is "damage." The ambiguity in this case is a patent ambiguity that involves ambiguous language. On the one hand, the word "damage" could have a connotation of physical injury to property; if so, the lawsuit does not allege property damage because no property was physically affected by the manufacturer's insulation. On the other hand, the word "damage" could also refer to harm to property of any type and diminution in the value of property is a harm to property that therefore falls within the ambit of the term "property damage."*

2. Craig worked as an insurance agent for an insurance company. His contract states that he is entitled on "retirement" to receive a percentage of the renewal commissions on business he generated while working for the company. "Retirement" is defined as "disengagement from the insurance industry at age 65 or after 10 years of service with the company whichever is later". Another clause in the contract records that in the event of retirement the agent is entitled to receive 100% of renewal commissions after seven years of service. Craig retires on his sixty-fifth birthday after completing eight years of service. He claims he is entitled to all of his renewal commissions. The insurance company refuses to pay. What part of the contract is ambiguous and why is it ambiguous?

3. Killer Cable Corporation (KCC) represented 960 cable television companies across the United States; 354 of those companies subscribed through KCC to MTV Network (MTVN), a television network that shows music videos. KCC and MTVN entered into an agreement in which, among other things, KCC agreed to occasional rate increases by MTVN under specified circum-

stances. The rate increase contract term stated: "Upon no less than sixty (60) days prior written notice to Affiliate, MTVN shall have the right to increase [the rate], from time to time during the Term hereof, as part of an industry-wide rate increase or modification." Two years into the contract, MTVN gave KCC 60-day notice of a planned rate increase in accordance with the 60-day notice provision. 90% of MTVN's affiliates were affected by MTVN's rate increase. MTVN was the only network that had a rate increase. What part of the contract is ambiguous and why is it ambiguous?

4.   Jonathan rented an apartment in Los Angeles, California. He contracted with Dan for a five-year lease. In the section of the contract labeled "Operating Services, Utilities and Reserved," the contract provided: "Dan shall provide and pay for all necessary current repairs, maintenance, and replacements of project property including the Member's dwelling, except that the Member shall be responsible for all interior repairs and all interior painting and decorating." About a month after signing the lease, Jonathan noticed a decrease in the hot water supply in his bathroom. He later found out that a pipe connecting the tub to the main supply system (risers) had corroded. The pipe, part of the so-called "feeder system," lay directly under the bathroom floor. Jonathan demanded that Dan pay for repairs. Dan refused. What part of the contract is ambiguous and why is it ambiguous?

5.   A construction contract provided that the contractor was required to "use copper for all sewer piping and for all culinary piping above ground." The contractor did not use copper for the underground sewer piping. The owner sued for breach. What part of the contract is ambiguous and why is it ambiguous?

6.   Chris worked at a paper manufacturing company. Chris purchased disability insurance which provided that he would be entitled to "66% of his earnings in the month prior to the incident" if he was injured and declared disabled. During the month of March, Chris made $8,000. However, in April, Chris took unpaid vacation from April 1 through April 14. Three days after returning to work, on April 17, Chris was injured while operating a forklift. Chris's doctor declared him physically disabled and the insurance company sent him a check that was equal to 66% of his earnings from March 17 through April 17th. Chris believes he has been underpaid. What part of the contract is ambiguous and why is it ambiguous?

7.   Dad entered into a separation agreement with his wife, Sarah. Dad and Sarah had a son, Enrique. The agreement provided that Dad "wanted to make sure Enrique received full and top quality treatment at the 'Feel Better Facility.'" The agreement further provided that Dad would pay "the expenses for Enrique's conclusion of treatment at the Feel Better Facility." The total cost of Enrique's stay at the treatment facility turned out to be $4,000, $250 of which was directly related to Enrique's final evaluation, his medical checkout, and the finalizing paperwork. All other amounts bore no relation to Enrique's completion of treatment but, instead, reflected the cost of his food, lodging, and therapy. When Sarah forwarded the $4,000 bill for the Feel Better Facility to Dad, Dad refused to pay the entire amount; instead, he sent Sarah a check for $250. What part of the contract is ambiguous and why is it ambiguous?

8.   Tessa owned a laundry facility which she leased to Chris for a six-year term. The term began in January 1995 and was to end in January 2001. The par-

ties also agreed that, "if, by December 1, 2000 (one month prior to the term ending), neither party has given notice that he or she does not intend to renew the contract for another six-year term, the contract automatically will renew for another six-year term." By the December 1, 2000 deadline, neither party had given notice not to renew. In mid-December, the parties signed an "addendum" by which Chris agreed to install additional dryers. The contract also stated "the Lease agreement shall be extended for a three-year period commencing the first day of the month following the installation of the additional new dryers." It also stated that this new agreement would "supersede and prevail over the language used in the main body of the lease in the event of any conflict." The additional dryers were installed on December 31, 2000. In 2003, Tessa leased the building to someone else and told Chris to vacate the premises. Chris asserts that the lease will be in force until 2010. What part of the contract is ambiguous and why is it ambiguous?

9. Sam owned a large plot of land that was zoned for retail development. He sold one parcel of the land to Carol for the operation of a KFC fast food restaurant. The contract for the sale of the parcel states that "Seller [Sam] will not after the date of this agreement, sell, lease, or permit to be occupied any real estate which Seller owns, manages or otherwise controls within one mile [of the parcel] for the purpose of constructing, or having conducted thereon, any fast food restaurant or restaurant facility whose principal food product is chicken on the bone, boneless chicken or chicken sandwiches." Sam wants to sell another parcel of land, less than half a mile away, to Bob. Bob plans to open a full-service bar diner with bone-in and boneless chicken wings as its main menu item. Carol objects. What part of the contract is ambiguous and why is it ambiguous?

10. Now that you have practiced identifying ambiguity, create your own plan of attack for identifying ambiguity. What will you do to minimize the risk that you miss an ambiguity? Now, create your own contract ambiguity and demonstrate how someone can use your method to spot the ambiguity. We recognize the task of making up a contract ambiguity can be particularly challenging so we encourage you to work with one or more of your peers in your contracts class. Try starting with a contract you have signed, such as a lease agreement or a car purchase contract.

Interpretation of Ambiguous Contracts

Once a court has concluded that a writing is ambiguous, the court must try to resolve that ambiguity. In other words, the court must determine what the contract means. As you complete the exercises and materials that follow, you should learn how courts interpret ambiguous contracts.

Exercise 11-3: Interpretation of Ambiguities

Re-read *Pacific Gas & Electric Co. v. G.W. Thomas Drayage & Rigging Co.* in Chapter 10 and identify the types of evidence the California Supreme Court ultimately allowed the defendant to introduce to prove the meaning of the word "indemnify."

Exercise 11-4: Contract Interpretation Rules

There are many rules—fifteen to twenty—that courts use to interpret contracts. The most important ones that you need to know are stated in Table 11-6 below. Answer the following questions regarding the rules in Table 11-6.

1. To what extent does the evidence at issue in *Pacific Gas & Electric Co.* fall within the categories stated in the rules?

2. The rules are presented more or less in order of preference. Explain the rationales underlying the order of preference. For example, why do courts prefer course of performance evidence above all other evidence of contract meaning? As another example, why is "*contra proferentem*" a rule of last resort? Make sure you explain the placement of each rule.

3. From among the four policies we studied at the outset of this course, what is the policy for the "*contra proferentem*" rule?

4. Has the state in which you plan to practice law codified any of these rules? Where?

Table 11-6: Contract Interpretation Rules

1. The best evidence of a contract's meaning is evidence of the parties' "course of performance." Course of performance refers to how the parties actually performed the contract at issue.

2. The next best evidence of a contract's meaning is evidence of the parties' "course of dealing." "Course of dealing" refers to how the parties' performed prior contracts containing the term at issue.

3. Evidence of admissions and other significant statements made by the parties during their negotiations is often treated as being as persuasive as or even more persuasive than evidence of "course of dealing."

4. The next best evidence is evidence of a "trade usage." "Trade usage" refers to a term or phrase that expresses a meaning in a trade that has reached a level of standard usage. In other words, all who practice in the trade could be expected to know the meaning. Whether a particular alleged usage has reached the required level of adoption is often a subject of dispute. In addition, whether a particular party who is relatively new to an industry should be treated as a member of the trade also can become an issue.

5. Absent evidence of a course of performance, a course of dealing, negotiations, or a trade usage, courts prefer to interpret contracts to make them reasonable and consistent with public policy and to interpret them in a way that reconciles any seeming inconsistencies among the terms.

6. As a last resort, courts apply the doctrine of "*contra proferentem*" in interpreting contracts. "*Contra proferentem*" means the agreement should be interpreted against the person who drafted it.

Exercise 11-5: *Frigaliment* and *Landon*

The next two cases, *Frigaliment Importing Co. v. B.N.S. International Sales Corp.* and *Landon v. Twentieth Century-Fox Film Corp.*, are two trial court opinions that, together, address many of the contract interpretation principles described above. As you read the cases, consider the following:

1. Identify each contract interpretation principle discussed by each court and explain what the courts said about applying each principle to the facts of the cases.

2. The *Frigaliment* court ultimately decides the case in a way that can only be described as unclear and subtle. See if you can figure out the ultimate basis of the court's decision.

Frigaliment Importing Co v. B.N.S. International Sales Corp.

190 F. Supp. 116 (S.D.N.Y. 1960)

Friendly, Circuit Judge. The issue is, what is chicken? Plaintiff says "chicken" means a young chicken, suitable for broiling and frying. Defendant says "chicken" means any bird of that genus that meets contract specifications on weight and quality, including what it calls "stewing chicken" and plaintiff pejoratively terms "fowl." Dictionaries give both meanings, as well as some others not relevant here. To support its, plaintiff sends a number of volleys over the net; defendant essays to return them and adds a few serves of its own. Assuming that both parties were acting in good faith, the case nicely illustrates Holmes' remark "that the making of a contract depends not on the agreement of two minds in one intention, but on the agreement of two sets of external signs — not on the parties' having meant the same thing but on their having said the same thing." The Path of the Law, in Collected Legal Papers, p. 178. I have concluded that plaintiff has not sustained its burden of persuasion that the contract used "chicken" in the narrower sense.

The action is for breach of the warranty that goods sold shall correspond to the description, New York Personal Property Law, McKinney's Consol. Laws, c. 41, §95. Two contracts are in suit. In the first, dated May 2, 1957, defendant, a New York sales corporation, confirmed the sale to plaintiff, a Swiss corporation, of:

US Fresh Frozen Chicken, Grade A, Government Inspected, Eviscerated 2½–3 lbs. and 1½–2 lbs. each all chicken individually wrapped in cryovac, packed in secured fiber cartons or wooden boxes, suitable for export scheduled May 10, 1957 pursuant to instructions from Penson & Co., New York.

75,000 lbs. 2½–3 lbs ...   @$ 33.00
25,000 lbs. 1½–2 lbs ...   @$ 36.50
per 100 lbs. FAS New York

The second contract, also dated May 2, 1957, was identical save that only 50,000 lbs. of the heavier "chicken" were called for, the price of the smaller birds was $37 per 100 lbs., and shipment was scheduled for May 30. The initial shipment under the first contract was short but the balance was shipped on May 17. When the initial shipment arrived in Switzerland, plaintiff found, on May 28, that the 2½–3 lbs. birds were not young chicken suitable for broiling and frying but stewing chicken or "fowl"; indeed, many of the cartons and bags plainly so indicated. Protests ensued. Nevertheless, shipment under the second contract was made on May 29, the 2½–3 lbs. birds again being stewing chicken. Defendant stopped the transportation of these at Rotterdam.

This action followed ...

Since the word "chicken" standing alone is ambiguous, I turn first to see whether the contract itself offers any aid to its interpretation. Plaintiff says the 1½–2 lbs. birds necessarily had to be young chicken since the older birds do not come in that size, hence the 2½–3 lbs. birds must likewise be young. This is unpersuasive—a contract for "apples" of two different sizes could be filled with different kinds of apples even though only one species came in both sizes. Defendant notes that the contract called not simply for chicken but for "Fresh Frozen Chicken, Grade A, Government Inspected." It says the contract thereby incorporated by reference the Department of Agriculture's regulations, which favor its interpretation; I shall return to this after reviewing plaintiff's other contentions.

The first hinges on an exchange of cablegrams which preceded execution of the formal contracts. The negotiations leading up to the contracts were conducted in New York between defendant's secretary, Ernest R. Bauer, and a Mr. Stovicek, who was in New York for the Czechoslovak government at the World Trade Fair. A few days after meeting Bauer at the fair, Stovicek telephoned and inquired whether defendant would be interested in exporting poultry to Switzerland. Bauer then met with Stovicek, who showed him a cable from plaintiff dated April 26, 1957, announcing that they "are buyer" of 25,000 lbs. of chicken 2½–3 lbs. weight, Cryovac packed, grade A Government inspected, at a price up to 33 cents per pound, for shipment on May 10, to be confirmed by the following morning, and were interested in further offerings. After testing the market for price, Bauer accepted, and Stovicek sent a confirmation that evening. Plaintiff stresses that, although these and subsequent cables between plaintiff and defendant, which laid the basis for the additional quantities under the first and for all of the second contract, were predominantly in German, they used the English word "chicken"; it claims this was done because it understood "chicken" meant young chicken whereas the German word, "Huhn," included both "Brathuhn" (broilers) and "Suppenhuhn" (stewing chicken), and that defendant, whose officers were thoroughly conversant with German, should have realized this. Whatever force this argument might otherwise have is largely drained away by Bauer's testimony that he asked Stovicek what kind of chickens were wanted, received the answer "any kind of chickens," and then, in German, asked whether the cable meant "Huhn" and received an affirmative response. Plaintiff attacks this as contrary to what Bauer testified on his deposition in March, 1959, and also on the ground that Stovicek had no authority to interpret the meaning of the cable. The first contention would be persuasive if sustained by the record, since Bauer was free at the trial from the threat of contradiction by Stovicek as he was not at the time of the deposition; however, review of the deposition does not convince me of the claimed inconsistency. As to the second contention, it may well be that Stovicek lacked authority to commit plaintiff for prices or delivery dates other than those specified in the cable; but plaintiff cannot at the same time rely on its cable to Stovicek as its dictionary to the meaning of the contract and repudiate the interpretation given the dictionary by the man in whose hands it was put. [Citations omitted.] Plaintiff's reliance on the fact that the contract forms contain the words "through the intermediary of:", with the blank not filled, as negating agency, is wholly unpersuasive; the purpose of this clause was to permit filling in the name of an intermediary to whom a commission would be payable, not to blot out what had been the fact.

Plaintiff's next contention is that there was a definite trade usage that "chicken" meant "young chicken." Defendant showed that it was only beginning in the poultry trade in 1957, thereby bringing itself within the principle that "when one of the parties is not a member of the trade or other circle, his acceptance of the standard must be made to appear" by proving either that he had actual knowledge of the usage or that the usage is "so generally known in the community that his actual individual knowledge of it may be inferred." [Citation omitted.] Here there was no proof of actual knowledge of the alleged usage; indeed, it is quite plain that defendant's belief was to the contrary. In order to meet the alternative requirement, the law of New York demands a showing that "the usage is of so long continuance, so well established, so notorious, so universal and so reasonable in itself, as that the presumption is violent that the parties contracted with reference to it, and made it a part of their agreement." [Citation omitted.]

Plaintiff endeavored to establish such a usage by the testimony of three witnesses and certain other evidence. Strasser, resident buyer in New York for a large chain of Swiss cooperatives, testified that "on chicken I would definitely understand a broiler." However, the force of this testimony was considerably weakened by the fact that in his own transactions the witness, a careful businessman, protected himself by using "broiler" when that was what he wanted and "fowl" when he wished older birds. Indeed, there are some indications, dating back to a remark of Lord Mansfield ... that no credit should be given "witnesses to usage, who could not adduce instances in verification." [Citations omitted.] While Wigmore thinks this goes too far, a witness's consistent failure to rely on the alleged usage deprives his opinion testimony of much of its effect. Niesielowski, an officer of one of the companies that had furnished the stewing chicken to defendant, testified that "chicken" meant "the male species of the poultry industry. That could be a broiler, a fryer or a roaster," but not a stewing chicken; however, he also testified that upon receiving defendant's inquiry for "chickens," he asked whether the desire was for "fowl or frying chickens" and, in fact, supplied fowl, although taking the precaution of asking defendant, a day or two after plaintiff's acceptance of the contracts in suit, to change its confirmation of its order from "chickens," as defendant had originally prepared it, to "stewing chickens." Dates, an employee of Urner-Barry Company, which publishes a daily market report on the poultry trade, gave it as his view that the trade meaning of "chicken" was "broilers and fryers." In addition to this opinion testimony, plaintiff relied on the fact that the Urner-Barry service, the Journal of Commerce, and Weinberg Bros. & Co. of Chicago, a large supplier of poultry, published quotations in a manner which, in one way or another, distinguish between "chicken," comprising broilers, fryers and certain other categories, and "fowl," which, Bauer acknowledged, included stewing chickens. This material would be impressive if there were nothing to the contrary. However, there was, as will now be seen.

Defendant's witness Weininger, who operates a chicken eviscerating plant in New Jersey, testified "Chicken is everything except a goose, a duck, and a turkey. Everything is a chicken, but then you have to say, you have to specify which category you want or that you are talking about." Its witness Fox said that in the trade "chicken" would encompass all the various classifications. Sadina, who conducts a food inspection service, testified that he would consider any bird coming within the classes of "chicken" in the Department of Agriculture's regulations to be a chicken. The specifications approved by the General Services Administration include fowl as well as broilers and fryers under the classification "chickens." Statistics of the Institute of American Poultry Industries use the phrases "Young chickens" and "Mature chickens," under the general heading "Total chickens," and the Department of Agriculture's daily and weekly price reports avoid use of the word "chicken" without specification.

Defendant advances several other points which it claims affirmatively support its construction. Primary among these is the regulation of the Department of Agriculture, 7 C.F.R. § 70.300–70.370, entitled, "Grading and Inspection of Poultry and Edible Products Thereof" and in particular 70.301 which recited:

Chickens. The following are the various classes of chickens:

(a) Broiler or fryer ...

(b) Roaster ...

(c) Capon ...

(d) Stag ...

(e) Hen or stewing chicken or fowl ...

(f) Cock or old rooster ...

Defendant argues, as previously noted, that the contract incorporated these regulations by reference. Plaintiff answers that the contract provision related simply to grade and Government inspection and did not incorporate the Government definition of "chicken," and also that the definition in the Regulations is ignored in the trade. However, the latter contention was contradicted by Weininger and Sadina; and there is force in defendant's argument that the contract made the regulations a dictionary, particularly since the reference to Government grading was already in plaintiff's initial cable to Stovicek.

Defendant makes a further argument based on the impossibility of its obtaining broilers and fryers at the 33 cents price offered by plaintiff for the 2½–3 lbs. birds. There is no substantial dispute that, in late April, 1957, the price for 2½–3 lbs. broilers was between 35 and 37 cents per pound, and that when defendant entered into the contracts, it was well aware of this and intended to fill them by supplying fowl in these weights. It claims that plaintiff must likewise have known the market since plaintiff had reserved shipping space on April 23, three days before plaintiff's cable to Stovicek, or, at least, that Stovicek was chargeable with such knowledge. It is scarcely an answer to say, as plaintiff does in its brief, that the 33 cents price offered by the 2½–3 lbs. "chickens" was closer to the prevailing 35 cents price for broilers than to the 30 cents at which defendant procured fowl. Plaintiff must have expected defendant to make some profit—certainly it could not have expected defendant deliberately to incur a loss.

Finally, defendant relies on conduct by the plaintiff after the first shipment had been received. On May 28 plaintiff sent two cables complaining that the larger birds in the first shipment constituted "fowl." Defendant answered with a cable refusing to recognize plaintiff's objection and announcing "We have today ready for shipment 50,000 lbs. chicken 2½–3 lbs. 25,000 lbs. broilers 1½–2 lbs.," these being the goods procured for shipment under the second contract, and asked immediate answer "whether we are to ship this merchandise to you and whether you will accept the merchandise." After several other cable exchanges, plaintiff replied on May 29 "Confirm again that merchandise is to be shipped since resold by us if not enough pursuant to contract chickens are shipped the missing quantity is to be shipped within ten days stop we resold to our customers pursuant to your contract chickens grade A you have to deliver us said merchandise we again state that we shall make you fully responsible for all resulting costs."[1] Defendant argues that if plaintiff was sincere in thinking it was entitled to young chickens, plaintiff would not have allowed the shipment under the second contract to go forward, since the distinction between broilers and chickens drawn in defendant's cablegram must have made it clear that the larger birds would not be broilers. However, plaintiff answers that the cables show plaintiff was insisting on delivery of young chickens and that defendant shipped old ones at its peril. Defendant's point would be highly relevant on another disputed issue—whether if liability were established, the measure of damages should be the difference in market value of broilers and stewing chicken in New York or the larger difference in Europe, but I cannot give it weight on the issue of interpretation. Defendant points out also that plaintiff proceeded to deliver some of the larger birds in Europe, describing them as "poulets"; defendant argues that it was only when plaintiff's customers complained about this that plaintiff developed the idea that "chicken" meant "young chicken." There is little force in this in view of plaintiff's immediate and consistent protests.

When all the evidence is reviewed, it is clear that defendant believed it could comply with the contracts by delivering stewing chicken in the 2½–3 lbs. size. Defendant's subjective intent would not be significant if this did not coincide with an objective meaning of "chicken." Here it did coincide with one of the dictionary meanings, with the definition in the Department of Agriculture Regulations to which the contract made at least oblique reference, with at least some usage in the trade, with the realities of the market, and with what plaintiff's spokesman had said. Plaintiff asserts it to be equally

---

1. These cables were in German; "chicken," "broilers" and, on some occasions, "fowl," were in English.

plain that plaintiff's own subjective intent was to obtain broilers and fryers; the only evidence against this is the material as to market prices and this may not have been sufficiently brought home. In any event it is unnecessary to determine that issue.

For plaintiff has the burden of showing that "chicken" was used in the narrower rather than in the broader sense, and this it has not sustained. This opinion constitutes the Court's findings of fact and conclusions of law. Judgment shall be entered dismissing the complaint with costs.

Landon v. Twentieth Century-Fox Film Corp.
384 F. Supp. 450 (S.D.N.Y. 1974)

Lasker, District Judge. In 1944 Margaret Landon entered into an agreement with Twentieth Century-Fox Film Corporation (Fox) to sell, among other things, "motion picture rights" to her book entitled *Anna and the King of Siam*. In 1972 Fox produced 13 films which were broadcast on the CBS Television network as a weekly serial entitled "Anna and the King."

This suit presents the question whether the 1944 agreement between Landon and Fox authorized Fox to produce and exhibit the 1972 series through defendant CBS. [Landon claims, among other things,] that the series infringed her copyright in the literary property *Anna and the King of Siam*.

Landon moves for summary judgment only as to the infringement claim ... Defendants move for summary judgment as to all claims against them ...

The heart of Landon's contention that the series infringed her copyright is that the granting language of the 1944 agreement gave Fox the right to produce only motion pictures of feature length intended for first exhibition in movie theaters, and not those intended for first exhibition on television. The grant clauses of the agreement provide, in relevant part:

> "FIRST: The Owner does hereby grant, convey and assign unto the Purchaser, its successors and assigns forever:
>
> (a) The sole and exclusive motion picture rights and motion picture copyright throughout the world in and to said literary property....
>
> (c) The sole and exclusive right to make, produce, adapt, sell, lease, rent, exhibit, perform and generally deal in and with the copyright motion picture versions of said literary property, with or without sound accompaniment and with or without the interpolation of musical numbers therein, and for such purposes to adapt one or more versions of said literary property, to add to and subtract from the literary property, change the sequence thereof, change the title of said literary property, use said title, or any of its components, in connection with works or motion pictures wholly or partially independent of said literary property, change the characters in said literary property, change the descriptions of the said characters, and use all thereof in new versions, adaptations and sequels in any and all languages, and to register and obtain copyright therein, throughout the world...."

(f) The sole and exclusive right to broadcast by means of the method generally known and described as television, or any process analogous thereto, any of the motion picture versions of said literary property produced pursuant hereto. The Owner specifically reserves to herself the right to broadcast the literary property by television direct from living actors; provided, however, that the Owner agrees that, for a period from the date hereof until eight (8) years after the date of general release of the first motion picture produced by the Purchaser based upon the literary property, or until ten (10) years after the date hereof, whichever period first expires, she will not exercise or grant the right to broadcast the literary property, or any part thereof, by television, or by any other device now known or hereafter to be devised by which the literary property may be reproduced visually and audibly for an audience not present at a performance thereof and with living actors speaking the roles thereof. The Owner grants to the Purchaser the exclusive option to license, lease and/or purchase said reserve rights to broadcast the literary property by television from living actors, or otherwise, at the same price and upon such bona fide terms as may be offered to the Owner by any responsible prospective buyer and which shall be acceptable to the Owner.

(g) The right to broadcast by means of radio processes, portions of said literary property, or the motion picture version or versions thereof, in conjunction with or exploitation of or as an advertising medium or tie-up with the production, exhibition and/or distribution of any motion picture based on said literary property, provided that, in exercising said radio broadcasting rights, Purchaser shall not broadcast serially an entire photoplay produced hereunder. Except as herein stated, the Owner agrees that she will not permit the said literary property or any part thereof to be broadcast by any method or means until two years after the general distribution date of the first motion picture made by the Purchaser based upon the said literary property, or four years after the date hereof, whichever period first expires. This restriction on broadcasting, however, shall not in anyway way affect or restrict the rights on television herein granted.

(h) The right to publish, copyright or cause to be published and copyrighted in any and all languages, in any and all countries of the world, in any form or media (including, but not limited to, press books, press notices, trade journals, periodicals, newspapers, heralds, fan magazines and/or small separate booklets) synopses revised and/or abridged versions of said literary property, not exceeding 7,500 words each, adapted from the said literary property or from any motion picture and/or television version thereof, with or without sound accompaniment, produced, performed, released or exhibited pursuant hereto."

It is evident that the grant clauses are broadly drafted and do not contain or suggest the purported distinction between motion pictures made for first exhibition on television and those made for theater presentation. Clause (c) expressly grants to Fox the sole right to "make" and "generally deal in" an apparently unlimited number of "motion picture versions" of the property. It confers the right to use and modify the plot, characters and title in "new versions, adaptations, and sequels," again without apparent limit on the number of such versions. Clause (f) cedes the "exclusive" right to broadcast on television "any of the motion picture versions" of the property produced pursuant to the agreement.

The broad construction of the phrase "motion picture versions" to include the 1972 series is confirmed by related provisions of the agreement. These indicate that when the parties sought to reserve to Landon certain rights, they did so carefully and specifically. Such reservations are themselves strong evidence that if Landon had intended to reserve the right to make and exhibit filmed television versions of the property, she and her noted and experienced literary agents, the William Morris Agency, knew how to do so. For example, Clause (g) gives Fox the right to broadcast by radio portions of the property for advertising or promotional purposes, but by express language states that Fox "shall not broadcast serially an entire photoplay...." Significantly the provision states that "this restriction on broadcasting ... shall not in any way affect or restrict the rights on television herein granted." Clause (f), the television clause, specifically reserves to Landon the right to "broadcast the literary property by television direct from living actors," but contains a covenant providing that she shall not exercise even that limited right for a period of years. In view of this covenant obviously drafted to protect Fox from Landon's competition with Fox's own films, it is far-fetched to believe that the parties so carefully restricted Landon's right to exhibit live television performances only to leave her completely free to show an unlimited number of filmed television versions of the property. The construction Landon seeks was squarely rejected in *Wexley v. KTTV, Inc.*, 108 F. Supp. 558 (S.D. Cal.1952), *aff'd*, 220 F.2d 438 (9th Cir. 1955), in which the court considered almost identical contractual provisions and stated:

> The obvious reason for applying the fifteen year restriction "to live television" only, was because it was considered the most serious competition to the exhibition of motion pictures. If it were intended to leave in the grantor the right to exhibit motion pictures on television, the parties unquestionably would have applied the fifteen year restriction to such right.

108 F. Supp. at 560. Moreover, assuming *arguendo* that Landon did indeed reserve the right to exhibit motion pictures on television, she had no right to make or produce them: Clauses (h) and (c) clearly grant to Fox the "sole and exclusive" right to "make, produce, adapt ... exhibit, perform and generally deal in motion picture versions."

We conclude that the only reasonable construction of the 1944 agreement is that Fox was granted the right to make an unlimited number of motion picture versions of the property, without limitation as to length, or place of first exhibition. This conclusion is consistent with the law in this Circuit as to the interpretation of copyright grants. *Bartsch v. Metro-Goldwyn-Mayer, Inc.*, [citation omitted], is precisely in point. There the copyright owners of a musical play assigned to Bartsch in 1930 the "motion picture rights" in the play together with the right to "copyright, vend, license and exhibit" motion picture photoplays throughout the world. There was no television clause in the assignment. Later in 1930, Bartsch assigned his rights to Warner Brothers, which in turn transferred its rights to MGM. MGM produced and distributed a feature-length motion picture based on the musical play in 1935. In 1958 MGM licensed the picture for exhibition on television and Bartsch's widow, to whom his copyright interest had devolved, sued to enjoin the broadcast. The issue was comparable to ours: whether, under the terms of original grant by the copyright authors to Bartsch in 1930, (and then from Bartsch to Warner) the right to "copyright, vend, license and exhibit ... motion picture photoplays" included the right to license a broadcaster to exhibit the picture on television without a further express grant by the copyright owner (Bartsch). In deciding that the grant did include such a right, Judge Friendly emphasized that Bartsch's assignment to Warner was "well designed to give (Warner) the broadest rights" with respect to the right to produce motion pictures, and noted that "'exhibit' means to 'display' or to 'show' by any method, and nothing in the rest of the grant sufficiently reveals a contrary intention." 391 F.2d at 154. The court stated the rule which controls the present case:

> As between an approach that "a license of rights in a given medium (e.g., 'motion picture rights') includes only such uses as fall within the unambiguous core meaning of the term (e.g., exhibition of motion picture film in motion picture theaters) and exclude any uses which lie within the ambiguous penumbra (e.g., exhibition of motion picture film on television)" and another whereby "the licensee may properly pursue any uses which may reasonably be said to fall within the medium as described in the license," [Professor Nimmer)] prefers the latter. So do we.... If the words are broad enough to cover the new use, it seems fair that the burden of framing and negotiating an exception should fall on the grantor; if Bartsch or his assignors had desired to limit "exhibition" of the motion picture to the conventional method where light is carried from a projector to a screen directly beheld by the viewer they could have said so.

391 F.2d at 155. There was no question in *Bartsch* that the parties were aware of the possibilities of television even in 1930. In the present case, involving a 1944 agreement, there is, of course, no question on that score either; the Landon contract is sprinkled with references to television and one does not have to roam far into the penumbral meanings of "motion picture versions" to conclude that the term was intended by the parties to embrace rather than exclude the right to produce a television series. Indeed, Clause (h) of the agreement, (to which, curiously, the parties pay only passing attention) expressly refers to "any motion picture and/or television version ... produced, performed, released or exhibited pursuant hereto...."

We have carefully considered Landon's argument that, at the least, the presence of genuine issues as to material facts precludes the grant of summary judgment to Fox. Apart from the fact that such an assertion is undercut by her own motion for similar relief, the argument is without merit. Landon contends first that Fox's contracting practices as reflected in a number of other agreements drafted during the 1940's demonstrate that Fox often and explicitly contracted for the right to produce "television versions," and that its failure to do so here is probative of its intent as to the 1944 agreement. The contention is effectively rebutted by the undisputed facts that (1) Fox maintained both East coast and West coast legal departments, each with its own drafting style, and (2) Landon's contract was drafted in the office which, as a matter of consistent practice, did not use the magic words "television versions" to acquire the rights in issue here, relying instead on general language to achieve the same result.[2] In any event, contracts made between Fox and other copyright owners have little probative value as to what Fox and Landon intended in their particular agreement, *see Bartsch v. Metro-Goldwyn-Mayer, supra*, 391 F.2d at 154–155.

Landon also contends that "motion picture versions" is a term of art whose meaning can be established only by extrinsic "technical evidence." It is, of course, a familiar principle that where the terms of a contract are ambiguous, such evidence may be introduced, not to vary the meaning of a contract but to establish the intent of the parties. But in the context here, the terms of the contract are not ambiguous and do not raise a triable issue of fact.

We note, parenthetically, that both the copyright law, 17 U.S.C. §5, and related regulations, 37 C.F.R. §202.15, and the Copyright Office publication, *The Compilation of Copyright Office Practices* (1973 ed., at P2.14.1, p. 2-573) define "motion picture" to include "filmed television plays" or filmed pictures "transmitted by means of television," respectively. The relevant case law bears out these definitions. [Citations omitted.]

Plaintiff also argues that it was not her intention to grant to Fox the right to make television versions of the property. She takes the position that her intentions in 1944 present an issue of disputed fact requiring a trial on the merits. The argument is wide of the mark for two reasons. First, it is axiomatic that evidence of plaintiff's intent is admissible only insofar as it was expressed to Fox. Her affidavit is silent on the question whether she ever expressed to Fox in 1944 the construction of the agreement she presses on the present motions, and it is undisputed that she had very little, if any direct contact with Fox at all. Albert B. Taylor, an executive with William Morris Agency (plaintiff's literary agents) with some familiarity with the negotiation of the 1944 agreement, does not state that he, or any other employee of the Agency communicated Landon's understanding of the agreement to Fox. More to the point, the opposing affidavit of Helen Strauss, who was personally responsible for plaintiff's account and for negotiation on Landon's behalf of the Fox agreement, states that in 1944 Strauss understood the agreement to convey to Fox all film rights, including television rights, while reserving to Landon 'dramatic rights,' including the right to televise a 'live' dramatic rendition of the property.

In sum, there is no genuine issue as to any material fact and defendants are entitled to summary judgment as to the infringement claim....

---

2. Landon's submissions on the present motions include as exhibits a group of Fox contracts (the Exhibit F contracts) in which the granting clause contains language granting to Fox the right to make 'motion picture and television versions' of a literary property. The 'F' contracts were drafted by the Fox West coast legal department in Los Angeles. Landon contrasts those contracts with another group of contracts (the Exhibit E contracts) which, like the agreement in issue here, do not include the phrase 'television versions.' However, it is undisputed that the 'E' contracts were all prepared by the Fox East coast legal department.

Exercise 11-6: *Landon* and *Frigaliment* Revisited

1. If the buyer in *Frigaliment* had refused to pay for the chicken and the seller therefore had been the party that sued for breach of contract, could the seller have sustained its burden of proof?

2. Each of the problems below recalls one of the ambiguity identification hypotheticals you analyzed in Exercise 11-2, and describes some evidence bearing on the resolution of the ambiguity. For each hypo, classify the evidence described and determine which interpretation a court would be most likely to adopt.

    a. An insurance company and an insulation manufacturer entered into an insurance contract by which the insurer insured the manufacturer against legal defense costs and damages judgments in connection with any lawsuit for "liability to others for property damage caused by the manufacturer's insulation products." During the policy period, a homeowner installed insulation in his home that was made by the manufacturer. The insulation contained asbestos (which we have since learned is a very dangerous substance). The insulation, because it is undamaged and fully functional, has not caused any health injuries, but the presence of the insulation has reduced the property value of the home. The homeowner sued the manufacturer to recover for his lost property value. The insurance company refused the manufacturer's request that the insurer defend the lawsuit and pay any judgment if one was awarded. The manufacturer sued the insurer for breach.

        Assume the manufacturer introduced evidence that the insurer had not denied coverage for loss-in-value claims, notwithstanding an absence of physical damage, under past contracts between the insurer and other insureds. Assume the insurer introduced evidence that all other insurance companies interpret contracts the same way this insurance company is arguing it should be interpreted.

    b. Killer Cable Corporation (KCC) represented 960 cable television companies across the United States. 354 of those companies subscribed through KCC to MTV Networks (MTVN). KCC and MTVN entered into an agreement in which, among other things, KCC agreed to occasional rate increases by MTVN under specified circumstances. The rate increase contract term stated: "Upon no less than sixty (60) days prior written notice to Affiliate, MTVN shall have the right to increase [the rate], from time to time during the Term hereof, as part of an industry-wide rate increase or modification." Two years into the contract, MTVN gave KCC 60-day notice of a planned rate increase in accordance with the 60 day notice provision. 90% of MTVN's affiliates were affected by MTVN's rate increase. MTVN was the only network that had a rate increase.

        Assume that KCC introduces evidence that, in another clause of the contract, the parties also used the term "industry" in such a way that it only could be referring to the network industry. Assume that MTVN introduces evidence that shows that KCC drafted the contract.

    c. Jonathan rented an apartment in Los Angeles, California. He contracted with Dan for a five-year lease. In the section of the contract labeled "Operating Services, Utilities and Reserved," the contract provided "Dan shall provide and pay for all necessary current repairs, maintenance and replacements of project property including the Member's dwelling, except that the Member shall be responsible for all interior repairs and all interior painting and decorating." About a month after signing the lease, Jonathan noticed a decrease in the hot water supply in his bathroom. He later found out that a pipe connecting the tub to the main supply system (risers) had corroded. The pipe, part of the so-called feeder system, lay directly under appellee's bathroom floor. Dan refused to pay for the repairs.

Assume that Dan proves that Jonathan was an experienced renter and that, in the apartment-rental industry, "interior" includes everything other than the exterior walls, roof, and foundation of an apartment building. Assume Jonathan proves that, during negotiations, Jonathan asked what would happen if the apartment had an electrical problem with the wiring (which is in the walls) and Dan said, "That would be my responsibility."

d. Chris worked at a paper manufacturing company. Chris purchased disability insurance which provided that he would be entitled to "66% of his earnings in the month prior to the incident" if he was injured and declared disabled. During the month of March, Chris made $8,000. However, in April, Chris took unpaid vacation from April 1 through April 14. Three days after returning to work, on April 17, Chris was injured while operating a forklift. Chris's doctor declared him physically disabled and the insurance company sent him a check that was equal to 66% of his earnings from March 17 through April 17th. Chris believes he has been underpaid.

Assume that Chris introduced evidence that he understood "month" to refer to a calendar month. The insurance company introduced evidence that it meant to refer to a month's worth of days (*i.e.*, 30 or 31 days). A state statute requires employers to provide disability insurance and declares that "the purpose of this statute" is "to ensure that all employees who become disabled receive at least 2/3 of their income."

e. Sam owned a large plot of land that was zoned for retail development. He sold one parcel of the land to Carol for the operation of a KFC fast food restaurant. The contract for the sale of the parcel states that "Seller [Sam] will not after the date of this agreement, sell, lease, or permit to be occupied any real estate which Seller owns, manages or otherwise controls within one mile [of the parcel] for the purpose of constructing, or having conducted thereon, any fast food restaurant or restaurant facility whose principal food product is chicken on the bone, boneless chicken or chicken sandwiches." Sam wants to sell another parcel of land, less than half a mile away, to Bob. Bob plans to open a full-service bar diner with bone-in and boneless chicken wings as its main menu item. Carol objects.

Assume that there is a written memorial of the parties' negotiations that suggests that Carol was only prepared to do the deal if the contract protected her against competition from any kind of restaurant that serves primarily chicken. Assume that the contract also contains additional language that the prohibited business would include, but not be limited to, an enumerated list of specific restaurant franchises which are all fast food restaurants.

Exercise 11-7: *Raffles v. Wichelhaus*

The next case, *Raffles v. Wichelhaus*, is short and old, making it a little challenging to follow. The bottom line is that the court agreed with the last argument made right before the line by which the court issued its decision. As you read *Raffles*, consider the following two questions:

1. How is the problem in this case different from the problem in *Frigaliment* and in *Landon*?

2. Generalize a rule from *Raffles*. After you have done so, see if you can find the Restatement rule addressing the issue in this case. Do you like how the Restatement frames the rule?

Raffles v. Wichelhaus

159 Eng. Rep. 375 (1864)

To a declaration for not accepting Surat cotton which the defendant bought of the plaintiff "to arrive ex 'Peerless' from Bombay," the defendant pleaded that he meant a ship called the "Peerless" which sailed from Bombay, in October, and the plaintiff was not ready to deliver any cotton which arrived by that ship, but only cotton which arrived by another ship called the "Peerless," which sailed from Bombay in December ...

Declaration. For that it was agreed between the plaintiff and the defendants, that the plaintiff should sell to the defendants, and the defendants buy of the plaintiff, certain goods, to wit, 125 bales of Surat cotton ... to arrive ex "Peerless" from Bombay; and that the cotton should be taken from the quay, and that the defendants would pay the plaintiff for the same ... at the rate of 17 pence per pound, within a certain time then agreed upon after the arrival of the said goods in England.

Averments: that the said goods did arrive by the said ship from Bombay in England and the plaintiff was then and there ready and willing and offered to deliver the said goods to the defendants ...

Breach: that the defendants refused to accept the said goods or pay the plaintiff for them.

Plea. That the said ship mentioned in the said agreement was meant and intended by the defendants to be the ship called the "Peerless," which sailed from Bombay ... in October; and that the plaintiff was not ready and willing and did not offer to deliver to the defendants any bales of cotton which arrived by the last mentioned ship, but instead thereof was only ready and willing and offered to deliver to the defendants 125 bales of Surat cotton which arrived by another and different ship, which was also called the "Peerless," and which sailed from Bombay ... in December ...

Demurrer and joinder therein.

Milward, in support of the demurrer. The contract was for the sale of a number of bales of cotton of a particular description, which the plaintiff was ready to deliver. It is immaterial by what ship the cotton was to arrive, so that it was a ship called the "Peerless." The words "to arrive ex 'Peerless,'" only mean that if the vessel is lost on the voyage, the contract is to be at an end.... [Pollock, C.B. It would be a question for the jury whether both parties meant the same ship called the "Peerless."] That would be so if the contract was for the sale of a ship called the "Peerless;" but it is for the sale of cotton on board a ship of that name ... [Pollock, C.B. The defendant only bought that cotton which was to arrive by a particular ship. It may as well be said, that if there is a contract for the purchase of certain goods in warehouse A., that is satisfied by the delivery of goods of the same description in warehouse B.] In that case there would be goods in both warehouses; here it does not appear that the plaintiff had any goods on board the other "Peerless ..." [Martin, B. It is imposing on the defendant a contract different from that which he entered into ...] The defendant has no right to contradict by parol evidence a written contract good upon the face of it. He does not impute misrepresentation or fraud, but only says that he fancied the ship was a different one. Intention is of no avail, unless stated at the time of the contract ... [Pollock, C.B. One vessel sailed in October and the other in December.] The time of sailing is no part of the contract.

Mellish (Cohen with him), in support of the plea. There is nothing on the face of the contract to show that any particular ship called the "Peerless" was meant; but the moment it appears that two ships called the "Peerless" were about to sail from Bombay there is a latent ambiguity, and parol evidence may be given for the purpose of showing that the defendant meant one "Peerless," and the plaintiff another. That being so, there was no consensus ad idem and therefore no binding contract ...

Judgment for the defendants.

Exercise 11-8: *Raffles* Revisited

1. The most challenging task in thinking about the *Raffles* case is to synthesize it with the list of rules for resolving ambiguities. When do courts abandon all those rules and decide cases in the way the *Raffles* court decided that case?

2. Take one more look at the Restatement's approach to ambiguity. Change the facts of *Raffles* again and again so that you can make the case fit each of the exceptions.

While Exercise 11-8 marks the end of your initial study of ambiguity, it is crucial that you continue to attend to the issue of identifying ambiguity and to the principles courts use to resolve ambiguity. Many of the problems you will deal with in the rest of this book and as a practicing attorney require you to understand and use these principles.

Identifying and Filling Contract Gaps

Your final topic in the context of contract interpretation is gap filling. Recall that, in *Wood v. Lucy*, the contract was silent as to the duties of Mr. Wood. The court held there was an implied duty to use reasonable efforts to obtain endorsements on Lady Duff-Gordon's behalf. Likewise, in the *Omni Group* case, a contract term conditioned the buyer's duty to perform on obtaining satisfactory architect's and engineer's reports. The court held that the contract included an implied promise to make reasonable efforts to obtain the reports and a promise to evaluate whether the buyer was satisfied in good faith. In both cases, the courts implied duties to fill in gaps in the parties' agreements. What other contract terms do courts imply?

Exercise 11-9: Standardized Implied Terms

1. What does "good faith" mean?

   a. Is it bad faith for a party to argue for an interpretation of a contract term that favors itself? What if the parties had discussed an alternative interpretation during negotiations?

   b. Is it bad faith for a party to insist that the other party perform the contract if, during the time between when the parties made their contract and the time for performance, market forces have made the contract price very unfair?

2. Take a look at Article 2 of the U.C.C. and list all of the contract terms courts are authorized to imply under Article 2.

Exercise 11-10: *Haines v. City of New York*

The next case, *Haines v. City of New York*, addresses the issue of implied terms. As you read the case, consider the following questions:

1. The court implies two different terms. In each instance, determine the basis on which the court did so.

2. Could the court have reached a better conclusion as to the proper terms to imply under these circumstances? Why or why not?

Haines v. City of New York
364 N.E.2d 820, 41 N.Y.2d 769 (1977)

Gabrielli, Judge. In the early 1920s, respondent City of New York and intervenors, Town of Hunter and Village of Tannersville, embarked upon negotiations for the construction of a sewage system to serve the village and a portion of the town. These negotiations were prompted by the city's need and desire to prevent the discharge of untreated sewage by residents of the area into Gooseberry Creek, a stream which fed a reservoir of the city's water supply system in the Schoharie watershed.

In 1923, the Legislature enacted enabling legislation authorizing the city to enter into contracts with municipalities in the watershed area "for the purpose of providing, maintaining (and) operating systems and plants for the collection and disposal of sewage...."

The negotiations culminated in an agreement in 1924 between the city and intervenors. By this agreement, the city assumed the obligation of constructing a sewage system consisting of a sewage disposal plant and sewer mains and laterals, and agreed that "all costs of construction and subsequent operation, maintenance and repair of said sewerage system with the house connections thereof and said disposal works shall be at the expense" of the city. The agreement also required the city to extend the sewer lines when "necessitated by future growth and building constructions of the respective communities." The village and town were obligated to and did obtain the necessary easements for the construction of the system and sewage lines.

The Board of Estimate, on December 9, 1926, approved the agreement and authorized the issuance of $500,000 of "corporate stock" of the City of New York for construction of the system by appropriate resolution. A modification of the original agreement occurred in 1925 wherein the village agreed to reimburse the city for a specified amount representing the expense of changing the location of certain sewer lines. The plant was completed and commenced operation in 1928. The city has continued to maintain the plant through the ensuing years and in 1958 expended $193,000 to rehabilitate and expand the treatment plant and facilities.

Presently, the average flow of the plant has increased from an initial figure of 118,000 gallons per day to over 600,000 gallons daily and the trial court found that the plant "was operating substantially in excess of design capacity." It is not disputed by any of the parties in this action, that the system cannot bear any significant additional "loadings" because this would result in inadequate treatment of all the sewage and consequently harm the city's water supply. The instant controversy arose when plaintiff, who is the owner of a tract of unimproved land which he seeks to develop into 50 residential lots, applied to the city for permission to connect houses, which he intends to construct on the lots, to existing sewer lines. The city refused permission on the ground that it had no obligation to further expand the plant, which is presently operating at full capacity, to accommodate this new construction.

Plaintiff then commenced this action for declaratory and injunctive relief maintaining that the 1924 agreement is perpetual in duration and obligates the city to expend additional capital funds to enlarge the existing plant or build a new one to accommodate the present and future needs of the municipalities. Both the trial court and the Appellate Division, by a divided court, held in favor of plaintiff and intervenors concluding, that, while the contract did not call for perpetual performance, the city was bound to construct additional facilities to meet increased demand until such time as the village or town is legally obligated to maintain a sewage disposal system ...

We conclude that the city is presently obligated to maintain the existing plant but is not required to expand that plant or construct any new facilities to accommodate plaintiff's substantial, or any other, increased demands on the sewage system. The initial problem encountered in ascertaining the nature and extent of the city's obligation pursuant to the 1924 agreement, is its duration. We reject, as did the courts below, the plaintiff's contention that the city is perpetually bound under the agreement. The contract did not expressly provide for perpetual performance and both the trial court and the Appellate Division found that the parties did not so intend ...

On the other hand, the city's contention that the contract is terminable at will because it provides for no express duration should also be rejected. In the absence of an express term fixing the duration of a contract, the courts may inquire into the intent of the parties and supply the missing term if a duration may be fairly and reasonably fixed by the surrounding circumstances and the parties' intent ...

Thus, we hold that it is reasonable to infer from the circumstances of the 1924 agreement that the parties intended the city to maintain the sewage disposal facility until such time as the city no longer needed or desired the water, the purity of which the plant was designed to insure. The city argues that it is no longer obligated to maintain the plant because State law now prohibits persons from discharging raw sewage into streams such as Gooseberry Creek. However, the parties did not contemplate the passage of environmental control laws which would prohibit individuals or municipalities from discharging raw, untreated sewage into certain streams. Thus, the city agreed to assume the obligation of assuring that its water supply remained unpolluted and it may not now avoid that obligation for reasons not contemplated by the parties when the agreement was executed ...

Having determined the duration of the city's obligation, the scope of its duty remains to be defined. By the agreement, the city obligated itself to build a specifically described disposal facility and to extend the lines of that facility to meet future increased demand. At the present time, the extension of those lines would result in the overloading of the system. Plaintiff claims that the city is required to build a new plant or expand the existing facility to overcome the problem. We disagree. The city should not be required to extend the lines to plaintiffs' property if to do so would overload the system and result in its inability to properly treat sewage. In providing for the extension of sewer lines, the contract does not obligate the city to provide sewage disposal services for properties in areas of the municipalities not presently served or even to new properties in areas which are presently served where to do so could reasonably be expected to significantly increase the demand on present plant facilities ...

Exercise 11-11: *Haines* Revisited

In 1935, Railroad Company entered into a contract with City in which City granted Railroad permission to use a bridge owned by City for a railroad line. Railroad agreed to maintain the bridge. The arrangement had no ending date. This arrangement worked perfectly fine until 2007, when Railroad decided to abandon the line and remove its tracks from the bridge. Railroad did so and left the bridge in good repair. By 2009, the bridge needed repairs again. The City demanded that Railroad make the necessary repairs. Must Railroad make the repairs?

Chapter Problem Revisited

Return to the Chapter Problem at the beginning of this chapter and complete it. As you do so, keep in mind that, as in-house counsel, your concerns extend far beyond the particular legal question raised by the facts. You need to consider broader company concerns such as the amount of money involved, the costs of litigation, the short-term business issues, any potential impact on sales if the company fights the issue, whether a quick and generous settlement might encourage future claims, as well as other long-term business implications of settling or fighting the threatened lawsuit. The memo you write must justify your recommendations, yet it cannot be very long because your boss, the president of the company, has only a limited time to evaluate this issue.

Professional Development Reflection Questions

1. Empirical research in the field of positive psychology demonstrates that it is possible to increase your level of happiness in just a couple of months with just a little effort and commitment. What percent of your happiness do you think you can control? How much do you think it is possible to increase your level of happiness?

2. Positive psychologists have empirically studied happiness-increasing strategies and proven that such strategies increase happiness—not just temporarily, but with lasting effects. Such strategies can be learned by anyone and can become habits. In question three below and in the next two chapters, we introduce you to several happiness strategies that we hope you will try. Please be aware that, because of individual preferences, some people find certain strategies more helpful than others. Accordingly, as you learn about happiness strategies, pay attention to which ones fit you best and try to vary your use of strategies to keep them fresh.

3. One strategy for increasing your happiness is to cultivate a sense of gratitude by thinking about things in life you have to be grateful about. Positive psychologists have empirically studied this strategy using a "Three Good Things" exercise. As the label implies, "Three Good Things" means writing down three things in your life that you are grateful for, including the reasons why you are grateful and why the good things happened. Take a few minutes now to do the "Three Good Things" exercise yourself.

4. Imagine that you are a second-year associate who drafted a contract for a client as one of your first assignments after starting your first law firm job. You have now heard that the parties to the contract are in a dispute and accusing each other of breaching the contract. You have repeatedly woken up in the middle of the night in a panic, wondering if you failed to properly draft the contract and are worried about a malpractice suit before your career gains momentum. To what standard of care will you be held? How should you best deal with your anxiety so that it doesn't continue to interfere with your sleep?

CONTRACT PERFORMANCE AND NON-PERFORMANCE

In what order were the parties to perform, and is there any justification for any non-performance?

Chapter 12

Express Conditions, Constructive Conditions, and Excuse and Discharge

Exercise 12-1: Chapter Problem

Task I: Understanding a Contract

You are an attorney. Your client is Pippi Landbuyer, a successful business-woman who has a bachelor's degree in accounting. Landbuyer is considering entering into the contract reproduced on the next page. The other party to the proposed contract is David Decorator, a professional home decorator. Pippi has hired you to analyze objectively the contract law implications of this proposed contract based on what you have learned about contract law. Write Ms. Landbuyer a letter in which you communicate your analysis of the contract law implications of the contract. *At this time, you are not authorized by your client to redraft any terms of the contract.* Assume that, at all relevant times, Pippi has owned Pippi'sOldHouse.

Please also submit a two-page memorandum to your senior partner in which you explain your thinking in drafting the letter, *i.e.*, any choices between trade-offs, any issues you did not discuss (and why not), and anything else you think your supervisor should know about the letter you wrote.

Task II: Redrafting a Contract

After you have completed your letter and memorandum, you will have an opportunity to meet with your client and discuss the issues you have identified. Make sure you determine what the client wants you to do to address the issues you have raised. Then, rewrite the contract to address all those issues.

Agreement

Whereas Pippi Landbuyer ("Pippi") desires to purchase DecoratorHouse from David Decorator ("David) and to secure David's home decorating services for DecoratorHouse and Pippi'sOldHouse;

Whereas David desires to sell DecoratorHouse and to decorate DecoratorHouse and Pippi'sOldHouse and be paid for doing so;

Therefore, Pippi and David agree as follows:

1. Pippi needs another $100,000 to buy DecoratorHouse without dipping into her vacation savings. Accordingly, the parties' duties under this contract are tied to Pippi's expected inheritance of $100,000 from her recently deceased grandmother, Old Mother Landbuyer.

2. On June 1, _____, for $200,000, Pippi covenants to buy DecoratorHouse, located at 0001 State Street, and David covenants to transfer title to DecoratorHouse.

3. David will start and complete the decoration of DecoratorHouse within one year, beginning after Pippi takes title to DecoratorHouse. David will design all aspects of the home decoration and negotiate the prices of the furniture, lighting, window-coverings, paint, wallpaper, carpeting and other decorating items ("The Supplies") for DecoratorHouse. Pippi will pay for The Supplies up to a maximum cost of $100,000 and pay David, for his services, an amount equal to the total discount from the marked price on The Supplies that David is able to negotiate.

4. David will start and complete the decoration of Pippi'sOldHouse located at 0002 State Street within one year, beginning immediately. David will design all aspects of the home decoration and negotiate the prices of The Supplies for Pippi'sOldHouse. Pippi will pay for The Supplies up to a maximum cost of $85,000 and pay David, for his services, an amount equal to the total discount from the marked price on The Supplies that David is able to negotiate.

5. The parties to this contract agree that time is of the essence with respect to all terms of this contract.

6. If either party to this contract is prevented from the performance of any obligation through no fault of her or his own by reason of adverse weather, earthquakes, fires, volcanic eruption, flood or other such cause, the performance of such obligation shall be excused.

7. This writing contains the entire agreement of the parties. All previous discussions and understanding shall be deemed merged into this writing.

Dated: May 1, _____

_____   _____

Pippi Landbuyer   David Decorator

Introduction to Transactional Law Practice

As you consider these tasks, you also need to reorient your understanding of how lawyers think about problems. So far in law school, you mostly have been trained to think like a lawyer who does appellate, trial, and pre-trial work. The questions on which you have focused have been questions of liability (Was there a breach? Did she commit the crime? Was it a tort? What litigation strategy would work best here? How can I prove it?). As you move into learning how to interpret and draft conditions and other contract provisions, you need to add to your repertoire and learn to think like a lawyer who drafts contracts. Professor Tina Stark calls this skill "Thinking Like a Deal Lawyer."[1] Below are some excerpts from Professor Stark's article by that name in which she explains this skill. Please pay particular attention to the ideas in this article because this book will refer to them in several other places.

Tina L. Stark, *Thinking Like a Deal Lawyer*

54 J. Legal Educ. 223 (2004)
Copyright © 2004 Association of American Law Schools
(reprinted with permission)

Deal lawyers start from the business deal. The terms of the business deal are the deal lawyer's facts. The lawyer must then find the contract concepts that best reflect the business deal and use those concepts as the basis of drafting the contract provisions. I call this skill "translating the business deal into contract concepts." Mastering it is the first steppingstone to becoming a deal lawyer. All else flows from this skill. It is the foundation of a deal lawyer's professional expertise and problem-solving ability. Without it, negotiating and drafting are abstractions....

[Deal lawyers know there] is an underlying similarity to all contracts. Their structure is composed of representations, warranties, covenants, and conditions precedent. They are the contract's building blocks....

Translating the business deal into contract concepts is only one aspect of thinking like a deal lawyer. The better deal lawyers are able to look at a transaction from the client's perspective and add value to the deal. Looking at a contract from the client's perspective means understanding what the client wants to achieve and the risks it wants to avoid. "Adding value to the deal" is a euphemism for "finding and resolving business issues." These skills are problem-solving skills and are an integral component of a deal lawyer's professional expertise. They require a sophisticated understanding not only of substantive law, but also of business, the client's business, and the transaction at hand. At a law firm, having these skills is generally the province of the partners, and not necessarily all of them ...

A careful analysis of a cross-section of agreements reveals that five business issues recur in most agreements. With an understanding of these issues, the student (or lawyer) is better able to analyze the transaction and to recognize how each of the issues manifests itself in a particular agreement. The five issues are money, risk, control, standards, and endgame. They are the five prongs of the business issue framework.

Virtually all agreements have issues related to *money*: purchase price, interest rates, time value of money, or earn-out calculations. Lawyers can often add value by using their

---

1. Tina L. Stark, *Thinking Like a Deal Lawyer*, 54 J. Legal Educ. 223 (2004). Reprinted with permission.

practice-specific expertise. For example, if a corporation is entering into a broker arrangement in connection with the purchase of a jet, the lawyer may be able to draw upon her expertise and note that the brokerage fee is outside the normal range.

The second prong is *risk*. Representations and warranties, covenants, and conditions precedent are all risk allocation mechanisms. How they are negotiated directly affects a client's risk in a transaction. Risk can also manifest itself in multiple other ways in a transaction. First, a contract can raise the specter of tort liability—fraudulent inducement, product liability, or tortious interference with contract. Second, the provisions can create contract risk. For example, a noncompete, liquidated damages, or an indemnity provision could be unenforceable. Third, a contract could create the risk of statutory liability. A classic example is liability under the securities laws. Finally, risk could be inherent in the transaction. Credit risk is a salient example.

Ferreting out risks is not usually a problem for most lawyers. They have been taught issue spotting. But if that is all that a lawyer does, she will justly earn a reputation as a deal killer. To be effective, she must assess the probability that a risk will occur and, if it is significant, find a way to limit it.

The third business issue is *control*. In analyzing control as a business issue, the initial inquiry must be whether having control is good or bad from a client's perspective. The answer is fact dependent. For example, limited partners are entitled to limited liability because they exercise no control over the limited partnership. In this context, lack of control is good. But limited partners generally do not want to abdicate to the general partner all control over their investment. They want the right to make decisions to protect their investment. Therefore, the limited partners will seek as much control as the general partner will tolerate and as much as they can accrete without becoming general partners under the relevant state law. Control is a two-edged sword for limited partners....

Control is always an issue when there is risk. To add value, a deal lawyer must recognize the risk and then determine how to control or diminish it.

The fourth prong of the framework is *standards*. Virtually every word in a contract is a standard. There are both macro and micro standards. For example, every representation and warranty establishes a standard of liability. If the standard is not met, the recipient of the representation and warranty may sue the maker. This is a macro standard. But that macro standard can be changed at the micro level. By changing a word or a phrase in a representation and warranty, the standard changes. Are property, plant, and equipment in *good* repair, *customary* repair, or *in compliance with industry standards?*

Covenants and conditions precedent are also standards, as is every adjective (*material* contracts) and adverb (*promptly* deliver). Definitions are also standards (how a financial ratio is defined determines the standard to be incorporated into a loan covenant). A deal lawyer adds value by recognizing when a standard is inappropriate and by negotiating an alternative that more accurately reflects the client's business goals.

The last prong is *endgame*. Every transaction ends. It may end happily or unhappily. The relationship between a banker and its borrower can end with the loan repaid in full (happy) or with the borrower in default (unhappy). If a trademark license agreement ends, the contract must provide for, among other things, a mechanism for determining how and when the licensee should make the final payments, as well as instructions for what the licensee should do with any remaining merchandise. Endgame provisions are some of the most significant provisions in a contract because they often involve money—a topic near and dear to most clients' hearts.

Introduction

Part VI of this text focuses on a large body of specialized and important contract terms collectively referred to as "conditions." You will continue working with and studying actual contracts, such as the Widgets, Inc.-Schmo contract. By the end of your study of Part VI, you should be able to read a contract and explain its terms to a layperson.

Imagine a client has come to you. She tells you that she agreed to buy a house and some land. She also says the seller promised to remove an ugly old shed before the sale closed, and she reports that the seller has not done so and, therefore, she does not think she should have to go forward with the purchase. Must she? We know that if the promise to remove the shed is a part of the contract, the seller's failure to do so is a breach of the contract. But what is the significance of that failure? Can your client get out of the contract altogether or is she still obliged to go through with the purchase and can only claim damages from the seller for the breach?

We will start by evaluating the significance of contract breaches. To analyze the significance of a contract breach, we need to learn about the law of conditions. In particular, after starting with a general introduction to the idea of conditions, we will learn how the parties to a contract can create a particular type of condition, an express condition, and we will learn the effect of doing so. Later, we will learn that courts can also create conditions, called constructive conditions, and we will consider the effect of the courts doing so. Finally, we will explore a wide variety of mechanisms used by the courts to ameliorate the sometimes harsh effects of conditions.

In Part V of this book, you learned that contract lawyers frequently focus on four broad issues:

(1) What terms do courts treat as part of the contract for the purposes of determining what each party has promised? (In other words, what is the contract?)

(2) How do courts determine what the words of a contract obligate the parties to do? (In other words, what does the contract mean?)

(3) Did the parties properly and fully perform? (In other words, did either party breach?)

(4) Assuming either party did not properly do everything she promised to do, what is the consequence of any breach?

Part V focused on the first two questions. You learned how to determine which terms are parts of the parties' contract and which terms are not. You also learned how to identify contractual ambiguities and how courts resolve those ambiguities through various canons of interpretation or by implying unstated terms.

Part VI, which consists entirely of this chapter, continues our study of the second question and also focuses on the third and fourth questions. First, the question of whether the parties have created a condition or whether the court should do so is a matter of contract interpretation—the court must determine whether the words communicate what they need to communicate for the courts to apply either the "express condition" or the "constructive condition" label. Second, we must determine whether any such condition is both a condition and a promise or just a condition. Constructive conditions, those created by the courts, are always based on promises, but express conditions may or may not also be promises. Third, we need to determine whether every promise was performed and whether every condition occurred. Finally, we must evaluate the consequences of any failure to perform a promise or any non-occurrence of a condition—we have to evaluate the impact that any breach and/or non-occurrence has on the other party's duty to perform.

Introduction to Conditions

Section 224 of the RESTATEMENT SECOND OF CONTRACTS states that **a condition is "an event, not certain to occur, which must occur ... before performance under a contract becomes due."** We have already studied several examples of conditions. First, in the *Omni Group* case, a buyer of land included the following clause in its contract with the seller:

> "This transaction is subject to purchaser receiving an engineer's and architect's feasibility report ... If said report is satisfactory to purchaser, purchaser shall so notify seller in writing within fifteen (15) days ... If no such notice is sent to seller, this transaction shall be considered null and void."

The *Omni Group* court held that this clause created "two conditions precedent to Omni's duty to buy the Clark's property," a condition of getting the report and a condition of "satisfaction." Also in connection with our discussion of illusory promises, we discussed the example of a home purchaser conditioning her duty to buy a home on getting a home loan and a car purchaser conditioning her duty to buy the car on getting a car loan.

All of these examples fall within the above definition. First, in *Omni Group*, getting the report was an event (something that can happen) that was uncertain to occur (the architect and the engineer may refuse to deliver a report or no architect or engineer may be asked to make a report). By the terms of the clause, that event had to occur before the buyer's performance (the duty to buy the land) became due, because the transaction was "subject to" (meaning "dependent" or "conditional upon") getting the report. Likewise, the buyer being satisfied was an event (something that may happen) that was uncertain to occur (the buyer might not be satisfied with the feasibility of the project for any number of reasons, for example, the land may require special engineering or the local government may have imposed stringent zoning regulations), and, by the terms of the clause, if the buyer is not satisfied, the deal would be "null and void" (meaning the event must occur for performance to be due).

Similarly, a promise to buy a house or a car only if one gets a home or car loan identifies an event (getting the loan), that may not occur (many loan applicants are turned down, for credit or income reasons) and, such clauses make it clear that, if the event does not occur, the deal is off (the event must occur before performance is due).

Keep in mind one other crucial point alluded to above. A condition may also be a promise, but it is not **always** a promise. Likewise, a promise may also be a condition, but it is not **always** a condition. This distinction among contract terms that are *conditions and promises*, terms that are *conditions but not promises*, and terms that are *promises but not conditions* has important ramifications. **If a contract term is just a condition (and not a promise) and the condition does not occur, the parties' duties of further performance are excused and neither may sue the other for breach. If a contract term is just a promise (and not a condition) and the promise is not performed, the failure to perform is a breach but the parties' duties of further performance are not excused.** Finally, **if a contract term is both a promise and a condition, non-occurrence of the condition excuses the parties' duties of further performance *and* constitutes a breach of contract.**

To understand these distinctions and their implications, compare the following three contract clauses:

(1) The clause at issue in the *Omni Group* case.

(2) "I have purchased a lottery ticket for this week's state lottery. I will buy your land for $250,000 only if that lottery ticket proves to be a winner."

(3) "I promise to sell you my house, Greenacre, for $250,000 and I will also wash the floors of the house before I move out."

Recall that the *Omni Group* court held that the architect and engineer report condition "requires Omni to attempt, in good faith, to obtain ... [the report]." In other words, the **condition** of getting the report included an **implied promise** to make a reasonable effort to get the report. Likewise, the court held the satisfaction **condition** also included an **implied promise** (court said "duty" but the only duties in connection with contracts are duties undertaken as promises in the parties' contract) to make a good faith determination of whether the promisor was satisfied. Thus, both terms were conditions AND promises. The fact the promises were implied does not change the analysis; implied promises carry exactly the same weight and binding effect as express promises, and the result in the case would have been exactly the same if Omni Group had expressly promised to make a reasonable effort to get the report and to evaluate its satisfaction in good faith. If Omni Group had not obtained the report because it had made no effort to do so, the fact that the report was not obtained would have been a breach of the implied promise to make a reasonable effort to get the report and therefore a breach of contract. Similarly, if Omni had acted in "bad faith" in claiming dissatisfaction, Omni's bad faith would have been a breach of the contract, entitling the seller to a remedy. While the *Omni Group* case represents one way to have a condition that also is a promise, we will learn about other ways.

In contrast, the lottery condition above is NOT a promise to win the lottery and is not even a promise to use good faith in trying to win the lottery because, having already purchased a ticket, the speaker has no control AT ALL over who wins. Thus, the speaker's good or bad faith would be irrelevant. Thus, if the buyer did not win the lottery, the lottery condition would be deemed not to have occurred. Because that condition did not occur, the buyer's duty to buy the land would be excused. The seller could not sue the buyer for breach of a promise to win the lottery.

Finally, in the third example above, the **promise** to wash the floors is NOT a condition; there is nothing in it to suggest that the duty to buy the home **depends** on whether the seller washes the floors. Rather, the promise to wash is just a promise. Accordingly, if the seller did not mop the floors, that failure would be a breach of contract, but, because mopping the floors is NOT a condition, the buyer's duty to buy would not be excused by the seller's failure to mop. The buyer would still be obliged to close the deal.

Types of Conditions

There are two principal types of conditions and a third type, which we will consider but on which we will not focus a lot of attention. The two principal types of conditions, as noted above, are "express conditions" and "constructive conditions." **Express conditions are conditions actually stated as terms of the parties' contract. Constructive conditions are conditions imposed by the courts in connection with bilateral contracts to achieve justice between the parties.** Finally, the third type of conditions, implied-in-fact

Diagram 12-1: Contract Law Graphic Organizer

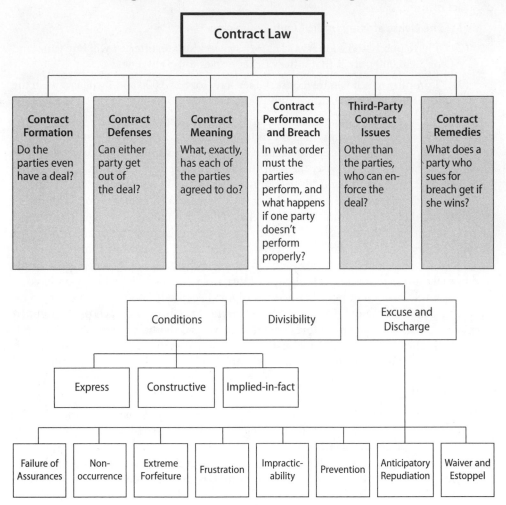

conditions, are necessary conditions the court concludes that the parties must have intended to be part of their deal but did not expressly state in their agreement.

Diagram 12-1 is the Contract Law Graphic Organizer; it depicts where this body of law fits within the larger scheme of contract law and the major sub-topics within this body of law.

Overview of Chapter 12

Chapter 12 addresses a significant number of closely related issues. The chapter has been organized so that you study the materials in an order you might follow in analyzing a contract performance problem. Thus, the chapter begins with the background information about the lawyer's role as a dealmaker and the introduction to conditions (see above).

The chapter then proceeds in four parts. The first part focuses on express conditions and addresses three sub-topics: (1) creation of express conditions; (2) occurrence of express conditions; and (3) three express condition problems that regularly arise: "pay when paid" clauses, "satisfaction" clauses, and "time is of the essence" clauses. The first two sub-topics will be considered together.

The second part of the chapter focuses on constructive conditions. This part also has three sub-parts. The first sub-part of the materials focuses on the circumstances in which courts choose to create constructive conditions, and the second part discusses the test by which common law courts evaluate whether constructive conditions have occurred. The third part addresses the U.C.C. Article 2 approach to contract performance.

The third part of the chapter looks at the circumstances under which, notwithstanding the fact that the parties have chosen to include multiple promises from both parties in a single contract, the courts will treat the contract as divisible, that is, as two or more independent contracts.

The final lengthy part of the chapter discusses the various ways courts have ameliorated the sometimes harsh effects of conditions law. As reflected in the chart above, there are nine such ameliorating doctrines: waiver, estoppel, non-occurrence of a prior condition, prevention, extreme forfeiture, anticipatory repudiation, failure of assurances, impracticability and impossibility, and frustration of purpose.

Express Conditions

Creation of Express Conditions

As noted above, an express condition is a condition actually stated as a term of the parties' agreement. Determining whether a particular term creates an express condition is a matter of **contract interpretation**. Because, as you know, parol evidence may be relevant to the process of interpreting a contract, an express condition issue may also raise a **parol evidence rule** issue. In determining whether a particular contract term is an express condition, courts assess whether the **language** used communicates an intent to require the event described in the term to occur as a prerequisite to further performance of the contract. In other words, whether the language used communicates an intent to make further performance dependent on the occurrence of the event.

Let's return to our examples. Note the process of analysis demonstrated below so you can emulate the process on your exams and assignments.

First, the term in *Omni Group* requiring the reports is an express condition because the parties used a phrase "subject to." Courts uniformly have agreed that the words "subject to" suffice to communicate an intent to create an express condition.

Second, the term requiring satisfaction uses the word "if." On the one hand, by using the word "if," the contract does not unequivocally state that performance depends on the buyer's satisfaction. On the other hand, the word "if" usually connotes "conditional on" and the clause also states "the transaction will be null and void" if the buyer is not satisfied. Because the non-occurrence of an express condition has the **effect** of making a contract "null and void," the statement to that effect in the clause communicates the desired effect of the clause is for it to be an express condition. Also, satisfaction clauses tend to be treated as express conditions. Accordingly, the satisfaction clause does create an express condition.

Please avoid a common student error and remember that express terms (terms stated in a contract) are not the same thing as express conditions. Notice, for example, that the promise to mop in the third example above is an express term of the contract; in other words, the contract expressly states the seller's promise to mop. As noted above, this express term is NOT an express condition. For an express term to be an express condition, the term must expressly communicate that the duty of further performance depends on the occurrence of the event referenced in the term. Thus, for example, if the term had stated that the buyer's duty to buy was "expressly conditioned" on the seller mopping the floor, the term would have been an express condition.

Types of Express Conditions

As noted above, our focus for now is on express conditions. As we will learn, express condition issues may arise in any contract performance dispute. At the same time, there are three recurring express conditions issues with which you should be familiar: "pay when paid" clauses, "time is of the essence" clauses and "satisfaction" clauses. You already know something about satisfaction clauses; we will learn more. We will also study the other two types of recurring express conditions issues.

Creation and Occurrence of Express Conditions

Exercise 12-2: *Tacoma Northpark, LLC v. NW, LLC* and *Howard v. Federal Crop Insurance Corp.*

The first two cases address the type of language the parties must use for a court to conclude that the parties have created an express condition. As you read these cases, consider the following questions:

1. Identify the key facts in both the *Tacoma* case and the *Howard* case. In particular, make sure you identify all of the language on which the court relies in its decision.

2. The *Tacoma* court lists some of the words and phrases that courts have concluded suffice to create express conditions. However, some of the words and phrases on the *Tacoma* court's list are more debatable. The court also leaves out words and phrases that other courts have concluded unambiguously create express conditions, such as "if and only if" and expressly conditioned on." Which of the words on the *Tacoma* court's list seem to you to unambiguously communicate an express condition? Which do not? Why?

3. The *Tacoma* court concludes that the language in the contract sufficed to create an express condition. Why?

4. According to the *Tacoma* court what is the significance of a determination that a contract term is either a promise or a condition. How does that determination bear on the dispute in this case?

5. From where does the *Tacoma* court get the idea that the contract required NW to make even a good faith effort to get plat approval? (Hint: On this point, you may find it helpful to take another look at the *Omni Group* case.)

6. Was the plat approval term merely a condition or was it both a condition and a promise?

7. The *Howard* court concludes the term at issue was NOT an express condition.

    a. The court relied primarily on a body of law we already have studied in this book. On what body of law did the court rely?

b. Identify all the rules upon which the court relied.

c. Explain how the court applied the rules you identified in response to the previous question.

d. The *Howard* court devotes considerable time to distinguishing the *Fidelity-Phoenix* case. Be prepared to explain the bases on which the *Howard* court distinguished the *Fidelity-Phoenix* case.

e. According to the *Howard* court, what is the significance of a determination that a contract term is either a promise or a condition?

Tacoma Northpark, LLC v. NW, LLC
96 P.3d 454 (2004)

Quinn-Brintnall, C.J.

[...] On November 22, 1999, O'Connor entered into an agreement to purchase property from NW. NW had filed a preliminary plat with the City that proposed to divide the property into 23 lots for future residential development. After completing the land purchase, O'Connor planned to build homes for sale.

One of the purchase agreement's addenda stated that the offer was subject to final plat approval and that NW warranted that final plat approval would occur prior to the closing date:

> This Offer is subject to Seller providing the final plat approval by City of Tacoma and engineering as-built for this plat and deliver to Buyer (23) buildable lots to include all curbing, paved roadway, and all utilities to the lots.
>
> ...
>
> This offer is subject to Buyer obtaining Financing for construction loans.
>
> ...
>
> The transaction is contingent upon the Purchaser obtaining engineer's and/or architect's feasibility reports, utility agreements, percolation tests, if required and determining the availability of permits for construction.

[...] Closing was originally set for February 15, 2000. On December 21, 1999, both parties agreed to put the feasibility study on hold pending the City's final plat approval. But the City did not approve the final plat and closing was further delayed.

NW and O'Connor eventually agreed to close on four lots on June 15, 2000; six lots on August 15, 2000; eight more lots on December 1, 2000; and the last five lots on February 1, 2001. The City never issued final plat approval and the sale did not close. But O'Connor assigned two of the future lots to United Builders of Washington, Inc. (United) anyway. To effect these transfers, NW signed two statutory warranty deeds conveying four lots by metes and bounds: two lots were conveyed to O'Connor and two lots were conveyed to United.

The City issued building permits under the Model Home Ordinance that allowed O'Connor and United to build four model homes on these lots.

NW hired the engineering firm Larson and Associates Land Surveyors and Engineers, Inc. (Larson) to complete the platting process and obtain final plat approval from the City. But NW encountered financial difficulties and could not pay to complete the platting process. NW then offered to sell the property to O'Connor "as is"—with O'Connor being required to complete the plat process. O'Connor declined the offer and NW sold the land to Tacoma Northpark. NW did not inform Tacoma Northpark of its prior purchase agreement with O'Connor.

On August 31, 2001, Tacoma Northpark filed a quiet title action against several parties, including O'Connor, NW, United, and several lending organizations. O'Connor and United counterclaimed against Tacoma Northpark and cross claimed against NW for breach of contract. Trial was to the court which found that NW had not breached the property sale agreement with O'Connor because NW acted with "good faith" in unsuccessfully attempting to secure final plat approval. O'Connor and United appeal....

O'Connor contends that the trial court erred by holding that NW's good faith effort excused its failure to obtain final plat approval and erred in finding that NW had not breached the purchase agreement. O'Connor argues that to prevail against its breach of contract claim, NW had to prove that circumstances beyond its control made it impossible for it to obtain final plat approval and that NW's financial difficulties did not satisfy this impossibility standard.

But whether NW was required to prove impossibility of performance, or only that it had made a good faith effort to obtain final plat approval, depends on whether the addendum to the purchase agreement dealing with "final plat approval" is a promise (contractual duty) or an express condition precedent. [Citation omitted.] If it is a promise or contractual duty, NW must prove impossibility of performance. And mere financial difficulty is not sufficient to prove such impossibility of performance. [Citation omitted.] But if it is a condition precedent, NW need only establish that it made a good faith effort to satisfy the condition by obtaining final plat approval.

"Conditions precedent" are "those facts and events, occurring subsequently to the making of a valid contract, that must exist or occur before there is a right to immediate performance, before there is a breach of contract duty, before the usual judicial remedies are available." [Citation omitted.] In contrast, a breach of a contractual obligation subjects the promisor (NW) to liability for damages, but it does not necessarily discharge the other party's (O'Connor's) duty of performance. But the nonoccurrence of a condition precedent prevents the promisor (NW) from acquiring a right (to require O'Connor to purchase the property) or deprives it of one, but it does not subject the promisor (NW) to liability. [Citation omitted.] (Whether a provision in a contract is a condition, the nonfulfillment of which excuses performance, depends upon the intent of the parties, to be ascertained from a fair and reasonable construction of the language used in the light of all the surrounding circumstances.) [Citations omitted.]

It is clear that NW's failure to procure final plat approval excused O'Connor from any contractual obligations. But NW is not seeking to enforce the purchase agreement. Instead, is O'Connor entitled to damages for breach of the contract when NW's financial difficulties caused it to fail to obtain final plat approval? If final plat approval is a contractual obligation, O'Connor can recover damages because financial difficulties do not establish impossibility of performance. [Citation omitted.] If, however, final plat approval is a condition precedent, and NW acted in good faith in attempting to obtain final plat approval, O'Connor is not entitled to recover damages. [Citation omitted.]

The construction of a contract provision is a matter of law and our review is de novo. [Citation omitted.]Whether a contract provision is a condition precedent or a contractual obligation depends on the intent of the parties. We determine this intent from a fair and reasonable construction of the language used, taking into account all the surrounding circumstances. [Citations omitted.] Where it is doubtful whether words create a promise (contractual obligation) or an express condition, we will interpret them as creating a promise. [Citation omitted.] But words such as "provided that," "on condition," "when," "so that," "while," "as soon as," and "after" suggest a conditional intent, not a promise. [Citations omitted.] ...

Although the addendum does not use the express words identified in [above], the words "subject to" and "contingent upon" leave no doubt that at the time of execution the parties intended that no sale would take place until these conditions were satisfied. [Citation omitted.] Thus, until NW satisfied the condition of obtaining final plat approval for 23 buildable lots from the City, the offer did not ripen into a promise. Under the O'Connor/NW purchase agreement, final plat approval was a condition precedent, not a contractual promise....

Good faith is the standard that governs review of NW's failure to satisfy the condition precedent that it obtain final plat approval for 23 buildable lots ... we hold here that the proper standard to review a promisor's failure to fulfill a condition precedent is good faith ...

Here substantial evidence supports the trial court's finding that NW made a good faith, albeit unsuccessful, effort to secure final plat approval for 23 buildable lots. Therefore, the trial court correctly applied the appropriate standard when it held that NW did not breach the purchase agreement and O'Connor was not entitled to damages for NW's failure to satisfy a condition precedent to the offer for sale of the property ...

The trial court properly applied the good faith standard to its review of NW's failure to fulfill a condition precedent to its purchase agreement with O'Connor, and we affirm.

Howard v. Federal Crop Ins. Corp.

540 F.2d 695 (1976)

Widener, Circuit Judge. Plaintiff-appellants sued to recover for losses to their 1973 tobacco crop due to alleged rain damage. The crops were insured by defendant-appellee, Federal Crop Insurance Corporation (FCIC). Suits were brought in a state court in North Carolina and removed to the United

States District Court. The three suits are not distinguishable factually so far as we are concerned here and involve identical questions of law. They were combined for disposition in the district court and for appeal. The district court granted summary judgment for the defendant and dismissed all three actions. We remand for further proceedings. Since we find for the plaintiffs as to the construction of the policy, we express no opinion on the procedural questions.

Federal Crop Insurance Corporation, an agency of the United States, in 1973, issued three policies to the Howards, insuring their tobacco crops, to be grown on six farms, against weather damage and other hazards.

The Howards (plaintiffs) established production of tobacco on their acreage, and have alleged that their 1973 crop was extensively damaged by heavy rains, resulting in a gross loss to the three plaintiffs in excess of $35,000. The plaintiffs harvested and sold the depleted crop and timely filed notice and proof of loss with FCIC, but, prior to inspection by the adjuster for FCIC, the Howards had either plowed or disked under the tobacco fields in question to prepare the same for sowing a cover crop of rye to preserve the soil. When the FCIC adjuster later inspected the fields, he found the stalks had been largely obscured or obliterated by plowing or disking and denied the claims, apparently on the ground that the plaintiffs had violated a portion of the policy which provides that the stalks on any acreage with respect to which a loss is claimed shall not be destroyed until the corporation makes an inspection.

The holding of the district court is best captured in its own words:

> "The inquiry here is whether compliance by the insureds with this provision of the policy was a condition precedent to the recovery. The court concludes that it was and that the failure of the insureds to comply worked a forfeiture of benefits for the alleged loss."

There is no question but that apparently after notice of loss was given to defendant, but before inspection by the adjuster, plaintiffs plowed under the tobacco stalks and sowed some of the land with a cover crop, rye. The question is whether, under paragraph 5(f) of the tobacco endorsement to the policy of insurance, the act of plowing under the tobacco stalks forfeits the coverage of the policy. Paragraph 5 of the tobacco endorsement is entitled *Claims*. Pertinent to this case are subparagraphs 5(b) and 5(f), which are as follows:

> 5(b) *It shall be a condition precedent* to the payment of any loss that the insured establish the production of the insured crop on a unit and that such loss has been directly caused by one or more of the hazards insured against during the insurance period for the crop year for which the loss is claimed, and furnish any other information regarding the manner and extent of loss as may be required by the Corporation. (Emphasis added.)

> 5(f) The tobacco stalks on any acreage of tobacco of types 11a, 11b, 12, 13, or 14 with respect to which a loss is claimed *shall not be destroyed until the Corporation makes an inspection.* (Emphasis added.)

The arguments of both parties are predicated upon the same two assumptions. First, if subparagraph 5(f) creates a condition precedent, its violation caused a forfeiture of plaintiffs' coverage. Second, if subparagraph 5(f) creates an obligation (variously called a promise or covenant) upon plaintiffs not to plow under the tobacco stalks, defendant may recover from plaintiffs (either in an original action, or, in this case, by a counterclaim, or as a matter of defense) for whatever damage it sustained because of the elimination of the stalks. However, a violation of subparagraph 5(f) would not, under the second premise, standing alone, cause a forfeiture of the policy.

Generally accepted law provides us with guidelines here. There is a general legal policy opposed to forfeitures. [Citations omitted.] Insurance policies are generally construed most strongly against the insurer. [Citations omitted.] When it is doubtful whether words create a promise or a condition precedent, they will be construed as creating a promise. [Citation omitted.] The provisions of a contract will not be construed as conditions precedent in the absence of language plainly requiring such construction. [Citations omitted.]

Plaintiffs rely most strongly upon the fact that the term "condition precedent" is included in subparagraph 5(b) but not in subparagraph 5(f). It is true that whether a contract provision is construed as a condition or an obligation does not depend entirely upon whether the word "condition" is expressly used. [Citation omitted.] However, the persuasive force of plaintiffs' argument in this case is found in the use of the term "condition precedent" in subparagraph 5(b) but not in subparagraph 5(f). Thus, it is argued that the ancient maxim to be applied is that the expression of one thing is the exclusion of another.

The defendant places principal reliance upon the decision of this court in *Fidelity-Phoenix Fire Insurance Company v. Pilot Freight Carriers*, 193 F.2d 812 (4th Cir. 1952). Suit there was predicated upon a loss resulting from theft out of a truck covered by defendant's policy protecting plaintiff from such a loss. The insurance company defended upon the grounds that the plaintiff had left the truck unattended without the alarm system being on. The policy contained six paragraphs limiting coverage. Two of those imposed what was called a "condition precedent." They largely related to the installation of specified safety equipment. Several others, including paragraph 5, pertinent in that case, started with the phrase, "It is further warranted." In paragraph 5, the insured warranted that the alarm system would be on whenever the vehicle was left unattended. Paragraph 6 starts with the language: "The assured agrees, by acceptance of this policy, that the foregoing conditions precedent relate to matters material to the acceptance of the risk by the insurer." Plaintiff recovered in the district court, but judgment on its behalf was reversed because of a breach of warranty of paragraph 5, the truck had been left unattended with the alarm off. In that case, plaintiff relied upon the fact that the words "condition precedent" were used in some of the paragraphs but the word "warranted" was used in the paragraph in issue. In rejecting that contention, this court said that "warranty" and "condition precedent" are often used interchangeably to create a condition of the insured's promise, and "manifestly the terms 'condition precedent' and 'warranty' were intended to have the same meaning and effect." 193 F.2d at 816.

Fidelity-Phoenix thus does not support defendant's contention here. Although there is some resemblance between the two cases, analysis shows that the issues are actually entirely different. Unlike the case at bar, each paragraph in *Fidelity-Phoenix* contained either the term "condition precedent" or the term "warranted." We held that, in that situation, the two terms had the same effect in that they both involved forfeiture. That is well established law.

(citation omitted). In the case at bar, the term "warranty" or "warranted" is in no way involved, either in terms or by way of like language, as it was in *Fidelity-Phoenix*. The issue upon which this case turns, then, was not involved in *Fidelity-Phoenix*.

The RESTATEMENT OF THE LAW OF CONTRACTS states:

§ 261. INTERPRETATION OF DOUBTFUL WORDS AS PROMISE OR CONDITION.

Where it is doubtful whether words create a promise or an express condition, they are interpreted as creating a promise; but the same words may sometimes mean that one party promises a performance and that the other party's promise is conditional on that performance."

Two illustrations (one involving a promise, the other a condition) are used in the RESTATEMENT:

2. A, an insurance company, issues to B a policy of insurance containing promises by A that are in terms conditional on the happening of certain events. The policy contains this clause: 'provided, in case differences shall arise touching any loss, *the matter shall be submitted to impartial arbitrators*, whose award shall be binding on the parties.' This is a promise to arbitrate and does not make an award a condition precedent of the insurer's duty to pay.

3. A, an insurance company, issues to B an insurance policy in usual form containing this clause: 'In the event of disagreement as to the amount of loss it shall be ascertained by two appraisers and an umpire. The loss shall *not be payable until 60 days after the award of the appraisers when such an appraisal is required.*' This provision is not merely a promise to arbitrate differences but makes an award a condition of the insurer's duty to pay in case of disagreement. (Emphasis added)

We believe that subparagraph 5(f) in the policy here under consideration fits illustration 2 rather than illustration 3. Illustration 2 specifies something to be done, whereas subparagraph 5(f) specifies something not to be done. Unlike illustration 3, subparagraph 5(f) does not state any conditions under which the insurance shall "not be payable," or use any words of like import. We hold that the district court erroneously held, on the motion for summary judgment, that subparagraph 5(f) established a condition precedent to plaintiffs' recovery which forfeited the coverage.

From our holding that defendant's motion for summary judgment was improperly allowed, it does not follow the plaintiffs' motion for summary judgment should have been granted, for if subparagraph 5(f) be not construed as a condition precedent, there are other questions of fact to be determined. At this point, we merely hold that the district court erred in holding, on the motion for summary judgment, that subparagraph 5(f) constituted a condition precedent with resulting forfeiture ...

The explanation defendant makes for including subparagraph 5(f) in the tobacco endorsement is that it is necessary that the stalks remain standing in order for the Corporation to evaluate the extent of loss and to determine whether loss resulted from some cause not covered by the policy. However, was subparagraph 5(f) inserted because without it the Corporation's opportunities for proof would be more difficult, or because they would be impossible? Plaintiffs point out that the Tobacco Endorsement, with subparagraph 5(f), was adopted in 1970, and crop insurance goes back long before that date. Nothing is shown as to the Corporation's prior 1970 practice of evaluating losses. Such a showing might have a bearing upon establishing defendant's intention in including 5(f). Plaintiffs state, and defendant does not deny, that another division of the Department of Agriculture, or the North Carolina Department, urged that tobacco stalks be cut as soon as possible after harvesting as a means of pest control. Such an explanation might refute the idea that plaintiffs plowed under the stalks for any fraudulent purpose. Could these conflicting directives affect the reasonableness of plaintiffs' interpretation of defendant's prohibition upon plowing under the stalks prior to adjustment?

We express no opinion on these questions because they were not before the district court and are mentioned to us largely by way of argument rather than from the record. No question of ambiguity was raised in the court below or here and no question of the applicability of paragraph 5(c) to this case was alluded to other than in the defendant's pleadings, so we also do not reach those questions. Nothing we say here should preclude FCIC from asserting as a defense that the plowing or disking under of the stalks caused damage to FCIC if, for example, the amount of the loss was thereby made more difficult or impossible to ascertain whether the plowing or disking under was done with bad purpose or innocently. To repeat, our narrow holding is that merely plowing or disking under the stalks does not of itself operate to forfeit coverage under the policy.

The case is remanded for further proceedings not inconsistent with this opinion.

Exercise 12-3: *Oppenheimer v. Oppenheim*

The next case, *Oppenheimer*, addresses the standard courts use to determine whether an express condition has occurred. The case also distinguishes this standard from the substantial performance standard courts use in determining whether constructive conditions have occurred. As you read the case, consider the following questions:

1. Why did the court conclude the terms at issue were express conditions?

2. What policy supports the rule that the court applies to determine whether the express condition had occurred in this case?

3. If the defendant had sued for breach of contract and sought damages because the notice condition was not met, what would have been the result?

Oppenheimer v. Oppenheim

660 N.E.2d 415 (N.Y. 1995)

CIPARICK, Justice. The parties entered into a letter agreement setting forth certain conditions precedent to the formation and existence of a sublease between them. The agreement provided that there would be no sublease between the parties "unless and until" plaintiff delivered to defendant the prime landlord's written consent to certain "tenant work" on or before a specified deadline. If this condition did not occur, the sublease was to be deemed "null and void." Plaintiff provided only oral notice on the specified date. The issue presented is whether the doctrine of substantial performance applies to the facts of this case. We conclude it does not for the reasons that follow.

I.

In 1986, plaintiff Oppenheimer & Co. moved to the World Financial Center in Manhattan, a building constructed by Olympia & York Company (O & Y). At the time of its move, plaintiff had three years remaining on its existing lease for the 33rd floor of the building known as One New York Plaza. As an incentive to induce plaintiff's move, O & Y agreed to make the rental payments due under plaintiff's rental agreement in the event plaintiff was unable to sublease its prior space in One New York Plaza.

In December 1986, the parties to this action entered into a conditional letter agreement to sublease the 33rd floor. Defendant already leased space on the 29th floor of One New York Plaza and was seeking to expand its operations. The proposed sublease between the parties was attached to the letter agreement. The letter agreement provided that the proposed sublease would be executed only upon the satisfaction of certain conditions. Pursuant to paragraph 1(a) of the agreement, plaintiff was required to obtain "the Prime Landlord's written notice of confirmation, substantially to the effect that [defendant] is a subtenant of the Premises reasonably acceptable to Prime Landlord." If such written notice of confirmation were not obtained "on or before December 30, 1986, then this letter agreement and the Sublease ... shall be deemed null and void and of no further force and effect and neither party shall have any rights against nor obligations to the other."

Assuming satisfaction of the condition set forth in paragraph 1(a), defendant was required to submit to plaintiff, on or before January 2, 1987, its plans for "tenant work" involving construction of a telephone communication linkage system between the 29th and 33rd floors. Paragraph 4(c) of the letter agreement then obligated plaintiff to obtain the prime landlord's "written consent" to the proposed "tenant work" and deliver such consent to defendant on or before January 30, 1987. Furthermore, if defendant had not received the prime landlord's written consent by the agreed date, both the agreement and the sublease were to be deemed "null and void and of no further force and effect," and neither party was to have "any rights against nor obligations to the other." Paragraph 4(d) additionally provided that, notwithstanding satisfaction of the condition set forth in paragraph 1(a), the parties "agree not to execute and exchange the Sublease unless and until the conditions set forth in paragraph (c) above are timely satisfied."

The parties extended the letter agreement's deadlines in writing and plaintiff timely satisfied the first condition set forth in paragraph 1(a) pursuant to the modified deadline. However, plaintiff never delivered the prime landlord's written consent to the proposed tenant work on or before the modified final deadline of February 25, 1987. Rather, plaintiff's attorney telephoned defendant's attorney on February 25 and informed defendant that the prime landlord's consent had been secured. On February 26, defendant, through its attorney, informed plaintiff's attorney that the letter agreement and sublease were invalid for failure to timely deliver the prime landlord's written consent and that it would not agree to an extension of the deadline. The document embodying the prime landlord's written consent was eventually received by plaintiff on March 20, 1987, 23 days after expiration of paragraph 4(c)'s modified final deadline.

Plaintiff commenced this action for breach of contract, asserting that defendant waived and/or was estopped by virtue of its conduct from insisting on physical delivery of the prime landlord's written consent by the February 25 deadline. Plaintiff further alleged in its complaint that it had substantially performed the conditions set forth in the letter agreement.

At the outset of trial, the court issued an order *in limine* barring any reference to substantial performance of the terms of the letter agreement. Nonetheless, during the course of trial, the court permitted the jury to consider the theory of substantial performance, and additionally charged the jury concerning substantial performance. Special interrogatories were submitted. The jury found that defendant had properly complied with the terms of the letter agreement, and answered in the negative the questions whether defendant failed to perform its obligations under the letter agreement concerning submission of plans for tenant work, whether defendant by its conduct waived the February 25 deadline for delivery by plaintiff of the landlord's written consent to tenant work, and whether defendant by its conduct was equitably estopped from requiring plaintiff's strict adherence to the February 25 deadline. Nonetheless, the jury answered in the affirmative the question, "Did plaintiff substantially perform the conditions set forth in the Letter Agreement?," and awarded plaintiff damages of $1.2 million.

Defendant moved for judgment notwithstanding the verdict. Supreme Court granted the motion, ruling as a matter of law that "the doctrine of substantial performance has no application to this dispute, where the Letter Agreement is free of all ambiguity in setting the deadline that plaintiff concededly did not honor." The Appellate Division reversed the judgment on the law and facts, and reinstated the jury verdict. The Court concluded that the question of substantial compliance was properly submitted to the jury and that the verdict should be reinstated because plaintiff's failure to deliver the prime landlord's written consent was inconsequential.

This Court granted defendant's motion for leave to appeal and we now reverse.

II.

Defendant argues that no sublease or contractual relationship ever arose here because plaintiff failed to satisfy the condition set forth in paragraph 4(c) of the letter agreement. Defendant contends that the doctrine of substantial performance is not applicable to excuse plaintiff's failure to deliver the prime landlord's written consent to defendant on or before the date specified in the letter agreement and that the Appellate Division erred in holding to the contrary. Before addressing defendant's arguments and the decision of the court below, an understanding of certain relevant principles is helpful.

A condition precedent is "an act or event, other than a lapse of time, which, unless the condition is excused, must occur before a duty to perform a promise in the agreement arises" [Citations omitted.] Most conditions precedent describe acts or events which must occur before a party is obliged to perform a promise made pursuant to an existing contract, a situation to be distinguished conceptually from a condition precedent to the formation or existence of the contract. [Citation omitted.] In the latter situation, no contract arises "unless and until the condition occurs." [Citation omitted.]

Conditions can be express or implied. Express conditions are those agreed to and imposed by the parties themselves. Implied or constructive conditions are those "imposed by law to do justice." [Citation omitted.] Express conditions must be literally performed, whereas constructive conditions, which ordinarily arise from language of promise, are subject to the precept that substantial compliance is sufficient. The importance of the distinction has been explained by Professor Williston:

> "Since an express condition ... depends for its validity on the manifested intention of the parties, it has the same sanctity as the promise itself. Though the court may regret the harshness of such a condition, as it may regret the harshness of a promise, it must, nevertheless, generally enforce the will of the parties unless to do so will violate public policy. Where, however, the law itself has imposed the condition, in absence of or irrespective of the manifested intention of the parties, it can deal with its creation as it pleases, shaping the boundaries of the constructive condition in such a way as to do justice and avoid hardship".

[Citations omitted.]

In determining whether a particular agreement makes an event a condition courts will interpret doubtful language as embodying a promise or constructive condition rather than an express condition. This interpretive preference is especially strong when a finding of express condition would increase the risk of forfeiture by the obligee. [Citation omitted.]

Interpretation as a means of reducing the risk of forfeiture cannot be employed if "the occurrence of the event as a condition is expressed in unmistakable language." RESTATEMENT SECOND OF CONTRACTS § 229, comment a, at 185; see § 227, comment b (where language is clear, "(t)he policy favoring freedom of contract requires that, within broad limits, the agreement of the parties should be honored even though forfeiture results"). Nonetheless, the nonoccurrence of the condition may yet be excused by waiver, breach or forfeiture. The Restatement posits that "[t]o the extent that the non-occurrence of a condition would cause disproportionate forfeiture, a court may excuse the non-occurrence of that condition unless its occurrence was a material part of the agreed exchange." RESTATEMENT SECOND OF CONTRACTS § 229.

Turning to the case at bar, it is undisputed that the critical language of paragraph 4(c) of the letter agreement unambiguously establishes an express condition precedent rather than a promise, as the parties employed the unmistakable language of condition ("if," "unless and until"). There is no doubt of the parties' intent and no occasion for interpreting the terms of the letter agreement other than as written.

Furthermore, plaintiff has never argued, and does not now contend, that the nonoccurrence of the condition set forth in paragraph 4(c) should be excused on the ground of forfeiture. Rather, plaintiff's primary argument from the inception of this litigation has been that defendant waived or was equitably estopped from invoking paragraph 4(c). Plaintiff argued secondarily that it substantially complied with the express condition of delivery of written notice on or before February 25th in that it gave defendant oral notice of consent on the 25th.

Contrary to the decision of the Court below, we perceive no justifiable basis for applying the doctrine of substantial performance to the facts of this case. The flexible concept of substantial compliance "stands in sharp contrast to the requirement of strict compliance that protects a party that has taken the precaution of making its duty expressly conditional" (citation omitted). If the parties "have made an event a condition of their agreement, there is no mitigating standard of materiality or substantiality applicable to the non-occurrence of that event." RESTATEMENT SECOND OF CONTRACTS § 237, comment d, at 220. Substantial performance in this context is not sufficient, "and if relief is to be had under the contract, it must be through excuse of the non-occurrence of the condition to avoid forfeiture." [Citations omitted.]

Here, it is undisputed that plaintiff has not suffered a forfeiture or conferred a benefit upon defendant ...

The essence of the Appellate Division's holding is that the substantial performance doctrine is universally applicable to all categories of breach of contract, including the nonoccurrence of an express condition precedent. However, as discussed, substantial performance is ordinarily not applicable to excuse the nonoccurrence of an express condition precedent....

Our precedents are consistent with this general principle. In *Maxton Bldrs. v. Lo Galbo,* ... 502 N.E.2d 184 (1986), the defendants contracted on August 3 to buy a house, but included in the contract the condition that if real estate taxes were found to be above $3,500 they would have the right to cancel the contract upon written notice to the seller within three days. On August 4 the defendants learned that real estate taxes would indeed exceed $3,500. The buyers' attorney called the seller's attorney and notified him that the defendants were exercising their option to cancel. A certified letter was sent notifying the seller's attorney of that decision on August 5 but was not received by the seller's attorney until August 9. We held the cancellation ineffective and rejected defendants' argument that reasonable notice was all that was required, stating: "It is settled ... that when a contract requires that written notice be given within a specified time, the notice is ineffective unless the writing is actually received within the time prescribed." *Id.* at 186. We so held despite the fact that timely oral notice was given and the contract did not provide that time was of the essence.

III.

In sum, the letter agreement provides in the clearest language that the parties did not intend to form a contract "unless and until" defendant received written notice of the prime landlord's consent on or before February 25, 1987. Defendant would lease the 33rd floor from plaintiff only on the condition that the landlord consent in writing to a telephone communication linkage system between the 29th and 33rd floors and to defendant's plans for construction effectuating that linkage. This matter was sufficiently important to defendant that it would not enter into the sublease "unless and until" the condition was satisfied. Inasmuch as we are not dealing here with a situation where plaintiff stands to suffer some forfeiture or undue hardship, we perceive no justification for engaging in a "materiality-of-the-nonoccurrence" analysis. To do so would simply frustrate the clearly expressed intention of the parties. Freedom of contract prevails in an arm's length transaction between sophisticated parties such as these, and in the absence of countervailing public policy concerns there is no reason to relieve them of the consequences of their bargain. If they are dissatisfied with the consequences of their agreement, "the time to say so [was] at the bargaining table." [Citation omitted.] ...

Accordingly, the order of the Appellate Division should be reversed, with costs, and the complaint dismissed.

"Pay When Paid" Clauses

Exercise 12-4: *Southern States Masonry v. J.A. Jones Construction*

Southern States Masonry and the cases that follow all address particularized express condition issues that are frequently litigated. The first issue involves "pay when paid" clauses. "Pay when paid" clauses are contract terms, frequently included in contracts between general contractors and subcontractors, which have language communicating that the general contractor will pay the subcontractor "when" or "as" or "after" the general contractor is paid by the owner. As you read the *Southern States Masonry* case, consider the following questions:

1. The court frames the issue as whether the terms at issue are "suspensive" conditions. How does the idea of suspensive conditions relate to the idea of express conditions?

2. The court's conclusion, which is consistent with the overwhelming majority rule, also reflects a policy choice. What is the policy for placing the loss caused by the insolvent owner on the contractor rather than the subcontractor?

Southern States Masonry v. J.A. Jones Construction
507 So. 2d 198 (1987)

CALOGERO, Justice. These disputes between general contractors and subcontractors arose after the owner of the 1984 Louisiana World's Fair, Louisiana World Exposition, Inc. (LWE), filed for bankruptcy before having fully paid its general contractors. In each case, LWE entered into a construction contract with a general contractor. The general contractor, in turn, subcontracted out portions of the work. After LWE failed, the subcontractors demanded payment for the work they had satisfactorily completed. The contractors, relying on certain provisions in the subcontracts, refused to make final payment. The Fifth and Fourth Circuit Courts of Appeal ruled in favor of the general contractors in the respective cases, holding that the effect of the payment provisions in the subcontracts made payment by the owner to the contractor a suspensive condition to the contractor's obligation to make payment to its subcontractor. In effect, the rulings of the Courts of Appeal relieved the general contractors of making further payments to the subcontractors because LWE had defaulted in paying them. We granted writs of review and now reverse both Court of Appeal judgments. Our conclusion is that the contract provisions reciting essentially that the subcontractor would receive payment after receipt of payment by the general contractor from the owner (the so-called "pay when paid" clauses) are not suspensive conditions, but rather terms for payment which only delay the execution of the respective general contractors' obligations to make payment, and then only for a reasonable period of time.

In the Southern States Masonry case, J.A. Jones Construction Company (Jones) entered into a construction contract with LWE on October 1, 1982. Jones, in turn, entered into a subcontract with Southern States Masonry (Southern) on October 6, 1983, wherein Southern agreed to furnish concrete masonry work on the International Pavilion, the U.S. Pavilion, and the Amphitheatre.

Jones was paid by LWE for work billed and completed only through March, 1984. LWE's insolvency has prevented Jones' receipt of a portion of the contract price due them from LWE. After LWE filed for a Chapter 11 reorganization, Jones filed a proof of claim in the bankruptcy proceedings and has taken other steps in an effort to recover the remaining contract payment, but to date without avail.

On October 1, 1985, Southern filed suit, seeking recovery of all amounts owed it by Jones on the subcontract. Jones admittedly refused to make any payments to Southern for work for which Jones had not already been paid by LWE. Jones based its refusal on the articles of the subcontract, which provide, in pertinent part:

> 2. *Price.* Subject to all of the other provisions of this Subcontract, Contractor shall pay to Subcontractor for the due and full performance of the Work the Subcontract Price....

> 3.... Contractor shall pay to Subcontractor, *upon receipt of payment from the Owner,* an amount equal to the value of Subcontractor's completed work, to the extent allowed and paid by Owner on account of Subcontractor's Work....

> 4. *Final payment.* A final payment, consisting of the unpaid balance of the Price, shall be made within forty-five (45) days after the last of the following to occur: (a) full completion of the Work by Subcontractor, (b) final acceptance of the work by the Architect and Owner[,] (c) *final payment by Owner to Contractor under the Contract....* (Emphasis added)

Exceptions of prematurity and no cause of action, together with a motion for summary judgment, were filed by Jones and its surety, Fidelity and Deposit Company of Maryland. The trial court granted the exception of prematurity and dismissed Southern's suit, holding that these contract provisions *conditioned* payment by Jones to Southern on further payment to Jones by LWE. As we have noted, this judgment was affirmed by the Fifth Circuit Court of Appeal.

A similar factual scenario developed in the Strahan/Landis matter. In that case, Landis Construction Company, Inc., after entering into a building contract with LWE, subcontracted with Strahan Painting Company for painting and other related work on the World's Fair Wonder Wall. In its petition, Strahan alleged it had not been paid $23,449.62, a portion of the fully earned contract price. Landis refused to pay and argued that it was not obligated to make payments unless and until it received corresponding funds from LWE. Landis premised its refusal on the following provision of its subcontract:

> IN CONSIDERATION WHEREOF, The said Contractor agrees that he will pay to the said Sub-Contractor the sum of Five Thousand Nine Hundred Thirty-Six Dollars ($5,936.00) for such materials and work, said amount to be paid as follows: ninety per cent (90%) of the value of the work completed and accepted each month *for which payment has been made by said Owner to said Contractor,* to be paid on or about the twentieth of the following month, except that *final payment will be made* by said Contractor to said Sub-Contractor *immediately following* final completion and acceptance of such materials and work by the Architect, and *final payment received by said Contractor,* and after satisfactory evidence has been furnished to said Contractor by said Sub-Contractor that all labor and material accounts for use on this particular work have been paid in full. (Emphasis added)

Strahan thereupon filed a Motion for Summary Judgment. The trial court granted partial summary judgment in favor of Strahan in the amount of $22,551.82. In a five-member Fourth Circuit decision, the appeal court reversed, depriving Strahan of that district court judgment, and held that further payment by Landis to Strahan was conditioned upon further payment to Landis by LWE. One judge dissented.

It is axiomatic in Louisiana that courts are bound to give legal effect to written contracts according to the true intent of the parties. [Citations omitted.] Where the words of a contract are clear and explicit, the intent of the parties is to be determined from the contract itself. [Citation omitted.] However, if a provision in a written contract is doubtful or ambiguous, the provision must be interpreted against the party who prepared the agreement [Citation omitted.] Finally, contractual provisions are construed as *not* to be suspensive conditions whenever possible. [Citation omitted.]

The appeal courts found the respective quoted payment provisions clear and unambiguous, such that the effect of the provisions was to make payment by the owner to the contractor a suspensive condition to the contractor's obligation to make payment to its subcontractor. With this conclusion we disagree.

The recitations in both contracts were clear that the subcontractors would perform certain work, while the general contractors would make certain payments. In neither subcontract was it recited, or clearly implied, that the subcontractor was, in effect, an insurer of LWE's solvency. In neither subcontract was there any suggestion or implication that LWE's possible insolvency was even given consideration by the parties. In short, that LWE would pay the general contractor was presumed. In such circumstances, we conclude that the payment provisions do not constitute suspensive conditions which negate any obligation on the part of the general contractors until they are paid by the owner. Rather, the better reasoned view is that the provisions create terms for payment which at most retard the execution of the contractor's obligation for a reasonable time. [Citations omitted.][2]

This court is addressing this issue for the first time. There is admittedly conflict among our courts of appeal concerning the effect of similar "pay when paid" clauses. In *Miller v. Housing Authority,* 175 So.2d 326 (1965), modified on other grounds, 190 So.2d 75 (1966), the pertinent contract provided that "On the 10th day of each month, the Subcontractor shall present to the Contractor a statement of the work done during the preceding month, which statement when checked and approved by the Contractor, will be paid within 10 days after receipt of payment from the Owner." *Miller,* 190 So.2d at 77 n. 3. In *Miller* the court of appeal found this provision constituted a suspensive condition as to the general contractor's obligation to its subcontractor:

> This provision was obviously intended to prevent the prime contractor from being compelled to assume the obligation of financing the construction of the Project in the event of default by the Owner. *Miller,* 175 So.2d at 331.

While the *Miller* language favors the position taken by the general contractors, the case is distinguishable on its facts. The solvency of the owner in *Miller* was never at issue. In fact, our decision there after the grant of writs indicates that the Fourth Circuit's decision was rendered *after* the general contractor had been paid. *Miller,* 190 So.2d at 79 n. 1. The central issue in *Miller* involved simply a determination of the appropriate point in time from which to award legal interest. It was this interest issue which prompted our grant of writs in *Miller.*

More recent Louisiana Court of Appeal decisions (with the obvious exception of the two before us) have not followed the holding of the Fourth Circuit in *Miller.* In fact, the Fourth Circuit itself, in *Pelican Construction Co. v. Sewerage and Water Board,* 240 So.2d 556 (1970), did not mention, or follow, *Miller.* In *Pelican,* the pertinent agreement stated the contractor would pay plaintiff "within five days after receipt of payment by owner." The agreement further noted that plaintiff "agrees to receive payments earned and due him at such time payments are received from [the] Sewerage and Water Board of New Orleans." *Pelican,* 240 So.2d at 557. In *dicta* the Fourth Circuit expressed doubt that the aforementioned clauses constituted a suspensive condition:

> [W]e consider it unlikely that the parties intended to make [the contractor's] obligation to pay [plaintiff] depend on a suspensive condition; we think it more likely that the obligation was merely intended to be modified so as to make the implied reasonable-time term, C.C. art. 2050, relate to the time when "in the usual course of events" (compare C.C. art. 1776) payment by Laguna or the Board would ordinarily occur or at least be exigible.

240 So.2d at 559.

---

2. As will be discussed further, the subcontracts evidence the parties' intent that payments would be forthcoming when, in the usual course of events, the general contractor would be paid by the owner. The time period has since become indeterminable. Thus, the inference will be supplied that the parties intended the obligation to be performed within a reasonable time.

The dicta in *Pelican* was followed by the First Circuit in *Chartres Corp. v. Charles Carter and Co.*, 346 So.2d 796 (1977). In *Chartres,* the agreement provided that the subcontractor would receive payment "within five (5) days after receipt of payment from Owner" and it further provided that "final payment ... shall be made after ... full payment therefor by Owner." *Chartres,* 346 So.2d at 797. Without mentioning *Miller,* the First Circuit found it was "unable to conclude that the parties intended that the defendant could always refuse to pay the plaintiff as long as any money was supposedly outstanding from the owner." 346 So.2d at 797–798. Analogous case law has supported the rationale in *Pelican* and *Chartres.* [Citations omitted.]

[A Louisiana statute] defines conditional obligations as those "made to depend on an uncertain event." [Another Louisiana statute] notes that an obligation subject to a suspensive condition "depends ... on a future and uncertain event." Moving from the precepts outlined in these codal articles, [one court] ... noted that "when an obligation is subject to a suspensive condition, the very existence of the obligation depends upon the occurrence of the event." [Citations and emphasis omitted.] Whether the parties intended to create a condition, or only to modify the obligation without making its existence depend on the event, is determined in doubtful cases by applying the rules established for the interpretation of obligations. [Citation omitted.]

A term, in contrast to a condition, may consist of a determinate lapse of time or of an event, "provided that [the] event be *in the course of nature,* certain." [Citation to Louisiana statute omitted.] The ... qualifying verbiage seems to underscore that human element which caused Benjamin Franklin to write that "in this world nothing is certain but death and taxes." As this applies to the controversy at hand, it is reasonable to assume that the general contractors and their subcontractors were reasonably certain that the normal course of events would follow, and the contractor would in fact be paid by LWE when and as contemplated by provisions of the contract between LWE and the general contractor. Further, even if we were to interpret LWE's duty to make payment to the general contractors as a precipitating event which should be characterized in a sense as "uncertain," the language of [the Louisiana statute] ... "envisions the possibility of an obligation being *modified* by an uncertain event which nevertheless does not affect, suspensively or resolutorily, the *existence* of the obligation." *Pelican,* 240 So.2d at 558. In all events the duty of payment by LWE to the general contractors was not viewed as an uncertain event, the occurrence of which, in the contemplation of the parties, would be required in order to trigger the reciprocal obligations....

The clauses in this case, therefore, did not suspensively condition the contractors' obligation to make payments until the contractors were in fact paid by the owner. They merely dictated when the contractor's payment should occur. The payment provisions of both subcontracts indicates that payment by the owner (LWE) was viewed as a reasonably certain event. Payment by LWE was only uncertain to the extent that all human events are uncertain. Thus, the terms for payment were defined by a more or less certain event (as envisioned by the parties), an event which, to the dismay of the parties, did not come to pass. It is not reasonable to infer from the language used in these contracts that the parties either agreed, or contemplated, that should LWE not pay the general contractors, then in that event the subcontractors would not have to be paid by the general contractors.[3]

We take especial note of the fact that in the case before us payment provisions in both subcontracts are couched in mandatory terms.[4] The question in both subcontracts relative to payment by the contractor is not "if" the subcontractors will be paid, but, rather, "when" they will be paid. The clauses in question therefore relate to the time when contractor must pay, and not the fact or certainty of such payment.

The foregoing analysis leads us to conclude that the payment clauses constituted terms relating to the time of payment which served to retard or delay the general contractor's payment until the occurrence of an event (owner's payment to contractor), contemplated surely to take place in the anticipated normal course of events. The unanticipated failure to pay on the part of the owner changed the fundamental premise on which the parties were relying. That unanticipated occurrence thereupon made the time for performing the payment obligation unascertainable, or uncertain, requiring the obligation be performed within a reasonable time.

The proper interpretation to be given to the so-called "pay when paid" provisions in construction contracts has been discussed at some length in other state and federal decisions. A leading case in this area is *Thomas J. Dyer Co. v. Bishop International Engineering Co.*, 303 F.2d 655 (1962). In *Dyer,* the defendant general contractor entered into a contract with the Kentucky Jockey Club, Inc. in connection with the construction of the Latonia Race Track in Boone County, Kentucky. The defendant then entered into a subcontract with the plaintiff, the terms of which, with perhaps even stronger pro-contractor language than that employed in the two cases under consideration here, provided as follows:

> The total price to be paid to Subcontractor shall be ... ($115,000.00) ... no part of which shall be due until five (5) days after Owner shall have paid Contractor therefor. . . .

303 F.2d at 656.

On December 4, 1958, the Jockey Club filed for reorganization under the provisions of federal bankruptcy law. When the contractor refused to make further payments to the subcontractor, the lawsuit was instituted. The contractor argued that payment from the owner was a condition precedent[5] to its obligation to make further payment to the subcontractor. Using language with which we are in agreement, the United States Court of Appeals for the Sixth Circuit affirmed the trial court judgment in favor of the subcontractor:

---

3. As we have noted, if such was the intent of the parties it should have been expressed in clearer and more explicit language.

4. The Strahan/Landis subcontract states that Contractor "will pay." The Southern/Jones subcontract states that contractor "shall pay" and that final payment "shall be made."

5. The common law "condition precedent" is analogous to the civilian "suspensive condition." *City of New Orleans v. Texas and Pacific Railway Company,* 171 U.S. 312, 18 S.Ct. 875, 43 L.Ed. 178 (1898).

It is, of course, basic in the construction business for the general contractor on a construction project of any magnitude to expect to be paid in full by the owner for the labor and material he puts into the project. He would not remain long in business unless such was his intention and such intention was accomplished. That is a fundamental concept of doing business with another. The solvency of the owner is a credit risk necessarily incurred by the general contractor, but various legal and contractual provisions, such as mechanics' liens and installment payments, are used to reduce this to a minimum. These evidence the intention of the parties that the contractor be paid even though the owner may ultimately become insolvent.

This expectation and intention of being paid is even more pronounced in the case of a subcontractor whose contract is with the general contractor, not with the owner. In addition to his mechanic's lien, he is primarily interested in the solvency of the general contractor with whom he has contracted. He looks to him for payment. Normally and legally, the insolvency of the owner will not defeat the claim of the subcontractor against the general contractor. Accordingly, in order to transfer this normal credit risk incurred by the general contractor from the general contractor to the subcontractor, the contract between the general contractor and subcontractor should contain an express condition clearly showing that to be the intention of the parties....

In the case before us we see no reason why the usual credit risk of the owner's insolvency assumed by the general contractor should be transferred from the general contractor to the subcontractor. It seems clear to us under the facts of this case that it was the intention of the parties that the subcontractor would be paid by the general contractor for the labor and materials put into the project. We believe that to be the normal construction of the relationship between the parties. If such was not the intention of the parties it could have been so expressed in unequivocal terms dealing with the possible insolvency of the owner.... [T]he subcontract does not refer to the possible insolvency of the owner. On the other hand, it deals with the amount, time and method of payment, which are essential provisions in every construction contract, without regard to possible insolvency. In our opinion ... the subcontract is a reasonable provision designed to postpone payment for a reasonable period of time after the work was completed, during which the general contractor would be afforded the opportunity of procuring from the owner the funds necessary to pay the contractor.... To construe it as requiring the subcontractor to wait to be paid for an indefinite period of time until the general contractor has been paid by the owner, which may never occur, is to give to it an unreasonable construction which the parties did not intend at the time the subcontract was entered into. (citations omitted)....

The ambiguity in both contracts may have been somewhat alleviated had either general contractor used the conjunction "if" in the payment provisions of the subcontract. The use of "if" in these provisions might have evidenced the parties' intention to condition receipt of payment by the subcontractor upon receipt of payment from the owner to the general contractor....

Exercise 12-5: *Southern States Masonry* Revisited

1. Read section 227 of the SECOND RESTATEMENT OF CONTRACTS and Illustrations 1–3 thereto. If your statutory supplement does not include these Illustrations, find them online or in your law library and answer the following questions:

    a. Explain Illustration 1.

    b. Explain Illustration 2.

    c. Explain Illustration 3 and reconcile it with Illustrations 1 and 2.

2. Paula was a real estate agent. Paula entered into a contract with Solomon by which Paula agreed to serve as the real estate agent for the sale of LongAcre, a tract of vacant land owned by Solomon. The contract provided that, if Paula sold the house on behalf of Solomon, Paula would be paid her real estate agent fee "when Seller (Solomon) was paid the purchase price at the close of escrow for such sale." One week later, with Paula's professional and highly competent assistance, Solomon and a buyer named Barb entered into a contract for the purchase and sale of LongAcre. Close of escrow was scheduled for one month later. However, at the last possible moment, Barb backed out of the deal. Paula sued Solomon for her fee, citing cases including the *Southern States Masonry* case. Who would win and why?

"Time Is of the Essence" Clauses

A "time is of the essence" clause explicitly states, "time is of the essence." Many, many contracts include "time is of the essence" clauses. In fact, so many contracts include "time is of the essence" clauses that such clauses are considered "boilerplate" contract terms. Boilerplate terms are contract terms that people frequently include in contracts without necessarily considering their implications. Of course, you, having been trained otherwise, would not mindlessly include any clause in a contract.

Exercise 12-6: *Pederson v. McGuire*

Pederson describes one common approach to "time is of the essence" clauses. As you read the case, consider the following questions:

1. Imagine a contract in which Contractor, promises to build a bridge for a town. Assume the contract provides, "Contractor's performance is due January 1, 2015." All courts would agree that this term is *not* an express condition but is a promise. Why?

    Note that it *would* be a breach of contract if Contractor completed Contractor's performance on January 20, 2015, but that breach almost certainly would *not* excuse the other party's performance because, using the substantial performance test referenced above and explained below, if Contractor's performance is otherwise perfect, Contractor almost certainly has substantially performed.

2.   Why have some courts concluded, unlike the *Pederson* court, that "time is of the essence" clauses always create express conditions? (Hint: Interpret the language to develop your argument.)

3.   Why have other courts agreed with the *Pederson* court's approach?

Pederson v. McGuire

333 N.W.2d 823

HENDERSON, Justice.... This action revolves around a tract of commercial property and a building known as Cargill Tract # 1 in the Northeast Quarter (NE 1/4) of Section Sixteen (16), Township One Hundred One (101) North, Range Forty-nine (49) West, Minnehaha County, South Dakota, also known as 707 Weber Avenue, Sioux Falls, South Dakota (Cargill Tract # 1).

On August 26, 1946, the City of Sioux Falls, South Dakota, by ordinance, granted to the Chicago and Northwestern Transportation Company (the Railroad) an irrevocable easement for a railway right-of-way on Weber Avenue which is contiguous with Cargill Tract # 1. The sole method of ingress and egress to Cargill Tract # 1 is over the Railroad easement. Railroad traffic on the easement ceased in 1975. Appellees Pedersons acquired Cargill Tract # 1 in 1978 and negotiated an agreement with the Railroad granting a license to install a private roadway crossing over the easement. Numerous conditions upon appellees and their successors in interest were contained in the license, including the ability of the Railroad to cancel the license on 30 days' notice. The agreement was filed on public record with the Minnehaha County Register of Deeds on February 17, 1978. A major portion of the railroad track was removed in 1980.

On February 23, 1981, appellant Sioux Sound Co. executed a real estate purchase agreement for Cargill Tract # 1. Closing was set for May 1, 1981, with appellees to place appellant in possession on closing. Appellees were required to furnish title insurance showing good and merchantable title on closing. Additionally, appellees were to provide a warranty deed upon full payment of the purchase price which was not due at closing. The agreement provided: "TIME is the essence of this contract."

Appellant's attorney discovered the 1946 easement and 1978 license when he reviewed the title insurance policy during April of 1981. Although appellees never mentioned the 1978 license to appellant or the realtor, appellant's president, Mr. McGuire had previously visited Cargill Tract # 1 several times and had observed a portion of railroad track in the parking area of the tract. On May 7, 1981, appellant notified the realtor that because of the 1978 license, closing was cancelled and appellant was cancelling the purchase agreement. Appellees proposed to amend the 1978 license to remove the 30-day cancellation clause and reduce the insurance requirements. Appellant responded in a May 15, 1981 letter to the realtor that appellees' proposals were unacceptable.

On June 10, 1981, appellees offered to have the 1978 license terminated, and on August 19, 1981, appellees filed with the Register of Deeds an addendum to the 1978 license which granted a permanent roadway crossing. Appellees' measures did not satisfy appellant and a trial ensued. The trial court's reconsideration opinion required appellees, at their own expense, to terminate the Railroad's interest in the easement. On July 23, 1982, appellees filed with the Register of Deeds an agreement to cancel the right of the Railroad in the easement ...

Appellant was to purchase Cargill Tract # 1 for $135,000.00. Payment terms called for: (1) $1,000.00 in earnest money at the signing of the agreement; (2) $29,000.00 cash on closing; (3) a $42,000.00 first mortgage to be obtained from First Service Mortgage Corporation with no specified date for payment of proceeds to appellees; and (4) the balance of the purchase price, approximately $63,000.00, to be carried by appellees as a second mortgage.

Appellees agreed to "execute and deliver a good and sufficient Warranty Deed upon payment of the full purchase price called for herein." Undoubtedly, by the terms of the agreement, appellees' obligation to deliver a warranty deed was tied to the ambiguous date for disbursement of the first mortgage proceeds. Therefore, although the purchase agreement explicitly stated that time was of the essence, the performance of its critical obligations, tender of deed, and payment of the full purchase price were indefinite.

SDCL 53-10-3 provides: "Time is never considered as of the essence of the contract, unless by its terms expressly so provided." A determination whether or not time is of the essence depends upon the intention of the parties and the purpose of the contract, rather than printed contract clauses claiming time to be of the essence. *Farmers Coop. Ass'n v. Dobitz,* 240 N.W.2d 116 (1976); *Phillis v. Gross,* 143 N.W. 373 (1913);[6] *W. Town Site Co. v. Lamro Town Site Co.,* 139 N.W. 777 (1913).[7] *See also, Jackson v. Holmes,* 307 So.2d 470 (Fla.App.1975). In *Boekelheide v. Snyder,* 26 N.W.2d 74, 76 (1947), we held that when a real estate contract fails to set a time for full payment, we will imply that payment is to be made within a reasonable time. Since the terms of parties' contract were indefinite as to when tender of deed and full payment were to occur, we are unable to hold that time was of the essence as regards tender and full payment. The import of this holding is that appellees had a reasonable time to cure any title defects.

Specific performance is an equitable remedy addressed to the sound discretion of the trial court, to be granted or denied according to the facts and circumstances in each case. [Citations omitted.] SDCL 21-9-6 provides: "An agreement for the sale of property cannot be specifically enforced in favor of

---

6. In *Phillis,* the printed contract form provided that time was of the essence, and the parties added that all overdue sums of money would draw interest. We responded by holding time was not of the essence due to the intention of the parties.

7. In *W. Town Site,* 31 S.D. at 57, 139 N.W. at 779, we held: "It is a question of construction, and, unless it plainly appears that the object and purpose of the contract depends upon its being performed by a given date, time will never be construed to be of the essence of the contract."

a seller who cannot give to the buyer a title free from reasonable doubt." In ... [another case], we interpreted the predecessor of SDCL 21-9-6, which is identical, and held: "This refers to the condition of title at the time fixed for performance ..." [Citation omitted.]

Terms of the purchase agreement did require that on closing appellees were to place appellant in possession of Cargill Tract # 1 and furnish title insurance covering a good and merchantable title of record, "free and clear of all encumbrances unless otherwise agreed to herein." The title insurance company excepted the 1978 license from its coverage. However, earlier language of the purchase agreement made the sale subject to "Conditions, Restrictions and Easements of record, if any ..." Therefore, by the very terms of the purchase agreement, appellant agreed to purchase Cargill Tract # 1 subject to the easement and 1978 license, as both were of public record when the purchase agreement was signed.

Ample evidence further exists in the record of appellees' diligent efforts, and eventual success, in clearing the title of Cargill Tract # 1 within a reasonable time. A contract vendee may not rescind as long as the vendor is sincerely acting to perform his duty to perfect the title. [Citation omitted.] Here, appellees did cancel the easement in its entirety. Any claimed defect was cured. The reconsideration opinion and judgment of the trial court are affirmed upon this issue.

Affirmed ...

Exercise 12-7: *Pederson v. McGuire* Revisited

The City of Columbia has been chosen as the site of the Super Bowl in the year 2018. You are the city attorney and you have been directed to prepare a contract with Connie's Construction, a construction firm that the city has hired to build a new football stadium. The stadium **must be** completed by January 19, 2018, or the city will be humiliated on a national scale and suffer enormous financial losses. The city wants to be assured that the stadium is completed on time, and that it has no obligation to pay if the stadium is not completed on time. Draft an appropriate contract clause to accomplish the city's goals. Then explain how your chosen clause meets the city's needs. **Please note: There are many possible solutions to this problem. Be creative.**

"Satisfaction" Clauses

Exercise 12-8: *Mattei v. Hopper*

You already are familiar with "satisfaction" clauses; you learned about them in connection with your study of illusory promise. You may recall the *Omni Group* case, in which the buyer of land promised to buy on the condition that it obtain feasibility reports from an architect and from an engineer that were "satisfactory" to the buyer.

"Satisfaction" clauses always seem to use the word "satisfy" or "satisfied" or "satisfaction" (although a synonym probably would be treated similarly); like the clause in *Omni Group*, they state that the party will only perform if that party (or a third-party designee, such as the party's engineer or architect) is satisfied with the work or with some issue with respect to going forward with the deal. Courts overwhelmingly treat "satisfaction" clauses as express conditions. The tricky issue, addressed in *Mattei v. Hopper*, deals with the standards courts use to determine whether the satisfaction condition has been met. As you learned in connection with the *Omni Group* case, courts need a standard to determine whether the clause has been met because, absent a standard, the word "satisfied" would leave the promisor free to perform or withdraw without liability. *Mattei v. Hopper* does a good job explaining the two standards and when courts use each one. Make sure you get those points from the case.

Mattei v. Hopper
330 P.2d 625 (1958)

SPENCE, Justice.

Plaintiff brought this action for damages after defendant allegedly breached a contract by failing to convey her real property in accordance with the terms of a deposit receipt which the parties had executed. After a trial without a jury, the court concluded that the agreement was "illusory" and lacking in "mutuality." From the judgment accordingly entered in favor of defendant, plaintiff appeals.

Plaintiff was a real estate developer. He was planning to construct a shopping center on a tract adjacent to defendant's land. For several months, a real estate agent attempted to negotiate a sale of defendant's property under terms agreeable to both parties. After several of plaintiff's proposals had been rejected by defendant because of the inadequacy of the price offered, defendant submitted an offer. Plaintiff accepted on the same day.

The parties' written agreement was evidenced on a form supplied by the real estate agent, commonly known as a deposit receipt. Under its terms, plaintiff was required to deposit $1,000 of the total purchase price of $57,500 with the real estate agent, and was given 120 days to "examine the title and consummate the purchase." At the expiration of that period, the balance of the price was "due and payable upon tender of a good and sufficient deed of the property sold." The concluding paragraph of the deposit receipt provided: "Subject to Coldwell Banker & Company obtaining leases satisfactory to the purchaser." This clause and the 120-day period were desired by plaintiff as a means for arranging satisfactory leases of the shopping center buildings prior to the time he was finally committed to pay the balance of the purchase price and to take title to defendant's property.

Plaintiff took the first step in complying with the agreement by turning over the $1,000 deposit to the real estate agent. While he was in the process of securing the leases and before the 120 days had elapsed, defendant's attorney notified plaintiff that defendant would not sell her land under the terms contained in the deposit receipt. Thereafter, defendant was informed that satisfactory leases had been obtained and that plaintiff had offered to pay the balance of the purchase price. Defendant failed to tender the deed as provided in the deposit receipt.

Initially, defendant's thesis that the deposit receipt constituted no more than an offer by her, which could only be accepted by plaintiff notifying her that all of the desired leases had been obtained and were satisfactory to him, must be rejected. Nowhere does the agreement mention the necessity of any such notice. Nor does the provision making the agreement "subject to" plaintiff's securing "satisfactory" leases necessarily constitute a condition to the existence of a contract. Rather, the whole purchase receipt and this particular clause must be read as merely making plaintiff's performance dependent on the obtaining of "satisfactory" leases. Thus a contract arose, and plaintiff was given the power and privilege to terminate it in the event he did not obtain such leases. [Citation omitted.] This accords with the general view that deposit receipts are binding and enforceable contracts. [Citation omitted.]

However, the inclusion of this clause, specifying that leases "satisfactory" to plaintiff must be secured before he would be bound to perform, raises the basic question whether the consideration supporting the contract was thereby vitiated. When the parties attempt, as here, to make a contract where promises are exchanged as the consideration, the promises must be mutual in obligation. In other words, for the contract to bind either party, both must have assumed some legal obligations. Without this mutuality of obligation, the agreement lacks consideration and no enforceable contract has been created. [Citation omitted.] Or, if one of the promises leaves a party free to perform or to withdraw from the agreement at his own unrestricted pleasure, the promise is deemed illusory and it provides no consideration. [Citation omitted.] Whether these problems are couched in terms of mutuality of obligation or the illusory nature of a promise, the underlying issue is the same — consideration. [Citation omitted.]

While contracts making the duty of performance of one of the parties conditional upon his satisfaction would seem to give him wide latitude in avoiding any obligation and thus present serious consideration problems, such "satisfaction" clauses have been given effect. They have been divided into two primary categories and have been accorded different treatment on that basis. First, in those contracts where the condition calls for satisfaction as to commercial value or quality, operative fitness, or mechanical utility, dissatisfaction cannot be claimed arbitrarily, unreasonably, or capriciously [citation omitted], and the standard of a reasonable person is used in determining whether satisfaction has been received. [Citations omitted.] ... However, it would seem that the factors involved in determining whether a lease is satisfactory to the lessor are too numerous and varied to permit the application of a reasonable man standard as envisioned by this line of cases. Illustrative of some of the factors which would have to be considered in this case are the duration of the leases, their provisions for renewal options, if any, their covenants and restrictions, the amounts of the rentals, the financial responsibility of the lessees, and the character of the lessees' businesses.

This multiplicity of factors which must be considered in evaluating a lease shows that this case more appropriately falls within the second line of authorities dealing with "satisfaction" clauses, being those involving fancy, taste, or judgment. Where the question is one of judgment, the promisor's determination that he is not satisfied, when made in good faith, has been held to be a defense to an action on the contract. [Citations omitted.] Although these decisions do not expressly discuss the issues of mutuality of obligation or illusory promises, they necessarily imply that the promisor's duty to exercise his judgment in good faith is an adequate consideration to support the contract ...

The judgment is reversed.

Exercise 12-9: *Mattei v. Hopper* Revisited

1. Buyer purchased a washing machine on the condition that it worked to his "satisfaction." If Buyer were to later claim dissatisfaction, return the washing machine, and refuse to pay for it, which of the two standards discussed in *Mattei* would the court use to determine whether the buyer has breached the contract?

2. Owner entered into a contract with Contractor for Contractor to extend Owner's house by building Owner a conservatory. Owner agreed to pay on the condition that his architect certifies in writing that he was "satisfied" with the workmanship. Contractor built the conservatory. Because of relatively minor defects, which did not significantly affect the value or use of the conservatory, but which could not be repaired without tearing down the conservatory and starting over, the architect refused to certify that he was "satisfied." Owner therefore refused to pay.

   a. Issue 1: Which of the two standards discussed in *Mattei* would the court use to determine whether Owner has breached the contract?
   b. Issue 2: Under the standard you identified above, argue both sides of the issue as to whether Owner has breached.

Express Condition Review

Exercise 12-10: Express Condition Problems and Exercises

1. Analyze the following mini-hypotheticals. In each of the following cases, determine whether the duties that arise out of the promises described are conditional or unconditional. You may wish to refer back to the Restatement's definition of a condition. (Assume in each case that the promise is supported by consideration.)

   a. A promise to pay $100 after a specified date.

   b. A promise to pay $100 if Ms. Z is elected Governor.

   c. A and B enter into a contract pursuant to which A agrees to sell B A's home. The contract provides that A will install a sprinkler system "before close of escrow."

2. Analyze in writing the following longer problem:

    Ima Inventor was an experienced construction contractor. She had an idea for a new construction process (pre-fabrication in a manufacturing plant), which, if successful, would revolutionize the construction industry by reducing construction costs while increasing quality. On June 1, 2013, Ima brought her idea to Linda Landowner, a wealthy land developer who owned some nearby, undeveloped land and was planning to build houses on the land. Ima and Linda discussed Ima's need for financing for her dream project and Linda's somewhat conflicting need to be sure the construction contractor she hired would complete the job. The parties therefore agreed that they would not allow Ima simply to "walk away" if Ima did not get the funding she desired. The parties also discussed the uncertainties involved in the development of any new process and Linda's willingness to be flexible in terms of a completion date for her project, and they agreed their contract also would address this issue.

    Linda then prepared a written contract, which both parties signed on July 1, 2013. The valid, enforceable contract consisted of 30 pages. The contract provided, among other things, that Ima would build 100 houses on Linda's land and according to Linda's specifications (which were attached to the contract). It also provided that Ima would complete construction within two years of the date of the contract and Linda would pay Ima $500,000. The contract also contained, among others, the following relevant clauses (Professor's note: THE CLAUSES QUOTED BELOW ARE THE **ONLY** RELEVANT CLAUSES IN THE PARTIES' WRITING):

    > Ima Inventor will begin construction only following her receipt of an 8% interest rate loan from Ima's bank to fund her development of the manufacturing plant and construction process contemplated by this agreement.

    > This agreement is final but the parties recognize provisions of this agreement may need to be revised to accommodate Ima's progress in developing her construction innovations.

    After trying as hard as was humanly possible, Ima was unable to get a loan from her bank (or from any of the ten other banks to which she applied for a loan for the project) at an interest rate below 9%. She therefore telephoned Linda and said, "I'm sorry, but I couldn't get the loan we agreed I'd need to go forward with our project. I hope we can work together on some future project." Ima never built the houses. Linda sued Ima for breach of contract.

    Discuss all the issues raised by the question of whether Ima breached the contract.

3. So far, we have identified some words and phrases that all courts would agree create express conditions (*e.g.*, "on the condition that"), some that all courts would agree do not create express conditions (*e.g.*, "I promise"), and some about which reasonable lawyers and judges could argue either way (*e.g.*, "when").

    a. Review all the cases, hypotheticals and examples we have studied regarding express conditions. Identify and classify all the examples into one of the three above categories: (1) words and phrases all courts would agree create express conditions, (2) words and phrases all courts would agree do not create express conditions, and (3) words and phrases about which reasonable lawyers could disagree.

b. Review the lists you created in response to the previous question. Working with a dictionary or thesaurus, brainstorm as many additional possible examples in each category as you can.

Constructive Conditions

Review of Introduction to Contract Meaning and Contract Performance

Imagine again the client who came to you to enforce an alleged promise to remove an old shed where the promise to remove the shed was not contained in the parties' writing. As we discussed, by applying what we have learned about the parol evidence rules, you would be able to assess whether a court would conclude the alleged oral promise to remove the storage shed was part of the parties' contract. Assume that, for one reason or another, you determine a court likely would conclude that the oral promise was a part of the contract. Also assume that, based on contract interpretation, you can determine that the party breached the contract by knocking down the shed but not removing the debris. However, knowing that the promise was a part of the contract and knowing that the failure to remove the debris was a breach does NOT tell you what the legal consequences are.

In the materials that follow, we will continue working on evaluating the significance of contract breaches. So far we have looked at conditions in general and at express conditions, that is, terms that parties expressly include in their contracts to create conditions. Next, we will consider when courts will impose conditions in contracts where the parties have not expressly done so. In other words, we will consider the law of constructive conditions.

As you may recall, we are focusing on the following issues:

(1) What terms do courts treat as part of the contract for the purposes of determining what each party has promised? (In other words, what is the contract)

(2) How do courts determine what the words obligated the parties to do? (In other words, what does the contract mean?)

(3) Did the parties properly and fully perform? (In other words, did either party breach?)

(4) Assuming either party did not properly do everything she promised to do, what is the consequence of any breach?

The topic of constructive conditions involves further consideration of the second, third and fourth of these questions. The second question is relevant because courts determine whether to impose a condition based, in large part, on their interpretation of the parties' intent. The third question is relevant because in order to determine whether there has been a breach, particularly in cases where neither party has performed, we need to know who was supposed to go first or whether the parties were supposed to start performing at the same time. Finally, the fourth question is relevant because, once we decide that a party breached the contract, we still need to figure out the legal consequence of that breach. Does the breach excuse the other party's duty to perform as well as giving rise to a claim for a remedy or does the breach give rise to a claim for a remedy but not excuse the other party's performance? The answer to this question, we will learn, depends on the seriousness of the breach.

Introduction to Constructive Conditions

Imagine the following scenario: Jenny and Helen enter into a law school success joint venture agreement pursuant to a detailed written contract. The contract lays out a list of 30 contractual duties (15 duties owed by each party [briefing, outlining, writing practice exams]). The agreement includes no express conditions. Both parties do nothing and both sue the other for breach. Why might a court want to imply conditions here? Because conditions will allow the court to determine the order of performance, *i.e.*, who was supposed to do what and when she was supposed to do it, so the court can determine who is breach—one, neither, or both parties.

In many bilateral contracts, the parties simply lay out each party's obligations and make no mention as to the order in which the parties must perform. This omission, as the preceding hypothetical suggests, has the potential to create chaos because, where the parties are agreeing to many performances under the contract, no one knows who must do what first. Through the device of creating constructive conditions, courts impose an order of performance. In other words, courts determine who was supposed to go first. In such cases, courts say they are imposing "constructive conditions precedent." Sometimes, however, parties intend their performances to have occurred at the same time. In such a case, a court still would impose conditions, but the conditions the courts would impose would be labeled "constructive conditions concurrent." A constructive condition concurrent requires each party, if she wishes to have the other party deemed in breach, to perform (render) or to offer (tender) her performance. Finally, parties sometimes intend a promise or set of promises to be "independent". This means that the promisor must perform the independent promise regardless of whether the other party has performed any of his or her promises. Promises that are also constructive conditions precedent, for example, are **always** independent promises— the party who must go first has made a promise that must be performed before the other party is obliged to do anything. While many contracts include independent promises, contracts in which all of the parties' obligations are independent are rare. These ideas can be expressed as a set of rules, set forth below, that describe the effect of constructive conditions.

Once you grasp the practical significance of the question of whether a promise is independent, a constructive condition precedent, or a constructive condition concurrent, you are ready to tackle the more challenging issue: How do courts determine what the parties intended in terms of order of performance? In other words, how do courts decide which party was supposed to go first, second, third, etc. or determine that the parties' performances were to have been rendered simultaneously? The materials and cases below develop those rules and demonstrate their application.

After a court has determined it will impose a constructive condition, the court must then determine whether the construction condition has occurred. When we studied express conditions, we learned that the standard for evaluating whether an express condition has occurred is "strict compliance" (perfect performance). The standard for measuring the occurrence of constructive conditions is a different one—"substantial performance." As we will learn, to determine whether there has been substantial performance (*i.e.*, to determine whether a constructive condition has occurred), courts weigh five factors.

Finally, after a court has determined that a party has or has not substantially performed a promise that is also a constructive condition, the court must then determine the consequence of the success or failure to substantially perform. You actually know the answer to this last point. As we learned in connection with express conditions, if ANY kind of condition does not occur, it excuses the performance of any promise dependent on the occurrence of that condition.

Effect of Constructive Conditions

Exercise 12-11: Effect of Constructive Conditions

1. Below are the three rules that describe the effect of constructive conditions. Make sure you understand these rules. You will see them lurking and/or stated in most of the constructive conditions cases you will be reading.

Rules Regarding the Effect of Constructive Conditions

(1) If the court determines the parties intended that one party go first, it will impose a "constructive condition precedent," which means that the party whose performance must happen second has no duty to perform unless the other party has performed.

(2) If the court determines the parties intended that both parties perform at the same time, it will impose a "constructive condition concurrent," which means that each party must perform (render) or offer to perform (tender) for the other party to have a duty to perform.

(3) If the court determines the parties intended that a promise or set of promises must be performed regardless of whether any other performance is rendered first, the court will deem that promise "independent," which means that the promisor must perform the promise regardless of whether the other party has performed any of his or her promises.

2. A crucial step in understanding constructive conditions law is making sure you are comfortable with the varied terminology used by the courts to express their analysis. Many of these terms appear in the above discussion. Review the three columns of terminology and draw lines to match the terms from each of the three columns to their equivalents in the other two columns.

Dependent	Unconditional	Other party must go first
Independent	Constructive condition precedent	Both parties must render or tender performance
Mutually dependent	Constructive condition concurrent	Promisor goes first

Creation of Constructive Conditions

Our next step is to identify the rules that govern the creation of constructive conditions and to see how courts apply those rules. There are five rules you need to know; translate each rule below into your own words.

Rules Regarding the Creation of Constructive Conditions

(1) As a general rule, to determine the order of performance, courts impose constructive conditions on bilateral contracts.

(2) If the parties' contract specifies dates and/or times or relative dates and/or times (e.g., "after" "before") for performance, those specified dates/relative times determine the order of performance and the creation of constructive conditions.

(3) If both parties can perform at the same time, they must perform at the same time and each must perform (render) or offer to perform (tender) to put the other party in breach.

(4) If one party's performance requires a period of time and the other's can be performed all at once, the party whose performance requires a period of time must perform first.

(5) If the order of performance is unclear, courts create constructive conditions based on the nature of the transaction and what the parties must have intended given the deal they made.

Exercise 12-12: Creation of Constructive Conditions: *Kingston v. Preston*

As you read *Kingston v. Preston*, consider the following questions:

1. To understand the constructive conditions cases (and exam questions and real contracts), it is crucial that you identify all of the promises made by the parties. The most effective way to do so is to create a "Contract Obligations Chart" like the chart at the top of the facing page for *Kingston v. Preston*. Therefore, to be prepared for class with respect to any of the constructive conditions cases, you should create a "Contract Obligations Chart."

Contract Obligations Chart
Kingston v. Preston

Π's DUTIES	Δ's DUTIES
Serve D as an apprentice (servant) for next 1 and 1/4 years	Pay P 200 pounds/year while P is an apprentice
Buy D's business with (D's designee) from D, paying fair value for D's stock	Sell P and D's designee (probably D's nephew) D's business and stock
Execute a 14-year partnership agreement with D's designee	Let P and D's designee use D's house to carry on the business
Pay D 250 pounds per month until the value of the stock is reduced to 4,000 pounds	
Give D good and sufficient security (before the sealing and delivery of D's deeds)	

2. Aside from the contract terms, identify all of the additional relevant facts in *Kingston v. Preston*.

3. Given what you learned about express conditions, why didn't the court just conclude that the plaintiff's delivery of security was an express condition, the non-occurrence of which excused defendant's duty to sell?

4. What did the court conclude was the legal significance of plaintiff's failure to deliver the security?

5. The court identifies three types of covenant. What are those three types and what does the court say are the legal ramifications of each of them?

6. The court said the security was the "essence of the agreement" and therefore was a condition precedent to defendant transferring title to the business to plaintiff. Why did the court reach this conclusion? Explain the court's reasoning in your own words.

7. In which of the court's three categories, therefore, does the court conclude the promise to deliver the security falls? What does the label mean?

8. Why do we allow the courts to "impose" conditions "in absence of or irrespective of the manifested intention of the parties"? In other words, what is the policy for allowing courts to create conditions?

Kingston v. Preston

(1773) 2 Doug. 690

It was an action of debt, for non-performance of covenants contained in certain articles of agreement between the plaintiff and the defendant. The declaration stated:

> That, by articles made the 24th of March, 1770, the plaintiff, for the considerations therein-after mentioned, covenanted, with the defendant, to serve him for one year and a quarter next ensuing, as a covenant-servant, in his trade of a silk-mercer, at £200 a year, and in consideration of the premises, the defendant covenanted, that at the end of the year and a quarter, he would give up his business of a mercer to the plaintiff, and a nephew of the defendant, or some other person to be nominated by the defendant, and give up to them his stock in trade, at a fair valuation; and that, between the young traders, deeds of partnership should be executed for 14 years, and from and immediately after the execution of the said deeds, the defendant would permit the said young traders to carry on the said business in the defendant's house.

Then the declaration stated a covenant by the plaintiff, that he would accept the business and stock in trade, at a fair valuation, with the defendant's nephew, or such other person, &c. and execute such deeds of partnership, and, further, that the plaintiff should, and would, at, and before, the sealing and delivery of the deeds, cause and procure good and sufficient security to be given to the defendant, to be approved of by the defendant, for the payment of £250 monthly, to the defendant, in lieu of a moiety of the monthly produce of the stock in trade, until the value of the stock should be reduced to £4000.

Then the plaintiff averred, that he had performed, and been ready to perform, his covenants, and assigned for breach on the part of the defendant, that he had refused to surrender and give up his business, at the end of the said year and a quarter.

The defendant pleaded, 1. That the plaintiff did not offer sufficient security; and, 2. That he did not give sufficient security for the payment of the £250, &c.

And the plaintiff demurred generally to both pleas.

On the part of the plaintiff, the case was argued by Mr. Buller, who contended, that the covenants were mutual and independent, and, therefore, a plea of the breach of one of the covenants to be performed by the plaintiff was no bar to an action for a breach by the defendant of one of which he had bound himself to perform, but that the defendant might have his remedy for the breach by the plaintiff, in a separate action.

On the other side, Mr. Grose insisted, that the covenants were dependent in their nature, and, therefore, performance must be alleged: the security to be given for the money, was manifestly the chief object of the transaction, and it would be highly unreasonable to construe the agreement, so as to oblige the defendant to give up a beneficial business, and valuable stock in trade, and trust to the plaintiff's personal security, (who might, and, indeed, was admitted to be worth nothing,) for the performance of his part.

In delivering the judgment of the Court, Lord Mansfield expressed himself to the following effect: There are three kinds of covenants: 1. Such as are called mutual and independent, where either party may recover damages from the other, for the injury he may have received by a breach of the covenants in his favour, and where it is no excuse for the defendant, to allege a breach of the covenants on the part of the plaintiff. 2. There are covenants which are conditions and dependent, in which the performance of one depends on the prior performance of another, and, therefore, till this prior condition is performed, the other party is not liable to an action on his covenant. 3. There is also a third sort of covenants, which are mutual conditions to be performed at the same time; and, in these, if one party was ready, and offered, to perform his part, and the other neglected, or refused, to perform his, he who was ready, and offered, has fulfilled his engagement, and may maintain an action for the default of the other; though it is not certain that either is obliged to do the first act.

His Lordship then proceeded to say, that the dependence, or independence, of covenants, was to be collected from the evident sense and meaning of the parties, and, that, however transposed they might be in the deed, their precedency must depend on the order of time in which the intent of the transaction requires their performance. That, in the case before the Court, it would be the greatest injustice if the plaintiff should prevail: the essence of the agreement was, that the defendant should not trust to the personal security of the plaintiff, but, before he delivered up his stock and business, should have good security for the payment of the money. The giving such security, therefore, must necessarily be a condition precedent.

Judgment was accordingly given for the defendant, because the part to be performed by the plaintiff was clearly a condition precedent.

Exercise 12-13: Creation of Constructive Conditions (cont'd): *Kingston v. Preston* Revisited and *Price v. Van Lint*

1. If the plaintiff in Kingston had been wealthy and had possessed more than enough assets to pay all of the money due under the parties' contract, would the result in this case have been any different?

2. As you read *Price v. Van Lint*, look for answers to the following questions:

    a. Create a "Contract Obligations Chart" for *Price v. Van Lint*.

    b. Identify the key facts of the *Price* case in addition to those stated in the parties' agreement.

    c. The *Price* court concludes that the defendant did have a duty to lend the plaintiff the funds notwithstanding the fact that the plaintiff had not given the defendant the required security. Reconcile this outcome with the outcome in the *Kingston* case.

    d. On what rules regarding conditions did the court rely?

    e. How did the court apply the rules you identified in response to the previous question to the facts of the case?

    f. What's the policy reason for the court's conclusion in this case?

Price v. Van Lint
120 P.2d 611 (1941)

SADLER, Justice.

In the trial of this action the district court had before it for construction the following agreement in writing, signed by the plaintiff and by the defendant, for claimed breach of which the former sought damages, to-wit:

> Cimarron, N.M. 12-23-1939
>
> This agreement, entered into by V. J. Van Lint party of the first part and C. S. Price, party of the second part,
>
> First party agrees to deposit the sum of fifteen hundred on or before the first day of February, A. D. 1940 for which security said party of the second part agrees to give mortgage-deed and insurance for the full sum of fifteen hundred dollars and agrees to use the above named amount for erecting a building on the land purchased from the Maxwell Land grant Company for which a warranty-deed will be executed and delivered. Party of the second part agrees to keep all taxes and insurance paid up to date on the above described property.
>
> Party of the second Part   Party of the first Part.
>
> (Sgd.) C.S. Price   (Sgd. V.J. Van Lint)

This inartificially drawn contract resulted from the joint efforts of the parties thereto, the plaintiff having contributed its phraseology in seemingly extemporaneous dictation to the defendant who furnished the mechanical skill of reducing it to form on the typewriter. The parties to the contract and to this action both resided at Cimarron, in Colfax County, New Mexico. The defendant was local agent for Maxwell Land Grant Company at the time of the contract but without authority to execute a deed on its behalf. The plaintiff, desiring to purchase a small tract of land near Cimarron and to construct a building thereon in which to conduct a business, negotiated with the defendant touching the matter. The contract in question resulted. It embodies mutual covenants and reflects the plaintiff's plan for financing both the purchase of the site and the construction of the building.

Anticipatory of the loan mentioned in the writing, the defendant advanced for the plaintiff's account the sum of $134, the agreed sale price of the tract being purchased as a site, repayable from the proceeds of the loan. This sum, along with a deed prepared by the defendant, in due course was dispatched to Amsterdam in the Kingdom of Netherlands. Likewise and in due course, said deed was returned from Amsterdam, apparently the residence of officials of the grantor with authority to act in this connection, and duly delivered to the plaintiff in the early part of March, 1940. Both parties were aware of the necessity of these steps being taken to consummate the purchase and that a considerable time would necessarily elapse before the deed could be delivered to the plaintiff.

In the meantime, the plaintiff seemed anxious to proceed with the construction of the proposed building. The defendant had left Cimarron in late December for a sojourn of more than two months at Corpus Christi, Texas. Apparently, meeting with disappointment in realizing funds from which to make the agreed loan, the defendant sought release from the contract under which he obligated himself to make it. This is shown by the correspondence passing between the parties. Indeed, the tenor of defendant's letters to him was such that the plaintiff very well might have elected to claim an anticipatory breach of the agreement. But he did not do so. On the contrary, he refused to release defendant from the contract and on January 16, 1940, caused his attorney to make telegraphic demand on defendant for performance, declaring: "Your contract has not been canceled and Price (the plaintiff) will hold you liable to any actual damages which may result to him by your failure to comply with agreement.... If money agreed to be loaned not here by February first you will be held liable for actual damages."

No mutual rescission thus having resulted and the plaintiff not having elected to claim an anticipatory breach of the agreement, the defendant also employed an attorney who, prior to February 1, 1940, the date upon which the defendant promised to deposit the amount of the loan, conferred with the plaintiff's attorney regarding the matter. At this conference, both attorneys treated the loan agreement as still in force and subject to performance, disagreeing only as to what should be deemed proper performance thereof.

Eliminating recital of the steps by which the parties arrived at their respective positions, it appears from a finding based on the letter of January 24, 1940, from defendant's attorney to plaintiff's attorney, that prior to February 1, 1940, the date on or before which the defendant was required to "deposit" the amount of the loan, he made the following offer of performance to the plaintiff, to-wit: " ... that he (defendant) deposit in First National Bank in Raton before February 1, 1940, the full sum of the contemplated loan (that is to say, $1,500.00

less the $134.00 already advanced), this amount to be made available to the plaintiff as soon as the plaintiff should receive his deed to the property in question and as soon as the plaintiff and his wife should give a suitable first mortgage deed as security for the money, the money to be disbursed in any reasonable manner satisfactory to both parties, guaranteeing that it would be used to pay off all possible material and labor claims which might give rise to mechanic's liens so as to insure that the mortgage would be a first lien."

The plaintiff refused this tender of performance and through his attorney by letter of January 24, 1940, advised defendant's attorney as follows: "If Mr. Van Lint will deposit and make available to Mr. Price for the purpose of paying bills on or before the first day of February, 1940, the sum of $1,366. plus $72.00 to cover a portion of the actual expense which his announced failure to comply with his agreement has caused Mr. Price, Price and his wife will sign the note for $1,500.00 according to the terms and on the form shown you this afternoon, and will also execute and acknowledge a formal written contract to execute and deliver a mortgage upon the tract of land purchased from the Maxwell Land Grant, including of course the new improvements being now constructed thereon, and as security for said note, and will waive any and all other damages which he feels he has obviously suffered in connection with this matter."

After receipt of the letter of January 24, 1940, just quoted, the defendant's attorney on January 29, 1940, addressed the following communication to the plaintiff's attorney: "Since you and Mr. Price have rejected in advance a literal compliance with the contemplated loan arrangement, it would be a useless and futile thing for Mr. van Lint to arrange for depositing the money along the lines which I suggested to you. Accordingly, Mr. van Lint will not arrange for the deposit of the money and will not advance any more money to Mr. Price."

Touching these matters, the trial court made the following additional findings:

> "That the defendant has never receded from his position as expressed in the letters of January 24, 1940, and January 29, 1940, written by his attorney, and the plaintiff has never receded from his position as expressed in the letter of January 24, 1940, written by his attorney.
>
> That the plaintiff has never tendered to the defendant any mortgage deed; that the defendant has never offered to or been willing to advance to the plaintiff the balance of the agreed loan prior to the receiving from the plaintiff of a valid mortgage deed on said premises; that the plaintiff has never repaid to the defendant the sum of $ 134.00 advanced to him by the defendant or any part thereof or any interest thereon."

For such weight as they properly may have in construing the contract involved, the substance of other findings should be stated at this time. They stand unchallenged. Indeed, none of the facts found by the court as hereinabove recited, are excepted to by either party.

The court found that the loan was to be for a period of two years; that the loan was to bear interest at the rate of 10% per annum; that the mortgage was to cover the land being purchased by the plaintiff from Maxwell Land

Grant Company; and that the "deposit" was to be made at First National Bank in Raton.

It further found that prior to his departure for Corpus Christi, Texas, the defendant informed Lorenzo Rosso of Cimarron, New Mexico, doing business as Cimarron Mercantile Company, and R. E. Adams of Springer, New Mexico, doing business as R. E. Adams Lumber Company, of his agreement to make a loan of $1,500 to the plaintiff; that on January 9, 1940, the defendant wrote and mailed a letter to said Lorenzo Rosso at Cimarron, New Mexico, stating that the contemplated loan to plaintiff was not going through due to unforeseen difficulties met with by the defendant; that a similar notice was given by defendant to R. E. Adams Lumber Company; and "that some time thereafter both Cimarron Mercantile Company and R. E. Adams Lumber Company refused to extend any substantial further credit to the plaintiff."

It was also found that because of defendant's refusal to advance the amount of the loan to plaintiff on or before February 1, 1940, the plaintiff was compelled to suspend construction work on his building; that but for said refusal, the building would have been ready for use and occupancy by February 10, 1940, instead of April 27, 1940.

The trial court concluded: "That the written agreement made and entered into by and between the plaintiff and defendant, a copy of which is attached to the plaintiff's Complaint and marked Exhibit A, when properly construed, required the defendant to deposit the balance of the agreed loan on or before February 1, 1940, and that the amount so deposited should be immediately paid to the plaintiff, whether or not the plaintiff should at that time have received a deed to the real estate, and whether or not the plaintiff should at that time be the legal owner or the record owner of said real estate, and whether or not the plaintiff at that immediate time should be able to give a valid mortgage, and whether or not the real estate at that time should be free from liens and encumbrances; that the defendant, in refusing to deposit said balance for the plaintiff's immediate use on or before February 1, 1940, breached said agreement, and the defendant is liable to the plaintiff for the damages resulting therefrom."

Having thus concluded, the court rendered judgment in plaintiff's favor for $543.55, being the aggregate amount of plaintiff's damage as ascertained in specific findings, after deducting therefrom $134 advanced by defendant to cover the purchase price of the real estate with accrued interest thereon.

We have, then, the case of an agreement by the defendant to make a loan to the plaintiff in the sum of $1,500 for two years at a specified rate of interest; to deposit the amount thereof in a certain bank on or before a fixed date; and to have as security for the loan a mortgage lien on a certain tract of land then being purchased by the plaintiff from a third party, whose deed to plaintiff, it was known to the parties, necessarily could not be delivered for some time, although neither party to the contract doubted its ultimate delivery. The trial court construed the relative obligations of the parties under this agreement as set forth in its conclusion of law hereinabove quoted. The court held in substance and effect that the written agreement, interpreted in the light of the unchallenged findings, imposed upon the defendant the obligation to deposit to the plaintiff's credit in the bank named the amount of the loan, notwithstanding the fact that because of the delayed delivery of the deed, the plaintiff could not then deliver to the defendant the mortgage which was to furnish the security for the loan.

The correctness of the trial court's ruling on this question presents the main point for decision in the case. It involves the determination whether the plaintiff's promise to give a mortgage to secure the promised loan and the defendant's promise to make the loan are dependent or independent covenants of the contract. If the former, then the plaintiff's failure to allege performance denies him the right of recovery. If the latter, the defendant was under obligation to perform his covenant and look to his remedy for any breach of performance on the plaintiff's part. [Citations omitted.]

The rule of decision is not to construe promises as independent unless the nature of the contract or the surrounding circumstances compel a contrary inference. In other words, interpretation favors the conclusion of an agreed exchange of performance as the true intent of the parties unless such a construction does violence to the language employed in the light of known facts and circumstances.... "It is a general rule that covenants are to be construed to be either dependent or independent of each other, according to the intention and understanding of the parties and the common sense of the case."

... "Where a contract contains mutual promises to pay money or perform some other act, and the time for performance for one party is to, or may, arrive before the time for performance by the other, the latter promise is an independent obligation, and nonperformance thereof merely raises a cause of action in the promisee, and does not defeat the right of the party making it to recover for a breach of the promise made to him. Contract construed, and agreement held to be independent."

When we apply [this] to the situation disclosed by the contract in question, interpreted in the light of the findings made, we are compelled to hold with the trial court that the mutual covenants are independent of each other.

We are not unfamiliar with the rule that where the mutual covenants go to the entire consideration on both sides, they are considered mutual conditions and dependent unless there are clear indications to the contrary. [Citation omitted.] We seek, then, in the findings, something to support the trial court's conclusion that the covenants are independent. The contract in question was made on December 23, 1939. It obligated the defendant to deposit in First National Bank in Raton, New Mexico, the amount of the loan on or before February 1, 1940. It obligated the plaintiff to give as security a mortgage on the land he was purchasing from Maxwell Land Grant Company. It was well known to both parties that the deed must go to Amsterdam in the Kingdom of the Netherlands for execution by proper officers of the corporate grantor and that a considerable period would "necessarily elapse before said deed could be delivered to the plaintiff". While it may be said to have been within the contemplation of the parties that by expedient passage and return, a delivery could occur before the defendant was called upon to perform by depositing the loan in the bank agreed upon; nevertheless, and necessarily, the parties must have known that the day for performance by defendant might arrive before the plaintiff would be in a position to give the promised mortgage following delivery of his deed upon its return from abroad. This brings the case squarely within the test ...

Exercise 12-14: *Ziehen v. Smith* **and** *Stewart v. Newbury*

Ziehen v. Smith and *Stewart v. Newbury* illustrate the two rules addressed in Restatement Second of Contracts Section 234. As you read *Ziehen* and *Stewart*, consider the following questions:

1. Read and paraphrase section 234.

2. Create a "Contract Obligations Chart" for *Ziehen v. Smith*.

3. Identify the key facts of the *Ziehen* case in addition to those stated in the parties' agreement.

4. The *Ziehen* court concluded that the existence of the unknown mortgage and foreclosure action did not excuse the plaintiff's failure to render or tender performance.

    a. The court began its analysis by affirming the trial court's conclusion that all the parties' obligations other than the plaintiff's duty to make the $500 downpayment were due on September 15, 1892. On what basis did the court reach that conclusion?

    b. What rules did the court state in reaching its conclusion?

    c. How did the court apply the rules you identified in response to the previous question?

    d. Why does the court conclude that the defendant could have removed the encumbrance?

    e. Surely, it would have taken the defendant time to pay off that loan; in other words, the defendant could not have paid it off in time to perform on September 15. Why doesn't that fact excuse the plaintiff's tender duty? Reconcile the outcome in the *Ziehen* case with the outcome in *Price v. Van Lint*.

5. Create a "Contract Obligations Chart" for *Stewart v. Newbury*.

6. Identify the key facts of the *Stewart* case in addition to the terms stated in the parties' agreement.

7. Why wasn't Stewart entitled to be paid for the work he had done between July and September?

Ziehen v. Smith

148 N.Y. 558

O'BRIEN, J.

The plaintiff, as vendee, under an executory contract for the sale of real estate, has recovered of the defendant, the vendor, damages for a breach of the contract to convey, to the extent of that part of the purchase money paid at the execution of the contract, and for certain expenses in the examination of the title. The question presented by the record is whether the plaintiff established at the trial such a breach of the contract as entitled him to recover.

By the contract, which bears date August 10th, 1892, the defendant agreed to convey to the plaintiff by good and sufficient deed the lands described therein, being a country hotel with some adjacent land. The plaintiff was to pay for the same the sum of $3,500, as follows: $500 down, which was paid at the time of the execution of the contract, $ 300 more on the 15th day of September, 1892. He was to assume an existing mortgage on the property of $1,000, and the balance of $1,700 he was to secure by his bond and mortgage on the property, payable, with interest, one year after date. The courts below have assumed that the payment of the $300 by the plaintiff, the execution of the bond and mortgage, and the delivery of the conveyance by the defendant, were intended to be concurrent acts, and, therefore, the day designated by the contract for mutual performance was the 15th of September, 1892. Since no other day is mentioned in the contract for the payment of the money, or the exchange of the papers, we think that this construction was just and reasonable, and, in fact, the only legal inference of which the language of the instrument was capable. It is not alleged or claimed that the plaintiff on that day, or at any other time, offered to perform on his part or demanded performance on the part of the defendant, and this presents the serious question in the case and the only obstacle to the plaintiff's recovery. It is, no doubt, the general rule that in order to entitle a party to recover damages for the breach of an executory contract of this character he must show performance or tender of performance on his part. He must show in some way that the other party is in default in order to maintain the action, or that performance or tender has been waived. But a tender of performance on the part of the vendee is dispensed with in a case where it appears that the vendor has disabled himself from performance, or that he is on the day fixed by the contract for that purpose, for any reason, unable to perform. The judgment in this case must stand, if at all, upon the ground that on the 15th day of September, 1892, the defendant was unable to give to the plaintiff any title to the property embraced in the contract, and hence any tender of performance on the part of the plaintiff, or demand of performance on his part, was unnecessary, because upon the facts appearing it would be an idle or useless ceremony.

It appeared upon the trial that at the time of the execution of the contract there was another mortgage upon the premises of $ 1,500, which fact was not disclosed to the plaintiff, and of the existence of which he was then ignorant. That on or prior to the 21st of July, 1892, some twenty days before the contract was entered into, an action was commenced to foreclose this mortgage, and notice of the pendency of the action filed in the county clerk's office; that on the 30th of September following judgment of foreclosure was granted and entered on the 31st of October thereafter, and on the 28th of December the property was sold to a third party by virtue of the judgment, and duly conveyed by deed from the referee. It appears that the defendant was not the maker of this mortgage and was not aware of its existence, but it was made by a former owner, and the defendant's title was subject to it when he contracted to sell the property to the plaintiff.

The decisions on the point involved do not seem to be entirely harmonious. In some of them it is said that the existence, at the date fixed for performance, of liens or encumbrances upon the property is sufficient to sustain an action by the vendee to recover the part of the purchase money paid upon the contract. [Citations omitted.] The general rule, however, to be deduced from an examination of the leading authorities seems to be that in cases where by the terms of the contract the acts of the parties are to be concurrent, it is the duty of him who seeks to maintain an action for a breach of the contract, either by way of damages for the non-performance, or for the recovery of money paid thereon, not only to be ready and willing to perform on his part, but he must demand performance from the other party. The qualifications to this rule are to be found in cases where the necessity of a formal tender or demand is obviated by the acts of the party sought to be charged as by his express refusal in advance to comply with the terms of the contract in that respect, or where it appears that he has placed himself in a position in which performance is impossible. If the vendor of real estate, under an executory contract, is unable to perform on his part, at the time provided by the contract, a formal tender or demand on the part of the vendee is not necessary in order to enable him to maintain an action to recover the money paid on the contract, or for damages. [Citations omitted.]

In this case there was no proof that the defendant waived tender or demand either by words or conduct. The only difficulty in the way of the performance on his part was the existence of the mortgage which the proof tends to show was given by a former owner and its existence on the day of performance was not known to either party. In order to sustain the judgment we must hold that the defendant on the day of performance was unable to convey to the plaintiff the title which the contract required, simply because of the existence of the encumbrance. We do not think that it can be said upon the facts of this case that the defendant had placed himself in such a position that he was unable to perform the contract on his part and that his title was destroyed or that it was impossible for him to convey within the meaning of the rule which dispenses with the necessity of tender and demand in order to work a breach of an executory contract for the sale of land. It cannot be affirmed under the circumstances that if the plaintiff had made the tender and demand on the day provided in the contract that he would not have received the title which the defendant had contracted to convey. The contract is not broken by the mere fact of the existence on the day of performance of some lien or encumbrance which it is in the power of the vendor to remove. That is all that was shown in this case, and hence the judgment was recovered in violation of an important principle of the law governing contracts.

For this reason the judgment should be reversed and a new trial granted, costs to abide the event. All concur. Judgment reversed.

Stewart v. Newbury

115 N.E. 984

CRANE, J. The defendants are partners in the pipe fitting business under the name of Newbury Manufacturing Company. The plaintiff is a contractor and builder residing at Tuxedo, N. Y. The parties had the following correspondence about the erection for the defendants of a concrete mill building at Monroe, N. Y.:

> Alexander Stewart, Contractor and Builder, Tuxedo, N. Y., *July* 18*th*, 1911. Newbury Mfg. Company, Monroe, N. Y.:
>
> Gentlemen. — With reference to the proposed work on the new foundry building I had hoped to be able to get up and see you this afternoon, but find that impossible and am, in consequence, sending you these prices, which I trust you will find satisfactory. I will agree to do all excavation work required at sixty-five ($ .65) cents per cubic yard. I will put in the concrete work, furnishing labor and forms only, at Two and 05-100 ($2.05) Dollars per cubic yard. I will furnish labor to put in reenforcing at Four ($4.00) Dollars per ton.
>
> I will furnish labor only to set all window and door frames, window sash and doors, including the setting of hardware for One Hundred Twelve ($112) Dollars. As alternative I would be willing to do any or all of the above work for cost plus 10 per cent., furnishing you with first class mechanics and giving the work considerable of my personal time.
>
> Hoping to hear favorably from you in this regard, I am, Respectfully yours,
>
> (signed) ALEXANDER STEWART.
>
>
> The Newbury Mfg. Co.,
> Steam Fittings, Grey Iron Castings,
> Skylight Opening Apparatus,
> Monroe, N. Y.
> Telephone Connection. Monroe, N. Y., *July* 22, 1911."
>
> Alexander Stewart,
> Tuxedo Park, N. Y.:
>
> Dear Sir. — Confirming the telephone conversation of this morning we accept your bid of July the 18th to do the concrete work on our new building. We trust that you will be able to get at this the early part of next week.
>
> Yours truly,
>
> THE NEWBURY MFG. CO.,
> H. A. Newbury.

Nothing was said in writing about the time or manner of payment. The plaintiff, however, claims that after sending his letter and before receiving that of the defendant he had a telephone communication with Mr. Newbury and said: "I will expect my payments in the usual manner," and Newbury said, "All right, we have got the money to pay for the building." This conversation over the telephone was denied by the defendants.

The custom, the plaintiff testified, was to pay 85% every thirty days or at the end of each month, 15% being retained till the work was completed.

In July the plaintiff commenced work and continued until September 29th, at which time he had progressed with the construction as far as the first floor.

He then sent a bill for the work done up to that date for $896.35. The defendants refused to pay the bill and work was discontinued.

The plaintiff claims that the defendants refused to permit him to perform the rest of his contract, they insisting that the work already done was not in accordance with the specifications. The defendants claimed upon the trial that the plaintiff voluntarily abandoned the work after their refusal to pay his bill.

On October 5, 1911, the defendants wrote the plaintiff a letter containing the following: "Notwithstanding you promised to let us know on Monday whether you would complete the job or throw up the contract, you have not up to this time advised us of your intention.... Under the circumstances we are compelled to accept your action as being an abandonment of your contract and of every effort upon your part to complete your work on our building. As you know, the bill which you sent us and which we declined to pay is not correct, either in items or amount, nor is there anything due you under our contract as we understand it until you have completed your work on our building."

To this letter the plaintiff replied the following day. In it he makes no reference to the telephone communication agreeing, as he testified, to make "the usual payments," but does say this: "There is nothing in our agreement which says that I shall wait until the job is completed before any payment is due, nor can this be reasonably implied.... As to having given you positive date as to when I should let you know what I proposed doing, I did not do so; on the contrary I told you that I would not tell you positively what I would do until I had visited the job, and I promised that I would do this at my earliest convenience and up to the present time I have been unable to get up there."

The defendant Herbert Newbury testified that the plaintiff "ran away and left the whole thing." And the defendant F. A. Newbury testified that he was told by Mr. Stewart's man that Stewart was going to abandon the job; that he thereupon telephoned Mr. Stewart, who replied that he would let him know about it the next day, but did not.

In this action, which is brought to recover the amount of the bill presented, as the agreed price and $95.68 damages for breach of contract, the plaintiff had a verdict for the amount stated in the bill, but not for the other damages claimed, and the judgment entered thereon has been affirmed by the Appellate Division.

The appeal to us is upon exceptions to the judge's charge. The court charged the jury as follows: "Plaintiff says that he was excused from completely performing the contract by the defendants' unreasonable failure to pay him for the work he had done during the months of August and September.... Was it understood that the payments were to be made monthly? If it was not so understood the defendants' only obligation was to make payments at reasonable periods, in view of the character of the work, the amount of work being done and the value of it. In other words, if there was no agreement between the parties respecting the payments, the defendants' obligation was to make payments at reasonable times.... But whether there was such an agreement or not, you may consider whether it was reasonable or unreasonable for him to exact a payment at that time and in that amount."

The court further said, in reply to a request to charge: "I will say in that connection, if there was no agreement respecting the time of payment, and if there was no custom that was understood by both parties, and with respect to which they made the contract, then the plaintiff was entitled to payments at reasonable times."

The defendants' counsel thereupon made the following request, which was refused: "I ask your Honor to instruct the jury that if the circumstances existed as your Honor stated in your last instruction, then the plaintiff was not entitled to any payment until the contract was completed."

The jury was plainly told that if there were no agreement as to payments, yet the plaintiff would be entitled to part payment at reasonable times as the work progressed, and if such payments were refused he could abandon the work and recover the amount due for the work performed.

This is not the law. Counsel for the plaintiff omits to call our attention to any authority sustaining such a proposition and our search reveals none. In fact the law is very well settled to the contrary. This was an entire contract. [Citation omitted.] Where a contract is made to perform work and no agreement is made as to payment, the work must be substantially performed before payment can be demanded....

The judgment should be reversed, and a new trial ordered, costs to abide the event.

Exercise 12-15: *Ziehen v. Smith* and *Stewart v. Newbury* Revisited

1. What if the buyer in *Ziehen* had just notified the seller that it was ready to perform?

2. What if the buyer in *Ziehen* had just contacted the seller on September 15th and demanded performance?

3. Laura Landowner hired Constance Contractor to build Laura a house on land owned by Laura for $100,000. They agreed to the following performance schedule. Explain the order of performance. (Note: This contract is more typical of the real world.)

   $20,000 on completion of the foundation

   $20,000 on completion of the framing

   $20,000 on completion of the roof and walls

   $20,000 on completion of the house

   $20,000 on final approval by the City

Occurrence of Constructive Conditions

It is not sufficient to establish that a promise is also a constructive condition. To complete the analysis, you must also determine whether the constructive condition has occurred. Consider the following hypothetical:

A parent promises to pay a child her allowance if she fully cleans her room. The child makes her bed, vacuums the carpet, and dusts the furniture but misses two sheets of scrap paper that have fallen behind her desk. Should she get her allowance?

As we have learned, because cleaning a room requires a period of time, the child must perform first; in other words, the child's duty to clean is also a constructive condition precedent of the parent's duty to pay. However, as you learned from the *Oppenheimer* case, while express conditions require perfect performance, constructive conditions require substantial performance.

Exercise 12-16: Substantial Performance

Section 241 of the Second Restatement of Contracts states the substantial performance test. Read the section and answer the following questions:

1. Section 241 refers to the "circumstances significant in determining whether a failure is material." What is the relationship between substantial performance and material breach?

2. Are the circumstances labeled (a)–(e) in section 241 elements or factors?

3. Restate each circumstance, (a), (b), (d) and (e) in your own words and explain the relationship of that circumstance to the overall question of whether a party has substantially performed. (**For example:** circumstance (c) refers to whether the breaching party "will suffer forfeiture." The court will consider the harm to the breaching party were the court to determine that the breaching party has not substantially performed. In other words, because a determination that a party has materially breached means the other party's duty to perform is excused, a court will consider the extent of loss the breaching party will suffer. If the breaching party will lose a lot, her performance appears more substantial; if that party will lose only a little, her performance appears more insubstantial).

Exercise 12-17: *Plante v. Jacobs*

1. Summarize the key facts of *Plante v. Jacobs*.

2. Based on what you have learned about the creation of constructive conditions, what was the order of performance of the contract in *Plante* and why?

3. The court concluded that the plaintiff in *Plante* substantially performed. Why does it matter whether the plaintiff substantially performed? What would the legal consequences have been if the court had concluded that the plaintiff had not substantially performed?

4. Apply the substantial performance standard from section 241 to the facts of *Plante*. Be sure to evaluate and weigh each of the section 241 factors.

5. Which of the section 241 factors seems most significant given the *Plante* court's analysis of that case?

6. Reconcile separately the boiler, boathouse and paint cases discussed by the court in *Plante*.

7. The *Plante* court also analyzes what the plaintiff should get as a remedy.

a. What damages rules did the court use?

b. How did the court apply those rules to the facts of the case?

c. Would the result have been the same if the misplaced wall in *Plante* had caused a $4,000 diminution in value?

Plante v. Jacobs

103 N.W.2d 296 (1960)

HALLOWS, Justice.

The defendants argue the plaintiff cannot recover any amount because he has failed to substantially perform the contract. The plaintiff conceded he failed to furnish the kitchen cabinets, gutters and downspouts, sidewalk, closet clothes poles, and entrance seat amounting to $1,601.95. This amount was allowed to the defendants. The defendants claim some 20 other items of incomplete or faulty performance by the plaintiff and no substantial performance because the cost of completing the house in strict compliance with the plans and specifications would amount to 25 or 30 per cent of the contract price. The defendants especially stress the misplacing of the wall between the living room and the kitchen, which narrowed the living room in excess of one foot. The cost of tearing down this wall and rebuilding it would be approximately $4,000. The record is not clear why and when this wall was misplaced, but the wall is completely built and the house decorated and the defendants are living therein. Real estate experts testified that the smaller width of the living room would not affect the market price of the house.

The defendants ... [argue] there can be no recovery on the contract as distinguished from *quantum meruit* unless there is substantial performance. This is undoubtedly the correct rule at common law.... The question here is whether there has been substantial performance. The test of what amounts to substantial performance seems to be whether the performance meets the essential purpose of the contract. In the ... [cited] case the contract called for a boiler having a capacity of 150 per cent of the existing boiler. The court held there was no substantial performance because the boiler furnished had a capacity of only 82 per cent of the old boiler and only approximately one-half of the boiler capacity contemplated by the contract. In ... [another case], the contract provided the plaintiff was to drive pilings in the lake and place a boat house thereon parallel and in line with a neighbor's dock. This was not done and the contractor so positioned the boat house that it was practically useless to the owner. [A third case] ... involved a contract to paint a house and to do a good job, including the removal of the old paint where necessary. The plaintiff did not remove the old paint, and blistering and roughness of the new paint resulted. The court held that the plaintiff failed to show substantial performance.... [A fourth case] involved a contract to install a heating and ventilating plant in the school building which would meet certain tests which the heating apparatus failed to do. The heating plant was practically a total failure to accomplish the purposes of the contract....

Substantial performance as applied to construction of a house does not mean that every detail must be in strict compliance with the specifications and the plans. Something less than perfection is the test of specific performance unless all details are made the essence of the contract. This was not done here. There may be situations in which features or details of construction of special or of great personal importance, which if not performed, would prevent a finding of substantial performance of the contract. In this case the plan was a stock floor plan. No detailed construction of the house was shown on the plan. There were no blueprints. The specifications were standard printed forms with some modifications and additions written in by the parties. Many of the problems that arose during the construction had to be solved on the basis of practical experience. No mathematical rule relating to the percentage of the price, of cost of completion or of completeness can be laid down to determine substantial performance of a building contract. Although the defendants received a house with which they are dissatisfied in many respects, the trial court was not in error in finding the contract was substantially performed.

The next question is what is the amount of recovery when the plaintiff has substantially, but incompletely, performed. For substantial performance the plaintiff should recover the contract price less the damages caused the defendant by the incomplete performance.... [T]he correct rule for damages due to faulty construction amounting to such incomplete performance ... is the difference between the value of the house as it stands with faulty and incomplete construction and the value of the house if it had been constructed in strict accordance with the plans and specifications. This is the diminished-value rule. The cost of replacement or repair is not the measure of such damage, but is an element to take into consideration in arriving at value under some circumstances. The cost of replacement or the cost to make whole the omissions may equal or be less than the difference in value in some cases and, likewise, the cost to rectify a defect may greatly exceed the added value to the structure as corrected. The defendants argue that ... their damages are $10,000. The plaintiff on review argues the defendants' damages are only $650. Both parties agree the trial court applied the wrong rule to the facts.

The trial court applied the cost-of-repair or replacement rule as to several items, relying on ... [a case that held that,] when there are a number of small items of defect or omission which can be remedied without the reconstruction of a substantial part of the building or a great sacrifice of work or material already wrought in the building, the reasonable cost of correcting the defect should be allowed. However, ... when the separation of defects would lead to confusion, the rule of diminished value could apply to all defects.

In this case no such confusion arises in separating the defects. The trial court disallowed certain claimed defects because they were not proven. This finding was not against the great weight and clear preponderance of the evidence and will not be disturbed on appeal. Of the remaining defects claimed by the defendants, the court allowed the cost of replacement or repair except as to the misplacement of the living-room wall. Whether a defect should fall under the cost-of-replacement rule or be considered under the diminished-value rule depends upon the nature and magnitude of the defect. This court has not allowed items of such magnitude under the cost-of-repair rule as the trial court did. Viewing the construction of the house as a whole and its cost we cannot say, however, that the trial court was in error in allowing the cost of repairing the plaster cracks in the ceilings, the cost of mud jacking and repairing the patio floor, and the cost of reconstructing the non-weight-bearing and nonstructural patio wall. Such reconstruction did not involve an unreasonable economic waste.

The item of misplacing the living room wall under the facts of this case was clearly under the diminished-value rule. There is no evidence that defendants requested or demanded the replacement of the wall in the place called for by the specifications during the course of construction. To tear down the wall now and rebuild it in its proper place would involve a substantial destruction of the work, if not all of it, which was put into the wall and would cause additional damage to other parts of the house and require replastering and redecorating the walls and ceilings of at least two rooms. Such economic waste is unreasonable and unjustified. The rule of diminished value contemplates the wall is not going to be moved. Expert witnesses for both parties, testifying as to the value of the house, agreed that the misplacement of the wall had no effect on the market price. The trial court properly found that the defendants suffered no legal damage, although the defendants' particular desire for specified room size was not satisfied....

On review the plaintiff raises two questions: Whether he should have been allowed compensation for the disallowed extras, and whether the cost of reconstructing the patio wall was proper. The trial court was not in error in disallowing the claimed extras. None of them was agreed to in writing as provided by the contract, and the evidence is conflicting whether some were in fact extras or that the defendants waived the applicable requirements of the contract. The plaintiff had the burden of proof on these items. The second question raised by the plaintiff has already been disposed of in considering the cost-of-replacement rule.

It would unduly prolong this opinion to detail and discuss all the disputed items of defects of workmanship or omissions. We have reviewed the entire record and considered the points of law raised and believe the findings are supported by the great weight and clear preponderance of the evidence and the law properly applied to the facts.

Judgment affirmed.

Exercise 12-18: *Plante v. Jacobs* Revisited

1. Would the result in this case have been different if the contract had provided, "Contractor promises to strictly comply with all terms and conditions in this contract and all specifications attached hereto"?

2. Analyze the problems below. Ignore the impossibility issues in both hypotheticals.

   a. A service station operator enters into two contracts with a major oil company: (1) a lease agreement for the premises where the service station is located, pursuant to which the operator is obligated to make monthly rental payments to the oil company; and (2) a contract pursuant to which the operator agrees to purchase at least 200,000 gallons of gasoline from the oil company per year, and the oil company agrees to supply all of the operator's gasoline requirements, not to exceed 500,000 gallons per year. In July, the oil company failed to fill the operator's requirements for that month, citing a request from the Federal Energy Office to allocate its existing gasoline supply among its dealers. In August, the operator failed to make its lease rental payment, citing the oil company's failure to perform under the requirements contract. The parties sue for declaratory relief. Discuss whether the operator is obligated to make the August rental payment under the lease.

b. On August 1, 2014, Alex, an experienced trial attorney, hired Bianca, an appeal specialist, to draft an appellate brief for one of Alex's clients. Bianca agreed to complete the brief "absolutely no later than October 1, 2014." Alex agreed to "pay Bianca $5,000 for the brief, with the stipulation that the brief must be in final form." Bianca reviewed the trial transcript, researched the issues, drafted the brief, and rewrote her draft five times. On September 15, Bianca mailed the brief to Alex together with a cover letter and an invoice. The letter described the brief as being "complete" and "final" in accordance with the contract. The letter also sought payment of the enclosed invoice. Alex reviewed the brief and telephoned Bianca to discuss Alex's comments. At the end of the discussion, Bianca agreed to research one more point, which Alex and Bianca had agreed might affect a portion of the brief. Before Bianca began the research, however, the President appointed Bianca to the Seventh Circuit Court of Appeals. As a result, Bianca could not complete the brief. Must Alex pay Bianca?

Performance under Article 2 of the U.C.C.

Introduction

The purpose of this section of the chapter is two-fold. First, the materials are designed to teach you the key points of law with respect to contract performance under Article 2 of the U.C.C. A full treatment is beyond the scope of this book, but you can expect to gain a good sense of the major issues from these materials. Second, these materials are designed to continue your development of statutory construction skills. In prior chapters of this book, you developed your skill in outlining and applying statutes. However, in most of those exercises, we directed you to particular sections of the U.C.C. As you now have a bit more experience, the problems that follow are more challenging. Each one requires you to find the relevant section or sections of the U.C.C. and then read, interpret, and apply that section or sections. Some of the problems include hints to get you started.

Exercise 12-19: Contract Performance under Article 2 of the U.C.C.

1. Manufacturing, Inc. entered into a written contract with Widgets Corp. to buy 500,000 widgets from Widgets for $500,000.

    a. Assume neither party did anything.

       i. If Widgets sued Manufacturing for breach, what result? (*Hint: Start with the index to Article 2 of the U.C.C. While the U.C.C.'s label for the part in which the key statute appears is quite helpful, the particular section on point is harder to find. There are two applicable sections—one for buyers and one for sellers.*)

      ii. Based on the rules you found in response to the previous question, what types of condition(s) does the U.C.C. create?

    b. Assume the contract included the following term: "Delivery C.O.D." Then assume the following chain of events. Seller tendered the goods. Buyer insisted on looking over the goods before deciding whether to pay. Seller refused to allow Buyer to inspect unless Buyer pays first. Who is in breach? (*Hint: Make sure you identify the normal rule and any possible exception implicated by the "Delivery C.O.D." clause.*)

    c. Assume the contract included the following term: "The parties agree that Widgets' duty to deliver the widgets described in this contract is expressly conditional on Manufacturing paying the contract price ($500,000) in full." Assume neither party did anything. If Manufacturing sued Widgets for breach, what would be the result?

    d. What if both parties in problem 1.a properly offered to perform but neither did anything else? (*Hint: This problem implicates several sections.*)

2.   Seller contracted to deliver to Buyer 50,000 widgets (at a price of $10 per widget) delivery to be made on July 1, 2015. A widget is a precision component used by Buyer, a manufacturer, to manufacture Buyer's main product.

    a. On June 1, 2015, Seller delivered the widgets but each one had a small defect that would slow down Buyer's manufacturing process by 50%. Buyer rejected the widgets specifying the problem arising from the defect.

       i. Is Buyer's rejection proper?

      ii. Does Seller have any rights?

    b. What if, in the previous hypothetical, Buyer, who needed to manufacture its product for a big order, sent the same rejection but used 10,000 of the widgets for its big order?

    c. If, in the previous hypothetical, the defect in the widgets had no effect on Buyer's manufacturing process but it meant that each widget differed from the specifications and requirements stated in the parties' contract, can Buyer lawfully reject by e-mailing Seller a rejection? Assume that the defect would have no effect on Buyer's ability to sell its products.

    d. Assume that Seller shipped the widgets to Buyer's business, and Buyer spent two months after delivery inspecting each widget. Buyer then returned the widgets to Seller after identifying a genuine defect in every widget that made the widgets half as valuable to Buyer. The defect was only discoverable upon microscopic inspection. Seller claims Buyer accepted the goods and can recover damages but cannot return the widgets. Is Seller correct?

Divisibility

Exercise 12-20: *Sterling v. Gregory* and *Tipton v. Feitner*

Read section 240 of the SECOND RESTATEMENT OF CONTRACTS and the *Sterling* and *Tipton* cases and then answer the following questions:

1. Section 240 tells you the test for determining whether a contract is "divisible." Restate section 240 into your own words.

2. Apply section 240 to the facts of both cases. Make sure you can reconcile the results of the two cases.

3. Based on what you learned from *Tipton*, of what effect is a material breach of one but not both parts of a contract divisible into two parts?

4. What fact, not discussed by the *Tipton* court, might have led a different court to have reached a different result?

Sterling v. Gregory

85 P. 305 (1906)

SLOSS, J.

Action for damages for breach of contract. The plaintiff was the owner of certain orange groves in San Bernardino county, known as the 'Upper Orchard,' and alleges an agreement with defendant, by the terms of which the latter agreed to buy all the oranges grown on this orchard at the price of 1¼ cents per pound. After the contract was partly executed, the defendant refused to accept or pay for any more fruit, and the plaintiff, after selling the remaining fruit for less than the contract price, brings this action to recover the difference. The answer denies that the contract was merely for the purchase and sale of the oranges grown on the groves described in the complaint, and alleges that the agreement between the parties was that defendant should handle, pack, ship and sell for the account of plaintiff all the oranges grown on two other orchards belonging to plaintiff, and known as the 'Triangle' and 'Klondike' groves; that as part of the same contract and in consideration of having the handling of the crops from said groves the defendant agreed to buy all the oranges on the 'Upper Orchard' at 1¼ cents per pound. The answer then goes on to allege that before the deliveries from the 'Upper Orchard' were complete, the plaintiff broke his contract as to the 'Triangle' and 'Klondike' groves by selling the fruit grown on those groves to other parties; that thereby there was a partial failure of consideration as to the defendant, and he promptly rescinded the contract and restored to plaintiff everything of value which he had received from him. The findings on these issues were in favor of defendant, and he had judgment for his costs. Plaintiff appealed from the judgment within 60 days, and brings up the evidence by means of a bill of exceptions.

The appellant contends that the findings as to the contract between the parties are unsustained by the evidence. But this contention cannot prevail. While the plaintiff testified that he made no agreement regarding the fruit on the 'Triangle' and 'Klondike' groves other than he would give the handling of it to the defendant in case he should decide to ship it, two witnesses, in addition to the defendant himself, testified to an unconditional agreement that the defendant was to have the handling of the fruit from these groves at 50 cents per box, and was to buy the fruit from the 'Upper Orchard' at 1 ¼ cents per pound. And the further finding that the purchase and sale of the oranges from the 'Upper Orchard' was a part of the contract for the handling of the fruit from the other groves, and was made in consideration of defendant's having the handling of such fruit, also finds sufficient support in the record. There is testimony to the effect that the agreed price of 50 cents per box for handling would have allowed the defendant a profit of 25 cents per box. And the defendant, in stating the conversation between himself and the plaintiff regarding the transaction, gave this version: 'I told him ... that a cent and a quarter was full market value at that time; but inasmuch as I would have the privilege of shipping the two other orchards below the railroad, the Klondike and the Triangle, that would realize me some profit that we would be sure of, as we were not taking the chances of the market on these two orchards, and that I thought I could handle the other orchards, paying him the cent and a quarter with this understanding, ... Mr. Sterling accepted my proposition.' This testimony, if believed by the trial court, as it evidently was, fully justified the finding.

The appellant's main contention is that the contract, assuming it to have been made as found by the court, was not an entire contract; that the stipulation for the sale of fruit from the 'Upper Orchard' and the one regarding the handling of other fruit, were distinct and severable, and that, therefore, a breach of one furnished no ground for rescinding the other. It may readily be conceded that if the evidence went no further than to show that, at one and the same time, the parties agreed that the plaintiff should sell to the defendant, at a given price, the oranges from one grove, and that he should deliver to the defendant for handling, the oranges from other groves, for a compensation of 50 cents per box, the agreement for sale and the agreement for handling, would form separate and independent undertakings, and a breach of one would not authorize a rescission of the other. The several things required to be done by plaintiff were to be done at different times, and the money consideration to be paid for them was not entire, but was apportioned to each of the items to be performed. There is ample authority for the proposition that in such case the stipulations are ordinarily regarded as severable and independent.... But it must be remembered that the question whether a contract is entire or whether its various stipulations are to be regarded as severable is a question of construction. The court seeks to determine the intent of the parties from a consideration of all the circumstances surrounding the making of the contract. The rule is ... as follows: "A contract is entire, and not severable, when by its terms, nature, and purpose it contemplates and intends that each and all of its parts, material provisions and the consideration, are common each to the other and independent.... On the other hand, a severable contract is one in its nature and purpose susceptible of division and apportionment, having two or more parts, in respect to matters and things contemplated and embraced by it, not necessarily dependent upon each other, nor is it intended by the parties that they shall be.... It is sometimes difficult to determine whether the contract is entire or severable in such cases, and there is great diversity of decisions on the subject, but on the whole, the weight of opinion, and the more reasonable rule would seem to be that where there is a purchase of different articles at different prices at the same time, the contract would be severable as to each article, unless the taking of the whole was rendered essential either by the nature of the subject-matter or by the act of the parties. This rule makes the interpretation of the contract depend on the intention of the parties as manifested by their acts and the circumstances of each particular case." And the cases relied on by appellant, in which this court has declared certain contracts to be severable, all recognize that the intention of the parties governs and that stipulations apparently distinct and separate may, by the agreement of the parties, be made to be mutually dependent and to form parts of an entire contract....

The case at bar differs in its facts from all those cited in that the answer alleged and the court found that the two undertakings of the plaintiff as to the different groves were, in fact, by the agreement of the parties, made parts of one contract, and the agreement to buy the oranges from one grove was in consideration of defendant's having the handling of the oranges from the other groves. This was in effect an allegation and finding that the contract was entire and not severable. Such finding being, as we have seen, sustained by the evidence, it follows that on the refusal by the plaintiff to fully perform his part of the contract, there was a partial failure of consideration, which ... gave the defendant the right to rescind.... By the judgment, the defendant recovered costs against the plaintiff....

Tipton v. Feitner
20 NY 423 (1859)

APPEAL from the Supreme Court. Action to recover the price of certain slaughtered hogs, sold by the plaintiffs to the defendant. It was defended on the ground that they were purchased under a special contract with the plaintiffs, which had been violated on their part. The case, according to the finding of the referee, before whom it was tried, was as follows: On the 3d day of February, 1855, at the city of New York, the plaintiffs agreed with the defendant, by parol, by one and the same contract, to sell the defendant eighty-eight dressed hogs, then at the slaughter-house of a third person, in the city, at 7 cents per pound; and also certain live hogs of the plaintiffs, which were being driven, and were then on their way from the State of Ohio to New York, at 5 1/4 cents per pound live weight, the defendant agreeing on his part to buy the dressed and live hogs at these prices. The dressed hogs were to be delivered immediately after the sale, and the live ones on their arrival at the city, where they were expected, and did arrive some days afterwards. The dressed hogs were delivered on the same day, but were not paid for by the defendant. The live hogs arrived five days afterwards; they were not delivered to the defendant, but were slaughtered by the plaintiffs, and by them sold to other parties. The defendant insisted that the plaintiffs could not recover for the dressed hogs, on the ground that they had failed to perform their agreement as to the live ones. The referee however held, that the plaintiffs were entitled to recover the price of the dressed hogs, deducting the damages which the defendant had sustained for the breach of the other branch of the contract; and he reported accordingly. The dressed hogs came to $1,182.57; deducted for defendant's damages, $401, leaving $780.38, for which judgment was given, which was affirmed at a general term. The defendant appealed....

DENIO, J.

It is not universally true that a party to a contract who has himself failed to perform some of its provisions is thereby precluded from recovering damages for a breach committed by the other party. The question in such cases is, whether the stipulation which the plaintiff has failed to observe was a condition precedent to the performance by the defendant; and whether it is of that character or not depends upon the general scope and intention of the agreement, to be gathered from its several provisions. If the parties have in terms stipulated that the defendant's performance shall be dependent or conditional upon something to be done by the plaintiff, the case is a plain one. It is equally so where the act to be done by the plaintiff must naturally precede, in the order, of time what the defendant is called upon to do, and where the former is necessary to be done to enable the defendant to perform; and also where the defendant's performance is the payment or equivalent for something which he is to receive from the plaintiff, unless, in the latter case, it is provided that such equivalent is to be rendered in advance of what is to be received on account of it, credit being given for the latter.

In contracts for the purchase of property, real or personal, where there is no stipulation for credit or delay on either side, the delivery of the property (or its conveyance where it is of a nature to pass by grant), and the payment of the price are each conditions of the other, and neither party can sue for a breach without having offered performance on his part. Such was the nature of the contract in this case. The plaintiffs had slaughtered hogs and also live hogs to dispose of, and the defendant agreed to purchase the whole of both kinds, and to pay a certain price per pound, discriminating, however, as to price between the two species of property. There was no agreement for credit for any part of the property for any time; and in the absence of such a stipulation we must consider that it was to be paid for on delivery, and that the delivery of the property and the payment of the price were to be concurrent acts. But a question then arises, whether the contract was entire in the sense that a delivery of the whole — the live hogs as well as the dressed meat — was to precede the payment for the latter; and it is upon the answer to that inquiry, as I think, that this case depends. And I am of the opinion that the bargain respecting the several kinds of property, in regard to the payment for each, is to be taken distributively. The dressed hogs were to be delivered immediately, while those which were alive, and were on their way from Ohio, were to be delivered when they should arrive. It would not be unreasonable for the parties to have agreed that payment for those first delivered should be postponed until the others came to hand, so that there should be one settlement for the whole; but it would be a more probable mode of adjustment for the purchaser to agree to pay for the parcel which he was to receive at once, and for the other when he should receive it. In that way neither of the parties would be called upon to trust the other — and there being nothing in the contract which looked to credit, we cannot, I think, reasonably hold that any was contemplated. The difference in the kind of property, in the price, and in the time of delivery showed such a diversity in the two operations as to preclude any necessary or probable inference that the one first to be consummated by delivery was to be suspended, as to its liquidation, for the period, more or less uncertain, which might elapse before the other would be ready for adjustment. Upon the construction of so peculiar an agreement a precise precedent is not to be expected. . . .

Assuming that I am right in the construction of the contract, I am of opinion that the defendant cannot refuse to pay for the dressed hogs delivered, on the ground that the plaintiff has broken his contract respecting the live ones. The only condition upon which the payment for the former depended, was their delivery. The payment might have been required to be made concurrently with the delivery; but that being waived, the plaintiff might have sued immediately afterwards, and before the time for the delivery of the other property had arrived. It is true, that before this action was commenced the plaintiff was in default for not delivering the other parcel of the property; but for that wrong the defendant had his remedy, either by separate action or by a recoupment in the plaintiff's action; and the referee has allowed him the benefit of it in the latter form. The law no doubt intends to discourage men from breaking their engagements, but this is not generally accomplished by visiting them with a penalty beyond the damages sustained by the party injured. If I am right in my construction of the agreement, there can be no pretence that the delivery of the hogs coming from Ohio was a precedent condition to the payment for the others; and if this were not so when the agreement was made, it did not become so by the facts which afterwards took place.

The defendant's counsel referred to an opinion ... in which ... [the] judge said, that a party who had advanced money or done an act in part performance of an agreement, and then stopped short and refused to proceed to the ultimate conclusion of the agreement, the other party being willing to proceed and fulfill all his stipulations according to the contract, could never be suffered to recover for what had been thus advanced or done. This dictum, taken broadly, would always preclude a party from recovery for anything done under a contract, where he had himself violated any of its provisions; but the case before the court was that of a vendee in an executory contract for the purchase of land, who had paid a part of the price, and refused, without cause, to make the final payment and receive a deed. When applied to such a case, the doctrine was perfectly correct. But it would not hold where a vendee should, by a single contract, agree to sell one piece of land for $1,000, to be conveyed and paid for in one month, and a different parcel for another sum, to be in like manner conveyed and paid for in two months, and should entitle himself to be paid for the first parcel by a strict performance, but should make default in conveying the other, and should then bring his action for the price of the first piece — though it would be embraced in the generality of the expression used by the judge ...

[S]uppose a contract for a year, the employers agreeing to pay the servant ten dollars at the end of each month; and a part performance and subsequent breach by the servant, the employer being in arrear for several full months. In such a case, I conceive that the servant should be permitted to recover for the wages earned, subject to a recoupment of the master's damages for the time covered by the breach. I am ignorant of any principle upon which it could be held that he could not recover anything. It certainly cannot be upon the ground of the nonperformance of a condition precedent; for it is absurd to say, that under such a contract, serving the last month was a condition to the payment for the first. In the case of contracts for personal services, the death of the servant we have seen would enable his representatives to recover a pro rata compensation …

The position, that one who has violated a contract on his own part, cannot recover for the breach of any of its stipulations by the other party, however disconnected with the one he has broken, cannot be sustained.

Exercise 12-21: *Sterling v. Gregory* and *Tipton v. Feitner* Revisited

1. If the *Tipton* court had concluded the contract was "entire," which party would have been in breach and why?

2. Would either case have come out differently under Article 2 of the U.C.C.? Why or why not? (*Hint: Two sections of the U.C.C. are implicated by this question. It may be helpful to know that the U.C.C. uses the terms "lots" and "installments" to refer to issues relating to divisibility.*)

3. Contractor agreed to build a house on Owner's land for $100,000. The parties agreed to the following payment schedule:

   $10,000 to Contractor on signing the contract

   $10,000 after foundation is poured

   $20,000 after framing is completed

   $30,000 after plumbing and electricity are completed

   $30,000 upon final approval from the local housing inspector

   If Contractor's foundation, framing and plumbing fully comply with the plans and specifications, but Contractor's electrical work is so defective that it cannot be made to work at all without starting over, and Contractor refuses to do so, may Owner terminate the contract without further liability? In other words, is the contract divisible such that a breach of one part does not excuse the other party's performance of the rest of the contract or is it entire so that a material breach excuses performance of all dependent duties?

4. Could you change the facts of the hypo in the previous question to reach the opposite result on the divisibility question? If so, how?

Excuse of Conditions and Discharge of Obligations

Introduction

Imagine a client has come to you for help enforcing an oral contract term that allegedly required another party to remove an old shed in connection with that party's sale of a house and land to your client. Assume that the alleged term was not contained in the parties' writing. By applying what you have learned about the parol evidence rules, you would be able to assess whether a court would conclude that the alleged oral promise to remove the shed was part of the parties' contract. Assume that, for one reason or another, you determine a court likely would conclude that the term was part of the contract. Also assume that, based on contract interpretation, you can determine that knocking down the shed but not removing the debris does not comply with what the term requires. Thus, you know that if the term were deemed an express condition, the condition would be deemed not to have occurred because the performance was imperfect and, if the term were a mere promise, the failure to remove the debris would be a breach (and, based on its relative magnitude, probably not a material breach). However, what if the buyer was the owner of the only dumpsite within 500 miles of the property and had refused to allow the seller to leave the debris at the buyer's dumpsite? What if the shed had been declared an historical monument before the seller began knocking it down so that the seller, wanting to avoid breaking the law, had not knocked it down or removed the debris? In other words, what if the seller claims the court should excuse her failure to knock down the shed and remove the debris?

In the materials that follow, we will focus on issues relating to the excuse and discharge of conditions. In discussing these materials, keep the context in mind. For the purposes of this discussion, we are assuming we can determine both that the contract includes a condition and that the condition has not occurred. Our focus therefore is on the consequences of material breaches and of non-occurrences of conditions. Sometimes, courts excuse or discharge the non-occurrence of conditions. Table 12-1 on the facing page is a list of the excuses/grounds for discharge and the gist of each. We will develop the elements of each excuse as we work through them. Nevertheless, you will find it extremely helpful to familiarize yourself with this list by way of an overview.

It is also helpful to understand, before you get further along, some key terminology and its relationship to the above grounds. Three terms are key: breach, discharge and excuse. The term "breach" refers to any deviation from perfect performance of any contract obligation. It includes both what we previously called "non-performance" and "defective performance." The term "discharge" refers to the liberation of a party's contract obligations. Discharge occurs most commonly when a party fully and perfectly performs his or her contractual duty. However, discharge is also used to describe the release of a contract obligation based on some of the grounds listed in Table 12-1. In other words, a party's duty also may be liberated (discharged) in defined circumstances. Finally, "excuse" refers to a situation where the court will treat as irrelevant or will put aside a condition upon which a duty is dependent so that, even if the condition did not occur, the dependent duty is not released.

Thus, for example, imagine a contract where one party agrees to build a gazebo in the other party's back yard and the other party agrees to pay the builder $5,000. Also assume the parties agree that their duties are "expressly conditioned" on the homeowner getting a loan at an 8% interest rate. As we have learned, absent other terms,

Table 12-1: List of Excuses and Grounds for Discharge and Gist of Each

Grounds for Non-Performance or Non-Occurrence	Gist of Ground
Non-occurrence of a prior condition	A condition due before the obligation at issue did not occur
Waiver	Beneficiary of condition intentionally gave up her right to enforce the condition
Estoppel	Beneficiary of condition takes action indicating an Intent not to enforce the condition and that action causes the other party to rely
Prevention/Failure to Cooperate/Bad Faith	Beneficiary of the condition causes the condition not to occur or otherwise has breached her duty of good faith in connection with the occurrence of the condition
Extreme forfeiture	Excusing the beneficiary of the condition based on its non-occurrence would be extremely unfair to the other party
Impracticability/Impossibility	An unforeseen event changes things such that the promise or condition no longer can occur
Frustration	An unforeseen event causes the party's entire reason for making the contract to no longer exist
Anticipatory repudiation	Before the time for performing, other party clearly communicates a refusal to perform
Failure to Give Adequate Assurances	Other party fails, in response to a justified demand for reassurance, to provide sufficient confirmation that her performance will be forthcoming

the homeowner's duty to pay would be constructively conditioned on the builder's duty to build, and both parties' duties are expressly conditioned on the homeowner getting the loan. Imagine the homeowner can only get a loan at an 8¼% interest rate, and the homeowner tells the builder that the 8¼% rate is "close enough." That statement would likely be deemed a waiver and would *excuse* the non-occurrence of the 8% interest rate express condition. If the government then exercised its right of eminent domain and assumed ownership of the homeowner's land, both parties' duties under the contract would be deemed *discharged* by the impossibility of the builder now performing his contractual duty to build the gazebo for the homeowner on the homeowner's land. Each party's duties also would be *discharged* by full performance by that party. Of course, if the builder built the gazebo poorly, there would be a *breach* by defective performance. Finally, if the builder refused to perform or delayed the project beyond all reasonable boundaries, the builder would be in *breach* and the homeowner's duty to pay also would be deemed *excused*.

Table 12-2 lists the various grounds for non-performance and non-occurrence and identifies the effect of each.

Table 12-2: Effect of Various Grounds of Discharge

Grounds for Non-Performance or Non-Occurrence	Effect
Non-occurrence of a condition	Discharge or excuse and breach
Waiver	Excuse
Estoppel	Excuse
Prevention/Failure to Cooperate/Bad Faith	Depending on the significance, may be excuse but usually is discharge
Extreme forfeiture	Excuse
Impracticability/Impossibility	Depending on the significance, may be excuse but usually is discharge
Frustration	Discharge
Anticipatory repudiation	Discharge and breach
Failure to Give Adequate Assurances	Discharge and breach

Non-Occurrence of a Condition

Of all the grounds discussed in this chapter, the most commonly litigated ground is non-occurrence of a condition. As noted above, non-occurrence discharges or excuses any duty made dependent on the occurrence of that condition. In fact, most of the cases we have read so far have involved a party asserting that he or she had no duty to perform because of the non-occurrence of either an express or constructive condition.

Exercise 12-22: Non-Occurrence as a Ground for Discharge

Review all of the cases you have read so far in this chapter.

1. Which of those cases involved a party claiming that a duty to perform was discharged or excused by the non-occurrence of a prior condition. What was the condition in each of those cases?

2. What did the court conclude on the question of discharge or excuse in each of the cases you identified in response to the previous question?

Waiver, Estoppel, and Prevention/Failure to Cooperate/Bad Faith

A non-occurrence of a condition can be excused by waiver or through estoppel **but only if the condition deals with an issue that is relatively minor**. A waiver is **an intentional relinquishment of a known right**. In the context of a condition, a party that is waiving its rights communicates an intent to perform a duty notwithstanding the non-occurrence of the condition. Thus, for example, if an insured under a car insurance policy were to fail to comply with an express condition requiring notice of an accident within 30 days and the insurer were to promise to "cover the accident anyway," the insurer likely would be deemed to have waived the non-occurrence of the express condition.

A party is estopped from asserting the non-occurrence of a condition **if the party misstates or fails to disclose a fact, and the other party justifiably relies on the impression thereby created to her detriment.** Thus, if the insurer in the previous paragraph had represented to the insured that notice need only be provided within 90 days and the insured had provided such notice within 90 days but not within 30 days, the insurer likely would be estopped from asserting the non-occurrence of the 30-day notice express condition.

Prevention/Failure to Cooperate/Bad Faith (hereinafter just "bad faith") operates somewhat differently. As you already know, **every contract includes an implied promise of good faith and fair dealing.** In the context of conditions, **bad faith can be a ground for discharge, or it can be an excuse for the non-occurrence of a condition.** If one party acts to thwart the other party's ability to perform the contract at all, bad faith results in the discharge of the other party's duty. If a party prevents an express condition from occurring, bad faith may excuse the non-occurrence of the condition. For example, if a party agrees to buy a painting subject to her being satisfied with the painting, but she then refuses to inspect the painting, her bad faith may well excuse the non-occurrence of a condition with the consequence that she would be in breach of contract unless she closes out the purchase.

While these rules are relatively easy to state, their application in particular cases tends to be more complicated. In many instances, it's hard to tell where waiver leaves off and estoppel begins. *Shultz* provides a murky application of waiver or estoppel of an express condition and a fairly straightforward application of bad faith as a ground for discharge. *Prousi* also blurs the clear waiver/estoppel line. And *Fay v. Moore* provides a useful illustration of both waiver and bad faith excusing the non-occurrence of a condition.

Exercise 12-23: *Shultz v. Los Angeles Dons, Inc.; Prousi v. Cruisers Div. of KCS Intern., Inc.;* and *Fay v. Moore*

1. In *Schultz*, the defendant argues non-occurrence of both an express condition and a constructive condition.

    1.1. Make sure you can identify both conditions and explain why they are conditions.

    1.2. Make sure you also understand why the non-occurrence of the express condition is excused and why the non-occurrence of the constructive condition is discharged.

    1.3 Is *Schultz* a waiver case, or an estoppel case, or both?

2. As you read *Prousi*, consider whether the court's analysis is consistent with a waiver theory, an estoppel theory or both.

3. In the course of its opinion, the *Fay* court includes discussions of substantial performance, waiver and bad faith. Make sure you identify and understand each point.

Shultz v. Los Angeles Dons, Inc.

238 P.2d 73 (1951)

VICKERS, Justice pro tem.

The plaintiff-respondent Schultz alleged in his complaint that on July 2, 1948, he and the defendant-appellant corporation entered into a written contract under which he agreed to play professional football for the appellant for the season of 1948 for which the defendant-appellant agreed to pay $8,000; that on July 14, 1948, he reported to the training camp of appellant; that on August 12, 1948, he was discharged without cause or justification by the appellant; that he had "done and performed any and all conditions and covenants on his part to be done and performed under said contract"; that on September 25, 1948, he notified the appellant that he was ready, able and willing to perform the services required under the contract; that the defendant failed and refused to permit such performance and that he was only paid $500 by respondent; and was thereby damaged in the sum of $7,500. By its answer the appellant admitted the execution of the contract and that respondent reported for training as alleged and was discharged; appellant denied that the termination was without cause or justification. Appellant's answer also admitted the receipt of the notification of September 25th and that there was no acceptance of respondent's services thereafter, but denied performance of the contract by respondent and that there was damage to respondent. By its answer the appellant also pleaded a number of affirmative defenses among which were fraud on the part of respondent in failing to disclose that his physical condition, due to prior injury, was such as to make it impossible for him to perform as required by the contract and that, if in good physical condition, respondent could have obtained employment with another professional football club and received compensation equal to that called for by the contract.

From the transcript it appears that there was little dispute in regard to the evidentiary facts except as to the cause and extent of the physical disability suffered by the respondent. Respondent had been a professional football player for approximately seven years. During the 1946 or 1947 football seasons, while playing with the Los Angeles Rams, he was partially incapacitated from a back injury. On June 28, 1948, he was examined by appellant's physician, who reported to it that he was in excellent physical condition and that there was no evidence of prior injury to his back or otherwise. On July 14, 1948 (12 days after the execution of the contract) he was examined by another physician on behalf of the appellant who certified to the appellant that respondent was in excellent condition and there were no symptoms of previous back injury. Between July 14th and July 18th respondent engaged in the regular training activities in Ventura, with the rest of the team and took part in two vigorous scrimmages. On July 18th respondent developed a pain in the back of his leg and numbness in his foot which greatly interfered with his attempts to run and he immediately reported his condition to the team trainer, William Kapela, and the team head coach, James Phelan. During the next few days the trainer gave respondent treatments to alleviate the condition but with little or no success. The trainer made full written reports of respondent's condition to the insurance carrier, it being one of his duties. Shortly after July 18th, under the coach's instructions, respondent was examined by three orthopedic specialists who, after examination, reported to appellant that the respondent was suffering from a herniated disc in his lower back and sometime prior to August 12th informed appellant that it would be very dangerous for him to attempt to play football and that it was doubtful, if not certain, that his playing days were over. Between July 18th and August 12th the respondent reported for practice in proper attire but was not able to engage in the more strenuous activities and was not taken with the team on August 8th when it went to another city to engage in a practice game. Shortly prior to August 12th Mr. Benjamin F. Lindheimer, one of the successors of the club corporation and former chairman of the Board instructed Mr. Don Ameche, President of appellant, to discharge respondent. On August 12th respondent received from Coach Phelan a letter, the body of which read as follows:

> "Under the terms of your contract you agreed to be in proper physical condition to play professional football for our club. Our doctors medical report indicates that you are not in proper physical condition."

> "We wish therefore, to advise you that your contract is terminated effective immediately."

On August 20th respondent received from appellant a more formal notification of discharge. Prior to this, on August 12th, Coach Phelan suggested to the respondent that he see another orthopedic specialist named Dr. Billig. He did so and Dr. Billig examined and treated him thereafter. Dr. Billig found him to be suffering from sciatic neuritis and under the doctor's treatment his condition rapidly improved. On August 23rd Dr. Billig released him to resume his activities as a football player and on September 23rd discharged him as fully recovered without fear of recurrence. On August 12th respondent had protested being discharged and thereafter on many occasions had conferences with Coach Phelan and with officers of appellant informing them of Dr. Billig's reports of his condition and attempted to have himself reinstated and allowed to perform his contract. Appellant refused both requests. Respondent attempted to secure employment with some of the other clubs of the same football league without success and was informed in September by Mr. Lindheimer that he could not play with "The Chicago Rockets" (one of such clubs) and, "to get back to Los Angeles." On September 25th respondent's attorney, by letter to appellant, declared the disability was sustained by respondent while acting in the service of appellant and that respondent was then ready, able and willing to perform under the contract. On October 25th the complaint was filed.

The trial court found that on July 14th, respondent was examined by appellant's physician and found by him to be in excellent physical condition; that such physician was at that time informed of respondent's previous back injury "to-wit, a slipped disc." The court further found that on August 12th, appellant notified respondent his contract was terminated; that respondent "has done and performed any and all conditions and covenants on his part to be done and performed under said contract, and in accordance with the terms and provisions thereof." The court also found that appellant did not terminate the contract for "good and sufficient reason or cause"; that prior to and at the time of the signing of the contract in question respondent did not make any false or fraudulent representation to appellant; that as a result of the termination respondent was damaged in the sum of $7,500; and that none of the allegations in the affirmative defenses were true.

Appellant's principal attack upon the judgment centers about the finding of full performance quoted above and relies upon the rule ... that a complaint based upon a contract must allege either performance or a valid excuse for non-performance; that the one is not the same as the other and if the plaintiff did not perform the contract but relies upon an excuse for non-performance he must set forth the excuse in his complaint; further, that evidence of excuse will not support a finding of performance. We have no quarrel with this rule. However, it cannot avail appellant in this case. Under the allegations of the complaint and the findings of the court it was established that the contract was executed; that respondent commenced performance; that he was discharged and prevented from performing by appellant; that such discharge was without good or sufficient cause; and that appellant failed to pay $7,500 of the contract price and that respondent was damaged in that sum. Each of such findings is supported by substantial evidence and by inferences reasonably to be drawn therefrom. They are therefore binding on appeal ... Appellant having discharged respondent without good cause and prevented him from performing, no further performance or offer to perform by respondent was required. [Citation omitted.] He was entitled to treat the contract as at an end, insofar as performance was concerned, and sue for his lost profits. [Citation omitted.] The finding of full performance was therefore unnecessary and may well be considered as immaterial and disregarded. [Citation omitted.] It is difficult to understand why such allegation and finding were made. It is clear that during the trial respondent at no time contended that he had done all the things referred to in the contract, such as engaging in exhibition and league games. However, it may be that the pleader and the court considered that respondent had fully performed in that he had done substantially everything requested of him by appellant and that that was all that was required of him under the contract. Our examination of the transcript has revealed no instance in which respondent failed or refused to comply with any request by appellant. It is implicit in a contract of this character that the player can perform only those services that the coach of his team permits or requests him to perform and it is a matter of common knowledge that a player is under the complete control of his coach.

If we assume appellant made no requests for specific services from respondent after July 18th because of respondent's incapacity from injury, such injury and incapacity were not a ground under the contract for respondent's discharge. The court found that respondent's injury, causing his incapacity, was incurred while he was performing the services required of him. This finding is more fully considered hereafter. Such injury and incapacity was a risk which appellant specifically assumed under paragraph 7 of the contract. This paragraph reads in part as follows: "If this contract is terminated by Club by reason of Player's failure to render his services hereunder due to disability resulting directly from injury sustained in the performance of his services hereunder and written notice of such injury is given by the Player as provided in Regulation 6, Club agrees to pay Player at the rate stipulated in paragraph 2 [$8,000]...." Paragraph 7 further provides that in all other cases, if the contract is terminated during the training season, the player will receive only his expenses.

Appellant further contends that it is relieved from liability because respondent admittedly failed to give the written notice required by paragraph

7 and regulation 6. With this we cannot agree. Regulation 6 reads as follows: "Written notice of any injury sustained by Player in rendering services under his contract, stating the time, place, cause and nature of the injury, shall be delivered to Club by Player within 10 days of the sustaining of the injury. In the absence of such notice, disability of Player to perform his services resulting from such injury shall be cause for termination of Player's contract by Club without liability for payment beyond the date of termination." The apparent purpose of the required notice was to make certain that appellant was promptly and fully informed of any such injury so that it could take the necessary steps to have its trainer and doctors treat the injury and protect its investment in respondent. It may also have had some relation to the insurance carried on respondent by appellant. The evidence clearly establishes that respondent promptly gave appellant, through its trainer and coach, all information in his possession in regard to the injury and that appellant took full advantage of it by having respondent treated by its trainer and examined and treated by one of its doctors on July 19th and shortly thereafter by two others, and that these doctors made written reports to appellant of their findings. By so doing appellant waived the requirement of written notice. In addition, the trainer sent reports about the injury to the insurance company. Appellant was therefore as fully protected as if the required information had been given in writing. A written notice from respondent would have been an idle act ...

The judgment is affirmed.

Prousi v. Cruisers Div. of KCS Intern., Inc.

975 F. Supp. 768 (1997)

LOUIS H. POLLAK, District Judge.

In this case, plaintiff Andrew S. Prousi (hereinafter "Prousi") has brought warranty claims against defendants Cruisers, a Division of KCS International, Inc. ("Cruisers") and Crusader Marine Engines ("Crusader") in connection with plaintiff's purchase of a yacht manufactured by defendant Cruisers. Cruisers has moved for summary judgment ...

I. Background

In passing on a motion for summary judgment, the court must review the evidence in the light most favorable to the non-moving party, in this case Prousi. So viewing the record, it appears that on April 11, 1995, Prousi purchased a yacht from Greenwich Boat Works in New Jersey, an authorized dealer of Cruisers boats. The boat was manufactured by Cruisers in all respects other than that of the engine, which was manufactured and warranted separately by defendant Crusader. The vessel was launched in Greenwich in May 1995; thereafter Prousi hired Tim Silvio to pilot the boat to Delaware and eventually to Maryland. Prousi testified in his deposition that the vessel stalled several times in the course of its journey and that he reported this to Greenwich Boat Works.

In July 1995, Prousi notified Kenneth Hayes, an agent of Cruisers, of several minor problems he was having with his boat. Prousi had these problems repaired by local mechanics. After Prousi notified Cruisers of these problems, Cruisers sent parts at no charge and notified Greenwich Boat Works that Cruisers would reimburse Prousi for his other expenses if Greenwich Boat Works, whom Cruisers believed was responsible, did not ...

In October, Prousi contracted with Annapolis Motor Yachts ("AMY") to move the boat to Annapolis. AMY found that the starboard engine was not functioning properly and had local mechanic Tom Vogel inspect the engine. Vogel reported that the valves in the starboard engine were rusted and sticking as a result of water having intruded into the engine. After further inspection, Vogel opined that the water probably came in through the exhaust system, which was installed by and presumably warranted by Cruisers. On October 13, 1995, Prousi notified Cruisers by fax of the problem with the engine. Cruisers responded that the engine was warranted by Crusader and referred Prousi thereto for warranty service. On the 16th Prousi sent a letter to Crusader with the same request for warranty work. Crusader apparently authorized Vogel to continue his inspection of the engine. On October 26, 1995, Prousi directed Vogel to cease work on the engine.

On October 18, 1995, Prousi filed this lawsuit alleging three counts of warranty violations ... The gist of Prousi's complaint is that a defect in either the installation of or peripheral attachments to the engine (warranted by Cruisers) caused water to intrude into the engine, eventually making it inoperable. Prousi complains that Cruisers refused to honor its warranty by seeing that the damage was repaired or the engine replaced.

II. Discussion

Summary judgment will be granted if there is no genuine issue of material fact. [Citation omitted.] In the motion before the court, Cruisers argues that Prousi did not deliver the vessel to an authorized dealer as required by the warranty and did not permit warranty work to be effected on the engine ...

A. Failure to Perform Condition Precedent

Cruisers argues that Prousi never presented the boat to an authorized Cruisers dealer for warranty work and consequently failed to perform a condition precedent to Cruisers' warranty obligations. Prousi does not contest Cruisers' factual contention. If meritorious, Cruisers' argument would support summary judgment for defendant irrespective of other contested issues, for even if Prousi did not affirmatively prevent warranty work, his failure to perform a condition precedent would bar recovery.

The warranty explicitly states that "[f]or warranty service, the boat must be delivered to the selling dealer." However, the issue remains whether Cruisers is entitled to rely on this condition. Cruisers may not rely on the condition if it has waived its right to do so. From the record before the court, viewed as it must be in the light most favorable to the plaintiff, it is apparent that a fact-finder could reasonably conclude that defendant has waived reliance on this condition. Under Pennsylvania law, a waiver of legal rights can arise by "a clear unequivocal, and decisive act of the party claimed to have waived its rights, with knowledge of such right and evident purpose to surrender it." [Citations omitted.] Waiver may be effected by a party's words or conduct. When waiver is implied from conduct, it applies in those situations that would support equitable estoppel. [Citations omitted.] Thus for an implied waiver to be operative, the person charged with waiver must have by conduct manifested an intent to relinquish the right and the party claiming the benefit of the waiver must show that he or she was "misled and prejudiced" by the conduct. [Citation omitted.] ...

In this case plaintiff has undertaken to establish, or at least has alleged with support and without contradiction by defendant, all of the elements of a waiver of legal rights (albeit without arguing the point). According to the pleadings, documents, and affidavits supplied by both parties, it appears that Cruisers (1) provided Prousi with replacement parts at no charge, and (2) reimbursed or promised to reimburse plaintiff for work performed by people other than authorized Cruisers dealers, despite the fact that the boat was not brought to a dealer. [Citation to record omitted.] Furthermore, Prousi has alleged that he was never shown the written warranty, an allegation that has not been denied by Cruisers' agent Hayes. [Citation to record omitted.] Consequently, Prousi's only guidance in understanding the warranty would be defendant's conduct. Thus plaintiff has made a sufficient showing to support the proposition that defendant's conduct — namely, honoring [a] minor warranty [claim] without requiring that Prousi deliver the vessel to the New Jersey dealer — could be found by a fact-finder to have led Prousi reasonably to believe that bringing the boat from Maryland to the dealer in New Jersey was unnecessary. But for this apparent waiver prejudice would result from the conduct because plaintiff did not deliver the vessel to the dealer within the warranty's time limit. Accordingly, defendant is not entitled to summary judgment on the basis of plaintiff's failure to perform a condition precedent ...

Fay v. Moore

104 A. 686 (1918)

FRAZER, J. Plaintiff, a contractor, sues to recover from the owner a balance alleged to be due under a contract for the erection of a building. The defense is that plaintiff failed to complete the work in accordance with the specifications, whereby defendant was obliged to take possession of the building and finish it at an expense beyond the contract price. Plaintiff having died while the action was pending, his wife was substituted on the record as administratrix of his estate. The case has been tried three times, the result of the last trial being a verdict and judgment for plaintiff, from which defendant appealed.

The first two assignments of error are to the refusal of the court below to give binding instructions and subsequently to enter judgment for defendant non obstante veredicto. The contract required payments to be made only upon the certificate of the architect. When the building was practically completed, and a certificate for final payment requested, the architect notified plaintiff in writing that the work was not performed in accordance with the contract in certain specified particulars. Plaintiff contends the defects enumerated by the architect were rectified by him, while defendant avers such was not the case, but, on the contrary, he was obliged to employ another contractor to complete the work.

The first objection is that corner beading was omitted. The specifications call for "wood corner beads on all exposed angles," but failed to set forth the particular kind of beading to be used. Plaintiff's son, who had charge of the construction work, testified beads were put on at exposed corners, and this does not seem to be denied; the contention being a different style of beading should have been supplied, as appears in a subsequent letter from the architect, in which he states the owner —

> "has instructed me to put on beads in accordance with his desire, although I have never seen that kind of bead which he desires, at the same time he states that nothing else [will] be accepted by him; so there is no other alternative, and therefore I am compelled to instruct you to make them different from what I would personally select."

In another letter, written a few days later, the architect says:

> "I am perfectly aware that the bead Mr. Moore desires is impractical, as well as impossible; but as Mr. Moore gave me no other alternative in the matter, and the best I could do was to give his instructions verbatim to you."

And in a third letter says he had again taken the matter up with the owner —

> "and asked him to give me instructions for the regular old-fashioned wood corner bead put on, which is the only thing that can be accomplished outside of the covered bead, which you have at present, and which Mr. Moore does not want."

Under these circumstances the jury were warranted in finding the architect, in condemning the bead used by plaintiff, was not acting upon his own impartial judgment as to the sufficiency of the work, but at the dictation and to satisfy the whim of the owner.

Another objection is the window sashes were of chestnut instead of white pine lumber, as called for in the contract. With respect to this item, the testimony on behalf of plaintiff is to the effect the architect instructed him to use chestnut instead of pine, so as to conform to the interior finish of the house. The owner visited the work almost daily, and with the architect made up lists of matters to be attended to or corrected, among which appears a memorandum to the effect that the owner would consider the matter of using chestnut instead of white pine sash. While it is true the contract provides that no alterations should be made, except on the written order of the architect, the parties had the right to waive the provision. [Citation omitted.] And this the verdict indicates they did. Furthermore, there is no attempt in this case to charge for extra work.

As to the various items of which complaint is made, the testimony on behalf of plaintiff is to the effect that portions of the work, the details of which were not mentioned in the specifications, were done under the direction of the architect, and that other variations and defects were remedied after complaint was received. The architect having persisted in refusing a certificate of completion, giving as an excuse for his action the owner's dissatisfaction with the work, and the contractor continuing to claim a completion of the contract, the owner procured a bid and entered into a contract for the additional work on the house he deemed necessary to complete the contract according to specifications, paying therefor the sum of $819, and for other items the sum of $220, which amounts were deducted from the contract price, and the architect signed a certificate to the effect that, after deducting such items, a balance of $1,100 remained due the contractor.

While the testimony on behalf of plaintiff was contradicted by the architect and other witnesses for defendant, the case was necessarily for the jury, to whom it was submitted by the trial judge with instructions to consider the decision of the architect conclusive, unless they found from the circumstances in the case his decision was the result of collusion with the owner, and not a fair and impartial one. The court also left to the jury to say whether the contractor faithfully, honestly, and substantially complied with the provisions of his contract, and further charged, if they so found, and minor defects or deficiencies existed, such defects would not prevent a recovery for the amount due under the contract, less a reasonable allowance for the cost of remedying the imperfections.

The provision in the contract requiring the production of the certificate of the architect, showing completion of the work, is intended as a protection to the owner against unjust claims by the contractor and to see that the latter properly carries out his agreement and in cases where the evidence establishes refusal of the architect to be capricious, fraudulent, or based on collusion with the owner, his withholding the certificate will not prevent the contractor from recovering the amount due him. [Citation omitted.] There also being evidence in the case to support the conclusion of the jury of there being no willful or intentional departure from the terms of the contract, the doctrine of substantial performance was applicable, and was properly stated by the trial judge ...

The assignments of error are overruled and the judgment affirmed.

Exercise 12-24: *Shultz, Prousi* and *Fay* Revisited

1. What, if anything, could the Dons have done differently to avoid a claim of waiver?

2. Besides strictly adhering to the terms of the warranty, what else could Cruisers have done to protect itself against a claim of waiver or estoppel?

3. The architect's letters end up creating a significant evidentiary problem for the defendant in *Fay*. Would the defendant have prevailed if the architect had not written those letters?

4. In 2014, Midwest Manufacturing ("Midwest") entered into a five-year contract with Regal Retailing ("Regal") to sell Regal widgets in 2,000-widget bundles "at market price as determined by an official industry publication". The contract included the following clause: "Midwest's duty to ship the widgets is expressly conditioned on Regal making a 25% down payment by cer-

tified check." In 2014, after 20 instances in which Midwest delayed delivery until it had received the required down payment by certified check, Midwest's shipping department twice shipped widgets to Regal even though Regal failed to provide the required down payment. When, Regal again demanded shipment and Midwest refused, asserting that Regal had not provided the required down payment, Regal insisted that Midwest ship the widgets (which Regal desperately needed for one of its most important customers) immediately, claiming that Midwest had waived the requirement or was estopped to assert it. Is Regal correct?

Extreme Forfeiture

Exercise 12-25: *Alcazar v. Hayes*

1. Read section 229 of the RESTATEMENT (SECOND) OF CONTRACTS and then paraphrase the rule in your own words.

2. Give an example of a forfeiture caused by the non-occurrence of a condition that is a material part of the agreed exchange and an example of a forfeiture that is not a material part of the agreed exchange.

3. The *Alcazar* court adopts a new rule for the Tennessee courts relating to prejudice in the context of insurance contracts containing express conditions requiring notice. Should the rule in *Alcazar* be used outside the insurance context? Why or why not?

Alcazar v. Hayes

982 SW2d 845 (1998)

DROWOTA, Justice.

This suit arose from a motor vehicle accident in which plaintiff David Alcazar was injured. Alcazar appeals from the Court of Appeal's affirmance of the trial court's award of summary judgment to defendant Government Employees Insurance Company ("GEICO"). The sole issue for our determination is whether an insurance policy is automatically forfeited when the insured does not comply with the policy's notice provision, regardless of whether the insurer has been prejudiced by the delay ...

I. FACTS & PROCEDURAL HISTORY

On November 3, 1995, plaintiff Alcazar and defendant Christopher Hayes were working in chicken houses on a farm in Bradley County owned by Alcazar's mother. Alcazar asked Hayes for a ride to pick up Alcazar's truck. Hayes agreed under the condition that Alcazar ride on the trunk of the car, since he was extremely dirty. Alcazar acquiesced and during the drive Alcazar was flung from the trunk, striking his head on the paved roadway. Alcazar, who was eighteen years old and living with his mother, was hospitalized for a couple of days and then returned home. Alcazar alleges that he suffers injuries as a result of the accident, including permanent brain damage.

At the time of the accident, Alcazar was covered under a "Family Automobile Insurance Policy" issued by GEICO to Alcazar's mother, Deborah Wheatley. An "uninsured motorist coverage" provision in this policy includes the following clauses:

1. Notice

As soon as possible after an accident notice must be given us or our authorized agent stating:

(a) the identity of the *insured*;

(b) the time, place and details of the accident; and

(c) the names and addresses of the injured, and of any witnesses.

. . .

3. Action Against [GEICO]

Suit will not lie against [GEICO] unless the *insured* or his legal representative have fully complied with all the policy terms.

(Italics in original.) It is undisputed that Alcazar qualified as an "insured" under the policy.

Although the exact date that GEICO received notice of the accident is somewhat uncertain, it is clear that notice was not provided until approximately one year after the accident. At this time, Alcazar filed a Complaint seeking damages for his personal injuries suffered as a result of the accident.... Alcazar and Wheatley testified that notice was not provided to GEICO earlier because they mistakenly assumed that the policy did not apply since Alcazar was not the driver of the automobile involved in the accident. Wheatley also testified that she did not intend to make a claim on the insurance policy until nearly a year after the accident, because she did not learn until this time the extent of Alcazar's brain injury.

GEICO filed a motion for summary judgment, asserting that under the terms of the policy, they could not be sued since the notice provision was breached. Alcazar insisted that notice was provided "as soon as possible" and, alternatively, argued that the policy could not be forfeited since there was no evidence that GEICO was prejudiced by the delay. The trial court granted summary judgment to GEICO and Alcazar appealed. The Court of Appeals affirmed, finding that GEICO could not be listed as a party defendant since Alcazar breached the notice provision. Although finding plaintiff's "no prejudice" argument "appealing," the Court of Appeals ... held that prejudice to the insurer is immaterial to the issue....

II. ANALYSIS

The sole issue for our review concerns whether an insured, who fails to comply with the notice provision of his or her insurance policy, may nevertheless enforce the policy in the event that the insurer has not been prejudiced by the delay.

Construction of Insurance Contracts

In general, courts should construe insurance contracts in the same manner as any other contract.... .[Citations omitted.] [W]e stated:

> The cardinal rule for interpretation of contracts is to ascertain the intention of the parties and to give effect to that intention ... [i]t is the Court's duty to enforce contracts according to their plain terms.... [Citations omitted.]

Tennessee, like most states, recognizes the validity of conditions precedent for insurance coverage, including uninsured motorist coverage. [Citations omitted.] In the instant case, GEICO contends that Alcazar's compliance with the notice provision was a condition precedent for coverage. Because Alcazar failed to provide notice "as soon as possible" pursuant to the insurance contract, GEICO asserts that coverage was automatically forfeited.

Traditional Approach

For years Tennessee has consistently adhered to the traditional common law approach that:

> (1) notice is a condition precedent to recovery under the policy and
> (2) there need not be any showing of prejudice.

[Citations omitted.] Although this approach is grounded on a strict contractual interpretation methodology, this Court has acknowledged underlying public policy rationales that serve as the basis for the inclusion of this "vital and indispensable condition precedent" in an insurance policy:

> [W]e recognize that the notice requirement of an insurance policy providing uninsured motorist coverage based on hit-and-run incidents, while founded in contract, also are deeply rooted in public policy considerations. Not only is the insurer entitled to notice in order that it may make prompt investigation and prepare for the defense of the claim, it is entitled to protect its interests in an area susceptible to the presentation of spurious claims. Also, it is in the public interest that litigation be minimized and, to this end, it is essential that the insurance company be in a position to settle claims on a knowledgeable basis.

[Citations omitted.] It has been noted:

> The purpose of a policy provision requiring the insured to give the company prompt notice of an accident or claim is to give the insurer an opportunity to make a timely and adequate investigation of all the circumstances. An adequate investigation often cannot be made where notice is long delayed, because of the possible removal or lapse of memory on the part of witnesses, the loss of opportunity for examination of the physical surroundings and making photographs thereof for use at the trial, and the possible operation of fraud, collusion, or cupidity. Such a requirement tends to protect the insurer against fraudulent claims, and also against invalid claims made in good faith. If the insurer is given the opportunity for a timely investigation, reasonable compromises and settlements may be made, thereby avoiding prolonged and unnecessary litigation.

[Citations omitted.]

Modern Trend

While once the overwhelming majority approach in this country, the number of jurisdictions that still follow the traditional view has dwindled dramatically. [Citations omitted.] In recent years a "modern trend" has developed, and a vast majority of jurisdictions now consider whether the insurer has been prejudiced by the insured's untimely notice. ([Citations omitted.] [A] review of these cases indicates that three rationales are particularly pervasive: 1) the adhesive nature of insurance contracts; 2) the public policy objective of compensating tort victims; and 3) the inequity of the insurer receiving a windfall due to a technicality.

Many states have recognized the adhesive nature of insurance contracts as a justification for a more liberal approach. In reality, most insurance policies are form contracts drafted by the insurer, and the insured has little, if any, bargaining power....

Another predominant basis for the modern trend is that it advances the public policy goal of compensating accident victims, including innocent third parties.

A third popular rationale supporting the modern trend focuses on the intent of the inclusion of the notice provision in the insurance contract. It is reasoned that notice requirements are devised in order to insulate the insurer from prejudice and, thus, in the absence of prejudice the notice provisions should not be strictly enforced....

Consequently, courts have shifted away from the technical aspects of contractual interpretation so that an insurer can not take advantage of "an undeserved windfall" as a result of forfeiture [Citations omitted.]

Public Policy

... Although the determination of public policy is primarily a function of the legislature, the judiciary may determine public policy in the absence of any constitutional or statutory declaration. [Citations omitted.]

Unless a private contract tends to harm the public good, public interest, or public welfare, or to conflict with the constitution, laws, or judicial decisions of Tennessee, it does not violate public policy. The reverse is also true: A contract with a tendency to injure the public violates public policy.

We believe that the public policy of Tennessee is consistent with the overwhelming number of our sister states that have adopted the modern trend....

... It is a general principle, pervading the law of all forms of insurance, that policies shall be liberally construed in favor of the insured. This because courts do not shut their eyes to realities; they know that the policy is a contract of "adhesion," i.e. not one which the parties have reached by mutual negotiation and concession, not one which truly expresses any agreement at which they have arrived, but one which has been fixed by the insurer and to which the insured must adhere, if he chooses to have insurance. [Citations omitted.]

In addition, the public policy of this State has long promoted the notion that victims of torts should recover compensation for their injuries. [Citations omitted.]

Third, we agree with our sister states that it is inequitable for an insurer that has not been prejudiced by a delay in notice to reap the benefits flowing from the forfeiture of the insurance policy. In light of the adhesive nature of such contracts as well as our inclination to construe these contracts against the drafter/insurer, we believe that this State's public policy disfavors the ability of an insurer to escape its contractual duties due to a technicality ...

Burden of Proof

After resolving to join the modern trend, we must now determine how to incorporate the consideration of prejudice into our analysis. In the process, we must balance the equities between the parties. States that consider prejudice essentially follow one of three different approaches: 1) once it is shown that the insured has breached the notice provision, the contract is, nevertheless, effective unless the insurer shows that it has been prejudiced by the delay; 2) once it is shown that the insured has breached the notice provision, a rebuttable presumption exists that the insurer has been prejudiced by the delay; and 3) prejudice to the insurer is considered as a factor in the initial inquiry of whether the insured provided timely notice. [Citations omitted.]

A clear plurality of states hold that once it is demonstrated that the insured breached the notice provision, the burden of proof is allocated to the insurer to prove that it has been prejudiced by the breach. [Citations omitted.] Many of these states reason that it is more equitable to place the burden on the insurer, since the insurer is the entity that seeks to repudiate its obligations under an adhesive contract. [Citations omitted.] Furthermore, it is reasoned that the insurer is in a much better position to prove that it has been prejudiced, especially since the insured would otherwise be forced to prove a negative: that the insurer was not prejudiced. As the Supreme Court of Kentucky stated in [*Jones v. Bituminous Cas. Corp.*, 821 S.W.2d 798 at 803 (Ky.1991)]:

> There are two reasons for imposing the burden on the insurance carrier to prove prejudice, rather than imposing on the claimant the burden to prove no prejudice resulted. The first is the obvious one: it is virtually impossible to prove a negative, so it would be difficult if not impossible for the claimant to prove the insurance carrier suffered no prejudice. Secondly, the insurance carrier is in a far superior position to be knowledgeable about the facts which establish whether prejudice exists. Indeed, it is difficult to imagine where the claimant would look for evidence that no prejudice exists.

...

Some jurisdictions hold that when the insured fails to comply with the notice requirements, it is presumed that the insurer is prejudiced by the breach. Thus, the insured bears the burden of rebutting this presumption. [Citations omitted.] ...

Tennessee Approach

[W]e believe that the rebuttable presumption rule is the soundest approach in the context of an uninsured/underinsured motorist policy as it provides the best balance between the competing interests ... [The] instant issue is akin to unjust enrichment law: in both instances, an undeserving party seeks forgiveness for his or her own breach. [Citation omitted]. Therefore, once it is determined that the insured has failed to provide timely notice in accordance with the insurance policy, it is presumed that the insurer has been prejudiced by the breach. The insured, however, may rebut this presumption by proffering competent evidence that the insurer was not prejudiced by the insured's delay.

Although summary judgment is not proper in the present case, we recognize that summary judgment may, nevertheless, be appropriate in some circumstances. We quote approvingly the following non-exclusive guidelines for determining whether the insurer has been prejudiced:

> the availability of witnesses to the accident; the ability to discover other information regarding the conditions of the locale where the accident occurred; any physical changes in the location of the accident during the period of the delay; the existence of official reports concerning the occurrence; the preparation and preservation of demonstrative and illustrative evidence, such as the vehicles involved in the occurrence, or photographs and diagrams of the scene; the ability of experts to reconstruct the scene and the occurrence; and so on. [Citations omitted.]

We acknowledge that attempting to prove what information the insurer would have been able to discover had notice been promptly provided would be difficult for either party. [Citations omitted.] However, we are less sympathetic to the insured in this instance, since the insured bears sole responsibility for breaching a term of the contract that was intended to preserve fairness to the insurer.

III. CONCLUSION

In sum, we overrule ... cases in this State holding that prejudice to the insurer is irrelevant to whether forfeiture of an insurance contract results from the insured's breach of a notice provision. Instead, the appropriate inquiry is: 1) Did the insured provide timely notice in accordance with the contract? 2) If not, did the insured carry its burden of proving that the insurer was not prejudiced by the delay? This standard shall apply to (1) all cases tried or retried after the date of this opinion, and (2) all cases pending on appeal in which the prejudice issue was raised in the trial court. Consequently, the decisions of the lower courts granting summary judgment to GEICO are reversed. This case is remanded to the trial court for findings consistent with this opinion ...

Exercise 12-26: *Alcazar v. Hayes* Revisited

1. Given the court's resolution of the burden of proof issue, how great a victory for insureds is *Alcazar*? Consider, in particular, the court's explanation as to why some courts assign the burden to the insurer to prove prejudice.

2. Igor signed a one-year employment contract with California Construction to be a framing supervisor. The contract included an express condition requiring Igor to: (1) provide written notice of any claim against California "arising out of or relating to this contract" within 30 days of the events that give rise to the claim, and (2) delay instituting suit until six months after the occurrence of the events that give rise to the claim. Two months into the contract, California fired Igor. Assume that Igor gave the notice 35 days after he was fired and filed suit five months after he was fired.

   a. Did the condition(s) occur? Why or why not?

   b. Assume the condition(s) did not occur. Analyze the two grounds Igor would assert to justify the non-occurrence.

Anticipatory Repudiation and Failure of Assurances

We now turn to the question of what a party should do and should not do if she is faced with a likelihood of not getting what she was supposed to get from the other party because there is some prospect that the other party will be unable or unwilling to perform. In other words, we will look at the topics of anticipatory repudiation and failure to provide adequate assurances. In connection with these topics we will look at two questions:

1. What constitutes an anticipatory repudiation and what are its legal effects?

2. What is the relationship between the doctrine of anticipatory repudiation and the doctrine of failure of assurances?

Introduction

There are two elements to a claim for anticipatory repudiation: (1) **there must be a repudiation, which is** *an unequivocal manifestation of intent not to render the promised performance,* **and** (2) **the repudiation must be anticipatory, i.e.,** *it must arise before the time for performance is due.* **An anticipatory repudiation has the effect of** *discharging any duty legally dependent on the repudiated obligation.* Of course, a repudiation made at or after the time for performance also discharges a dependent duty; it's just not an anticipatory repudiation. We encountered anticipatory repudiation briefly in Chapter 6 when we were considering the avoidability limitation on damages. In *Rockingham County v. Luten Bridge Co.*, when Rockingham County notified Luten Bridge Co. that it should proceed no further with the construction of the bridge, this was an anticipatory repudiation of the county's obligation to pay for the completed bridge.

Exercise 12-27: *Wallace Real Estate Investment, Inc. v. Groves*

Wallace provides an illustration of anticipatory repudiation. Make sure you understand why the court concluded that Wallace repudiated its obligations under the contract.

Wallace Real Estate Investment, Inc. v. Groves
881 P.2d 1010 (1994)

MADSEN, Justice ...

Joanna Groves and her cousins, Charles and James Siler (the sellers), own 10 acres of undeveloped commercial property in Everett. On August 1, 1989, the sellers entered into an agreement with Roddy Cox whereby Cox agreed to pay $1,520,000 for the property. Real estate prices were in flux at the time, and the sellers established the purchase price to encourage a quick, cash sale. The sellers also needed the funds that the sale would generate. [Ed.'s note: All references to the record on appeal have been deleted.]

Cox gave the sellers a $20,000 note as a down payment. The agreement gave Cox 30 days to conduct a feasibility study for the potential development of an apartment complex. After this 30-day period, Cox could either abandon the property and receive back its note, or exchange the note for cash. If Cox went ahead with the sale, it would close within 60 to 90 days. A standard form liquidated damages provision applied to the deposit, stating that "[i]n the event of default by Buyer, Seller shall have the election to retain the earnest money as liquidated damages."

An addendum to the purchase and sale agreement added extension periods for closing. For each additional 30-day delay, Cox agreed to pay $15,000. This amount was suggested by Cox. The $15,000 amount represented the lost investment value of the purchase price, calculated at 12 percent simple interest on the investment value not realized. The interest component thus compensated the sellers for holding the property off the market. The addendum authorized up to 12 extensions of 30 days each, and stated that the deposit and extension payments were nonrefundable.

Cox negotiated this agreement with the intention of assigning his interest to Wallace Real Estate Investment, Inc., which he did in September 1989. During the negotiations, Cox consulted with William Wallace, president of Wallace Real Estate Investment, Inc., about the sellers' objectives and terms, including the purpose of the extension payments.

After the last $15,000 extension payment permitted by the addendum, the parties negotiated a second addendum.... Wallace countersigned the second addendum, which provided for $30,000 extension payments for October and November 1990 and established December 17, 1990, as the new closing date.

The liquidated damages provision to the second addendum provided as follows:

> Liquidated damages: The parties hereto agree that in the event Buyer or its assign fails to comply with the terms of this Agreement ... Seller shall retain all payments made to date ... as liquidated damages and not as penalty, in order to indemnify the Seller against loss as a result of breach of this agreement. It is agreed that damages that result to Seller include: freezing the purchase price at a time when real estate land values were escalating at unprecedented rates; compensating seller for holding the property off the market and losing the time value of its property were the property liquidated and funds invested; lost opportunity for larger profits; and related costs.... It is further agreed that the damages that may result from a breach of this agreement are uncertain and difficult to ascertain any more than Seller and Buyer have done, and that the agreed amount is a reasonable estimate of the probable damages to Seller.

On December 13, 1990, William Wallace wrote the sellers, stating that he could not close on December 17 and requesting "a new agreement with everyone to close on or about January 7, 1991." The sellers refused and, in a December 14, 1990, letter, informed Wallace that they were prepared to close as scheduled on December 17, 1990.

On December 17, Joanna Groves and Charles Siler attended the closing. James Siler, who lived in Oregon, could not attend because of a back injury. Wallace also did not attend, though he did fax a letter stating that closing could not take place as scheduled because of two problems with the title. Despite Wallace's absence, Groves express mailed the deed and closing papers to James Siler. Siler signed and returned the documents to Groves, who delivered them to escrow on December 21, 1990.

On December 24, 1990, the escrow agent received the sellers' notice of cancellation, which they had executed on December 21, 1990. The sellers then retained the $260,000 in earnest money and extension payments as liquidated damages. Wallace filed suit seeking to recover the moneys paid....

The trial court ruled in favor of the sellers and awarded them reasonable attorneys' fees and costs. The Court of Appeals affirmed.

I

In Washington, a provision for liquidated damages will be upheld unless it is a penalty or otherwise unlawful. [Citations omitted.] This court follows the United States Supreme Court's view that liquidated damages agreements fairly and understandingly entered into by experienced, equal parties with a view to just compensation for the anticipated loss should be enforced. [The court analyzed and upheld the liquidated damages clause.]

II

Also at issue is whether Wallace is entitled to a return of the payments forfeited because the sellers failed to concurrently perform under the purchase and sale agreement. Wallace argues here, as he did in both courts below, that the sellers' failure to perform as required on December 17, the date of closing, places the sellers in default and warrants a return of all payments made to them.

If a contract requires performance by both parties, the party claiming nonperformance of the other must establish as a matter of fact the party's own performance. [Citations omitted.] A vendor selling land may not put the buyer in default until the vendor has offered to perform; the payment of the purchase price and the delivering of the deed are concurrent acts.

Both the trial court and Court of Appeals concluded that Wallace's December 13 letter to the sellers constituted an anticipatory breach of the contract and relieved the sellers of any duty to perform, [it stated in part]:

> "I am prepared to close with all the sellers on the same date. This would have been done on December 17, 1990 had not (i) the Phase I sellers unexpectedly demanded a January closing, and (ii) Cox's attempts to prevent my closing unless I pay him more money than he had agreed to.... I request a new agreement with everyone to close on or about January 7, 1991."

Wallace contends that his December 13 letter did not constitute an anticipatory breach, and cites as support ... *Lovric v. Dunatov*, 18 Wash.App. 274, 282 (1977). *Lovric* states that an anticipatory breach occurs when one of the parties to a bilateral contract either expressly or impliedly repudiates the contract prior to the time of performance. A party's intent not to perform may not be implied from doubtful and indefinite statements that performance may or may not take place. *Id*. at 282. Rather, an anticipatory breach is a "'positive statement or action by the promisor indicating distinctly and unequivocally that he either will not or cannot substantially perform any of his contractual obligations.'" [The Lovric] case [does not] present a communication similar to Wallace's December 13 letter. In ... *Lovric*, a letter stating that the defendants "may" not be able to perform also did not constitute an anticipatory breach. Wallace's letter stated that he could not perform on December 17 and requested a new agreement. In the words of the trial court, the letter "was clearly an anticipatory breach."

The sellers would have been perfectly entitled in not even showing up themselves on the 17th. They were not required to do a useless act. They were told that payments into escrow would not be made; that the defendant would not tender into closing; and they were entitled to rely on that information. Everything in the history of their dealing with this purchaser supported the conclusion that when he said he wasn't going to be there with his $1.5 million, then he wasn't going to be there. Their performance, in a sense, was excused by the prior breach, the anticipated breach, by the buyer/plaintiff.

We agree with both the trial court and the Court of Appeals that Wallace's December 13 letter constituted an anticipatory breach.

Exercise 12-28: *Wallace Real Estate Investment, Inc. v. Groves* Revisited

1. Arguably, Wallace should have won this case. Wallace's main argument was that his letter of December 13 was equivocal (like the letter in *Lovric*) rather than unequivocal as the rule requires. We think there was a better argument available that the letter was not an anticipatory repudiation. Can you see what that argument might be? [Hint: It has something to do with the repeated extension of the closing date.]

2. Apply the repudiation element of anticipatory repudiation to the following hypotheticals (assume all of the following statements were made before the time for performance was due):

    a. A party to a contract says, "I refuse to perform my contract obligation."

    b. A party to a contract says, "I might have a problem giving you the deed on the day we agreed on, but I should be able to get it to you one day later."

    c. A party to a contract says, "I'm thinking about taking a vacation to Europe instead of fulfilling my promise to be your contracts tutor."

    d. At 11:00 p.m. eastern on the night before the contracts final, a contracts tutor who is a party to a tutoring contract (to be performed in Pittsburgh, Pennsylvania) calls to say, "It doesn't look like I will be able to meet with you tomorrow morning as per our tutoring schedule because I will be in Japan visiting my sick grandmother. I'm just arriving in the Tokyo airport right now."

Exercise 12-29: *K & G Construction Co. v. Harris*

As you read this case, consider the following questions:

1. Based on what you have learned about constructive conditions law, state the order of performance created by the contract in *K & G Construction Co. v. Harris* and be prepared to explain your reasoning.

2. Was the contract in *K & G Construction Co.* divisible? Why or why not?

3. On what basis did the court conclude that the defendant was in repudiatory breach? Why was this breach anticipatory?

4. Could the plaintiff in *K & G Construction Co.* have kicked the defendant off the job once the defendant refused to pay the damages caused by the bulldozer accident? Why or why not?

K & G Construction Co. v. Harris

164 A.2d 451 (1960)

PRESCOTT, Judge.

Feeling aggrieved by the action of the trial judge of the Circuit Court for Prince George's County, sitting without a jury, in finding a judgment against it in favor of a subcontractor, the appellant, the general contractor on a construction project, appealed.

The principal question presented is: Does a contractor, damaged by a subcontractor's failure to perform a portion of his work in a workmanlike manner, have a right, under the circumstances of this case, to withhold, in partial satisfaction of said damages, an installment payment, which, under the terms of the contract, was due the subcontractor, unless the negligent performance of his work excused its payment?

The appeal is presented on a case stated in accordance with Maryland Rule 826 g.

The statement, in relevant part, is as follows:

> " ... K & G Construction Company, Inc. (hereinafter called Contractor), plaintiff and counter-defendant in the Circuit Court and appellant herein, was owner and general contractor of a housing subdivision project being constructed (herein called Project). Harris and Brooks (hereinafter called Subcontractor), defendants and counter-plaintiffs in the Circuit Court and appellees herein, entered into a contract with Contractor to do excavating and earth-moving work on the Project. Pertinent parts of the contract are set forth below:
>
> "Section 3. The Subcontractor agrees to complete the several portions and the whole of the work herein sublet by the time or times following:

"(a) Without delay, as called for by the Contractor.

"(b) It is expressly agreed that time is of the essence of this contract, and that the Contractor will have the right to terminate this contract and employ a substitute to perform the work in the event of delay on the part of Subcontractor, and Subcontractor agrees to indemnify the Contractor for any loss sustained thereby, provided, however, that nothing in this paragraph shall be construed to deprive Contractor of any rights or remedies it would otherwise have as to damage for delay.

"Section 4. (b) Progress payments will be made each month during the performance of the work. Subcontractor will submit to Contractor, by the 25th of each month, a requisition for work performed during the preceding month. Contractor will pay these requisitions, less a retainer equal to ten per cent (10%), by the 10th of the months in which such requisitions are received.[8]

"(c) No payments will be made under this contract until the insurance requirements of Sec. 9 hereof have been complied with.

"Section 5. The Contractor agrees—

"(1) That no claim for services rendered or materials furnished by the Contractor to the Subcontractor shall be valid unless written notice thereof is given by the Contractor to the Subcontractor during the first ten days of the calendar month following that in which the claim originated....

"Section 8.... All work shall be performed in a workmanlike manner, and in accordance with the best practices.

"Section 9. Subcontractor agrees to carry, during the progress of the work, ... liability insurance against ... property damage, in such amounts and with such companies as may be satisfactory to Contractor and shall provide Contractor with certificates showing the same to be in force." ...

"While in the course of his employment by the Subcontractor on the Project, a bulldozer operator drove his machine too close to Contractor's house while grading the yard, causing the immediate collapse of a wall and other damage to the house. The resulting damage to contractor's house was $3,400.00. Subcontractor had complied with the insurance provision (Sec. 9) of the aforesaid contract. Subcontractor reported said damages to their liability insurance carrier. The Subcontractor and its insurance carrier refused to repair damage or compensate Contractor for damage to the house, claiming that there was no liability on the part of the Subcontractor.

"Contractor gave no written notice to Subcontractor for any services rendered or materials furnished by the Contractor to the Subcontractor....

"Contractor was generally satisfied with Subcontractor's work and progress as required under Sections 3 and 8 of the contract until Sep-

---

8. This section is not a model for clarity.

tember 12, 1958, with the exception of the bulldozer accident of August 9, 1958.

"Subcontractor performed work under the contract during July, 1958, for which it submitted a requisition by the 25th of July, as required by the contract, for work done prior to the 25th of July, payable under the terms of the contract by Contractor on or before August 10, 1958. Contractor was current as to payments due under all preceding monthly requisitions from Subcontractor. The aforesaid bulldozer accident damaging Contractor's house occurred on August 9, 1958. Contractor refused to pay Subcontractor's requisition due on August 10, 1958, because the bulldozer damage to Contractor's house had not been repaired or paid for. Subcontractor continued to work on the project until the 12th of September, 1958, at which time they discontinued working on the project because of Contractor's refusal to pay the said work requisition and notified Contractor by registered letters of their position and willingness to return to the job, but only upon payment. At that time, September 12, 1958, the value of the work completed by Subcontractor on the project for which they had not been paid was $1,484.50.

"Contractor later requested Subcontractor to return and complete work on the Project which Subcontractor refused to do because of nonpayment of work requisitions of July 25 and thereafter. Contractor's house was not repaired by Subcontractor nor compensation paid for the damage.

"It was stipulated that Subcontractor had completed work on the Project under the contract for which they had not been paid in the amount of $1,484.50 and that if they had completed the remaining work to be done under the contract, they would have made a profit of $1,340.00 on the remaining uncompleted portion of the contract. It was further stipulated that it cost the Contractor $450.00 above the contract price to have another excavating contractor complete the remaining work required under the contract. It was the opinion of the Court that if judgment were in favor of the Subcontractor, it should be for the total amount of $2,824.50.

" ... Contractor filed suit against the Subcontractor in two counts: (1), for the aforesaid bulldozer damage to Contractor's house, alleging negligence of the Subcontractor's bulldozer operator, and (2) for the $450.00 costs above the contract price in having another excavating subcontractor complete the uncompleted work in the contract. Subcontractor filed a counter-claim for recovery of work of the value of $1,484.50 for which they had not received payment and for loss of anticipated profits on uncompleted portion of work in the amount of $1,340.00. By agreement of the parties, the first count of Contractor's claim, i.e., for aforesaid bulldozer damage to Contractor's house, was submitted to jury who found in favor of Contractor in the amount of $3,400.00. Following the finding by the jury, the second count of the Contractor's claim and the counter-claims of the Subcontractor, by agreement of the parties, were submitted to the Court for determination, without jury. All of the facts recited herein above were stipulated to by the parties to the Court. Circuit Court Judge Fletcher found for counter-plaintiff Subcontractor in the amount of $2,824.50 from which Contractor has entered this appeal."

The $3,400 judgment has been paid.

It is immediately apparent that our decision turns upon the respective rights and liabilities of the parties under that portion of their contract whereby the subcontractor agreed to do the excavating and earth-moving work in "a workmanlike manner, and in accordance with the best practices," with time being of the essence of the contract, and the contractor agreed to make progress payments therefor on the 10th day of the months following the performance of the work by the subcontractor. The subcontractor contends, of course, that when the contractor failed to make the payment due on August 10, 1958, he breached his contract and thereby released him (the subcontractor) from any further obligation to perform. The contractor, on the other hand, argues that the failure of the subcontractor to perform his work in a workmanlike manner constituted a material breach of the contract, which justified his refusal to make the August 10 payment; and, as there was no breach on his part, the subcontractor had no right to cease performance on September 12, and his refusal to continue work on the project constituted another breach, which rendered him liable to the contractor for damages. The vital question, more tersely stated, remains: Did the contractor have a right, under the circumstances, to refuse to make the progress payment due on August 10, 1958?

The answer involves interesting and important principles of contract law …

In the early days, it was settled law that covenants and mutual promises in a contract were prima facie independent, and that they were to be so construed in the absence of language in the contract clearly showing that they were intended to be dependent … The modern rule, which seems to be of almost universal application, is that there is a presumption that mutual promises in a contract are dependent and are to be so regarded, whenever possible. [Citations omitted.]

While the courts assume, in deciding the relation of one or more promises in a contract to one or more counter-promises, that the promises are dependent rather than independent, the intention of the parties, as shown by the entire contract as construed in the light of the circumstances of the case, the nature of the contract, the relation of the parties thereto, and the other evidence which is admissible to assist the court in determining the intention of the parties, is the controlling factor in deciding whether the promises and counter-promises are dependent or independent. [Citations omitted.]

Considering the presumption that promises and counter-promises are dependent and the [facts of this case], we have no hesitation in holding that the promise and counter-promise under consideration here were mutually dependent, that is to say, the parties intended performance by one to be conditioned on performance by the other; and the subcontractor's promise was, by the explicit wording of the contract, precedent to the promise of payment, monthly, by the contractor. In [a recent case], we stated that it is the general rule that where a total price for work is fixed by a contract, the work is not rendered divisible by progress payments. It would, indeed present an unusual situation if we were to hold that a building contractor, who has obtained someone to do work for him and has agreed to pay each month for the work performed in the previous month, has to continue the monthly payments, irrespective of the degree of skill and care displayed in the performance of work, and his only recourse is by way of suit for ill-performance. If this were the law, it is conceivable, in fact, probable, that many contractors would become insolvent before they were able to complete their contracts. As was stated by the Court in [another case]: "Covenants are to be construed as dependent or independent according to the intention of the parties and the good sense of the case."

We hold that when the subcontractor's employee negligently damaged the contractor's wall, this constituted a breach of the subcontractor's promise to perform his work in a "workmanlike manner, and in accordance with the best practices." [Citations omitted.] And there can be little doubt that the breach was material: the damage to the wall amounted to more than double the payment due on August 10. [Citation omitted.] 3A Corbin, Contracts, § 708, says: "The failure of a contractor's [in our case, the subcontractor's] performance to constitute 'substantial' performance may justify the owner [in our case, the contractor] in refusing to make a progress payment ... If the refusal to pay an installment is justified on the owner's [contractor's] part, the contractor [subcontractor] is not justified in abandoning work by reason of that refusal. His abandonment of the work will itself be a wrongful repudiation that goes to the essence, even if the defects in performance did not." [Citations omitted.] Professor Corbin, in § 954, states further: "The unexcused failure of a contractor to render a promised performance when it is due is always a breach of contract.... Such failure may be of such great importance as to constitute what has been called herein a 'total' breach.... For a failure of performance constituting such a 'total' breach, an action for remedies that are appropriate thereto is at once maintainable. Yet the injured party is not required to bring such action. He has the option of treating the nonperformance as a 'partial' breach only...." In permitting the subcontractor to proceed with work on the project after August 9, the contractor, obviously, treated the breach by the subcontractor as a partial one. As the promises were mutually dependent and the subcontractor had made a material breach in his performance, this justified the contractor in refusing to make the August 10 payment; hence, as the contractor was not in default, the subcontractor again breached the contract when he, on September 12, discontinued work on the project, which rendered him liable (by the express terms of the contract) to the contractor for his increased cost in having the excavating done—a stipulated amount of $450. [Citation omitted.]

The appellees suggest two minor points that may be disposed of rather summarily. They argue that the contractor "gave no written notice to subcontractor for any services rendered or materials furnished by the contractor to the subcontractor," in accordance with the terms of the contract. It is apparent that the contractor's claim against the subcontractor for ill-performance did not involve, in any way, "services rendered or materials furnished" by the contractor; hence, the argument has no substance. They also contend that the contractor had no right to refuse the August 10 payment, because the subcontractor had furnished the insurance against property damage, as called for in the contract. There is little, or no, merit in this suggestion. The subcontractor and his insurance company denied liability. The furnishing of the insurance by him did not constitute a license to perform his work in a careless, negligence, or unworkmanlike manner; and its acceptance by the contractor did not preclude his assertion of a claim for unworkmanlike performance directly against the subcontractor.

Judgment against the appellant reversed; and judgment entered in favor of the appellant against the appellees for $450, the appellees to pay the costs.

Exercise 12-30: *Cobb v. Pacific Mutual Life Insurance Co.*

The next anticipatory repudiation case, *Cobb v. Pacific Mutual Life Insurance Co.*, deals with an exception to the anticipatory repudiation rule. Most law students find the rationale behind this exception elusive, if not completely bizarre. Consider yourself successful if you identify the nature of the exception. Consider yourself wildly successful if you can articulate the rationale for this exception.

Cobb v. Pacific Mutual Life Insurance Co.
51 P.2d 84 (1935)

SEAWELL, Justice.

Plaintiff and respondent, Augustus M. Cobb, will be referred to, when not designated by name, as the insured or respondent. The Pacific Mutual Life Insurance Company, a corporation, will be referred to as the company, or as insurer, or as appellant. Respondent, Cobb, brought this action against the Pacific Mutual Life Insurance Company, corporation, upon two policies of insurance issued by said company to insured, Cobb, during the month of August, 1929. One of said policies was upon the life of the insured, and therefore it is only collaterally involved in the action. The other, known as non-cancelable income policy, is the policy which furnishes the bases of the action and it is brought to our attention by this appeal. By its terms the company obligated itself to pay indemnity on account of disability resulting from sickness or accidental means, at the rate of $250 per month for the period throughout when such disability "consists of continuous, necessary and total loss of all business time."

[The] [t]wo policies above mentioned are in fact reissues of an original policy issued by [the] company to respondent, Cobb, on March 15, 1926. [The] original policy was not only a life policy, but it also contained a provision known as a business, permanent total disability provision, which provided for health indemnity payment in a lump or gross sum of $15,000 in the event the insured should become totally, continuously, and irrevocably disabled as a result of sickness. The original policy of 1926 insured against two elements of risk, death and health disability. In 1929 two separate policies were issued to take the place of the 1926 policy; one being issued solely upon the life of the insured and the other ... being issued as a noncancelable income policy, providing for the payment of health indemnity at the rate of $250 per month "for the period throughout which disability described above [in said policy] consists of continuous, necessary and total loss of business time...." The original policy was canceled upon the issuance and acceptance of the 1929 policies. The main difference between the indemnity provisions of the 1926 and 1929 policies is apparent. The earlier one provided that [the] policy would fully mature upon either the death of the holder or upon total and irreparable disability suffered by the insured, payable in a gross or lump sum. The policy of August, 1929, in effect at the time of breach, provided for monthly payments of $250 so long as the insured should remain physically disabled to the extent expressly stated therein. Two and one-half years after the 1929 indemnity policy was issued, the insured became wholly, permanently, and incurably disabled from the disease known as encephalitis or sleeping sickness. That the disabling effects of [the] disease has rendered the insured totally and permanently incapacitated within the terms of the policy and constitutes a continuous loss of "business time," and that its course is progressive and cannot be cured or arrested, is conclusively established by all of the medical testimony in the case, and this prognosis of the medical experts is not disputed by either of the parties to the action. This being true, the insured was entitled to receive a monthly payment of $250 per month, provided he had made no fraudulent misrepresentations nor withheld any material information from the company's medical examiner as to the state of his health or made any statement as to facts which were not true and which, if fully and truthfully given, would have probably caused [the] company to reject [the] applicant as not being an acceptable or desirable risk. The insured became totally disabled so as to suffer the loss of all business time on March 14, 1932. Proper notice as to disability was given to the company and demand was made for monthly indemnity at the rate of $250 per month as provided in the contract of insurance, but the company repudiated its contract by giving notice of rescission and by refusing to pay any amount thereunder, claiming fraudulent representations and the suppression of material information bearing on the state of health of the insured during a definite period of time both immediately before and on the day he was examined and interrogated by the examining physician on behalf of the company on matters affecting his health and physical condition. The company's repudiation was complete and absolute, as it was made by written notice offering to restore all the premiums it had received from the insured, with interest, which amount it afterwards deposited in court. [The] repudiation was again set up by its cross-complaint, wherein it sought rescission and prayed for a cancellation of the policy on the ground that it had been fraudulently procured. Quoting from Williston on Contracts, volume 3, § 1325, citing sustaining authorities, it is said: "So denying the validity of the contract between the parties, or insisting that its meaning or legal effect are different in a material particular from the true meaning or effect, coupled with the assertion, express or implied in fact, that performance will be made only according to the erroneous interpretation," amounts to total repudiation. In the instant case the validity of the contract was vigorously assailed by the company. The contract of insurance having been repudiated, the insured filed his complaint containing three counts. The prayer of the first, as set forth in paragraph 1, asks for indemnity at the rate of $250 per month, and paragraph 2 thereof prays for judgment in the gross sum of plaintiff's life [expectancy], amounting to $54,270. The second cause of action prays for indemnity at the rate of $250 per month as in [the] policy provided, but does not make any claim for damages caused by a breach of the policy. It is a straight action on the contract. The third cause of action is grounded upon the policy of 1926, and judgment is asked at the rate of $250 for three months, plus the aggregate gross sum of $15,000 as provided in [the] 1926 policy. This policy was superseded by [the noncancelable policy], issued in 1929.

Upon the trial of the case, the jury rendered a verdict in favor of the insured, and in the words of the verdict assessed "his damages in the amount of the present worth of payments of $250 per month for a life expectancy of fifteen years." According to the American mortality tables, the life expectancy of a person in reasonably good health of the age of the insured was a fraction above eighteen years. The trial court, treating the verdict of the jury as advisory, found that the policy and contract of insurance had been repudiated by the insurer without legal cause, and adopted the terms of the policy for the payment of monthly indemnity at the rate of $250 per month during the period of disability, and decreed that the contract had been breached and that the insured was entitled to be indemnified in damages for "the present worth of the sum of $250 per month for the period of plaintiff's life expectancy of fifteen years and that the present worth of [the] sum was $30,830." Judgment was accordingly entered in [the] sum, together with interest thereon a the rate of 7 [percent annually] from the 19th of May, 1932, together with plaintiff's costs of suit.

The trial court in its findings reviews at some length the charges that the insured procured [the] policy by fraudulent misrepresentations and by willfully suppressing material information bearing upon the health of the insured, and concludes that, while it is a fact that certain answers made by the insured as to questions bearing upon his health were not correctly given and certain facts within the scope of the medical examination were not disclosed by the insured, none of the acts or omissions complained of was "material to the acceptance of the risk and hazard assumed by defendant," and none of the erroneous answers made to questions asked or failure to give requested information was omitted with intent to deceive the insurer.

An appeal was taken from said judgment by the insurer to the District Court of Appeal ... and that portion of the judgment which applied the doctrine of anticipatory breach to the case and consequently allowed the insured a judgment for a sum equal to the present value of the monthly payments for the length of time that the insured at the time of the trial would be reasonably expected to live (fifteen years) was reversed and the insured was remitted to the amount of the accrued installments. The finding that the policy had not been fraudulently or wrongfully procured was sustained.

Upon the petition of the insured a hearing was granted.... We are in accord with the view expressed by the District Court of Appeal to the effect that the verdict of the jury finding against fraudulent procurement on the part of the insured is amply supported by the evidence.

The single question presented by this appeal is whether the doctrine of anticipatory breach is applicable to a policy of insurance which provides for payment of installments of indemnity for disabilities in the manner herein set forth, even though the insurer repudiates the contract on the grounds that it would not have issued the policy had the appellant given truthful answers to the medical examiner and full information germane to the condition of his health, and which, if so given, may have reasonably resulted in his rejection as an insurable risk.

The rule as accepted by this state is decisively stated in a number of decisions of this court, the most recent of which is *Brix v. People's Mutual Life Insurance Co.*, 41 P.2d 537, 541 (1935). In that case the insurance company by way of cross-complaint alleged that the policy upon which the action was brought was procured by the insured by means of material false representations made by the insured, and because of such it prayed for its cancellation and rescission. The court made findings against the company on the allegations of misrepresentations; thus taking notice of the issue of repudiation. The court gave judgment for plaintiff, at the rate of $100 per month during the remainder of his life. The judgment was modified on appeal by striking therefrom the portion which gave to plaintiff $100 per month for the remainder of his life. The decision nowhere recognizes the right of the insured to obtain judgment for future benefits either in monthly payments or for a gross sum. On this branch of the law we said:

"The books are filled with cases in which actions have been brought to recover upon insurance policies similar to the one here involved in which the insured has attempted to recover judgment not only for accrued payments, but has also sought an adjudication as to installments not yet due. While the decisions upon the right of the plaintiff in such character of actions to recover for installments which have not yet accrued are not entirely uniform, the great weight of authority is to the effect that, in such actions, recovery cannot be had for any installments falling due in the future. [Citations omitted]. In *Atkinson v. Railroad Employees Mutual Relief Society*, 22 S.W.2d 631, 634, the court declared the law as follows: 'While the benefit certificate issued to complainant constitutes an entire contract, the obligation thereby cast upon the society is severable, with a right of action accruing to the holder for each benefit installment payable and in default.' (Citation omitted). So it is generally held that, in an action at law for breach of a contract of insurance, payable in weekly or periodic installments, only those installments in default at the time suit was brought may be recovered." [Citation omitted.]

Howard v. Benefit Ass'n of Railway Employees, 39 S.W.2d 657, is directly in point. It is there held that, upon repudiation by an insurer of its obligation under a health insurance policy to make stipulated monthly payments so long as the insured shall continuously suffer total disability, the insured may not treat the entire contract as breached and sue for gross damages based upon his alleged expectancy of life.... We are mindful that there are many decisions which hold to the contrary view. It would be an interminable and delicate task to attempt even to sketch the origin, development, and application of the doctrine of anticipatory damages for the breach of contracts ... The difficulty lies not so much in the elucidation of the doctrine as it does with a knowledge as to the time and things to which it should be applied. There can be no anticipatory breach of a unilateral contract. WILLISTON ON CONTRACTS, Vol. 3, § 1328.... It is also the law that a bilateral contract becomes unilateral when the promisee has fully performed. In the case at bar the promisee had fully performed. He was exempt from future performance so far as dues or assessments were concerned. The fact that he was required or requested to submit to reasonable future medical examinations or furnish an occasional health report is too trivial and inconsequential to be regarded as an unperformed obligation on the part of the insured. He was therefore within the exception stated in the rule which holds that no repudiation can amount to an anticipatory breach of the rest of the installments not yet due. There is yet another obstacle in the way of plaintiff's right to recover future benefits in a gross sum ... He did not rely solely upon the right of election to declare a breach of the contract, but ... affirmed the contract and prayed for judgment in accordance therewith. This alone would be sufficient to hold him to an action on the contract.

The principle upon which the right to declare a contract at an end without a provision to do so and to sue for a breach of contract differ so fundamentally and widely from a contract of indemnity to pay a definite fixed sum in money during health disability that doctrine of anticipatory breach would seem to be an inept and in many cases an unjust doctrine to invoke.

The action is based upon contract for the payment of money, not unlike a promissory note providing for installments or the payment of rent. The installments as they become due are but debts. Yet, if the insurer in good faith and with color of right challenges the good faith of the insured and fails to prevail in an action, he is required to pay a large gross amount, although the insured is suffering from a permanent progressive disease and will not probably live the period of expectancy that a person in normal health would live.

To apply to this case the principle contended for by the insured would, in effect, penalize the company for asserting its defense if it did not prevail in a controversial matter even if made in good faith and with color of reason, notwithstanding the fact that the insured expressly agreed that "the falsity of any statement in the application materially affecting either the acceptance of the risk or the hazard assumed ... or made with the intent to deceive, shall bar all right to recovery under this contract." It is admitted that there is some authority for the application of this rule in cases so clearly within the doctrine of anticipatory breach that there is no room for question, but at best it is a drastic rule and should not be applied to a contract in which the parties impliedly recognize the right of contest.

The insured urges the application of the doctrine on the theory that, if the company becomes unfriendly or hostile to the insured, it may compel him to bring an action on every installment falling due, possibly for the purpose of harassing the insured, thereby causing a multiplicity of actions. It would seem that a reasonably sound business policy would of itself be a sufficient consideration to deter an insurer against practices which could not do otherwise than bring discredit to it. Besides, the law ought to be able to offer relief where compensation is willfully and contumaciously withheld. In the instant case, however, the situation cannot occur. It is admitted that the insured is totally and incurably ill with a progressive and totally [incapacitating] disease. The decision as to the validity of the contract has become final, and there is nothing left to be done but the payment of the indemnity as expressly provided by the parties thereto.

The tendency of this court has consistently been opposed to the application of the doctrine of anticipatory damages to cases involving fixed installment money payments which arise in the manner set forth in the contract herein....

The cause is remanded to the trial court, with leave to respondent, Cobb, to file a supplemental complaint including all payments due, and interest thereon, at the time of filing the complaint herein. That portion of the judgment which allows respondent damages for breach of said contract for the present worth of the sum of $250 per month for plaintiff's life expectancy of fifteen years, estimated to be the gross sum of $30,830, is reversed. In all other respects the judgment is affirmed. Let proceedings be had consistent with the views expressed and conclusions reached by this decision.

Exercise 12-31: *Cobb v. Pacific Mutual Life Insurance Co.* Revisited

Tenant signs a ten-year lease with Landlord to rent a small building for Tenant's business. As part of the agreement, Landlord remodels the building to suit Tenant's needs (a common practice in business leasing). Tenant anticipatorily repudiates the contract even before moving in, and Landlord sues Tenant, seeking 10-year's worth of rent. Citing *Cobb*, Tenant argues Landlord should only be awarded past due rent and should not be awarded future rent. Landlord argues *Cobb* is distinguishable. Who is right and why?

Exercise 12-32: *Drake v. Wickwire*

The next case raises both anticipatory repudiation and failure of assurances, the next ground for discharge, in a very interesting context: a suit for legal malpractice. The client argued, in effect, that her attorney had failed to learn what you are supposed to be learning right now! As you read the case, consider the following questions:

1. Why did the court conclude that the attorney had committed malpractice as a matter of law? Make sure you identify the principle of anticipatory repudiation law the attorney should have known and applied.

2. Do you agree with the court?

3. Why do you think the trial court granted summary judgment to the attorney?

4. Express the rule stated in section 251 of the Restatement Second of Contracts in your own words. It is identical to U.C.C. §2-609, the U.C.C. rule on point.

5. If the client's only claim had been that the attorney had failed to demand adequate assurances, would the court have found that the attorney had committed malpractice as a matter of law?

Drake v. Wickwire

795 P.2d 195 (1990)

MATTHEWS, Chief Justice.

This is a malpractice action against an attorney for allegedly inducing his client to break an earnest money sales agreement. The underlying facts are set forth in *Drake v. Hosley*, 713 P.2d 1203 (Alaska 1986). We excerpt them at this point:

On March 5, 1984, Paul Drake signed an exclusive listing agreement with The Charles Hosley Company, Realtors (hereafter "Hosley"). The agreement authorized Hosley to act as Drake's agent until March 30, 1984, to sell some land Drake owned in North Pole, Alaska. The agreement provided for payment of a ten percent commission if, during the period of the listing agreement, 1) Hosley located a buyer "willing and able to purchase at the terms set by the seller," or 2) the seller entered into a "binding sale" during the term set by the seller.

Hosley found a group of three buyers, Robert Goldsmith, Dwayne Hofschulte and David Nystrom (hereafter "buyers"), who were interested in the property. On March 23, 1984, Drake signed a purchase and sale agreement, entitled "earnest money receipt," in which he agreed to sell the land to the buyers at a specified price and terms. The buyers also signed the agreement. It provided that closing would occur "within 10 days of clear title" and "ASAP, 1984." A typed addendum stated that Drake agreed to pay Hosley a commission of ten percent of the price paid for the property. Both Drake and Hosley signed the addendum.

On April 3, 1984, Hosley received a preliminary commitment for title insurance. The title report listed a judgment in favor of Drake's ex-wife as the sole encumbrance on the title. The next day Hosley called Drake's attorney, Tom Wickwire, to ask about the judgment. Wickwire stated that the judgment would be paid with the cash received at closing.

Two or three days later, attorney Wickwire called Hosley and stated that his client (Drake) wanted the sale closed by April 11. Wickwire explained that he had negotiated a discounted settlement with Drake's ex-wife that required payment by April 11. Wickwire claims that Hosley agreed to close by April 11. Hosley disagrees, and claims he merely stated that he would try to close as quickly as possible.

When Hosley became concerned that the buyers would not be able to close on April 11, he telephoned the attorney for Drake's ex-wife and learned that the April 11 deadline for payment of the judgment had been extended to the end of the month.

On April 11, Wickwire called Hosley to set up the closing. Hosley told Wickwire that the buyers could not close that day because they did not have the money and would not have it before May 1. Wickwire indicated that he would advise Drake to call off the sale because the buyers had refused to perform. Wickwire mailed a letter to Hosley, dated April 11, stating that Drake's offer to sell was withdrawn. Hosley received the letter on approximately April 18. On April 12, Drake sold his property through another broker to different buyers.

On April 12, Hosley went to Wickwire's office to close the sale and submitted checks from the buyers totaling $33,000 for the down payment. Wickwire refused the checks, stating that another buyer already had purchased the property. Id. at 1204–05 [Footnote omitted.]

In *Drake*, Hosley sued Drake for his real estate commission. The trial court granted summary judgment to Hosley. On appeal we affirmed, holding that

Hosley was Drake's agent, not the agent of the buyers and thus would have had no authority to change the deadline for closing from April 12 or 13 to April 11 as Drake contended. We concluded:

> Hosley found a group of buyers who were willing and able to perform in accord with the terms set by the seller, but they were prevented from doing so by the seller's frustrating conduct. The buyers tried to perform by tendering checks for the down payment "within 10 days of clear title," as required by the earnest money agreement. The sale did not take place because the seller, Drake, sold the property to a third party during the ten-day closing period.

Id. at 1208.

In the present action, Drake alleges that Wickwire was negligent in advising him that he could sell his property to another buyer on April 11. Wickwire moved for summary judgment. Wickwire contended that he believed that there had been an anticipatory breach of the earnest money agreement when Hosley told him the buyer would not have the money until May 1 and that his conduct "did not fall below an acceptable standard of care." He supported this contention with the affidavits of two attorneys. Drake filed a memorandum in opposition to the motion for summary judgment but did not submit testimony or affidavits from attorneys opining that Wickwire had been negligent.

The trial court granted Wickwire's motion in a written decision which adopted a rule requiring expert evidence to establish a breach of an attorney's duty of care, except in non-technical situations where negligence is evident to lay people or where the fault is so clear as to constitute negligence as a matter of law. After adopting this rule the court applied it to the facts of this case, finding that Wickwire's negligence, if any, was not so obvious that it could be determined as a matter of law, nor was the subject matter non-technical so that negligence might be evident to lay people. The court therefore concluded that expert testimony from Drake was required. Since none was presented by Drake, summary judgment was granted.

The court stated:

> Defendant contends that expert testimony is required. He notes that the case involves issues of anticipatory repudiation of a contract, earnest money agreements, real estate brokers, and closing dates in the context of a $330,000 raw land sale transaction. Plaintiff alleges that the defendant's breach of duty was so obvious that expert testimony is not required. Plaintiff portrays the issues as simple mathematics (adding 10 days to April 2 or 3), and not selling land to a party after you have promised to sell to another party. Plaintiff also argues that the issue of anticipatory repudiation has already been decided by the Alaska Supreme Court in *Drake v. Hosley*, 713 P.2d 1203 (Alaska 1986). The court concludes that the alleged breach, or lack thereof, is not so obvious that it may be determined as a matter of law nor is it within the ordinary knowledge of laypersons. Thus, expert testimony is required. Anticipatory repudiation is an issue in this case; the Supreme Court's decision in *Drake v. Hosley* is not dispositive. The issue in this case is not whether the anticipatory repudiation did or did not occur, but whether a reasonable attorney under

the existing circumstances could reasonably have made such a determination. There is also a complex agency issue involving the conduct of the real estate broker. Neither issue is within the ordinary knowledge of laypersons.

On appeal, Drake does not take issue with the rule of law adopted by the court. Instead, he argues that this case involves obvious breaches of duty on the part of Wickwire and, in addition, urges us to "find negligence as a matter of law as [we] did in Drake v. Hosley." Concerning the latter case, Drake argues:

> This court (in *Drake v. Hosley*, supra) has already determined that there is no material issue of fact and that reasonable minds cannot differ with respect to the question of whether an anticipatory breach took place. It did not. These findings were made against a layperson (Drake), relying on an attorney's advice, after repeated urging that a question of fact existed in that reasonable minds could differ. *A fortiori*, the same ruling must apply to Wickwire where the standard is obviously higher.

In response, Wickwire argues issues going to anticipatory repudiation:

> The judgment exercised by Wickwire was not a matter of counting, but (1) whether Hosley had apparent authority to deliver word from the buyers regarding the sale and (2) whether Wickwire could reasonably rely on the admission of Hofschulte, as conveyed by Hosley, that the buyers could not perform until May 1.

We agree with the rule of law adopted by the superior court in this case ... [Discussion of supporting authority omitted.]

However, we are of the view that Wickwire was negligent as a matter of law. In Drake's brief, authored by Wickwire, in the case of *Drake v. Hosley*, the critical conversation between Hosley and Wickwire relating to the alleged anticipatory repudiation is set forth as follows:

> [O]n the morning of April 11 [Wickwire] called Hosley to select a specific time and place for closing. But Hosley's response was that his buyers could not close on that day as they did not have the money but would need until May 1 to get it. Wickwire asked Hosley if the problem was just getting the time to get the money out of the bank or did they not have the downpayment. Hosley replied that the buyers in fact had the money but were "resisting the pressure to close."

The law of anticipatory repudiation is set forth in sections 253, 250 and 251 of the RESTATEMENT SECOND OF CONTRACTS (1981) (hereafter RESTATEMENT). Section 253(1) of the RESTATEMENT provides:

> Where an obligor repudiates a duty before he has committed a breach by non-performance and before he has received all of the agreed exchange for it, his repudiation alone gives rise to a claim for damages for total breach.

The concept of repudiation is explained in § 250 as follows: "A repudiation is (a) a statement by the obligor to the obligee indicating that the obligor will commit a breach that would of itself give the obligee claim for damages...."

The commentary to this section explains that a statement, in order to qualify as a repudiation, must be reasonably clear:

> In order to constitute a repudiation, a party's language must be suf-
> ficiently positive to be reasonably interpreted to mean that the party
> will not or cannot perform. Mere expression of doubt as to his will-
> ingness or ability to perform is not enough to constitute a repudia-
> tion, although such an expression may give an obligee reasonable
> grounds to believe that the obligor will commit a serious breach and
> may ultimately result in a repudiation under the rule stated in § 251.
> However, language that under a fair reading "amounts to a statement
> of intention not to perform except on conditions which go beyond
> the contract" constitutes a repudiation.

RESTATEMENT § 250, comment b. [Citation omitted.]

In our view, Wickwire did not act reasonably in treating Hosley's statement as a repudiation. As recited by Wickwire, it was ambiguous on its face.
Hosley first indicated that the buyers would need until May 1 to get the money.
Later, though, Hosley indicated that the buyers had the money but were "resisting the pressure to close." The latter statement itself is ambiguous in that
it is unclear whether the buyers were resisting the pressure to close on April
11 as Drake desired, or on April 12 or 13 as the contract required.

If the former meaning was intended, there would have been no anticipatory repudiation because the buyers had no contractual obligation to close
on the 11th. If the latter meaning was intended, Wickwire would have had at
most reasonable grounds to believe that the buyers would breach the contract. Neither meaning justifies treating the statement as a repudiation. Instead,
Wickwire could have sought assurances of performance under the rule stated
in § 251 of the Restatement. That rule states:

(1) Where reasonable grounds arise to believe that the obligor will com-
    mit a breach by nonperformance that would of itself give the obligee
    a claim for damages for total breach ... the obligee may demand ad-
    equate assurance of due performance and may, if reasonable, sus-
    pend any performance for which he has not already received the
    agreed exchange until he receives such assurance.

(2) The obligee may treat as a repudiation the obligor's failure to provide
    within a reasonable time such assurance of due performance as is
    adequate in the circumstances of the particular case.

Wickwire's negligence in this case was in advising precipitate conduct in the
face of an ambiguous statement which was insufficient to indicate that the
buyers would breach the contract.

The judgment is reversed and this case is remanded for further proceedings consistent with this decision.

Exercise 12-33: *AMF v. McDonalds*

As you read *AMF v. McDonald's*, please consider the following questions:

1. Why did the *AMF* court conclude that McDonald's had reasonable grounds
    for insecurity?

2. The court concludes, without much analysis, that the demands that Mc-Donald's made were reasonable. What did McDonald's demand by way of assurance? Was that demand reasonable? Why?

AMF, Inc. v. McDonald's Corp.

536 F.2d 1167 (1976)

CUMMINGS, Circuit Judge.

AMF, Incorporated, filed this case in the Southern District of New York in April 1972. It was transferred to the Northern District of Illinois in May 1973. AMF seeks damages for the alleged wrongful cancellation and repudiation of McDonald's Corporation's ("McDonald's") orders for sixteen computerized cash registers for installation in restaurants owned by wholly-owned subsidiaries of McDonald's and for seven such registers ordered by licensees of McDonald's for their restaurants. In July 1972, McDonald's of Elk Grove, Inc. sued AMF to recover the $20,385.28 purchase price paid for a prototype computerized cash register and losses sustained as a result of failure of the equipment to function satisfactorily. Both cases were tried together during a fortnight in December 1974. A few months after the completion of the bench trial, the district court rendered a memorandum opinion and order in both cases in favor of each defendant. The only appeal is from the eight judgment orders dismissing AMF's complaints against McDonald's and the seven licensees. We affirm.

The district court's memorandum opinion and order are unreported. Our statement of the pertinent facts is culled from the 124 findings of fact contained therein or from the record itself.

In 1966, AMF began to market individual components of a completely automated restaurant system, including its model 72C computerized cash register involved here. The 72C cash register then consisted of a central computer, one to four input stations, each with a keyboard and cathode ray tube display, plus the necessary cables and controls.

In 1967 McDonald's representatives visited AMF's plant in Springdale, Connecticut, to view a working "breadboard" model 72C to decide whether to use it in McDonald's restaurant system. Later that year, it was agreed that a 72C should be placed in a McDonald's restaurant for evaluation purposes.

In April 1968, a 72C unit accommodating six input stations was installed in McDonald's restaurant in Elk Grove, Illinois. This restaurant was a wholly-owned subsidiary of McDonald's and was its busiest restaurant. Besides functioning as a cash register, the 72C was intended to enable counter personnel to work faster and to assist in providing data for accounting reports and bookkeeping. McDonald's of Elk Grove, Inc. paid some $20,000 for this prototype register on January 3, 1969. AMF never gave McDonald's warranties governing reliability or performance standards for the prototype.

At a meeting in Chicago on August 29, 1968, McDonald's concluded to order sixteen 72C's for its company-owned restaurants and to cooperate with

AMF to obtain additional orders from its licensees. In December 1968, AMF accepted McDonald's purchase orders for those sixteen 72C's. In late January 1969, AMF accepted seven additional orders for 72C's from McDonald's licensees for their restaurants. Under the contract for the sale of all the units, there was a warranty for parts and service. AMF proposed to deliver the first unit in February 1969, with installation of the remaining twenty-two units in the first half of 1969. However, AMF established a new delivery schedule in February 1969, providing for deliveries to commence at the end of July 1969 and to be completed in January 1970, assuming that the first test unit being built at AMF's Vandalia, Ohio, plant was built and satisfactorily tested by the end of July 1969. This was never accomplished.

During the operation of the prototype 72C at McDonald's Elk Grove restaurant, many problems resulted, requiring frequent service calls by AMF and others. Because of its poor performance, McDonald's had AMF remove the prototype unit from its Elk Grove restaurant in late April 1969.

At a March 18, 1969, meeting, McDonald's and AMF personnel met to discuss the performance of the Elk Grove prototype. AMF agreed to formulate a set of performance and reliability standards for the future 72C's, including "the number of failures permitted at various degrees of seriousness, total permitted downtime, maximum service hours and cost." Pending mutual agreement on such standards, McDonald's personnel asked that production of the twenty-three units be held up and AMF agreed.

On May 1, 1969, AMF met with McDonald's personnel to provide them with performance and reliability standards. However, the parties never agreed upon such standards. At that time, AMF did not have a working machine and could not produce one within a reasonable time because its Vandalia, Ohio, personnel were too inexperienced. After the May 1st meeting, AMF concluded that McDonald's had cancelled all 72C orders. The reasons for the cancellation were the poor performance of the prototype, the lack of assurances that a workable machine was available and the unsatisfactory conditions at AMF's Vandalia, Ohio, plant where the twenty-three 72C's were to be built.

On July 29, 1969, McDonald's and AMF representatives met in New York. At this meeting it was mutually understood that the 72C orders were cancelled and that none would be delivered.

In its conclusions of law, the district court held that McDonald's and its licensees had entered into contracts for twenty-three 72C cash registers but that AMF was not able to perform its obligations under the contracts.... Citing Section 2-610 of the Uniform Commercial Code [citation to Illinois statute omitted][9] and Comment 1 thereunder, the court concluded that on

---

9. Section 2-610 provides: "Anticipatory Repudiation. When either party repudiates the contract with respect to a performance not yet due the loss of which will substantially impair the value of the contract to the other, the aggrieved party may (a) for a commercially reasonable time await performance by the repudiating party; or (b) resort to any remedy for breach (Section 2-703 or Section 2-711), even though he has notified the repudiating party that he would await the latter's performance and has urged retraction; and (c) in either case suspend his own performance or proceed in accordance with the provisions of this Article on the seller's right to identify goods to the contract notwithstanding breach or to salvage unfinished goods (Section 2-704)."

July 29, McDonald's justifiably repudiated the contracts to purchase all twenty-three 72C's.

Relying on Section 2-609 and 2-610 of the Uniform Commercial Code [citation to Illinois statute omitted],[10] the court decided that McDonald's was warranted in repudiating the contracts and therefore had a right to cancel the orders by virtue of Section 2-711 of the Uniform Commercial Code. [11] [Citation to Illinois statute omitted.] Accordingly, judgment was entered for McDonald's.

The findings of fact adopted by the district court were a mixture of the court's own findings and findings proposed by the parties, some of them modified by the court. AMF has assailed ten of the 124 findings of fact, but our examination of the record satisfies us that all have adequate support in the record and support the conclusions of law.

Whether in a specific case a buyer has reasonable grounds for insecurity is a question of fact. [Citations omitted.] On this record, McDonald's clearly had "reasonable grounds for insecurity" with respect to AMF's performance. At the time of the March 18, 1969, meeting, the prototype unit had performed unsatisfactorily ever since its April 1968 installation. Although AMF had projected delivery of all twenty-three units by the first half of 1969, AMF later scheduled delivery from the end of July 1969 until January 1970. When McDonald's personnel visited AMF's Vandalia, Ohio, plant on March 4, 1969, they saw that none of the 72C systems was being assembled and learned that a pilot unit would not be ready until the end of July of that year. They were informed that the engineer assigned to the project was not to commence work until March 17th. AMF's own personnel were also troubled about the design

---

10. Section 2-609 provides: "Right to Adequate Assurance of Performance. (1) A contract for sale imposes an obligation on each party that the other's expectation of receiving due performance will not be impaired. When reasonable grounds for insecurity arise with respect to the performance of either party the other may in writing demand adequate assurance of due performance and until he receives such assurance may if commercially reasonable suspend any performance for which he has not already received the agreed return. (2) Between merchants the reasonableness of grounds for insecurity and the adequacy of any assurance offered shall be determined according to commercial standards. (3) Acceptance of any improper delivery or payment does not prejudice the aggrieved party's right to demand adequate assurance of future performance. (4) After receipt of a justified demand failure to provide within a reasonable time not exceeding 30 days such assurance of due performance as is adequate under the circumstances of the particular case is a repudiation of the contract."

11. Section 2-711 provides: "Buyer's Remedies in General; Buyer's Security Interest in Rejected Goods. (1) Where the seller fails to make delivery or repudiates or the buyer rightfully rejects or justifiably revokes acceptance then with respect to any goods involved, and with respect to the whole if the breach goes to the whole contract (Section 2-612), the buyer may cancel and whether or not he has done so may in addition to recovering so much of the price as has been paid (a) 'cover' and have damages under the next section as to all the goods affected whether or not they have been identified to the contract; or (b) recover damages for non-delivery as provided in this Article (Section 2-713). (2) Where the seller fails to deliver or repudiates the buyer may also (a) if the goods have been identified recover them as provided in this Article (Section 2-502); or (b) in a proper case obtain specific performance or replevy the goods as provided in this Article (Section 2-716). (3) On rightful rejection or justifiable revocation of acceptance a buyer has a security interest in goods in his possession or control for any payments made on their price and any expenses reasonably incurred in their inspection, receipt, transportation, care and custody and may hold such goods and resell them in like manner as an aggrieved seller (Section 2-706)."

of the 72C, causing them to attempt to reduce McDonald's order to five units. Therefore, under Section 2-609 McDonald's was entitled to demand adequate assurance of performance by AMF.[12]

However, AMF urges that Section 2-609 of the U.C.C.... is inapplicable because McDonald's did not make a written demand of adequate assurance of due performance. In *Pittsburgh-Des Moines Steel Co. v. Brookhaven Manor Water Co.*, [citation omitted], we noted that the Code should be liberally construed and therefore rejected such "a formalistic approach" to Section 2-609. McDonald's failure to make a written demand was excusable because AMF's Mr. Dubosque's testimony and his April 2 and 18, 1969, memoranda about the March 18th meeting showed AMF's clear understanding that McDonald's had suspended performance until it should receive adequate assurance of due performance from AMF [Citations to record omitted.].

After the March 18th demand, AMF never repaired the Elk Grove unit satisfactorily nor replaced it. Similarly, it was unable to satisfy McDonald's that the twenty-three machines on order would work. At the May 1st meeting, AMF offered unsatisfactory assurances for only five units instead of twenty-three. The performance standards AMF tendered to McDonald's were unacceptable because they would have permitted the 72C's not to function properly for 90 hours per year, permitting as much as one failure in every fifteen days in a busy McDonald's restaurant. Also, as the district court found, AMF's Vandalia, Ohio, personnel were too inexperienced to produce a proper machine. Since AMF did not provide adequate assurance of performance after McDonald's March 18th demand, U.C.C. Section 2-609(1) permitted McDonald's to suspend performance. When AMF did not furnish adequate assurance of due performance at the May 1st meeting, it thereby repudiated the contract under Section 2-609(4). At that point, Section 2-610(b) ... permitted McDonald's to cancel the orders pursuant to Section 2-711 ...

Judgment Affirmed.

Exercise 12-34: *AMF v. McDonald's* Revisited

Assume that you represent McDonald's. Draft a written demand for assurances on behalf of McDonald's that both meets the concerns of McDonald's and would survive 2-609 scrutiny.

---

12. McDonald's was justified in seeking assurances about performance standards at the March 18th meeting. The parts and service warranty in the contracts for the twenty-three 72C's was essentially a limitation of remedy provision. Under U.C.C. §2-719(2) [citation to Illinois statute omitted.], if the 72C cash registers failed to work or could not be repaired within a reasonable time, the limitation of remedy provision would be invalid, and McDonald's would be entitled to pursue all other remedies provided in Article 2. [Citations omitted.]. Because McDonald's would have a right to reject the machines if they proved faulty after delivery and then to cancel the contract, it was consistent with the purposes of Section 2-609 for McDonald's to require assurances that such eventuality would not occur. See Comment 1 to U.C.C. §2-719.

Impracticability/Impossibility and Frustration of Purpose

Impracticability

Exercise 12-35: Introductory Impracticability Hypothetical

Jenny and Helen entered into a contract by which Jenny and Helen agreed to share their briefs, course outlines, and practice exams during their second semester of law school. Both parties entered into the contract because they regarded the other as intelligent and thoughtful and as possessing excellent listening and teaching skills. Unfortunately, before performance was due under the contract, Jenny died, and so Jenny did none of the work she had contracted to do. Helen, who has never offered to give Jenny's estate her (Helen's) briefs, outlines and practice exams, sued Jenny's estate for breach.

Based on what you have learned about constructive conditions, did Helen have to render or tender her performance to put Jenny's estate in breach?

Also, based on what you have learned, in Helen's suit against Jenny's estate, is it clear that, unless Jenny's performance is **discharged**, Jenny materially breached the contract?

If your answer to the previous two questions is "yes," the only question would be whether Jenny's death excuses Jenny's estate's performance. As we will learn, Jenny's death would discharge the performance. Likewise, as we will learn, the fact that Jenny's performance became impossible also means Helen's obligation to render or tender her performance would also be discharged.

Here are the elements of impracticability:

1. Occurrence of an unforeseen event.

2. Which event makes a party's performance impracticable, that is, so vitally different from what was expected as to alter the essential nature of the performance.

3. Non-occurrence of the event was a basic assumption on which the parties made the contract.

4. The party claiming impracticability had no fault in causing the event.

5. The party claiming impracticability did not assume the risk because:

   a. The contract does not assign her the risk, OR

   b. She could not foresee the event and therefore did not choose to undertake the risk, OR

   c. The event was not within her control and she was therefore not in the best position to avoid the loss.

Here are the rules that address the effect of impracticability.

- If the impracticable performance is a material part of the agreed exchange, it is excused and the rest of the contract is discharged.

- If the impracticable performance is not a material part of the agreed exchange, it is excused but the rest of the parties' respective obligations remain due.

Notice that, although the rule only requires impracticability, in the above example, the required performance is not merely impracticable but is, in fact, impossible. What would be the result in the Jenny-Helen hypo above if Jenny "merely" suffered a head injury in a car accident and therefore withdrew from the agreement because she needed to approach studying in a different way to accommodate her injury? Do not attempt to answer this question now. Rather, keep this question in mind as your read the assigned materials.

Also notice that, in both of the above hypotheticals, there is no basis for saying that the contract allocated the risk of impracticability. What would be the result in the second hypo if the contract stated that: "Jenny assumes the risk of any illness or injury"? Do not attempt to answer this question now. Rather, keep this question in mind as your read the assigned materials.

Finally, notice that impracticability is a ground for discharge of an obligation. It functions this way in the first Jenny-Helen hypo (Jenny's death discharges her obligation to perform). However, impracticability can also be a ground for excusing the non-occurrence of a condition that is a non-material part of a contract. For example, if the buyer of a parcel of land conditions her duty to buy on the seller first demolishing an unsightly building owned by the seller that overlooks the land, the condition might be excused if the building were declared a national monument thus making its demolition legally impossible. In these circumstances, a court would likely conclude that the demolition of the building was a non-material condition and excuse its non-occurrence but not discharge the parties. Whether a particular instance of impracticability excuses the non-occurrence of a condition or discharges both parties' duties to perform depends on whether the court deems the condition material or non-material. In other words, once we decide a party's performance is impracticable, we still have a crucial question: What's the effect of the impracticability on both parties' future performances? The answer to that question, as we will learn, depends on the nature of the promise the performance of which has become impracticable.

Exercise 12-36: *Taylor v. Caldwell*

As you read *Taylor v. Caldwell*, consider the following questions:

1. When was each party's performance due in *Taylor*?
2. Was the contract in *Taylor* divisible?
3. Was the issue of divisibility relevant in *Taylor*?
4. How could you change the facts in *Taylor* and make divisibility relevant?
5. Apply the above list of elements to the facts of *Taylor*.
6. What is the policy for excusing performance based on impracticability?

Taylor v. Caldwell
3 Best & S 826 (1863)

The declaration alleged that by an agreement, bearing date the 27th May, 1861, the defendants agreed to let, and the plaintiffs agreed to take, on the terms therein stated, The Surrey Gardens and Music Hall, Newington, Surrey, for the following days, that is to say, Monday the 17th June, 1861, Monday the 15th July, 1861, Monday the 5th August, 1861, and Monday the 19th August, 1861, for the purpose of giving a series of four grand concerts and day and night fêtes, at the Gardens and Hall on those days respectively, at the rent or sum of 100 pounds. for each of those days. It then averred the fulfilment of conditions etc., on the part of the plaintiffs; and breach by the defendants, that they did not nor would allow the plaintiffs to have the use of The Surrey Music Hall and Gardens according to the agreement, but wholly made default therein, etc.; whereby the plaintiffs lost divers moneys paid by them for printing advertisements of and in advertising the concerts, and also lost divers sums expended and expenses incurred by them in preparing for the concerts and otherwise in relation thereto, and on the faith of the performance by the defendants of the agreement on their part, and had been otherwise injured, etc....

On the trial, before Blackburn J., at the London Sittings after Michaelmas Term, 1861, it appeared that the action was brought on the following agreement:

"Royal Surrey Gardens,

"27th May, 1861.

"Agreement between Messrs. Caldwell & Bishop, of the one part, and Messrs. Taylor & Lewis of the other part, whereby the said Caldwell & Bishop agree to let, and the said Taylor & Lewis agree to take, on the terms hereinafter stated, The Surrey Gardens and Music Hall, Newington, Surrey, for the following days, viz.:

"Monday, the 17th June, 1861,

Monday the 15th July, 1861,

Monday the 5th August, 1861,

Monday the 19th August, 1861,

for the purpose of giving a series of four grand concerts and day and night fêtes at the said Gardens and Hall on those days respectively at the rent or sum of 100 pounds for each of the said days. The said Caldwell & Bishop agree to find and provide at their own sole expense, on each of the aforesaid days, for the amusement of the public and persons then in the said Gardens and Hall, an efficient and organised military and quadrille band, the united bands to consist of from thirty-five to forty members; al fresco entertainments of various descriptions; coloured minstrels, fireworks and full illuminations; a ballet or divertissement, if permitted; a wizard and Grecian statues; tight rope performances; rifle galleries; air gun shooting; Chinese and Parisian games; boats on the lake, and (weather permitting) aquatic sports, and all and every other entertainment as given nightly during the months and times above mentioned. And the said Caldwell & Bishop also agree that the before mentioned united bands shall be present and assist at each of the said concerts, from its commencement until 9 o'clock at night; that they will, one week at least previous to the above mentioned dates, underline in bold type in all their bills and advertisements that Mr. Sims Reeves and other artistes will sing at the said gardens on those dates respectively, and that the said Taylor & Lewis shall have the right of placing their boards, bills and placards in such number and manner (but subject to the approval of the said Caldwell & Bishop) in and about the entrance to the said gardens, and in the said grounds, one week at least previous to each of the above mentioned days respectively, all bills so displayed being affixed on boards. And the said Caldwell & Bishop also agree to allow dancing on the new circular platform after 9 o'clock at night, but not before. And the said Caldwell & Bishop also agree not to allow the firework display to take place till a quarter past 11 o'clock at night. And, lastly, the said Caldwell & Bishop agree that the said Taylor & Lewis shall be entitled to and shall be at liberty to take and receive, as and for the sole use and property of them the said Taylor & Lewis, all moneys paid for entrance to the Gardens, Galleries and Music Hall and firework galleries, and that the said Taylor & Lewis may in their own discretion secure the patronage of any charitable institution in connection with the said concerts. And the said Taylor & Lewis agree to pay the aforesaid respective sum of 100 pounds in the evening of the said respective days by a crossed cheque, and also to find and provide, at their own sole cost, all the necessary artistes for the said concerts, including Mr. Sims Reeves, God's will permitting. (Signed)

"J. CALDWELL."
Witness "CHAS. BISHOP.
(Signed) "S. Denis."

On the 11th June the Music Hall was destroyed by an accidental fire, so that it became impossible to give the concerts....

The judgment of the Court was now delivered by Blackburn J. In this case the plaintiffs and defendants had, on the 27th May, 1861, entered into a contract by which the defendants agreed to let the plaintiffs have the use of The Surrey Gardens and Music Hall on four days then to come, viz., the 17th June, 15th July, 5th August and 19th August, for the purpose of giving a series of four grand concerts, and day and night fêtes at the Gardens and Hall on those days respectively; and the plaintiffs agreed to take the Gardens and Hall on those days, and pay 100 pounds for each day.

The parties inaccurately call this a "letting," and the money to be paid a "rent;" but the whole agreement is such as to shew that the defendants were to retain the possession of the Hall and Gardens so that there was to be no demise of them, and that the contract was merely to give the plaintiffs the use of them on those days. Nothing however, in our opinion, depends on this. The agreement then proceeds to set out various stipulations between the parties as to what each was to supply for these concerts and entertainments, and as to the manner in which they should be carried on. The effect of the whole is to shew that the existence of the Music Hall in the Surrey Gardens in a state fit for a concert was essential for the fulfilment of the contract,—such entertainments as the parties contemplated in their agreement could not be given without it.

After the making of the agreement, and before the first day on which a concert was to be given, the Hall was destroyed by fire. This destruction, we must take it on the evidence, was without the fault of either party, and was so complete that in consequence the concerts could not be given as intended. And the question we have to decide is whether, under these circumstances, the loss which the plaintiffs have sustained is to fall upon the defendants. The parties when framing their agreement evidently had not present to their minds the possibility of such a disaster, and have made no express stipulation with reference to it, so that the answer to the question must depend upon the general rules of law applicable to such a contract.

There seems no doubt that where there is a positive contract to do a thing, not in itself unlawful, the contractor must perform it or pay damages for not doing it, although in consequence of unforeseen accidents, the performance of his contract has become unexpectedly burthensome or even impossible ... But this rule is only applicable when the contract is positive and absolute, and not subject to any condition either express or implied: and there are authorities which, as we think, establish the principle that where, from the nature of the contract, it appears that the parties must from the beginning have known that it could not be fulfilled unless when the time for the fulfilment of the contract arrived some particular specified thing continued to exist, so that, when entering into the contract, they must have contemplated such continuing existence as the foundation of what was to be done; there, in the absence of any express or implied warranty that the thing shall exist, the contract is not to be construed as a positive contract, but as subject to an implied condition that the parties shall be excused in case, before breach, performance becomes impossible from the perishing of the thing without default of the contractor. There seems little doubt that this implication tends to further the great object of making the legal construction such as to fulfil the intention of those who entered into the contract. For in the course of affairs men in making such contracts in general would, if it were brought to their minds, say that there should be such a condition....

There is a class of contracts in which a person binds himself to do something which requires to be performed by him in person; and such promises, e.g. promises to marry, or promises to serve for a certain time, are never in practice qualified by an express exception of the death of the party; and therefore in such cases the contract is in terms broken if the promisor dies before fulfilment. Yet it was very early determined that, if the performance is personal, the executors are not liable; [citations omitted] "Thus, ... if an author undertakes to compose a work, and dies before completing it, his executors are discharged from this contract: for the undertaking is merely personal in its nature, and, by the intervention of the contractor's death, has become impossible to be performed." ... In *Hall v. Wright* (E.B. & E. 746, 749), Crompton J., in his judgment, puts another case. "Where a contract depends upon personal skill, and the act of God renders it impossible, as, for instance in the case of a painter employed to paint a picture who is struck blind, it may be that the performance might be excused."

It seems that in those cases the only ground on which the parties or their executors, can be excused from the consequences of the breach of the contract is, that from the nature of the contract there is an implied condition of the continued existence of the life of the contractor, and, perhaps in the case of the painter of his eyesight ...

These are instances where the implied condition is of the life of a human being, but there are others in which the same implication is made as to the continued existence of a thing. For example, where a contract of sale is made amounting to a bargain and sale, transferring presently the property in specific chattels, which are to be delivered by the vendor at a future day; there, if the chattels, without the fault of the vendor, perish in the interval, the purchaser must pay the price and the vendor is excused from performing his contract to deliver, which has thus become impossible....

The principle seems to us to be that, in contracts in which the performance depends on the continued existence of a given person or thing, a condition is implied that the impossibility of performance arising from the perishing of the person or thing shall excuse the performance.

In none of these cases is the promise in words other than positive, nor is there any express stipulation that the destruction of the person or thing shall excuse the performance; but that excuse is by law implied, because from the nature of the contract it is apparent that the parties contracted on the basis of the continued existence of the particular person or chattel. In the present case, looking at the whole contract, we find that the parties contracted on the basis of the continued existence of the Music Hall at the time when the concerts were to be given; that being essential to their performance.

We think, therefore, that the Music Hall having ceased to exist, without fault of either party, both parties are excused, the plaintiffs from taking the gardens and paying the money, the defendants from performing their promise to give the use of the Hall and Gardens and other things.

Consequently the rule must be absolute to enter the verdict for the defendants. Rule absolute.

Exercise 12-37: *Taylor v. Caldwell* Revisited

1. How could you change the facts to make defendants liable?

2. What if the music hall itself had not been damaged in the fire but a special room the parties had planned to use for a post-concert wine-and-cheese reception had been destroyed?

3. Consider the following hypotheticals:

   a. Arnie contracts to produce a movie for Brian. As Brian knows, Arnie's only source for funding is a $100,000 deposit in Columbia Bank. Columbia bank fails, and Arnie does not produce the movie. Is Arnie excused based on impracticability?

   b. Farmer contracts to sell Bread Company all of Farmer's wheat production but not less than 500 bushels. Farmer's wheat crop is destroyed because of a disease that was not caused by any fault of Farmer's. Is Farmer excused based on impracticability?

   c. Would the result be the same if Farmer had simply contracted to sell Bread Company all of Farmer's wheat production?

d. Alyssa and Brooke contract for Brooke to work for Alyssa in Alyssa's business under a two-year contract for $50,000 per year. After one year, Alyssa fires Brooke and closes her business citing as the reason for closure the introduction of a new government regulation the costs of complying with which would wipe out the profitability of the business. Is Alyssa excused from further performance of her obligations under the contract with Brooke based on impracticability?

Exercise 12-38: *National Association of Postmasters of the United States (NAPUS) v. Hyatt Regency Washington*

The next case has several important lessons to teach. As you read the case, consider the following questions:

1. The court rejects NAPUS' argument that the court should discharge NAPUS' duty to perform based on the "For Cause" cancellation provision in the contract. Almost all courts would characterize this clause as a "force majeure" clause.

   a. Why does the court conclude that the clause does not excuse the union's duty to perform?

   b. Why does the court invoke dictionary definitions in its analysis?

2. NAPUS also argued that it should be excused based on the impracticability rule. In the final footnote to the opinion, the court rejects this argument. Why?

National Association of Postmasters of the United States v. Hyatt Regency Washington
894 A.2d 471 (2006)

FISHER, Associate Judge:

In this contract dispute, the National Association of Postmasters of the United States (NAPUS) and Hyatt Regency Washington (Hyatt) each sought summary judgment in relation to the cancellation of two NAPUS conferences to be held at Hyatt. The trial court granted judgment for Hyatt, holding that NAPUS was not permitted to cancel the conferences without paying liquidated damages because it had not given notice within the time limits established by the contract. We affirm the trial court's ruling, on alternative grounds ...

I.

This dispute arose from a multi-year contract in which Hyatt agreed to provide blocks of rooms and other amenities for the annual leadership conference held by NAPUS. The contract, entered into in February of 2001, set specific dates for the 2002, 2003, and 2004 conferences. In each of those years, the gathering was to be held in mid-February, as it had been for many years.

After this contract was executed, a federal arbitrator, ruling on a collective bargaining agreement between two entities not parties to this appeal or the underlying suit, ordered the U.S. Postal Service to move the 2003 and 2004 Rural Mail Count[13] from its usual time in September to a new time in February. The dates selected by the arbitrator, February 15 through March 15, 2003, and February 14 through March 6, 2004, substantially conflicted with the dates of the 2003 and 2004 leadership conferences, which were to be held February 12–21, 2003, and February 11–20, 2004.

Because postmasters play a central role in conducting the Rural Mail Count, this newly-emerged conflict at the very least made it inadvisable to hold the leadership conferences for 2003 and 2004 on the dates previously scheduled. NAPUS learned of the change in dates and resulting conflict on February 4 or 5, 2002, and it verified on February 17, 2002, that a substantial number of postmasters would be unable to attend the 2003 and 2004 conferences due to the conflicting obligation. On February 7, 2002, NAPUS orally informed the Hyatt that there was a conflict with the 2003 and 2004 leadership conference dates. On February 8, NAPUS began exchanging e-mails with Hyatt in an attempt to identify new dates for the conference. Hyatt indicated that it would charge increased rates for the days it proposed, but NAPUS was unwilling to pay those increased rates. Unable to find dates and prices that fit, NAPUS sent a letter on February 25, 2002, terminating the contract for 2003 and 2004.

NAPUS sought a declaratory judgment absolving it of any liability for terminating the contract, relying upon a "For Cause" cancellation clause and also asserting the impracticability of performance. Hyatt counter-sued for liquidated damages under the "Cancellation Option"... Both parties moved for summary judgment, and the Superior Court granted judgment in favor of Hyatt, finding that NAPUS owed liquidated damages in the amount of $257,617 because it did not strictly comply with the notice requirements of the "For Cause" cancellation clause.

II.

... "[S]ummary judgment is appropriate where a contract is unambiguous since, absent such ambiguity, a written contract duly signed and executed speaks for itself and binds the parties without the necessity of extrinsic evidence." [Citation omitted.] Although the parties have engaged in a spirited debate about the meaning of their agreement, "[c]ontracts are not rendered ambiguous by the mere fact that the parties do not agree upon their proper construction." Id. Moreover, a contract "is not ambiguous where the court can determine its meaning without any other guide than a knowledge of the simple facts on which, from the nature of language in general, its meaning depends." Id. [Internal quotation marks and citation omitted.] Our analysis reveals that the remaining factual disputes are not material and that this case therefore was ripe for summary judgment.

---

13. As NAPUS explains, "[t]he Rural Mail Count measures the volume of mail delivered along the nation's rural mail routes and the effort required to perform various tasks necessary to deliver that mail. The results of the Rural Mail Count determine the compensation paid to rural mail carriers."

A. Cancellation of the Contract

Two cancellation provisions in the contract are at the center of controversy in this case. The first of these is a "Cancellation Option." It allows either party to cancel the contract upon written notice to the other, but requires the cancelling party to pay liquidated damages in the amount found in an accompanying graduated scale:

> [e]ither the Hotel or the Group may cancel any one or all of the dates stated as "definite" in this contract without cause upon written notice to the other party at any time prior to the arrival of the event room block and upon payment of an amount based on the [graduated] scale.

Hyatt claims that NAPUS' cancellation falls within this broad provision. NAPUS, on the other hand, claims that the rescheduling of the Rural Mail Count created an emergency it could not foresee and, therefore, the cancellation of the conference falls within the "For Cause" provision. The "For Cause" clause is much narrower than the "Cancellation Option," but permits cancellation without liability:

> [t]he parties' performance under this Contract is subject to acts of God, war, government regulation, terrorism, disaster, strikes, civil disorder, curtailment of transportation facilities, or any other emergency beyond the parties' control, making it inadvisable, illegal or which materially affects a party's ability to perform its obligations under this Contract. Either party may terminate this Contract for any one or more of such reasons upon written notice to the other party within three (3) days of such occurrence or receipt of notice of any of the above occurrences.[14]

NAPUS asks us to hold that the rescheduling of the Rural Mail Count is covered by the "For Cause" cancellation clause. If that clause applies, we then must decide whether NAPUS gave proper and timely notice in compliance with the contract. We conclude that the rescheduling of the Rural Mail Count was not covered by the "For Cause" cancellation provision and, therefore, need not reach the second issue.

The "For Cause" clause begins by enumerating several circumstances in which the contract can be cancelled for cause: "acts of God, war, government regulation, terrorism, disaster, strikes, civil disorder, [and] curtailment of transportation facilities." NAPUS does not argue that the rescheduling of the Rural Mail Count falls within any of these specifically enumerated categories.[15] It does contend, however, that this change of circumstances fits within the

---

14. Such provisions are often called force majeure clauses, but attaching that label does not assist in our analysis. We still must "look to the language that the parties specifically bargained for in the contract to determine the parties' intent concerning whether the event complained of excuses performance." [Citation omitted.]

15. NAPUS does claim that the rescheduling of the Rural Mail Count by the federal arbitrator was a "government mandate[ ] of the 'same type' as the 'government regulation' set forth in the Agreement." Nevertheless, it is not a government regulation, so it is not one of the events enumerated in the contract. Nor, as we explain below, does the arbitrator's ruling constitute "any other emergency."

residual category of "any other emergency beyond the parties' control, making it inadvisable, illegal or which materially affects a party's ability to perform its obligations under this Contract."

We decline to interpret the "any other emergency" provision so broadly. A common aid for interpreting both statutes and contracts is ejusdem generis: "Where general words follow specific words in a[n] ... enumeration, the general words are construed to embrace only objects similar in nature to those objects enumerated by the preceding specific words." [Citations omitted.]

The events specifically enumerated in the "For Cause" clause of the contract are qualitatively different from the rescheduling of the Rural Mail Count. It was not a war, an act of God, or an act of terrorism; it was not a strike, civil disorder, or a curtailment of transportation facilities. This unexpected conflict of schedules was not "of the same kind" as the events listed. It would excuse the payment of liquidated damages only if it qualifies as "any other emergency" under the residual exception. However, the word "emergency" describes an unexpected development urgently requiring a prompt response, not one where the effects will be felt in a year's time or two years' time. See WEBSTER'S II NEW RIVERSIDE UNIVERSITY DICTIONARY 427 (1994) (defining "emergency" as "[a]n unexpected, serious occurrence or situation urgently requiring prompt action" (emphasis supplied)); AMERICAN HERITAGE DICTIONARY OF THE ENGLISH LANGUAGE 602 (3d ed.1992) (defining "emergency" as "a serious situation or occurrence that happens unexpectedly and demands immediate action"). NAPUS learned of the rescheduling of the Rural Mail Count a full year in advance of the 2003 leadership conference and two years in advance of the 2004 leadership conference. The rescheduling of the Rural Mail Count may be an inconvenience or even make compliance with the contract inadvisable, but without an urgent need for prompt reaction, it cannot be considered an "emergency" as that term is properly understood.[16]

During oral argument, NAPUS suggested that the rescheduling was inherently urgent because prompt action was required under the "three day written notice" provision. If this kind of urgency were enough, however, then every unforeseen event making compliance with the contract inadvisable would be an emergency. Under this theory, it is not the unforeseen event, but rather the contract itself and the desire to avoid paying liquidated damages that create the "emergency." This interpretation would render the "Cancellation Option" superfluous, as it is human nature to want to avoid paying liquidated damages and any reason for cancellation would become an "emergency" requiring prompt reaction. We therefore conclude that the "Cancellation Option" applies and that NAPUS owes Hyatt liquidated damages according to the graduated chart found in the contract.[17] We affirm the ruling of the trial court to that effect.

---

16. Indeed, NAPUS devotes much of its brief to arguing that the conflict made it "inadvisable" to hold the leadership conference on the dates previously scheduled or "materially affect[ed]" its ability to do so. This may be true, but it is not sufficient. In order to invoke the "For Cause" clause, NAPUS must also demonstrate that the conflict was either an enumerated event or "any other emergency."

17. NAPUS argues, in the alternative, that cancellation was permitted by the common law doctrine of commercial impracticability. To establish commercial impracticability, a party must show (1) the unexpected occurrence of an intervening act; (2) the risk of the unexpected occurrence was not allocated by agreement or custom; and (3) the occurrence made performance impractical. [Ci-

Exercise 12-39: *National Association of Postmasters of the United States v. Hyatt Regency Washington* Revisited

1. Defendant contractor agreed to build a house on land owned by Plaintiff, and Plaintiff agreed to pay Defendant $100,000. After Defendant was two-thirds finished with construction, the partially constructed building was destroyed by fire. Defendant refused to start over, and Plaintiff sued Defendant for breach of contract. D's impracticability claim will fail. Why? (*Hint: Look at the elements of impracticability stated above.*)

2. Defendant contractor agreed to add a sunroom onto an existing house owned by Plaintiff. After Defendant was two-thirds finished with construction, the house was destroyed by fire. Defendant refused to start over, and Plaintiff sued Defendant for breach of contract. Defendant's impracticability claim will succeed. Why? Reconcile your answer to this hypothetical with your answer to the previous hypothetical.

Exercise 12-40: *American Trading and Production Corp. v. Shell International Marine, Ltd.* (a/k/a the Suez Canal case) and *Mineral Park Land Co. v. Howard*

Read and consider the following questions regarding the Suez Canal case and the *Howard* case.

1. The first question the Suez Canal case court addresses is whether the contract made the Suez Canal the exclusive means for performing the contract.

    a. This issue is of a type we already have studied. What type of issue is this question?

    b. What was the plaintiff's tactical reason for trying to persuade the court that the parties had agreed that the Suez Canal would be the exclusive means for performing the contract?

    c. How did the court resolve this issue? Why did the court reach the conclusion it reached?

2. The second question in the Suez Canal case focuses on whether the performance of the plaintiff's obligations as defined in connection with the first issue became impracticable.

    a. On which of the elements set forth above does the case turn?

    b. How did the court analyze that element?

---

tations omitted] In the instant agreement, however, the contract has allocated the risk for every situation in which a party cancels. For those reasons that are enumerated or otherwise constitute an "emergency," the parties have determined that both share the risk. For all other reasons, the risk is allocated to the cancelling party. That is the very point of the "Cancellation Option" and liquidated damages chart. As the situation presented here fails to meet the second prong of the commercial impracticability test, this doctrine does not excuse NAPUS' refusal to pay damages according to the "Cancellation Option."

3. Is *Howard* really an impracticability case?
4. Reconcile *Howard* with the Suez Canal case.

American Trading & Production Corp. v. Shell International Marine, Ltd.

453 F.2d 939 2d. Circuit (1972)

MULLIGAN, Circuit Judge:

This is an appeal by American Trading and Production Corporation (hereinafter "owner") from a judgment entered on July 29th, 1971, in the United States District Court for the Southern District of New York, dismissing its claim against Shell International Marine Ltd. (hereinafter "charterer") for additional compensation in the sum of $131,978.44 for the transportation of cargo from Texas to India via the Cape of Good Hope as a result of the closing of the Suez Canal in June, 1967. The charterer had asserted a counterclaim which was withdrawn and is not in issue....

The owner is a Maryland corporation doing business in New York and the charterer is a United Kingdom corporation. On March 23, 1967 the parties entered into a contract of voyage charter in New York City which provided that the charterer would hire the owner's tank vessel, Washington Trader, for a voyage with a full cargo of lube oil from Beaumont/Smiths Bluff, Texas to Bombay, India. The charter party provided that the freight rate would be in accordance with the then prevailing American Tanker Rate Schedule (ATRS), $14.25 per long ton of cargo, plus seventy-five percent (75%), and in addition there was a charge of $.85 per long ton for passage through the Suez Canal. On May 15, 1967 the [vessel] departed from Beaumont with a cargo of 16,183.32 long tons of lube oil. The charterer paid the freight at the invoiced sum of $417,327.36 on May 26, 1967. On May 29th, 1967 the owner advised the [vessel] by radio to take additional bunkers at Ceuta due to possible diversion because of the Suez Canal crisis. The vessel arrived at Ceuta, Spanish Morocco on May 30, bunkered and sailed on May 31st, 1967. On June 5th the owner cabled the ship's master advising him of various reports of trouble in the Canal and suggested delay in entering it pending clarification. On that very day, the Suez Canal was closed due to the state of war which had developed in the Middle East. The owner then communicated with the charterer on June 5th through the broker who had negotiated the charter party, requesting approval for the diversion of the [vessel], which then had proceeded to a point about 84 miles northwest of Port Said, the entrance to the Canal. On June 6th the charterer responded that under the circumstances it was "for owner to decide whether to continue to wait or make the alternative passage via the Cape since Charter Party Obliges them to deliver cargo without qualification." In response the owner replied on the same day that in view of the closing of the Suez, the [vessel] would proceed to Bombay via the Cape of Good Hope and "[w]e [are] reserving all rights for extra compensation." The vessel proceeded westward, back through the Straits of Gibraltar and around the Cape and eventually arrived in Bombay on July 15th (some 30 days later than initially expected), traveling a total of 18,055 miles instead of the 9,709 miles, which it would have sailed had the Canal been open. The owner billed $131,978.44 as extra compensation which the charterer has refused to pay.

On appeal and below the owner argues that transit of the Suez Canal was the agreed specific means of performance of the voyage charter and that the supervening destruction of this means rendered the contract legally impossible to perform and therefore discharged the owner's unperformed obligation. RESTATEMENT OF CONTRACTS § 460. Consequently, when the [vessel] eventually delivered the oil after journeying around the Cape of Good Hope, a benefit was conferred upon the charterer for which it should respond in *quantum meruit.* The validity of this proposition depends upon a finding that the parties contemplated or agreed that the Suez passage was to be the exclusive method of performance, and indeed it was so argued on appeal. We cannot construe the agreement in such a fashion. The parties contracted for the shipment of the cargo from Texas to India at an agreed rate and the charter party makes absolutely no reference to any fixed route. It is urged that the Suez passage was a condition of performance because the ATRS rate was based on a Suez Canal passage, the invoice contained a specific Suez Canal toll charge and the vessel actually did proceed to a point 84 miles northwest of Port Said. In our view all that this establishes is that both parties contemplated that the Canal would be the probable route. It was the cheapest and shortest, and therefore it was in the interest of both that it be utilized. However, this is not at all equivalent to an agreement that it be the exclusive method of performance. The charter party does not so provide and it seems to have been well understood in the shipping industry that the Cape route is an acceptable alternative in voyages of this character.

The District of Columbia Circuit decided a closely analogous case, *Transatlantic Financing Corp. v. United States.* [Citation omitted.] There the plaintiff had entered into a voyage charter with defendant in which it agreed to transport a full cargo of wheat ... from a United States port to Iran. The parties clearly contemplated a Suez passage, but on November 2, 1956 the vessel reduced speed when war blocked the Suez Canal. The vessel changed its course in the Atlantic and eventually delivered its cargo in Iran after proceeding by way of the Cape of Good Hope. In an exhaustive opinion Judge Skelly Wright reviewed the English cases which had considered the same problem and concluded that "the Cape route is generally regarded as an alternative means of performance. So the implied expectation that the route would be via Suez is hardly adequate proof of an allocation to the promisee of the risk of closure. In some cases, even an express expectation may not amount to a condition of performance." [Citation omitted.]

Appellant argues that *Transatlantic* is distinguishable since there was an agreed upon flat rate in that case unlike the instant case where the rate was based on Suez passage. This does not distinguish the case in our view. It is stipulated by the parties here that the only ATRS rate published at the time of the agreement from Beaumont to Bombay was the one utilized as a basis for the negotiated rate ultimately agreed upon. This rate was escalated by 75% to reflect whatever existing market conditions the parties contemplated. These conditions are not stipulated. Had a Cape route rate been requested, which was not the case, it is agreed that the point from which the parties would have bargained would be $17.35 per long ton of cargo as against $14.25 per long ton.

Actually, in *Transatlantic* it was argued that certain provisions in the P. & I. Bunker Deviation Clause referring to the direct and/or customary route required, by implication, a voyage through the Suez Canal. The court responded "[a]ctually they prove only what we are willing to accept—that the parties expected the usual and customary route would be used. The provisions in no way condition performance upon non-occurrence of this contingency." [Citation omitted.] We hold that all that the ATRS rate establishes is that the parties obviously expected a Suez passage but there is no indication at all in the instrument ... that it was a condition of performance.

This leaves us with the question as to whether the owner was excused from performance on the theory of commercial impracticability. Restatement of Contracts § 454. Even though the owner is not excused because of strict impossibility, it is urged that American law recognizes that performance is rendered impossible if it can only be accomplished with extreme and unreasonable difficulty, expense, injury or loss. There is no extreme or unreasonable difficulty apparent here. The alternate route taken was well recognized, and there is no claim that the vessel or the crew or the nature of the cargo made the route actually taken unreasonably difficult, dangerous or onerous. The owner's case here essentially rests upon the element of the additional expense involved—$131,978.44. This represents an increase of less than one third over the agreed upon $417,327.36. We find that this increase in expense is not sufficient to constitute commercial impracticability under either American or English authority.

Mere increase in cost alone is not a sufficient excuse for non-performance. RESTATEMENT OF CONTRACTS, § 467 ... It must be an "extreme and unreasonable" expense. *Id.* at § 454.... Appellant further seeks to distinguish *Transatlantic* because in that case the change in course was in the mid-Atlantic and added some 300 miles to the voyage while in this case the [vessel] had traversed most of the Mediterranean and thus had added some 9000 miles to the contemplated voyage.... Aside from this however, it is a fact that the master of the [vessel in this case] was alerted by radio on May 29th, 1967 of a "possible diversion because of Suez Canal crisis," but nevertheless two days later he had left Ceuta (opposite Gibraltar) and proceeded across the Mediterranean. [There] does not seem to be any question but that the master here had been actually put on notice before traversing the Mediterranean that diversion was possible. Had the [vessel] then changed course, the time and cost of the Mediterranean trip could reasonably have been avoided, thereby reducing the amount now claimed. RESTATEMENT OF CONTRACTS, § 336, comment d to subsection (1) ...

Matters involving impossibility or impracticability of performance of contract are concededly vexing and difficult. One is even urged on the allocation of such risks to pray for the "wisdom of Solomon." 6 A. CORBIN, CONTRACTS, § 1333, at 372 (1962). On the basis of all of the facts, we affirm.

Mineral Park Land Co. v. Howard
156 P. 458 (1916)

SLOSS, J. The defendants appeal from a judgment in favor of plaintiff for $3,650. The appeal is on the judgment roll alone.

The plaintiff was the owner of certain land in the ravine or wash known as the Arroyo Seco, in South Pasadena, Los Angeles county. The defendants had made a contract with the public authorities for the construction of a concrete bridge across the Arroyo Seco. In August, 1911, the parties to this action entered into a written agreement whereby the plaintiff granted to the defendants the right to haul gravel and earth from plaintiff's land, the defendants agreeing to take therefrom all of the gravel and earth necessary in the construction of the fill and cement work on the proposed bridge, the required amount being estimated at approximately 114,000 cubic yards. Defendants agreed to pay 5 cents per cubic yard for the first 80,000 yards, the next 10,000 yards were to be given free of charge, and the balance was to be paid for at the rate of 5 cents per cubic yard.

The complaint was in two counts. The first alleged that the defendants had taken 50,131 cubic yards of earth and gravel, thereby becoming indebted to plaintiff in the sum of $2,506.55, of which only $900 had been paid, leaving a balance of $1,606.55 due. The findings support plaintiff's claim in this regard, and there is no question of the propriety of so much of the judgment as responds to the first count. The second count sought to recover damages for the defendants' failure to take from plaintiff's land any more than the 50,131 yards.

It alleged that the total amount of earth and gravel used by defendants was 101,000 cubic yards, of which they procured 50,869 cubic yards from some place other than plaintiff's premises. The amount due the plaintiff for this amount of earth and gravel would, under the terms of the contract, have been $2,043.45. The count charged that plaintiff's land contained enough earth and gravel to enable the defendants to take therefrom the entire amount required, and that the 50,869 yards not taken had no value to the plaintiff. Accordingly the plaintiff sought, under this head, to recover damages in the sum of $2,043.45.

The answer denied that the plaintiff's land contained any amount of earth and gravel in excess of the 50,131 cubic yards actually taken, and alleged that the defendants took from the said land all of the earth and gravel available for the work mentioned in the contract.

The court found that the plaintiff's land contained earth and gravel far in excess of 101,000 cubic yards of earth and gravel, but that only 50,131 cubic yards, the amount actually taken by the defendants, was above the water level. No greater quantity could have been taken "by ordinary means," or except by the use, at great expense, of a stream dredger, and the earth and gravel so taken could not have been used without first having been dried at great expense and delay. On the issue raised by the plea of defendants that they took all the earth and gravel that was available the court qualified its findings in this way: It found that the defendants did take all of the available earth and gravel from plaintiff's premises, in this, that they took and removed "all that could have been taken advantageously to defendants, or all that was practical to take and remove from a financial standpoint"; that any greater amount could have been taken only at a prohibitive cost, that is, at an expense of 10 or 12 times as much as the usual cost per yard. It is also declared that the word "available" is used in the findings to mean capable of being taken and used advantageously. It was not "advantageous or practical" to have taken more material from plaintiff's land, but it was not impossible. There is a finding that the parties were not under any mutual misunderstanding regarding the amount of available gravel, but that the contract was entered into without any calculation on the part of either of the parties with reference to the amount of available earth and gravel on the premises.

The single question is whether the facts thus found justified the defendants in their failure to take from the plaintiff's land all of the earth and gravel required. This question was answered in the negative by the court below. The case was apparently thought to be governed by the principle — established by a multitude of authorities — that where a party has agreed, without qualification, to perform an act which is not in its nature impossible of performance, he is not excused by difficulty of performance, or by the fact that he becomes unable to perform. [Citations omitted.]

It is, however, equally well settled that, where performance depends upon the existence of a given thing, and such existence was assumed as the basis of the agreement, performance is excused to the extent that the thing ceases to exist or turns out to be nonexistent. [Citation omitted.] Thus, where the defendants had agreed to pasture not less than 3,000 cattle on plaintiff's land, paying therefor $1 for each and every head so pastured, and it developed that the land did not furnish feed for more than 717 head, the number actually put on the land by defendant, it was held that plaintiff could not recover the stipulated sum for the difference between the cattle pastured and the minimum of 3,000 agreed to be pastured. [Citation omitted.] ... There are many other cases dealing with mining leases of this character, and the general course of decision is to the effect that the performance of the obligation to take out a given quantity or to pay royalty thereon, if it be not taken out, is excused if it appears that the land does not contain the stipulated quantity. [Citations omitted.]

We think the findings of fact make a case falling within the rule of these decisions. The parties were contracting for the right to take earth and gravel to be used in the construction of the bridge. When they stipulated that all of the earth and gravel needed for this purpose should be taken from plaintiff's land, they contemplated and assumed that the land contained the requisite quantity, available for use. The defendants were not binding themselves to take what was not there. And, in determining whether the earth and gravel were "available," we must view the conditions in a practical and reasonable way. Although there was gravel on the land, it was so situated that the defendants could not take it by ordinary means, nor except at a prohibitive cost. To all fair intents then, it was impossible for defendants to take it.

"A thing is impossible in legal contemplation when it is not practicable; and a thing is impracticable when it can only be done at an excessive and unreasonable cost." [Citation omitted.] We do not mean to intimate that the defendants could excuse themselves by showing the existence of conditions which would make the performance of their obligation more expensive than they had anticipated, or which would entail a loss upon them. But, where the difference in cost is so great as here, and has the effect, as found, of making performance impracticable, the situation is not different from that of a total absence of earth and gravel.

On the facts found, there should have been no recovery on the second count.

The judgment is modified by deducting therefrom the sum of $2,043.45, and, as so modified, it stands affirmed.

Exercise 12-41: *American Trading and Production Corp. v. Shell International Marine, Ltd.* (a/k/a the Suez Canal case) and *Mineral Park Land Co. v. Howard* Revisited

1. How could you change the facts of each of these cases to reach a different result in each one?

2. Consider the following hypotheticals:

   a. Alex contracts to ship logs from a logging site to Brad's sawmill in exchange for $10,000. The contract nowhere mentions a specific river, but the parties know there is only one river between the logging site and the sawmill. An extraordinary drought dries up the river, making it impassable. Is performance of Alex's obligation impracticable? Is the Suez Canal case distinguishable?

   b. Would the result be the same if Alex could rent trucks at a total price of $40,000 to get the logs from the logging site to the sawmill?

Exercise 12-42: *Mutual Life Insurance Co. of New York v. Johnson*

1. You learned already that impracticability can either be a ground for discharge or excuse, depending on the materiality of the condition at issue.

For each of the impracticability cases you have studied in this chapter, determine whether the potential effect of the alleged impracticability was discharge or excuse. In particular, analyze the materiality of the condition at issue in each of the cases.

2. What was the basis of the insured's claim of impracticability in *Johnson*?

3. Why does the court conclude that performance of the obligation at issue in *Johnson* was impracticable?

4. What was the effect of the impracticability in *Johnson*? Explain the effect in terms of the materiality test you considered in 1. above.

Mutual Life Ins. Co. of New York v. Johnson
293 U.S. 335 (1934)

Mr. Justice CARDOZO delivered the opinion of the Court.

On May 16, 1930, the petitioner, the Mutual Life Insurance Company of New York, issued in Virginia to Benjamin F. Cooksey, who resided in that state, a policy of life insurance in the amount of $4,500 with disability benefits. Upon the face of the policy, it is provided that, if the insured is totally and permanently disabled before the age of 60, the company will pay him "forty-five dollars monthly during such disability, … besides waiving premium payments, all upon conditions set forth in section 3." The conditions thus incorporated by reference are these: "If before attaining the age of sixty years, and while no premium on the policy is in default, the insured shall furnish to the company due proof that he is totally and permanently disabled, … the company will grant the following benefits during the remaining lifetime of the insured as long as such disability continues. Benefits (a) … The company will pay a monthly income to the insured of the amount stated on the first page hereof … beginning upon receipt of due proof of such disability…. (b) Waiver of Premium. The Company will also, after receipt of such due proof, waive payment of each premium as it thereafter becomes due during such disability." There is also a provision that the policy will be reinstated within six months after a default if proof is given within that time that at the date of the default the insured was totally disabled and has continuously remained so.

A quarterly premium became payable under this policy upon November 16, 1931, subject, however, to a period of grace of thirty-one days, whereby the time for payment was extended until December 17. This premium was never paid by the insured, though all earlier premiums had been paid as they matured. On December 17, the date of the default, the insured, who was under 60, was confined to his bed, a sufferer from chronic nephritis, which on January 20, 1932, resulted in his death. There is evidence by concession that as early as December 14, 1931, he was totally and permanently disabled, not only physically, but mentally, to such an extent that he was unable to give notice to the insurer in advance of the default, and thus procure the waiver called for by the policy. The company takes the ground that, because of the omission of that notice, the default is unexcused and the policy has lapsed.

In this action by the administrator the District Court upheld the company's position, and directed a verdict for the defendant. The Court of Appeals for the Fourth Circuit reversed, and remanded the cause for trial. 70 F.(2d) 41. For the defendant it was argued that insanity is no more an excuse for the failure to give a notice that will cause the payment of the premiums to be waived than for the failure to make payment of the premiums when waiver is not a duty, either conditional or absolute. [Citation omitted.] For the plaintiff it was argued that, waiver having been promised, though subject to a condition as to notice, there must be a liberal construction of a requirement that is merely modal or procedural, and the insurer will not be deemed, in respect of matters of that order, to have exacted the impossible. The controversy is one as to which the courts of the country are arrayed in opposing camps.... The case is here on certiorari.

We think the contract is to be interpreted in accordance with the law of Virginia where delivery was made. [Citations omitted.] As to the meaning and obligation of such a policy, the highest court of the state has spoken [citation omitted], construing a provision substantially the same as the one in controversy here. The ruling there was that notice was excused by physical and mental incapacity to give it. "When the disability of the insured occurred while the policy was in force, he was entitled to have his premiums waived until his death, for his disability continued until his death. He had paid for this right, and to say that he should lose the benefit of his policy because he failed through mental or physical incapacity to present proofs would be harsh and unreasonable under the circumstances."...

The judgment is affirmed.

Frustration of Purpose

Exercise 12-43: Introduction to Frustration of Purpose

Introductory hypothetical: On January 2, 2014, at a time before the Spring semester started, Student entered into a contract with Supertutor for personal tutoring in contracts during the spring semester because she had heard that contracts is a hard subject and that her particular contracts professor is a hard teacher. At that point in time, Student had not yet received her fall grades. Three weeks later, she received her fall grades, which reflected a 1.3 grade point average. The grades were accompanied by a letter informing Student that she had been academically dismissed. Student therefore did not attend law school that semester and informed Supertutor that Student would not be needing Supertutor's services. Supertutor sued Student for breach.

1. To prevail, must Supertutor render or tender performance?

2. If Student asserted impracticability in an effort to discharge her liability under the contract, her claim would fail. Why?

3. As we will learn, although Student's impracticability claim would fail, her performance probably would be discharged based on frustration of purpose because an unforeseen event, the academic dismissal, made Supertutor's performance valueless to Student.

4. **Below are the elements of frustration of purpose.** Note the similarities between frustration of purpose and impracticability. Save for one, both claims have the same elements. Also note that frustration has only one possible effect: discharge. Frustration always discharges both parties whereas impracticability discharges the parties only if the excused performance was material.

1. Occurrence of an unforeseen event.

2. Which event substantially frustrates a party's principal purpose in making the contract (the transaction no longer makes any sense).

3. Non-occurrence of the event was a basic assumption on which the contract was made.

4. The party claiming frustration had no fault in causing the frustrating event.

5. The party claiming frustration did not assume the risk because:

   a. The contract does not assign her the risk, OR

   b. She could not foresee the event and therefore did not choose to undertake the risk, OR

   c. The event was not within her control and she was therefore not in the best position to avoid the loss.

Exercise 12-44: *Krell v. Henry*

As you read the *Krell* case, consider the following questions:

1. What was the order of performance in the *Krell* case? How do we know? On what constructive conditions rule does your answer rely?

2. Did the condition to P's duty to let the premises occur?

3. The *Krell* court suggests that the issue in *Krell* is the same issue as the question in *Taylor*. Is the court right? Has D's performance been rendered impracticable? Why or why not?

4. Apply the frustration elements stated above to the facts of *Krell*.

5. Reconcile the *Krell* court's discussion of the cab hypothetical with the result in *Krell*.

6. Would the result in the *Krell* case have been the same if the coronation had gone forward but it had been so foggy on the day of the coronation that the defendant couldn't really see much of the procession?

Krell v. Henry

2 K.B. 740 (1903)

The plaintiff, Paul Krell, sued the defendant, C. S. Henry, for 50 pounds, being the balance of a sum of 75 pounds, for which the defendant had agreed to hire a flat at 56A, Pall Mall on the days of June 26 and 27, for the purpose of viewing the processions to be held in connection with the coronation of His Majesty. The defendant denied his liability, and counter-claimed for the return of the sum of 25 pounds, which had been paid as a deposit, on the ground that, the processions not having taken place owing to the serious illness of the King, there had been a total failure of consideration for the contract entered into by him.

The facts, which were not disputed, were as follows. The plaintiff on leaving the country in March, 1902, left instructions with his solicitor to let his suite of chambers at 56A, Pall Mall on such terms and for such period (not exceeding six months) as he thought proper. On June 17, 1902, the defendant noticed an announcement in the windows of the plaintiff's flat to the effect that windows to view the coronation processions were to be let. The defendant interviewed the housekeeper on the subject, when it was pointed out to him what a good view of the processions could be obtained from the premises, and he eventually agreed with the housekeeper to take the suite for the two days in question for a sum of 75 pounds.

On June 20 the defendant wrote the following letter to the plaintiff's solicitor:—

> "I am in receipt of yours of the 18th instant, inclosing form of agreement for the suite of chambers on the third floor at 56A, Pall Mall, which I have agreed to take for the two days, the 26th and 27th instant, for the sum of 75 pounds. For reasons given you I cannot enter into the agreement, but as arranged over the telephone I inclose herewith cheque for 25 pounds. as deposit, and will thank you to confirm to me that I shall have the entire use of these rooms during the days (not the nights) of the 26th and 27th instant. You may rely that every care will be taken of the premises and their contents. On the 24th inst. I will pay the balance, viz., 50 pounds, to complete the 75 pounds agreed upon."

On the same day the defendant received the following reply from the plaintiff's solicitor:

> "I am in receipt of your letter of to-day's date inclosing cheque for 25 pounds deposit on your agreeing to take Mr. Krell's chambers on the third floor at 56A, Pall Mall for the two days, the 26th and 27th June, and I confirm the agreement that you are to have the entire use of these rooms during the days (but not the nights), the balance, 50 pounds, to be paid to me on Tuesday next the 24th instant."

The processions not having taken place on the days originally appointed, namely, June 26 and 27, the defendant declined to pay the balance of 50 pounds. alleged to be due from him under the contract in writing of June 20 constituted by the above two letters. Hence the present action.

Darling J., on August 11, 1902, held, upon the authority of *Taylor v. Caldwell* and *The Moorcock* that there was an implied condition in the contract that the procession should take place, and gave judgment for the defendant on the claim and counter-claim. The plaintiff appealed.

...

Vaughan Williams, L.J.

... The real question in this case is the extent of the application in English law of the principle of the Roman law which has been adopted and acted on in many English decisions, and notably in the case of *Taylor v. Caldwell*, 40 3 B. & S. 826. That case at least makes it clear that "where, from the nature of the contract, it appears that the parties must from the beginning have known that it could not be fulfilled unless, when the time for the fulfillment of the contract arrived, some particular specified thing continued to exist, so that when entering into the contract they must have contemplated such continued existence as the foundation of what was to be done; there, in the absence of any express or implied warranty that the thing shall exist, the contract is not to be considered a positive contract, but as subject to an implied condition that the parties shall be excused in case, before breach, performance becomes impossible from the perishing of the thing without default of the contractor." Thus far it is clear that the principle of the Roman law has been introduced into the English law. The doubt in the present case arises as to how far this principle extends.... English law applies the principle not only to cases where the performance of the contract becomes impossible by the cessation of existence of the thing which is the subject-matter of the contract, but also to cases where the event which renders the contract incapable of performance is the cessation or non-existence of an express condition or state of things, going to the root of the contract, and essential to its performance. It is said, on the one side, that the specified thing, state of things, or condition the continued existence of which is necessary for the fulfillment of the contract, so that the parties entering into the contract must have contemplated the continued existence of that thing, condition, or state of things as the foundation of what was to be done under the contract, is limited to things which are either the subject-matter of the contract or a condition or state of things, present or anticipated, which is expressly mentioned in the contract. But, on the other side, it is said that the condition or state of things need not be expressly specified, but that it is sufficient if that condition or state of things clearly appears by extrinsic evidence to have been assumed by the parties to be the foundation or basis of the contract, and the event which causes the impossibility is of such a character that it cannot reasonably be supposed to have been in the contemplation of the contracting parties when the contract was made. In such a case the contracting parties will not be held bound by the general words which, though large enough to include, were not used with reference to a possibility of a particular event rendering performance of the contract impossible. I do not think that the principle of the civil law as introduced into the English law is limited to cases in which the event causing the impossibility of performance is the destruction or non-existence of something which is the subject-matter of the contract or of some condition or state of things expressly specified as a condition of it. I think that you first have to ascertain … from necessary inferences, drawn from surrounding circumstances recognised by both contracting parties, what is the substance of the contract, and then to ask the question whether that substantial contract needs for its foundation the assumption of the existence of a particular state of things. If it does, this will limit the operation of the general words, and in such case, if the contract becomes impossible of performance by reason of the non-existence of the state of things assumed by both contracting parties as the foundation of the contract, there will be no breach of the contract thus limited.

Now what are the facts of the present case? The contract is contained in two letters of June 20 which passed between the defendant and the plaintiff's agent, Mr. Cecil Bisgood. These letters do not mention the coronation, but speak merely of the taking of Mr. Krell's chambers, or, rather, of the use of them, in the daytime of June 26 and 27, for the sum of 75 pounds, 25 pounds then paid, balance 50 pounds to be paid on the 24th. But the affidavits, which by agreement between the parties are to be taken as stating the facts of the case, show that the plaintiff exhibited on his premises, third floor, 56A, Pall Mall, an announcement to the effect that windows to view the Royal coronation procession were to be let, and that the defendant was induced by that announcement to apply to the housekeeper on the premises, who said that the owner was willing to let the suite of rooms for the purpose of seeing the Royal procession for both days, but not nights, of June 26 and 27. In my judgment the use of the rooms was let and taken for the purpose of seeing the Royal procession. It was not a demise of the rooms, or even an agreement to let and take the rooms. It is a licence to use rooms for a particular purpose and none other. And in my judgment the taking place of those processions on the days proclaimed along the proclaimed route, which passed 56A, Pall Mall, was regarded by both contracting parties as the foundation of the contract; and I think that it cannot reasonably be supposed to have been in the contemplation of the contracting parties, when the contract was made, that the coronation would not be held on the proclaimed days, or the processions not take place on those days along the proclaimed route; and I think that the words imposing on the defendant the obligation to accept and pay for the use of the rooms for the named days, although general and unconditional, were not used with reference to the possibility of the particular contingency which afterwards occurred. It was suggested in the course of the argument that if the occurrence, on the proclaimed days, of the coronation and the procession in this case were the foundation of the contract, and if the general words are thereby limited or qualified, so that in the event of the non-occurrence of the coronation and procession along the proclaimed route they would discharge both parties from further performance of the contract, it would follow that if a cabman was engaged to take one to Epsom on Derby Day at a suitable enhanced price for such a journey, say 10 pounds, both parties to the contract would be discharged in the contingency of the race at Epsom for some reason becoming impossible; but I do not think this follows, for I do not think that in the cab case the happening of the race would be the foundation of the contract. No doubt the purpose of the engager would be to go to see the Derby, and the price would be proportionately high; but if the cab had no special qualifications for the purpose which led to the selection of the cab for this particular occasion. Any other cab would have done as well. Moreover, I think that, under the cab contract, the hirer, even if the race went off, could have said, "Drive me to Epsom: I will pay you the agreed sum; you have nothing to do with the purpose for which I hired the cab," and that if the cabman refused he would have been guilty of a breach of contract, there being nothing to qualify his promise to drive the hirer to Epsom on a particular day. Whereas in the case of the coronation, there is not merely the purpose of the hirer to see the coronation procession, but it is the coronation procession and the relative position of the rooms which is the basis of the contract as much for the lessor as the hirer.... It could not in the cab case be reasonably said that seeing the Derby race was the foundation of the contract, as it was of the licence in this case. Whereas in the present case, where the rooms were offered and taken, by reason of their peculiar suitability from the position of the rooms for a view of the coronation procession, surely the view of the coronation procession was the foundation of the contract ... Each case must be judged by its own circumstances. In each case one must ask oneself, first, what, having regard to all the circumstances, was the foundation of the contract? Secondly, was the performance of the contract prevented? Thirdly, was the event which prevented the performance of the contract of such a character that it cannot reasonably be said to have been in the contemplation of the parties at the date of the contract? If all these questions are answered in the affirmative (as I think they should be in this case), I think both parties are discharged from further performance of the contract. I think that the coronation procession was the foundation of this contract, and that the non-happening of it prevented the performance of the contract; and, secondly, I think that the non-happening of the procession ... was an event "of such a character that it cannot reasonably be supposed to have been in the contemplation of the contracting parties when the contract was made, and that they are not to be held bound by general words which, though large enough to include, were not used with reference to the possibility of the particular contingency which afterwards happened." [Citation omitted.] The test seems to be whether the event which causes the impossibility was or might have been anticipated and guarded against. It seems difficult to say, in a case where both parties anticipate the happening of an event, which anticipation is the foundation of the contract, that either party must be taken to have anticipated, and ought to have guarded against, the event which prevented the performance of the contract.... *The Moorcock* is of importance in the present case as shewing that ... one must ... look not only at the words of the contract, but also at the surrounding facts and the knowledge of the parties of those facts.... It is not essential to the application of the principle of *Taylor v. Caldwell* that the direct subject of the contract should perish or fail to be in existence at the date of performance of the contract. It is sufficient if a state of things or condition expressed in the contract and essential to its performance perishes or fails to be in existence at that time. In the present case the condition which fails and prevents the achievement of that which was, in the contemplation of both parties, the foundation of the contract, is not expressly mentioned either as a condition of the contract or the purpose of it; but I think for the reasons which I have given that the principle of *Taylor v. Caldwell* ought to be applied ...

[Appeal dismissed].

Exercise 12-45: *Krell v. Henry* Revisited

Analyze the following hypotheticals:

1. Angelo leases a gas station to Brandon. A new traffic regulation so impacts Brandon's business that he can only operate at a loss. Must Brandon continue to pay rent?

2. What if a new zoning regulation forbade the selling of gasoline at the location?

3. Would the result in the previous hypothetical be the same if B also provided repair services at his station?

Exercise 12-46: *Aluminum Co. of America v. Essex Group, Inc.*

The final case in this chapter is the very interesting and very challenging trial court opinion in *Aluminum Co. of America v. Essex Group, Inc.* The case is interesting because it appears that the former chairman of the Federal Reserve, Alan Greenspan was the architect of the error that led to this litigation. It is of further interest because the court finds mistake, impracticability, and frustration in circumstances where many other courts may not have done so, and then grants a remedy, reformation, never before granted in this type of mistake case, or in an impracticability or frustration case. As you read the case, consider the following questions:

1. Why is the court's conclusion on impracticability suspect? (Hint: Pay particular attention to the assumption of risk discussion.) Nevertheless, do you think the court was right?

2. Why is the court's conclusion on frustration even more suspect? Nevertheless, do you think the court was right?

3. What do you think about the court's decision to reform the contract?

Aluminum Co. of America v. Essex Group, Inc.

499 F.Supp. 53 (1980)

MEMORANDUM OPINION AND ORDER

TEITELBAUM, District Judge.

Plaintiff, Aluminum Company of America (ALCOA), brought the instant action against defendant, Essex Group, Inc. (Essex), in three counts. The first count requests the Court to reform or equitably adjust an agreement entitled the Molten Metal Agreement entered into between ALCOA and Essex ... Essex ... counterclaims that ALCOA is liable to it for damages based on ALCOA's failure to deliver to Essex the amounts of molten metal ALCOA is contractually obligated to deliver under the Molten Metal Agreement and seeks entry of an order specifically enforcing its right to receive molten aluminum from ALCOA in the amounts requested ...

In 1966 Essex made a policy decision to expand its participation in the manufacture of aluminum wire products. Thus, beginning in the spring of 1967, ALCOA and Essex negotiated with each other for the purpose of reaching an agreement whereby ALCOA would supply Essex with its long-term needs for aluminum that Essex could use in its manufacturing operations.

By December 26, 1967 the parties had entered into what they designated as a toll conversion service contract known as the Molten Metal Agreement under which Essex would supply ALCOA with alumina which ALCOA would convert by a smelting process into molten aluminum. Under the terms of the Molten Metal Agreement, Essex delivers alumina to ALCOA which ALCOA smelts (or toll converts) into molten aluminum at its Warrick, Indiana, smelting facility. Essex then picks up the molten aluminum for further processing.

The price provisions of the contract contained an escalation formula which indicates that $.03 per pound of the original price escalates in accordance with changes in the Wholesale Price Index-Industrial Commodities (WPI) and $.03 per pound escalates in accordance with an index based on the average hourly labor rates paid to ALCOA employees at the Warrick plant. The portion of the pricing formula which is in issue in this case under counts one and two is the production charge which is escalated by the WPI. ALCOA contends that this charge was intended by the parties to reflect actual changes in the cost of the non-labor items utilized by ALCOA in the production of aluminum from alumina at its Warrick, Indiana smelting plant. In count one of this suit ALCOA asserts that the WPI used in the Molten Metal Agreement was in fact incapable of reasonably reflecting changes in the non-labor costs at ALCOA's Warrick, Indiana smelting plant and has in fact failed to so reflect such changes.

It is ALCOA's contention in count one of its complaint that the shared objectives of the parties with respect to the use of the WPI have been completely and totally frustrated, that both ALCOA and Essex made a mutual mistake of fact in agreeing to use the WPI to escalate non-labor costs at Warrick. ALCOA is seeking reformation or equitable adjustment of the Molten Metal Agreement so that pursuant to count one of its complaint, the pricing formula with respect to the non-labor portion of the production charge will be changed to eliminate the WPI and substitute the actual costs incurred by ALCOA for the non-labor items used at its Warrick, Indiana smelting plant. Essex opposes relief under count one contending that: 1) ALCOA cannot obtain reformation of the Molten Metal Agreement on the grounds of mutual mistake since ALCOA has failed to establish any antecedent agreement on pricing not expressed in the Molten Metal Agreement; 2) ALCOA assumed the risk that its prediction as to future costs would be incorrect; 3) ALCOA has failed to prove that enforcement of the Molten Metal Agreement would be unconscionable ...

As previously indicated, Essex has filed a counterclaim to the ALCOA complaint. The original counterclaim of Essex contends that under the terms of the Molten Metal Agreement as implemented during the years 1977, 1978 and the first six months of 1979, ALCOA has, on numerous occasions, breached the Molten Metal Agreement by improperly failing to deliver the amounts of molten aluminum required by the contract. This first counterclaim asks that Essex be awarded damages in an amount as to fully compensate it for the failure of ALCOA to deliver molten aluminum in accordance with the terms of the Molten Metal Agreement....

The Court finds, based upon consideration of all the evidence, that ALCOA is entitled to reformation of the Molten Metal Agreement....

COUNT ONE

ALCOA's first count seeks an equitable modification of the contract price for its services. The pleadings, arguments and briefs frame the issue in several forms. ALCOA seeks reformation or modification of the price on the basis of mutual mistake of fact, unilateral mistake of fact, unconscionability, frustration of purpose, and commercial impracticability.

A.

The facts pertinent to count one are few and simple. In 1967 ALCOA and Essex entered into a written contract in which ALCOA promised to convert specified amounts of alumina supplied by Essex into aluminum for Essex. The service is to be performed at the ALCOA works at Warrick, Indiana. The contract is to run until the end of 1983. Essex has the option to extend it until the end of 1988. The price for each pound of aluminum converted is calculated by a complex formula which includes three variable components based on specific indices ...

The indexing system was evolved by ALCOA with the aid of the eminent economist Alan Greenspan. ALCOA examined the non-labor production cost component to assure that the WPI-IC had not tended to deviate markedly from their non-labor cost experience in the years before the contract was executed. Essex agreed to the contract including the index provisions after an examination of the past record of the indices revealed an acceptable pattern of stability.

ALCOA sought, by the indexed price agreement, to achieve a stable net income of about 4¢ per pound of aluminum converted. This net income represented ALCOA's return (i) on its substantial capital investment devoted to the performance of the contracted services, (ii) on its management, and (iii) on the risks of short-falls or losses it undertook over an extended period. The fact that the non-labor production cost component of ALCOA's costs was priced according to a surrogate, objective index opened the door to a foreseeable fluctuation of ALCOA's return due to deviations between ALCOA's costs and the performance of the WPI-IC. The range of foreseeable deviation was roughly three cents per pound. That is to say that in some years ALCOA's return might foreseeably (and did, in fact) rise to seven cents per pound, while in other years it might foreseeably (and did, in fact) fall to about one cent per pound....

Essex sought to assure itself of a long term supply of aluminum at a favorable price. Essex intended to and did manufacture a new line of aluminum wire products. The long term supply of aluminum was important to assure Essex of the steady use of its expensive machinery. A steady production stream was vital to preserve the market position it sought to establish. The favorable price was important to allow Essex to compete with firms like ALCOA which produced the aluminum and manufactured aluminum wire products in an efficient, integrated operation.

In the early years of the contract, the price formula yielded prices related, within the foreseeable range of deviation, to ALCOA's cost figures. Beginning in 1973, OPEC actions to increase oil prices and unanticipated pollution control costs greatly increased ALCOA's electricity costs. Electric power is the principal non-labor cost factor in aluminum conversion, and the electric power rates rose much more rapidly than did the WPI-IC. As a result, ALCOA's production costs rose greatly and unforeseeably beyond the indexed increase in the contract price ...

During the most recent years, the market price of aluminum has increased even faster than the production costs. At the trial ALCOA introduced the deposition of Mr. Wilfred Jones, an Essex employee whose duties included the sale of surplus metal. Mr. Jones stated that Essex had resold some millions of pounds of aluminum which ALCOA had refined. The cost of the aluminum to Essex (including the purchase price of the aluminum and its transportation) was 36.35 cents per pound around June of 1979. Mr. Jones further stated that the resale price in June 1979 at one cent per pound under the market was 73.313 cents per pound, yielding Essex a gross profit of 37.043 cents per pound. This margin of profit shows the tremendous advantage Essex enjoys under the contract as it is written and as both parties have performed it. A significant fraction of Essex's advantage is directly attributable to the corresponding out of pocket losses ALCOA suffers. ALCOA has sufficiently shown that without judicial relief or economic changes which are not presently foreseeable, it stands to lose in excess of $75,000,000 out of pocket, during the remaining term of the contract....

C.

ALCOA initially argues that it is entitled to relief on the theory of mutual mistake. ALCOA contends that both parties were mistaken in their estimate of the suitability of the WPI-IC as an objective index of ALCOA's non-labor production costs, and that their mistake is legally sufficient to warrant modification or avoidance of ALCOA's promise ... [Editor's Note: In a long and thoughtful analysis, the court concluded that ALCOA had made out the elements of mutual mistake and did not assume the risk of mistake. While that discussion is not reproduced here, it is worth pausing to ask whether the court was right on both counts. There are good arguments that the mistake was not a mistake as to a basic assumption and, in any event, that ALCOA assumed the risk of the mistake.]

D.

ALCOA argues that it is entitled to relief on the grounds of impracticability and frustration of purpose. The Court agrees.

In broad outline the doctrines of impracticability and of frustration of purpose resemble the doctrine of mistake. All three doctrines discharge an obligor from his duty to perform a contract where a failure of a basic assumption of the parties produces a grave failure of the equivalence of value of the exchange to the parties. And all three are qualified by the same notions of risk assumption and allocation. The doctrine of mistake of fact requires that the mistake relate to a basic assumption on which the contract was made. The doctrine of impracticability requires that the non-occurrence of the "event" ... or the non-existence of the "fact" ... causing the impracticability be a basic assumption on which the contract is made. The doctrine of frustration of purpose similarly rests on the same "non-occurrence" or "non-existence", "basic assumption" equation ...

... [T]he non-occurrence of an extreme deviation of the WPI-IC and ALCOA's non-labor production costs was a basic assumption on which the contract was made. And it is clear that ALCOA neither assumed nor bore the risk of the deviation beyond the foreseeable limits of risk .

[Editor's note: The following discussion of assumption of risk, taken from the court's mistake discussion, is moved here so that readers get the benefit of studying the court's and the parties' interesting analyses of this issue.]

The Restatements and ... cases reveal four facets of risk assumption and risk allocation under the law of mistake. First, a party to a contract may expressly assume a risk. If a contractor agrees to purchase and to remove 114,000 cubic yards of fill from a designated tract for the landowner at a set price "regardless of subsurface soil and water conditions" the contractor assumes the risk that subsurface water may make the removal unexpectedly expensive.

Customary dealing in a trade or common understanding may lead a court to impose a risk on a party where the contract is silent. Often the result corresponds to the expectation of both parties, but this will not always be true. [Citation omitted.] ...

Third, where neither express words nor some particular common understanding or trade usage dictate a result, the court must allocate the risk in some reasoned way. Two examples from the RESTATEMENT SECOND OF CONTRACTS § 296 illustrate the principle. A farmer who contracts to sell land may not escape the obligation if minerals are discovered which make the land more valuable. And in the case of the sale of fill stated above, if there is no express assumption of the risk of adverse conditions by the contractor, he may still bear the risk of losing his expected profits and suffering some out of pocket losses if some of the fill lies beneath the water table. These cases rest on policies of high generality. Contracts are—generally—to be enforced. Land sales are—generally—to be treated as final.

Fourth, where parties enter a contract in a state of conscious ignorance of the facts, they are deemed to risk the burden of having the facts turn out to be adverse, within very broad limits. Each party takes a calculated gamble in such a contract. Because information is often troublesome or costly to obtain, the law does not seek to discourage such contracts.[18] Thus if parties agree to sell and purchase a stone which both know may be glass or diamond at a price which in some way reflects their uncertainty, the contract is enforceable whether the stone is in fact glass or diamond. If, by contrast, the parties both mistakenly believe it to be glass, the case is said not to be one of conscious ignorance but one of mutual mistake. Consequently the vendor may void the contract.

In this case Essex raises two arguments. First, it asserts that ALCOA expressly or by fair implication assumed the risk that the WPI-IC would not keep up with ALCOA's non-labor production costs. Second, it asserts that the parties made a calculated gamble with full awareness that the future was uncertain, so the contract should be enforced despite the mutual mistake. Both arguments are correct within limits, and within those limits they affect the relief ALCOA may receive. Both arguments fail as complete defenses to ALCOA's claim.

Essex first asserts that ALCOA expressly or implicitly assumed the risk that the WPI-IC would not track ALCOA's non-labor production costs. Essex asserts that ALCOA drafted the index provision; that it did so on the basis of its superior knowledge of its cost experience at the Warrick Works; and that ALCOA's officials knew of the inherent risk that the index would not reflect cost changes. Essex emphasizes that, during the negotiation

_____

18. Editor's footnote: The court's discussion of conscious ignorance is included because the issue is so similar to the assumption of risk by foreseeability issue under impracticability and frustration law.

of the contract, it insisted on the inclusion of a protective "ceiling" on the indexed price of ALCOA's services at 65% of a specified published market price. Essex implies that ALCOA could have sought a corresponding "floor" provision to limit its risks.

Essex' arguments rely on two ancient and powerful principles of interpretation. The first is reflected in the maxim "expressio unius est exclusio alterius." The second is the principle that a contract is to be construed against its drafter. To agree to an indexed price term subject to a ceiling but without a floor is to make a deliberate choice, Essex argues. It is to choose one principle and to reject another. The argument is plausible but not sufficient. The maxim rules no farther than its reason, and its reason is simply this: often an expression of a rule couched in one form reflects with high probability the rejection of a contradictory rule. Less often it reflects a probable rejection of a supplementary rule. To know if this is true of a particular case requires a scrupulous examination of the thing expressed, the thing not expressed, and the context of the expression. The question here is precisely this: By omitting a floor provision did ALCOA accept the risk of any and every deviation of the selected index from its costs, no matter how great or how highly improbable? The course of dealing between the parties repels the idea. Essex and ALCOA are huge industrial enterprises. The management of each is highly trained and highly responsible. The corporate officers have access to and use professional personnel including lawyers, accountants, economists and engineers. The contract was drafted by sophisticated, responsible businessmen who were intensely conscious of the risks inherent in long term contracts and who plainly sought to limit the risks of their undertaking. The parties' laudable attention to risk limitation appears in many ways: in the complex price formula, in the 65% ceiling, in the "most favored customer" clause which Essex wrote into the contract, and in the elaborate "force majeure" clause favoring ALCOA. It appears as well in the care and in the expense of the negotiations and drafting process. Essex negotiated with several aluminum producers, seeking a long term assured supply, before agreeing to the ALCOA contract. Its search for an assured long term supply for its aluminum product plants itself bespeaks a motive of limiting risks. Essex settled on ALCOA's offer rather than a proffered joint venture on the basis of many considerations including the required capital, engineering and management demands of the joint venture, the cost, and the comparative risks and burdens of the two arrangements. When ALCOA proposed the price formula which appears in the contract, Essex's management examined the past behavior of the indices for stability to assure they would not cause their final aluminum cost to deviate unacceptably from the going market rate. ALCOA's management was equally attentive to risk limitation. They went so far as to retain the noted economist Dr. Alan Greenspan as a consultant to advise them on the drafting of an objective pricing formula. They selected the WPI-IC as a pricing element for this long term contract only after they assured themselves that it had closely tracked ALCOA's non-labor production costs for many years in the past and was highly likely to continue to do so in the future. In the context of the formation of the contract, it is untenable to argue that ALCOA implicitly or expressly assumed a limitless, if highly improbable, risk. On this record, the absence of an express floor limitation can only be understood to imply that the parties deemed the risk too remote and their meaning too clear to trifle with additional negotiation and drafting.

The principle that a writing is to be construed against its maker will not aid Essex here. That principle once sounded as a clarion call to retrograde courts to pervert agreements if they could. Today it is happily domesticated as a rule with diverse uses. In cases involving issues of conscience or of strong policy, such as forfeiture cases, the principle complements the familiar doctrine of strict construction to favor lenient results. In other cases it serves as an aid in resolving otherwise intractable ambiguities. This case presents neither of these problems. The question of defining the risks ALCOA assumed is one of interpretation. It implicates no strong public policy. Neither does it present an intractable ambiguity.

Neither is this a case of "conscious ignorance" as Essex argues. Essex cites many cases which establish the general rule that mistaken assumptions about the future are not the sort of mistaken assumptions which lead to relief from contractual duties ... The general rule is in fact as Essex states it. But that rule has limited application. The new Restatement notes that the rule does not apply where both parties are unconscious of their ignorance — that is, where both mistakenly believe they know the vital facts. [Citations omitted.]

This distinction is sufficient to settle many cases but it is framed too crudely for sensible application to cases like the present one. The distinction posits two polar positions: certain belief that a vital fact is true and certain recognition that a vital fact is unknown. Such certainties are seldom encountered in human affairs. They are particularly rare in the understanding of sophisticated businessmen....

Once courts recognize that supposed specific values lie, and are commonly understood to lie, within a penumbra of uncertainty, and that the range of probability is subject to estimation, the principle of conscious uncertainty requires reformulation. The proper question is not simply whether the parties to a contract were conscious of uncertainty with respect to a vital fact, but whether they believed that uncertainty was effectively limited within a designated range so that they would deem outcomes beyond that range to be highly unlikely. In this case the answer is clear. Both parties knew that the use of an objective price index injected a limited range of uncertainty into their projected return on the contract. Both had every reason to predict that the likely range of variation would not exceed three cents per pound. That is to say both would have deemed deviations yielding ALCOA less of a return on its investment, work and risk of less than one cent a pound or of more than seven cents a pound to be highly unlikely. Both consciously undertook a closely calculated risk rather than a limitless one. Their mistake concerning its calculation is thus fundamentally unlike the limitless conscious undertaking of an unknown risk which Essex now posits ...

The focus of the doctrines of impracticability and of frustration is distinctly on hardship. Section 281 declares a party is discharged from performing a contract where a supervening event renders his performance impracticable. Comment d discusses the meaning of "impracticability." The comment states the word is taken from Uniform Commercial Code § 2-615(a). It declares that the word denotes an impediment to performance lying between "impossibility" and "impracticality".

Performance may be impracticable because extreme and unreasonable difficulty, expense, injury, or loss to one of the parties will be involved....

A mere change in the degree of difficulty or expense due to such causes as increased wages, prices of raw materials, or costs of construction, unless well beyond the normal range, does not amount to impracticability since it is this sort of risk that a fixed-price contract is intended to cover. RESTATEMENT SECOND OF CONTRACTS § 281 com. (d).

Similarly, § 285 declares a party is discharged from performing his contract where his principal purpose is substantially frustrated by the occurrence of a supervening event. The extent of the necessary frustration is further described in comment a: "(T)he frustration must be substantial. It is not enough that the transaction has become less profitable for the affected party or even that he will sustain a loss. The frustration must be so severe that it is not fairly to be regarded as within the risks that he assumed under the contract."

Professor Corbin explained this requirement of a severe disappointment by relating this doctrine to the broad public policies that parties should generally be required to perform their contracts.

> Variations in the value of a promised performance, caused by the constantly varying factors that affect the bargaining appetites of men, are the rule rather than the exception. Bargainers know this and swallow their losses and disappointments, meantime keeping their promises. Such being the business mores, court decisions that are not in harmony with them will not make for satisfaction or prosperity. Relief from duty, outside of the bankruptcy court, can safely be granted on the ground of frustration of purpose by the rise or fall of values, only when the variation in value is very great *73 and is caused by a supervening event that was not in fact contemplated by the parties and the risk of which was not allocated by them. CORBIN ON CONTRACTS § 1355.

This strict standard of severe disappointment is clearly met in the present case. ALCOA has sufficiently proved that it will lose well over $60 million dollars out of pocket over the life of the contract due to the extreme deviation of the WPI-IC from ALCOA's actual costs.[19]

Is this, then, a case of impracticability, of frustration, or both? The doctrine of impracticability and of frustration focus on different kinds of disappointment of a contracting party. Impracticability focuses on occurrences which greatly increase the costs, difficulty, or risk of the party's performance. RESTATEMENT SECOND OF CONTRACTS § 281.

The doctrine of frustration, on the other hand, focuses on a party's severe disappointment which is caused by circumstances which frustrate his principal purpose for entering the contract. [Citation omitted.] The doctrine of frustration often applies to relieve a party of a contract which could be performed without impediment; relief is allowed because the performance would be of little value to the frustrated party. Illustration 1 of the new RESTATEMENT abstracted from the Coronation Cases typifies this aspect of the doctrine of frustration.

> A and B make a contract under which B is to pay A $1,000 and is to have the use of A's window on January 10 to view a parade that has been scheduled for that day. Because of the illness of an important official, the parade is cancelled. B refuses to use the window or pay the $1,000. B's duty to pay $1,000 is discharged, and B is not liable to A for breach of contract.

Nothing impedes the full performance of this contract. B is able to pay $1,000 and to use the window despite the cancellation of the parade. But B's purpose to observe the spectacle has been frustrated.

In the present case ALCOA has satisfied the requirements of both doctrines. The impracticability of its performance is clear. The increase in its cost of performance is severe enough to warrant relief, and the other elements necessary for the granting of relief have been proven. Essex argues that the causes of ALCOA's losses are due to market price in-

---

19. The Court recognizes the additional requirement that the frustration or impracticability must not be the fault of the party who seeks relief. RESTATEMENT SECOND OF CONTRACTS §§ 281, 285. Essex has not claimed or shown that ALCOA's dealings during the contract caused or contributed to ALCOA's losses. The record sufficiently proves that the great cost increases of some of the non-labor cost components (power, electrolytes, carbon) were beyond ALCOA's control. This distinguishes the present case from *Iowa Elec. Light & Power Co. v. Atlas Corp.*, 467 F.Supp. 129 (N.D.Iowa 1978) where the court concluded that it was not clear that Atlas, a uranium supplier, could not have protected itself contractually from some of the risk which caused its loss. Id. at 129.

creases to which the doctrine of impracticability does not apply ... The official comment to [U.C.C.] § 2-615 lends strength to Essex's claim.

> 1. This section excuses a seller from timely delivery of goods contracted for, where his performance has become commercially impracticable because of unforeseen supervening circumstances not within the contemplation of the parties at the time of contracting.

However,

> 4. Increased cost alone does not excuse performance unless the rise in cost is due to some unforeseen contingency which alters the essential nature of the performance. Neither is a rise or a collapse in the market in itself a justification, for that is exactly the type of business risk which business contracts made at fixed prices are intended to cover. But a severe shortage of raw materials or of supplies due to a contingency such as war, embargo, local crop failure, unforeseen shutdown of major sources of supply or the like, which either causes a marked increase in cost or altogether prevents the seller from securing supplies necessary to his performance is within the contemplation of this section.

Several of the cases cited by Essex rely on comment 4 in denying claims for relief. [Citations omitted.] Each is distinguishable from the present case in the absolute extent of the loss and in the proportion of loss involved.

In [one case cited by Essex], the defendant Union Carbide had contracted in 1972 to sell ethanol in specified quantities over a three year period to the plaintiff. The price was set by a formula, adjusted annually to reflect the seller's cost for raw materials, and subject to a ceiling on adjustment increases. The raw materials were derivatives of natural gas; their price soared beginning in 1973 as did ALCOA's energy costs. The seller's costs for ethanol rose from 21.2 cents a gallon in 1973 to 37.2 cents per gallon in mid-1974. The ceiling contract sales price was then 26.5 cents per gallon. The seller's loss of 10.7 cents per gallon led to a projected aggregate loss of $5.8 million. The court refused to relieve the seller. It found that the ceiling provision constituted an intentional allocation of the "risk of a substantial and unforeseen rise in cost" to the seller. It based this finding in part on the twenty-five percent rise in prices by OPEC in 1971 which made future cost increases highly foreseeable. The court addressed the degree of loss issue, declaring:

> We are not aware of any cases where something less than a 100% cost increase has been held to make a seller's performance 'impracticable.'

> ... '(T)here must be more of a variation between expected cost and the cost of performing by an available alternative than is present in this case, where the promisor can legitimately be presumed to have accepted some degree of abnormal risk, and where impracticability is urged on the basis of added expense alone.' Id. at 992.

[This case] is clearly distinguishable from the present case respecting the degree of loss which the seller suffered in comparison to what it foresaw at the time of contracting. The fact that the contract [in the other case] was made after the substantial price increase of 1971 may justify the court's finding that the seller had assumed the risk of further large price increases. The contract in the present case antedated the 1971 price increase. There is no similar factual basis for finding that ALCOA assumed the risk of the full loss which it is experiencing ...

Here ALCOA's loss is more than a thousand times greater than the carrier's loss. And the circumstances surrounding the contract show a deliberate avoidance of abnormal risks ...

Courts must decide the point at which the community's interest in predictable contract enforcement shall yield to the fact that enforcement of a particular contract would be commercially senseless and unjust. The spirit of the Code is that such decisions cannot justly derive from legal abstractions. They must derive from courts sensitive to the mores, practices and habits of thought in the respectable commercial world.

If it were important to the decision of this case, the Court would hold that the foreseeability of a variation between the WPI-IC and ALCOA's costs would not preclude relief under the doctrine of impracticability. But the need for such a holding is not clear, for the Court has found that the risk of a wide variation between these values was unforeseeable in a commercial sense and was not allocated to ALCOA in the contract.

The Court holds that ALCOA is entitled to relief under the doctrine of impracticability. The cases Essex relies on and the other cases discovered by the Court are all distinguishable with respect to the gravity of harm which the aggrieved contracting party was liable to suffer. Except for *Transatlantic Financing*, they are also distinguishable with respect to the question of allocation of the risk, inferred from the circumstances known to the parties at the time of the contract and from the contract terms.

ALCOA's claim of frustration requires more discussion. ALCOA's "principal purpose" in making the contract was to earn money. This purpose has plainly been severely disappointed. The gravity of ALCOA's loss is indisputably sufficient to meet the stern standard for relief. But the question remains whether the law will grant relief for the serious frustration of this kind of purpose, i.e., for the conversion of an expected profit into a serious loss. All of the new Restatement illustrations center on purposes other than making a profit. However most of them bear on some stage of a profit-oriented activity. Illustrations 2-7 describe profit-oriented business activities which contribute to the success of enterprises though they are not themselves directly profitable. In each, the question is whether the immediate end of this discrete contract is frustrated, without regard to the impact of the frustration on the more remote end of earning profits. Thus illustration 4 involves a lease of a neon sign to a business. A subsequent governmental regulation prohibits illuminating the sign. The Restatement declares the lessee's duty to pay rent to be discharged. Here the lessee's most immediate principal purpose is night-time advertising ...

In § 1360 Professor Corbin demonstrates that at times courts should treat loss avoidance as a principal purpose of a party. That section deals with frustration of purpose caused by inflationary depreciation of money. Corbin demonstrates that the decisions are not uniform on this subject, but he rejects as reprehensible the nominalist rule that a dollar's a dollar no matter how small. The injustice of the nominalist position was clearly recognized in the case of *Anderson v. Equitable Life Assurance Society*, 134 L.T. 557, 42 T.L.R. 302 (1926). The facts in Anderson were these: In 1887 an Englishman in Russia took out a twenty-premium life insurance policy with premiums and benefits payable in German marks. The policy benefit was 60,000 marks. The premiums were paid from 1887 to 1907 and were converted, as both parties understood they would be, into pounds. Their value came to £2,377. The insured died in 1922 at the height of the German hyperinflation. At that time the value of 60,000 marks was less than an English penny. The insurer argued that it owed nothing on the contract, for it could not be required to pay a fraction of a cent. Astonishingly, the court agreed. Under English law the obligation to pay in foreign currency was absolute and unqualified by variations in exchange rates. The judges noted the harshness of the result and pressed upon the company its moral obligation to make some payment which they held the law would not compel.

Happily some American cases and the law of many foreign countries take a different view of the problem. The problem of serious, sustained inflation is not unique to modern America. During the Revolution and the Civil War, America witnessed serious inflation. And several other nations have recently experienced more severe inflation than America has. When the problem has arisen, here and abroad, courts and legislatures have repeatedly acted to relieve parties from great and unexpected losses. [Citations omitted.] The exact character of the relief granted is not important here. Neither is the exact explanation of the decisions found in the cases, because even the Civil War cases antedate the evolution of the distinct doctrine of frustration. What is important is this: first, the results of those decisions would be readily explained today in terms of frustration of purpose. Corbin discusses them in his chapter on Frustration of Purpose. And second, the frustration which they involved was a frustration of the purpose to earn money or to avoid losses. Thus it appears that there is no legitimate doctrinal problem which prevents relief for frustration of this sort. There remain the customary strictures concerning risk allocation and gravity of injury. Those have been addressed above and need not be considered again here. The Court holds ALCOA is entitled to relief on its claim of frustration of purpose.

E.

This leaves the question of framing a remedy for ALCOA. Essex argues that reformation is not available. It cites many Indiana cases declaring that reformation is only available to correct writings which, through mistake, do not reflect the agreement of the parties. The declarations to that effect are clear. [Citations omitted.]

But the point is immaterial here. This case does not fall within reformation as a traditional head of equity jurisprudence. It does fall within the more general rules of equitable restitution. Courts have traditionally applied three remedial rules in cases of mistake, frustration and impracticability. In some cases courts declare that no contract ever arose because there was no true agreement between the parties, [citation omitted], or because the parties were ignorant of existing facts which frustrated the purpose of one party or made performance impracticable. [Citation omitted.] In some other cases, courts hold that a contract is voidable on one of the three theories. In these cases the customary remedy is rescission. In both classes of cases where one or both parties have performed under the supposed contract, the courts award appropriate restitution in the light of the benefits the parties have conferred on each other. The aim is to prevent unjust enrichment ...

The same ends can be achieved under a long term executory contract by a similar remedy. To decree rescission in this case would be to grant ALCOA a windfall gain in the current aluminum market. It would at the same time deprive Essex of the assured long term aluminum supply which it obtained under the contract and of the gains it legitimately may enforce within the scope of the risk ALCOA bears under the contract. A remedy which merely shifts the windfall gains and losses is neither required nor permitted by Indiana law ...

[Editor's Note: The court then created a new price structure for the contract.]

Exercise 12-47: Distinguishing Impracticability from Frustration

The next set of problems has been designed to help you develop your ability to distinguish impracticability from frustration.

1. What is the essence of each of these two claims? In other words, how will you distinguish these two claims?

2. Amelia owns a hotel and Ben owns a nearby country club. Amelia agrees to pay Ben $1,000 per month for five years to allow Amelia's hotel guests to play Ben's golf course free of charge. Amelia's hotel burns down. Ben sues Amelia for breach when Amelia stops paying. Is Amelia's claim impracticability or frustration?

3. Same contract as in the previous hypothetical. Assume that the golf course burns down and the hotel remains fine so that this time it is Ben who does not perform. Amelia sues Ben for breach. Is Ben's claim impracticability or frustration?

4. Same contract as in the previous two hypotheticals. Assume that, because of a grass disease that is transmitted via golf clubs, Ben now must spray the grass with a special spray every time a player uses the golf course. This triples Ben's costs. Ben therefore tripled the green fees he charges his regular customers and is refusing to perform the contract with Amelia anymore. Amelia sues Ben for breach. Is Ben's claim impracticability or frustration?

5. Same contract as in the previous three hypotheticals. Assume the grass on Ben's golf course becomes diseased and therefore so ugly that Amelia's guests have no desire to play golf on it and Amelia therefore stops paying Ben. Ben sues Amelia for breach. Is Amelia's claim impracticability or frustration?

Chapter Problem Revisited

Task 1: Make sure you consider the contract law application of all the clauses in the contract and not just the clauses about which you have learned in this chapter.

Task 2: The second task involves meeting with your client to ask questions and take instructions and then rewriting the contract to accomplish the client's objectives. Make sure you prepare a list of questions in advance of your meeting with the client. While you need to ask questions that will allow you to clarify every issue implicated by your analysis in Task 1, make sure you consider the possibility of other issues not addressed at all in the contract.

Professional Development Reflection Questions

1. When you met with your client in connection with the Chapter Problem, she asked you to leave one clause deliberately ambiguous. Why did she ask you to do so? How did her request make you feel? Is it ethical to leave a clause deliberately ambiguous at the request of your client?

2. In Chapter 11's reflection questions, you learned about a few happiness strategies. This chapter's reflection questions introduce you to more happiness strategies. For example, one strategy that you can use to increase your level of happiness is to learn about happiness. Take a few minutes to browse some positive psychology Web sites. Or, pick up and start reading one of the many positive psy-

chology books. Two that we recommend are: Martin Seligman, AUTHENTIC HAP-PINESS, and Sonya Lybormirsky, THE HOW OF HAPPINESS.

3.   Another strategy that is scientifically proven to increase your level of happiness is called the "gratitude visit." To use this strategy, think of someone to whom you are grateful but have never properly thanked. Write a letter to that person in which you specifically express what you are grateful for and what that person has meant to you. Then, arrange a visit to that person and read your letter to them.

4.   One more strategy you can use to increase your level of happiness is called the "three doors." As we go through life, we all experience "doors" shutting in our faces — no one is exempt from losses, rejections, or plans that collapse. To use the three-doors strategy, specifically identify three "doors" that have closed in your life and reconstruct those memories by focusing on what other doors opened as a result. For example, what good resulted or how did you grow?

Non-Party Contract Rights
Other than the parties, who else can enforce a deal?

PART SEVEN

NON-PARTY CONTRACT RIGHTS

Other than the parties: Who else can enforce a deal

Chapter 13

Third-Party Beneficiaries

Exercise 13-1: Chapter Problem

You are a first-year associate working for a law firm that handles personal injury cases. You are about to meet with a new client. Your paralegal spoke to the potential client on the phone. Her notes of that phone call report the following:

> 16 months ago, the potential client was a passenger in her best friend's car when it was struck by someone driving another car whom the potential client believes was uninsured or underinsured. Her friend was not significantly injured, but she (the potential client) suffered severely broken bones in her right leg and ribs and a lacerated spleen. Her friend is wealthy and has told your potential client that she had uninsured and underinsured motorists' coverage.

Prepare a list of questions in anticipation of your upcoming initial client interview. (Hint: Unlike in law school, cases do not come to you with labels; no client comes to you and says, "I would like you to bring a torts claim for negligence based on res ipsa loquitur." Moreover, almost all cases require you to use your knowledge from multiple law school disciplines. This problem is such a problem. Make sure your questions draw from what you have learned in both contracts and torts.)

Overview of Chapter 13

So far, we have focused on the two (or more) parties who make a contract, *e.g.*, seller and buyer or contractor and owner. This chapter brings in a new group of parties; parties who may have rights even if the contract does not bind them to do anything other than enjoy the benefits of one party's contract performance. As you know, a contract usually only creates rights in the parties to that contract. There are three situations, however, when nonparties may become involved and acquire rights and/or liabilities. Those situations involve: (1) third-party beneficiaries; (2) assignments of rights and delegations of duties; and (3) novations. This chapter focuses on third-party beneficiaries. Assignments, delegations, and novations are addressed in Chapter 14.

In this chapter, you will learn about third-party beneficiaries. In the first part of the chapter, you will be introduced to the ideas and terminology used in third-party beneficiary contract law. In the second part of this chapter, you will learn the tests courts use to evaluate whether a party who claims to be a third-party beneficiary has such rights. In the third part of this chapter, you will explore issues relating to efforts to modify a third-party beneficiary's rights. Finally, the chapter concludes with a discussion of defenses to third-party beneficiary claims.

Contract Law Graphic Organizer

Diagram 13-1 shows where third-party beneficiaries fit within the big picture of contract law. As the diagram shows, "Third-Party Contract Issues" is the fifth major contract issue. That issue is addressed in three sections: "Third-Party Beneficiaries," "Assignment and Delegation," and "Novation." This chapter addresses third-party beneficiaries.

Diagram 13-1: Contract Law Graphic Organizer

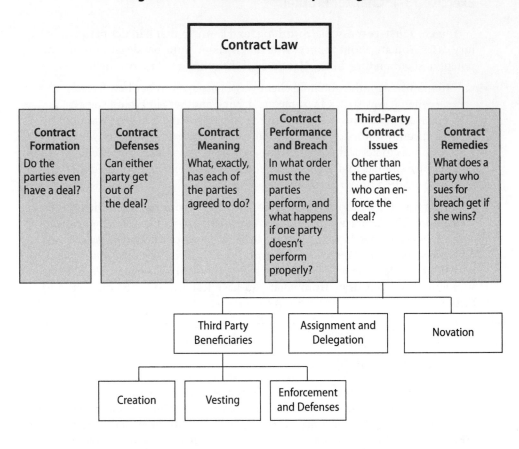

Exercise 13-2: Preliminary Questions

The main issues in third-party beneficiary law can be expressed in the following three questions. Try to predict the answers.

1. Does a contract create rights in a third party who is not a party to the contract?

2. Have those rights vested in the third party or may those rights be modified?

3. What rights does the third party have against the promisor or promisee, what rights does the promisee have against the promisor, and what defenses can a promisor assert?

Introduction to Third-Party Beneficiary Contracts and Terminology

Two parties form a contract. One party, the promisee, provides consideration for and extracts a promise from the other party, the promisor. In the context of a third party beneficiary contract, the promisor promises to bestow a benefit to a third party who is not a party to the contract. The third-party beneficiary is not a party to the contract, but the parties intend that person to benefit from performance of the promisor's promise.

For example, assume Sheila is a first-year law student who wants to sign up for a bar review course so she can obtain free first-year study aids available to all new registrants. However, Sheila cannot afford it. Sheila's favorite aunt, Amelia, offers to buy the bar review course for Sheila as a birthday present. Amelia therefore signs a contract with the bar review listing Sheila as the bar review student and pays the fee. In this example, as to the third party promise, Amelia is the promisee — the party providing consideration and extracting a promise of return performance for a third party, Sheila. The bar review is the promisor — the party receiving consideration and promising to bestow a benefit on a third party who is not a party to the contract. Sheila is the third-party beneficiary. Although Sheila is not a party to the contract, the parties intend the contract to benefit her, and she has rights under the contract. This relationship can be depicted using the following two graphics. The first, Diagram 13-2, shows the relationship between the bar review and Amelia.

Diagram 13-2: Basic Promissory Relationships between Parties to a Third-Party Beneficiary Contract

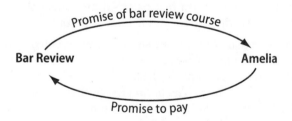

Note that, as to the promise of a bar review course, the bar review is the promisor, and Amelia is the promisee. As to the promise to pay, Amelia is the promisor and the bar review is the promisee. In other words, in every bilateral contract, both parties are promisors and both are promisees.

Now, we can add Sheila to the picture. Diagram 13-3 (on the next page) shows how Sheila fits in. Whereas Diagram 13-2 shows the promises, Diagram 13-3 depicts to whom the promised performances must be rendered.

Note that, with respect to the promise to provide the bar review course, while Amelia is still the promisee as depicted in Diagram 13-3, Sheila is the third party beneficiary because the bar review will be rendering its performance to Sheila.

Diagram 13-3: Performances Due Under a Third-Party Beneficiary Contract

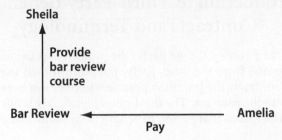

As you read the cases and problems in this chapter, make sure you always identify the promisees, promisors, and third-party beneficiaries. As you do so, draw diagrams depicting the relationships of the parties. Doing so will help you understand the materials in this chapter because many of the rules are framed in terms of these labels, and courts use the terms without explanation.

In addition, this chapter will use the term "promisee" to refer to the party who extracts a third party beneficiary promise from the other party. While, as noted above, both parties to a contract are promisees and promisors, our word choices will focus mostly on the parties to the third party beneficiary promise.

There are two other situations that raise third-party issues that you should be aware of and become able to distinguish from third-party beneficiary situations: assignments of rights and delegations of duties; and novations. In an assignment of rights, two parties form a contract that neither party intends to benefit or obligate a third party. After the parties form their contract, one of the parties (known as the assignor or delegator) then forms a new contract with a third party that requires the third party (who is known as an assignee or delegatee) to perform that party's duties under the original contract or conveys, to the third party, that party's rights under the contract.

For example, assume that Nhu is a law student who executed a contract to purchase a particular bar review's California bar review course, and Nhu paid for the course in full when she was a first-year law student. In the fall of her third year of law school, Nhu accepted a job with a Texas law firm. The bar review provider, however, does not offer its services in Texas. Nhu's friend, Roberto, took a job in California and has not yet registered for any bar review course. Nhu and Roberto agree that Nhu will sell her bar review course to Roberto. Nhu and Roberto sign a contract by which Nhu assigns her rights under the bar review contract to Roberto, and Roberto agrees to pay Nhu the same price that Nhu had already paid to the bar review provider. In this situation, Nhu is an assignor and Roberto is an assignee of the contract rights between the bar review provider and Roberto. If Nhu had signed the contract but not paid for the bar review course, her contract with Roberto would also delegate her duty to pay the bar review provider instead of requiring Roberto to pay Nhu.

In a novation situation, two parties form a contract that neither party intends to benefit a third party. Later, one party decides he wants out of the contract and finds another party to take his place. The parties then execute a new contract that releases the first party from the original contract and substitutes the new party as the other party to the contract.

For example, assume that Nhu has one year left on her apartment lease when she graduates. Although she originally intended to stay in California and continue her lease, she no longer needs to stay in her apartment another year because she is moving to Texas. Although her lease permits assignments, Nhu does not want to have any lingering responsibilities when she moves out of state. Nhu convinces Roberto, who has taken a job with a big California law firm, to take over her lease. Roberto and Nhu's landlord sign a new lease for the same apartment Nhu had leased and for the time remaining on Nhu's lease. The new lease expressly states that Nhu is being released from all obligations under her lease with the landlord. The new contract is a novation contract. Nhu no longer owes any contractual obligations to the landlord, and the landlord no longer owes any contractual duties to Nhu.

Exercise 13-3: Third-Party Beneficiary Contract versus Assignment and Delegation versus Novation

The following hypotheticals involve a third-party beneficiary, an assignment and/or a delegation, or a novation. It is critical that you be able to speedily distinguish these situations because the rules that apply to each are so dramatically different. Look back at the above examples to help you.

1. Donatella owes Christy $10,000. Donatella, Christy, and Pierre enter into a contract in which Pierre agrees to pay the $10,000 to Christy, and Christy agrees to release Donatella from her obligation.

2. Anastasia enters a contract with Insurance Company. Anastasia promises to pay an annual premium until her death, and Insurance Company promises to pay Anastasia's designated beneficiary, Marcello, $200,000 upon Anastasia's death.

3. Pedro, who serves our country in the Navy Reserves, is called to active duty overseas. Unfortunately, he recently signed a one-year lease to rent fancy golf clubs from Rent-a-Club. Pedro enters into a contract with Felice by which Felice agrees to pay Pedro's rental fee amount to Rent-a-Club, and Pedro agrees to allow Felice to use the golf clubs.

Creation of Third-Party Beneficiaries

The first issue that you must address in any third-party beneficiary problem is whether a contract actually creates any rights in the alleged third-party beneficiary. This question is often framed as a question of whether the third party has standing to sue. A third party has standing if the contract meets the requirements courts have created for determining that the third party is an intended beneficiary (has standing) rather than an incidental beneficiary (lacks standing).

Historically, the rights of contract beneficiaries have been the subject of doctrinal difficulties. The history of third-party beneficiary law has been described as "troubled," "tortured," and "formalistic."[1] In early common law cases, English courts frequently denied parties who were neither promisors nor promisees the right to recover under contracts.

---

1. CORBIN ON CONTRACTS, section 41.1.

The English experience was largely replicated in early American cases. Gradually, however, American law developed two categories of third persons that were entitled to recover under contracts: donee beneficiaries and creditor beneficiaries. These categories helped but courts continued to struggle. These difficulties have now been largely resolved by recognizing the power of contracting parties to create rights in a beneficiary by manifesting an intention to do so.

In this section, you will first learn the general rules relating to the creation of third-party beneficiaries. Then, three specific situations will be examined: (1) third-party beneficiaries of attorney-client contracts; (2) third-party beneficiaries of government contracts; and (3) the statutory creation of third-party warranty beneficiaries under the U.C.C.

Intended Third-Party Beneficiaries

Lawrence v. Fox is an early case, included in nearly all contracts texts, involving the issue of whether a contract confers any rights on a third party who stands to benefit under the contract. The case should give you a sense of how courts struggled on a doctrinal level when addressing this issue.

Exercise 13-4: *Lawrence v. Fox*

As you read *Lawrence*, consider the following questions:

1. Identify and draw a diagram depicting the promisor, promisee, and alleged third-party beneficiary.

2. Why have courts struggled to determine when a third party should or should not have rights under a contract?

3. What theories have courts applied in an attempt to allow third parties to recover?

4. *Lawrence* is a landmark case because of the rule it states and applies. What is that rule?

5. How is that rule applied to the facts in *Lawrence*?

6. What policy rationales support recognizing contract rights in third-party beneficiaries?

7. Does the rationale of *Lawrence* support limiting its application to creditor-beneficiary cases?

Lawrence v. Fox

6 E.P. Smith 268, 20 N.Y. 268 (1859)

H. Gray, J. The first objection raised on the trial amounts to this: That the evidence of the person present, who heard the declarations of Holly giving directions as to the payment of the money he was then advancing to the defendant, was mere hearsay and therefore not competent. Had the plaintiff sued Holly for this sum of money no objection to the competency of this evidence would have been thought of; and if the defendant had performed his promise by paying the sum loaned to him to the plaintiff, and Holly had afterwards sued him for its recovery, and this evidence had been offered by the defendant, it would doubtless have been received without an objection from any source. All the defendant had the right to demand in this case was evidence which, as between Holly and the plaintiff, was competent to establish the relation between them of debtor and creditor. For that purpose the evidence was clearly competent; it covered the whole ground and warranted the verdict of the jury.

But it is claimed that notwithstanding this promise was established by competent evidence, it was void for the want of consideration. It is now more than a quarter of a century since it was settled by the Supreme Court of this State — in an able and pains-taking opinion by the late Chief Justice Savage, in which the authorities were fully examined and carefully analysed [sic] — that a promise in all material respects like the one under consideration was valid; and the judgment of that court was unanimously affirmed by the Court for the Correction of Errors. (*Farley v. Cleaveland*, 4 Cow. 432; *same case in error*, 9 id. 639.) In that case one Moon owed Farley and sold to Cleaveland a quantity of hay, in consideration of which Cleaveland promised to pay Moon's debt to Farley; and the decision in favor of Farley's right to recover was placed upon the ground that the hay received by Cleaveland from Moon was a valid consideration for Cleaveland's promise to pay Farley, and that the subsisting liability of Moon to pay Farley was no objection to the recovery.

The fact that the money advanced by Holly to the defendant was a loan to him for a day, and that it thereby became the property of the defendant, seemed to impress the defendant's counsel with the idea that because the defendant's promise was not a trust fund placed by the plaintiff in the defendant's hands, out of which he was to realize money as from the sale of a chattel or the collection of a debt, the promise although made for the benefit of the plaintiff could not inure to his benefit. The hay which Cleaveland delivered to Moon was not to be paid to Farley, but the debt incurred by Cleaveland for the purchase of the hay, like the debt incurred by the defendant for money borrowed, was what was to be paid. That case has been often referred to by the courts of this State, and has never been doubted as sound authority for the principle upheld by it. [Citation omitted.] It puts to rest the objection that the defendant's promise was void for want of consideration. The report of that case shows that the promise was not only made to Moon but to the plaintiff Farley.

In this case the promise was made to Holly and not expressly to the plaintiff; and this difference between the two cases presents the question, raised by the defendant's objection, as to the want of privity between the plaintiff and defendant. As early as 1806 it was announced by the Supreme Court of this State, upon what was then regarded as the settled law of England, "That where one person makes a promise to another for the benefit of a third person, that third person may maintain an action upon it." ...

In this case the defendant, upon ample consideration received from Holly, promised Holly to pay his debt to the plaintiff; the consideration received and the promise to Holly made it as plainly his duty to pay the plaintiff as if the money had been remitted to him for that purpose, and as well implied a promise to do so as if he had been made a trustee of property to be converted into cash with which to pay. The fact that a breach of the duty imposed in the one case may be visited, and justly, with more serious consequences than in the other, by no means disproves the payment to be a duty in both. The principle illustrated by the example so frequently quoted (which concisely states the case in hand) "that a promise made to one for the benefit of another, he for whose benefit it is made may bring an action for its breach," has been applied to trust cases, not because it was exclusively applicable to those cases, but because it was a principle of law, and as such applicable to those cases ...

The judgment should be affirmed.

Johnson, Ch. J., Denio, Selden, Allen, and Strong, Js., concurred. Johnson, Ch. J., and Denio, J., were of opinion that the promise was to be regarded as made to the plaintiff through the medium of his agent, whose action he could ratify when it came to his knowledge, though taken without his being privy thereto.

Comstock, Dissenting. The plaintiff had nothing to do with the promise on which he brought this action. It was not made to him, nor did the consideration proceed from him. If he can maintain the suit, it is because an anomaly has found its way into the law on this subject.

In general, there must be privity of contract. The party who sues upon a promise must be the promisee, or he must have some legal interest in the undertaking. In this case, it is plain that Holly, who loaned the money to the defendant, and to whom the promise in question was made, could at any time have claimed that it should be performed to himself personally. He had lent the money to the defendant, and at the same time directed the latter to pay the sum to the plaintiff. This direction he could countermand, and if he had done so, manifestly the defendant's promise to pay according to the direction would have ceased to exist. The plaintiff would receive a benefit by a complete execution of the arrangement, but the arrangement itself was between other parties, and was under their exclusive control. If the defendant had paid the money to Holly, his debt would have been discharged thereby. So Holly might have released the demand or assigned it to another person, or the parties might have annulled the promise now in question, and designated some other creditor of Holly as the party to whom the money should be paid. It has never been claimed, that in a case thus situated, the right of a third person to sue upon the promise rested on any sound principle of law. We are to inquire whether the rule has been so established by positive authority ...

The cases in which some trust was involved are also frequently referred to as authority for the doctrine now in question, but they do not sustain it. If A delivers money or property to B, which the latter accepts upon a trust for the benefit of C, the latter can enforce the trust by an appropriate action for that purpose. [Citation omitted.] If the trust be of money, I think the beneficiary may assent to it and bring the action for money had and received to his use. If it be of something else than money, the trustee must account for it according to the terms of the trust, and upon principles of equity. There is some authority even for saying that an express promise founded on the possession of a trust fund may be enforced by an action at law in the name of the beneficiary, although it was made to the creator of the trust ...

In the case before us there was nothing in the nature of a trust or agency. The defendant borrowed the money of Holly and received it as his own. The plaintiff had no right in the fund, legal or equitable. The promise to repay the money created an obligation in favor of the lender to whom it was made and not in favor of anyone else ...

Exercise 13-5: *Seaver v. Ransom*

Lawrence illustrates one of the classic beneficiary categories—creditor beneficiaries—recognized in early American law. Post-*Lawrence*, many courts limited the case to its narrow holding and continued to struggle with the recognition of any other types of beneficiaries.

The next case, *Seaver v. Ransom*, is another case commonly read by law students. It addressees the same issue as *Lawrence*—when does a contract create rights in a third party—but in a non-creditor context. As you read *Seaver*, consider the following questions:

1. What are the relevant facts?

2. Identify and draw a diagram depicting the promisor, promisee, and alleged third-party beneficiary.

3. The court also discusses several situations in which courts have enforced the rights of third-party beneficiaries. Explain those situations.

4. What is your reaction to the court's discussion about protecting third parties who are in close relationships with a promisee—specifically, spouses, fiancés, and children? Do these categories conform with close relationships in modern American life? If not, how should our legal standards define the concept of close relationships?

5. What did the *Seaver* court hold?

6. Recall what you learned in Chapter 3 about consideration and the rule that promises to make gifts do not constitute enforceable contracts. As a matter of contract doctrine, can you reconcile that rule with the result in favor of the donee beneficiary in *Seaver*?

Seaver v. Ransom

120 N.E. 639, 224 N.Y. 233 (1918)

Pound, J. Judge Beman and his wife were advanced in years. Mrs. Beman was about to die. She had a small estate, consisting of a house and lot in Malone and little else. Judge Beman drew his wife's will according to her instructions. It gave $1,000 to plaintiff, $500 to one sister, plaintiff's mother, and $100 each to another sister and her son, the use of the house to her husband for life, and remainder to the American Society for the Prevention of Cruelty to Animals. She named her husband as residuary legatee and executor. Plaintiff was her niece, 34 years old, in ill health, sometimes a member of the Beman household.

When the will was read to Mrs. Beman, she said that it was not as she wanted it. She wanted to leave the house to plaintiff. She had no other objection to the will, but her strength was waning, and, although the judge offered to write another will for her, she said she was afraid she would not hold out long enough to enable her to sign it. So the judge said, if she would sign the will, he would leave plaintiff enough in his will to make up the difference. He avouched the promise by his uplifted hand with all solemnity and his wife then executed the will. When he came to die, it was found that his will made no provision for the plaintiff.

This action was brought, and plaintiff recovered judgment in the trial court, on the theory that Beman had obtained property from his wife and induced her to execute the will in the form prepared by him by his promise to give plaintiff $6,000, the value of the house, and that thereby equity impressed his property with a trust in favor of plaintiff. Where a legatee promises the testator that he will use property given him by the will for a particular purpose, a trust arises. [Citations omitted.] Berman received nothing under his wife's will but the use of the house in Malone for life. Equity compels the application of property thus obtained to the purpose of the testator, but equity cannot so impress a trust, except on property obtained by the promise. Beman was bound by his promise, but no property was bound by it; no trust in plaintiff's favor can be spelled out.

An action on the contract for damages, or to make the executors trustees for performance, stands on different ground. [Citation omitted.] The Appellate Division properly passed to the consideration of the question whether the judgment could stand upon the promise made to the wife, upon a valid consideration, for the sole benefit of plaintiff. The judgment of the trial court was affirmed by a return to the general doctrine laid down in the great case of *Lawrence v. Fox*, 20 N.Y. 268, which has since been limited as herein indicated.

Contracts for the benefit of third persons have been the prolific source of judicial and academic discussion. Williston, *Contracts for the Benefit of a Third Person*, 15 HARV. L. REV. 767; Corbin, *Contracts for the Benefit of Third Persons*, 27 YALE L. REV. 1008. The general rule, both in law and equity was that privity between a plaintiff and a defendant is necessary to the maintenance of an action on the contract. [Citations omitted.] The consideration must be furnished by the party to whom the promise was made. The contract cannot be enforced against the third party, and therefore it cannot be enforced by him.

On the other hand, the right of the beneficiary to sue on a contract made expressly for his benefit has been fully recognized in many American jurisdictions, either by judicial decision or by legislation, and is said to be "the prevailing rule in this country." [Citations omitted.] It has been said that "the establishment of this doctrine has been gradual, and is a victory of practical utility over theory, of equity over technical subtlety." BRANTLY ON CONTRACTS (2d ed.) p. 253. The reasons for this view are that it is just and practical to permit the person for whose benefit the contract is made to enforce it against one whose duty it is to pay. Other jurisdictions still adhere to the present English rule that a contract cannot be enforced by or against a person who is not a party. [Citations omitted.]

In New York the right of the beneficiary to sue on contracts made for his benefit is not clearly or simply defined. It is at present confined: First to cases where there is a pecuniary obligation running from the promisee to the beneficiary, "a legal right founded upon some obligation of the promisee in the third party to adopt and claim the promise as made for his benefit." *Lawrence v. Fox, supra.* [Citations omitted.] Secondly to cases where the contract is made for the benefit of the wife, affianced wife, or child, of a party to the contract. [Citations omitted.] The close relationship cases go back to the early King's Bench case (1677), long since repudiated in England of *Dutton v. Poole.*... The natural and moral duty of the husband or parent to provide for the future of wife or child sustains the action on the contract made for their benefit. "This is the farthest the cases in this state have gone," says Cullen, J., in the marriage settlement case of *Borland v. Welch,* 162 N.Y. 104, 110, 56 N.E. 556.

The right of the third party is also upheld in, thirdly, the public contract cases where the municipality seeks to protect its inhabitants by covenants for their benefit; and, fourthly, the cases where, at the request of a party to the contract, the promise runs directly to the beneficiary although he does not furnish the consideration. [Citations omitted.] It may be safely said that a general rule sustaining recovery at the suit of the third party would include but few classes of cases not included in these groups, either categorically or in principle.

The desire of the childless aunt to make provision for a beloved and favorite niece differs imperceptibly in law or in equity from the moral duty of the parent to make testamentary provision for a child. The contract was made for the plaintiff's benefit. She alone is substantially damaged by its breach. The representatives of the wife's estate have no interest in enforcing it specifically ... It was, however, the love and affection or the moral sense of the husband and the parent that imposed such obligations in the cases cited, rather than any common-law duty of husband and parent to wife and child.

If plaintiff had been a child of Mrs. Beman, legal obligation would have required no testamentary provision for her, yet the child could have enforced a covenant in her favor identical with the covenant of Judge Beman in this case. [Citation omitted.] The constraining power of conscience is not regulated by the degree of relationship alone. The dependent or faithful niece may have a stronger claim than the affluent or unworthy son. No sensible theory of moral obligation denies arbitrarily to the former what would be conceded to the latter. We might consistently either refuse or allow the claim of both, but I cannot reconcile a decision in favor of the wife in *Buchanan v. Tilden,* based on the moral obligations arising out of near relationship, with a decision against the niece here on the ground that the relationship is too remote for equity's ken. No controlling authority depends upon so absolute a rule ...

Kellogg, P. J., writing for the court below well said: "The doctrine of *Lawrence v. Fox* is progressive, not retrograde. The course of the late decisions is to enlarge, not to limit, the effect of that case." The court in that leading case attempted to adopt the general doctrine that any third person, for whose direct benefit a contract was intended, could sue on it. The headnote thus states the rule ...

But, on principle, a sound conclusion may be reached. If Mrs. Beman had left her husband the house on condition that he pay the plaintiff $6,000, and he had accepted the devise, he would have become personally liable to pay the legacy, and plaintiff could have recovered in an action at law against him, whatever the value of the house. [Citations omitted.] That would be because the testatrix had in substance bequeathed the promise to plaintiff, and not because close relationship or moral obligation sustained the contract. The distinction between an implied promise to a testator for the benefit of a third party to pay a legacy and an unqualified promise on a valuable consideration to make provision for the third party by will is discernible, but not obvious. The tendency of American authority is to sustain the gift in all such cases and to permit the donee beneficiary to recover on the contract. [Citations omitted.] The equities are with the plaintiff, and they may be enforced in this action, whether it be regarded as an action for damages or an action for specific performance to convert the defendants into trustees for plaintiff's benefit under the agreement.

Judgment affirmed.

Exercise 13-6: Intended versus Incidental Beneficiaries[2]

Under the RESTATEMENT (FIRST) OF CONTRACTS, which is still used by some courts in third-party beneficiary cases, courts classify alleged third-party beneficiaries as creditor beneficiaries, donee beneficiaries, or incidental beneficiaries. Either a creditor beneficiary or a donee beneficiary has a right to recover. A donee beneficiary is someone to whom the promisee wishes to confer a gift or a right against the promisor. A creditor beneficiary is someone to whom the promisee does not intend to give a gift but, instead, is someone for whom the promisor's performance will satisfy a real or supposed obligation.

1. Under the RESTATEMENT SECOND OF CONTRACTS, what standards are used to determine if a third party has a right to recover under a contract?

2. Apply both the first and second RESTATEMENT standards to *Lawrence* and *Seaver*. What results would have been reached under the RESTATEMENTS?

3. Dave's son Riley is indebted to Blake. With the purpose of assisting Riley, Dave secures from Zacharius a promise to pay the debt to Blake. Are there any intended beneficiaries under the SECOND RESTATEMENT approach? If so, under which subsection? Would Blake have a right to sue under the RESTATEMENT (FIRST)? Would Riley have a right to sue under the RESTATEMENT (FIRST)?

4. Charlie, the operator of a chicken processing and fertilizer plant, contracts with City to use City's sewage system. With the purpose of preventing harm

---

2. The examples in problems 3-8 are based on Illustrations to sections 302 and 308 in the RESTATEMENT SECOND OF CONTRACTS. *See* section 302, Illustrations 3-4, 6-8, 10, and section 308, Illustration 1.

to landowners downstream, City extracts a promise from Charlie to remove specified types of waste from its deposits into the system. Hannah owns land downstream. Is Hannah an intended beneficiary under the RESTATE-MENT SECOND? If so, under which subsection?

5. Blake owes Jacob $100 for money lent. Megan promises Blake to pay Jacob $200, both as a discharge of the debt and as an expression of Blake's grati-tude to Jacob for making the loan. Is there an intended beneficiary under the RESTATEMENT SECOND?

6. Mike buys a life insurance contract from LifeTrust Company and agrees to pay premiums. LifeTrust Company agrees to provide the life insurance pol-icy and pay the proceeds from the policy to the beneficiary named by Mike. Mike names the beneficiary as "my daughter." Has a third-party beneficiary been created?

7. Bernard promises Amy to pay whatever debts Amy incurs in a certain un-dertaking. In the undertaking, Amy incurs debts to Lisa, Stacey, and Fred. Are Lisa, Stacey, and Fred protected beneficiaries?

8. Archie conveys land to Bob in consideration of Bob's promise to pay $15,000 as follows: $5,000 to Connie, Archie's wife, on whom Archie wishes to make a settlement; $5,000 to Mallory to whom Archie is indebted in that amount; and $5,000 to Annuity Insurance Company, to purchase an an-nuity payable to Archie during his life. Are Connie, Mallory, or Annuity protected beneficiaries?

9. Mike makes a contract with Kendra to tutor Kendra for 100 hours in con-tract law. Kendra agrees to pay Mike $1,000 for his tutoring services. Saman-tha is very happy with this contract because Mike is very smart and Kendra is in Samantha's study group. Samantha believes she will benefit from the con-tract and master contracts better, too. Can Samantha sue Mike if Mike doesn't perform?

10. The University of Iowa lost a basketball game to Purdue University when a referee called a foul on an Iowa player resulting in Purdue's last-minute vic-tory, thereby eliminating Iowa from the "Big Ten" championship. Duane and Ruth, the owners and operators of a store specializing in Iowa sports mem-orabilia, assert that they are third-party beneficiaries under the contract be-tween the university and the athletic conference and sue the referee for breaching his contract to be a competent referee. Are Duane and Ruth pro-tected beneficiaries?

11. Draft a contract provision (or two) for the contract described in problem 8 above that make(s) it clear that Connie and Mallory are protected benefici-aries and Annuity is not.

Third-Party Beneficiaries of Attorney-Client Contracts

Has it ever occurred to you that, as a practicing attorney, you may have legal duties to parties other than your clients? Specifically, have you considered that you may have du-ties to third parties who stand to benefit from your services?

Exercise 13-7: *Heyer v. Flaig*

The next case, *Heyer v. Flaig*, addresses that situation, although the precise issue addressed is when the statute of limitations begins to run. The case is also instructive about your responsibilities as an attorney. As you read *Heyer*, consider the following questions:

1. What are the relevant facts?

2. What theories of liability does the court discuss? What are the differences between those theories of liability?

3. Why does the court consider the daughters to be intended beneficiaries?

4. Why wasn't the executor of the estate a plaintiff?

5. What level of performance is owed by an attorney when handling a client's matter?

6. What is *Heyer*'s lesson for you as an attorney in training?

Heyer v. Flaig
449 P.2d 161, 70 Cal. 2d 223 (1969)

Tobriner, Justice. This case presents a single, basic question: When does the statute of limitations commence to run against an intended beneficiary of a will who ... acquires a right of action against an attorney for malpractice in negligently failing to fulfill the testamentary directions of his client? Under the alleged facts of this case, we conclude that the limitations period starts from the date that the cause of action accrues: namely, the incidence of the testatrix'[s] death when the negligent failure to perfect the requested testamentary scheme becomes irremediable and the impact of the injury occurs. Accordingly, the trial court erroneously sustained a demurrer to plaintiff's complaint on the ground that the statute of limitations bars the present action brought later than two years after the defendant drafted the will. Since the plaintiffs filed their complaint within two years of the testatrix'[s] death, the cause avoids the statutory bar.

The plaintiffs' complaint sets forth inter alia the following allegations: In December 1962 Doris Kilburn, the testatrix, retained defendant Flaig to prepare her will. She told defendant that she wished all of her estate to pass to her two daughters, plaintiffs in this action. She also told him that she intended to marry Glen Kilburn. On December 21, 1962, Doris Kilburn executed a will prepared by defendant. On December 31, 1962, she married Glen Kilburn.

The will purports to leave the entire estate of Doris Kilburn to the plaintiffs. The testament however, does not mention the testatrix'[s] husband, except that it names him executor. On July 9, 1963, Doris Kilburn died; thereafter the Los Angeles County Superior Court admitted to probate the above-described document as her last will and testament. In these probate proceedings,

Glen Kilburn claimed a portion of the estate as a post-testamentary spouse under Probate Code section 70.

Plaintiffs allege that defendant negligently failed to advise Doris Kilburn of the consequences of a post-testamentary marriage, and negligently failed to include in the will any provision as to the intended marriage. Plaintiffs allege further that, subsequent to the marriage, and up until the date of testatrix'[s] death, the defendant negligently failed to advise her of the legal consequences of omitting from the will any provision relative to her husband's claim to a share of her estate. Plaintiffs allege that this negligence caused them to suffer damages in the amount of $50,000. They also pray for $50,000 punitive damages on the ground that defendant proceeded maliciously, in wanton disregard of their rights....

An attorney who negligently fails to fulfill a client's testamentary directions incurs liability in tort for violating a duty of care owed directly to the intended beneficiaries. In the case of *Lucas v. Hamm,* 56 Cal.2d 583, 15 Cal.Rptr. 821, 364 P.2d 685 (1961), we embraced the position that an attorney who erred in drafting a will could be held liable to a person named in the instrument who suffered deprivation of benefits as a result of the mistake. Although we stated that the harmed party could recover as an intended third-party beneficiary of the attorney-client agreement providing for legal services, we ruled that the third party could also recover on a theory of tort liability for a breach of duty owed directly to him. At the heart of our decision in *Lucas v. Hamm* lay this recognition of duty.

In the earlier case of *Biakanja v. Irving,* 49 Cal. 2d 647, 320 P.2d 16 (1958), we had held that a notary public who negligently failed to direct proper attestation of a will became liable in tort to an intended beneficiary who suffered damage because of the invalidity of the instrument. In that case, the defendant argued that the absence of privity deprives a plaintiff of a remedy for negligence committed in the performance of a contract. In rejecting this contention we pointed out that the inflexible privity requirement for such a tort recovery has been virtually abandoned in California. [Citation omitted.] We then analyzed the bases for imposing such a duty:

> The determination whether in a specific case the defendant will be held liable to a third person not in privity is a matter of policy and involves the balancing of various factors, among which are the extent to which the transaction was intended to affect the plaintiff, the foreseeability of harm to him, the degree of certainty that the plaintiff suffered injury, the closeness of the connection between the defendant's conduct and the injury suffered, the moral blame attached to the defendant's conduct, and the policy of preventing future harm.

Applying the *Biakanja* criteria to the facts of *Lucas,* the court found that attorneys incur a duty in favor of certain third persons, namely, intended testamentary beneficiaries. In proceeding to discuss the contractual remedy of such persons as the plaintiffs in *Lucas,* we concluded that "as a matter of policy, ... they are entitled to recover as third-party beneficiaries." 56 Cal. 2d at 590, 364 P.2d at 689. The presence of the *Biakanja* criteria in a contractual setting led us to sustain not only the availability of a tort remedy but of a third-party beneficiary contractual remedy as well....

Turning to the present case we therefore concentrate on the tortious aspect of defendant's conduct. We inquire as to whether there was such a duty; the breach, if any; the possibility of the bar of the statute of limitations. When an attorney undertakes to fulfill the testamentary instructions of his client, he realistically and in fact assumes a relationship not only with the client but also with the client's intended beneficiaries. The attorney's actions and omissions will affect the success of the client's testamentary scheme; and thus the possibility of thwarting the testator's wishes immediately becomes foreseeable. Equally foreseeable is the possibility of injury to an intended beneficiary. In some ways, the beneficiary's interests loom greater than those of the client. After the latter's death, a failure in his testamentary scheme works no practical effect except to deprive his intended beneficiaries of the intended bequests. Indeed, the executor of an estate has no standing to bring an action for the amount of the bequest against an attorney who negligently prepared the estate plan, since in the normal case the estate is not injured by such negligence except to the extent of the fees paid; only the beneficiaries suffer the real loss. We recognized in *Lucas* that unless the beneficiary could recover against the attorney in such a case, no one could do so and the social policy of preventing future harm would be frustrated.

The duty thus recognized in *Lucas* stems from the attorney's undertaking to perform legal services for the client but reaches out to protect the intended beneficiary. We impose this duty because of the relationship between the attorney and the intended beneficiary; public policy requires that the attorney exercise his position of trust and superior knowledge responsibly so as not to affect adversely persons whose rights and interests are certain and foreseeable.

Although the duty accrues directly in favor of the intended testamentary beneficiary, the scope of the duty is determined by reference to the attorney-client context. Out of the agreement to provide legal services to a client, the prospective testator, arises the duty to act with due care as to the interests of the intended beneficiary. We do not mean to say that the attorney-client contract for legal services serves as the fundamental touchstone to fix the scope of this direct tort duty to the third party. The actual circumstances under which the attorney undertakes to perform his legal services, however, will bear on a judicial assessment of the care with which he performs his services.

We now examine the complaint in the present case. The complaint alleges that defendant negligently prepared a will purporting to carry out the testatrix'[s] testamentary intention, to give her entire estate to the plaintiffs. The defendant's alleged negligence consisted of his omitting from the will any language which would defeat the rights of the testatrix'[s] husband who could claim a statutory share of the estate as a post-testamentary spouse under Probate Code section 70.

In rendering legal services, an attorney must perform in such manner as "lawyers of ordinary skill and capacity commonly possess and exercise." [Citation omitted.] A reasonably prudent attorney should appreciate the consequences of a post-testamentary marriage, advise the testator of such consequences, and use good judgment to avoid them if the testator so desires. In the present case, defendant allegedly knew that the testatrix wished to avoid such consequences. Despite his knowledge that the testatrix intended to marry following the execution of the will, the attorney drafted a will which arguably lacked adequate provision against such consequences. [Citation omitted.] Furthermore, the complaint alleges that the defendant negligently failed to advise the testatrix that she should change her will after her marriage and continued this negligent omission until the time of her death. The complaint states a sufficient cause of action in tort under the doctrine of *Lucas*; we proceed, therefore, to determine when the cause of action accrued so as to commence the running of the statute of limitations....

An intended testamentary beneficiary acquires no recognized legal rights under a will until the testator dies, at which time his interest will vest or, indeed, possibly fail. [Citation omitted.] Before her death, the testatrix in the present case could have altered her will at any time and for any reason. Furthermore, she could have changed her testamentary intention to conform to the actual disposition of her estate under the "defective" will; in such a case, the plaintiffs here would have suffered no actionable injury. Before the testatrix'[s] death, the plaintiffs can state no cause of action because until that time there can be no injury....

We cannot accept defendant's argument that the application to the instant case of the present rule with respect to legal malpractice actions, *i.e.*, that the statutory period commences to run from the time of the negligent act....

A rule placing the beneficiary in the same position as the testatrix as to the running of the statute of limitations would be viable only if an action by either were equally available and vindicated identical substantive rights. We have noted that the intended beneficiary of a will acquires no cause of action until his testator's death, whereas the prospective testator may sue immediately to recover the cost of drafting the will. Furthermore, the interests at stake in an action by the intended beneficiary and in an action by the testator differ. The former seeks to recover an intended bequest which has been denied him because of the attorney's negligence. The latter seeks to perfect his testamentary scheme, now defective because of the attorney's negligence. In the latter case, the plaintiff's damages will be slight and the consequences of finding a statutory bar will be mild since the testator can create a new and effective estate plan.[3]

The intended beneficiary, on the other hand, suffers a great and irrevocable loss: he has nowhere to turn but to the attorney for compensation. Indeed, *Lucas* recognizes that unless the beneficiary can recover from the attorney the beneficiary suffers a wrong without a compensating remedy. The duty which the attorney owes the beneficiary is separate and distinct from the duty owed the client; so, too, are the remedies for breaches of these duties.... [4]

In the present case we have determined that the plaintiffs' action would have been premature until the testatrix'[s] death and that the defendant's negligence was continuing and incomplete until that time. Hence the statute of limitations does not commence to run until the testatrix'[s] death and con-

---

3. After the testator's death, no one but the intended beneficiary has an interest in the defeated bequest. The estate could sue only for the attorney's fees expended since presumably there will have been no other diminution of the estate funds due to the error.

4. In any event, in the present case we have found, for the reasons expressed in the text, that, with respect to the intended beneficiaries of a will, the statute of limitations for attorney negligence cannot commence to run before the testatrix'[s] death.

sequently the trial judge erroneously sustained defendant's general demurrer on the ground of the bar of the statute of limitations.... The judgment of dismissal is reversed....

Third-Party Beneficiaries of Government Contracts

Imagine the following situation: The United States government loans money to Abe, an apartment builder and property manager. Abe promises to keep the rental rates for the completed apartments within prescribed limits. After six months, Abe raises the rental rates above the prescribed limits. Do the tenants have standing to sue Abe?

This scenario introduces a new twist into the third-party beneficiary situation. Specifically, it raises the issue of how the third-party rules apply to contracts between the government and private parties. Because government exists for the benefit of its citizens, are citizens intended beneficiaries of government contracts? Before you read further, consider whether government contracts should be treated similarly to or differently from other contracts. What policy rationales support your position?

Exercise 13-8: *H.R. Moch Co. v. Rensselaer Water Co.*

The next case, *H.R. Moch Co. v. Rensselaer Water Co.*, involves a third party who did not have legally enforceable rights as a beneficiary of a government contract. As you read the case, consider the following points:

1. What are the relevant facts?

2. Identify and diagram the relationships of the parties involved.

3. What rule does the court state and apply?

4. The court specifically notes that the third party cannot recover based on *Lawrence*. Why not?

5. Does the court's reasoning make sense to you? Why or why not?

6. What public policy rationale does the court's result undermine? What public policy rationale does the court's result promote?

H.R. Moch Co. v. Rensselaer Water Co.
159 N.E. 896, 247 N.Y. 160 (1928)

Cardozo, C.J. The defendant, a waterworks company under the laws of this state, made a contract with the city of Rensselaer for the supply of water during a term of years. Water was to be furnished to the city for sewer flushing and street sprinkling; for service to schools and public buildings; and for service at fire hydrants, the latter service at the rate of $42.50 a year for each hydrant. Water was to be furnished to private takers within the city at their homes and factories and other industries at reasonable rates, not exceeding a stated schedule. While this contract was in force, a building caught fire. The flames, spreading to the plaintiff's warehouse nearby, destroyed it and its contents.

The defendant, according to the complaint, was promptly notified of the fire, "but omitted and neglected after such notice, to supply or furnish sufficient or adequate quantity of water, with adequate pressure to stay, suppress, or extinguish the fire before it reached the warehouse of the plaintiff, although the pressure and supply which the defendant was equipped to supply and furnish, and had agreed by said contract to supply and furnish, was adequate and sufficient to prevent the spread of the fire to and the destruction of the plaintiff's warehouse and its contents." By reason of the failure of the defendant to "fulfill the provisions of the contract between it and the city of Rensselaer," the plaintiff is said to have suffered damage, for which judgment is demanded. A motion, in the nature of a demurrer, to dismiss the complaint, was denied at Special Term. The Appellate Division reversed by a divided court ...

We think the action is not maintainable as one for breach of contract. No legal duty rests upon a city to supply its inhabitants with protection against fire. [Citation omitted.] That being so, a member of the public may not maintain an action under *Lawrence v. Fox* against one contracting with the city to furnish water at the hydrants, unless an intention appears that the promisor is to be answerable to individual members of the public as well as to the city for any loss ensuing from the failure to fulfill the promise. No such intention is discernible here. On the contrary, the contract is significantly divided into two branches: One a promise to the city for the benefit of the city in its corporate capacity, in which branch is included the service at the hydrants; and the other a promise to the city for the benefit of private takers, in which branch is included the service at their homes and factories. In a broad sense it is true that every city contract, not improvident or wasteful, is for the benefit of the public.

More than this, however, must be shown to give a right of action to a member of the public not formally a party. The benefit, as it is sometimes said, must be one that is not merely incidental and secondary. [Citation omitted.] It must be primary and immediate in such a sense and to such a degree as to bespeak the assumption of a duty to make reparation directly to the individual members of the public if the benefit is lost. The field of obligation would be expanded beyond reasonable limits if less than this were to be demanded as a condition of liability. A promisor undertakes to supply fuel for heating a public building. He is not liable for breach of contract to a visitor who finds the building without fuel, and thus contracts a cold. The list of illustrations can be indefinitely extended. The carrier of the mails under contract with the government is not answerable to the merchant who has lost the benefit of a bargain through negligent delay. The householder is without a remedy against manufacturers of hose and engines, though prompt performance of their contracts would have stayed the ravages of fire. "The law does not spread its protection so far." [Citation omitted.]

So with the case at hand. By the vast preponderance of authority, a contract between a city and a water company to furnish water at the city hydrants has in view a benefit to the public that is incidental rather than immediate, an assumption of duty to the city and not to its inhabitants. Such is the ruling of the Supreme Court of the United States. [Citation omitted.] Such has been the ruling in this state though the question is still open in this court.

[Citations omitted.].... Such with few exceptions has been the ruling in other jurisdictions. WILLISTON, CONTRACTS § 373,.... The diligence of counsel has brought together decisions to that effect from 26 states.... Only a few states have held otherwise. PAGE, CONTRACTS § 2401....

An intention to assume an obligation of indefinite extension to every member of the public is seen to be the more improbable when we recall the crushing burden that the obligation would impose. [Citation omitted.] The consequences invited would bear no reasonable proportion to those attached by law to defaults not greatly different. A wrongdoer who by negligence sets fire to a building is liable in damages to the owner where the fire has its origin, but not to other owners who are injured when it spreads. The rule in our state is settled to that effect, whether wisely or unwisely. [Citations omitted.] If the plaintiff is to prevail, one who negligently omits to supply sufficient pressure to extinguish a fire started by another assumes an obligation to pay the ensuing damage, though the whole city is laid low. A promisor will not be deemed to have had in mind the assumption of a risk so overwhelming for any trivial reward.

The cases that have applied the rule of *Lawrence v. Fox* to contracts made by a city for the benefit of the public are not at war with this conclusion. Through them all there runs as a unifying principle the presence of an intention to compensate the individual members of the public in the event of a default. For example, in *Pond v. New Rochelle Water Co.*, 183 N.Y. 330, 76 N.E. 211, the contract with the city fixed a schedule of rates to be supplied, not to public buildings, but to private takers at their homes. *In Matter of International R. Co. v. Rann*, 224 N.Y. 83, 85, 120 N.E. 153, the contract was by street railroads to carry passengers for a stated fare. In *Smyth v. City of New York*, 203 N.Y. 106, 96 N.E. 409, and *Rigney v. New York Cent. & H.R.R. Co.*, 217 N.Y. 31, 111 N.E. 226, covenants were made by contractors upon public works, not merely to indemnify the city, but to assume its liabilities. These and like cases come within the third group stated in the comprehensive opinion in *Seaver v. Ransom*, 224 N.Y. 233, 238, 120 N.E. 639. The municipality was contracting in behalf of its inhabitants by covenants intended to be enforced by any of them severally as occasion should arise ...

The judgment should be affirmed, with costs.

Exercise 13-9: *Martinez v. Socoma Companies, Inc.*

Many government contract cases, such as the *Martinez v. Socoma Companies, Inc.* case that follows, involve the rights of poor people as potential third-party beneficiaries of social services contracts. *Martinez* also illustrates the importance of the terms in government contracts and the statutory authority underlying such contracts. As you read *Martinez*, consider the following questions:

1. What are the relevant facts?

2. Identify and diagram the relevant parties' relationships.

3. The court states: "Unquestionably plaintiffs were among those whom the Government intended to benefit through defendants' performance of the

contracts...." Nevertheless, the court holds that the plaintiffs were only incidental beneficiaries with no standing to sue. Explain this result, identifying the rules the court applied and how the court applied those rules to the facts of the case.

Martinez v. Socoma Companies, Inc.
521 P.2d 841, 11 Cal. 3d 394 (1974)

Wright, Chief Justice. Plaintiffs brought this class action on behalf of themselves and other disadvantaged unemployed persons, alleging that defendants failed to perform contracts with the United States government under which defendants agreed to provide job training and at least one year of employment to certain numbers of such persons. Plaintiffs claim that they and the other such persons are third party beneficiaries of the contracts and as such are entitled to damages for defendants' nonperformance. General demurrers to the complaint were sustained without leave to amend, apparently on the ground that plaintiffs lacked standing to sue as third party beneficiaries. Dismissals were entered as to the demurring defendants, and plaintiffs appeal.

We affirm the judgments of dismissal. As will appear, the contracts nowhere state that either the government or defendants are to be liable to persons such as plaintiffs for damages resulting from the defendants' nonperformance. The benefits to be derived from defendants' performance were clearly intended not as gifts from the government to such persons but as a means of executing the public purposes stated in the contracts and in the underlying legislation. Accordingly, plaintiffs were only incidental beneficiaries and as such have no right of recovery.

The complaint names as defendants Socoma Companies, Inc. ("Socoma"), Lady Fair Kitchens, Incorporated ("Lady Fair"), Monarch Electronics International, Inc. ("Monarch"), and eleven individuals of whom three are alleged officers or directors of Socoma, four of Lady Fair, and four of Monarch. Lady Fair and the individual defendants associated with it, a Utah corporation and Utah residents respectively, did not appear in the trial court and are not parties to this appeal.

The complaint alleges that under 1967 amendments to the Economic Opportunity Act of 1964 (81 Stat. 688–690, 42 U.S.C. §§ 2763–2768, repealed by 86 Stat. 703 (1972)), "the United States Congress instituted Special Impact Programs with the intent to benefit the residents of certain neighborhoods having especially large concentrations of low income persons and suffering from dependency, chronic unemployment and rising tensions." Funds to administer these programs were appropriated to the United States Department of Labor. The department subsequently designated the East Los Angeles neighborhood as a "Special Impact area" and made federal funds available for contracts with local private industry for the benefit of the "hardcore unemployed residents" of East Los Angeles.

On January 17, 1969, the corporate defendants allegedly entered into contracts with the Secretary of Labor, acting on behalf of the Manpower Administration, United States Department of Labor (hereinafter referred to as the "Government"). Each such defendant entered into a separate contract and all three contracts are made a part of the complaint as exhibits. Under each contract the contracting defendant agreed to lease space in the then vacant Lincoln Heights jail building owned by the City of Los Angeles, to invest at least $5,000,000 in renovating the leasehold and establishing a facility for the manufacture of certain articles, to train and employ in such facility for at least 12 months, at minimum wage rates, a specified number of East Los Angeles residents certified as disadvantaged by the Government, and to provide such employees with opportunities for promotion into available supervisorial-managerial positions and with options to purchase stock in their employer corporation. Each contract provided for the lease of different space in the building and for the manufacture of a different kind of product. As consideration, the Government agreed to pay each defendant a stated amount in installments. Socoma was to hire 650 persons and receive $950,000; Lady Fair was to hire 550 persons and receive $ 999,000; and Monarch was to hire 400 persons and receive $800,000. The hiring of these persons was to be completed by January 17, 1970.

Plaintiffs were allegedly members of a class of no more than 2,017 East Los Angeles residents who were certified as disadvantaged and were qualified for employment under the contracts. Although the Government paid $712,500 of the contractual consideration to Socoma, $299,700 to Lady Fair, and $240,000 to Monarch, all of these defendants failed to perform under their respective contracts, except that Socoma provided 186 jobs of which 139 were wrongfully terminated, and Lady Fair provided 90 jobs, of which all were wrongfully terminated.

The complaint contains 11 causes of action. The second, fourth, and sixth causes of action seek damages of $3,607,500 against Socoma, $3,052,500 against Lady Fair, and $2,220,000 against Monarch, calculated on the basis of 12 months' wages at minimum rates and $1,000 for loss of training for each of the jobs the defendant contracted to provide. The third and fifth causes of action seek similar damages for the 139 persons whose jobs were terminated by Socoma and the 90 persons whose jobs were terminated by Lady Fair. The first, seventh, and eighth causes of action seek to impose joint liability on Socoma, Lady Fair, and Monarch as joint venturers, alleging that they negotiated the contracts through a common representative and entered into a joint lease of the Lincoln Heights jail building ...

Each cause of action alleges that the "express purpose of the [Government] in entering into [each] contract was to benefit [the] certified disadvantaged hard-core unemployed residents of East Los Angeles [for whom defendants promised to provide training and jobs] and none other, and those residents are thus the express third party beneficiaries of [each] contract."

The general demurrers admitted the truth of all the material factual allegations of the complaint, regardless of any possible difficulty in proving them, but did not admit allegations which constitute conclusions of law or which are contrary to matters of which we must take judicial notice. [Citations omitted.] When a complaint is based on a written contract which it sets out in full, a general demurrer to the complaint admits not only the contents of the instrument but also any pleaded meaning to which the instrument is reasonably susceptible. [Citation omitted.] Moreover, where, as here, the general demurrer is to an *original* complaint and is sustained without leave to amend, "the issues presented are whether the complaint states a cause of action, and, if not, whether there is a reasonable possibility that it could be amended to do so." [Citations omitted.] Thus, we must determine whether the pleaded written contracts support plaintiffs' claim either on their face or under any interpretation to which the contracts are reasonably susceptible and which is pleaded in the complaint or could be pleaded by proper amendment. This determination must be made in light of applicable federal statutes and other matters we must judicially notice. [Citation omitted.]

Plaintiffs contend they are third party beneficiaries under Civil Code section 1559, which provides: "A contract, made expressly for the benefit of a third person, may be enforced by him at any time before the parties thereto rescind it." This section excludes enforcement of a contract by persons who are only incidentally or remotely benefited by it. [Citation omitted.] American law generally classifies persons having enforceable rights under contracts to which they are not parties as either creditor beneficiaries or donee beneficiaries. [Citations omitted.] California decisions follow this classification. [Citations omitted.]

A person cannot be a creditor beneficiary unless the promisor's performance of the contract will discharge some form of legal duty owed to the beneficiary by the promisee. [Citations omitted.] Clearly the Government (the promisee) at no time bore any legal duty toward plaintiffs to provide the benefits set forth in the contracts and plaintiffs do not claim to be creditor beneficiaries.

A person is a donee beneficiary only if the promisee's contractual intent is either to make a gift to him or to confer on him a right against the promisor. [Citation omitted.] If the promisee intends to make a gift, the donee beneficiary can recover if such donative intent must have been understood by the promise or from the nature of the contract and the circumstances accompanying its execution. *Lucas v. Hamm, supra.* This rule does not aid plaintiffs, however, because, as will be seen, no intention to make a gift can be imputed to the Government as promisee.

Unquestionably plaintiffs were among those whom the Government intended to benefit through defendants' performance of the contracts which recite that they are executed pursuant to a statute and a presidential directive calling for programs to furnish disadvantaged persons with training and employment opportunities. However, the fact that a Government program for social betterment confers benefits upon individuals who are not required to render contractual consideration in return does not necessarily imply that the benefits are intended as gifts.

Congress' power to spend money in aid of the general welfare, U.S. CONST., art. I, § 8, authorizes federal programs to alleviate national unemployment. [Citation omitted.] The benefits of such programs are provided not simply as gifts to the recipients but as a means of accomplishing a larger public purpose. The furtherance of the public purpose is in the nature of consideration to the Government, displacing any governmental intent to furnish the benefits as gifts. [Citations omitted.]

Even though a person is not the intended recipient of a gift, he may nevertheless be "a donee beneficiary if it appears from the terms of the promise in view of the accompanying circumstances that the purpose of the promisee in obtaining the promise ... is ... to *confer upon him a right against the promisor* to some performance neither due nor supposed or asserted to be due from the promisee to the beneficiary." RESTATEMENT OF CONTRACTS § 133, subd. (1)(a) (italics supplied). [Additional citation omitted.]

The Government may, of course, deliberately implement a public purpose by including provisions in its contracts which expressly confer on a specified class of third persons a direct right to benefits, or damages in lieu of benefits, against the private contractor. But a governmental intent to confer such a direct right cannot be inferred simply from the fact that the third persons were intended to enjoy the benefits. The Restatement of Contracts makes this clear in dealing specifically with contractual promises to the Government to render services to members of the public: "A promisor bound to the United States or to a State or municipality by contract to do an act or render a service to some or all of the members of the public, is subject to no duty under the contract to such members to give compensation for the injurious consequences of performing or attempting to perform it, or of failing to do so, unless, ... *an intention is manifested in the contract*, as interpreted in the light of the circumstances surrounding its formation, *that the promisor shall compensate members of the public for such injurious consequences....*" RESTATEMENT OF CONTRACTS § 145 (italics supplied).[5][citation omitted.]

The present contracts manifest no intent that the defendants pay damages to compensate plaintiffs or other members of the public for their nonperformance. To the contrary, the contracts' provisions for retaining the Government's control over determination of contractual disputes and for limiting defendants' financial risks indicate a governmental purpose to exclude the direct rights against defendants claimed here.

Each contract provides that any dispute of fact arising thereunder is to be determined by written decision of the Government's contracting officer, subject to an appeal to the Secretary of Labor, whose decision shall be final unless determined by a competent court to have been fraudulent, capricious, arbitrary, in bad faith, or not supported by substantial evidence. These administrative decisions may include determinations of related questions of law although such determinations are not made final. The efficiency and uniformity of interpretation fostered by these administrative procedures would tend to be undermined if litigation such as the present action, to which the Government is a stranger, were permitted to proceed on the merits.

In addition to the provisions on resolving disputes each contract contains a "liquidated damages" provision obligating the contractor to refund all amounts received from the Government, with interest, in the event of failure to acquire and equip the specified manufacturing facility, and, for each employment op-

---

5. The corresponding language in the Tentative Drafts of the RESTATEMENT (SECOND) OF CONTRACTS (1973), section 145, is: "[A] promisor who contracts with a government or governmental agency to do an act for or render a service to the public is not subject to contractual liability to a member of the public for consequential damages resulting from performance or failure to perform unless ... the terms of the promise provide for such liability...." The language omitted in this quotation and the quotation in the accompanying text relates to the creditor beneficiary situation in which the government itself would be liable for nonperformance of the contract. As noted earlier, plaintiffs do not claim to be creditor beneficiaries.

portunity it fails to provide, to refund a stated dollar amount equivalent to the total contract compensation divided by the number of jobs agreed to be provided. This liquidated damages provision limits liability for the breaches alleged by plaintiffs to the refunding of amounts received and indicates an absence of any contractual intent to impose liability directly in favor of plaintiffs, or, as claimed in the complaint, to impose liability for the value of the promised performance. To allow plaintiffs' claim would nullify the limited liability for which defendants bargained and which the Government may well have held out as an inducement in negotiating the contracts.[6]

It is this absence of any manifestation of intent that defendants should pay compensation for breach to persons in the position of plaintiffs that distinguishes this case from *Shell v. Schmidt,* 126 Cal. App. 2d 279, 272 P.2d 82 (1954), relied on by plaintiffs. The defendant in *Shell* was a building contractor who had entered into an agreement with the federal government under which he received priorities for building materials and agreed in return to use the materials to build homes with required specifications for sale to war veterans at or below ceiling prices. Plaintiffs were 12 veterans, each of whom had purchased a home that failed to comply with the agreed specifications. They were held entitled to recover directly from the defendant contractor as third party beneficiaries of his agreement with the government. The legislation under which the agreement was made included a provision empowering the government to obtain payment of monetary compensation by the contractor to the veteran purchasers for deficiencies resulting from failure to comply with specifications. Thus, there was "an intention ... manifested in the contract ... that the promisor shall compensate members of the public for such injurious consequences [of nonperformance]."[7]

---

6. Comment a of section 145 of the Tentative Drafts of the RESTATEMENT SECOND OF CONTRACTS points out that these factors—retention of administrative control and limitation of contractor's liability—make third party suits against the contractor inappropriate: "Government contracts often benefit the public, but individual members of the public are treated as incidental beneficiaries unless a different intention is manifested. In case of doubt, a promise to do an act for or render a service to the public does not have the effect of a promise to pay consequential damages to individual members of the public unless the conditions of Subsection (2)(b) [including governmental liability to the claimant] are met. Among factors which may make inappropriate a direct action against the promisor are *arrangements for governmental control over the litigation and settlement of claims, the likelihood of impairment of service or of excessive financial burden,* and the availability of alternatives such as insurance." (Italics supplied.)

7. In contrast to *Shell, supra,* is *City & County of San Francisco v. Western Air Lines, Inc., supra,* 204 Cal. App. 2d 105. There, Western Air Lines claimed to be a third party beneficiary of agreements between the federal government and the City and County of San Francisco under which the city received federal funds for the development of its airport subject to a written condition that the airport "be available for public use on fair and reasonable terms and without unjust discrimination." Western Air Lines asserted that it had been charged for its use of the airport at a higher rate than some other air carriers in violation of the contractual condition, and therefore was entitled to recover the excess charges from the city. One of the reasons given by the court on appeal for rejecting this contention was the absence of any provision or indication of intent in the agreements between the government and the city to compensate third parties for noncompliance. The court said: "The granting agreement in each instance entitles the [federal] administrator to recover all grant payments made where there has been any misrepresentation or omission of a material fact by the sponsor [*i.e.,* the city]. We find no other provision for recovery of funds by the administrator and none whatsoever permitting recovery of money or excess rates by a private party. Indeed the language of the granting agreement itself appears to us to point up that it is simply and entirely a financial arrangement between two par-

Plaintiffs contend that section 145 of the RESTATEMENT OF CONTRACTS, previously quoted, does not preclude their recovery because it applies only to promises made to a governmental entity "to do an act or render a service to … the public," and, plaintiffs assert they and the class they represent are identified persons set apart from "the public." Even if this contention were correct it would not follow that plaintiffs have standing as third party beneficiaries under the Restatement. The quoted provision of section 145 "is a special application of the principles stated in §§ 133 (1a), 135 [on donee beneficiaries]," RESTATEMENT OF CONTRACTS § 145, com. a, delineating certain circumstances which preclude government contractors' liability to third parties. Section 145 itself does not purport to confer standing to sue on persons who do not otherwise qualify under basic third party beneficiary principles.[8] As pointed out above, plaintiffs are not donee beneficiaries under those basic principles because it does not appear from the terms and circumstances of the contract that the Government intended to make a gift to plaintiffs or to confer on them a legal right against the defendants.

Moreover, contrary to plaintiffs' contention, section 145 of the RESTATEMENT OF CONTRACTS does preclude their recovery because the services which the contracts required the defendants to perform *were* to be rendered to "members of the public" within the meaning of that section. Each contract recites it is made under the "Special Impact Programs" part of the Economic Opportunity Act of 1964 and pursuant to a presidential directive for a test program of cooperation between the federal government and private industry in an effort to provide training and jobs for thousands of the hard-core unemployed or under-employed. The congressional declaration of purpose of the Economic Opportunity Act as a whole points up the public nature of its benefits on a national scale. Congress declared that the purpose of the act was to "strengthen, supplement, and coordinate efforts in furtherance of [the] policy" of "opening to everyone the opportunity for education and training, the opportunity to work, and the opportunity to live in decency and dignity" so that the "United States can achieve its full economic and social potential as a nation." 42 U.S.C. § 2701.

In providing for special impact programs, Congress declared that such programs were directed to the solution of critical problems existing in particular neighborhoods having especially large concentrations of low-income persons, and that the programs were intended to be of sufficient size and scope to have an appreciable impact in such neighborhoods in arresting tendencies toward dependency, chronic unemployment and rising community tensions. 42 U.S.C. former § 2763. Thus the contracts here were designed not to benefit individuals as such but to utilize the training and employment of disadvantaged persons as a means of improving the East Los Angeles neighborhood. Moreover,

---

ties. As the agreement states, it constitutes 'the obligations and rights of the United States and the Sponsor with respect to the accomplishment of the Project.…'" 204 Cal. App. 2d at 120.

8. The same is true of the Tentative Draft of section 145 of the RESTATEMENT (SECOND) OF CONTRACTS which declares that the general rules on third party beneficiaries "apply to contracts with a government or governmental agency except to the extent that application would contravene the policy of the law authorizing the contract or prescribing remedies for its breach" and that "[in] particular" the limitations of section 145, including those set forth in footnote 2, *supra*, apply to a government contractor's liability to a member of the public for nonperformance of a service to the public.

the means by which the contracts were intended to accomplish this community improvement were not confined to provision of the particular benefits on which plaintiffs base their claim to damages—one year's employment at minimum wages plus $1,000 worth of training to be provided to each of 650 persons by one defendant, 400 by another, and 550 by another. Rather the objective was to be achieved by establishing permanent industries in which local residents would be permanently employed and would have opportunities to become supervisors, managers and part owners. The required minimum capital investment of $5,000,000 by each defendant and the defendants' 22-year lease of the former Lincoln Heights jail building for conversion into an industrial facility also indicates the broad, long-range objective of the program. Presumably, as the planned enterprises prospered, the quantity and quality of employment and economic opportunity that they provided would increase and would benefit not only employees but also their families, other local enterprises and the government itself through reduction of law enforcement and welfare costs.

The fact that plaintiffs were in a position to benefit more directly than certain other members of the public from performance of the contract does not alter their status as incidental beneficiaries. *See* RESTATEMENT OF CONTRACTS § 145, illus. 1 (C, a member of the public cannot recover for injury from B's failure to perform a contract with the United States to carry mail over a certain route).[9] For example, in *City & County of San Francisco v. Western Air Lines, Inc., supra,* 204 Cal. App. 2d 105, the agreement between the federal government and the city for improvement of the airport could be considered to be of greater benefit to air carriers using the airport than to many other members of the public. Nevertheless, Western, as an air carrier, was but an incidental, not an express, beneficiary of the agreement and therefore had no standing to enforce the contractual prohibition against discrimination in the airport's availability for public use. The court explains the distinction as follows: "None of the documents under consideration confers on Western the rights of a third-party beneficiary. The various contracts and assurances created benefits and detriments as between only two parties—the United States and the City. Nothing in them shows any intent of the contracting parties to confer any benefit directly and expressly upon air carriers such as the defendant. It is true that air carriers, including Western, may be *incidentally* benefited by City's assurances in respect to nondiscriminatory treatment at the airport. They may also be incidentally benefited by the fact that, through federal aid, a public airport is improved with longer runways, brighter beacons, or larger loading ramps, or by the fact a new public airport is provided for a community without one. The various documents and agreements were part of a federal aid program directed to the promoting of a national transportation system. Provisions in such agreements, including the nondiscrimination clauses, were intended to advance such federal aims and not for the benefit of those who might be affected by the sponsor's failure to perform." 204 Cal. App. 2d at 120.

For the reasons above stated we hold that plaintiffs and the class they represent have no standing as third party beneficiaries to recover the damages

---

9. This illustration is repeated in Tentative Drafts, RESTATEMENT (SECOND) OF CONTRACTS, section 145, illustration 1.

sought in the complaint under either California law or the general contract principles which federal law applies to government contracts.

The judgments of dismissal are affirmed.

Exercise 13-10: Third-Party Beneficiaries and Government Contracts

1. Read section 313 in the RESTATEMENT (SECOND) OF CONTRACTS. Outline that section.

2. Mail Carrying, Inc. contracts with the United States to carry mail over a certain route. Lidia, a member of the public, is injured by Mail Carrying, Inc.'s failure to perform its contract. Does Lidia have standing to sue Mail Carrying, Inc.?[10]

3. Answer the problem posed at the beginning of this section: The United States government loans money to Abe, an apartment builder and property manager. Abe promises to keep the rental rates for the completed apartments within prescribed limits. After six months, Abe raises the rental rates above the prescribed limits. Do the tenants have standing to sue Abe?

Statutory Third-Party Beneficiaries

In some situations, overriding social policies result in the creation of statutory rights for third parties (and, consequently, limitations on parties' freedom of contract). This section will examine one example of that situation: third-party beneficiaries of warranties under the U.C.C.

As you know from Chapter 1, the U.C.C. applies to transactions in goods. Almost all of us have purchased goods that we did not use ourselves. For example, groceries and household products are commonly consumed and used by third parties in your home who did not purchase them. Gift purchases also raise this issue. May these third parties recover as beneficiaries of the contracts you made with your sellers? May they also sue a remote manufacturer up the supply chain in addition to the more immediate seller?

U.C.C. section 2-318 extends sellers' warranties to third parties as beneficiaries of buyer-seller contracts. Section 2-318 provides three alternative provisions (A, B, and C). Some jurisdictions have legislatively modified their chosen alternative even further. Thus, recovery in a given jurisdiction will depend on the version adopted as well as the judicial construction of that version. Exercise 13-11 gives you an opportunity to learn more about third-party beneficiaries under section 2-318.

Exercise 13-11: U.C.C. Warranty Beneficiaries

1. Look up and read U.C.C. section 2-318.

2. What are the differences among alternatives A, B, and C?

---

10. This example is based on Illustration 1 to section 313 in the RESTATEMENT SECOND OF CONTRACTS.

3. Find your state's version of 2-318. Which alternative did your state adopt? Did your state modify that alternative?

4. Stacey buys groceries from Grocer for household use, including a six-pack of Drinka Cola, relying on Grocer's express warranty. Once home, Kendra, Stacey's minor child, took a bottle of Drinka Cola out of the grocery bag. Suddenly, the bottle of Drinka Cola exploded. Jagged pieces of glass caused Kendra severe injuries. Can Kendra recover from Grocer and from Drinka?[11]

5. Assume the same facts as in problem 4, except the injured child is a neighbor's son, Paul. Can an action be brought on Paul's behalf to recover from Grocer based on the warranty? How about an action against Drinka?

Vesting of Third-Party Beneficiaries' Rights

Courts and attorneys often label the second major issue raised in third-party beneficiary situations as a question of "vesting." Ordinarily, when two parties make a contract, they may change their minds and agree to a modification or rescission of their contract. However, there are limits on parties' rights to make contractual modifications that change the rights of a third-party beneficiary.

Unless a contract specifically makes third-party rights irrevocable, beneficiaries do not have any enforceable rights until their rights vest. Until vesting, promisors and promisees can modify or even rescind their contracts without regard to the rights of any third-party beneficiaries. Consequently, it is important to identify when third-party beneficiary rights vest.

Exercise 13-12: *Robson v. Robson*

The next case, *Robson v. Robson*, addresses whether the third-party beneficiary's rights had vested or whether an attempted modification of those rights by the promisor and promisee was valid. As you read *Robson*, consider the following questions:

1. What are the relevant facts? Pay particular attention to the timing of the events described in the facts.

2. Identify and diagram the parties' relationships.

3. Why does the court find that the wives were intended beneficiaries?

4. What rules does the court state and apply?

5. What would the result have been if the third party had demonstrated that she relied on the contract? What evidence could the third party produce to prove reliance?

6. What rationales support the *Robson* rules regarding modification?

---

11. This problem is based on Illustration 15 to section 302 of the RESTATEMENT SECOND OF CONTRACTS.

Robson v. Robson

514 F. Supp. 99 (N.D. Ill. 1981)

Aspen, District Judge. Plaintiff Birthe Lise Robson ("Birthe") brought this action against her father-in-law, Raymond F. Robson, Sr. ("Ray, Sr.") in order to obtain his performance under a contract entered into between Ray, Sr. and Birthe's husband, R.F. Robson, Jr. ("Ray, Jr."). Plaintiff asserts that under the terms of the contract, she is a third-party beneficiary with vested rights that are being infringed by the failure of Ray, Sr. to perform under the terms of the agreement. This matter is currently before the Court on cross motions for summary judgment.

The following facts are undisputed. Ray, Sr. and Ray, Jr. each owned fifty percent of the outstanding shares of P.B. Services, Inc. On July 23, 1975, they entered into a written contract in order to satisfy a twofold purpose: (1) to establish a retirement payment schedule for Ray, Sr., and (2) to provide for the ownership of their stock certificates in the eventuality of their deaths. The contract provides that each party would continue to own fifty percent of P.B. Services, Inc.; Ray, Jr. would be obligated to maintain the operation of the business; and Ray, Sr.'s only compensation from the operation of the business would be an allotment of $1,000 per month for the duration of his life. In the event of Ray, Sr.'s death, his stock certificates were to become the property of Ray, Jr., who was obliged to pay $500 per month from the proceeds of the company to his father's spouse for the duration of her life. In the event of Ray, Jr.'s death, his shares were to become the property of Ray, Sr., who thereafter was to pay $500 per month from the proceeds of the company to his son's wife (the plaintiff) for the five years immediately following Ray, Jr.'s death or until plaintiff remarried, whichever first occurred.

Subsequent to the execution of the contract, Ray, Jr. and Birthe experienced marital problems and separated, and in 1977, Ray, Jr. filed a Petition for Divorce. On February 21, 1979, Ray, Jr. and Ray, Sr. attempted to modify their contract by deleting that portion of the agreement which provided for any payment to Birthe. Ray, Jr. drew a line through the applicable portions of the contract in the presence of three witnesses and the change was initialed by both Ray, Jr. and Ray, Sr. Two days later Ray, Jr. died of cancer. Plaintiff now seeks enforcement of the provisions of the original contract that require Ray, Sr. to pay her $500 per month for five years or until she remarries.

Under Illinois law, plaintiff has standing to sue as a third-party beneficiary under the original contract. As the Illinois Supreme Court stated in *Carson Pirie Scott & Co. v. Parrett*, 346 Ill. 252, 257, 178 N.E. 498, 501 (1931):

> [I]f a contract be entered into for a direct benefit of a third person not a party thereto, such third person may sue for breach thereof. The test is whether the benefit to the third person is direct to him or is but an incidental benefit to him arising from the contract. If direct he may sue on the contract; if incidental he has no right of recovery thereon.

A contract need not be entered into for the sole benefit of the third person in order to enable him to enforce it, so long as it is clear that the contracting parties intended him to benefit directly. *Id.* [other citations omitted.]

The contracting parties in the case at bar clearly intended the contract to directly benefit not only themselves, but also their wives, with respect to whom specific provisions were drafted.

The more difficult question, and the one that as far as our research discloses, has never been faced by an Illinois court, is whether contracting parties may discharge, rescind, or revoke the benefit promised to a third-party donee beneficiary prior to the vesting of the beneficiary's rights, where the beneficiary has not detrimentally relied upon receiving the benefit. Although some authorities have stated that the promisor in a third-party beneficiary contract has no right to deprive the beneficiary of his vested rights therein, these authorities have no bearing on the case at bar because they fail to distinguish between creditor beneficiaries and donee beneficiaries (at issue in the instant case), and because plaintiff's rights in the instant case had not vested at the time the contracting parties attempted to discharge Birthe's interest. [Citations omitted.]

A donee beneficiary of a contract is a third-party to whom the promised beneficial performance comes without cost as a donation or gift. 4 CORBIN ON CONTRACTS sec. 782. In contrast, if a promisee enters into a contract with a promisor with the express intent that the performance contracted for is to satisfy and discharge a pre-existing duty or liability, the third-party to whom the pre-existing duty or liability is owed is a creditor beneficiary. 4 CORBIN ON CONTRACTS sec. 787. In the typical creditor beneficiary case, A and B enter into a contract and thereafter B and C contract to have C perform B's obligation to A. A then becomes the third-party beneficiary to the contract between B and C.

In such creditor beneficiary cases, Illinois courts have held that the party procuring the promise (B) has no legal right to discharge the person who made the promise (C) from his liability to the beneficiary (A). [Citations omitted.] Underlying this doctrine is the fact that the beneficiary obtains a vested right as against the promisor at the instant the promisor agrees to undertake the promisee's duty or liability to the beneficiary. Because creditor beneficiary cases only involve situations where a pre-existing duty or liability is contractually transferred to a new party, there is never any question that the third-party beneficiary's rights vest as soon as the contract is executed. Also underlying this doctrine is the belief that the beneficiary will relax his efforts to obtain performance from the promisee upon discovering that it is now the promisor who is obligated to perform the task. [Citation omitted.] The third-party beneficiary's reliance upon the performance of the promisor thus can be presumed in creditor beneficiary cases, due to the nature of the transaction. In such cases, Illinois courts have refused to let B discharge C's duty to perform, because A, although not a party to the B/C contract, obtained a vested right in the contract and will be harmed by the discharge of C. The harm, however, does not arise because A has not received his due from C; that problem arose long before the B/C contract. It arises, rather, because the B/C contract created a time-consuming diversion, during which A looked to C for performance. Were B allowed to constantly change the cast of characters on A, contracting for and then discharging his obligations to a steady stream of Ds, Es, Fs, and Gs, A, without any right to interfere in B's collateral contracts, would be impotent to stop B's diversionary and dilatory tactics. Thus, Illinois courts have consistently held that a third-party creditor beneficiary obtains an immediate vested right as against a promisor, and this right, once given, deprives the promisor of any interest or right in the subject matter of the promise, including the right to alter, rescind, or revoke it. [Citation omitted.]

Donee beneficiaries present very different considerations. Their interests do not vest automatically upon execution of the B/C contract because they were not owed any pre-existing duty or liability. Indeed, prior to the B/C contract, the donee beneficiary may have had no relationship whatsoever with B or C. Similarly, unlike the creditor beneficiary situation, there is no reason for the Court to presume that a donee beneficiary would act in reliance upon the B/C contract. Indeed, a donee beneficiary may acquire rights even though he is unaware that he has been made a beneficiary to the B/C contract. Thus, because there is no pre-existing duty or liability owed to the donee beneficiary, there is no reason for courts to presume that a donee beneficiary acted in reliance upon being named as a third-party beneficiary to a contract.

One reason for the analytical distinction between the rights of creditor beneficiaries and donee beneficiaries is their disparate heritage. The rights of a creditor beneficiary derive directly from contract law. It is by virtue of his contract rights against the debtor that the creditor beneficiary acquires a right to sue against the new promisor. WILLISTON ON CONTRACTS, 3d ed. §§ 364, 368. Determining the rights of a donee beneficiary, however, is conceptually more akin to the law of gifts than it is to the law of contracts. In that context, it is elementary that when a donor has delivered a gift to C for the benefit of A, the gift is not revocable by the donor after such delivery, even if A is unaware of it. [Citations omitted.] But where the gift has not been delivered, and moreover, where the gift is made conditional upon subsequent events which may or may not occur, that gift may be revoked by the donor at any time prior to its vesting; for until delivery there exists no gift, but rather, merely the promise of a gift. [Citations omitted.]

Although commentators have recognized the analogy between the rights of a donee beneficiary and the rights of one receiving a gift of property, they fail to follow the analogy through to its necessary conclusion. [Citations omitted.] Instead, both Williston and Corbin indicate that a donee beneficiary acquires a right at once upon the making of the contract and that right becomes immediately indefeasible. *Id.* The commentators, however, fail to consider a situation such as the one at bar. Where the donee beneficiary's right is contingent upon the occurrence of certain events, it does not vest until the occurrence of those events. [Citations omitted.] Until the donee beneficiary obtains vested rights, he is without power to affect the decisions made by the contracting parties.

Regardless of whether contract principles, gift principles, or estates principles are applied, Ray, Sr. and Ray, Jr. had a right to alter, rescind, or revoke any or all of their contract prior to the time that the contract vested rights in the donee beneficiaries. Had the donee beneficiary acted to her detriment in reliance upon a promise contained in the agreement, this would be a very different case. There has been no evidence presented to the Court, in affidavit form or otherwise, to indicate that plaintiff acted in reliance upon the contract entered into by Ray, Sr. and Ray, Jr. However, where the contract rights of a donee beneficiary have not yet vested and where the beneficiary has not detrimentally relied upon a promise contained in the contract, this Court will not subvert the intent of the contracting parties when it is clear that they desired to alter the terms of their contract.

Finally, plaintiff argues that the modification of the contract is invalid for lack of consideration. This argument must fail for a variety of reasons. First, lack of consideration is an argument which goes to an attempt by one party to enforce a contract against another party. In the case at bar, nobody is seeking to enforce the terms of the modified contract. Moreover, plaintiff, with no rights in the modified contract, and with only contingent unvested rights in the original contract, is in no position to challenge the adequacy of consideration. [Citation omitted.] Indeed, even if this were a proper challenge to consideration and if plaintiff was a proper party to assert the challenge, the Illinois Supreme Court has stated that a contract modification that has been executed by the parties will not be disturbed by the court, even in the absence of consideration. [Citations omitted.] Moreover, it is apparent that the modified contract did involve adequate consideration for both the contracting parties. Ray, Jr. benefitted by discharging the contingent rights of a wife for whom he no longer cared and Ray, Sr. benefitted by being released from a potential obligation to make monthly payments to the plaintiff.

For the foregoing reasons, plaintiff's motion for summary judgment is denied and defendant's motion for summary judgment is granted. It is so ordered.

Exercise 13-13: Vesting of Third Party Rights[12]

1. Read section 311, subsections 1–3, in the RESTATEMENT SECOND OF CONTRACTS (ignore subsection 4). Create an outline that paraphrases the section 311 rules.

2. In *Lawrence*, after making the contract, could Holly and Fox have changed their minds and agreed that Fox would just pay Holly instead of Lawrence? What would the answer be under the SECOND RESTATEMENT?

3. What would have been the result in *Robson* if the second Restatement's modification rule had been applied?

4. Rick and Ellen make a contract in which Ellen promises to maintain Rick's car for Rick if Rick will leave ten acres of land to Ellen's son, Sammy. Ellen performs as promised. Three years after the contract was made, Rick and Ellen modify the contract to provide that Sammy will only get five acres of land, and the American Society for the Prevention of Cruelty to Animals will get the other five acres. Ellen continues to perform as promised. Rick dies and Sammy tries to enforce the original contract for ten acres. Will Sammy be successful in obtaining the ten acres?

---

12. Problems 7–8 are based on Illustrations in section 311 of the RESTATEMENT SECOND OF CONTRACTS.

5. Steve takes out a life insurance policy and lists Gracie as the beneficiary. The policy contains a standard clause reserving a power to modify. Two years later, Steve changes the beneficiary to Stacey. When Steve dies, who gets the money, Gracie or Stacey?

6. Assume the same facts as in problem 5, except the policy omits the standard clause reserving a power to modify. Does Gracie have any rights as a third-party beneficiary?

7. Jeff insures his life for $1,000,000 with Secure Insurance Company, designating Dana as the beneficiary but reserving power to change the beneficiary. The policy provides for surrender of the policy by the insured for a stated cash value. Subsequently, Jeff irrevocably designates Grace as the beneficiary. One year later, Jeff surrenders the policy to Secure for the stated cash value. Should Secure pay the cash value to Jeff?

8. Bonita contracts with Fred to pay Samantha $2,000, which Fred owes to Samantha. In exchange, Fred agrees to tutor Bonita in Calculus. Before Samantha learns of the Bonita-Fred contract, in consideration of a horse worth $2,000, Fred releases Bonita from her promise to pay Samantha. Does Samantha have any enforceable rights against Bonita?

9. Assume the same facts as in problem 8, except Samantha files a lawsuit to enforce her rights before receiving notification of the release. Does Samantha have any enforceable rights?

10. Assume you are an attorney drafting the original Rick-Ellen contract in problem 4. Draft a contract clause that will ensure that Sammy's right to the ten acres of land is irrevocable. Now, draft a contract clause preserving Rick and Ellen's right to modify the contract they make.

Enforcement of Rights and Defenses

The third major issue raised in third-party beneficiary situations is enforcement and defenses. As you have already learned, incidental beneficiaries have no enforceable rights. In contrast, intended beneficiaries have enforceable rights, and those rights become irrevocable after they vest. The three enforcement issues that will be examined in this section are: (1) whom a third party can sue, (2) a promisee's rights against a promisor, and (3) defenses a promisor can assert.

Enforcement by Third-Party Beneficiaries

In third-party beneficiary situations, third parties are often the parties most interested in the performance of contracts made for their benefit. Exercise 13-14 will explore third parties' enforcement rights.

Exercise 13-14: Enforcement by Third-Party Beneficiaries

1. Why can a third party like Lawrence sue a promisor like Fox directly? (Hint: See section 304 of the RESTATEMENT SECOND OF CONTRACTS.)

2. In *Lawrence*, assume that Fox went bankrupt before paying the $300 to Lawrence. Could Lawrence sue Holly for the money instead? (Hint: See comment c to section 304.)

3. Ann owes Chris $10,000. For consideration Ben promises Ann to pay the debt. Ben breaks his contract. Whom can Chris sue to recover the $10,000?

4. Abby gives money to Bill, her son, who for consideration promises to pay Abby's daughter, Clara, $50,000 on Abby's death. Abby dies and Bill fails to pay Clara. Can Clara recover the $50,000? If so, whom can she sue?

5. Andy's son Cameron is indebted to Doug. With the purpose of assisting Cameron, Andy secures from Barb, for consideration, a promise to pay the debt to Doug. Can Doug enforce the promise?

6. Ali, a stockholder of X Corporation, guarantees payment of a debt owed by X to Cindy. Ali sells her stock to Brandy, who agrees to assume and pay Ali's obligation on the guaranty. Brandy fails to pay, and Cindy sues Ali on the guaranty. What options does Ali have for avoiding paying the debt? (Hint: See section 307 of the RESTATEMENT (SECOND) OF CONTRACTS.)

7. Alexis owes Chanel $100,000. For consideration Bob promises Alexis to pay the debt. Bob breaks his contract. Can Chanel recover? If so, whom can she sue?

8. Arnie owes Carin a debt of $10,000, secured by a mortgage on Arnie's land. Arnie sells Arnieacre to Blair, who assumes and agrees to pay the mortgage debt. Carin, knowing of this assumption, releases a portion of the mortgaged premises from the lien of the mortgage. At the time of the release, the remaining portion of Arnieacre is worth $12,000, but at the date of maturity of the mortgage it has declined in value to only $8,000. At the date of maturity of the mortgage the released land is worth $2,000. Blair defaults in paying the debt. Carin sues Arnie. How much can Carin recover?

Promisees' Rights Against Promisors

In addition to a third party's action against a promisor who breaches a contract, a promisee can also assert her rights against a promisor who breaches. Exercise 13-15 explores a promisee's rights.

Exercise 13-15: Promisees' Rights

1. Andrew's son, Christopher, owes Doug $10,000. To help his son out, Andrew and Bailey agree, for consideration, that Bailey will pay the $10,000 to Doug. Bailey fails to pay the $10,000 as agreed. What options does Doug have with regard to enforcing the agreement made?

2. Alex owes Chad $10,000. For consideration, Brad promises Alex that he (Brad) will pay the debt. Brad breaches the contract.

   a. Chad does not enforce the contract. What are Alex's options?

   b. Chad sues Alex, gets a judgment for $10,000, and collects the judgment from Alex. What are Alex's options?

Promisors' Defenses

The third issue that frequently arises in the enforcement of third-party beneficiary contracts is the issue of promisors' defenses.

Exercise 13-16: *Rouse v. United States*

The next case, *Rouse v. United States*, addresses the issue of promisors' defenses. *Rouse* is a factually complex case. Make sure to take the time to understand the factual situation and the contracts involved. As you read *Rouse*, answer the following questions:

1. What are the relevant facts?

2. Identify the third-party beneficiary contract and which parties are the promisor, promisee, and third-party beneficiary. Diagram the relationships among the parties.

3. The court quotes a provision of the contract that states that the parties are not "bound by any terms, conditions, statements, warranties or representation, oral or written" not contained in it. What is that clause called? What is its effect?

4. What rule does the court state regarding what defenses a promisor may assert?

5. What defenses did Rouse assert against the United States?

6. Why was it an error to strike Rouse's first defense? What rationale supports that result?

7. Why was it proper for the court to strike Rouse's second defense? What rationale supports that result?

Rouse v. United States

215 F.2d 872 (D.C. Cir. 1954)

Edgerton, Circuit Judge. Bessie Winston gave Associated Contractors, Inc., her promissory note for $1,008.37, payable in monthly installments of $28.01, for a heating plant in her house. The Federal Housing Administration guaranteed the note and the payee endorsed it for value to the lending bank, the Union Trust Company.

Winston sold the house to Rouse. In the contract of sale Rouse agreed to assume debts secured by deeds of trust and also "to assume payment of $850 for heating plant payable $28 per mo." Nothing was said about the note.

Winston defaulted on her note. The United States paid the bank, took an assignment of the note, demanded payment from Rouse, and sued him for $850 and interest.

Rouse alleged as defenses: (1) that Winston fraudulently misrepresented the condition of the heating plant; and (2) that Associated Contractors did not install it satisfactorily. The District Court struck these defenses and granted summary judgment for the plaintiff. The defendant Rouse appeals.

Since Rouse did not sign the note he is not liable on it. D.C. Code 1951, Sec. 28-119; N.I.L. Sec. 18. He is not liable to the United States at all unless his contract with Winston makes him so. The contract says the parties to it are not "bound by any terms, conditions, statements, warranties or representation, oral or written" not contained in it. But this means only that the written contract contains the entire agreement. It does not mean that fraud cannot be set up as a defense to a suit on the contract. Rouse's promise to "assume payment of $850 for heating plant" made him liable to Associated Contractors, Inc., only if and so far as it made him liable to Winston; one who promises to make a payment to the promisee's creditor can assert against the creditor any defense that the promisor could assert against the promisee. Accordingly Rouse, if he had been sued by the corporation, would have been entitled to show fraud on the part of Winston. He is equally entitled to do so in this suit by an assignee of the corporation's claim. It follows that the court erred in striking the first defense. We do not consider whether Winston's alleged fraud, if shown, would be a complete or only a partial defense to this suit, since that question has not arisen and may not arise.

We think the court was right in striking the second defense. "If the promisor's agreement is to be interpreted as a promise to discharge whatever liability the promisee is under, the promisor must certainly be allowed to show that the promisee was under no enforceable liability.... On the other hand, if the promise means that the promisor agrees to pay a sum of money to A, to whom the promisee says he is indebted, it is immaterial whether the promisee is actually indebted to that amount or at all.... Where the promise is to pay a specific debt ... this interpretation will generally be the true one."

The judgment is reversed and the cause remanded with instructions to reinstate the first defense. Reversed and remanded.

Exercise 13-17: Promisors' Defenses

1. In a suit by a party like Lawrence, could a party like Fox assert the following defenses regarding the promisee's contract with the third-party beneficiary?

    a. That the promisee's obligation to the third party was induced by fraud?

    b. That the promisee-third-party contract failed to comply with an applicable statute of frauds?

    c. That the promisee-third-party contract is excused by impracticability?

    d. That the third party materially breached the promisee-third-party contract?

2. In a suit by Lawrence, could Fox assert the following defenses based on the Fox-Holly contract:

    a. That Fox's promise to Holly was induced by fraud?

    b. That the Fox-Holly contract failed to comply with an applicable statute of frauds?

    c. That the Fox-Holly contract is excused by impracticability?

    d. That Holly materially breached the Holly-Fox contract?

3. Abigail owes Clara $10,000. For consideration, Blake promises Abigail: "I will pay Clara the $10,000." Before Blake pays Clara, the statute of limitations bars an action by Clara against Abigail to recover the debt. Can Blake assert the statute of limitations as a defense in an action against him by Clara?

4. Jacob orally promises Annecy that he will convey Blackacre to Megan. Jacob's promise to Annecy is unenforceable because it is not in writing. If Megan files an action against Jacob, can Jacob assert any defenses?

5. Assume the same facts as in problem 4, except after Jacob's oral promise, he delivers a written memorandum of his promise to Annecy. Can Megan maintain an action based on Jacob's promise?

Chapter Problem Revisited

Because you will be conducting a client interview, some materials on conducting client interviews would be helpful.

"A simple checklist of the concerns that may also be addressed during [an] interview are ... :

1. Elicit pertinent facts being sure to fill in who, what, where, when, why and how the present situation came to arise.

2. Make an initial determination as to what the client really hopes to achieve. This can be accomplished by asking the question to consider what his or her interests are in the outcome and by discussing the client's underlying motives, needs and interests.

3. Discuss whatever alternatives the client may have already considered, while being careful not to inflate the client's expectations.

4. Discuss the process, what the attorney will try to accomplish and how, explaining procedural phases and the expected time frame.

5. Discuss how and at what points the client may ... be involved at various stages in the process.

6. Establish ongoing means of communication, defining when the client can expect to receive status reports and whether copies of correspondence and/or pleadings should be sent to the client on a routine basis."

Ted A. Donner, *Six Steps of Planning*, ATTORNEY'S PRACTICE GUIDE TO NEGOTIATIONS § 1.3 (Database updated April 2008).

"The initial interview is a tool to determine whether counsel will proceed with representation. This is why an attorney in the law firm should meet with the potential client at the initial interview. First impressions mean a lot to insurance adjusters, judges and juries. So summing up a "first impression" of this new client gives the attorney an opportunity to make some notes on non-legal issues. These include the client's demeanor, dress, education level, how the client presents himself when discussing the event that may lead to the representation, and other pertinent observations that are only present during the initial interview."

"In addition, even what appears to be the most straightforward, minor damages case deserves an attorney's attention. Only in rare circumstances should someone in the firm other than an attorney conduct the initial client interview. Some attorneys believe that their staff can handle this paperwork competently. However, it is recommended that an attorney handle the initial meeting with the client. The initial interview is arguably the most important part of the case. It doesn't have to be time-consuming, but it will prove to be one of the most time efficient tasks counsel does for and with the client, if it is conducted correctly."

Eva Marie Mancuso and Sonja L. Deyoe, *Preliminary considerations—Initial interview*, ATLA's Litigating Tort Cases (Database updated June 2007).

Initial Client Interview Checklist[13]

_____ **A. Identify Potential Parties ...**

    _____ 1. [buyer, seller, etc.]

    _____ 2. sureties, guarantors, indemnitors, insurance companies

    _____ 3. financing institutions

    _____ 4. check for conflicts

_____ **B. Obtain Initial Information on Client**

    _____ 1. names, addresses, phone numbers

    _____ 2. related businesses

    _____ 3. state of incorporation

    _____ 4. principal place of business

    _____ 5. financial condition

    _____ 6. prior legal counsel (if any)

    _____ 7. prior legal advice (if any)

    _____ 8. who, what, and how much involved

    _____ 9. identify and request relevant documents

    _____ 10. discuss and confirm the fee[14]

_____ **C. Pre-Conference Document Review**

    _____ 1. contracts ...

    _____ 2. pay requests ...

    _____ 3. significant correspondence

_____ **D. Location, Attendees, and Documents ...**

    _____ 1. key personnel to attend

    _____ 2. contracts, subcontracts, and purchase orders

    _____ 3. correspondence files ...

_____ **E. Preliminary Legal Issues**

    _____ 1. what law governs

    _____ 2. validity of exculpatory clauses [if any] ...

    _____ 3. ADR procedures

    _____ 4. arbitration vs. litigation

---

13. This checklist has been edited and renumbered.

14. Please note: students will not be required to discuss their fee with this client.

_____   5. jurisdiction and venue
_____   6. statutes of limitation and repose
_____   7. liquidated vs. actual damages
_____   8. consequential damages ...

_____ **F. Establish a Game Plan**
_____   1. identify the desired result
_____   2. involvement of client personnel
_____   3. involvement of experts and consultants
_____   4. timetable for preparing or reviewing claims
_____   5. negotiated settlement, mediation, arbitration, or litigation

Thomas J. Kelleher, Jr., Brian G. Corgan and William E. Dorris, *Checklist for Initial Interviews*, CONSTRUCTION DISPUTES: PRACTICE GUIDE WITH FORMS (2006).

Professional Development Reflection Questions

1. This chapter's first four reflection questions provide you three more ways to increase your level of happiness. The first strategy is to keep a gratitude journal. Write down three things for which you are grateful. Try doing so again tomorrow. If you like it, try keeping a gratitude journal for 21 days.

2. Another way to increase your level of happiness is by eschewing comparisons, unless they are a source of inspiration for you. Remember that authentic happiness comes from raising the bar for yourself.

3. You also can increase the level of happiness you feel by intentionally engaging in active and constructive responding. To do so, stop and listen when people you care about report good events or news to you and go out of your way to respond enthusiastically. Notice the other person's response to you and the mutual energizing that results.

4. Happy people know where they want to go and have the organizational and time management skills necessary to plan to reach their goals. Accordingly, you can also increase your level of happiness by setting personal goals and working on increasing the effectiveness of your organizational and time management efforts.

5. You have been retained to draft a contract for a client who wants to provide you a benefit under the contract as a third-party beneficiary. Should you continue to represent the client and draft the third-party beneficiary clause?

Chapter 14

Assignment, Delegation, and Novation

Exercise 14-1: Chapter Problem — Memorandum 1

You are an associate at a law firm and your supervising partner has just sent you Memorandum 1, which is provided in Table 14-1. As you will see, your supervising partner would like you to complete three tasks.

As you read this chapter, keep these tasks in mind. When you are finished learning the materials in this chapter, you will be asked to complete the three projects. By the end of this chapter, you will be able to do so.

MEMORANDUM 1

To: Associate Attorney
From: Darci Partner, Esq.
Date: May 7, 20XX
Re: Contract Between Widgets, Inc. and Josephina Schmo (JS), Inc.

As you know, Widgets. Inc. is a long-term client of our firm. You have a draft of the contract that I banged out a few weeks ago. Widgets, Inc. is very concerned that JS, Inc. might delegate its duties under the contract to a subcontractor. Can JS do so under the general rules that govern the delegation of duties? Can JS do so given the existing language of the contract? Finally, please draft a contract clause for the Widgets, Inc. — JS, Inc. contract that unmistakably prohibits delegation of duties.

Exercise 14-2: Memorandum 2

A couple of months have passed, and the clients wish to revise their contract. To do so, you will need to draft one or more new contract provisions. Memorandum 2, which is provided in Table 14-1, details your drafting task(s).

MEMORANDUM 2

To: Associate Attorney
From: Darci Partner, Esq.
Date: July 27, 20XX
Re: Contract Between Widgets, Inc. and Josephina Schmo (JS), Inc.

Widgets, Inc. has asked JS, Inc. to now undertake governmental lobbying responsibilities in addition to the duties outlined in the above-referenced contract. I explained to our client that there is an argument that the term "public relations" encompasses lobbying, but our client asked me not to press that issue because the parties' working relationship is excellent and the contract has proven to be a good one for our client. In exchange, JS has asked us to revise the contract to allow JS to delegate purely administrative aspects of its duties (in contrast with JS's creative, advisory, and analytical duties). Please revise the prohibition against delegation clause to allow such delegation, but make sure our client gets to approve any delegate.

Overview of Chapter 14

In the last chapter, you learned about one situation where contracts create rights in third parties who are not parties to the contracts—third-party beneficiaries. This chapter examines two more situations in which nonparties to original contracts become involved in those contracts: (1) assignments of rights and delegations of duties, and (2) novations.

In this chapter, you will begin with an introduction to assignments and delegations. You will then learn what rights may be assigned and what duties may be delegated. After you learn what may be assigned and delegated, you will learn the requirements for effective assignments and delegations. The discussion of assignment and delegation concludes with materials addressing the rights and liabilities of parties involved with assignments and delegations. The chapter concludes with a short discussion of novations.

Contract Law Graphic Organizer

Diagram 14-1 shows where assignments, delegations, and novations fit within the big picture of contract law. As Diagram 14-1 shows, "Third-Party Contract Issues" is the fifth major contract issue. That issue is addressed in three sections: "Third-Party Beneficiaries," "Assignments and Delegations," and "Novations." Assignments, delegations, and novations are the topics examined in this chapter.

Diagram 14-1: Contract Law Graphic Organizer

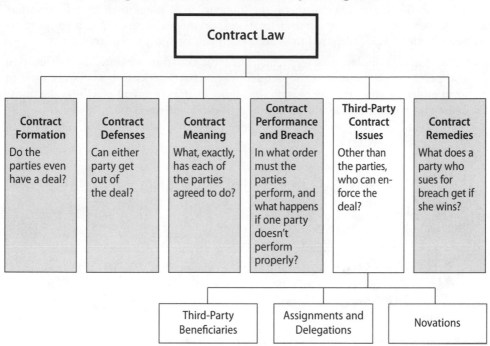

Introduction to Assignments and Delegations and Novations

Toward the beginning of Chapter 13, in the section entitled "Introduction to Third-Party Beneficiary Contracts and Terminology," we introduced you to third-party beneficiaries and assignments, delegations, and novations. Take a few minutes to review that section of Chapter 13 and Exercise 13-2. Then, complete exercise 14-3.

Exercise 14-3: Third-Party Beneficiaries, Assignments, Delegations, and Novations

1. In what ways are third-party beneficiary, assignment, and novation situations similar?

2. How are third-party beneficiary situations different from both assignment and novation situations?

3. How are assignments and novations different from each other?

Assignments of Rights and Delegations of Duties

The basic situation presented by an assignment involves two parties who make a contract. Subsequently, one party seeks to transfer her rights or duties under the contract to a third party. In a transfer of rights, the party transferring her rights is the "assignor." The party to whom the rights are transferred is the "assignee." The party who owes the right due on the underlying contract is the "obligor." If an assignment lawfully transfers a right or benefit, the assignment or delegation is deemed "effective." If an attempt to assign is not effective, it is referred to as an "attempted" or "purported" transfer.

Delegations are similar to assignments. The basic situation presented by a delegation is: Two parties make a contract. Subsequently, one party seeks to transfer her duty to perform under the contract. There is no such thing as an assignment of a duty; the transfer of the duty is called a "delegation." The original party who owed the duty is the "obligor" and "delegator." The party to whom the duty is transferred is the "delegate." The party to whom the duty is owed is the "obligee."[1]

What Rights May Be Assigned and What Duties May Be Delegated?

Exercise 14-4: *Globe & Rutgers Fire-Insurance Co. v. Jones*

The first case you will read in this section, *Globe & Rutgers Fire-Insurance Co. v. Jones*, addresses the issue of what rights may be assigned. As you read *Globe*, consider the following questions:

1. What are the relevant facts?

2. Identify and diagram the relationships of the parties.

3. What is the issue addressed by the court?

4. What rule did the court apply?

5. How did the court apply that rule to the facts of the case?

Globe & Rutgers Fire-Insurance Co. v. Jones

89 N.W.2d 580, 129 Mich. 664 (1902)

Moore, J. This is an action for money had and received. The defense is a set-off for damages from a breach of contract alleged by defendant to have been committed by the plaintiff.

Prior to March 1, 1898, the defendant, James A. Jones, was the local agent in Detroit for the Rutgers Fire-Insurance Company. On that date he was ap-

---

1. *See* RESTATEMENT SECOND OF CONTRACTS, section 316, comment c; section 317, comment a. Note that courts and parties frequently use imprecise language, which causes confusion in learning about this topic. For example, parties often use the term "assignment" when they are actually referring to a delegation or a combined assignment and delegation. By using correct terminology, you can ensure that you will perform well on your contract exam and represent your clients effectively in practice.

pointed general agent of the same company for the State of Michigan, under a written contract. The term of the appointment and the contract was five years from March 1, 1898. The defendant worked under the appointment from its date until about March 1, 1899, continuing his local agency for the same company. By the contract he was to render an account to the company monthly "on or before the 20th, and forward to said Rutgers Fire-Insurance Company a check for the balance within 60 days of the close of each month." Defendant, Jones, rendered statements of account as required by the contract, showing balances aggregating $1,464.01, but failed to make remittance to the company. The balances are the amounts, less all deductions, except for the returned premiums, of which there were $62.50 in March and April, and $295.32, Jones' contingent commission of 10 per cent on net profits at the end of each year, provided he continued in the performance of his duties under the contract. The balance due, allowing the items just mentioned, is $1,106.19, with interest from March 1, 1899.

On the 20th day of December, 1898, the Globe Fire-Insurance Company and the Rutgers Fire-Insurance Company, both corporations of the State of New York, doing business in the city of New York, were consolidated and merged in the Globe & Rutgers Fire-Insurance Company, the plaintiff in this case. This consolidation was effected under section 129, chap. 38, 2 Rev. Stat. N.Y., the material portion of which is as follows: ...

> Upon such merger, all the rights, franchises, and interests of the merging corporations in and to every species of property and things in action belonging to them, or either of them, shall be deemed to be transferred to and vested in the new corporation, without any other deed or transfer, and the new corporation shall hold and enjoy the same to the same extent as if the merging corporations, or either of them, should have continued to retain the title and transact business. The new corporation shall succeed to all the obligations and liabilities of the merging corporations, or either of them, and shall be held liable to pay and discharge all such debts and liabilities in the same manner as if they had been incurred or contracted by it. The stockholders of the merging corporations shall continue subject to all the liabilities, claims, and demands existing against them, or either of them, at or before such merger.

The defense to the plaintiff's claim is that the Rutgers Fire-Insurance Company ceased to do business in the State of Michigan on or about the 30th day of December, 1898, and afterwards, by its voluntary act and deed, became consolidated with the Globe Fire-Insurance Company of New York, and the said Rutgers Fire-Insurance Company wholly incapacitated itself by its voluntary act from performing its contract aforesaid. The defendant claimed to have heard rumors in September or October, 1898, that the stock of the Rutgers Fire-Insurance Company was to be purchased by persons connected with the Globe; that he first learned that the Rutgers had ceased to do business in Michigan in March, 1899, and learned about the same time of the consolidation; that he then—in March, 1899—stopped all business under his contract, and took up all policies he had written in 1899.

The general agency contract ran for five years from March, 1898. By it Mr. Jones was to be general agent for the Rutgers Company during that period.

That company's State license expired January 31, 1899, and was never re-newed. The plaintiff did not qualify itself in Michigan till April 17, 1899, and its license expired January 31, 1900, and was never renewed. Mr. Jones had long been local agent for the Rutgers Company, and general agent from March, 1898. He testified the officers of that company were fine men, and the company a fine company, while he had objection to the men in control of the Globe. He said their reputation was that of wreckers, and that he objected to the character and reputation of the whole concern. He declined the general agency of the new company when offered him in May, 1899, after he had sev-ered his connection with the company in March, when he recalled the poli-cies written during that year. Mr. Jones did not pay over to the company any of the moneys in his hands after October, 1898, and did not notify the com-pany of any reason for failure to do so. The circuit judge ruled that the con-solidation of the Rutgers Fire-Insurance Company with the Globe Fire-Insurance Company on the 20th of December, 1898, was a breach of the contract on its part, and that the defendant was entitled to recover damages therefor to the amount of the plaintiff's claim against him for its money which he had withheld, if the jury found he had sustained that amount of damages.

Counsel for plaintiff says in his brief: "The only question, then, to be re-viewed on this record is: Was the consolidation of these two New York cor-porations a breach of the contract of March 1, 1898, between the Rutgers Fire-Insurance Company and the defendant, Jones?"

The following request states the claim of the plaintiff:

> The Rutgers Fire-Insurance Company is a corporation under the laws of New York. The defendant, in dealing with that company, and in making the contract of March 1, 1898, must be conclusively pre-sumed to have dealt with the said company with full knowledge of its power and rights under the laws of the State of New York, and any act of said company authorized by the law of New York cannot constitute a breach of this contract.

It will be noticed that, by the terms of the New York statute, the two cor-porations were merged in the corporation provided for in the agreement. This made a new corporation. [Citations Omitted.] Is it true, as contended here, that, because one has contracted to render personal service for one corporation for a definite period of time, his contract for personal service may pass to a new corporation, made up of two or more corporations, by virtue of the merger of the two or more companies? In WOOD, MAST. & S. §91, it is said:

> When a person contracts to work for another for a term, the par-ties are treated as having contracted in reference to the personal qual-ities of each other, and the master cannot shift his liability by turning the servant over to another master before the term is ended, nor can the servant compel the master to accept the services of another per-son in lieu of his own. The consent of the parties is essential to ef-fect a substitution, and this is true even though the servant is ill, and unable to labor himself. [Citations omitted.]

Everyone knows that insurance companies, like individuals, differ in rep-utation and methods of doing business. An insurance agent of large experi-ence might be quite willing to act as state agent for one insurance company, when he would not be willing to work for another upon any terms. He has a right to say for whom he will work, and under a contract to work for one company he cannot be required to work for an entirely different company.

Judgment is affirmed.

Exercise 14-5: *The Macke Co. v. Pizza of Gaithersburg, Inc.*

The next case, *The Macke Co. v. Pizza of Gaithersburg, Inc.*, addresses an issue similar to the issue in *Globe*: what contractual duties may be delegated. As you read *Macke*, consider the following questions:

1. What are the relevant facts?

2. Identify and diagram the key parties.

3. What issue does the court address?

4. The court quotes a now-famous rule about the assignment of contracts from a California case, *Taylor v. Palmer*. Identify that rule.

5. How does the court apply that rule and what result does it reach?

Macke Co. v. Pizza of Gaithersburg, Inc.

259 Md. 479, 270 A.2d 645 (Md. App. 1970)

Singley, J. The appellees and defendants below, Pizza of Gaithersburg, Inc.; Pizzeria, Inc.; The Pizza Pie Corp., Inc. and Pizza Oven, Inc., four corporations under the common ownership of Sidney Ansell, Thomas S. Sherwood and Eugene Early and the same individuals as partners or proprietors (the Pizza Shops) operated at six locations in Montgomery and Prince George's Counties. The appellees had arranged to have installed in each of their locations cold drink vending machines owned by Virginia Coffee Service, Inc., and on 30 December 1966, this arrangement was formalized at five of the locations, by contracts for terms of one year, automatically renewable for a like term in the absence of 30 days' written notice. A similar contract for the sixth location, operated by Pizza of Gaithersburg, Inc., was entered into on 25 July 1967.

On 30 December 1967, Virginia's assets were purchased by The Macke Company (Macke) and the six contracts were assigned to Macke by Virginia. In January, 1968, the Pizza Shops attempted to terminate the five contracts having the December anniversary date, and in February, the contract which had the July anniversary date.

Macke brought suit in the Circuit Court for Montgomery County against each of the Pizza Shops for damages for breach of contract. From judgments for the defendants, Macke has appealed.

The lower court based the result which it reached on two grounds: first, that the Pizza Shops, when they contracted with Virginia, relied on its skill, judgment and reputation, which made impossible a delegation of Virginia's duties to Macke; and second, that the damages claimed could not be shown with reasonable certainty. These conclusions are challenged by Macke.

In the absence of a contrary provision—and there was none here—rights and duties under an executory bilateral contract may be assigned and delegated, subject to the exception that duties under a contract to provide personal services may never be delegated, nor rights be assigned under a contract where *delectus personae* was an ingredient of the bargain. [Citations omitted.] *Crane Ice Cream Co. v. Terminal Freezing & Heating Co.*, 147 Md. 588, 128 A. 280 (1925) held that the right of an individual to purchase ice under a contract which by its terms reflected a knowledge of the individual's needs and reliance on his credit and responsibility could not be assigned to the corporation which purchased his business. In *Eastern Advertising Co. v. McGaw & Co.*, 89 Md. 72, 42 A. 923 (1899), our predecessors held that an advertising agency could not delegate its duties under a contract which had been entered into by an advertiser who had relied on the agency's skill, judgment and taste.

The six machines were placed on the appellees' premises under a printed "Agreement-Contract" which identified the "customer," gave its place of business, described the vending machine, and then provided:

Terms

1. The Company will install on the Customer's premises the above listed equipment and will maintain the equipment in good operating order and stocked with merchandise.

2. The location of this equipment will be such as to permit accessibility to persons desiring use of same. This equipment shall remain the property of the Company and shall not be moved from the location at which installed, except by the Company.

3. For equipment requiring electricity and water, the Customer is responsible for electrical receptacle and water outlet within ten (10) feet of the equipment location. The Customer is also responsible to supply the Electrical Power and Water needed.

4. The Customer will exercise every effort to protect this equipment from abuse or damage.

5. The Company will be responsible for all licenses and taxes on the equipment and sale of products.

6. This Agreement-Contract is for a term of one (1) year from the date indicated herein and will be automatically renewed for a like period, unless thirty (30) day written notice is given by either party to terminate service.

7. Commission on monthly sales will be paid by the Company to the Customer at the following rate:....

The rate provided in each of the agreements was "30% of Gross Receipts to $300.00 monthly, 35% over $300.00," except for the agreement with Pizza of Gaithersburg, Inc., which called for "40% of Gross Receipts."

We cannot regard the agreements as contracts for personal services. They were either a license or concession granted Virginia by the appellees, or a lease of a portion of the appellees' premises, with Virginia agreeing to pay a percentage of gross sales as a license or concession fee or as rent ... and were assignable by Virginia unless they imposed on Virginia duties of a personal or unique character which could not be delegated. [Citation omitted.]

The appellees earnestly argue that they had dealt with Macke before and had chosen Virginia because they preferred the way it conducted its business. Specifically, they say that service was more personalized, since the president of Virginia kept the machines in working order, that commissions were paid in cash, and that Virginia permitted them to keep keys to the machines so that minor adjustments could be made when needed. Even if we assume all this to be true, the agreements with Virginia were silent as to the details of the working arrangements and contained only a provision requiring Virginia to "install ... the above listed equipment and ... maintain the equipment in good operating order and stocked with merchandise." We think the Supreme Court of California put the problem of personal service in proper focus a century ago when it upheld the assignment of a contract to grade a San Francisco street:

> All painters do not paint portraits like Sir Joshua Reynolds, nor landscapes like Claude Lorraine, nor do all writers write dramas like Shakespeare or fiction like Dickens. Rare genius and extraordinary skill are not transferable, and contracts for their employment are therefore personal, and cannot be assigned. But rare genius and extraordinary skill are not indispensable to the workmanlike digging down of a sand hill or the filling up of a depression to a given level, or the construction of brick sewers with manholes and covers, and contracts for such work are not personal, and may be assigned.

Taylor v. Palmer, 31 Cal. 240 at 247–48 (1866). [Further citation omitted.]

Moreover, the difference between the service the Pizza Shops happened to be getting from Virginia and what they expected to get from Macke did not mount up to such a material change in the performance of obligations under the agreements as would justify the appellees' refusal to recognize the assignment. [Citation omitted.]

In support of the proposition that the agreements were for personal services, and not assignable, the Pizza Shops rely on three Supreme Court cases.... We find none of these cases persuasive. *Burck v. Taylor,* 152 U.S. 634 (1894), held that the contractor for the state capitol in Texas, who was prohibited by the terms of his contract from assigning it without the state's consent, could not make a valid assignment of his right to receive three-fourths of the proceeds. In *Delaware County Comm'rs v. Diebold Safe & Lock Co.,* 133 U.S. 473 (1890), Diebold Safe and Lock, which was a subcontractor in the construction of a county jail, was barred from recovering from the county commissioners for its work on the theory that there had been a partial assignment of the construction contract by the prime contractor, which had never been assented to by the commissioners. This result must be limited to the facts: *i.e.,* to the subcontractor's right to recover under the assignment, and not to the contractor's right to delegate. [Citation omitted.] *Arkansas Valley Smelting Co. v. Belden Mining Co.,* 127 U.S. 379 (1888), which held invalid an attempt to assign a contract for the purchase of ore, is clearly distinguishable, because of a contract provision which stipulated that payment for the ore was to be made after delivery, based on an assay to be made by the individual purchaser named in the contract. The court concluded that this was a confidence imposed in the individual purchaser's credit and responsibility and that his rights under the contract could not be transferred to another....

We find more apposite two cases which were not cited by the parties. In *The British Waggon Co. & The Parkgate Waggon Co. v. Lea & Co.,* 5 Q.B.D. 149 (1880), Parkgate Waggon Company, a lessor of railway cars, who had agreed to keep the cars "in good and substantial repair and working order," made an assignment of the contract to British Waggon Company. When British Waggon Company sued for rent, the lessee contended that the assignment had terminated the lease. The court held that the lessee remained bound under the lease, because there was no provision making performance of the lessor's duty to keep in repair a duty personal to it or its employees.

Except for the fact that the result has been roundly criticized, *see* Corbin, *supra*, at 448–49, the Pizza Shops might have found some solace in the facts found in *Boston Ice Co. v. Potter,* 123 Mass. 28 (1877). There, Potter, who had dealt with the Boston Ice Company, and found its service unsatisfactory, transferred his business to Citizens' Ice Company. Later, Citizens' sold out to Boston, unbeknown to Potter, and Potter was served by Boston for a full year. When Boston attempted to collect its ice bill, the Massachusetts court sustained Potter's demurrer on the ground that there was no privity of contract, since Potter had a right to choose with whom he would deal and could not have another supplier thrust upon him. Modern authorities do not support this result, and hold that, absent provision to the contrary, a duty may be delegated, as distinguished from a right which can be assigned, and that the promisee cannot rescind, if the quality of the performance remains materially the same.

RESTATEMENT OF CONTRACTS § 160 (3) (1932) reads, in part:

> Performance or offer of performance by a person delegated has the same legal effect as performance or offer of performance by the person named in the contract, unless:

> (a) performance by the person delegated varies or would vary materially from performance by the person named in the contract as the one to perform, and there has been no ... assent to the delegation....

In cases involving the sale of goods, the Restatement rule respecting delegation of duties has been amplified by Uniform Commercial Code § 2-210 (5) ... which permits a promisee to demand assurances from the party to whom duties have been delegated. [Citations Omitted.]

As we see it, the delegation of duty by Virginia to Macke was entirely permissible under the terms of the agreements. In so holding, we do not put ourselves at odds with *Eastern Advertising Co. v. McGaw, supra,* 89 Md. 72, for in that case, the agreement with the agency contained a provision that "the advertising cards were to be 'subject to the approval of Eastern Advertising Company as to style and contents,'" which the court found to import that reliance was being placed on the agency's skill, judgment and taste. [Citations omitted.]

Having concluded that the Pizza Shops had no right to rescind the agreements, we turn to the question of damages....

To recover direct profits in a case such as this, the measure of damages is the difference between what it would have cost Macke to perform and what it would have received had the Pizza Shops not repudiated....

We cannot agree with the lower court's conclusion that the claim for damages could not be shown with reasonable certainty because it was based on conjecture. For this reason, we propose to remand the case in order that damages may properly be assessed....

Judgment reversed as to liability; judgment entered for appellant for costs, on appeal and below; case remanded for a new trial on the question of damages.

Exercise 14-6: *Globe* and *Macke* Revisited

1. Do the results reached in *Globe* and *Macke* make sense to you? If so, explain why. If not, why not?

2. Under the common law, contracts could not be assigned. That common law rule has been progressively narrowed. Today, the general rule is that contracts are freely assignable. What is the rationale underlying the shift in rules regarding assignability?

3. What policies does the result in *Globe* promote or undermine?

4. What policies does the result in *Macke* promote or undermine?

5. In *Globe*, Mr. Jones testified about the men in control of Globe, stating that "their reputation was that of wreckers, and that he objected to the character and reputation of the whole concern." How important was that testimony? For example, what would have been the result if Mr. Jones had not testified as quoted, and, instead testified that he just didn't want to work for a new employer?

6. Assume you were the lawyer for Mr. Jones before he entered the general agency contract with Rutgers. Assume Mr. Jones hired you to review the contract and asked you to ensure that, under the contract, he would never have to work for any employer other than Rutgers. Draft a contract provision that would have protected Mr. Jones.

7. In *Macke*, The Pizza Shops argued that they "had dealt with Macke before and had chosen Virginia because they preferred the way it conducted its business." Specifically, they said that "service was more personalized, since the president of Virginia kept the machines in working order, that commissions were paid in cash, and that Virginia permitted them to keep keys to the machines so that minor adjustments could be made when needed." What if The Pizza Shops had expressed an even stronger negative view toward Macke—for example, that they were "wreckers" just as Mr. Jones testified in *Globe*. Would stronger testimony have changed the result in *Macke*?

8. In *Macke*, the court did not regard the contracts between The Pizza Shops and Virginia as ones for personal services and considered the delegation effective. Did the court provide any other explanation for the result it reached?

9. The *Macke* court also notes the general rule that, in the absence of a contrary provision, rights under an executory bilateral contract may be assigned and delegated (with some exceptions). Assume that you were the attorney for The Pizza Shops when they entered the agreements with Virginia. Draft a contract clause you could have insisted upon to protect your clients from the outcome in *Macke*.

10. The Restatement (Second) of Contracts has many sections that refer to assignments and delegations. What types of assignments and delegations are subject to the Restatement's rules?

11. In *Macke*, the court cites section 160 from the Restatement (First) of Contracts, which addressed the delegation of duties. What is the rule in the Restatement (Second) of Contracts regarding when duties are delegable?

12. What is the U.C.C.'s rule about when duties can be delegated in a sales contract?

13. Abigail owes Ben $100. Abigail asks Cindy to pay Ben instead. Is the delegation effective under the common law?

14. Andy contracts to deliver coal to Brad. The type and quality of coal is specified in their agreement. Andy delegates the performance of his duty to Carl. Is the delegation effective?

15. WeBuild, Inc., a general contractor, contracts to build a building for Tower Associates in accordance with detailed specifications. WeBuild delegates the plumbing work to WaterWorks, a plumbing subcontractor. Is the delegation effective?

16. Christine contracts with Radio Corp. to sing three songs over the radio as part of advertisements for three of Radio's advertising clients. Christine delegates her duties to Montego. Is the delegation effective?

17. Mike enters a contract with Doug to have Doug "personally cut the grass on Mike's meadow" for the entire summer for $800. Doug delegates his duty to his son, Jacob. Is the delegation effective?

18. Assume the same facts as in problem 16. When Montego showed up, Christine said, "That's great. I love your voice, Montego." Montego then proceeded to sing the songs. Is the purported delegation effective?

19. What exceptions to the rule of free assignability are contained in the Restatement (Second) of Contracts?

20. Dawn owns a stationary store. She leased a piece of commercial property for her store and, among other things, obtained an insurance policy to insure against any losses arising from a fire on the premises. Assume that Dawn closes her store and sublets her space to a new tenant, Blake, who plans to open a pizza shop. Dawn also assigns her rights under her fire insurance policy to the Blake. Is the assignment effective?

21. Danielle enters an agreement to buy a bedroom suite from Ruth. Their contract contains a provision stating that "the contract may not be assigned." Subsequently, Danielle assigns the contract to Darci. Is the assignment effective?

22. Assume the same facts as in question 21, but the contract provision states, "the parties' rights under the contract are not assignable and any attempted

assignment is void." Subsequently, Danielle assigns the contract to Darci. Is the assignment effective?

Requirements for Effective Assignments and Delegations

Exercise 14-7: *Baker v. Eufaula Concrete Co.*

The next case, *Baker v. Eufaula Concrete Co.,* examines what is necessary for an effective assignment. As you read the case, consider the following points:

1. What are the relevant facts?

2. Identify and diagram the parties' relationships.

3. Identify the non-assignment provision in the Baker-Eufaula lease.

4. What rules does the court state regarding the requirements for effective assignments?

5. Was there an effective assignment?

Baker v. Eufaula Concrete Co.

557 So. 2d 1228 (Ala. 1990)

Jones, Justice. Guy M. Baker appeals from a judgment entered on a directed verdict in favor of Eufaula Concrete Company, Inc., Hugh Stephenson, and Kenneth D. Stephenson (hereinafter collectively referred to as "Eufaula Concrete"). Baker sought a judgment declaring that Eufaula Concrete had wrongfully assigned a lease, entered into between the parties, in violation of its non-assignment provision. He also sought an accounting and money damages for breach of contract and fraud. Because there are triable issues of material fact, we reverse and remand.

In 1980, Baker and his wife, owners of a 30-acre parcel of land, entered into a 10-year written lease with Eufaula Concrete. Pursuant to the lease, Eufaula Concrete was given the right to "mine, process, and remove sand, gravel, and/or field dirt" from the subject land. Eufaula Concrete was obligated to pay Baker $ .25 per cubic yard for the materials removed from the land during the first five years of the lease and $ .35 per cubic yard during the remaining five years of the lease. The following non-assignment clause was also contained in the lease: "The Grantee [Eufaula Concrete] agrees not to assign or sub-let this lease, without the permission of the Grantors [the Bakers]."

Through 1986, Eufaula Concrete mined the property and the Bakers received their royalties in accordance with the provisions of the lease. In 1987, Williams Brothers, Inc., another company in the concrete business, proposed to purchase substantially all of the assets of Eufaula Concrete. Eufaula Concrete was unsuccessful in obtaining the Bakers' consent to an assignment of the lease.

On March 11, 1987, an acquisition agreement was executed between Eufaula Concrete and Williams Brothers, whereby Williams Brothers agreed to purchase the assets and to assume the liabilities of Eufaula Concrete. After the acquisition by Williams Brothers, Mr. Baker noticed that Williams Brothers' equipment and employees were being used to mine the property.

Being unable to determine the status of the lease or who was mining the property, Baker sued Eufaula Concrete, Hugh and Kenneth Stephenson, and Williams Brothers. Baker sought a declaration that Eufaula Concrete had assigned the lease to Williams Brothers in violation of the lease provisions. The case was tried before a jury. At the close of Baker's evidence, the trial court granted Eufaula Concrete's motion for a directed verdict pursuant to Rule 50(a), A.R. Civ. P.[2] Baker appeals.

> The general rule is that, in order to work an assignment of a chose in action, or contract…, there must be an absolute appropriation by the assignor of the debt or fund sought to be assigned to the use of the assignee. The intention of the assignor must be to transfer a present interest in the … subject matter of the contract. If this is done, the transaction is an assignment; otherwise not. It is further held that what amounts to a present appropriation, which constitutes an assignment, is a question of intention to be gathered from all the language, construed in the light of attendant circumstances. Where the transaction is evidenced by a written agreement or stipulation in writing, it depends upon the intention of the parties as manifested in the writing, and construed in the light of such extrinsic circumstances as, under the general rules of law, are admissible in aid of the interpretation of written instrument.

Andalusia Motor Co. v. Mullins, 28 Ala. App. 201, 205, 183 So. 456, 460 (1938). [Further citation omitted.]

Pursuant to the acquisition agreement between Williams Brothers and Eufaula Concrete, Williams Brothers not only purchased the assets of Eufaula Concrete, but also purchased the good will and the name of Eufaula Concrete. The Stephensons executed a non-competition agreement whereby they agreed not to compete with Williams Brothers and Williams Brothers agreed to employ the Stephensons. In regard to the Baker lease, the acquisition agreement listed the lease as an asset to be purchased by Williams Brothers, but Article 2, § 8(b), in pertinent part, provided: "To the extent that any of the … leases … that this Agreement contemplates are to be assigned to the Purchaser [Williams Brothers] are not assignable without the consent of another party, this Agreement shall not constitute an assignment or attempted assignment of such Agreements and Rights if such consent is not obtained." However, in an at-

---

2. It is apparent from the record that the trial court, in directing a verdict in favor of Eufaula Concrete, construed the acquisition agreement between Eufaula Concrete and Williams Brothers as not constituting an assignment in violation of the lease agreement between Eufaula Concrete and Baker; thus, we address only the threshold issue of assignment and not the merits of Baker's separate claims.

tempt to offset the effect of this language, Eufaula Concrete and Williams Brothers provided in § 8(b) of the acquisition agreement as follows:

> If such consent shall not be obtained, the Seller [Eufaula Concrete] and the Principal Shareholder [the Stephensons] agree to cooperate with the Purchaser in implementing any reasonable arrangement designed to provide for the Purchaser the benefits under any such Agreements and Rights, including purchasing under outstanding purchase orders and reselling to the Purchaser at invoice price (without any charge for such service) or exercising rights with respect to the Assets or the Assumed Liabilities (whether under indemnification agreements with parties from whom the Seller acquired such rights or otherwise) so that the Purchaser obtains the benefit of such unassigned item.

After the execution of the acquisition agreement, Williams Brothers began to mine the property and, at the entrance of the property, erected a "no trespassing" sign. Williams Brothers paid Baker the royalties for the month of May (which was the first month that royalties were due for mining done by Williams Brothers), but paid it late. Because Baker expected prompt payment of the royalties at the first of the month, Eufaula Concrete resumed paying Baker the monthly royalty. Hugh Stephenson, in pertinent part, testified:

Q: Will you tell me who paid Mr. Guy M. Baker, Jr., for the ... [May] 1987, royalty.

A: I believe that is the one month that Williams Brothers sent a check direct to the Bakers for the royalties on the property. The check was late getting there. The Bakers—they wanted their money on the 1st and not on the 5th or the 10th, and Eufaula Concrete Company always got it to them at that time. Williams Brothers was somewhere in the neighborhood of two weeks getting their money to them. From that time on we paid them on time, and they reimbursed us for that material that was hauled off of that place.

Furthermore, in regard to payment, Kenneth Stephenson testified as follows:

Q: And who got paid when the material went through the gates?

A: We paid the Bakers for what they had that went through the gate. We paid them thirty-five cents a yard for every yard, whoever was in there removing it.

Q: Did Mr. Couch [an independent hauler] have to pay anybody anything for the privilege of removing the sand, gravel, or fill dirt from the property?

A: Yes, he paid us for it.

Q: He paid—who is us?

A: Eufaula Concrete.

Q: Eufaula Concrete from 4-1-87 to 12-31-87?

A: No, he paid Williams Brothers and Williams Brothers reimbursed us.

Also, driver reports used in accounting for the amount of materials extracted from the Baker property were made on Williams Brothers stationery. Further, Kenneth Stephenson testified:

Q: And did you give Williams Brothers all the benefit of the Lease like the agreement says you are supposed to do?

A: Correct.

Q: And you intentionally did that?

...

A: Yes, we intentionally did that.

After reviewing the evidence of record, we hold that the trial court should have let the case go to the jury. Eufaula Concrete did not demonstrate that there was a lack of a genuine issue of material fact and that it was entitled to a judgment as a matter of law. [Citation Omitted.] We cannot accept, as did the trial judge, Eufaula Concrete's contention that the language of the acquisition agreement (a contract to which Baker was not a party) forecloses all future inquiry on the assignment issue.

There is no requirement that magical words be used to accomplish an assignment, and an assignment may be written, parol, or otherwise. Courts look to substance rather than form. The test, as set forth in *Andalusia Motor Co., supra*, is whether the purported assignor intended to transfer a present interest in the subject matter of the contract. This is a question of fact to be determined under the attendant circumstances.

Although the acquisition agreement stated that it was not to be construed as an assignment of the lease, there was sufficient evidence presented upon which reasonable persons could infer that an assignment had in fact occurred. Indeed, under the totality of the circumstances, we seriously question whether the jury could have reasonably concluded to the contrary. Nonetheless, it is not within our prerogative to judge the weight of the evidence. Because there was ample evidence for the submission of the assignment issue to the jury, the motion for a directed verdict was improperly granted.

The judgment appealed from is due to be, and it hereby is, reversed, and the cause is remanded for a trial on all of the issues.

Reversed and remanded.

Exercise 14-8: Mode of Assignment

1. In *Baker*, the Baker-Eufaula contract contained a provision prohibiting assignment without consent. Why wasn't that clause determinative? What policy rationales were promoted or undermined by the result in this case?

2. Assume you were the attorney for the Bakers and reviewed the Baker-Eufaula contract before it was executed. Draft a clause that would have ensured that Eufaula had neither the right nor the power to assign the contract.

3. Under the RESTATEMENT (SECOND) OF CONTRACTS, what is necessary for an effective assignment?

4. In *Baker*, assume that there was no provision prohibiting assignment without consent and that the acquisition agreement between the William Brothers and Eufaula Concrete provided that "Eufaula hereby conveys its rights in the Baker-Eufaula contract to Williams." Would that clause result in an effective assignment?

5. In *Baker*, assume that the acquisition agreement between William Brothers and Eufaula Concrete provided that "Eufaula plans to convey its rights in the Baker-Eufaula contract to Williams." Would that clause result in an effective assignment?

6. Jeff, of Jeff's Landscaping Services, is owed $4,000 from landscaping services performed for Dawn and Doug. Jeff orally assigns his rights under the contract to Dave. Is there an effective assignment?

7. An effective assignment requires a present intent to transfer a party's interest in a contract to another party. How is intent determined? Who decides what a party's intent was?

8. Digital Outfitters contracts to buy ten model ES computers from Computing, Inc. Subsequently, Digital Outfitters executes an "assignment of rights under the contract" to D & J Associates. Is there an effective assignment or delegation or both?

9. Blake owes Annecy $5,000. Annecy assigns her rights to the $5,000 to her sister, Emmaline, "based on her love and affection for Emmaline." Is there an effective assignment?

Rights and Liabilities of Parties Involved with Assignments and Delegations

Exercise 14-9: *Imperial Refining Co. v. Kanotex Refining Co.*

In this section, you will learn about one final topic regarding assignments and delegations: the rights and liabilities of the parties involved. The next case you will read, *Imperial Refining Co. v. Kanotex Refining Co.*, examines that topic. As you read *Imperial*, consider the following questions:

1. What kind of contract was the original contract between Fern Oil and Imperial?

2. How did Kanotex get involved with the contract?

3. *Imperial* discusses two lawsuits. Who were the parties and what was the cause of action in the first lawsuit?

4. Who were the parties and what was the cause of action in the second lawsuit?

5. Diagram and label the relationships among the three parties.

Imperial Refining Co. v. Kanotex Refining Co.

29 F.2d 193 (8th Cir. 1928)

Booth, Circuit Judge. This is a writ of error to a judgment dismissing a cause, after an order had been entered sustaining a demurrer to the complaint, and after plaintiff had declined to plead further. The questions raised by the demurrer were: (1) Whether the complaint stated facts sufficient to constitute a cause of action; and (2) whether the complaint showed on its face that the alleged cause of action was barred by the statute of limitations of the state of Kansas. Jurisdiction was based on diversity of citizenship and the requisite amount involved.

The complaint alleged in substance as follows: That the plaintiff, Imperial Refining Company, a corporation, had on May 28, 1919, made a written contract with Fern Oil Company, a joint-stock association, whereby plaintiff agreed to purchase from Fern Oil Company and that company agreed to sell to plaintiff for a period of one year commencing June 4, 1919, all of the seven-eighths of the oil produced and saved from a certain oil and gas lease owned by the Fern Oil Company; that on the same day plaintiff assigned the contract and all its rights thereunder to the defendant herein, the Kanotex Refining Company, by written instrument duly signed by plaintiff, and duly accepted in writing by the Kanotex Company; that at the time when the contract and the assignment were made the Fern Oil Company was operating and developing the leased premises for oil and gas, and did thereafter obtain oil in paying quantities on the premises; that, after the assignment was made, defendant, acting under it and under the rights conferred by the contract, caused pipe line connections to be made to the leased premises, and made all necessary preparations to run and take the oil which was being produced at the time from the premises; that defendant, after making the pipe line connections, refused to run the oil then being produced; that as a result of the actions of defendant in making the pipe line connections, and then refusing to run the oil, the Fern Oil Company and its assignees sustained damages; that thereafter the Fern Oil Company and its assignees commenced suit in the state court of Oklahoma against plaintiff as the original promisor to recover damages for breach of the contract; that plaintiff herein immediately notified defendant herein of the suit brought by the Fern Oil Company and requested defendant to defend the same; that, though defendant did not employ counsel to defend the suit, yet it did advise with plaintiff relative thereto, and furnished certain of its employees as witnesses at the trial, and its counsel was present at the trial; that plaintiff herein defended the suit with diligence, but nevertheless judgment was obtained against it in the amount of $18,000; that plaintiff promptly notified defendant herein of the judgment and preserved the right to appeal, and notified defendant that it did not desire to appeal, but that, if defendant desired to appeal, plaintiff would cooperate, and that plaintiff expected defendant to protect it against the judgment obtained; that defendant disregarded the notice sent by plaintiff, and took no steps to perfect an appeal; that plaintiff has paid and satisfied the judgment, and has paid the attorney's fees and costs incident to the suit; that by reason of the fact that defendant was the assignee of the contract with the Fern Oil Company, and succeeded to plaintiff's rights and obligations under the same, and by reason of the acts of defendant heretofore recited, plaintiff is entitled to recover from defendant the amount of the judgment, attorney's fees, and costs paid by plaintiff as before stated. Attached to the complaint as exhibits were copies of the contract with the Fern Oil Company, of the assignment to the defendant and of the journal entry of the judgment obtained against plaintiff in the state court.

One of the points raised by the demurrer to the complaint was that the contract with the Fern Oil Company was invalid, because of indefiniteness of description of the leased premises.... We think there is no merit in this point of the demurrer.

The next point of the demurrer is that the contract with the Fern Oil Company was void for lack of mutuality, and that, since the contract was void, no obligation in reference to it were assumed by the Kanotex Company. It may be conceded that, unless the contract between the Imperial Company and the Fern Company was valid, no duty in reference thereto rested on the Kanotex Company under the assignment. Two questions therefore arise: (1) Was the contract with the Fern Company invalid for lack of mutuality? (2) Was the Kanotex Company under any obligation to the Imperial Company to carry out the contract?

As to the first question, it is claimed that by the terms of the contract the Fern Company was not bound to sell any oil to the Imperial Company; that in this respect the contract was subject wholly to the wish or whim of the Fern Company. The language of the contract is as follows:

> ... The Seller [the Fern Company] hereby offers and agrees to sell and deliver to the 'Company' [the Imperial Company] his, or their seven-eighths (7 / 8ths) part of all oil produced and saved from wells No. 1, and up on the following described property, ... for the period beginning 7 a.m. June 4th, 1919, and ending 7 a.m. June 4th, 1920. And the Company hereby agrees to accept and purchase said oil subject to the following conditions:

> 7. The Seller and Company further agree that this contract shall be in force and effect for the full term hereof and be binding on their successors, assigns, heirs or administrators.

We construe this language to mean that, if any oil was produced on the land in question and during the period named, the Fern Oil Company was bound to sell and deliver it to the Imperial Company. While no exact number of gallons is specified, yet all of the output belonging to the Fern Company during the named period is covered, and the Fern Company disqualifies itself to sell to any one else than the Imperial Company or its assigns. The books are full of cases involving questions relating to the mutuality of contracts....

In the case at bar, while the complaint does not allege that the Fern Company had producing wells on the premises described at the time of making the contract, yet the complaint does allege that the Fern Company owned the oil lease on the premises and was operating and developing the same to produce oil, and thereafter did produce oil in paying quantities. By the contract the Fern Company promised to sell and the Imperial Company promised to buy the oil produced. The price was fixed; the duration of the contract was fixed; the amount of oil was fixed by the output. We are clearly of the opinion that ... the contract involved did not lack mutuality and was valid....

By previous language in the contract, as we have already seen, the Imperial Company bound itself to purchase all of the output belonging to the Fern Company during the period named....

The next question is: Was the defendant Kanotex Company under any obligation to the Imperial Company to carry out the provisions of the Fern Oil Company contract, by reason of the assignment of that contract to defendant by the Imperial Company? It is a general rule that the right of one party to a contract to its performance by the other may be assigned, absent any provision to the contrary in the contract or by statute, and excepting contracts involving relations of personal confidence or calling for personal services. 5 C.J. pp. 874–82, §§ 44–47. The contract in the case at bar did not forbid an assignment, and no statute is pointed out having such effect; nor did the contract fall within the excepted classes. That it was the intention of the parties to the assignment that the original contract should be carried out is apparent from the terms of the assignment. It provides:

> It is understood and agreed that a part of this consideration is that the said Kan-O-Tex Refining Co. will mail its check to the said Imperial Refining Co., at its office in Fort Worth, Texas, on the lst of each month for an amount equal to 10 cts. per barrel for each and every barrel of crude oil taken from the lease belonging to the Fern Oil Co. in block 84. The said Kan-O-Tex Co. agrees to connect their pipe lines to two five hundred barrel steel tanks and one sixteen hundred barrel wood tank, said tanks being on the lease of the Fern Oil, by Tuesday night, June 3d, 1919. This transfer and assignment is made subject to the contract made and entered into the 28th day of May, 1919, by and between Imperial Refining Co. and the Fern Oil Co.

By this assignment from the Imperial Company to the Kanotex Company, the latter company acquired the right of the Imperial Company in the contract. This is conceded. But this was not the only effect of the assignment. The Imperial Company by the assignment not only transferred its rights in the contract, but it also delegated its duties, and the Kanotex Company by accepting the assignment accepted the delegation of the duties. It accepted the burdens with the benefits. As between the Imperial Company and the Kanotex Company, a primary duty rested upon the latter company to perform the contract, and the Imperial Company stood toward the Kanotex Company in the nature of a surety for the performance of the contract. We think the weight of authority sustains these views.

In 5 C.J. 976, it is said: "As between the assignee and the assignor, the assignee is bound to carry out the provisions of the assigned contract and in all respects to comply with the terms of the assignment, and the assignor may recover from him the damages he sustained by reason of the failure of the assignee to comply with the contract."

In *Cutting Packing Co. v. Packers' Exchange,* 86 Cal. 574, 25 P. 52, the Cutting Company had contracted with one Blackwood to purchase from him certain apricots. [Parallel citation omitted.] The Cutting Company assigned its interest in the contract to Packers' Exchange. Blackwood refused to accept the Packers' Exchange in place of the Cutting Company, but delivered the apricots to the Cutting Company, according to the contract. The Cutting Company received the apricots and paid for them, and tendered them to the Packers' Exchange; but the latter refused to accept them. Thereupon the Cutting Company sold them to the best advantage, but sustained a loss, for which it sued Packers' Exchange. It was held that the original contract was assignable; that the assignment did not relieve the Cutting Company from its obligation to Blackwood; that the refusal of Blackwood did not relieve Packers' Exchange from its obligation to the Cutting Company under the assignment. The court in its opinion said:

> So far as the parties to this suit are concerned, the appellant [Packers' Exchange] contracted with the respondent [the Cutting Company] to accept and pay for the fruit Blackwood had contracted to deliver to the latter. It could make no difference, therefore, whether the fruit was delivered to the appellant by Blackwood directly or by the respondent. As between the parties to this suit, the appellant was bound to receive and accept the fruit, and it cannot relieve itself from this obligation by showing that Blackwood had refused to relieve the respondent from its obligation to him.... We therefore think it plain that as the plaintiff, as assignor, was still bound to Blackwood to pay the price stipulated in the contract, notwithstanding the assignment, and as the defendant, as assignee, assumed such obligation, the plaintiff, as between it and the defendant, stood in the nature of a surety for the latter for the performance of the obligation. If this be correct, it then follows that from the assignment an implied contract arose between the plaintiff and defendant, whereby the latter became bound to the former to receive and pay for the apricots, according to the terms of the original contract....

From the foregoing discussion, we think it is plain that there was a duty under the Fern Oil Company contract on the part of the Imperial Company toward the Fern Company to carry out the terms of that contract, and that it is equally plain that there was also a duty, under the assignment of that contract, on the part of the Kanotex Company toward the Imperial Company to carry out the terms of the same contract. The allegations of the complaint are that the terms of the contract were not carried out. The default was by the Kanotex Company. The Imperial Company thus became liable to the Fern Company, and in turn the Kanotex Company became liable to the Imperial Company. The Imperial Company was sued by the Fern Company. Its liability under the contract was established; judgment was obtained against it, and it paid the judgment. Notice of the suit was given by the Imperial Company to the Kanotex Company, and demand was made that the latter company come in and defend. Under these circumstances we think that the Kanotex Company is bound by the judgment obtained against the Imperial Company.

In *Washington Gas Light Co. v. District of Columbia*, 161 U.S. 316, 16 S. Ct. 564, 40 L. Ed. 712, the court quoted with approval from the opinion of the court in *Littleton v. Richardson*, 34 N.H. 179, 187, 66 Am. Dec. 759, as follows:

> When a person is responsible over to another, either by operation of law or by express contract, and he is duly notified of the pendency of the suit, and requested to take upon him the defense of it, he is no longer regarded as a stranger, because he has the right to appear and defend the action, and has the same means and advantages of con-

troverting the claim as if he were the real and nominal party upon the record. In every such case, if due notice is given to such person, the judgment, if obtained without fraud or collusion, will be conclusive against him, whether he has appeared or not....

There remains for consideration the question of the statute of limitations. The applicable statute is section 60-306, Revised Statutes of Kansas (1923).... It is conceded by plaintiff in error that the three-year and not the five-year provision applies.

The present suit was started at least as early as November 16, 1926. When did the cause of action arise? Defendant in error contends that it arose when the Kanotex Company failed to carry out the terms of the Fern Oil Company contract, which was at least prior to February 28, 1920. If this contention is correct, then the cause of action was plainly barred. Plaintiff in error contends that the cause of action arose when it was compelled to pay the judgment which the Fern Oil Company obtained, or at least not earlier than the date when the judgment was entered, which was April 20, 1925. If this contention prevails, the cause of action was not barred.

We think the latter contention is the correct one. The cause of action of the Imperial Company against the Kanotex Company, set out in the complaint, was not primarily for breach of contract, nor for injury to property rights, but was for reimbursement of moneys which the Imperial Company had been compelled to pay or had become liable to pay because of the default of the Kanotex Company. As between the Imperial Company and the Kanotex Company, as above stated, the primary liability to perform the contract rested on the Kanotex Company. The liability of the Imperial Company was secondary. The latter company having been forced to respond in damages for the breach of the contract, it could recover from the Kanotex Company on the broad equitable principles of indebitatus assumpsit, the amount so paid. The right to sue for this reimbursement did not arise until the payment had been made by the Imperial Company, or at least not until the liability of that company to pay the money had been determined by entry of judgment against it. [Citations omitted.]

Our conclusion is that the sustaining of the demurrer to the complaint and the entering of judgment dismissing the cause constituted error, and that the judgment should be reversed. It is so ordered.

Exercise 14-10: *Imperial Refining* Revisited

1. On what basis was Imperial held liable to Fern Oil after the contract was assigned and Kanotex became the obligor?

2. On what basis was Kanotex liable to Imperial?

3. Could Fern Oil have short-circuited the process and sued Kanotex directly?

4. After the assignment, would Fern Oil have had the right to refuse to accept performance from Kanotex?

Exercise 14-11: Rights and Liabilities

1. Able is under a contract to build a house for Blake for $10,000. Able assigns his rights under the contract to Chad, who agrees to assume Able's duty to build the house. Blake is informed of the assignment and assumption, and makes no objection. Chad builds half of the house, and then quits. Does Blake have any rights against Able?

2. Assume that in problem 1, Able withdraws from the construction business and informs Blake that he will not take any further responsibility for Chad's performance. Blake makes no objection and Chad proceeds to build the house. After Chad is three-fourths of the way finished with the house, he never shows up again and does not finish the house. Does Blake have any rights against Able?

3. When an assignment is made, what warranties does an assignor make to an assignee?

4. Alexis has a right to $1,000, which is owed to her by Brittany. Alexis assigns her right, for value, to Cindy. Thereafter, Alexis gives Brittany a release. Does Cindy have any rights against Alexis?

5. In problem 4, assume instead that Brittany repudiated the contract with Alexis without any excuse. Thereafter, Alexis assigned her right to Cindy for value without disclosing Brittany's repudiation. Does Cindy have any rights against Alexis?

6. Arnie reasonably, and in good faith, believes he has a right to collect $1,000 from Barb. Arnie assigns the right, as an actual right, to Cameron for value. In fact, Arnie's right does not exist. Does Cameron have any rights against Arnie?

7. Ann believes that there is only a slight possibility that she may have a right against Bradley. Ann assigns to Chris, for value, "any claim or right which I may have against Bradley." When doing so, Ann does not disclose how seriously she doubts the validity of the claim. Ann's claim turns out to be invalid. Does Chris have any rights against Ann?

8. Annie has a right to a payment of $1,000 from Beatrice. Subsequently, Annie assigns her right, for value, to Christine. Annie then tells Christine, "I am hereby revoking my assignment." Does Christine have any rights as an assignee?

9. Annie has a right to a payment of $1,000 from Beatrice. Annie orally assigns her right to Christine as a gift. Subsequently, Annie also assigns the right to Dawn, who gives value but knows of the assignment to Christine. To whom does Beatrice owe the $1,000?

10. Assume the same facts as in question 9, except Annie assigned her right to Christine for consideration. To whom does Beatrice owe the $1,000?

Novations

Novation is the third major issue listed under "Third-Party Issues" in Diagram 14-1. The basic situation presented by a novation involves two parties who make a contract. Subsequently, one party seeks to transfer her responsibilities under the contract to a new party and the other party to the contract consents to release the original party to the contract.

Exercise 14-12: Novations

1. What is a "novation" and what is its effect under the RESTATEMENT (SEC-OND) OF CONTRACTS?

2. Annecy owes Ben $10,000. Ben promises Annecy that he will discharge Annecy's debt immediately if Cameron will promise Ben to pay Ben $10,000. Cameron promises to pay Ben the $10,000. Is there an effective novation?

3. Assume the same situation as in problem 2, except Ben promises Cameron that he will discharge Annecy's debt immediately if Cameron promises to pay Ben the $10,000. Cameron promises to pay Ben the $10,000, intending to benefit Annecy. Is there an effective novation?

4. Again, assume that Annecy owes Ben $10,000. Annecy asks Ben if he will discharge her from the debt if Cameron promises to pay the debt. Ben says that he will think about it. Cameron then promises both Annecy and Ben that she will pay Ben the $10,000. Is there an effective novation?

5. Dave owns a bike store, which sells and services a broad range of bikes and exercise equipment. Mike owns a health club. Dave and Mike enter a contract in which Dave promises to service all the machines in Mike's health club monthly for one year. Dave sells part of his business to Riley, who promises Dave that he will assume Dave's service contract with Mike if Mike promises to accept service from Riley immediately and in substitution for Dave's duty. Mike promises Dave he will do so. Is there an effective novation?

6. Andy owes Beatrice $1,000. Beatrice promises Andy that she will discharge the debt immediately if Andy promises Cindy to weed, fertilize, mulch, and water Cindy's landscaping. Andy promises to perform those services to Cindy. Is there an effective novation?

7. Blake owes Jacob $1,000. Blake convinces Megan to pay the debt to Jacob instead.

    a. Assume that Jacob is fine accepting payment from Megan, but wants to ensure that Blake also remains liable on the debt. As the attorney for Jacob, draft a contract clause that will ensure that Jacob can recover from either Blake or Megan.

    b. Assume that Jacob is happy to accept Megan as the new obligor because Jacob knows that Blake doesn't have the assets necessary to repay him. As the attorney for Blake, draft a contract clause that ensures that Blake will no longer be liable for the debt and that Jacob can only recover from Megan.

Chapter Problems Revisited

You should now know enough to complete Exercises 14-1 and 14-2 presented at the beginning of this chapter.

Professional Development Reflection Questions

1. As you might imagine, "happiness" is a scientifically unwieldy term. Researchers who study "happiness" break the concept down into more specific constructs. In the area of positive psychology, psychologists conceptually parse "happiness" into three constructs: (1) the pleasant life (maximizing positive emotions and minimizing negative emotions); (2) the engaged life (using your strengths in activities that are engaging); and (3) the meaningful life (using your strengths to serve something larger than yourself such as legal education, your community, or our free society). Is the way positive psychologists think about happiness consistent with your own personal definition of happiness?

2. When positive psychologists refer to your "strengths," they are frequently referring to the "Classification of Strengths" developed by Peterson and Seligman. Take a half hour to complete the Values-in-Action Inventory of Strengths to identify your five greatest strengths. There are many web sites where the public can take the Values-in-Action Inventory for free. (For example, try accessing www.viacharacter.org or www.authentichappiness.sas.upenn.edu/questionnaires.aspx.)

3. Once you have identified your five greatest strengths, take a few minutes to consider how you can use your strengths more frequently in the main domains of your life (at school, at work, in your relationships, and at home). Finding new ways to use your strengths in the main domains of your life is another strategy which has been scientifically demonstrated to increase levels of happiness.

4. Imagine you are an attorney representing a party to a contract who is deciding whether to agree to a novation or to insist on full performance of the original contract. What factors will you advise your client to consider before agreeing to the novation?

PART EIGHT

CONTRACT LAW PROBLEMS

*How do contract lawyers use contract law
to analyze and solve client problems?*

Chapter 15

Contract Law Problem-Solving

Our final topic of study is contracts problem-solving. Because this chapter is so different from all of the previous chapters in this book and because it also is the most ambitious chapter in the book in terms of what we hope you will learn, it is helpful to start by considering what we hope you will learn in this chapter.

Explanation of Objectives

This chapter really has two purposes: (1) to assist you in synthesizing what you have learned about contract law and prepare you to analyze contract law-specific problems (the types of problems you are likely to encounter on your contracts final examination), and (2) to continue your preparation for the practice of contract law by introducing you to the types of considerations and problems you might encounter as a practicing contracts lawyer. In other words, this chapter is designed to facilitate your efforts to transfer (apply) what you have learned in the context of your prior study of the various individual doctrinal categories (*e.g.*, damages, conditions, etc.) to solve two types of problems:

1. The narrow, highly structured problems fitting squarely within the contract law discipline (you might think of this goal as "near transfer"), and

2. The broad, unstructured, unlabeled problems characteristic of law practice (you might think of this goal as "far transfer").

Overview of Chapter 15

This chapter begins by assisting you in your efforts to synthesize and remember all the contract law you have learned. You will then learn how to combine all the concepts to solve contract-specific problems and have the opportunity to practice your skills in doing so in connection with a number of practice questions. Having learned how to analyze contracts-specific problems, you will then have the opportunity to begin developing your skill in handling multi-disciplinary problems that require you not only to know and understand contract law but also to know and understand other bodies of law you have been studying during your first year of law school. These problems also require you to know and consider your client's interests and objectives.

Analyzing Contracts-Specific Problems

Syntheses of Contract Law

Exercise 15-1: Synthesis Exercises

1. Prepare a one-page substantive law summary sheet on which you include broad references to all the contract law concepts you have learned. You cannot use the back of the page or a second page.

2. Prepare five questions regarding one, some, or all of the following topics: (1) issue spotting with respect to **specific** issues, (2) what you need to know about the content **of specific** rules we have studied, (3) application of **specific** rules we have studied, (4) how **specific** areas of law (*e.g.*, remedies and formation, remedies and contract performance, parol evidence and contract performance) may be combined in an examination question, (5) exam approaches with respect to broad areas of law (*e.g.*, contract meaning, contract formation) or with respect to narrower issues (*e.g.*, frustration of purpose, substantial performance, degree of integration).

3. According to experts in how humans learn, human beings store knowledge in organized structures. This theory explains why using organizational strategies, such as outlining or creating graphic organizers, help you remember knowledge. Experts in learning also explain that the more mental paths you have to a piece of knowledge, the more likely you are to recall it when you need it. For example, you might recall the name of a novel because you enjoyed it a lot so it's among your list of favorites, but you would be more likely to recall the name of the novel if you also mentally associated the novel with its author, genre (*e.g.*, historical novel or western) and publication era (*e.g.*, recent or the 1950s). Just as having multiple ways of getting to work helps you get to work on time on those days when your favorite route is blocked, having multiple mental paths helps you recall knowledge when you are mentally blocked.

    So far, your study of contract law, as reflected in the "Contract Law Graphic Organizer," has mostly been a cradle-to-grave subject in which we have asked you to consider each topic in isolation (for example, contract defenses). On a few occasions, we also have asked you to consider a topic in the context of its direct relationship to a closely related topic (for example, the parol evidence rule and interpretation). This exercise will ask you to re-organize a significant chunk of what you have learned in contract law.

    The practice of contract law, as you have learned, frequently involves language interpretation. In other words, you have developed the skill of identifying ambiguous language and using interpretive tools to resolve such ambiguities. For example, in connection with contract formation, you have learned to identify ambiguities in parties' formation communications and resolve such ambiguities. As a second example, you have learned that a large body of contract law is contained in the Uniform Commercial Code; the U.C.C., which like any set of statutes, is subject to interpretation.

    Diagram 15-1 (on the next page), the Contract Interpretation Hierarchy Chart, depicts graphically the relationships among all the types of contrac-

Diagram 15-1: Contract Law Graphic Organizer

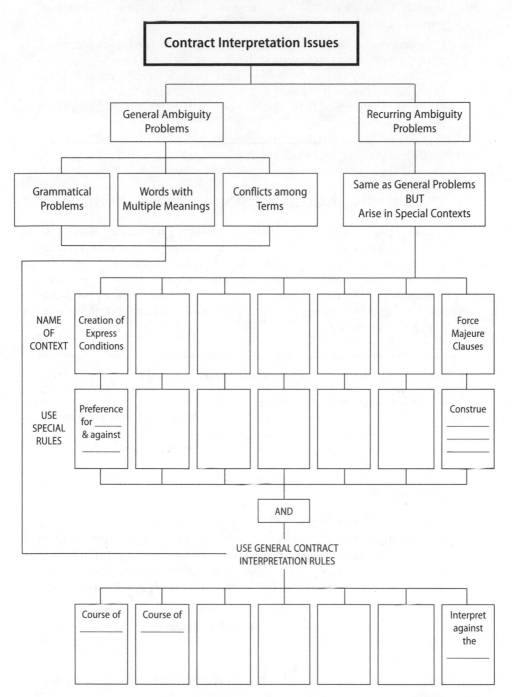

tual ambiguities we have studied and the rules courts use to resolve those ambiguities. Complete this chart; to assist your efforts, we have completed a small portion of the chart.

4. Now that you have reorganized your learning under the topic of language interpretation, see if you can come up with another broad topic within which you can fit many of the concepts we have learned. Keep in mind that the mental effort involved in doing this reorganization is at least as important if not more important than whether your particular reorganization effort is an optimal one.

Analysis of Contracts-Specific Problems

Below are suggested approaches to analyzing contract performance issues and contract interpretation issues. First, Table 15-1 depicts ten steps you might take in analyzing contract performance questions. Table 15-2 then depicts eleven steps you might take in identifying and resolving contract ambiguities. Afterwards, to assist you in developing your skills in applying these approaches to exam-like problems, we have provided a sample exam problem and an in-depth description of how we would think about and write our analysis of the hypothetical.

Table 15-1: Analyzing Contract Performance Essay Exam Questions

Note: The list below assumes you have already done any necessary formation, contract defenses, parol evidence rule and contract interpretation analyses and that you will analyze any remedial issues afterward. Nearly all exam questions will require you to skip some of these steps so please do not try to use all of these steps on all exam questions. IF YOU TRIED TO IMPLEMENT ALL OF THESE STEPS ON EVERY CONTRACT PERFORMANCE QUESTION, YOU WOULD NOT FINISH YOUR EXAM.

1. Create a "contract obligations map" to show the parties' obligations.

2. Identify, if possible, a party who did not perform at all, but rather refused to perform when her time to perform arrived or who anticipatorily repudiated. Explain that such party's conduct would be a breach unless the breach were to be excused. If you cannot identify any such party or both parties refused to perform, skip to step 4.

3. Identify all possible excuses for the breach you identified in response to the previous question. One likely excuse will be non-occurrence of a prior condition.

4. Analyze all the excuses you identified in response to the previous question except non-occurrence of a prior condition.

5. Identify and then analyze the existence of all possible express conditions.

6. Determine whether any such express conditions have occurred.

7. Identify and then analyze any excuses for the non-occurrence of any express conditions.

8. Determine the order of performance of all remaining promises using the constructive condition rules.

9. Determine whether all constructive conditions occurred. In other words, determine whether any party who breached the contract materially breached. Use substantial performance factors and then weigh them. Do not do a substantial performance analysis in all instances. You are wasting your time if you are analyzing whether a party who did not perform at all materially breached; of course, that party materially breached.

10. Identify and analyze all possible grounds for discharge and excuses.

Table 15-2: Analyzing Contract Interpretation Issues

1. Look at the call of the question to see if it directly raises a general interpretation issue or if it raises one of the recurring contract interpretation issues (express conditions; divisibility; creation of third party beneficiaries; application of *force majeure* clauses; contractual prohibitions of assignment or delegation; interpreting whether a party has delegated duties, assigned rights or done both; contractual assignments of risk of unforeseen events).

2. Create a "contract obligations map" to show the parties' obligations.

3. Look for facts giving rise to each of the recurring contract interpretation issues.

4. Look in the facts for what caused the parties to get into a dispute, *i.e.*, where in the fact pattern did the parties' relationship break down.

5. Find which word or words in the contract constitute the basis for either party's contention or for both parties' contentions.

6. Jot down the first definition that occurs to you for the word or words involved and then brainstorm and jot down alternative definitions. Assume the issue is either a minor one or that there must be a language basis for the parties' actions.

7. Develop a hypothesis as to why each contract term was included in the fact pattern.

8. Recall the rules specific to each of the recurring interpretation issues in the problem and search for facts relevant to each one.

9. Recall the general rules of contract interpretation and search for facts relevant to each rule.

10. Weigh the application of the various rules against each other.

"Think Aloud" Demonstration

Students often struggle with contract interpretation and contract performance issues. Because these issues so pervade contracts law as it is practiced and tested, below you will find a hypothetical and a "think aloud" analysis of that hypothetical for which one of us explicitly "talks through" (writes out) how he would read through the hypothetical, identify issues, and plan an analysis/exam answer. A "think aloud" is an effort by an expert in a field to articulate all of the thoughts, ideas, and hypotheses the expert has as he or she reads through and analyzes a problem (including all the thoughts, ideas, and hypotheses the expert rejected). The problem is in Exercise 15-2, and the "think aloud" appears in Exercise 15-3.

Exercise 15-2: Sample Problem — *Bob v. Felicia*

Felicia and Bob, whom Felicia knew was a land speculator, entered into a valid and enforceable, written contract for the purchase by Bob of Felicia's land for $100,000. The contract required Bob to pay $10,000 on closing and to pay the remainder plus 8% interest per year in equal monthly installments over a ten-year period. To secure Bob's duty to pay, Bob agreed to give Felicia a deed of trust. In describing Felicia's duties under the contract, the contract, which Felicia prepared, contained the following three clauses, among others:

...

3. Felicia's duty to sell is expressly conditioned on Bob demonstrating to the satisfaction of an accountant designated by Felicia that Bob has the ability to make the required payments.

4. Felicia must sell the land to Bob, with the restriction that Bob pay Felicia the down payment and Bob spend one day trying to help Felicia find a new home.

5. Bob expressly represents that he has been employed by IBM for the past twenty years.

Assume the parties have stipulated that Bob satisfactorily demonstrated to Felicia's designated accountant that Bob had the ability to make the monthly payments and that Bob paid the $10,000 on closing, but Bob repeatedly refused to help Felicia find a new home. Also assume that (i) Felicia refused to sell her land, (ii) the fair market value of the land at the time Felicia refused to perform was $90,000, (iii) Bob sued Felicia for breach of contract, and (iv) Bob had made an undisclosed contract to resell the land to Adam, a client of Bob's, for $110,000, and that, after Felicia refused to perform, Bob made no effort to find substitute land for Adam to buy, but, instead, agreed to pay Adam $5,000 because he did not want to take any chance that Adam might get mad and no longer wish to continue being Bob's client.

Question 1: Is Felicia liable to Bob for breach of contract?

Question 2: Assume, for the purposes of this question only, that Felicia did breach the contract. Analyze Bob's remedies.

Exercise 15-3: Think-Aloud Analysis of *Bob v. Felicia* Problem

Introductory Note:

A "think aloud" analysis, unlike a model answer, includes the author's thinking process in evaluating the question and preparing a written analysis. In the context of real problems, many of the mental steps described below occur almost automatically, without much conscious thought. **Thus, keep in mind the importance of developing for yourself a high level of automaticity in your knowl-**

edge of the material in this course (and any other law school course for that matter) and of how to perform good legal analysis. This "think aloud" uses a convention of distinguishing thinking process points from the written answer by placing the former in *italic* font. Try to answer the question yourself before reading the think aloud below.

Think Aloud:

In looking over the problem, I notice a few things right away. The call of the first issue provides a hint as to the nature of the dispute. Obviously, Bob is claiming Felicia breached a contract with Bob. The facts also state Felicia "refused to sell her land." I therefore recall and note that Bob will win his lawsuit, unless Felicia can show she and Bob did not form a contract, that she has a contract defense or that she has an excuse for not performing.

I note the second issue expressly raises remedies issue(s). I quickly recall the three basic remedies for breach of contract: damages, restitution and specific performance and make a mental note to look for facts relevant to each as I review the facts.

I begin to look over the facts. The first sentence tells me the dispute is not a contract formation dispute because the facts state the parties "entered into a ... contract," and the contract is described as "valid and enforceable." I therefore conclude the issue in question 1 is a contract defense, a contract interpretation and/or a contract performance issue. I notice the facts tell me Felicia prepared the contract and recall the contra proferentem *doctrine and that such a fact would be relevant only if the facts raise a contract interpretation issue.*

I also note that the contract is for the sale of land and quickly recall the fact that courts universally conclude that land is unique and therefore it will be easy to establish that the remedy at law is inadequate.

I notice the facts include an excerpt from the parties' contract. I know the language doesn't raise a formation issue because I have determined the facts state the parties formed a valid contract. The inclusion of quoted contract language makes it seem even more likely the question involves a performance issue, an interpretation issue or both. I also notice the question gives me no information about the parties' negotiations, making a contract formation defense issue or a parol evidence rule issue unlikely. I also notice the reference to the contract being written and for the sale of land, suggesting the author did not want me to consider any statute of frauds defense. I am becoming convinced the issue is either a performance issue or an interpretation issue.

I begin to read with more focus. As I read the description of the contract, I create the following "contract map" on my scratch paper:

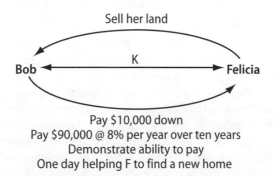

I notice the phrase "expressly conditioned" with respect to contract clause number 3, circle it, and then write "EC" above it immediately to remind myself that this clause likely creates an express condition. I tell myself that I should study the facts below to make sure that this condition occurred exactly as stated because I recall that express conditions must occur exactly as stated in the parties' contract.

As I read contract clause #4, I am drawn to the phrase "with the restriction that." I notice how similar the phrase "with the restriction that" is to the phrase "on the condition that." I therefore circle the words and write "EC?" above them to signal to myself that there might be an express condition issue here. At this point, I have a strong suspicion that at least one issue will be whether clause #4 creates an express condition.

Contract clause #5 appears to be a simple express representation going to Bob's creditworthiness. The inclusion of this fact raises the possibility of a misrepresentation defense; I will look for facts indicating this representation was not true at the time Bob made it.

I read the next paragraph, noting that it reports Bob's perfect performance with respect to clause #3. I therefore dismiss in my mind the possibility that the issue here revolves around clause #3 and become even more convinced the issue revolves around clause #4. I then confirm my suspicion when I read that Bob refused to help Felicia find a new home. I become convinced the issue is a creation of express condition issue because, in addition to the language point made above, I have noted that Bob only agreed to help Felicia for one day. I recall that, if clause #4 is not an express condition, it must be a promise and may be a constructive condition and the standard for performance of constructive conditions is "substantial performance." I feel confident that all courts would conclude that Bob's overall contract performance would be deemed "substantial" because Bob's failure to honor a one-day obligation is coupled with perfect performance of all of Bob's other obligations. Thus, Felicia's only hope of prevailing is to show that clause #4 is an express condition such that Bob's failure to help caused the non-occurrence of an express condition and therefore excused Felicia's performance.

Now that I know there is an issue as to whether #4 is an express condition, I know I must interpret the phrase "with the restriction that." I therefore draw two lines from my "EC?" at the end of which I plan to write possible interpretations. I then try to brainstorm competing definitions of the word "restriction." Because the words reminded me of words of express condition, I first try to generate a definition that makes the clause seem more like an express condition. I write down "limit." I also write down, on the other line, the other definition that immediately occurred to me, "requirement." I mentally note I will need more thinking work here later and I go on.

I note the remainder of the facts provide information regarding Bob's alleged losses. Thus, I note that Bob did make the $10,000 payment and write "restitution?" and "essential reliance" above that statement in the facts. I also note Bob's planned resale and write "consequential" above the facts that reference Bob's anticipation of a $10,000 profit on the resale. I also note that the resale is described as "undisclosed." Whenever I see a reference to a failure to disclose, I think of an affirmative claim for non-disclosure or of foreseeability re damages. Here, I zero in on foreseeability given the second call of the question referencing damages and the absence of any requirement that a party disclose their plans for using the contract consideration, or any other basis for requiring Bob to disclose his plans to Felicia. I then look for other facts relevant to whether Felicia could have known about Bob's resale. First, I note the fact that the fair market value was $90,000 and the contract price was $100,000. This fact suggests Felicia would not have guessed Bob could have made such a profitable resale because Felicia was already making $10,000 on the deal. I therefore write "foreseeability when buyer already paying more than FMV?" over the $90,000 in the facts. I also then recall that this fact also means Bob's general damages would be zero and write "losing K" over the $90,000. In addition, I note that Felicia knows Bob is a "land speculator" and ask myself whether knowing the other party is a land speculator would allow you to anticipate a resale at $20,000 over market price and $10,000 over the contract price. I write "foreseeability?" over the words referring to Felicia knowing Bob was a land speculator. Finally, I note a reference to Bob's failure to look for a replacement property and his quick settlement with Adam (for business purposes). Both facts strike me as relating to the question of actions Bob possibly could have taken to minimize his losses and therefore strike me as avoidability facts. I therefore write "avoidability" over both facts.

Finally, I see no facts indicating Bob lied when he represented that he had been employed by IBM for 20 years; I have decided the clause is irrelevant. I am fairly confident now that the only issue in question 1 is whether clause #4 is an express condition. The one question in my mind is why clause #3 was included. I recall my certainty that clause #3 creates an express condition and the rule that a contract generally should be interpreted to be consistent with itself. I write "clear EC — compare clause #4 to clause #3."

I re-read the facts one more time to make sure there aren't any contract defenses or any additional contract performance facts. There aren't any, so I jot down an outline of my answer.

My outline looks like this:

I. Question 1: Breach by F?
   A. No formation or defenses issues.
   B. Breach unless excused. — Non-o of prior cond. as excuse
      1. No CC issues
      2. EC in contract?
         a) #3 (yes) but occurred
         b) #4?
            (1) Pro-EC interp. — "limit"
            (2) Con-EC interp. — "requirement"
            (3) Specific interp. rule — pref. for prom.
            (4) General interp. rules:
               (a) Make consistent — #3
               (b) Felicia drafted — contra proferentem
            (5) Reconcile principles and conflict in interpretation
      3. Occur
         a) #3 occurred
         b) #4 d/n occur
II. Question 2:
   A. Damages to B
      1. Generals (none b/c losing K)
      2. Specials
         a) Downpayment ($10k)
         b) $5k settlement to Adam

   c) Consequential (lost resale to Adam)
  B. Rest. ($10k down)
  C. Specific perf.
   1. Inadequacy (land)
   2. Discretionary factors (no facts)

I realize at this point in my outline that I saw no facts that raised any of the discretionary factors in my mind. I therefore run through the factors in my head and compare the facts to those factors on a checklist basis (undue burden on the D [no facts I can see], undue burden on the court [I think this is a one-time transaction where there are no personal relations at all so easy to administer]), public policy [I recall I can always argue a public policy of enforcing contracts to move property from one who desired it less to one who desired it more but see nothing else], and adequacy of consideration [deal does not appear overly one-sided]. I therefore would only add public policy to the discretionary factors in II.C.2 I plan to discuss.

Finally, I realize I did not check that no other excuses were present, so I run through my mental list of excuses to make sure none are raised by the facts. None are so raised. I also realized I did not make sure none of the other general contract interpretation principles were raised by the facts. I again make a mental comparison of the facts to my list and conclude none of the other issues are present.

I conclude my thinking by considering how I might reconcile the three relevant contract interpretation principles before me. I recall that the preference for a promise conclusion in connection with express condition issues stems from courts seeking to avoid forfeitures wherever possible and that contra proferentem *is generally a contract interpretation principle of last resort.*

I feel ready to write.

Comments Regarding the above "Think Aloud"

A few things should stand out to you about the "think aloud" demonstration. Legal problems require the learner to possess quick and full recall of the relevant doctrine; to dialogue with the text, making predictions as to the issues and testing those predictions; to keep moving mentally back and forth between recall of the doctrine and review of the facts; to determine the purpose for the inclusion of each fact included in the fact pattern; and to think a lot before starting to write.

You are now ready to handle your own problems.

Problems

For each of the problems, you will learn most by writing out a full analysis, and, in fact, you will learn even more by doing your own "think aloud" with a peer, your professor or an academic support professional.

Exercise 15-4: Contract-Law-Specific Problem 1

On March 1, 2015, Miguel entered into a valid, enforceable agreement with his brother Esteban. Miguel agreed to provide legal services in drafting a set of standard form contracts for Esteban's business, and Esteban agreed to assist Miguel in certain projects around Miguel's house. The contract stated that the brothers agreed the total value of each brother's obligations was $60,000 and, more specifically, provided:

1. Miguel will prepare an employment agreement for use in Esteban's business. Esteban then will review the agreement, and, if it satisfies him, this contract will proceed in accordance with paragraphs 2–4 below.

2. Esteban will assist Miguel in tiling Miguel's kitchen floor (using Miguel's tools and materials), and Miguel will prepare a home sales agreement.

3. Esteban will assist Miguel in landscaping Miguel's backyard (using Miguel's tools and materials), and Miguel will prepare a form subcontractor agreement.

4. Esteban will assist Miguel in building a small, two-story guesthouse in Miguel's backyard, and Miguel will draft a form for Esteban's real property purchases.

On March 15, Miguel completed the employment agreement, and, one week later, Esteban showed up at Miguel's house to help Miguel with the tiling. Esteban said, "Frankly, Miguel, I hate the agreement you wrote. You misspelled the company's name, you have 65 typos, you forgot to include the kind of arbitration clause I asked for, and you wrote the agreement in such a way that, according to my friend, Anna (who is also an attorney), you have me guaranteeing permanent jobs to all my employees. I assume you'll fix these problems while you're working on the home sales agreement, so I'm here. Let's get this done so you can get started on fixing the employment agreement and on drafting the home sales agreement." Miguel agreed the employment agreement was wholly substandard and promised to fix it as soon as they finished the tiling.

When Miguel and Esteban finished the tiling, they agreed it was perfect. Miguel then prepared the home sales agreement, revised the employment agreement, and sent both to Esteban. When Esteban saw the agreements, he became furious. He said, "This deal is over. I'm done. The employment agreement still has five typos and the wrong kind of arbitration clause, and the home sales agreement is 15 pages long and still doesn't even have a liquidated damages clause, a force majeure clause, or a merger clause." The brothers then sued each other for breach of contract. Discuss the parties' claims. **DO NOT DISCUSS ANY REMEDIES ISSUES.**

Exercise 15-5: Contract-Law-Specific Problem 2

Kendra solicited bids for the new mansion she wanted built on land she already owned. Hagi Construction's $800,000 bid was $200,000 less than the bid of the next lowest bidder. Hagi was able to underbid its competitors by so much and still reserve itself a $100,000 profit because Hagi's owner had designed a construction method that reduced Hagi's labor costs substantially. The method involved building a steel foundation and prefabricating large parts of the home out of steel, instead of wood. Kendra, who knew Hagi had submitted the bid based on its "new method," awarded the contract to Hagi. Hagi and Kendra signed a valid written contract on June 1, 2015. The contract required Hagi to complete construction of the mansion in accordance with the plans and specifications by May 20, 2017. The parties knew that Kendra had a desperate need to move into the house by June 1, 2017 because she had to be out of her current house by that date. Assume there are no other relevant terms of the Hagi-Kendra contract.

Hagi began construction on June 15, 2015. Hagi quickly ran into problems. The steel did require much less labor to erect, but it required additional special machinery. Hagi had based his bid on the cost of the machines at the time he signed the contract. Unfortunately, an increased demand for steel erection machinery because of a boom in the commercial construction industry caused the price of the machinery to increase by $150,000. In addition, because of the boom, the machines could not be delivered to the job site when Hagi had planned. They could only be delivered two months later than Hagi had planned. Hagi therefore telephoned Kendra and told her that Hagi would not build the mansion unless Kendra agreed to pay Hagi an extra $100,000. Kendra refused. Kendra then demanded, in writing, that Hagi (1) perform the contract notwithstanding his increased costs and (2) agree to pay her cost of renting a substitute mansion if Hagi did not complete her mansion by May 20, 2017 as promised. Hagi refused Kendra's requests. Kendra then kicked Hagi off the job.

Assume Kendra has sued Hagi for breach of contract. Also assume Hagi did not file a counterclaim. Discuss. **DO NOT DISCUSS ANY REMEDIES ISSUES.**

Exercise 15-6: Contract-Law-Specific Problem 3

Ship Owner and Car Manufacturer, both of which are multi-million dollar businesses, entered into a contract whereby Ship Owner agreed to deliver 5,000 cars made by Car Manufacturer (you may assume 5,000 cars reflects a full ship load of cars) from Car Manufacturers' manufacturing plant in Northern California to Venezuela (which is on the east coast of South America). During negotiations, the parties exchanged e-mails discussing the fact that Ship Owner was planning to take the only logical route—through the Panama Canal. They also discussed, by e-mail, the fact that Panama and Colombia were threatening to go to war, which would close the Panama Canal. Finally, by e-mail, they agreed that Ship Owner would not have to perform the contract if Panama and Colombia went to war. They then jointly drafted and signed the contract, which was dated June 1, 2015. The contract, which was 50 pages in length, contained the following terms (which are indented below). You may assume the contract contained **no other** relevant terms, the contract addressed all of the issues one would except to see in such a contract, but the contract did not address the Panama Canal issue discussed above. You also may assume that neither party was represented by counsel in connection with the negotiation or drafting of the contract.

> On June 30, 2015, Ship Owner will transport 5,000 cars delivered by Car Manufacturer to Ship Owner's Dock at the San Francisco Bay in California to Ship Owner's Dock at the Port of Cumano, Venezuela. The parties expect the cars to arrive at the Port of Cumano no later than August 1.

> Car Manufacturer will pay Ship Owner $5,000,000 when the cars safely arrive to the Port of Cumano.

On June 28, 2015, Panama and Columbia declared war on each other, and the Panama Canal was closed to all traffic. Ship Owner immediately informed Car Manufacturer it would not be able to transport the cars as promised. Car Manufacturer then sued Ship Owner for breach of contract. Assume that, if Ship Owner had to travel from San Francisco to Cumano by any route other than through the Panama Canal, it would cost Ship Owner $20,000,000. (**Exam Hint: Do Question 1 below first.**)

Question 1: For this question ONLY, assume the parties' e-mails discussed in the first paragraph above are **NOT** admitted into evidence and that Ship Owner asserts the only excuse available to it. Discuss only the element(s) of that excuse that explain why a court would refuse to excuse Ship Owner's performance.

Question 2: Ignore the assumptions for the previous issue. Assume that Ship Owner seeks to introduce the parties' e-mail exchange as evidence and Car Manufacturer objects to this evidence. Fully analyze whether the evidence will come in. Assume the case will be heard in a Williston jurisdiction.

Exercise 15-7: Contract-Law-Specific Problem 4

On February 15, 2015, Sally Slatelover entered into a valid, enforceable, written and signed contract with Carol Construction Company (CCC) whereby Sally agreed to pay CCC $20,000, and CCC agreed to install landscaping (plants, trees, and flowers) and hardscaping (concrete, slate, built-in barbecue, etc.) in Sally's backyard. The contract described in detail the plants and materials to be used in the design and included the following term:

> CCC acknowledges that Sally is fanatical about the look of manufactured Ragastration Slate and therefore understands that it will get payment once it uses manufactured Ragastration Slate on the barbecue and planters in Sally's backyard (as detailed elsewhere in this contract).

At the time the parties made this contract, both understood that, while CCC had once manufactured Ragastration Slate on its own premises, CCC was planning to import the needed slate from Ragastratia, a small European country, because manufacturing the slate cost CCC 15 times more than importing it. The parties also understood that the final step in the construction process involved installing the slate.

CCC immediately commenced construction and ordered the slate from its supplier in Ragastratia. Unfortunately, three days before the slate was scheduled to arrive from Ragastratia, and after CCC had completed all of the work on the project, the United States decided that Ragastratia was a "rogue nation" and barred all imports from Ragastratia.

CCC immediately ordered American Slate, which is similar to manufactured Ragastration Slate in appearance and price, from a local manufacturer and installed it in Sally's backyard in every location where the contract called for Ragastration Slate. Assume that Sally has refused to pay CCC anything and CCC has sued Sally for breach. Finally, assume that the parties knew, at all relevant times, that the total fair market value of CCC's services and materials was $17,000. Discuss. **DO NOT DISCUSS ANY PARTY'S REMEDIES AND ASSUME ALL OF THE EVIDENCE REFERENCED IN THE ABOVE FACTS IS ADMITTED.**

Exercise 15-8: Contract-Law-Specific Problem 5

Alice entered into negotiations with Bee Goode, the producer of a reality television show called "The Single, Unattached Guy" to be a contestant on the show. "The Single, Unattached Guy" is a contest where 15 female contestants vie for a date with a single guy. The guy asks contestants questions, and, based on their answers, asks the ones he doesn't like to leave at the end of that episode. During the negotiations Alice repeatedly told Bee, "I am doing this to raise money to support my boyfriend, C. Me, who needs money to open a sunglasses store." Each time Alice mentioned this goal, Bee replied, "OK with me." Bee, for her part, repeatedly told Alice that Bee had had bad experiences with contestants who had claimed Bee had made promises that "weren't even in the contract they signed." Bee therefore informed Alice that "we both need to understand that any promise that is not in the writing isn't a part of the deal." Each time Bee said this, Alice replied, "OK."

Bee and Alice then signed a valid and enforceable written contract. The contract was 10 pages long. It included, among other things, the following provisions:

> Alice agrees to participate as a contestant on the television series "The Single, Unattached Guy" for the Fall 2015 season.

> Bee agrees to pay Alice $1,000 per episode so long as Alice remains a contestant.

Assume the contract did not contain any other provisions relevant to the issues addressed below. Also assume that, after signing the contract, Bee decided that Alice simply was not right for the show and fired her before the first episode was filmed. Assume further that C. Me has sued Bee for breach of contract. Discuss.

Exercise 15-9: Contract-Law-Specific Problem 6

Willie's Wedding Services ("WWS") entered into a valid written agreement with Ima Parent in which WWS agreed to provide catering and related wedding services for the wedding reception of Ima's son, and Ima agreed to pay WWS $125,000. WWS' services were to include, among other things, preparing and serving the food, setting the tables, providing a sound system for the wedding reception ceremonies (*e.g.*, the speeches, cutting the cake, throwing the bouquet), and arranging the flowers.

The contract included, among others, the following provisions:

...

10. All of WWS' services shall strictly follow, without deviation, the standards and practices set forth in *The Handbook for Happy Wedding Receptions*.

11. The main dish, Chicken Cordon Bleu, shall be prepared in accordance with the best standards of French cooking. Ima shall have no duty to pay WWS if she is not personally satisfied with the chicken.

12. Ima will select the types of flowers to be used in the floral arrangements and must do so within one week of the wedding day.

The Handbook for Happy Wedding Receptions provides, among other things not relevant here, that reception flower arrangements shall be "attractively arranged to tantalize the eye," and that a sound system for a reception must be "sufficient to allow all guests to hear and enjoy in the proceedings."

One week before the arrangements, Ima made her flower selections. Over WWS' vehement objections, Ima insisted that WWS use only blue carnations in the flower arrangements. (Carnations are a relatively inexpensive flower and are considered unattractive, and blue did not match the rest of the reception decorations.)

On the day before the wedding, a truck crashed into WWS' place of business, destroying the building and all of its contents. WWS quickly replaced all of its wedding reception supplies, except its sound system. Two years before the crash, WWS has purchased its $16,000 sound system via the Internet because doing so saved WWS $9,000. WWS ordered a replacement system from the same mail order company and received the same savings. Unfortunately, the Internet seller could not deliver the replacement system in time for the wedding. Had WWS purchased its replacement system at a local store, it could have had the system available for use in time for the wedding. For the wedding, WWS rented the best system it could get, for which WWS paid $1,000.

The wedding took place as scheduled, and the wedding guests seemed to enjoy themselves. Because the flower arrangements only used the blue carnations, the guests agreed the arrangements were unattractive and boring. Many of the guests also complained that they could not hear significant parts of the festivities; the sound system simply was not adequate for the space. The bride, however, must have heard enough of the best man's toast; she decided she liked him more than her new husband, Ima's son, and she ran off with the best man.

On Monday morning, as her son sobbed in the next room, Ima called WWS and said, "I will not pay you one penny for your foul services. Not only were the flower arrangements dull, but also the sound system was useless and the chicken was totally unacceptable."

Discuss the issues that might be raised in any lawsuit between WWS and Ima.

Exercise 15-10: Contract-Law-Specific Problem 7

On April 15, Rich Vacationer entered into negotiations with The Terrific Tourguides (TTT), a company that arranges hotel rooms for and gives private limousine tours to visitors to New York City. During the discussions, Vacationer explained his need for a hotel room that has a whirlpool bath; he said, "if I cannot take a whirlpool bath each night my back stiffens up and I suffer from painful back spasms, which would put a real damper on my whole vacation." TTT therefore agreed to "put something in the contract to clearly protect you against not having a whirlpool bath in your room." Vacationer also said he couldn't go through with the contract if he didn't get an expected $15,000 bonus from his employer, which was due April 30th. The parties thereafter entered into a valid and enforceable written contract. The contract included the following terms, among others (assume the terms below are the only terms relevant to the issues before you):

...

(3) It shall be an express condition precedent to formation of this contract that Vacationer receives a $15,000 bonus from his employer no later than April 30.

(4) Vacationer will pay TTT $15,000 for TTT's services as described below upon arriving at his hotel room and determining that the room has a whirlpool bath.

(5) For Vacationer's two-week visit from June 1–June 14 to New York City, TTT will arrange accommodations in a hotel room that has a whirlpool bath and will provide private, TTT-led, limousine tours of the major New York tourist attractions.

On April 30, Vacationer received a $15,000 bonus from his employer and therefore informed TTT to make the hotel reservations for his trip. TTT then made the reservations. However, when Vacationer arrived in New York on June 1, things with Vacationer's room went badly. Although TTT had requested and obtained for him a room with a whirlpool bath (and had, in fact, emphasized to the front desk of the hotel that "this is crucial to our customer") and, even though the hotel had the best possible reputation for excellence in hotel services, the whirlpool bath was broken and therefore did not work at all. Unfortunately, no hotel room with a whirlpool bath was available in the entire city and the whirlpool bath in his room, according to the hotel manager, could not be repaired until June 20. The next morning, Vacationer telephoned TTT and repudiated the parties' contract. He then checked out of the hotel and took the next flight home. Discuss whether Vacationer is liable for breach of contract. **ASSUME THE COURT WILL ADMIT ALL PAROL EVIDENCE. DO NOT DISCUSS IMPRACTICABILITY OR FRUSTRATION.**

Practicing Contract Law with Professionalism

Introduction to Practicing Contract Law with Professionalism

The practice of contract law. This short introduction is designed to introduce you to some basic concepts of practicing contracts law and to draw together and reinforce the professionalism principles addressed throughout this book. This discussion is not intended to be an exhaustive exploration of either contract law practice or of professionalism, and we therefore encourage you to find and study supplemental resources addressing both topics.

Most experts agree that the ideal in law practice is "client-centered lawyering." Being client-centered is often juxtaposed against being lawyer-centered. The difference stems from the lawyers' orientation in connection with decision-making. Many resources on law practice, and quite a few lawyers, assert that clients should make business decisions and lawyers should make strategic and drafting decisions. This division of duties works well for many lawyering problems, but, in many instances, it leads lawyers to make decisions contrary to their clients' preferences.

For example, a lawyer may make a strategic decision to subpoena a particular witness to testify; the client, however, might not want to involve the witness for personal reasons—for example, because the witness is his boss or his sister. A lawyer-centered practitioner might make the decision to call the witness without consulting with the client, seeing the issue as one of strategy and, therefore, within the practitioner's decision-making domain. Such a lawyer might ask for the client's opinion but would override the client's objection. A client-centered lawyer might approach the problem from an opposite perspective; the client-centered lawyer would lay out the risks of not calling the witness, but leave the decision to the client.

In the contract drafting context, these same issues play out in negotiating the relationship between the lawyer's goal of protecting the client and the client's goal of making the contract. A lawyer-centered practitioner might be more likely to include every term she feels is necessary to protect her client's interests whereas a client-centered lawyer would recommend each such clause, encourage the client to include it by explaining the consequences of its omission but, in the end, defer to the client's choice not to include the term if the client were to make that decision.

In its most extreme forms, client-centered lawyering might lead a lawyer to follow a client's wishes to engage in behavior contrary to the lawyer's personal values and sense of professionalism. For example, the client might ask the lawyer to engage in litigation behavior, such as propounding abusive discovery solely to gain a strategic advantage, or a client might ask the lawyer to draft a contract clause that is unenforceable, or even illegal, if the client knows the other party would not know the term is unenforceable and would therefore comply with it.

Professionalism. While some extreme proponents of client-centered lawyering might advocate following the client's wishes in the above matters, most lawyers believe that the lawyer's duty to the legal system and to herself would commend raising the issue with the client, and, if necessary, withdrawing from the representation. In other words, you should never abandon your sense of professionalism and your values. In the long run, those touchstones will serve you much better than meeting a client's wishes you regard as inappropriate or unethical.

Some of the problems throughout this book include challenges that require you to balance your clients' interests and your sense of professionalism.

Professionalism certainly includes these considerations, but it also includes a much broader set of concerns. For example, professionalism should lead you to manage your time and workload in ways that may be new to you. While you may have succeeded in college (and might succeed in law school) notwithstanding a tendency to procrastinate, lawyers cannot afford to do so. As a lawyer, it is very hard to know when a new matter will come into your office and require your full attention or when an existing matter will, as lawyers say, "blow up." Consequently, what may have appeared to be a light calendar may have you working day and night. If you also have procrastinated unpleasant tasks, your license, or, at least, your clients' satisfaction with your work will be at risk. Your obligation to manage your time and work professionally, in other words, is critical.

We encourage you, as you work the problems that follow, to plan your work so that you have plenty of time not only to complete these projects but also to rethink your work and revise it as necessary.

Professionalism also connotes expertise. The idea of expertise requires lawyers not to take on matters beyond their reasonable capabilities and to make sure, when they do take on matters that require specialized legal knowledge, to know when they do not know what they need to know, to learn what they need to know, and to seek consultation when they need it. At the same time, the notion of expertise also requires professionals to be able to work independently and autonomously and to take pride in their work.

Some of the problems below require you to recognize your lack of expertise and to conduct the legal research you need to be able to complete the assigned tasks.

Not only does professionalism require lawyers to possess expertise, it also requires lawyers to engage in continuous self-improvement. As you probably have noticed, many of the reflection questions in this text ask you to reflect on what you have learned and your own growth as a learner and future lawyer.

Finally, professionalism requires lawyers to act with a lack of self-interest, to place their clients' interests and the interests of the legal system ahead of the lawyer's interests.

As you work on the following problems, we encourage you to keep all these considerations in mind.

Problems

Exercise 15-11: Practice Problem 1 — Objective Memorandum*

BUELLER AND GOODSON

ATTORNEYS AT LAW
1060 WEST COMMERCIAL
FAIRVIEW, KS 66425

September 29, 2015

To: Junior Associate
From: Tom Bueller
Re: Representation of Shirk Bros. Contracting

This case involves one of our long-time clients, Shirk Bros. Contracting. They are probably going to be sued by homeowners Walter Fielding and Anna Crowley for some work that they did on the house a year ago. Apparently, the staircase that they renovated collapsed and caused a large amount of damage to the house. They had Commercial General Liability insurance at the time of the renovation through Crimson Permanent Assurance Company. However, that policy expired a week before the staircase collapsed. Because of the policy's expiration, and because Crimson believes that there was no "occurrence" within the policy's definition, Crimson has denied coverage.

I'd like you to take a look at this case to determine whether we have a chance of getting coverage for the Shirk Brothers through the Crimson policy. I've enclosed the pertinent documents here. If you need more, let me know. The Shirk Brothers get sued quite a bit, so they are pretty good clients. Do what you can. I'd like to see something by October 23.

Tom

---

* This problem is courtesy of Michael Schwartz's former colleague at Washburn University College of Law, Jeffrey Jackson, and is used with his permission.

Shirk Bros. Contracting

Most Jobs Done in Two Weeks
123 East Commercial
Fairview, KS 66425
(785) 467-8762

September 26, 2015

Tom Bueller
Bueller & Goodson
1060 West Commercial
Fairview, KS 66425

Tom,

Well old buddy, it looks like I need your help again. Walt Fielding and Anna Crowley are gonna sue me over some work that Brad and I did on their house. We repaired the grand staircase for them soon after they moved in in June of 2014. It was a tough job, because the old staircase was a complete mess and a lot of it had to be gutted. I think it took us the better part of two months. I thought we did a good job.

Unfortunately, it seems that the staircase sort of collapsed. I don't know why, but Walt and Anna seem to think that it has something to do with the way we built it. They've even hired this other contractor to look at it and he says that it's all our fault. Something about how we didn't brace it correctly and how it was "exceedingly dangerous" and such. I'm not mad at Walt. Heck, if I got mad at everyone who threatened to sue me, I wouldn't get anything else done. I'm really mad at my insurer, though. I figured this was just the kind of thing that you buy insurance for. However, when I asked them about the claim, they said that I wasn't covered. I just don't understand this. I pay my premiums, and I don't have to tell you how expensive those are. Part of the problem, I guess, is that I cancelled the policy right before all of this happened. I meant to get another policy from another insurer, but I just hadn't gotten around to it by the time the staircase collapsed. Really, though, why shouldn't I be protected? We were insured when we built the thing.

As you know, I don't really understand all the legal implications here. I just build quality things at good prices. I'm hoping you can make sure this is covered.

Thanks,

Art

The Crimson Permanent Assurance Company

221 W. Electric Road
Fairview, KS 66425
"Your Friend and Neighbor"

September 20, 2015
Art Shirk
President,
Shirk Bros. Contracting
123 East Commercial
Fairview, Kansas 66425

Dear Mr. Shirk:

We have received your inquiry asking whether we would provide coverage and a defense for the possible liability incurred by your company for work done on the house at 221 Maple Street. A staircase at the house collapsed on January 6, 2015.

Section I, Coverage A, paragraph (a) of Crimson Permanent Commercial General Liability, in effect from January 1, 2013 to December 31, 2014, clearly states:

    a.   We will pay those sums that the insured becomes legally obligated to pay as damages because of "bodily injury" or "property damage" to which this insurance applies.

Paragraphs (b)(1) and (2) state:

    b.   This insurance applies to "bodily injury" and property damage only if:
       (1) the "bodily injury" or "property damage" is caused by an "occurrence" that takes place in the "coverage territory."
       (2) the "bodily injury " or "property damage" occurs during the policy period.

Section V, subsection 13 defines an "occurrence" as:

    c.   an accident, including continuous or repeated exposure to substantially the same harmful conditions.

Because the collapse of the staircase was not an accident, but instead the natural consequences of your faulty workmanship, there was no "accident" as required by the policy. Further, even if the collapse of the staircase could be termed an "occurrence," this occurrence happened on January 6, 2015, after the cancellation of the policy. As a result, we are denying coverage and will not furnish a defense in this matter.

As a valued former customer, your business is important to us. If we can be helpful in any way, please don't hesitate to let us know.

Your Friend and Neighbor,

John Macy
Regional Agent

DEMOTT & WINSLOW

ATTORNEYS AND COUNSELORS AT LAW

H. GEORGE DEMOTT
FRANKLIN WINSLOW
JON VAN DREELEN
Douglass Watson
Henry Baker
Ronald Foster
Peter Richardson
George L. Demott
Adam Clark

401 BANK TOWER
341 W. COMMERCIAL
FAIRVIEW, KS 66425

Conner Smith
Edwin Willmarth
H. Tier Avalon
F. Llock Haven
Matthew Cowls
Douglas Plavin
Michael Tremont
Edward Winslow
Reginald Parker
Jonah Markham
Alfred Winslow

August 15, 2015

Art Shirk
President, Shirk Bros. Contracting
123 East Commercial
Fairview, Kansas 66425

Dear Mr. Shirk:

I have been retained to represent Mr. Walter Fielding, Jr. and Ms. Anna Crowley. You performed work for them from June 12, 2014 to November 16, 2014 on their residence at 221 Maple Street, Fairview, Ks. Despite your repeated assurances that all repairs would be performed within "two weeks," the actual renovations took almost six months.

A problem has occurred with the main grand staircase that you replaced. On January 6, 2015, the staircase collapsed without warning while Mr. Fielding was ascending it. It was only through great good fortune that Mr. Fielding escaped without major injury. As it was, he suffered some injury as well as great emotional distress. I shudder to think what might have happened if Ms. Crowley had also been on the staircase.

Mr. Fielding and Ms. Crowley have obtained a report on the damage from Zenger Construction. The report is attached to this letter. In sum, the report states that your work on the staircase was grossly deficient and constituted a dangerous condition.

In order to avoid unnecessary expense, Mr. Fielding and Ms. Crowley have authorized me to offer to settle their claim against you for the liability. Upon receipt of damages, in the amount of $25,000.00, they will execute a release from liability on your behalf. If this offer is not accepted within 30 days, I will be forced to take other measures, up to and including filing a lawsuit for the full replacement cost of the staircase as well as other damages to which Mr. Fielding and Ms. Crowley may be entitled.

Yours Very Truly,

A. Winslow

Alfred Winslow
Attorney at Law

Z E G N E R
C O N S T R U C T I O N

Licensed Residential Contractor
1 Rocklin Road
Fairview, KS 66425
785·266·0829

February 7, 2015

Mr. Walter Fielding, Jr.
211 Maple St.
Fairview, KS 66425

Dear Mr. Fielding:

At your request, I examined the staircase at your home at 211 Maple St. My opinion follows.

From an examination of the wreckage of the staircase, it is apparent that the workmanship was defective and caused the collapse and resultant damage. The staircase in question was built, along with the house, in 1950. Renovations were undertaken in 2014. While the original workmanship on the staircase is of high-quality, the recent 2014 additions are obviously defective. In my professional opinion, these additions led to the collapse of the staircase.

Many of the 2014 additions were cosmetic. While these additions did not contribute to the actual collapse, they are indicative of the type of work that was performed. For instance, the rails and balustrades, rather than being secured with glue and supporting fasteners, appear to have been affixed together through the use of a bonding product similar to StickyPutty, which is advertised on late-night infomercials. Because this product is brittle over time, it is not a proper product to use in fastening. No doubt this is why you experienced rails and balustrades all falling apart as you ascended the staircase.

The main problem, however, occurred in the underpinning of the staircase. It is clear that, in replacing the supports for the staircase, the renovator neglected to securely fasten the braces, or to include enough braces to adequately support the weight of the staircase, especially with the new additions, which added considerable weight to the staircase. As a result, the weight of the staircase would have began putting undue strain on the remaining supports immediately, and they would have begun to crack. Eventually, they broke completely under the strain, and the collapse of the entire staircase was a direct result. Frankly, I'm quite surprised that the supports lasted as long as they did, given the weight that they had to bear.

In my opinion, this work is not up to professional standards and does not comply with building codes in effect at the time the work was performed. The work done in 2014 was grossly deficient, and constituted a dangerous condition that was bound to cause damage.

If I can be of any more help to you, or in repairing the damage, please let me know.

Sincerely,

John Peter Zegner
KS License #28756

Exercise 15-12: Practice Problem 2: Draft a Client Engagement Letter

You are a partner in a small, two-person firm that you created two years after you graduated from law school with a friend you made in law school. Annie Smith, the sole shareholder and president of Smith Fine Carpentry, Inc., is your firm's first client. In Exercise 15-13 below, you will be evaluating a contract Smith is planning to sign. Before you do so, you need to create a standard-form client engagement letter for your law firm and modify that form to address your relationship with Smith. For now, she has asked you only to represent her in connection with *evaluating* the contract. In fact, she has told you expressly that she does **not** want you to rewrite the contract to better protect her interests. Your partner has assured Smith that you can review the contract for $1,000.

You believe that, if all you do is evaluate the contract and explain its implications to your client, $1,000 would be fair compensation. You have some concern, however, that, once you identify any deficiencies in the contract, your client may ask you to rewrite the contract and even, possibly, to negotiate the rewrite with the other contracting party or its attorney. If so, the $1,000 will become a very poor business deal for the firm.

Below are some general principles of contract drafting and a form client engagement letter your new partner got from his father, who has retired from the practice of law. Create a client engagement letter and modify the letter to address the arrangement between you and Smith.

Principles for contract drafting

Goals. What should your goals be in drafting any contract? (Keep in mind that these concerns are just as significant when you are drafting a contract, such as a client engagement letter, to which you are a party.) First, you should accurately describe the agreements made. The most important criterion for any contract is whether it correctly and unambiguously articulates the parties' agreement. As you have learned, the task of drafting unambiguous contract obligations is harder than you might have imagined before you started studying contract law.

Second, because both parties to any contract have made the contract to acquire the other party's performance, the contract you draft should encourage full and flawless performance. Certainly, there are terms you can add that will encourage such performance, such as liquidated damages clauses, express conditions, and warranties. Of course, because parties often view such terms as increasing their risk, they will treat such terms as "deal points" and negotiate trade-offs, such as increases (or decreases) in the contract price.

Third, the contract you draft should at least make some effort to minimize your client's chances of ending up in litigation with the other party and minimize the cost and business implications of the contract becoming adversarial. Dispute resolution clauses, while helpful in minimizing litigation costs once the parties are in litigation, have no effect on whether the parties end up in litigation. Attorney's fees clauses can actually encourage litigation because each party may believe that the other party will cover its fees. The best way to discourage future litigation is to make sure the contract achieves your client's goals, is clear, and, even when your client has greater bargaining power, isn't such a harsh bargain that the other party would be unlikely to achieve its goals or will resent your client's choice to exploit its bargaining advantage. For these reasons, good contracts almost always are what lawyers call "win-win deals."

Fourth, the contract you draft should anticipate possible future problems and address them. This task is the key to what you, as a lawyer, bring to the table. It is also the area in which you are most likely to be sued for malpractice if you make a mistake and fail to protect your client against a particularly foreseeable problem. When parties are about to enter into a contract, their focus is on what they would receive under the contract and on what the contract requires them to do. In many instances, clients also see contracts as a part of a longer-term relationship with the other party, and, in fact, clients are often willing to live with less-than-optimal contracts or, at least, less-than-optimal contract terms in exchange for building a business relationship with the other party. As a result of the conflict between the client's business interests and your goal of minimizing the client's risk (and, thereby, minimizing your malpractice risk), contract drafting is a trickier and more delicate enterprise than you might now imagine. In fact, negotiating the boundary between your client's business goals and protecting your client's other interests often tests your client counseling skills.

Finally, lawyers know that if they do their job well, if they draft contracts that meet their clients' needs and do so efficiently, they can not only obtain return business from their clients, but also attract future clients by creating good references.

Steps in drafting contracts. The most important thing contract drafters need to know is **the facts**. Practicing lawyers always start with the facts. While it may seem that litigation matters require a greater command of the facts, contract drafting is equally fact sensitive. Knowing the factual context, including: the relationship between the parties, each party's goals in making the contract, the client's general business needs and practices, the usages of the trade, and past contractual dealings between the parties, can assist the lawyer in avoiding ambiguities and anticipating contingencies.

In many instances, careful lawyering may require lawyers not only to conduct an initial client interview regarding the facts, but also to ask follow-up questions, clarify understandings, and confirm goals. You may even have to research your client's field, to make sure you possess the necessary background. New lawyers tend to be anxious about asking their clients questions; they assume more experienced lawyers would not need to ask such questions. An experienced lawyer recognizes that getting answers to questions will help the lawyer avoid errors and avoid having to re-draft the contract.

Identifying the facts will lead the lawyer to **conduct legal research**. Drafting contracts almost always involves identifying possible legal issues and researching those issues. Sometimes, the research involves determining the enforceability of a particular clause desired by a client. In other instances, the research focuses on potential outcomes of a variety of alternative approaches.

In many instances, law firms have developed form contracts designed to facilitate the lawyer's drafting efforts. Some lawyers have published form contracts in books. Forms save clients money by reducing drafting time and minimizing the need for research. The key to **effectively using forms** is to use them thoughtfully, critically, and reflectively.

Below, in Table 15-3, are a list of questions you should ask yourself when you are using a form.

Table 15-3: Questions You Should Ask Yourself When Using a Form

1. Do I understand the reason underlying each of the terms I am copying? Sometimes, it is hard to determine why the person who created a particular form chose to include a particular term. In such instances, ask yourself:

   a. Is the term legally required?

   b. Is the term the product of the drafter's eccentricity?

   c. Is the term a matter of tradition within your law firm? Among lawyers? In the industry?

   d. Is the term the product of a particular factual situation significantly similar to or different from your client's situation?

   e. Does the term reflect a mistake?

   f. Does the term reflect a negotiated concession?

2. Does each term actually achieve what the drafter designed it to achieve? Is it well written? Is it clear and concise?

3. Is each term relevant and necessary to this matter?

4. Does the term reflect current law?

The most important thing you can do to increase the likelihood that you produce a contract that achieves the client's goals while protecting the client's interests is to reserve plenty of time for **drafting, editing, re-drafting, and re-editing**. Time between each review of the draft increases the likelihood you will catch errors.

It is also important that, where possible, you choose **plain language** to express the agreement. Plain language increases clarity so that the parties' negotiations focus on issues and interests, ensures predictability by allowing the parties to reliably anticipate how a court would interpret the contract, and improves understanding between the parties. On some occasions, parties choose to eschew plain language. For example, parties may choose technical legal language when they intend a technical legal effect, or they may choose language that, while seemingly unclear, has been fully vetted by the courts to mean what the parties intend. Parties may even choose to deliberately leave a term, even a key term like price, ambiguous where a rule such as U.C.C. 2-305 will provide a term.

By and large, **there are some terms you always should include** and **some you always should consider including**. Generally, all contracts should include the parties, the parties' respective obligations, the times and places for both parties' performances, the date of the contract, and the parties' signatures. Nearly all contracts also should include recitals, which are terms that identify the parties' respective over-arching objectives, and most contracts should include a section addressing how parties should notify each other of important matters, and a section labeled "definitions," a section that defines the key terms in the contract.

The terms worth considering include all of the terms you have learned about in this text, including clauses addressing:

1. Modification (how the parties can modify the contract)

2. Merger

3. Attorney's fees and costs clauses if the parties get into a dispute

4. Dispute resolution

5. Force majeure

6. Assignment and delegation

7. Liquidated damages

8. Warranties

9. Express conditions

10. Order of performance

11. Choice of law.

Table 15-4: Client Engagement Letter Form

LAW OFFICES OF _____

_____ __, 20__

Re: Fee Arrangement Regarding _____.

Dear _____:

You have asked our firm to represent _____ with respect to matters concerning _____.

1.   Scope of Work. Our work is to be limited to the above-described work.

2.   Fees. Legal services will be billed on an hourly basis at our then-prevailing rates for attorney, paralegal, law clerk and word processing time. At present, rates for attorneys range from _____ to _____ per hour, depending upon the attorney and work involved. While others in the firm may assist with your work, I will supervise and be in overall charge. My hourly rate for this matter will be $ _____.

3.   Costs. You will be asked to advance funds or to reimburse our firm for costs incurred in handling the matter. Typical cost items include copying, long-distance calls, fax, filing service and recordation fees, and word processing time.

4.   Billings. We will send the monthly statements itemizing our work and costs incurred but updated with all payments received through the date of the statement. We expect payment within 20 days of your receipt of this statement. We will gladly answer any questions you might have concerning our charges. We acknowledge receipt from you of a $_____ retainer check. Any amount unused as a result of this engagement will be returned to you.

5.   Late Payments. We are confident that our clients make every effort to pay us promptly and know that you will do so. Occasionally, however, a client has difficulty in making timely payment. To avoid the necessity of increasing our fees to all clients to cover the added costs we incur due to clients who are delinquent, a monthly service charge will be added for late payments. This charge will be assessed on the last day of each month against all unpaid fees and costs which were billed for the preceding month. The monthly service charge is calculated at the rate of .83 percent per month on the unpaid balance.

6.   <u>Arbitration</u>. ALL DISPUTES, CLAIMS AND CONTROVERSIES, INCLUDING, BUT NOT LIMITED TO, THOSE REGARDING FEES, MALPRACTICE, BREACH OF FIDUCIARY DUTY, BREACH OF CONTRACT, NEGLIGENCE OR OTHER TORT (INTENTIONAL OR UNINTENTIONAL) AND/OR DECLARATORY OR OTHER EQUITABLE RELIEF ARISING UNDER OR CONCERNING THE PERFORMANCE OF THIS AGREEMENT BY EITHER [NAME OF FIRM] OR CLIENT SHALL BE SUBMITTED TO BINDING ARBITRATION. IN THE EVENT THE PARTIES DO NOT AGREE UPON AN ARBITRATOR WITHIN TEN (10) DAYS AFTER ANY PARTY DEMANDS ARBITRATION, THEN THE JUDICIAL ARBITRATION & MEDIATION SERVICES, INC. ("JAMS") SHALL PROVIDE TO EACH THE NAMES OF THREE (3) AVAILABLE RETIRED JUDGES ON ITS STAFF AND EACH PARTY SHALL BE ENTITLED TO STRIKE ONE (1) NAME. THE REMAINING JUDGE SHALL BE THE SELECTED ARBITRATOR. IF EITHER SIDE REFUSES TO STRIKE AN ARBITRATOR WITHIN TEN (10) DAYS FROM THE SERVICE OF THE NAMES OF THE ARBITRATORS, THEN JAMS SHALL DECIDE WHICH OF THE REMAINING TWO (2) SHALL BE SELECTED. THE FINDINGS, ORDERS OR AWARD OF THE ARBITRATOR(S) MAY THEREAFTER BE ENTERED AS A JUDGMENT UPON PETITION TO A COURT HAVING JURISDICTION OVER THE PARTIES AND THE MATTER.

CLIENT UNDERSTANDS AND AGREES THAT BY CONSENTING TO ARBITRATE ALL DISPUTES AND CONTROVERSIES, INCLUDING THOSE INVOLVING FEES AND ALLEGED MALPRACTICE, CLIENT AGREES TO WAIVE TRIAL BY JURY. PLEASE INITIAL THIS PARAGRAPH SIGNIFYING YOUR UNDERSTANDING OF THIS AGREEMENT TO ARBITRATE.

7.   <u>Attorneys' Fees</u>. If arbitration or litigation is instituted to enforce or interpret this Agreement, the prevailing party shall recover its reasonable attorneys' fees and all costs.

If this Agreement is satisfactory, please sign the enclosed copy of this letter and return it to me. Please also initial Paragraph 6 above. I have enclosed a stamped return envelope for your convenience. The signed original will serve as your counterpart. If you have any questions, please give me a call.

We appreciate the opportunity to work with you on this matter.

Sincerely,

_____

[Name of Attorney in Firm] for

[NAME OF FIRM]

The foregoing terms and provisions are acceptable.

DATED: _____, 20___   _____

[Name of Client]

Exercise 15-13: Practice Problem 3: Evaluate a Client's Proposed Contract

You are a partner in a small, two-person firm that you created, two years after you graduated from law school, with a friend you made in law school. Annie Smith, the sole shareholder and president of Smith Fine Carpentry, Inc., is your firm's first client. Smith Fine Carpentry, Inc. and Carmelo Construction, Inc. are planning to sign the contract reproduced on the next two pages. Smith has asked you to "review" the contract. She has told you that she has been in business for five years. This contract is her first with Carmelo Construction, a large real estate developer with whom Smith hopes to do a lot of business in the future. Her last words to you as she left the room were, "Look, we need this deal. Carmelo Construction told me that this is their 'form contract.' Just tell me what I am getting myself into. I am not going back to Carmelo with a bunch of lawyer fine print."

Assume the plans and specifications were not attached to the following contract. When you asked about the plans and specifications, Smith said, "I'll worry about the construction issues; you worry about the legal issues."

Respond to Smith. Decide for yourself whether your response should be oral or in writing or both.

Agreement

Whereas Smith Fine Carpentry, Inc. (Subcontractor) is an expert with respect to constructing built-in cabinetry and bookshelves; and

Whereas Carmelo Construction, Inc. (Contractor) has agreed to build a house for Andrea Amercua (Owner) on a lot located at 1111 State Street in New York, New York ("The House") and the contract between Owner and Contractor requires Contractor, among other things, to construct built-in cabinetry and bookshelves in the kitchen, bathroom, office, and library (the "Fine Carpentry Work") of The House;

The parties agree as follows:

1. **Constructive Conditions.** The parties' duties under this contract are subject to the following:

    1.1. By May 1, 2016, Subcontractor must obtain a performance bond providing $100,000 of insurance to Contractor if Subcontractor fails to complete her duties described below.

Page 1 of 2

1.2. By May 1, 2016, Contractor must obtain a payment bond providing $100,000 of insurance to Subcontractor if Contractor fails to complete his duties described below.

1.3. Timely performance by both parties.

2. **Subcontractor's Duties.** Subcontractor will perform all Fine Carpentry Work called for by the Plans and Specifications attached to this contract in accordance with those Plans and Specifications and will complete this work within 90 days of Contractor's performance of his duties described below in paragraph 3.

3. **Timing.** When Contractor has completed all work on The House that must be completed before Subcontractor can start the Fine Carpentry Work, Contractor will notify Subcontractor. Subcontractor will then have thirty days in which to purchase all the materials and other supplies needed for the Fine Carpentry Work.

4. **Payment by Contractor.** Contractor will compensate Subcontractor for the Fine Carpentry Work as follows:

   4.1 Within two days of submission, by Subcontractor, of receipts showing payment by Subcontractor for all the materials and other supplies needed for the Fine Carpentry Work, Contractor shall repay Subcontractor for purchasing the materials and supplies.

   4.2 Thereafter, Contractor shall build a five-room cabin on Lakeland Acres according to the plans and specifications attached to this contract. The parties agree and acknowledge that Lakeland Acres is owned by Jones Starr, to whom Subcontractor owes $100,000.

5. **No oral modifications.** This contract can only be modified in a writing signed by both parties.

6. **Cancellation and Assignment.** Neither party shall have the right to cancel or assign this contract.

7. **Force Majeure.** If events or conditions beyond the control of either party, such as fires, floods, terrorist attacks, earthquakes, or other Acts of God prevent either party from performing any obligation due under this contract or delay timely performance of any such obligation, that party will not be liable for such breach of contract.

8. **Merger.** This agreement contains the entire agreement of the parties. There are no promises, representations, assurances, or other terms not contained in this writing.

_____ __/ __/ 20__   _____ __/ __/ 20__

For Subcontractor   For Contractor

Exercise 15-14: Practice Problem 4: Drafting a Motion to Dismiss for Failing to State a Cause of Action[*]

DARROW & DARROW, ATTORNEYS AT LAW

INTEROFFICE MEMORANDUM

TO: Andrea Associate
FROM: Rachel Darrow
DATE: May ___, 20___
SUBJECT: *Smith v. Golden Rule Construction Company*
OUR FILE No.:   GRCC 102.11

As you know, Betty Golden, who does business under the name Golden Rule Construction Company (GRCC), is one of our best clients. GRCC has been sued by Jeremiah Smith for breach of a construction contract and for intentional infliction of emotional distress. I attach the complaint. I believe both causes of action are faulty, and Smith cannot truthfully amend the complaint to state a claim for relief. Please draft a motion, pursuant to FRCP section 12(b)(6), to dismiss both claims. The second claim strikes me as particularly suspect. Thus, even if the plaintiff were allowed to amend his first claim for relief, I doubt he will be allowed to amend his second claim. Moreover, if we can knock out that claim, we may also be able to challenge jurisdiction. Make sure your motion also moves for dismissal based on a lack of jurisdiction under 12(b)(1).

---

[*]   Professor Rory Bahadur of Washburn University School of Law assisted in the drafting of this complaint.

IN THE UNITED STATES DISTRICT COURT
FOR THE DISTRICT OF KANSAS
CASE NO. 2015-098-78651

JEREMIAH SMITH,

       Plaintiff,

vs.

BETTY GOLDEN d/b/a GOLDEN
RULE CONSTRUCTION
COMPANY,

       Defendant.

COMPLAINT

COMES NOW, the Plaintiff, JEREMIAH SMITH, by and through the undersigned counsel, and sues the Defendant, BETTY GOLDEN d/b/a GOLDEN RULE CONSTRUCTION COMPANY, alleging as follows:

GENERAL ALLEGATIONS

1. This action is a diversity action where the matter in controversy exceeds the sum or value of $75,000, exclusive of interest and costs, and is between a citizen of California and a citizen of Kansas and falls within the class of actions allowed under 28 USC 1332(a)(1-4) and Federal Jurisdiction is therefore proper under 28 USC § 1332.

2. Plaintiff is entitled to, and demands, a trial by jury pursuant to 28 USC § 1332.

3. At all times material hereto, Plaintiff was a citizen of the state of Kansas.

4. At all times material hereto, Defendant was a citizen of the state of California, doing business in California as a construction general contractor.

COUNT I — BREACH OF CONTRACT AGAINST GOLDEN
on behalf of JEREMIAH SMITH

Plaintiff re-alleges paragraphs one (1) through four (4) above and further alleges as follows:

5. On or about December 15, 2014, Plaintiff and Defendant entered into a contract whereby Defendant was to add a sunroom to Plaintiff's existing residence at 1221 State Street in Topeka, Kansas. A copy of the contract is attached hereto and incorporated by reference.

6. On or about December 16, 2014, and continuously thereafter until the date of filing of this complaint, Defendant breached the contract described in paragraph 5 by failing to perform any of its obligations under the contract.

7.   Defendant's breach of contract was material and in no way constituted substantial performance of the contract.

COUNT II—INTENTIONAL INFLICTION OF EMOTIONAL DISTRESS AGAINST GOLDEN on behalf of JEREMIAH SMITH

Plaintiff re-alleges paragraphs one (1) through seven (7) above and further alleges as follows:

8.   At all times material hereto, Defendant possessed full knowledge that Plaintiff was looking forward to using the room Defendant had promised to build and would become greatly upset and angry if Defendant breached the contract.

9.   Notwithstanding this knowledge, Defendant has acted outrageously by failing to perform any of its obligations under the contract described in paragraph 5.

10. As a result, Plaintiff has sustained great emotional suffering, including problems with vomiting and persistent headaches, for which Plaintiff has sought and received medical treatment.

WHEREFORE, the Plaintiff, JEREMIAH SMITH, demands judgment for damages against the Defendant, BETTY GOLDEN,

a.   In the amount of $25,000 on Count I, representing the excess cost of having another contractor complete the work Defendant promised to complete, exclusive of fees and costs

b.   In an amount in excess of Seventy-Five Thousand Dollars ($75,000.00) on Count II, exclusive of fees and costs

c.   Plus all other awards, including but not limited to interest and punitive damages, and a trial by jury.

Respectfully Submitted,
Dayton & Associates, P.A.
Ron D. Dayton, Esq.
7501 19th Street
Topeka, KS, 66621
Telephone No.: (785) 444-4444
ron.dayton@daylaw.com

_____

Ron D. Dayton, Esq.
Kansas Bar No.: 123456

Golden Rule Construction Company

Construction Contract

This agreement is made this <u>15th</u> day of <u>December</u>, <u>2014</u>:

Recitals

Whereas <u>Jeremiah Smith</u> ("Owner") desires to have a <u>Golden Rule Type S Sunroom</u> added to his residence at <u>1221 State Street in Topeka, Kansas</u> (the "Project"), and

Whereas Golden Rule Construction Company ("Contractor") is an expert with respect to constructing sunrooms of the type desired by Owner and is the designer of the Sunroom;

Agreements

In consideration of the mutual promises set forth below and good and valuable consideration, the parties agree as follows:

1. **Express Condition Precedent.** Contractor's duties under this contract depend on and shall ONLY arise if Owner provides Contractor with a $35,000 payment bond.

2. **Contractor's Duties.** Beginning December 20, 2014 Contractor will build a <u>Golden Rule Type S Sunroom</u> at Owner's residence located at <u>1221 State Street in Topeka, Kansas</u>.

3. **Payment by Owner.** When Contractor has completed all work on The Project, Owner will pay Contractor $35,000.

4. **Waiver of Consequential Damages.** Contractor and Owner hereby waive all of their rights to consequential damages arising out of the other party's breach of contract.

5. **Indemnification.** Owner promises to indemnify Contractor and hold Contractor harmless against any claims brought by third parties alleging any breach of duty, negligence, or intentional wrongdoing committed by Owner.

6. **No oral modifications.** This contract may only be modified in a writing signed by both Owner and Contractor.

7. **Merger.** This writing contains the entire agreement of the parties. All prior agreement are deemed merged into this writing, and there are no promises, representations, or assurances not reflected in this writing.

<u>*Betty Golden*</u>　　<u>12-15-2014</u>　　　　　　　<u>*Owner*</u>　　　　　　<u>12/15/2014</u>

By Betty Golden for　　　　　　　　　　　　By Owner
Golden Rule Construction Company

Exercise 15-15: Practice Problem 5: Tribal Coal Mining Contract Analysis and Drafting*

LAW OFFICES OF ANGELIQUE BEGAY

I N T E R O F F I C E   M E M O R A N D U M

TO: Albert Associate
FROM: Angelique Begay
DATE: May ___, 20__
SUBJECT: Two Drafting Issues for Proposed Coal Mining Contract between the
                    Northern Cheyenne Tribe and Shell Oil Company*
OUR CLIENT: The Northern Cheyenne Tribe   OUR FILE No.: NCT303.02

As you know, the Northern Cheyenne Tribe, located in Montana, has enormous coal and methane gas reserves on its 445,000-acre reservation. For a long time, the Tribe has resisted development of these resources because of the belief that developing the coal would betray the Tribe's duty to protect the Earth. Two forces have caused the Tribal community to reconsider the issue. First, concerns about reliance on foreign sources of energy have elevated the value of these reserves such that all of the major energy producers have approached the Tribe about purchasing the right to mine the tribe's vast coal resources. Second, poverty and unemployment on the reservation are rampant; a good deal would create jobs and bring in enormous revenue. For example, the Navajo Nation's efforts to exploit its coal resources are expected to create 3,000 jobs and bring in $54,000,000 in revenue to that tribe.

Shell Oil has made the Tribe a very attractive offer to mine the coal. I am working on most of the issues with respect to this contract, but I need you to research two issues, write up an objective analysis, and, if necessary, draft appropriate contract clauses.

First, my recollection is that all tribes enjoy sovereign immunity. Does this immunity extend to contracts? To contracts signed on non-tribal property? My recollection is that the leading case involves the Kiowa Tribe. Shell has proposed the dispute resolution clause below. If the Tribe signs the clause, has it waived its sovereign immunity?

> Shell and the Tribe promise to attempt in good faith to resolve through negotiation any dispute, claim, or controversy arising out of or related to this agreement. If any such dispute arises, both parties agree to meet at least twice to try to resolve the dispute informally through negotiation. If the parties cannot resolve such a dispute through negotiation, both parties agree to participate in a one-day mediation in accordance with the rules and procedures of the Judicial Arbitration and Mediation Service (JAMS). The parties agree to cooperate in selecting a JAMS neutral mediator, and, if they are unable to agree upon a JAMS mediator, agree to allow JAMS to select a suitable neutral mediator. The fees and expenses of the mediator and of JAMS shall be borne equally by the parties.

---

* Professor Schwartz thanks Professor Angelique Townsend EagleWoman of the University of Idaho for providing the idea that formed the basis of this problem and helping him develop it.

This first issue is a tricky one because I am not certain our client wishes to waive its sovereign immunity if it has immunity for this contract, and I am not sure that it would be in the client's best interest to do so. At the same time, I suspect Shell is proceeding delicately. On the one hand, Shell surely wants an outlet for the resolution of disputes and is proposing this clause because it believes, if the Tribe agrees, Shell can later argue that agreeing to mediate waives the Tribe's sovereign immunity. On the other hand, Shell knows this entire project is a controversial one within the Tribe and wants to avoid protracted negotiations.

The second issue is at least as challenging. To accommodate the concerns of the large number of Tribal members who object to the proposed contract as a violation of the Tribe's duties to the Earth, the contract needs a clause or a set of clauses that unambiguously requires Shell to fully reclaim the land after the mining is complete. The problem is that the cost of reclamation is likely to greatly exceed the increase in value of the land that such reclamation would produce. I recall from my contracts class that this differential might be problematic. Your memo should confirm my understanding of this issue and the likelihood the Tribe would lose if the issue were litigated, and you should draft a reclamation clause and any additional clause or clauses needed to solve this problem. Make sure you explain why your efforts achieve the client's objectives.

Professional Development Reflection Questions

1. The third component of positive psychologists' definition of happiness (introduced to you in Chapter 14) is a "meaningful life"—creating a deeply satisfying and meaningful life by using your strengths to serve something larger than yourself (for example, the legal profession, your local community, or our democratic society). Consider how this component is different from the first two components of happiness you have already learned about (the "pleasant life" and the "good life").

2. Review your top signature strengths (which you identified when completing the questions at the end of Chapter 14). Are you currently using any of your signature strengths in service of something larger than yourself? Which strengths? How are you using them?

3. Empirical research demonstrates that one way to increase your sense of meaningfulness is to find new ways to use your signature strengths. Identify three new ways that you can use your signature strengths in service of something larger than yourself. Then, give them a try! We wish you success in creating a life that you find deeply meaningful and satisfying.

4. If you are reading these questions, you probably are close to finishing your first semester or first year of law school. How has law school changed you? Are you comfortable with the ways law school has changed you? Have your goals, career or otherwise, changed?

5. Where do you see yourself in ten years?

6. Imagine you are about to retire from your law practice and just returned from attending a retirement party in your honor. Write yourself a letter in which you describe what people will say about you. Now, give the letter to a friend or relative to hold for you until you graduate from law school.

Index